Nineteenth-Century Literature Criticism

Guide to Gale Literary Criticism Series

For criticism on	Consult these Gale series
Authors now living or who died after December 31, 1999	*CONTEMPORARY LITERARY CRITICISM (CLC)*
Authors who died between 1900 and 1999	*TWENTIETH-CENTURY LITERARY CRITICISM (TCLC)*
Authors who died between 1800 and 1899	*NINETEENTH-CENTURY LITERATURE CRITICISM (NCLC)*
Authors who died between 1400 and 1799	*LITERATURE CRITICISM FROM 1400 TO 1800 (LC)* *SHAKESPEAREAN CRITICISM (SC)*
Authors who died before 1400	*CLASSICAL AND MEDIEVAL LITERATURE CRITICISM (CMLC)*
Authors of books for children and young adults	*CHILDREN'S LITERATURE REVIEW (CLR)*
Dramatists	*DRAMA CRITICISM (DC)*
Poets	*POETRY CRITICISM (PC)*
Short story writers	*SHORT STORY CRITICISM (SSC)*
Literary topics and movements	*HARLEM RENAISSANCE: A GALE CRITICAL COMPANION (HR)* *THE BEAT GENERATION: A GALE CRITICAL COMPANION (BG)* *FEMINISM IN LITERATURE: A GALE CRITICAL COMPANION (FL)* *GOTHIC LITERATURE: A GALE CRITICAL COMPANION (GL)*
Asian American writers of the last two hundred years	*ASIAN AMERICAN LITERATURE (AAL)*
Black writers of the past two hundred years	*BLACK LITERATURE CRITICISM (BLC)* *BLACK LITERATURE CRITICISM SUPPLEMENT (BLCS)* *BLACK LITERATURE CRITICISM SUPPLEMENT: CLASSICAL AND EMERGING AUTHORS SINCE 1950 (BLC-2)*
Hispanic writers of the late nineteenth and twentieth centuries	*HISPANIC LITERATURE CRITICISM (HLC)* *HISPANIC LITERATURE CRITICISM SUPPLEMENT (HLCS)*
Native North American writers and orators of the eighteenth, nineteenth, and twentieth centuries	*NATIVE NORTH AMERICAN LITERATURE (NNAL)*
Major authors from the Renaissance to the present	*WORLD LITERATURE CRITICISM, 1500 TO THE PRESENT (WLC)* *WORLD LITERATURE CRITICISM SUPPLEMENT (WLCS)*

ISSN 0732-1864

Volume 215

Nineteenth-Century Literature Criticism

Criticism of the
Works of Novelists, Philosophers, and Other
Creative Writers Who Died between 1800
and 1899, from the First Published Critical
Appraisals to Current Evaluations

Kathy D. Darrow
Project Editor

GALE
CENGAGE Learning·

Detroit • New York • San Francisco • New Haven, Conn • Waterville, Maine • London

Nineteenth-Century Literature Criticism, Vol. 215

Project Editor: Kathy D. Darrow

Editorial: Dana Barnes, Elizabeth Cranston, Kristen Dorsch, Jeffrey W. Hunter, Jelena O. Krstović, Michelle Lee, Thomas J. Schoenberg, Lawrence J. Trudeau

Data Capture: Katrina D. Coach, Gwen Tucker

Rights and Acquisitions: Margaret Abendroth, Sari Gordon, Aja Perales

Composition and Electronic Capture: Gary Oudersluys

Manufacturing: Cynde Bishop

Associate Product Manager: Marc Cormier

For product information and technology assistance, contact us at
Gale Customer Support, 1-800-877-4253.
For permission to use material from this text or product,
submit all requests online at **www.cengage.com/permissions.**
Further permissions questions can be emailed to
permissionrequest@cengage.com

While every effort has been made to ensure the reliability of the information presented in this publication, Gale, a part of Cengage Learning, does not guarantee the accuracy of the data contained herein. Gale accepts no payment for listing; and inclusion in the publication of any organization, agency, institution, publication, service, or individual does not imply endorsement of the editors or publisher. Errors brought to the attention of the publisher and verified to the satisfaction of the publisher will be corrected in future editions.

Gale
27500 Drake Rd.
Farmington Hills, MI, 48331-3535

LIBRARY OF CONGRESS CATALOG CARD NUMBER 84-643008

ISBN-13: 978-1-4144-3849-8
ISBN-10: 1-4144-3849-4

ISSN 0732-1864

Printed in the United States of America
1 2 3 4 5 6 7 13 12 11 10 09

Contents

Preface vii

Acknowledgments xi

Literary Criticism Series Advisory Board xiii

Preface

Since its inception in 1981, *Nineteenth-Century Literature Criticism* (*NCLC*) has been a valuable resource for students and librarians seeking critical commentary on writers of this transitional period in world history. Designated an "Outstanding Reference Source" by the American Library Association with the publication of is first volume, *NCLC* has since been purchased by over 6,000 school, public, and university libraries. The series has covered more than 500 authors representing 38 nationalities and over 28,000 titles. No other reference source has surveyed the critical reaction to nineteenth-century authors and literature as thoroughly as *NCLC*.

Scope of the Series

NCLC is designed to introduce students and advanced readers to the authors of the nineteenth century and to the most significant interpretations of these authors' works. The great poets, novelists, short story writers, playwrights, and philosophers of this period are frequently studied in high school and college literature courses. By organizing and reprinting commentary written on these authors, *NCLC* helps students develop valuable insight into literary history, promotes a better understanding of the texts, and sparks ideas for papers and assignments. Each entry in *NCLC* presents a comprehensive survey of an author's career or an individual work of literature and provides the user with a multiplicity of interpretations and assessments. Such variety allows students to pursue their own interests; furthermore, it fosters an awareness that literature is dynamic and responsive to many different opinions.

Every fourth volume of *NCLC* is devoted to literary topics that cannot be covered under the author approach used in the rest of the series. Such topics include literary movements, prominent themes in nineteenth-century literature, literary reaction to political and historical events, significant eras in literary history, prominent literary anniversaries, and the literatures of cultures that are often overlooked by English-speaking readers.

NCLC continues the survey of criticism of world literature begun by Gale's *Contemporary Literary Criticism* (*CLC*) and *Twentieth-Century Literary Criticism* (*TCLC*).

Organization of the Book

An *NCLC* entry consists of the following elements:

- The **Author Heading** cites the name under which the author most commonly wrote, followed by birth and death dates. Also located here are any name variations under which an author wrote, including transliterated forms for authors whose native languages use nonroman alphabets. If the author wrote consistently under a pseudonym, the pseudonym will be listed in the author heading and the author's actual name given in parenthesis on the first line of the biographical and critical information. Uncertain birth or death dates are indicated by question marks. Single-work entries are preceded by a heading that consists of the most common form of the title in English translation (if applicable) and the original date of composition.

- The **Introduction** contains background information that introduces the reader to the author, work, or topic that is the subject of the entry.

- The list of **Principal Works** is ordered chronologically by date of first publication and lists the most important works by the author. The genre and publication date of each work is given. In the case of foreign authors whose works have been translated into English, the list will focus primarily on twentieth-century translations, selecting those works most commonly considered the best by critics. Unless otherwise indicated, dramas are dated by first performance, not first publication. Lists of **Representative Works** by different authors appear with topic entries.

- Reprinted **Criticism** is arranged chronologically in each entry to provide a useful perspective on changes in critical evaluation over time. The critic's name and the date of composition or publication of the critical work are given at the beginning of each piece of criticism. Unsigned criticism is preceded by the title of the source in which it appeared. All titles by the author featured in the text are printed in boldface type. Footnotes are reprinted at the end of each essay or excerpt. In the case of excerpted criticism, only those footnotes that pertain to the excerpted texts are included. Criticism in topic entries is arranged chronologically under a variety of subheadings to facilitate the study of different aspects of the topic.

- A complete **Bibliographical Citation** of the original essay or book precedes each piece of criticism.

- Critical essays are prefaced by brief **Annotations** explicating each piece.

- An annotated bibliography of **Further Reading** appears at the end of each entry and suggests resources for additional study. In some cases, significant essays for which the editors could not obtain reprint rights are included here. Boxed material following the further reading list provides references to other biographical and critical sources on the author in series published by Gale.

Indexes

Each volume of *NCLC* contains a **Cumulative Author Index** listing all authors who have appeared in a wide variety of reference sources published by Gale, including *NCLC*. A complete list of these sources is found facing the first page of the Author Index. The index also includes birth and death dates and cross references between pseudonyms and actual names.

A **Cumulative Nationality Index** lists all authors featured in *NCLC* by nationality, followed by the number of the *NCLC* volume in which their entry appears.

A **Cumulative Topic Index** lists the literary themes and topics treated in the series as well as in *Classical and Medieval Literature Criticism, Literature Criticism from 1400 to 1800, Twentieth-Century Literary Criticism,* and the *Contemporary Literary Criticism* Yearbook, which was discontinued in 1998.

An alphabetical **Title Index** accompanies each volume of *NCLC*, with the exception of the Topics volumes. Listings of titles by authors covered in the given volume are followed by the author's name and the corresponding page numbers where the titles are discussed. English translations of foreign titles and variations of titles are cross-referenced to the title under which a work was originally published. Titles of novels, dramas, nonfiction books, and poetry, short story, or essay collections are printed in italics, while individual poems, short stories, and essays are printed in roman type within quotation marks.

In response to numerous suggestions from librarians, Gale also produces an annual paperbound edition of the *NCLC* cumulative title index. This annual cumulation, which alphabetically lists all titles reviewed in the series, is available to all customers. Additional copies of this index are available upon request. Librarians and patrons will welcome this separate index; it saves shelf space, is easy to use, and is recyclable upon receipt of the next edition.

Citing *Nineteenth-Century Literature Criticism*

When citing criticism reprinted in the Literary Criticism Series, students should provide complete bibliographic information so that the cited essay can be located in the original print or electronic source. Students who quote directly from reprinted criticism may use any accepted bibliographic format, such as University of Chicago Press style or Modern Language Association style.

The examples below follow recommendations for preparing a bibliography set forth in *The Chicago Manual of Style,* 14th ed. (Chicago: The University of Chicago Press, 1993); the first example pertains to material drawn from periodicals, the second to material reprinted from books:

Franklin, J. Jeffrey. "The Victorian Discourse of Gambling: Speculations on *Middlemarch* and *The Duke's Children*." *ELH* 61, no. 4 (winter 1994): 899-921. Reprinted in *Nineteenth-Century Literature Criticism.* Vol. 168, edited by Jessica Bomarito and Russel Whitaker, 39-51. Detroit: Thomson Gale, 2006.

Frank, Joseph. "*The Gambler*: A Study in Ethnopsychology." In *Freedom and Responsibility in Russian Literature: Essays in Honor of Robert Louis Jackson,* edited by Elizabeth Cheresh Allen and Gary Saul Morson, 69-85. Evanston, Ill.: Northwestern University Press, 1995. Reprinted in *Nineteenth-Century Literature Criticism.* Vol. 168, edited by Jessica Bomarito and Russel Whitaker, 75-84. Detroit: Thomson Gale, 2006.

The examples below follow recommendations for preparing a works cited list set forth in the *MLA Handbook for Writers of Research Papers,* 6th ed. (New York: The Modern Language Association of America, 2003); the first example pertains to material drawn from periodicals, the second to material reprinted from books:

Franklin, J. Jeffrey. "The Victorian Discourse of Gambling: Speculations on *Middlemarch* and *The Duke's Children*." *ELH* 61.4 (winter 1994): 899-921. Reprinted in *Nineteenth-Century Literature Criticism.* Eds. Jessica Bomarito and Russel Whitaker. Vol. 168. Detroit: Thomson Gale, 2006. 39-51.

Frank, Joseph. "*The Gambler*: A Study in Ethnopsychology." *Freedom and Responsibility in Russian Literature: Essays in Honor of Robert Louis Jackson.* Eds. Elizabeth Cheresh Allen and Gary Saul Morson. Evanston, Ill.: Northwestern University Press, 1995. 69-85. Reprinted in *Nineteenth-Century Literature Criticism.* Eds. Jessica Bomarito and Russel Whitaker. Vol. 168. Detroit: Thomson Gale, 2006. 75-84.

Suggestions are Welcome

Readers who wish to suggest new features, topics, or authors to appear in future volumes, or who have other suggestions or comments are cordially invited to call, write, or fax the Associate Product Manager:

Associate Product Manager, Literary Criticism Series
Gale
27500 Drake Road
Farmington Hills, MI 48331-3535
1-800-347-4253 (GALE)
Fax: 248-699-8054

Acknowledgments

The editors wish to thank the copyright holders of the criticism included in this volume and the permissions managers of many book and magazine publishing companies for assisting us in securing reproduction rights. Following is a list of the copyright holders who have granted us permission to reproduce material in this volume of *NCLC*. Every effort has been made to trace copyright, but if omissions have been made, please let us know.

COPYRIGHTED MATERIAL IN *NCLC*, VOLUME 215, WAS REPRODUCED FROM THE FOLLOWING PERIODICALS:

American Scholar, v. 72, summer, 2003 for "At Large and At Small: Embedding Trollope," by Phyllis Rose. Copyright © 2003 by the United Chapters of the Phi Beta Kappa Society. Reproduced by permission of the author.—*ARIEL: A Review of International English Literature,* v. 13, January, 1982 for "Anthony Trollope: The Compleat Traveller" by Helen Heineman; v. 27, July, 1996 for "The Empire Turned Upside Down: The Colonial Fictions of Anthony Trollope" by Nicholas Birns. Copyright © 1982, 1996 The Board of Governors, The University of Calgary. Reproduced by permission of the publisher and the respective authors.—*British Library Journal,* v. 8, autumn, 1982. Copyright © 1982 The British Library Board. Reproduced by permission.—*Contemporary Review,* v. 278, February, 2001. Copyright © 2001 Contemporary Review Company Ltd. Reproduced by the permission of Contemporary Review Ltd.—*Criticism: A Quarterly for Literature and the Arts,* v. 36, summer, 1994. Copyright © 1994 Wayne State University Press. Reproduced with permission of the Wayne State University Press.—*ELH,* v. 62, summer, 1995; v. 67, summer, 2000. Copyright © 1995, 2000 The Johns Hopkins University Press. Both reproduced by permission.—*English Literature in Transition, 1880-1920,* v. 47, 2004. Copyright © 2004 *English Literature in Transition: 1880-1920.* Reproduced by permission.—*Journal of the History of Ideas,* v. 13, June, 1952. Copyright © 1952 *Journal of History of Ideas.* Copyright © renewed 1980 by the *Journal of History of Ideas.* All rights reserved. Reprinted by permission of the University of Pennsylvania Press.—*New Criterion,* v. 26, October, 2007 for "Trollope & the Law" by Marc Arkin. Copyright © 2007 by The Foundation for Cultural Review. Reproduced by permission of the author.—*Nineteenth-Century Fiction,* v. 6, September, 1951 for "Anthony Trollope's Younger Characters" by Russell A. Fraser. Copyright © 1951 by The Regents of the University of California. Copyright © renewed 1979 by the University of California Press. Reproduced by permission of the publisher and the author.—*Novel: A Forum on Fiction,* v. 28, spring, 1995; v. 33, fall, 1999. Copyright © NOVEL Corp., 1995, 1999. Both reproduced with permission.—*South Atlantic Review,* v. 51, January 19, 1986. Copyright © 1986 by the South Atlantic Modern Language Association. Reproduced by permission.—*Studies in English Literature 1500-1900,* v. 30, autumn, 1990. Copyright © 1990 by The Johns Hopkins University Press. Reproduced by permission.—*Studies in Short Fiction,* v. 30, winter, 1993. Copyright © 1993 by Newberry College. Reproduced by permission.—*Studies in the Novel,* v. 38, summer, 2006. Copyright © 2006 by the University of North Texas. Reproduced by permission.—*Texas Studies in Literature and Language,* v. 45, autumn, 2003 for "Partying with the Opposition: Social Politics in *The Prime Minister*" by Courtney C. Berger. Copyright © 2003 by the University of Texas Press. All rights reserved. Reproduced by permission of the publisher and the author.—*Toronto Slavic Quarterly,* Summer, 2005 for "Derzhavin's Monuments: Sculpture, Poetry, and the Materiality of History" by Luba Golburt. Copyright © 2005 *Toronto Slavic Quarterly.* Reproduced by permission of the author.—*Utopian Studies,* v. 10, 1999. Copyright © 1999 by Society for Utopian Studies. Reproduced by permission.—*Victorian Studies,* v. 44, autumn, 2001; v. 45, autumn, 2002; v. 45, winter, 2003. Copyright © 2001, 2002, 2003 by Indiana University Press. All reproduced by permission.

COPYRIGHTED MATERIAL IN *NCLC*, VOLUME 215, WAS REPRODUCED FROM THE FOLLOWING BOOKS:

Brown, William Edward. From *A History of 18th Century Russian Literature.* Ardis, 1979. Copyright © 1979 by Ardis Publishers. All rights reserved. Reprinted by permission of Ardis/Overlook.—Crone, Anna Lisa. From *The Daring of Derzhavin: The Moral and Aesthetic Independence of the Poet in Russia.* Slavica, 2001. Copyright © 2001 by Anna Lisa Crone. All rights reserved. Reproduced by permission of the author.—Dale, Peter Allan. From "George Lewes' Scientific Aesthetic: Restructuring the Ideology of the Symbol," in *One Culture: Essays in Science and Literature.* Edited by George Levine and Alan Rauch. Copyright © 1988 by the Board of Regents of the University of Wisconsin System. Reproduced by permission of the University of Wisconsin Press.—Friedrich, Paul. From *Music in Russian Poetry.* Peter Lang,

Gale Literature Product Advisory Board

The members of the Gale Literature Product Advisory Board—reference librarians from public and academic library systems—represent a cross-section of our customer base and offer a variety of informed perspectives on both the presentation and content of our literature products. Advisory board members assess and define such quality issues as the relevance, currency, and usefulness of the author coverage, critical content, and literary topics included in our series; evaluate the layout, presentation, and general quality of our printed volumes; provide feedback on the criteria used for selecting authors and topics covered in our series; provide suggestions for potential enhancements to our series; identify any gaps in our coverage of authors or literary topics, recommending authors or topics for inclusion; analyze the appropriateness of our content and presentation for various user audiences, such as high school students, undergraduates, graduate students, librarians, and educators; and offer feedback on any proposed changes/enhancements to our series. We wish to thank the following advisors for their advice throughout the year.

Gavriil Romanovich Derzhavin
1743-1816

Russian poet, critic, and autobiographer.

The following entry presents an overview of Derzhavin's life and works.

INTRODUCTION

Widely recognized as the most important Russian literary figure before Alexander Pushkin, Gavriil Derzhavin departed from the prevailing styles of his time and brought a highly personalized and inventive approach to the practice of poetry. Like other literary figures in eighteenth-century Russia, he wrote by avocation rather than profession, and his successes in the government of Catherine II provided him with rank, income, and audiences. Conversely, his talent as a poet frequently enabled him to survive the vicissitudes of Russian political life. A colorful personality—persistently outspoken, opinionated on almost every matter, and cheerfully epicurean—Derzhavin was politically conservative: he supported monarchism and serfdom, but his poetry reflected the belief that implementation of the system was corrupted by vain courtiers and inept bureaucrats. Throughout his career, Derzhavin sought to balance philosophy and poetry, public service and private experience, and though his fame was initially based on the panegyric odes written during his association with the imperial court, a large part of his abundant production was devoted to lyrics celebrating the joys of life and reflecting on the fate of man.

In the history of Russian literature, Derzhavin's importance centered on his rejection of the strict rules for composition that had been imposed by the extremely influential poet Mikhail Lomonosov (1711-65) in favor of a style that used both "high" (literary) and "low" (folk) language, blending lofty subjects with mundane details and mixing adulation with skillful satire. He is credited with revitalizing a moribund poetic tradition in Russia by introducing language variation and sensual imagery. His use of language—and indeed, his whole approach to poetry—were so idiosyncratic that no school grew up around him, though he both gave and received influence as part of the Lvov Circle; later, in the early-twentieth-century "Silver Age" of Russian poetry, Derzhavin was rediscovered by such poets as Marina Tsvetaeva, Osip Mandelstam, and Vladimir Mayakovsky. Although his poetry has sometimes been characterized as showing pre-Romantic influences, he was for the most part opposed to the Europeanizing currents beginning to affect Russian literature. Derzhavin was the first Russian author to be translated into more than a dozen other languages (including Japanese) during his lifetime.

Derzhavin's best-known works—"Felitsa" (1782; "Felitsa"), "Bog" (1784; "God"), and "Vodopad" (1794; "The Waterfall")—stand alone, neither elaborating past works nor prefiguring future movements. The same can be said for other important but lesser-known works, such as "Priglashenie k obedu" (1795; "Invitation to Dinner"), "Evgeniu. Zhizn' Zvanskaya" (1807; "To Eugene. Life at Zvanka"), "Videnie Murzy" (1783-84; "A Murza's Vision"), "Na vzyatie Izmaila" (1790; "On the Taking of Izmail"), and certain of the *Anakreonticheskiia pesni* (1804; *Ancreontic Songs*), all of which reflect in some way Derzhavin's thematic reflections on time and man's fate.

BIOGRAPHICAL INFORMATION

Derzhavin was born in 1743 in Kazán, a city in central European Russia that had been historically inhabited by Tatars, a Turkic ethnic group. Derzhavin's family was among the landed gentry but by the time of his birth had become quite poor. Derzhavin received rudimentary tutoring and attended a local gymnasium for a few years; he acknowledged in an autobiography, however, that his education had been limited and of inferior quality. In 1762, at the age of eighteen, he was conscripted into the military and left Kazán as a private in the Preobrazhensky Guards. After serving with the regiment for ten years, during which time he devoted some of his free time to drinking and gambling and some to reading and to the imitation of Russian and German verse (he had learned a little German during his brief education), Derzhavin finally received a commission as an ensign in 1772. By the time of his discharge two years later, he had attained a rank equivalent to lieutenant colonel and was granted a large estate (with 300 serfs) in Belorussia. This rapid rise was due to the initiative and cleverness he displayed during an action to quell the peasant uprising led by Pugachev, but was also marked by the first in a lifelong series of career complications: Derzhavin avoided a court-martial for insubordination only by a nearly accidental intervention from the empress.

To some extent Derzhavin's lack of formal education proved an advantage in that he was not indoctrinated with the classicist views dominating Russian literature in the eighteenth century. He did, in his early work, follow the approved practice of imitating well-known writers of the past, but in the process he determined that his own abilities were poorly suited to the reproduction of formulaic works. As a consequence he began to develop a personal style and voice, which appeared in nascent form in his first published volume, *Ody perevedennyia i sochinennyia pri gore Chitalagae 1774 goda* (1774). Although the collection was published anonymously and was later disparaged by its author, it revealed a certain amount of originality—especially in its best-known poem, "Na smert Generala-Enshefa Bibikov" ("Ode on the Death of General Bibikov"), which was unrhymed. During this period of imitative study, Derzhavin also wrote songs, some of which were published twenty years later in his only other poetry collection, *Anacreontic Songs.*

Derzhavin's marriage to the accomplished young Catherine Bastidon in 1778 provided him with connections in the intellectual world, and he became acquainted with the circle of artists and writers surrounding noted architect and poet Nicolai Lvov. The group introduced Derzhavin to some of the historical background and critical insights that had been absent from his self-education, but for the most part, Derzhavin's own iconoclastic temperament seems to have been the driving factor in his stylistic development. A complex personality, Derzhavin was noted throughout a long public career for absolute commitment to his own ideals and opinions, even when these were at odds with prevailing standards or with the orders of his superiors. He is reputed to have been sharp-tongued, impulsive, and entirely without tact, so it is not surprising that his political fortunes were mixed. He enjoyed a series of significant positions, including a period in the Senate (1782), the governorship of two provinces (Olonets, 1785, and Tambov, 1786-88), a term as Empress Catherine's personal secretary of petitions (1791), and appointments as president of the department of commerce (1794) in the brief reign of Emperor Paul and minister of justice (1802) under Paul's successor, Emperor Alexander I. Each of these tenures was marked by quarrels and ended in dismissal, however. In 1803 Derzhavin was firmly retired from public service; he spent the last thirteen years of his life writing and entertaining guests at Zvanka, his estate near Novgorod.

The determined spirit with which Derzhavin approached his military and administrative duties also shaped his literary life. He refused to be restrained by traditional conventions, and though he received some criticism for mixing genres and breaking forms, his exceptional talent as a poet was acknowledged even by detractors. Popular recognition of his work began in 1779, the year

after his marriage, with the publication of his poem celebrating the birth of the future Emperor Alexander. "Stikhi na rozhdenie v Severe porfirorodnago otroka" ("On the Birth of a Royal Son in the North") is noteworthy as the first example of Derzhavin's most famous tactic: the mixing of high and low forms. In the same year, which Derzhavin himself described as a "turning point" in his search for a personal style, "Na smert' kniazia Meshcherskogo" ("On the Death of Prince Meshchersky") was published. Acknowledged as one of his greatest odes, this work skillfully employed a traditional form and a common theme (the inevitability of death) but was infused with powerful originality by Derzhavin's choice of language and imagery.

The next advance in Derzhavin's poetic development also proved to be a crucial step in his political career. In 1782, apparently moved by a sincere admiration for Catherine II (whom he had not yet met), Derzhavin constructed an extremely clever literary homage to the empress. The title of the ode, "Felitsa," was the name of a character who represented the empress in a fairy tale that Catherine herself had written for her grandson. Derzhavin's combination of everyday detail and lofty praise, along with his juxtaposition of adulation for Catherine and satirical depictions of her courtiers, made "Felitsa" an immediate sensation, delighting the empress and opening new levels of career opportunities for Derzhavin. In the following years, as he moved in the imperial circle, Derzhavin reused this poetic strategy more than once to enhance or repair his relationship with the empress with offerings that included several fairly ordinary tributes, along with the beautifully original lyric, "A Murza's Vision." As he later admitted in his autobiography, however, the more he observed his subject, the less inspiration he could find for poetic flattery. By 1793 his relations with the empress had entirely deteriorated, due in part to his difficult personality and in part to the continuing dramas that afflicted the imperial court. In spite of a scorn for the Russian aristocracy sometimes revealed in both his manner and his poetry, Derzhavin remained a staunch monarchist and political conservative.

During his politically active years, Derzhavin wrote two poems considered to be among his greatest, "God" and "The Waterfall." The first is noteworthy not only for its poetic daring but also for its spiritual intensity, while the second demonstrates Derzhavin's masterful use of descriptive language and nature imagery. In 1794 Derzhavin's beloved wife (whom he had celebrated in a number of minor lyrics during their sixteen-year marriage) died; a year later he married one of her friends, a daughter of the literary patron Senator Dyakov. After Empress Catherine's death in 1796, Derzhavin maneuvered his way through the brief tenure of Paul and the beginning of Alexander's reign, apparently too busy to write much poetry. Following his retirement in 1803, however, he began a new phase of his literary life during which he published a book of odes on various pleasures of human life, wrote several pieces of prose (including autobiographic material and a lengthy essay on his poetics), and made a few attempts at drama.

The most famous of Derzhavin's later works was a graceful account of life at his country estate, "To Eugene. Life at Zvanka." He maintained a very active life, often entertaining his fellow advocates of literary tradition and sometimes the younger proponents of literary experimentation as well. In fact, Derzhavin was present at a school poetry recital by the young Alexander Pushkin, and this symbolic—but somewhat accidental—event came to be regarded as a passing of the mantle from the greatest Russian poet of one century to the greatest of the next. The following year, in 1816, the prolific Derzhavin died suddenly, reputedly while working on a poem. Its beginning lines, now known as "Reka vremen v svoem stremlenii" ("The River of Time in Its Ceaseless Course"), are said to have been found on a slate near his body.

MAJOR WORKS

Derzhavin characterized his 1774 *Ody perevedennyia i sochinennyia pri gore Chitalagae 1774 goda* as a failed attempt to reach the poetic heights attained by Lomonosov, Russia's most influential poet at the time. Yet even in his earliest work, Derzhavin demonstrated a degree of talent that would enable him to eclipse Lomonosov's reputation in just a few years. By 1780, after the publication of his odes on the birth of Alexander and the death of Prince Meshchersky, Derzhavin was widely considered the leading Russian poet. Although there is no formal critical consensus on the categorization of Derzhavin's poetic works, a reasonable overview can be constructed by dividing them into five groups.

The seriocomic odes exhibit the mixture of high and low styles for which Derzhavin is most famous. The Felitsa cycle (which includes "Felitsa" and two other poems addressed to the Empress in her Felitsa persona, as well as "A Murza's Vision" and a few occasional pieces) demonstrates his development of this original poetic type, also evident in his reworking of a traditional ode on nobility, which he had written in 1778, into the much more successful "Vel'mozh" (1794; "The Nobleman").

The panegyric odes, which commemorate personalities and events, include most notably (in addition to "On the Death of Prince Meshchersky" and "On the Birth of a Royal Son in the North") the poems "On the Taking of Izmail," "Na vozvrashchenie Grafa Zubova iz Persii"

(1797; "On the Return of Count Zubov from Persia"), and "Osen' vo vremia osady Ochakova" (1788; "Autumn during the Siege of Ochakov"). These works are more consistently faithful to the formal tradition than most of Derzhavin's poems, but they, too, frequently violate the classicist rules of style and genre.

The spiritual odes include Derzhavin's two most famous works, "God" and "The Waterfall," along with the controversial "Oda. Prelozhenie 81-go psalma" ("Ode. Transposition of Psalm 82"), which later became known as "Vlastiteliam i sudiiam" ("To Rulers and Judges"—the title of an address that heads the poem). Derzhavin's version of Psalm 82 was suppressed in 1780 for its supposedly antimonarchist implications, and even seven years later, when it was eventually published, Derzhavin had to defend the work against Catherine's displeasure, a series of events that demonstrates the difficulty of combining his public career with the honest work of observation he believed was incumbent upon the poet. In fact, after 1779 Derzhavin did not sign any of his odes until the entirely uncontroversial "God" was published in 1784 under his own name. Even "The Waterfall," which in its entirety is an ode on the death of Grigory Potemkin in 1794, faced some political scrutiny, since the complex Potemkin was in disfavor at the time.

The Horatian odes follow Horace's example in reflecting on human life and especially on the role of the poet. In "Pamiatnik" (1795; "The Monument") and "Lebed" (1804; "The Swan"), Derzhavin freely translated poems by Horace, and in both he contemplates the probability that his poetry will prove far more important than his public service. The earlier "Moi Istukan" (1794; "My Bust") presents a similar theme.

The Anacreontic odes were inspired by another poet of the classical age, Anacreon. Noted for his light-hearted lyrical poetry, Anacreon celebrated the joys of everyday life. Derzhavin began writing in this style early on, composing drinking songs during his military days. He began to shift his attention back toward this style in the 1790s, producing one of his most skillful poems, "Priglashenie k obedu" (1795; "Invitation to Dinner"), in praise of food. In 1804 he published a volume containing 109 poems in the Anacreontic style, including two masterful short lyrics, "Russkie devuski" ("Russian Maidens") and "Cyganskaja pljaska" ("Gypsy Dance"). His best-known poem in this style is "To Eugene. Life at Zvanka."

In all these categories Derzhavin developed common themes, notably the passage of time, the inevitability of death, the limitations of human nature, the enjoyment of life, and the grandeur of nature. He frequently utilized two powerful techniques: linguistic excess and profusions of sensory stimulation. Employing the combination of folk Russian and Church Slavic vocabulary and grammar in diverse mixtures, along with inversions of word order, complex syntax (for example, ten subjects for one verb or ten predicates for one subject), and cascades of imagery evoking color and sound, Derzhavin created what scholar Lisa Crone has called an "aesthetics of excess." Derzhavin himself discussed this approach in his theoretical work *Rassuzdenie o liriCeskoj poezii ili ob ode* (1811; *Discourse on Lyric Poetry or on the Ode*), wherein he distinguished two purposes of writing, the most important of which—and therefore the purview of the ode—was inspiration. In addition, Derzhavin indicated both in this work and in several of his poems that he considered poetry to have a moral purpose and the poet an obligation to be a truthful observer. Detailed expositions of all these topics, along with other material important to the study of Derzhavin, were published in a pair of his prose works: *Ob'isaneniia* (1809-10; *Explanations of Derzhavin's Works*), made up of his own commentaries on his poetry; and *Zapiski* (1810-13; *Notes*), a mainly political autobiography.

CRITICAL RECEPTION

In Russia Derzhavin was widely admired during his lifetime; he was considered not only to have surpassed Lomonosov's mastery of the ode with works such as "God" and "The Waterfall" but also to have brought a new liveliness to Russian panegyric poetry in "Felitsa" and other poems that mixed lofty praise with mischievous satire. Even before his death, however, Derzhavin's work was beginning to be regarded as old-fashioned. His attempt to enlarge the lexicon of Russian poetry by adding aspects of colloquial and folk language gathered no adherents, and Karamzin's movement to transform literary Russian by aligning syntax and style more closely with the French model prevailed. Derzhavin, who knew neither French nor the classical languages and was persistently conservative in his view of Russian culture, remained resistant to this trend. Not coincidentally, the earliest criticism of Derzhavin centered on his use of language, and Pushkin (in a letter of 1825) observed that Derzhavin "knew neither the Russian ABCs nor the spirit of the Russian language." Yet the younger poet admitted that Derzhavin's work contained "thoughts, pictures, and movements which are truly poetic."

British linguist and writer John Bowring, in his volume of translations *Specimens of the Russian Poets* (1821), was prescient in asserting that Derzhavin deserved first rank among eighteenth-century Russian poets. In the nineteenth century, however, Pushkin's influence hugely overshadowed the memory of Derzhavin, and for a time he received little critical attention. Although several sets

of Derzhavin's *Sochineniia* (collected works) were issued in the first part of the century, it was the publication of Jakov Grot's definitive nine-volume collection (1864-83), which includes Grot's annotations and a substantive biography, that prepared the way for a renewed interest in the poet's work. In 1882 scholar Charles Turner offered a thorough, balanced, and generally appreciative discussion of Derzhavin's writings in his *Studies in Russian Literature*.

Nevertheless, the scope and value of Derzhavin's work was widely misunderstood well into the twentieth century, as evidenced by the description in Peter Kropotkin's *Russian Literature: Ideal and Reality* (1916), which dismisses Derzhavin as "the poet-laureate of Catherine" who "sang in pompous odes the virtues of the ruler and the victories of her generals." Yet even Kropotkin acknowledged that Derzhavin displayed true poetic skill and sensibility in a few poems (mentioning "God" and "The Waterfall"). By midcentury D. S. Mirsky, in his authoritative *History of Russian Literature* (1949), characterized Derzhavin not only as "towering above" all other Russian poets of the eighteenth century but as "one of the greatest and most original of all Russian poets." The 1960s saw a significant increase in attention to Derzhavin among Russian and Eastern European critics; in 1978 Pierre Hart published a well-received critical biography, *G. R. Derzhavin: A Poet's Progress,* and an extensive chapter was devoted to Derzhavin in William Edward Brown's 1980 study, *A History of Eighteenth Century Russian Literature.* By the 1990s the groundwork had thus been laid for publication of substantive Derzhavin scholarship in English, both in translation and as original work. Notable examples are the discussions of Derzhavin's work in Paul Friedrich's *Music in Russian Poetry* (1998) and Harsha Ram's *The Imperial Sublime* (2006); a substantive examination of Derzhavin's poetics in Anna Lisa Crone's *The Daring of Derzhavin* (2001); and the publication in journals and anthologies of several articles exploring various aspects of Derzhavin's work. In addition, poet Vasily Khodasevich's 1931 biography of Derzhavin—especially noteworthy in that it casts Derzhavin as a model for the future development of Russian poetry—was published in English in 2007.

Over time, critical attention has shifted from a preoccupation with Derzhavin's panegyric and spiritual odes to include the Anacreontic odes and a deeper exploration of the poet's dual identity as civil servant and literary figure during a dramatic period of Russian history. Topics of contemporary critical discussion include Derzhavin's self-identification as a poet and his interpretation of the poet's role in society; the evaluation of Derzhavin's achievements in the context of Catherinian Russia and the decline of classicism; and the personal beliefs he either disguised or revealed in his poetry. Derzhavin criticism shows increasing energy among specialists, but in 2001 Crone argued that "scholarly literature is still rife with facile and misinformed notions about Derzhavin."

PRINCIPAL WORKS

"Na smert Generala-Enshefa Bibikov" ["Ode on the Death of General Bibikov"] (poem) 1774

*Ody perevedennyia i sochinennyia pri gore Chitalagae 1774 goda (poetry) 1774

"Na znatnost" ["On Nobility"] (poem) 1778

"Na smert' kniazia Meshcherskogo" ["On the Death of Prince Meshchersky"] (poem) 1779

"Stikhi na rozhdenie v Severe porfirorodnago otroka" ["On the Birth of a Royal Son in the North"] (poem) 1779

"Felitsa" ["Felitsa"] (poem) 1782

"Videnie Murzy" ["A Murza's Vision"] (poem) 1783-84

"Bog" ["God"] (poem) 1784

†"Oda. Prelozhenie 81-go psalma" ["Ode. Transposition of Psalm 82"] (poem) 1787; subsequently known as "Vlastiteliam i sudiiam" ["To Rulers and Judges"]

"Osen' vo vremia osady Ochakova" ["Autumn during the Siege of Ochakov"] (poem) 1788

"Na vzyatie Izmaila" ["On the Taking of Izmail"] (poem) 1790

"Moi Istukan" ["My Bust"] (poem) 1794

‡"Vel'mozh" ["The Nobleman"] (poem) 1794

"Vodopad" ["The Waterfall"] (poem) 1794

"Pamiatnik" ["The Monument"] (poem) 1795

"Priglashenie k obedu" ["Invitation to Dinner"] (poem) 1795

"Na vozvrashchenie Grafa Zubova iz Persii" ["On the Return of Count Zubov from Persia"] (poem) 1797

§*Anakreonticheskiia pesni* [*Anacreontic Songs*] (poetry) 1804

"Evgeniu. Zhizn' Zvanskaya" ["To Eugene. Life at Zvanka"] (poem) 1807

‖*Ob'isaneniia* [*Explanations of Derzhavin's Works*] (autobiography) 1809-10

#*Zapiski* [*Notes*] (autobiography) 1810-13

Rassuzdenie o liriCeskoj poezii ili ob ode [*Discourse on Lyric Poetry or on the Ode*] (criticism) 1811

**"Reka vremen v svoem stremlenii" ["The River of Time in Its Ceaseless Course"] (poem) 1816

*This work (the title of which may be rendered into English as Odes Translated and Composed at Chitalagay Hill in 1774) contains translations of works by Frederick II of Prussia.

†*This poem was scheduled for publication in the Saint Petersburg Herald in November 1780, but it was deleted because of its allegedly anti-monarchist sentiments and was not published until seven years later.*

‡*This poem is a major reworking of the more traditional 1778 ode "On Nobility."*

§*This work contains 109 poems written over the course of many years. Among them are the well-known lyrics "Lebed" ("The Swan"), "Cyganskaja pljaska" ("Gypsy Dance"), "K lyre" ("To My Lyre"), and "Russkie*

devuski" ("Russian Maidens"). Though they may have appeared before 1804, these poems are usually dated by their publication in *Anakreonticheskiia pesni.*

‖*An earlier version of this work, written in 1805 but not published in its original form until the 1970s (after being rediscovered in a Kiev archive), is known in English as "Something About Derzhavin."*

#*An earlier version of this work, written in 1805 but not published in its original form until the 1970s (also found in the Kiev archive), is known in English as Footnotes.*

*Although the lines contained in this poem, purported to have been written in the moments before Derzhavin's death, presumably constitute only the beginning of the intended work, they have been given a title and are generally treated as a poem rather than as a fragment.

CRITICISM

John Bowring (essay date 1821)

SOURCE: Bowring, John. Introduction to *Specimens of the Russian Poets,* translated by John Bowring, pp. vii-xxxv. London: Printed for the Author, 1821.

[*In the following excerpt, Bowring characterizes Derzhavin as preeminent among Russian poets and discusses several of his poems.*]

But of all the poets of Russia, Derzhavin is in my conception entitled to the very first place. His compositions breathe a high and sublime spirit; they are full of inspiration. His versification is sonorous, original, characteristic; his subjects generally such as allowed him to give full scope to his ardent imagination and lofty conceptions. Of modern poets, he most resembles Klopstock: his ***Oda Bog, Ode on God,*** with the exception of some of the wonderful passages of the Old Testament, "written with a pen of fire," and glowing with the brightness of heaven, passages of which Derzhavin has frequently availed himself, is one of the most impressive and sublime addresses I am acquainted with, on a subject so pre-eminently impressive and sublime. The first poem which excited the public attention to him was his ***Felitza.***

Charles Edward Turner (essay date 1882)

SOURCE: Turner, Charles Edward. "Derzhavin." In *Studies in Russian Literature,* pp. 74-94. London: Sampson Low, Marston, Searle, and Rivington, 1882.

[*In the following excerpt, Turner offers an overview of Derzhavin's work, highlighting the social context and philosophical background of his poetry.*]

To the number and variety of his works we may probably attribute the different and at times radically opposed criticisms that have been passed on the poetry of Derzhavin. If we consider it merely as the product of the eighteenth century, it cannot but possess a high value in our eyes; whereas, if we regard it from a strictly æsthetical point of view, we shall find that a large number of his compositions scarcely rise above the level of the ordinary verses of a Sumarokoff or a Tredyakoffsky. But, to judge the genius of Derzhavin fairly, we must take into account the character of the times in which he lived. That from a very early age he felt those rare and special impulses of the fancy and imagination which distinguish genius from bare talent, we have abundant evidence in the stories related of his infancy and youth. The child, who in his nurse's arms gazed wonderingly for a few minutes at the comet of 1746, and then lisped out the word "God,"[1] was in truth father of the poet who some forty years later wrote the world-famous **"Ode to God."** But the form and shape which these poetic impulses assumed could only be in accordance with the literary traditions and spirit of the age. At the time when he began writing, Russia could not boast of more than one poet, and it would have been next to impossible for Derzhavin to do otherwise than take Lomonosoff as his model and master. And even when he felt, to refer once more to words that have been already quoted, the impossibility of maintaining the lofty style peculiar to the Russian Pindar, and "struck out for himself a completely new path," we must not suppose that he altogether escaped the influence of his great precursor. Derzhavin in point of date is the first Russian poet-artist, and in some of his works we observe an originality both in the choice and in the treatment of his subject, but in general his verse preserves that didactic and rhetorical character which is the dominant trait in the poetry of Lomonosoff.[2]

Nor must it be forgotten that these bursts of rhetoric and these moral tags, which excite a smile or oftener provoke a yawn on the part of modern readers, were the necessary adjuncts of all Russian poetry in the earlier stages of its development. The poet then held a position quite different from that which he now occupies. He was expected to show a reason for the existence of his art. It was not enough to sing, for then he would only rank in public estimation among the ordinary caterers for the amusement of royalty and the aristocracy; but if the poet wished to obtain any real hold on the national mind, it was necessary first to prove that his art was beneficial and useful to the country at large. Art as mere art was not understood, still less appreciated; the beautiful was considered to be a vain thing, unless it could be shown to be also profitable; and accordingly we find Derzhavin and his contemporaries constantly insisting on the utility of the fine arts. It is for this reason that in **"An Invitation to Dinner,"** after having promised his guest the most varied and luxurious dishes,

the enumeration of which alone would have whetted the appetite of a Lucullus, he concludes with the copybook reflection that "happiness does not consist in sumptuous fare, and that moderation is the best of feasts." Many of his so-called odes are not odes at all, but simply moral homilies; and his celebrated **"Ode to God"** is for the most part an exposition in rhyme of the subtlest dogmas of the Christian faith, reminding us alternately of Klopstock's "Messias" and Young's "Night Thoughts." "To read such pieces," Belinsky remarks, "is dull work enough, and is very like reading a rhymed manual of arithmetic; we of course agree with the author that two and two make four, but none the less regret that such simple venerable truths are not set forth in plain prose rather than in ornate verse."[3] But such was the literary creed, and Poushkin is the first of Russian poets who departed from the tradition that poetry must be moral and didactic.

Derzhavin is the chronicler of Russian life in the eighteenth century. While reading him, we become acquainted with its habits and customs, take part in its triumphs, mix with its chief characters, and men like Suvaroff, Potemkin, and Kutusoff, cease to be mere historical figures. They stand out the more clearly in his pages, with all that strange feverish energy of theirs which made them to be at one and the same time heroes and sensualists, magnanimous and paltry, chivalrous and savage, because he has given us portraits rather than psychological analyses. The humanity of the poet is, however, circumscribed by reason of the low intellectual condition in which the Russian people then and long afterwards were sunk. We must not expect to find in Derzhavin descriptions of the humble struggling life of the poor. Beyond the limits of the court all was an unknown and unexplored region of barbarous ignorance and sloth; and the civilization of Western Europe had as yet penetrated only among the higher classes of society. A Kolzoff,[4] in the reign of Catherine, would have been an anachronism. The poet of the poor was the product of a later age, when the theories of liberal thinkers had begun, however imperfectly, to be put into practice. "Happy is the man," exclaims the poet in his ode **"To my First Neighbour,"** "whose whole life is one uninterrupted round of gaiety;" and "Drink, eat, and be merry, neighbour, for the time of our life on earth is short and uncertain," is the Epicurean advice in which he counsels his friend to make the best of the good things of this world. To enjoy wealth was then regarded to be the end and aim of existence. Fabulous sums were squandered at court and by the nobility on passing amusements, as when (to cite only one of a hundred instances that might be given) Prince Galitzin celebrated his marriage by the erection on the Neva of an ice palace, in which a series of balls and masquerades was given. The most exalted personages gladly lent themselves to sports and pastimes in which we should have thought children alone could have found any pleasure;

and Derzhavin relates how, "whilst the Empress Anne was one morning attending service in the palace chapel, two or three court favourites squatted down in large wicker baskets in a room through which her Majesty had to pass on her return and saluted her appearance with a clucking chorus, which excited loud and general mirth."[5]

It is then the frivolities, riot, and dissipations of aristocratic society, portrayed with something of the grace Horace has given to his pictures of Roman life, that form the favourite theme of Derzhavin's poetry. But his descriptions are mostly coloured with a tone of melancholy suggested by the thought that all the pleasures of life are transitory and ephemeral. At each of those gay banquets, where mirth and laughter seem to be the only guests, death with his scythe is present, and "where but now the feast was spread there stands a coffin." Of course, any such antitheses must strike us as being a rhetorical affectation that has long lost whatever power it might once possess to touch or even instruct the reader. But rhetoric played so important a part in the literature of the eighteenth century, that the contemporaries of Derzhavin expected a writer to indulge in these cheap contrasts, and believed them to form the necessary constituents of all true poetry. "To a modern poet," as Belinsky has shrewdly remarked, "the puzzle of life presents itself under a different aspect."[6] But, true to his age and to the traditions of the life he enjoyed, it is the death of the rich man, and never of the beggar, that Derzhavin describes. He writes of that which his own experiences had taught him, and he treats of themes likely to interest the narrow circle to whom a poet could then address himself.

But if these constitute the dominant traits of Derzhavin's poetry, they are accompanied with other qualities of a higher and rarer order, springing like the first from his own actual experience and knowledge of life. The dignity of man in the abstract, apart from any accidental favours that fortune may shower upon him, is never lost sight of by the poet. The rise and fall of favourites at court, the capricious inconstancy of sovereigns that makes of yesterday's idol the disgraced of to-day, and like casualties which he had himself so often witnessed, forced the poet to search for something durable, solid, and true in the midst of all this change and deception. Beneath the weaknesses and inconsistencies that mar the best of us, he recognizes the presence of those aspirations that lend a dignity to human nature. Nor does he, like many of his contemporaries in Western Europe, fall into a tone of sentimental exaggeration, but his eulogy of the manly is invariably expressed in a manly and simple way. His conception of human perfection is based on the harmony of the instincts of our nature with the conduct of our life, in whose regulation duty is

our sovereign and truth our god. And this is the ideal that he proposes to himself in his charming poem, entitled **"My Bust"**:—

> Honest fame is to me a joy;
> I wish to be a man,
> Whose heart the poison of passion
> Is powerless to corrupt;
> Whom neither gain can blind,
> Nor rank, nor hate, nor the glitter of wealth;
> Whose only teacher is truth;
> Who, loving himself, loves all the world,
> With a pure enlightened love,
> That is not slothful in good works.

In the same spirit, and with all the force of our own Burns, he elsewhere ridicules the titled fool who imagines that rank can condone for folly, and in **"The Grand Signor"** bitterly exclaims:—

> The ass will still remain an ass,
> Although you load him with stars,
> And, when you want him to use his mind,
> He can only just prick up his ears.

Nor is it from any lofty pedestal of self-assumed superiority that he preaches the exercise of virtue; but, conscious how sadly he had come short of the standard he had set for his guidance, confesses—

> I have fallen and sunk to the level of my age:
> Forbear, stern sage, to cast stones upon my grave,
> Unless thou thyself be more than man.

With such views of life and such an appreciation of human nature, it was impossible for Derzhavin to be narrow-minded or intolerant in questions and dogmas of religion. Indeed, to judge from certain passages occurring in his **"Autobiographical Sketches,"** we may conclude that at a comparatively early period in his life Derzhavin was inclined to scepticism; and, though in pieces like his **"Ode to God"** he proclaimed his adherence to the nicest doctrines of Christianity, many of his later compositions are characterized by that spirit of doubt which was as natural to Derzhavin's age as it is to our own. None of his poems produced a stronger or more favourable impression on his contemporaries than the ode just referred to. It was quickly translated into nearly every European language, and was even put into Japanese by Admiral Golovine during his captivity at Jeddo.[7] That the ode is in places marked by a rare boldness and majesty of language, few who have ever read it will be disposed to deny; but it is far too declamatory, and, if it exhibits the power of the lyrical poet, it not seldom—as in the line which so sorely puzzled the poor Japanese to whom Golovine read his translation, where God is declared to be "impersonal in the three Persons of the Godhead"—lacks that simplicity of conception which should underlie the exposition of a faith. The very emphasis of his belief, as expressed in this ode, stands out in such striking contrast with the dreamy mystic scepticism which characterized the later years of his life, that we are almost tempted to suspect the poet of trying to force himself into the belief that he believed. Passages like the following, which is taken from his **"Lines in Memory of Kutusoff,"** written as late as 1813—

> And this was the genius that made his age a glorious
>   one!
> But where is now the soul, the fire, the strength?
> And what is man,
> Whose final end is the grave,
> Whose whole being is a patch of earth?—

impress us as being more in accordance with the poet's natural bent of mind. And this same tone of feeling runs through his **"Monody on Prince Mestchasky,"** the finest and most characteristic of all his compositions:—

> O iron tongue of Time, with thy sharp metallic tone,
> Thy terrible voice affrights me!
> Each beat of the clock summons me,
> Calls me, and hurries me to the grave.
> Scarcely have I opened my eyes upon the world,
> Ere Death grinds its teeth,
> And with his scythe, that gleams like lightning,
> Cuts off my days, which are but grass.
>
> Not one of the horned beasts of the field,
> Not a single blade of grass escapes,
> Monarch and beggar alike are food for the worm.
> The noxious elements feed the grave,
> And Time effaces all human glory;
> As the swift waters rush towards the sea,
> So our days and years flow into Eternity,
> And Empires are swallowed up by greedy Death.
>
> We crawl along the edge of the treacherous abyss,
> Into which we quickly fall headlong:
> With our first breath of life we inhale death,
> And are only born that we may die.
> Stars are shivered by him,
> And suns are momentarily quenched,
> Each world trembles at his menace,
> And Death unpityingly levels all.
>
> The mortal scarcely thinks that he can die,
> And idly dreams himself immortal,
> When death comes to him as a thief,
> And in an instant robs him of his life.
> Alas, where fondly we fear the least,
> There will Death the sooner come;
> Nor does the lightning-bolt with swifter blast
> Topple down the towering pinnacle.
>
> Child of luxury, child of freshness and delight,
> Mestchasky, where hast thou hidden thyself?
> Thou hast left the realms of light,
> And withdrawn to the shores of the dead;
> Thy dust is here, but thy soul is no more with us.
> Where is it? It is there. Where is there? We know not.
> We can only weep and sob forth,
> Woe to us that we were ever born into the world!

> They who are radiant with health,
> Love and joy and peace,
> Feel their blood run cold
> And their souls to be fretted with woe.
> Where but now was spread a banquet, there stands a
>   coffin:
> Where but now rose mad cries of revelry,
> There resounds the bitter wailing of mourners;
> And over all keeps Death his watch:
>
> Watches us one and all,—the mighty Tsar
> Within whose hands are lodged the destinies of a
>   world;
> Watches the sumptuous Dives,
> Who makes of gold and silver his idol-gods;
> Watches the fair beauty rejoicing in her charms;
> Watches the sage, proud of his intellect;
> Watches the strong man, confident in his strength;
> And, even as he watches, sharpens the blade of his
>   scythe.
>
> O Death, thou essence of fear and trembling!
> O Man, thou strange mixture of grandeur and of
>   nothing-ness!
> To-day a god, and to-morrow a patch of earth:
> To-day buoyed up with cheating hope,
> And to-morrow, where art thou, man?
> Scarce an hour of triumph allowed thee,
> Ere thou hast taken thy flight to the realms of Chaos,
> And thy whole course of life, a dream, is run.
>
> Like a dream, like some sweet vision,
> Already my youth has vanished quite.
> Beauty no longer enjoys her potent sway,
> Gladness no more, as once, entrances me,
> My mind is no longer free and fanciful,
> And all my happiness is changed.
> I am troubled with a longing for fame;
> I listen; the voice of fame now calls me.
>
> But even so will manhood pass away,
> And together with fame all my aspirations.
> The love of wealth will tarnish all,
> And each passion in its turn
> Will sway the soul, and pass.
> Avaunt happiness, that boasts to be within our grasp!
> All happiness is but evanescent and a lie:
> I stand at the gate of eternity.
>
> To-day or to-morrow we must die,
> Perfilieff, and all is ended.
> Why, then, lament or be afflicted
> That thy friend did not live for ever?
> Life is but a momentary loan from heaven:
> Spend it then in resignation and in peace,
> And with a pure soul
> Learn to kiss the chastening rod.[8]

Derzhavin was regarded by his contemporaries as the poet of the court, and Gogol has aptly styled him "the panegyrist of the great."[9] He himself counted it as his highest honour "to have sung the glory of three sovereigns," and in one of his odes dedicated to Catherine boasts that "linked with thy name mine shall be immortal." We have nearly outlived the fashion of palace and laureate singers, but in the age of Derzhavin, as with us under Elizabeth and the Georges, poets were expected to be courtly and to find in the reigning sovereign a model of every Christian virtue. There is, moreover, a great difference to be observed in the tone and style of his odes to Catherine, when compared with the poems in which he celebrates some national event or some incident of court life. In the former the eulogy is as honourable to the writer as it is to the person to whom it is offered. The playfulness with which he describes the pursuits and character of the Empress in **"Felicia"**—a poem, it must be remembered, which was not intended for publication[10]—and the entire absence of that fulsome adulation with which despotic sovereigns are habitually approached, amply testify the sincerity of the poet's praise. "Though I have written," says Derzhavin in his **Memoirs,** "many poems in her honour, yet I never failed, by means of allegory or under some such slight veil, to tell her plain truths, for which reason I imagine my verses were not altogether pleasing to her."[11] The latter, on the contrary, are nothing more than official tributes of homage, and it would be as unjust to dwell upon their insincerity as it would be ridiculous to expect to find in them real poetry. The trivial circumstances that frequently formed a pretext for their composition—as, for example, the arrival of a Grand Duchess in St. Petersburg from a tour abroad—sufficiently measure their true value. The poet himself would seem to have felt this, since he has made his style to reflect the difference; the language of the Catherine odes being as light, unaffected, and graceful, as that of the panegyrical odes is stilted, artificial, and sonorous. Nor should we forget that the poems which most offend in this respect were written towards the close of his literary career. In his earlier days, before he was obliged to flatter the great or to lose his reward, he disdained to offer adulation that could only be considered an unworthy and interested homage; and in his **"Epistle to Schuvaloff"** he proudly refuses to play the sycophant's part.

> Pardon me, that I dare to speak with such rude boldness;
> But the smooth harmony of lying verse is like the charm of Circe.
> Words of adulation addressed in praise of the great,
> Unaccompanied by wise counsel, are a poisonous incense.

Derzhavin, not altogether without reason, prided himself on having been "the first who dared in humorous verse to sing of Felicia's virtues, in simple language of the heart to speak of God, or laughingly to tell the truth to Tsars." This boast is, of course, applicable only to certain of his poems, but in his best compositions it is impossible not to be struck with the colloquialness of his diction. "My muse," he tells us, "cares not to deck herself in gorgeous robes, and I sing no pompous song." He constantly employs words taken from the speech of the people, and does not scruple, in order to render the

idea more picturesque, to invent an expressive term. Thus, in **"Felicia,"** speaking of his heroine's sobriety of manners, he eulogizes her in that she is not too fond of masquerades, and does not care, at the sacrifice of dignity, to *donquixotize* herself. Occasionally, this simplicity of language is pushed to an extravagance, as when, in the same poem, Felicia is represented as finding "poetry to be as pleasant, sweet, and useful as a draught of lemonade in summer heat." The same mixture of the lofty and trivial, admissible in a light sketch similar to **"Felicia,"** characterizes some of the graver poems, in one of which, speaking of the pride that fills a man when, some great work accomplished, he looks back on all the difficulties he has surmounted, the poet adds: "And even whilst thou art contentedly twirling thy moustaches, death awaits thee for his guest." But, as has been already observed, we must not suppose that Derzhavin altogether abandoned the use of that inflated diction which was in his age thought to be the essence of true poetry. It is in his patriotic odes, as we should expect, that his style becomes most strained and bombastic; and to heighten their effect, the poet executed a number of designs intended to illustrate his descriptions of Russian heroism. In one of the engravings Vesuvius is represented as being in a state of eruption, and we have a Russian grenadier marching against the revolutionary volcano with fixed bayonet; the brave hero having already overthrown the pillars of Hercules, the ruins of which are depicted in the background.

Such extravagances, however, must not blind us to the grandeur of conception, the vivacity of style, and the lofty moral tone that characterize the principal poems and odes of Derzhavin. Intimately connected with the events of his own life, or with the more striking incidents of contemporary history, their historical signification and moral value have remained unimpaired by any changes that have come over Russian society, belief, or customs; and they still aid in the interpretation of those great deeds which made the age of Catherine the most glorious epoch in the annals of the poet's country.

Notes

1. [Gavriil Romanovich Derzhavin] *Works* [*Sochineniia Derzhavina,* edited by Ia. K. Grot (Sanktpeterburg: Izd. Imp. Akademii nauk, 1864-83], iii. 476.

2. [V. G.] Belinsky, *Collected Works* [*Sochineniia V. G. Bielinskago* (Kiev: Tip. F. A. Iogansona, 1902)], vii. 84.

3. *Collected Works,* vii. 71.

4. Those of my readers who wish to know more of Kolzoff (1809—1842), "the Russian Burns," as Bodenstedt has styled him, are referred to Mr. Ralston's interesting article, "A Russian Poet," in the *Fortnightly Review* for September 15, 1866.

5. *Works,* iii. 482.

6. *Collected Works,* vii. 116.

7. *Works,* i. 134.

8. Prince Mestchasky, president of the magistracy at St. Petersburg, was noted for the luxurious life he led, and died very suddenly in 1779, when Derzhavin wrote this ode to his memory, dedicating it to General Perfilieff, the prince's most intimate friend.

9. Gogol's *Works* (St. Petersburg Edition of 1867), iii. 505.

10. *Works,* i. 91.

11. Galachoff, "History of Russian Literature," i. 527.

Peter Kropotkin (essay date 1905)

SOURCE: Kropotkin, Peter. Introduction to *Russian Literature: Ideals and Realities,* pp. 1-39. London: Duckworth and Company, 1916.

[*In the following excerpt, originally published in 1905, Kropotkin remarks briefly on the faults and virtues of Derzhavin's poetry.*]

The poetry of Derzhávin certainly does not answer our modern requirements. He was the poet-laureate of Catherine, and sang in pompous odes the virtues of the ruler and the victories of her generals and favourites. Russia was then taking a firm hold on the shores of the Black Sea, and beginning to play a serious part in European affairs; so that occasions for the inflation of Derzhávin's patriotic feelings were not wanting. However, he had some of the marks of the true poet; he was open to the feeling of the poetry of nature, and capable of expressing it in verses that were positively good (**"Ode to God," "The Waterfall"**). Nay, these really poetical verses, which are found side by side with unnatural, heavy lines stuffed with obsolete pompous words, are so evidently better than the latter, that they certainly were an admirable object-lesson for all subsequent Russian poets. They must have contributed to induce our poets to abandon mannerism. Púshkin, who in his youth admired Derzhávin, must have felt at once the disadvantages of a pompous style, illustrated by his predecessor, and with his wonderful command of his mother tongue he was necessarily brought to abandon the artificial language which formerly was considered 'poetical'—he began to write as we speak.

V. V. Vinogradov (essay date 1969)

SOURCE: Vinogradov, V. V. "The Mid-Eighteenth Century: Normalization and Disintegration of the Three Styles." In *The History of the Russian Literary Language from the Seventeenth Century to the Nineteenth,* translated and adapted by Lawrence L. Thomas, pp. 55-85. Madison: University of Wisconsin Press, 1969.

[*In the following excerpt, Vinogradov surveys linguistic aspects of Derzhavin's poetry.*]

12. Intrusion of the Colloquial Language into the Middle and High Styles. The Language of Deržavin

The question of redistribution of functions between the high Slavonic style and living speech (which sometimes shifted into peasant dialect) had an original solution in the language of a great poet of the end of the eighteenth century, G. R. Deržavin. In his language, one may note a number of grammatical devices which clearly "simplify" and "lower" the high style. They are a far cry from the refinements of the fashionable, noble salon.

In the first place, Deržavin used reflexive forms of verbs which, according to Lomonosov's theory, should not have them. Lomonosov preferred that reflexive forms be restricted to Slavonic verbs; Deržavin used them with conversational verbs which had a concrete, everyday meaning (Сколько с Нею Ни *делюсь* [instead of разделен]; Лель упорстбом *рассердился*). He used the colloquial form of the present adverbial participle even with verbs from the high and middle styles (блистаючи, побеждаючи). He formed adverbial participles in -*я, -а* not only from prefixed verbs in -*ить,* but also from verbs of other categories, regardless of whether they were Russian or Slavonic (разлиясь, низбержась). He also had a mixture of forms, of various stylistic coloring, in his participles. Alongside archaic Slavonic participles like тборяй, создабьый, седящ, ядущий, one finds participial formations from conversational verbs. Deržavin frequently used colloquial declensional forms of neuter nouns of the type бремя (б бодах и б *пламе*; жниц с *знамем* идуюих). He employed genitive plurals in -*еб, -об* from feminine and neuter nouns (зданиеб, стихиеб, кикимороб). And he used such colloquial numerical constructions as На сорок дбух столпах and пребудут б тысячи беках. In regard to conjunctions, it is sufficient to point out the causative use of что, as in these lines from **"Na smert' Bibikova"**:

> Он берно любит добродетель,
> Что пишет ей сбои стихи.

Even more striking is the mixture of Slavonicisms and colloquial terms in Deržavin's lexicon. Alongside expressions like На карты нам плебать пора, one finds Slavonicisms like дщерь, сих утех, предстань. This kind of mixture of high and low style was observed by Gogol': "His style is outstanding as is that of none of our poets; if you open it with a scalpel, you will see that this comes about because of an unusual combination of the very highest words with the very lowest and simplest:

И смерть как гостью ожидает,
Крутя задумабжись усы.

Who, besides Deržavin, would dare to connect such a matter as expectation of death with such a paltry act as the twirling of one's moustache?"

In Deržavin's language, the colloquial appears in all its everyday, familiar impudence; a good example may be found in the poem **"Želanie zimy"**:

На кабаке Борея
Эол ударил б нюни:
От бяхи той бледнея,
Бог хлада слякоть, слюни
Из глотки источил,
Бсю землю замочил.
Узря ту Осень шутку,
Их б прабду драться нудит,
Подняб пред нами юбку,
Дожди, как реки, прудит,
Плеща им б рожи грязь,
Как дуракам смеясь . . .

Deržavin also combined Slavonic and Russian expressions in parodistic antithesis; he provided humorous examples of intimate dialogue; and he occasionally used terms from regional dialects.

An interesting characterization of Deržavin's language is provided by V. G. Belinskij:

In Deržavin's poetry one already hears and feels the sounds and pictures of Russian nature—but mixed with some sort of Greek mythology distorted in the French manner. For example, let us take the beautiful ode **"Osen' vo vremja osady Očakova."** What a strange picture of purely Russian nature with Lord knows what kind of nature, of charming poetry with incomprehensible rhetoric:

Спустил седой Эол Борея
С цепей чугунных из пещер;
У жасные крыле расширя,
Махнул по сбету богатырь;
Погнал стадами боздух синий,
Сгустил туманы б облака,
Дабнул—и облака расселись.
Спустился дождь и босшумел.

What are Aeolus, and Boreas, and caverns, and cast-iron chains doing here? Don't ask: why were powder, beauty-spots, and farthingales necessary? Because, in those days, you couldn't show your face without them. And how that Russian word "bogatyr'" clashes with that foreigner "Boreas"!

The living language, before Puškin, did not directly submit to organic unification with the literary language. It was not organized, not adapted to the expression of abstract ideas. It could not, in its raw state, become the semantic center of a complexly structured literary language. Moreover, the everyday colloquial language

seemed too low and coarse for the society of the salon. The upper levels of society, toward the end of the eighteenth century, thus came to the conclusion that the bonding element which would unite national Russian speech and unavoidable Slavonicisms into a literary language would be French—the leading language of European civilization.

Pierre R. Hart (essay date 1978)

SOURCE: Hart, Pierre R. "Songs of Simple Pleasures." In *G. R. Derzhavin: A Poet's Progress*, pp. 99-137. Columbus, Ohio: Slavica Publishers, Inc., 1978.

[*In the following excerpt, Hart analyzes Derzhavin's Anacreontic poetry and provides close readings of several poems. Hart's book also presents an overview of Derzhavin's poetic development.*]

ANACREONTIC VERSE

We have already noted several early instances of Derzhavin's use of Anacreontic verse, but he did not begin to cultivate the genre intensively until the 1790's. In part, his increased interest resulted from N. A. Lvov's translation of the *Anacreonta* in 1794; this collection served as the basis for Derzhavin's subsequent translations, as well as his variations on the original poems. Before that time, he seems to have been inspired by a variety of works in the Anacreontic vein produced by his contemporaries. According to the poet, one of his very first love lyrics—**"To Nina,"** written while he was still a soldier in 1770—was an imitation of an ode by the German poet Friedrich Klopstock, although we do not know which one. Whatever his first sources, Derzhavin's early Anacreontic verse was quite imitative and appeared more of a literary exercise than anything else. Only an occasional bit of detail hints at the immediate emotional involvement which would distinguish the Anacreontic poetry of his later years. In its tenor, the early poetry produced that slightly learned effect that has consistently rendered the *Anacreontea* suspect as truly expressive lyric verse.[1] The mature poet's work in this genre, however, seems closer in spirit to the surviving fragments of Anacreon's own poetry on which the later *Anacreontea* were based.[2] There is a sense of immediacy in the poet's description of those objects and activities which attest to the splendor of life. Whether he is conveying his feelings for his beloved or simply expressing delight at the sight of young maidens dancing, Derzhavin is convincingly concrete.

Derzhavin regarded a wide range of expression as appropriate to Anacreontic verse, for he included one hundred and nine poems in the separate volume of ***Anacreontic Songs***.[3] We should, however, note that the collection does not contain all the Anacreontic verse he had written up to then. One very significant omission is **"An Excursion in Tsarskoe Selo,"** which, in addition to its skillful recall of pleasurable experience in the royal gardens, is important as the first of Derzhavin's Anacreontic poems to use the iambic trimeter favored by both Lomonosov and Sumarokov for this genre.[4] On the other hand, he included some works which hardly qualify as Anacreontic verse, for instance the fifteen poems immediately following the dedication, "A Present to Beauties," which are occasional verse written in celebration of royal events. Although Derzhavin claimed that they were composed for his own satisfaction and without the knowledge of the court,[5] they are public declamations reminiscent of the solemn ode. The first of these, **"On the Birth of a Royal Son in the North,"** is, as we have already seen, a product of the period in which its author was still actively experimenting with the ode; but the others fall between 1793 and 1801, when Derzhavin was gradually dissociating his poetic from his civic role. It is therefore necessary to assess the relative weight of continued civic involvement indicated by the inclusion of these fifteen poems as contrasted with the disavowal of civic intentions which figures rather prominently in the remainder of the collection.

Among those works more readily associated with the *Anacreontea,* several groupings can be distinguished. The "direct" translations are of primary interest as examples of the poet's effort to create equivalent forms for the Greek verse accessible to him only through Lvov's Russian renderings. Those written as "imitations" of particular poems in the *Anacreontea* are both more numerous and more intriguing: his "To a Little Dove," which he labelled an imitation of Ode IX (15),[6] exploits the central image of the bird for totally different purposes. Derzhavin transforms the dove, a willing captive of Apollo in the original, into a symbol for the defense of serfdom! Derzhavin's tendency to adapt themes to his own purposes is equally apparent in other works which, although not labeled imitations, take their inspiration from specific poems in the *Anacreontea.* **"To the Lyre"** is an adaptation of the ode previously used by Lomonosov in pressing his case for civic verse in his "Conversation with Anacreon." While we cannot be certain that Derzhavin's choice of models was deliberate, his restatement of the original opposition of private and public sentiment invites comparison with Lomonosov's approach.

Finally, there is a considerable body of poetry which, in varying degree, reflects Derzhavin's creative assimilation of the Anacreontic spirit. The best of these verses may employ themes that are quite insignificant in the *Anacreontea,* but they convey the same *joie de vivre.* The visual and aural representation of dancing maidens in **"Russian Maidens,"** for example, is among

Derzhavin's finest achievements in the genre. Here, as elsewhere in the collection, a sense of personal witness makes the poem very effective. The "occasional" nature of the first fifteen odes is, in fact, a distinguishing feature of the entire collection. Whether the event is public or private, it is usually presented as a single, sharply delineated moment, and this infuses a feeling of immediacy into Derzhavin's verse that is conspicuously lacking in the vague accounts of frolics of handsome youths and charming maidens in the *Anacreontea.*

In their thematic diversity, the **Anacreontic Songs** represent the culmination of the genre's evolution over half a century. Virtually from the time of its introduction into Russian literature, Anacreontic verse had served as a vehicle for the treatment of subjects other than the traditional wine, women, and song. During the 1760's, for example, M. M. Kheraskov and poets close to him wrote meditations on philosophic questions cast in this genre. Masonic conviction led them ultimately to reject worldly pleasure in favor of more enduring spiritual values, but they accomplished this in their verse without abandoning the Anacreontic form.[7] This early propensity to dissociate what René Wellek and Austin Warren term the "outer" from the "inner" form raises the question of the genre's integrity.[8] G. A. Gukovsky contended that the Russian Anacreontic, unlike its European counterparts, could only be defined in terms of its distinctive metric features, so diverse were its themes.[9] Gukovsky's discussion is flawed, however, by his studious omission of any works by Derzhavin which retain the thematic conventions of the Anacreontic while dispensing with the features he defines as essential. Nonetheless, Gukovsky's remarks are valuable for their emphasis upon the significance of vocabulary, syntax, and verse structure in evoking the Anacreontic spirit. In works such as **"On the Birth of a Royal Son in the North,"** Derzhavin effectively exploited these features to elaborate upon a theme which had traditionally been regarded as within the province of the solemn ode.

To appreciate better the fashion in which Derzhavin modified Anacreontic verse while retaining its distinctive spirit, we might briefly summarize the genre's prosodic features in Russian verse of the eighteenth century. As C. L. Drage has pointed out,[10] Lomonosov, despite his declared aversion to the themes of the *Anacreontea,* rendered the verse forms of the original Greek quite successfully with iambic trimeters in his first two original responses of the "Conversation with Anacreon." Since the iambic meters had been preferred to the trochaic before the 1760's, when the Anacreontic first became popular, its specific metrical scheme would appear to be of less significance than its relatively short line. The great majority of Anacreontic poems were composed in either trimeter or tetrameter. Derzhavin departed from this practice by writing half of his poems in trochaic tetrameter, but they produce the same effect of light, rapid movement. The relative brevity and lack of stanzaic divisions in the original *Anacreontea* further contributed to their lyric mood. Although these conventions were widely accepted by Russian poets, Derzhavin sometimes used stanzas, and he frequently violated the practice of employing unrhymed lines with fixed feminine endings as an approximation of the original Greek verse form.[11]

Derzhavin's early preference for the solemn ode prompted him to incorporate features from other genres into it instead of experimenting with various lyric forms as independent entities. In both **"On the Birth of a Royal Son in the North"** and **"Felitsa,"** he was partially successful; but his lapse into the conventions of the panegyric in the latter half of each ode indicates that he found such fusions difficult to sustain. Derzhavin made a further attempt to combine Anacreontic features with those of the panegyric during the 1780's: while **"A Portrayal of Felitsa"** is decidedly less successful than either of the earlier works, it is of interest as a response to Lomonosov's prescription of civic themes for the genre. The product of that difficult period in 1789 when Derzhavin's performance as a provincial administrator was under investigation, the ode is an obvious attempt to win Catherine's favor through flattery. Yet its artistic weakness stems less from its underlying conceit than its execution as an extremely lengthy and tedious work. Lomonosov, we will recall, had taken issue with the *Anacreontea*'s praise of feminine beauty in Ode XXVIII (16), summoning the Russian poets to concentrate instead upon the praise of their native land. In the first seven stanzas of **"A Portrayal of Felitsa,"** Derzhavin combines the original's praise of particular beauty with Lomonosov's civic recommendation by creating a portrait of Catherine that symbolizes the glory of the Russian state. As does the original, he appeals to the painter to produce a visual image which will convey all his subject's most striking qualities. To be sure, the Greek poet speaks of those features relating to pleasurable sensual experience, as in the lines:

> For her cheeks and nose to render
> Mingle rose-leaves with the cream;
> And that the lip like hers may seem,
> Make it what Persuasion's is,
> Provocation to a kiss.[12]

Derzhavin's instructions to the painter Raphael stress the necessity of capturing moral qualities by visual means. The couplet on the rendering of Catherine's lips, for example, recommends a fusion of the physical with the abstract: "Show how wisdom and love are to her lips / As the fragrance of a rose" (I, 273). The composite is, then, a compromise between the grand abstractions of the conventional panegyric and the intimate detail of the love lyric.

It is especially noteworthy that Derzhavin deliberately attempted to realize Lomonosov's prescription for the Anacreontic at such a late date. As our analysis of **"A Mirza's Vision"** suggests, an element of dissatisfaction with the poet's role as civic spokesman began to appear in Derzhavin's verse toward the end of the 1780's, at which point he began asserting the poet's importance in his verse instead of contenting himself with the panegyrist's impersonal stance. The "jocular Russian style" of **"Felitsa"** gave way to a sharper and more self-assertive tone as Derzhavin strove to transmit to his reader a more personal view of life and society. His renewed interest in the *Anacreontea,* roughly simultaneous with this shift, might be considered a further attempt at adequate expression of personal sentiment within the genres he had previously favored. Anacreontic poetry became an important forum through which Derzhavin offered his reflections on the conflict between the self-denial of public service and private fulfillment. In a series of such poems, written over some fifteen years, his initial irresolution yielded to clear assertion of the legitimacy of emotional experience as one basis for artistic expression.

We can better gauge the change in Derzhavin's attitude by comparing **"A Portrayal of Felitsa"** with another poem, inspired by Lomonosov's "Conversation with Anacreon" written in 1797. **"To the Lyre"** is an adaptation of the second Anacreontic ode in which Lomonosov had set forth the necessity for choice between public and private themes. In the context of Derzhavin's poetry, **"To the Lyre"** may be seen as the result of a deliberate decision as to his artistic direction. Though the work contains elements of both the Anacreontic and the panegyric, they are assessed quite differently than in either **"On the Birth"** [**"On the Birth of a Royal Son in the North"**] or **"A Portrayal of Felitsa."** **"To the Lyre"** ends by rejecting the proposition that the original impulses of the *Anacreontea* should be harnessed in the service of civic verse.

In its presentation, the poem moves from the panegyric's impersonal celebration of heroic deeds to the lyric's expression of private emotional experience. The poet strengthens his suggestion of changing preferences by effectively dividing the poem into equal parts through the use of past and future tenses. The first half offers a retrospective view of the author's original plan and of those historical events which had prevented its realization. The remaining lines, by contrast, anticipate Derzhavin's subsequent awareness of the difficulties facing the civic poet. Described as a "paeon" (*pokhvala*) to two of the author's favorite heroes, Generals Rumyantsev and Suvorov, the poem in its opening lines creates a mood appropriate to the solemn ode. A lyre resounds with thunder and fire flashes from its strings. The effect can scarcely be mistaken for the gentle lyre's sound in the original Anacreontic ode. The sense of the opening lines is appropriate to the glorification of statesmen. At the same time, the trochaic tetrameter line characteristic of Derzhavin's Anacreontic verse creates the same dissonance between style and theme as that observed in the latter half of **"On the Birth of a Royal Son in the North."** In the present instance, however, the problem does not persist for, just when the poem has reached the point of filling Lomonosov's civic prescription, it abruptly shifts thematically.

The immediate explanation for Derzhavin's abandonment of his original theme was Rumyantsev's death and Suvorov's imperial disfavor.[13] But the poet was obviously aware of these facts from the outset, and since he still chose to praise the two men, the break only serves to accentuate the deliberate nature of the poem's construction. "Jealous fate" *(zavistlivaia sud'ba),* which Derzhavin blames for his heroes' change of fortune, may be responsible for affecting the poet's activity as well. Without directly implicating the throne, Derzhavin makes it clear that external circumstances have prevented the further development of his intended theme. The remainder of the poem then advocates an entirely different sort of poetry, much closer in spirit to that of the opening lines of **"On the Birth of a Royal Son in the North."**

The assertion of interest in poetry based upon emotion at the conclusion of **"To the Lyre"** is most important, for it continues as a dominant element in the verse written in the final two decades of Derzhavin's career. The juxtaposition of civic and personal considerations differs in its implication from that found in either the original *Anacreontea* or in Lomonosov's "Conversation with Anacreon." Each of the latter presumed that the poet, when confronted by the necessity of voicing either public or private sentiments, would respond instinctively in an unambiguous manner. Thus, while Lomonosov admitted that he was subject to the same sort of personal feeling that had inspired the original poet, he still declared that his own inspiration stemmed from the heroic accomplishments of great men:

> Although I am not lacking
> Love's heartfelt tenderness,
> I am more inspired
> By heroes' eternal glory.[14]

Derzhavin's poem, on the other hand, does not treat the question of inspiration directly, and the poet has chosen his themes quite deliberately, as the final lines of "To the Lyre" indicate. At first glance, the poet's position seems self-deprecating, as though he were doubtful of his ability to enhance the glory of public figures: "Without us the world will not forget / Their immortal deeds" (255). This very statement, however, calls attention to their accomplishments without becoming a panegyric to the disgraced Suvorov, which would only incur the monarch's disfavor. Derzhavin redirects his attention to songs of love, then, for that is both politically expedient

and poetically more productive. The poet might pursue private themes with equanimity, investing in them a talent and inspiration which might be wasted or severely compromised in the realm of civic verse.

This was not the first occasion on which Derzhavin had appealed to the Anacreontic in considering the various functions of verse. One of his first attempts to deal with this problem was the deceptively playful **"Philosophers, Drunken and Sober,"** which, Derzhavin maintained, was composed for no other purpose than to represent the opposing philosophies of Aristippus and Aristides. Derzhavin uses the lives of the hedonistic philosopher and the Athenian statesman, rather than any explicitly articulated code of conduct attributable to them, as the basis for his poem. As they are presented, the alternative life styles are universal in their application—and yet we sense an element of the poet's personal uncertainty. The poem remained unfinished, but such things as the incomplete stanza that was to continue the drunken philosopher's argument contain much to suggest that Derzhavin was partial to the hedonist's position.[15]

The work consists of alternating statements by the two philosophers, in which each attempts to convince the other of the validity of his position. The drunken philosopher initiates the debate by rejecting the conventional values of wealth, fame, and rank in favor of the life of pleasure. His sober counterpart immediately defends these goals as worthy of human ambition, so long as they are pursued in moderation. In ensuing stanzas the discussion treats the more specific question of service to one's country in time of war, and the final pair of stanzas deals with the administration of justice. On both issues, the sober philosopher rebuts criticisms of the existing order or encourages its reform. At this point the poem abruptly ends without resolution, except that the sober philosopher has had (in the published version at least) the last word.

The primary point at issue here, then, is the individual's civic obligation. The drunken philosopher makes it clear that his awareness of society's corruption is as much a cause of his attitude as is his positive appreciation of life's pleasures. That awareness complicates what might otherwise be regarded as a straightforward opposition of values. If society is corrupt, one may either participate in its reform or withdraw from it. The sober philosopher urges the former course of action, but his opponent speaks in disillusionment: he has turned to the more rewarding pursuit of pleasure after having been frustrated in his attempts to serve. Thus the poem contains, on the one hand, the sober philosopher's appeal to patriotism and self-sacrifice, which must certainly have struck a responsive chord among the nationally conscious readers of eighteenth century Russia; and, on the other, the drunken philosopher's argument that society's faults quite justify the individual's withdrawal from it especially when there are such attractive alternatives. The latter concludes each of his statements with a bacchanalian chant emphasizing wine's palpable qualities, in characteristic Anacreontic style:

> How wonderfully foams the wine!
> What taste, bouquet, and color it has!
> Why should the hours be lost in vain?
> Let's pour, my dear neighbor!

> (130)

Wine, not the "bestial poison" of fame, is the preferred drink of this philosopher. The choice posed in such jocular fashion here anticipates the more serious consideration of the same alternatives which would subsequently appear in Derzhavin's verse.

Perhaps the poet's improved fortunes in the early 1790's caused him temporarily to discontinue exploring the possibility of a life independent of the court. But it is noteworthy that in 1797, the year following Catherine's death, Derzhavin vigorously renewed his poetic consideration of this possibility. Aside from **"To the Lyre,"** he wrote several additional verses in which he set forth the positive value of pleasure in the artist's life. In **"The Gift"** the alternatives confronting the poet are the same as in **"To the Lyre,"** but the poet places greater emphasis on moral considerations as they relate both to the artist's message and his audience's response. As Apollo informs him, the poet must address his songs to the nobility and rulers if he wishes to receive the rewards of wealth and fame. The alternative is to be "loved by beauty" for his praise of pleasure, tranquility, and love. Faced with this choice, the poet invokes truth as the basis for all his works, irrespective of their content:

> I seized the lyre and began to sing,
> The strings began to sound with truth,
> Who wished to heed me?
> Only beautiful women did.

> (261)

Were it not for the mention of "truth", this poem might be simply a restatement of the concluding sentiment of **"To the Lyre."** Here, however, Derzhavin avoids the either/or proposition put to him by Apollo in another, and equally subtle manner—by introducing the notion of artistic integrity as the necessary concomitant of all verse. Presumably the poet may choose to sing of anything which moves him, so the question of response to his song becomes paramount. The claim that only beautiful women appreciate his songs of truth serves indirectly to indict others who have chosen to disregard his verses. Derzhavin's declaration of satisfaction with his lot in the final stanza seems once again to have been dictated by circumstances beyond his control. As in **"To the Lyre,"** the pragmatist in him stresses those means by which artistic goals can be most effectively realized.

"The Laurels of Immortality" (also 1797) is Derzhavin's culminating testament to the value of pleasurable pursuits in the artist's life, and it concludes the ***Anacreontic Songs.*** The figure of Anacreon is closely identified with the poem's narrator, who looks favorably upon many of the activities traditionally celebrated in such verse: the play of beautiful young maidens, the leisurely enjoyment of nature, the company of a handsome youth, and a cup of golden mead. Of particular significance is the fact that this pattern of life has been specifically preferred to wealth and rank. No ruler can offer rewards sufficient to induce the poet to abandon the "tranquility, love, and freedom" which he presently enjoys. While the first two nouns are common in Anacreontic verse, the added mention of freedom underscores the poet's awareness of the particular social conditions necessary for the development of his talent. The proof of his belief in the link between a life of pleasure and creativity lies in the concluding assertion that the poet's claim to immortality is founded precisely upon the cultivation of earthly delights. The figure of Anacreon in this poem may thus represent the artist whose involvement in sacred play is ultimately more productive than any concern with affairs of state.

His increased confidence in the creative stimulus of pleasure may also help to explain those works in which Derzhavin categorically rejects civic involvement. **"Freedom,"** written shortly after Derzhavin's forced retirement, is constructed on approximately the same model as **"To the Lyre,"** although it is divided into stanzas. The trochaic tetrameter with alternating masculine and feminine lines provides the same metric unity. Thematically, the first stanza reinforces the meter's suggestion of mood. Nature provides the setting for the poet's "sweet sleep": the generally tranquil landscape reflects Sentimentalism's influence upon Derzhavin's later verse.[16] Far from being sensually intoxicated, the poet rests in quiet harmony with his surroundings. The initial scene, in which theme and meter combine to produce an impression of serenity, is totally disrupted by the poet's vision in the next two stanzas. All the emotions evoked by the introduction vanish as the poet finds himself standing on an elevation, gazing out over the surrounding landscape. The manner of his description makes it clear that Derzhavin is recalling the heady experience of bureaucratic power which he had so recently known. Yet the vision—a familiar one of title, wealth, and honor—lasts but a short time. As he awakens, the poet disclaims any interest in a position which might deprive him of his freedom and tranquility.

As both **"On the Birth of a Royal Son in the North"** and **"To the Lyre"** have revealed, internal changes of tone are a recurring feature of Derzhavin's works. In **"Freedom,"** however, it is not the panegyrist's rhetoric which alters the prevailing mood; rather the poet's concern with conscience prompts him to speak forcefully about his own situation. The playful poet of the previous decade is no longer evident in the stern speaker who concludes **"Freedom"**: "Then is my power great / If I do not power seek" (292). The cynical reader might be inclined to explain this singular assertion as a mere rationalization, since the poet had so recently been removed from office. We have seen, however, that there is reason to believe that this was a logical, if somewhat strident, culmination to a change in esthetic attitude which had been in the making over the final decade of Derzhavin's career as a civil servant.

Derzhavin's position was not totally consistent in this respect, however. His increasing tendency to disavow any wish for public recognition is not in accord with his continued composition of verses in praise of royalty. He offers his most explicit justification of such writing in **"Conversation with a Genius,"** the last of the fifteen works at the beginning of his *Anacreontic Songs.* This poem is to those preceding it roughly as **"The Laurels of Immortality"** is to the larger group of Anacreontic poems on personal themes: in both instances the poet has a dream conversation with an idealized figure (the genius tsar, Anacreon) in which he reflects upon problems explored previously. In this case, the poet is "enraptured" by his vision of a youthful ruler, who encourages the aging poet once again to use his gifts for the celebration of his rule. The poet unhesitatingly complies. His ethical doubts expressed in other works vanish when the monarch offers him words of confidence, and at the end the poet states his willingness to sing the praises of both the ruler and the nation.

The fact that this conversation occurs in a dream is of particular note in this instance, for, as the poet had previously demonstrated in **"A Mirza's Vision,"** he sometimes employed such a device in order to depict an ideal which might be quite unrealized in fact. The figure of the tsar in **"Conversation with a Genius"** has all the attributes Derzhavin might have envisaged, but his instructions to the elderly poet hint at a disparity between fantasy and reality. In urging the writer to serve him, he first attempts to erase the negative impression possibly left by the actual record of his rule: "I am not the terrible thunderer, / [But] a gentle tsar and man" (II, 390). The particular circumstances which gave rise to this poem[17] do much to explain the combination of reassuring tsar and responsive poet. And while neither this nor the works preceding it in the *Anacreontic Songs* should be ignored, they do not provide a reliable measure of their author's continuing civic conviction. As the products of momentary surges of enthusiasm, they represent the poet's wishful identification of royalty with literary models, including those provided by the *Anacreontea,* and are not necessarily supported by the examples of the rulers themselves.

On another plane, however, Derzhavin's manner of portraying the nation's leaders in his Anacreontic verse attests to an increasing interest in the setting for such figures rather than in the subjects themselves. It is not simply a matter of drawing comparisons between reigning monarchs and mythological figures such as was common in the solemn ode; an examination of the poem **"Ruins"** shows, for example, that Derzhavin transforms the traditional landscape of Anacreontic verse into a realistic depiction of the natural world at Tsarskoe Selo and, with its aid, recalls the image of the departed Catherine. Moreover, if we compare the detail of this work with a similar one of more exclusively personal dimension, **"An Excursion in Tsarskoe Selo,"** the fine gradation between publicly and privately oriented verse becomes apparent. In both instances, the poet's perceptual experience is important to the poem's construction, with other elements depending directly upon it for their effect.

Strangely enough, while Derzhavin included the elegiac **"Ruins"** in *Anacreontic Songs,* he omitted **"An Excursion in Tsarskoe Selo"** despite the latter's more obvious capture of the spirit appropriate to Anacreontic verse. Written five years prior to Catherine's death, in 1791, **"An Excursion in Tsarskoe Selo"** reflects all of the splendor of her favorite residence with only fleeting allegorical mention of the monarch herself. The poem's focus remains firmly fixed on the poet and his beloved "Plenira" (see below) as they revel in the warmth and beauty of a spring day. It is certainly one of Derzhavin's most sprightly and vivid representations of the physical world, and the iambic trimeter in which the poem is written effectively enhances its joyous mood. Abandoning the Anacreontic's stylized references to nature, Derzhavin instead portrays a familiar Russian landscape at a particular moment in time. Beginning with a formal view of the royal buildings and statues as reflected in the water, he passes to visual and aural details which nobody but the perceptive observer might note. Only at the very conclusion does his emphasis shift momentarily, when he pays his respects to God and tsar. This flaw is a minor one, however, and in the poem's final couplet, Derzhavin directs his attention to another author interested in the subjective portrayal of nature, Nikolay Karamzin.

In recalling the cruise which he has enjoyed with his wife, the poet sets the mood for the remainder of his description:

> At evening tide
> Withdrawing from all,
> My young Plenira and I,
> Riding in a little boat
> Went cruising on the little lake:
> She sat in the stern,
> And in the middle, I.
>
> (172)

A reduction in scale, here effected by the use of the diminutives *lodochka* (little boat) and *ozerko* (little lake), is apparent throughout the work. The park is pictured with a panoply of detail which attests to the sensitivity of the poet's perception. Derzhavin's selection of an aquatic vantage point enables him to depict the interplay of water and sky at close range. His preference for metallic colors, on the one hand, and the rich tones of red and purple, on the other, expresses itself in the silver of the water, the ruby of the clouds, the crimson gold of the gilded roofs, and the clear royal purple of the air. Equally pleasurable are the sounds of the splashing fish, the echo of laughter, the trumpeting of horns, and the whisper of brooks. The total effect resembles that of some of Derzhavin's "gourmet" scenes: for him, colors, textures, odors, and sounds are valuable as sensual stimuli, independently of the objects with which they are associated. The poem's concluding apostrophe to Karamzin, while unanticipated, is consistent with the highly subjective nature of the entire poem. Derzhavin exhorts Karamzin to sing so that the nightingale's voice may also be heard in prose, thus implying that every literary genre should bear witness to the pleasures of the senses so central to this poem.

The muted recall of similar sensations informs **"Ruins,"** a poem written shortly after Catherine's death. Using the past tense in all but the final six lines, Derzhavin again depicts the sights and sounds of Tsarskoe Selo, partly from the vantage point of a participant in the courtly life and partly through Catherine's eyes. The result is a more formal portrait than that of **"An Excursion in Tsarskoe Selo"**, but his treatment of the nobility at play is still distinctly positive. Instead of contrasting the late ruler's industry with her courtiers' indolence, Derzhavin creates an idyllic scene in which Catherine participates in the same enjoyable pastimes as her subjects. Once again we hear the distant music of the horns and the cascading sound of the brooks; once again we see some of the same landscape as in **"An Excursion in Tsarskoe Selo."** The primary difference in descriptive emphasis—a direct consideration of official buildings in **"Ruins"**—is consistent with this work's more public orientation. Catherine's inspection of a monument to a military hero, A. G. Orlov-Chesmesky, provides the occasion for a digression on the accomplishments of her military commanders in general. But Derzhavin restrains the panegyric impulse, and so avoids the abrupt shift from jocularity to rhetorical earnestness found in the earlier works. Instead, the poem maintains a stylistic and thematic equilibrium as it commemorates Catherine's rule by briefly describing a variety of physical artifacts. Although the poem's final lines remind us that these are all but pleasant remnants of the past, the body of **"Ruins"** offers an interesting example of Derzhavin's capacity to combine elements of the Anacreontic and the elegy.

Among the Anacreontic themes, Derzhavin exhibits particular originality in his celebration of feminine beauty,

whereas he subdues his praise of the pleasures of drink. Wine and drinking are mentioned, but often in connection with other themes which draw attention away from the notion of intoxication as pleasurable. In the drunken philosopher's chant cited earlier, for example, the wine is praised for its color, taste, and bouquet rather than for its effect, so it might be considered merely one of a vast array of sensual pleasures in which the speaker takes delight. Another poem, **"Various Wines"** of 1782, combines the two themes of wine and women. Each of the stanzas is similarly constructed. It opens with a brief description of a particular wine appropriate for toasting a certain type of woman. The second couplet of the stanza reinforces the sensual link between the two subjects with the mention of a kiss. In each of the first two stanzas, the color of the lips bestowing the kiss complements that of the wine. The poet's delight results from their combined effect: "How sweet it [the wine] is to our heart / With the kiss of crimson lips" (97). The concluding invitation to a kiss focuses the poem more fully on the pleasure provided by a woman's company; the wine theme has now served its purpose. Although the poem is a slight one, it does indicate Derzhavin's early interest in Anacreontic themes without the complication of civic sentiment.

With time, the poet's capacity for unabashed surrender to the spirit of the genre became more evident. Dance, although frequently mentioned in the *Anacreontea*, plays but a minor part in the thematic development of any of the original poems. Thus Derzhavin's exploitation of dance as a means of exhibiting feminine grace and beauty must be regarded as an innovation which enhances the esthetic effect of the genre as a whole. Three poems written between 1796 and 1805 offer instructive examples of the poet's continuing efforts to achieve a more expressive union of theme and form. Viewed collectively, **"The Graces,"** **"Russian Maidens,"** and **"Gypsy Dance"** trace the evolution of Derzhavin's interest in complementing visual effects with the feeling of graceful motion. From his initial account of a dance at the Winter Palace in St. Petersburg, he subsequently moved to the representation of dance as a purely esthetic experience, without reference to the particular circumstances of its performance.

Derzhavin's divorce of panegyric from artistic purposes is especially evident in the comparison of **"The Graces"** and **"Russian Maidens."** The two poems, remarkably similar in form, are written without stanzaic division in trochaic tetrameter. The alternating masculine and feminine lines contribute to the sensation of dancing by lending a pronounced, regular rhythm to each work. Moreover, both poems begin with a reference to Anacreon as a model whom the poet intends either to imitate or surpass. In **"The Graces"** however, Derzhavin still shows his awareness of the royal audience for which he had written so many of his previous poems.

After witnessing a performance by Catherine's grand-daughters, he suggests they compare favorably with the dancing graces. The comparison comes only at the poem's conclusion, however, following a lengthy description of the goddesses. Though somewhat ethereal, they still display several of the attributes that Derzhavin would use to greater effect in his account of the Russian maidens. In both instances, there is an element of inner tranquility which finds external expression in quiet gazes and fluid movements. The total effect is one of pleasure more than ecstasy. It might be argued that only the former was appropriate to an implied portrayal of royalty; but the content of the two later poems indicates that Derzhavin was becoming increasingly cognizant of the value of moderation. Once free of the constraints of the panegyric, he simply expanded his frame of reference to include all of Russia's maidens.

At the start of **"Russian Maidens"** the poet emerges as a patriot, challenging Anacreon, the "Teian singer," to compare the spectacle of dancing Russian beauties with that of ancient Greek maidens. The poet concludes his work in confidence that the young woman here depicted are superior to the Greeks:

> Were you [Anacreon] to see these lovely maidens,
> You would forget the Grecian girls,
> And your Eros to them would be chained
> On his sensuous wings.

(282)

Derzhavin supports this contention by presenting both the dancers' features and the motions they describe in dancing the *bychok,* a form of peasant round dance. Initially he focuses upon their movements. In so doing, Derzhavin relies heavily on verbs, thus imparting a dynamic quality to his work far greater than that to be found in descriptions of dance in the *Anacreontea.* Fluid body motions and the staccato stamp of feet create the impression of a stylized but still expressive dance:

> Have you seen, Teian singer,
> How in spring the Russian maidens
> Dance the *bychok* in the meadow
> To the shepherd's pipe?
> How they pass with heads inclining,
> And with *bashmaki* stamp time,
> How their hands quietly direct their gaze,
> And their shoulders speak?

(280)

The vitality conveyed through the patterns of dance is complemented by the collective portrait of the dancers. Although the poet describes the fair flush of their exertion in rather conventional terms, his additional mention of their "sable brows" (*brovi soboliny*) and "falcon gaze" (*sokolii vzgliad*) lends a distinctive folk quality to their physical portrayal. These, together with the mention of such decidedly Russian details as the *bychok* it-

self (the particular dance) or the *bashmaki* (peasant footwear), create a particular sense of time and place for the poem without detracting from its affirmation of the universally recognized pleasure of dance.

The third poem on this same theme, **"Gypsy Dance,"** was written about a year later. It is decidedly more exuberant in tone. In order to evoke the unbridled enthusiasm of gypsy dance, the poet utilizes visual and aural effects suggesting frenzy rather than grace. Little of the feeling of intimate pleasure found in **"Russian Maidens"** remains; the exclamations and imperatives predominant in the first five stanzas create a mood closer to that of the dithyramb. The gestures are bolder and the sensuality more intense than in the two earlier poems. In the opening stanza, the poet urges the gypsy woman, filled with "voluptuous fever," to seize her guitar and strike its strings. Her purpose should be to revive the emotions cultivated in the ancient Bacchanal. The dance rhythms which she stamps out are so intense as to disturb the deathly silence of the night; her cry of frenzy has an animal-like quality about it. Each of these descriptive stanzas closes with a refrain stressing the intoxicating effect of such a performance: "Ignite souls, cast fire into the heart / From your swarthy face" (30).

Suddenly, as if recognizing that he has reached the limits of descriptive intensity, Derzhavin alters his tone at the beginning of the final stanza. Now he reverts to the more tranquil rhythms of **"Russian Maidens"** in his culminating statement on the esthetic effect of dance:

> No, stop temptress! That is sufficient!
> Spare modest muses further fright,
> But decorously, poised, and graceful
> Dance on like a Russian maid.

(306-308)

Reference to the "modest muses" and to the example of his earlier poem brings back his concern for moderation as the best guarantee of enduring pleasure.[18]

The notion of restraint in the cultivation of sensual pleasures is best illustrated by Derzhavin's Anacreontic verse on love themes. While the playful, sometimes ironic stance assumed by the lover in the *Anacreontea* is adopted in some of Derzhavin's early, imitative works, it is gradually modified by his growing appreciation of a more profound sort of emotional experience. **"To Nina"** is an early harbinger of Derzhavin's later attitudes about love. The poet urges that his kisses be accepted as those of a brother, fearing that an excess of emotion might lead to satiation:

> Most tender passion's flame is modest,
> And if it burns excessively,
> And fills us with a feeling of satisfaction,
> Then it quickly dies and passes.

(78)

We may contrast the caution voiced in this poem with the surrender to love's irresistible appeal concluding **"Anacreon by the Stove,"** a poem of 1795 which relies more heavily upon the Anacreontic conventions. It is constructed about the established conceit of the moth flying into the flame, a symbol of love's consuming nature. The fateful object of attraction, Maria, is endowed with the usual charms: her heavenly blue eyes and rosy lips scarcely distinguish her from countless other such beauties. It is rather the very title's incongruous combination of ancient Greek poet and Russian *pechka* (stove) which lends a certain vitality to the work. By substituting so prosaic an object for the usual meadows of the *Anacreontea*, Derzhavin prompts his reader to view the poem as an expression of his compatriot's lightly ironic experience of love's torments.[19]

Marriage ultimately provided the poet with the enduring emotional satisfaction he sought. Although he wrote only a few separate poems to either his first or second wife, Derzhavin frequently refers to his domestic bliss in other poems. A truly delightful expression of this feeling concludes **"To Myself"**, which he wrote both to indicate his dissatisfaction with court life under Paul and to declare his increasing devotion to a life centering about the home and his art. Work shades imperceptibly into play as the muse and his wife alternate in giving him pleasure:

> About three times a week I'll sport
> With my dear muse in the morning;
> Then again return to bed
> And with my wife embrace.
>
> (273)

It is not simply the jocular eroticism of this passage which is important to its effect. In the poet's estimate, genuine emotional experience and creative expression are closely related.

Since the celebration of life was the hallmark of his Anacreontic verse, Derzhavin predictably turned to that genre in seeking to assuage his apprehension about death. The theme of age confronted by reminders of temporal beauty links the poems **"The Old Man"** and **"To Lucy,"** which are fairly direct translations of Odes 7 and 51 respectively. Both works attest to that intensified appreciation of beauty which often accompanies the awareness of personal physical decline. Despite his outward appearance, the old man maintains that he is not "grey in soul" and that death's approach will simply spur him to enjoy life more actively. As in the *Anacreontea*, death remains beyond the poem's boundaries as a force of inevitable consequence, one which can be rendered less ominous only momentarily, by an assertion of faith in the sensations of this world. Several of Derzhavin's more original poems develop the "eat, drink, and be merry" philosophy with considerable suc-

cess, and may be regarded as evidence of his ability to create variations on established Anacreontic themes.

"The Nightingale in a Dream" is especially noteworthy for its integration of images and sound patterns in support of the pleasure theme. It is one of several Anacreontic verses in which Derzhavin deliberately avoided using the letter "r," and is quite mellifluous in tone. This impression is strengthened by a descriptive concentration on the constantly varied and lilting quality of the nightingale's song which suffuses the first stanza. The effect diverges from that produced by the birds of the *Anacreontea*, which are populated by cooing doves and twittering swallows. By his choice of birds Derzhavin draws attention to hearing as one of life's joys. The following stanza makes it clear that the sleeping poet's ability to appreciate the music is more important than the song itself: his present condition is contrasted with the "tedious endless sleep of death." There is no suggestion of spiritual recompense for the physical silence of the grave. At the poem's conclusion, the poet's recollection of life's pleasurable experiences takes on a particular urgency:

> If I shall no longer hear
> Sounds of merriment and play,
> Sounds of dance, of choirs, of glory—
> Then I shall enjoy this life,
> Kiss my beloved more frequently,
> Listen to the nightingale's songs.
>
> (267)

With the noteworthy exception of the "sounds of glory," all the pleasures cited here are those which the poet might most readily find within the realm of private experience.

Notes

1. Carol Maddison, *Apollo and the Nine* [Baltimore, Md., 1960], pp. 19-20, remarks on the modern Anacreontic: "No matter how simple and song-like some of the ancient Greek poems may have been, modern poems written in imitation of them are, from the very fact that they are imitations, ceremonious and learned, and not the impulsive expression of individual emotion but the traditional expression of universal human experience."

2. Albin Lesky, *A History of Greek Literature* (New York, 1966), p. 176, draws a clear distinction between Anacreon's love poetry and that of his later Classical imitators. The superiority of the former is evident from his characterization of Anacreon: "The poet who hates all excess and maintains such a careful balance between love and indifference, between drunkenness and sobriety, is always master of his medium; yet the magic of his art lies in that gentle resignation which invests everything

with an unconscious inevitability." Lesky's remarks are equally applicable to Derzhavin's best
Anacreontics, but there is no evidence that the
Russian poet was aware of any models other than
those in Lvov's translation of the *Anacreontea.*
The similarities between his works and surviving
fragments of Anacreon's original poetry thus appear to be the result of temperament and the influence of Horace, rather than any conscious design.

3. Derzhavin's introduction to this volume, "To the
Readers," displays the same mixture of artistic
and patriotic impulses as the works themselves: "I
wrote these songs for amusement, in my youth, at
idle moments, and finally, for the pleasure of
members of my household. Out of love for my native language, I wished to show its richness, its
versatility, lightness, and in general, its capacity
for expressing the most tender feelings, which are
scarcely to be found in other languages" (VIII,
512). As one proof of Russian's richness and softness, Derzhavin included 10 poems in which he
deliberately avoided the consonant "r". Among
them is a strident political statement in "Freedom", which shows that the poet could unhesi-
tantly pursue several disparate purposes simultaneously.

4. C. L. Drage, "The *Anacreontea* and 18th-Century
Russian Poetry," *Slavonic and East European Review,* 41 (1962-63), p. 134, finds that eight of the
thirteen poems which these two authors wrote are
in iambic trimeter, although it should be added
that Sumarokov's eight works are equally divided
between this metric scheme and trochaic tetrameter, the latter being by far the most common in
Derzhavin's Anacreontic verse as well (46 of 94).
Drage's article is in general useful for its description of the way various Russian authors, beginning with Kantemir, adapted the Anacreontic to
the established metrical patterns of Russian verse.

5. In the table of contents for *Anacreontic Songs,*
Derzhavin inserted a statement to this effect immediately after "Conversation with a Genius,"
thus separating this initial group from the remaining 93 poems. This is not to say that other poems
do not relate to events at court. "Anacreon in a
Gathering," for example, was composed in honor
of Potemkin's capture of Izmail and ostensibly depicts events on a holiday to mark this victory. In
fact, however, the poem primarily celebrates feminine beauty.

6. The numbering system in common usage among
writers of the eighteenth century was that employed by Anne Dacier in her 1716 translation,
Les Poesies d'Anacreon et de Sapho. Although
this translation was unavailable to me, I have retained the roman numerals indicating the sequence
of odes in that volume. To facilitate the reader's

use of a more accessible translation, I have also
included arabic numbers in parentheses to indicate
the sequence in *Elegy and Iambus,* trans. J. M.
Edmonds, II (New York, 1931).

7. Doris Schenk, *Studien zur anakreontischen Ode in
der russischen Literatur des Klassizismus und der
Empfindsamkeit* [Frankfurt am Main, 1972], has
an excellent chapter on the Anacreontic verse of
Kheraskov and his followers. Regrettably, Schenk
did not devote a similar survey chapter to
Derzhavin, although she recognizes his Anacreontic verse as the culmination of that genre's development in 18th century Russian poetry.

8. René Wellek and Austin Warren, *Theory of Literature* (New York, 1956), p. 221.

9. G. A. Gukovskii, "Ob anakreonticheskoi ode,"
Russkaia poeziia XVIII veka (Leningrad, 1927),
pp. 103-50. Gukovskii bases his conclusions on a
selective study of poems labelled "Anacreontics"
by their authors. His unquestioning acceptance of
such works as examples of the genre vitiates much
of his analysis.

10. C. L. Drage, "The *Anacreontea* and 18th Century
Russian Poetry," p. 119.

11. C. L. Drage, "The *Anacreontea* and 18th-Century
Russian Poetry," p. 122, identifies Sumarokov's
1775 Anacreontic verse as being the first to use
unrhymed feminine endings as the syllabotonic
equivalent of the original Greek.

12. *Elegy and Iambus,* II, 41-42.

13. The poem appeared after Suvorov had been exiled
to his native village for making unfavorable remarks about Paul.

14. M. V. Lomonosov, *Polnoe sobranie sochinenii* (10
vols., Moscow-Leningrad, 1950-57), VIII, 762.

15. Grot includes the unfinished stanza in which the
drunken philosopher maintains that he had intended to serve the tsar and to "speak the truth" to
him but found this impossible (I, 264). The poet's
direct statements to this effect elsewhere support
this identification with the drunken philosopher. It
is curious that Derzhavin chose the epithet
"drunken" (*p'ianyi*) for the title of the finished
poem, for as Grot notes, his first draft characterized this philosopher as "luxury-loving"
(*roskoshnyi*). The latter more accurately reflects
Derzhavin's own attitude toward life.

16. G. N. Ionin, "Anakreonticheskie stikhi Karamzina
i Derzhavina," *XVIII vek,* sb. 8 (1969), 162-78,
makes a number of interesting observations on the
similarities and differences in the two authors' use
of the Anacreontic. While Ionin is correct in his
general statement that Derzhavin stressed nature's

vitality, as opposed to the melancholy characteristic of Karamzin's moonlit landscapes, he fails to recall Derzhavin's use of precisely this setting, with somewhat similar effect, in such diverse poems as "A Mirza's Vision" and "Freedom."

17. According to Grot (II, 458), Derzhavin wrote this poem after having been personally ordered by Alexander, who had but recently ascended the throne, to investigate certain administrative irregularities in one of the provinces. The poet was obviously heartened by this expression of royal confidence in his abilities, for during Paul's reign he had often thought that his talents were ignored.

18. This poem was a response to one written by his friend, I. I. Dmitriev, which portrayed the gypsies in a fashion that did not fully satisfy Derzhavin. Dmitriev is the "tender poet" of the final line, and the preceding description of dance was intended for his edification.

19. Here, as in several other poems, Derzhavin deliberately identified himself with Anacreon. The occasion for this poem was a harp recital of 1795 by Marya Naryshkina.

William Edward Brown (essay date 1980)

SOURCE: Brown, William Edward. "Gavriil Romanovich Derzhavin and the Beginnings of Sentimentalism." In *A History of Eighteenth Century Russian Literature,* pp. 378-415. Ann Arbor, Mich.: Ardis, 1980.

[*In the following excerpt, Brown provides an extensive and substantive overview of Derzhavin's poetic achievements. Brown investigates form in several of Derzhavin's poems and discusses connections between Derzhavin's writings and the works of Horace and Edward Young.*]

The precise position which Derzhavin occupies in the history of Russian literature is a matter of considerable concern to Russian critics, and one seemingly quite impossible to define. Derzhavin cannot be pigeon-holed. As Professor Berkov[1] points out ironically, he has been called a classicist, a romantic, a pre-romantic, and even a representative of the Baroque! The last mentioned classification, nonsensical though it is, has actually had some quite reputable adherents. It is perfectly indefensible: the Baroque is a period style, and to move it from the seventeenth to the end of the eighteenth century deprives it of all meaning whatever. Neither can Derzhavin be put down as a genuine and unalloyed classicist. Perhaps the pre-romantic label comes a little closer to the truth than the others—but it is, after all, best to eschew the attempt to label. Derzhavin is a transitional figure, both in point of time and in poetical practice; there are

elements in his work which show unmistakably his close connection with the classical poetical system. There are, however, other elements which link him just as certainly to the beginnings of romanticism. The number and importance of the classical norms which he repudiated, both theoretically and in practice, was impressive. Other poets of his own age, and even of his own literary circle—Lvov, Kapnist, Khemnitser *et al.*—are far more traditional and conservative in this regard than Derzhavin. Why is this so?

Two reasons can be advanced for Gavriil Derzhavin's cavalier treatment of the revered norms of classical verse composition. The first is a fact of his environment and early life; the second of his psychological make-up. Derzhavin had, for his time, a very deficient education: his earliest tutors were country ignoramuses—a local sexton, a tyrannical German exile, and an army artilleryman. He later had a few years of "high school" education in the Kazan Gymnasium, where everything was taught by one, not universally competent, teacher. He did not even finish the Gymnasium course, but was called up for army duty at the age of eighteen, and spent the next fourteen years in military uniform. As a result of this early background, Derzhavin had no knowledge of the classical languages or of French; he had learned conversational German from Herr Rose. He was, however, by ignorance of the essential languages of classicism, cut off from the originals and obliged to rely on such mediocre translations as were available. But he did not even have any literary training at all, even in Russian, beyond the reading of the Slavonic Scriptures which his mother insisted on. In fact, literature did not at first attract him—he wanted to be a scientist! He came to literature as an outsider—a badly educated soldier, completely ignorant of everything that his contemporaries took for granted as the necessary preparation for a literary career. When he did, about 1777, at the beginning of his civilian career, come for the first time in contact with a genuinely cultured literary group, the circle that had formed around Nikolai Alexandrovich Lvov (1751-1803)—Lvov himself, Kapnist, Khemnitser, Muraviev and others—these men were already touched by the new literary currents that we associate with pre-romanticism. Thus, Lvov "translated" a typical, and popular, quasi-Scandinavian piece, "The Song of the Norseman Harald the Brave"; he translated the *Odes of Anacreon*; and he was strongly attracted to Russian popular song, under the influence of Herder, and made a collection of such songs together with the tunes. All this means that the literary influences which reached Derzhavin just at the time when, according to his own testimony, he was first beginning to find his own personal way (1770), were not the strictly classical ones which he would have felt had he been educated properly.

As for the second, psychological, factor in Derzhavin's literary nonconformity, it needs only a glance at his biography to convince one that he was by temperament a man who could never brook coercion or arbitrary dictation. Even in military service he was not willing to accept orders which he considered unreasonable, and suffered accordingly; and it would be difficult to point to a single superior in all his long and very successful administrative career, from the Empress on down, with whom he did not quarrel. That he should have tamely accepted the dictates of normative eighteenth century taste is as unthinkable as that he should carry out the arbitrary orders of Catherine II about planting trees in Olonets province! His attitude toward the "rules of taste" and their makers is revealed in his angry note protesting the rejection of a young playwright's effort by a pedantic director on the grounds of its "bad taste": "Who gave the right to this dictatorial tone?"

What has been said above does not of course mean that Derzhavin had no literary schooling whatever. He learned to read from his boorish tutors, and he did read, rather undiscriminatingly. Of course the poetic models that at once offered themselves to his eye were the poems of Lomonosov and Sumarokov. It was a fundamental dictum of classicism that a poet must *imitate*: and what should he imitate but the great masterworks of the past—primarily the Latin writers of the Augustan age, then the great French classics of the age of Louis XIV, and finally in Russia, the acknowledged Russian classics, who would, of course, be Lomonosov (died 1765) and Sumarokov (died 1777). Derzhavin began by imitating, and the first collection of his verse to see the light, published anonymously in 1774 while the author was still in the Volga country hunting Pugachev, is, as should be expected, immature and imitative. Derzhavin himself spoke of the book very disparagingly, as the work of an aspiring poet who tried to soar with Lomonosov, but lacked the genius. Actually, these *Odes, Translated and Composed at Chitalagay Hill* show a surprising amount of originality; for example, his very sincere and quite moving **"Ode on the Death of General-in-Chief Bibikov,"** though written in the traditional ten-line strophe of iambic tetrameter, is unrhymed! Derzhavin explained that he thought the embellishment of rhyme inappropriate to the expression of sorrow. So, incidentally, did Edward Young; but whether Derzhavin had encountered the *Conjectures on Original Composition* at this date is not certain. The influence of Lomonsov is, however, apparent everywhere in these odes. At the same time he was also writing songs, which he did not publish separately, but incorporated over twenty years later in his volume *Anacreontic Songs* of 1804. In this genre his model was of course Sumarokov, and it must be said that he came closer to his prototype here than he did to Lomonosov in his "odes." In accordance with accepted eighteenth century practice he was following different models for different genres, and himself employing two consciously different styles.

The classical poet of the eighteenth century followed unquestioningly the principle that every poetical genre has its own appropriate style, and its own appropriate poetic *persona*. The poet who writes an elegy, for example, assumes the mask of an ardent lover facing separation from his mistress; he may himself be a happily married man, no matter; the elegist must be a melancholy bachelor. The writer of Anacreontic verse must put on the mask of the old toper from Teos; the satirist must borrow Juvenal's indignation and thunder against the depravity of the times. As Sumarokov's example shows, the same poet can wear all these, and numerous other, masks—but successively. What his own personality is like he will not have any occasion to reveal. This is not to say that the classical poet is necessarily insincere; the mask of the passionate patriot and inspired prophet which Lomonosov wears in his great odes corresponds truly to his own personality, and doubtless the same is true of the pungent satirist which his "Ode to the Beard" reveals. The conventional faces which tradition accepted for the tragic poet, the satirist, the writer of comedy, of ode, of elegy, and all the rest, were all normal human varieties of personality and such as any individual might assume at different times. The patriot may also be a lover, the harsh critic of society may in another mood be a tolerant wit. But for the classicist these conventional masks may no more be combined and confused than the genres of poetry themselves, which the usage of the ancients has once and for all set apart in impermeable compartments.

Derzhavin repudiated all this. He rode rough-shod over the entire eighteenth century genre system, and the personality which he exhibited, though there are still differences between the solemn manner of such poems as **"The Waterfall"** and the intimacy of **"To Eugene. Life at Zvanka"** or the Epicureanism of **"The Bath of Aristippus,"** is still recognizably the same, and is not dictated by the kind of verse he is writing. The first intimation of this significant revolution may be found in a poem of 1779: **"On the Birth in the North of a Porphyrogennete Child."**[2]

In the notes which Derzhavin wrote many years later for an edition of his works which did not materialize, he makes this significant statement about this poem; he, it appears, like several other poets, wrote an ode to commemorate the birth of the prince who was to become Alexander I, "but in a style not in conformity with the author's gifts, but in that of Lomonosov, for which he felt himself unsuited; this ode accordingly has not been printed in his works, and the present one was written later."[3] The "ode in the style of Lomonosov" has apparently not survived; the existing verses were published in the *St. Petersburg Herald* in 1779, with a full title which explains the poetical device which the poet employs in constructing his piece: **"Verses on the Birth in the North of a Porphyrogennete Child on**

the Twelfth Day of December, on Which the Sun Begins his Return from Winter to Summer." Alexander Pavlovich was born December 12, 1777 OS, equivalent to December 23 NS; the winter solstice is on December 22, so the 23rd is in fact the date "on which the sun begins his return from winter to summer." Whether the original ode utilized this device is unknown; in any case the inflated, pompous style of Lomonosov, "for which" Derzhavin "felt himself unsuited" was rejected, and a poem written in a style as different from it as possible. The meter is not the iambic tetrameter of the ode, but trochaic tetrameter, traditionally associated with songs and Anacreontics; there is no strophic division, and the rhyme scheme is a simple alternation: aBaB. Most significantly, the poetic mask of the author is almost playful rather than solemn and prophetic. The poem begins with a fairly realistic description of a northern winter, with, however, some oddly incongruous mythological elements in the classical style: thus the white-haired, gray-bearded Boreas makes all nature tremble:

> The earth is turned to stone by his chill hand; the beasts have fled into holes, the fish have hidden themselves in the depths, the choirs of birds dared not sing, the bees have huddled in their hives; out of boredom the nymphs have fallen asleep amid caves and rushes, and the satyrs have gathered around fires to warm their hands.

At the moment of the birth of the "porphyrogennete child," however, "Boreas ceased to roar. . . . and the beautiful sun turned back toward spring." Around the child's cradle gathered various "genii" in classical style to confer their gifts—wealth, the glory of the purple, joys and delight, peace and repose, etc. Finally the last genius, Virtue, gives the crowning gift: "Be master of your passions, be a man ["chelovek"] upon the throne!"

The poem shows clearly the classical inheritance—the allegory of winter, the intrusive mythology, etc.; at the same time it flagrantly transgresses the classical canons of style by employing a light, dance-like meter for a "lofty" subject. Other poems of the same year 1779, which Derzhavin himself considered the turning-point in his search for a style of his own, show the same combination of classical and anti-classical elements.

Such a poem is **"The Spring"** ("Kliuch"),[4] with its three rather oddly assorted and not very harmonious elements. It begins with a neo-classical picture, which Professor I. Z. Serman,[5] certainly rightly, regards as suggested to Derzhavin by the writings of his friend N. A. Lvov on sculpture:

> Seated, crowned with sedge, in the shade of branching trees, leaning with one hand on an urn, showing the face of the heavens—such is the beautiful spring which I see.

The pose of the figure and its attributes—the urn, the crown of sedge—are precisely those of the conventional classical allegory of the fountain. Then comes a description, beautifully realized of a *real,* not allegorical fountain:

> When upon your silvery arcs the red dawn gleams, what fiery purples and flaming roses roll, burning, with the fall of your waters!

> * * *

> Your bank becomes purple when the sun is descending from the heavens; your crystal is set afire by his rays; in the valley the forest begins to turn blue, and a sea of mists spreads out.

Here we may see, incidentally, an early example of Derzhavin's wonderful sense of color and an anticipation of the gorgeous description of **"The Waterfall."** But by the eighth strophe of **"The Spring"** we become dimly aware that there is more to this fountain than meets the eye:

> Burning with a poet's passion, I come to you, O rill; I envy the fortune of the bard who has tasted of your waters, [the poet] crowned with Parnassus's laurel.

> Give me to drink, give me to drink of you, and I shall sing similarly, and my thought in songs shall be comparable with your pure stream, and [my] lyre's voice with your striving.

> May your honor pass through all barriers, as echo from the mountains through the slumberous forest: sacred fountain of Grebenevo, you have given the creator of the immortal *Rossiad* [Mikhail Kheraskov] to drink of the water of poetry.

It is with some shock that we finally recognize that the prettily described fountain is no other than Castalia, in a Russian disguise! Awkwardly as the elements of sculptural emblem, realistic description and classical allegory are combined, they show clear evidence of Derzhavin's impatience with the classical prescriptions that would keep them isolated.

The greatest of the 1779 poems and one of Derzhavin's masterpieces is **"Ode on the Death of Prince Meshchersky."**[6] Here we are closer to the traditional form: the meter is iambic tetrameter, in eight-line strophes, rhyming *AbAbCddC*. The theme is one of the commonest of classical themes, although significantly, not one found in Lomonosov—the inevitability of death, which brings poor and great to the same end. Two famous poems of Horace (Odes I, 24 and II, 14) are almost the canonical examples of it, and Derzhavin's poem follows the Horatian construction so faithfully that one wonders if he had not been by this time introduced to the great Latin poet—the more so as **"The Spring"** has such an obvious similarity with Horace's *O fons Bandusiae* (III, 13). The Derzhavin ode, however, is powerfully original, even when it makes use of the trite allegory of Death as "the grim reaper"; Edward Young's *Night Thoughts,* especially his *First Night,* played a part in Derzhavin's development but, as we shall see, a chiefly negative one.

O word of time![7] Metallic peal! Your dread voice confounds me; Your groan calls me, calls me, calls—and brings me nigh to the grave. Hardly have I seen this light, when Death gnashes his ["Death" in Russian is feminine, but it seems best in translating to follow the gender familiar in English] teeth; his scythe flashes like lightning, and cuts down my days as grass.

None escapes from his fatal claws, no creature. Monarch and captive are food for the worm, the grave's malevolence devours the elements; time gapes to blot out glory; as swift waters pour into the sea, so days and years pour into eternity; greedy Death swallows kingdoms.

Only the mortal thinks not to die, and fancies he is immortal; Death comes to him like a thief and of a sudden steals his life. Alas! where we fear it least, there may Death soonest appear; no more swiftly do the thunders fly down upon proud mountain peaks.

And so the great chant goes on, every stanza marked by the word "death" or a related idea. The words are solemn and the solemnity is heightened by the echoes of Scripture: "Cuts down my days *as grass*"; Death comes to him *like a thief,* etc. Ideas are pounded home by constantly repeated words: *Zovet menia, zovet* tvoi ston, *zovet*—i k grobu priblizhaet (strophe 1), or I ves', *kak son,* proshel tvoi vek, *Kak son,* kak sladkaia mechta," etc. (strophes 8 and 9) ["And, *like a dream,* all your life has gone by, *Like a dream,* like a sweet vision"]. And then, suddenly, at the end, following immediately upon the superb line: "Ia v dveriakh vechnosti stoiu," "I stand at the door of eternity," comes a strophe that seems to clash most dissonantly with all that has preceded:

To die, today or tomorrow, Perfilev, is of course the destiny of us all. Why then torment yourself and mourn that your mortal friend did not live eternally? Life is heaven's momentary gift; arrange it for your own repose, and with your pure soul bless the blow of the fates.

Such an Epicurean admonition after the magnificent picture of all-conquering death is disconcerting, to say the least—but perhaps not more so than the last two lines of Horace's ode on the death of Quintilius (I, 24), which follow four strophes that reiterate with all manner of mythological examples the notion that Death is inexorable: "durum, sed levius fit patientia quidquid corrigere est nefas"—"It's hard; but patience makes easier whatever cannot be corrected." Horace's example was probably in Derzhavin's mind in ending his poem thus; almost certainly he was also in a way engaging in a polemic with Edward Young. The English poet's deep dejection at the omnipotence of death leads him to admonish his reader to think only of the inevitable end and abandon concern for the ephemeral pleasures of life that are so soon to be snatched away. For Derzhavin's lusty, life-affirming nature such an attitude was intolerable, and he adds his final strophe almost as an act of defiance.

* * *

The year 1779 marked a turning point in Derzhavin's verse; but the poems of that year, fine as they are, still show certain awkwardnesses and uncertainties. The poems of 1782, however, are fully and triumphantly mature, and usher in the series of odes on which Derzhavin's fame securely rests. The first of these is an example of a familiar eighteenth-century genre, the "paraphrase of a Psalm." In this case the Psalm is No. 81 (82 in our numeration).[8] Dissatisfied with his first version, he made two others: the final one was published in the *St. Petersburg Herald* in 1780. The issue in which it appeared, however, was ordered suppressed, and a new page substituted for that which contained the poem. Derzhavin was put to some trouble to convince the authorities that "King David was not a Jacobin," and that the paraphrase was perfectly innocent. It was not issued for the public until 1787. The paraphrase is headed: **"To Potentates and Judges" ["Vlastiteliam i sudiiam"]:**

The Most High God has arisen to judge the gods of earth [i.e., kings] in their assembly: "How long," He says, "how long shall you continue to spare the unrighteous and wicked?

Your duty is to maintain the laws, to regard not the faces of the mighty, not to leave orphans and widows without aid, without defence.

Your duty is to save the innocent from tribulation, to give shelter to the unfortunate; from the powerful to protect the powerless, to snatch the poor from [their] chains."

They do not heed! They see, and do not realize! Their eyes are covered with lucre; evil-doers make the earth to tremble, unrighteousness rocks the heavens.

Kings! ["Tsari"] I deemed ye were mighty gods, no one a judge over you; but ye are moved by passion, even as I, and likewise mortal, even as I.

And even as I, ye fall, as the withered leaf falls from the tree! And ye die even as your lowliest slave dies!

Arise, O God! God of the just! And give ear to their prayer; come hither, pass judgment, chastise the crafty, and be sole king of the earth!

The paraphrase is in fact very close to the original, but Derzhavin has in a few places allowed himself to interpret a somewhat obscure text; thus the first verse of the original reads: "God arose in the assembly of gods; amid the gods he has pronounced judgment." The phrase "earthly gods" as a synonym for "kings" is an eighteenth-century commonplace, and comes very naturally here, whatever the Hebrew may have meant. The original of the third verse contains only an imperative; Derzhavin has added the phrase, doubtless offensive to Catherine: "your duty is." In the fifth verse "their eyes are covered with lucre ["mzdoiu," "reward," that is, "bribe"]" corresponds to the original "they walk in darkness." Finally, in verse 6, the line "but you are moved by passions, even as I, and likewise mortal, even as I," is entirely a Derzhavin interpolation; the original reads: "I said: ye are gods, and sons of the Most High, all of you."

Whatever embarrassment his "Jacobin" version of the Psalm may have caused Derzhavin was erased by the signal success of his **"Ode to Felitsa"** of 1782, which found such favor with Catherine that the poet was presently promoted and most handsomely rewarded. Since this is Derzhavin's most famous poem, and shows with particular clarity the decisive break between his poetical system and the norms of classical usage, it will be well to consider it in some detail.

The background of the **"Ode to Felitsa"** is the following. In 1782 there appeared, in a restricted edition, a didactic fairy-tale for children which Catherine II had written for her little grandson, Prince Alexander Pavlovich—the "Porphyrogennete child" of Derzhavin's earlier poem. "The Tale of Prince Khlor"[10] describes the mission of the Prince (Alexander) to discover "the rose without thorns." He accomplishes his task through the aid of Queen Felitsa of "the Kirghiz-Kaizak Horde" (the tale is laid in the East). Felitsa, in Catherine's allegory, represents "Reason," by whose assistance the young prince at last finds at the top of a mountain "the rose without thorns," i.e., Virtue. Doubtless Felitsa in Catherine's intention is also a disguise for herself: her flatterers habitually called her "Minerva." Derzhavin's bold and original idea was to utilize this tale of Catherine's own making in order to eulogize her in, as it were, an Oriental masquerade. His secondary, and even more revolutionary, idea was to compose his eulogy of the Empress—"Felitsa"—by the device of contrasting her virtues with the weaknesses of the great noblemen of her entourage, whom he calls "murzas," in accord with the assumed Oriental location of Queen Felitsa's realm. Thus, in the ode form most commonly used by Lomonosov and associated with solemn panegyric in exalted style, Derzhavin, assuming as his own poetic mask the person of one of Queen Felitsa's "murzas," describes the Queen's hard-working, beneficent, abstemious mode of life as a contrast to the idleness, luxury and parasitism of her courtiers. Not only is the device of an Oriental masquerade in an ode unheard-of, but by the admixture of the accusatory elements of satire in the picture of the "murzas" the inflexible classical prohibition against genre mixture is broken. Further to affront the classicist, the hierarchic distinctions of language levels is also broken: in the passages which concern "Felitsa," i.e., Catherine, Derzhavin's language belongs to the level classified as "middle" by Lomonosov, while in the "murza" passages it is decidedly "low," with the startling appearance of an everyday vocabulary undreamed of before in an ode—"tobacco," "coffee,"

"fools" (a card game), etc. Less obtrusive, but still a decided break with tradition is the intrusion of the poet's own personality, even though disguised under the mask of a "murza," and the half-playful, light tone of the whole. Derzhavin had indeed performed the perilous feat of "pouring new wine into old bottles," and with brilliant success. A few strophes of the long ode (260 lines), will illustrate the various novelties just discussed. The poem begins with a strophe that at once sets the tone:

> Godlike queen of the Kirghiz-Kaizak Horde! Whose incomparable wisdom revealed the true path to young Prince Khlor, to ascend to that lofty mountain where grows the rose without thorns, where Virtue dwells—she captivates my mind and spirit: let me find her counsel.

> Give [me], O Felitsa! instruction: how to live both splendidly and justly, how to tame the agitation of the passions, and be happy in the world! Your voice arouses me, your son [i.e., Khlor] leads me on; but I am [too] weak to follow him. Confused by life's vanity, today I am master of myself, but tomorrow I am a slave to caprice.

The contrast between Queen and courtiers is immediately drawn, and the language descends a level accordingly; the "common" words are underlined:

> Not imitating your murzas, you often walk *on foot*, and the simplest food is usually on your *table*; not valuing your ease, you read, write at your *desk*, and from your pen pour out happiness for all mortals. You do not, like me, *play cards* from morning to morning.

Presently the satiric element takes over entirely, and strophes 5-10 take the form of confessions by the murza-poet of the frivolous ways in which "he" wastes his time. Actually, the descriptions of these several kinds of dissipation fitted individual magnates of Catherine's court so precisely—as they were meant to—that it is said that the Empress took pleasure in sending each of those described a marked copy of the poem! Potemkin, naturally, occupies first place, followed by Alexei Orlov, Peter Panin, Semen Naryshkin and Prince Vyazemsky. It scarcely needs to be said that the Empress' delight in the new ode was not shared by her courtiers, and Derzhavin's popularity with his fellow peers, never very great, disappeared in a wave of indignant outrage. A good example of the homely, "vulgar" but realistic pictures which the poet paints is strophe 6:

> Or I am at a sumptuous banquet, where they are giving a toast for me, where the table glitters with silver and gold, [and] where there are thousands of different dishes: there is the famous Westphalian ham, there are the slices of Astrakhan fish [i.e., sturgeon], there stand pilau and pasties, I wash down waffles with champagne; and I forget everything on earth, amid the wines, the sweets and the perfumes.

The picture of imperial virtues which Derzhavin sketches hardly conforms to the notion of later generations about Catherine the Great, but was probably at this date in the poet's life quite sincere (he became disillusioned later):

> To you alone, O Queen, it belongs to create light out of darkness: dividing Chaos harmoniously into spheres, to strengthen the entirety by union [supposed to refer to Catherine's creation of the administrative districts called "governments"]; from discord, harmony, and from greedy passions you alone are able to create happiness. Thus the helmsman, sailing over the deep, catching the roaring wind in his sail, is skilled to guide his ship.
>
> You alone do not offend, do no one an injury; you look through your fingers at foolishness—evil alone you do not tolerate. You correct faults with indulgence, you do not oppress people as a wolf does sheep, you truly know their worth. They are subject to the will of kings, but yet more to the just God who lives in their [i.e., the kings'] laws.

(strophes 13-14)

As he nears the end of his ode, the poet, who has for some time forgotten his Oriental locale, returns suddenly to it, and asks (strophes 25-26):

> But where in the world does your throne gleam? Where, O heavenly branch, do you bloom? In Baghdad, Smyrna, Kashmir? Hearken, wherever you live-in noting my praises of you, do not suppose that I wanted hats or jackets from you for them. To feel the charm of good, such is the wealth of the soul, the like of which even Croesus did not amass.
>
> I pray the great prophet that I may touch the dust of your feet, and delight myself with the most sweet flow of your words and the sight of your face! I pray the heavenly powers that, spreading out their sapphire wings, they may invisibly keep you from all sickness, evils and sorrow; that the noise of your deeds in posterity may shine forth like the stars in the heavens.

The device of flattery which Derzhavin hit upon in "Felitsa" he made use of several times again, it seems not without Catherine's prompting. In 1783 he wrote his **"Thanks to Felitsa"**[11] for her munificent rewards, and in the same year or the next **"The Murza's Vision,"**[12] in which "Felitsa," now in the pose and costume of Levitsky's famous painting of Catherine II, appears to her faithful courtier in a dream of the night. In the same year, probably at a hint from Potemkin, he wrote **"To Reshemysl,"**[13] using the second of Catherine's children's stories, "Tale of Prince Fevei," in which Potemkin appears in the guise of the wise Reshemysl. In 1789 he wrote another long ode (464 lines), **"Portrait of Felitsa."**[14] Thereafter, however, as he notes in his autobiography, he was unable to find inspiration in the subject again, and dropped it, despite Catherine's hints that she would like it revived.

The **"Verses on the Birth in the North of a Porphyrogennete Child"** are, in form, a radically novel variation on a common classical genre, the congratulatory ode. The poem **"To Potentates and Judges"** is a Psalm paraphrase differing from others of its kind only in its boldly denunciatory language; **"Felitsa"** is in form a perfectly classical ode, but in content a completely unorthodox combination of eulogy and satire. In 1784 Derzhavin laid hands on another favorite eighteenth-century genre, the religious ode, with results hardly less innovative. The ode entitled **"God"**[15] utilizes, as did **"Felitsa,"** the Lomonosov stanza—ten lines of iambic tetrameter, rhyming *aBaBccDeeD*. It begins, in quite orthodox fashion:

> O thou, infinite in extension, living in the motion of substance, eternal by the flow of time, without person, in three persons of Godhead! Being spirit everywhere and unique, who has neither place nor cause, whom no one has been able to reach, who fills everything with himself, embraces, creates, preserves—whom we call God.

Then the poet proceeds through five further stanzas to emphasize the infinitude of God and the insignificance of all creation in comparison—a theme already familiar from Lomonosov's "Meditations." In strophe 6 comes the word which stands as a pivot in the whole composition—"nothing":

> As a drop lost in the sea is all this firmament before Thee. But what is the universe that I behold? And what, before Thee, am I? In that aerial ocean worlds multiplying other worlds by the hundred million—and this, when I dare compare it with Thee, will be but a pinprick; and I, before Thee—am nothing.

The next strophe begins with the same word—"Nothing!" But now the emphasis is shifted: man is God's image, and God lives in him—so he is not "nothing," but shares in the divine infinitude:

> Nothing! But Thou shinest in me with the magnitude of Thy goodness; in me Thou dost reflect Thyself, as the sun in a tiny drop of water. Nothing! But I feel life, with a certain unsated soaring I am ever flying aloft; my soul trusts in Thy existence, probes, thinks, reasons; I am—and so Thou are too!
>
> Thou art!—my heart knows the order of nature, proclaims this to me, my reason affirms, Thou art—and I am no longer nothing! I am a particle of the entire universe, set, it seems to me, in that honored center of existence where Thou didst end Thy bodily creation, and where begin the heavenly spirits, and with me Thou didst link the chain of all beings.
>
> I am the connector of worlds everywhere existing, I am the utmost step of matter, I am the midpoint of living things, the initial stroke of Godhead; I moulder with my body in the dust, [but] in mind I give orders to the thunders. I am king, I am slave, I am worm, I am God! But being so wondrous, whence have I come? It is unknown; but of myself I could not exist.
>
> Thy creation I am, O Creator! I am the creature of Thy wisdom, Thou source of life, giver of good, soul of my soul and king! Thy justice would needs have it so, that

my immortal being should traverse the abyss of mortality; that my spirit should be clouded in mortality and that through death I should return, O Father!—into Thy deathlessness.

Inscrutable, unfathomable! I know that my soul's imaginings are powerless to sketch even Thy outlines; but if blessing be one's duty, then for weak mortals it is impossible to honor Thee by any other means than only for them to raise themselves to Thee, to lose themselves in [Thy] measureless diversity, and to shed tears of gratitude.

This ode represents just as drastic a departure from classicism as **"Felitsa,"** but here the novelty is in the thought rather than the form. The theme of man's insignificance in comparison with the Infinite is a Biblical one (e.g., the Book of Job), and traditional to the religious ode. A good deal of the matter in Derzhavin's 8th and 9th stanzas on the human paradox was borrowed, as his contemporaries were quick to note, from Edward Young's *Night Thoughts*. Compare Young's "Night First," lines 68-82:[16]

> How poor, how rich, how abject, how august,
> How complicate, how wonderful is man!
> How passing wonder He who made him such!
> Who centered in our make such strange extremes!
> From different natures so marvelously mix'd,
> Connexion exquisite of distant worlds!
> Distinguish'd link in being's endless chain!
> Midway from nothing to the Deity!
> A beam ethereal, sullied and absorb'd!
> Though sullied and dishonor'd, still divine!
> Dim miniature of greatness absolute!
> An heir of glory! a frail child of dust!
> Helpless immortal! insect infinite!
> A worm! a god!—I tremble at myself,
> And in myself am lost! etc.

But there is nothing essentially unorthodox in the famous theme of "the great chain of being." The development, which would, I think, have startled the good English clergyman as much as it must have Derzhavin's countrymen, *is* unorthodox. I exist, therefore God exists! The traditional reasoning could hardly be more boldly violated. Where is "faith" in this meditation? Everything is subjected to reasoning—and reason declares that I—the human being—have only one duty: to raise myself to divinity! Presumption unheard-of! Where is the doctrine of original sin, of the essential imperfectability of man? Where is the redemption? Where is grace? Derzhavin is reasoning like a man of the enlightenment, not a Christian. Man is *perfectible,* and his purpose in life is to make himself divine. Deistic optimism is triumphant.

* * *

One of the eighteenth-century varieties of the lyric most frequently cultivated by Lomonosov and his imitators, such as V. P. Petrov, was the ode in commemoration of

great military victories. Derzhavin wrote a few such odes, grandiose and inflated in style, such as the one **"On the Capture of Izmail"** (1790 or 1791).[17] They seem to be evidently concessions to popular taste, and show little of Derzhavin's originality, although in the Izmail ode there are traces already of Ossianic influence. Much more characteristic, indeed, one of his best poems, is the 1788 ode **"Autumn During the Siege of Ochakov".**[18] It was written while Derzhavin was governor of Tambov, in the neighborhood of which was the estate of Prince S. F. Golitsyn, who was actively engaged in the siege of Ochakov, a Turkish fortress west of the Crimea, guarding the approaches to the Dnieper River. The ode was composed early in November; Ochakov fell to the Russians in December. It is notable in this very unorthodox ode that it is neither General-in-Chief Potemkin, who was nominally in charge of operations in the Crimean campaign, nor Golitsyn, who was the actual commander at Ochakov, but the ordinary, anonymous Russian soldier who is glorified—and far less space is devoted to "the siege of Ochakov" than to attendant circumstances: the autumn at Tambov, where Derzhavin and Princess V. V. Golitsyna, the General's wife, were anxiously awaiting news from the front; and the domestic picture of the General's family. In this poem, as in so many of Derzhavin's, the eighteenth century conventional "description through mythology" stands in incongruous juxtaposition to actual, realistic genre scenes of Russian life, not entirely unlike the masterly sketches of autumn and winter in *Eugene Onegin*. Such a medley would have been unthinkable to Lomonosov or Sumarokov, or indeed to any of Derzhavin's own contemporaries. The ode begins:

> Gray-haired Aeolus has let Boreas loose from his iron chains out of the caverns; spreading wide his fearful pinions ["krile"—accusative dual number! an unexampled Slavonicism, said to have been suggested to Derzhavin by the poet I. I. Dmitriev], the doughty warrior ["bogatyr"] has flapped over the world; he has driven the blue air in herds, he has thickened the mists into clouds; he has pressed, and the clouds have settled, rain descended and drummed.

> Already ruddy Autumn is carrying the golden sheaves to the threshing-floor, and luxury with greedy hand is demanding the grapes for wine. Already the flocks of birds are crowding, the feather-grass is silver on the steppes; rustling red and yellow leaves are scattered everywhere on the paths.

The picture of the autumn rains is wholly mythological, but with the curiously unlikely identification of the Greek wind-god Boreas with a Russian *bogatyr*! The second strophe begins with a quite conventional personification and a *classical* description of autumn activities. The "golden sheaves" may answer to Russian realities, but most certainly the grapes do not; as Belinsky impatiently notes:[19] "Beautiful verses too—but where they take us, God knows!" The excuse that Derzhavin is describing the natural scene at Ochakov, where grapes might grow, is ingenious, but unconvincing. The rest of his description is obviously north Russian. The flocks of birds ready for migration, the feather-grass and the autumn leaves fallen on the paths belong to the real world of Russian experience. Noteworthy once again is Derzhavin's keen sense of color—he even creates the compound adjective "red-yellow" ["krasno-zheltyi"] to describe the leaves. The third strophe moves us entirely into Russian reality, with no classical conventions and with a homely vocabulary startling in a formal ode: "On the forest edge lies the swift-footed hare, having settled like the spoonbill; the hunting-horns resound, and the baying and clamor of hounds peals out. The peasant, having laid in his store of bread, eats good cabbage-soup ["shchi"] and drinks beer; enriched by generous heaven, he sings the happiness of his days." The next strophe once more brings in Boreas and personifications of Autumn and Winter; then another genre picture: "On the carpets of the green fields the white down lies scattered; deserts and dales mourn, and hungry wolves howl in them"; then another strophe (No. 6) which combines the two disparate elements: "The reindeer has gone out into the mossy tundras and the bear has lain down in his den; in the villages the loud-voiced nymphs [here obviously just the village girls] have stopped singing in round-dances; the houses smoke with gray smoke ["dymiatsia serym dymom"], the traveler hastens on his path; the Mars of the heavens [not war-god, but the Star] has laid aside his thunders, and lain down in the mists to rest." Mention of Mars is introduced in order to bring in, in strophe 7, "The Russian Mars, Potemkin," the Crimean campaign and the siege of Ochakov; but Potemkin has no great place in the ode (nor had in the siege); after this polite reference he disappears, and at Ochakov it is "the invincible Russian [soldier]" who "in the frost reaps green laurels, scorns the gray storms, flies against ice, against trenches, against thunder, [and] amid water and fire thinks: he will either die or win victory." Derzhavin then, in two strophes (9 and 10) addresses the Russian heroes directly: "Be men, you Russian Achilleses, sons of the northern goddess [i.e., Catherine]; though you were not dipped in the Styx [as the Greek Achilles was], yet by your deeds you are immortal." Then he turns to his friend General Golitsyn with the exhortation: "Bring back to your home the laurel with the olive." The mention of Golitsyn's home then at once introduces his anxious wife and family: "When with warmth you shall embrace your seven sons, you will cast tender glances at their mother and in your joy seek no words." The tender scene of husband and wife reunited is then elaborated with homely details extraordinary in a classical ode:

Hasten, husband, to your faithful wife, be joyful yourself and give her joy; she is thoughtful, sorrowful, in simple attire, her hair scattered over her brow in disarray, she sits on the sofa at a little table, and her light-blue ["sveto-golubye"] eyes are always shedding tears.

There are fifteen strophes in Derzhavin's ode **"Autumn During the Siege of Ochakov,"** and of these four are devoted to the siege and military exploits, while two others refer to the delights of listening to tales of prowess at the hero's home-coming—surely a quite extraordinary proportion for a "triumphal ode!"

Derzhavin's universally recognized masterpiece is the great ode entitled simply **"The Waterfall,"**[20] written during the years 1791-1794. The ode was occasioned by the sudden death in 1791 of the most spectacular magnate of Catherine's reign, Grigory Potemkin. Derzhavin of course knew Potemkin and had very ambivalent feelings about him. Unnamed, but identifiable by unmistakable allusions, he is the first of Catherine's "murzas" to be satirized in **"Felitsa";** and he appears often enough elsewhere in the poems, but never with any great adulation. Even in **"Reshemysl"** the portrait of the ideal courtier is evidently not meant to be identified with Potemkin. The man was an enormous force in his time; a magnificent, magnetic, overpowering personality, devoured by ambition and obsessed with the most visionary and fantastic schemes, such as the recovery of Constantinople for Christianity and the reestablishment, under a Russian protectorate, of a Greek "Byzantine Empire." But he was capricious, vain, petty, and an intriguer; he was inordinately fond of luxury and extravagance, and in the last decade of his life, when he was dominant over even the Empress and perhaps actually her morganatic husband, he was a ruthless tyrant. And yet with all his negative qualities, Potemkin was such a titanic figure that the ordinary criteria of morality seemed hardly to apply to him—or so it appeared to Derzhavin.

The ode on Potemkin's death is dominated by the image of the "waterfall,"—a very real waterfall, in fact, which Derzhavin had encountered during his Olonets governorship; it is called Kivach and is on the Suna river, which flows into Lake Onega, northeast of St. Petersburg. The ode opens with a splendid, realistic description of the cataract itself, with Derzhavin's usual eye for color:

A mountain of diamonds pours down from the height in four cliffs [i.e., the waterfall makes four successive leaps]; an abyss of pearl and silver boils below, and beats aloft in hillocks; a dark-blue hill of spray stands high, and the roar thunders afar through the forest.

The noise goes up, and then is lost in the depths amid the thick woods; the sun's ray glances quickly through the torrent; beneath the pliant vault of trees, as though roofed with a dream, the waves pour quietly, drawn together in a milky stream.

The stupendous power of the waterfall is then briefly noted, and the terror which it inspires in three symbolic animals that visit its bank—the wolf, fallow-deer and horse (malice, meekness and pride, Derzhavin tells us). Then comes an Ossianic vision: an old man, with spear and shield and helmet at his feet, sits under a low-hanging cedar tree, on the bank overlooking the waterfall, and meditates. An unmistakable allusion in a simile of the "red" ["rumianoi"] sunset identifies this spectator as General Peter Alexandrovich Rumiantsev (1725-1796), hero of the Seven Years War and of the first of Catherine's wars against Turkey. Rumiantsev, whom the envious Potemkin had intrigued to disgrace, was universally regarded at this time as the model of self-effacing, patriotic heroism. Watching the noisy waterfall the old man is moved to make it a symbol of human life: "Is it not thus that time pours down from heaven, the torrents of the passions seethe, fame spreads abroad, the fortune of our days flashes past, whose beauty and joy are darkened by griefs, sorrows, and old age." Again the theme of universal death emerges, with the same kind of development as in the **"Verses on the Death of Prince Meshchersky":**

> Into this maw does not king fall from throne, and friend of kings? They fall—and, commander invincible, Caesar fell in the Senate House amid his praises, at the very moment when he desired the diadem—and covered his face with his cloak. [His] projects, hopes disappeared, and the eyes covetous for a throne were closed.

So far in the ode everything has been general and there has been nothing to hint at Potemkin's death—but the *exemplum* of Julius Caesar, followed by that of Belisarius, unmistakably points to another mortal of insatiable ambition, cut down at the moment of triumph by inexorable death. Then, after some melancholy reflections on his own vanished glory and present frustration: "[My] strength weakened, the tempest wrenched the spear from my hands, and hale though my spirit is still, fate has deprived me of victories," the old man falls asleep. His dream of his own glorious career is suddenly interrupted—and again the influence of the dark Ossianic poetry is very apparent—by natural signs that portend some ominous event:

> He listens: the fir-tree is riven, the company of ravens awakes, the stony hill breaks in a terrible fissure, the mountain with its riches falls, echo rumbles through the mountains, like thunder rolling upon thunder ["kak grom gremiashchi po gromam"].

Culminating the ominous dream comes a vision of a black-clad woman with a scythe—Death. Awakened from his vision, the old man proclaims: "Surely, some chieftain has died!" Then follows a strophe that could hardly have been interpreted as unqualified praise of the "chieftain" Potemkin: "Blessed is he if, in striving after glory, he has maintained the general good, been merci-ful in bloody war, and spared the lives of his very enemies; blessed among later ages be this friend of men!" The next strophe ends with the line "if. . . . he did not seek for false glory!" This leads to the comparison which is the central theme of the ode:

> O glory, glory in the world of the mighty! You are exactly this waterfall. By the torrent of its abundant waters and the noise of the pouring coolness it is magnificent, bright, beautiful, wondrous, mighty, thunderous, clear;

> It gathers people about it in crowds for constant admiration; but if with its water it does not give all to drink comfortably, if it bursts its banks and if there is no profit from its swiftness—ah! would it not be better to be less famous, but more useful? Like the charming little brooks to sprinkle fields, meadows, gardens, and from a distance with gentle murmur to attract the notice of posterity ["potomstvo": cf. Potemkin]?

The old man's speech ends with another guarded benediction for the still unknown hero: "Oh! Be immortal, warlike knight, *if* you have maintained all your duty!"

Then again an Ossianic passage, as the poet, now in his own person, sees a great shade "hastening over the clouds to mansions aloft." "The wind is too slow to flow by his paths; he surveys the kingdoms round about, he clamors, and glitters like a star, and scatters sparks in his wake." A vision of the corpse on the steppe, and the poet cries:

> Whose bier is the earth—whose baldequin the blue air, whose palace the sights of the desert about you—Are you not the son of Fortune, son of Glory, magnificent Prince of Tavrida? Was it not you who from the summit of honors fell suddenly amidst the steppes?

The last portion of the ode is largely a fairly conventional glorification of the dead hero, mourned by his army, by Catherine herself, by poets and preachers:

> A single hour, a single moment are capable of smiting kingdoms, a single breath of the elements of converting giants to dust! Their places are sought, but not found, and the dust of heroes is trampled upon.

> Of heroes? No! But their deeds gleam forth from the dusk and the centuries; [their] memory uncorrupted, their praises fly forth even from ruins; their tombs blossom like hills. Potemkin's labor shall be recorded.

At last, as though almost against his intention, Derzhavin, returning again to his key metaphor, sees in the noisy waterfall now only beauty:

> Roar, roar, O waterfall! Touching the regions of the air, gladden hearing and sight by your torrent, bright, noisy, and in mankind's memory live hereafter only by your beauty.

Most of Derzhavin's poetical work from his debut in 1779 until about 1795 was public and monumental—great odes, commemorative poems, satires such as **"The**

Magnate" (1794)[21] and the like. These poems, as we have noted, were for the most part highly innovative and stylistically quite far from the models created by Lomonosov and Sumarokov, but they nevertheless belonged to the same class of public document, the utterances of a Russian patriot speaking as the mouthpiece of the people. In the latter part of his life, however, Derzhavin came more and more to dissociate himself from such public themes and to speak increasingly in his own personal quality. It has been noted before that he was attracted to the so-called poems of Anacreon, especially after a translation of these had been published by his close friend Nikolai Alexandrovich Lvov (in 1794). Derzhavin of course had no knowledge of Greek, but using his friend's version (in unrhymed verse) as a point of departure, he "translated" quite successfully some of the Anacreontea. More significantly, he began to imitate "Anacreon," and in 1804 published a collection of translations and imitations which even contained some of his earliest songs, written long before he had even known of the Greek poet.[22] The concerns of this Anacreontic *persona* are entirely private, like those of his model—chiefly Epicurean delight in the innocent pleasures of eating, drinking and love-making. A healthy, life-affirming hedonist by temperament, Derzhavin felt a natural affinity for such themes.

Other private concerns, however, make their appearance in Derzhavin's later poetry. Mention has been made earlier of the evident influence of Horace on such a poem as **"Verses on the Death of Prince Meshchersky."** The Roman poet is almost the only writer from classical antiquity, except the spurious "Anacreon," who seems to have had a genuine influence on Derzhavin. One of Horace's most famous poems, the last of the first published collection of *Carmina* (III, 30) is the confident proclamation of his poetical immortality: "Exegi monumentum aere perennius"—"I have reared a monument more enduring than bronze." In 1795 Derzhavin wrote his imitation of this Latin ode; it is entitled simply **"Monument"**;[23] it may be remembered that Lomonosov had translated the same poem.

> I have reared me a monument wondrous, eternal; it is stronger than metal and higher than the pyramids. Neither tempest nor swift thunder shall break it, and the flight of time shall not destroy it.
>
> Yes! I shall not wholly die, but a great part of me, escaping corruption, shall live after death, and my fame shall grow, unwithering, as long as the universe shall honor the race of the Slav.
>
> * * *
>
> For I first, in entertaining Russian style, dared to proclaim the virtues of Felista, in sincere simplicity to converse about God, and with a smile to tell the truth to kings.

The odes **"Felitsa"** and **"God"** evidently constitute the poet's chief claim to immortality in his own opinion,

and whether we share this opinion or not, Derzhavin's contemporaries certainly did.

In 1794 Derzhavin's beloved first wife died. They had been married in 1778, and the poet and his "Plenyra," as he affectionately disguised her in his love poetry, had been a model couple. The little six-stanza poem which he wrote **"On the Death of Katerina Iakovlevna [Bastidon], Occurring on the 15th Day of July, 1794"**[24] he never published; it was evidently too personal a revelation. Professor G. A. Gukovsky published it in 1933, in his selection of Derzhavin's verse. The poem has a strong flavor of Russian popular verse, with its lines of irregular metrical structure and frequent dactylic rhymes; the very fact of its lack of polish makes it more effective. The emblem of the swallow has a connection with a poem, published in 1792, called **"The Swallow,"**[25] to which, after his wife's death, Derzhavin added two wistful last lines. The unpublished poem **"On the Death of Katerina Iakovlevna"** reads as follows:

> No longer the sweet-voiced swallow, the household [guest], from the eaves—oh! my dear one, my beautiful one, she has flown away—and my joy with her.
>
> The moon's pale radiance does not shine from the cloud in the terrible darkness—oh! her body lies dead, like a bright angel in sound slumber.
>
> The dogs are digging the ground, of a sudden they begin to howl, the wind howls, the house howls; they do not waken my dear one. The thunder shatters my heart!
>
> O you, gray-winged swallow! You will return to my house in the spring; but you, my wife, my dear one, will be seen with me no more forever.
>
> My loyal friend is no more, my good wife is no more, my priceless comrade is no more—oh! they are all buried with her.
>
> Everything is desolate! How can I bear life? Great anguish has devoured me. Farewell, the half of my heart, the half of my soul! The coffin planks have hidden you.

Derzhavin's Epicurean outlook on life and at the same time his sharp break with eighteenth-century decorum that barred from poetry such vulgarly specific items as foods and drinks may be seen in his **"Invitation to Dinner"**[26] of 1795. It begins:

> The golden sterlet of the Sheksna, clabbered cream ["kaimak"] and borsht are already standing [in preparation]; in the carafes wine and punch allure, one sparkling with ice, the other with flame; from the censers pour perfumes; fruits are smiling in baskets, the servants do not dare even to breathe, as they await you around the table; the shapely young mistress [Derzhavin's second wife, Daria Alexeevna Diakova, whom he married early in 1795] is ready to stretch out her hand.

The banquet, like Horace's, is to be "a feast of reason and the flow of soul," not a vulgar drinking-bout; but the poet, again like Horace, is moved to admonish his guests to enjoy themselves while they can:

To my friends I dedicate this day, to my friends and to beauty; I know the value of merits, and I know this, that our life is a shadow; that scarcely have we passed our childhood when we have already arrived at old age, and death is peeping at us through the fence. Alack! Then why not become philosophers, garland ourselves, if but once, with flowers, and leave off our gloomy looks!

Even kings, it appears, are not always happy—"He that is eternally on duty is as pitiable as a poor sentryman!" The final strophe of the **"Invitation"** [**"Invitation to Dinner"**] ends with the perfectly Horatian sentiment: "Happiness is not in the gleam of purple, nor in the savor of foods, nor in the delight of the ear; but in soundness and repose of spirit; moderation is the best banquet." It may be noted that the **"Invitation to Dinner,"** in marked contrast of its form to the homely vocabulary and easy, unconstrained tone, is in the strictest ode form: Lomonosov's ten-line iambic tetrameter strophe, rhyming *aBaBccDeeD!*

* * *

One of Derzhavin's masterpieces, and the most complete example of his delight in the beauties of life and his consummate ability to enshrine them in vivid word pictures is the epistle: **"To Eugene. Life at Zvanka."**[27] The addressee was Derzhavin's close friend Bishop Eugene Bolkhovitinov (1767-1837), a learned historian, archaeologist and literary critic. Zvanka was Derzhavin's fine estate in Novgorod province on the Volkhov river, to which he retired in 1803. The epistle, written in 1807 and published in the same year, is quite long (252 lines), in four-line strophes which consist of three Alexandrines followed by a four-beat iambic line; the rhymes are alternate masculine and feminine: *AbAb*. The strophic division is irregular for an epistle, which is normally in straight Alexandrines.

The poem describes what presumably might be a typical day at Zvanka during the summer, from the moment of rising to the reveries of evening. All the pictures are sharp and clear:

I hear close at hand the call of the shepherd's horn, and at a distance the dull drumming of grouse, "lambs in the air" [i.e., snipe, which have a bleating call like lambs], the whistling of nightingales in the bushes, the lowing of cows, the thundering of woodpeckers and the neighing of horses. I note how the swallow twitters on the roof—and from the house is wafted the vapor of Manchuria [tea] or the Levant [coffee]. I go to the round table: and there there is a chattering about dreams, the gossip of the city and of the peasants.

* * *

From the cow-barns, bee-hives and ponds I look at gold covered with leaves—now of butter and now of honey-comb; at the purple of berries, the velvet down of mushrooms, and the silver of threshing bream.

* * *

The hour of midday strikes, they run to serve at table; the mistress with a chorus of her guests goes to the dining-room. I inspect the table—and see a flower-garden of various dishes, set out in a pattern.

Pink ham, green cabbage-soup with the yellow of egg, reddish-yellow pasty, white cheese, red crayfish, caviar like pitch or like amber—and there the varicolored pike with blue fin—beautiful!

* * *

Or standing we note the sound of the green and black waves; how the plow mounds up the turf; how the ripe heads of the hay fall under the scythe, the gold of the cornlands under the sickle—and how, full of aromas, the wind takes flight amidst the rows of nymphs [i.e., the reaping women].

Or we watch how beneath a black cloud the shadow races over the ricks, over the sheaves, over the yellow-green carpets; and how the sun descends to its lowest step toward the blue-black hills and groves.

As usual, the precise color words, often compound adjectives put together as a painter might mix his paints on a palette, are prominent in these scenes; the still-life of the dining table is justly famous. But the other senses are not neglected; there are more precise words describing bird sounds—drumming, whistling, thundering, twittering—then are to be found in all Russian literature before Derzhavin; and indoors we hear "the thunder from the resonant harp, that penetrates the soul, the soothing, melting tones" that "flow from the strings of the pianoforte ["tikhogrom"]."

The gentle, pastoral repose of **"Life at Zvanka"** [**"To Eugene. Life at Zvanka"**] is interrupted here and there by meditation; the poet retires in the forenoon to his study, and perusal of history shows him "nothing but the self-love and wrangling of men." "'All is vanity of vanities,' think I, sighing; but casting my eyes on the radiance of the noon-day sun—O how beautiful is the world! Why should I burden my soul? The universe is in the Creator's keeping." As the day wanes, melancholy returns: "What is our worthless life? My fragile lyre? Alas! Even the dust of my bones Saturn will sweep away with his wings from this world of corruption. This house will be torn down, forest and garden will wither, nowhere will there be even a remembrance of the name of Zvanka; but the fire-green eyes of hoot-owls and barn-owls [will peer] from the hollows, and perhaps smoke will roll up from a mud hut." But at the last the poet reminds himself that his younger friend Eugene will not let his name pass into oblivion: "Waking with your pen our descendants from slumber, near to the capital of the north, you shall whisper in the wanderer's ear, like quiet thunder in the distance: 'Here lived the singer of God—and of **"Felitsa."**'"

The peculiarities of Derzhavin's linguistic practice have been pointed out in nearly every poem discussed, and it need only be remarked, by way of summary, that he treated the hierarchies of language with as little respect as he did other eighteenth-century poetical conventions. Champagne, playing cards, tobacco, Westphalian ham in an ode, side by side with solemn Slavonicisms—a bewildering medley. Nor is his grammar always conventional, although it would be too difficult to document this for an English reader. Pushkin, much too harshly, remarks in a letter to his friend Anton Delvig:[28] "So help me, this genius thought in Tatar—he hadn't the time to be bothered with Russian grammar." Actually, Derzhavin's deviations are not so much grammatical solecisms as a tendency, seen also in vocabulary, to employ the language of the common people.[29]

Much has also been said about his use of meter. Most notable, probably, is the appearance in so many of his poems of a perfectly classical form, as for example the Lomonosov strophe, in a thoroughly uncanonical ode, such as **"Felitsa"** or **"Invitation to Dinner."** But he is also experimental in metrical matters: the use of a slightly irregular "popular" line in the poem on his wife's death has been noted. A much more determined—and published—effort in the popular direction is his **"Maiden-Tsar"** [**"Tsar'-Devitsa"**][30] of 1812, written in the spirit of a popular ballad, and employing the quasi-popular four-line stanza of trochaic tetrameter rhyming *aBaB*. But perhaps his greatest metrical experiment, and an extremely successful one, is the famous **"Gypsy Dance"**[31] of 1805. This is written in six stanzas of six lines each, of which the last two lines in each stanza constitute an ever-repeated refrain: "Set souls aflame, hurl fire on hearts from [your] swarthy face." The first four lines are amphibrachic trimeters, with alternating feminine and masculine rhyme. Zhukovsky and the romantic poets came to use this triple measure quite extensively, but the amphibrach is a great rarity in Russian verse before this time. Derzhavin's metrical *tour de force* was intended to transfer to verse the curious syncopated beat of gypsy music. A metrical analysis of the first strophe will make this clearer:

> Бозьми, еипттянка, гитару,
> У дарь по струнам, босклицак;
> Исполнясл сладострастна жару,
> Тбоей бсех пляской босхишай.
> 　Жги душу, огнь бросай б сердца
> 　от смугдого лица.

> * * *

> Take the guitar, Gypsy maiden,
> Strike on the strings, cry out;
> Filled with voluptuous fire,
> Entrance all with your dance.
> 　Set souls aflame, hurl fire on hearts,
> 　From [your] swarthy face.

Our discussion of Derzhavin's lyric poetry has emphasized throughout the simultaneous presence in it of elements characteristic of the classical system of verse composition, and of elements antithetical to that system. Let us now attempt to summarize these disparate elements in Derzhavin's style, beginning with the classical inheritance.

It hardly needs to be said that much of Derzhavin's verse is, as Belinsky quite unjustly said of it all, rhetoric. So, of course, is Lomonosov's or Sumarokov's. In an age when verse composition was regarded as a form of intellectual exercise, and reason its guide, all poetry, with rare exceptions, tends to take the form of rhetoric. Too often for modern tastes the best efforts of a poet become merely moral or philosophical discourse in metrical form. What else is there, indeed, in the verse of Pope, or of Voltaire? Derzhavin's verse is, however, in this as in most other respects, transitional—and his poetical theory, as we shall presently discover, equally vacillating. **"The Waterfall," "God," "The Magnate,"** etc., are indeed rhetoric, versified reasoning, with little basis in or appeal to the emotions. **"Life at Zvanka," "On the Death of Katerina Iakovlevna," "Gypsy Dance,"** and many other of the smaller lyrics are, however, no more rhetorical than, let us say, the lyrics of such pre-romantics as Batiushkov or Zhukovsky. But in the prevalence of rhetoric in his verse Derzhavin is truly a representative of his age.

In another regard too we may consider Derzhavin typically classical—his didacticism. Classical theories of poetry always assume that art must teach, must be aimed primarily at inculcating a lesson. Very typical of this side of Derzhavin's verse is the short piece called **"The Peacock."**[32] It begins with a minute and sharply observed description of the gorgeous bird, with Derzhavin's usual painterly eye for color:

> What proud creature, spreading his tail magnificently, displays, sparkling, the black-green feathers with loose fringe behind his scaly body, like some proud and wondrous shield?

> Azure-gray-turquoise shadowy circles on the end of each feather, new waves of undulating gold and silver; he bends—and emeralds glitter! He turns—and sapphires burn!

Then follow the ironically phrased expectations aroused by the peacock's beauty:

> Is not this the famous feathered king? Is not this the paradisal Fire-bird, whose so rich adornment inspires creation with wonderment? Where he steps, rainbows play! Where he stands, there is radiance around!

> Surely in his wings are the strength and soaring of eagles, in his sweet mouth the trumpet's voice, the song of the swan—and the pelican's virtue in his heart and soul!

The last strophe pounds home the, by now obvious, "message" of the poem, with all the insistence of a schoolmaster: "But what an extraordinary phenomenon!

I hear a sort of strange screech! This Phoenix has suddenly lowered his plumes at sight of the ugliness of his feet. O magnificence! How you blind [people]! A witless nobleman ["baryn"] is a peacock."

There is a good deal of didacticism in Derzhavin, not often as obtrusive as this. Many also of the habitual classical procedures of verse description may be found in his poetry; they must have been almost automatic. Such is the mythological ornamentation: late autumn or winter is ushered in by Boreas, the god of the Northwind (**"Verses on the Birth in the North of a Porphyrogennete Child"**; **"Autumn During the Siege of Ochakov"**); nymphs and satyrs inhabit the woods; Mars presides over battles, Venus over scenes of love, etc. But this convention is so deep-rooted in European verse from the Renaissance on, that it is not even wholly accurate to call it merely classical. In this connection it is worth noting that some Russian eighteenth-century poets, uncomfortably aware of the incongruity of a Greek pantheon in the Slavic world, but still feeling the indispensability of mythology as a poetic instrument, tried to find a native substitute, and *faute de mieux,* to create one. Such is the love-god Lel', assumed to be identical with Cupid, whom Derzhavin sees in a vision in the poem **"The Cupid of Falconet".**[33]

The classical elements in Derzhavin's style are unobtrusive and omni-present—but it would be a great mistake for this reason to regard him as a typically classical poet. Too many features of his verse are precisely anti-classical, as is his poetical theory, as we shall see. Two of these anti-classical elements have been frequently commented upon above—the naturalism of his descriptions and his disregard of genre distinctions. Classical theory required the elimination of all specific details in description: a group of trees is "a shady grove," not "a clump of birch and alders!"; a table is set "with savory viands and sparkling wine," not with "Westphalian ham and champagne," etc. The goal is to make everything universal. We have seen how antithetical to this is Derzhavin's practice. Especially, as has so often been pointed out, is this true of his use of color designations. Where the autumn leaves would perhaps be called "motley" or "varicolored" ["pestrye"] by a classical poet at his most specific, Derzhavin makes them "red-yellow." His peacock has "azure-gray-turquoise" circles on his tail feathers, etc. This specificity is equally noteworthy in words denoting sounds—the peacock's voice is "a strange screech," the bleating call of the snipe makes them "lambs in the air," etc. Derzhavin is a poet of the senses, and he refuses to blur the impressions which his senses bring him in order to create a universally intelligible picture.

Notes

1. Berkov, P. N. "Problemy Izucheniia russkogo klassitsizma," XVIII VEK, Sbornik VI (1964), p. 29.

2. Derzhavin, [*G.R. Stikhotvoreniia* (L. Biblioteka poeta. Bol'shaia seriia. 1957] 398.

3. Ibid., 369.

4. Ibid., 83-85.

5. IRP [*Istoriia russkkoi poezii.* T.I.L. Isdatel'stvo "Nauko," 1968], p. 130 (I. Z. Serman).

6. Derzhavin, pp. 85-87.

7. Young uses the metaphor of the bell as the tongue of time: "The bell strikes one! We take no note of time, But from its loss: to give it then a tongue, Is wise in man." Edward Young, The Complaint and the Consolation, or Night Thoughts. (London, 1797), p. 3.

8. Derzhavin, p. 92.

9. Ibid., 97-104.

10. This tale is printed in Manning [*Anthology of Eighteenth Century Russian Literature,* New York: King's Crown Press, 1951], I, 85-90.

11. Derzhavin, pp. 104-05.

12. Ibid., 109-13.

13. Ibid., 106-09.

14. Ibid., 133-47.

15. Ibid., 114-16.

16. Young, pp. 3-4.

17. Derzhavin, pp. 156-66.

18. Ibid., 121-24.

19. Belinskii, V. G. *Sobranie sochinenii v trekh tomakh* (M. 1948), II, 504.

20. Derzhavin, pp. 178-90.

21. Ibid., 211-16.

22. Some of Derzhavin's anacreontics may be found in the *Stikhotvoreniia* volume on pp. 79, 97, 171, 226, 233, 245, 255, 259, 268.

23. Derzhavin, p. 233.

24. Ibid., 207.

25. Ibid., 207-08.

26. Ibid., 223-25.

27. Ibid., 326-34.

28. Pushkin, A. S. *Polnoe sobranie sochinenii* (M. 1962), 10, 162.

29. Vinogradov, V. V. *Ocherki po istorii russkogo literaturnogo iazyka xvii-xix vv* (Leiden: Brill, 1950), pp. 139-43.

30. Derzhavin, pp. 352-58.

31. Ibid., 306-08.

32. Ibid., 232.

33. Ibid., 305.

Paul Friedrich (essay date 1996)

SOURCE: Friedrich, Paul. "Gavrilo Derzhavin (1743-1816)." In *Music in Russian Poetry,* pp. 31-6. New York: Peter Lang, 1998.

[*In the following essay, originally published in 1996, Friedrich compares Derzhavin with Pindar, appraising Derzhavin's contribution to the musical tradition in Russian poetry.*]

> The tongue of time! the metal's clang!

Gavrilo Derzhavin stands foremost in a century when poets were initiated in musical culture as well as searching to integrate and harmonize music and poetry (Livanova 1952-53 [*Russkay a muzykal'naya kul'tura XVIII*]: 150, 188). In my terms, he was both linguistically and literally musical and, in his linguistic music, Russian-specific rather than universal. He possessed a never-to-be-surpassed ear for the primal musical value of Russian sounds as phonic images that, especially in his opening lines, hit like an aural blow. The Russian of the epigraph above and its stanza goes:

> Glagol vremën! Metalla zvon!
> Tvoy strashnyy glas menya smushchaet;
> Zovët menya, zovët tvoy ston,
> Zovët—i k grobu priblizhaet.

By the time Derzhavin appeared on the literary scene, there were four main types of ode (Titunik 1985 ["Odes"]: 313-14), and he created major poems in all of them. The ode of praise or panegyric ode was brilliantly exemplified by his **"On the Death of Prince Meshchersky,"** just quoted. The spiritual ode on a lofty or sacred theme was fully realized in "God": "I decompose in earthly dust . . . I'm tsar, I'm slave, / A worm, I'm God!" Light and often amorous, anacreontic odes emerged in his later years, as in his **"Gypsy Dance"**: "Take up your guitar, Gypsy woman!" (written to defend some Gypsies who were keeping his neighbors awake). The Horatian ode is addressed to the human condition, above all, to the inevitability of death and oblivion. It is best illustrated by his free paraphrase of Horace's *Exegi Monumentum.* Derzhavin invented a new type of ode with his serio-comic **"Felitsa,"** and there were blends and degrees of ode such as **"Waterfall"** (his finest achievement in the opinion of many poets, written in the early 1790s).

Here is the celebrated first stanza, which, in the style of translation from the Chinese, I will first render more or less literally:

> Алмазна сыплется гора
> Diamond splashes-down mountain
>
> С бысот четыремя скалами,
> From heights down between four rockfaces
>
> Жемчугу Бездна и сребра
> Of-pearl abyss and of-silver
>
> Кипит бнизу, Бьет бберх Буграми;
> Boils below, beats upwards in/like hills
>
> От брызгоб синий холм стоит,
> From (drops-of-) spray dark-blue stands
>
> Далече рзб б лесу гремит.
> Farther roar in forest thunders.

And here is a poetic translation:

> Mountain of diamonds pouring down
> Through four rockbound crags on high:
> An abyss of silver ore and pearl
> Boils up below, explodes as hills.
> Drop fragments form in a knoll of blue;
> The roar, far off in the woods, resounds.

The next stanza is worth quoting to give a fuller context:

> Makes tumult and then dies away
> Amid the thick forest's undergrowth.
> A ray darts swiftly through the stream
> Beneath a rippling dome of trees, by dreams
> It's covered as the waves flow soft
> Drawn onward by their milky way.

> Бодопад
>
> Алмазна сыплется гора
> С бысот четыремя скалами,
> Жемчугу Бездна и сребра
> Кипит бнизу, Бьет бберх Буграми;
> От Брызгоб синий холм стоит,
> Далече рзб б лесу гремит.
>
> Шумит, и средь густого Бора
> Теряется б глуши потом;
> Луч чрез поток сберкает скоро;
> Под зыбким сбодом дреб, как сном
> Покрыты, болны тихо льются,
> Рекою млечною блекутся.

In a century when the ode was the dominant and most popular genre in Russian, Derzhavin surpassed all others in all of the established variants as well as in coining some new ones. And yet despite its formal diversity, the ode had come to be practiced mainly in terms of two functions. It was the vehicle for intrigue and adulation. Second, for religious purposes and ceremonial occasions it had been cultivated, notably by Lomonosov, to a majestic if often ponderous level.

The great achievement of Derzhavin was the way he took the ode, or rather the odic genre and principles of its composition, and, in his rough and ready way, reconnected them to the feel and structure of the ultimate odist, Pindar (518-438 b.c.). Pindar's odes, in apt words that would remind any Russianist of Derzhavin, are characterized by diverse linguistic irregularities, unexpected shifts of theme and lexicon, and startling "blinding" moves by association (Fogle 1974 ["Ode"]: 585). Derzhavin's syntax was not only fractured, but unhinged to the point of veering toward, even into, what has been interpreted as ungrammatical (Grot 1864 [*Sochineniya Derzhavina*]: 333-55). This syntax is part of a dialectic between two forces. Centripetal ones, such as parallelism or repetition of the same part of speech, pull toward the center while centrifugal forces spin away from it (for example, drastically marked inversion, or extreme discontinuity between coupled forms such as a noun and its adjective). The way Derzhavin delays resolution to conflicts created by these two processes forces us, among other things, to listen to the sound of his poems. His resolutions also force us to integrate separate lexical and syntactic levels (Crone 1994a ["The Chiasmic Structure of Derzhavin's 'Bog'"])—levels which his eighteenth-century listeners felt to be as different and distinguishable from each other as the sections of an orchestra.

Derzhavin may have gotten his intuition of an authentically Pindaric ode from wide reading in criticism, or from Pindar's odes themselves in German translations (his only foreign language), or from stray conversations with literary people. But how he got it matters little compared with the way he used such intuitions to suggest combinations of musical order and musical chaos. His great odes, like Blok's "Twelve," combine forces of building up and tearing down in a way that is at the heart of much great poetry and its music (Friedrich 1986 [*The Language Parallax*]: 133-35). My positive reading here contradicts the familiar negative ones, be it Pushkin's quip that Derzhavin's language was of a "Tatar," or Dmitri Mirsky's grandiloquent contention that "His style is a continuous violence to the Russian tongue, an uncertain, vigorous, personal, virile, but often cruel, deformation of it" (1958 [*A History of Russian Literature*]: 51). Thus, while Lomonosov was dubbed "The Russian Pindar," he was actually guided by German odists and inspired by German and Latin odes. It is Derzhavin who is the more Russian Pindar of the two and the closest thing to Pindar since Pindar (just as Tsvetaeva was to be the closest thing to Sappho since Sappho; see "Tsvetaeva" below).

Eighteenth-century Russian odes were usually intended to be sung with the intonation of "a powerful choir with orchestra, or of a choral cantata" (Livanova 1952-53:

186). Derzhavin's main composer for this associated music was surely Bach, but more research is needed on his debt to the poet Friedrich Klopstock (1724-1803), whose Musical Odes he probably knew just as he did know much Klopstock-influenced German music (for instance, Christoph Glück). Nor is there a sharp line between his poetry and opera, a genre in which—after his retirement—he composed seven works and translated two. These range from tasteless vaudeville to failed attempts to create a national style. All of them evidence his commitment to music and his interest in structuring a poetic form in terms of a musical one (for example, the choral response in his *Pozharsky*).

Derzhavin was exceptionally musical in his personal culture: in his marital life (his first wife was a pianist, the second a harpist); in the innumerable musical happenings in his home; in using his governmental appointments to promote music (for example, importing Italian teachers); in his references to music, musical instruments, and the musical sounds of things in his writings; in the way the spirit of music informed his poetry. The Gypsy poems written during his retirement in Zvanka were not only about Gypsies, but reflected the way he was, like so many of his successors, inspired by Russian Gypsy music.

The contributions of our poet to the musical tradition of Russian poetry, partly described above, were profound and often innovative. His technique was "surprisingly in advance of its time" (Unbegaun 1956 [*Russian Versification*]: 144): (1) in its fractured, centripetal/centrifugal syntax; (2) in its mysterious devices for achieving grand vocalic resonances, (3) in its use of approximate and otherwise inexact rhyme (Kholshevnikov 1972 [*Oshovy Stikhove deniya*]: 91); (4) in the ways it advanced Sumarokov's experiments with drawing-room language for light themes (as in his **"Nightingale in a Dream,"** written without *r*'s "to prove the mellifluousness of the Russian language"); and, above all, (5) as noted, in its virtuoso variations on the odic genre, ranging from praise poems in the standard iambic tetrameter and *ababcc* rhyme format to anacreontic variants in irregular amphibrachic quatrains (with a refrain couplet in iambic). It is these lighter works, incidentally, that have been set to music most often (G. Ivanov 1966 [*Russkaya poeziya*]: 116-17).

At a deep psychological and etymological, almost Jungian, level, Derzhavin seems to have felt that the base of his own name (*derzhava*), which means "power," underlay an implicit analogy between himself, the greatest power in (the music of) Russian poetry, and the political power of Russia and Russians that he variously admired, struggled for, and contended with. **"The Waterfall,"** so often extolled by poets and critics for its music and other formal qualities of its language, even for its depiction of a specific waterfall in the Olonets area, is also a 74-stanza political allegory centered on the be-jewelled image of the court politico and generalissimo, Grigory Potymkin, and of Potymkin's villages (Crone 1994b [*Doing Justice to Potemkin*]). The music of Derzhavin's poems was often entangled with politics, or, commuting this, the "aural blow" which has been striking his readers for two centuries was often the expression of profoundly political sentiments.

References

Crone, Anna Lisa. 1994a. "The Chiasmic Structure of Derzhavin's 'Bog': Poetic Realization of the 'Chain of Being.'" *Slavic and East European Journal* 38, no. 3 (Fall): 407-18.

———. 1994b. "Doing justice to Potemkin: paradox, oxymoron, and two voices in Derzhavin's 'Waterfall.'" *Russian History* 21, no. 3: 1-26.

Fogle, Stephen F. 1974. "Ode." In *Princeton Encyclopedia of Poetry and Poetics,* edited by Alex Preminger, pp. 585-86. Princeton, NJ: Princeton University Press.

Friedrich, Paul. 1986. *The Language Parallax.* Austin: University of Texas Press.

Grot, Yakov Karlovich. 1864. *Sochineniya Derzhavina s ob''yasnitel'nymi primechaniyami Ya. Grota,* Volume 9. St. Petersburg: Akademiya Nauk.

Ivanov, Georgiy Konstantinovich. 1966. *Russkaya poeziya v otechestvennoy muzyke (do 1917 goda).* Moscow: Muzyka.

Kholshevnikov, Vladislav Evgenevich. 1972. *Osnovy Stikhovedeniya. Russkoe Stikhoslozhenie.* Leningrad: Izdatel'stvo Leningradskogo Universiteta.

Livanova, Tamara. 1952-53. *Russkaya muzykal'naya kul'tura XVIII Veka v eë svyazyax s literaturoy, teatrom, i bytom; Issledovaniya i materialy.* Vols. 1 and 2: Muzykal'noe Izdatel'stvo.

Mirsky, Dmitriy Petrovich. 1958. *A History of Russian Literature from the Beginning to 1900.* Edited by Francis J. Whitfield. New York: Random House: Vintage Russian Library.

Titunik, I. R. 1985. "Odes." In *Handbook of Russian Literature,* edited by Victor Terras, pp. 313-14. New Haven: Yale University Press.

Unbegaun, Boris O. 1956. *Russian Versification.* Oxford: Clarendon Press.

Anna Lisa Crone (essay date 2001)

SOURCE: Crone, Anna Lisa. "Both the Voice of God and the Voice of the People: Deržhavin's Independence in Language." In *The Daring of Derzhavin: The Moral and Aesthetic Independence of the Poet in Russia,* pp. 33-62. Bloomington, Ind.: Slavica, 2001.

[*In the following essay, Crone explores in detail Derzhavin's fusion of "high" and "low" language, focusing on the relationship between style and content. Crone also examines Derzhavin's response to the principles of Lomosovian classicism and evaluates Derzhavin's poetic and philosophic development within the context of Russian history.*]

The most noted area of Deržavin's independence was and is his new odic style. His peculiar mix of high style words—the language of God—and very low style ones—the language of the Folk, was considered a stylistic strength by Nikolaj Gogol':

> His style is so grand, unlike the style of all our other poets. This is owing to the unusual combination of the very highest words with the very lowest and simplest.
>
> And he awaits death like a lady friend
> Pensively tweaking his mustache.
>
> Who besides Deržavin would dare to link a matter like awaiting death with something so mundane as tweaking a mustache?[1]

The reason for Deržavin's attempt to integrate the language of the real Russian people with that of the Church Books—two styles that had pretensions to being a "language of Truth"—is all too often analyzed exclusively on the basis of artistic decisions, and too rarely in terms of the poet's moral/ethical aims. Aesthetically, Deržavin had a residual love for Lomonosovian high style, especially in odes, but, as we have seen above in the first ode to Catherine (stanza 2), if that style is only beautiful and entertaining and not *true,* it holds little charm for him as artist.

I agree with those scholars who feel Deržavin's artistic preferences in odes remained largely Lomonosovian.[2] His 1811 treatise *Discourse on Lyric Poetry or about the Ode* is at once his primer on what lyric poetry should be and a post-factum justification of his own odes. There Deržavin takes over 90 percent of his illustrative examples from the verse of Lomonosov.[3]

Like most poets whose careers began in the period of Classicism, Deržavin wrote serious verse with moral-edificatory aims. Scholarship has tended to overemphasize either Deržavin's literary aims or his moral/ethical ones, failing to treat both as inextricably bound. The first emphasis may have resulted from the Formalist approach, whose dominance, evinced in Èjxenbaum's article of 1916, "Deržavin," upon the centennial of the poet's death, coincided with a rebirth of interest in his poetry. Owing to Formalist treatment, Deržavin's innovations have often been seen as arising from a self-conscious desire to parody the style of his odic predecessors-fathers.[4] Evidence from other areas of Deržavin's activity renders it highly unlikely that he violated Lomonosov's prescriptions for style with alacrity and for purely aesthetic (literary-evolutionary) reasons. Richard Wortmann, in an essay astutely analyzing

Deržavin's character, "Russia's First Minister of Justice," shows the poet to be quite traditionalist in mentality, a believer in tradition and the rule and even sanctity of established law and custom.[5] We see from Deržavin's administrative practice that when he broke laws he tended to do so openly, and only because he felt they were inapplicable in the given case or not conducive to the public good. Such open violation of precedent led to Deržavin's being frequently charged with insubordination in the service, and I believe the best description for Deržavin as stylist is still an "insubordinate Lomonosovian." He was a selective law-breaker in his administrative life, and in literature he hardly viewed himself as a revolutionary or great reformer.

One must not look at Deržavin's violation of Lomonosov in isolation. At the time when Deržavin's poetic license allowed him to take liberties with Lomonosov's prescriptions, Karamzin's advocation of a homogeneous, aristocratic-based middle style with French syntax and massive calquification from the French was a truly revolutionary reform, and a much greater threat to the Lomonosovian system. Deržavin's albeit far-reaching modifications of Lomonosov represented a conservative alternative to Karamzin's ultimately successful assault on the theory of three styles.

It is essential to appreciate the language crisis of the late Neo-Classical period and the truly revolutionary changes wrought by Nikolaj Karamzin. Historians of language Vinogradov and Efimov do not mince words on this point: "he [Karamzin] produced a new grammatical reform in the Russian language by abrogating the obsolete norms of Lomonosov's grammar of three styles."[6]

Karamzin and his young followers, members of the Arzamas group, so destroyed the Lomonosovian system of poetic language that even as perceptive a reader as Puškin declared Lomonosov a "non-poet." His aesthetic judgment of Deržavin was biting but less harsh; he called Deržavin's original odes "poor translations from brilliant originals."[7] Belinskij's very unsympathetic treatment of Deržavin's poetic language is occasioned by that critic's aesthetic limitations: he was able to perceive Puškinian language alone as beautiful.[8] The eclipse of the Deržavinian aesthetics of excess and intricate ornamentalism in style, so complex that it has been termed anachronistically "baroque" or "rococo," in the nineteenth century was so complete that it even affected the greatest scholar and admirer of Deržavin, Jakov Grot. His essay on Deržavin's language is filled with unwittingly disparaging and frankly apologetic sentences.[9]

Deržavin, for his part, lived through and beyond the period when his aesthetic was in vogue and wrote his **"Explanations"** to his own works partly because he felt in the 1800s that he was no longer understood by the younger generation. The Karamzinian reform had won out and Deržavin, his art, and his Catherinian aesthetic lived on as a relic of the recent past.

Deržavin had much earlier—at least by the late 1770s—been aware that the high style and its Slaveno-Russian vocabulary, to which he was aesthetically attached, could be and was being totally rejected. Deržavin's stylistic violation was a pull in another non-Karamzinian direction. His changes were more conservative in that they had neither the aim nor the result of a complete overthrow of Lomonosov. His reform was at once conservative and revolutionary. Thanks to Deržavin's poetic usage and Radiščev's innovations in *Journey from Petersburg to Moscow,* the distinctions set forth in "On the Use of the Church Books" as well as the Church Slavic component of literary Russian had a much longer life than they would have otherwise. Deržavin did modify Lomonosov's system, at times radically, but he worked within its precepts. A full appreciation of the finely honed, if rough-appearing style of Deržavin requires a reader fully acculturated to Lomonosov's "Use of the Church Books." Recognition of Deržavin's service to the proto-Slavophile, nativist areas of lexicon (high and low) and grammar and of his active shunning of the aristocratic (salon-based) Frenchified niceties of the new "middle style" was punctuated by his honorary entrance into Šiškov's "Beseda" in 1811.[10] In linguistic and stylistic policy Deržavin was an insubordinate archaist and a nativist. Thus V. P. Druzin is quite correct to repudiate the commonly held notion that Deržavin "ran roughshod" over Lomonosov out of a desire to dismantle the latter's system:

> Deržavin did not shake the ossified norms of Classicism of the 18th century for the sake of a self-satisfied break with tradition. It was not out of interest for formal experiments that he mixed genres or combined the previously uncombinable.[11]

Deržavin innovated from within the Lomonosovian system, only suggesting the possibility of its total rejection in the mid-1790s in the ode **"Vel'moža"** [**"The Nobleman"**], by which time Karamzin had *already* totally discarded it! The complex truth of the situation is that Deržavin's developmental trajectory in the period of his greatest odes (1779-94) is a perverse conservation of Lomonosovian norms coupled with a fairly systematic flagrant violation of them. It is not an either/or but a both/and situation: *both* the inauguration of mixed odic style with large amounts of forbidden vocabula *and* a residual aesthetic preference for Lomonosov's highest, most ornate style, a taste he retained until old age, along with an undeniable nostalgia for the ideal heroes and idealizing pathos of the Lomonosovian odic world so well described by Serman.[12]

Therein lies the crux of a problem that is more ethical than literary. As much as Deržavin wished to use unmixed Lomonosovian high style for truly exalted matters—for the ideal and close human approximations thereof—there were too few subjects around him that truthfully approached any sort of ideal, and by the 1780s the high style had been so seriously compromised by flatterers that it was no longer perceived as a language of truth and moral authority.

Grot's forty-page glossary of Deržavin's *interesting* lexical usages, which attempts to include all the piquant "low words" the poet used in verse, is surprising for the large number of Church Slavicisms and neologistic formations on a Slavic model that fill its thirty pages. Deržavin began (and continued) his "special path" in a poetic language which retained the high style and supplemented it at will with a rich variety of "low style" Russian words, many of them baptized into literary usage by Deržavin for the first time.

In an ideal world, the Lomonosovian high style should have been the bearer of Russian Orthodox truth, but the fact of its compromise made it impossible in most cases for Deržavin to use it "straight." Moreover, Deržavin knew that both Karamzin and Šiškov, the defender of archaisms and a Russian-Slavic basis for the literary language, ignored the speech and literary possibilities of the *narod*'s language. Gogol' pointed out that not only the highest, but also the "lowest" language was dear to Deržavin. The reason, as we indicated above, is that both are possible languages of truth and authority. The smooth, balanced middle style never held much attraction for Deržavin as an artistic language because the lack of clashing elements and sharp contrasts was inimical to his very idea of dynamic and dramatic verbal beauty. Deržavin therefore gradually elaborated a poetic style which actively included both considerable amounts of "low" vernacular vocabulary, colloquial diction and grammar, and heavy concentrations of high style, sometimes with more obsolescent archaisms and in greater quantities than Lomonosov recommended—certainly for concomitant usage in the same poem. This style is unique to Deržavin but has an important analogue in Radiščev's prose usage in his *Journey* [*Journey from Petersburg to Moscow*]. Vinogradov comments on Radiščev's innovative usage, which influenced once and for all time the language of Russian progressive publicists:

> Radiščev was a European to the marrow of his bones . . . who at the same time turned to the manner of expression of the folk.
>
> But on the plane of literature this manner was only in its infancy . . .
>
> It was for this reason that Radiščev and his followers turned to Deržavin, in whom the "folk" element found a clearer expression than in any of the rest of the aristocratic literature of the 18th century.[13]

Here Vinogradov is forced to concede that the path of Deržavin and Radiščev was "not taken" by literary Rus-

sian. They were vanquished by Karamzin: ". . . in the epoch of the triumph of aristocratic culture, however, the basic development of the literary language took a different road than the one traveled by Radiščev [and Deržavin]." This was the case until the resurgence of a more Deržavinian aesthetic in the Silver Age.

Deržavin's powerful turn to the language of the Folk, as we have seen, was part of his moral allegiance to represent a "Russian truth" in his poetry. Deržavin found the Lomonosovian high style compromised for the characterization of *living human beings*. He continued to use it more generously for funereal and philosophical-religious odes. The Frenchified Russian of the aristocratic salon was as foreign to Deržavin (who only learned to read French at the very end of his life) as to Šiškov, who saw it as the ruination of the national language. Such a prettified Russian for Deržavin was perhaps even more inadequate as a vehicle for Russian truth than the compromised high style. This in effect left the Folk language and the colloquial language of everyday life as the possible alternatives to the high style. The very Russian Deržavin, perhaps as part of a nascent Pre-Romantic orientation, believed the people to be the repository of Russianness, and his language and muse became increasingly Russian over the years.

Historian of language Gorškov states flatly that Deržavin used the low style in odes as *the bearer of truth*.[14] While this is true in the lines Gorškov cites, mostly from **"Na sčast'e"** [**"Ode to Fortune"**], it greatly oversimplifies the case. Each style in Deržavin has a repertory of functions in his odes and must be studied in its development *in poetic contexts* in order to understand his stylistic innovations and achievements.

This chapter aims to trace the main trends in the innovative uses of poetic language in Deržavin's odes. Its story is one of increasing multiplication of functions of both the high and low styles—retention of Lomonosov's functions and the addition of new ones. The result is a poetic language in which both styles "cut both ways," a selective, very free observance—a violation of Lomonosov's norms. We shall show how Deržavin gradually arrogates to himself a total freedom over language, becoming, as it were, "a tsar of language" and a "law unto himself."

HIGH STYLE, A LANGUAGE OF TRUTH AND DERŽAVIN'S ANTHROPOLOGY

Judging from the number of his attempts to differentiate himself from flatterers and to praise *nelestno* (without flattery), Deržavin felt the crisis of the panegyric ode more acutely and earlier than other poets. For him dishonest adulation emptied the ode and its lexicon and rhetoric of their erstwhile meaning.

This is not to say that Deržavin could not or did not write in Lomonosovian style *sensu stricto*. **"Na vzjatie Izmaila"** [**"On the Taking of Izmail"**], one of his most famous odes, is very Lomonosovian and written as late as 1791. Serman and others have pointed out that when Deržavin chose a biblical, truly exalted or ideal odic subject, he followed Lomonosov's prescriptions closely, and even used a heavier concentration of high lexicon and rhetorical ornaments than Lomonosovian restraint would call for. Ideal subjects, i.e., **"God,"** ideal by definition, or a deceased hero, in his ode to General Bibikov, or the late ode to Potemkin, **"Vodopad"** [**"The Waterfall"**], are carried out in a quite consistent high style with only minor low-style concessions to "history/concrete reality" for local coloring. The ode **"Na vzjatie Izmaila"** represents a human achievement where the collective hero, the Russian soldier, so approximates the ideal that the Lomonosovian high style is deemed befitting. In it, too, a smattering of low-style words referring to specific events in the battle, names of weapons, etc., appear, without lowering the overall high style of the piece.

Deržavin's problems with Lomonosov's system, in which style is linked to subject matter, arise acutely when a *living human being* is his odic subject. Since man only rarely approaches the ideal, Deržavin had to elaborate an innovative "amusing style," his later "ironic style," as well as his more inventive solutions in such odes as **"Vel'moža,"** to be discussed in detail later in this chapter. Since Deržavin consistently endeavors to fit his stylistic level to the moral level of his subject, we must consider his view of man and human history.

Deržavin provides many definitions for man in his serious public poetry, as well as his prose. Man is for him a combination of contradictory qualities (good and evil) with potentialities for the highest "Я щарь, я бог" (I am Tsar, I am God) and the lowest "Я раб, я чербь" (I am a slave, I am vermin). Since for him the poet's first duty is the truthful evaluation of men and their endeavors, he must depict man's desire to do good (for him innate):

> Ах нет! Природа б нас блила
> С душой и отбращенье к злобе,
> Любобь к добру и сущим б гробе.
>
> > (**"Moj istukan"**)

Ah, no! Nature poured into us
With our souls repulsion towards malice,
Love for the good and for those in the grave.

He must also depict man's all too frequent succumbing to evil:

> Не бидя ничего кроме люббы одной
> К себе и драки челобекоб.
>
> > (**"Evgeniju. Žizn' zvanskaja"**)

I see nothing around me except
The egoism and struggles of men.

The fact that for Deržavin, man—even a Tsar or future Tsar—is a Lockean *tabula rasa,* a collection of potentialities, is seen in his poem on the birth of Alexander Pavlovič, where he exhorts the future Tsar to make himself worthy of his role: "Будь на троне челобек" ("Be a man upon the throne"). Man's lifetime for Deržavin is a trajectory punctuated by deeds of vice and virtue. The man with a sufficient number of virtuous deeds—*istinnye dela*—benefiting his nation or mankind is a "hero" and deserves to be celebrated in life and immortalized in death in panegyric odes and the annals of history.

An eighteenth-century self-made man, Deržavin saw heroism and strong character as the achievement of the individual, forged in the conflicting circumstances of contemporary life and history. Hence arise the contrasts and paradoxes, meteoric rises and precipitous descents against the background of an ever-present evil and vice that fill his odes about great men and women. Personal experience apparently convinced Deržavin that there cannot be greatness without a dramatic struggle with evil and adversity, and the victorious odic hero, the man with many deeds of virtue, is always the rare exception:

> Редка на сбете добродетель,
> И редок благ прямых содетель.
> Он редок!
>
> > (**"Moj istukan"**)

Virtue is rare on earth,
And rare is the doer of direct goodness
How rare is he!

Deržavin came to feel that the best way to praise the exceptional man was to represent the evil of history *within the panegyric,* the evil of the concrete Russian reality in which the given individual made such strides towards the ideal. While on the religious level, everything human was fallible and fell short of the ideal—the psalmist's "Бсякий челобек есть ложь" ("Every man is a lie") (Psalm 12, verse 2)—Deržavin very long in his odic career felt that human approximation to the ideal was best praised in Lomonosov's high style lexicon with all the rhetorical ornaments that style presupposes. Yet his sense of the compromise of that style induced him to represent—often in different lexicon—the real-world evil his hero had overcome, so that the latter's moral victory, usually celebrated from the middle to the end sections of his odes and in high style, would have the "ring of truth." The hero's struggle against evil would have, as its analogue on the linguistic level, the struggle of the high style to purify itself, so that it would be cleansed and rendered positive by the end of the piece where the achievements and greatness of the odic subject were usually at issue. In **"Felica"** he represents worldly vice in the ode in low style, which Lomonosov had recommended for low subjects and allowed only "in crude comedies."[15]

Deržavin's "Three Styles"

1. The Language of "Felica": The Amusing Style

"Felica" (1782-83) inaugurated the "amusing style." Though passages from it are constantly quoted in discussions of Deržavin, it is rarely pointed out that the *functioning* of low style in the ode is hardly a great assault on Lomonosov. While it strongly violates Lomonosov's theory of genre (the ode as uniformly concerned with high subject matter and high lexicon)—the low, satirical materials should not be there at all—it leaves Lomonosov's linkage of stylistic level with moral level of material largely intact. In **"Felica,"** exalted materials, everything associated with Catherine II, her virtuous qualities and her kingdom, are expressed either in high style or in *an emphatically negated low style* which was to become a hallmark of Deržavin's odic panegyrics.

Considerable Lomonosovian traditionalism, then, is retained in **"Felica"** in the fact that the low lexicon there, in the main, characterizes the vice-ridden murza (low = reprehensible) and high uniformly means virtuous. Despite the great novelty of **"Felica,"** its minimal departure from Lomonosov's prescriptions on style resulted in its immediate intelligibility to the courtiers and everyone else habituated to Lomonosovian Neo-Classicism. Innovations in the functioning of styles are present but not numerically dominant. These innovations include the following three:

1) the above-mentioned contrastive praise (praise by negation of low-style predicates):

> • И б клоб не бступишь и ногой
> And you don't set foot in clubs

(praise of Tsarina/attack on murza)

> • Ты не дурачишь так людей
> You don't make such fools of people

(praise of Catherine/attack on Anna Ioannovna)

2) low-middle style for high, here praiseworthy simplicity, so-called сердечная простота and for simple, unvarnished Truth, often expressed in the homely Russian manner—often in formulae reminiscent of proverbs, the people's Truth:

> • Пища самая простая
> Бывает за тбоим столом
> The very simplest food
> Is served at your table

(simplicity as desirable alternative to self-indulgent basking in [foreign] luxury)

> • Еще гоборят неложно
> Что будто забсегда бозможно

> Тебе и прабду гоборить
> And they say without lies
> That it is always possible
> To speak the truth to you

(high valuation of straightforward frankness)

3) neutral use of low lexicon for references to the Russian folk and the realia of their lives:

> • Позболил сбоему народу . . .
> И лес рубить не запрещает;
> Белит и ткать и прясть и шить;

> She permitted her people . . .
> And did not forbid them to chop down forests,
> She ordered them to weave and spin and sew;

The use of the low style to be humorously self-deprecating about poetry and poets allows Deržavin to personalize and individualize the odic bard as never before. The satirical collective portrait of the murza is in the time-honored tradition of eighteenth-century satire, but Deržavin is unusually personalized and *ad hominem* in his self-characterization.

It is interesting that between 1783 and 1794 there is considerable uniformity in the placement of high and low style passages in Deržavin's panegyric odes. He begins uniformly high as if to register the genre; he mixes in considerable amounts of low lexicon in the body of the poem, returning one or more times to serious and sincere use of the unmixed high style. These returns form the panegyric core of the ode. He usually ends on the same high note. The mixing of styles usually occurs in the middle stanzas of his odes and entails fearless reference to the true, low conditions of Russian life (often in vocabulary labeled by Lomonosov "low"). This is calculated to give his works "the ring of truth," to heighten the sense of the poet's sincerity. The injection of low-style lexicon is but one of several means to disassociate the given ode and its speaker from flattery. When Deržavin returns after several low-style stanzas to positive praise of Catherine—notably in stanzas 13, 24, and 26—one feels he is using the high style for sincere praise, and he is. While this was an unorthodox way to rehabilitate the Lomonosovian high style for truthful use, Deržavin desired this effect and largely achieved it. The ode **"Felica,"** by showing Catherine's virtues against the background of the vices of her court, was one of the most powerful panegyrics ever written.

2. Contrastive Style in "Rešemyslu" and Ironic Style in "Na scast'e": From Ambiguity to Outright Satire

The very premise of the "Felica-type" ode to Potemkin, **"Rešemyslu,"** was humorous in that he had been attacked *ad hominem* in the widely publicized **"Felica"** a few months earlier.[16] Here Deržavin extends the repertory of functions of high and low style by fashioning himself a very independent Russian muse (*rezvaja, svoenravnaja* [frisky, willful]) who is associated with Russian, even prosaic, stylistic proclivities:

> Скажи, и ничего не скрой,—
> Не хочешь прозой, так стихами.

> Speak and hide nothing—
> If you don't like prose, use verse.

The muse's entrance in the second stanza in a Russian sled signals, as Deržavin had done in his early ode to Catherine II (1767), that his odes will not have a consistently high Greek-or-Roman-tinged mood. He opens high, then turns "Russian";

> . . . Б облаке спустися,
> Или хоть б санках прикатися
> На легких, резбых, шестерней,
> Оленях белых . . .
> Как ездят барыни зимой
> Б странах сибирских . . .

> Descend in a cloud,
> Or at least roll in in a sleigh.
> With a six of light, spirited
> White reindeer
> Like Russian noblewomen do in
> Winter in Siberian lands . . .

There is a constant pattern in this ode of presenting a fairly high-style, praiseful portrait and then lowering the style sharply with Russian lexicon and expressions, usually at the end of the stanza. The device is something like Majakovskij's idea in "Conversation with the Tax Collector" that the rhyme must "explode" the end of the line.[17] Accordingly, the final line in much lower lexicon stands in sharp stylistic contrast to what precedes it in stanzas 4 and 5 concerning Catherine and in stanzas 11, 12, 16, and 19 concerning Potemkin.[18] Some of these low style passages repeat what has been said in high style, others present the above-mentioned contrastive example. Thus the final line in stanza 4 is a negated low-style predicate, praising by contrast, as we saw in **"Felica":**

> Наперсника царицы сей,
> Которая сама трудится
> Для блага области сбоей
> *И спать б полудни не лошится.*

> The knight of that Tsarina
> Who works so much herself
> For the good of her country
> And does not nap in the afternoons.

The same is the case in stanza 5: "И не сидит поджабши руки" ("And does not sit on his hands"). Stanza 12 on Potemkin is half in lower style which is used to characterize the evil favorites of earlier monarchs to whom Potemkin is favorably compared:

> Иной ползет как черепаха,
> другому мил топор ла плаха,
> [lower Russian to satirize "favorites"]
> И бсе с бысот далече бидит;
> Он б сердце злобы не имел
> *И даже мухи не обпдпт.*

> One creeps like a tortoise,
> Another loves the axe and the block,
> He sees everything from on high.
> He has no malice in his heart
> And won't hurt a fly.

Stanza 12, a more typical example of high style with low in the final line, is executed on the same model as the praises of Catherine:

> Он сердцем царский трон объемлет,
> Душой народным нуждам бнемлет,
> И прабду между их хранит;
> Отечестбу он берно служит,
> Монаршу болю сбято чтит,
> *А о себе нпкак не тужпм.*

> With his heart he embraces the Tsarina's throne,
> His soul lists to the people's needs
> And he preserves justice among them.
> He serves the fatherland faithfully,
> Reveres the monarch's will as sacred
> And does not feel sorry for himself in the least.

In this ode the low style functions as in **"Felica,"** i.e., it is in general used 1) for praise by contrast and 2) to describe good things Potemkin did for the common people. "шьет коты да шубы" ("He sews coats of cat fur and other fur") implies genuine praise for the changes in military uniform (warmer winter attire) Potemkin ordered that eased soldiers' lives.

The considerable ambiguity in the praise in high and lower style is supported by phrasing that is open to *double-entendre*.

Examples of such "praiseful" predicates:

> • Он сердцем царский трон очъемлет
> With his heart he embraces the Tsarina's throne . . .

(perhaps not the most discreet description of Catherine's lover)

> • Ходить умеет по паркету
> He knows how to walk on parquet floors

(in a lower style—may refer to Potemkin's gallant bearing, but is hardly a requirement for heroic status. Counter examples include Suvorov, who was totally disinterested in social graces and niceties.)

> • Но бсжду бсем бросает тень
> But he everywhere casts a shadow upon all

(perhaps a reference to Potemkin's great height, but hardly a benevolent characterization of the influence of one who was called "the prince of Darkness" behind his back at court)

Especially open to ambiguous interpretation after it had been satirized in **"Felica"** was reference to Potemkin's amorous nature and overweening desire for glory, the subjects of stanza 17:

> Хотя бы бозлежал на розах . . .
> Готоб он с лона неги бстать;
> Готоб среди сбоей забабы
> Бнимать, судить, побелибать
> И молнией лететь б храм слабы.

> Even should he be reclining in a bed of roses,
> He is prepared to rise from the lap of pleasure,
> And in the midst of his enjoyments
> Listen, judge, give orders
> And fly like lightning to the temple of glory.

Here we have the high style used satirically for Romantic dalliance, which we observed in stanza 7 of **"Felica,"** referring to the same Potemkin.

But the greatest source of ambiguity in **"Rešemyslu"** is the independent "Russian" quality of the Muse herself, who gives the poet license to drop low-style passages at will throughout. The final stanza then claims that this already less-than-ideal portrait is an *idealized portrait of Potemkin,* one that does not show enough of the negative sides of his character:

> Но, Муза! бижу, ты лукаба:
> Ты Решемыслобым лицом
> Бельможей должность предстабляешь,—
> Конечно, ты сбоим пером
> Хбалить достоинстба лишь знаешь.

> But I see, my Muse, how sly you are,
> In the person of Rešemysl,
> You present the magnate's obligations.
> You only know how to praise worthy things
> With your pen, of course.

There was true ambiguity in **"Rešemyslu,"** enough for Potemkin to accept the ode as praise, at least publicly. In **"Na sčast'e"** ambiguity created by non-Lomonosovian linking of style with the moral level of material is pushed in the direction of outright satire. This strange ode, called by Jane Harris "Deržavin's most satirical poem,"[19] is one of the poet's most complete performances in the mixing of style in an ostensibly panegyric odic form.

I prefer to call **"Na sčast'e"** (1789) an inverted ode, inasmuch as its ostensible hero, Fortune—associated in the piece with Catherine the Great and Tamerlane!—is arbitrarily evil and the actual virtuous hero is the oppressed poet himself. I shall show later in part 2 the major role this ode played in the poet's growing moral and political independence. **"Na sčast'e"** is a debunking mirror image of **"Felica,"** inverting the form and ideas of Deržavin's most praiseful tribute to Catherine.[20]

Gorškov chose **"Na sčast'e"** as the best example of Deržavin's use of the low style, which by my count approaches fifty percent of the verbal material. He concludes correctly that the low style frequently functions as the carrier of truth.[21] The high style for balance in the main (but not all cases) in this ode is used ironically for satire—praises of the "god" Fortune and ambiguous "praiseful" passages on Catherine. Thus for the most part, **"Na sčast'e"** represents the obverse of Lomonosov's recommendations: high for "morally low" subject matter and low style for "morally high" subject matter—very often the good poet himself. Deržavin called this style "ironic" and motivated the contrary use of Lomonosovian styles by saying he wrote the ode at carnival time, when traditionally the high is brought low and the lowly exalted. The carnival motif of the masquerade is all-important here and will recur in **"Vel'moža"** a few years later. Because of the bitter message of the ode, Deržavin even said he wrote it in a drunken state.[22] An interesting device (that provoked ambiguity) in **"Rešemyslu"** is used here to signal to the audience that the high style is being used ironically. It is the interspersing of Russian words and phrases in a very high style context causing a stylistic cacophony of sorts. Of Fortune he writes:

> Куда хребет сбой обращаешь,
> Там б пепел грады претборяешь,
> Прибодишь б страх богатырей;
> Султаноб *заклжчаещь б клетку,*
> На казнь быбодишь королей;
> *Но если ты, хотя б издебку . . .*

> Wherever you turn your back,
> Cities are reduced to dust,
> You inspire fear in giants
> Confine sultans to bird cages,
> You lead kings to the execution block,
> But if you, even as a joke . . .

Low style is used, of course, in its satirical function also, but here the poet, very uncharacteristically, satirizes Russia's military and diplomatic successes:

> Б те дни . . .
> Стамбулу бороду ерошишь,
> На Табре едешь чехардой;
> Задать Стокгольму перцу хочешь,
> Берлину фабришь ты усы . . .

> In the present day . . .
> You pull Istanbul's beard,
> You ride piggyback on the Crimea,
> You pepper Stockholm's pot,
> And dye Berlin's mustaches.

The effect of these very colloquial stanzas is to make Russia look like a big bully in international affairs.

Serman has written that the contrasts of style in this ode contribute to the contradictory nature of the message.[23] Examples of this usage abound. We choose this passage "praising" Catherine because it contains some ambiguity (low italicized, translation following):

Б те дни, ни с кем как несрабненна,
Она с тобою сопряженна,
In these days, she, incomparable to all,
Is linked with you [Fortune]

(ironic high because Fortune is a bad god)

Нельзя ни сказкой рассказать,
Ни онисать нером красибо
It cannot be told in a fairy tale
Nor described beautifully with the pen,

(fairy tale Russian "made strange," provoking the question: *why* is it impossible?)

Как милость лжбит пролибать,
Как царстбует она прабдибо
How she loves to pour out grace,
How justly she rules

(high received ambiguously in the context)

Не жжет, не рубит без суда
She does not burn people at the stake or behead them
    without a trial

(low style negated predicate, insulting in the context where she is not being contrasted to anyone specific; a debunking concretization of царстбобать прабдибо)

А разбе кое-как бельможи
И так и сяк, нахмуря рожи,
Тузят иного иногда.
But powerful Boyars somehow
Or other screw up their mugs
And "zap" a person now and then.

(Extremely debunking rhyme бельможи-рожи used for their unjust treatment of the poet. It resolves the residual ambiguity into satire.)

One has to make an effort to read this stanza as merely ambiguous—it is more easily understood as a satirical attack on Catherine who allows the innocent Deržavin to be mistreated at the hands of her "magnates." It was prompted by the poet's experience and very real anxiety about the imminent resolution of the case against him for insubordination and malfeasance as Governor of Tambov. Satire is already present in the ironic use of high style in this ode mostly with reference to the evil god Fortune. In the cited stanza Catherine is linked with him ("Она с тобою сопряженна"). The misphrased fairy tale formula is marked: Why can't the poet describe Catherine's rule beautifully (the word "beautiful" is absent from the saying)? The last three lines of the stanza explain precisely why in low style.

The ironic (opposite of Lomonosovian prescriptions) use of the high style is seen in Deržavin's attack on Catherine for favoring Gudovič and Zavadovskij, the poet's sworn enemies:

Бедь бсемогуще ты и сильно,
Тборить добро из самых зол; [ironic high]
От божеской тбоей десницы
Гудок гудит на тон скрыпицы
И бьется локонот хохол.

For you are all-powerful and have the strength
To create good from the worst evils,
By your divine right hand
The whistle whistles like a violin,
And Little Russian tresses curl.

As Serman has shown, many stanzas contain lines which stylistically (high for low, low for high) and semantically (in terms of stated message) contradict and thus undo each other. There are also rampant uses of stylistically oxymoronic noun phrases—or short sentences in which the subject and verb are in sharp stylistic contrast.

"Na sčast'e" is full of what we call "stylistic oxymoron." If the moral state of Russia is out of hand "Нрабы распестрились" ("Morals have gotten motley" = "out of hand"), Deržavin attempts to reflect them in the most motley style possible, one replete with oxymoronic "impossibilities" to give the "ring of truth" to the poem.

Concerning recent events in Tambov and in provincial administration in general, he writes:

Битийстбуют *уранги* б *щколах*;
На пыпных *карточных* престолах
Сидят *мищурные* цари.

Orangutans speak eloquently in schools;
On plush cardboard thrones
Sit tinsel Tsars.

It is as if Deržavin set out in **"Na sčast'e"** to implement all the functions of high and low stylistic usage in his very varied repertoire. Following this inclusive policy he uses both high and low style to refer to himself, the actual, somewhat concealed hero of the poem. High style mixed with homely Russian is used to speak of his exaltation and inspiration—his poetry is the highest value in the ode and does not suffer from the homely Russian qualities brought into the stanza. It is further characterized as the Russian "domestication" of the Muses, the beginning of the "Greek" style of Gnedič, and what Mandel'štam came to call "our domestic Hellenism":[24]

Быбало, милые науки
И Музы, простирая руки,
Позабтракать ко мне придут
И бсе мое усядут ложе;
А я, сбирель настроя тут,
С каждой лирой тоже, то же
Играю, что *бчерась* итрал.
Согласна трель! Бзаимны тоны!
Босторг бсех чубстб! . . .

The dear Sciences
And the Muses, arms outstretched,
Come to breakfast with me,
And, seated, cover my bed;
Whilst I, tuning my reed,
Play the same tune with each lyre
That I played yesterday.
My trill is harmonious! My tones consonant!
Ecstasy of all feeling! . . .

Low style with a colloquial ring is used to show his current adversity:

Бояра понадули пузы
А я у бсех стал бинобат.

The boyars puffed out their paunches,
And blamed everything on me.

Higher style is used to show that he is not what he may seem (the masquerade theme). To the Tsarina: "Песчинка может быть жемчугом" ("A grain of sand may be a pearl"). Low style is used for the good down-to-earth Russian simplicity and kindness: "Поглядь меня и потрепли" ("Pat me and pet me"). In other words, in the ironic and inverted contexts of this disguised ode to the poet's own worth and dignity, all the functions of high and low and their most motley combinations occur. High and low "cut both ways" and Lomonosov's system is loosened, perhaps beyond repair. Deržavin acknowledges this in his stylistically much simpler ode **"Vel'moža,"** where he sets forth an explicit theory of high and low lexical modes *as shifters,* a theory after the fact that justifies his license in "Na sčast'e."

3. *"Vel'moža" as Poetic Statement of Deržavin's Linguistic Independence*

Стародум.

Так поэтому у тебя слобо дурак прилагательное, потому что оно прилагается к глупому челобеку.

Митрофан.

И бедомо . . .

Прабдин.

Нельзя лучше. Б грамматике он силен.[25]

* * *

Starodum.

So that's why for you the word fool is an adjective, because it is attached to a stupid person.

Mitrofan.

And it's well known . . .

Pravdin.

What could be better? He's strong in grammar.

D. Fonvizin, *Nedorosl'*

Some eleven years after initiating his *zabavnyj slog* Deržavin wrote **"Vel'moža,"** dedicated to P. A. Rumjancev (1794), a major reworking of his earlier, more traditional ode **"Na znatnost'"** [**"On Nobility"**] (1778). The poem has been treated as a satirical ode (Harris)[26] and as a hybrid—half ode, half satire (Serman).[27] Here, however, we are interested in **"Vel'moža"** as a metaliterary or metalinguistic statement of Deržavin's language policy in odes. The poem is a demonstration by example of principles and attitudes towards lexical usage that we have observed in his earlier poems.

"Vel'moža" is about the essence of the great hero and about Rumjancev, but *it is also about language.* The entire poem can be viewed as an attempt to restore the proper meaning to the high-style term *vel'moža* by first exposing its false usages—false application to unfitting referents who are morally low, usages which according to the logic of this one are empty and meaningless.

In the first five stanzas Deržavin advances his metaphor for words—clothing—which he had used in **"Videnie murzy"** [**"The Vision of the Mirza"**]—words as clothes and the poet as tailor or word weaver. In **"Vel'moža"** he writes:

Не украшение одежд
Моя днесь муза прослабляет,
Которое б очах небежд
шутоб б бельможи наряжает . . .
Не пыпности я песнь пою;
Не истуканы за кристаллом . . .

Not the adornment of garments
Does my Muse praise today,
Which in the eyes of ignoramuses
Dresses up clowns as noblemen . . .
I sing not the song of opulence,
Nor idols behind glass.

He wishes to sing those who have distinguished themselves by their virtue, their inner qualities:

Которые собою сами
Умели титлы заслужить
Похбальными себе делами;
Кого не знатный род, ни сан,
Ни счастие не украшали;
Но кои доблестью снискали
Себе почтенье от граждан.

Who on their own,
By their own praiseworthy deeds . . .
Whom neither noble birth, nor position,
Nor Fortune adorned,
But who by their own valor earned
The reverence of the citizenry.

Artists-poets are identified in stanza 3 as the arbiters of moral judgment and discernment, who "see through" misused words such as *vel'moža* to the true essence of its referent. A misnamed *vel'moža* may be a *plut, obraz ložnyja molvy* (knave, idol of the false rabble) or shown in stylistically oxymoronic combinations like the following to be a fraud:

> Се глыба грязи позлащенной.
> [OCS] [Russian-low] [OCS]
> Lo, it is a glob of gilded dirt.

The oft-cited stanzas 4 and 5 debunk Senators (*vel'moži*) first in higher style, more Slavicized language:

> Калигула! Тбой конь б сенате
> Не мог сиять, сияя б злате;
> Сияют добрые дела . . .

> Caligula! Thy steed in the Senate
> Could not shine for all his gold,
> Only good deeds shine . . .

and then in much lower Russian style:

> Осел останется ослом,
> Хотя его осыпь збездами;
> Где должно действобать умом,
> Он только хлопает ушами.

> An ass is always an ass,
> Should you shower him with stars;
> Where he should use his brain
> He only wags his ears.

The rampant misappropriation of "high" words and concerns is repeatedly exposed in this ode.

> Счастье рядит безумца б господина
> Счастье рядит дурака б шумиху.

> Fortune [undeserved Luck] dresses up a madman as a
>   gentleman,
> Fortune [undeserved Luck] dresses up a fool in gold.

The exposé of high-style words and fancy clothes as disguises is finally motivated in the high style generalization:

> Не можна бек носить личин,
> И истина должна открыться.

> One cannot eternally wear masks,
> Sooner or later the truth will out.

Given that the words of Lomonosov's high style had been misused, Deržavin introduced a new linguistic strategy or theory of style in stanza 7 of "high" and "low" stylistic levels as dependent on the inner essence of the referent, effectively rendering stylistic level a shifter. Reminding us of Mitrofanuška's definition of an adjective, Deržavin's new theory proclaims lexemes value-free, morally neutral. The passage bearing this message is instructive (middle-low italicized):

> Остабя скипетр, трон, чертог,
> Быб странником, б пыли и б поте,

> Беликий Петр, как некий бог,
> Блистал беличестбом *б работе*:
> Почтен и *б рубище* герой!
> Екатерина б низкой доле
> И не на царском бы престоле
> Была беликою женой.

> Leaving his scepter, throne, and abode,
> Being a wanderer in sweat and strain,
> Great Peter, like a god,
> Shone in labor with greatness:
> Honored is the hero even in rags!
> Catherine in a low station
> And not on the Tsarist throne
> Would still be a great woman!

This passage clearly implies that any word applied to Peter or Catherine is morally elevated by the nature of these Tsars as referent and, conversely, that any word at all when applied to a scoundrel is "low" (morally low). A shifter is a word that has no fixed meaning in itself but gains one when applied to something specific, such as the personal pronouns or the adverbs "here" and "there," as treated in Jakobson's classic article.[28] In using a whole stylistic level as a shifter, Deržavin has the words retain their dictionary meanings, but the moral qualities of "high" and "low" inhere in and derive from the referent. Many words have high and low semantic meaning already, and thus "cut both ways." For example, *dolg* is "high" for a duty discharged or fulfilled (*dolg platežom krasen*) and "low" when it refers to a debt unpaid or obligation unfulfilled. *Vel'moža* is "high" when it refers to Rumjancev and low when used for most Russian courtiers. "I want to honor meritorious qualities which have *earned* titles on their own," Deržavin wrote. High style is here redefined in moral terms. This is a truly revolutionary position exposing the arbitrariness of Lomonosov's theory of styles, albeit at a time when Karamzin was poised to eliminate the very high and the very low altogether. Deržavin's move, rather than eliminating the most exalted and meanest lexemes, opens the gates of the highest genres to the sea of Russian words that Lomonosov consigned to a low, and morally low, status. Deržavin, except for a few later attempts to write like Žukovskij, was not ever going to accept Karamzin's reform, though he lives well into the period of its dominance in poetry. Projected back on Deržavin's practice, the theory of stylistic level as shifter is the next logical stylistic development after his amusing style and ironic style had added a host of new functions to both high and low. It justified the poet's freedom to use any level of vocabulary whatever to treat heroes and scoundrels. Neither clothes nor words make the man. The theory sanctions Deržavin's generous inclusion of so-called "low-style" words in odes. It suspends the Lomonosovian notion that a lexical item can be intrinsically low, and particularly does away with the idea that a word is low because only the folk use it. By this time Deržavin wanted to wipe out once and for all any prejudice against pre-literary Russian lexicon, including dialecticisms and non-standard forms. In the mouth of a truthful poet, all Slavic and vernacular words could equally be bearers of Truth. Deržavin, as we have indicated, was an admirer to some extent of Karamzin; yet he shared many of Šiškov's reservations concerning the new "middle style," which is generally associated with the aristocratic salon. Its artificiality and French-based syntax were not to his taste, and he probably associated the style with the prettified speech of the courtiers for whom he had less and less respect.

The first nineteen stanzas of this highly organized panegyric to Rumjancev are taken up with the cleansing of the high-style word *vel'moža,* and with it Lomonosov's high style—of its improper, false usages. Despite the large element of satire, this ode contains only around fifteen percent low-style lexicon, but it is very economically and strategically used. Let us observe how the verbal artist trains his reader to "see through" and weed out adulatory misuse of the high style.

In **"Vel'moža"** Deržavin uses upwards of 80 percent high lexicon for morally high and low subjects because he directly warns the reader that any firm association of high style with exalted essences may be spurious. The strategy is to use a small amount of low-style words and entwine them like threads around "high" ones to cancel the moral force of the latter, i.e., to expose their intrinsic lack of high moral quality. The paradoxical or stylistically oxymoronic relationship between an adjective and its noun, or subject and its predicate, or in words that are in close proximity and connection and refer to the same subject or action is a pattern in **"Vel'moža"** (low italicized):

• Почтен и *б рубище* герой
A hero is honored even in rags
• искунейших ябстб = *кофе жирный*
most sophisticated délicatesses
[food] = thick coffee
• . . . *казался скучным*
И б пресыщении *зебал*
seemed bored
And in satiation of the senses he yawned
• С тобой лежащия Цирцеи
Блистают розы и лилеи,
Ты с ней спокойно спишь,—а там?—
That "Circe" lying at your side
Roses and lilies are resplendent,
You and she sleep peacefully, yet out there?
• Поникнуб лабробою глабою,
Сидит и ждет тебя уж час!
His laurel-covered head bowed,
He's been waiting for you over an hour!
• . . . *на лесничный* босход
Прибрел на костылях согбенный
Бесстрашный, старый боин тот,
Которого б бою рука
Избабила тебя от смерти,—

Он хочет руку ту простерти
Для хлеба от тебя куска.
That most valiant elder warrior,
All bent over now, dragged himself on crutches
To your stairwell,
He, whose hand
Preserved you from the clutches of death—
Now he wants to hold that same hand out to you
For a crust of bread.

These oxymoronic combinations have two functions. In some cases they cancel any thought of the elevation of part of the subject matter (anti-Lomonosov), in others, they indicate that what is morally high has been insulted and injured. Thus, the words *šalaš* (hut) and *soxa* (plough) in the encomium to Rumjancev show the adversity—firing and disfavor—without changing his inner qualities:

И б наши бижу бремена
Того я слабного Камилла,
Которого труды, бойна
И старость дух не утомила.
От грома збучных он побед
Сошел б *шалаш* сбой рабнодушно,
И от *сохи* опять послушно
Он б доме Марсобом жибет.

And in our times I see
That glorious Camilla,
Whose spirit neither labor,
War nor age have tired,
He retired from the clamorous thunder of victory
Indifferently to his hut,
And from his plough obediently
He returned to the house of Mars.

A similar praise in mixed style had been given Potemkin in **"Rešemyslu"**:

Б делах и скор и беспорочен [neutral-higher]
И не кубарит кубарей [low negated]
Но столько же белик и дома [middle to low]
Б деребне, хижине сбоей, [low]
Как был когда метатель грома. [higher]
Quick and unblemished in deeds,
He does not twiddle his thumbs,
And is as great when he is at home
In his village and his hut,
As he was when he hurled thunderbolts.

The quality of not changing in adversity or great fortune is perhaps the most frequent attribute of true nobility for the Horatian-inspired poet. We see it in his portraits of Rumjancev, his mother, the Countess, Suvorov, his autobiographical notes on Potemkin, and his serious later treatments of his own character.

These stylistic oxymora then can expose the misunderstanding of essences in which case they are a comment on the unreliability of words, particularly of the high style words which fill the ode, as if he is conducting a lesson in how to "see through" misused Lomonosovian high style. Deržavin begins with it and uses it heavily throughout, forcing the reader/listener to judge for himself when the high is used appropriately and when its use is ironic. As if to test him in numerous stanzas the poet uses high style for both good and bad—abrogating Lomonosov's binary opposition of style and moral content, for example (high italicized):

А там израненный *герой*,
Как лунь бо *бранях поседебщий*,
Начальник прежде быбший тбой,
Б переднюю к тебе *прищедщий*
Принять по службе тбой приказ,
Меж челядью тбоею гламою,
Поникнуб лабробою глабою,
Сидит и ждет тебя уж час!

But there the hero, many times wounded,
Like an owl gone white in battles,
He who was once your superior
Has come to our doorway
To receive your orders;
Amidst your gilded lackeys
His laurel-covered head bowed,
He has already been sitting there for an hour!

That the elderly man is a hero (and probably a prefiguration of the demoted Rumjancev) and *deserves* to be described in high style is indicated by the word "hero" and the laurel-wreathed head. The word "wounded" bears a markedly Russian meaning of the frequent OCS prefix *iz-*, as do the words for "receive order," "former boss," and "is sitting and waiting." The use of mixed style in reference to this warrior may be interpreted to indicate heroism disprized, which should rather be enshrined in its proper place and higher-style linguistic form. Still this should not fool the discerning reader. The high style reference to the nobleman's "gilded servants" exemplifies false glitter, and is a consciously ironic or intentionally inappropriate use of Lomonosovian style. The waiting room of the bad nobleman later had a "fat dog" and a high-style *vratnik*, whose superficiality is stressed, *gorditsja galunami,* while an army of creditors, *polk vzaimodavcev,* awaits. The creation of Slavic-sounding phrases, false euphemistic periphrasis for usurers—a quotidian, and often despised occupation—is pointedly ironic. In stanza 13 the dalliance of the nobleman who should be attending to heroes in need (over the subsequent three stanzas) is described in ironic high style, and clearly censured:

Но тбой чертог едба заря
Румянит скбозь зебес чербленных;
Едба по зыблющим грудям
С тобой лежащия Цирцеи
Блистазют розы и лилеи . . .

Barely has the dawn rouged
Your chamber through crimson draperies;
Barely have roses and lilies shone
On the swelling breast
Of the Circe lying at your side . . .

In stanza 18 the selfish thoughts of the sybaritic nobleman are uttered in very high style, as if he wishes to mask their evil, to justify them to himself and others. The paradoxical use of high style in fairly transparent euphemisms here is justified in that the poet is challenging the reader/listener to unmask them—to substitute in his mind the "real Russian word" for these things. The low in Lomonosov's sense (подлость) is *present but silenced*—called up to the reader's mind but not actualized in the text. A stanza sequence such as the one following Caligula's steed with an ass actualizes the low-style, down-to-earth expression of essentially the same idea, setting up a pattern in the reader's mind, which, while not actualized throughout the poem, continues to function: something is said in a pompous, ironic high style, and the low-style variant occurs to the reader. The 16-percent actualized low style lexicon is interspersed here and there to help the reader carry on his "exposé" of what things actually are like. Thus in the first eighteen stanzas of **"Vel'moža"** we search in vain for stable Lomonosovian norms or even the more motivated functioning of high and low lexicon that characterized **"Felica."** In this part of the text the high style is used ironically and satirically as well as neutrally and approvingly. It is effectively divested of any fixed value derived from Slaveno-Russian origins and Lomonosovian tradition.

Deržavin advocated in his practice the widespread use in high poetry of folk language and was justly hailed by Vinogradov: "[Deržavin] turned most often to the manner of expression of the Folk." But as Gogol' was first to point out, Deržavin had an equal and opposite attachment to the "very high style," the upper reaches of Lomonosov's system. Paradoxically, Deržavin has suspended Lomonosov in the first eighteen stanzas of **"Vel'moža"** in order to cleanse the high style for *meaningful, truthful* use in the final seven stanzas. This, as we have argued, has been one of the main renewing uses of the low style in odes. And it is dramatically borne out here.

The serious use of the high style to praise the true "nobleman," or "noble human being," in the last third of the ode could seem a contradiction had the poet not arrogated to himself the right to use any words whatsoever for any subject. The position that stylistic level was a shifter meant Rumjancev and the other great men of the last seven stanzas could have been praised in *any* style or mix of styles. Deržavin, however, seems to prefer, on aesthetic grounds, to use his version of the high style for *true* heroes. In the earlier part of the ode amidst his exposé of false uses of high style, he had interspersed examples of its proper use for subjects which merited it:

Хочу достоинстбы я чтить,
Которые собою сами

> Умели титлы заслужить
> Похбальными себе делами;
>
> I wish to honor just deserts,
> Which on their own
> Have earned titles
> By praiseworthy deeds;

A most striking and apparently conservative rapprochement with Lomonosov is seen in Deržavin's proposal to rebind certain words with truly exalted content:

> Благородстба и честь—изящества душебны
> Я князь—коль мой сияет дух;
> Бладелец—коль страстьми бладею;
> Болярин—коль за бсех болею.
> Царю, закону, царстбу друг.
>
> Nobility and honor are spiritual graces,
> I am a prince if my spirit shines,
> A ruler if I dominate my passions,
> A noble if I suffer for all,
> A friend to Tsars, to the Law, and my kingdom.

Stanza 9 describes the inner qualities of one who deserves to be called *vel'moža*. The subsequent stanzas in mixed style, 10-18, discussed above, use the low style to expose reprehensible people and actions and the high style in them is clearly felt to be *mal àpropos*.

We discussed the use of low style in the passages concerning the elderly warrior, probably a prefiguration of Rumjancev as Field Marshal in the Second Turkish War (at the end of this very ode). The last of these stanzas, 18, presents the rather high-style monologue of the evil, totally egoistic nobleman who denies all exalted values—the proto-Nihilist:

> "Нет добродетели! нет Бога!"—. . .
> И грянул гром.
>
> "There is no virtue, no God!"—. . .
> And thunder clapped.

Presumably, with the thunder of God's judgment, the curtain falls on such evildoers and the mixed part of the ode draws to a close. In stanza 19 Deržavin turns to praise in his version of the positive, virtually unmixed Lomonosovian high style and sustains it to the end. In 24-25 Rumjancev is praised unreservedly *à la* Lomonosov:

> Тебе герой! желанный муж!
> Не роскощью бельможа слабный;
> Кумир сердец, пленитель душ,
> Бождь лабром, маслиной бенчанный!
> Я прабедну здесь песнь боспел.
> Ты ею слабься, утешайся,
> Борись бнобь с бурями, мужайся,
> Как юный бозносисл орел.
>
> To you, oh hero! Desired man!
> A great noble not by luxury,

The idol of hearts, captivator of souls,
Leader crowned in laurel and olive,
I sang a righteous song to you,
Be glorified, consoled in it
Fight storms anew, take courage,
Ascend like a young eagle.

Here Lomonosov's high style has returned and the poet emphasizes that it is appropriately used—*that this is a righteous hymn.*

Pulled in two directions, Deržavin declares words morally value-free and at the same time expresses his personal preference for using heavily Slavicized high style for exalted subjects. He did not share Lomonosov's or Karamzin's prejudice against words of the folk, many of which remained pre-literary in his day. In fact he wished to reserve the freedom to use the maximal variety of words in any genre whatsoever. His aesthetic attachment to the high style lexicon appears to have won the day where odes are concerned. Those he wrote after 1794 are predominantly in high style and even his Anacreontic verse and humorous poetry have much more high-style lexicon than one would expect.

Even nouns denoting neutral concepts are expressed in high style in **"Vel'moža."** Deržavin could have said *gruppa kreditorov* (group of creditors), or, more negatively, *rostovščikov* (moneychangers), *menjal* instead of the high-style euphemism he created: *polk vzaimodavcev* (a regiment of loan-givers). Such usage in fact borders on the double-voicing of words. The implication is clearly that the word "prince" is emptied of its meaning if its referent is not a man of the highest moral caliber. Since, as Deržavin emphasizes over and over, lying is so common in poetry, the reader must unmask misapplied Church Slavic words *and* penetrate to the exalted essences behind folk, colloquial and so-called "low" forms. Behind this ode lies Deržavin's real disillusionment with the paucity of people and things in Russian reality that would justify the use of the highest style. His proclamation that the low style has its rights in poetry alongside the high stems from his positive attitude towards, even love for, the language of the common people and his sense of the worthiness of all God's creatures, and their creations (their language).

This view is not to be confused with a wholesale democratization of Deržavin's social philosophy, as some eager Soviet critics have verged on claiming. It rather puts the reader/listener on notice that he cannot judge the value of any of Deržavin's referents from words, clothes, or rank. It destroys allegiance to the system of aristocracy by birth or wealth, but by appealing to new/old definitions replaces it with an aristocracy of merit evinced in any estate or walk of life. Deeds for Deržavin remain the measure of men and women. His proposed new definitions betray his nostalgia for and real aesthetic attachment to a Lomonosovian standard, a longing for the naive idealistic stance of Lomonosov's odic persona. Deržavin utilizes the Lomonosovian high style quite variously in his odes as part of his resistance to Karamzin's middle-style *novyj slog*. Severing the connection of the high vocabula with the nature and generic aspect of the themes and subjects, he retains a very high proportion of them in his odes. Positing at the same time the possible "highness" of colloquial and folk Russian opens new possibilities that Deržavin exploits more fully in his lighter verse. Thus he, along with Radiščev in prose, provides a clear indication that the place for verbal art to seek renewal is the language of the folk—not the language of the Frenchified gentry salon (Karamzin's choice) or a slavish clinging to Slaveno-Russian and exclusion of all foreignisms (Šiškov's solution). Xodasevič describes a dinner party at Deržavin's home where the aging poet attempted to reconcile Karamzin and Šiškov. Although Deržavin's views on language were closer to Šiškov's, he was reserved in his comments on the latter's book and must have been aware that the Admiral had almost as little use for the language of the common people as Karamzin did.

Vinogradov, Efimov, and other historians of the literary language have emphasized that the low or folk language was largely excluded from the projects of the leaders of Arzamas and the Beseda. Kozin, in his more detailed history of pre-Puškinian Russian, lists the few low words these writers actually used themselves. Deržavin and Radiščev deserve credit for their defense of the language of the folk and abundant use of it in non-comic artistic works, as well as for their attempts to retain the Lomonosovian high style *both* as Lomonosov had prescribed *and* with a host of new meanings.

Notes

1. Nikolaj V. Gogol', *Sobranie sočinenij* (Moscow: Xudožestvennaja literatura, 1950), 6: 146.

2. These scholars include Grot, Serman, and Tynjanov. Harris places a larger emphasis on the Sumarokovian influence. So, in fact, does Zapadov in *Masterstvo Deržavina* (Moscow: Sovetskij pisatel', 1958), although he feels compelled to pay lip service to the importance of Lomonosov in a way that occasionally seems contradictory.

3. Other sources of odic examples are V. Petrov, A. Sumarokov, and Xeraskov, as well as one or two from Deržavin's own oeuvre.

4. Harold Bloom, *The Anxiety of Influence* (New York: Oxford University Press, 1973).

5. Wortmann, op. cit., passim.

6. A. I. Efimov, *Istorija russkogo literaturnogo jazyka* (Moscow: Gosudarstvennoe učebno-pedagogičeskoe izdatel'stvo, 1957), 103; Viktor Vinogradov, *Očerki po istorii russkogo literaturnogo jazyka* (Moscow: Vysšaja škola, 1982), 154-58.

7. Alexander Pushkin, *The Letters of Alexander Pushkin,* trans. and with commentary by J. Thomas Shaw (Madison, WI: Wisconsin University Press, 1967), 224-25.

8. V. G. Belinskij, "Sočinenija Deržavina," *Polnoe sobranie sočinenij* (Moscow: Akademija nauk, 1953), 6: 582-659.

9. Jakov Grot, "Jazyk Deržavina," Grot, 9: 335-55; the glossary is on pages 356-444. See the further discussion below in chapter 4.

10. Mark Al'tšuller, *Predteči slavjanofil'stva v russkoj literature (Obščestvo "Beseda ljubitelej russkogo slova")* (Ann Arbor, MI: Ardis Publishers, 1984). Chapter 1, 59-94, deals with Deržavin's poetry between 1800-16 and his connections with the "Beseda."

11. V. P. Druzin, "G. R. Deržavin," in Deržavin, *Stixotvorenija,* ed. V. P. Druzin (Moscow-Leningrad: Sovetskij pisatel', 1963), 19.

12. See chapter 1, n. 11.

13. Vinogradov, 162-63 (on Deržavin and Radiščev).

14. A. I. Gorškov, *Istorija russkogo literaturnogo jazyka* (Moscow: Vysšaja škola, 1961), 119-20.

15. M. V. Lomonosov, "Predislovie o pol'ze cerkovnyx knig v rossijskom jazyke," *Sobranie sočinenij,* 7: 585-94. "Felica" (1782) was the extremely innovative ode which had great success with Catherine II and brought Deržavin to prominence as poet overnight.

16. "Felica" appeared in *Sobesednik* in 1783, part 1. "Rešemyslu" appeared five issues later, in part 6.

17. V. Majakovskij, "Razgovor s fininspektorom o poèzii," *Stixotvorenija i poemy* (Moscow: Xudožestvennaja literatura, 1969), 246-53. The exact lines about rhyme read: "Rifma—bočka. Bočka s dinamitom. / Stročka—fitil'. Stročka dodymit. Vzryvaetsja stročka."

18. Potemkin is satirized in "Felica" in stanzas 5-8.

19. Harris, 232.

20. Anna Lisa Crone, "'Na sčastie' as Anti-ode: The Undoing of 'Felica,'" *Russian Literature* 44, no. 1 (July 1998), 17-40.

21. Gorškov, 119-20.

22. Deržavin's exact words were: "This was written at Mardi Gras and when the author was in a state of drunkenness." See chapter 8, n. 4.

23. Serman, "Ot liričeskogo 'ja' . . . ," 87.

24. This concept is discussed in Osip Mandel'štam, "O prirode slova," *Sobranie sočinenij,* 2: 241-59. The definition of domestic Hellenism there is: "the Hellenistic nature of the Russian language can be identified with its daily-life (*bytovye*) qualities. The word in the Hellenistic understanding is active flesh, which resolves itself into events" (246). "Hellenism—is an oven pot, a crude vessel with milk, the utensils of the home, dishes, all which surrounds the body; Hellenism is the warmth of the hearth felt as something sacred, any property which brings part of the external world to man . . ." (253).

25. Denis Fonvizin, "Nedorosl'," *Pervoe polnoe sobranie sočinenij* (St. Petersburg: Samov, 1888), 103-56.

26. Harris, 220ff.

27. Serman, "Ot liričeskogo 'ja' . . . ," 90-91.

28. Roman O. Jakobson, "Šiftery, glagol'nye kategorii i russkij glagol," *Principy tipologičeskogo analiza jazykov različnogo stroja,* ed. Boris A. Uspenskij (Moscow, 1972).

Harsha Ram (essay date 2003)

SOURCE: Ram, Harsha. "The Ode and the Empress." In *The Imperial Sublime: A Russian Poetics of Empire,* pp. 63-120. Madison: University of Wisconsin Press, 2003.

[*In the following excerpt, Ram considers Derzhavin's transformational influence on the Russian ode, placing close readings of his major panegyrics in the context of a larger discussion on the relationship of poetry and politics in Russian history.*]

Derzhavin's role in transforming the panegyric ode and shattering the classicist system of poetic genres has long been acknowledged.[1] What Pushkin had once dismissed as Derzhavin's wildly uneven poetic culture can now be viewed as a radical if implicit assault on the stylistic markers of the Lomonosovian sublime.[2] Without ever calling the ode theoretically into question, Derzhavin renewed it from within by violating the distinction between the Pindaric ode, distinguished by what he called "flashes of piety and edifying lessons for the tsars," and the Horatian tradition, with its capacity to derive the "rules of wisdom" from contemplating "life's sweetness" (7:579). This led to a crisis of the "lofty" style that had typified the Russian ode, undermining, in turn, the thematic hierarchy that separated politics from the sensuous givenness of everyday life.

While never ceasing to praise the sovereign and the state, Derzhavin stretched the panegyric ode to accommodate sharply satirical asides against potentates and court favorites even as he also sought to provide new philosophical moorings for his own class, the post-Petrine service gentry.

Derzhavin was, in fact, to write relatively traditional Lomonosovian odes throughout his life, preserving the older tradition primarily for the theme of military victory. Celebrating Catherine's success in dividing Poland and rapidly extending Russia's southern borders, these poems are perhaps the least original of Derzhavin's major works.[3] Yet Derzhavin understood early on that the Lomonosovian ode in its traditional form was not to be his calling. From the hindsight of 1805, he wrote (speaking of himself in the third person) that he had initially "wanted to imitate Mr. Lomonosov, but . . . when desiring to soar, was unable continuously to sustain, through an attractive choice of words, the grandiloquence and sumptuousness that are unique to the Russian Pindar alone. For that reason, beginning in 1779, he chose a very specific path . . . imitating Horace most of all" (6:431).

Derzhavin's long quest to surpass Lomonosov began predictably with failed acts of homage. Among his juvenilia we find poetic effusions dedicated to the empress in the older odic vein. Although they count for little as poetry, they signal an early convergence of theme and geography that would leave a lifelong mark on Derzhavin's poetic dialogue with the empress. In 1767 Catherine undertook a journey of inspection through the Volga provinces to coincide with the elections to the Legislative Commission. Drawn from government institutions as well as all recognized social groups, including non-Russian *inorodtsy* (here "foreign subjects"), the Commission was a consultative body intended to elaborate the great legal and political reconceptualization of the Russian Empire that had been set out in Catherine's "Nakaz." Destined never to be formalized into a code of law, the "Nakaz" remained a set of ideal precepts whose real function, as Richard Wortman suggests, was to propagate an image of Catherine as ruler based on a "myth of universal justice": "The empress followed the myth of empire, not of the universal Christian Empire but a Roman Empire, led by an enlightened monarch and an enlightened administrative elite, bringing the benefits of law and improved material life to the new territories, as well as to the Russian provinces."[4]

Sailing down the Volga to Kazan in a flotilla of eleven galleys, the empress and her courtiers amused themselves by translating Jean-François Marmontel's controversial *Bélisaire* (1766), a historical novel set in Byzantium intended as a didactic parable for contemporary monarchs, and by observing the festive displays of regional color organized for them by the local nobility. In a letter to Voltaire written from Kazan, Catherine shared her impressions of Asiatic Russia:

> These laws, of which so much is being said at present, are not quite completed as of yet. . . . Consider only, if you will, that they are destined to serve both Asia and Europe: and what a difference there is between them in terms of climate, people, customs, and even ideas!
>
> Here I am finally in Asia; I have wanted so terribly to see it with my own eyes. There are in this city twenty different peoples who do not resemble one another in the least. We shall nonetheless have to design a garment that would fit them all. General principles can certainly be found, but what of the details? And what details! I was about to say: we will have to create, unify, and preserve a whole world.[5]

There is a certain poignancy to this letter, marking as it does the arrival of the Enlightenment in Russia's southern peripheries, and with it the familiar double-edged sword of the European civilizing mission. Catherine desires to acknowledge and permit those cultural and religious differences that she can classify, even as she seeks to establish an overarching commonality which would make that very diversity redundant. The attitude is one of cultural superiority, to be sure, but one that also admits to a taxonomist's lucid anxiety about "details," the refractory specificities of custom and religion that cannot be subsumed by the spectacles of picturesque natives organized on her behalf. As Catherine wrote with still greater candor two days later, "this is an Empire in itself and only here can one see what an immense enterprise it is as concerns our laws, and how little these conform at present to the situation of the Empire in general."[6]

This was also Derzhavin's homeland, and his earliest poems are, in fact, minor documents of Catherine's vision for the outlying Asiatic provinces. Commenting on a masquerade for the empress in which Nogays and other nomadic peoples danced and played before her on their instruments, the young poet wrote:

> Достойно мы тебя Минербой назыбаем
> На мудрые тбои законы как бзираем.
> Достойно мы тебя Астреею зобем:
> Под скипетром тбоим златые дни бедем.
> И дикие с степей сбегаются фауны
> И пляйут пред тобой, согласно дбижа струны.
> Россия! похбались бладычицей тбоей:
> И барбарски сердца уже пленились ей.
>
> (3:183-84)

It is fitting that we call you Minerva
When we gaze upon your wise laws.
It is fitting that we call you Astrea:
We live our Golden Age under your scepter.
And wild fauns come running from the steppe
And dance before you, striking strings in accord.

Russia! Well may you boast of your sovereign:
Even the hearts of barbarians have already fallen captive to her.

A Catherinian Golden Age is inaugurated here. Unlike the Elizabethan Golden Age of Lomonosov, it is presided over by the sovereign personified as imperial legislator, for whom the fate of the non-Russian peoples of the empire looms newly on the horizon. The poem establishes an abyssal gap between nature and culture—"wild fauns," on the one hand, and a Russia aligned with Greek gods, on the other—and then reconciles both through a hypostasis of universal law. According to Catherine's "Nakaz," the incorporation of the Turkic nomads, no less than the loyalty of the empress's Russian subjects, could be idealized as a voluntary submission to the law.

Even as he showered the empress with laudatory epithets, the young Derzhavin was already wary of surrendering entirely to the idiom of praise. Truth, he insisted, was his principal Muse; "what Russians feel," and not the dictates of eloquence, would guide his pen (3:184-85). Both Derzhavin's sincerity and the Catherinian myth of the Golden Age were powerfully tested with the Pugachev Uprising, the century's most significant internal challenge to imperial governmentality that brought unprecedented upheaval to Derzhavin's native region. The poet fought Pugachev as a nobleman and an officer committed to the monarchy and eager for the rewards that proven loyalty could bring. His "Chitalagai Odes" of the same period—a cycle of four translated and four original odes published in 1776—are a case in point.[7] Although the few explicit references to the Pugachev Uprising to be found in the "Chitalagai Odes" remain bound by the odic cliches of the time, other aspects of the cycle suggest that Derzhavin had found a more indirect way to register the limits of imperial control as well as the crises of his own career.

The translated odes of the cycle, written by King Frederick II of Prussia, were devoted to praising or denouncing virtues and vices such as flattery, calumny, or constancy. These odes evince a strong ethico-political and metaphysical orientation that would become a consistent feature of Derzhavin's work. Critical of power without ceasing to be monarchist, they provided an alternative model to Lomonosov's gingerly attempts at political didacticism. They urge sovereigns to be wary of the "false mirror" of flattery and denounce the arrogance of power that is the downfall of all rulers (3:207). Derzhavin's original poems of the **"Chitalagai"** cycle continue in the same vein. An ode to Catherine "composed during the revolt of 1774" focuses more on her spirit of mercy than on her military victory: the poem, comments Ronald Vroon, praises an "ideal model of behaviour prescribed by the poet" more than it commemorates Catherine's actual triumph over Pugachev.[8] In his

"**Oda na znatnost'**" ("**Ode on Nobility**") Derzhavin tellingly contrasts the formal titles of grandees with a nobility that is of the spirit: "I am a prince, if my spirit shines; / A master if I am master of my passions" (3:225-26). A few years later these lines resurfaced in the still more pointed context of a poem addressed to the newly born tsarevich Alexander, "**Na rozhdenie v Severe porfironosnogo otroka**" ("**On the Birth of a Royal Son in the North**") (1779): «Будь страстей тбоих блаиетель, / Будь на троне чело́бек!» (Be the master of your passions, / Be a human on the throne!) (1:51). These lines formulate the typically Derzhavinian strategy of *internalizing political power and the social world as an ethical facet of personality*. Self-control, not the domination of external reality, is seen as the supreme goal, and with this contrast is born the richly productive dialectic between the public and the private self.

Since Gukovskii, scholars of Derzhavin have rightly emphasized Derzhavin's discovery of personhood, while neglecting to account for the sublime as the continued locus of the encounter, in Derzhavin, between the individual and history.[9] One of Derzhavin's ongoing goals, in poetry as in life, was to negotiate between the public and the private persona. The political sphere embodied by the ceremonial ode had provided little space for the intimacy and leisure necessary for the articulation of private life. To push the ode beyond the rubric of the state without renouncing the defining sphere of public service was one of Derzhavin's primary poetic tasks. This he accomplished by redefining the place of the sublime as pertaining to an ontological realm that was at the same time greater and lesser than the political state.

Derzhavin and the Sublime

In the fourth of Derzhavin's "**Chitalagai Odes**," a prose translation of Frederick's ode, "Life Is a Dream," we read: "11. Land, titles, honors, power, you are deceptive like smoke. The mere glance of truth dissipates the luster of your transient beauty. There is nothing reliable in this world, and even the greatest kingdoms are the playthings of inconstancy. 12. . . . If we soar to the heavens and from this grandiose height cast our gaze down onto Paris, Peking, and Rome, then from this remote distance all those great things disappear. The entire earth resembles a point; and what of man himself? 13. Filled with vanity, we rush about between the abyss of the past and that of future centuries, which hurtle constantly onward" (3:219-20).

This awareness of the radical impermanence of worldly affairs was to become Derzhavin's philosophical motto. Like all poets of the sublime, the poet here soars to the heavens to contemplate the earth below, but this familiar vertical axis now yields the opposite lesson to

Lomonosov's odic maps of empire. The capital cities of nations become annihilated at this infinite remove of contemplation, dissolving the imperial state into a vaster movement of the cosmos. The experience being intimated here is no less quintessentially sublime, but it is configured ontologically rather than geopolitically, as the erasive force of time or fate. Derzhavin would return again and again to these concerns, as in "**Na smert' kniazia Meshcherskogo**" ("**On the Death of Prince Meshcherskii**") (1779):

> Монарх и узник—снедь чербей,
> Гробницы злость стихий снедает;
> Зияет бремя слабу стерть:
> Как б море льются быстры боды,
> Так б бечность льются дни и годы;
> Глотает царстба алчна смерть.
>
> (1:54)

> [Both] monarch and convict are food for worms,
> Tombs are devoured by the malice of the elements;
> Time yawns to erase fame:
> As fast-flowing waters pour into the sea,
> So the days and years pour into eternity;
> Kingdoms are swallowed by ravenous death.

Temporal infinity, rather than empire, is for Derzhavin the supreme sublimity, although he remained content to juxtapose both categories rather than abolish one in favor of the other. Time exposes the evanescence of empire and earthly power, and displaces the empress as the supreme arbiter of destiny. The sovereignty of fate resembles imperial rule in inducing fear and awe but also differs in functioning randomly and violating the distinctions of the social world. Whereas the rulers of the panegyric ode had presided over a relatively static universe, the Derzhavinian sublime creates a mobile hierarchy of being that contains elements both greater and lesser than the empire and the empress: «Сегодня бог, а забтра прах» (1:54) ["God today, ash tomorrow"]. The sublime is a relativistic force, but its energy is not simply destructive. It speeds things up, dislodges experiences, and uproots structures with the fury of a flash flood, making social stability, professional security, political glory, and ontological fixity seem like so much debris borne along by a rapid current. The sublimity of fate is the motor energizing much of Derzhavin's universe. Its effects can be felt in the metaphysical poems such as "**Bog**" ("**God**") (1784), where the poet declares in a famous line that he is, all at once, "tsar, slave, worm, and God" (1:132). In Derzhavin's world, hierarchy, be it metaphysical or political, is less a ladder than a roller coaster, allowing for the psychological extremes of exaltation and abasement, self-aggrandizement and abjection to exist contiguously rather than as opposites.

It is from this perspective that Derzhavin contemplates the distinction between the public and private. If Derzhavin's later collection of Anacreontic verse lends itself to Il'ia Serman's conclusion that, at least in the 1790s, Derzhavin "distanced himself from all politics and from history, and was drawn to the theme of a peaceful domestic life," then his earlier work suggests a more complex articulation of this polarity.[10] Far from contrasting the two as a simple binary opposition and securing the private world as a respite from politics, Derzhavin examines both from the radical infinity of Time as a sublime force.

Death touches the king and the householder equally, and it is this ontological dimension, not politics as such, that creates as its opposite the concrete dimension of lived life. The lyric subject in Derzhavin is born already knowing the brittleness of power and the voluptuous transience of the sensory world. Embodying both is the *vel'mozha*, the grandee or magnate of the Catherinian era whose mercurial career and sybaritic tastes Derzhavin will describe in numerous poems: it is the magnate, not the state or the empress, who generally provides a counterpoint to the poet's own life. While in the poem **"Na Novyi god"** (**"On the New Year"**) (1780-81) the magnate clambers up the sublime ladder of ambition—«Еще бельможа возбышаться, / Еще сильнее хочет быть» (The magnate desires to rise still higher / To be still stronger), the poet opts "not to chase happiness in the world / [But] to find it in himself" (1:76). For Derzhavin, to live inwardly is never an ascetic goal: it involves savoring the gamut of the senses even as one seeks to become reconciled ethically to the workings of fate.

Derzhavin's late essay, **"Rassuzhdenie o liricheskoi poèzii ili ob ode"** (1811-15) (**"Discourse on Lyric Poetry or on the Ode [1811-15]"**), his only substantial excursion into literary criticism, summarized his poetic debt to the odic past, as well as the revisions he brought to the discourse of the sublime. Here Derzhavin follows Trediakovskii in equating the ode and the psalm, and follows Lomonosov in viewing the ode as practically synonymous with the lyric. In the same essay, however, the poet goes on to distinguish explicitly "two kinds of sublimity (*vysokost'*)", one that is *sensuous* and consists of the lively representation of material substances . . . the incessant representation of a multitude of brilliant pictures and feelings in a sonorous, grandiloquent, flowery diction that induces rapture and astonishment." The other sublime is "*intellectual*, and consists of showing the actions of a lofty spirit, . . . the silent and peaceful movements of a great soul that is higher than others" (7:550). In this passage Derzhavin fails to identify the sublime as Time itself: instead, he dwells on its *effects*. First, it assails the senses as an experience of grandeur, combining beauty with terror in such a way as to induce "rapture." Its second dimension is intellectual or moral, embodied in the spiritual drama of the superior individual. This discussion corresponds strikingly to a passage in Ivan Martynov's heavily annotated

translation of Longinus's treatise on the sublime, then recently published. At one point Martynov comments that the sublime can be further separated into a "sublime of feelings" and a "sublime of thoughts" which is provoked by a "large physical or abstract object" such as "the firmament, high craggy cliffs, bottomless abysses, ruins, . . . the clash of troops, earthquakes, . . . hurricanes, noisily flowing rivers, and waterfalls." Both forms of the sublime are the property of "genius," distinguished by "grandeur of spirit."[11]

In Derzhavin's work, both the sensuous and the intellectual sublime are manifested in the life trajectory of the *vel'mozha*, the generals, courtiers, and functionaries of Catherinian Russia, as much as in the empress or her empire. It is their lifestyle, career, and ultimate fate that will compel the poet to ask the empress to teach him "how to live sumptuously and righteously" (**"Felitsa,"** 1:83).

We can say, then, that Derzhavin first "ontologized" the sublime as Time itself and then mapped its transformative effects on the privileged individual and his destiny. These innovations did not in themselves abolish the imperial theme that had been the ceremonial ode's essential core. Rather, it engendered a newly complex vision in which empire could be juxtaposed as an entity alongside the vaster reality of Time as well as the lesser but poetically essential dimension of the historical individual, be it the poet himself or his aristocratic peers.

THE SUBLIME INDIVIDUATED

Derzhavin's celebrated poem **"Vodopad"** (**"The Waterfall"**) (1791-94) is one poem that successfully combines all these elements. Conceived in response to the death of Prince Grigorii Potemkin, statesman, military commander, and a lover of Catherine, the poem begins by describing a waterfall that will provide an allegorical frame for the piece as a whole:

> Алмазна сыплется гора
> С бысот четыремя скалами,
> Жемчугу бездна и сребра
> Кипит бнизу, ввет бберх буграми;
> От брызгоб синий холм стоит,
> Далече реб б лесу шумит.
>
> (1:318)

> A diamond mountain is scattering
> [Plunging] from the heights along four ledges,
> A chasm [or multitude] of pearls and silver
> Seethes below and thrusts up mounds;
> A dark-blue hill stands [created by] the jets of water,
> Farther away a roar reverberates in the forest.

Derzhavin's waterfall generates yet another example of the mountainous sublime with which we are now well familiar. Indeed, this first stanza of **"Vodopad,"** and the poem as a whole, can be read as a complex parody of

Lomonosov's ode on Khotin. The latter began, we recall, with the poet's flight to the top of Mount Parnassus, from which he harkens to the visual and auditory details of a receding horizon: «Далече реб б лесу шумит» (*Further out* a roar resounds through the forest), says Derzhavin at the end of his first stanza; «Далече дым б полях курится» (*Further out* smoke curls along the fields), reads Lomonosov's equivalent line. Both poems begin with a figurative vertical axis that affords an experience of the sublime; both then use this vantage point to view and comment on an ongoing conflict between Russia and Ottoman Turkey.

Unlike Lomonosov's poem, however, **"Vodopad"** does not celebrate a single military victory nor does it articulate its theme in exclusively patriotic terms. Its allegorical premise is at once greater and smaller, and embraces a range of voices, human experiences, and philosophical conclusions. Long before the appearance of Potemkin or the theme of the second Russo-Turkish war of 1787-92, we encounter a "gray-haired man"—Count Rumiantsev, a respected army commander and civilian administrator of the time, whom Potemkin had sidelined from power during the recent war. Rumiantsev's function in the poem is didactic: his loss of political clout provides him with the moral distance necessary to interpret the poem's unfolding allegory. Seated by the waterfall clad in golden armor, he broodingly glosses the "terrible beauty" (*strashnaia krasa*) of the natural scene:

> Не жизнь чи челобекоб нам
> Сей бодопад изображает?
> Он также благом струй сбоих
> поит надменных, кротких, злых.
>
> Не так ли с неба бремя льется,
> Кипит стремление страстей,
> Честь блещет, слаба раздается,
> Мелькает счастье наших дней,
> Которых красоту и радость
> Мрачат печали, скорби, старость?
> Не упадает ли б сей зеб
> С престола царь и цруг цареб?

(1:319-20)

> Is not the life of humans
> Depicted for us by this waterfall?
> With its benign waters it too
> Provides drink for the haughty, the meek, and the evil.
>
> Does not time pour in a like way from heaven,
> The ambition of passions seethe,
> Honor gleam, and glory resonate,
> The happiness of our days flash,
> Whose beauty and joy
> Is obscured by sadness, grief, and old age?
> Do not the king and the king's friend
> Fall from the throne into these jaws?

The rush of water was one of Derzhavin's preferred metaphors: generally representing the all-consuming vortex of time, it was also likened metapoetically to the ode itself, which, like a fast river, "carries everything away in its wake" (7:593). Time's flow leaves nothing and no one untouched: it is the supreme force, shaping and smashing people's lives just as water might carve out or erode formations of rock. To interpret these shapes is to map the effects of time on the scale of life as it is lived by individuals. What results, in this poem as in many of Derzhavin's works, are lyric biographies: whereas Lomonosov gauged historical events in terms of the benefits accruing to the empress *qua* empire, Derzhavin particularizes these events as watersheds in the political life of the noblemen of his day. The heroes of Lomonosov's Khotin ode, we recall, were Ivan, Peter, and Anna, who were little more than the sum of their victories in battle. Derzhavin's heroes, by contrast, are very human; they are the Russian statesmen whose conflicting ambitions marked the course of the Turkish war. Unlike Lomonosov's ode, then, the imperial theme in **"Vodopad"** does not simply glorify Russian expansion; it establishes the context for the statesman's career that becomes the new matrix for understanding the relationship between the individual and the general.

"Vodopad" is a long poem, whose very diffuseness permits a series of protagonists, allegorical visions, and philosophical assertions that are only tenuously integrated, creating what Anna Lisa Crone calls a "reticulating and meandering effect."[12] Rumiantsev dominates only the first half, articulating a sense of the transience of glory whose pessimism is counterbalanced by a dream in which he revisits his heroic exploits. This structure of alternating negative and positive moments is repeated throughout the poem: the poet or his heroes acknowledge the impact of mortality only to wrest some compensatory consolation from the jaws of death. Thus Rumiantsev, on seeing the winged figure of death announce Potemkin's demise,

> sighs . . . :
> "Blessed is he who, in aspiring to glory, preserved the
>   common good,
> Was merciful in bloody war,
> And preserved the life of his very enemies."

(1:323)

Rumiantsev ultimately bridges the evident gap between his past glory and his present decline by projecting an alternative vision of his own posthumous fame, vouchsafed not only by martial valor but also by greatness of spirit (1:323).

Yet if Rumiantsev represents the ideal ethical reconciliation of personal glory (*slava*) and the general good (*pol'za*), then Potemkin is a less benign and more complex figure. Unlike Rumiantsev, who was deprived of royal favor, Potemkin represents a more compelling fusion of glory and good fortune (*schast'e*). Potemkin, again unlike Rumiantsev, does not speak and hence cannot provide his own life with any sense of philosophical closure. Potemkin is thus doubly enigmatic: his titanic persona, the meteoric extremes of his rise and fall, render him more compelling than Rumiantsev, yet his charisma remains a source of aesthetic wonderment rather than ethical synthesis.[13] Potemkin's alienation from his own destiny is underscored by the split between his spirit and his body, which the poet represents separately, and in turn. His "wondrous spirit" flies southward to the scene of his great victories against the Turks, reviewing the kingdoms he has conquered, while his "corpse" lies prostrate in the ground, fallen "abruptly among the steppes," his "deathbed the earth," his "palace the surrounding desolation" (1:324).

While Rumiantsev's words most closely match Derzhavin's philosophical conclusions, it is Potemkin's dead body that marks the beginnings of a new model for the imperial sublime. Marked by a restless sense of personal ambition, Potemkin's fate anticipates the narcissistic cult of the romantics (Potemkin's corpse is surely an intertext for Lermontov's great poem, "The Dream," with its description of a soldier's bleeding body lying in a valley of Daghestan, unburied and hence unreconciled with his homeland, a text we turn to in the next chapter). With Potemkin we have a man whose life and death appear suddenly coterminous with empire, which is now measurable in terms of personal loss or gain as much as territorial contraction and expansion. Derzhavin notes in his commentary that "none better than Prince Potemkin grasped Catherine's ambitious spirit and the might of her empire, on whose foundation he based his own great plans" (3:521). Here Derzhavin was referring to the "Greek Project," a plan to wrest Constantinople from Ottoman hands and establish there a fraternal Orthodox empire, which became closely identified with Potemkin's rise to power in 1774. As Andrei Zorin observes, such enterprises as the annexation of the Crimea in 1783 were perceived in certain quarters as "Potemkin's political adventure, undertaken despite the opposition of the entire cabinet of ministers, and whose outcome would determine the continuation of Catherine's favour and his influence."[14] Derzhavin's views reflect a similar ambivalence: in the following lines, the prestige of the sovereign and the state seem equally to be a platform for Potemkin's own ambitions:

Не ты ль, который бзбесить смел
Мощь Росса, дух Екатерины,
И опершись на них, хотел
Бознесть тбой гром на те стремнины,
На коих дребний Рим стоял,
И бсей бселенной колебал?

(1:324-25)

Is it not you who dared to weigh
The might of the Russian and the spirit of Catherine,
And leaning on them, wanted
To raise your thunder to that precipice
On which ancient Rome had stood
And swayed the entire universe?

While Rumiantsev's discourse remains essentially self-contained, Potemkin's "open but silent mouth" needs to be ventriloquized. The poet thus addresses Potemkin directly and revisits his exploits, which he had himself celebrated in the past:

Б созбучность громкого Пиндара
Мою настроить лиру мнил,
Боспел победу Измаила,
Боспел,—но смерть тебя скосила!

(1:325)

In consonance with loud Pindar
I thought to tune my lyre,
I celebrated your victory at Izmail,
I celebrated [it]—but death cut you down!

In recalling **"Na vziatie Izmaila"** (**"On the Taking of Izmail"**) (1790), the most famous and the most conventional of his victory odes, Derzhavin here signals its essential limits. In Derzhavin's work, the odic sublime is perpetually threatened by death and the evanescence of power. The strains of sustaining the odic enterprise of praise, and the glory of empire that is its object, are vividly manifest in the nervously rhetorical quality of the poem's final pages. Just as the poem as a whole seems to waver between ode and elegy, so, too, the poet repeatedly renounces his most pessimistic conclusions with a hasty "or no!"—much like a suicide who changes his mind at the edge of a cliff.

Derzhavin's **"Vodopad"** thus contains several heterogeneous elements: the traditional concerns of the ode (Russian "rapture" and Turkish "terror") coexist alongside a pessimism concerning the efficacy of human endeavor that threatens to negate all worldly affairs, while the piece finally concludes by returning to the poet's ethical agenda. The waterfall is reminded that its sublimity should only exist in proportion to its beneficial effects: «Чтоб был . . . сколь дибен, столь полезен» (May you be . . . as wondrous as you are useful) (1:329).

Given the importance of state service for Derzhavin's own career, it is not surprising that the career of the state functionary, subject to the whims of the sovereign and the tides of fortune, continued to provide a model for the poet's notion of selfhood. The concerns of **"Vodopad,"** which struggles to reconcile imperial policy with an ethics of public behavior, became an ongoing theme of Derzhavin's poetry. **"Na vozvrashchenie grafa Zubova iz Persii"** (**"On the Return of Count Zubov from Persia"**) (1797) and its immediate predecessor, **"Na pokorenie Derbenta" ("On the Conquest of Derbent")** (1796), are a case in point. Both poems are addressed to the young military commander Valerian Zubov, brother to another of Catherine's favorites, and address the vicissitudes of his career as a means of inserting a search for ethical norms into the ode's traditional celebration of military conquest.

Zubov's career had brought home yet again the extent to which empire could be made and unmade by the personality of the monarch and the shifting tides of royal favor. On ascending the throne, Catherine's son, Paul, decided to renounce his mother's ambitious southern policy: Zubov was ordered home in the midst of a successful campaign against Persia and then forced to live under police surveillance. Derzhavin's innovation was to contemplate this shift in imperial policy as a human and ethical problem rather than as a question of geopolitics. Motivated, like **"Vodopad,"** by a sympathy for the underdog, the ode to Zubov could neither be published at the time nor read at court: this itself suggests the extent to which the ode, even when marking Russia's imperial engagements, was outgrowing its ceremonial function.

Addressing Zubov on his return from Persia, the poem begins at a considerable philosophical remove from the count's recent campaign. The aim of life, we are told in the very first line, is peace of mind (*pokoi*). The poem figures life as a series of landscapes to be traversed in this search for ultimate peace, a journey in which a steep rise or descent is equivalent to temporary success or failure: «Сей с холма б пропасть упадает, / А тот бзойти спешит на холм» (This man falls from a hill into an abyss, / And that one races to climb the hill) (2:20). Yet true happiness involves abandoning the dizzying heights of the vertical sublime («За ней на бысоту не мчится» [does not pursue it by rushing to a high place]) for the calm certitudes of the "middle path." The poem thus begins by denying *philosophically* what would be its greatest *poetic* innovation: its vivid description, the first in Russian literature, of the Caucasus as a privileged locus of the sublime.

As the poet recalls Zubov's recent campaign in the Caucasus, the poem makes an abrupt shift from ethical detachment to aesthetic rapture:

> О юный бождь!—сберша походы,
> Прошел ты с боинстбом Кабказ,
> Зрел ужасы, красы природы:
> Как с ребр там страшных гор лиясь
> Ребут б мрак бездн сердиты реки:
> Как с чел их с грохотом снега
> Падут, лежабши целы беки;
> Как серны, бниз склониб рога,
> Зрят б мгле спокойно под собою
> Рожденье молний и громоб.
>
> (2:20-21)

O young leader!—in waging your campaigns,
You have marched through the Caucasus with your soldiery,
You have gazed upon the horrors, the beauties of nature:
The angry rivers, as they pour forth there from the ribs of terrifying mountains
As they roar into the gloom of abysses:
The snows as from their brows [of the hills] thunderously
They fall, after having lain there for whole centuries;
The chamois, their horns bent down,
View calmly in the gloom below them
The birth of lightening [*sic*] and thunder.

The Caucasus mountains and their region are presented here in a way that corresponds perfectly to Derzhavin's later definition of the sublime as being either "sensuous," "intellectual," or (occasionally) both (7:550). These lines are nothing if not "the incessant representation of a multitude of brilliant pictures"; as such they contain the germ of the Caucasian problematic that would become a major current of Russian romanticism. Derzhavin here signals the beginning of what is a more specifically sensuous or natural form of the imperial sublime, whose rich visual excess was definitively formulated for Russian poetry in Pushkin's southern verse. The luxuriant profusion of natural detail here is no longer abstractly symbolic (as with Lomonosov) and not yet simply picturesque or enumerative (as often with Pushkin). It is organized in strict accordance with the visual criteria of horror and beauty («ужасы, красы природы» [the horrors, the beauties of nature]), which the sublime will first juxtapose and then conflate. Descriptive detail proliferates up and down a sheer vertical drop that is contrasted with the horizontal perspective of the itinerant eye.

The stanzas devoted to describing the landscape of the Caucasus are structured as a series of vertical glances, arrested and then displaced, providing a series of vignettes that are recounted as part of the poem's account of Zubov's life as a career. This sequence of visions provides the natural counterpart to the intellectual sublime, the latter consisting of "showing the actions of a lofty spirit." A great soul is one who, having climbed the ladder of power and savored both success and failure, gains the self-mastery necessary to view his own destiny with detachment. Soaring ambition thus becomes the intellectual counterpart to the mountainous sublime:

> Ты домы зрел царей, бселенну,
> Бнизу, бберху ты бидел бсе;
> Упадшу спицу, бознесенну,
> Бертяше мира колесо.
>
> (2:21)

You saw the homes of tsars, the universe,
Above, below, you saw it all;

You saw the fallen spoke and the raised one,
The world's wheel turning.

The poem thus effectively creates two vertical axes, the *sensuous* sublime that celebrates the natural grandeur of the Caucasus mountains and the *intellectual* sublime that symbolizes the hierarchical power of kings and potentates "seated on the throne / high above mortals" (2:20). Both sublimities function to link the imperial metropolis to the colonial periphery, re-creating the typically Lomonosovian effect of imperial cartography. Yet, for Derzhavin, this map is not, at least here, a representation of the Russian state. It is a psychological lesson, serving as a guide to the individual's "victories over the self" (2:22), a gauge of one's capacity to survive the caprices of power and finally surrender the realm of politics for the "wisdom of other kingdoms." The glory of conquest is devalued in favor of self-control, and this introjection of power is what allows the imperial sublime to become psychologized as an ethical imperative.

This ethical vision permits Derzhavin to question the attractions of the vertical sublime without dismantling it. The latter is philosophically subordinated to the poet's search for a reflective equilibrium but, rhetorically speaking, remains the privileged mode of expressing that very search. This is why it is dismissed as transient or episodic in the ode to Zubov even as it rhetorically defines the poem's basic movement. What finally remains, the soul stripped of earthly illusions, can best be defined as a subtler version of what the poet once defined as the intellectual sublime:

> Сиянье бкруг тебя заснуло,
> Прошло,—остался только ты.
> Остался ты!—и та прекрасна
> Душа почтенна будет ббек . . .
>
> (2:22)

The luster about you has faded,
It has passed,—you alone remain.
You remain!—and that splendid
Soul will be esteemed forever.

The great soul is like the poem itself, an immortal residue that has survived the experience of the vertical sublime, to measure its rise and fall. . . .

ADDRESSING THE DESPOT

Derzhavin wrote a series of poems whose theme and central protagonists he culled from Catherine's "Tale of the Crown Prince Khlor." The first of these poems, **"Felitsa,"** succeeded spectacularly in establishing Derzhavin's poetic reputation as well as defining his political relationship to Catherine and her court. It was followed at varying intervals by the related poems **"Blagodarnost' Felitse"** (**"Gratitude to Felitsa"**) (1783), **"Videnie murzy"** (**"The Murza's Vision"**) (written in 1783-84, reworked and published in 1791), **"Izobrazhenie Felitsy"** (**"A Portrayal of Felitsa"**) (1789), and, much later, **"Poslanie indeiskogo bramina k tsarevichu Khloru"** (**"Epistle of an Indian Brahmin to the Crown Prince Khlor"**) (1802), a poem dedicated, appropriately enough, to Catherine's grandson, Alexander.

Critics have generally hailed the **"Felitsa"** cycle as Derzhavin's vindication of the individual personality. "Derzhavin's originality," writes Il'ia Serman, lies in "having placed himself" inside his portrait gallery of Catherine's noblemen.[15] Iurii Lotman writes, still more pointedly, that "Derzhavin paradoxically reversed the situation" of the Russian ode by "predicat[ing] the very possibility of odic poetry on the assumption that the tsarina was a private person, a human being and not an embodied principle. Derzhavin abolished the antithesis of the state and the private individual by subordinating the positive sphere of the former to the latter."[16] Yet was this inversion so absolute? That Derzhavin succeeded in personalizing his dialogue with power is beyond doubt, but was his individuation of the human persona an unequivocal triumph over the state? And how does his unsettling of these antinomies relate to the oriental tales that Catherine herself authored?

In writing **"Felitsa"** Derzhavin fulfilled his need to win the empress's favor and attention even as he reworked the genre of the panegyric ode. This double success, pragmatic and literary, is easily understood from the very title **"Felitsa."** A transient but crucial figure in the Khlor tale, Felitsa is the Kirgiz khan's daughter, a princess of "merry character and exceedingly pleasant," who provides Khlor with the kindly counsel he needs to find the thornless rose, and offers him her son, Reason, as his guide. In Felitsa the quintessential folkloric motif of the magical intercessor becomes a vehicle for Enlightenment ideology: her aid consists solely of fostering Khlor's innate capacity to discern what constitutes proper conduct and to persevere on the correct path. Derzhavin's brilliance consisted of recognizing Felitsa as the empress's own self-projection, and of magnifying and then turning back on Catherine the mirror she had crafted for herself. Overall the **"Felitsa"** cycle dramatized in poetic form the awkward reconciliation of "oriental" despotism and Enlightenment principles that had become identified as Catherinian ideology. This was a playful but forced marriage between a progressive European content and a regressive "oriental" form, one whose strains are evident throughout much of the cycle.

"Felitsa" begins by addressing Catherine as the "God-like Princess of the Kirgiz-Kaisak horde," imploring her to instruct the poet just as she had once taught the crown prince Khlor. In the course of the poem, the poet's self-representation acquires two dimensions. He is first an eager student, submitting like Khlor before him to the empress's discipline; second, he identifies himself as the Murza Lazybones, a genially indolent aristocrat who functions in Catherine's story as a minor obstacle to Khlor's quest for virtue. This second dimension sits awkwardly with the first and is a radical emendation of the original story: a reprobate and morally static character in Catherine's text, the Murza now abruptly turns to Felitsa in search of self-improvement:

> Подай, Фелица, настабленье,
> Как пышно и прабдибо жить,
> Как укрошать страстей болненье
> И счастлибым на сбете быть.
> Меня тбой голос бозбуждает,
> Меня тбой сын препробождает;
> Но им последобать я слаб:
> Мятясь житейской суетою,
> Сегодня бластбую собою,
> А забтра прихотям я раб.

> (1:83-84)

> Give me instructions, Felitsa,
> On how to live sumptuously and righteously,
> How to subjugate the agitation of the passions
> And be happy on the earth.
> Your voice makes me animated,
> Your son sends me off,
> But I am too weak to follow them:
> Rushing about absorbed in life's vain pursuits,
> Today I am in control of myself,
> But tomorrow I am a slave to my caprices.

The poem as a whole is not much more than a continuing elaboration of this initial contrast between benign instructress and errant pupil. The Murza presents himself as indolent and prone to sybaritic excesses, while exalting Felitsa for being a sovereign who is permissive in relation to others yet disciplined enough to be able herself to "subjugate the passions." The contrast between Felitsa and the Murza is more than a theme: it is also the structuring principle behind a new sense of lyric subjectivity. In a typically Derzhavinian gesture, the above lines turn the political realm inward, converting the imperial state into a psychic sovereignty over the self. The lyric subject is born in this quest for self-mastery but also, as we shall see, in the repeated failure of this quest.

The tone of bashful self-reproach that dominates the poem has been primarily read as a social satire of gentry mores; yet it might also be read in a more psychological vein, as the construction of a gentry selfhood reached through critical self-examination. (That Derzhavin was not a part of Catherine's inner circle when writing **"Felitsa,"** and hence not fully implicated in the Murza's self-deprecating confessions, makes the overlapping of collective and individual selves all the more complex.) In fact, as James Billington has observed, these two aspects, social and psychological, are deeply connected: "The personal moral crisis for the ruling aristocrat of Catherine's era was not, in the first instance, created by economic and political privilege but rather by the new style of life within the aristocracy itself: by the vulgar hedonism and imitative Gallomania of their own increasingly profligate lives."[17]

The Murza's aristocratic consciousness is precisely this: a self-reflexivity that turns inward to critique the indulgent rhythms of gentry life, and then looks for external models in order to overcome its malaise. While the details of the Murza's lifestyle have given rise to much critical discussion of Derzhavin's new individualism, it is worth noting that the poet's search seldom culminates in any real sense of personal autonomy. For Derzhavin there is always a higher authority to which the self is answerable. Felitsa is one image of this authority and, as such, has two hypostases, political and moral. As ruler, she has broadened the range of permitted behavior, knowing the "rights of both people and kings" and allowing at least her aristocratic subjects to "travel to foreign parts" (1:88-89). Ethically she functions as a model of proper conduct, a regulatory ideal to be absorbed and emulated:

> You do not play cards,
> Like me, from one morning to the next.

> (1:84)

These two hypostases are inflected in inverse ways: the political sphere is expansive and permissive whereas the moral sphere emphasizes restraint and self-discipline. These two spheres are not necessarily in contradiction: doctrinally speaking, the power of the absolute monarch was defined as unlimited, with any restriction on his power emanating from him alone, as an act of voluntary self-limitation. The sovereign's moral restraint, then, was the necessary complement to the political freedom of his subjects.

Although Derzhavin's civic odes can vary in terms of which hypostasis is dominant, it is generally true that the ethical aspect prevails in his verse. This moral strain corresponds to what many critics have seen as Derzhavin's "privatization" of politics, a process that merits more careful examination. Far from abandoning the state for the comforts of private life, Derzhavin introjects the state's authority, internalizing the sovereign as an ego-ideal that penetrates even the private sphere of domestic life. The enlightened despot, omnipotent but consciously self-limiting, is projected beyond the sphere of governance, to become an ethical ideal for the everyday life of the gentry. This regulatory model bears little resemblance to Catherine herself: operating externally as an exalted vision of the sovereign, it is also a moral imperative emanating from within the poet.[18]

In **"Videnie murzy,"** for example, Felitsa appears to the Murza in his chamber as a nocturnal vision and unexpectedly upbraids him for his facile panegyrics:

When
Poetry is not a whim,
But the highest of the gods' gifts, then
this gift of the gods should be used
only for honor
And for teaching their ways,
Not for flattery
And the perishable praise of people.

(1:109)

These words bear no relationship to Catherine's actual understanding of poetry, which was limited, or her relationship to poets, which was mainly instrumental. Yet if Derzhavin "literally puts words into [Catherine's] mouth," as Pierre Hart would have it,[19] then it is also true that the question of authorship and agency here becomes increasingly moot. Commenting on the closing lines of **"Videnie murzy,"** addressed by the Murza to Felitsa, «Пребознесу тебя, прослаблю / Тобой безсмертен буду сам!» (I shall exalt and praise you / Through you I myself shall be immortal!) (1:111), Hart suggests that it is the poet and his immortality that is privileged here, for which Felitsa is merely a vehicle.[20] Yet however bold these lines appear, they nonetheless perpetuate a condition familiar to us from Lomonosov's time: lyric subjectivity remains an extension of political subjecthood (*poddanstvo*). What is new here is the transformation and *internalization* of the monarch's voice: the enlightened despot is no longer just the empress— she is also the inner voice of the poet's own conscience, a superego if you will, urging the Murza to question his actions and test his motivations.

The inverse, however, is also true: taken as a whole, **"Videnie murzy"** can also be read as a sly message to Catherine on how to read and what to ask of poetry, a message that is then attributed to Felitsa herself. In this sense one might say that Derzhavin and Catherine were involved in a complex game of mutual ventriloquism. The **"Felitsa"** cycle invokes Catherine's writings as if it were yielding to a higher power but in quoting them ultimately turns their authority back on the empress. Given the discursive levels—fictional (Felitsa and the Murza) and authorial (the empress and the poet)— simultaneously present in Derzhavin's poems, it is not easy at any given time to discern who is speaking, and who is teaching whom.[21] Hence the strangely contradictory gestures of sycophancy and didactic presumption that typify Derzhavin's addresses to the empress. Derzhavin may well have achieved a personalized dialogue with the empress but one in which neither interlocutor possesses a distinctly individuated voice.[22]

The apotheosis of both hypostases of Felitsa, moral and political, was achieved in the poem **"Izobrazhenie Felitsy"** (1789). Derzhavin's longest poem, and by no means his most original, **"Izobrazhenie Felitsy"** was written in the hope—vain as it turned out—of securing the empress's personal intercession in the poet's career, which appeared particularly shaky after political intrigues deprived him of the governorship of Tambov Province. **"Izobrazhenie Felitsy"** rhetorically reposes the long-standing question of the odic representation of the monarch. The poem repeats the clichés of the panegyric tradition concerning the godlike nature of the empress, but also seeks to reconcile them with a typically Derzhavinian emphasis on the integrity of the artist. Claiming to be "enraptured" by Felitsa, the poet Murza feels he can continue to sing his "Tatar songs" in her praise with a "clear conscience" (1:201-2). For this to be so, Felitsa can no longer be "merely" a royal persona but a fundamental aspect of the poet's inner life:

Но что, Рафаэль, что ты пишешь?
Кого ты, где изобразил?
Не на холсте, не б красках дышишь,
И не металл ты ожибил: Я б сердце зрю алмазну
    гору;
На нем божестбенны черты
Сияют изступленну бзору;
На нем б лучах—Фелица, ты!

(1:202)

But what, Raphael, what is it you are painting?
Whom have you depicted, and where?
Not on a canvas, and not in paint do you breathe,
It was not to metal that you brought life: I see a dia-
    mond hill in my heart;
In it divine features
Shine before my ecstatic gaze;
In it, surrounded by rays [of light] are you, Felitsa!

However hyperbolic, these lines are not a mere rhetorical flourish: Felitsa is consistently presented as the "mistress of hearts" (1:191): her empire extends over the inner self as much as over physical territory. Her gaze is said to

swiftly penetrate thoughts
even in the most secretive of hearts;
so that from afar she might discern
whoever is innocent of all [crimes].

(1:196)

Felitsa's moral hypostasis allows Derzhavin to jointly articulate a range of apparently unconnected questions, from the fate of the odic poet to the status of the subject peoples of the Russian Empire. Both the artist and the non-Russian subject (and let us remember that the Murza is *both* a poet and a Tatar) submit voluntarily to Felitsa's sovereignty («обладать собой избрал» [1:191]). By surrendering their will to the "Felitsa within" («Стаб сами бы *себе* послушны» [1:192; my emphasis]) they translate the political dimension of imperial subjecthood into the psychic dimension of subjectivity. Just as the inner workings of conscience can reconcile individual will with moral constraint, so, too, the rule of the enlightened despot reconciles political freedom and imperial sovereignty.

"Izobrazhenie Felitsy" elaborates this idealized scenario in great detail; what results is the most sustained poetic treatment of what enlightened absolutism entails for empire and for poetry:

> Престол ее на Скандинабских,
> Камчатских и Златых горах,
> От стран Таймурских до Кубанских
> Постабь на сорок дбух столпах;
> Как босемь бы зерцал стояли
> Ее беликие моря;
> С полнеба збезды осбещали,
> Бокруг—багряная заря.
>
> Средь дибного сего чертога
> И белелепной бысоты
> Б беличестбе, б сияньи Бога
> Ее изобрази мне ты;
> Чтоб, сшед с престола, подабала
> Скрыжаль запобедей сбятых;
> Чтобы бселенна принимала
> Глас Божий, глас природы б них.
>
> Чтоб дики люди, отдаленны,
> покрыты шерстью, чешуей,
> Пернатых перьем испещренны,
> Одеты листьем и корой,
> Сошедшися к ее престолу
> И кроткий бняб законоб глас
> По желто—смуглым лицам долу
> Струили токи слез из глаз;
>
> Струили б слезы и, блаженство
> Сбоих проразумея дней,
> Завыли бы сбое рабенстбо
> И были бсе подбластны ей:
> Финн б море бледный, рыжебласый,
> Не разбибал бы кораблей,
> И узкоглазый Гунн жал класы
> Среди седых, сухих зыбей.

(1:192-93)

Place her throne on the hills of Scandinavia,
Kamchatka and the Golden Hills,
from the countries of Timur to the Kuban
On forty-two columns;
Like eight mirrors
Her great seas would stand;
Stars covering half the sky would illuminate [them],
All round—a purple dawn.

In the midst of this splendid palace
And magnificent elevation
In her grandeur and divine luster
Depict her for me;
So that, descending from her throne, she might offer
The tablet of sacred commandments;
So that the universe might accept
The voice of God and the voice of nature in them.

So that distant and savage people,
Covered in furs and scales,
Speckled with the feathers of birds,
Clothed in leaf and bark,
Converging on her throne
And hearing the voice of gentle laws
Might shed streams of tears
Down their swarthily yellow faces.

They would shed tears, and foreseeing the bliss
Of their [future] days,
Would forget their own equality
And all submit to her:
The pale and red-haired Finn,
Would not destroy ships at sea,
and the slant-eyed Hun would reap the ears of grain
Among the dry, gray rippling [fields].

In typical odic fashion, these lines project the sovereign's body onto the realm she rules, so that her throne appears physically to straddle Russia's forty-two provinces, transforming terrain into territory. At this point, however, the allegory becomes historically more precise. Derzhavin's own notes (3:494) identify the above passage as a reference to the Legislative Commission of 1767, an emblematic moment in the early years of Catherine's reign which Derzhavin had also celebrated in his youth. The commission, we remember, had marked a historic first encounter between the European Enlightenment and the peoples of Russia's outlying provinces, whose significance had been confirmed by Catherine's journey of discovery down the Volga. Signaling a symbolic convergence between the ruler and the ruled, the commission promised a new legal covenant that would supersede the politics of conquest and coercion. Returning to this early and unfulfilled promise to reconcile a multinational empire to the rule of law, Derzhavin depicts Catherine as a second Moses, and her Nakaz as a secular revelation binding the racially marked bodies of the subject peoples to the sovereign who rules over them. In the new dispensation, submission takes the place of subjugation: Catherine's subjects, the Finn and the "Hun" (the Turk?) are shown willingly abandoning their primitive freedoms to become subject to the legal constraints of empire. V. M. Zhivov has called these lists of "savage peoples" the "ethnographic correlative" to the geographical markers of empire that were a long-established odic topos: "in geographical space the monarch appears in the hypostasis of Mars," the god of war, "while in ethnographic space she appears in the hypostasis of Minerva," the goddess of wisdom.[23]

The Legislative Commission, as an early watershed in Catherine's reign and as a topos in Derzhavin's poetry, might well be reexamined as a way of historicizing the figures of Felitsa and the Murza, which critics have often viewed as nothing more than playful literary masks.[24] Catherine had consistently nurtured territorial ambitions as well as a civilizational vision for Russia's southern peripheries, which were noted for their ethnic and religious diversity. Two prolonged wars against Ottoman Turkey, the annexation of the Crimea, a steady advance through the Kuban into the Northern Caucasus, and the ambitious if unrealized "Greek Project" to retake Constantinople were the milestones of a southern policy that was one of the guiding principles of Catherine's rule. This extraordinary chapter in the history of Russian expansionism paradoxically coincided with a rare period of domestic tolerance toward people of other faiths. Abandoning overt coercion for bureaucratic assimilation, Catherine sought to stabilize the volatile borderlands by absorbing the local nobility as well as the Muslim clergy into the Russian state apparatus. The Tatars of Kazan, as the most assimilated non-Russian community of the time, played a significant role as intermediaries in this new dispensation.[25] As a native of Kazan claiming noble Tatar ancestry, an active participant in quelling the Pugachev Revolt, and the owner of several villages in the Orenburg district bordering the Kirgiz horde over which Felitsa's father was said to have ruled, Derzhavin would have been acutely aware of the immense stakes of Catherine's southern policy.[26] His choice of the Murza as a lyric persona might well be seen as a lyric refraction of this historical moment, when the civilizational discourse of the European Enlightenment, adopted and modified for the Russian autocratic tradition, created a new kind of pacified imperial subject. The Murza gives voice to a specifically Russian imperial variant of enlightened absolutism, juxtaposing the predicament of the odic poet alongside the impact of imperial rule on Russia's *inorodtsy*. These are the beginnings of a persistent analogy found in Russian literature: the relationship between the emperor and his empire is seen as parallel to the one obtaining between the emperor and the writer as subject.

While Derzhavin's **"Felitsa"** cycle contributed enormously to the consolidation of an official Catherinian myth, the orientalist fantasy that was its basis paradoxically foregrounded the underlying contradictions of the odic tradition. Whereas Felitsa was intended to symbolize the triumphant application of Enlightenment principles to an Asiatic empire, the figurative elaboration of the oriental despot inevitably exacerbated the tension between the ode's newly professed ideology and its rhetorical form. The Enlightenment ideals of human dignity, civic merit, and law-based rule were difficult enough to express through the traditional apparatus of panegyric description and address but appeared even more incongruous alongside the playful evocations of murzas, pashas, sultans, and harems. Nevertheless, Derzhavin's **"Felitsa"** cycle represents the most vivid and sustained attempt at resuscitating what was an increasingly moribund genre. Its stylized orient was a subtle means of updating the ode's historical content, evoking an imaginary geography in which the Russian autocratic state could continue its southward expansion while retaining its claim to European modernity.

More than one generation of poets after Derzhavin would intuit the layered and allegorical nature of the Felitsa/Murza encounter, embracing as it does the broader question of autocracy and empire, and the specifically literary dimension of the poet's subjective relation to political power and literary genius. As a brief index of its reverberations we might cite the celebrated Pushkin poem "Prorok" ("The Prophet") (1826), which echoes several elements (including one rhyming sequence, albeit with different stress) from **"Videnie murzy."** Says Felitsa to the Murza in that ode:

«*Во*трепещи, мурза несчастный!
И страшны истины *внемли*,
Которым стихотборцы страстны
Едва ли берят на *земли*.»
"Tremble, unfortunate Murza!
And hearken to terrible truths,
Which passionate poets
On earth scarcely believe."

And in "Prorok" Pushkin's God exclaims:

«*Во*сстань, пророк, и биждь и *внемли*,
Исполнись болею моей,
И, обходя моря и *земли*,
Глаголом жги сердца людей.»
"Arise, o prophet, both see and harken
Be filled with my will
And, traversing sea and land,
Burn the hearts of men with the word."

The sublime confrontation between ruler and subject remained the context in which the prophetic sublime was to evolve in Russian romantic poetry. To restore the romantic poet-prophet to this imperial context will be one of our tasks in the chapters to come.

Derzhavin's reworking of the imperial sublime was not limited to the **"Felitsa"** cycle or to those poems that satirize or exalt the gentry culture of the time. His poem, **"Vlastiteliam i sudiiam" ("To Rulers and Judges")**, a blunt condemnation of social injustice first published in 1780, continues the tradition of using the Psalms of David as a vehicle for dissent. More interesting are the two short poems **"Pamiatnik" ("The Monument")** (1795) and **"Lebed'" ("The Swan")** (1804), both translations of Horace, which strikingly anticipate what the imperial sublime will become in the romantic era. Both poems assert the Horatian topos of poetic immortality with a confidence new to Russian verse, locating the poet's sense of his life's accomplishments and posthumous future in a new vision of imperial space.[27] Each poem erects its own sublime vertical axis—a monument "higher than the pyramids" and a swan that soars far above the earth—but for an entirely new purpose. Where the vertical sublime formerly yielded maps of empire, replete with toponyms and ethnonyms, whose sole purpose was to elaborate the glory of the empress and the state, now the same map charts the poet's vision of his *own* greatness. **"Pamiatnik"** declares that the poet's glory "will grow undiminished / as long as the race of Slavs is honored by the universe" and that news of him "will spread from the waters of the White Sea to the Black," where every man "among innumerable peoples" will remember his achievements (1:534). **"Lebed"** elaborates Derzhavin's "poetic empire" with still greater boldness. The poet-swan leaves behind the "dazzle of kingdoms" and the rewards of courtly life to establish a new relationship to the earth below:

> С Курильских остробоб до Буга,
> От Белых до Каспийских бод,
> Народы, сбета с полукруга,
> Состабибшие россоб род,
>
> Со бременем о мне узнают:
> Слабяне, гунны, скифы, чудь,
> И бсе, что бранью днесь пылают,
> Покажут перстом—и рекут:
>
> «Бот тот летит, что, строя лиру,
> Языком сердца гоборил,
> И, пропобедуя мир миру,
> Себя бсех счастьем беселил.»

(2:315)

> From the Kurile Islands to the River Bug,
> From the waters of the White Sea to the Caspian,
> The peoples from half the circumference of the earth
> Who compose the Russian race,
>
> Will learn of me in time:
> The Slavs, the Huns, the Scythians, and the Chud,
> And all those who today are aflame with [the fire of] war,
> Will point their finger and say:
>
> "Behold him flying who, tuning his lyre,
> Spoke the language of the heart,
> And, propagating peace to the world,
> Made himself and everyone merry with happiness."

The odic markers of geography and ethnicity are all present here, but as witness to the poet's glory. However bound to empire, the poet renounces the odic celebration of conquest, pointing to a future reconciliation of all the peoples of Russia that is the utopian political correlative to his own poetic immortality. **"Pamiatnik"** and **"Lebed"'** are two audacious and early examples of a fissure between Russian literature and the state that would only grow wider during the course of the nineteenth century. Yet it is also worth recalling that, like all symmetrical reversals, these poems remain indebted to the model they implicitly critique. Neither denies empire as the sole matrix of fame and glory—they merely crown the poet in place of the tsar. This gesture strikingly anticipates the poetry of the Decembrists who will literalize—and politicize—a usurpation of power that remains a literary conceit in Derzhavin's hands.[28]

Empire and poetic language were established almost simultaneously in eighteenth-century Russia. This fact, generally acknowledged yet unstudied in all its ramifications, was the object of the last two chapters. In Lomonosov's theory and odic practice, a parallel dynamic of poetic inspiration and political power came together as the imperial sublime. Implicitly assimilating questions of territory to poetics and selectively adapting newer European models to the older panegyric tradition, Lomonosov succeeded in establishing a poetic language equal to the post-Petrine model of imperial statehood.

The Lomonosovian sublime is at the same time the most consistent of models as well as the most primitive in its absence of nuances. Often little more than a prolonged exclamation of praise and wonderment, its vision does not intimate the real complexities of war, statecraft, or court life under the empresses Anna and Elizabeth. Nonetheless, its very idealization of state policy contains prescriptive elements that sound a note of subtle dissent. As Iurii Lotman notes, independent literary culture was first manifested in Russia as a utopian vision of the state that was clearly opposed to the realities of empire.[29] Despite these veiled disagreements with imperial policy, the ode as a genre necessarily generated a lyric self that was intimately connected to the empress and her empire. Indeed, we might say that a new lyric subjectivity was born out of the dynamic of supplication that bound the poet to the monarch and was then projected onto the horizontal stretch of conquered territory. The narrow range of emotions available to the odic poet, from dread to rapturous enthusiasm, corresponds in the main to this imperial context.

It was Derzhavin's task to transform and personalize the abstract limitations of the Lomonosovian sublime. Although Derzhavin was deeply engaged in the realities of imperial administration, his poetry was never limited to being a crudely celebratory mouthpiece, hailing a victory won or a treaty signed. It achieved a distance on the politics of the day by widening the ode beyond the defining matrix of the state. Sublimity, for Derzhavin, was the impact of force in general, be it the sovereign will or the vaster workings of time: individuality is what absorbs and survives the shattering experience of the sublime in one of its many forms. The ethical dimension typical of Derzhavin's poetry is a result of this transformative internalization, in which the political or ontological dimension of power is contemplated and then introjected to become a regulating mechanism within the human personality.

The life story thus becomes a necessary foil to the abstractions of empire, and many of Derzhavin's odes are, in fact, short lyric biographies. As the vicissitudes of ambition and the struggles of conscience loom larger in the poet's consciousness, the fortunes of empire are gauged less for their importance to Russia than as benchmarks in the career of the Russian statesman. This vocational aspect of empire, typified by such figures as Rumiantsev, Potemkin, or V. Zubov, was to have a profound impact on the next literary generation (namely, Griboedov, the Decembrists, Pushkin, and then Lermontov) all of whom would experience, in poetry or in battle, the imaginative pull of Russia's southern borderlands. It was Derzhavin who first intuited the natural sublimity of the Caucasus as a *subjective* experience that is felt through and beyond its picturesque value. Celebrating the Caucasus (and before it the Kivach waterfall) as the aesthetic fusion of horror and beauty, Derzhavin was also able to draw the more sobering lesson that self-mastery is a greater accomplishment than foreign conquest. It is this inward turn that translates the imperial sublime into an ethical dilemma for the gentry intellectual.

This internalizing mechanism is most evident in Derzhavin's poetic dialogue with the empress. The individuation of both the empress and the poet is accomplished allegorically, through the use of oriental literary masks. In historical terms, the image of Felitsa proclaims the myth of the enlightened despot who can reconcile omnipotence and self-restraint, imperial rule and political freedom. Psychologically speaking, the same myth permits the despot to function internally as an ego-ideal to which the poet willingly submits. To the extent that it repeatedly dramatizes the encounter between the self and a vaster power, Derzhavin's poetry remains deeply engaged in the workings of the sublime. Yet the poet's ultimate response is as much a philosophical reconciliation as an act of political submission: in this way the Derzhavinian sublime greatly surpasses in subtlety the older model of Lomonosov's, even as it lacks the volatility of the romantic sublime to come.

Notes

1. Belinskii believed that Derzhavin had reconciled Kantemir's satire and Lomonosov's ode; Gukovskii suggested that Derzhavin had replaced genre and concept with the human persona; Tynianov spoke of Derzhavin's "destruction of the ode as a closed, canonical genre."

   See Belinskii, "Vzgliad na russkuiu literaturu 1847 g. (stat'ia 1-aia)," in *Èstetika i literaturnaia kritika v dvukh tomakh,* 2:652; Gukovskii, "O russkom klassitsizme," 24; and Tynianov, "Oda kak oratorskii zhanr," in *Arkhaisty i novatory,* 75. Cf. also Hart, "Continuity and Change in the Russian Ode," 45-62; and Stennik, "Lomonosov i Derzhavin," 235-67. See also Mayer's doctoral dissertation, "Models for Creativity and the Image of the Author in the Poetry of G. R. Derzhavin," for a useful summary of the critical debates.

2. Pushkin, in a letter to A. A. Del'vig, June 1825, polemically dismisses Derzhavin for his defiance of grammar and euphony (*Perepiska A. S. Pushkina v dvukh tomakh,* 1:381).

3. In *Sochineniia Derzhavina* cf. "Na priobretenie Kryma" ("On Acquiring the Crimea") (1784), *Sochineniia* [*Derzhavina*], 1:126-28; "Na vziatie Izmaila" ("On the Taking of Izmail") (1790), 1:237-47; "Na vziatie Varshavy" ("On the Taking of Warsaw") (1794), 1:443-49; "Na pokorenie Derbenta" ("On the Subjugation of Derbent") (1796), 1:507-8; "Na perekhod Al'piiskikh gor" ("On Crossing the Alps") (1799), 2:173-82. Other odes of empire, such as "Osen' vo vremia osady Ochakova" ("Autumn during the Seige of Ochakova") (1788), 1:156-59, involve transformations of the older imperial theme that I will treat shortly.

4. Wortman, *Scenarios of Power,* 1:122-23, 138-39.

5. Reddaway, Letter XV (29 May / 9 June 1767), in *Documents of Catherine the Great,* 17-18; see also Madariaga, *Russia in the Age of Catherine the Great,* 150; and Alexander, *Catherine the Great,* 107-12.

6. Quoted in Alexander, *Catherine the Great,* 109.

7. On the "Chitalagai" odes, see Hart, *G. R. Derzhavin,* 19-27; Etkind, "Rozhdenie 'krupnogo sloga,'" 163-84; and Vroon, "'Chitalagaiskie ody,'" 185-201.

8. Vroon, "'Chitalagaiskie ody,'" 195.

9. Gukovskii, *Russkaia literatura XVIII veka,* 416-17; Blagoi, "Gavrila Romanovich Derzhavin," 29; Serman, *Derzhavin,* 108-9.

10. Serman, "Derzhavin v novom veke," 27:56.

11. Longinus, *O vysokom ili velichestvennom,* 46-47.

12. Crone, "Doing Justice to Potemkin," 393-418.

13. Cf. Serman, *Derzhavin,* 67-68; Zapadov, *Gavrila Romanovich Derzhavin,* 97-104; and Kondrashov, "'Plan obshirnyi ob'' emletsia smelost'iu zamysla,'" 31-42. See also Khodasevich, *Derzhavin,* 138-39.

14. See Zorin, "Krym v istorii russkogo samosoznaniia," 124. See also Zorin, "Russkaia oda kontsa," 5-29; and Schönle, "Garden of the Empire," 1-23.

15. Serman, *Russkii klassitsizm,* 82.

16. Lotman, "Ocherki po istorii russkoi kul'tury," 105-6.

17. Billington, *The Icon and the Axe,* 233.

18. My argument here has benefited from Judith Butler's *The Psychic Life of Power.*

19. Hart, *G. R. Derzhavin,* 57. Much has been made of the prose and the poetic variants of "The Murza's Vision," the former far bolder than the latter: see Makogonenko, *Ot Fonvizina do Pushkina,* 376-431. The gap between the two suggests the limits of the ceremonial ode in realizing an autonomous literary or political vision.

20. Hart, *G. R. Derzhavin,* 58.

21. Most critics either defend Derzhavin's didacticism as proof of his independence, for example, Zapadov, *Masterstvo Derzhavina,* or Makogonenko, *Ot Fonvizina do Pushkina,* 367-431, or (less frequently) condemn his panegyrics as proof of his political venality: yet surely neither extreme is really true.

22. The most sophisticated analysis of the ambiguities of Derzhavin's "self" is I. Z. Serman's, in *Russkii klassitsizm* (80-96), and *Derzhavin* (108-9), but even Serman does not go beyond a model based on a "complex system of relations between the "I, the ode's narrator, and a concrete embodiment of the odic ideal—Felitsa" (89).

23. Zhivov, "Gosudarstvennyi mif," 4:672-73. E. Ia Dan'ko, in "Izobrazitel'-noe iskusstvo v poèzii Derzhavina," 243-44, has suggested that Derzhavin's pictorial representations of ethnicity derive from a porcelain dinner set commissioned between 1780 and 1790 for the Russian court.

24. Cf. Blagoi, *Istoriia russkoi literatury XVIII veka,* 293, who describes the Murza as an "artificial 'Tatar' disguise." Richard Wortman also discusses another journey of 1787 which took Catherine as far as the recently conquered territories on the Black Sea and whose objective was to present a "spectacular confirmation of the motifs of conquest and transformation" (*Scenarios of Power,* 1:141); for another perspective on this journey, see Panchenko, "'Potemkinskie derevni' kak kul'turnyi mif," 93-104. This journey might have provided an additional historical precedent for aspects of "Izobrazhenie Felitsy."

25. On the details of Catherine's policy toward the Tatar Muslims, and the role of the Legislative Commission in the evolution of her ideas, see Fisher, "Enlightened Despotism," 4:552-53; Kappeler, *Russlands erste Nationalitäten,* esp. 298-307, 370-77; and Barthold, *La Découverte de l'Asie,* 249-50.

26. It has long been suggested that Derzhavin's choice of the Murza as a lyric persona has a biographical basis (see Grot's notes in Derzhavin, 1:91, 94), but the broader historical significance of the lyric persona has been neglected.

27. In Horace's original poems (*Odes,* III:30 and II:20) references to empire serve only to corroborate the breadth of the poet's fame; in Derzhavin, empire is the poet's inhabited space and an integral part of his literary mission.

28. Derzhavin's posthumously published poem, "Lirik" (dated approximately between 1801-1816), bridges the gap between the eighteenth-century perception of King David's "psalmic odes" and the Decembrist notion of the poet-prophet: "Did not a pastor, through his rapture, / Become king, establishing commerce with God himself?" (3:411).

29. Lotman, "Ocherki po istorii russkoi kul'tury," 4:95.

Bibliography

Alexander, John T. *Catherine the Great: Life and Legend.* New York: Oxford University Press, 1989.

Barthold, V. V. *La Découverte de l'Asie. Histoire de l'orientalisme en Europe et en Russie.* Paris: Payot, 1947.

Belinskii, V. G. *Èstetika i literaturnaia kritika v dvukh tomakh.* 2 vols. Moscow: GIKhL, 1959.

Billington, James. *The Icon and the Axe: An Interpretive History of Russian Culture.* New York: Vintage, 1970.

Blagoi, D. D. *Istoriia russkoi literatury XVIII veka.* Moscow: Izdatel'stvo Narkomprosa RSFSR, 1945.

———. "Gavrila Romanovich Derzhavin." In *G. R. Derzhavin. Stikhotvoreniia,* 5-30. Leningrad: Sovetskii pisatel', 1957.

Butler, Judith. *The Psychic Life of Power: Theories in Subjection.* Stanford: Stanford University Press, 1997.

Crone, Anna Lisa. "Doing Justice to Potemkin: Paradox, Oxymoron, and Two Voices in Derzhavin's 'Waterfall.'" *Russian History* 21, no. 4 (winter 1994): 393-418.

Dan'ko, E. Ia. "Izobrazitel'noe iskusstvo v poèzii Derzhavina." *XVIII vek.* 2 (1940): 243-44

Derzhavin, G. R. *Sochineniia Derzhavina s ob''iasnitel'nymi primechaniiami Ia. Grota.* 7 vols. 2nd ed. St. Petersburg: Tipografiia Akademiia nauk, 1868-78.

Etkind, Efim. "Rozhdenie 'krupnogo sloga.' Derzhavin i poèziia Fridrikha Vtorogo Prusskogo." In *Symposium Dedicated to Gavriil Derzhavin: Norwich Symposia on Russian Literature and Culture,* 4:163-84. Northfield, Vt.: The Russian School of Norwich University, 1995.

Fisher, Alan W. "Enlightened Despotism and Islam under Catherine II." *Slavic Review* 27, no. 4 (December 1968): 542-64.

Gukovskii, G. A. "O russkom klassitsizme." In *Poètika. Vremennik otdela slovesnykh iskusstv gosudarstvennogo instituta istorii iskusstv. Vypusk V,* 21-65. Leningrad: Academia, 1929.

———. *Russkaia literatura XVIII veka.* Moscow: Uchpedgiz, 1939.

Hart, Pierre R. "Continuity and Change in the Russian Ode." In *Russian Literature in the Age of Catherine the Great: A Collection of Essays,* ed. A. G. Cross, 45-62. Oxford: Willem A. Meeuws, 1976.

———. *G. R. Derzhavin: A Poet's Progress.* Columbus, Ohio: Slavica, 1978.

Kappeler, Andreas. *Russlands erste Nationalitäten. Das Zarenreich und die Völker der Mittleren Volga vom 16. bis 19. Jahrhundert.* Cologne: Böhlau Verlag, 1982.

Khodasevich, V. *Derzhavin.* Moscow: Kniga, 1988 [1931].

Kondrashov, S. N. "'Plan obshirnyi ob" emletsia smelost'iu zamysla.' (Nekotorye sotsial'no-èticheskie motivy stikhotvoreniia G. R. Derzhavina 'Vodopad')." In *Zhanrovoe svoeobrazie russkoi poèzii i dramaturgii,* 31-42. Kuibyshev: Kuibyshevskii gosudarstvennyi pedagogicheskii institut, 1981.

Longinus. *O vysokom ili velichestvennom. Tvoreniia Dionisa Longina.* Translated by I. I. Martynov. St. Petersburg: n.p., 1803.

Lotman, Iu. M. "Ocherki po istorii russkoi kul'tury XVIII-nachala XIX veka." In *Iz istorii russkoi kul'tury (XVIII-nachalo XIX veka),* 4:13-337. Moscow: Shkola "Iazyki russkoi kul'tury," 1996.

Madariaga, Isabel de. *Russia in the Age of Catherine the Great.* New Haven: Yale University Press, 1981.

Makogonenko, G. P. *Ot Fonvizina do Pushkina. Iz istorii russkogo realizma.* Moscow: Khudozhestvennaia literatura, 1969.

Mayer, Alis Gayle. "Models for Creativity and the Image of the Author in the Poetry of G. R. Derzhavin." Ph.D. dissertation, Brown University, 1997.

Panchenko, A. M. "'Potemkinskie derevni' kak kul'turnyi mif." *XVIII vek. Sbornik 14. Russkaia literatura XVIII-nachala XIX veka v obshchestvenno-kul'turnom kontekste* (1983): 93-104.

Pushkin, A. S. *Perepiska A. S. Pushkina v dvukh tomakh.* 2 vols. Moscow: Khudozhestvennaia literatura, 1982.

Reddaway, W. F., ed. *Documents of Catherine the Great.* Cambridge: Cambridge University Press, 1931.

Schönle, Andreas. "Garden of the Empire: Catherine's Appropriation of the Crimea." *Slavic Review* 60, no. 1 (spring 2001): 1-23.

Serman, I. Z. *Derzhavin.* Leningrad: Prosveshchenie, 1967.

———. *Russkii klassitsizm. Poèziia, drama, satira.* Leningrad: Nauka, 1973.

———. "Derzhavin v novom veke." *Novoe literaturnoe obozrenie* 27 (1997): 54-67.

Stennik, Iu. V. "Lomonosov i Derzhavin." In *Lomonosov i russkaia literatura,* 235-67. Moscow: Nauka, 1987.

Tynianov, Iurii. "Oda kak oratorskii zhanr." In *Arkhaisty i novatory,* 48-56. Munich: Wilhelm Fink Verlag, 1967 [1929].

Vroon, Ronald. "'Chitalagaiskie ody.' (K istorii liricheskogo tsikla v russkoi literature XVIII veka)." *A Symposium Dedicated to Gavriil Derzhavin: Norwich Symposia on Russian Literature and Culture,* 185-201. Northfield, Vt.: Russian School of Norwich University, 1995.

Wittfogel, Karl A. *Oriental Despotism: A Comparative Study in Total Power.* New Haven: Yale University Press, 1957.

Wortman/Richard. *Scenarios of Power: From Peter the Great to the Death of Nicholas I.* Vol. 1. Princeton, N.J.: Princeton University Press, 1995.

Zapadov, A. V. *Masterstvo Derzhavina.* Moscow: Sovetskii pisatel', 1958.

———. *Gavrila Romanovich Derzhavin. Biografiia.* Moscow: Prosveshchenie, 1965.

Zhivov, V. M. "Gosudarstvennyi mif v èpokhu prosveshcheniia i ego razrushenie v Rossii kontsa XVIII veka." In *Iz istorii russkoi kul'tury,* 4:657-85. Moscow: Shkola, 1996.

Zorin, Andrei. "Russkaia oda kontsa 1760-kh-nachala 1770-kh godov, Vol'ter i 'grecheskii proèkt' Ekateriny II." *Novoe literaturnoe obozrenie* 24 (1997): 5-29.

———. "Krym v istorii russkogo samosoznaniia." *Novoe literaturnoe obozrenie* 31 (1998): 123-44.

Luba Golburt (essay date summer 2005)

SOURCE: Golburt, Luba. "Derzhavin's Monuments: Sculpture, Poetry, and the Materiality of History." *Toronto Slavic Quarterly,* no. 13 (summer 2005): no pagination.

[*In the following essay, Golburt studies Derzhavin's poetry and thought in relation to changing views of art and history in Russia after Peter the Great.*]

Derzhavin's famous 1796 restatement of the Horatian *Exegi Monumentum* has been traditionally interpreted as a sign of the growing significance of literary authorship in Derzhavin's oeuvre and in the Russian culture of the pre-Romantic decades. Most recently, for instance, Derzhavin's monument poems (**"Moi Istukan"** (1794), **"Pamiatnik"** (1796)) were described as his "treatment of the vital national importance of the poet's verbal deeds."[1] While thus emphasizing the hubristic message of the poems and rightly marking their self-reflexive interest in texts as "verbal deeds," these readings overlook the novelty of another, the sculptural, metaphor for end-of-the-eighteenth-century Russia. Granted that **"Pamiatnik"** was an imitation of an overused classical text and, by extension, of the Horatian tradition that especially in the eighteenth century had come to be exploited throughout Europe as a mediator between writers' civic, poetic, and domestic callings, the appearance of Derzhavin's poem in late Enlightenment Russia has an added significance that calls to be unpacked.

If in the West the reception of Horace's text placed it within a cultural tradition equally accustomed to representing history through narrative and through the visual media, in Russia, by contrast, sculpture became a legitimate and widespread form of expression only with Peter the Great's (r. 1689-1725) massive importation of Western cultural practices and institutions. In pre-Petrine Russia, sculpture (except for bas-reliefs) was treated as an essentially idolatrous art. The few high-relief or round representations bore the imprint either of the Slavic pagan and folk traditions, or of a later influence of Polish Catholicism, and were mostly executed as wood carvings rather than marble or bronze statues typical of Renaissance and post-Renaissance Europe. Sculpture's status changed only as the elite speedily consented to Peter's comprehensive secularization and westernization packet, in which sculpture was only one of the more harmless yet conspicuous accessories.[2] The Orthodox ban on graven images remained in force only in the consecrated church areas where sculpture made a cautious and slow entry even as it virtually invaded Russian secular spaces: gardens, palaces, and the rising St. Petersburg cityscape.

Even if not completely universal, the effect of Peter's innovations was so fast and the popularity of statuary in Enlightenment Europe so extensive that by the end of the eighteenth century sculpture became the vogue of the day among Catherine II's courtiers. Already during Peter's reign, his courtiers' desire for self-aggrandizement and commemoration brought some lucrative commissions to the sculptors the first Emperor had imported from the West. Still rare in the early 1700s, these commissions could no longer surprise anyone by the end of the eighteenth century. In the late Enlightenment Russia, sculpture was fully placed at the disposal of biography and history.

The novelty of Derzhavin's poems, remarkable in their elevation of the poet's status, consists also in his perceptive consideration of the methods for preserving this poetic status and legacy in history. Needless to say, portraying hitherto marginalized, private literary achievements as worthy of commemoration could become possible only in a Russia that had already seen its most illustrious figures, including its Empress, enthusiastically endorse and even dabble in belles-lettres. This confidence in one's posthumous fame could, furthermore, seem doubly suggestive precisely at the conclusion of the Russian Enlightenment project. In the 1790s, the French *philosophes* had lost official esteem as their ideas were reified, even if misinterpreted and transformed, in the terrors of the French Revolution. On the other hand, Peter's westernization and the literary activity of Catherine II's reign had by then produced a number of educated readers who could appreciate Derzhavin's poetic hubris and its Horatian endorsement.[3]

Importantly, the sculptural metaphor as well could come to the fore only in this period when throughout Europe sculpture came to occupy the imaginations of the likes of Diderot, Winckelmann, and Lessing. Whether put forward to be doggedly imitated or confidently surpassed, antique sculpture and its interpretations provided a model for engaging with the past and in fact gave form to one of the central metaphors for shaping history, both national and personal. In Russia, where sculpture was hurriedly appropriated as a form of the new, secularized culture, the very word "pamiatnik" ("monument") acquired its dominant sculptural meaning only in the course of the eighteenth century. As we shall see, when Derzhavin erected a verbal monument to himself, he was not only echoing the Classicist topos or placing authorship on a pedestal traditionally reserved for Russian czars and military leaders. Quite significantly, he was also elaborating the latest model of historical memory, which greatly relied upon sculptural and architectural imagery.

Only some half a century before the appearance of Derzhavin's **"Pamiatnik,"** Lomonosov in his first-ever Russian translation of Horace's text ("Я знак бессмертия себе боздбигнул . . . ," "I have erected a sign of immortality to Myself," 1747) could not yet render *monumentum* as *pamiatnik* even though the Russian *pamiatnik* comes closest to the Latin term since both have their origin in the terminology of memory ("monere"—to remind, warn, advise; "pamiat'"—memory).[4] *Pamiatnik* had not yet acquired its sculptural connotation, and Lomonosov translated the Latin word with the less literal and more abstract "znak bessmertiia" ("sign of immortality"). As a result of this abstraction, Lomonosov's translation elides Horace's central opposition between sculpture and writing; in fact, it is unclear why it is so important that the sign of immortality be higher than the pyramids, for the reader has no definite image of this elusive sign. Horace's *monumentum* stages within itself the rivalry of the written and the sculptural memorial, in which sculpture takes a subordinate position because of its very materiality—its fixed location and capacity for physical decay. Lomonosov's "znak bessmertiia," by contrast, contains no double meaning and lacks this internal polemic. Similarly, the fame of Lomonosov's poet resounds in an Italian landscape, disengaged from any immediate Russian reality: the speaker claims immortality by virtue of his introduction of "Aeolian verse to Italy" ("бнесть б Италию стихи эольски"), a direct transposition of topography and imagery that explicitly draws the readers' attention to the poem's translated, foreign quality. The poet's accomplishment as well as the means he proposes for its memorialization are thus unmistakably an import. The poem's speaker, furthermore, is not directly Lomonosov, but Horace who appears as an unnamed transcendent figure and whose memory is claimed to be preserved through an equally recondite sign, in an equally idealized landscape. An anachronistic semiotic reading would most likely privilege Lomonosov's translation as aware of the abstract qualities of historical commemoration, a text that attempts to engrave a sign of immortality that evades and transcends the question of medium, or concrete signifier.

As a rendition of Horace, however, Derzhavin's imitation, not intended as a direct translation, paradoxically is more faithful to the Latin original as well as more revealing of the author's self-identification within Russian landscape and late-Enlightenment culture. Unlike his celebrated predecessor's, Derzhavin's imagery foregrounds the conflict between sculptural and verbal monuments and projects an informed reader who would no longer categorize the claims of the Horatian text as an outlandish import. The Russian reading elite has by the end of the eighteenth century naturalized both secular sculpture and secular literature. As a result, Derzhavin's magisterial ascent over the sublime landscape of the Russian empire can appear at once presumptuous and unique, yet by comparison to Lomonosov's Italian topography, more contextually grounded and less of a foreign import. What happened, then, between Lomonosov's and Derzhavin's renditions of **"Exegi Monumentum"** to make the Russian reader understand sculpture and writing as the two legitimate yet rival forms of historical and personal commemoration?

PAMIATNIK: A HISTORY OF THE TERM AND THE TERMINOLOGY OF HISTORY

In *The Dictionary of the Russian Language of the 11th-17th Centuries,* the word *pamiatnik* still carries only one meaning, of a "commemorative note or inscription; a testimony."[5] From the examples cited in the dictionary, it follows that before the eighteenth century, pamiatnik referred primarily to a written historical document. Although the word has preserved this meaning until the present (e.g. in such collocations as "pamiatnik

epokhi," "literaturnyi pamiatnik," "pamiatnik kul'tury," etc.[6]), during the eighteenth century pamiatnik slowly moved away from the semantic field of specifically narrative history where it had belonged together with the chronicle, into the realm of art history and particularly sculpture. There it assumed its place next to such previously distant semantic units as "istukan," "kumir," "izvaian," and "idol,"[7] and to the Latinate borrowings, such as "statue" ("статуя") and "monument" ("монумент"). In Russia, the evolution of *pamiatnik's* new meaning required first a recognition and assimilation of European secular sculpture as a valid and valuable art form. Russian Orthodoxy, unlike Catholicism, was essentially against three-dimensional images, which it associated directly with idolatry and paganism.[8] It is not by accident that the terms used as late as the end of the eighteenth century to describe statuary are the same words that a hundred years earlier had unequivocally designated pagan idols: «истукан», «кумир», «избаян», «болбан» and «идол». As these words slowly shed some of their derogatory associations with unorthodox religious practices, they could still not be used neutrally though some attempts were made ("истукан" as "bust" or "кумир души моей" as a calque from the French "l'idole de mon âme," etc.). While secularization of terminology followed a more significant secularization of both the practices and the uses of art, sculptural vocabulary of paganism came to be employed in depicting sculpture in an ironic light. As we shall see, the commemorated figure in Derzhavin's **"Moi Istukan"** provokes a much more ambiguous and potentially ironic reaction than does the lyrical persona of **"Pamiatnik."** With its initial association with documentary textual history, the latter term more comfortably invoked the newly appropriated artifacts of secular sculpture.

The mechanism of memory, central to both meanings of *pamiatnik,* facilitated this semantic shift. Both narrative and sculptural monuments were intended to memorialize the past, to serve as concrete metonyms of a greater history. *Pamiatnik* was a fortunate native term that not only could adequately render and indeed bring to the fore the memorial function of monuments, but also altogether overwrote and dispensed with the religious uneasiness surrounding lifelike corporeal representations. Formerly a term attached to documentary testimony, *pamiatnik* as a sculptural object could now indeed stand as a disembodied and less morally dubious sign or *"znak bessmertiia."*

Even as history and sculpture were thus terminologically wedded, the act of commemoration itself occurred differently on a page of an ancient document and in marble or bronze. While a textual document claimed to give adequate representation to a factual reality, a sculptural monument, in the absence of an inscription, loomed as a silent symbol in need of an imaginative decoding. This semiotic ambiguity of statuary was fully recognized already in the Renaissance when the interest toward sculptural antiques demanded for the statues' subject matter to be explained and stabilized in a title: it mattered whether a given marble body belonged to Pompey, Augustus, Julius Cesar, Domitian or Trajan because this information could shed light on the statue's expressivity and execution.[9] What this paper ultimately thematizes is the growing awareness and attraction on the part of Russian writers of the late 1700s toward the symbolic rather than documentary demands of history and toward sculpture's capacity for responding to these demands in ever-ambiguous yet evocative forms.

The transformation in *pamiatnik*'s semantics offers only a superficial view of a more profound shift in Russian academic historiographical practices as well as in the notions of the past, memory and historical narrative prevalent in Russian elite culture of the eighteenth century. In the 1700s, new Western historical genres had irrevocably replaced the traditional annalistic forms of the Russian chronicles. Now writers of Russian history increasingly inscribed historical events within a more linear progression, which disposed of the annalistic segmentation of the chronicles in favor of narrative coherence and interpretation, centered on individual biography and accomplishment.[10] To use terms from narratology, the historiographer thus exploited the vantage point of an omniscient narrator, who had the power to "narrate" as well as to "describe." Russian academic historiography was at first largely a foreign venture, dominated by German or German-trained historians.[11] Only in the early 19th century did Karamzin, one of the greatest practitioners of Russian sentimental prose, write the first nationally significant work of Russian historiography, *The History of the Russian State* (1818-24).[12] It was not by accident that this history came from the pen of the first Russian author who repeatedly considered sculptural and architectural remnants of the past and their sentimental impact.

In addition to the new genres of academic historiography and more central to this article and to Russian literature of the eighteenth century, historical writing and especially interpretation of recent events surfaced as a principal—albeit unadvertised—task of odic poetry. Even as they ostensibly only sang a celebratory refrain to the recent past of conquests and jubilees, and praised the given ruler, panegyric odes crafted their own historical narratives. Ode-writers, unlike their academic counterparts, united historical events not only through a specific plot—e.g. a chain of victories, or the sequential account of a certain imperial celebration—but also through a symbolic system which bound the achievements of Russian military leaders to mythical feats, and contemporary heroes to those from classical mythology: Peter I to Jupiter, Catherine II to Minerva. Such comparisons allowed ode writers to shed only partial light

on the details of the contemporary subject, and even to conceal the real behind the ideal. Once the reader beheld Catherine in the guise of a Minerva, Astreia, or Felitsa, he could decode both the authorial and official versions of the events, which often but not always coincided, and fill in the blanks prudently left vacant by the ode-writer.[13] Even as in academic historiography the laconic chronicle entries were reshaped into a narrative and thereby explicated and transformed, odes encrypted idiosyncratic, if in most cases laudatory, interpretations of current politics by means of a repertory of symbols, allegories, and legendary names. The reader then took pleasure in extricating the signified reading of historical events from layers of allegorical signifiers. For instance, the ode **"Felitsa,"** so pivotal in Derzhavin's career, invited the reader and especially the poet's royal addressee to observe and revere Catherine II as a paragon of virtuous simplicity whereas comparisons with Minerva elevated her military and juridical successes. Different allegorical portrayals could reveal different visages, and elicit the patron's favor, disdain, or indifference. In the process of such decoding, readers inevitably, if unintentionally, transformed the history plotted by the ode-writers. The same verbal monuments could now legitimately yield very different testimony. The new multiplicity of classical parallels and a panoply of available historical genres (ranging from historiography to panegyric ode) turned historical commemoration away from documentary and toward symbolic monumental forms.

Meanwhile, throughout Europe, sculpture and fine arts were also being questioned as bearers of history. As in the solemn odes, history appeared before the viewers of historical paintings or statuary clad in increasingly ambiguous classical plots.[14] One could make sense of these plots not only by heeding color, light, and compositional cues, but also by marking and pondering the specific point within the classical narrative selected by the artist in order to embody and represent the narrative whole. It was precisely the selection of this specific point, or "significant moment," that was to stand for the entire plot and direct the viewer's imagination toward recreating both ancient and contemporary history in the narrative form, and which was furthermore to determine the audience's emotional response.[15] Gotthold Ephraim Lessing, who in his *Laocoon: An Essay on the Limits of Painting and Poetry* (1766), famously advanced the distinction between the poetic temporal progression and the spatial stasis of painting, thus describes the effect of the painter's choice of a specific moment on the imagination of the viewer:

> If the artist can never make use of more than a single moment in ever-changing nature, and if the painter in particular can use this moment only with reference to a single vantage point, while the works of both painter and sculptor are created not merely to be given a glance but to be contemplated—contemplated repeatedly and

at length—then it is evident that this single moment and the point from which it is viewed cannot be chosen with too great a regard for its effect. But only that which gives free rein to the imagination is effective.[16]

The significant moment thus encapsulated and promised not only specifically the greater occluded narrative, but more significantly the viewer's personal imaginative engagement with the art object. Accustomed to viewing history through the prism of such symbolic stand-ins—antiquity for modernity, significant moments for complete story lines, mythical ideal heroes for contemporary flawed sovereigns and generals—the viewers of historical art as well as the readers of historical odes learned to participate in history-writing, which was no longer based on documents as in the medieval *pamiatniki,* in the chronicles, or even in academic historiography, but hinged upon their own historical erudition and imagination.

A special inspiration for such creative historical reconstruction based upon antique fragments came with the excavation of Herculaneum and Pompeii in the mid-eighteenth century. To the delectation of the enthusiastic impression-seeking public, these sites offered ruins and shards of a bygone era, which promised to render historical reconstruction ever more plausible and exciting. On the one hand, these discoveries led to a growing popularity of fragmentary genres both in the fine arts (sketches, sculptural fragments) and in belles-lettres (anthologies and lyrical fragments).[17] On the other, it became even less clear what kind of testimony was inscribed on the monuments of the past, what fortuitous laws guided history and what could ultimately be preserved for posterity.

For a sentimental sensibility then in fashion, antiquity seemingly yielded ruins and fragments rather than monuments and edifices. Precisely in contemplating these ruins, whether archaeological or imaginary, the viewer projected the ultimate destruction of the artifacts of his own time and relished his sublime fear. Even such an acute critic of art as Diderot surrenders to this historical paranoia before Hubert Robert's ruined landscapes, rightly prophesying a grand career of a ruin-painter for this young artist. If only the painter, later aptly nicknamed "Robert des Ruines," would banish most of his contemporary figures from his canvas, instructs Diderot, the experience of the sublime in his ruins would be complete. Diderot waxes rhapsodical in his expressions of this experience: "O les belles, les sublimes ruines![. . .] Quel effet! Quelle grandeur! Quelle noblesse!"[18] But his enthusiasm also has a more articulate explanation; ruins afford the viewers a glimpse of the destruction of their own civilization: "Nous anticipons sur les ravages du temps, et notre imagination disperse sur la terre les édifices mêmes que nous habitons."[19] Yet, if ruins survive, their function is not merely

to presage universal annihilation, but to convey historical knowledge and to inspire the viewer to memorialize his epoch in addition to, as Diderot suggests, anticipate its decay.

Rescued from destructive natural forces, the fragments of the marvelous world of classical antiquity thus inflected the act of poetic and sculptural history-writing with a task of synecdochal commemoration. Winckelmann projected from the surviving monuments of Greek antiquity—or to be more precise, from the Roman copies he could actually observe—an entire, superior, classical world, and impelled his contemporary artists, sculptors and poets alike (an important distinction for Lessing, but not for Winckelmann) to create by imitation: "There is but one way for the moderns to become great, and perhaps unequalled, I mean, by imitating the ancients."[20] Meanwhile, the task of the odic historian became to compress an actual, lived world of eighteenth-century experience and history to their synecdoche or symbol: a few significant moments-monuments. While historical writing and art was thus reductive, posterity was invited to effect an archaeological excavation, reconstruction and expansion of the century from its skillfully planted splinters. To artists and writers of the late eighteenth century, then, Herculaneum and Pompeii were not simply a display of volcano-spared ruins, but more significantly, served as a poignant metaphor for the fragmentary state of all historical knowledge, and authorized imaginative expansion and generalization by authors and their audiences as a legitimate path toward an artistic representation of history.

Conceived and written in the very same years that Derzhavin took to imitating Horace, Petr Slovtsov's "Drevnost'" (1793-6) also uses a sculptural metaphor commemorating the passing age. Slovtsov (1767-1843), a minor poet whose career was tragically tarnished by his unswerving faith in Enlightenment ideals (he spent most of his life in exile, first under Catherine II, then under Alexander I and Nicholas I), can serve as an indicative foil to the successful maitre Derzhavin. "Drevnost'," his most evocative ode, can be read in three parts: an elegiac rumination at a gravesite, Slovtsov's idiosyncratic selection and lionization of the heroes of the passing Age of Enlightenment, and finally his critique of Catherine's foreign policy and the partitions of Poland. Writing in the tradition of the much-translated ode "Sur La Fortune" by Jean-Baptiste Rousseau, which insisted on privileging feats of the intellect over the bloody exploits of war, Slovtsov strives to discern those few symbols of his age that could merit being chiselled on the "bas-relief" of "antiquity," which can in this context be read as History itself. His prophetic answer favours three figures of the European Enlightenment:

Франклин, преломивши скиптр британской,
Рейналь с хартией б руке гражданской,

Как оракул больныя страны,
И Мурза б чалме, пебец Астреи,
Под бенком дубобым, б грибне с шеи
Будут у тебя иссечены.[21]

Although the official heroic pantheon, which had been just in those years marshalled together to adorn the newly-built Cameron Gallery in Catherine's suburban residence of Tsarskoe Selo, included only Lomonosov as its eighteenth-century Russian of distinction and thus reflected the evolving official cult of this poet, Slovtsov chooses Derzhavin for his pantheon.[22] This choice hinged not only upon Derzhavin's widely acknowledged poetic achievements, but even more importantly on his contentious position as a self-proclaimed upholder of truth in state service, which in Slovtsov's evaluation made the Bard of Felitsa an ideological equal to Franklin and Raynal and a partisan of Slovtsov's own Enlightenment-influenced moral agenda. Thus, when the ode proceeds to criticize the recent partitions of Poland, which for the author had irrevocably blemished the image of the century and of the Russian Enlightenment, Franklin, Raynal, and Derzhavin—unlikely bedfellows in any other context—give Slovtsov their unanimous support.

Along with the blood-spattered ghost of Poland hovering over the Carpathian ridges, the central image that lingers with the reader at the ode's conclusion is the dispassionate—albeit suspiciously quick to accommodate Slovtsov's judgment—bas-relief of history-cum-antiquity.

Дребность, мабзолей сбой украшая,
Лишь над нами упражняет гнеб
И, осьмнадцатый бек удушая,
Бысечет лишь нобый барельеф.[23]

If at the outset, Slovtsov is keen on distinguishing on the basis of antiquity's unintelligible inscriptions the virtuous from the evil characters of the past, his ultimate ambition is to engrave his Enlightened verdict for some future archaeologist's edification. What starts out as an elegiac rumination on the language of unassuming tombstones of his contemporaries develops into a grandiose odic commemoration of modernity that blends the sculptural and poetic in the monumental figure of antiquity's bas-relief. For Slovtsov, Enlightenment prevails over despotism as past and future are allegorically bound in a covenant of peace:

Мирна радуга для них [гениеб] ябилась,
)Полобиной б дребность наклонилась,
А другой б потомстбе оперлась.[24]

Unlike Horace, whose sculptural monuments are susceptible to decay precisely by virtue of their materiality, Slovtsov sees in sculptural materiality an unyielding solidity and capacity for conserving powerful visual im-

agery. Furthermore, it is important to note that the symbolic logic of Slovtsov's ode most likely was influenced by Masonic symbolism, which pictures the Mason's work on the human soul as masonry or work with stone. This is yet another, cryptic, layer in the complex semantics of statuary during the late Russian Enlightenment, which here can be noted only in passing. By 1796, when such allusions to Freemasonry were certainly unwelcome, Slovtsov's Masonic sculptural metaphor works to compound the censuring thrust of his version of eighteenth-century Russian history.

While there is no doubt that "Drevnost'" mistakenly enlists Derzhavin in the service of Slovtsov's outspoken subversive ideology, we will see that these authors, nonetheless, shared a common strategy for metaphorizing history, if not for its evaluation. For both, the monumental form is a site of historical inscription, which in generic terms, perpetually hesitates between elegiac melancholy and odic commemorative vigour.

If in the Renaissance a fascination with monuments of antiquity informed the development of the humanistic tradition, which looked to Greek and Roman sculpture for knowledge of the human form and, by extension, of human psychology, the upsurge of interest toward deciphering antiquity in the eighteenth century had historical narrative rather than the human figure as its main protagonist.[25] Monuments *qua* documentary testimonies morphed into monuments as fragmentary stimuli for the historical imagination. While ancient *pamiatniki* could reveal or inspire visions of the past, their contemporary counterparts loomed as tangible guarantees of posthumous survival. From an anonymous and neutral testimony, both the term and its corresponding notion thus evolved and could be manipulated to service various national and personal aspirations.

Particularly during the reign of Catherine the Great, sculpture had assumed a conspicuous place in the limited but speedily growing art world in Russia. Just as any enlightened capital city, St. Petersburg acquired its own sculpture garden and a towering equestrian statue intended to rival and surpass the Roman *Marcus Aurelius*. The parks of suburban royal and noble palaces, too, housed numerous figures inspired by or copied from those of antiquity. Catherine II fully recognized the symbolic and instructive power of statuary, and commissioned the casting of some eighty figures from Classical mythology as well as heroes and thinkers of the antiquity and a few noteworthy contemporaries.[26] As the selection of these figures was to embody the empress's philosophy of power, so did Falconet's *Bronze Horseman*—in its form and in the history of its commission and construction—testify to the fundamental alliance of Catherine's national and personal pursuits in her sculptural projects.[27] The immense scope and protracted duration of Falconet's work reveal the central place this sculpture must have come to occupy in the imaginations not only of artistically-minded nobles, but of simple passers-by who for a decade had to walk or drive past the monument at various stages of completion.[28] Ever since the death of Peter I in 1725, each successive rule invented itself in relation to Russia's first Emperor.[29] Not only the discourses of power, but the general historical discourse established Peter as the center of all Russian history, the demiurge of Russian modernity, regardless of whether this was judged a pleasing or alarming development. With the erection of Peter's colossal statue, all the discussions on Russian modern history found a tangible and visible physical representation in St. Petersburg's cityscape. And so did the Russian eighteenth century, which was aptly if willfully summed up in Catherine's dedication: "Petro Primo Catarina Secunda." As a result, a permanent bond had been forged between the contemporary moment of Derzhavin and Slovtsov and the mythical, if recent, past of the demiurge Peter. Falconet's and his Imperial Commissioner's acumen for visual allegory—a grand natural rock, a rearing horse, a trampled snake—had definitely surpassed that of their potential detractors (e.g. Slovtsov who spared no place for Peter and no admiration for Catherine). Russian history had finally attained a monumental figure, and the term *pamiatnik,* too, had permanently assumed its new, sculptural definition and ousted the rival pagan terminology to the margins of discourse. Peter's colossus was unquestionably, if menacingly, a *pamiatnik* or monument rather than an *istukan* or idol.

To conclude this section, a record of this semantic transformation and of the various strains in its colorful history is preserved in the *Dictionary of the Russian Academy,* another Enlightenment project initiated during Catherine's reign. In its second edition (1806-1822), the original definition of *pamiatnik* as a textual document is altogether absent, supplanted by two new denotations that point precisely to the Enlightenment transformation of sculpture's role in Russia, which I have outlined in this section. As a "commemorative edifice," *pamiatnik* is cited in the context of the monument to Peter and of a tombstone, and as a "relic testifying to the past glory of a place," it qualifies the ruins of ancient Rome: "The ruins of ancient Rome are monuments to its former magnificence."[30] Thus, gravestones and monuments, ruins and edifices were aligned most obviously in the Russian linguistic practice as well as in the burgeoning historical imagination at the dawn of the nineteenth century. *Pamiatnik,* the term and the artifact, was called to perform a complex work of mourning, documenting, and memorializing the past.

DERZHAVIN'S MONUMENTS TO PETER I AND PRINCE REPNIN

As Falconet's ambitious Petersburg project slowly neared its completion, Derzhavin, ever sensitive to his-

tory's representational demands, penned two poems in honor of Peter the Great, **"Monument Petra Velikogo"** and **"Petru Velikomu"** (both dated 1776). The poems, classified by their author as drinking songs ("застольные песни"), make no open reference to sculpture. It is understood that **"The Monument to Peter the Great"** is not an ekphrastic tribute to Falconet, but rather Derzhavin's own unmediated commemoration of the Monarch, his bid in the competition for an enduring monument to Peter.[31] If one is to heed Lessing's judgment, Derzhavin shows himself a true poet in avoiding a facile description of Falconet's monument and instead relying fully on devices appropriate and unique to poetry. Organized through a similar pattern of pairing increasingly eulogistic quatrains with a fixed refrain, the two songs aurally reiterate Peter's significance for posterity:

Тбоя пребудет добродетель,
О *Петр*! дюбезна бсем бекам;
Храни, храни бсегда, Содетель,
Его б преемниках Ты нам!

(«Монумент Петра Беликого»)

Неси на небо гласы, бетр:
Бессмертен ты, Беликьи *Петр*!

(«Петру Беликому»)[32]

Although Derzhavin was prone to incorporating descriptive imagery inspired by the visual arts, from paintings to fine china, into his poetry,[33] the monuments to Peter flaunt their independent poetic technique, which privileges exhortatory speech acts and the commemorative power of voices over ekphrasis ("Да ббек *Петру* гремит баш хор!").[34] Just as Falconet's monument creates a community of viewers by virtue of its central locale, grandiose stature, and powerful symbolism, Derzhavin's texts call for a community of drinking fellows or at least for a social gathering to rehearse both Peter's name and deeds. Incidentally, in his ***Primechaniia,*** Derzhavin notes that the songs enjoyed popularity in the Masonic lodges.[35] Famous for celebrating Imperial holidays together with the pleasures of domestic life, Derzhavin here again locates his verbal memorial to Peter at a festive table rather than on a public square and shapes it in the low genre of a drinking song. If Derzhavin does not want to recreate Falconet's monument in his verse, he also avoids openly declaring the poetic medium superior to sculpture, a recurrent move in his other monument poems and one that is justifiable for odes, but not for drinking songs. After all, to undermine the lasting impact of the officially sponsored equestrian statue by picturing it crumbling while the verbal monuments still stand would have been a risky enterprise. Yet, this was precisely the age-old idea Derzhavin upheld when his poems competed against monuments to personages of lesser eminence. There Derzhavin complicated his odic register with elegiac ruminations on the monuments' physical and representational disintegration.

Inasmuch as they serve the purposes of commemoration, sculptural monuments in Derzhavin and in much of late-eighteenth-century literature are also elegiac loci of decay, sites of mourning, paradoxically vulnerable both to semiotic petrification and material fragmentation. In sentimental and Gothic fiction, for example, the surviving monuments were interpreted as melancholy, ever-ambiguous ruins. As we have already seen in Diderot's reactions to Hubert Robert's landscapes, ruins "demonstrated the entropy of being, a visible break with the past and the logic of progress. Yet, simultaneously they fostered the imagination and even testified to its immense potential, casting doubt upon man's alleged ethics of systematic dismantling of myths."[36] As a potential generator of myths, every ruin concealed and promised a former or future monument, and this ambivalent relationship between entropy and memory lay at the core of late-eighteenth-century attempts to cast poetic history in sculptural form and threaded together Derzhavin's monument poems. The monument for Derzhavin becomes precisely the site where ode meets elegy, as the nostalgic wordless gravesites are reinvented in the form of future-oriented historical narratives and as the lament becomes also the act of memorialization.

In **"Pamiatnik Geroiu"** (1791), a poem dedicated to Prince Repnin, Derzhavin invites the Muse to consider what appears to be Repnin's tombstone:

> Бождя при памятнике дпбном
> Боссядь, - и б пении унv1бном
> Бещай: сей столп побергнет бремя,
> Разрушит.[37]

At first, the Muse in **"Pamiatnik Geroiu"** seems to be an elegiac one. Derzhavin surveys the questionable legacy of military heroes, who themselves produce and hand down ruins: "разбалины, могилы, пепел, черепья, кости им подобных."[38] Is this the patrimony of heroes, queries Derzhavin, only more strikingly to switch to the odic register and extol the heroic feats of virtue (добродетель) and conscience (собесть). The hero Repnin emerges as a man who has nothing to fear from the destructive onslaught of time, for his monument, much like Derzhavin's own *monumentum* several years later, will survive in speech and not in ephemeral marble:

> Такого мужа обелиски
> Не тем слабны, что к нечу члизки,
> Не мрамором, не медью тберды,
> Пускай их разрушает бремя,
> Но бобсе истребить не может;
> Жибет б преданьах добродетель.[39]

Even as Derzhavin repeatedly disparages the media of sculptural commemoration as presumptuous and inadequate (see also his **"Monument miloserdiiu,"** 1804), he nevertheless is to a striking degree partial to the sculptural metaphor. In a letter to N. M. Karamzin who was to publish the poem in *Moskovskii Zhurnal,* Derzhavin coyly excuses his anonymity by the modesty of his illustrious hero, "б честь которого сооружен им [Держабиным] сей памятник."[40] By the 1790s, it is definitely no longer possible to use *pamiatnik* in constructions with verbs of writing even if writing in fact is at stake: Derzhavin erects (сооружает) his monument. His Muse, too, is summoned to build rather than to guide his pen: "Строй, Муза, памятник Герою."[41] The metaphor points in two directions: on the one hand, the poetic Muse relinquishes its ephemeral verbal tools, to take up those of a master builder, a sculptor or an architect; on the other, the sculptural record is belittled in favor of the poetic. That Derzhavin grew disillusioned with his eulogized Hero, Prince N. V. Repnin, several years after the ode's publication in a sense does not matter, for by apostrophizing both the Muse and Repnin, the ode immortalizes not primarily the general's military *virtu,* but more significantly the text's very ability to erect a verbal monument, "more durable than brass."

DERZHAVIN'S AUTOBIOGRAPHICAL MONUMENT

Derzhavin's interactions with sculpture were not limited to the Horatian paradigm of valorization of the verbal over the material. Keeping a keen eye on the new sculptures imported from abroad and cast in Russia proper, Derzhavin entertained the thought of modeling his own likeness in bronze to place next to Lomonosov's in the Cameron Gallery. He commissioned the sculptor J.-D. Rachette (1744-1809), the head of the sculpture workshop at the Imperial Porcelain Factory, with a pair of busts of himself and his wife.[42] The final product, completed in late 1793, inspired Derzhavin to offer his most elaborate rumination on sculpture in the service of personal history, the poem **"Moi Istukan"** (**"My Idol,"** 1794).

While complementing Rachette's Praxitelean naturalism in his execution of the bust, Derzhavin without any delay puts forward sculpture's general representational deficiencies. Sculpture, he believes, is too open to interpretation, or alternatively conveys no certain message:

> Но мне какою честью льститься
> Б бессмертном истукане сем?
> Без слабных дел, гремящих б мире,
> Ничто и Царь б сбоем кумире.
> Ничто! И не жибет тот смертный,
> О ком ни малой нет молбы.[43]

According to Derzhavin, it is deeds that garner acclaim and immortality for a mortal, and furthermore, it is through verbal tributes that a man's deeds can be properly memorialized. Fame can crown both the virtuous and evil; therefore, without a corresponding text, statuary signifies little and can be manipulated for the achievement of any ends. Like Catherine II, who decided against the inclusion of her own bust in the Cameron gallery and, furthermore, rejected casts of those figures of antiquity who could be interpreted as potentially undermining the monarchic order or endorsing the French Revolution, Derzhavin, too, works through an inventory of the statues he knows to select those few heroes who in his view deserve a commemoration of their virtues. In addition to ancient leaders, Derzhavin nominates several of his own countrymen: Peter I together with his father and grandfather, Pozharski, Minin, and Filaret are his heroes. But it would be presumptuous to pretend to equal them, Derzhavin reasons, and consequently, the bust should be destroyed: "Разбей же, мой бторой создатель, Разбей мой истукан, Рашет!"[44] But Derzhavin abruptly reconsiders, and proceeds to examine an already familiar repertory of his poetic accomplishments: his compelling images of Felitsa and his discernment of virtue. In the sudden elation at the recognition of his own worth, Derzhavin's ambitious imagination transfers his bust to the Cameron Gallery ("чтобы на ней меня бместить, забистникоб моих к досаде, б ез [Екатерины] прекрасной колоннаде"[45]). Even this vision, however, is soon shattered as Derzhavin projects a less than indulgent reassessment of his contributions by some future generation.[46]

Envisioning his own formerly dignified image as a silly, bald monkey exposed to the derision of children, or tumbling off the colonnade and trampled in obscurity, Derzhavin removes his bust from the public sphere of great men on exhibit in the royal gardens. The bust, significantly, is not a *pamiatnik,* a deserving form of commemoration, but an *istukan* and even *bolvan,* an idolatrous graven image that turns the man Derzhavin into a monkey, a ludicrous ape of the real being. A conventional figure of demure self-effacement in Derzhavin's poem, the image of the monkey also appeared in contemporary Russian discourse in connection to the mindless imitators of the West; the satirical thrust, for instance, of Karamzin's nickname "Popugai Obezyaninov" ("Parrot Monkeyson") is well known. Commonly dubbed as monkeys or apes of the Enlightenment, the pretentious Russian elite plays at casting their own images in bronze, but these representations only betray their clumsy westernizing mimicry and are doomed to posterity's derision.

Derzhavin judiciously yet playfully concludes that the proper place for his image is next to his wife's in her boudoir, where he would be on view only for his spouse, family and friends. Thus, he again, as in many of his odes, carves out a private domain where even the public genre of sculpture finds its intelligible niche. In his home, the bust evokes a living body in the affectionate eyes of Derzhavin's friends, while outside of this secluded private space, Rachette's well-executed creation is subject to "entropy of meaning." Unlike painting or printed text, sculpture lacks a frame and fully enters the semantics of its present surroundings. Paradoxically, just as any idol, it can thus be physically touched, trampled and overthrown, rather than contemplated as an artifact or admired as a likeness of its original model.

A sensitive observer of the ancient monuments' vulnerability to destruction, fragmentation, and misinterpretation, Derzhavin projects a similar fate for his own bust and concludes that sculpture needs necessarily to be accompanied by text in order to provide adequate representation in the public sphere. Meanwhile, poetry escapes this fate and can stand on its own. And herein lies Derzhavin's contribution to Lessing's project of establishing and defining the distinctive spheres for the arts. If for Lessing the difference between verbal and visual art gives rise to distinctive modes of imaginative reception as the former unfolds in time and the latter in space, for Derzhavin sculpture and poetry reveal their true significance only in the retrospective evaluation of posterity. In this rivalry, statuary comes out as opaque in the absence of text.

It is precisely in this context that two years after **"Moi Istukan,"** a rendition of the Horatian *Exegi Monumentum* is striking in its definitiveness. In **"Pamiatnik"** (1796), where sculpture's commemorative might is again placed below that of poetry, Derzhavin does not even attempt to smuggle in a fragment of his domestic, private space. Grandiloquent in its formulations, the poem displays a vast Russian terrain for public view. Derzhavin's fame resonates through all this space, heedless of any obstacle or disclaimer:

> Слух пройдет обо мне от Белых бод до Черных,
> Гле Болга, Гон, Неба, с Рифея дьет Урал.

It is important to note that the critique of sculpture in **"Moi Istukan"** is couched in terms that had only recently belonged to the lexicon of paganism: "istukan," "kumir," "bolvan," all objects of misplaced adoration and victims of violent demolition. Meanwhile, the discursive monument, one that is ultimately capable of fashioning a satisfactory historical narrative of the self, is termed *pamiatnik.* It is the only term that can boast sufficient semantic capacities for transcending sculpture and adequately accommodating representation. For ultimately, at stake in the revamped eighteenth-century contest of sculpture and poetry as repositories of history was the vexed question of the transparency of representation, which so concerned Enlightenment thinkers from Rousseau to Diderot. Which medium is capable of conveying more accurately and effectively personal and national history: the image, which leaves an immediate but unspoken and therefore unexplained impression on the viewer, or the word, which strives to fix and define meaning but is itself intangible? More significantly, will any medium successfully prevail over what Diderot called "the ravages of time"?

I have argued that in the eighteenth-century Russia, this age-old contest acquired an added urgency. As we have seen, in the late 1700s, Russian elite's relationship toward sculpture and history, of which Derzhavin was an eloquent mouthpiece, was certainly inflected by widespread Enlightenment ideas on ruins, historical commemoration, and the respective domains of the arts. More significantly, however, the discourse of novelty and rupture promulgated by Peter I and his ideologues had spotlighted the difficulty and exigency of historical representation, one that until the late 1700s was expected to displace ruins of the past in favor of the monuments of the eulogized present, and, furthermore, to ignore the ruin within the monument. The new cityscape of Saint Petersburg was a particularly appropriate locale for experiencing and questioning these monumental workings of recent Russian history. Rising out of nowhere, Petersburg immediately assumed monumental dimensions, which were constantly threatened by erasure from elemental forces or future iconoclasts. The critic of Peter's reforms, Prince M. M. Scherbatov, famously pictured Petersburg in shambles and old Moscow alive and bustling with activity, in his unfinished utopian novel *The Land of Ophir* (1784).[47] Diderot, upon his arrival at Catherine's Petersburg court, was surprised to discover a city devoid of city life, but instead filled with barracks and palaces, both sites of merely temporary power.[48] Thus, even the new capital's monumental form, which was intended to surpass in longevity and splendor the overwhelmingly wooden architecture of pre-Petrine Russia, was subject to obliteration, if not by fire then by imagination and history. By displacing the old capital and unseating traditional Russian lifestyles, Peter I dangerously opened a possibility for recurring destructive changes. Diderot's remark on ruins, which, as we remember, inspired their observer to anticipate a similar collapse of his own epoch's artifacts, thus translated well into the context of the Russian eighteenth century. Only for an inhabitant of Saint Petersburg, destruction lurked not simply behind the aestheticized medieval ruins, of which there were known but few physical specimens in Russia, but rather behind the newly constructed monuments of Peter's capital and Peter's modernity. As their turn-of-the-century dictionary definition attests, these new monumental figures—from Falconet's colossus to Rachette's modest bust of Derzhavin—could equally mark a gravesite and a triumphal bas-relief of History.

Notes

1. Crone, *The Daring of Derzhavin,* 186

2. For a well-documented and thoughtful story of Peter's transformations in the visual arts, see Craft, *The Petrine Revolution* [*in Russian Imagery*]. The most illuminating for our purposes is a brief chapter on sculpture (pp. 220-231). It is worth noting that even relatively late into Peter's reign, sculpture continued to be an ideological battleground. While Stefan Iavorskii, who exercised considerable influence on Peter I in the early 1700s, did not openly object to the appearance of statuary in consecrated spaces, his opponent Feofan Prokopovich, once he assumed power, brought about the Synod's ban on church sculpture in 1722. See Preskov, "Skul'ptura," 430.

3. In a recent article, Joachim Klein traces the Russian pre-history of poetic self-glorification and draws out the specific Russian context of the late eighteenth century, in which Derzhavin's poem appeared. (Klein, "Poet-samokhval," 148-170). These claims to poets' elevated status, the scholar demonstrates, received a predominantly critical reception from the readers until the virtual canonization of Lomonosov during Catherine's reign. Part of the daring of such claims lay in the limited scope of Russian Enlightenment, which made it possible for only a limited group within the reading public to even consider these declarations seriously. In this reading, Klein is supported by the statistics Gary Marker collects in his by-now-classic *Publishing, Printing, and the Origins of Intellectual Life in Russia, 1700-1800.* Behind the various literary projects of Catherine's era—the Society for Translation of Foreign Books into Russian (f. 1768), the many short-lived "moral weeklies" (whose number and popularity peaked in 1769 and early 1770s), the Empress's personal involvement in theater and correspondence with European luminaries, which had all helped raise the cultured public's esteem for literature, Marker discerns a veritable dearth of educated readers and cultural institutions. Most recently, Thomas Barran provides a summary of various scholarly calculations of the number of educated Russian readers in the introduction to his *Russia Reads Rousseau,* xx.

4. Lomonosov, *Izbrannye proizvedeniia,* 255

5. *Slovar' russkogo iazyka XI-XVII vv,* vol. 14: 138: "Памятникъ—памятная запись, сбидетельстбо." The latest example in the dictionary is from 1553: «Намъ . . . до аржимарита Иеба . . . дѣла нѣтъ бо бсякихъ земскихъ податѣхъ по розрубнымъ спискомъ и по паметникомъ и по кабаламъ съ тѣхъ полуторы деребни за прошлые годы. А. Уст. П, 71, 1553г . . .»

6. "Monument of the epoch," "literary monument," "cultural monument."

7. All of these words denote a "pagan idol."

8. Free-standing statuary was rare in pre-Petrine Russia. Decorative wooden sculpture on the izba facades and bas-reliefs were by far the most prevalent types of sculpture.

9. Haskell and Penny, *Taste and the Antique,* 296

10. Non-annalistic historiography appeared already before Peter; what distinguishes post-Petrine historiography, however, is the sheer number of texts as well as the centrality of biographical narrative as historiographies' structuring device.

11. S. L. Peshtich offers a comprehensive picture of historiography in 18th-century Russia in *Russkaia Istoriogragfiia XVIII veka.*

12. I am grateful to V. M. Zhivov for alerting me to the connection between sentimental and nationalist historiographical prose.

13. For a recent elaboration of the political connotations of one such symbolic disguise, see Proskurina, "Mif ob Astreiie [iruskii prestol]," 153-185.

14. By mid-eighteenth century, academic history painting had traveled a long way from the cold and clear linear narratives of Poussin. Painting and sculpture now acquired multiple meanings, could be read along multiple axes, and were placed in multiple conceptual and spatial contexts, which called for an informed viewer's interpretation. In his series of essays on "The Pleasures of the Imagination," Addison located the stimuli for imaginative responses in visual objects. Several decades later, Denis Diderot sauntered through the Salon exhibits and composed his passionate analyses, amalgams of erudition and imagination, which were to become the early samples of professional art criticism. For the first time, art openly required an interpretation. Ronald Paulson has aptly referred to this period as "an age of art works of great mobility and shifting intentionality." (Paulson, *Emblem and Expression,* 18.)

15. For a stimulating discussion of the narrative "significant moment" in eighteenth-century art, see Dowley, "The Moment in Eighteenth-Century Art Criticism," 317-336.

16. Lessing, *Laocoon,* 19. For a superb, highly contextualized reading of *Laocoon,* consult Wellbery, *Lessing's Laocoon.*

17. While Lessing drew a distinction between poetry which worked on the imagination through an explicit temporal progression of plot, and visual arts which seized on a fragment of plot to inspire the viewer's fancy, the fascination with ruins and fragments motivated a similar kind of imaginative response in consumers of both visual and verbal arts. This similarity becomes especially apparent in the topoi of sentimental prose and in Romantic elegy. Monika Greenleaf outlines a connection between statuary and poetry in her chapter on the genealogy of Romantic fragment in *Pushkin and Romantic Fashion,* 30-36. In "draw[ing] a genealogical dotted line between the discovery of the sculptural fragment at the beginning of the eighteenth century and the invention of the poetic fragment toward its end," the scholar elaborates an analogy between the sculptural/architectural fragments and the poetic ones: "If the muteness of sculptural and architectural fragments invited a complementary interior monologue from the viewer, fragments of ancient texts stimulated readers to picture the context from which they had been torn, for which they served as an inscription." I would argue that monuments too came to be fashioned as inscriptions analogous to ruins and fragments.

18. Diderot, *Oeuvres esthétiques,* 462. "O beautiful, sublime ruins! [. . .] What effect! What grandeur! What nobility!"

19. *Ibid,* 461. "We anticipate the ravages of time, and our imagination disperses upon the earth the very edifices in which we dwell."

20. Winckelmann, "On the Imitation of the Painting and Sculpture of the Greeks," 61.

21. Slovtsov, "Drevnost'" (*Poetry 1790-1810-kh godov*), 214-220.

> You will have carved out
> Franklin, who fractured the British scepter,
> Raynal the upholder of a civic charter,
> As an oracle of a free nation,
> And Murza in a turban, the bard of Astreia,
> In an oak wreath and a grivna on his neck.
>
> [translation is mine—LG]

Grivna was a metal decoration, similar to a medal, and served as a token of distinction.

22. In addition to Lomonosov's in the Cameron Gallery, Sumarokov's bust deservedly adorned the Hermitage Theater.

23. Antiquity, adorning its mausoleum,
Exercises its wrath only upon us,
And strangling the eighteenth century,
Will carve out merely a new bas-relief.

24. A peaceful rainbow for them [Enlightened geniuses] appeared,
One half bent toward antiquity,
The other resting upon posterity.

25. In their acclaimed *Taste and the Antique,* Francis Haskell and Nicholas Penny trace different receptions and re-appropriations of antiquity from the

Renaissance to the Modernist fin-de-siècle. Leonard Barkan paints a fascinating picture of the discovery and appropriation of the Antiquity in the Italian Renaissance in *Unearthing the Past* (1999).

26. On the history of sculptures in the Cameron gallery, see two articles in a recent volume dedicated to Russian museum collections: Neverov, "Skul'pturnyi Dekor [Kameronovsi galerei i ego programma]," 9-15 and Stepanenko, "Skul'pturnaia [Kollektsiia Kameronovoi galerie kak otrazhenie mentaliteta imperatritsy Ekatering II]," 15-27.

27. Alexander Schenker tells a fascinating story of all the stages of the monument's creation in his recent *The Bronze Horseman*. Despite the book's title, what comes out of the history it weaves is that at least in the initial years of Falconet's work in Petersburg, the monument could be called Catherine's as much as Falconet's. In fact, the politics around the shape and the inscription on the monument reveal Catherine's deliberate attention to her personal as well as her Empire's national history.

28. Here one would be obliged to mention the centrality of the monument to the Petersburg text and recall its long literary genealogy from Pushkin through Bely and beyond. However, for the purposes of this article significant is the sense of novelty that such a huge sculptural specimen must have inspired in its eighteenth-century contemporaries when only a century earlier sculpture altogether had been essentially allied with idolatry.

29. See Wortman, *Scenarios of Power,* 1995.

30. The full entry from the Dictionary (*Slovar' Akademii Rossiiskoi,* 1822: 784) reads: "Памятник—1) Сооружение боздбигнутое торжестбенно б боспоминание и честь какой-либо особы, или знаменитого деяния, происшестбия для памяти б позднейшем потомстбе; *Петру I воздвигнут памятник Императрицею Екатериною II; Боздвигнуть памятник в честь героя; памятник надгробный*; 2) бещи, остатки, напоминающие, сбидетельстбующие прошедшую слабу, знаменитость, беличие какого-либо места; *Разбалины древнего Рима суть памятнуки бывиего его беличия.*"

31. There is no mention of Falconet in these two poems; however, we know that Derzhavin admired Falconet's art and dedicated one of his later poems to Falconet's Cupid ("Fal'konetov Kupidon," 1804). In that poem dream meets reality as a flesh-and-blood boy congeals in Falconet's breathing

statue. This lighthearted poem pays tribute to Falconet's art by means of a widespread eighteenth-century trope: the dead form of sculpture approximates life so closely that it appears to breathe and move (see, for instance, Lessing's descriptions of Classical statuary).

32. "Your virtue, Peter! shall be pleasing to all ages; Preserve, preserve forever, o Creator, Him in our posterity!" ("Monument to Peter the Great") and "Raise voices to the sky, o wind! You are immortal, o Great Peter!" ("To Peter the Great"). Derzhavin, *Sochineniia,* 169-172.

33. For a convincing demonstration of Derzhavin's stylistic reliance upon the visual media, see Dan'ko, "Izobrazitel'noe iskusstvo [v poezii Derzhavina]," 166-247. The scholar characterizes Derzhavin's poetic technique as "speaking painting" ("govoriashchaia zhivopis'") (174). Reading Derzhavin's oeuvre through the topos of *ut pictura poesis,* Dan'ko writes: "Derzhavin in his "Treatise on Lyrical Poetry" (1811) pays a lot of attention to the questions of poetic pictoriality [kartinnost'] [. . .] Derzhavin's genius was not that of rhetorical poetry. His paragon was Horace who likened poetry to painting." (178-9)

34. Here Derzhavin addresses all Russians ("o Россы!"): "Let your choir praise Peter forever!"

35. "Песнь сия была б беликом употреблении б ложах у масоноб." Quoted in Derzhavin, *Sochineniia,* 586.

36. Schoenle, "Mezhdu 'novoi' i 'drevnei' Rossiei," 136.

37. Derzhavin, *Sochineniia,* 121. "Sit next to the wonderful monument of the leader,—and in your mournful song convey: this pillar shall be crushed by time, destroyed."

38. "ruins, graves, ashes, skulls, and bones of their equals."

39. "The obelisks of such a man emit glory not because of their proximity to the heavens, stand firm not in their marble or brass. Let time destroy them, but it can't annihilate them altogether: virtue survives in legend."

40. "in whose honor the author had erected this monument." Quoted in Derzhavin, *Sochineniia,* 572.

41. "Build, Muse, a monument to the Hero."

42. See the section "Derzhavin and Rachette" in Dan'ko, "Izobrazitel'noe iskusstvo," 230-247.

43. Derzhavin, *Sochineniia,* 195

44. "Break then, my second creator, break my bust, Rachette!" Incidentally, a curious parallel to these

lines appears in Diderot's *Salons.* Diderot records that Falconet, recognizing the superiority of Collot's bust of Diderot over his own, shatters the uninspired likeness he had produced. "Ce Falconet, cet artiste si peu jaloux de la réputation dans l'avenir, ce contempteur si déterminé de l'immortalité, cet homme si disrespectueux de la postérité, délivré du souci de lui transmettre un mauvais buste." (Diderot, *Oeuvres Esthétiques,* 514) The shattered bust reveals a fine pair of ears that would have been concealed if not for Falconet's iconoclastic act. Diderot is pleased to see his own false public representation yield an object for private jokes and private admiration. Similarly, we will see that Derzhavin too is pleased to locate his bust in the domain of private aesthetic consumption. For further discussion of the passage from the *Salons,* consult Brewer, "Portraying Diderot," 44-59.

45. "so as to include me, to the chagrin of my detractors, in her [Catherine's] beautiful colonnade."

46. Such turns toward posterity were characteristic of Enlightenment thinking. Daniel Brewer shows Diderot in a quandary over the representational power of portraiture. He finds this concern in several Diderot passages: "Quand l'homme n'est plus, nous supposons la ressemblance." "C'est la figure . . . peinte qui restera dans la mémoire des hommes à venir." Brewer elaborates: "In time the portrait always comes to take the place of its original; it's what remains in the absence of its model. The model is just remains, remaining, remembered, but only because of its place within representation." (Brewer, "Portraying Diderot," 49).

47. Shcherbatov, "*Puteshestvie v Zemliu Ofirskuiu.*"

48. See Diderot, *Mémoires pour Catherine II,* 55-56.

Bibliography

Barkan, Leonard. *Unearthing the Past: Archaeology and Aesthetics in the Making of Renaissance Culture.* New Haven: Yale University Press, 1999.

Barran, Thomas. *Russia Reads Rousseau, 1762-1825.* Evanston, Il: Northwestern University Press, 2002.

Brewer, Daniel. "Portraying Diderot." In *Diderot, Digression and Dispersion: A Bicentennial Tribute,* edited by Jack Undank and Herbert Josephs, 44-59. Lexington, KY: French Forum, 1984.

Cracraft, James. *The Petrine Revolution in Russian Imagery.* Chicago and London: The University of Chicago Press, 1997.

Crone, Anna Lisa. *The Daring of Derzhavin: The Moral and Aesthetic Independence of the Poet in Russia.* Bloomington, Indiana: Slavica Publishers, 2001.

Dan'ko, E. Ia. "Izobrazitel'noe iskusstvo v poezii Derzhavina." *XVIII vek: stat'i i materialy,* vol. 2, 166-247. Moskva, Leningrad: Izdatel'stvo Akademii Nauk SSSR, 1940.

Derzhavin, G. R. *Poetic Works: A Bilingual Album,* trans. Alexander Levitsky and Martha Kitchen. Providence: Brown University, 2001.

———. *Sochineniia,* Sankt-Peterburg: Akademicheskii Proekt, 2002.

Diderot, Denis. *Mémoires pour Catherine II.* Paris: Editions Garnier Frères, 1966.

———. *Oeuvres esthétiques.* Paris: Editions Garnier Frères, 1965.

Dowley, Francis. "The Moment in Eighteenth-Century Art Criticism," in *Studies in Eighteenth-Century Culture,* vol. 5, edited by Ronald C. Rosbottom, 317-336. Madison: University of Wisconsin Press, 1976.

Greenleaf, Monika. *Pushkin and Romantic Fashion: Fragment, Elegy, Orient, Irony.* Stanford: Stanford University Press, 1994.

Haley, Bruce. *Living Forms: Romantics and the Monumental Figure.* Albany: SUNY Press, 2003.

Haskell, Francis and Nicholas Penny. *Taste and the Antique: The Lure of Classical Sculpture, 1500-1900.* New Haven: Yale University Press, 1981.

Klein, Joachim. "Poet-samokhval: 'Pamiatnik' Derzhavina i status poeta v Rossii XVIII veka." *Novoe Literaturnoe Obozrenie* 65 (2004): 148-170.

Lomonosov, M. V. *Izbrannye proizvedeniia.* Leningrad: Sovetskii pisatel', 1986.

Lessing, Gotthold Ephraim. *Laocoon: An Essay on the Limits of Painting and Poetry.* Baltimore and London: Johns Hopkins University Press, 1984.

Madariaga, Isabel de. *Russia in the Age of Catherine the Great.* New Haven: Yale University Press, 1981.

Marker, Gary. *Publishing, Printing, and the Origins of Intellectual Life in Russia, 1700-1800.* Princeton: Princeton University Press, 1985.

Neverov, O. Ia. "Skul'pturnyi dekor Kameronovoi galerei i ego programma." In *Sud'by muzeinykh kollektsii,* Sankt-Peterburg: Tsarskoe Selo, 2000, pp. 9-15

Paulson, Ronald. *Emblem and Expression: Meaning in English Art of the Eighteenth Century.* London: Thames and Hudson, 1975.

Peshtich, S. L. *Russkaia Istoriogragfiia XVIII veka.* Leningrad: Leningradskii Gosudarstvennyi Universitet, 1961-71.

Preskov, G. M. "Skul'ptura." In *Istoriia russkogo iskusstva,* edited by I. E. Grabar', 429-499. Moskva: Izdatel'stvo Akademii Nauk, 1960.

Proskurina, Vera. "Mif ob Astreiie i russkii prestol." *Novoe Literaturnoe Obozrenie* 63 (2003): 153-185.

Schenker, Alexander. *The Bronze Horseman: Falconet's Monument to Peter the Great.* New Haven: Yale University Press, 2003.

Schoenle, Andreas. "Mezhdu "novoi" i "drevnei" Rossiei: ruiny u rannego Karamzina kak mesto modernity." *Novoe Literaturnoe Obozrenie* 59 (2003): 125-141.

Shcherbatov, M. M. "Puteshestviie v Zemliu Ofirskuiu," In *Russkaia Literaturnaia Utopiia,* edited by V. P. Shestakov. Moskva: Izdatel'stvo Moskovskogo Universiteta, 1986.

Shell, Marc. *The Economy of Literature.* Baltimore: Johns Hopkins University Press, 1978.

Slovar' Akademii Rossiiskoi po azbuchnomu poriadku raspolozhennyi, vol. 4. Sankt Peterburg: Pri Imperatorskoi Akademii Nauk, 1806-22 [Odense: University Press, 1971].

Slovar' russkogo iazyka XI-XVII vv, vol. 14. Moskva: Nauka, 1988.

Slovtsov, Petr. "Drevnost'." In *Poety 1790-1810-kh godov,* edited by Iu. M. Lotman, 214-220. Leningrad: Sovetskii Pisatel', 1971.

Stepanenko, I. G. "Skul'pturnaia kollektsiia Kameronovoi galerei kak otrazhenie mentaliteta imperatritsy Ekateriny II." In *Sud'by muzeinykh kollektsii: materialy VI Tsarskoselskoi nauchnoi konferentsii,* 15-27. Sankt-Peterburg: Tsarskoe Selo, 2000.

Wellbery, David. *Lessing's Laocoon: Semiotics and Aesthetics in the Age of Reason.* Cambridge, New York: Cambridge University Press, 1984.

Winckelmann, Johann Joachim. "On the Imitation of the Painting and Sculpture of the Greeks." In *Writings on Art,* edited by David Irwin, 61-86. London: Phaidon Publishers, 1972.

Wortman, Richard. *Scenarios of Power: Myth and Ceremony in Russian Monarchy.* Princeton: Princeton University Press, 1995.

FURTHER READING

Bibliographies

Crone, Anna Lisa. "Gavrila Romanovich Derzhavin, 1743-1818." In *Reference Guide to Russian Literature,* edited by Neil Cornwell and Nicole Christian, pp. 241-43. London: Taylor and Francis, 1998.

Presents a selected bibliography of English and non-English Derzhavin criticism, with a brief introductory essay.

Derzhavin, G. R. *Poetic Works: A Bilingual Album,* edited by Alexander Levitsky; translated by Alexander Levitsky and M. T. Kitchen. Providence, R.I.: Brown University, 2001, 590 p.

Includes both English and Russian versions of selected poems by Derzhavin, along with some bibliographic information.

Segel, Harold B. *The Literature of Eighteenth-Century Russia,* Vol. 2. New York: Dutton, 1967, 448 p.

Offers translations of various Russian poems from the eighteenth century, with short critical introductions to each.

Biographies

Bethea, David M. *Realizing Metaphors: Alexander Pushkin and the Life of the Poet.* Madison: University of Wisconsin Press, 1998, 244 p.

Considers Derzhavin's influence on Pushkin and subsequent Russian poets, with extensive biographical information on both poets.

Khodasevich, Vladislav. *Derzhavin: A Biography,* edited by Angela Brintlinger. Madison: University of Wisconsin Press, 2007, 344 p.

Provides an English translation of Khodasevich's authoritative 1931 biography of Derzhavin.

Criticism

Beaver, Aaron. "Derzhavin's Metaphysics of Morality." *The Russian Review* 66 (summer 2007): 189-210.

Argues that Derzhavin's poetry consistently connects metaphysical and moral beliefs.

Brintlinger, Angela. "Searching for a Hero: Khodasevich and his Derzhavin." In *Writing a Usable Past: Russian Literary Culture, 1917-1937,* pp. 62-89. Evanston, Ill.: Northwestern University Press, 2000.

Introduces Khodasevich's biography of Derzhavin and includes a translated excerpt.

Byrd, Charles. "Thunder Imagery and the Turn Against Horace in Derzhavin's 'Evgeniyu. Zhizn' Zvanskaya' (1807)." In *Russian Literature and the Classics,* edited by Peter I. Barta, David H. J. Larmour, and Paul Allen Miller, pp. 13-34. Amsterdam: Harwood Academic Publishers, 1996.

Traces the use of thunder imagery in Derzhavin's poetry, advancing a complex interpretation of poetic influence in the psychological factors underlying Derzhavin's originality.

Crone, Anna Lisa. "From King-as-Poet to Poet-as-King: Gavrilla Derzhavin between Friedrich of Prussia and Catherine II." In *Cold Fusion: Aspects of the German Cultural Presence in Russia,* pp. 34-50. New York: Berghan Books, 2000.

Analyzes Derzhavin in the context of eighteenth-century political influences on poetry.

Harris, Jane Gary. "Before 'Felica': The First Signs of G. R. Derzhavin's Odic Voice." *Russian Language Journal* 41, nos. 138-139 (January 1987): 69-81.

Examines Derzhavin's early poems as building blocks for his mature poetic voice.

Harvie, J. A. "In Defence of Derzhavin's Plays." *New Zealand Slavonic Journal,* no. 2 (1975): 1-15.

Asserts that Derzhavin's plays have been unjustly overlooked in twentieth-century scholarship.

Jakobson, Roman. "Derzhavin's Last Poems and M. Halle's First Literary Analysis." In *Language, Sound, Structure: Studies in Phonology Presented to Morris Halle by His Teacher and Students,* edited by Mark Aronoff and Richard T. Oehrle, pp. 1-4. Cambridge, Mass.: MIT Press.

Presents a linguistic analysis of Derzhavin's "On Perishability," focusing on Morris Halle's observations on the poem's acrostic elements.

Lilly, Ian K. "Russian Word-Play Poetry from Simeon Polotskii to Derzhavin: Its Classical and Baroque Context." *Slavonic and East European Review* 72, no. 3 (July 1994): 500-01.

Traces the classical and baroque backgrounds of experimental or unorthodox language in Russian poetry.

Loewen, Donald. "Questioning a Poet's Explanations: Politics and Self-Presentation in Derzhavin's 'Footnotes' and Explanations." *Russian Review* 64, no. 3 (July 2005): 381-400.

Discusses Derzhavin's autobiographic prose, arguing that these materials present a consistent tendency to privilege his political identity over his role as a poet.

Mirsky, D. S. "The Age of Classicism." In *A History of Russian Literature: From Its Beginnings to 1900,* edited by Francis J. Whitfield, pp. 40-70. New York: Alfred A. Knopf, 1960.

Outlines Derzhavin's life and work, analyzing his strengths and weaknesses as a poet.

Pushkin, Alexander. "Exile Under Double Surveillance—Mikhaylovskoe, August 1824-December 1825." In *The Complete Works of Alexander Pushkin,* Volume 10: *Letters: 1815-1826,* translated by J. Thomas Shaw, pp. 181-300. Norfolk, Va.: Milner and Company Limited, 2002.

Provides a concise personal opinion on Derzhavin's language and thought.

Waszink, Paul M. "New Love or Old Flower? Kant and Schelling in Derzhavin's and Baratynsky's Poetry." *Australian Slavonic and East European Studies* 9, no. 2 (January 1995): 1-26.

Considers the influence of German Idealism on the poetry of Derzhavin and Baratynsky.

George Henry Lewes
1817-1878

English philosopher, critic, biographer, essayist, historian, novelist, and dramatist.

The following entry presents an overview of Lewes's life and works. For additional discussion of Lewes's career, see *NCLC*, Volume 25.

INTRODUCTION

Although he is primarily remembered as the common-law husband of novelist George Eliot, George Henry Lewes was a prominent and prodigious man of letters in his own right, producing a diverse body of work that includes philosophical treatises, literary and drama criticism, biographies, scientific studies, explorations in psychology, novels, and a play. An astute editor, he held senior editorial positions at two prominent periodicals: the *Leader,* which he helped establish in 1851, and the *Fortnightly Review* in its early years. Throughout his career, Lewes examined the philosophical concept of positivism, which argued that knowledge could only be derived through the rigorous application of the scientific method. The most thorough presentation of Lewes's philosophical and scientific beliefs is his five-volume treatise *Problems of Life and Mind* (1874-79), regarded by the majority of modern critics as a notable addition to the histories of philosophy and psychology. Lewes's literary criticism was also guided by positivism and the belief that the scientific principles of analysis and verification could be applied to all forms of intellectual inquiry. His critical evaluations, expressed in witty and sometimes acerbic language, are appreciated by literary commentators even today. Scholar Diana Postlethwaite has argued that Lewes's essay "Spinoza's Life and Works" (1843) was the "cornerstone of his early thought." The biographical study *The Life and Works of Goethe* (1855) was probably his best-known text in his own era.

BIOGRAPHICAL INFORMATION

George Henry Lewes, the son of John Lee and Elizabeth Ashweek Lewes, was born in London on April 18, 1817. Both Lewes's father and his grandfather, Charles Lee Lewes, were actors, and many commentators have argued that his theatrical background influenced Lewes's later critical interest in the art of acting. His early education was somewhat aimless: he attended schools in London, Jersey, Brittany, and Greenwich before leaving the academic world to pursue a vocation. After working in a notary's office and performing duties as a clerk in a Russian merchant house, Lewes turned his attention to the field of medicine. After visiting several hospitals, however, he discovered that he could not stand the sight of blood in the operating room. He nevertheless acquired a theoretical knowledge in anatomy and physiology that proved vital to his later scientific studies. Meanwhile, Lewes began to meet regularly with like-minded intellectuals, including Leigh Hunt, Charles Dickens, Thomas Carlyle, and John Stuart Mill, to discuss literary and philosophical ideas. In 1838 he visited Germany, where he gained an appreciation for European literature and philosophy. By 1840 Lewes had begun submitting essays and reviews to a number of prominent periodicals, but because he had neither family connections nor a substantial university career to recommend him, he had little immediate success, despite his impressive knowledge of European literature. His essay "The French Drama: Racine and Victor Hugo" was accepted by the *Westminster Review* in September 1840. At about this time Lewes was working as an English tutor in the household of Swyfen Jervis of Chatcull, Staffordshire. He fell in love with Mr. Jervis's daughter, Agnes, and the two were married in February 1841.

As the 1840s progressed, Lewes began to achieve some success. The periodicals were increasingly interested in his literary criticism; his philosophical views provided him with a distinct approach to literature that focused on the general principles governing the novel form. His critiques of the late 1840s and early 1850s established his subsequent reputation as one of foremost exponents of realism in the Victorian period; his insistence on analytical rigor influenced not only his scientific work but also his literary criticism and in particular his emphasis on the "reality" of experience as represented in theater. While he adopted the realist position throughout the 1850s, he did insist that the authenticity in a given work relate to the writer's actual experience. Indeed, Lewes reserved his harshest criticism for novels that imitated other novels and for stereotypes of character and incident. Many critics have noted that his theory demanded "sincerity" as much as reality. Through his reviews, Lewes was responsible for attracting attention to numerous European authors, including Johann Wolfgang von Goethe, Benedict de Spinoza, and Jean Racine. He also reviewed novels by many of his English contemporaries, including Anthony Trollope, William Thackeray, Charlotte and Emily Brontë, Charles Dickens, and Elizabeth Gaskell.

The initial volume of Lewes's *Biographical History of Philosophy,* his first significant publication, came out in 1845. Lewes followed this accomplishment with two novels, *Ranthorpe* (1847) and *Rose, Blanche, and Violet* (1848), which the budding novelist Charlotte Brontë enthusiastically reviewed upon their publication. Pursuing his interest in the theater, Lewes wrote a play titled *The Noble Heart: A Tragedy, in Three Acts* (1849), acted in Charles Dickens's private company, and contributed his theater reviews to several prestigious Victorian periodicals, including the *British Quarterly Review,* the *Westminster Review,* and *Fraser's Magazine.* Over the course of the decade, Lewes and Agnes had four children. The couple espoused a belief in free love, and friends were struck by Lewes's bohemianism and the freedom of his conversation, a reaction likely accentuated by his homely appearance. Together with Thornton Hunt, the son of critic and writer Leigh Hunt, Lewes established the *Leader,* a liberal-minded weekly, publishing the first edition in 1851. Before the end of the year, it came out that Hunt and Agnes were engaged in an affair that ultimately resulted in the birth of a child. Lewes did not request a divorce but separated from his wife in October 1851.

Despite the domestic crisis, Lewes continued to fulfill his editorial duties at the *Leader* and to contribute essays to the periodical. Under the assumed alter ego "Vivian," Lewes wrote brilliant and sometimes scathing reviews of contemporary literature, criticized British conservatism, and offered valuable and witty observations on current plays. As a number of critics have noted, Vivian's typically airy tone became serious when he reviewed the acting of a great artist, such as the French actress Rachel. In these instances Vivian revealed Lewes's passion for "natural" acting—that is, for the authentic representation of human nature. In the company of his friends, he maintained Vivian's ebullient charm and a certain humorous audacity. It may have been his boldness in conversation that so offended George Eliot when her close friend Herbert Spencer introduced her to Lewes in 1851. Evidently, she gradually came to enjoy Lewes's company, as she confided to Cara Bray in an 1853 letter: "Mr. Lewes [. . .] has quite won my regard, after having had a good deal of my vituperation. Like a few other people in the world, he is much better than he seems. A man of heart and conscience wearing a mask of flippancy." Postlethwaite notes that between 1851 and 1853, Lewes, Spencer, and Eliot were something of an "intellectual *ménage à trois.*" Through winter and spring 1854, Lewes and Eliot became intimate. By summer they had decided to defy Victorian convention and live together in a common-

law arrangement. Visiting Germany with Eliot that same summer, Lewes gathered research for his upcoming book, *The Life and Works of Goethe,* which he published in 1855.

Upon the couple's return to England in March 1855, Lewes discovered in Eliot a refreshing change from his previously discordant domestic lifestyle. Because he and Agnes had come to a mutual agreement regarding the separation, his eventual union with Eliot stemmed from common sense rather than recklessness. Over the next several years, Lewes devoted most of his time to scientific study, producing three works on biology and physiology: *Sea-Side Studies at Ilfracombe, Tenby, the Scilly Isles, and Jersey* (1858), *The Physiology of Common Life* (1859-60), and *Studies in Animal Life* (1860). He ultimately gained the respect of professional scientists, including the young biologist T. H. Huxley, for the veracity and discipline of his original research. The works reflect Lewes's wish to become an expert vivisectionist and microscopist. He was one of the foremost defenders of the surgical practice during the furious antivivisectionist debates of the late 1850s. Contemporary critics still agree, however, that Lewes's greatest contribution of the decade was his intellectual and moral support of Eliot's writing career. With Lewes's encouragement Eliot published *Scenes of Clerical Life,* a trilogy of short novels, in 1858 and *Adam Bede* in 1859. Over the course of her writing career, Eliot took Lewes's comments on portions of her work, and he protected Eliot from negative reviews of her novels. Author Barbara Smalley argues that Eliot's novels were influenced by Lewes's own "fascination with problems in human motivation."

By the 1860s Lewes was engaged in the ambitious project of writing a history of science. He completed the first volume, *Aristotle: A Chapter in the History of Science,* in 1864. By Lewes's own account, his initial research into anatomy, physiology, pathology, insanity, and the science of language ultimately prepared him for the study of the principles of psychology. Accordingly, he interrupted his history of science in 1862 to begin work on his most profound contribution to modern psychology, *Problems of Life and Mind.* As in the previous decade Lewes was active in multiple fields, dividing his time between his philosophical and scientific endeavors, assuming senior editorial responsibilities for the new periodical the *Fortnightly Review* between 1865 and 1866, and contributing his own articles to the *Fortnightly,* the *Pall Mall Gazette,* and *Cornhill Magazine.*

Health problems in the late 1860s forced Lewes to abandon most of his writing activity, and as a result the first series of *Problems of Life and Mind, The Foundations of a Creed,* did not appear until the mid-1870s. Lewes delayed the completion of this project further by turning his attention back to the theater; the result was a collection of essays, *On Actors and the Art of Acting* (1875). Twentieth-century commentators have granted Lewes's study a prominent position in theater criticism, noting the author's unique psychological approach to acting and his emphasis on the actor's "range of expression." Lewes devoted the rest of his life to finishing *Problems of Life and Mind*; the second series, *The Physical Basis of Mind,* came out in 1877. Lewes was working on the third series when he died on November 30, 1878. The following year Eliot used Lewes's notes to complete this series, and it was published in 1879 in two volumes: *Problems of Life and Mind. Third Series, Problem the First: The Study of Psychology, Its Object, Scope, and Method* and *Problems of Life and Mind. Third Series, Problem the Second: Mind as a Function of Organism. Problem the Third: The Sphere of Sense and Logic of Feeling. Problem the Fourth: The Sphere of Intellect and Logic of Signs.*

MAJOR WORKS

Throughout his writing career, Lewes made it his mission to critique one of the dominant schools of philosophical thought in the nineteenth century: the obsession with metaphysics, or the search for a transcendental truth that purportedly existed beyond the realm of experience. Lewes's approach may not be surprising given his interest in the other dominant school, which espoused the theory of positivism developed by French philosopher and scientist Auguste Comte. Lewes's first published investigation into positivism was his *Biographical History of Philosophy,* a work that contributed intelligently to a variety of fields, among them philosophy, biology, and especially psychology. He pursued his exploration of positivism in *Comte's Philosophy of the Sciences* (1853). Most critics agree that Lewes's doctrines did not present a slavish acceptance of positivism but instead sought a synthesis between empirical and transcendental philosophy. Lewes called his system empirical metaphysics, acknowledging that while there are certain unknown principles in nature, there are no unknowable truths because experience is infinite.

Lewes digested and reformulated the principles of other leading thinkers as well. While many philosophers in the nineteenth century still believed that the mind was an absolute entity, Lewes strove to demonstrate that it was part of the nervous system and therefore associated with the other sensations of the body. He consistently explored the correlation between mental phenomena and physiology, developing a school that twentieth-century philosophers named evolutionary associationism. In rejecting such dualities as German theorist Immanuel Kant's noumena and phenomena (ideas and sense perceptions, or mind and body), Lewes argued that the two sides are not separate but are rather aspects

of the same process. His essays "Spinoza's Life and Works" and "Spinoza" (1866) confirm that Lewes resonated more with the Dutch philosopher's view that mind and matter are one ultimate principle, but he revised Spinoza's ideas by adding material on the interconnections between space, time, matter, force, and motion and by attempting to prove that the developing mind was an important part of the evolutionary progress of the human species. Lewes's doctrine, which became known as the double aspect theory, served as the guiding principle of his major work, *Problems of Life and Mind.*

Lewes's *The Life and Works of Goethe* was the first biography of Goethe written in English and was regarded by his contemporaries, and by succeeding generations, as the best account of the German author. Lewes had multiple motivations for writing such a work. While Goethe was clearly of literary interest, he was a "poetical scientist," embracing both the arts and the sciences. A major portion of Lewes's intellectual activity was devoted to uniting science and humanism, and Goethe provided the model for such a project. Additionally, as Postlethwaite has argued, Lewes saw in Goethe's explorations of the divine energy of the universe a "genius in the Spinozist mold." Throughout the 1860s and 1870s, Lewes approached all literature from a scientific point of view, praising novels that presented a reality that could be empirically validated. Lewes's later literary reviews were seen as overly stringent, perhaps as the result of the dominance of his scientific perspective. The most notable example is his controversial critique, in the essay "Dickens in Relation to Criticism" (1872), of what he considered Dickens's implausible characterizations. Lewes's *Principles of Success in Literature* (1891) provides a valuable sampling of his unique style of literary criticism, but most critics agree that the best expression of his critical criteria is to be found in his many reviews scattered throughout Victorian periodicals.

CRITICAL RECEPTION

It has been generally believed that Lewes stood in the shadow of his confidante, George Eliot, during his lifetime. While Eliot received almost immediate success, Lewes's accolades were few and belated. Some commentators were disdainful of his early work: philosopher W. R. Sorley called the first edition of *The Biographical History of Philosophy* slender and, to some degree, specious; and biologist T. H. Huxley criticized *Comte's Philosophy of the Sciences* as riddled with errors and generally the work of an amateur. Huxley was, however, one of the first authorities to commend Lewes's next scientific work, *Sea-Side Studies.* By 1878, the year of Lewes's death, historian Frederic Harrison could claim that "what cultivated Englishmen know of philosophy and of science is in great part due to the popular treatises of Mr. Lewes."

The twentieth century brought a recognition that Lewes's scientific and philosophical studies offered a unique exploration of positivism and that they had made a crucial impact on the evolutionary psychology of prominent biologist-philosopher Herbert Spencer. Raymond St. James Perrin devoted three chapters of his study *The Evolution of Knowledge: A Review of Philosophy* (1905) to Lewes, tracing his efforts to tackle the metaphysical problem from an evolutionary perspective. In *A History of the Association Psychology* (1921), Howard C. Warren highlighted Lewes's psychological studies, demonstrating that Lewes was "an acute and logical thinker" and lamenting in a footnote that his work would have had a greater impact if he had been less verbose and, more significantly, if later studies in psychology had not veered away from associationism. Jack Kaminsky reinforced Lewes's role as a "renegade positivist" in his 1952 article "The Empirical Metaphysics of George Henry Lewes" and maintained that Lewes was appreciated by many of his contemporaries, including Huxley and Frederic Harrison.

As late as 1979, however, critic Diderik Roll-Hansen [see Further Reading] objected to the persistence of the misinformed view that Lewes was simply a helpmate for Eliot. The many claims for Lewes—his position within the history of science, philosophy, and psychology; his prominence as a theater critic and as an exponent of realism—suggest a different story. More recent studies in Victorian history and culture, such as Diana Postlethwaite's book *Making It Whole: A Victorian Circle and the Shape of Their World* (1984) and Paul White's essay "Cross-Cultural Encounters: The Co-production of Science and Literature in Mid-Victorian Periodicals" (2002), have confirmed this position of prestige. Despite the fact that Lewes would be overshadowed by Herbert Spencer and, in the United States, William James, his contributions to evolutionary psychology make him a prominent figure in the history of philosophy. In "George Lewes' Scientific Aesthetic: Restructuring the Ideology of the Symbol" (1987), scholar Peter Allan Dale has gone so far as to call Lewes "the Victorians' foremost philosopher of science after Mill."

PRINCIPAL WORKS

"The French Drama: Racine and Victor Hugo" (essay) 1840; published in journal *Westminster Review*

"Spinoza's Life and Works" (essay) 1843; published in journal *Westminster Review*

A Biographical History of Philosophy. 4 vols. (history and philosophy) 1845-46; revised as *The Biographical History of Philosophy from Its Origins in Greece Down to the Present Day,* 1857 and as *The History of Philosophy from Thales to Comte,* 1867

The Spanish Drama: Lope de Vega and Calderon (history and criticism) 1846

Ranthorpe (novel) 1847

Rose, Blanche, and Violet. 3 vols. (novel) 1848

The Noble Heart: A Tragedy, in Three Acts (play) 1849

Comte's Philosophy of the Sciences: Being an Exposition of the Principles of the "Cours de Philosophie Positive" of Auguste Comte (philosophy) 1853

The Life and Works of Goethe (biography) 1855; revised as *The Life of Goethe,* 1864

Sea-Side Studies at Ilfracombe, Tenby, the Scilly Isles, and Jersey (nonfiction) 1858

The Physiology of Common Life. 2 vols. (nonfiction) 1859-60

Studies in Animal Life (nonfiction) 1860

Aristotle: A Chapter in the History of Science (history) 1864

"Spinoza" (philosophy) 1866; published in journal *Fortnightly Review*

"Dickens in Relation to Criticism" (criticism) 1872; published in journal *Fortnightly Review*

Problems of Life and Mind. First Series: The Foundations of a Creed. 2 vols. (nonfiction) 1874-75

On Actors and the Art of Acting (criticism) 1875

The Physical Basis of Mind, Being the Second Series of Problems of Life and Mind (nonfiction) 1877

Problems of Life and Mind. Third Series. 2 vols. (nonfiction) 1879

The Principles of Success in Literature (criticism) 1891

Dramatic Essays [with John Forster] (criticism) 1896

Literary Criticism of George Henry Lewes (criticism) 1964

CRITICISM

Anthony Trollope (essay date 1 January 1879)

SOURCE: Trollope, Anthony. "George Henry Lewes." *Fortnightly Review* 25, no. 145 (1 January 1879): 15-24.

[*In the following essay, Trollope offers one of the first biographical sketches of Lewes. Written as a eulogy, the article places Lewes in the context of Victorian culture and science, and it lists and briefly evaluates Lewes's principal literary, philosophical, and scientific works.*]

On Wednesday the 4th of December a few loving friends stood over the grave in the Highgate Cemetery which received the body of George Henry Lewes, who was the first Editor of this Review. The papers of the day generously and for the most part correctly recorded the leading incidents of his peculiarly valuable literary life. But as he was our Editor when we first established this periodical, having undertaken the duty in compliance with my urgency, and as he was to me personally a most dear friend and a cherished companion, I purpose to say a few words in these pages as to his life and work.

He was born in April, 1817, in London, and was the grandson of Charles Lee Lewes, the well-known comedian. His father, I think, left no special mark in the world. His education was desultory, but wonderfully efficacious for the purposes of his life. Among many schools he was longer at Dr. Burney's at Greenwich than at any other. A part of his early years he spent at the Channel Islands, having been at school at Jersey, and a part in Brittany. To the latter was probably due his idiomatic knowledge of French. On leaving school he made various essays in life, going first into a notary's office and then as a clerk into a Russian merchant's house;—but with no serious intent on his own part to adhere to the work to which he was there expected to apply himself. From the nature of the books which he then bought when he could buy a book, and of the studies to which he really gave himself, it is manifest that philosophical research had fixed itself in his mind as the pursuit which would be dear to him. But philosophical research does not promise as a profession an early income, and George Lewes took to walking the hospitals with the purpose of joining the studies which he loved with the necessary work of earning his living. But here he was met by a physical weakness which he was unable to overcome. The horrors of the operating-room were too powerful for him, and he found himself able to study anatomy and physiology only as a part of his general education. In 1838 he went to Germany, still teaching himself, still apparently unfixed as to his future career, but with a vague conviction on his mind that if he would give himself to mental work, mental work would make to him some great return. He was one of those who have been gradually carried up into a career of literature by the tide of their own fitness. The progress of the tide has been certain; but there have been the painfully receding waves which have seemed at the time to deny rather than to promise advance. Nevertheless the water has run up and has filled its allotted space up to the brim.

As far as I can learn his earliest work,—earliest written though by no means the first published,—was the Tragedy in Three Acts called the *Noble Heart.* This was written as early as 1841, when he was twenty-four years old, and was published in 1850 with a dedication to his friend Mr. Helps. The dedication is remarkable for its indignant protest against those pruderies in literature, which through his whole life were odious to his taste. It was not however acted till 1849, when the author himself took the part of Don Gomez in the theatres at Manchester and Liverpool. I do not know enough of theatrical matters to be aware whether the piece is now held to be useful for stage purposes; but I am sure that it contains much fine poetry; as for instance,

GOMEZ.

> Oh! ye great glories of our race look down
> And bid me not forget from whence I sprang!
> Ye, who have lived and loved as princes should,
> Who never let your passions weaken pride,
> But kept, unswerving, on your noble course;
> Eagles who never mated but with those
> Who could confront the sun!

From this it will be seen that Lewes played on the public stage; but I believe I am right in saying that he never did so except in his own play, and then not for a salary. He played afterwards in Charles Dickens's private troupe, and throughout life was devoted to the stage as a poet and a critic.

Previous to the publication of the *Noble Heart,* but after the writing of it, he published a volume on the Spanish Drama in 1846, and two novels,—*Ranthorpe* in 1847, and *Rose, Blanche, and Violet,* in 1848. In 1848 he also published a *Life of Robespierre.* In the short space of these few pages it is impossible to offer anything of criticism on all these various works. Within the last day or two I have re-read *Ranthorpe,* and find it to be a tale, crude indeed with the hitherto unsatisfied ambition of a literary aspirant, but full of strong character. I have heard it spoken of as a failure,—one of the lost labours of the day. It was translated into German, and re-published by Tauchnitz; two facts which prove that it was not regarded as a failure by judges at the time who may be supposed to have known their business.

It might be presumed from these earlier published volumes that Lewes began his literary career with an intention of devoting himself to light literature. Some too may have been led to think so from remembering the success of his comedy, *The Game of Speculation,* which though published under the name of Slingsby Lawrence was well known to have been written by him. It is probable that many English ladies and gentlemen were intimately acquainted with *The Game of Speculation,* which first came out in 1851; and were conversant with the author's true name, who had never heard of the *Biographical History of Philosophy.* It would be natural to suppose that the young poet, the young novelist, the young dramatist was following his chosen avocation. But it was not so. From a period previous to the dates above given he had devoted himself to those philosophical researches on the foundation of which his honour and renown will stand. There was present to him always that necessity of working hard; and beyond that, more powerful even than that, there was a vivacity in the man, an irrepressible ebullition of sarcasm mixed with drollery, of comic earnestness and purpose-laden fun, which we who knew him never missed in his conversation even when his health was at the lowest and his physical sufferings were almost unbearable. These together,—the early want of an income and his own love of tragedy, satire and comedy,—induced those who saw only the palpably visible outside of the man to think that the philosophy of which they heard was, or at any rate in early years had been, only a second part with him. On this point I will quote here a passage from a short notice which appeared in the *Academy,* immediately after Lewes's death, written by Frederic Harrison:—

> If, as some writers have reminded us, Mr. Lewes began life as a journalist, a critic, a novelist, a dramatist, a biographer, and an essayist, it is as well to remember that he closed his life as a mathematician, a physicist, a chemist, a biologist, a psychologist, and the author of a system of abstract general philosophy.

To speak the whole truth, however, of our friend, it has to be added to this that while he was working as journalist, critic, and novelist, he was becoming the mathematician, the physicist, and the chemist whom the world has since recognised.

From the year 1841, down even to 1878, he supplied matter on various topics of general interest, literary, philosophical, historical, and scientific, to a world of magazines and reviews. *The Edinburgh* knew him, *The Foreign Quarterly, The British Quarterly, The Westminster, Knight's Cyclopædia, Fraser, Blackwood, The Cornhill, The Pall Mall, The Saturday,* and our own *Fortnightly.* From the old-established *Buff and Blue* coming out at three months' serious interval, down to the light evening sheet, there was no form of literary expression in which he did not delight and instruct. How little do they know, who talk of the padding of our periodicals, how much of the best thought which the nation produces is given to make up the cheap morsel of ephemeral literature which the recurring day puts into their hands with undeviating regularity! From 1851 to 1854 Lewes was editor of *The Leader,* and devoted himself very thoroughly, though not exclusively, to a paper which was thoroughly honest in its intention and deserved a better fate than was accorded to it. It was thus that he was earning his bread while he was doing his great work.

In 1845 and 1846 appeared in its first form,—in Knight's Cyclopædia,—the **Biographical History of Philosophy.** In 1857, in 1867, and again in 1871, this now appreciated work was again brought out, and at each time with elaborate revision. I annex here, also from the pen of Frederic Harrison, a statement of the effect produced by this great book. Our readers will agree that I could have applied to no fitter writer to speak on a subject which I am not able to treat worthily myself.

> Mr. Lewes opened his career in speculative thought by the four small volumes originally published by Knight, the **Biographical History of Philosophy.** This astonishing little work was designed to be popular, to be readable, to be intelligible. It was all of these in a singular degree. It has proved to be the most popular account of philosophy of our time; it has been republished, enlarged, and almost rewritten, and each re-issue has found new readers. It did what hardly any previous book on philosophy ever did—it made philosophy readable, reasonable, lively, almost as exciting as a good novel. Learners who had been tortured over dismal homilies on the pantheism of Spinoza, and yet more dismal expositions of the pan-nihilism of Hegel, seized with eagerness upon a little book which gave an intense reality to Spinoza and his thoughts, which threw Hegel's contradictories into epigrams, and made the course of philosophic thought unfold itself naturally with all the life and coherence of a well-considered plot. It was designed, we have said, to make philosophy intelligible, and this it undoubtedly accomplished. Tiros, learners, the long-suffering 'general reader,' even students, began to see that these strange peripeties of human thought—the fantastic, as it seemed, and perverse 'systems' of so many acute minds 'from Thales to Comte'—all meant something, could be explained as most ingenious attempts to answer very formidable problems: nay, that these systems, however antagonistic, and, it appeared, however disparate, grew out of one another in a reasonable sequence of human thought. It began to be clear what Pyrrho meant, when he said that we can know nothing but appearance, and even how Berkeley came to deny that we have any knowledge of matter. These whims, as it used to be thought, of great minds, all came to have a certain truth in them: and, what was more, they all had a very close relation to each other, a relation in part of cause and effect.

There can be no possible doubt as to the success of this method. Men to whom philosophy had been a wearisome swaying backwards and forwards of meaningless phrases, found something which they could remember and understand. Professors and professed students, of whatever special school, frowned, shook their heads, and were inclined to think that their mysteries were being trifled with, and their trade undermined. But, in spite of official discouragement and learned doubts, the new book triumphed. Students who forbore to quote it got their real information from it; professors and examiners looked askance, but they found their subject invested with a new interest, and they found in their pupils a new understanding of the matter. For a generation this little, unrecognised, 'entirely popular' book, saturated the minds of the younger readers. It has done as much as any book, perhaps more than any, to give the key to the prevalent thought of our time about the metaphysical problems. We have it on the authority of the *Times,* an authority not given to defy the dominant opinion of the day, that what cultivated Englishmen know of philosophy and of science is in great part due to the popular treatises of Mr. Lewes.

The question arises—Was he right? Was his method sound? Was his brilliant explanation of systems in accordance with sober judgment and ripe knowledge? As to this, of course, opinions must differ; and it cannot be denied that many stout and learned philosophers indignantly answer, No. It is the settled conviction of this present writer, who has studied these books again and again, now for thirty years, that, in the true sense of the term, the right answer is, Yes. If he did not know his books, ancient and modern, if he were merely making a light magazine paper of his philosophers, if his amusing tragi-comedy of the metaphysical imbroglio were a *jeu d'esprit,* or a clever paradox—then, undoubtedly, the book of Mr. Lewes was worthless, and worse than worthless. But it was not so. It has stood the test of time. Public opinion has accepted the substance of these brilliant analyses. They were based on real, though, of course, not specialist knowledge. The method of concatenation was sound. It was the invincible method of the Positive Philosophy. The book may have been an *aperçu,* and, perhaps, often *too* lively, *too* obvious: but it was the *aperçu* of a man of real genius, thoroughly master of a true method.

That such a book should have had such a triumph was a singular literary fact. The opinions frankly expressed as to theology, metaphysics, and many established orthodoxies; its conclusion, glowing in every page, that Metaphysic, as Danton said of the Revolution, was devouring its own children, and led to self-annihilation; its proclamation of Comte as the legitimate issue of all previous philosophy, and Positive Philosophy as its ultimate *irenicon*—all this, one might think, would have condemned such a book from its birth. The orthodoxies frowned; the professors sneered; the owls of metaphysic hooted from the gloom of their various jungles; but the public read, the younger students adopted it, the world learned from it the positive method; it held its ground because it made clear what no one else had made clear—what Philosophy meant, and why Philosophers differed so violently. Profound specialism continued its mission of making chaos more void and dark than it was from eternity. But the little half-crown book had simply killed Metaphysic. Its burial is a long and wearisome ceremony.

The popular treatises on Science did something of the same kind for Science that the *Biographical History* [*Biographical History of Philosophy*] had done for Philosophy. But there was not a tenth part of the same work to do. And Mr. Lewes was far more eminent in Philosophy than in Science. But there too his work will be memorable, in breaking up superstitions, in coordinating ideas, in suggesting new paths. Of his latest and mature work on Philosophy we do not now propose to speak. It has been in part examined at length in this Review, and we hope to continue the examination in detail. It was, in short, the special and mature exposition of the principles of which the *History of Philosophy* [revised title of *Biographical History of Philosophy*] had shown the building up in the entire course of human thought. We cannot forget that the work is yet incomplete, nor can we forget that we hope to read it completed, when animated and re-arranged by one to whom he intrusted at his death the great work of his life.

In 1853 Lewes published *Comte's Philosophy of the Sciences,* and in 1855 the first edition of his *Life of Goethe.* It is by this biography, perhaps, that he is best known to general readers. As a critical biography of one of the great heroes of literature it is almost perfect. It is short, easily understood by common readers, singularly graphic, exhaustive, and altogether devoted to the subject. It is one of those books of which one is tempted to say that he who has it before him to read, is to be envied. In 1858 followed the *Seaside Studies*; in 1859 and 1860, the *Physiology of Common Life,* and in 1862 the *Studies in Animal Life.* These last appeared first in the *Cornhill Magazine,*—in 1860,—running through the six first numbers of that periodical, and they mark the period when I first knew the friend whom I have lost. They were not republished till a year had elapsed. In 1864 he brought out his *Aristotle,* a chapter from *The History of Science* [*Aristotle: A Chapter in the History of Science*]. He says in his preface, "I have for many years prepared myself to attempt a sketch of the Embryology of Science, so to speak,"—did ever a man lay out for himself a more aspiring or a more difficult task,—"an exposition of the great *Momenta* on scientific development, and the present volume is the first portion of such an exposition, which I publish separately, because in itself it forms a monograph, and because I may never live to complete the larger scheme." That larger scheme was afterwards made to give way to the more constructive work to which the latter years of his life were devoted, and which has been published, as yet only partially, under the name of *Problems of Life and Mind.*

In 1874 came out the first volume, or rather the first series, of the *Problems of Life and Mind,—The Foundations of a Creed*—as the author entitles it. A review of this first volume will be found in our periodical, July, 1874, by Frederic Harrison. The second and third volumes appeared in 1875 and 1877, and the author was engaged on the fourth when he died. He has left it unfinished, but he had long been labouring on it, and it is trusted that it is in a state so far advanced, that far the larger portion may be presented to the public in a form closely accordant with his intentions. For the nature and position of a work of such wonderful scope in philosophical research I must refer our readers to that review in our own pages to which I have alluded.

In 1875 also there was published a volume entitled, *Actors and Acting,* which was a reprint of articles written in previous years.

I will now come to the connection which George Lewes had with this Review and the work he did for it. Early in the year 1865 a few men, better perhaps acquainted with literature than trade, conceived the idea,—an idea by no means new,—of initiating a literary "organ" which should not only be good in its literature, but strictly impartial and absolutely honest. This is not the place to point out what are perhaps sometimes imagined to be defects in other periodical reviews and magazines; but we were determined to avoid all such defects if such defects existed. We would get the best literature we could, and pay well for what we got whether good or bad. We would be thoroughly eclectic, opening our columns to all opinions. We would in all cases require the signature of the author for open publication, and we would think more of reputation than of profit. The enterprise was to belong to a Company, "Limited," which was duly formed, and was to be published by a publisher whose property in it was to be confined to the share which he might hold. That upon the whole the enterprise succeeded is proved by the existence, position and character of the Review at the present moment. Financially, as a Company, we failed altogether. We spent the few thousands we had collected among us, and then made over the then almost valueless copyright of the Review to the firm of publishers which now owns it. Such failure might have been predicted of our money venture without much sagacity from the first. But yet much was done. While our funds were gradually disappearing, the periodical was obtaining acknowledgment and character. That dream of eclecticism had to pass away. No Review can stand long which shall be colourless. It must be either with, or must be against some recognised set of opinions, either as to religion, politics, philosophy or other subject of commanding interest. It must be admitted of the Review as it now works, that it is very much with, and also very much against certain views on matters of commanding interest. Our present Editor is a man of opinions too far settled to admit of eclectic principles in literature. But the determination to produce good steady work, of whatever colour, has I think been recognised, and I think it may be granted that the Review has done very much towards introducing the French system of adding the signature of the authors to magazine writing.

Our first difficulty when we began our work in 1865 was to find an Editor fit for the task which was to be confided to him. Mr. Lewes's name was soon adopted by us, but there was much to be done in inducing him to undertake the work. To the proposal he lent all his heart, but he doubted his power to give us sufficient of his strength. To me it has often been a marvel that he should have lived and worked, and thoroughly enjoyed his life,—as he did with a relish beyond that of most healthy men,—when I have observed the frailness of his physical nature. It was for me to persuade him to undertake the office, if it might be so, and, anxious as I was, I could not but shrink from pressing him when he told me that he doubted his health. But at last, having taken a few days for final thought, he yielded, and on

15th of May, 1865, he brought out the first number of the Review. As long as he remained with us, he was indefatigable, enthusiastic, and thoroughly successful as to the matter which he produced for the public. He remained our Editor till the end of 1866, when he was forced to resign, wisely feeling that on behalf of Philosophy he was bound to husband what strength remained to him for higher work than that even of editing the *Fortnightly*. The Review then went into the hands of the present Editor—of whose merits it is not becoming that I should speak in his own paper.

But Lewes's connection with the Review was not then brought to an end,—has been brought to an end indeed only by the hand of death,—as may be seen by a paper from him on the **"Dread and Dislike of Science,"** which was published in the June number of 1878. Were I to speak of the lucidity of expression shown in the few pages which it fills, I should seem to imply some diminution in his capacity for lucid work as he drew near his end. Nothing could be more untrue of him. For ten days he was ill, painfully dangerously ill;—but up to that time he was free for his work with no slightest lessening of his brain power.

I have extracted a list of all that he wrote for the *Fortnightly*; but I do not know that a mere catalogue would serve our readers. There is a series of articles on the Principles of Success in Literature which I hope may be republished as a whole. There is criticism descending from Mr. Grote's Plato to the last new novel. There is biography, free inquiry into philosophical truths and untruths, and there is that pleasant chit chat with which most editors love occasionally to indulge themselves and their readers.

I will allude specially to a criticism on the works of Charles Dickens which appeared in the July number of 1872, because I think there is to be found in it the best analysis we have yet had of the genius of that wonderful man, and it displays at its best not only the critical acumen of the writer, but that special lucidity of expression from the want of which critical acumen so often becomes comparatively valueless. It may be remembered by those who have read Forster's *Life of Dickens*,—and who has not!—how angry that staunchest of biographers and most loving of friends was made, because the critic pointed out how Dickens by the strength of his imagination so subordinated his readers that they do not perceive, or at any rate do not suffer from, that want of reality which pervades his characters. With Lewes at the time I discussed very fully the passage in Forster's biography. He was greatly hurt by the charge made against him, because it seemed to indicate unfairness towards a fellow-author who was dead. John Forster is dead also. They were two loving honest friendly men, both of them peculiarly devoted to genius wherever they could find it. On behalf of Lewes I find myself bound to say that his was the simple expression of his critical intellect dealing with the work of a man he loved and admired,—work which he thought worthy of the thoughtful analysis which he applied to it.

Such is a short record of the work of him whom we have lost, and I think it will be admitted that we have to deplore the end of a career which has been most valuable to the world at large. I am sure that those who knew him personally as I did, will feel that a large portion of their life's pleasure has been taken away from them. To me personally Lewes was a great philosopher only because I was told so. When he would acquaint me with some newly found physical phenomenon, as that a frog could act just as well without his brains as with them,—I would take it all as gospel, though a gospel in which I had no part myself. When he would dilate on the perspicuity or the inaccuracy of this or the other philosopher,—in my presence, though probably for the advantage and delight of some worthier listener,—I would be careless as to his subject, though I loved his zeal. But though the philosopher was lost upon me, the humourist was to me a joy for ever. Sure no one man told a story as he did. To see him gradually rise from his chair and take his place standing between two or three of us! He must have known, though he never looked as though he knew it, that he was going to act a great part in mixed comedy and satire. Then by degrees he would pile up little incident on incident, the motion of his fingers assisting the peculiar fire of his eye, till in two minutes the point would have been made and the story told with all the finish of a jeweller's finest work. His personal appearance was admirably fitted for such scenes! His velvet coat and his neat slippers and the rest of his outward garniture looked,—as a man's clothes always should look,—as though they were there by chance, there of necessity but not much to be thought of; but they helped to make him a man peculiarly pleasant to the eye in conversation. No one could say that he was handsome. The long bushy hair, and the thin cheeks, and the heavy moustache, joined as they were, alas! almost always to a look of sickness, were not attributes of beauty. But there was a brilliance in his eye, which was not to be tamed by any sickness, by any suffering, which overcame all other feeling on looking at him. I have a portrait of him, a finished photograph, which he gave me some years since, in which it would seem as though his face had blazed up suddenly, as it often would do, in strong indignation against the vapid vauntings of some literary pseudo-celebrity. But the smile would come again, and before the anger of his sarcasm had had half a minute's play, the natural drollery of the man, the full overflowing love of true humour, would overcome himself, and make us love the poor satirised sinner for the sake of the wit his sin had created.

Perhaps it may be felt that in saying these last words almost over the grave of one so well beloved, and one so glorious for high acquirements and high achievements, I might better have abstained from such memorials of his lighter hours. I must excuse myself by saying that I have wanted to paint George Lewes as I knew him. Nor will those who think of him solely as a student in philosophy, of one who has devoted his life to research at the cost of lighter joys, understand his full character any better than he who shall imagine that, because he began his literary life with a few novels and a few dramas, he found in those the occupation most congenial to his soul. There was never a man so pleasant as he with whom to sit and talk vague literary gossip over a cup of coffee and a cigar. That he was a great philosopher, a great biographer, a great critic there is no doubt;—and as little that he has left behind him here in London no pleasanter companion with whom to while away an hour.

Raymond St. James Perrin (essay date 1905)

SOURCE: Perrin, Raymond St. James. "George Henry Lewes." In *The Evolution of Knowledge: A Review of Philosophy,* pp. 268-304. New York: Baker and Taylor, 1905.

[*In the following excerpts, Perrin appraises Lewes's achievement as an evolutionary philosopher, focusing primarily on Lewes's goal of fusing ideas of mind and matter into "one ultimate principle." Perrin illustrates how Lewes sought to replace the metaphysical belief in an "absolute or immutable type" with the evolutionary theory of the organic development of both animal and human species.*]

THE PRINCIPLES OF PSYCHOLOGY

George Henry Lewes directed the best efforts of his life to researches in mental phenomena. He felt that there was no hope of understanding consciousness until the metaphysical problem was solved. To solve this most difficult of all problems is to show that mind and matter are forms of one ultimate principle.

The philosophic system of Lewes bears the general name of *Problems of Life and Mind.* Two volumes are entitled *Foundations of a Creed,* and explain the nature of belief. The third volume deals with *Mind as the Function of the Organism,* and shows the identity of physical and mental energy. This volume constitutes an introduction to the posthumous works, entitled *The Physical Basis of Mind,* and *The Study of Psychology.*

In the preface to the opening volume Lewes says:

"In 1862 I began the investigation of the physiological mechanism of Feeling and Thought, and from that time forward have sought assistance in a wide range of research. Anatomy, Physiology, Pathology, Insanity and the Science of Language have supplied facts and suggestions. . . . The first result was such a mutual illumination from the various principles arrived at separately, that I began to feel confident of having something like a clear vision of the fundamental inductions necessary to the constitution of Psychology. The second result, which was independent of the first, arose thus: Finding the exposition obstructed by the existence of unsolved metaphysical problems, . . . and knowing that . . . the conceptions of Force, Cause, Matter and Mind, were vacillating and contradictory, I imagined that it would be practicable . . . at least to give such precise indications of the principles adopted throughout my exposition as would enable the reader to follow it untroubled by metaphysical difficulties."[1]

Here then, at the very outset, the metaphysical difficulty is encountered, but, as will later appear, instead of a positive a negative solution will be offered.

In the opening of Lewes' argument the following significant quotation from Mill occurs: "England's thinkers are again beginning to see, what they had only temporarily forgotten, that the difficulties of Metaphysics lie at the root of all Science; that those difficulties can be quieted only by being resolved, and that until they are resolved, positively whenever possible, but at any rate negatively, we are never assured that any knowledge, even physical, stands on solid foundations." Lewes was unable to offer a positive solution of the metaphysical problem because of his tentative acceptance of the theory of an unknowable, which implies a fundamental mystery. He was convinced, however, that both religion and science demand a positive solution of the problem of existence. In other terms, he held that so long as all avenues of research lead to mystery, it is impossible to unify knowledge. As will be shown, Lewes goes farther than any other writer, except, perhaps, Spencer, toward demonstrating the unity of knowledge.

The deep conviction that both religion and science require a positive solution of the metaphysical problem Lewes expressed in the following impressive words: "Assuredly some mighty new birth is at hand. Not only do we see Physics on the eve of a reconstruction through Molecular Dynamics, we also see Metaphysics strangely agitated, and showing symptoms of a reawakened life. After a long period of neglect and contempt, its problems are once more reasserting their claims. And whatever we may think of those claims, we have only to reflect on the important part played by Metaphysics in sustaining and developing religious conceptions, no less than in thwarting and misdirecting scientific conceptions, to feel assured that before Religion and Science can be reconciled by the reduction of their principles to a common method, it will be necessary to transfer Metaphysics or to stamp it out of existence.

There is but this alternative. At present Metaphysics is an obstacle in our path: it must be crushed into dust and our chariot-wheels must pass over it, or its forces of resistance must be converted into motive powers, and what is an obstacle become an impulse."[2]

As previously demonstrated, the metaphysical problem or the question of existence resolves itself into that of motion. Lewes vainly endeavored to divide this problem into the soluble and the insoluble. The insoluble part of the metaphysical problem he denominated *Metempirics,* or beyond experience. Now this term means precisely the same thing as metaphysics, for the physical is the world of sensible experience, and beyond sensible experience is mental experience, which is the field of metaphysics. As explained in Chapter IX, there are many unsolved but no insoluble problems. All problems can be reduced to one final relation, in the objective and subjective terms of which will be found its solution.

Those who examine the writings of Lewes will become convinced that consciousness is no longer a mystery. They will cease to regard the mind as an absolute entity, defying analysis, for Lewes demonstrates that consciousness is a phenomenon, or, in other terms, an individual expression of universal force.

Lewes removes the term Cause from the list of ultimates by showing that it denotes one aspect of every phenomenon, the other being Effect. He thus bequeaths to our age five universals, namely, Space, Time, Matter, Force and Motion. Matter he proves to be indistinguishable from space, because force in its deepest sense means motion; and in its restricted sense means motion considered apart from its material or space aspect; or simply Time. These conclusions are not given in direct terms, but that they are fair inferences from the course of reasoning pursued by Lewes the reader will have an opportunity of judging.

Although unable to refute it, Lewes instinctively opposed the theory of an unknowable. "A traditional perversion," says he, "makes the essence of a thing to consist in the relations of that thing to something . . . unknowable, rather than in its relations to a known or knowable—*i. e.,* assumes that the thing cannot *be* what it *is* to us and other known things, but must be something 'in itself,' unrelated, or having quite other relations to other unknowable things. In this contempt of the *actual* in favor of the vaguely imagined *possible,* this neglect of reality in favor of a supposed deeper reality, this disregard of light in the search for a light behind the light, metaphysicians have been led to seek the 'thing-in-itself' beyond the region of Experience."[3] Thus Lewes identifies the belief in an unknowable which is the root of all skepticism with the *à priori* philosophy, or the theory that all questions of phenomena are fundamentally insoluble, there being no real knowledge of external nature.

"The initial condition of metaphysical inquiry," says Lewes, "is that of separating the insoluble from the soluble aspects of each problem—but the question everywhere arises: What is insoluble? There are problems which are recognized as insoluble because of their conditions. For example, it is impossible to extract the square root of a number which is not made by the multiplication of any whole number or fraction by itself. To all eternity this must be impossible."

Now there is no doubt of the impossibility of extracting the square root of a number not made by multiplying any whole number or fraction by itself, because the impossibility has been purposely imposed. If an object weighs one hundred pounds, the impossibility of its weighing two hundred pounds is a matter of construction, it is the function of its weight, or, in other terms, of its conditions. This is all the impossibility and all the insolubility that exists in any question. No question rationally stated is impossible of solution, because every question is a form of the ultimate relation and can be reduced to its simplest terms. Hence, there are no insoluble, there are only unsolved questions.

Following this attempt at a metaphysical analysis are the chapters on the Principles of Psychology. In the opening chapter, Lewes says, that it would be premature to attempt a systematic treatise on Psychology, as there are still unsolved biological and metaphysical questions which it is necessary first to settle. In short, Lewes, who, on account of his great generalizing power and his familiarity with the structural and functional aspects of thought, was perhaps the best equipped man of his time to deal with the problems of Psychology, frankly admitted that the most important materials for the undertaking were lacking. He begins a "sketch of the programme of Psychology," with the reminder that Man is not simply an Animal Organism, but is also a unit in the Social Organism. He reminds us that Psychology occupies itself with the study of Consciousness: beyond this fact it is not obliged to look. This means that the psychologist feels no obligation to account for consciousness, although it is from this fact that he evolves his science. The psychologist regards mind; the mathematician regards motion; the physicist, force, and the biologist, life, as the ultimate fact in their respective fields of inquiry; but, according to Lewes, these scientists feel no necessity of affiliating this ultimate with universal change.

It is scarcely necessary to say that, although the mathematician may profess indifference as to the meaning of motion, and although the physicists may make no attempt to define force, or the biologists life, all this indifference is assumed. The last fact in each field of inquiry should be understood, that is to say, should be correlated with the ultimate reality. Nothing can exceed in importance this unification of knowledge, for it has the power of illuminating all research.

Psychology has no firm ground to stand on until mind and matter are reduced to a single principle. It is now well known that there can be no function without structure, which means that mind is a part of nature. The relation called gravitation, suggesting activities which are infinite, those relatively constant types of energy known as the chemical elements, the adjustments of organism and environment, including the development of feeling and thought from lower forms of life,—this vast plexus of conditions must be correlated before we can perceive the meaning of consciousness. Thus intelligence is taxed to its uttermost to comprehend its own nature, but it is finally persuaded that its functions and structures are an inseparable part of the universal economy.

It will be found that "The Programme of Psychology" as presented by Lewes is of commanding interest. Although the mind is an evolution of nature, it cannot be fully accounted for by a biological analysis, because both thought and feeling are more than the activity of a personal organism. The ordinary meaning of "person" must be greatly extended before it can be made to include all the phenomena of the intellect as well as of the emotions. The psychologist is aware that feeling is the source of thought, and that it is also the activity of a personal organism, but he is at a loss to explain the development of the one into the other without first comprehending the nature of language, that medium through which individuals of various times and places are brought into permanent relationship. Now the study of the relationship of individuals is known as sociology, an inquiry made possible by the evolution of language. Thus language accounts for the development of the life of the family into that of society. Words and sentences constitute the psychoplasm from which the individual draws its sustenance, bringing it into relation with its surroundings. To understand the structures and functions of mind, therefore, it is necessary to resolve consciousness into its biological and its sociological factors, and from the isolated views thus obtained to reconstruct a symmetrical whole. If the biological factors of consciousness offer only a partial explanation of mind, they at least supply us with the fundamental conditions of its theory. Of these substructures of the intellect Lewes says:

> Theoretically taking the organism to pieces to understand its separate parts, we fall into the error of supposing that the organism is a mere assemblage of organs, like a machine which is put together by juxtaposition of different parts. But this is radically to misunderstand its essential nature and the universal solidarity of its parts. The organism is not made, not put together, but evolved; its parts are not juxtaposed,

but differentiated; its organs are groups of minor organisms, all sharing in a common life, *i. e.,* all sharing in a common substance constructed through a common process of simultaneous and continuous molecular composition and decomposition; precisely as the great Social Organism is a group of societies, each of which is a group of families, all sharing in a common life—every family having at once its individual independence and its social dependence through connection with every other. In a machine, the parts are all different, and have mechanical significance only in relation to the whole. In an organism, *the parts are all identical in fundamental characters and* diverse only in their superadded differentiations: each has its independence, although all co-operate. The synthetical point of view, which should never drop out of sight, however the necessities of investigation may throw us upon analysis, is well expressed by Aristotle somewhere to the effect that all collective life depends on the separation of offices and the concurrence of efforts. In a vital organism, every force is the resultant of *all* the forces; it is a disturbance of equilibrium, and equilibrium is the equivalence of convergent forces. When we speak of Intelligence as a force which determines actions, we ought always to bear in mind that the efficacy of Intelligence depends on the organs which co-operate and are determined: it is not pure Thought which moves a muscle, neither is it the abstraction Contractility, but the muscle which moves a limb.[4]

The crisis of the argument then comes in these words: "That Life is Change, and that Consciousness is Change, has always been affirmed. It remains only to add that the changes are serial, and convergent through a *consensus determined by essential community of structure.*"[5] Thus Lewes reveals the identity of physical and mental function by pointing out the community of physical and mental structure.

The aim of Psychology is to show that mental life is a part of nature. Tennyson's idea that "The thoughts of men are widened by the process of the suns" means that body and mind are inseparable parts of the cosmos. To express this truth in the simplest terms, organic movements, which include all mental phenomena, are distinguished from inorganic movements only by their higher complexity.

Biology follows the development of organisms from the monad to the man, and also from the germ to the adult in each type. This science, however, confines itself to the individual and its physical medium. The psychical medium of each organism is language, the most potent of all structural developments, because it brings individual minds into communication. Biology investigates the relation of the organism and its physical medium; psychology the relation of the organism and its mental medium. The primary law of biology is that "Every vital phenomenon is the product of the two factors, the Organism and its Medium." The primary law of psychology is that "Every mental phenomenon is the prod-

uct of the two factors, subject and object." Now it is to be observed that these two sets of terms are in the deepest sense identical. They are distinguishable only relatively, as are mind and matter.

Thus biology and psychology are reciprocal. They investigate respectively the physical and the mental aspects of life showing that the relation of the individual and its environment is only another name for that of subject and object. "Modern psychology," says Lewes, "replaces the old dualism in which subject and object were two independent and unallied existences, by a Monism, in which only one existence, under different forms, is conceived. The old conception was of life in conflict with the external; the new conception recognizes their identity, and founds this recognition on the demonstrable fact that external forces instead of tending to destroy Life (according to Bichat's view), are the very materials out of which Life emerges, and by which it is sustained and developed."[6]

Lewes reminds us, however, that a complete psychology is impossible "until there is something like a general agreement concerning many questions of fundamental importance, these being partly biological and partly metaphysical."

It is to be observed that all biological and metaphysical questions can be solved by the unification of mind and matter or of subject and object. This unification depends upon our ability to prove that both subject and object occupy space as well as time, a proof that can be reached only by an analysis of our ideas of space and time. In order to see the connection between time and the subjective, and between space and the objective aspect of existence, it is necessary to observe that the subject occupies space, and, therefore, has space relations; and that the object occupies time, and, therefore, has time relations. The idea of space is generated by attending to co-existence or existences considered simultaneously (or apart from time). The idea of time is generated by considering sequence, or a serial existence as distinguished from all other existences (or apart from space). It is clear that the only existence we can realize apart from all other existences, is our own; but we must remember that to each individual the power that others have of being conscious is a part of objective nature, only relatively separable from the cosmos.

Thus we get an idea of how the primordial notions of time and space, the most abstract forms of subject and object, are formed. In forming this dual idea, however, we have been employing symbols, or language, that medium which brings individuals into communication.

Language springs from the attempt to compare and to communicate images. Upon this subject Lewes says: "It was perfectly clear that in imagination must be sought the first impulse toward explanation; and, therefore, all primitive explanations are so markedly imaginative. Images being the subjective or ideal form of Sensation, the Logic (or sequence) of Images is the first stage of intellectual activity; and is, therefore, predominant in the early history of individuals and of nations. The first attempt to explain a phenomenon must be to combine the images of past sensations with the sensations now felt, so as to form a series. In the next stage, words, representatives of abstractions (of experience), take the places of both images and objects. Thus the Logic of Signs (or language) replaces the Logic of Images, as the Logic of Images replaces the Logic of Sensation."[7] By means of images or symbols, therefore, that higher medium called language is formed. In every sentence subject and object unite in the verb, which is the symbol of action or being, and separate as its aspects, time and space. Thus mind and matter are the unity and the variety of nature, the subjective and objective terms of the universal relation.

EXPERIENCE AND BELIEF

Such is the continuity of mind that those apparently widely separate phases of consciousness known as experience and belief can be shown to have the same ultimate meaning; that is to say, they are both forms of feeling and therefore of universal change.

"The absolute," says Lewes, "is known to us in feeling which in its most abstract expression is change." Not only are experience and belief interdependent forms of this ultimate relation, but the problem of proof or of reality which is at the very basis of psychology can be reduced to that of motion.

No philosophical question is more often agitated, than the nature of belief. It is generally supposed that credence is voluntary, or, in other words, that conviction is given or withheld at will, but there is no greater delusion, for as will later appear, belief is determined by influences far beyond our control. We imagine that faith is free because it is an evolution of feeling, and that the will is free because it springs from the same source. We have only to realize that by far the greater part of our intellectual activities are unconscious to become convinced that opinions are formed of their own accord.

Belief is never at rest. Though the movements are at times imperceptible, conviction rises and falls with the tide of investigation and verification. The only belief that is unchangeable is that of change itself.

Belief is the voice of experience; or a result of the actions and reactions of individual and environment. To comprehend how it is formed, we must learn to affiliate our experiences with universal energy; that is to say, we must reduce to their prime factors those organic actions and reactions from which both feeling and thought are evolved.

Every influence affecting the organism, whether exerted during life, or throughout that vast series of lives leading up to each individual, is in the deepest sense a factor of mind, and, therefore, of belief. If experiences were always conscious, we could easily discern their origin, but only an infinitesimal part of them are sufficiently centralized to constitute attention. Consciousness is an equilibrium moving over the sentient deep. The waves of sentiency are forms of universal force.

For the same reason that there is no ultimate difference between matter and force, there is none between body and mind,—terms which represent respectively the structural and functional aspects of the sensorium. There is no more direct way of gaining a comprehension of the nature of experience and belief than by following the investigations of Lewes in neural phenomena, because they identify the activities of body and mind.

As explained in the previous chapter, the fundamental question of psychology is that of subject and object. To correlate these opposite aspects of existence is to unify knowledge.

> "We cannot," says Lewes, "stir a step in the exposition of subject and object without presupposing to be already settled fundamental questions which are still under discussion. No explanation can be given of matter which does not involve a conception of force."

What Lewes means by the above is that we cannot explain consciousness until we perceive that the matter and force of mind are identical with matter and force in general.

> "The main question," continues Lewes, "must remain nebulous so long as we are without a precise definition of Experience. The term is very variously and very laxly used. I have defined it as 'the Registration of Feeling.' And what is Feeling? It is the reaction of the sentient Organism under stimulus. Observe, it is not the reaction of an organ, but of the Organism—a most important distinction, and rarely recognized.
>
> "The response of a sensory organ . . . is not an *experience,* unless it be *registered* in a modification of structure, and thus be *revivable,* because a statical condition is requisite for a dynamical manifestation. Rigorously speaking, of course, there is no body that can be acted on without being modified; every sunbeam that beats against the wall alters the structure of that wall; every breath of air that cools the brow alters the state of the organism. But such minute alterations are inappreciable for the most part by any means in our possession, and are not here taken into account, because, being annulled by subsequent alterations, they do not become *registered* in the structure. We see many sights, read many books, hear many wise remarks; but, although each of these has insensibly affected us, changed our mental structures, so that 'we are a part of all that we have met,' yet the registered result, the *residuum,* has perhaps been very small. While, therefore, no excitation of Feeling is really without some corresponding

modification of Structure, it is only the excitations which produce lasting modifications that can be included under Experience. A feeling passed away and incapable of revival, would never be called an experience by any strict writer. But the feelings registered are psycho-statical elements, so that henceforward when the organism is stimulated it must react along these lines, and the product will be a feeling more or less resembling the feeling formerly excited."[8]

Hence the organism as a whole responds to each stimulus and if the response can be revived, however, faintly, it can be regarded as an experience, because it has educated or modified, or as the psychologists would say, it can be remembered. Observe, however, that in the deepest sense, all the modifications of an organism, and hence all the activities of that organism, whether conscious or unconscious, belong directly or indirectly to the sum of its experiences and its beliefs.

"Mind," says Lewes, "is commonly spoken of in oblivion of the fact that it is an abstract term expressing the sum of mental phenomena. As an abstraction, it comes to be regarded in the light of an entity, or separate *source* of the phenomena which *constitute* it. In like manner a thought, which as a product is simply an *embodied process,* comes to be regarded in the light of something distinct from the process; and thus two aspects of one and the same phenomenon are held to be two distinct phenomena. Because we abstract the material of an object from its form, considering each apart, we get into the habit of treating form as if it were in reality separable from material. By a similar illusion we come to regard the process (of thinking) apart from the product (thought), and, generalizing the process, we call it Mind, or Intellect, which then means no longer the mental phenomena condensed into a term, but the *source* of these phenomena. . . .

"It is experiment and verification which convince us that the air is a material object capable of being weighed and measured. It is experiment and verification which convince us that thought is an embodied process, which has its conditions in the history of the race no less than in that of the individual."[9]

The prevailing method of teaching psychology is dwelt upon with no little scorn by Lewes. Everything, says this author, is prepared in advance for the student. The physical activities are carefully demarcated from the mental. These demarcations are more than analytical; they are made to appear fixed, if not absolute, and they are never removed in order to afford a synthetic view of the operations of the sensorium as a whole.

In the analysis of feeling, thought and action given in a previous chapter, the artificiality of the distinctions made between the different phases of nervous action was pointed out. The idea that mind means something wholly different from body has become so prevalent that, until the futility of the distinction is exposed, too much emphasis cannot be laid upon the error. For instance, some psychologists believe that the cerebral hemispheres are the seat of combination for all the senses. That is to say, all the co-ordinations of sense resulting in consciousness are believed to take place in the brain. It is said that only in these brain structures are sensations transformed into thoughts.

"The cerebral hemispheres," says Lewes, "considered as organs, are similar in structure and properties to the other nerve-centres; the laws of sensibility are common to both; (and) the processes are alike in both; in a word, the Brain is only one organ (a supremely important one!) in a complex of organs, whose *united* activities are necessary for the phenomena called mental. . . . The assignment of even Thinking (exclusively) to the cerebral hemispheres is purely hypothetical. Whatever may be the evidence on which it rests, it must still be acknowledged to be an hypothesis awaiting verification. This may seem incredible to some readers, accustomed to expositions which do not suggest a doubt— expositions where the course of an inexpression is described as progressing, from the sensitive surface along the sensory nerve to its ganglion, from thence to a particular spot in the Optic Thalamus (where the impression is said to become a sensation), from that spot to cells in the upper layer of the cerebral convolutions (where the sensation becomes an idea), from thence downward to a lower layer of cells (where the idea is changed into a volitional impulse), and from thence to the motor-ganglia in the spinal cord, where it is reflected on the motor-nerves and muscles.

"Nothing is wanting to the *precision* of this description. Everything is wanting to its *proof.* The reader might suppose that the course had been followed step by step, at least, as the trajectory of a cannon-ball, or the path of a planet is followed: and that where actual observation is at fault, calculation is ready to fill up the gap. Yet what is the fact? It is that not a single step of this involved process has ever been observed; the description is imaginary from beginning to end."[10]

Lewes does not question the fact that the grey matter of the brain performs by far the greater part of the work known as thought. Since the composition of the grey matter indicates that it contains the highest molecular multiples, competent authorities now agree that the mind is that part of the sensorium capable of the greatest molecular activity. What Lewes would emphasize is the solidarity or interdependence of the whole nervous system. Evidence is yet to be adduced that any part of the sensorium is exempt from participation in the operation known as thought. In *The Physical Basis of Mind* Lewes shows that after the brain of a certain animal has been removed, sensations, emotions, instincts, and even volitions are manifested. Hence it is impossible to sustain the theory that the brain is the exclusive seat of either feeling or thought. Since all the operations of the mind are from moment to moment dependent upon physical conditions, every activity of the organism is a more or less direct factor of consciousness. Not only are mental aberrations traceable to functional disorders, but all moral derelictions can be shown to be the consequence of abnormal conditions. No tissue or organ of the body is without influence in its intellectual and, therefore, in its moral determinations.

Although not the sole organ of mind, the brain is by far the most important one. "We must," says Lewes, "no longer isolate the cerebrum from the rest of the nervous system, assigning it as the exclusive seat of sensation, nor suppose that it has laws of grouping which are not at work in the other centres. . . . The soul is a history, and its activities the product of that history. Each mental state is a state of the whole sensorium; one stroke sets the whole vibrating."[11]

In the widest sense, therefore, the sensorium is the whole living organism. So delicately are its many parts adjusted that all vibrate to every stimulus. Although various combinations of nerve fibrils, fibres, and cells form nerve and ganglia, and as such are easily distinguishable, still, considered as a whole, the nervous system has no absolute demarcations from the organism. As it is impossible to determine where nerve ends and muscle begins, so it is impossible to isolate nervous from physical excitement. In this connection Spencer says, "that throughout the entire fabric of Mind, the method of composition remains the same from the formation of its simplest feeling up to the formation of those immense and complex aggregates of feelings characterizing its highest developments."[12]

From a functional point of view, therefore, the sensorium is that part of the organism capable of the greatest molecular activity, which definition, as above indicated, is also applicable to mind. Hence when we trace the development of the nervous system from rudimentary forms of life to the highest types it becomes manifest that the progress of thought is identical with that of physical organization.

In explaining reflex action, the attempt is often made to isolate the nervous arc from the rest of the system; or, in other terms, to demarcate reflex action from its surrounding states. The discovery that in certain animals, after the removal of the brain, co-ordinated movements take place in the extremities, indicates that co-ordinations do not originate in the brain. In fact, "when isolated from the organism, no single organ has a function at all." This principle, differently expressed, is that no activity, whether physical or mental, can be separated (otherwise than ideally) from the complex of activities known as individual life.

"The brain," says Lewes, "is simply one element in a complex mechanism, each part of which is a component of the Sensorium or Sentient Ego. We may consider the several elements as forming a plexus of sensibilities, the solidarity of which is such that while each in a particular way may be stimulated separately, no one of them can be active without involving the activity

of all the others. . . . Hence, when we reduce the abstract term Mind to its concretes, namely, states of the sentient mechanism, the 'power of the Mind' simply means the stimulative and regulative processes which ensue on sentient excitation. We may now formulate a conclusion: Sensibility is the special property of the nervous tissue. Every bit of that tissue is sensitive in so far that it is capable of entering as a *sensible component* into a group the resultant of which is a *feeling—i. e.,* a change in the state of the sentient organism. *The Sensorium is the whole which reacts on the stimulation of any particular portion of the whole.*"[13] Now this generalization of Lewes brings into view the vast mechanism of thought and feeling acting and reacting with the unity and the variety characteristic of nature.

The aversion to the theory that all intellectual and moral activities are governed by mechanical laws is the result of a cramped and inadequate idea of the character and extent of mechanics. For instance, the most devout person would not object to the assertion that all the activities of nature, from the evolutions of the heavenly spheres to the life of plants and animals, are guided by the hand of God, and that this same guidance is manifested in every feeling and thought. And yet these words may be interpreted as meaning that Motion is the ultimate fact in all phenomena, whether subjective or objective, uniting mind and matter, or consciousness and nature.

Lewes fixed upon feeling as the ultimate of experience, and upon experience as the ultimate of belief. Thus he expanded the meaning of feeling so as to include on the one hand sensation, and upon the other thought. In their most abstract form experience and belief are changes in the sentient mechanism. This idea Lewes expressed as clearly as was possible without employing the instrument of an ultimate analysis. It can be seen from his argument on the "Principles of Certitude" that he practically rejected the unknowable in favor of the unknown. By rejecting the theory of an unknowable, he has shown that experience is infinite, or that the conscious and the unconscious are only opposite views of universal energy.

The Greeks evolved the science of logic from analogy, the moderns from identity. In the deepest sense these methods are one, for all analogies the simplest is the identity of subject and object, or of space and time, the opposite aspects of the ultimate relation. Thus the terms of all equations can be reduced to the subjective and the objective aspects of motion.

According to Lewes, "Truth is the equivalence of the terms of a proposition; and the equivalence is tested by the reduction of the terms to an identical proposition."[14] Is it not clear that this "identical proposition" is the ultimate generalization? Spencer said that the final test of truth is indirect or negative; by which he meant that the ultimate of proof is that equilibrium expressed in our inability to doubt. Instead of being a conscious determination, therefore, belief is for the most part involuntary. Our opinions are formed of their own accord. Belief, or the satisfaction of doubt, is simply the balance of internal and external forces through the medium of language, a balance formed for the most part without our consent.

"All knowledge," says Lewes, "begins with the discernment of resemblances and differences; it is necessarily polar, resemblance being impossible except on a background of difference, and difference being impossible except on a background of resemblance. While knowledge begins here, it ends with the equation. The resemblances abstracted from all accompanying differences, and reduced to the identity of equivalence."[15]

From the foregoing it can be seen that consciousness is the evolution of identity from difference; of unity from variety, or of subject from object.

The wonder concerning Lewes' philosophy is, that he could have been so explicit in identifying the matter and force of mind with matter and force in general, declaring them to be aspects of motion, and yet that he should never have hit upon the idea of identifying space with matter and time with force, thus bringing the most general terms of existence into interdependence. This wonder increases as we read such luminous definitions of Motion as the following: "Here arises a complication which will beset the whole discussion unless we form distinct ideas of the separation of matter and force as a purely analytical artifice. The two abstractions are but two aspects of the same thing; a separation rendered inevitable by the polarity of Experience, which everywhere presents Existence under passive and active aspects. Force is not something superadded to Matter, it is Reals viewed in their dynamic aspect; Matter is not something different from Force, but Reals viewed in their statical or passive aspect; *either is unthinkable without the other.* Force is immanent in Matter, and Matter is immanent in Force. The schoolmen called Matter *potentia passiva,* and Force *virtus activa.*" Only logically can they be considered apart.[16]

Here Lewes clearly recognized that Motion is the union of the dynamical and the statical aspects of nature, or the one relation of which time and space are respectively the subjective and the objective terms. Although the most advanced physicists recognize this principle of the universality of Motion, they are far from rendering it in simple and concise language. Thus we read in the well-known work of Thomson and Tait: "We cannot, of course, give a definition of matter which will satisfy the metaphysician, but the naturalist may be content to know matter as *that which can be perceived by the*

senses, or as *that which can be acted upon by* or *can exert force.* The latter, and indeed the former also, of these definitions involves the idea of Force."[17]

In the treatise of Lewes on the Nature of Matter, in Problem IV., we have an example of the lengths to which these discussions are carried. Here the extension, impenetrability, infinite divisibility, indestructibility, gravity, and inertia of matter are considered, the one definite conclusion arrived at being that matter is the symbol of all objectivity, which is equivalent to its identification, first, with extension, or space, and, finally, with motion.

Problem V. is entitled "Force and Cause," and VI. "The Absolute in the Correlations of Feeling and Motion." The former shows conclusively that Cause and Effect are the opposite views of every phenomenon, and therefore imply each other.

In closing Problem VI., we find Lewes again triumphant over all difficulties. After many failures he at last reaches the universal principle, enabling us to overlook the futile attempts of previous chapters to coordinate universals. Although failing to perform this last analysis by showing the relationship of ultimate terms, by another route, he arrives at the same result. Witness the closing words of Problem VI., which is without doubt the best attempt thus far made to describe thought without the aid of that most fundamental of all experiences and beliefs, our consciousness of existence as the ultimate generalization.

> "Existence"—the Absolute—is known to us in feeling, which in its most abstract expression is Change, external and internal. The external changes are symbolized as motion, because that is the mode of Feeling into which all others are translated when objectively considered; objective consideration being the attitude of *looking at* the phenomena, whereas subjective consideration is the attitude of any other sensible response, so that the phenomena are different to the different senses. There is no real break in the continuity of Existence; all its modes are but differentiations. We cannot suppose the physical organism and its functions to be other than integrant parts of the Cosmos from which it is formally differentiated; nor can we suppose the psychical organism and its functions to be other than integrant parts of this physical organism from which it is ideally separated. Out of the infinite modes of Existence a group is segregated, and a planet assumes individual form; out of the infinite modes of this planetary existence smaller groups are segregated in crystals, organisms, societies, nations. Each group is a special system, having forces peculiar to it, although in unbroken continuity with the forces of all other systems. Out of the forces of the animal organism a special group is segregated in the nervous mechanism, which has its own laws. If ideally we contrast any two of these groups—a planet with an organism, or an organism with a nervous mechanism—their great unlikeness seems to for-

bid identification. They are indeed different, but only because they have been differentiated. Yet they are identical, under a more general aspect. In like manner, if we contrast the world of Sensation and Appetites with the world of Conscience and its Moral Ideals, the unlikeness is striking. Yet we have every ground for believing that Conscience is evolved from Sensation, and that Moral Ideals are evolved from Appetites; and thus we connect the highest mental phenomena with vital Sensibility, Sensibility with molecular changes in the organism, and these with changes in the Cosmos.

This unification of all the modes of Existence by no means obliterates the distinction of modes, nor the necessity of understanding the special characters of each. Mind remains Mind, and is essentially opposed to Matter, in spite of their identity in the Absolute; just as Pain is not Pleasure, nor Color either Heat or Taste, in spite of their identity in Feeling. The logical distinctions represent real differentiations, but not distinct existents. If we recognize the One in the many, we do not thereby refuse to admit the Many in the One.[18]

Here the term absolute (or time) is used in the place of motion or the ultimate reality, but the unity of the argument rises above this verbal defect. The idea which Lewes seeks to convey is that the most general terms of life and mind are modes of a single principle, to which they bear a definite and comprehensible relation.

THE UNITY OF MIND AND MATTER

The remaining three volumes of Lewes' system were written not in the attempt to find an ultimate analysis, but as a treatise upon physiological Psychology. They contain little, therefore, that is strictly metaphysical. The first is entitled the **Physical Basis of Mind,** and presents the following problems: "The Nature of Life;" "The Nervous Mechanism;" "Animal Automatism," and "The Reflex Theory." The second deals with the problems: "Mind as a Function of the Organism;" "The Sphere of Sense and the Logic of Feeling;" "The Sphere of Intellect and the Logic of Signs," and the last is the brief work entitled **The Study of Psychology.**

Those who look deeply into organic life find it difficult to avoid the theory of a design in nature. The form of imagery, known as design, is so closely associated with all human effort that we are apt to attribute it to the efforts of nature.

As a rule, the theory of design has been adopted by zoölogists. Thus Von Baer, in his great work, has a section entitled "The Nature of the Animal Determines its Development." This author affirms that every stage in development is made possible by its pre-existing condition, but nevertheless the entire development is determined by the *nature* of the animal which is about to be. As will appear by reference to his work when he uses the term *nature* Von Baer means an absolute or immutable type. "The form which this superstition generally

takes," says Lewes, "is the belief that an organism is determined by its type, or, as the Germans say, its idea. All its parts take shape according to this ruling plan; consequently, when any part is removed, it is reproduced according to the idea of the whole of which it forms a part.

"At first the Type or Idea was regarded as an objective reality, external to the organism that it was supposed to rule. Later on this notion was replaced by an approach to the more rational interpretation, that is to say, the Idea was made an internal, not an external, force, and was incorporated with the material elements of the organism, which were said to 'endeavor' to arrange themselves according to the Type. Thus Treveranus declares that the seed "dreams of the future flower."

Lewes characterizes this theory as "eminently metaphysical" (superstitious), because, as he says, it refuses to acknowledge the operation of immanent properties,—refuses to admit that the harmony of a complex structure results from the mutual and natural relations of its parts, and seeks *outside* the organism for some mysterious force, some plan, not otherwise specified, which regulates and shapes the parts. The meta-physiologists admit "that *every separate stage* in development is the necessary sequence of its predecessor, but declare nevertheless that the *whole of the stages* are independent of such relations and inherent properties."

By attacking the "superstition of the nerve-cell," that theory of peculiar vital forces "wholly unallied with the primary energy of motion," Lewes illuminates the whole subject of organic development. He points out the relation existing between the high molecular complexity of protoplasm, and the less complex structure of inorganic substances. He maintains that the difference in the activities of the two classes of substances represents their degrees of structural complexity. So far-reaching are its consequences that this generalization is not readily appreciated.

Natural selection operates through assimilation and reproduction, and is, therefore, necessarily associated with the emotions, but this force reaches far beyond the emotions, to chemical and to cosmical attractions. In fact, all organic development is a selection operating along lines of least resistance. The struggle for existence or the competition and antagonism of organisms extends to the "competition and antagonism" of *tissues and organs* for existence. The potentialities of tissues and organs is, therefore, inherent in their chemical and cosmic conditions. That is to say, cosmic or universal force is expressed in chemical energy, which in turn expresses itself in organic as well as in super-organic life.

"When a crystalline solution takes shape," says Lewes, "it always takes a definite shape, which represents what may be called the *direction* of its forces, the polarity of its constituent molecules. In like manner when an organic plasmode takes shape—crystallizes, so to speak—it always assumes a specific shape dependent on the polarity of its molecules. Crystallographers have determined the several forms possible to crystals; histologists have recorded the several forms of Organites, Tissues, and Organs. Owing to the greater variety in elementary composition, there is in organic substance a more various polar distribution than in crystals; nevertheless there are sharply defined limits never overstepped, and these constitute what may be called the specific forms of Organites, Tissues, Organs, Organisms."[19]

As held by the extreme school, the theory of the origin of living things is that all animal life has descended from a single organic point, and that the subsequent differences are the result of modifications in the environment, resulting in differences in the descendants of this first organism. The less extreme school holds that (to use Darwin's words) "animals have descended from at most only *four or five progenitors,* and plants from an equal or less number."

In examining both of these positions, Lewes asks for a more thorough analysis of the facts than is given by either school. He held Darwin in affectionate reverence, and regarded his great work as indispensable, inasmuch as it gave the first adequate presentation of that aspect of organic development now known as Natural Selection. Lewes shows, however, that the Darwinian theory accounts for only a part of the facts. Striking as are the points of resemblance between plants and animals, the *differences* are irreconcilable with a theory of common descent from a single cell at a single point upon the earth's surface. Throughout all stages of its past metamorphosis, the proportion of the principal organic elements on the earth's surface has been relatively constant. There is no reason to doubt, therefore, that the beginnings of terrestrial life were both wide-spread and multifarious. The kinship of the inorganic and the organic is a fact quite as remarkable as that of the plant and the animal kingdoms. Surely the evolution of solar and of stellar systems can account for the changes which have taken place upon a single planet, including all the phases of its inorganic, its organic and its social phenomena. If we view the facts from a sufficiently remote point in the cosmos, therefore, there will be no need of introducing any mysterious beginning to terrestrial life, for it is manifestly a consequence of universal conditions.

"Upon what principle," inquires Lewes, "are we to pause at the cell or protoplasm? If by a successive elimination of differences we reduce all organisms to the cell, we must go on and reduce the cell itself to the chemical elements out of which it was constructed; and inasmuch as these elements are all common to the inorganic world, the only difference being one of synthesis, we reach a result which is the stultification of all classification, namely, the assertion of a kinship which is universal."

Passing from general to intellectual phenomena, Lewes exposes the assumption so often made by writers on mental physiology. Although his explanation of this assumption is somewhat elaborate for so brief a review, it is nevertheless of sufficient importance to warrant the following reproduction:

"The most abridged expression of the action observed in the sensorium is, by common consent, called the nervous arc. Anatomists note that the motor nerves issue from the anterior side of the spinal cord (that which in animals is the under side), and that the sensory nerves issue from the posterior side, (that which in animals is the upper side). Like the cerebrum, the spinal cord is a double organ, but in the former the gray structure is mainly external, while in the spinal cord it is internal. In the development of the nervous system from the embryo, "the outermost layer of the germinal membrane of the embryo develops a groove, which deepens as its sides grow upward and finally close over and form a canal. Its foremost extremity soon bulges into three well-marked enlargements which are then called the *primitive* cerebral vesicles. The cavities of these vesicles, known as the Fore-brain, Middle-brain and Hind-brain are continuous, and the continuity of the walls and cavities of these vesicles is never obliterated throughout the subsequent changes. This continuity is also traceable throughout the medulla spinalis."

"Microscopic investigation reveals that underneath all the morphological changes the walls of the whole cerebrospinal axis are composed of similar elements on a similar plan. The conclusions which directly follow from the above are, first, that *since the structure of the great axis is everywhere similar, the properties must be similar;* secondly, that *since there is structural continuity, no one part can be called into activity without at the same time more or less exciting that of all the rest.*"

When we consider the continuity of structure and function throughout the sensorium and the inevitable dependence of all its constituent elements upon chemical and cosmical conditions, we begin to realize that our feelings and thoughts form an inseparable part of the rhythms of nature. There are those, however, who feel degraded by the thought that they are an integral part of the economy of the universe. They believe that their individuality is of a higher order than that of nature.

Lewes complains of the tendency to draw absolute dividing lines between the various functions of the sensorium. When a stimulus is applied to the skin it is followed by a muscular movement or a glandular secretion accompanied by various degrees of consciousness. These familiar experiences are interpreted by neurologists as neural processes. All the other processes are left out of account. Even in the neural process the organs are neglected for the sake of the nervous *tissue,* and the nervous tissue for the sake of the *nerve-cell.*

Whether it be a muscular movement, a glandular secretion, an emotion, or a thought, the neurologist represents the activity of the sensorium about as follows: "The nerve-cell is the supreme element, the origin of the nerve-fibre, and the fountain of nerve-force. The cells are connected one with another by means of fibres, and with muscles, glands, and centres, also by means of fibres, *which are merely channels for the nerve-force.* A stimulus at the surface is carried by a sensory fibre to a cell in the centre; from that point it is carried by another fibre to another cell; and from that by a third fibre to a muscle; a reflex action results;— this is the elementary nervous arc." The passage of an excitation, therefore, into the labyrinths of the sensorium and out again (until it emerges in action) is said to describe the nervous arc.

Briefly stated the theory of the nervous arc is, "that one fibre passes into the spinal cord, and, that another passes out of it, and that a movement is produced usually preceded by a sensation and sometimes by a thought." But investigation proves that the continuity of the nerve-fibre, from cell to cell, through the spinal cord, which is supposed to separate the simpler reflexes from consciousness, is purely imaginary. In other terms, the path of energy in the sensorium is governed by the same laws of polarity or attraction as those that prevail in the inorganic world. Hence whether the action is that of the formation of a crystal in the mother liquid, or that of a frog after the brain has been removed, repelling the point of the scalpel from one leg by pushing it away with the other, or that of a statesman endeavoring to solve some problem of government, the same order of structure acts and reacts with the same order of environment, the same potentialities are called into play. The efforts of the inorganic, of the organic and of the social worlds are, therefore, distinguished ultimately only by the degrees of their complexity, degrees which can be expressed in terms of time and space. In short, physiologists, as well as neurologists, are beginning to perceive that it is impossible to isolate reflex action upon the one hand from sensibility and thought, and upon the other from inorganic nature.

Assuming that consciousness has its seat in the brain, sensation in the base of the brain (the medulla oblongata), and the simplest reflexes in the spinal cord, the manner in which sensations mingle with consciousness is explained as follows: The most widely accepted theory is, that the wave of excitation must pass onward to the central convolutions of the brain, and that there,

in the excitation of the *cells,* it first becomes sensation—consciousness is first aroused. This theory regards consciousness and sensation as nearly identical, and locates them both in the brain. In all these theories, however, sensation is made the middle term between the most unconscious actions and thought. The theories differ only in the distance supposed to intervene between the central convolutions of the brain and the seat of *sensation.* . . .

All the actions of the sensorium, therefore, are *Reflex* actions; and the degree of *centralization,* or dependence upon the brain, determines the degree of consciousness accompanying them. If physiologists could only agree concerning the facts upon which they base their theory of the nervous arc, the path of the student would be greatly facilitated.

According to Van Deen, reflection takes place without *Volition,* but not without *Sensation.* Budge thinks that it takes place without Perception (Vorstellung). Marshall Hall and Muller divide actions into four distinct classes, the voluntary, the involuntary, the respiratory, and the purely reflex. The purely reflex actions he compares to an ordinary mechanism because they depend wholly upon excito-motor nerves.

"It is needless nowadays," says Lewes, "to point out that the existence of a distinct system of excito-motor nerves belongs to imaginary anatomy; but it is not needless to point out that the Imaginary Physiology founded on it still survives. . . . We have already seen that what anatomy positively teaches is totally unlike the Reflex mechanism popularly imagined. The sensory nerve is not seen to enter the spinal cord at one point and pass over to a corresponding point of exit; it is seen to enter the gray substance, which is continuous throughout the spinal cord; it is there lost to view, its course being untraceable."[20]

It is safe to say, therefore, that, notwithstanding its incompleteness, Lewes has given the clearest view of mental phenomena thus far offered to the world. The conclusion to be drawn from his work is, that mind has a basis far wider and deeper than organic life, or, in other terms, that consciousness is the function of universal conditions.

The aim of Lewes was to identify mind and matter by reducing thought and feeling to one principle. This aim was interfered with by his theory of an unknowable which postulates an ultimate mystery. He then turned to the study of the functions and structures of the sensorium in the hope of explaining the physical basis of mind. In this undertaking he was successful. The identity of mind and matter is clearly indicated by his great dictum, "Motor perceptions are condensed in intuitions and generalized in conceptions."

Notes

1. *Problems of Life and Mind,* Vol. I., Preface.

2. *Problems of Life and Mind,* Vol. I., p. 4.

3. *Problems of Life and Mind,* Vol. I., pp. 58, 59.

4. *Problems of Life and Mind,* Vol. I., pp. 103-105.

5. *Problems of Life and Mind,* Vol. I., p. 113.

6. *Problems of Life and Mind,* Vol. I., p. 113.

7. *Problems of Life and Mind,* Vol. I., p. 155.

8. *Problems of Life and Mind,* Vol. I., p. 188.

9. *Problems of Life and Mind,* Vol. I., pp. 193, 195.

10. *Problems of Life and Mind,* 3rd Series, p. 65.

11. *Problems of Life and Mind,* 3rd Series, pp. 69, 71, 102.

12. Herbert Spencer, *Principles of Psychology,* Vol. I., p. 184.

13. *Problems of Life and Mind,* 3rd Series, pp. 77, 82.

14. *Problems of Life and Mind,* 1st Series, p. 78.

15. *Problems of Life and Mind,* Vol. II., pp. 79, 81, 83.

16. *Problems of Life and Mind,* Vol. II., p. 206.

17. Thomson and Tait: *Natural Philosophy,* Vol. I., p. 161.

18. *Problems of Life and Mind,* Vol. II., pp. 449, 451.

19. *Physical Basis of Mind,* pp. 101 to 125.

20. *Physical Basis of Mind,* pp. 480, 481.

Howard C. Warren (essay date 1921)

SOURCE: Warren, Howard C. "Evolutionary Associationism." In *A History of the Association Psychology,* pp. 118-53. New York: Charles Scribner's Sons, 1921.

[*In the following excerpt, Warren demonstrates the ways in which Lewes shaped the tradition of English philosophy through his incorporation of recent findings in biological research and evolution theory. Warren considers Lewes's significant contribution to a variety of psychological theories, including those treating associationism, logical grouping, and the distinction between memory and perception.*]

6. THE PSYCHOLOGY OF G. H. LEWES

George Henry Lewes (1817-1878), a writer in many fields of literature, editor for some time of the *Fortnightly Review,* and domestic helpmate of the novelist Mary Ann Evans ('George Eliot'), is known in philosophy and psychology by his *Biographical History of Philosophy* (1854-6),[1] his *Physiology of Common Life* (1859-60), and a series of volumes entitled *Problems of Life and Mind* (1874-9).[2] This last work develops in detail his views of the nature of mind and his system of psychology. The final volume was never revised by the author; it is not arranged in proper sequence and contains many redundancies. But it is quite readable and complete with the exception of the last Problem; this was written shortly before the author's death and is merely a sketch.

Lewes is an acute and logical thinker, and his *Problems* [*Problems of Life and Mind*] carry the associational analysis to its historical culmination. One could only wish that he had written a briefer statement of his position in one or two volumes, taking up the analysis in a single, orderly sequence with less discussion and fewer illustrative examples. The inner consistency and force of his system would then have appeared to better advantage, and Lewes would probably have exerted a greater influence on the development of psychology in England.[3] The fact remains that Lewes's system has not been noticed to the extent of Bain's or Spencer's, although it seems to deserve greater attention on the part of psychologists on account of its striking adaptation of the traditional English position to the new results of biological research and to the evolution theory.

Besides several notable advances in the manner of performing the mental analysis and some improvements in nomenclature, Lewes makes two original contributions to the analysis itself. In the first place, he lays special emphasis upon the *social* side as a factor in mental evolution; and second, in place of the usual distinction between sensations and ideas, he adopts a threefold division into sensations (or feelings), images, and ideas (or conceptions), attributing a special symbolic character to the third.

(1) Lewes's conception of the special importance of social phenomena for mental science is traceable to Auguste Comte. But in opposition to Comte he insists that we must treat psychology as an independent science. The data of psychology, he affirms, are contributed by biology and sociology. The biological data furnish the starting-point of both animal and human psychology. The sociological data appear only in the human sphere and form the basis of the human intellectual and moral life, as distinguished from the animal sentient life.[4] Such diverse phenomena as folk-customs, traditions, arts, tools, science-lore, literature, depend on the system of intellectual signs known as *language;* and language exists only as a social function.[5]

(2) The primary form of sensibility, which Lewes calls *feeling,*[6] includes sensibility resulting from external stimulation (*special sensations,* the 'sensations' of ear-

lier psychologists), and sensibility due to systemic stimulation (systemic sensations or *emotion*). A reproduced feeling constitutes an *image*. But when the image has lost its original value and has become merely a sign or symbol of some feeling different from itself, it then becomes an idea or conception.[7] This triple division he also borrows from Comte,[8] though the third element is found implicitly in most of the associationists.[9] The manner in which the image is transformed into the idea and the role of ideas in psychological evolution will be examined presently. The important point here is that Lewes regards ideas or conceptions as essentially a social product and instrument; they are *signs,* whose objective expression is *language.*

While Lewes agrees with Spencer in laying special stress on physiology and biological evolution as a basis of explanation for psychological phenomena, he does not go to Spencer's length of regarding the biological standpoint as furnishing the only scientific element in psychology. He endeavors to maintain an equilibrium between the objective and subjective sides of the science, and puts forth an earnest plea for introspection as an instrument of research.[10] He claims that what the data of introspection lack in quantitative *exactness* they make up for in possessing the highest degree of *certainty;* the results of external observation or objective analysis, on the other hand, though preeminently exact, lack this element of surety or conviction.[11]

7. ASSOCIATION AND LOGICAL GROUPING

Lewes starts with sensibility, which he uses as a general term for the material of psychology. The psychical organism evolves from 'psychoplasm,' or 'sentient material.' The psychoplasm is ever fluctuating; it is constantly being renewed, and these movements constitute the function of sensibility.[12] Sensibility is the internal factor, to which corresponds, on the physiological side, "the successions of neural tremors variously combining into neural groups";[13] it includes both consciousness and subconsciousness.[14]

There are three fundamental laws of sensibility: (1) *Interest*: "We see only what interests us, know only what is sufficiently like former experiences to become, so to speak, incorporated with them—assimilated by them."[15]

(2) *Signature*: Every feeling "has its particular signature or mark in consciousness, in consequence of which it acquires its objective localization, i.e., its place in the organism or in the cosmos."[16] Signature is Lewes's term for the individuality or specific identity of each particular sensation or experience.

(3) *Experience, or registration of feeling*: "Through their registered modifications, feelings once produced are capable of reproduction, and must always be reproduced, more or less completely, whenever the new excitation is discharged along the old channels."[17]

Sensibility becomes organized into definite mental states along with the evolution of the physical organism, and in modes best described by reference to the corresponding biological processes. In physiological reaction we find a threefold process—stimulation, coordination, and discharge; the psychological equivalents of these are *sensible affection, logical grouping,* and *impulse*.[18] The sensible affection includes, as we have seen, sensibility resulting from both external and systemic stimulation.[19] But "no reaction on a stimulation can be called forth without revival of residua of past stimulations."[20] These revival states or images arise according to two fundamental processes, irradiation and restriction, whose laws may be stated on the physiological side as follows: (1) *Irradiation.*—Every wave impulse is irradiated and propagated throughout the system. (2) *Restriction.*—Every impulse is restricted, and by its restriction a group is formed.[21]

Revival states, or reinstatements, are due physiologically to the irradiative tendency, by which any given neural process tends to re-excite those processes which formerly were excited in conjunction with it, or which are anatomically linked with it.[22] On the subjective side this means that a sensation formerly connected with the given sensation may be reproduced with fainter energy as an image.[23] Physiologically, the irradiative tendency is limited by the definite pathways of discharge cut by previous stimulations—the law of restriction;[24] on the psychological side this means that the given sensations will tend to re-excite certain groups of fainter feelings of previous impressions, so that they are grouped into a judgment or perception.[25]

Irradiation and restriction work together in the process of *Reinstatement,* whose law is as follows: "Every mental state will be reinstated whenever the conditions of its production are reproduced; and the reinstatement will be more or less complete according to the more or less perfect reproduction of the original conditions."[26] The directly excited feeling (*sensation* or *presentation*) is distinguished by its greater vividness from the indirectly excited or reproduced feeling (*image* or *representation*). The former is fitly considered *real,* because it has objective reality (*res*) for its antecedent stimulus; the latter is *ideal,* because its antecedent is a subjective state.[27]

Association, according to Lewes, is a special form of the process of Reinstatement. Reinstatement is grouping; association is "the grouping of groups which are not connected by any necessary anatomical links. Processes which depend on the native mechanism, although dependent on the connection of groups, are not called associative processes. Association is acquisition."[28] Without discussing the laws of this restricted type of association at all systematically, Lewes refers his readers to Bain's exhaustive analysis, which he accepts in the main. He notes, however, two phenomena of association which Bain fails to take properly into account: (1) "The enormous influence of the emotional factor . . . in determining the reinstatement of images and ideas." (2) "The influence of obscure organic motors, manifested in the sudden irruption of incongruous states—the orderly course of association being burst in upon by images and ideas having none of the normal associative links."[29]

It is not clear why Lewes restricts the meaning of the term *association* to such narrow limits. He goes even further than Spencer in this respect. Spencer limits the term to revival by similarity. Lewes makes it a sort of adventitious revival; he harks back to Locke's notion of a connection "wholly owing to chance or custom." His broad treatment of the process, however, fully warrants us in considering Lewes an associationist, in spite of his peculiar restriction of the term. Historically, *association* corresponds closely to what Lewes calls *grouping,* or *logical process.* And this logic, or grouping of elements, enters fundamentally into his system, as we shall see; it begins at the lowest and simplest states and follows through to the highest and most complex.

The grouping or coordination of experience can be understood only when interpreted as part of the entire reactive process, whose three terms on the psychological side are *affection, grouping,* and *impulse.* The grouping process is of significance only as it leads to some new or more integrated form of impulse and activity. And just as grouping determines impulse, so it is determined by affective data. The modifications of neural structure caused by past impressions are what determine the specific neural grouping; on the subjective side it is the residua of former experiences that determine the specific mode of grouping in any instance.

Grouping, then, depends not only on the stimulus at the present moment, but also on the entire condition of the organism as determined by its past history—in other words, it depends on the *self,* as determined by the individual's whole past experience, as truly as on the given presentation.[30] "When once a neural group, however complex, has been formed, it operates like a simple unit, and enters as such into the combination of other groups." So, on the subjective side, sensations which were originally independent are "brought into such convergence by intermediate links that they now coalesce and act together without the need of such intermediation"; for example, visual and tactile sensations combine to form "an intuition of form and size of an object; but these having coalesced, and the intuition being effected, we no longer need the intermediate process."[31] This is the simultaneous aspect of grouping.

The serial aspect is more important. In accordance with the law of irradiation, "one excitation of the sensorium sets going associated excitations, the associations rising out of prior modifications."[32] This results in a *series* of images and ideas, whose specific course is determined according to the law of restriction. Restriction operates in accordance with two distinct factors: the specific revival depends (1) on the harmony of the image to be revived with the ground-tone of feeling or mental predisposition at the time, and (2) on the energy of the image.[33] This grouping of experiences in serial order is what Lewes terms the *logical process,* or in brief, *logic.* As a psychological process, logic is "not simply the process of reasoning, but that which is common to reasoning and to all other modes of combination belonging to mental states. This common process is *coordination,* or grouping of neural elements."[34] One mental state thus determines its successor, and is included in it.[35]

All experience, even its lowest forms, involves coordination. On the physiological side, this process of coordination results from the tendency of stimuli to general irradiation and restriction of such irradiation by previous modifications of structure to more or less habitual paths. On the mental side, therefore, the experience grouped with the given experience would be one that had been *contiguous* to it in some past primary experience. And since the associated element is always a revival—a reinstatement, not a mere *copy*[36]—only the law of contiguity would seem to apply; in other words, the law of similarity would appear to have no place in association. Lewes is apparently mistaken in believing that he agrees with Bain in this part of his analysis, since the latter admits both contiguity and similarity as associative principles. He differs with Bain still further in assuming an association by contrast.[37] It should be noticed, however, that Lewes admits these principles only as laws of 'casual' association, not of the general logical process.[38]

* * *

While he does not expressly admit that the synthetic process yields anything really new in chemistry or in mental grouping,[39] several passages show that Lewes recognizes a qualitative variation; he concedes that the effect of mental synthesis is, in appearance at least, similar to what chemical synthesis appears to be. Causation, he says, is of two sorts: the effect may be "the *resultant* of its components, the product of its factors"; or, in cases of cooperation of things of unlike kinds, the effect is an *emergent,* that is, it is 'qualitatively unlike' the causes.[40] Quality is a primary fact of feeling which enters into every subjective synthesis;[41] and no matter how much we strive to reduce psychology to quantitative terms, "no variation of undulations will really correspond with variation in color, unless we reintroduce the suppressed *quality* which runs through all color."[42]

8. Lewes's Analysis of Mental Phenomena

Lewes attributes not only the higher types of experience, but *all* definite experience, including sensation itself, to the grouping or logical process. "A sensation is a group of neural tremors."[43] Given the hypothetical simple element underlying experience, which he calls a neural tremor, such tremors are grouped into definite sensations by the irradiative tendency which unites to them the residua of past tremors.[44] A perception is "the synthesis of all the sensations we have had of the object in relation to our several senses";[45] this includes secondary elements (images) as well as primary (sensations).

The application of the grouping principle to space perception is typical: extension is perceived as a continuum, he says, inasmuch as by irradiation "there is a necessary blending of the discrete points, a fusion of the similar tremors."[46] And the observed temporal unity of consciousness admits of explanation in the same way, the serial order of conscious experiences being the result of serial irradiation.[47]

A remembered sensation is something more than a repetition of the sensation: the repetition of the stimulus causes in addition a stimulation of residua, which furnish 'an escort of other states.'[48] Memory differs from perception in the character of this escort: in memory the escort is of states constituting the field of personal experience, in perception the escort lacks that definite personal character.[49] Memory is a grouping of image elements as they occurred in the past. Imagination differs from memory in that its personal escort has reference to the present or future, not to the past.[50] In plastic or constructive imagination the image elements are grouped in new ways.[51] "Images, although reproductions of perceptions, possess a property not possessed by perceptions, namely, that of *facultative reproduction,* which enables them to be abstracted from the sensible order of presentation, and combined and recombined anew."[52] Emotions are to be regarded under two aspects—as sensations and as impulses which guide action; under the former aspect "they belong to the systemic more than to the special affections, but are complexes of both."[53]

All the above-named forms of grouping belong to the *logic of feeling,* or to its subdivision, the *logic of images.* The grouping of ideas, or symbols, or conceptions, constitutes the *logic of signs.*[54] In the mode of grouping known as logic of images, the image becomes the representative of its sensation; it is a sort of substitute, but a substitute which is more or less *equivalent* to the thing signified.[55]

With the growth of organization "these images may be replaced by signs which have no trace of the sensations signified";[56] they are substitutes of sensations, not reinstatements.[57] This higher type of reproductive states Lewes calls *ideas,* as distinguished from *images.*[58] Words are signs of this sort; the auditory symbol *horse* has no likeness to the visual or other sensations which the idea symbolizes—it may not even awaken a visual

image of the horse; yet such verbal symbols "operate quite as effectually as the images."[59] Verbal symbols (language) arise as a result of social intercourse—they could not have arisen without it.[60] For this reason and also because a high degree of nervous organization is requisite for the production of words, language belongs solely to the human species.[61]

Ideas, with all their substitutive and symbolic value, could never have developed *ab initio* in an individual's single lifetime. But according to the evolution theory they are not innate in the older sense—rather, they are con-nate.[62] The advent of language introduces a new factor into the environment—namely, the social medium.[63] In the higher stages of mind, where ideas exist, we find a social as well as a physical environment, an ideational as well as affective self.[64]

Ideas group themselves according to the same principles as images. Serial groupings of ideas constitute *thought,* or the logic of signs. Since ideas are general and flexible, while images and perceptions are always particular and fixed,[65] we are able in thought to pass rapidly and easily from one term to another, in a way that would be impossible were it necessary to translate each idea into a specific image.[66] It is this use of the general symbol that constitutes the superiority of the human over the animal mind.[67] The logic of signs enables man to act with reference to more distant ends, as the symbols become further removed from direct correspondence to sensations;[68] whereas, the 'reasoning' of animals is always in terms of sensations and images.[69] 'Associations' in the narrower sense are generally symbolic, whence the phrase *association of ideas.*[70]

The developed processes of thought form the *intellect,* or rational functions, or reflection.[71] All these processes—judgment, induction, deduction—are reducible to the 'logic of signs';[72] they culminate in the *laws of thought,* which Lewes focuses into a single *principle of equivalence*[73]—an affirmative counterpart of the criterion of certitude which Spencer states in negative form as the inconceivability of the contrary.

The consciousness of volition includes two factors according to Lewes: (1) the feeling of effort in attention, which is reducible to muscle sensations;[74] (2) an innervation feeling, due to the irradiation of the outgoing motor impulse *back toward the center.*[75] But the consciousness attending volition is merely an incidental feeling linked with it;—the motor side of subjective phenomena is impulse or action, rather than feeling. The grouping or coordinating process is the guide which controls the impulse, and thereby regulates conduct. In the broadest view of psychology "the significance of mental phenomena is their relation to conduct."[76]

9. Lewes's Contributions to the Problem

The main features of Lewes's psychology, in so far as they bear on the association problem, may be summed up as follows: (1) He takes the concept of biological evolution from Darwin and Spencer, and carries it out on the psychological side more fully than they.

(2) He interprets the laws of nervous irradiation and restriction in mental terms, under the single law of *Reinstatement,* which serves to account at once for (*a*) the distinction between primary and secondary feeling, or sensation and image, and for (*b*) the grouping or associative function of mental phenomena, which he terms *logic.*

(3) The *grouping tendency* accounts for all complex forms of experience, from sensation upwards, the only datum not attributable to grouping being the hypothetical underlying element, the neural tremor.

(4) The tendency to use part of a complex experience as a sign for the whole, which is a general phenomenon of mental activity, evolves to a higher form in the *human* mind. In man arbitrary associated elements (ideas) come to be used as symbolic signs for sensations and images which they in no wise resemble. This *symbolism* and *logic of signs* arises out of social intercourse, for which words and language afford a convenient, flexible, and adequate medium.

(5) Images are individual, concrete, specific—ideas are general, abstract. The sequence of ideas, or logic of signs, is therefore more facile and more adaptable than the logic of feeling or the logic of images. Ideas and ideational processes constitute the intellectual side of the mental life, and *intellect* is its highest form.

(6) An established group, which has become a single experience (intuition), is characterized by a higher degree of *belief,* conviction, certainty, than a group in the making (inference); intuitions of sensations and images (called perceptions) are distinguished from intuitions of ideas (conceptions); and inferences of sensations and images (memories, hallucinations, imaginations) are distinguished from inferences of ideas (judgment, reasoning).

(7) Lewes applies the term association in an unusual way to that special sort of grouping in which the elements are casually brought together by contiguity, similarity, or interest. Grouping in general, which he calls logic, proceeds by the revival of identical elements in the form of images, the revival operating from one element to another according to the principle of contiguity only. He applies Bain's treatment of association in general to his own 'casual associations.'

To appreciate the breadth of Lewes's viewpoint we should also note several other points which bear on our problem only slightly. (1) His conception of the cooperation of organism and environment in experience. The present stimulus and the self due to one's entire past experience work together; any given experience is a resultant of these two factors. (2) His extension of the nervous arc concept to psychology. Feeling or affection, logic or grouping, impulse or action, are the mental equivalents of the three sides of the nervous arc; they form the psychological spectrum, whose combination constitutes mentality. (3) His endeavor to give proper weight to both the subjective and objective sides of psychology—to the method and data of introspection as well as to the method and data of external observation. (4) His demarcation between external sensations and the systemic sensations. This distinction deserves special notice on account of the prominent role which he assigns to the latter.

To grasp Lewes's system as a whole requires considerable effort. His style is prolix and his development is not always systematic. He is careless of detail, inconsistent on some points, and obscure in his treatment of others. Yet upon close examination he proves to be the most consistently *associational* of all psychologists. Lewes deserves far more study than has been accorded him by recent writers; and especially does he deserve the attention of genetic psychologists. Those who wish to know at first hand the *evolutionary* associationism at its best, should read his final volume.[77] Though not a complete exposition, it contains most of the essential points of his psychology, and corrects many of his earlier inconsistencies.

Notes

1. Revised editions to 1880.

2. The first series of the *Problems* [*Problems of Life and Mind*], Vols. I and II, with subtitle *Foundations of a Creed,* includes Introduction, Psychological Principles (Psy. Pr.), and six Problems. The second series, Vol. III, entitled *The Physical Basis of Mind,* with the serial title subordinate, contains four Problems (1-4). The third series (posthumous), embracing Vols. IV and V, takes the serial title again, and contains four Problems; the subtitle of Vol. IV is *The Study of Psychology,* from the problem discussed—Vol. V has no subtitle. In citing this work the *volume* (from I to V), *problem,* and *section* are given. Section numbers run through each 'problem' separately.

3. Lewes would probably have been more carefully studied, in spite of his prolixity, had not the general trend of psychology during the next decades been away from associationism. See Chapter VIII.

4. 'Probs.,' Vol. I, Psy. Pr., § 1.

5. *Ibid.,* § 10.

6. V, Prob. 2, §§ 3-5.

7. I, Psy. Pr., §§ 44, 64-5, 25; V, Prob. 4, §§ 26-8; V, Prob. 2, § 7.

8. V, Prob. 3, note following § 14.

9. It is to be regretted that Lewes did not work out more fully and consecutively his distinction between *image* and *idea*. He emphasizes the striking difference in their associative value ('logic'), but his discussion of the *nature* of symbolic experience is scattered about in various parts of his work.

10. IV, Prob. 1, §§ 50-1, 62-6.

11. *Ibid.*

12. I, Psy. Pr., § 6; *cf.* III, Prob. 1, § 60.

13. I, Psy. Pr., § 6; *cf.* V, Prob. 2, § 33.

14. I, Psy. Pr., § 33; *cf.* III, Prob. 3, §§ 50-2.

15. Psy. Pr., § 9; *cf.* V, Prob. 2, §§ 74-6.

16. I, *loc. cit.; cf.* V. Prob. 3, §§ 117-8.

17. I, *loc. cit.; cf.* V, Prob. 2, ch. 4.

18. V, Prob. 2, § 33.

19. I, Psy. Pr., § 28.

20. V, Prob. 2, § 35.

21. *Ibid.,* § 36.

22. I, Psy. Pr., § 37.

23. § 42.

24. § 35.

25. I, Psy. Pr., § 38.

26. V, Prob. 2, § 80.

27. I, Psy. Pr., § 43.

28. V, Prob. 2, § 94. In this passage Lewes accepts Spencer's conception of 'association,' not the wider connotation of earlier writers.

29. *Ibid.,* § 95.

30. I, Psy. Pr., § 9—law of exp.; V, Pr. 2, §§ 42, 77, 166-72.

31. V, Prob. 2, § 136.

32. V, Prob. 2, § 42.

33. *Ibid.,* 102.

34. V, Prob. 3, § 2. Lewes uses the term *neural element* here and frequently elsewhere to denote the primitive, unanalyzable element of *experience.*

35. *Ibid.*

36. V, Prob. 4, § 8.

37. V, Prob. 2, §§ 100-1.

38. Possibly Lewes would have reduced these "groupings of groups which are not connected by any necessary anatomical links" to irradiation and restriction also, and attributed all association to contiguity, had he repeated for himself Bain's analysis.

39. See I, Psy. Pr., § 88.

40. II, Prob. 5, §§ 65-6.

41. II, Prob. 2, § 31.

42. III, Prob. 3, § 5.

43. V, Prob. 2, § 35; *cf.* I, Psy. Pr., § 24.

44. As already noted, the term *neural tremor* is used subjectively.

45. I, Psy. Pr., § 25.

46. Psy. Pr., § 35.

47. *Ibid.,* § 36.

48. V, Prob. 2, § 82. This 'escort' corresponds to what William James later called the "fringe of consciousness."

49. *Ibid.,* § 87.

50. § 92.

51. § 93.

52. I, Psy. Pr., § 64.

53. V, Prob. 3, § 154.

54. I, Psy. Pr., § 25.

55. *Ibid.;* V, Prob. 2, § 137; Prob. 4, § 28.

56. V, Prob. 2, § 137.

57. V, Prob. 4, § 26.

58. *Ibid.* This gives still another meaning to the much-defined term *idea*. It would seem more in keeping with historic usage to make *idea* the generic term, including *imagery* and *thought* as its species; thought would be the *symbolic type of ideation.*

59. V, Prob. 2, § 137.

60. I, Psy. Pr., §§ 10, 54, 63; V, Prob. 4, ch. 6.

61. *Ibid.*

62. I, Psy. Pr., §§ 57, 60; *cf.* § 8.

63. *Ibid.,* §§ 10, 57.

64. V, Prob. 2, §§ 168, 171-2.

65. I, Psy. Pr., § 25; V, Prob. 4, § 27.

66. V, Prob. 4, § 61; *cf.* chs. 5, 6.

67. *Ibid.,* §§ 45-8.

68. I, Psy. Pr., § 27.

69. V, Prob. 4, §§ 40-4.

70. V, Prob. 2, § 94.

71. In several passages Lewes makes *discrimination* the fundamental fact of intellect; he appears to use the term to denote the selective or restrictive effect of grouping. Though he does not explicitly say so, he apparently applies the term *discrimination* to the subjective aspect of 'restriction' and *selection* to its objective or neural aspect. (See I, Psy. Pr., § 17; III, Prob. 4, §§ 51, 53; V, Prob. I, §§ 104, 151.)

72. II, Prob. 2, chs. 2-4.

73. II, Prob. 2, chs. 4, 5.

74. V, Prob. 2, § 157.

75. V, Prob. 3, §§ 82-91, esp. 87.

76. *Ibid.,* § 15.

77. *Problems of Life and Mind,* Vol. V.

Edwin Mallard Everett (essay date 1939)

SOURCE: Everett, Edwin Mallard. "An Independent Review." In *The Party of Humanity: The* Fortnightly Review *and Its Contributors, 1865-1874,* pp. 28-73. Chapel Hill: University of North Carolina Press, 1939.

[*In the following excerpts, Everett outlines the history and content of the* Fortnightly Review, *devoting attention to Lewes's involvement as senior editor between 1865 and 1866. Everett characterizes the* Fortnightly's *reactions to crucial social events of the day, including labor disputes, slavery and the American civil war, British politics, and the Jamaican uprising of 1865.*]

Among the many minds contributing to the first issue of the *Fortnightly Review* were Anthony Trollope, Walter Bagehot, George Eliot, Frederic Harrison, and the editor himself [George Henry Lewes]. The place of honor was given to Bagehot, the first chapter of whose *English Constitution* appeared as the leading article. Trollope's *Belton Estate* was the novel chosen for serial publication.[1] Frederic Harrison furnished a long article on trade unions, and George Eliot reviewed Lecky's *Spirit of Rationalism in Europe.* Lewes, besides editorially charging the late Confederate States of America with the recent murder of President Lincoln, contributed a short popular article on a scientific subject and

the first chapter of his *Principles of Success in Literature.* There was a very favorable review article by J. Leicester Warren (Lord de Tabley) on Swinburne's *Atalanta in Calydon.* Science, criticism, and reminiscence completed the table of contents. There were two regular departments: "Public Affairs," unsigned but presumably written by the editor, and "Notices of New Books," containing signed short reviews of books not considered important enough to merit a whole article. The new review was bound in a cream-colored back; it carried various advertisements of books, wines, furniture, musical instruments, and paper hangings; and it sold for two shillings.

The editor had begun well. His contributors were prominent, and their subjects were appropriate to public interest. Trollope and George Eliot were near the height of their careers as novelists, Bagehot and Lewes were both well known in the periodical world, and Frederic Harrison was just coming to be recognized as one of the most earnest defenders of the unions in their struggle against the capitalists. Except in "Notices of New Books" there was hardly an unknown name among the contributors. The interest in science, the discussion of the labor question, and the approval of such new literature as Swinburne's *Atalanta* showed an eagerness on the part of the editor to keep pace with his times.

Lewes was not new at the business of journalism and editorship. Before the *Fortnightly* [*Fortnightly Review*] was conceived he had already written for most of the English reviews—for the *Edinburgh,* the *Westminster,* the *British and Foreign* and the *Foreign Quarterly* reviews. He had written for the magazines, chiefly for *Blackwood's, Fraser's,* and the *Cornhill;* and among the weekly and daily journals he had contributed to the *Saturday Review* and the *Pall Mall Gazette.* He had, in fact, appeared in almost every one of them, as he told Espinasse, "except the damned old *Quarterly.*"[2] His contributions to the *Edinburgh* alone "ranged from the *mise en scène* of the London theaters to disquisitions on Arabian philosophy." As early as 1850, when he was twenty-eight years old, he had begun his career as an editor. For four years, a period ended by his departure to Germany with Marian Evans, he and Thornton Hunt were co-editors of the *Leader,* Hunt managing the political departments of this magazine and Lewes the literary. Here he wrote to his heart's content on science, education, communism, and the philosophy of Auguste Comte; and besides, in the character of "Vivian"—a flippant and sophisticated young man—he conducted a regular column of informal chatter about the classics, the church fathers, and the stage. His criticism in this column was excellent, particularly his strictures on the drama and acting in an age when those arts were barren. It was the work of these years, especially of those on the *Leader,* that led Carlyle to call Lewes "The Prince of Journalists."[3]

Again, in 1862, Lewes was attracted to editorial work, for when Thackeray resigned the editorship of the *Cornhill Magazine,* George Smith offered the position to Lewes. But for some time now his health had been unusually bad, and he had been constantly seeking cures both at home and abroad. George Eliot's journal and letters of these years and Lewes's diary, especially for the year 1864, make frequent reference to headaches, fainting spells, and watering places.[4] The consequence was that, although, because of his poor health, he refused the editorship of the *Cornhill,* he did accept a position as its chief literary adviser at a salary of £600 a year. But even the work of criticizing manuscripts was too arduous; and his ill health continuing, in October, 1864, he resigned this position. The fact that the work was "light and agreeable" and paid for with a handsome salary is enough to indicate his weakness of body and spirit. But in the very face of this weakness Anthony Trollope within a few months was able to persuade him to assume an even more onerous and exacting task than the one he had just resigned—the editorship of the *Fortnightly Review.*

Lewes's contemporaries were agreed that he was a man of brilliance and versatility. His mind was unorthodox, as his life had been. As a young boy he had received his earliest schooling in London, in Brittany, and at St. Helier on the island of Jersey. Later he had attended Dr. Burney's school at Dulwich.[5] He read Latin and Greek; and although he was not a university man he was familiar with classical literature in a homespun way. He told Espinasse that he read Greek three hours a day—but he did not say how long he continued the practice.[6] He had some knowledge of Hebrew, which George Eliot had taught him so that they might converse together without being understood by the waiters of European hotels. His knowledge of the languages and literatures of France, Germany, Italy, and Spain, his experience with the theater both as critic and amateur actor, his extensive travels on the continent, his scientific fervor contracted from Herbert Spencer, and his studies in biology—all these more than compensated for his lack of a university degree; for like Robert Browning, also irregularly educated, he recognized no bounds to his interest in the teeming world around him. He was indeed what one of his younger contemporaries long after called him, "that wonder of versatile talents."[7]

Already in 1865 Lewes was the author of two well-known books and many scientific and literary studies. His ***Biographical History of Philosophy,*** published serially in 1845 and 1846, survived many editions and revisions and has continued of interest to modern students.[8] His life of Goethe, completed in 1855, was the first in the English language and is still in print. He published two novels, of which he was never very proud; a rather unsuccessful play; and a number of studies of such varied subjects as Aristotle, Robespierre, the Spanish drama, marine life, and physiology. When Espinasse showed surprise at the conjunction of two such literary tasks as the lives of Robespierre and Goethe, Carlyle explained to him, "Lewes is not afraid of any amount of work."[9] He was an earnest student of psychology, a subject to which he made definite contributions in his ***Problems of Life and Mind,*** published late in his life. His philosophical studies were stimulated by an early interest in Spinoza, and he was one of the first English adherents of Auguste Comte and one of the most effective popularizers of his Positive Philosophy. In the early forties, when Comte and his work were known to only a few Englishmen, Lewes published his first account of the Frenchman's philosophy. In 1853 he wrote for the *Leader* a series of articles entitled ***Comte's Philosophy of the Sciences***; and in the conception and execution of his ***Biographical History*** [***Biographical History of Philosophy***] the part played by Comte's philosophy was an important one.

But if it was Comte who influenced Lewes's thinking more than any other, it was John Stuart Mill who first convinced him of the value of Comte's Positivism.

> Although Mill was the first and principal medium of making Comte and his doctrines familiar to the public [wrote one of Mill's followers], he was soon followed by George Henry Lewes, who was beginning his literary career, as a writer in reviews, about the year 1841. I met Lewes frequently when I was first in London in 1842. He sat at the feet of Mill, read the logic with avidity, and took up Comte with equal avidity. These two works, I believe, gave him his start in philosophy.[10]

Like many another in the middle of the nineteenth century Lewes owed an incalculable debt to the friendship and guidance of Mill. The earliest personal association of the two men seems to have occurred at the end of 1840 when Lewes sent to the *Westminster Review* an article on Shelley.[11] Mill, who had just relinquished the editorship of the review but who still apparently engaged in editorial advising, wrote Lewes a criticism of his contribution, warning the young author particularly against any imitation of the style of Carlyle. As he continued to criticize Lewes's work, a strong friendship grew up between them. And at about this time Mill published his *Logic.* It is more than likely that this book, published in 1843, and Comte's *Cours de philosophie positive,* brought to England in 1837, both of which Lewes read at the beginning of his literary career, fixed the stout rationalist mold in which his mind had begun to set. It is just as likely that they changed a young man of Bohemian and dilettante propensities into something of less doubtful spiritual significance.[12] . . .

[F]rom the very first Anthony Trollope seemed to like Lewes. They met in January, 1860, at one of the *Cornhill* dinners given by George Smith to the contributors to his new magazine.[13] In the same year Lewes's son

Charles obtained a position at the Post Office "through Anthony Trollope's kindness."[14] By Trollope's influence Lewes lectured at the Post Office in 1861; and that year the Leweses, who did very little visiting, called upon the Trollopes at Waltham Cross. "I like him very much," said Lewes of Trollope, "so wholesome and straightforward a man."[15] After that there were frequent visits to the Trollopes'; and when the *Fortnightly* was projected, Trollope, convinced that he knew his man, was determined to have Lewes for editor. And he would have him in spite of Lewes's talk of illness and incapability, and in spite of his own conscience. "It was for me," he says, "to persuade him to undertake the office, if it might be so, and, anxious as I was, I could not but shrink from pressing him when he told me that he doubted his health."[16] Certainly the salary offered him, £600, could have been no great inducement, for it was no more than he had got for his work on the *Cornhill*; and besides, these years were among the fat years of Lewes's income. Possibly the intimacy of Trollope and Lewes and the remembrance of Trollope's kindness to Charles Lewes led Lewes finally to accept the position. Possibly the "wholesome and straightforward" Trollope was accustomed to getting what he set out to get.

Lewes's diary shows that as early as December 30, 1864, he had given Trollope his "provisional promise" to become editor;[17] and in January Lewes and George Eliot made a quick trip to Paris, where amidst great bustle of opera-going and sight-seeing and visits to the home of Comte, Lewes made special observation of the working of the *Revue des Deux Mondes*. George Eliot wrote to Sara Hennell: "A little business was an excuse for getting a great deal of pleasure."[18] And in the same letter she wrote: "There is great talk of a new periodical—a fortnightly apparition, partly on the plan of the *Revue des Deux Mondes*. Mr. Lewes has consented to become its editor if the preliminaries are settled so as to satisfy him." Just what those preliminaries were there is no telling; but by March they must have been settled to Lewes's liking, for he was "all activity, yet in very frail health,"[19] and he had begun to write letters to ask for contributions to the review. To Thomas Adolphus Trollope in Florence he wrote: "We rejoice in the prospect of your 'History of Florence,' and I am casting about, hoping to find somebody to review it worthily for the *Fortnightly Review*. By the way, would you or your wife help me there also? Propose your subjects!"[20] In May he was dining with Herbert Spencer and some of his scientific brethren getting promises of articles.[21] Apparently then Lewes made up his mind about the matter shortly after the trip to Paris; and the whole task of producing a first number, from the time that Trollope approached the prospective editor, occupied almost five months. On Sunday afternoon, May 14, the day before the first issue appeared, there was celebration at the

Priory. Spencer was there, and Lord Houghton, Bagehot, and Fitzjames Stephen; and they "kept up talk and tea from 3 to 7!"[22]

Lewes edited the review through the issue of December 1, 1866, when ill health forced him to retire. During the twenty months of his administration the review grew more and more liberal. The policy of independence was from time to time proclaimed to its readers; and the review was willing to print replies to its articles and to give the other man his say. But if willingness to be impartial was present, the other man was too often absent; and it became obvious before very long that, for one reason and another, the *Fortnightly Review,* if it was to attain any success at all, must do so as an organ of liberal opinion.

But Lewes worked hard to establish the principles of the founders. He himself wrote for the review a series of articles, **The Principles of Success in Literature,** in which he stressed particularly the principle of sincerity, and in which a reader might have discovered the desire for earnestness and honesty that seemed to characterize the *Fortnightly* itself. Concerning this series and the purposes of the review, George Eliot wrote to a friend:

> I am glad you have been interested in Mr. Lewes's article. His great anxiety about the *Fortnightly* is to make it the vehicle for sincere writing—real contributions on important topics. But it is more difficult than the inexperienced could imagine to get the sort of writing that will correspond to that desire of his.[23]

At times it became more difficult than even the experienced could imagine. How much success Lewes had in his effort to establish an impartial review may be seen in an examination of those articles that were either controversial or contrary to the editor's own liberal opinions, of the liberal articles that were published, and of the editorial policy of the department of "Public Affairs."

Opposition and controversy were aroused by the very first issue of the review, in which there appeared a long and earnest article by Frederic Harrison[24] on the Iron-Masters' Trade Union. Harrison was incensed by the growing use of the lockout; he was particularly solicitous for the plight of the Staffordshire iron-workers. Basing his argument on the economics of Adam Smith, he contended that combinations of masters are more reprehensible, because less just, than combinations of workmen. Strikes, he explained, are a simple and logical expedient to test the price of labor; whereas the lockout is not at all the opposite of the strike, but rather a measure of force and punishment. The lockout, in fact, is the complete denial of the rule that wages naturally follow supply and demand.

> In reality no lock-out was ever attempted except when the employers were tolerably certain that no labourers can be found on the offered terms. The more certain

they are that labourers are in the market and ready to come in the less likely they are to resort to the expense and risk of a lock-out, in the attempt to compel them. They do so because they believe that violent pressure alone will force the labourers to terms. That is to say, they only lock out to enforce terms which the state of the market by itself will not justify. . . . Morally it is nothing but avarice working, through cruelty, on a scale and with a system which throws into the shade the worst excesses of the workmen at the worst times of trade selfishness. It exhibits in its most stupendous form, in the natural heads of society, a wanton contempt of every true social duty, which threatens the existence of society itself.[25]

This was a rather free casting about of charges, accusing as social menaces the very authors of British prosperity; and the charge did not long remain unanswered. The *Fortnightly* published a well-written reply, which contended not only that the strikers were wrong but that strikes were harmful to the workmen as well as to the masters because the masters had always won.[26] The large sums of money lost in wages by strikers was calculated, and the inefficiency of the strike as a social instrument was stressed. But Harrison returned to the attack more expansive than ever, covering the general subject of trade unionism.[27] He discussed the character of the societies and their leaders; and he not only emphasized the desirability of getting at the truth about the success or failure of strikes, but also brought evidence to show that some strikes do succeed. Here was a mixture in the *Fortnightly* of both liberal and conservative doctrines; but one must remember that Harrison and his editor were both Positivists, that they were, besides, very close friends, and that, whatever the cause, Harrison had the last word.

The review, in the meantime, had further demonstrated its eclecticism. When, for instance, the new Clerical Subscription Act was passed, relaxing the oath of the clergy, the *Fortnightly* published on this question a very reactionary article, which expressed the fear that the bars had been too carelessly let down.[28] The rigidity of the old oath and the flexibility of the new were compared at considerable length, and the heedlessness of the bishops and laymen who had so blindly made the change was decried. But for all its conservatism the article ended with the admission that "this new measure will not only relieve many tender consciences from a cruel burden, but will tend to maintain the connection between the established church and the enlarged thought and stirring intellect of the age." But these very words proposed the theme that other contributors were to expand to show that a too great rigidity in such matters was very bad. Later, the author of the original protest against the new oath returned to the review to lament the fact that the Church was gradually driving young men into secular professions, whereas it should appeal especially to young persons, particularly in "an age of dawning brightness, both as to the moral and physical

condition of mankind." Just how he managed to reconcile the religious eclipse that he deplored with the dawning brightness of which he was so proud is not quite clear.

Church doctrine as well as Church practice was both defended and assailed in the new review, conservatives and liberals dividing their dogmas between them. The publication in Paris in 1866 of Ernest Renan's *Les Apôtres* was a signal for critical strife in the *Fortnightly*. The book was attacked by Henry Rogers,[29] whose object was to show that a history of the first days of Christianity, if M. Renan's view of his materials be correct, is impossible; and that if such a history were possible it is still incredible that Renan's history should be the true one.[30] Rogers was in turn attacked by the young American historian John Fiske in a very modern rationalist manner as dogmatic in its own way as the views attacked. Rogers had complained of Renan for assuming that miracles are invariably to be rejected. "Certainly a historian of the present day," wrote Fiske, "who should not make such an assumption would betray his lack of the proper qualifications for his profession."[31] Although there was little argument in all this talk of assumptions, especially from a scientific historian, Fiske's article had its better parts. "Of all history," he wrote, "the miraculous part should be attested by the strongest testimony, whereas it is invariably attested by the weakest. And the paucity of miracles wherever we have contemporary records, as in the case of primitive Islamism, is a most significant fact."[32] One other contributor engaged frequently in these religious jousts, Peter Bayne,[33] who never avoided an opportunity to confute those who, like Fiske, were disrespectful toward the miraculous. "Christ's miracles," he wrote, "admit, I believe, of proof as valid as that of any scientific or historical facts, and all hypothesis on the subject is superfluous."[34] He spoke at least with admirable assurance, especially in the face of the scientific fervor of contributors like Huxley and John Tyndall.

There were other controversies, usually carried on by the disputants with polite deference to each other, over such questions as reform of the franchise and control of crime, or over historical and literary problems like the authenticity of the Paston Letters. Occasionally the editor published articles which, from his own point of view, came, as it were, directly from the camp of the enemy. American affairs offer a good illustration.

In its articles on the United States of America, most of which dealt with some aspect of the struggle between the North and the South, the *Fortnightly* applauded the success of the North. Lewes and his friends, sympathetic with the antislavery movement and exultant at its success, were opposed to the South. And yet Lewes, in spite of his own feelings, published a paper entitled "The Last Six Days of Secessia," which recounted with something like romantic sympathy the retreat of Lee from Petersburg and Richmond to Amelia Court House and then the surrender at Appomattox.[35] The author was an admirer of General Lee, whom he ranked, as a soldier, with Marlborough, Cromwell, and Bonaparte. Another piece, "President Johnson and the Reconstruction of the Union," was written with strong sympathy for the defeated South and with admiration for the President's stand against the Radicals in the American Senate.[36] The publication of these articles alone was sufficient exemplification of Lewes's avowed fight upon partisan journalism, especially if one contrasts with them the work of Moncure Conway, who served the *Fortnightly* as a kind of specialist on American affairs. Conway, a Virginian by birth, had left America to live in London, where his abolitionist sentiments were more popular than in his native state; and the delight with which he mutilated the dead corpse of slavery in the pages of the *Fortnightly* was almost pathological.[37]

These references are enough to show that the *Fortnightly Review* did mean to open its pages to liberals and conservatives alike, to progressives and reactionaries, to any one who had a thing to say and could say it. But the liberal editorial policy manifested in the important department of "Public Affairs" did not at all accord with the professed independence of the founders. The obvious incongruity between the sentiment of the partisan editorials and the ideal of eclecticism must have alienated many who might have thought well of the review and helped to make it a forum for Victorian thought.

But that liberal sentiment of the editorials might have been expected from a man of Lewes's temperament and experience. His association in his younger days with Leigh Hunt and his family, and his unfortunate marital life, in which Leigh Hunt's son Thornton played so important and unconventional a part, had led to ideas hardly consonant with the standard amenities. His friendship with Mill, his enthusiasm for Comte, and his interest in the new science had made him quite disregardful of authority and orthodoxy. As to his previous journalistic experience—his work on the *Leader* had been chiefly radical criticism, he and Thornton Hunt having consistently attacked established interests, ecclesiastical, educational, and economic. His common-law marriage to George Eliot was only a part of his general attitude toward the Victorian world around him. He was undoubtedly a man who had instincts toward indiscriminate iconoclasm but who was saved for human usefulness by the earnestness of his character, the vitality of his intellect, and the felicity of his friendships. The editorials that he wrote for the *Fortnightly,* however cogent his yearning for impartiality, must inevitably have composed a body of liberal doctrine.

Under Lewes then the *Fortnightly Review* supported the Liberal Party in politics—when it was not berating that

party for not working with greater harmony to accomplish changes opposed by the Conservatives. To him the party of Lord John Russell and Mr. Gladstone was, in its social outlook, sound and beneficent. Had it not "converted the country from what it was in the dark days of the Prince Regent and Fourth George to what it had become in the days of Queen Victoria"?[38] The Conservatives, and especially Disraeli, were merely Eldon Tories in disguise; their professed humanity was only skin deep. Not to be duped, the *Fortnightly* announced:

> Mistrust, fear, love of monopoly, intolerance, a leaning toward coercion—these, as of old, are the characteristics of your Tory, rounded and worn a little, no doubt, by time and circumstance, but as hard, unpleasant, and barren as the shingle on the beach. Arid and unfruitful, to Toryism is left the function of supplying that amount of resistance which makes life, movement, what we call progress, possible, but which is not progress itself. Resistance is a good thing in its way, but a thing of which we have had a little too much in the history of England.[39]

The chief subject of most of Lewes's editorials was reform of the franchise. After the general election in September, 1865, the *Fortnightly* discussed the moral results to be expected of reform, which had been much in the air during the election. "The index," wrote Lewes, "points to reform." And for a leader there was Mr. Gladstone with his new Lancashire constituency—although he had lost Oxford to Mr. Gathorne Hardy and the Carlton Club.

> Mr. Gladstone's position in relation to the Liberal party [wrote Lewes] was conspicuous enough before; it is far more conspicuous now. In this struggle it is Mr. Gladstone's name which has risen above all others. The University of Oxford, instead of driving him into the wilderness, has driven him into the leadership of the Liberal party in the House of Commons.[40]

And that was as far as anyone, even Mr. Gladstone, might be expected to go.

When Palmerston died the next month, the *Fortnightly* suggested that perhaps now the state machinery would work more effectively. And when Lord Russell was given the task of forming a cabinet, Lewes talked of his "great services and historical renown and indubitable patriotism and sound Liberal convictions." As for the coming session, "it would redound to the honour of the new Parliament as well as to the new Government, were it possible to frame a measure, which, while it would represent the triumph of liberal opinions and principles, would not represent the triumph of a party."[41] Reform, after all, was greater than any party. When in December it was announced that the ministers would bring in a Reform Bill, Lewes wrote: "There can be no doubt about it. This time there will be no coquetting with Reform, no sham fights. The measure is now in course of preparation."[42] But he thought that the measure must be broad enough to satisfy the country and wise enough to conciliate the interests: a measure that would bring the representative machinery into harmony with the vast changes that have occurred since 1832, and would elicit from the thoughtful as well as from the masses, a sufficient demonstration of opinion and force at the back of it, to secure the passing of the Bill through Parliament.[43]

What the *Fortnightly* wanted was a bill "to put Reform to sleep, so that Parliament might set to work on the great social and political business of the nation, undisturbed by discussions on the constitutional machinery."

But when Mr. Gladstone brought in his bill, it proved to be "avowedly not an attempt to effect a complete settlement"; and the *Fortnightly* began to demur.

> What the country wanted, in so far as it wanted anything, was a settlement. What has been presented to it—no matter how good it may be in itself—is not a settlement. . . . It does open the door to many now shut out. But it should have been accompanied by other arrangements; it should have been part of a great whole. As it stands it is to be feared that it will fail, and as the ministers stand or fall with it, there is a chance that they may fall.[44]

When the bill did fail, and the ministers fell with it, the *Fortnightly* blamed the Prime Minister. Again, as in the case of the Corn Laws in 1846, Lord John had "upset the coach," this time, ironically enough, by too closely following the radical Mr. Bright. Dissension among the Liberals had caused their downfall, and Lord Derby and Mr. Disraeli came into power. Concerning the Liberal Party Lewes now somewhat ruefully commented:

> There are many who think that the time has come when each man must think for himself, and that the line taken by the Liberal chiefs has been so mistaken and unsuccessful that it is unsafe to follow them without a careful examination of their views and the means by which they intend to carry them out. These opinions have been much strengthened by the violent language of Mr. Bright and the adhesion of so important a person as Mr. Mill to the extreme and violent party—and the consequence is that however ardently a small knot of persons may desire to return to office, we believe that when Parliament meets they will find themselves obliged by public opinion to give the Conservatives a really fair chance of showing what they can do in the difficult task of national administration.[45]

The failure of the Liberals, however, did not prevent the *Fortnightly* from continuing to harp upon the subject of Reform. There was never any doubt in Lewes's mind that reform of the franchise was desirable: he simply begged the whole question, addressing himself rather to the means by which the end was to be consummated—even if that means must be the Conservative Party. He was impatient at having to write about the franchise when he might be giving more space to those matters that were organic rather than mechanical, to those reforms that really needed championing. But, at that, he did find space to instruct Parliament and the nation in their social duties, for when Lord Derby came into office Lewes was ready with his questions:

> Both sides will probably concur in amending the treatment of the sick in workhouses, and in a new bankruptcy law; but how about a Reform Bill? of the relations of landlord and tenant in Ireland? of making the Universities really national institutions instead of confining their governments and emoluments to those only who profess one particular creed? On the great questions of civil and religious liberty the difference between parties is almost as great as ever.[46]

Only the Liberals, apparently, could see the necessity for reforms that the *Fortnightly* desired—and especially was this true with respect to education, dominated since man could remember by the Lords and the Church. Though neither public school man nor university man, Lewes had definite ideas for the improvement of both organization and curriculum of the schools. They showed, according to him, "disgraceful deficiencies, with vested interests standing in the way of reforms." Eton, for example, was "an aristocratic nursery for idleness . . . where the rich tradesman who sends his son to learn aristocratic habits has rather Lord Dundreary placed before him as a model than Sir Philip Sidney."[47] He pointed out the conspicuous examples of the United States, Scotland, and Prussia. Noblemen's sons and their education were responsible to a great extent for the bad state of affairs in England:

> They can scarcely be said at our public schools and universities to have ever been taught the value of a thoroughly good training and education. Indeed, the principal lesson a nobleman's son learns at school or college is that he may safely depend upon his natural, untutored nobility; that with his class ordinary rules are not to be enforced; that he may amuse himself while others work; that the mere fact of his birth is sufficient to make him respected and bowed down to even by his tutors.[48]

One chief trouble in English education, he thought, was that young men spent years composing Greek and Latin poetry when they might better be studying those forces that were beginning to come alive in their own day: physics, for instance, and psychology. Lewes complained, with some justice, that a man preparing to study medicine studied no science until he actually began his professional training. But vested interests and the Church stood in the way of educational reform, especially the Church, with its Thirty-Nine Articles, which Lewes called "a set of complicated and contradictory propositions representing the progress of the sixteenth century."

And the Church, according to the *Fortnightly,* obstructed social reform not only in England but in Ireland, where it shared with the English landlord the abuse of English liberal critics bent upon improving the conditions among the Catholic tenants. "Until in some way or other," Lewes wrote, "we become reconciled with the Irish people, Ireland will be a just reproach to us in the mouths of foreign nations."[49] But the problem was a difficult one, made doubly difficult for patriotic English editors by the outrages of equally patriotic Irish revolutionaries.

Young men in the southern counties of Ireland, who rejoiced in the "strange appellation of Fenians," were reported to be practicing military drill at night. In September, 1865, the *Fortnightly* noticed them briefly:

> Of course no apprehension is felt about these Fenians by any sensible person. The first sign of overt action would bring down upon them sharp punishment, and if not instant extinction, at least complete repression. A Fenian republic is a simple impossibility. The loyal Irishmen alone, without the aid of troops, would suffice to settle accounts with these misguided men, whose smattering of military drill will, if they ever break out, only help them the more effectively to their ruin.[50]

But two weeks later "these misguided men," about whom no sensible person could feel apprehensive, became the main editorial consideration in the *Fortnightly Review*. Fenians had been arrested in both Ireland and England. What had begun rather quietly two weeks before now became "another chapter in human folly." But the review contained no wholesale indictment of Ireland, merely pity for the great body of Irish, who were considered innocent of any complicity. The review pleaded for peaceful constitutional settlement of Irish grievances and expressed its confidence in the Government's ability to deal justly with the Fenian plotters. Throughout the series of disorders the *Fortnightly* showed its disapproval of Fenianism; but it refrained with admirable restraint from imputing to the Irish as a whole any blame for the ill-advised excesses of a small part of their countrymen. But Ireland was not the only part of the Empire that was having its troubles with revolts.

On November 15, 1865, the *Fortnightly* carried its first notice of the vigorous suppression by Governor Eyre of a supposed incipient uprising of the Negroes of Jamaica. Although few facts had been published in England when that first notice went to press, the *Fortnightly* from the very beginning embraced the cause of the Negroes. "The colony," it said, "has long been a scandal and a disgrace, and now that it has become the scene of a horrible rebellion, perhaps the Imperial Parliament may be moved to strike at the evil."[51] When it was learned how and to what extent the Governor had punished the Negroes, Lewes's complaints and charges began to grow more specific:

> The outrages of the negroes at Morant Bay have sunk into the background, and the foreground is now filled by the spectacle of the punishments inflicted indis-

criminately on the coloured race of the two parishes in the east end of the island by the Governor, by the white West Indians, by officers of Her Majesty's regular Army, and by their dark allies, the Maroons, for the crimes committed in Morant Bay, and the subsequent ravages of plantations. . . . Standing out in bold relief, like a giant figure against a lurid sunset, is one distinct act of proscription committed in defiance of all law. The figure of Mr. George Gordon, swinging on a gibbett in Morant Bay, with a background of massacre, has made an impression on the public mind. . . . These are strong assertions, and these assertions we mean to justify out of the official despatches. For the honour and credit and good name of England are involved, and these must be vindicated, either by the production, on the part of the Jamaica authorities, of ample warrant for what they have done, or by a disavowal of what they have done on the part and in the name of the Imperial Government.[52]

The case of George Gordon was unusual. He was a colored man—nearly white—with an English wife; and as a member of the Assembly he had become obnoxious in Jamaica as "opposition" and as a defender of the Negroes in endless quarrels. At the time of the trouble in Morant Bay, which had been placed under martial law, Gordon was at Kingston. Eyre, claiming that Gordon was the chief cause of the uprising at Morant Bay "through his own misrepresentation and seditious language," had him arrested, carried to Morant Bay, tried by court-martial, and hanged on the twenty-third of November "beneath the great arch of the burnt courthouse."

> Now this [said Lewes] is a proceeding which can find its justification in no rule or principle of law. Governor Eyre had no authority to send Mr. Gordon to Morant Bay for trial; the Brigadier and his militia officers had no authority to try him, and consequently neither the Governor nor the so-called court had any authority to hang him. Mr. Gordon has been slain in violation of the law. He may have been guilty of all that is charged against him—of that we know nothing; but Governor Eyre and Brigadier Nelson have been guilty of a crime quite as great as that imputed to Gordon—they have taken life by an illegal process; they have in the name of the Queen, and by misusing the powers entrusted to them by the Queen, committed a judicial murder. Unless these men are called to a strict account, it will be impossible to say that any man is safe in any British possession or even in Great Britain itself. . . . Governor Eyre ought to be recalled, and those officers, who, on their own showing, did flagrantly illegal acts, should be directed to report to the Horse Guards. The public conscience demands satisfaction and will have it.[53]

The appointment of a commission of inquiry was applauded by the *Fortnightly,* which at the same time deplored the conduct of those who "at first tried to bully the public and then to burke the facts." All the editorial comment of the review was based upon the official despatches from Jamaica, that is upon the reports made by Eyre himself; and the very words of those reports were quoted in denunciation of Eyre's conduct. The review called for evidence that Eyre and his associates, by the harshness of their punishments, had forestalled rebellion.

> The questions, then, to be dealt with first are, not the causes of the alleged rebellion, not the conduct of Mr. Cardwell [Colonial Secretary]—upon whom the Tories boast they will fasten the odium of the whole business—not the character of the Jamaica negro, not the proceedings of the Baptists, but these:—1st. Was there any rebellion; and, if so, did its character and extent warrant an application of the law of self preservation, so bloody and savage as to fill the world with horror; and, 2nd, is there any justification for the judicial killing of Mr. Gordon, legal or otherwise? *After* these points have been investigated to the satisfaction of the public conscience, then we may go to the causes of the rebellion, the conduct of the dissenting missionaries, and the character of the black and white people who live in Jamaica.[54]

Finally about a year after the hanging of Gordon the Commission made its report, and national excitement subsided. The Commission found that punishment of Negroes had been excessive, and the punishment of death unnecessarily frequent; that the burning of houses and the floggings had been wanton and barbarous; that martial law had "almost precluded a calm inquiry into each man's guilt or innocence"; that it had been unreasonable to send officers to quell rebellion without very specific instructions; and that the evidence had been insufficient to establish the charge on which Gordon had stood trial. In the minority report of those who had desired strong action against Eyre it was conceded that good had been achieved in demonstrating that men in Eyre's position would thenceforth be held responsible to juries of their countrymen for any excesses of conduct.[55] Although no attempt was made to punish Eyre or the military officers, the *Fortnightly* endorsed the work of the Commission and withdrew from the whole affair with something surprisingly like an anticlimactic gesture of good will toward Eyre himself.

> Governor Eyre [said the *Fortnightly*] is a man who bears the highest character, and doubtless he now regrets much which took place in Jamaica. He has been, however, most severely tried and punished already; and we doubt the expediency, at any rate, of the Government bringing him to trial for the murder of Mr. Gordon. . . . Meanwhile the effect of the discussion of the subject, and the condemnation of the cruelty of the officials by public opinion in England, will have a great effect, and make our authorities abroad justly careful in the exercise of power placed in their hands.[56]

This softening toward Eyre is hard to reconcile with the bitterness of the review in its earlier editorials.[57]

In its general attitude, then, toward the famous case of Governor Eyre, which for over a year divided English thinkers into hostile camps, the *Fortnightly Review* took the same liberal part taken by such men as John Stuart Mill, Herbert Spencer, Huxley, and Darwin. It was militantly opposed to the well-known views of Carlyle, who, on the whole "Nigger Question," was scornful of what he considered sentimental liberalism.

In the eyes of English Liberals black slavery loomed large enough to obscure any clear vision of the North American continent. The sympathy of the *Fortnightly Review* for the free Negroes of the West Indies extended to the recently liberated blacks of the southern United States. The party of humanity could hardly be mistaken about so palpable an issue as slavery; and that issue determined for many an Englishman his view of American politics during and after the Civil War. Besides, the position of the *Fortnightly* as a social force was in perfect accord with the division of classes in England as to their American sympathies. The upper classes naturally sided with the Southerners in their struggle with the business men of the North, for it was these same kinds of tradesmen who were more and more making inroads upon the rights of English agrarians. The English capitalist manufacturers were led by economic interest to sympathize with the cotton-producing South. On the other hand, the reforming element of English society and the English lower classes, themselves somewhat in the position of industrial slaves, had had the strongest desires to see complete abolition of slavery in America. These classes wanted to see the South fail in its efforts to destroy a union that would be, if the North triumphed, a model of democratic government: Europe in the middle of the nineteenth century could learn much from such a model. Very naturally and comfortably, then, the *Fortnightly,* in its character of reformer and defender of the workingman, fitted into this scheme of things. Its first issue, coming out on the very heels of Appomattox and the assassination of President Lincoln, contained five and a half editorial pages—of small type—excoriating the Southern states and exalting the humanitarian virtues of Mr. Lincoln. The assassination was "one of those great crimes in high places which are at once recognized by the common instinct of mankind as land marks in history." And as for those people of the South—

> There will be no decided manifestation of feeling on the part of the Southern leaders respecting the crime, or we are much mistaken; and if the murderers have been discovered, it has not been by Southern aid. Let it be remembered how absolutely personal the animosity of the people of the slave states is in all its characteristics. They hated such men as Lincoln and Seward with an intensity not to be credited by those ignorant of the passion which animated the hand that struck Sumner to the ground in the Senate, and that sought, in many a debate before secession, to adjust political differences on the field of honour.[58]

Then followed grave fears concerning the period of reconstruction after the war. The editorial ended with a word of good will toward the new president, Mr. Johnson. All this, in its first issue, left no doubt about the stand of the *Fortnightly* on American affairs. Every subsequent issue, for a while, carried some comment on the progress of reconstruction and the tribulations of President Johnson. Exactly what to do with Jefferson Davis was also a problem that vexed Lewes, as it vexed some others.

> If Mr. Davis had any guilty knowledge of Mr. Lincoln's murder, let him die the death. All the world will cry, "Amen." But to execute Mr. Davis for his acts in relation to secession would be an outrage to public opinion all over the world. . . . The greatest punishment that could be inflicted on Mr. Jefferson Davis would be to let him live in obscurity among the ruins of his hopes and fortunes.[59]

That was a fair enough comment, and the attitude of the review toward the amnesty and its exemptions was in the same spirit. If the amnesty exemptions purposed to keep out a vote on slavery, that was as it should be; but if they were punitive, then they were reprehensible.

Slavery and democracy were the twin sanctions of Lewes's criticism of America; and though he quarreled with John Bright for being too inexpediently eloquent about American democracy, he realized the value in English politics of Bright's extreme views. A certain degree of democracy in Europe was just as desirable to Lewes as it was to Bright, though Lewes had less confidence than Bright in the political acumen of the uneducated. Nevertheless, toward the end of 1866 Lewes appealed to the Tories to observe American success with universal suffrage:

> The United States have exhibited a wealth, a strength, and organization, a temperance and moderation after their great successes, which show that universal suffrage and the freest institutions are compatible with a well-ordered state, where life and property are secure, and that an elected president is able to sustain the honour of the country, and to keep up a military and a naval array which can vie with those of the proudest monarchies of Europe.[60]

In its whole attitude toward Europe the review persisted in this humanitarian tradition. A people—no matter who—struggling for independence, for unity, for freedom of expression, was assured of support from Lewes's *Fortnightly*. The oppressions of Bismarck were denounced, as were the imperial antics of Napoleon III. Venetia was supported against Austria, Austria against Prussia. Little sympathy was wasted upon Maximilian's venture in Mexico, a project which would have depended for success upon the oppression of the Mexicans and the existence just north of Mexico of a slave state as a buffer against the operation of the Monroe Doctrine.

This survey, then, of Lewes's editorials shows the liberal tendency that marked the policy of the *Fortnightly* from its beginning. How Lewes's liberalism spread

through the whole review may be seen by examining the articles that he published. The question of Parliamentary reform, for example, was a favorite subject among contributors to the review, in the second issue of which appeared a defense of those political principles which ultimately made the Reform Bill of 1867.[61] This article was an answer to a speech in Parliament by Robert Lowe, who had stood against reform, saying that the people were excellently governed already and that there was no reason for a change. The *Fortnightly* pointed out that England was already a democracy, and that consequently all movement in the direction of democracy was only organic development. Lewes prophesied manhood suffrage.

But usually the issue was not simply reform; that necessity was being granted even by most Conservatives. The contributors to the review, like the editor, simply took reform as a matter of course. It was special plans for reform that they proposed, plans for instance, like Thomas Hare's for the representation of minorities.[62] In its early days Hare contributed two papers to the *Fortnightly*: one of them proposed that members of unrepresented political minorities might register in a general electoral college and elect a number of special candidates determined by the size of the registration;[63] the other suggested a plan that would give the voter a more comprehensive choice of candidates, the old choice between Tweedledum and Tweedledee being not to his liking.[64] Another Parliamentary reformer proposed that the United Kingdom be divided "into several large electoral provinces as nearly as possible on the basis of population to return each a member to represent great leading interests"—among the constituents of these interests being clerks, tenant farmers, unskilled laborers, and women.[65] "The Just Demand of the Working Man" proposed to divide the country into four electoral groups, each to send members to Parliament: these groups were property, the professions, trade, and labor.[66] Feeling, like Lewes, that no reform should be passed that did not attempt a permanent settlement, the author of this paper attacked the Bill of 1832 and called for a new order.

> What is needed is not the preponderance of any one class or any united classes in this or that county or borough; but such arrangements for voting as shall enable each of the four distinct classes of English life to control one fourth of the Parliamentary representation. . . . And now that the hour for action has come, the real demand of the artisan ought to be, not a quarter, or a third, or a half of the voting power in this or that borough or county, but the power of practically nominating one fourth of the members of the House of Commons.[67]

This proposal was reinforced by an imaginary appeal from the working man:

> Without us and our daily labours the greatness of England would vanish tomorrow. Give us, then, our legiti-

mate share in the legislation and the government of England; or tell us, in so many words, that we are the Pariahs of our generation. Show us that the vices, the crimes, the bigotries, the extravagances of the age, are all our own, and that peers, gentlemen, and shopkeepers are all pure while we are vile; or else grant us that position in the rule of our common country which we ask, and which we will never rest until we obtain.[68]

But the most generally harassing question of the time, the relation of science and religion, elicited the greatest amount of plain speaking in the *Fortnightly Review*.[69] Very early an article by Thomas Henry Huxley on the methods and results of ethnology set a style to be followed by the others who wrote on science and religion. In this article Huxley advocated and endorsed the theory of natural selection as a plausible and useful scientific principle, and at the same time he paid a Victorian scientist's respects to the book of Genesis. Speaking of those who represented "the most numerous, respectable, and would-be orthodox of the public," who might be called "'Adamites' pure and simple," he wrote:

> They believe that Adam was made out of earth somewhere in Asia about six thousand years ago; that Eve was modeled from one of his ribs; and that the progeny of these two having been reduced to the eight persons who were landed on the summit of Mount Ararat after an universal deluge, all the nations of the earth have proceeded from these last, have migrated to their present localities, and have become converted into negroes, Australians, Mongolians, etc., within that time. Five sixths of the public are taught this Adamitic monogenism as if it were an established truth, and believe it. I do not; and I am not acquainted with any man of science, or duly instructed person, who does.[70]

Exactly six months later the *Fortnightly* published Huxley's first Lay Sermon, which had been delivered at St. Martin's Hall on Sunday, January 7, 1866. This so-called sermon "On the Advisableness of Improving Natural Knowledge," well known today and containing little to startle the twentieth century, must have been to its Mid-Victorian audience a hard crystallization of the various ethical implications of the new science. This new attack upon authority was a forceful sequel to Huxley's first article in the *Fortnightly*. What, Huxley asked, were the moral convictions most fondly held by barbarous peoples?

> They are the convictions that authority is the soundest basis of belief; that merit attaches to a readiness to believe; that the doubting disposition is a bad one and scepticism a sin; that when good authority has pronounced what is to be believed, and faith has accepted it, reason has no further duty. There are many excellent persons who hold by these principles, and it is not my present business or intention to discuss their views. All I wish to bring clearly before your minds is the unquestionable fact that the improvement of natural knowledge is effected by methods which directly give the lie to all these convictions, and assume the exact reverse of each to be true.

The improver of natural knowledge absolutely refuses to acknowledge authority, as such. For him scepticism is the highest of duties; blind faith the one unpardonable sin. And it cannot be otherwise, for every great advance in natural knowledge has involved the absolute rejection of authority, the cherishing of the keenest scepticism, the annihilation of the spirit of blind faith; and the most ardent votary of science holds his firmest convictions, not because the men he most venerates hold them; not because their verity is testified by portents and wonders; but because his experience teaches him that whenever he chooses to bring these convictions into contact with their primary source, nature—whenever he thinks fit to test them by appealing to experiment and observation—nature will confirm them. The man of science has learned to believe in justification, not by faith, but by verification.[71]

Another scientist, John Tyndall, writing on the constitution of the universe, pointed out the scientific attitude toward the relation of miracles to prayer. Those who devised prayers for rain, he said, admitted that the age of miracles was passed; yet in the same breath they petitioned for the performance of miracles. They would not, however, ask that water might flow uphill.

> The man of science [he explained] clearly sees that the granting of the one petition would be just as much of an infringement of the laws of conservation as the granting of the other. . . . And if our spiritual authorities could only devise a form in which the heart might express itself without putting the intellect to shame, they might utilise a power which they now waste, and make prayer, instead of a butt to the scorner, the potent inner supplement of noble outward life.[72]

Those articles, on the other hand, which may be considered to have presented the other side of this argument usually issued in a compromise. They did not present an extremely conservative point of view, for their authors either advocated changes within the Church or manifested far from conservative tolerance in handling liberal matters. Even Peter Bayne, for instance, in proposing a "Neo-Evangelism," defined a religion that would include the ideas of both Mr. Carlyle and Mr. Mill. Furthermore he reviewed Strauss's *New Life of Christ* and Seeley's *Ecce Homo* in a spirit incompatible with popular feeling about historical criticism—and Bayne was perhaps the most conservative of the *Fortnightly* writers. He enjoined his public to adjust its spiritual concepts to include the new ideas of the assailants of orthodox Christianity. He considered natural selection reconcilable with theism and called Seeley's book a contribution to "constructive Christianity." "When the brains are out," he warned the faithful, "a church will die."

Concerning the precarious hold of the English Church upon the public, the most forthright language of all is found in two articles by Viscount Amberley, oldest son of Lord John Russell.[73] Amberley was not opposed to a church establishment, but because he desired to see a church that was truly national he was opposed to the Anglican establishment of his day. Considering different religious points of view, he defined the Liberal as one who "will uphold the claims of the Nation at the expense of the Church," the Conservative as one who will "uphold the privileges of the Church at the expense of the Nation." None of the reforms brought about by the Liberal Party, he contended, have ruined the nation; on the contrary it is tacitly admitted that these reforms were right. And yet Oxford and Cambridge were still closed against Dissenters; an insulting oath was imposed upon Roman Catholic Members of Parliament; and unbaptized persons were refused Christian burial. Like Peter Bayne he felt that the Church must make a place for the liberal thinker and for all dissenting sects.

> Above all, if the creed supported by the state includes dogmas which can no longer be believed; if therefore the Church has ceased to express the religious feeling of the nation; if the best and wisest men in the nation find that her doors are closed against them, or can only be entered by contortions of conscience, then it is evident that either the connection should be altogether severed, or the conditions exacted from the clergy be so modified as to suit the growing intelligence and the broader opinions of the people.[74]

He thought they ordered things better than this in sixteenth-century Spain, where convictions were less diffident than in Victorian England.

> Philip II was no less warmly attached to his church than Mr. Disraeli and his followers are to theirs. But he proved his devotion in a much more thorough as well as a more consistent manner. Refusing to accord Christian burial to a Baptist or to a Unitarian may be a noble and dignified way of protesting against dissent. There is something almost superhuman in that heroic hatred of error which extends its animosity even to the bodies of the dead. Compared, however, with the proceedings of Phillip II, this is but a feeble attempt to discourage heresy and schism. Refusing to allow dissenters to exist at all is a much more effective plan than insulting them when dead. The principle is substantially the same, but the advantage in point of practice must be conceded to Phillip II and the Inquisition.[75]

It was perfectly evident, thought Amberley, what the English Church actually accomplished by its half-hearted strictures:

> So far as the necessity of conforming to the Thirty-Nine Articles and the Liturgy operates at all, it operates to narrow the field from which the clergy are selected; to exclude the learned, the intellectual, the profound; and instead of them, to fill the Church with ignorant and narrow-minded men, who are totally unable to influence the educated classes of their countrymen, who cannot sympathise with the feelings of those around them, and whose best excuse is that they are melancholy examples of the results of a mistaken system.[76]

Any institution upholding medieval doctrines contradictory to the science of the day and to the spirit of progress, Amberley concluded, must do so at its own peril.

Open discussion of the Church in England led, of course, to consideration of the Church in Ireland—and ultimately to the whole Irish question. The best treatment of Irish affairs in the review was contributed by James Godkin in a series of five articles.[77] Discussing the Church and the land, he appealed to the country during the election of 1865 to return a Liberal Government because Liberals alone had done justice to Ireland in the past; and attacking the Anglican establishment, he prophesied its early doom. He thought that Ireland without a Church establishment would be "a more religious, a more united, a more peaceable, and a more prosperous country than ever it had been since the days of Saint Patrick."[78] In his article "The Irish Presbyterians" he showed that Ulster alone had a Protestant population outside the Establishment nearly equal to all the members of the established Church in Ireland.[79] Where then was the argument that defended the English Church in Ireland as a necessary bulwark against Catholicism? Finally he attacked the Conservative Party and pointed to the Liberals as the only hope in any solution of the Irish problem.

> During the last century England has been endeavoring slowly but steadily, and always under the pressure of agitation, to atone for past wrongs to Ireland. But every single measure of concession, every act of justice and sound policy, though the withholding of it threatened the dismemberment of the empire, has been resisted strenuously, passionately, by the Tory party, the representatives of the old English interest or Protestant ascendency, in the name of which so much Irish blood has been shed, so much national poverty and suffering inflicted. There are signs that the great work of reconciliation between the two nations is about to be repeated, and that Mr. Gladstone is destined to be the providential instrument in solving "the Irish difficulty."[80]

In the same spirit Anthony Trollope discussed the Irish Church,[81] and Marmion Savage attacked the Irish judicial system.[82] "The smaller island," said Savage, "is as much over-wigged as she is over-mitred and over-churched."[83] He viciously attacked the Royal Commission that had reported that it was not expedient to reduce the number of Irish judges. He scoffed at the report: "Not expedient to reduce a Bench three times too numerous for its work. . . . Not expedient to reduce the number of Irish judges, when it is notorious that frequently in mid-terms they take their seats at eleven o'clock to hear the voice of the crier at one proclaiming 'Tomorrow! God Save the Queen!'"[84] In 1867 the intense interest in reform of the franchise drove the Irish articles from the review—for a while.

Although there was not so much discussion of industrial problems as their prominence seemed to demand, during the first half year of the review Frederic Harrison wrote four excellent papers on the subject.[85] He discussed strikes and lockouts, co-operation, trade unions, and the "limits of political economy." His article on co-operation moved George Eliot to write to him of the delight and gratitude she felt in reading it. "Certain points," she wrote, "admirably brought out in that article, would, I think, be worth the labour of a life if one could help in winning them thorough recognition."[86] Although he attacked the Utilitarian economics, Harrison praised John Stuart Mill, because he considered Mill's political economy merely a special phase of a much broader social philosophy. The average economist, he said, lacked the philosophical background of a Mill. "With the moral doctrine of self interest," he wrote, "and the political doctrine of *laissez-faire* (vaguely understood) the pure statistician thinks himself prepared for investigating production."[87] Harrison argued in favor of a humane social philosophy; and, like Carlyle and Ruskin, he denounced the economics of acquisition. Political economy, he thought, should have backgrounds and associations, for had not Auguste Comte written, "the phenomena of society being more complicated than any other, it is irrational to study the industrial apart from the intellectual and the moral"? Industry needed correcting, purifying, guiding. There were things in it, otherwise, that made one look upon material progress as a curse.

The whole "condition of England" question was a favorite one for liberal treatment in the *Fortnightly Review*. Trollope discussed the public schools; others the Church schools. Mining, the poor, state hospitals, the Civil Service, the Army, sanitation, banking, and the currency—all these received publicity in Lewes's pages, and that publicity was marked by a distinctly liberal tone. Dissatisfaction with the *status quo* was very much in evidence.

This survey of Lewes's *Fortnightly* shows clearly that in the year and a half of Lewes's editorship there was not so much diversity of opinion as the editor and proprietors had desired. Lewes, for one, was not completely satisfied with the liberal turn that affairs were taking, for even before the review had run its first year he made a direct plea to his public to recognize, and act upon, his desire for impartiality:

> It is our constant endeavor to get men of various views to express their views firmly, yet distinctly. To a great extent we have succeeded, as the list of our contributors sufficiently shows: but there are many who withhold their services from a half suspicion that because their views are not for the government, or against it, not in harmony with those of the editor or of some well-known contributors, they would on that account be unacceptable. Nothing of the kind. Our first question

is, have you any decided opinions, or any special knowledge? not what are your opinions?[88]

Some writers, he thought, might have contributed but for the publicity of their authorship; but with respect to the signed article the editor had steered his course straight and kept his colors flying. His appeal, however, having brought no greater diversity of opinion than was already apparent, he had to rest satisfied with things as they were. And as the months passed it became obvious that the number of liberal articles was increasing and that the *Fortnightly Review* was gradually losing its fight for impartiality.

But if Lewes was not completely satisfied with the fading of his ideal, at least one of the founders was downright resentful. Conservative proprietors and radical editors may not actually have clashed, but in the *Fortnightly* office there must have been some dissension. Anthony Trollope and perhaps some others were undoubtedly beginning to wonder what sort of journalistic Tartar they had caught. Trollope's latest biographer has an interesting contribution on this subject:

> Trouble was due and trouble came. There is a pleasant irony in the thought that, while the *Belton Estate*—that smooth, enchanting, but most unprovocative story— was completing its gentle serialisation in the magazine, its author was growling uneasily behind the scenes in the center of a crowd of contemptuous doctrinaires, who thought his novel a lump of spongy commonplace, and for all their great personal liking for him—said as much.[89]

Trollope himself complains against no one—whining was not his way—but his autobiography gives a summary of that whole matter which is as shrewd in analysis as it is generous in omitting personal accusation:

> That theory of eclecticism was altogether impracticable. It was as though a gentleman should go into the House of Commons determined to support no party, but to serve his country by individual utterances. Such gentlemen have gone into the House of Commons, but they have not served their country much. Of course the project broke down. Liberalism, free-thinking, and open inquiry will never object to appear in company with their opposites, because they have the conceit to think that they can quell those opposites; but the opposites will not appear in company with liberalism, free-thinking, and open inquiry.[90]

And when one considers the background of English journalistic tradition, one must admit that this explanation is as good as any. The dissatisfaction in the *Fortnightly* office is evidence that some thought that Lewes was bent upon turning the review into liberal channels; and if he was really, consciously or unconsciously, leaning to the left, he would certainly have attracted the liberal rather than the conservative contributor. And having once attracted the Liberals, the review, as Trollope explains, would have had increasing difficulty luring the Conservatives. What the founders might have considered from the start is that eclecticism is basically liberal in spirit—they had even called it liberalism in their prospectus. Independence of authority *is* liberalism; so it is not surprising that the Conservatives considered the review sectarian. In so far as the *Fortnightly* failed to gain conservative approval it seems to have failed in its attack upon the Victorian tradition of authority in journalism, but in its determination to speak plainly and openly on divers matters it succeeded, most eminently.

Its success in plain-speaking based upon signature and personal responsibility was a blow to the tradition of anonymity. Every article published by Lewes carried the name of its author—with three exceptions. The first unsigned contribution was entitled "Recent Austrian Policy,"[91] at the end of which, instead of the usual signature, there were four asterisks and this note: "Reasons of a diplomatic nature render it desirable, in this instance, to withhold the writer's name. The Editor, therefore, departs from his rule, and assumes the responsibility which would otherwise have fallen on the contributor"—and, he might have added, on the British diplomatic service. The second anonymous article, "Inedited Letters of Louis Philippe," appeared about six months later.[92] Again foreign diplomacy seemed to Lewes to justify the anonymity. Shortly before he relinquished the editorship the last unsigned article appeared: "The Army: By a (Late) Common Soldier."[93] On this occasion the editor's footnote explained: "For reasons easily divined the name of the writer of this paper is withheld; but the Editor testifies to the important fact that the writer, an acquaintance of his, was formerly a common soldier, and that his statements, therefore, deserve that attention which *bona fide* complaint may always claim." It was a good article attacking obvious abuses in the Army. The reasons for anonymity are, as Lewes said, very easily divined.

A review that had published only three unsigned articles in a year and a half and which continued to command contributions from prominent writers would seem to have succeeded in its fight against anonymity, and Lewes and his circle were proud of that success. As early as December 17, 1865, George Eliot wrote to M. d'Albert:

> The *Fortnightly* is a great *succès d'estime*. The principle of signature never before thoroughly carried out in England, has given it an exceptional dignity, and drawn valuable writers. It is a thoroughly serious periodical, intended for the few who will pay a high price and is supported by proprietors unconnected with the publishing trade. It is still a question whether it will succeed commercially.[94]

This letter alone seems to indicate that Lewes and his friends considered their use of signature a success; and

another letter, from Lewes to Thomas Adolphus Trollope, shows that there was little difficulty finding writers of signed articles.

> Thank Signor ———— for the offer of his paper, and express to him my regret that in the present crowded state of the *Review* I cannot find a place for it. Don't you, however, run away with the idea that I don't want your contributions on the same ground. The fact is ————'s paper is too wordy and heavy and not of sufficient interest for our publication; and as I have a great many well on hand, I am forced to be particular. Originally my fear was lest we should not get contributors enough. That fear has long vanished.[95]

This new kind of review, furthermore, appealed to intelligent readers. George Eliot wrote in her journal, November, 1865, "The success of the *Fortnightly* with the part of the reading public Lewes cared most about was a gratification to him"; and in his own private summary of the year 1865 Lewes notes, "Gratifying success of the *Fortnightly*."[96] But more conclusive than all this is what Lewes wrote in his **"Farewell Causerie,"** December 1, 1866:

> As this is the last number of the Review which will appear under my editorship, I wish in saying farewell to my friendly readers who have shown much sympathy with a novel and difficult undertaking, to thank the many and admirable contributors, for the most part strangers to me, whose labours have given the Review its eminent position. That we have been able to bring together men so various in opinion and distinguished in power, has been mainly owing to the principle adopted of allowing each writer perfect freedom; which could only have been allowed under the condition of personal responsibility. The question of signing articles has long been debated; it has now been tested. The arguments in favour of it were mainly of a moral order; the arguments against it, while admitting the morality, mainly asserted its inexpediency. The question of expediency has, I venture to say, been materially enlightened by the success of the Review.[97]

Any survey of Lewes's work on the *Fortnightly* would be incomplete without some consideration of that circle of authors whom Lewes gathered about him and who gave the review its eminent position; and in that consideration the part played by George Eliot must not be overlooked. She did not write for the *Fortnightly* after the first number, but by her intellectual charm she attracted to herself and to Lewes many who did. Quite logically Lewes at first appealed to his friends and to hers for assistance and contributions, to Trollope—very naturally, as a founder of the review—to Herbert Spencer, and to Frederic Harrison. Soon he began to attract to himself and to George Eliot a large group of the most prominent writers of the time, who spent many a Sunday afternoon at the Priory, where the Leweses had set up literary housekeeping in 1863, and where they dispensed tea and artistic atmosphere. It is hard to distinguish between the group of eminent visitors to the

Priory and the group of contributors to the *Fortnightly,* as hard as it is to avoid believing that both the review and the Sunday afternoons contributed each to the success of the other. The receptions at the Leweses' were in a way the social aspect of the *Fortnightly Review.* Among the visitors were scientists like Spencer (an old friend), Huxley, and Tyndall; the Positivists Harrison and the Congreves; and the poets Browning, Tennyson, Rossetti, and the young Robert Buchanan. Lord Houghton represented the aristocracy. Then there were a host of miscellaneous personalities: the Positivists Beesly and Crompton, who, like Harrison, were interested in the problems of labor; the scholar Emanuel Deutsch; the banker and critic, Walter Bagehot; and young men like John Dennis, Leslie Stephen, and John Morley. Almost all of these—and there were many more—contributed to the review, either in Lewes's time or later. The most industrious of all contributors were Lewes, Trollope, George Meredith, and Dennis—Trollope and Meredith swelling their list by the serial publication of a novel each, and Dennis, who was Lewes's assistant, appearing as the author of innumerable short reviews. It is significant that most of these men were pronouncedly liberal in their opinions.

Although the *Fortnightly* was in many respects an imitator of the *Revue des Deux Mondes,* Lewes was hardly an imitator of Buloz; for Lewes, unlike Buloz, wrote for his review and wrote copiously. He published serially his **Principles of Success in Literature,** he wrote articles on science and philosophy, and in almost every issue he reviewed at least one book, usually a scientific or classical work. Perhaps his best single contribution was a review article in which he discussed the philosophy of Auguste Comte. The writing of editorials alone must have consumed much of his time, for his department of "Public Affairs" always contained from eight to twelve pages of small type. How much help he had with this part of the work is impossible to ascertain; but his assistant, John Dennis, was probably of some aid to him in preparing this material. Throughout the whole of 1866 he conducted a department called "Causeries," under which head he found it convenient "to chat occasionally with readers and contributors; to comment on passing events in Literature, Science, and Art; and to mention briefly the appearance of works for which there is not space in our critical notices, or which may have to be postponed for some time before they can be noticed." In these "Causeries" Lewes could air his feelings more intimately than he could in the bonds of a formal editorial. His private tastes in books and the sciences were given frequent expression, and it was in this department that he appealed to the public to help the *Fortnightly* to be independent and impartial.

Next to Lewes, Anthony Trollope was certainly the most important contributor. Whereas Lewes was only a paid official with nothing to risk but his office and repu-

tation, Trollope was one of the founders of the review with £1250 at stake. As it was to his advantage that the review should prosper, he felt it necessary to take an active part in its work. He contributed the first serial novel, and during most of the first year he contributed an article about once a month. Among other things he discussed anonymous literature, the Irish Church, public schools, the Civil Service, and the Scotch Sabbath; and he rather testily reviewed Ruskin's *Sesame and Lilies* and *Crown of Wild Olive,* advising Mr. Ruskin to keep to his art criticism and not to spread his talents over too many fields. His growing dissatisfaction with the turn of affairs in the office of the editor perhaps explains why it was that Trollope appeared in the review more than twenty-three times during the first six months and only three times during the next twelve. But as long as he wrote for the *Fortnightly* he wrote good sound articles that had the ring of his own good sound convictions; and his observations on Ireland and the public school system and the Fourth Commandment were in very obvious accord with the liberalism of those same "contemptuous doctrinaires" who took so unkindly to his "unprovocative story." But it is hardly likely that these discords had any relation to the changes that occurred at the end of 1866.

Lewes's health, it must be remembered, was bad at the time he assumed the editorship, and it did not improve. In the autumn of 1865 he left England for a month, traveling in Normandy and Brittany. In June, 1866, he and George Eliot made a two months' trip to the continent in an effort to improve his health. Later he tried Tunbridge Wells. Editing the *Fortnightly* and his work upon a new book were too great a strain for his constitution to bear. Finally George Eliot persuaded him to abandon so rigorous a program. "George's increasing weakness," she wrote to Mrs. Congreve, "and the more and more frequent intervals in which he became unable to work, made me at last urge him to give up the idea of 'finishing' which often besets us vainly."[98] He surrendered before her urging: he stopped work on the new edition of his **History of Philosophy** and in December resigned his position as editor of the *Fortnightly Review.* At the end of the month he and George Eliot left England for the continent.

But those apprehensions already mentioned by George Eliot concerning the commercial success of the review, were, in the meantime, beginning to be fulfilled. The capital of the proprietors began to melt away. Espinasse suggests that the management of the finances being in the hands of authors exclusively, nothing else was to be expected; and Trollope gives the same explanation. These authors were, nevertheless, determined to salvage what they could, and they found a ready purchaser near at hand. They sold the copyright to their publishers, Chapman & Hall; but just before they abandoned the review they changed it to a monthly publication because the magazine dealers did not like to handle a fort-nightly. The issue of November 15 was the first mid-month issue to be discontinued; and Lewes's last issue of the review appeared December 1, 1866. The new owners chose John Morley as Lewes's successor.

Notes

With Morley's editorship, the numbering of the *Fortnightly Review* begins anew. All Morley's issues are designated "New Series" (N.S.). The *Fortnightly* is referred to as *F. R.*

1. Trollope says that he unsuccessfully opposed the Board of Managers in its determination to run part of a novel in each issue of the review.—*An Autobiography* [New York, 1883], p. 176.

2. Francis Espinasse, *Literary Recollections and Sketches* [London, 1893], p. 276.

3. *Ibid.,* p. 282.

4. Anna T. Kitchel, *George Lewes and George Eliot* [*: A Review of Records.* New York, 1933], pp. 27 ff.: John W. Cross, *George Eliot's Life as Related in Her Letters and Journals* [3 vols. New York, 1885], II, 277-85.

5. Espinasse says Greenwich, but see Kitchel, *George Lewes and George Eliot,* pp. 8 f.

6. Espinasse, *Literary Recollections,* p. 273.

7. John, Viscount Morley, *Recollections* [2 vols. New York, 1917], I, 85.

8. "Even today," writes Miss [Anna T.] Kitchel (*George Lewes and George Eliot* [New York, 1933], p. 46), "it proves a ready help to a student hard pressed to find his way through the mazes of the 'divine science.' To my disappointed query of a book dealer in Charing Cross as to why it was so hard to find a copy of the *Biographical History* [*Biographical History of Philosophy*] nowadays, he replied, 'We can't keep them in stock, madam. The London University students buy them up. You see, madam, they can understand Lewes.'"

9. Espinasse, *Literary Recollections,* p. 280.

10. Alexander Bain, *John Stuart Mill, A Criticism with Personal Recollections* [New York, 1882], p. 76 n.

11. Kitchel, *George Lewes and George Eliot,* pp. 27 f.

12. For a fuller account of Lewes's relations with Mill, including some interesting letters from Mill, see *ibid.,* pp. 27-40.

13. Anthony Trollope, *Autobiography* [New York, 1883], p. 134.

14. Kitchel, *George Lewes and George Eliot,* p. 204.

15. *Ibid.,* p. 208.

16. "George Henry Lewes," *F. R.* [*Fortnightly Review*], N.S. XXV (Jan., 1879), 22.

17. Kitchel, *George Lewes and George Eliot,* p. 231.

18. Cross, *George Eliot's Life* [*as Related in Her Letters and Journals*], II, 286; see also Blanche Colton Williams, *George Eliot* [New York, 1936], p. 215.

19. Cross, *George Eliot's Life,* II, 290.

20. Thomas Adolphus Trollope, *What I Remember* [New York, 1888], p. 480.

21. Kitchel, *George Lewes and George Eliot,* p. 232.

22. *Ibid.* This proves that the review did not come out on Saturday, May 13, as the advertisements had said that it would.

23. Cross, *George Eliot's Life,* II, 293.

24. Frederic Harrison (1831-1923), lawyer and journalist, devoted most of the energy of his long life to propagating in England the doctrines of Auguste Comte. A graduate of Wadham College, Oxford, he early became interested in the struggle of trade unionism. Because of his legal position and his knowledge of unions he was appointed to the Trade Union Commission of 1867-1869. He wrote the Trade Union Bill which established the policy of the state toward labor. He was co-founder of the *Positivist Review,* president of the English Positivist Committee from 1880 to 1905, and founder and head of Newton Hall, where he lectured regularly on Positivism. He was a "Little Englander" and a strong supporter of France during the Franco-German War. Among his long list of books are biography, history, and literary criticism. Perhaps his best known work is *The Choice of Books* (1886). At the age of eighty he wrote his *Autobiographic Memoirs* (1911), and twelve years later he died—on the eve of publication of his last work, *De Senectute.*—*Encyclopaedia Britannica,* 14th ed.; *Autobiographic Memoirs.*

25. *F. R.,* I (May 15, 1865), 115-16.

26. William Robinson Hopper, "An Iron-Master's View of Strikes," *F. R.,* I (Aug. 1, 1865), 742-56.

27. "The Good and Evil of Trade Unionism," *F. R.,* III (Nov. 15, 1865), 33-54.

28. G. D. Haughton, "The New Clerical Subscription Act," *F. R.,* I (July 15, 1865), 551-60.

29. Henry Rogers (1806-1877) was turned from surgery to the Congregationalist ministry on reading

John Howe's *The Redeemer's Tears Wept Over Lost Souls.* He was professor of English Language and Literature at University College, London, and then at Springhill College, Birmingham. In 1858 he was elected president of Lancashire Independent College, where he held the chair of Theology until 1871. He was author of a book of poems, a biography of John Howe, and three volumes of essays reprinted from the *Edinburgh Review.* His best work, *The Eclipse of Faith* (1852), was enjoyed by the pious but attacked by Francis Newman. Perhaps his most remarkable achievement was his editing *The Christian Correspondent* (1837), a classified collection of 423 letters "by eminent persons of both sexes, exemplifying the fruits of holy living and the blessedness of holy dying."—*DNB* [*Dictionary of National Biography*].

30. "Les Apôtres," *F. R.,* V (July 15, 1866), 513-36.

31. "Miracles No Proofs," *F. R.,* VI (Sept. 15, 1866), 356.

32. *Ibid.*

33. Peter Bayne (1830-1896) abandoned the Presbyterian ministry for journalism when bronchitis impaired his preaching. At different times he was editor of the *Witness;* the *Dial,* an unsuccessful newspaper; and the *Weekly Review,* organ of the Presbyterians, from which he resigned when he proved unsound on inspiration. A liberal evangelical, he contributed religious and literary papers to the prominent journals, and produced a long succession of books that included theology, drama, history, and literary criticism, among these, biographies of Hugh Miller and Martin Luther, and a history of the Free Church of Scotland. For a while he was popular in Scotland and America as a moral writer.—*DNB.*

34. "Critical Notices," *F. R.,* VI (Oct. 15, 1866), 639.

35. Francis Lawley, *F. R.,* II (Aug. 15, 1865), 1-10.

36. Charles Mackay, *F. R.,* IV (April 1, 1886), 477-90.

37. Moncure Daniel Conway (1832-1907), son of Virginia Methodist slave owners, experienced conversion to Methodism while a student at Dickinson College (Pennsylvania) and was led into the ministry by reading Emerson. Finding Methodism unsatisfying, he entered Harvard Divinity School, where he met the Cambridge and Concord abolitionists. He preached as Unitarian and Congregationalist, contributed to the *Atlantic Monthly,* and edited the *Dial* (1860) and the abolitionist *Commonwealth* (1862). Visiting England in 1863 to lecture for the Northern cause, he became pastor of the ultraliberal South Chapel, Finsbury, return-

ing to America in 1884. He made researches into demonology and oriental mysteries and wrote over seventy books and pamphlets, among them two novels; lives of Hawthorne, Carlyle, and Tom Paine, whose works he edited (1892); and *Autobiography, Memories and Experiences* (1904).—*DAB* [*Dictionary of American Bibliography*]; *Autobiography.*

38. "Public Affairs," *F. R.,* I (Aug. 1, 1865), 761.

39. *Ibid.,* I (July 1, 1865), 500.

40. *Ibid.,* I (Aug. 1, 1865), 762.

41. *Ibid.,* III (Nov. 15, 1865), 115.

42. *Ibid.,* III (Dec. 15, 1865), 364.

43. *Ibid.,* III (Feb. 1, 1866), 761.

44. *Ibid.,* IV (March 15, 1866), 370.

45. *Ibid.,* VI (Oct. 15, 1866), 622.

46. *Ibid.,* V (July 15, 1866), 624.

47. *Ibid.,* VI (Aug. 15, 1866), 105.

48. *Ibid.,* VI (Nov. 1, 1866), 747.

49. *Ibid.,* VI (Aug. 15, 1866), 106.

50. *Ibid.,* II (Sept. 15, 1865), 375.

51. *Ibid.,* II (Nov. 15, 1865), 116.

52. *Ibid.,* III (Dec. 1, 1865), 240.

53. *Ibid.,* pp. 244 f.

54. *Ibid.,* III (Dec. 15, 1865), 363.

55. Sir Spencer Walpole, *The History of Twenty-five Years* [London, 1904], III, 122-29.

56. "Public Affairs," *F. R.,* VI (Aug. 15, 1866), 107.

57. Possibly Lewes did not write this final comment, for it appeared August 15, 1866, when he had just returned from a long visit to the continent.—J. W. Cross, *George Eliot's Life As Related in Her Letters and Journals,* II, 312 f. He had left England on June 7th, and he returned August 2nd. Besides, the careless construction of the last sentence is not characteristic of him.

58. ["Public Affairs," *F. R.*], I (May 15, 1865), 117.

59. *Ibid.,* I (June 1, 1865), 247.

60. *Ibid.,* VI (Sept. 15, 1866), 358.

61. Sheldon Amos, "Democracy in England," *F. R.,* I (June 1, 1865), 228-38.

62. Thomas Hare (1806-1891), legal writer and active member of the Charities Commission, labored to devise a plan to secure for all classes, especially

minorities, representation in Parliament and other elected bodies. In 1857 appeared the first statement of his views, *The Machinery of Representation,* followed in 1859 by his more fully developed *Treatise on the Election of Representatives, Parliamentary and Municipal* (revised in 1861, 1865, and 1873). Although many regarded his system as impracticable, John Stuart Mill and his disciple, Henry Fawcett, ardently endorsed it.—*DNB.*

63. "An Electoral Reform," *F. R.,* II (Oct. 1, 1865), 439-42.

64. "The Keystone of Parliamentary Reform," *F. R.,* III (Jan. 15, 1866), 559-65.

65. Edward Wilson, "Principles of Representation," *F. R.,* IV (April 1, 1866), 421-36.

66. J. M. Capes, *F. R.,* IV (April 15, 1866), 560-68.

67. *Ibid.,* p. 566.

68. *Ibid.,* p. 568.

69. It is impossible here to do more than indicate the direction of the articles on science in Lewes's *Fortnightly,* for the subject was so frequently discussed that it is perhaps best presented as a part of the general treatment of science and rationalism. See below, Chapter IV.

70. *F. R.,* I (June 15, 1865), 273.

71. *F. R.,* III (Jan. 15, 1866), 636-37.

72. 'The Constitution of the Universe," *F. R.,* III (Dec. 1, 1865), 144.

73. John Russell, Lord Amberley (1842-1876), and Katharine Stanley (1842-1874), daughter of Lord Stanley of Alderley, were married in 1864 and for ten years were a radical sensation. In their brief but idyllic lives, influenced by John Stuart Mill, they embraced such radical causes as birth control and women's rights. They traveled in America, visiting Concord, Oberlin College, and other points of radical interest. Amberley was M. P. for Nottingham in 1867 but next year was defeated for South Devon for his Malthusian views. Lady Amberley lectured on women's rights and supported the movement for Girton College. Most of their friends were radicals of one sort or another: Mill, Helen Taylor, Harriet Grote, Henry Crompton, Jowett, and the Carlyles.—Bertrand and Patricia Russell, *The Amberley Papers: The Letters and Diaries of Bertrand Russell's Parents* [1937].

74. "Liberals, Conservatives, and the Church," *F. R.,* II (Sept. 1, 1865), 164.

75. *Ibid.,* p. 167.

76. "The Church of England as a Religious Body," *F. R.,* VI (Dec. 1, 1866), 784.

77. James Godkin (1806-1879), Irish journalist, for a while served the Irish Evangelical Society as a missionary to Roman Catholics. He attacked Romanism in two works: *A Guide from the Church of Rome to the Church of Christ* (1836) and *Apostolic Christianity, or the People's Antidote against Puseyism and Romanism* (1842). In 1847 he went to London as a journalist but returned in 1849 to Ireland, where he edited newspapers, served as Dublin correspondent for the *Times,* and became an active member of the Irish Tenant League. He wrote three books on Irish problems: *Ireland and Her Churches* (1867), *The Land War in Ireland* (1870), and *Religious History of Ireland; Primitive, Papal, and Protestant* (1873). In 1873 he was pensioned by the Queen.—*DNB.*

78. "Ireland without a Church Establishment," *F. R.,* II (Sept. 15, 1865), 298.

79. *F. R.,* III (Nov. 15, 1865), 89-111.

80. "The Case of Ireland," *F. R.,* IV (March 15, 1866), 298.

81. "The Irish Church," *F. R.,* II (Aug. 15, 1865), 82-90.

82. Marmion Savage (1803-1872), Irish novelist, went in 1856 to London, where for three years he was editor of the *Examiner.* He was the author of six novels, the best of which was *The Bachelor of the Albany* (1847). His last work, *The Woman of Business, or the Lady and the Lawyer* appeared serially in the *Fortnightly Review* (1869-70).—*DNB.*

83. "The Irish Judicial System," *F. R.,* IV (March 1, 1866), 137.

84. *Ibid.,* p. 139.

85. "The Iron Masters' Trade Union," I (May 15, 1865), 96-116; "The Limits of Political Economy," I (June 15, 1865), 356-76; "The Good and Evil of Trade Unionism," III (Nov. 15, 1865), 33-54; and "Industrial Co-operation," III (Jan. 1, 1866), 477-503.

86. Cross, *George Eliot's Life,* II, 303.

87. *F. R.,* I (June 15, 1865), 376.

88. "Varia," *F. R.,* III (Jan. 1, 1866), 512.

89. Michael Sadleir, *Anthony Trollope* [: *A Commentary.* Boston and New York, 1927], p. 256.

90. Trollope, *Autobiography,* p. 172.

91. *F. R.,* III (Nov. 15, 1865), 55-74.

92. *F. R.,* IV (May 1, 1866), 729-44.

93. *F. R.,* VI (Oct. 1, 1866), 435-45.

94. Kitchel, *George Lewes and George Eliot,* pp. 235 f.

95. T. A. Trollope, *What I Remember,* p. 481.

96. Kitchel, *George Lewes and George Eliot,* p. 236.

97. *F. R.,* VI (Dec. 1, 1866), 890.

98. Cross, *George Eliot's Life,* II, 323.

Jack Kaminsky (essay date June 1952)

SOURCE: Kaminsky, Jack. "The Empirical Metaphysics of George Henry Lewes." *Journal of the History of Ideas* 13, no. 3 (June 1952): 314-32.

[*In the following essay, Kaminsky assesses Lewes's efforts to solve metaphysical problems with an empirical rather than a transcendental approach. Kaminsky also studies the influence of Auguste Comte on Lewes's desire to "unify the sciences."*]

English philosophy in the nineteenth century was characterized by two opposing tendencies. On the one hand, the advance in science captured the philosophic imagination and produced the empirical-positivistic views of John Stuart Mill and Herbert Spencer. On the other hand, scientific progress produced a philosophic reaction exemplified by Carlyle's transcendentalism, Newman's Catholicism, and Green's idealism. Because these two philosophic positions appeared to be incompatible, philosophers generally allied themselves with either one or the other.

However, not all philosophers were willing to accept either a purely positivistic or a purely metaphysical approach. The deficiencies as well as the merits of both views suggested to one renegade positivist, George Henry Lewes, the possibility of producing a successful synthesis. He urged that a resuscitated and modernized Aristotelianism might heal the bifurcation in philosophy, and that the study of metaphysical problems might be pursued with an empirical rather than a transcendental method. Perhaps it was possible to achieve a new metaphysics—an empirical kind that would include within itself the steadily developing body of scientific data. George Henry Lewes deserves recognition today as the first noteworthy exponent of an empirical metaphysics.

George Henry Lewes was born on April 18, 1817. Little is known of his childhood or of his parents except that his father was an actor and a writer, and his mother was a woman of strong temperament whom Lewes held in high esteem. His early education was erratic; he studied in various schools in London, Jersey, Brittany, and Greenwich. After this period his formal education appears to have ended, and he began drifting desultorily from one occupation to another. He worked as a clerk in a notary's office, served as an assistant in the counting room of a Russian merchant, studied medicine, and discussed philosophical issues with students at Red Lion Square. In 1838, at the age of twenty-one, he visited Germany. But in 1840 he was back in London struggling for a foothold in the journalistic world. The following year he married Agnes, the daughter of Swyfen Jervis of Chatcull, Staffordshire, a member of Parliament. Lewes was writing a great deal during this period in all fields ranging from drama to philosophy. In 1845 his first book, *The Biographical History of Philosophy,* appeared. This was followed by several novels, dramas, and literary critiques. In 1850 he launched the Socialist newspaper, *The Leader,* which was probably the most liberal newspaper of the Victorian period. Finally, in 1851 occurred the most important event in his life; he was introduced to George Eliot.

By 1851 Lewes' relationship to his wife was far from satisfactory. It was evident that Agnes no longer loved him. The breaking point was finally reached with Lewes' discovery that she had been having an affair with his friend, Thornton Hunt. Lewes left his wife, but for reasons that are not quite clear he never obtained a divorce. He was genuinely hurt, but he found consolation and understanding in his friendship with George Eliot. Finally, on July 20, 1854, Lewes and George Eliot made the decision to live together in a common law marriage. It was an ideal companionship and for twenty years their relationship thrived in the closest love and happiness.

During this twenty-year period with George Eliot Lewes produced his most important writings: *Comte's Philosophy of the Sciences* (1853), *The Life and Works of Goethe* (1855), *Sea-Side Studies of Ilfracombe, Tenby, the Scilly Isles and Jersey* (1858), *The Physiology of Common Life* (1860), *Studies in Animal Life* (1862), *Aristotle* (1864), and the many literary criticisms he regularly contributed to periodicals. But the essential fruit was his final work, *Problems of Life and Mind.* Until the last days before his death Lewes continued to add to an enormous amount of psychological, biological, and physical data which he had accumulated primarily through his own research and experimentation. But it remained for George Eliot to proofread and publish the final manuscript. On November 28, 1878, after a short period of illness, Lewes died.[1]

Lewes' position in philosophy has been sorely neglected. Overshadowed by the literary accomplishments of his famous partner, his name has usually been recalled only in connection with George Eliot's personal life. Modern philosophers have little if any knowledge of Lewes, although he received some fine tributes in the past. Lewes' personal friends considered him one of the shining lights of the nineteenth century. William Bell Scott remarked, "He is nearly the only man among all my friends who has never ceased to advance. At first he was only the clever fellow . . . then the able investigator, and lastly the scientific thinker and philosopher, one of the most trenchant and advanced minds in the science of this country."[2] Thomas Henry Huxley spoke very highly of him as a philosopher.[3] Frederic Harrison thought that the ***Biographical History of Philosophy*** "has acted on the mind of this generation almost more than any single book except Mr. Mill's *Logic*."[4] Even the arrogant Thomas Carlyle had to be wary of Lewes, who "was too apt to puncture the balloons of prophecy that Carlyle was fond of blowing up. . . ."[5] An early twentieth century commentator asserted that "Lewes has given the clearest view of mental phenomena thus far offered to the world."[6] John Fiske called Lewes' ***Aristotle*** an "excellent work" and praised his essays on Darwinism.[7] William James spoke with approval of Lewes' views on cognition and perception, while J. T. Merz declared that Lewes had "a vastly superior knowledge of the natural, especially the biological sciences, than Mill possessed."[8] More recently Lloyd Morgan claimed that Lewes was far ahead of his time in recognizing the distinction to be made between an emergent and a resultant.[9] But in spite of such commendatory evaluations Lewes' name has not been rescued from oblivion. Only in recent years has there been a renascence of interest in Lewes' accomplishments.[10]

Generally Lewes' thought is strongly permeated by positivistic opinions. Influenced by Mill and Comte,[11] he became a lifelong exponent of scientific method and analytic rigor. His ***Biographical History of Philosophy,*** although specious in its earlier editions,[12] never wavered from the primary goal of endeavoring to render obsolete any thinking that could not abide by scientific standards. The rigor and precision of the scientific method, he declared in that work, is "the only Method adapted to human capacity, the only one on which truth can be found."[13] Reasoning, he stated elsewhere, is to be considered valid only if it is "rigorously subordinated to Verification."[14] And verification to Lewes was "the grand characteristic distinguishing Science from Philosophy, modern inquiry from ancient inquiry."[15] The method of science, therefore, was the proper one and only through such a method was valid reasoning about the world capable of being differentiated from the invalid.

Such a view appeared to imply a complete condemnation of metaphysical schemes. And there is little question that Lewes was genuinely opposed to most of the metaphysics of his day. It is our strength, he stated in an early article, that "we reject as frivolous all metaphysics."[16] In later works he insisted that "I reject all ontological schemes"[17] and that "the condemnation of metaphysics is inevitable."[18] This same disapprobation of metaphysics is to be found in all his works, and it is

thus not difficult to understand the traditional view that regards Lewes as a strict positivist.

However, a closer examination of Lewes' work reveals that his criticism was not directed against the subject matter of metaphysics. He was not in opposition to metaphysical speculation *per se*. Rather he was opposed to the means that he felt had been traditionally used in attempts to resolve metaphysical issues. A strong interest in metaphysics pervaded his article on Spinoza and he frankly admitted that Spinoza's pantheism did assume "an aspect of science."[19] But his own empirical and scientific bias made him suspicious of most metaphysical systems, and he recognized clearly that although the problems of metaphysics might be considered legitimate, the solutions of such problems frequently led to the most transcendental and mystical conceptions. He was aware of these deficiencies in many metaphysical schemes, and he attributed them to a defective method of analysis.

Even in this very early work on Spinoza, in which Lewes is trying to clarify fully the precise nature of his objections to metaphysics, the question of methodology is an important one for him. He is very conscious of the evil that attaches to any confused method, and he is constantly reiterating that the application of a bad or uncritical method to a problem negates the quality of the problem. "A Method," he declares, "is the vital principle of all science; it is only by method that science is possible."[20] In the same article he asserts, "It is one of the curious points in the history of humanity that *methods* are so seldom altered. Each man follows his father, and endeavors to succeed where generations have failed; he never once suspects the nature of the method he employs—*that* he takes for granted; yet, in most cases, it is precisely there that the cause of failure lies."[21]

Later, he specifically states that this cause of failure arises "from not distinguishing between Metaphysical and Philosophical Method."[22] Lewes proclaims that the metaphysical method with its inclusion of transcendental features has caused most of the woes found in metaphysics. The subject matter of metaphysics and the problems with which it deals should most assuredly be analyzed and resolved. Such inquiry is legitimate. But the method that has been used is illegitimate. The fundamental difference between scientific and metaphysical speculation "does not lie in their objects, but in their method,"[23] he asserts in his supposedly anti-metaphysical ***Biographical History of Philosophy.*** And what this means is that Lewes is not concerned with repudiating metaphysics as a realm for inquiry, since the aims of metaphysics and science are not fundamentally different. But he is concerned with rejecting the method which he believes has been steadily employed in metaphysical investigations. Once this distinction between subject matter and method is made, the way lies open for the introduction of an empirical metaphysics.

It was probably his strong interest in all phases of science that made Lewes aware of the unquestioned and frequently ambiguous categories employed by scientists. Matter, reality, substance, and force were only a few of the concepts utilized in the sciences without a clear cognizance of the meanings they contained and the problems they presented. Such seemingly simple terms like events, things, and properties were freely inserted into scientific theories without any recognition of the paradoxical and difficult issues implicit in the usage of these terms. Lewes felt that such an uncritical approach towards the fundamental data of any scientific hypothesis revealed an inadequacy in scientific knowledge which was otherwise characterized by rigorous scrutiny and experimentation. Nor was this all. Since these undefined terms were central to all the sciences, the possibility suddenly presented itself of accomplishing what Comte and the entire positivist school had desired to accomplish for years, *viz.*, the unification of the sciences. Lewes, as a positivist, was in accord with the Comtist aim to unify the sciences,[24] and he felt that the study of these basic terms underlying and incorporated into the individual sciences would not only result in such a unification, but would also bring the subject matter of metaphysics into the realm of scientific interrogation. Thus the study of metaphysics would be the study of just those general undefined terms that were inherent in the sciences. Lewes believed that a subject matter of this nature could utilize the same method applied to the natural sciences. Then metaphysics, in the company of those sciences, would follow their example and reject transcendental concepts.

Metaphysics, therefore, is not inherently other-worldly or transcendental. If a distinction were made between the subject matter of metaphysics and its method, Lewes asserts in his *Problems of Life and Mind*,[25] we would find that the method, not the subject itself, entails transcendental conceptions. The vanity of metaphysics "lies in its Method, not in its aims."[26] It is the "Metaphysical Method that has been relinquished"[27] in Lewes' new construction of metaphysics, not metaphysics itself. If metaphysics is "ever to reach a solution of its problems, it must relinquish that Method altogether for the Method of Science which has proved its power."[28] Scientific method, therefore, is not simply to be identified with what is applied in the natural sciences, and Lewes, in one of his last articles, declares that "We are slowly beginning to recognize that there may be a science of History, a science of Language, a science of Religion, in fact, that all knowledge may be systematized in a common Method."[29] This method is to be used for all problems, and Lewes himself points out that his attack against metaphysics has always been against its method, not against its problems. "This is not a retreat, but a change of front. Throughout my polemic against Metaphysics, the attacks were directed against the irrational Method, as one by which *all* problems whatever must be insoluble."[30]

The new metaphysics will thus be a scientific one, and how this is to be accomplished becomes the major problem of *Problems of Life and Mind*:

> It is towards transformation of Metaphysics by reduction to the Method of Science that these pages tend. Their object is to show that the Method which has hitherto achieved such splendid success in Science needs only to be properly interpreted and applied, and by it the inductions and deductions from experience will furnish solutions to every metaphysical problem that can be rationally stated; whereas *no* problem, metaphysical or scientific, which is irrationally stated, can receive a rational solution. I propose to show that metaphysical problems have, rationally, no other difficulties than those which beset all problems; and, when scientifically treated, they are capable of solutions not less satisfactory and certain than those of physics.[31]

Now the first step in this undertaking is to discover whether metaphysics is capable of being investigated in a scientific manner. Lewes, of course, has implicitly assumed this all along, and it remains now for him to justify this assumption. A science exists, he asserts, "(1) when it has a clearly defined *object*; (2) when it has a clearly defined *place* in the region of research, a place not occupied by any other; and (3) when it has a clearly defined Method of applying the results of experience to the extension of Experience."[32] All these characteristics are clearly to be found in the domain of metaphysics:

> Its object is the disengagement of certain most general principles such as Cause, Force, Life, Mind, etc., from the sciences which usually imply these principles, and the exposition of their constituent elements—the *facts,* sensible and logical, which these principles involve, and the relations of these principles. Its place, as a special discipline, is that of an Objective Logic. Its method is that of dealing exclusively with the known functions of unknown quantities, and at every stage of inquiry separating the empirical from the metempirical data.[33]

Consequently, Lewes felt justified in attempting to treat metaphysics as a science. It had all the necessary prerequisites. But if it were eventually to realize its potentialities it would have to repudiate the "inanity of Scholasticism"[34] which had so heavily burdened metaphysics with metempirical or unknowable elements. Just as scientific inquiry was characterized by a method that carefully differentiated between empirically warranted and empirically unwarranted assertions, so metaphysics was to undergo the same type of strict analysis in which only what was empirically warranted would be considered relevant. Such analysis of the sensible and logical grounds for the general undefined principles of the sciences would make up what Lewes calls his Objective

Logic. Such a study would certainly not be metempirical, since it would be dependent on scientific developments. Nor would it be strictly deductive, in the Hegelian sense, since its results would be corrigible in the light of future scientific discoveries.

Lewes was well aware that metaphysics would always have those exponents who would insist on the metempirical elements, but he felt that "this like all inquiries so pursued is necessarily fruitless."[35] Only a metaphysics that could meet the rising tide of scientific rigor would remain vital, and he believed that his own theory of metaphysics could do precisely that. His ontology was "Abstract Science, which is occupied with the general laws of Being."[36] It was this type of ontology that Lewes labelled "Empirical Metaphysics." And since it "is the science of those highest generalities which emerge from the study of Things, . . . there can be no difference between Science and Metaphysics except in the degree of generality."[37] This empirical kind of metaphysics would not be detached from the sciences, as Lewes believed it had been traditionally. Rather the material of metaphysical investigation would consist of the conclusions and data yielded by the sciences. From the "laws of the Cosmos discovered by Science it elicits certain general relations, which are then visible in phenomena, just as the theory of Gravitation, originated by inductions from terrestrial physics, was confirmed by inductions from celestial physics, and when thus established, was afterwards reflected back on terrestrial physics, disclosing unexpected relations there."[38]

Thus, for example, in order to give a suitable explanation to the problem of causation, the metaphysician would be required (1) to investigate the use of such a concept in the sciences, (2) to reveal the logical difficulties and experiential paradoxes that such a concept may imply, and (3) to attempt, by empirical and scientific data, to resolve these difficulties and paradoxes. Completely endorsing the Aristotelian definition, Lewes concluded, ". . . our definition of empirical Metaphysics (we recognize no other) will be 'the science of the most general principles.'"[39]

The full import of Lewes' views on metaphysics was completely lost to nineteenth-century philosophers. Frederic Harrison, although he thought highly of Lewes, probably spoke for all his contemporaries when he said that Lewes' "attempt to revive Metaphysics under a scientific aspect has deservedly failed."[40] Except perhaps for the youthful C. S. Peirce,[41] few were aware of the significance of Lewes' suggested integration of science and metaphysics. The epitome of oversimplification was implicit in one commentator's glib statement that "Lewes began his labors as a physiological interpreter of metaphysics; he closed them as a metaphysical interpreter of physiological phenomena."[42]

As we have seen, Lewes, in opposition to the strictly positivistic platform, contends that metaphysics is a legitimate domain of inquiry. But methods that "delude the mind with unverified, unverifiable assumptions"[43] are to be avoided, and we are no longer to tolerate the type of ontology that "sees God everywhere and in everything,"[44] and whose truths or falsehoods "are supposed to be involved in the assumption of their loftiness and cheerlessness."[45] Any method that "rests contented with its own verdicts without seeking the verification of facts, or seeking only a partial confrontation with facts,"[46] is to be completely repudiated. The new metaphysics will avoid all these pitfalls, and will include only what can be substantiated by empirical verification. There will no longer be a transcendental aura about metaphysics, but instead it will be just what "comes after physics" in the same strict sense implicit in the Aristotelian philosophy. The aims of science are directed towards attaining laws of phenomena, but the aims of an empirical metaphysics are "not these, but laws of the laws."[47] In short, metaphysics will begin with the data of grounded scientific assertions and attempt to answer its problems precisely by means of such data. This will not only produce a metaphysics based on science, but it will also do a great deal to unify the results of science.

Now that Lewes has justified the possibility of an empirical metaphysics, he is ready to take another step in developing his theory. Such a step, he feels, will consist in demonstrating that the various dualisms of mind and body, of subjective and objective, that have persisted as basic assumptions in philosophic systems, are to be rejected. Such a demonstration is required because dualism, in one form or another, has constantly challenged any attempts to construct a scientific metaphysics. The curious problems about the relation of phenomena to noumena, of consciousness to existence have raised numerous barriers to the possibility of making metaphysical assertions that have the same objectivity as scientific assertions. Scientists, Lewes contends, are correct in disregarding such problems and relegating them "to Metaphysics for such minds as choose to puzzle over questions not amenable to experiment."[48] But the new metaphysics will also be justified in disregarding these questions, since, as Lewes will endeavor to show, they are not really problems at all. Rather they pertain to possible logical, not real, divisions of one unified and continuous experience. It is because philosophers have mistaken logical divisions for real ones that the objectivity of metaphysical statements has frequently been challenged. How can metaphysical statements be grounded on experience, when the experience itself is objective and yet subjective, existential and yet mental? These dualisms, Lewes claims, have been thorns in the side of a possible empirical and scientific metaphysics. They must now be resolved once and for all.

A major emphasis in Lewes' philosophy and one that has been most clearly noted by his commentators,[49] is his insistence on man's continuity with all other forms of life. Life, Lewes states, "is an evolution, not a separate creation";[50] therefore, he rejects "the irrational effort of theologians and metaphysicians, to sever nature from all *community* with animal nature."[51] It must be recognized that we "must study man first as an animal,"[52] as the Darwinian findings had so brilliantly illustrated. However, this does not mean that man is simply an animal organism with no other outstanding characteristics than a few more highly specialized organs. Man is also "a unit in a social organism. He leads an individual life which is also a collective life."[53] Lewes agrees that "From man to animal, from animal to plant, and from plant to crystal, there is a descending scale of intensity and complexity in vital and psychical phenomena, but nowhere is there more than a difference of degree."[54]

But although there is this continuity of life, Lewes is careful to point out that man is uniquely distinguished from all other forms of life by his participation in a social life. Society is "inseparable from man. . . . It is the element in which he can freely move."[55] This social environment is of great importance to Lewes' analysis, and he constantly reiterates that man is "distinctively a social being."[56] He lives in society, is mentally developed by it and for it."[57] All philosophies, therefore, that bifurcate man from nature or man from his society are already creating unwarranted dualisms. There is neither man *and* society, nor man *and* nature. Man and his social-physical environment are too inextricably intertwined to be viewed in isolation.[58] The organism, Lewes asserts, "adjusts itself to the external medium; it creates and is in turn modified by the social medium, for Society is the product of human feelings, and its existence is *pari passu* developed with the feelings which in turn it modifies and enlarges at each stage."[59] By the very nature of his constitution man is "forced to live for others and in others."[60] To isolate man from society "is almost as great a limitation of the scope of Psychology, as to isolate him from Nature."[61]

Thus the distinction that is made between man and his environment is not an actual one. Man can never be separated from his social-physical environment. His relations to that environment are intrinsic, not extrinsic. It is quite true that the simplification of research often demands that man be treated as a unique substance capable of being extracted from the medium in which he thrives. But Lewes warns that we must not confuse logical categories for real ones. For purposes of biological research we may frequently ignore man's social relations, but we must be constantly aware that to understand man as he actually is we would be required to investigate not simply his biological structure but his social environment as well. Any attempt to regard man's

physical and social aspects as independent entities in a real sense is false, for man is neither a social nor a physical animal; he is both.

With these comments on the nature of man, Lewes prepares a similar analysis of the subjective-objective paradoxes that seem to arise within experience. Just as an understanding of an organism entails an understanding of the conditions under which it lives, so also is there a similar involvement of the subjective and objective aspects found in an experiential whole. We do differentiate between that which appears to be *inside* of our brains and that which appears to be *outside*. But Lewes maintains that this does not imply a difference in kind. It is within an experience itself that such a dichotomy occurs. The dichotomy does not point to a combination of two incompatible subject matters. Rather the distinction "is simply that of aspects."[62] Every experience presents "a Twofold Aspect, real and ideal, actual and virtual."[63] This twofold aspect is ultimate in all experiential material. Regarded in one light experience becomes mental or strictly phenomenal; regarded from another aspect the same experience is not mental at all, but objective and seemingly outside of phenomena. But Lewes declares that although such distinctions are made, it is false to think that there are really two substances—that which is experienced on the one hand, and that which experience signifies on the other. Experience, as experience, Lewes claims, is characterized by certain major divisions, "the broadest of which is that into external and internal, object and subject."[64] But such a division is not a division between experience and what is not experience. The division is within what is experienced. It is one experience that is objective in one light and subjective in another. Similarly we know ourselves as "Body-mind; we do not know ourselves as Body *and* Mind, if by that be meant two coexisting independent Existents."[65] We may allude to body in one content, or its mental correlate in another, but this should not be taken to imply an existential difference between the two. Such a separation, Lewes insists, "is a logical artifice."[66]

> Ideally, and for our convenience, we dissociate the objective from the subjective aspect; but when we suppose that a real separation corresponds with the ideal distinction, we are thrown back upon the mystery of how a material process can become a mental process, how vibrations become sensations. The mystery is an illusion. There is no such transformation. What is called the material process is simply the objective aspect of the subjective mental process.[67]

This rejection of basic philosophic dualisms is carried over by Lewes into all areas of thinking. We must not accept the Kantian confusion of phenomena and noumena. The existence of the thing-in-itself "is not to be granted."[68] We are no longer to study phenomena in order "to discover the realities of underlying phenomena."[69] Scientific research is to be directed towards the examination and classification of experience under its two aspects, "the subjective and personal, the objective and impersonal."[70]

Having overcome the question of dualism, Lewes believes metaphysics can now formulate general laws of Being without worrying about whether such laws are illusions, or noumena, or forms in a Platonic world. The construction of an Objective Logic is now to proceed without the problem of its objectivity or subjectivity. Metaphysics will refer to given experience in the same way that science does. Just as science is concerned with problems within experience without becoming involved in the subjective or objective aspect of such experience, so metaphysics is to be concerned with experience in a similar fashion. The laws of Being will turn out to be the laws of experience.

Lewes now proceeds to demonstrate how a metaphysics of the kind that he proposes would cope with certain traditional questions in metaphysics. Two of these questions deal with the notions of matter and substance.

Now the term "matter" has always been an ambiguous term, and Lewes lists several traditional views of the nature of matter.[71] To all of these he objects on the grounds that such views have usually resorted to transcendental and unverifiable conceptions in order to give meaning to the notion of matter. He declares that the conception of matter must be validated, if it is to be validated at all, within an experiential context. Does experience vouch for this conception? Lewes answers that it does, and proceeds to outline the meaning that must be given to matter when it is regarded empirically.

The term "matter," Lewes maintains, refers to several different situations within experience which must be fully distinguished if we are to grasp the different connotations of matter. First of all, there is the common sense notion of matter. This refers to those general symbols that we use which "though intelligible and definite . . . are synthetical expressions, which often turn out to be confused and even chaotic, when we attempt to reduce them by analysis to their component experiences, and to specify *what* and *how much* the symbols really signify."[72] Thus, for example, even the peasant has an awareness of matter, but he knows it in "First Notions, which he is unable to analyze with any precision."[73] Such first notions consist of perceptions like light, sound, heat, and so forth. Generally, if you asked him to define matter he would tell you that it is "that which he sees, handles, tastes, moves, treads upon etc.; in a word, it is that of which all his materials are formed."[74] Such general, confused first notions usually "suffice for all his needs."[75]

However, Lewes also designates an "extra-sensible Matter."[76] It is matter in this latter sense that concerns scientists and philosophers. The philosopher is not simply concerned with just the bare givenness, or first notions, of things. He wishes to understand what matter is, what its essential properties are, and as a result "the First Notions of Common Knowledge are raised into the definite conceptions of Scientific Theory."[77] The basic uncriticized data that appear to the layman are not sufficient for the scientist and the philosopher. Such data, under scientific investigation, are made to reveal numerous other facts, especially the subjective-objective aspect of all experience. The analysis of first notions picks out what is and what is not part of the objective quality of experience, and then proceeds to discover the characteristics of this quality of experience. It is still true that "one and the same group of phenomena is objectively expressible in terms of Matter and Motion, and subjectively in terms of Feeling,"[78] but the scientific investigation of matter is primarily concerned with the objective expression of phenomena. Matter, Lewes states, "is for us the Felt,"[79] but it is the felt as contrasted with the feeling, which is the subjective component of an experience. Both aspects are part and parcel of any experience, but the problems of science are directed towards that which is considered objective. But Lewes warns that the final validity of any scientific conceptions rests in its capacity to become translatable into Feeling. Thus Lewes, when he rejects the attempt to bifurcate force from matter, declares:

> We logically separate the Felt from the Feelings; and in the Felt distinguish one group as Matter, another as Force. Both, however, are indissoluble in Feeling and in the Felt; and the conceptions by which we symbolize these feelings, like the extra-sensibles by which we extend the sensibles, are only artifices of interpretation, and only valid in so far as they are rigorously equivalent with actual feelings.[80]

Hence matter is not some unknown substratum for Lewes. Rather it is what is given within experience; but it is the objective element in experience. It becomes the task of science to discover the properties that all objective experience reveals, and the task of the empirical metaphysician to analyze any logical and sensible paradoxes such properties might involve.

This statement of matter as objective experience fully accords with Lewes' desire to make his metaphysics both corrigible and developmental in the same fashion as other sciences. Since matter is objective experience, the more we learn about such experience, the more we will know about matter. And we learn about matter by learning about the properties science has found in it. Lewes lists several such properties, *e.g.,* extension, impenetrability, infinite divisibility, indestructibility, gravity, and inertia.[81] The task of metaphysics is to examine these properties and analyze the problems they present. In this way metaphysics becomes an Objective Logic and uses the results of science for constructing its own theories.

Lewes thinks that the nature of matter can never be fully understood. Only corrigible assertions can be made about its basic properties. He carefully points out that "A complete solution of the Problem of Matter is, of course, hopeless, since our knowledge of the properties is always advancing, and with each step in advance, a variety of new problems present themselves."[82] Lewes gives the following general summary of his position on the concept of matter:

> Metaphysics, accepting the generalized results . . . reached in the several departments of research, coordinates them into a system. That the metaphysical system will vary with the varying materials furnished it by Science, is inevitable; and since we cannot imagine a limit to the progressive discovery of more and more objective relations, we must be content with solutions that are but approximations. The general question, What is Matter? is answered once and for all when we define Matter, the Passive Aspect of Existence. The particular questions respecting the Properties of Matter, and their mutual dependence, can only be answered by confining them to the Properties known at the time; and we must always be prepared for fresh extensions of knowledge, as more and more of the illimitable Unknown is brought within the range of Experience.[83]

With these words Lewes concludes his discussion on matter and proceeds to investigate the question of substance. Lewes acknowledges the intrinsic importance of the question of substance, and to this extent he is not a complete positivist. But, as we shall see, his solution to the problem relegates substance to the status of a logical category.

Traditionally, the question of substance revolves about the curious paradoxes that arise in describing things. When an attempt is made to specify any given thing, the specification is found to consist not of the thing itself, but of the properties of the thing. In short, we never seem to reach that point where we can designate the thing in which attributes or qualities inhere. We seem to be aware only of properties, and yet there is some certainty that these properties are together in the way that they are because they are united by some substance. Yet this substance never appears in experience. This apparent contradiction in experience that was of primary interest to Aristotle and the Scholastics Lewes now prepares to meet.

Lewes completely rejects the substance-attribute interpretation of experience. What we call a thing, he declares, is not some hidden factor in experience, but "*is* what it *appears*. It is the expression of a particular history of events, the group of conditions which are said to determine it."[84] Thus a thing is "a group of relations [which] varies under varying conditions."[85] The distinction that is made between the thing and its perceived properties, Lewes states, indicates that "we regard the thing as the group of all its known relations, and its ap-

pearances or manifestations here and there, as specifications of one or more of these relations; when we say the stone *appears* large or small, gray or hard, cold or rough, but that it is far more than these, we might equally well say that the stone *is* these in relations."[86] The thing "is what it is felt to be."[87] We perceive a cluster of qualities and these are the thing itself. But when we speak of the substance of these perceived qualities, when we seek the substatize that supposedly brings these qualities together, we should not think that we are seeking some thing-in-itself. Rather when we use the term "substance" we mean, Lewes asserts, "the abstract possibility of one factor of a product entering into relations with some different factors, when it will exist under another form. Oxygen, when combined with sulphur, *is* not anything which it *may be* in other combinations. The objective factor, which is stone, when in relation to sense, may be, *must be* something else in another relation."[88]

It is this *possibility* of presented experience to be other than it is, that results in the postulation of things-in-themselves or other unknowable substances. This thing-in-itself that Kant mentions, Lewes declares, is not an existential entity; rather it is "simply the symbol of that *otherness of relation* which the Thing we perceive may be *inferred* to present when it is no longer in relation to us, or is considered in relation to something else."[89] Because "we conceive the Thing as *capable* of other relations which are not definitely specified, or as existing in indeterminately fluctuating relations—a mere possibility of appearance,"[90] we hypostatize this belief by conceiving of some substance that underlies the relations and qualities that are given in experience and which is capable of appearing with other relations and other qualities in other experiences. It is simply the possibility of the presented to be other than what it is that produces the idea of some underlying substance. But such an idea only calls attention to the fact that knowledge is never conclusive. There are always further relations and further qualities to be discovered in what is presented. The difficulties of substance only arise when we think of substance as existential, and not as a logical category that calls attention to the possibility of experience changing under different conditions. The task of scientific research, Lewes declares, "is to fix precisely the conditions of each successive appearance, not to go in quest of the phantom *Thing-in-itself*, which never can appear."[91] Substance, then, for Lewes is not properly the subject matter of metaphysics since it only states that experience points to further possible experiences. What would be important for the empirical metaphysician would be an investigation of precisely what possibilities could be inferred from the data given in the present.

With such an interpretation of the meaning of dualism, matter, and substance, Lewes attempted to introduce feasible solutions to the paradoxes of reality without inserting transcendental elements. He conceived of these solutions as embodied in an empirical metaphysics. With the advent of Lewes' philosophy, the nineteenth century first saw the possibility of a scientific metaphysics constructed from experience. That such a philosophy was ignored or misinterpreted in a positivistic and transcendental age is understandable. Only in the contemporary period, with the theories of such philosophers as Pepper, Stace, and Hofstadter,[92] has empirical metaphysics achieved recognition and respectability as a new and swiftly developing philosophy. In the light of this development, George Henry Lewes becomes an important figure in the history of philosophy. Contemporary historians of philosophy cannot exclude reference to a man who foresaw a metaphysics based on empirical scientific principles, and should remove the veil which has unfortunately obscured his importance.

Notes

1. For further biographical material see the following: Articles on George Henry Lewes in the *Dictionary of National Biography* and the *Encyclopaedia Britannica;* Francis Espinasse, *Literary Recollections and Sketches* (London, 1889); Anna T. Kitchel, *George Lewes and George Eliot* (New York, 1933); an unpublished dissertation by Robert Doremus, "George Henry Lewes: A Descriptive Biography" (Harvard, 1940) 2 vols.

2. William Bell Scott, *Autobiographical Notes* (New York, 1892), II, 245.

3. Sir Mountstuart E. Grant Duff, *Notes from a Diary: 1873-1881* (London, 1898), II, 88, Dec. 16, 1878.

4. "George Henry Lewes," *Academy,* 14 (Dec. 7, 1878), 543.

5. Kitchel, 61.

6. Raymond St. James Perrin, *The Evolution of Knowledge* (New York, 1905), 304.

7. *Outlines of Cosmic Philosophy* (New York, 1903), I, 145; II, 398.

8. *The Principles of Psychology* (New York, 1905), I, 270-71; Merz, *A History of European Thought in the Nineteenth Century* (Edinburgh, 1914), III, 314.

9. *The Emergence of Novelty* (London, 1933), 31.

10. Proof of this is evident in "Research in Progress," *PMLA* LXIV (1949); Robert B. Doremus, Univ. of Wisconsin, and Gordon S. Haight, Yale, are preparing biographies of Lewes; Morris Greenhut, Univ. of Michigan, and Alice R. Kaminsky, New York Univ., are investigating Lewes' literary criticism.

11. His book, *Comte's Philosophy of the Sciences* (London, 1890) is still an excellent digest of Comte's leading ideas. See also "Auguste Comte," *Fortnightly Review* III (1895-96), 385-410; "Comte and Mill," *Fortnightly Review* VI (1866), 385-406.

12. W. R. Sorley correctly evaluates the book when he states that "the first edition of *The Biographical History of Philosophy* in 1845 was slight and inaccurate, but that later editions remedied many blemishes and "showed the author's ability to appreciate other points of view than that from which he started."—*A History of English Philosophy* (Cambridge, 1937), 273.

13. *The Biographical History of Philosophy* (New York, 1885), 784.

14. *Aristotle* (London, 1864), 57.

15. *The Biographical History of Philosophy* (1885 Edition), p. xxx.

16. "Spinoza's Life and Works," *Westminster Review* XXXIX (1843), 406.

17. "Spinoza," *Fortnightly Review* IV (1866), 399.

18. *Biographical History* [*Biographical History of Philosophy*] (1885 Edition), p. xxx.

19. "Spinoza's Life and Works," 405.

20. *Ibid.,* 384.

21. *Ibid.,* 403.

22. "Goethe as a Man of Science," *Westminster Review* LVIII (1852), 491. See also "The Modern Metaphysics and Moral Philosophy of France," *British and Foreign Review* XV (1843), 400, where the necessity for a single method is again stressed.

23. *Biographical History* (1885 Edition), p. xxx.

24. See *Comte's Philosophy of the Sciences,* 8ff.; also "On the Dread and Dislike of Science," *Fortnightly Review* XXIX (1878), 805-15.

25. *Foundations of a Creed,* I, 14. *Problems of Life and Mind* consists of the following five volumes: *The Foundations of a Creed* (Boston, 1891), 2 Vols.; *The Physical Basis of Mind* (Boston, 1891); *The Study of Psychology* (Boston, 1879); *Mind as a Function of the Organism* (Boston, 1880).

26. *Aristotle,* 66.

27. "Mr. Grote's Plato," *The Fortnightly Review* II (1865), 171.

28. *Foundations,* II, 103.

29. "On the Dread and Dislike of Science," 809.

30. *Foundations* [*The Foundations of a Creed*], I, 5.

31. *Ibid.,* I, 4-5.

32. *Ibid.,* I, 73.

33. *Ibid.,* I, 73-74.

34. *Aristotle,* 382. Lewes maintains that Aristotle would have been completely opposed to Scholasticism. The Scholastics practised "a different method than his."—*Ibid.,* 113. In fact, Bacon did not "attack the Method which Aristotle *taught;* indeed, he was very imperfectly acquainted with it. He attacked the Method which the followers of Aristotle *practised.*"—*Ibid.*

35. *Foundations,* I, 60.

36. *Ibid.,* I, 60.

37. *Ibid.,* I, 62.

38. *Ibid.,* I, 63.

39. *Ibid.,* I, 62. Lewes admits that the metaphysics he is introducing is by no means original. However, it is now "for the first time . . . definitely expressed in its principles and bearings."—*Ibid.,* I, 76.

40. *The Philosophy of Common Sense* (New York, 1907), 116-17.

41. Peirce was in all likelihood acquainted with the *Problems of Life and Mind,* since he speaks approvingly of Lewes' principle of verification as it appeared in the *Aristotle.* See *Collected Papers,* ed. Hartshorne & Weiss (Cambridge, 1931), I, 14.

42. *Principles of Success in Literature,* ed. Fred N. Scott, 3rd Edition (Boston, 1894), 12.

43. *Aristotle,* 31.

44. *Mind as a Function of the Organism,* 19.

45. "Causeries," *The Fortnightly Review* XII (1865-66), 770-71.

46. "Goethe as a Man of Science," 491.

47. *Foundations,* I, 62.

48. *The Physical Basis of Mind,* 347.

49. See W. H. Sorley, *A History of English Philosophy,* 274; also Carveth Read, "G. H. Lewes' Posthumous Volumes," *Mind* VI (1881), 498; Raymond St. James Perrin, *The Evolution of Knowledge,* 304.

50. *Comte's Philosophy of the Sciences,* 161.

51. *The Study of Psychology,* 122.

52. *The Study of Psychology,* 38.

53. *Foundations,* I, 101.

54. *Mind as a Function of the Organism,* 20.

55. "The Modern Metaphysics and Moral Philosophy of France," 355.

56. *The Study of Psychology,* 5.

57. *The Study of Psychology,* 38.

58. For this reason Lewes had previously declared that he could no longer agree with Mill that psychology should be a completely separate science. He now recognized clearly that "Biology could not be a perfect science, it would not be a science at all, without including psychical phenomena; the separation of vital from psychical (in an animal organism) is a scientific artifice, not a real distinction."—"Comte and Mill," 390.

59. *The Study of Psychology,* 71-72.

60. *The Study of Psychology,* 41.

61. *The Study of Psychology,* 78.

62. *Foundations,* I, 171-72.

63. *Foundations,* II, 15.

64. *The Physical Basis of Mind,* 396.

65. *The Physical Basis of Mind,* 396.

66. *The Physical Basis of Mind,* 397.

67. "Spiritualism and Materialism," *The Fortnightly Review* XXV (1876), 480.

68. *Foundations,* II, 393.

69. *Aristotle,* 122.

70. *The Study of Psychology,* 49.

71. *Foundations,* II, 203ff.

72. *Ibid.,* II, 223.

73. *Ibid.,* II, 223.

74. *Ibid.,* II, 224.

75. *Ibid.,* II, 224.

76. *Ibid.,* II, 230.

77. *Ibid.,* II, 224.

78. "Spiritualism and Materialism," 480.

79. *The Physical Basis of Mind,* 351.

80. *Foundations,* II, 281.

81. *Ibid.,* II, 238ff.

82. *Ibid.,* II, 274.

83. *Ibid.,* II, 302-303.

84. *Ibid.,* I, 331.

85. *Ibid.,* II, 38.

86. *Ibid.,* II, 39.

87. *Ibid.,* II, 392.

88. *Ibid.,* II, 392.

89. *Ibid.,* II, 404.

90. *Ibid.,* II, 39-40.

91. *Ibid.,* II, 40.

92. Stephen C. Pepper, *World Hypotheses* (Berkeley, 1948); W. T. Stace, *The Theory of Knowledge and Existence* (Oxford, 1932); Albert Hofstadter, "A Conception of Empirical Metaphysics," *Journal of Philosophy* XLV (1948), 421-35.

Nadine Miles (essay date March 1958)

SOURCE: Miles, Nadine. "Books in Review." *Educational Theatre Journal* 10, no. 1 (March 1958): 73-87.

[*In the following essay, Miles evaluates Lewes's work* On Actors and the Art of Acting *(1875), commending his vivid and provocative analysis of an actor's "range of expression," particularly in the case of Edmund Kean, a great tragic actor of the era.*]

Over thirty years ago, no courses in acting being offered at my college, I took private lessons with Katharine Wick Kelly, a very wonderful actress at the Cleveland Play House. Miss Kelly recommended two writers to me, Colley Cibber and George Henry Lewes. I look at the extensive reading lists we give our students in college today, and I wonder if a thorough, thoughtful reading of one or two fine books might not be better. Some passages of this book [*On Actors and the Art of Acting*] I know almost by heart. I really do not know any of all the excellent books that have been published in recent years which says wiser things about the actor's art.

In his *New Yorker* (November 28) review of *Time Remembered,* Woolcott Gibbs speaking of Helen Hayes' performance says, "The educated critical terms used to describe a player's technique are still beyond me, but I'm sure hers is as nearly perfect as any you'll ever see."

I suppose by "educated critical terms" Mr. Gibbs means pretentious phrases, cant, coterie, jargon, some sort of language too inflated for his modest assessment of the actor's performance. He describes what he sees, and how the actor creates his performance remains the actor's and the pretentious expert's secret. Mr. Lewes

does as Mr. Gibbs does. He describes what he sees to make one see the performer as he has seen him. He also believes that he understands and can analyse the art of the actor.

No fine actors had performed in London for years. The critical audience with trained judgements had disappeared. With Salvini drawing large audiences to *Hamlet* and *Othello* and with a play by Tennyson promised for the next season, Lewes hoped that a new day was dawning in the theatre. He gathered some of his writings together for publication. In the ***Epistle to Anthony Trollope*** he says:

> I only wanted to indicate that the object of here reprinting remarks, made at various times and in various periodicals, is to call upon the reflective part of the public to make some attempt at discriminating the sources of theatrical emotion. I want to direct attention not simply to the fact that acting is an art, but that, like all other arts, it is obstructed by a mass of unsystematized opinion, calling itself criticism.

The volume was published in 1875. There are fifteen essays, analyses of the performances of Edmund Kean, Charles Kean, Rachel, Macready, Farren, Charles Matthews, Frédéric Lemâitre, Fechter, Ristori, Salvini, and others. In the chapter, ***Shakespeare as Actor and Critic,*** Lewes gives his answer to the question, "In how far does an actor feel the emotion he expresses?" The essay ***On Natural Acting*** answers an attack from a critic who disagreed with him on the question of "naturalness." Visiting theatres on the continent, he writes of the drama in Paris in 1865, Germany and Spain in 1867.

Lewes has no respect for the critics who "confine their remarks to the general impression of a performance and do not analyse it." The actor's "range of expression" is a term he uses often. He analyses the art of each actor, describing successes and failures. His judgments are made after seeing the actor over a number of years, in many parts, and in each part many times. He seldom judges from a single performance. He saw Salvini during the summer of 1875, twice in *Othello,* once in *The Gladiator,* twice in *Hamlet;* but he says that this is not enough for a critical estimate, and that he will therefore only set down first impressions.

Here is one of my favorite paragraphs; he is writing of Edmund Kean:

> Kean was not only remarkable for the intensity of passionate expression, but for a peculiarity I have never seen so thoroughly realized by another, although it is one which belongs to the truth of passion, namely, the expression of subsiding emotion. Although fond, far too fond, of abrupt transitions—passing from vehemence to familiarity, and mingling strong lights and shadows with Caravaggio force of unreality—nevertheless his instinct taught him what few actors are taught—

that a strong emotion, after discharging itself in one massive current, continues for a time expressing itself in feebler currents. The waves are not stilled when the storm has passed away. There remains the ground-swell troubling the deeps. In watching Kean's quivering muscles and altered tones you felt the subsidence of passion. The voice might be calm, but there was a tremor in it; the face might be quiet, but there were vanishing traces of the recent agitation.

If there are such things as "educated critical terms" they could not describe any more clearly this "peculiarity" in Kean's technique, nor give a better lesson in acting.

I am glad that this book is in print again. Our 1878 library copy fell to pieces some years ago.

Richard Stang (essay date 1959)

SOURCE: Stang, Richard. "The Sacred Office: The Critics"; "The Craft of Fiction"; and "Mid-Victorian Realism: Real Toads in Real Gardens." In *The Theory of the Novel in England, 1850-1870,* pp. 46-190. New York: Columbia University Press, 1959.

[*In the following excerpts, Stang addresses Lewes's use of the theory of realism in his literary criticism. Stang analyzes in detail Lewes's various reviews of his contemporaries, including Charlotte Brontë.*]

Like Stephen, George Henry Lewes formulated a distinct critical programme, but Lewes considered the novel primarily as a work of art, and in discussing any art one must always refer to the absolute standards which govern it. 'The art of novel-writing, like the art of painting, is founded on general principles, which, because they have their psychological justification, because they are derived from tendencies of the human mind, and not, as absurdly supposed, derived from "models of composition", are of universal application.'[1] The discussion of Lewes' very definite formal criteria for the criticism of novels will be reserved for a later chapter, as well as his interesting theory of realism, but it is important to notice in this context that he believed novel criticism, if it was to have any value, must confine itself chiefly to questions of form. Too much contemporary criticism seemed irrelevant to him because it resolved itself into matters of taste. One can say that he likes a book because it is amusing, but that kind of statement admits of no discussion; 'those whom it amuses *are* amused' and there is an end to the matter.[2] In the same way there is the reader who can not become interested in Wordsworth's potters and waggoners just because potters and waggoners cannot excite his imagination. For Lewes these judgments cannot be considered criticism and admit of no rejoinder. But he does insist that 'when a question of Art comes to be discussed, it must not be confounded with a matter of individual feeling; and it requires a distinct reference to absolute standards'.[3] Thackeray's statement, which had become a critical cliché by this time, that *Tom Jones* 'as a work of art . . . is absolutely perfect', can thus be very easily refuted by showing that Fielding violates the all-important law of artistic economy. Lewes would admit that *Tom Jones* shows humour, 'a real talent for story-telling—for presenting the various elements of a story in an animated succession of illustrative scenes—an eye for characteristics in person, manner, and speech, and a style easy, idiomatic and vigorous'. But none of these merits makes a masterpiece. 'They are none of them high or rare merits.'[4]

It was only Jane Austen, among English novelists, whom Lewes would call a perfect artist: 'if the *truest* representation, effected by the *least expenditure* of means, constitutes the highest claim of art, then we may say that Miss Austen has carried the art to a point of excellence surpassing that reached by any of her rivals.' George Eliot, who was at the beginning of her career as a novelist at the date of this essay (["**The Novels of Jane Austen,**"] July, 1859), Lewes found superior to Jane Austen in 'culture, reach of mind, and depth of emotional sensibility', but Jane Austen's superiority in 'the art of telling a story; and generally . . . the "economy of art",' makes her the more perfect artist, simply *qua* artist.[5]

But there are other criteria one can use for works of art. Even though Jane Austen may be a perfect artist, greatness is dependent on other qualities as well. When it is admitted that Jane Austen has limited herself to 'quiet scenes of everyday life, with no power over the more stormy and energetic activities which find vent even in everyday life . . . [and that] she never stirs the deeper emotions, . . . never fills the soul with a noble aspiration, or brightens it with a fine idea . . . , we have admitted an objection to rank her among the great benefactors of the race. . . .'[6]

Lewes firmly believed that a novelist's choice of subject matter was extremely important in deciding his ultimate rank. 'It is obvious that the nature of the thing represented will determine degrees in art. Raphael will always rank higher than Teniers. . . . It is a greater effort of genius to produce a fine epic, than a fine pastoral; a great drama, than a perfect lyric . . . the higher the aims, the greater is the strain, and the nobler the success.' But he also believed that 'no art can be high that is not good. A great subject ceases to be grand when its treatment is feeble.'[7] His belief in the importance of subject matter in a work of art is clearly opposed to most modern aesthetic speculation: 'A well-painted table-cover is better than an ill-painted face; but a well-painted face, with a noble expression is the highest reach of art, as the human soul is the highest thing we know.'[8]

As an extremely prolific critic of novels,[9] it is surprising how wide was the range of Lewes' tastes, and how many of his judgments have been verified by posterity, especially when we remember that most of his essays were written as reviews of novels as they came out. The only demands he made on the book under consideration were that it be original and that it have imaginative power, and so he was especially severe on the writer of tame domestic novels who thought they were in the tradition of Jane Austen. 'It is only plenitude of power that restrains her from the perils of the form she has chosen—the perils, namely of tedium and commonplace. . . . She makes her people speak and act as they speak and act in everyday life; and she is the only artist who has done this with success. . . .' Furthermore the imitators of Jane Austen invariably fail because 'they cannot keep to the severe level of prose; they rise above it and the result is incongruity; or they fall below it, and the result is tediousness'.[10] Of *Kathie Brand,* by Holme Lee, a popular novelist usually placed in the 'school of Miss Austen', he wrote, 'None of the characters impresses us with any vivid sense of their reality; they are pale water-colour sketches, when not conventional novel types.' Miss Lee lacks a 'keen sense of reality, or the power of vivid representation of reality, which alone can make quiet everyday life interesting. . . .'[11] Mrs. Gaskell was one of the few English writers who had this power for Lewes, especially in *Cranford,* and that was why he predicted it would be 'more permanent than the others [of Mrs. Gaskell's novels up to 1853], though less noisy in reputation'. Because of the way her material was rendered, it 'stands out in the memory like an experience. . . . Provincial life in its ineffable dullness moves before us; we enjoy every detail of the pageant as heartily as we should detest the reality!'[12]

When *Moby Dick* was published in England in 1851 under the title of *The Whale,* it passed almost unnoticed or was damned as rant. But Lewes in the *Leader* cited it, along with the prose of Poe and Hawthorne, as the real beginning of a genuine American literature. For him it was 'a strange, wild, weird book, full of poetry, and full of interest. . . . The daring imagery often grows riotous and extravagant. . . . Criticism may pick holes in this work, but no criticism will thwart its fascination.'[13]

When Lewes received a review copy of *Jane Eyre* by the unknown writer Currer Bell from Smith, Elder and Company in 1847, he became so enthusiastic that he wanted to write a long article on it in *Fraser's Magazine.* The editor, however, objected that it might seem foolish to devote so much space to a book no one had ever heard of and whose reception was far from certain.[14] As a result Lewes had to include several other novels in the same essay under the heading of 'Recent Novels: French and English'; but the other books were

huddled into two pages, and nine were spent praising *Jane Eyre.* He pointed out that though the author was obviously addicted to 'melodrama and improbability which smack of the circulating library', she was 'unquestionably setting forth her own experience' by means of 'the machinery of the story'. 'Unless a novel be built out of real experience, it can have no real success.' Currer Bell had almost all he required of a novelist: 'perception of character, and power of delineating it; picturesqueness; passion; and knowledge of life'. But the quality he prized most in this new book was the sense that an individual wrote it. 'It has the capital point of all great styles in being *personal,*—the written speech of an individual, not the artificial language made from all sorts of books.'[15] *Shirley,* which Lewes reviewed in the *Edinburgh* in 1850, he found a falling off in power compared to *Jane Eyre.* Currer Bell had no real involvement in her social theme, the struggle between mill owners and their employees at the beginning of the nineteenth century.[16] *Villette,* however, he admired very much indeed. 'Here . . . is an *original* book. Every page, every paragraph, is sharp with *individuality.* It is Currer Bell speaking to you, not the Circulating Library reverberating echos, [*sic*] how *she* has looked at life . . . what she has thought, and felt, not what she thinks others will expect her to have thought and felt. . . .' And even though the book was lacking in unity and progression, Charlotte Brontë still had no living rival in passion and power.[17]

Cousin Pons was one of the French novels reviewed in the *Fraser's* article that acclaimed *Jane Eyre,* and Lewes could find no evidence of any decline in Balzac's amazing energy. 'Wonderful it is to see how with what marvellous power such a simple subject is wrought into a story of deep, unceasing interest. To those who prate about Balzac's having written himself out [Balzac was almost at the end of his career], we would oppose the first volume of *Le Cousin Pons* as a triumphant answer.'[18] In order to appreciate Lewes' critical acumen, we should read this criticism in the context of the kind of moralistic interpretation Balzac received in the English press during the forties.[19]

Lewes praised *Barchester Towers* too for its 'astonishing energy',[20] and nine years earlier he had noted the change in Thackeray with *Vanity Fair,* from a minor writer of travel books, *nouvelles,* and burlesques, to a major novelist. But characteristically in this review in *The Athenaeum* he disliked Thackeray's cavalier attitude towards his craft.[21]

As a result of Lewes' almost uncanny ability as a critic to pick out the important novels from the chaff, John Blackwood, with whom Lewes had had no previous dealings, immediately became very much interested when Lewes announced that he had discovered a new genius who had written the first story in a projected series, 'Scenes from Clerical Life'. And undoubtedly it was Lewes' encouragement and her faith in his critical ability that finally broke through the ice of George Eliot's doubts about her powers as a novelist.

It was unfortunate for Lewes' reputation as a critic of novels that probably his best known essay today is **'Dickens in Relation to Criticism'**, originally written in 1872 for the *Fortnightly Review.* Hutton was certainly right in calling it 'a mere blunder',[22] for Dickens was one of the few writers with whom Lewes was totally out of sympathy. He attributed Dickens' enormous popularity to 'overflowing fun' rather than humour, and to Dickens' 'marvellous vividness' of imagination, which he recognized as almost akin to the hallucinations of madness. But here Lewes was merely echoing Taine's famous essay on Dickens. Dickens' work was sure to be ephemeral because of his terrible limitation: 'the pervading commonness' and the lack of any thought or passion in his novels. In Dickens 'sensations never passed into ideas', and, as a result, compared with Thackeray's or Fielding's, his is 'a mere *animal* intelligence'. Lewes' insufferable condescension at the end of his essay—'He gave us his best. If the efforts were sometimes too strained, and the desire for effect too obtrusive, there was no lazy indulgence[23]—almost maddened John Forster, who attacked Lewes as a traitor in the second edition of his *Life of Dickens.* Lewes' very broad and catholic view of the novel had evidently, by 1872, become very restricted, probably because of the influence of George Eliot, who was now a universal yardstick for him. 'I do not suppose a single thoughtful remark on life and character can be found throughout the twenty volumes [of Dickens' collected works].' It was not only the 'marked absence of a reflective tendency' that bothered Lewes, but he could find no evidence that 'the past life of humanity . . . ever occupied him; keenly as he observes the objects before him, he never connects his observations into a general expression, never seems interested in the general relations of things'. Dickens was completely 'outside philosophy, science or higher literature' (this implication that novels were mere 'light literature' was very far from the Lewes who was a major critic of fiction in the forties and fifties), and he was shocked to see the state of Dickens' library—only novels, books of travel and presentation copies.[24] It must be remembered that for more than ten years Lewes had been an important writer on science and philosophy and had completely lost his interest in current imaginative literature. In 1858 James Cordy Jeaffreson's statement, in his *Novels and Novelists from Elizabeth to Victoria,* that G. H. Lewes was 'perhaps the best philosophical and critical essayist now living'[25] would not have found much disagreement among readers of Victorian periodicals, and Trollope was probably referring to the same period when he called Lewes 'the acutest critic' he knew.[26] Lewes' great critical reputation was also responsible for his being asked in 1862 to be-

come the editor of the *Cornhill Magazine* after Thackeray's resignation. Although he refused because of the pressure of his new scientific interests, he was retained as a consulting editor for several years at a high salary, and upon the formation of the *Fortnightly Review,* he became the first editor. . . .

The importance of unity and construction in the criticism of G. H. Lewes places him squarely in the tradition of mid-nineteenth-century classicism along with Matthew Arnold (in his 1853 preface), Walter Bagehot, Henry Taylor, and George Brimley. For Lewes, 'the object of construction is to free the story from all superfluity. Whatever is superfluous—whatever lies *outside* the real feeling and purpose of the work, either in incident, dialogue, description, or character—whatever may be omitted without in any degree lessening the effect— is a defect in construction.' Unity in a novel is no different in kind from unity in the drama, according to Lewes. 'The drama is more rigid in its requirements than the novel, simply because in the drama there is less time to tell the story in . . . ; moreover spectators are necessarily less patient than readers.' But, Lewes insists, 'the requirements as to construction . . . are the same in principle' for both forms. In the drama, any scene is purposeless if it does not 'directly tend to forward or elucidate the action'; if it can be 'cut out without rendering the story less intelligible, less effective, [such a scene] is an absolute defect, let it be never so splendidly written'. A purposeless scene is a 'serious mistake' not only because it occupies some of the dramatist's precious time allotment and causes him to skimp other scenes, but also because 'it helps to weary the spectator, by calling his attention away from the action, and by starting new expectations, which will not be fulfilled'.

> That which is true of whole scenes, is also true of parts of scenes, and of speeches. . . . Remarks *away* from the immediate business of the scene . . . are faults: they may be beautiful, they may be witty, they may be wise, but they are out of place; and the art of the dramatist consists in having everything in its proper place.

For Lewes even words and clauses that are superfluous are to be excised according to this same principle of economy.

But, according to Lewes, although 'the laws of economy are rigid, . . . the public must never feel the rigidity', hence the need for art which conceals art. All '"coincidences" and situations . . . introduced . . . for the sake of helping the author out of a difficulty' makes the machinery of the plot painfully evident and 'our illusion vanishes'. The construction of a play or a novel, even though it is in reality mechanical and artificial, must always seem 'natural' and 'organical', and this feat can only be accomplished by having 'all *secretly* and inevitably tending towards it. The artist must be careful in his selection, yet never suffer us to feel there has been a selection. . . .'[27]

The difference in the way these principles will be followed in plays and novels stems from the fact that 'in the novel the persons are *described* instead of being seen. . . .' Lewes realized that when he spoke about presentation as opposed to description, he was only using a metaphor; strictly speaking it is impossible literally to present a character in a novel. This condition

> renders it necessary that the author should supplement as far as possible this inferior vividness of presentation, by a more minute detail, both physical and moral. He must describe the tones and looks of his characters; on the stage these could be represented. He must make up for this inferiority of presentation by telling us more accurately the mental condition of his characters. Hence it is that the comments and reflections of the novelist are real aids to his effect, and become part of construction. Where, however, . . . he wanders into mere reflection and digression, suggested by, but not elucidating his characters and situations, he is guilty of a fault in construction. . . .

To illustrate his theories, Lewes examines the plot of *Tom Jones* and finds that 'far from being a masterpiece of construction', it is 'a very ill-constructed novel'. In the first place, Fielding relies too much on coincidence, and in the second—and this would condemn all picaresque novels—his plot is really made up of separate episodes and so lacks unity of action. It is true that this method gives variety to the story; but variety must be achieved in other ways. 'If Fielding is episodical, it is simply because he wanted to produce the effect of variety, and was not artist enough to make the variety spring from and tend to unity.' *Pride and Prejudice,* on the other hand, 'is a finely-constructed work' because 'the characters, scenes, and dialogues, in relation to each other and to the story' contain nothing superfluous. 'All this variety is secretly tending to one centre. . . .'[28]

Charles Kingsley, who agreed with Lewes that the drama should provide the standard of construction for the novel, complained that critics looked to the well-made French play rather than to Shakespeare for their ideas of unity. In Shakespeare, he pointed out to George Brimley,[29] there are characters and whole scenes which could be cut out without any damage to the plot.

> Now in the modern novel you ought to have all this, if it is to be a picture of actual life. You must have people coming in, influencing your principal characters for a while—as people do influence you and me, and then go on their way, and you see them no more. . . . You must . . . have people talk, as people do in real life, about all manner of irrelevant things, only taking care that each man's speech shall show more of his character, and that the general tone shall be such as never to make the reader forget the main purpose of the book.[30]

This very leisurely approach to the question of form in prose fiction, however, was rapidly becoming a thing of the past, and it was Lewes' much more stringent ideals that became dominant after 1870. . . .

In the 1850's G. H. Lewes, like George Eliot and Meredith, adopted a predominantly realistic position. He was, however, forced to modify it to such a degree that it bore very little relation to the ideas of those who demanded literal verisimilitude. One of Lewes' most reiterated points is that all successful novels must be based on the writer's actual experience. 'Unless a novel be built out of real experience, it can have no real success,'[31] he wrote in 1847, and in 1853 he still insisted: 'A novel must fuse one's own personal experience and observation' and not use material from other novels.[32] The worst thing he could say of a book is that it 'is not like life, but like novels',[33] and as a critic he waged a perpetual campaign against the stereotypes of character and incident in the fiction of the period.

When, however, Lewes reviewed *Modern Painters, Volume IV* in the *Leader,* June, 1856,[34] he felt called upon to qualify what he meant by experience. Lewes' essay is significantly entitled **'Imaginative Artists'** because many writers had mistakenly assumed that there was a conflict between imagination and real experience (a dichotomy which appears again towards the end of the century in Zola's 'Le roman experimental'). Charlotte Brontë, for instance, made Jane Eyre write, 'My imagination created, and narrated continuously; quickened with all of incident, life, fire, feeling, that I desired and had not in my actual existence.'[35] To this view of the imagination as a means of escape from a drab life into an exciting world of wish fulfilment, Lewes had opposed his own definition in his review of *Jane Eyre*: Imagination is 'that singular faculty of penetrating into most the secret recesses of the heart, and of showing a character in its inward and outward workings. . . .'[36] Far from helping us to escape from our experience, only through the imagination can we fully explore and understand reality. In his essay on **'Modern Painters'** Lewes observes that Ruskin's remarks apply to all the arts, not only to painting. 'When, for example, he lays down the canon, "It is always wrong to paint what you don't see," it is a canon as applicable to the poet (and novelist) as to the painter; and one, indeed, which has been iterated in these columns with almost wearisome pertinacity.' But to guard against a too simplistic idea of realism Lewes goes on to say, 'We have sometimes been misunderstood . . . to mean that only actual visible objects, or events actually experienced, should be chosen; whereas the vision and the faculty divine, although essentially consisting in *seeing* and in representing only what is seen, may be exercised upon things non-existent as well as existent.' Not all can see with the mind's eye. 'But no one should attempt to paint what he does *not* see; no one should feign to see or feel what he does not see or feel'—an injunction that can still sound revolutionary in Eastern Europe. '. . . If because *Jane Eyre* agitated novel readers, you, who never saw Mr. Rochester, and never were in love with your master, write Jane Eyrish novels, you are wasting your time and the reader's temper. Paint what you see, write what you have experienced, and the utmost success *possible for you* will be achieved,' he counsels the aspiring novelist.[37] Realism here is equivalent to sincerity, and this passage is almost a restatement of the Horatian maxim, 'Si vis me flere, dolendum est / Primum ipsi tibi.'

Lewes hated the prevailing form of idealism, especially popular in Germany, which stated that 'art must elevate the public by "beautifying" life'; this doctrine seemed to him 'the natural refuge of incompetence, to which men fly, impelled by a secret sense of their inability to portray Reality so as to make it interesting'. In his essay **'Realism in Art: Recent German Fiction'**, which appeared in the *Westminster* for October, 1858, he dismissed any distinction between art and reality as false, for 'Art is a Representation of Reality'. (Lewes in his critical writings seemed as unaware as most of his contemporaries of the pitfalls lying in the word reality, with or without a capital *r*.) The only legitimate distortion allowable is due to the nature of the medium—'The canvas of the painter, the marble of the sculptor, the chords of the musician, and the language of the writer, each brings its own peculiar laws. . . .' Lewes also apparently rejected the classical distinction between the real and the true—*le réel* and *le vrai*. 'Realism is thus the basis of all Art, and its antithesis is not Idealism, but *Falsism*.' The painter who gives 'regular features' and 'irreproachable linen' to his peasants and makes his milkmaids into 'Keepsake beauties', and the writer who makes 'Hodge . . . speak refined sentiments in unexceptional English' are alike guilty of falsification. 'Either give us true peasants, or leave them untouched; either paint no drapery at all, or paint it with the utmost fidelity, either keep your people silent, or make them speak the idiom of their class'—this is the ultimatum he gives the artist.[38]

True idealism, then, for Lewes, has nothing to do with *la belle nature* or generalized forms but is derived from a way of seeing reality. If a painter or writer discerns and can express the deepest emotional life of the people he is representing, can discern, in other words, the 'poetry' of his subject, then his treatment can be called 'ideal'. But 'the sentiment must be real, truly expressed as a sentiment, and as the sentiment of the very people represented; the tenderness of *Hodge* must not be that of *Romeo*. . . .' It is here that imagination and sympathy come into play; it is through them that the artist is enabled distinctly to 'see' his subject, and through them the antithesis between realism and idealism is broken down. The highest example, for Lewes, of an idealistic work of art, 'The Sistine Madonna', is also a work of the highest realism.

In the never-to-be-forgotten divine babe, we have at once the intensest realism of presentation, with the highest idealism of conception: the attitude is at once grand, easy, and natural; . . . in those eyes, and on that brow, there is an indefinable something which, greater than the expression of the angels, grander than that of pope or saint, is, to all who see it, a perfect *truth*; we feel that humanity in its highest conceivable form is before us, and that to transcend such a form would be to lose sight of the *human* nature there represented.[39]

With most products of Victorian realism, Lewes apparently had little sympathy. Instead of great subjects, grandly conceived, too many artists were spending their lives on trivia.

The rage for 'realism' [Lewes wrote in 1865] which is healthy in as far as it insists on truth, has become unhealthy, in as far as it confounds truth with familiarity, and predominance of unessential details. There are other truths besides coats and waistcoats, pots and pans, drawing-room and suburban villas. Life has other aims besides those which occupy the conversation of 'Society'.[40]

The same complaint had earlier been made by the *Prospective Review* in 1854: Too many novelists 'stifle . . . [themselves] with the minutiae of . . . [their] own experience' and show no imagination in their works.[41] Walter Bagehot in the *National Review,* October, 1855, had also complained of the 'strict experience school of writing' and the 'chatty school', both of which merely represented the 'surface of life'.[42] This kind of fiction, which depended on the accumulation of accurate details and in which verisimilitude was an end in itself, Lewes called 'detailism' to distinguish it from true realism.[43]

Through his distaste for novels which heaped up masses of detail, Lewes was often led to statements very close to a kind of neo-classicism. For example, of a novelist who tried to disarm his critics by claiming that all his events actually happened, he asserted, '. . . Incidents . . . must be true in *principle* rather than in fact.' The novelist must be able to present what is 'essential and typical in a subject [the last part of this quotation is very close to Sir Joshua Reynolds]'.[44] Earlier in the *Leader* Lewes had called art 'a selection of typical elements' from life, rather than a transcript of life or a mirror reflecting reality.[45] If the implications of such statements are developed fully, one would end up in the camp of the idealists.

Lewes found fault with many of the characters in *Shirley* because they were too strange, too unusual. And when Charlotte Brontë claimed that she had directly copied from nature precisely those characters who had been most objected to as unnatural, he replied, 'Art . . . deals with the broad principles of human nature, not with idiosyncracies. . . . The curious anomalies of life . . . are not suitable to a novel.' The characters of *Shirley,* moreover, were too harsh and too rude: 'They are, one and all, given to break out and misbehave themselves upon very small provocation. The manner and language of Shirley towards her guardian passes all permission.' Even if Yorkshiremen—and women—actually do talk in this way, decorum and propriety are here apparently more important for Lewes than realism: Currer Bell 'must learn . . . to sacrifice a little of her Yorkshire roughness to the demands of good taste, neither saturating her writings with such rudeness and offensive harshness, nor suffering her style to wander into such vulgarities as would be inexcusable—even in a man'.[46]

Lewes was most offended by the hero of the novel, Robert Moore, who 'is disgraced by a sordid love of money, and a shameless setting aside of an affection for Caroline in favour of the rich heiress'. Such behaviour may be true to nature, but it is not permitted in a hero, a figure whose position demands he have a 'noble' nature, be an 'ideal of manhood'.

> In a subordinate character such a lapse from the elevation of moral rectitude, might have been pardoned; but in a hero—in the man for whom our sympathies and admiration are almost exclusively claimed—to imagine it possible, is a decided blunder in art—as well as an inconsistency in nature. A hero may be faulty, erring, imperfect; but he must not be sordid, mean, wanting in the statelier virtues of our kind.[47]

The heroes of George Eliot's later novels, Felix Holt and Daniel Deronda, perfectly illustrate Lewes' idea of what a hero should be—figures deliberately drawn as ideals of manhood, and consequently never allowed lapses from 'the elevation of moral rectitude'.

Notes

1. *Blackwood's Edinburgh Magazine,* LXXXVI (July, 1859), 108.

2. *Ibid.,* LXXXVII (March, 1860), 331.

3. *Ibid.,* LXXXVI (July, 1859), 108.

4. *Ibid.,* LXXXVII (March, 1860), 331-3.

5. *Ibid.,* LXXXVI (July, 1859), 101-4.

6. *Ibid.,* pp. 112-13.

7. *Ibid.,* pp. 102-3.

8. *Westminster Review,* LXX (October, 1858), 499.

9. Lewes was weekly reviewer for the *Leader* from 1850 to 1857. He was also a contributor to most of the important periodicals of the period.

10. Anna Theresa Kitchell, *George Lewes and George Eliot, A Review of Records* (New York, 1933), pp. 103-4.

11. *Leader,* VII (November 15, 1856), p. 1097.

12. *Ibid.,* IV (July 2, 1853), 644.

13. Kitchell, *op. cit.,* p. 106. Compare the review in *The Athenaeum,* October 25, 1851, pp. 1112-13.

14. Franklin Gary, 'Charlotte Brontë and George Henry Lewes', *PMLA,* LI (1936), 518-42.

15. *Fraser's Magazine,* XXXVI (December, 1847), 691-3.

16. CLXXXIII (January, 1850), 159.

17. *Leader,* IV (February 12, 1853), 163.

18. *Fraser's Magazine,* XXXVI (December, 1847), 694.

19. See Clarence Decker, *The Victorian Conscience* (New York, 1952).

20. *Leader,* VIII (May 23, 1857), 497.

21. (August 12, 1848), 794-7.

22. *Contemporary Thought and Thinkers,* [Collections on Contemporary Thought and Thinkers, Selected from the Spectator. 2 vols. London: Macmillan, 1906], I, 89.

23. *Fortnightly Review,* XVII (1872), 144-52.

24. *Ibid.,* pp. 151-2.

25. (London, 1858), II, 368.

26. *Autobiography* (Berkeley and Los Angeles, 1947), p. 128.

27. *Blackwood's,* LXXXVII (March, 1860), 333-4.

28. *Blackwood's,* LXXXVII (March, 1860), pp. 335-6.

29. See above [in *Theory of the Novel in England*], p. 98.

30. [*His Letters and Memories of His Life,* edited by his wife. 4 vols. London: Macmillan, 1902], III, 40-1.

31. *Fraser's,* XXXVI (December, 1847), 691.

32. *Leader,* IV (January 8, 1853), 44.

33. *Ibid.,* V (January 21, 1854), 66.

34. *Ibid.,* VII (June 7, 1856), 545.

35. *Jane Eyre* (London, 1908), chap. XII, p. 104.

36. *Fraser's,* XXXVI (December, 1847), 687. See Franklin Gary, 'Charlotte Brontë and George Henry Lewes', *PMLA,* XI (1936), 518-54.

37. *Leader,* VII (June 7, 1856), 545.

38. LXX, 493.

39. LXX, pp. 493-6.

40. *Principles of Success in Literature* (London, n.d.), p. 81.

41. X, 473.

42. I, 337-40.

43. *Principles of Success in Literature,* p. 80.

44. *Leader,* V (December 2, 1854), 1144.

45. IV (July 30, 1853), 740.

46. *Edinburgh Review,* XCI (January, 1850), 160-1.

47. *Ibid.,* pp. 163-4.

Allan R. Brick (essay date March 1960)

SOURCE: Brick, Allan R. "Lewes's Review of *Wuthering Heights.*" *Nineteenth-Century Fiction* 14, no. 4 (March 1960): 355-59.

[*In the following essay, Brick discusses Lewes's positive review of Emily Brontë's* Wuthering Heights.]

When *Wuthering Heights* hazarded a second edition in December, 1850, George Henry Lewes became the first eminent critic to grant the strange novel, which revolted many, its due regard.[1] True, Sydney Dobell, critic for the *Palladium,* had lavished belated praise on the book three months before, thus winning Charlotte Brontë's undying affection. But Lewes was far more influential than Dobell: Lewes had over the previous decade established a reputation not only as journalist and reviewer, but also as scholar of European literature and philosophy; lately he had achieved some prominence as novelist, playwright, and, in the spring of 1850, literary editor of the new, avant-garde *Leader.* On December 28 his praise in that weekly of the "mastery" and "genius" of Ellis Bell must have been heard—though it has been since forgotten.

Charlotte Brontë's famous lament, in her Preface to this second edition, that the critics had been unjust in their treatment of *Wuthering Heights* has received necessary qualification.[2] Dobell's praise, on the other hand, has been deservedly exposed by Melvin R. Watson as far more rhapsodic than perceptive.[3] But Watson, describing all *Wuthering Heights* criticism before Swinburne's in 1888 as superficial, neglected Lewes's review, and thus left the impression that there was no more understanding shown in 1850 than the *Athenaeum*'s (December 28, 1850, p. 1369) stodgy acceptance of "this volume [*Wuthering Heights and Agnes Grey*], with its preface, as a more than usually interesting contribution to the history of female authorship in England."

On January 15, 1851, Charlotte Brontë wrote to James Taylor: "The only notices that I have seen of the new edition of *Wuthering Heights* were those in the *Exam-iner,* the *Leader,* and the *Athenaeum.* That in the *Athenaeum* somehow gave me pleasure: it is quiet but respectful—so I thought, at least."[4] Charlotte's preference of the *Athenaeum* review may be explained on the grounds that her sisters' novels were now shown proper respect, three columns deep, in the weekly which had long been pre-eminent arbiter in literature, music, and art. But it also may be explained by the fact that the *Athenaeum* review consisted largely of a reproduction of portions of her Preface, and thus put forward precisely the view of *Wuthering Heights* that she wanted taken: i.e., Emily's novel was a vigorous though immature work and its Heathcliff a powerful though unfortunate creation.

Charlotte's failure to cite the *Examiner* (December 21, 1850, p. 815) for a review which, while admitting the "loathsome" atmosphere of *Wuthering Heights,* went on to call the book "better in its peculiar kind than anything that had been produced since Fielding" is a more complicated matter. In so saying the *Examiner* was actually quoting the words of its own 1847 review and at the same time protesting against the implication in Charlotte's Preface that all the initial reviews had been unfavorable and unfair. Thus, that journal valued Emily's book far more than the *Athenaeum,* which reproduced, and Dobell, who anticipated, Charlotte's own attitude of "powerful but immature." Evidently, the authoress of *Jane Eyre,* effectual leader of Emily and Anne when they lived, was now proprietress of their reputations—which she would have neither under- nor over-valued. It was probably the insistent moderation of her own appraisal that kept her from rejoicing over the praise of the *Examiner* or even more over the enthusiasm of Lewes, whom she deeply admired, and of his *Leader,* to which she eagerly subscribed.[5]

Lewes opened his review with a mild vindication of the critics of the 1847 edition of *Wuthering Heights,* agreeing that "the error committed is an error in art—the excessive predominance of shadows darkening the picture." But, so much admitted, he hastened to his main points:

> And yet, although there is a want of air and light in the picture we cannot deny its truth; sombre, rude, brutal, yet true. The fierce ungoverned instincts of powerful organizations, bred up amidst violence, revolt, and moral apathy, are here seen in operation; such brutes we should all be, or the most of us, were our lives as insubordinate to law; were our affections and sympathies as little cultivated, our imaginations as undirected. And herein lies the moral of the book, though most people will fail to draw the moral from very irritation at it. . . .
>
> The power [of "vigorous delineation"], indeed, is wonderful. Heathcliff, devil though he be, is drawn with a sort of dusky splendour which fascinates, and we feel the truth of his burning and impassioned love for Cathe-

rine, and of her inextinguishable love for him. It was a happy thought to make her love the kind, weak, elegant Edgar, and yet without lessening her passion for Heathcliff. Edgar appeals for her love of refinement, and goodness, and culture: Heathcliff clutches her soul in his passionate embrace. Edgar is the husband she has chosen, the man who alone is fit to call her wife; but although she is ashamed of her early playmate, she loves him with a passionate abandonment which sets culture, education, the world at defiance. It is in the treatment of this subject that Ellis Bell shows real mastery, and it shows more genius, in the highest sense of the word, than you will find in a thousand novels.

Thus, after the polite gesture toward fellow-critics, Lewes went not into the "rhapsodies" which Watson finds typify the favorable criticisms preceding Swinburne's, but into the "analysis" which he finds they lacked. Brief it was, yet it included the novel's two salient themes: the psychological study of amorality and revolt, and the portrayal of Catherine Earnshaw torn between elemental Heathcliff and civilized Linton. If left alone, such analysis of *Wuthering Heights* in 1850 would have been miraculous.

However, it was in violation of his classicism that Lewes permitted himself to admire *Wuthering Heights.* Worshipper of Jane Austen, he had shocked Charlotte Brontë three years before by stating that he would rather have written *Pride and Prejudice* or *Tom Jones* than any of the Waverley Novels; and, indeed, while publicly praising *Jane Eyre* in *Fraser's Magazine* (December, 1847, pp. 690-694) for "perception of character," "passion," and "transcripts from the book of life," he had privately taken Charlotte to task for its "romanticism" and "melodrama."[6] Also, reviewing *Shirley* in the *Edinburgh Review* (January, 1850, pp. 81-92), he had belabored Currer Bell for the "sordid" and "repulsive" elements in her heroes. Charlotte's concern with Lewes's edicts, shown in her letters during 1848-1850 and perhaps reflected in 1853 by her relatively lifelike *Villette,* suggests that it was to some degree Lewes himself who had caused the creator of Rochester and his mad wife to make in the 1850 Preface to *Wuthering Heights* the following excuse for Heathcliff:

> Whether it is right or advisable to create beings like Heathcliff, I do not know: I scarcely think it is. But this I know: the writer who possesses the creative gift owns something of which he is not always master—something that, at times, strangely wills and works for itself. He may lay down rules and devise principles, and to rules and principles it will perhaps for years lie in subjection; and then, haply without any warning of revolt, there comes a time when it will no longer consent to "harrow the valleys, or be bound with a band in the furrow." . . . Be the work grim or glorious, dread or divine, you have little choice left but quiescent adoption. . . . If the result be attractive, the World will praise you, who little deserve praise; if it be repulsive the same World will blame you, who almost as little deserve blame.

In his *Leader* review Lewes quoted this entire paragraph, pointing out that Currer Bell shared with Plato's *Ion* the doctrine that "the artist does not possess, but is possessed":

> This is so true that we suppose every writer will easily recal his sensations of being "carried away" by the thoughts which in moments of exaltation possessed his soul—will recal the headlong feeling of letting the reins slip—being himself as much astonished at the result as any reader can be. There is at such time a *momentum* which propels the mind into regions inaccessible to calculation, unsuspected in our calmer moods.

Such inspiration might be tolerated if it were no more uncontrolled than in *Jane Eyre,* but in *Wuthering Heights* it was too wild. Lewes qualified his approval of Charlotte's explanation by insisting upon eighteenth-century humanity and restraint:

> The three sisters have been haunted by the same experience. Currer Bell throws more humanity into her picture; but Rochester belongs to the Earnshaw and Heathcliff family. Currer Bell's riper mind enables her to paint with a freer hand; nor can we doubt but that her two sisters, had they lived, would also have risen into greater strength and clearness, retaining the extraordinary power of vigorous delineation which makes their writings so remarkable.

While admitting and even analyzing the essential greatness of Ellis Bell's novel, Lewes revealed his own distaste—made necessary by the literature and philosophy which had formed his mind. Thus, in spite of insights unequaled by any other contemporary reviewer, his effect was divided. General readers, discovering their own preference for universalized humaneness as opposed to "animality," might have discounted too easily the praise. Charlotte Brontë might have derived too easily an added assurance that Rochester was more "true" than Heathcliff and that *Wuthering Heights* should be imprisoned within a minor shrine.

Notes

1. Lewes's review of *Wuthering Heights and Agnes Grey* appeared in the *Leader,* December 28, 1850, p. 953. For a description of the *Leader*'s influence upon nineteenth-century thought and of Lewes's role as its literary editor, see my dissertation, "The *Leader*: Organ of Radicalism" (Yale, 1957). See also Gordon S. Haight, "Dickens and Lewes," *PMLA,* LXXI (March, 1956), 166-179.

2. Edith M. Weir, "Contemporary Reviews of the First Brontë Novels," *Transactions and other Publications of the Brontë Society,* XI (1951), 88-96.

3. Melvin R. Watson, *"Wuthering Heights* and the Critics," *NCF* [*Nineteenth-Century Fiction*], III (March, 1949), 243-263.

4. *The Shakespeare Head Brontë,* ed. T. J. Wise and J. A. Symington (Oxford: Shakespeare Head Press, 1932), II, 200.

5. See Charlotte's many references to Lewes and the *Leader* in her letters (*Shakespeare Head Brontë*). Also see Franklin Gary, "Charlotte Brontë and George Henry Lewes," *PMLA,* LI (1936), 518-542.

6. See Charlotte's letter to Lewes on January 12, 1848 (*Shakespeare Head Brontë,* II, 179).

Diana Postlethwaite (essay date 1984)

SOURCE: Postlethwaite, Diana. "Synthetic Philosophy: George Henry Lewes and Herbert Spencer." In *Making It Whole: A Victorian Circle and the Shape of Their World,* pp. 164-231. Columbus: Ohio State University Press, 1984.

[*In the following excerpts, Postlethwaite seeks to give Lewes past due recognition. She stresses the importance of both Spinoza and Herbert Spencer in Lewes's thought.*]

I. The Heart and the Brain—George Henry Lewes: "Spinoza's Life and Works" (1843)

It has been said of George Henry Lewes that he "represented perhaps the more effervescent, more eccentric, and yet also the more truly philosophical aspects of the mid-Victorian mind."[1] A single chapter cannot do full justice to the breadth of Lewes's thought: he was a literary critic, a novelist, a playwright, an editor, a physiologist, a psychologist, a philosopher, an historian of ideas; a true Victorian polymath. What little attention has been paid to Lewes by previous scholars has tended to center on his relationship with George Eliot, or on his role as literary critic and man of letters. But Lewes viewed himself preeminently as a philosopher of science. My focus here will be on Lewes's earlier philosophical work, particularly in the field of psychology; those aspects of his intellectual biography that link him most closely with this Victorian circle.

Lewes called his final and most ambitious project, ***Problems of Life and Mind*** (5 vol., 1874-79), his "key to all Psychologies."[2] Therein, he attempted to resolve "the long debates respecting the true position of Psychology among the sciences," within a continuum of ideas from the 1840s and 1850s, freely acknowledging his debts to Comte, Mill, and Spencer as the thinkers with whom he was "most in agreement."[3] As we have seen, Lewes was an early disciple of Mill and Comte; but Herbert Spencer was his friend and intellectual equal. This chapter will establish some of the early sources of Lewes's and Spencer's ideas, and chronicle the path of their mutual intellectual development during the decade of the 1850s, their lively and reciprocal interplay of ideas. As with so many in this circle, it is often difficult to determine the exact origin of an idea. Spencer's greater philosophical fame has tended to obscure Lewes's own important contributions to nineteenth-century intellectual history—and to Herbert Spencer's intellectual history.

Lewes's debts to Mill and Comte notwithstanding, Johann Wolfgang von Goethe was his most-admired mentor. In his 1852 essay on **"Goethe as a Man of Science"** (the germ of Lewes's classic biography of Goethe), Lewes quotes Goethe speaking of a life "passed in creating and observing, in synthesis and analysis: the systole and diastole of human thought were to me like a second breathing process—never separated, ever pulsating."[4] The dual strands of philosophy and biology, synthesis and analysis, general and particular, span the decades of Lewes's intellectual development. Twenty-four years later, in an essay entitled **"Materialism and Spiritualism,"** which summarizes his work-in-progress on *Problems of Life and Mind,* Lewes would remember Goethe's words: "Analysis and synthesis are the systole and diastole of science."[5] It was Lewes's lifelong ambition to effect the perfect fusion of part and whole, that individuation in which each part is uniquely particular and yet fully subsumed within a greater unity. Like Herbert Spencer, Lewes would find the key that would unlock the apparent paradox of the many in the one, the one in the many, in evolutionary biology.

But in his search for this delicate balance, it has been Lewes's fate to be both oversimplified and misinterpreted. For example, Rosemary Ashton has difficulty reconciling Lewes's early enthusiasm for Hegel's aesthetics with his later embrace of Comte's positivism. She resorts to a simple dichotomy: "From 1843 on, Lewes ranged himself on the side of analysis, not synthesis in criticism, just as he stood for empiricism rather than *a priorism* in philosophy."[6] Similarly, Robert M. Young is incorrect in his interpretation of Spencer's debt to Lewes: "Just as the reading of Lyell's refutation of Lamarck turned Spencer *towards* belief in inheritance of acquired characteristics, the reading of Lewes's positivist polemics seemed to have turned him towards metaphysics."[7] In fact, Lewes was not an idealist turned empiricist; nor was he a positivistic polemicist who drove his friend to metaphysics.

To be fair, Lewes himself is partially responsible for the confusion: in the ***Biographical History of Philosophy,*** he argued emphatically for the death of metaphysics at the hand of positivistic natural science. But it should be clear from my discussion of Comte in chapter 1 that positivism is not simply to be allied with science in opposition to metaphysics. It occupies a middle ground between the two. Other critics have more correctly perceived the similar mediating tendencies in Lewes's work, but have incorrectly located their philosophical counterparts. In his essay on "The Empirical Metaphysics of George Henry Lewes," Jack Kaminsky divides nineteenth-century English philosophy into the "opposing tendencies" of "empirical positivism" (Mill and Spencer) and its "philosophic reaction" (exemplified in "Carlyle's transcendentalism, Newman's Catholicism, and Green's idealism"). Kaminsky correctly argues that Lewes sought to "heal the bifurcation in philosophy, [urging] that the study of metaphysical problems might be pursued with an empirical rather than a transcendental method." But Mill and Spencer themselves share many fundamental similarities with Lewes. Kaminsky considers Lewes "one renegade positivist," crying alone in a wilderness of skeptics and Roman Catholics, biologists and German idealists. In reality Lewes was far from solitary in his pursuit of a middle ground. Kaminsky ruefully concludes that "the full import of Lewes's views on metaphysics was completely lost to nineteenth-century philosophers."[8] Although it may be true that his ideas were not influential within the academy, the interconnections between Lewes and an important circle of Victorian minds were rich and pervasive.

One might expect that George Henry Lewes would have given a favorable review to Atkinson's and Martineau's *Letters on the Laws of Man's Nature and Development* in his three "Literature" columns in the *Leader* devoted to that subject in February and March 1851. Although Lewes did claim the *Letters* worthy of "serious discussion" and acknowledge them the "result of honest, independent thinking," he was otherwise highly critical. One immediate source of Lewes's disapprobation is suggested by his intolerance of phrenological faddism, mesmeric quacks, and pseudo-scientific notions of force—and indeed, "the mesmeric and clairvoyant revelations" of the pair do "excite [his] ridicule." But unexpectedly, Lewes is more critical of what could loosely be termed the theological aspects of the book than he is of its dubious scientific underpinnings: "We are among those who must unequivocally dissent from the opinions it ushers in": "the open avowal of Atheism and denial of Immortality." Lewes here sides with Froude and those critics who were offended by what they considered a dangerous materialism: "Reason is daylight; by it we see all that can be seen in daylight; but there *are* realities the perception of which daylight destroys, and among these are the stars."[9] These are hardly the words one might expect from a clear-eyed empiricist.

George Henry Lewes and Harriet Martineau have more in common than Lewes grants (as chapter 3 demonstrates). Although he misreads Martineau as a simple atheist, this misreading is highly illuminating of Lewes himself: *The soul is larger than logic,*" he argues; "there is . . . a logic of emotions, and a logic of instincts as well as a logic of ideas." George Henry Lewes, amateur scientist and positivist, five years after condemning metaphysics in the *Biographical History*

[*Biographical History of Philosophy*] and on the eve of his study of Comte, speaks in strikingly idealist terms: "We are not Kantists, but detect in his system the indistinct expression of that consciousness of a transcendental faculty we feel within ourselves."[10]

Although Lewes was never an orthodox religious believer, this transcendental streak was strong in him from the start. In his 1876 essay on **"Spiritualism and Materialism,"** Lewes indulges in a rare moment of autobiographical reminiscence:

> There was one brief period when I was very near a conversion. The idea of a noumenal Mind, as something distinct from mental phenomena—a something diffused through the Organism giving unity to Consciousness, very different from the unity of a machine, flashed upon me one morning with a sudden and novel force, quite unlike the shadowy vagueness with which it had heretofore been conceived. For some minutes I was motionless in a rapt state of thrilled surprise. I seemed standing at the entrance of a new path, leading to new issues with a vast horizon. The convictions of a life seemed tottering. A tremulous eagerness, suffused with the keen light of discovery, yet mingled with cross-lights and hesitations, stirred me; and from that moment I have understood something of sudden conversions. There was, as I afterwards remembered, no feeling of distress at this prospect of parting with old beliefs. Indeed it is doubtful whether sudden conversions are accomplished by pain, the excitement is too great, the new ideas too absorbing. The rapture of truth overcomes the false shame of having been in error. The one desire is for more light.[11]

Lewes's self-portrait here has much in common with Martineau's own rhapsodic account of her conversion to mesmerism, with its strong overtones of religious experience mingled with scientific conviction. Characteristically, Lewes asks for the "light" of intellectual illumination in the midst of this most emotional moment.

A brief scientific essay, **"The Heart and the Brain,"** which Lewes wrote for the *Fortnightly Review* in 1865, provides a theoretical analogue to his personal account of the interworkings of heart and brain. It is important to remember that for Lewes, as for Atkinson and Martineau, "transcendental faculties" were also biological phenomena. Much of **"The Heart and the Brain"** is, quite literally, a biological discussion of those two organs. "Heart and Brain are the two lords of Life," Lewes opens. But he immediately suggests that this statement may also be read figuratively: "In the metaphors of ordinary speech and in the stricter language of science, we use these terms to indicate two central powers, from which all motives radiate, to which all influences converge."[12]

The phrenologists had claimed that the brain was the organ of the mind, and were branded godless materialists. Lewes seems at first to disagree with phrenology, condemning as unscientific "the modern doctrine respecting the brain . . . as the exclusive organ of sensation." Lewes has come full circle within physiological psychology, "to appreciate the truth . . . in the ancient doctrine respecting the heart as the great emotional organ." But instead of repudiating the materialism of the phrenologists, Lewes actually enlarges their claims. The heart is physiologically the "great emotional center": "As the central organ of the circulation [it] is so indissolubly connected with every manifestation of Sensibility, and is so delicately susceptible to all emotional agitations." Heart does not replace brain as center; both are simply parts of a greater whole, "the vital activities of the whole organism."[13] Read figuratively (as Lewes invites), the "two lords of life," each equal in power yet interdependent, are the emotions and the intellect. Lewes insists that metaphor and fact, poetry and science, mirror one another. The transcendent logic of emotions has its correspondent physiology.

In this context I turn back to the 1840s, when Lewes was introduced to the study of philosophy by the work of Benedict Spinoza, a seventeenth-century Dutch philosopher who mechanized human passions in the form of geometrical propositions, and argued for the unification of mind and matter as manifestations of a single substance. In the philosophy of Spinoza, Lewes was to find both a solution and a dilemma: the prototype of his ideal philosophic temperament, and what he saw as the greatest obstacle to any philosophical endeavor.

Whether by fortunate coincidence or careful design, George Henry Lewes was asked to contribute to the "S" volume of the *Penny Cyclopaedia* in 1842; his task: to define the terms "Subject, Subjective," "Substance," and "Spinoza." His trip to Germany in 1838 had fueled Lewes's early fascination with German idealist philosophies; but even in these short entries, among his earliest published writing, we can see the characteristic bias of Lewes's mind. Lewes's definition of "subject" is inseparable from its polar antithesis: "The very subject itself (the mind) can become an object by being psychologically considered."[14] In his definition of "substance," Lewes similarly insists on a two-sided vision, the equivalence of subject and object: "The stronghold of Idealism is consciousness. In Consciousness there is nothing but transformations of itself—no substance, no external world is given. . . . But consciousness is equally the stronghold of Realism; for we are as conscious that what we call substance, or the world, is not ourselves, and does not depend on us, and is a distinct existence."[15]

Spinoza is identified with both subject and substance, closely linked with the idealist school: "All the German philosophers, from Kant downwards, owns [sic] him as its master."[16] Lewes confessed elsewhere that he considered Spinoza's "the grandest and most religious of philosophies."[17] The continuity of Lewes's interest in Spinoza is evident in his return to the philosopher in 1843 and again in 1866. In an autobiographical moment in the 1866 *Fortnightly Review* essay, Lewes travels to a small tavern in Red Lion Square in the mid-1830s, "where the vexed questions of philosophy were discussed with earnestness, if not insight," by young George, not yet twenty, and a mixed group of speculatively-minded friends. Supreme among them was a German Jew, a watchmaker named Cohn: "He remains in my memory as a type of philosophic dignity"; "I venerated his great calm intellect. He was the only man I did not contradict in the impatience of argument," Lewes recalls. It was Cohn who tutored the group weekly in Spinoza. Lewes's intense feelings for Spinoza were inextricably mixed with those for his mentor, Cohn: "I habitually think of him in connexion with Spinoza, almost as much on account of his personal characteristics, as because to him I owe my first acquaintance with the Hebrew thinker. My admiration for him was of that enthusiastic temper which in youth we feel for our intellectual leaders."[18] Lewes's essay on **"Spinoza's Life and Works"** in the *Westminster Review* (1843) came at a time when Spinoza was not translated into English, and was generally acknowledged as a ground-breaking attempt to bring this difficult philosopher to the attention of the English reading public.[19] I consider this essay the cornerstone of Lewes's early thought; it epitomizes both his characteristic frame of mind and his central intellectual dilemma at the time, to be resolved through his friendship with Herbert Spencer in the early 1850s.

Lewes's attraction to Spinoza is fraught with a most interesting tension: Lewes venerates Spinoza as a religious philosopher, and writes essays on the man at both ends of his career. Yet Lewes's early insistence in the **Biographical History** on the objective, psychological view, in contradistinction to the subjective, philosophical one, his assertion that consciousness is not all—this seems in conflict with Spinoza, by Lewes's own definition the forefather of Kantian idealism. Ashton argued that Lewes's early flirtation with German romanticism and *a priori* idealism gave way to the later empiricism of the **Biographical History.** And indeed that book does seem to support a reading of Lewes as an *a posteriori* empiricist. Lewes's fundamental disagreement with Spinoza in 1843 becomes the germ of his central argument throughout the 800-page history. The "fundamental error of Spinozism," Lewes writes, will be rectified by the objectivity of the new positivist psychology:

> It is our firm conviction that no believer in Ontology, as a *possible* science, can escape the all-embracing dialectic of Spinoza. To him who believes that the human mind can know *noumena*, as well as *phenomena*—who accepts the verdict of the mind as not merely the *relative* truth, but also the *perfect, absolute* truth—we see nothing, humanly speaking, but Spinozism as a philosophical refuge. . . . If you do not believe that your

knowledge is *absolute,* and not simply *relative,* you have no sort of ground for belief in the possibility of ontology.[20]

Lewes takes the latter position. In the ***Biographical History,*** the error of the ontologist becomes for scientific psychologist Lewes the fundamental error of *all* philosophers: the notion that the mind can intuitively, clearly and distinctly, know Truth, that Ideas exist independent of experience. "Spinozism or Skepticism?" Lewes demands; "choose between them, for you have no other choice."[21] But if Lewes was not a Spinozist, was he a Skeptic? I will look to both Lewes's 1843 essay and Spinoza's *Ethics,* and suggest two possible solutions to this dilemma: first, in the dialectic that Lewes sets up in that essay between the idealist, subjective Spinoza and the man Lewes considers his realist, objective polar antithesis, Francis Bacon; second, and more intriguing, in the philosophy of Spinoza itself, which in many ways attempts to reconcile antitheses in ways directly relevant to this Victorian circle.

"Spinoza's Life and Works" provides ample documentation of Lewes's continued attraction to the great philosopher since his student days in Red Lion Square. But Lewes's essay adopts a peculiar stratagem, given its ostensibly admiring stance towards Spinoza. Once Lewes has outlined Spinoza's life, he shifts unexpectedly to Francis Bacon, as a counterpoint to Spinoza: "From Bacon [comes] the whole school of scientific men, the materialists, Scotch physiologists, and political economists," in contradistinction to the "Cartesian" school, in which Lewes includes Spinoza, Kant, and Hegel. After Lewes's denunciation of the fundamental error of Spinozism, Bacon arises as the hero of a new, empirical psychology, which claims to escape the subjective boundaries of the reflective consciousness: "We might have gone on baffled, yet persisting, seeking the unknowable, and building palaces on air . . . had not Bacon arisen to point out that the method men were pursuing was not the path of transit to the truth, but led only to a land of chimeras." Bacon heralds the new spirit of Positive Science, and it is this nineteenth-century Baconianism, in opposition to the "arachnae philosophers of Germany," that Lewes praises throughout the ***Biographical History of Philosophy.***[22]

Yet to suggest that he simply abandoned Spinoza at this point belies the intensity of Lewes's fascination with the Dutch philosopher. Lewes not only returned to the subject of Spinoza in 1866, he also encouraged the earliest efforts to translate Spinoza into English. In January 1843 George Eliot had borrowed Spinoza's works from R. H. Brabant (who had been introduced to Spinoza by no less than Samuel Taylor Coleridge himself, in 1815-16[23]), and began a translation for her friend Charles Bray—probably the *Tractatus,* but also possibly "De Deo," the opening of the *Ethics.*[24] In February 1847 Eliot returned Brabant's copy of the philosopher's Latin

works and borrowed publisher John Chapman's.[25] Cara Bray wrote to Sara Sophia Hennell in the spring of 1849 of Eliot's "great desire to undertake Spinoza." It was to her translation of the *Tractatus* that Eliot turned while nursing her father through his final illness: "It is such a rest to her mind," Cara wrote.[26] But in the grief and aimlessness of those months following Robert Evans's death in May 1849, Eliot and Spinoza were "divorced"; though she agreed grudgingly to uphold her bargain with Chapman for a translation of the *Tractatus Theologico-Politicus,* to be published in conjunction with an American translation of the *Ethics*: "If you are anxious to publish the translation in question I could, after a few months, finish the Tractatus Theologico-Politicus to keep it company—but I confess to you, that I think you would do better to abstain from printing a translation." Grief may have dampened Eliot's energies, but her discouragement with the translation also took a more complex form: "What is wanted in English is not a translation of Spinoza's works, but a true estimate of his life and system. After one has rendered his Latin faithfully into English, one feels that there is another yet more difficult process of translation for the reader to effect, and that the only mode of making Spinoza accessible to a larger number is to study his books, then shut them and give his analysis."[27]

Spinoza was surely not the least of that community of intellectual interests that Eliot and Lewes found when they met and fell in love between 1851 and 1854; when they eloped to Germany in 1854, Eliot began a translation of the *Ethics* while Lewes labored on his ***Life of Goethe,*** and they returned to England to see both books through publication.[28] In October 1855 an announcement in Lewes's ***Goethe*** proclaimed that "Spinoza will ere long appear in English, edited by the writer of these lines," as a joint product of George Eliot and George Henry Lewes. Such was not to be: Lewes's agreement with publisher Bohn for his edition of Eliot's translation ended in acrimonious financial squabbles between Lewes and Bohn during the early weeks of June 1856.[29]

George Eliot's interest in the *Tractatus* was clearly of a piece with her translation of the German rationalist critics Strauss and Feuerbach. Spinoza is "Vater der Speculation unserer Zeit; er ist auch Vater der biblischen Kritik," Strauss himself wrote.[30] It was Lewes who turned Eliot to work on the *Ethics,* a book more directly relevant to my discussion here. For in the *Ethics* itself, we find many clear reasons for Spinoza's strong appeal to the frame of mind shared by this Victorian circle. . . .

III. STATICS AND DYNAMICS—TRANSCENDENTAL ANATOMY AND THE DEVELOPMENT HYPOTHESIS—SPENCER AND LEWES: ESSAYS, 1851-1857

All discovery must be the discovery either of a *fact* or of a *relation.* . . . The discovery of a fact may be a consequence of pre-eminent faculties in the discoverer, but it is not necessarily so. The discovery of a relation, on the contrary, is strictly and exclusively the consequence of pre-eminent faculties, or *power of origination.*

—George Eliot to George Combe, 22 April 1852

As Herbert Spencer recalled, the subject of his first conversation with George Henry Lewes in the spring of 1850 was not social statics, but the development hypothesis.[31] Thereafter, it was not backward to social theories inherited from the eighteenth century, but forward, to the exciting scientific developments of their own times, to which the new friends turned during the "long Sunday-rambles," beginning in the summer of 1851, which gradually grew into more wide-ranging excursions about the English countryside. One four-day journey up the valley of the Thames was especially significant: "It was to the impulse he received from the conversations during these four days that Lewes more particularly ascribed that awakened interest in scientific theories," writes Spencer. "And in me," he continues, "observation on the forms of leaves set going a train of thought which ended in my writing an essay on 'The Laws of Organic Form'; an extended exposition of which occupies some space in *The Principles of Biology*" (1864).[32]

In that essay, published in the *British and Foreign Medico-Chirugical Review* in 1859, Spencer reminisces about the same ramble, mentioning Lewes by name as his companion. He remembers picking a buttercup, gazing upon its form, and reflecting on the effects of soil and climate on structure. Spencer's interest is equally divided between the questions of environmental influence and the inherent structural principles within the plant itself. "The conditions are manifestly the antecedent, and the form the consequent," he concludes; "it may be fairly presumed that like relationship holds throughout the animal kingdom." Spencer is also impressed with the "universal harmony" of morphological forms, "the unity which pervades the organic creation."[33]

These were the same terms to which Spencer and Lewes would return again and again in their essays of the early 1850s: the unity of composition and the multiplicity of adaptation; in man, the animal kingdom, organic creation, and, in a grand progressive synthesis, the cosmos itself. Within the next year after that theory-hunting expedition, both Lewes and Spencer made public their adherence to the controversial "development hypothesis": Lewes first, the autumn after those summer rambles, in **"Lyell and Owen on Development"** (*Leader,* 18 October 1851); Spencer in the same journal in March 1852, on "The Development Hypothesis."

In his essay Lewes articulates his disagreement with particular scientific details in Lyell, Owen, and Robert Chambers. Yet he also argues for the larger ideological correctness of evolutionary theory: "The differences are reconcilable between all forms of the development hypothesis directly we substitute for it the more abstract and comprehensive formula of the law of Progressive Adaptation."[34] Although Spencer acknowledges that the theory of evolution is not yet "adequately supported by the facts" (many of which Darwin would provide), he also asserts unequivocally that "any existing species immediately begins to undergo certain changes of structure fitting it for new conditions." These changes follow the same pattern of progressive development that Spencer traced in *Social Statics*: "Complex organic forms have arisen by successive modifications out of simple ones."[35]

It is often remarked that during the decade before Charles Darwin's *Origin of Species,* evolution was "in the air." Chapter 2 demonstrated that Chambers's *Vestiges of Creation* was an important source of Lewes's and Spencer's early notions about evolution. Both men were also well-acquainted with the many other scientific guises in which precursors of Darwin appeared during the nineteenth century in the work of men such as Lyell, Owen, Lamarck. But it is important to remember that for both Lewes and Spencer, the faith preceded the facts. I have chosen Chambers as my prototypical Victorian evolutionist, precisely because he was, as Lewes said, the most "metaphysical" of these scientific theorists. For Lewes and Spencer began with certain beliefs about the order of things; when they read contemporary scientists, they sought the facts to fit those beliefs ("*tant pis pour les fleurs*").[36]

In the discussion of Lewes's and Spencer's evolutionary beliefs that follows, I make no claim to do full justice to the complex matrix of contemporary scientific developments that influenced these two Victorian thinkers. Rather, I will isolate the concepts I believe were central to their evolutionary cosmologies as they developed in the early 1850s, and suggest some of the sources for these concepts. They are: the unity of composition (from Goethe and St. Hilaire); the organism and the medium (from Comte); and the development from homogeneity to heterogeneity (from von Baer). The interrelation of these three concepts (and they were inseparable for Lewes and Spencer) reveals the thesis / antithesis / synthesis structure so characteristic of these Victorians: the static morphology of the unity of composition; the dynamic evolution of the developmental process; and what Lewes calls "the Staticodynamical view," in which the inherent "transcendent" structure of the individual organism is counterbalanced against the ever-changing forces of the medium as a whole.[37]

UNITY OF COMPOSITION

Lewes's choice of Goethe as the subject for a full-length biography (the first ever written on the German) was motivated by a subject who was scientific and philosophical, as well as literary. Lewes clearly saw

Goethe as a model for his own yearning to fuse science and humanism. Appropriately, Goethe was deeply involved in the rediscovery of Spinoza by the German romantics, praising Spinoza as one "who had wrought so powerfully on me, and who was destined to affect so deeply, my entire mode of thinking."[38] Goethe, like Herbert Spencer, was another genius in the Spinozist mold, the man of passionate emotions and far-reaching abstractions. In his *Life of Goethe,* Lewes singles out Goethe's ability to "[unite] the mastery of Will and Intellect to the profoundest sensibility of Emotion."[39] In an extended passage from that book, Lewes compares Goethe's "poetical Pantheism" to Spinoza's, with evolutionary overtones: "In it the whole universe was conceived as divine . . . as the living manifestation of divine energy . . . St. Paul tells us that God lives in everything and everything in God. Science tells us that the world is always *becoming* . . . the primal energies of Life are . . . issuing forth under new forms, through metamorphoses higher and higher."[40]

When Herbert Spencer writes in his *Autobiography* that "the inability of a man of science to take the poetic view simply shows his mental limitation; as the mental limitation of a poet is shown by his inability to take the scientific view. The broader mind can take both. Those who allege this antagonism forget that Goethe, predominantly a poet, was also a scientific inquirer," he unmistakably takes his cue from Lewes.[41] Goethe is not just a scientist who is also a poet; he is a poetical scientist. Head and heart, reason and imagination are fully integrated in him. As such Goethe epitomizes the intellectual temperament of both Lewes and Spencer themselves: "Do not mistake him for a metaphysician. He was a positive thinker on the *a priori* Method."[42]

Lewes's interest in Goethe germinated in the essay **"Goethe as a Man of Science,"** published in the *Westminster* under Eliot's editorship in 1852, which reappeared as chapter 9, book 5 in the *Life* [*Life of Goethe*], retitled "The Poet as a Man of Science." The seeds of Lewes's interest in Goethe were scientific, not literary. Lewes was the first to discuss seriously Goethe's work as a scientist on the metamorphosis of plants, the vertebral structure of the skull, and the discovery of the intermaxillary bone common to both man and animals. Lewes begins his essay by categorizing scientists as "analytical" or "synthetical" (those favorite Spencerian terms), as epitomized by Cuvier and St. Hilaire: "The former starts from Individuals in order to arrive at a Whole. . . . The latter carries within himself the image of this Whole, and lives in the persuasion that little by little the Individuals will be deduced from it."[43] He goes on to trace the similarities between the work of St. Hilaire and Goethe, arguing that Goethe, like St. Hilaire, is a "synthetical" scientist.

Lewes credits St. Hilaire with the grand concept of "Unity of composition," a notion not only of service to zoological studies, but of philosophical significance as well.[44] He would return to this same idea at length in an essay on the **"Life and Doctrine of Geoffroy St. Hilaire,"** again in the *Westminster,* in 1854: "What is his Doctrine? . . . That throughout the infinite variety of organic forms there runs one principle of composition: that there is one type underlying all diversities. This is . . . the greatest idea contributed by zoology to philosophy." St. Hilaire's "anatomy was philosophic, or transcendent, because *transcending* the vision of the eye, it had the vision of the mind"; it is "this addition of Reason to Observation which characterizes philosophic anatomy."[45] Herbert Spencer announced in his own essay on "Transcendental Physiology" in 1857 that he too was a "transcendental anatomist" who sought "general principles of structure common to vast and varied groups of organisms—the unity of plan discernible throughout multitudinous species."[46]

But Goethe was not merely "synthetical." He was also "eminently a positive thinker . . . the attitude of his mind, the organic tendency of his nature, was eminently scientific."[47] Revealingly, Lewes compares Goethe with Bacon as one "penetrated by the spirit of positive philosophy." In systole and diastole, Goethe descends from the philosophical generalization to the scientific fact, "and thus brings the whole diversity of forms within the unity of Life."[48] Lewes notes that Goethe himself was an early believer in the development hypothesis. Like Spencer, Goethe looks not just at static structure, but also to progressive development. In the *Life* Lewes quotes Goethe on the "law of Individuation," in language that bears an unmistakable similarity to Spencer's in *Social Statics*: "The more imperfect a being is, the more do its individual parts resemble each other, and the more do these parts resemble the whole. The more perfect the being, the more dissimilar are the parts. . . . The more the parts resemble each other, the less subordination is there of one to the other. Subordination of parts indicates high grade of organization."[49]

Lewes believes that Unity of Composition is a profound truth. Unity of Composition is the necessary starting point for an evolutionary biology; but taken by itself, it places too much emphasis on the static inherent order of the individual organism. It is not adequate to explain the changing nature of the universe. "It is only by connecting this theory with another, viewing it as the Statical Law of which the Development is the Dynamical Law, that, in our opinion, it can be accepted," Lewes concludes.[50] Lewes and Spencer found the key to progressive adaptation in the dynamic interrelationship of organism and medium.

ORGANISM AND MEDIUM

Writing on "The Natural History of German Life" in 1856, George Eliot made clear that she had thoroughly assimilated Herbert Spencer's movement from a biological to a social model in *Social Statics*: "The external conditions which society has inherited from the past are but the manifestation of inherited internal conditions in the human beings who compose it; the internal conditions and the external are related to each other as the organism and the medium; and development can take place only by the gradual constantaneous development of both."[51]

When Lewes investigated **"Mr. Darwin's Hypothesis"** in 1868, he credited French scientist Jean-Baptiste Lamarck (1744-1829) with the "law of Adaptation" that Charles Darwin enlarged into "natural selection," praising "the singular importance of Lamarck's hypothesis in calling attention to modifiability of structure through modifications of adaptation." Although Lamarck erred in placing too much emphasis on the medium at the expense of the organism, he provided a necessary corrective to the static viewpoint of transcendental anatomy. "Naturalists before his time had been wont to consider the Organism apart from the Medium in which it existed; [Lamarck] clearly saw that vital phenomena depended on the relation of the two."[52]

Auguste Comte's emphasis on the relationship of organism and medium developed the same idea.[53] Lewes found the most explicit statement of the concept in Comte's definition of life in the *Cours de philosophie positive*: "The idea of Life supposes the mutual relation of two indispensible elements—an organism and a suitable medium or environment."[54] Lewes returns to the concept repeatedly throughout his book on Comte: "So far from organic bodies being independent of external circumstances they become more and more dependent on them as their organization becomes higher, so that organism and a medium are the two correlative ideas of life."[55]

This same notion of mutual interdependence lies directly behind Herbert Spencer's famous definition of life in *The Principles of Psychology*: "the continuous adjustment of internal relations to external relations."[56] Lewes's own emphasis on the relationship between organism and medium as the cornerstone of his evolutionary philosophy never wavered. His final book, **Problems of Life and Mind,** echoes the ideas of twenty-five years earlier: *"Every vital phenomena is the product of two factors, the Organism and the Medium"*; "Life may be defined as the mode of existence of an organism in relation to its medium."[57]

HOMOGENEITY AND HETEROGENEITY

But taken by themselves, Unity of Composition and the interdependence of Organism and Medium do not necessitate a belief in progressive evolutionary development. The final seeds of Lewes's and Spencer's evolutionary theory were planted when Spencer reviewed W. B. Carpenter's *Principles of Physiology* in the autumn

of 1851. In reading Carpenter, writes Spencer, "I became acquainted with von Baer's statement that the development of every organism is a change from homogeneity to heterogeneity. The substance of the thought was not new to me, though its form was." The substance of von Baer's theory is anticipated in *Social Statics* as "an unshaped belief in the development of living things; including, in a vague way, social development."[58] Spencer's sociological notions of "individuation," in which each part becomes progressively more individualized and complex, yet simultaneously more interdependent with the whole, are given explicit scientific foundation by the German zoologist and embryologist Karl Ernst von Baer (1792-1876). Carpenter writes in the summary of von Baer that Spencer read: "The lower we descend in the scale of being, whether in Animal or in Vegetable series, the nearer approach do we make to that *homogeneousness* which is the typical attribute of organic bodies, wherein every particle has all the characters of individuality . . . as we ascend in the scale of being, we find the fabric—whether of the Plant or the Animal—becoming more and more heterogeneous."[59]

Reviewing Carpenter's book in 1855, T. H. Huxley claimed that von Baer's laws "are to Biology what Kepler's great generalizations were to Astronomy."[60] Spencer's application of von Baer gave the proof to Huxley's analogy. His researches in embryology led von Baer to conclude that development proceeds from the general to the more highly specialized. Not surprisingly, Herbert Spencer titled the 1857 essay that took von Baer's "homogeneity" and "heterogeneity" as its passwords "Progress: Its Law and Cause." Just as Spencer moved analogously from sociology to biology in *Social Statics,* so he made the even greater leap, in "Progress," from von Baer's embryology to a full-blown Victorian cosmology:

> The series of changes gone through during the development of a seed into a tree, or an ovum into an animal, constitute an advance from homogeneity of structure to heterogeneity of structure. . . . This is the history of all organisms whatever. . . . Now, we propose in the first place to show, that this law of organic progress is the law of all progress. Whether it be in the development of the Earth, in the development of Life upon its surface, in the development of Society, of Government, of Manufactures, of Commerce, of Language, Literature, Science, Art, this same evolution of the simple into the complex through successive differentiations, holds throughout.[61]

Spencer's intellectual kinship with Robert Chambers is most apparent in this essay. Chambers gathers the universe into "one majestic Whole," from the nebular hypothesis and the formation of the solar system to the mind of man, under the universal law of development.[62] In "Progress: Its Law and Cause," Spencer follows the same structural model as the *Vestiges,* tracing the "law of progress" (the development from homogeneity to heterogeneity) through the solar system, the formation of the earth, plants and animals, man, society, language, religion, and art.

George Henry Lewes and George Eliot were also much taken with von Baer. In June 1853 Lewes devoted an essay in the *Leader* to **"Von Baer on the Development Hypothesis,"** stressing "the law of *organic modification* in adaptation to circumstances."[63] Lewes also quotes the German scientist in his *Life of Goethe* in 1855: "The history of Development is the true torchbearer in every inquiry into organic bodies." Lewes continues in his own words, in terms that make clear that the notion of a broader, nonbiological application of von Baer's biological principles did not originate with Herbert Spencer in 1857: "In Geology, in Physiology, in History, and in Art, we are now all bent on tracing the phases of development. To understand the *grown* we try to follow the *growth*."[64] In that same year, Lewes notes that he and George Eliot are reading Carpenter's *Principles of Physiology* again—along with Gall's *Anatomie et physiologie du cerveau.*[65]

Of George Eliot's interest in von Baer, we have only a small but intriguing clue, to be found in the first of those three passionate love letters to Spencer in July 1852. The lovesick intellectual depicts herself filled with "a loathing for books," regressing on the scale of mental evolution: "You see I am sinking fast towards 'homogeneity,' and my brain will soon be a mere pulp unless you come to arrest the downward process."[66] Gordon Haight footnotes Spencer's essay on the "Development Hypothesis" of 20 March 1852 as the source of Eliot's "homogeneity"; but in fact "homogeneity" and "heterogeneity" do not make their first entrance in print until Spencer's essay on "The Philosophy of Style," in October 1852—and are not explicitly related to Spencer's evolutionary beliefs until "Progress," in 1857.[67] Spencer discovered von Baer's law while reading Carpenter in the autumn of 1851, and George Eliot offers a small but unmistakable clue that she was present at the creation. Eliot, like Herbert Spencer, was nurtured in the progressive cosmology of the phrenological world view; like Lewes, she met Spencer with an intellectual disposition ready to resonate with his. This was the woman who had opened her first essay for the *Westminster Review* in January 1851 "with a profound belief in the progressive character of human development."[68]

After 1859 Eliot, Lewes, and Spencer all accepted Darwin's evolutinary thesis—although each did so with qualifications. In the late 1860s, a congenial scientific correspondence between Charles Darwin and George Henry Lewes ensued, recently published in volume 8 of *The George Eliot Letters.* Lewes produced a series of lengthy essays on **"Mr. Darwin's Hypothesis"** in the *Fortnightly* in 1868 with the evolutionist's blessing:

"The articles strike me as *quite* excellent, and I hope they will be republished; but I fear they will be too deep for many readers," Darwin writes Lewes.[69]

Although much that he says about Darwin in 1868 is beyond the scope of this study, it is appropriate to note here that Lewes did not see Darwin's ideas as radically different from evolutionary predecessors like St. Hilaire, Lamarck, and Robinet. Lewes did argue that Darwin's unique contribution, natural selection, though only another hypothesis, is "the best hypothesis at present." He credits Darwin with a more explicit formulation of the "law of adaptation" than his predecessors, but he also finds reflected in Mr. Darwin's hypothesis much that should seem familiar to the reader of Herbert Spencer in the 1850s: "The evolution of Life is the evolution of the special from the general, the complex from the simple. An organism rises in power as it ramifies into variety. From a homogeneous organic mass a complex structure is evolved," writes Lewes—summarizing Darwin in very Spencerian language. Within Darwin's theory of natural selection, Lewes found a persuasive reformulation of his own dual emphasis on the dynamic interrelationship of "conditions" and "form," medium and organism: "Minds unconvinced [by previous theories] . . . were at once subdued by the principles of Natural Selection, involving as it did, on the one hand, the incontestible 'Struggle for Existence,' and on the other, the known laws of Adaptation and Hereditary Transmission."[70] But in the final analysis, the affinities between Herbert Spencer and Robert Chambers's *Vestiges* are much closer than any with Charles Darwin's *Origin.* Spencer is a cosmologist rather than a practicing scientist. He is interested in evolution as a universal process that could be applied not just to individual organisms, but to the solar system, social structures, and everything in between.

Spencer's second book, *The Principles of Psychology* (1855), takes the general evolutionary notions that first appeared in the social theory of *Social Statics,* and combines them with the scientific concepts of the early 1850s shared by Lewes and Spencer. The product: a model of the human mind that grows out of the distinctive intellectual matrix of this Victorian circle. For Herbert Spencer in the 1850s, the most productive application of the universal law of "progress" was to be found in the field of human psychology. This was to be Spencer's most original contribution to the history of ideas. It was Herbert Spencer, not Charles Darwin, who first conceptualized an adaptive, evolutionary psychology.[71]

IV. LIFE AND MIND—HERBERT SPENCER: THE
PRINCIPLES OF PSYCHOLOGY (1855)

Both George Eliot and George Henry Lewes were closely involved with the creation of *The Principles of Psychology.* Spencer's "general interest in mental phenomena" had been increased by reading Lewes's ***Biographical History of Philosophy*** in the autumn of 1851. He dated the inception of the *Principles* [*The Principles of Psychology*] from a letter to his father in March 1852 when he began his reading (starting with Mill's *Logic*, lent him by Eliot) for his "Introduction to Psychology."[72] The reader will remember that March 1852 dates the beginning of the most intense period of Eliot's and Spencer's relationship. Although the romance soon cooled, their continuing intellectual intimacy is evident in George Eliot's ecstatic letter to Sara Sophia Hennell in July 1854: "Herbert Spencer . . . will stand in the Biographical Dictionaries of 1954 as 'Spencer, Herbert, an original and profound philosophical writer, especially known by his great work XXX which gave a new impulse to psychology and has mainly contributed to the present advanced position of that science, compared with that which it had attained in the middle of the last century.'"[73]

After *The Principles of Psychology* was published in 1855, Eliot lent copies to her friends, and reported George Henry Lewes "*nailed* to the book by his interest in it."[74] Lewes, who had learned the art of adaptive survival of the fittest in the literary marketplace, wrote two quite different reviews of the book, one for the more conservative *Saturday Review*—"As the Saturday Review is not to be heterodox, he was necessarily gêné," explains Eliot[75]—the other, a series of three essays for the less orthodox *Leader.* Both are fascinating: the first for what it reveals of the impact of *The Principles of Psychology* on the general Victorian reader; the second for the clarity with which it represents Spencer's theories as the culmination of Lewes's search for the Victorian Spinoza.

The Principles of Psychology is grounded on the application of the physiological method to the study of the human mind: "He makes Psychology one of the great divisions of Biology," Lewes writes in the *Leader.*[76] The same readers who had been shocked by Combe, Chambers, and Martineau would respond in like manner to the *Principles,* as Lewes well knew when he wrote his "gêné" essay for the *Saturday Review*: "This is an exposition of psychical phenomena which will find little favor except with those who advocate materialism." Spencer's "denial of free-will" and "identification of mind with life" will be particularly controversial, observes Lewes; the *Principles* "cannot hope for much acceptance from the English public."[77] He was correct: "It does not appear to us scientific in character. . . . We are opposed to Mr. Spencer's fundamental principles," wrote the *British Quarterly Review.*[78] In the Unitarian *National Review,* R. H. Hutton entitles his essay "Atheism": "We find philosophers like Mr. Spencer, instead of *examining* the moral realities of human life, actually

dissipating or distorting them, in the hope of *deducing* them from physiological assumptions."[79] Such objections should by now sound familiar.

But when Lewes turns to his first essay in the *Leader,* **"Herbert Spencer's Psychology,"** the tactful mask of the common reader cast aside, the intensity of his intellectual excitement is unrestrained. Lewes designates Herbert Spencer as the third and culminating figure in a crucial process of scientific discovery, which begins with St. Hilaire's zoology and continues with Schwann's cell theory. Just as "Schwann set aside the old methods," writes Lewes, "and proved the Unity of Composition which really underlies all the variety of forms, so Herbert Spencer sets aside" the old philosophical psychology: "We may pause by the way to notice the stages of the history of this doctrine of Unity, which succeed each other according to the law of development, i.e. from general to particular. First comes Geoffrey St. Hilaire, who proclaims the Unity of Composition in the animal *forms*; then Schwann, who proves the Unity in the animal *tissues*; and finally, Herbert Spencer, who proves that Unity in the animal intelligence."[80]

Forms, tissues, intelligence—from the most homogeneous and general to the most particular, complex, and specialized forms of life; all are a part of that great Whole, that single Substance that constitutes the monist's universe. "The Law rules the whole, one process is seen amid the endless variety," writes Lewes. He reminds the reader of his 1851 review of *Social Statics,* and feels compelled to reiterate, even more emphatically, the analogy he drew there: "In reviewing Herbert Spencer's former work, we compared him with Spinoza: a comparison which seemed strange and even hyperbolical to those who knew nothing of the old Hebrew logician; but this *Principles of Psychology* is so like Spinoza in the mental qualities it exhibits, and frequently in the very doctrine it professes, that no one acquainted with the two can fail to perceive their kindred."[81]

In Spencer's *Principles of Psychology,* the positivist millennium has, in theory, arrived. Spencer has rescued British psychology from the airy insubstantialities of "arachnae" metaphysics. In editions of his ***Biographical History*** after 1855, Lewes added footnotes to that effect.[82] And thirty years after that first history of philosophy, he returns to the same subject in ***Problems of Life and Mind.*** Locke, Hobbes, Berkeley, and Hume "have produced essays, not systems. There has been no noteworthy attempt to give a conception of the World, of Man, and of Society, wrought out with systematic harmonizing of principles. . . . Mr. Herbert Spencer is now for the first time deliberately making the attempt to found a Philosophy."[83] This is a philosophy on the positive plan. At the heart of the *Principles* lies Spencer's most original contribution: he takes the biological principles he shared with Lewes during the early 1850s—the unity of composition, the organism and the medium, progressive adaptation from homogeneity to heterogeneity—and applies them to mental development: within the individual, but, with more far-reaching implications, to the human race as a whole.

George Henry Lewes entitled his third review essay of Spencer's *Principles,* **"Life and Mind,"** twenty years before his own *magnum opus* by that title. In order to appreciate Spencer's theories of mind, we must first state his definition of life. This subject has been discussed at some length in my prelude, in the context of Spencer's borrowings from Samuel Taylor Coleridge. Taken in conjunction with von Baer's development from homogeneity to heterogeneity, Spencer's "individuation" becomes an evolutionary process. This process is effected by the dynamic and adaptive interaction of organism and medium. Thus Spencer arrives at his "broadest and most complete definition of life": *"The continuous adjustment of internal relations to external relations."*[84]

This definition may strike the twentieth-century reader as less than earth-shaking. But we must place Spencer's definition against the psychology of Locke, Hume, Berkeley, and prior to Darwin's biology, to perceive its genuinely radical impact. In his own *Principles of Psychology,* William James paid homage to Spencer:

> At a certain stage in the development of every science a degree of vagueness is what best consists with fertility. On the whole, few recent formulas have done more real service of a rough sort in psychology than the Spencerian one that the essence of mental life and bodily life are one, namely, "the adjustment of inner to outer relations." Such a formula is vagueness incarnate; but because it takes into account the fact that minds inhabit environments which act on them and on which they in turn react; because, in short, it takes mind in the midst of all its concrete relations, it is immensely more fertile than the old-fashioned "rational psychology," which treated the soul as a detached existent, sufficient unto itself and assumed to consider only its nature and properties.[85]

According to Herbert Spencer, this adjustment of inner to outer, organism to medium, leads to "progressive adaptation."[86] When this adaptation is translated into psychological terms, Spencer arrives at his theory of mental inheritance, the cornerstone of *The Principles of Psychology.*

The Principles of Psychology is divided into four parts: the general analysis, special analysis, general synthesis, and special synthesis. In his preface Spencer explains that "the four parts of which this work consists, though intimately related to each other as different views of the same great aggregate of phenomena, are yet, in the main, severally independent and complete in them-

selves." The analysis deals with the study of human intelligence subjectively; the synthesis, objectively.[87] To translate this Spencerese: in his analysis, Spencer views the human mind philosophically, from the subjective, internal perspective, the single center of consciousness; in the synthesis, he views the same phenomena biologically, or objectively: each mind as a single part of a greater synthetic whole, the larger pattern of evolutionary development. The essence of *The Principles of Psychology* is to be found in the ingenious method by which Spencer mediates between analysis and synthesis, the claims of philosophy and biology, introspection and observation, intuition and experience; and asserts the harmonious coexistence and dynamic interpenetration of both.

Although Spencer claimed to ground his psychology on biology rather than metaphysical speculation, he did not believe that dissecting the brain like a turnip was any more efficacious, taken alone, than introspective cogitation. In claiming the unity of composition, that life and mind are one substance, Spencer did not intend simple materialism; like Spinoza, it is inaccurate to classify him as either materialist or idealist. In fact, what Spencer sought was a science of mind that would transcend biology; to unify the polarities of introspective idealists and their innate ideas (such as the "moral sense") with the empirical men of science, who grounded their utilitarian beliefs on sense experience. The hereditary transmission of innate mental characteristics was Herbert Spencer's key to all mythologies, his intended reconciliation of the Shaftesbury and the Benthamite schools; his chief claim to a science of mind that would combine the truths of the metaphysicians with the discoveries of the biologists.

In my discussion of Charles Bray and Harriet Martineau, I suggested that the bridge between Carlyle and Bentham for Bray, mystical experience and materialism for Martineau, was to be found in a blend of nineteenth-century romanticism with eighteenth-century rationalism, phrenology, and association psychology. In its original, "static," inception, Gall's phrenology argued for the unity of composition, mind as matter, innate mental characteristics determined in each individual at birth. But beginning with George Combe and Robert Chambers, these optimistic Victorian necessitarians added a "dynamic" belief in progress, adaptive change in accordance with circumstance. The law of universal causation remained invariable, as Mill and Comte had asserted; but the individual could also form new associative mental patterns, altering his innate constitution. And most significantly this new constitution could be passed on to the next generation.

George Henry Lewes's final words on the much-maligned science of phrenology were ones of praise: "Gall taught men the futility of looking inwards, and neglecting the vast mass of external observation which animals and societies afforded; he taught them *where* to seek the primary organic conditions—in inherited structures and inherited aptitudes. The effect of this teaching is conspicuous in modern works."[88] One of these modern works was *The Principles of Psychology.* The reader will recall that Spencer's introduction to psychology was phrenology during the decade of Charles Bray's *Philosophy of Necessity* and Robert Chambers's *Vestiges of Creation,* George Combe's proselytizing and Harriet Martineau's conversion. Robert M. Young argues persuasively that phrenology was also a seminal influence behind Spencer's psychological theories.[89] My discussion above of Combe and Chambers, Bray and Martineau, has suggested some of the ways in which Spencer's wedding of psychology to evolutionary biology was anticipated by other members of this Victorian circle, all of whom can be linked with phrenology.[90]

Hints of the evolutionary possibilities of phrenology can be found in the *Vestiges of Creation.* Chambers believes mental characteristics are innate: "The mental characters of individuals are inherently various . . . education and circumstance . . . are incapable of entirely altering these characters." And yet, he continues provocatively, "there is, nevertheless, a general adaptation of the mental constitution of man to the circumstances in which he lives." Might not environment alter heredity? And might not the development of the individual be parallel to that of the race?[91] Not surprisingly, young Charles Darwin took a strong interest in the evolutionary possibilities of phrenology: "One is tempted to believe phrenologists are right about habitual exercise of the mind, altering the head, & thus these qualities become hereditary," he writes in his notebooks in 1838. "To avoid stating how far I believe, in Materialism, say only that emotions, instincts, degrees of talent, which are hereditary are so because brain of child resembles parent stock.—(& phrenologists state that brain alters)."[92]

The phrenological cosmologies of Robert Chambers and George Combe, Charles Bray and Harriet Martineau, are intended to be equally biological and metaphysical; but prior to Herbert Spencer, the metaphysics clearly outweighed the biology. In 1855 Spencer not only had the phrenological background upon which to draw, but also the broader range of scientific sources he had explored with Lewes, from "transcendental anatomy" to the adaptation of the organism to the medium.

As early as 1841, in the *Philosophy of Necessity,* Charles Bray had anticipated Herbert Spencer's *Principles of Psychology*: "All moral rules are derived originally from Utility, but the pleasures and pains . . . on which they are based are transmitted to offspring and thus become intuitions."[93] But it is left to the reader of the *Philosophy of Necessity* to move inferentially from this statement to a reconciliation of Bray's transcendental with his empirical tendencies; Bray himself makes no overt connection. By contrast, in *The Principles of Psychology,* Spencer's synthesis is systematic and explicit, as he claims to "furnish a solution to the controversy between the disciples of Locke and those of Kant," combining "the experience-hypothesis and the hypothesis of the transcendentalists: neither of which is tenable by itself."[94]

"Before our generation," wrote William James in 1890, when empirical psychologists contended that sense experience was the basis of mental development, "it was the experience of the individual only that was meant." In his "brilliant and seductive" *Principles of Psychology,* Herbert Spencer wrought a seminal change: "When one nowadays says that the human mind owes its present shape to experience, he means the experience of ancestors as well. Mr. Spencer's statement of this is the earliest emphatic one."[95] In **Problems of Life and Mind,** George Henry Lewes rewrites Locke's famous metaphor in Spencerian terms: "The sensitive subject is no *tabula rasa*; it is not a blank sheet of paper, but a palimpsest."[96]

The heart of Spencer's argument for this new definition of an "experiential" school of psychology is to be found in chapter 3 of part 4 of *The Principles of Psychology,* the "Special Synthesis," "The Growth of Intelligence." There Spencer argues that all knowledge does come from experience, but expands the definition of experience to include "the experience of the *race* organisms forming its ancestry." Like the phrenologists Spencer believes in innate mental faculties; but he incorporates phrenology with association psychology, to arrive at the notion of mental development: "The familiar doctrine of association here undergoes a great extension. . . . The effects of associations are . . . transmitted as modifications of the nervous system."[97] Hereditary transmission is the key to this process by which each new mind is born, as a palimpsest, already imprinted with a rich mental heritage of so-called "innate" ideas: "Instinct may be regarded as a kind of organized memory."[98]

Spencer saves his biggest gun for the end: "As most who have read thus far have perceived," this notion of mental heredity implies "a tacit adhesion to the development hypothesis."[99] The racial mind of man develops over time, as its ancestral heritage grows ever more complex. What began as animal instincts evolve into higher mental processes: "That progressive complication of the instincts, which . . . involves a progressive diminution of their purely automatic character, likewise involves a simultaneous commencement of Memory and Reason."[100] Spencer's definition of life as "the continuous adjustment of internal relations to external relations" is thus central to the *Principles.* In her notebooks in the early 1870s, George Eliot demonstrated her familiarity with the vocabulary of the *Principles of Psychology*: "We have, as well as we can, to arrive at the classification which is called the distinction between the Static & Dynamic—between what is an inherent quality or characteristic or need of the human being . . . & what is modifiable or doomed to disappear under successive changes."[101]

The year after Spencer's *Principles of Psychology* was published, Lewes wrote his essay on **"Hereditary Influence, Animal and Human,"** which abounds with echoes of Spencer. Just as they had shared the unity of composition, the organism and the medium, and the development from homogeneity to heterogeneity between 1851-54, this intellectual friendship continued to be the source of rich reciprocation for both men. "We inherit the acquired experience of our forefathers—their tendencies, their aptitudes, their habits, their improvements," writes Lewes, commending to his readers the "original and remarkable *Principles of Psychology*": "In this work Heritage, for the first time, is made the basis of a psychological system; and we especially recommend any reader interested in the present article, to make himself acquainted with a treatise in every way so remarkable."[102] Twenty years later, in the five-volume ***Problems of Life and Mind,*** the influence of Spencer's evolutionary psychology continues to be strong and unmistakable: "Thought is an embodied process, which has its conditions in the history of the race no less than in that of the individual," writes Lewes. "We learn by individual experiences, registrations of feeling, rendered possible by ancestral experience."[103]

The Principles of Psychology completes the scientific argument of this study, closing a circle of thinkers that found its methodology in the universal causation of John Stuart Mill and the positivism of Auguste Comte, and its first practical application in the phrenologists' claim that the brain is the organ of the mind. Herbert Spencer's original contribution to the history of psychology grows directly out of the matrix of ideas shared by this Victorian circle: the *Principles* fuses holistic metaphysics with evolutionary biology in an exemplary incarnation of a distinctively Victorian frame of mind. But the final note of my history is to be sounded in a theological key: because for all these thinkers, science was ultimately the servant of a higher faith. Thus I conclude with what Spencer called the "ontological bearings" of the case.[104]

Notes

1. Hock Guan Tjoa, *George Henry Lewes: A Victorian Mind* (Cambridge, Mass., 1977), p. 135.

2. Lewes here playfully echoes the fictional Casaubon's "Key to All Mythologies" in *Middlemarch,* which Eliot was writing simultaneously with *Problems.* See [Gordon Haight, ed.], *George Eliot Letters,* 5:291, 350, 364, 370.

3. George Henry Lewes, *Problems of Life and Mind. Third Series. Problem the First. The Study of Psychology: Its Object, Scope and Method* (Boston, 1879), p. 54. In the preface to the first volume, Lewes says that "its origin may be said to go so far back as 1836" (*Problems* [*Problems of Life and Mind*]. *First Series. The Foundations of A Creed* [Boston, 1874-75], 1:v).

4. Johann Wolfgang von Goethe, quoted in "Goethe as a Man of Science," p. 261. Another German, Ludwig Feuerbach, uses the same metaphor in *The Essence of Christianity* (which Eliot was translating while Lewes researched his biography of Goethe). In Eliot's translation: "As the action of the arteries drives the blood into the extremeties, and the action of the veins brings it back again, as life in general consists in perpetual systole and diastole; so it is with religion. In the religious systole, man propels his own nature from himself, he throws himself outward; in the religious diastole, he receives the rejected nature into his heart again" (Feuerbach, *Essence,* trans. George Eliot [1854; rpt. New York, 1957], p. 468). Eliot herself uses the metaphor in *Middlemarch* (see "Finale," p. 249).

5. George Henry Lewes, "Spiritualism and Materialism," *Fortnightly Review* 25 (1876):713.

6. Rosemary Ashton, *The German Idea* (Cambridge, England, 1980), p. 121. In this study of Coleridge, Carlyle, Lewes, and Eliot, Ashton assumes Lewes's "permanent change of opinion away from the *a priori* philosophical approach" (p. 114).

7. Young, *Mind, Brain, and Adaptation,* p. 163.

8. Jack Kaminsky, "The Empirical Metaphysics of George Henry Lewes," *Journal of the History of Ideas* 13 (1952):314, 322. Similarly Tjoa accurately states that Lewes "earnestly tried to meet the two divergent intellectual demands of his age: the one a seasoned empiricism imposing procrustean measures upon all intellectual activity, and the other a swelling need for a kind of 'religious rationalism,' a meaningful vision of man and things (*Lewes* [*George Henry Lewes*], pp. 117-18). But he is skeptical of Lewes's optimism; his "positivistic enthusiasm" is "too extravagant" (p. 136). Tjoa incorrectly interprets this extravagant optimism as "the strained effort to put up a brave front" (p. 137).

9. George Henry Lewes, review of *Letters on the Laws, Leader,* 22 February 1851, p. 178; 8 March 1851, p. 227; 1 March 1851, pp. 201, 203, 202. Gordon Haight claims that Lewes's "devastating

reviews" of the book were the cause of hostility between Lewes and Martineau (see Haight, *George Eliot Letters,* 2:123n), fuel to the fire of her moral indignation in 1854.

10. Lewes, review of *Letters on the Laws, Leader,* 1 March 1851, p. 202. Compare this "transcendental faculty" with the "intuitive faculty" in the *Letters* [*Letters on the Laws of Man's Nature and Development,* Martineau and Atkinson] (p. 76).

11. Lewes, "Spiritualism and Materialism," p. 483. Lewes does not date this experience. George Levine writes perceptively of Lewes: he "is in the paradoxical position of any empiricist who seeks systemic wholeness. Committed to common sense, he finds himself in a reality that runs counter to what common sense reveals. . . . His language must move from appearances to realities in a rhythm that is so directly reminiscent of religious language that it is difficult to avoid the connection" ("George Eliot's Hypothesis of Reality," *Nineteenth Century Fiction* 35 [1980]:9).

12. George Henry Lewes, "The Heart and the Brain," *Fortnightly Review* 1 (1865):66. My attention was drawn to this essay by Bray's approving quotation of it (*On Force,* p. 20).

13. Lewes, "Heart and the Brain," p. 74.

14. George Henry Lewes, "Subject, Subjective," *Penny Cyclopaedia* (London, 1842), 23:185.

15. George Henry Lewes, "Substance," *Penny Cyclopaedia,* 22:198.

16. George Henry Lewes, "Spinoza, Spinozism," *Penny Cyclopaedia,* 22:351-52.

17. George Henry Lewes, marginalia on Hallam's *Introduction to the Literature of Europe,* quoted in *The George Eliot-George Henry Lewes Library,* ed. William Baker (New York, 1977), p. 85.

18. George Henry Lewes, "Spinoza," *Fortnightly Review* 4 (1866):386-87.

19. See Francis Espinasse, *Literary Recollections* (New York, 1938), p. 276n.

20. George Henry Lewes, "Spinoza's Life and Works," *Westminster Review* 39 (1843):397-98.

21. Lewes, *Biographical History* [The Biographical History of Philosophy], p. 493.

22. Lewes, "Spinoza's Life and Works," pp. 385, 404, 406.

23. Brabant's friendship with Coleridge was documented by his son-in-law, W. M. W. Call, in "Unpublished Letters, Written by Samuel Taylor Coleridge in 1815-16," *Westminster Review* 93, n.s. 37 (1870):341-64; 94, n.s. 38 (1870):1-24.

24. Haight, *George Eliot Letters,* 1:158n. Haight suggests that the work in question was the *Tractatus,* given Brabant's and Eliot's interest in the "higher criticism." He cites Mathilde Blind, *George Eliot* (London, 1883) as the source of the information that Eliot was translating "De Deo," chiding Blind for her ignorance that this is the opening chapter of the *Ethics*; and then implies that Blind's mistake undermines her credibility. But the source of Blind's information was probably W. M. W. Call's "George Eliot, Her Life and Writings," *Westminster Review* 116 (1881):154-98. Call writes: "Miss Evans had translated about ten years previously, the first part ('De Deo') of Spinoza's great treatise, for the edification of a philosophical friend" (161). As Brabant's son-in-law and a personal friend of Eliot, Call was in a good position to have accurate information. Given the "friend" Charles Bray's necessitarian interests, the *Ethics* was a likely subject. Regardless, it seems that Eliot would have known both *Ethics* and *Tractatus* in the early 1840s.

25. George Eliot to Sara Sophia Hennell, *George Eliot Letters,* 1:231.

26. Mrs. Charles Bray to George Eliot, *George Eliot Letters,* 1:280n.

27. George Eliot to Mr. and Mrs. Charles Bray, *George Eliot Letters,* 1:321. See Hilda Hulme, "Language of the Novel: Imagery," in *Middlemarch: Critical Approaches,* ed. Barbara Hardy (London, 1967), pp. 118-24 on Eliot and the *Ethics*; see also Dorothy Atkins, *George Eliot and Spinoza* (Salzburg, 1980).

28. The scandal raging over her liaison with Lewes may have been the source of Eliot's request to Bray in March 1856: "By the way, when Spinoza comes out, be so good as not to mention *my* name in connection with it. I particularly wish not to be known as the translator of the Ethics, for reasons 'too tedious to mention'" (Eliot to Bray, *George Eliot Letters,* 2:233; see also 2:197).

29. Haight, *George Eliot Letters,* 2:189n; see 8:156-60 for Lewes's correspondence with Bohn.

30. David Friedrich Strauss, quoted in Robert Willis, *Benedict de Spinoza: His Life, Correspondence, and Ethics* (London, 1870), 3:4n.

31. Spencer, *Autobiography,* 1:399.

32. Spencer, *Autobiography,* 1:436.

33. Herbert Spencer, "The Laws of Organic Form," *British and Foreign Medico-Chirurgical Review* 23 (1859):191, 198, 201.

34. George Henry Lewes, "Lyell and Owen on Development," *Leader,* 18 October 1851, p. 997.

35. Herbert Spencer, "The Development Hypothesis," *Leader,* 20 March 1852; rpt. in *Essays Scientific, Political, and Speculative* (New York, 1904), 1:5.

36. As J. D. Y. Peel writes: "Spencer's approach was unlike that of his biological contemporaries . . . in that he did not start off from a phenomenon to be explained, but from ethical and metaphysical positions to be established. Consequently, he was an evolutionist long before Lyell, Huxley, and Darwin" (*Herbert Spencer,* p. 132).

37. George Henry Lewes, "Mr. Darwin's Hypothesis," *Fortnightly Review* 4 (1868):497.

38. Johann Wolfgang von Goethe, quoted in George Henry Lewes, *The Life of Goethe,* 2d ed. (London, 1864), p. 170.

39. Lewes, *Life of Goethe,* p. 35. Similarly, in his novel *Ranthorpe,* Lewes's fictional hero Thornton muses: "Goethe, my young friend, was the last man in the world to deserve the epithet cold. What makes boobies call him so, is the magnificent supremacy which his reason always exercised over his passions" (*Ranthorpe* [1847; rpt. Athens, Ohio, 1974], p. 171).

40. Lewes, *Life of Goethe,* p. 520.

41. Spencer, *Autobiography,* 1:485. Though Lewes's claim is, characteristically, a more modest one: "The antithesis to Poetry, as Wordsworth felicitously said, is not Prose, but Science. Therefore have Poets and Men of Science, in all times, formed two distinct classes, and never, save in one illustrious example, exhibited the twofold manifestation of Poetry and Science working in harmonious unity: that single exception is Goethe" ("Goethe as a Man of Science," p. 258).

42. Lewes, *Life of Goethe,* p. 342.

43. Lewes, "Goethe as a Man of Science," p. 260.

44. Lewes, "Goethe as a Man of Science," p. 267.

45. George Henry Lewes, "Life and Doctrine of Geoffroy St. Hilaire," *Westminster Review* 61 (1854):178, 180.

46. Herbert Spencer, "Transcendental Physiology," *National Review,* October 1857, rpt. in *Essays,* 1:63. Similarly, in *The Principles of Psychology*: "There exists a *unity of composition* throughout all the phenomena of intelligence" (p. 329).

47. Lewes, "Goethe as a Man of Science," p. 261. Another interesting link between Goethe and this Victorian circle: Lewes writes that when phrenologist Gall visited Jena in 1805, Goethe attended his lectures: "Instead of meeting this theory with ridicule, contempt, and the opposition of ancient prejudices . . . Goethe saw at once the importance of Gall's mode of dissection . . . and of his leading views. . . . Gall's doctrine pleased him because it determined the true position of Psychology in the study of man . . . showing the identity of all mental manifestation in the animal kingdom" (*Life of Goethe,* p. 486).

48. Lewes, "Goethe as a Man of Science," p. 272.

49. Goethe, quoted in Lewes, "Goethe as a Man of Science," p. 268. In reworking this essay into "The Poet as a Man of Science" for the *Life,* Lewes gives a slightly different version of this passage, and also its source: *Zur Morphologie* (*Life of Goethe,* p. 355).

50. Lewes, "St. Hilaire" ["Life and Doctrine of Geoffroy St. Hilaire"], p. 189.

51. Eliot, "The Natural History of German Life," in Pinney [ed., *Essays of George Eliot,*], p. 287.

52. George Henry Lewes, "Mr. Darwin's Hypothesis," *Fortnightly Review* 3 (1868):356.

53. French historian Georges Banguilhem writes: "There was no biologist or physician in France between 1840 and 1860 who . . . did not have to deal either directly with the themes of Comte's biological philosophy [the dualism of life and matter, the correlation of organism and environment] or indirectly with that philosophy through the themes developed from it" ("La philosophie biologique d'Auguste Comte et son influence en France au xix siècle," quoted in Simon, *European Positivism,* p. 114).

54. Comte, *Cours* [*Cours de philosophie positive*], in Lenzer [ed., *Auguste Comte and Positivism*], p. 164.

55. Lewes, *Comte's Philosophy* [*Comte's Philosophy of the Sciences*], p. 167.

56. Spencer, *Principles of Psychology,* p. 374.

57. Lewes, *Problems of Life and Mind, The Foundations of a Creed,* 1:112; 2:21.

58. Spencer, *Autobiography,* 2:9, 14.

59. W. B. Carpenter, *Principles of Comparative Physiology,* new American edition, from 4th revised English edition (Philadelphia, 1854), p. 48. See Young, *Mind, Brain, and Adaptation,* p. 168n for a long and informative note on von Baer. In fact both Darwin and Spencer twisted von Baer to their own purposes: the German himself was opposed to the development hypothesis (Lewes does note this in his essay on von Baer).

60. T. H. Huxley, review of W. B. Carpenter's *Principles of* [*Comparative*] *Physiology,* "Science," *Westminster Review* 63 (1855):242.

61. Herbert Spencer, "Progress: Its Law and Cause," *Westminster Review* 67 (1857), rpt. in *Essays,* 1:10.

62. See Millhauser, *Just Before Darwin,* pp. 86-87, for a comparison of Chambers and Spencer.

63. George Henry Lewes, "Von Baer on the Development Hypothesis," *Leader,* 25 June 1853, p. 617.

64. Lewes, *Life of Goethe,* p. 354.

65. George Eliot to Sara Sophia Hennell, *George Eliot Letters,* 2:220.

66. George Eliot to Herbert Spencer, *George Eliot Letters,* 8:51.

67. See Spencer, *Autobiography,* 2:10 for Spencer's explanation of his earliest published use of the word "homogeneity."

68. Eliot, "The Progress of the Intellect," in Pinney, p. 29. In his essay on "Idea and Image in the Novels of George Eliot," W. J. Harvey writes: "All external evidence . . . points to Spencer rather than Darwin as the prime intellectual influence concerning [Eliot's] ideas on Evolution" (though he goes on, somewhat inaccurately, to add: "Spencer's claims to scientific seriousness are now completely exploded"). He also notes Eliot's close friendship with Robert Chambers and her familiarity with the *Vestiges* (in *Critical Essays on George Eliot,* ed. Barbara Hardy [London, 1970], p. 157). Since "The Progress of the Intellect" was written before she knew Spencer's work, Chambers must be considered a key source of Eliot's belief in development.

69. Charles Darwin to George Henry Lewes, *George Eliot Letters,* 8:425.

70. Lewes, "Mr. Darwin's Hypothesis," *Fortnightly Review* 3:355; 4:66; 3:356. Lewes's essays on Darwin appear in vols. 3 (1868):353-73, 611-29 and 4:61-80, 492-501. In "George Eliot's Hypothesis of Reality," George Levine states that "for Lewes and George Eliot, following Darwin, the highest organism is both the most complexly differentiated from its rudimentary origins and the most integrated in other organisms" (8). Levine is correct, but Spencer, not Darwin, is the source of this idea.

71. Peel sums up the distinction between Spencer and Darwin: "Darwin's theory accounted for the secular transformation of each species by the mechanism of natural selection, while Spencer's attempted to explain the total configuration of nature, physical, organic, and social, as well as its necessary process" (*Herbert Spencer,* p. 142). Young argues that Spencer was "more seminal than directly contributory," since he was not a practicing scientist; he notes Darwin's influential later work in evolutionary psychology. He draws a parallel between Gall and Spencer: "Both advocated studies which they did not successfully conduct themselves" (p. 190). Although Darwin had worked in the application of evolutionary theory of psychology in his early notebooks, he did not publish on the subject until 1871, in *The Descent of Man.*

72. Spencer, *Autobiography,* 1:453.

73. George Eliot to Sara Sophia Hennell, *George Eliot Letters,* 2:165.

74. George Eliot to Mrs. Wathen Mark Wilks Call, *George Eliot Letters,* 2:476; George Eliot to Sara Sophia Hennell, *George Eliot Letters,* 2:213. We catch a glimpse of Lewes's characteristic sense of humor in his letter to Spencer on the *Principles* [*Principles of Psychology*]: "I hope the book sells. If it can get a decent *nucleus* of a public it is sure to make its way; all that surrounds the nucleus being as you know a *sell*" (George Henry Lewes to Herbert Spencer, *George Eliot Letters,* 8:151).

75. George Eliot to Sara Sophia Hennell, *George Eliot Letters,* 2:228.

76. George Henry Lewes, "Life and Mind," *Leader,* 3 November 1855, p. 1,062. This is the third part of Lewes's review of Spencer's *Principles of Psychology,* preceded by "Herbert Spencer's Psychology" (*Leader,* 20 October 1855, pp. 1,012-13) and "History of Psychological Method" (*Leader,* 27 October 1855, pp. 1,036-37).

77. George Henry Lewes, "Herbert Spencer's *Principles of Psychology," Saturday Review,* 1 March 1856, pp. 353, 352.

78. Review of Herbert Spencer's *Principles of Psychology, British Quarterly Review* 22 (1855):598.

79. R. H. Hutton, "Atheism," *National Review* 2 (1856):122. See also the "Theology and Philosophy" section of the *Westminster Review* 65 (January, 1856):234-40 for a similar discussion.

80. Lewes, "Herbert Spencer's Psychology," p. 1,013.

81. Lewes, "Herbert Spencer's Psychology," p. 1,013.

82. See Lewes, *Biographical History,* pp. 602, 646, 744.

83. Lewes, *Problems of Life and Mind, Foundations of a Creed,* 1:77.

84. Spencer, *Principles of Psychology,* p. 374. The review of the *Principles* in the *British Quarterly Review* drew an explicit parallel between Spencer and Comte on this subject: the relation of life and

"outward environments" in the *Principles* is "precisely that put forth by the author of the Positive Philosophy" (p. 597).

85. William James, *The Principles of Psychology* (1890; rpt. New York, 1950), 1:6. The second edition of Spencer's *Principles* was James's textbook for his first class of undergraduates in psychology (see James Kennedy, *Herbert Spencer* [Boston, 1978], p. 47). Lewes praises Spencer's definition of life in the 1870s in *Problems of Life and Mind. Second Series. The Physical Basis of Mind* (London, 1877), p. 33. Bray quotes Spencer's definition several times in his autobiography, without citing Spencer as its author (was it so well-known that he need not do so?) (see *Phases of Opinion*, pp. 203, 207-9).

86. Spencer, *Autobiography,* 2:12.

87. Spencer, *Principles of Psychology,* "Preface," pp. iii-iv.

88. Lewes, *Problems of Life and Mind. Third Series. Problem the First. The Study of Psychology* (Boston, 1879), p. 77.

89. "Adaptation was a major issue in *Social Statics,* and Spencer's conception of it was derived directly from phrenology"; before Spencer, "no psychologists except Gall and his followers had so emphatically made the connection of mind with life, and the adaptation of the mental functions to the environment, central to their views" (Young, *Mind, Brain, and Adaptation,* p. 169).

90. In "a few remarks on the tenets of the phrenologists," Spencer attacks them as "wrong in assuming there is something specific and unalterable in the natures of the various faculties" (*Principles,* p. 610). Although this static view of the mind was true of Gall, modifiability of faculties became a central tenet from Combe onwards, as evidence in my discussion of Chambers, Bray, and Martineau.

91. Chambers, *Vestiges of Creation* [*Vestiges of the Natural History of Creation*], pp. 180, 181, 183.

92. Darwin, "M and N Notebooks," in [Howard E. Gruber,] *Darwin on Man,* pp. 271, 276.

93. Bray, *Philosophy of Necessity,* 2d ed., p. 87.

94. Spencer, *Principles of Psychology,* pp. 578, 581. Benn summarizes the obvious philosophical limitations of Spencer's grandiose claim: "Spencer believed that by his theory of inherited ancestral experience he had reconciled the opposing views of Kant and Mill. In reality he had done nothing of the kind. He had considerably extended the ground occupied by the empirical school, and furnished them with a plausible reply to one of the objections previously urged against their explanation of necessary truths; but he had done no more. The main contention of Kant and his followers, which is that no amount of experience can give universality and necessity to a proposition, still remained unanswered" (*History of [English] Rationalism,* 2:173).

95. James, *Principles of Psychology,* 2:625.

96. Lewes, *Problems of Life and Mind, Foundations of a Creed,* 1:149.

97. Spencer, *Principles of Psychology,* p. 526; summary of *Principles* in *Autobiography,* 1:548-49.

98. Spencer, *Principles of Psychology,* pp. 555-56.

99. Spencer, *First Principles* [*First Principles of a New System of Philosophy*], quoted in Bray, *Phases of Opinion,* pp. 98-99.

100. Spencer, *Principles of Psychology,* p. 556.

101. Eliot, "More Leaves" ["More Leaves from George Eliots Notebooks"], p. 373.

102. Lewes, "Hereditary Influence," 161n. Similarly, see Eliot in a letter to Bray on historian Henry Buckle: "He holds that there is no such thing as *race* or hereditary transmission of qualities!" (*George Eliot Letters,* 2:415).

103. Lewes, *Problems of Life and Mind, Foundations of a Creed,* 1:202, 220.

104. Spencer, "Progress," p. 60.

Bibliography

Ashton, Rosemary. *The German Idea: Four English Writers and the Reception of German Thought 1800-1860.* Cambridge, 1980.

Baker, William. *The George Eliot-George Henry Lewes Library: An Annotated Catalogue of Their Books at Dr. Williams' Library, London.* New York, 1977.

Benn, Alfred William. *The History of English Rationalism in the Nineteenth Century.* 2 vols. London, 1906.

Bray, Charles. *On Force, Its Mental and Moral Correlates; and on That Which is Supposed to Underlie All Phenomena; with Speculations on Spiritualism, and Other Abnormal Conditions of Mind.* London, 1866.

————. *Phases of Opinion and Experience During a Long Life: An Autobiography.* London, n.d.

————. *The Philosophy of Necessity; or, The Law of Consequences; As Applicable to Mental, Moral, and Social Science.* 2 vols. London, 1841.

Carpenter, W. B. *Principles of Comparative Physiology.* New American Edition, from 4th rev. English Edition. Philadelphia, 1854.

Chambers, Robert. *Vestiges of the Natural History of Creation. With a Sequel.* New York, 1859.

Comte, Auguste. *Cours de philosophie positive.* Translated by Harriet Martineau. In *Auguste Comte and Positivism, The Essential Writings.* Edited by Gertrud Lenzer. New York, 1975.

Eliot, George. *Essays of George Eliot.* Edited by Thomas Pinney. New York, 1963.

———. *Middlemarch: A Study of Provincial Life.* Edited by Gordon S. Haight. Boston, 1956.

———. "More Leaves from George Eliot's Notebook." Edited by Thomas Pinney. *Huntington Library Quarterly* 29 (1966):353-76.

Espinasse, Francis. *Literary Recollections.* New York, 1938.

Feuerbach, Ludwig. *The Essence of Christianity.* Translated by George Eliot. 1854. Reprint, New York, 1957.

Gruber, Howard E. *Darwin on Man: A Psychological Study of Scientific Creativity. Together with Darwin's Early and Unpublished Notebooks.* Transcribed and annotated by Paul H. Barrett. New York, 1974.

Haight, Gordon S. ed. *The George Eliot Letters.* 9 vols. New Haven, 1954-55, 1978.

Hardy, Barbara, ed. *Critical Essays on George Eliot.* London, 1970.

———. *"Middlemarch": Critical Approaches to the Novel.* London, 1967.

Hutton, R. H. "Atheism." *National Review* 2 (1856):97-123.

Huxley, T. H. Review of *Comparative Physiology,* by W. B. Carpenter. In "Science," *Westminster Review* 63 (1855):241-47.

James, William. *The Principles of Psychology.* 2 vols. 1890. Reprint, New York, 1950.

Kaminsky, Jack. "The Empirical Metaphysics of George Henry Lewes." *Journal of the History of Ideas* 13 (1952):314-32.

Levine, George. "George Eliot's Hypothesis of Reality." *Nineteenth Century Fiction* 35 (1980):1-28.

Lewes, George Henry. *The Biographical History of Philosophy.* Library Edition. New York, 1866.

———. *Comte's Philosophy of the Sciences: Being an Exposition of the Principles of the "Cours de philosophie positive" of Auguste Comte.* London, 1853.

———. "Goethe as a Man of Science." *Westminster Review* 58 (1852):258-72.

———. "The Heart and the Brain." *Fortnightly Review* 1 (1865):66-74.

———. "Herbert Spencer's *Principles of Psychology.*" *Saturday Review,* 1 March 1856, pp. 352-53.

———. "Herbert Spencer's Psychology." *Leader,* 20 October 1855, pp. 1,012-13.

———. "Hereditary Influence, Animal and Human." *Westminster Review* 66 (1856):135-62.

———. "History of Psychology Method." *Leader,* 27 October 1855, pp. 1,036-37.

———. Review of *Letters on the Laws of Man's Nature and Development,* by Harriet Martineau and Henry George Atkinson. *Leader,* 22 February 1851, p. 178; 1 March, 1851, pp. 201-3; 8 March 1851, pp. 227-28.

———. "Life and Doctrine of Geoffroy St. Hilaire." *Westminster Review* 61 (1854): 160-90.

———. "Life and Mind." *Leader,* 3 November 1855, pp. 1,062-63.

———. *The Life of Goethe.* 2d ed. London, 1864.

———. "Lyell and Owen on Development." *Leader,* 18 October 1851, pp. 996-97.

———. "Mr. Darwin's Hypothesis." *Fortnightly Review* 34 (1868):353-73, 611-29; 4 (1868):61-80, 492-501.

———. *Problems of Life and Mind. First Series. The Foundations of a Creed.* 2 vols. Boston, 1874-75.

———. *Problems of Life and Mind. Second Series. The Physical Basis of Mind.* London, 1877.

———. *Problems of Life and Mind. Third Series. Problem the First. The Study of Psychology: Its Object, Scope and Method.* Boston, 1879.

———. "Spinoza." *Fortnightly Review* 4 (1866):385-406.

———. "Spinoza, Spinozism." *Penny Cyclopaedia.* Vol. 22. London, 1842.

———. "Spinoza's Life and Works." *Westminster Review* 39 (1843):372-407.

———. "Spiritualism and Materialism." *Fortnightly Review* 25 (1876):479-93, 707-19.

———. "Subject, Subjective." *Penny Cyclopaedia.* Vol. 23. London, 1842.

———. "Substance." *Penny Cyclopaedia.* Vol. 22. London, 1842.

———. "Von Baer on the Development Hypothesis." *Leader,* 25 June 1853, pp. 617-18.

Martineau, Harriet, and Henry George Atkinson. *Letters on the Laws of Man's Nature and Development.* London, 1851.

Millhauser, Milton. *Just Before Darwin: Robert Chambers and the "Vestiges of Creation."* Middletown, Conn., 1959.

Peel, J. D. Y. *Herbert Spencer, The Evolution of a Sociologist.* New York, 1971.

Review of *Principles of Psychology,* by Herbert Spencer. *British Quarterly Review* 22 (1855):596-98.

Simon, W. M. *European Positivism in the Nineteenth Century: An Essay in Intellectual History.* New York, 1963.

Spencer, Herbert. *An Autobiography.* 2 vols. New York, 1904.

———. *Essays, Scientific, Political, and Speculative.* Vol. 1. New York, 1904.

———. *First Principles of a New System of Philosophy.* 3d ed. New York, 1879.

———. *"The Laws of Organic Form." British and Foreign Medico-Chirurgical Review* 23 (1859):189-202.

———. *The Principles of Psychology.* London, 1855.

Tjoa, Hock Guan. *George Henry Lewes: A Victorian Mind.* Cambridge, Mass., 1977.

Young, Robert M. *Mind, Brain, and Adaptation in the Nineteenth Century: Cerebral Localization and Its Biological Context From Gall to Ferrier.* Oxford, 1970.

J. Gill Holland (essay date January 1986)

SOURCE: Holland, J. Gill. "George Henry Lewes and 'Stream of Consciousness': The First Use of the Term in English." *South Atlantic Review* 51, no. 1 (January 1986): 31-9.

[*In the following essay, Holland argues that Lewes was the first English philosopher to use the phrase "stream of consciousness," a concept derived from the works of German philosopher Gustav Theodor Fechner.*]

In sorting out the confused parentage of the term "stream of consciousness" we have not given George Henry Lewes and Gustav Theodor Fechner, his German source, their due. Lewes, a well-known Victorian man of letters, editor of *The Fortnightly Review,* author of the first English biography of Goethe and various works of literary criticism, philosophy, and science, was less than fortunate in the neglect shown the posthumous fifth volume of his major undertaking, *Problems of Life and Mind.* In a volume unmentioned in the literature until 1921 (Warren [*A History of the Association Psychology*] 152), Lewes presented some four years before William James what seems to be the earliest full discussion of "stream of consciousness" in English (364-67).

Though Lewes had died in 1878, we know that the words were his own from the manuscript (*Notebook*) and from the "Preparatory Note" by the editor, the author's wife, George Eliot, who was assisted by Sir Michael Foster, then praelector of physiology at Trinity College, Cambridge, and James Sully, later Grote Professor of Philosophy at University College, London. Lewes's debt to Fechner, famous physicist and "psychophysicist" at the University of Leipzig, is clear from references in the text given below and from entries in Lewes's diary for the last year and a half of his life (8 June 1876, 9-10 September, 4-8 October 1877).

William James, heretofore credited with coining the term (Friedman [*Stream of Consciousness*] 2, Adams [*The Herbartian Psychology Applied to Education*] 78, Lloyd Morgan [*An Introduction to Comparative Psychology*] x), first mentioned "stream of consciousness" in print on the second page of his article "On Some Omissions of Introspective Psychology" (1884): "When we take a rapid general view of the wonderful stream of our consciousness, what strikes us first is the different pace of its different portions. Our mental life, like a bird's life, seems to be made of an alternation of flights and perchings."

Such variations as "stream of thought," "thought's stream," and "the subjective stream" appear throughout the article; "the continuity of the mental stream" is of paramount importance in his argument here on the nature of thought. With the further publication in 1890 of *The Principles of Psychology* (1: 224-90; *Psychology* 151-75) James came to be accepted as the first champion of the concept. He was seen to be the first to make the unbroken continuity of mental life the centerpiece of his system in the general debate over continuity versus discontinuity among the psychologists of the day. The French reviewer Marillier, for example, took the "stream" to be central to James's advance beyond the associationist school. In an early reaction in the United States, G. Stanley Hall said James was at his best on the subject of "the stream of thought" (though he rebuked him for not crediting Wilhelm Wundt for the image of flights and perchings). C. Lloyd Morgan, who "works out this figure [of the wave] in all its details, and even goes the length of giving a plan, elevation, and cross-section of the wave of consciousness" (Adams 78), bowed to the priority of James, "Whose conception of a wave of consciousness I have adopted" (x).

Of these early readers of the *Principles* [*The Principles of Psychology*], none I have found mentioned a source James might have used, and James gave none in his text. Though Lewes had published regularly in the pages of the journal *Mind,* where James first used the term, his posthumous discussion does not seem to have been known to James. Any debt to Fechner here is likewise difficult to pinpoint. James's principal attraction to

Fechner came with a broadening pursuit of psychical research later in his career from 1898 on (Perry [*The Thought and Character of William James*] 2: 132-33, 172). True, in 1867 he had been impressed by Fechner's attempt to make psychology more of a science (Perry 2: 3). Nevertheless, in *Principles* he astonished at least one reviewer with the harshness of his criticism of some of Fechner's notions (1: 545-49; Marty).

In contrast, the debt to Fechner is apparent the moment we look at Lewes's text. The term "stream of consciousness" makes its debut in an addendum to a problem of life and mind entitled **"The Sphere of Sense and Logic of Feeling"** (364-67), specifically in Paragraph 132. Just before, Paragraph 130 suggests Lewes's relation to Fechner and other researchers of the day:

130. There can be no sensation without adequate stimulation, and no stimulation without external stimulus. But the contact of a stimulus with a sensitive surface does not suffice for Sensation: it must have a certain energy to disturb the neural equilibrium, and produce an excitation; further, that excitation must reach a certain level of relative intensity to produce a change in the state of consciousness. Thus a stimulus may act without producing adequate excitation, or the excitation may discharge itself without producing sensation (*i.e.,* conscious sensation). This change of relative intensity is not produced simply by increasing the intensity of the stimulus: Sensation does not rise and fall *pari passu* with the rise and fall in the stimulus. The law of stimulation formulated by Fechner—that sensation is as the logarithm of stimulus—is an abstract ideal construction which may be accepted as such, although criticism has shown that as a concrete expression of the facts it is inaccurate. The law has to be supplemented by that of central reaction. The intensity of an excitation depends on the level of excitability and the psychostatical condition. Thus it is that the crash of a bullet may be unfelt.

Now just as the stimulations which do not reach the energy of excitation were nevertheless vital processes of the same kind as those which do reach it, and never lose their character of vital activity, so the excitations which do not reach the level of conscious states are neverthless sentient processes of the same kind as those which do; and they never lose this character to sink into merely physical processes. Sensibility, general or particular, may be represented by a curve: as it rises above the level of excitation it rises into the stage of consciousness, which having attained its maximum sinks into subconsciousness, and without changing its course falls to the level of unconsciousness, perhaps again to rise with like gradation.

"The law of stimulation formulated by Fechner" is the proposition Fechner himself called "Weber's Law," a formula that shows the relative intensity of stimulus and sensation (*Elements of Psychophysics* 1: 54, 198-99). Lewes, who was recognized as a follower of Fechner as opposed to the English tradition of J. S. Mill (Courtney ["The New Psychology"] 32: 319), took the

concept of the threshold of consciousness from this law (1: 199-212). Moreover, Fechner's frequent use of the metaphor of a mental wave (*Welle*) might have triggered Lewes's imagination with this image of waterways of the mind, though Lewes's image is not quite the same:

A metaphor: thought may be regarded as part of a stream of bodily processes itself [*Ich will ein Bild brauchen: mag der Gedanke am Flusse der körperlichen Thätigkeit selbst mitwirken*], and may be real only in terms of these processes, or it may need this stream only for steering as an oarsman steers his boat, raising only some incidental ripples with his oar. The conditions and laws of the river must be taken into account in both instances when the flow or progress of thought is concerned, though in each case from a quite different point of view, to be sure. Even the freest navigation is subject to laws, as to the nature of the elements and the means that serve it. Similarly, psychophysics will find it necessary, in any case, to deal with the relationship of higher mental activity to its physical base. From what point of view, however, and to what extent, psychophysics will one day have itself to decide.

(1: 13; *Elemente der Psychophysik* 1: 14)

The second paragraph of Par. 130 quoted above reflects Lewes's redefinition of psychology as "the science of the facts of Sentience" rather than "the science of the facts of Consciousness," the word *sentience* here including the subconscious and the unconscious; it is interesting to note that this plunge beneath the consciousness was thought by some to be "alien to English modes of thought," a phrase used in discussing the German philosopher J. F. Herbart's "assumption of mental modifications which are not objects of consciousness" (Stout ["Herbart Compared with English Psychologists and with Beneke"] 14: 9). The second paragraph of Par. 130 also provides an illustrative diagram reminiscent of Fechner's graphs—but only in the manuscript, just after the clause "sensibility, general or particular, may be represented by a curve." The image of the curve also suggests the continuity of mental life, which is spelled out clearly in Par. 132 below.

The importance of the metaphoric shift underway at this time is seen in an article in the *Encyclopaedia Britannica* in which the Cambridge philosopher and psychologist James Ward gave special prominence to "the unity or continuity of consciousness' (20: 42). The alarmed review of the Scottish psychologist Alexander Bain shows the urgency of the question at the time:

Mr. Ward's next important innovation in the treatment of fundamentals is his mode of expressing the unity of consciousness by the term "continuum," as a substitute for the old designations—train, series, sequence, transition. He thinks that by the usual modes, the discreteness of the successive individual presentations is made too much of, and the continuity too little. . . .

Now it is obvious that our language must provide for both the separateness and the unity or continuity of the stream of thought. Yet my fear is that "continuum" rather inclines us too much to the other extreme. More-over, I am not aware of any erroneous tendencies due to the previous phraseology; at all events, I think it could be used without implying any dangerous amount of independence among the terms of mental succession. A train of impressions, presentations, ideas, may have any amount of coherence and dependence, that we may choose to assign; while the word does not sink the circumstance of plurality.

(11: 460-61)

It is worthy of note that *continuum* is one of the very words James had earlier complimented Ward on using. In a letter of 27 February 1881 he wrote, "Your use of certain words [in your lectures], as *object* for *feeling, continuum,* etc., really puts a new power into our hands" (Perry 2: 58). About the article in the *Encyclopaedia Britannica* James wrote Ward on 29 July 1886, ". . . I think no competent person will deny that this article, by itself, marks the transition of English psychology from one epoch to another" (Perry 2: 59).

With his emphasis on sentience and continuity as new descriptions of the workings of the mind, Lewes was clearly in the vanguard of the day. He was defining for the first time in English that deep, fluid conception of mind which writers since have plumbed under the rubric of "stream of consciousness." His classic formulation appears in the next paragraphs of *Problems of Life and Mind*:

131. From first to last there has been an excitation which discharges or *tends* to discharge itself in a movement, and blends with other excitations into a group—sensation, emotion, idea, volition. Excitation then is the fundamental fact; consciousness, subconsciousness, and unconsciousness are its gradations of intensity, the ordinates of the curve. With this conception we have no difficulty in understanding how mental processes may pass unconsciously without losing their psychical character; for Consciousness is not an agent but a symptom, and a symptom not of any special organic process or of any constant energy of such process, but simply of the relation of that energy to simultaneous activities. A stimulation pursues its normal course, produces its normal effect, and is thus a factor in the working of the Sentient mechanism. If it is below the level, or if it has no escort of excitations above the level, it is then said to be "not accompanied by consciousness"; this means that in and for itself the movement has had neither the interest which connects it with Feeling, nor the significance which connects it with Thought. As an example, consider the somnambulist who moves securely through a crowded room, sees the objects and persons (since he avoids them) but is not conscious of them, they having no interest or significance for him; whereas he sees and is conscious of the objects which enter into his dream-pageant, and have an escort above the level.

132. That which is true of particular excitations, according to Fechner's law—namely, that the stimulation must reach a certain level (Fechner calls it the *Schwelle* or threshold of consciousness)—is true of the sum of

excitations which is the abstract Consciousness or Ego. Our mental activity is for ever alternating between the upper and under levels of excitation; and for every change in consciousness there is needed a rise in intensity on one side which involves a fall on the other. There is thus a stream of Consciousness formed out of the rivulets of excitation, and this stream has its waves and ground-swell: the curves are continuous and blend insensibly; there is no breach or pause. Any increase in the excitability of a particular organ, or neural group, will by raising its level give it a relative prominence, so that for the instant it will constitute the consciousness. And under the incessantly fluctuating waves of special sensation there is the continued ground-swell of systemic sensation, emotion, or ideal preoccupation, which from time to time emerges into the prominence of consciousness; and this, even when below the waves, is silently operating, determining the direction of the general current, and obscurely preparing the impulses which burst forth into action. Consciousness is composed of Feelings, and Feelings are composed of elementary excitations: besides the fluctuations of wandering attention raising the level now here and now there, we must take into account the fluctuations of Moods—each Mood being conditioned by residual feelings of systemic stimulation.

Behind these words we recognize Lewes's perennial mission throughout his work to refute the arguments of dualism. As he said a few pages later in *Problems of Life and Mind*:

We stand, then, on the position of Physiology that Sensibility is the physical side of Sentience, and that all the different forms of Feeling are different modes and complexities of Sensibility; and we are guided further by inductions which point to Sensibility as at first a general property of protoplasm, which becomes more various in its energies and modes as protoplasm becomes neuroplasm, and neuro-muscular tissues are differentiated and integrated into systems and organs.

(374)

On the one hand, there are mechanical, chemical "vital" phenomena in the body. On the other hand, there are subjective feelings known by the term "sentience," which, as we have seen in Par. 130 above, includes the consciousness, the subconsciousness, and the unconsciousness. The vital phenomena and the mental phenomena are but two "aspects" or "states" of the same activity. With this argument Lewes thus solved the mind-body problem to his own satisfaction. The issue is too complex to be elaborated here. Suffice it to say that the reviewers, including James Sully, one of the editors of Lewes's posthumous volume of *Problems of Life and Mind,* were not persuaded by his argument (Courtney 32: 323; "Reviews" ["Reviews: Lewes's *Problems of Life and Mind*"] 48: 84-85; Sully [Review of *Problems of Life and Mind*] 17: 308-9; Read ["G. H. Lewes's Posthumous Volumes"] 6: 489).

Regarding Par. 132 two observations need to be made. First, the metaphor of water as mind is not simply hinted at; it is elaborated in the fuller imagery of stream, wave, rivulet, and current. Indeed, the manuscript reveals that Lewes sought exact phraseology through revision. The draft of the key sentence reads thus: "There is thus a general [wave *crossed out*] curve formed out of the [*word illegible*: immeasurable? innumerable?] particular [waves *crossed out*] curves, a stream of consciousness formed out of the rivulets of excitation . . ." (*Notebook* VI, folder 32, 3-5). Second, the concept of "threshold of consciousness" points back to Johann Friedrich Herbart, whose importance in the rise of contemporary psychology was not yet recognized in England. Though Lewes like Sully cited Fechner, Herbart was the original coiner of the term (*OED* [*Oxford English Dictionary*] 11: 359; Herbart [*Psychologie als Wissenschaft*] 175). In his article in the *Encyclopaedia Britannica* Ward made the correct attribution (20: 47). By this time Herbart's work, in particular his contribution to the subject of consciousness, had become better known in England and throughout Europe (Dunkel [*Herbart and Herbartianism*] 4-5, 212; Adams 55, n. 1). Herbart contributed other language too; along with *Schwelle des Bewusstseyns,* the common imagery of *Steigen, Sinken,* and *Kraft* are already found in his writings (Herbart 176). On the other hand, the concept of time for Herbartians was still "discrete and not continuous," as Ward pointed out (20: 66); the continuity necessary for a *stream* of consciousness was a concept for the next generation.

In Par. 132 only one more textual matter remains to be noted. In the fifth sentence where the printed text reads, ". . . the continued ground-swell . . . is silently operating, determining the direction of the general current, and obscurely preparing the impulses which burst forth into action," Lewes's manuscript reads: ". . . obscurely preparing [for enough (*?*) *crossed out*] actions" (*Notebook* VI, folder 32, 5). The editors added the words *the impulses which burst forth into* and made *actions* singular. With or without the addition the sentence remains a provocative anticipation of the riches of future literature of stream of consciousness.

Works Cited

Adams, John. *The Herbartian Psychology Applied to Education: Being a Series of Essays Applying the Psychology of Johann Friedrich Herbart.* London: D. C. Heath, [1897].

Bain, Alexander. "Mr. James Ward's 'Psychology.'" *Mind* 11 (1886): 457-77.

Courtney, William L. "The New Psychology." *Fortnightly Review* 32 (1879): 318-28.

Dunkel, Harold B. *Herbart and Herbartianism: An Educational Ghost Story.* Chicago: U of Chicago P, 1970.

Eliot, George. "Preparatory Note." *Problems of Life and Mind, Third Series (Continued).* Boston: Houghton Osgood, 1880.

Fechner, Gustav. *Elemente der Psychophysik.* Erster Theil. Leipzig: Breitkopf und Härtel, 1860.

———. *Elements of Psychophysics.* Trans. Helmut E. Adler. Ed. Davis H. Howes and Edwin G. Boring. New York: Holt, Rinehart and Winston, 1966.

Friedman, Melvin. *Stream of Consciousness: A Study in Literary Method.* New Haven: Yale UP, 1955.

Hall, G. Stanley. Rev. of *Problems of Life and Mind,* by George Henry Lewes. *American Journal of Psychology* 3 (1890): 578-91.

Herbart, Johann Friedrich. *Psychologie als Wissenschaft: neu gegründet auf Erfahrung, Metaphysik und Mathematik.* Erster, synthetischer Theil. Königsberg: August Wilhelm Unzer, 1824.

James, William. "On Some Omissions of Introspective Psychology." *Mind* 9 (1884): 1-26.

———. *Psychology.* 1892. New York: Henry Holt, 1920.

———. *The Principles of Psychology.* 2 vols. 1890. [New York]: Dover, 1950.

Lewes, George Henry. *Diary.* George Eliot-George Henry Lewes Papers. Beinecke Rare Book and Manuscript Library. Yale U, New Haven, CT.

———. *Notebook.* George Eliot-George Henry Lewes Papers. Beinecke Rare Book and Manuscript Library. Yale U, New Haven, CT.

———. *Problems of Life and Mind, Third Series (Continued).* Boston: Houghton, Osgood, 1880.

Lloyd Morgan, C. *An Introduction to Comparative Psychology.* 1894. Washington, D. C.: University Publications of America, 1977.

Marillier, L. "La Psychologie de W. James." *Revue philosophique de la France et de l'étranger* 34 (1892): 449-70, 603-27; 35 (1893): 1-32, 145-83.

Marty, A. Rev. of *The Principles of Psychology,* by William James. *Zeitschrift für Psychologie und Physiologie der Sinnesorgane* 3 (1892): 297-333.

Perry, Ralph Barton. *The Thought and Character of William James.* 2 vols. Boston: Little, Brown, 1935.

Read, Carveth. "G. H. Lewes's Posthumous Volumes." *Mind* 6 (1881): 483-98.

"Reviews: Lewes's *Problems of Life and Mind.*" *Saturday Review* 48 (19 July 1879): 84-85.

Stout, G. F. "Herbart Compared with English Psychologists and with Beneke." *Mind* 14 (1889): 1-26.

Sully, James. Rev. of *Problems of Life and Mind,* by George Henry Lewes. *Academy* 17 (1880): 308-10.

"Threshold." *Oxford English Dictionary.* 1933.

Ward, James. "Psychology." *Encyclopaedia Britannica.* 1886.

Warren, Howard C. *A History of the Association Psychology.* New York: Charles Scribner's Sons, 1921.

Peter Allan Dale (essay date 1987)

SOURCE: Dale, Peter Allan. "George Lewes' Scientific Aesthetic: Restructuring the Ideology of the Symbol." In *One Culture: Essays in Science and Literature,* edited by George Levine and Alan Rauch, pp. 92-116. Madison: University of Wisconsin Press, 1987.

[*In the following essay, Dale presents an historical consideration of literary positivism in later nineteenth-century criticism. Dale entertains the possibility that Lewes's "discovery of the spirit of art in science" may be akin in some ways to contemporary deconstructionist theories.*]

> I believed . . . that I had caught nature in the lawful work of bringing forth living structures as the model for all artifice.
>
> —Goethe

"Since art and science move in entirely different planes, they cannot contradict or thwart one another."[1] The words happen to be Ernst Cassirer's, but they may stand apart from any particular author as an epitome of one of our most persistent modern beliefs about the relation, or rather nonrelation, between art and science. This belief has been a mainstay of both neo-Kantian (broadly speaking, New Critical) and phenomenological defenses of art in an increasingly technological age. In our more recent critical discourse the resistance to science's efforts to bring all human endeavor within its own methodological realm has become less compromising and more encompassing. Not only is current literary theory unlikely to allow science its separate plane (a point to which we must return), it jealously watches its own discourse, and that of the neighboring humanities, for signs of unconscious scientism. Indeed, the epithet "positivist" is now far more likely to be aimed at the work of fellow critics than at what the scientists are doing. Thus Jonathan Culler warns us against the "positivist claim" that criticism can attain a "true reading," an absolute interpretation of a text,[2] and J. Hillis Miller regrets that "'happy positivism'" by which we are "lulled into the promise of a rational ordering of literary study."[3]

The object of the present study is twofold. On the one hand, it is simply historical. I examine the phenomenon of literary positivism in the period, roughly the middle third of the past century, when it seemed to offer a new and exciting departure in criticism, when the notion of establishing a genuinely scientific or objective approach to art was as intellectually attractive as, say, our current

notion of an absolutely decentered and radically anti-objective criticism. But of course post-modernism has taught us nothing if not the naiveté of supposing one's studies of the past to be "simply historical," so I acknowledge at the outset that another purpose of the essay is revisionist. By resurrecting the dispute literary positivism had with the Romantic aesthetic that preceded it and by showing how this dispute crucially redefined contemporary concepts of imagination and symbolization, I hope to make a fair case for its intellectual respectability. My object is not to initiate a neopositivist movement in literary theory. One could scarcely imagine a more quixotic gesture. Rather, I seek, in some degree, to deliver what I take to be a very important theoretical movement from the marginalization, not to mention caricaturization, it has suffered at the hands of its modernist and postmodernist detractors.

We need, to begin with, a short and reasonably neutral definition of the phenomenon. By "positivism" I mean the belief that science or scientific method is the only reliable route to knowledge, not only of the natural world but also—and here we see its revolutionary import—of the cultural one.[4] As a philosophy in the hands, say, of Auguste Comte, John Stuart Mill, or Herbert Spencer it claimed nothing less than the regeneration of society. What concerns me here is one small part of that regenerative program, the effort to "scientize" the theory of art. In particular I am considering the work of George Henry Lewes (1817-79), whom we in literature know primarily as the companion of George Eliot and who, unfortunately, exists too much in the shadow of that great artist. In fact, Lewes was probably the Victorians' foremost philosopher of science after Mill, and one of their two or three most important psychologists. He was also a very talented and prolific literary critic, who needs to take second place to no one, including George Eliot, in the seriousness with which he engaged the problem of the relation between science and art. Still more particularly, I shall be looking at Lewes' concept of the literary symbol, an especially telling aspect of nineteenth- and early-twentieth-century efforts to define the meaning and function of art. What I hope to show is how Lewes' positivist aesthetic first disengages itself from the Romantic "ideology of the symbol" and then gradually reclaims the meaning of symbolic representation in a way that profoundly affects his concept not simply of artistic practice but of scientific method and social order as well. The result, as we shall see, is clearly anticipatory of Cassirer's philosophy of symbolic form and distantly (but interestingly) of our own "deconstructive turn."[5]

I

The expression, "ideology of the symbol," comes to me from Paul de Man's late article "Sign and Symbol in Hegel's Aesthetics." De Man is arguing that Hegel enshrines the Romantic doctrine of the beautiful as the symbolic and that "whether we know it or not" we are "most of us ["us" being literary critics] Hegelians and quite orthodox ones at that."[6] What de Man means by this, as I read him, is that we are most of us still essentially New Critics, Romantics manqués, if you like, who value literature because it is a sensuous, concrete representation of an inwardness, a consciousness that is, in some sense, deemed to be universal and, at the same time, beyond or behind language. De Man, of course, is rejecting this Romantic-cum-New Critical ideology of the symbol in favor of a Derridean grammatology, according to which language is not a symbol that refers to some ontological form of being other than itself, but a sign that has its meaning only as part of a larger linguistic system of differences. "Contrary to the metaphysical, dialectical, 'Hegelian' interpretation" of linguistic signs as deferring to an absent presence, writes Derrida, the only possible principle of signification lies in the differential relation of any given sign to the other terms of its language system: "Essentially and lawfully, every concept is inscribed in a chain or in a system within which it refers to the other, to other concepts, by means of the systematic play of differences."[7]

I shall come back to de Man's case against the ideology of the symbol. For the moment I want only to make the point that Lewes' positivist aesthetic, no less than de Man's deconstructionist one, begins with an attack on the Romantic ideology of the symbol although, of course, with a quite different philosophical end in view. For the positivist, no less than the deconstructionist, Romanticism is a metaphysical *ideology* (Lewes actually uses the word) whose cultural products—political, ethical, or, as in the present case, aesthetic—must be exposed as at once unrealistic and repressive. De Man would no doubt argue that the positivist's realism and the positivist's liberalism are themselves only expressions of another kind of metaphysics, but this need not concern us just yet.

Let me now briefly indicate Hegel's concept of the artistic symbol in the hope (following de Man) that it may be allowed fairly to represent not just an aspect of the Romantic aesthetic but its essence:

> [Art displays] the highest [reality] sensuously, bringing it thereby nearer to the senses, to feeling, and to nature's mode of appearance. What is [symbolically] displayed is the depth of a suprasensuous world which thought pierces and sets up as . . . a *beyond* . . .

> The external appearance [of art] has no immediate value for us [except as a representation of something else]; we assume behind it something inward, a meaning whereby the external appearance is endowed with the spirit. It is to this soul that the external points.

Through the faculty of imagination, the artist transforms "what exists in nature" into a symbol of the "something inward":

> Our imaginative mentality has in itself the character of universality, and what it produces acquires . . . thereby the stamp of universality in contrast to the individual thing in nature.[8]

To illustrate this doctrine in Romantic artistic practice is, of course, not difficult. I shall offer an example from Wordsworth (whom A. C. Bradley long ago connected with Hegel) in a moment.

Lewes' first substantive essay in criticism was, in fact, a review article on Hegel's *Aesthetics* (1842; so far as I know, he was the first to introduce this great Romantic text to England).[9] At the time he wrote the review, he was in the process of making a philosophical transition from his own youthful Romanticism (inspired mainly by Shelley) to positivism under the guidance first of Mill and subsequently of Comte. Three years later, with the publication of his famous *Biographical History of Philosophy,* it is clear that the transition is complete. "One Method must preside [over philosophy]," he writes at the close of that book. "Auguste Comte was the first to point out the fact. . . . When the positive method is universally accepted . . . then shall we again have unity of thought."[10] By the time he comes to the 1871 edition of the *History* [now called *The History of Philosophy from Thales to Comte*] (it went through four editions in his lifetime), he has a still sharper conception of the essential plot of nineteenth-century thought. Hegel, he writes, imagined that he had begun an epoch in philosophy. In fact, he merely closed out the latest epoch of metaphysics initiated by Fichte's misguided correction of Kant. Hegel, as well as the "incompetence" of metaphysics in general, has now been displaced by Comte's philosophy of science, which genuinely marks a new and, as far as Lewes is concerned, the ultimate epoch in philosophy.[11]

Lewes' application of the positivist philosophy to criticism is of a piece with his larger historical and epistemological argument. He evidently sees himself as doing in the sphere of aesthetics what Comte had done in general philosophy: overturning an "incompetent" mode of enquiry. Not surprisingly, Coleridge comes in for the brunt of Lewes' attack on the "abuses of English criticism."[12]

> Unless we are greatly deceived this [metaphysical] philosophy of art is a vain and misplaced employment of ingenuity. . . . To understand Nature, we must observe her manifestations, and trace out the laws of coexistence and succession of phenomena. And in the same way, to understand Art, we must patiently examine the works of art; and from a large observation of successful efforts deduce a general conclusion respecting the laws upon which success depends.[13]

Hegel's *Aesthetics* receives gentler treatment, but only because, at the time of writing about it, Lewes had not fully gone over to positivism. Yet even in this early, transitional phase of his thinking, he takes care to demystify Hegel's concept of mind, transforming the phenomenology of spirit into a psychological theory. What Hegel teaches us, finally, is that "the real way to set about [the] examination [of art] must be the investigation of those laws of the mind from whence it proceeds; . . . thus it becomes . . . a branch of psychology. . . . [Y]ou have only to translate [his] principle into your own formula, and the thing becomes intelligible" (**"Hegel's Aesthetics,"** pp. 43-44). In later, more informed treatments of Hegel, Lewes is less cavalier about the possibility of reconciling the German's "laws of mind" to a scientific philosophy. But one notes that what he is doing here is symptomatic of the reformation in aesthetics he is attempting to accomplish: metaphysical entities must be "translated" to psychological ones before we can hope to talk responsibly about art.

The attack on the Romantic metaphysic of art, when turned to questions of the *form* of art, becomes an attack on the idea that the essence of beauty is the symbolic. Preoccupation with the "symbolic in Art," Lewes writes in his book on Goethe (1855), reached its height in the Romantic school's desire to create "a new Religion, or at any rate, a new Mythology." But "the poet who makes symbolism the substance and purpose of his work has mistaken his vocation," symbolism "being in its very nature *arbitrary*—the indication of a meaning not directly expressed, but arbitrarily thrust *under* expression." Incidents "however wonderful, adventures however perilous, are almost as naught when compared with the deep and lasting interest excited by anything like a *correct representation of life*" (my emphasis).[14]

What is motivating Lewes here is the belief—we would now call it a realist or objectivist fallacy—that it is possible somehow to represent things as they are without the intervention of symbolic representation which distorts them into the shapes or forms we "arbitrarily" wish them to have. As Comte had said, "Le but le plus difficile et le plus important de notre existence intellectuelle consiste à transformer le cerveau humain en un miroir exact de l'ordre extérieur."[15] In effect, Lewes is collapsing the well-known Romantic distinction between the symbol as true representation of reality ("consubstantial" with it, as Coleridge insists) and the allegory as arbitrary or conventional and, hence, false representation. The Romantic symbol, for Lewes, is always only an allegory, the "thrusting under [concrete] expression" of beliefs about the world that have no scientific standing, that do not "mirror the external order." So, for example, Wordsworth's claim that a particular Alpine setting at a particular moment became for him the "type and symbol of Eternity," "the character of the great Apocalypse" (*The Prelude* [1850], 6.624 ff.) is simply an illusion, perpetrated by the poet's metaphysical-cum-theological belief that imagination is actually a divine power flowing through him, shaping

nature by means of his art to what it really means, "stamping" it, as Hegel says, with "universality." In fact, what Wordsworth calls symbolic is simply semiological. The Romantic poet, far from suffering from a "sad incompetence of speech," displays an excess of competence at connecting his speech with the ungrounded system of language (essentially scriptural language) that signifies divine presence.

Lewes' nineteenth-century positivism has not yet taken the "linguistic turn" of the Vienna circle, but it is clear from his discussion of Hegel that he considers the heart of the German's, and of Romanticism's, problem to be the merely verbal (symbolic) creation of nonexistent universals, "pseudo-concepts," as Carnap will later label them.[16]

> In his *Logic* [Hegel] makes it a special merit of the German language that more than all other modern languages it permits of ambiguity, many of its words containing not only different but directly opposed meanings "so that a speculative spirit in the language is not to be overlooked." . . .
>
> He is fond of revealing philosophic principles involved in ordinary terms [*aufheben* is Lewes', as it will later be Derrida's, principal example], and his derivations are often as ingenious as they are etymologically incorrect.
>
> (***History of Philosophy*** [***History of Philosophy from Thales to Comte***], 2: 628-29)

The Romantic symbol thus emptied of its metaphysical content is discarded in favor of the "correct representation of life," one that does not begin with what Lewes calls Hegel's "arbitrary suppression of concretes" (p. 638).

At this point, I have pressed the similarity between the positivist aesthetic and deconstructionism about as far as it will go. Lewes' notion that it is possible to have signs (aesthetic or otherwise) that represent some reality in the world obviously marks the parting of the ways. We now need to look at what exactly Lewes expects a realistic, nonsymbolic art to represent.

II

Passing over the many essays Lewes wrote in the 1840s and 1850s applying his positivist criteria to the discussion of particular works of art, I will note only that these essays make a case for essentially two things, that the novel is the genre most appropriate to the new scientific age and, what is closely related, that art must strive, above all, for *psychological* realism. (We may in passing distinguish Lewes' position from the positivist aesthetics of Hippolyte Taine and Emile Zola, both of whom show a characteristically French tendency to privilege the social rather than the psychological as the real.)

What Lewes means by the psychologically real, as we see from his essays on contemporary novels and poetry, is the deep elemental or instinctual nature of man. Balzac, for example, is admired for portraying the "secret springs" that determine action and, at the same time, criticized for allowing the intellect too large a role as cause of action. The French novelist's characters "calculate" too much; he overrates the "power of intelligence."[17] Again, Dickens is not a psychological realist because he does not understand how deeply rooted human motivation is, how inaccessible to conscious control. What Lewes is after in the literary presentation of human psychology is, in short, that which is furthest removed from the possibility of "intellectual conversion," the possibility, that is, of being controlled or transmuted by the reason.[18]

We may attribute Lewes' interest in the psychology of subrational motivation to his reading of Comte and the work of contemporary psychologists either directly influenced by Comte or working independently on positivist principles. One of the impulses behind Comte's work, as Marcuse has observed, was a desire to end the metaphysicians' and, in particular, Hegel's subordination of reality to "transcendental reason."[19] The foundations of human action, Comte insists, lie in biological or instinctual causes. As Lewes says, the *Politique positive* leads us to a "new cerebral theory"; Comte's reduction of psychology to biology has made a "philosophical revolution" and given the science of mind its proper basis.[20] The history of the rise of the "new cerebral theory" and its implications for nineteenth-century concepts of human behavior has been told elsewhere.[21] It is enough to note here that Lewes, as scientist, participated in that history to an extent beyond any of his British contemporaries, an extent still not properly recognized. He drew heavily upon the work of all the major continental figures, not only the pioneers—Gall, Cabanis, and Comte—but the later German animal and human physiologists, from Johannes Mueller to Fechner, Lotze, Helmholtz, and Wundt. The most important consequence of his study was to convince him that by far the greater and more influential part of human behavior is determined by unconscious (in his physiological and not, of course, Freud's psychoanalytical sense) motivation. This is the resounding conclusion of his first original scientific work, *The Physiology of Common Life* (1859-60), in which the study of animal physiology merges with that of human psychology. What we learn from exploring the continuum between animal and human physiology is that consciousness, pace Descartes and his many followers, forms but a small item in the total of human psychical processes.[22]

We need to bear in mind that Lewes' location of psychological reality in unconscious volition, while it may partake of a revolution in the theory of mind, does not represent a revolution in ethics in the way, for example,

Freud's concern with similar issues does. Unconscious volition, as Lewes understands it, is not without its Aristotelian *eidos*. The instincts have their form, and this form closely approximates certain moral presuppositions. Balzac, for example, is criticized for displaying instincts that go beyond the "natural" limit. Adultery is within that limit, but incestuous feelings are not (**"Balzac"** [**"Balzac and George Sand"**], pp. 269-73). Later, following Comte, Lewes will argue that there is in human nature a fundamental structure that makes for disinterested love or altruism, as opposed to self-interest or egoism.[23] The latter instinct, one notes, was the mainstay of the contemporary associationist or utilitarian school, against whose claims to being a scientific theory of mind Lewes and the Comteans were in conscious reaction.

Applying his psychological concepts to art, Lewes comes up in the 1850s with what he considers a properly scientific theory of artistic form. The form of art must mirror or reflect the essential structure of human feeling. The only "legitimate style of idealization," he writes in his 1858 essay **"Realism in Art,"** lies in representing the inner emotional structure of the human subject. His principal example of this, Raphael's "Madonna di San Sisto," is also a favorite of George Eliot's and figures importantly in her own realist efforts to express a "legitimate idealization." In Raphael's painting, says Lewes, we see "at once the intensest realism of presentation, with the highest idealism of conception." The Christ child expresses an "undefinable something" which we feel is a "perfect truth" of human nature: "we feel that humanity in its highest conceivable form is before us." The virgin mother's expression is also in the "highest sense ideal" precisely because "it is also in the highest sense real." This artistic "conception," as Lewes insists, is not grounded in any theological or metaphysical principle, but is the product of a "sympathetic," a purely psychological, projection of the artist's self into the unapparent emotional center of another human being. What is "ideal" is the sentiment felt by the artist in the actual human subjects and then "thrown into" the images on the canvas.[24] We note as well that in this particular image the emotional structure represented as ideal is a conspicuously altruistic one. Later, in *The Principles of Success in Literature* (1865), Lewes gives fuller theoretical attention to this issue of the ideal-cum-formal in art. There he objects to what he calls "the rage for 'realism.'" Realism is "healthy in as far as it insists on truth," but "unhealthy in as far as it confounds truth with . . . predominance of unessential details." A "rational philosophy" of art understands that the "natural means *truth of a kind,*" or, to use what has become for him an absolutely central concept, the truth of "type."[25]

Obviously, the more Lewes' notion of a legitimate idealization or truth of type seems to coincide with values that have their roots in the Judeo-Christian ethical tradition, the more we feel that, for all his positivist protestations, metaphysical presuppositions have seeped into his concept of realism. To understand what makes him so confident that this, in fact, has not taken place, that the forms of feeling or instinct which he seeks in art actually exist in human nature, we need to return to his work in scientific psychology.

Like many other contemporary researchers in the field, Lewes had come to believe one could find hard biological evidence of the reality of the psychological-cum-moral types that were the objects of the artist's vision. This is very much the sort of confidence we find in a modern biologist like Melvin Konner who, on seeing a photograph of the pyramidal brain cells, believes he has seen the essence of mind: "somehow it is structure—that most ancient of biological subjects—seen and drawn or photographed through the microscope—that most classic of tools—that persuades at last."[26] Lewes, of course, had no means of photographing, let alone seeing, the brain cells that determine thought. Yet by the close of the 1850s he was no less convinced than Konner that human consciousness is the result of typical neurological structures that are potentially observable.

Here Lewes' inspiration comes initially from Goethe, the one artist of the Romantic era whom he admires, the poet whose work in science taught him the necessity of an "objective" approach to art.[27] The German poet's greatest contribution to science was in formulating the principles of morphology, the "soul" of biological study, as Darwin says.[28] He was the first to express in definite terms the idea of the unity of plan or structure within all organic nature. His object, as he writes in the *Erster Entwurf einer allgemeinen Einleitung in die vergleichende Anatomie* (1795), is "to arrive at an anatomical *type* [anatomischer Typus], a general picture in which the forms of all animals are contained in potentia, and by means of which we can describe each animal in an invariable order" (my emphasis).[29]

There is no need to review here the story of Goethe's search for the fundamental organic type, the *Urbild,* from which all animal life has evolved. It is a commonplace at once of Goethe studies and the history of biology.[30] What we do need to note is that Lewes effectively made Goethe's theory the basis of all his work in physiology and psychology. "It is impossible," he writes in the **Life of Goethe,** "to be even superficially acquainted with biological speculations and not to recognise the immense importance of [the theory of] Type" (p. 351). By the time he comes five years later to the climactic chapter in **The Physiology of Common Life,** the chapter on the definition of life, he believes modern science has found that type in the cell, "the true biological atom," the structural unit from which all life derives

(**Physiology** [**The Physiology of Common Life**], 2: 357).[31] Is it any wonder that when George Eliot comes at last to give us a representative scientist in the figure of Tertius Lydgate, that scientist should be devoting his life work to the search for the "primitive tissue"? For Lewes, no less than Lydgate, the existence of a universal organic type at the source of all life argues the likelihood of a universal and scientifically demonstrable form of human consciousness.

Again we note that the form of consciousness Lewes, as well as George Eliot, wants most to demonstrate is that of an innate structural propensity for disinterested love:

> As the Aggressive Instinct springs from the Nutritive, so the Sexual Instinct springs from the Reproductive. It is the first of the sympathetic tendencies, the germ of Altruism. Love, which is the social motor, has this origin.
>
> (**Problems** [**Problems of Life and Mind**], 1st ser., 1:176)[32]

There is, of course, an important connection here with the Romantic aesthetic Lewes is seeking to displace, for no less than the Romantics he wants to affirm a vision of nature and mind united in an encompassing economy of love, to demonstrate, as Wordsworth has it, that "to love as prime and chief" we owe "all lasting [human] grandeur" (*The Prelude* [1850], 14.168-69). The difference is that Lewes seeks to ground that vision in the science of biology and not, like Wordsworth et al., in the phenomenology of spirit or imagination.

III

We come at this point to the classical disjunction in the positivist theory of mind, the disjunction that, in effect, generates the late-century neo-Kantian reaction to positivism, of which Cassirer, with whom we began, is a distinguished product. This reaction, in turn, leads to a revitalization of the concept of the symbol and a reassertion of its centrality in the aesthetic process. Mid-nineteenth-century "naturalistic theories of art," writes Cassirer, set out to refute "romantic conceptions of a transcendental" idea at the heart of the aesthetic. But

> they missed the principal point since they failed to recognize the symbolic character of art. . . . Art is, indeed, symbolism, but the symbolism of art must be understood in an immanent, not a transcendental sense.
>
> (*Essay* [*An Essay on Man*], p. 157)

What I now want to show is how Lewes, following out the logic of his own positivist theory of mind, or rather the breakdown of that logic, and influenced by one of Cassirer's own mentors, anticipates by a generation this critical modernist move toward a new, "immanent" understanding of the symbol.

The problem Lewes faces is that of moving from organic structures, which he can verify using ordinary scientific procedures, to psychological or mental ones, which he cannot verify by those procedures. Comte's assertion, for example, that the brain's physiological structure contains the germ of altruism is, as Lewes comes to understand, sheer speculation; it cannot be scientifically substantiated according to the principles of Comte's own method. Yet one contemporary psychologist seemed to Lewes to have approached a solution to this problem of moving from organic to mental forms. This was Hermann von Helmholtz, a man whom, in his later writing, he placed with Bacon, Newton, and Comte on his shortlist of the greatest thinkers of the modern world (*Problems,* 1st ser., 1:175),[33] the clear implication being that Helmholtz had become for him Comte's successor in science's effort to define the nature of mind.

A student of Kant and at the same time fully devoted to the natural sciences, Helmholtz made a critical contribution to the positivist theory of mind. In a word, he naturalized Kant's transcendental aesthetic, reducing the a priori forms of that aesthetic to physiological structures through the laboratory analysis of perception.

> Perceptions of external objects being . . . of the nature of ideas, and ideas themselves being invariably activities of our psychic energy, perceptions also can only be the result of psychic energy. Accordingly, . . . the theory of perceptions belongs properly in the domain of psychology. . . . [We] have to determine, scientifically as far as possible, what special properties of the physical stimulus and of the physiological stimulation are responsible for the formation of this or that particular idea as to the nature of the external objects perceived. . . . Thus, our main purpose will be simply to investigate the material of sensation whereby we are enabled to form ideas.[34]

As Cassirer has observed, with Helmholtz we have "a new and unique bond . . . forged between empirical science and philosophy."[35] For Lewes, Helmholtz's research seems to have come as a revelation, making for him the crucial connection between organic structure and thought.

We see clear evidence of Helmholtz's impact on Lewes in the latter's first theoretical treatise on psychology attached as "Prolegomena" to the 1867 edition of his *History of Philosophy,* the point presumably being to present his reader with the latest advance in that scientific psychology which the *History* announces as the goal of philosophy. The "sensationalist" (that is, the associationist or utilitarian) theory of mind must now, says Lewes, give way to an entirely new conception.

> The Sensational School [postulates an] unscientific conception of the mind as a *tabula rasa* upon which Things inscribe their characters—a mirror passively reflecting the images of objects. This presupposes that Consciousness is absolved from the universal law of action and reaction, presupposes that the Organism has no movement of its own. . . . The *a priori* [metaphysical] School commits the opposite mistake of conceiving Consciousness as a pure spontaneity, undetermined by the conditions of the Organism and its environment; a spontaneity . . . derived from a supra-mundane, supra-vital source.

> We cannot take a step unless we admit that Consciousness is an active reagent. . . . Nor is this all. Biology teaches that the Sensitive Organism inherits certain [mental] aptitudes. . . . Forms of Thought . . . are evolved, just like the Forms of other vital processes.

(***History of Philosophy,*** 1: xcv-xcvi)

In his criticism of Hegel at the close of the *History of Philosophy,* Lewes had focused on the German's metaphysical transmutation of the logical into the real. "How does the Logical become the Real, how are the Forms of Thought shown to be at the same time the Forms of Things?" Hegel, says Lewes, resolves this Kantian dilemma from the wrong direction by making the forms of thought prior to and productive of the forms of things (2:635). Using Helmholtz, with an admixture of Darwin, Lewes, as we see, believes he has established the proper relation of mental to external form: the forms of things are prior to and productive of the forms of thought, the latter being an evolution from the former.

This is a promising approach to anchoring mental structure in reality, to achieving Comte's goal, noticed earlier, of assimilating the shape of human thought to "l'ordre extérieur." If it can be made to work, one may (to return to our central concern) dispense with symbols, at least in the sense in which Lewes objected to them. Taking what Lewes himself comes to regard as the most fundamental institution of human thought, the structure of language, we see that by extending the spirit of Helmholtz's inquiry, one might, theoretically, reduce that structure to "un miroir exact" of the world in which there need be no symbolic, no merely "arbitrary," overdetermination of what "never was on sea or land." Indeed, this was to become the project of the Vienna positivists in our own century. But for Lewes, I may as well say at once, this move does not succeed. He is all right as long as, like Helmholtz, he is concerned only with forms of thought as sensuous *apperceptions* of the real. But when he tries to move from apperception to the forms of thought that really matter to him, both as psychologist and as critic, that is, *moral* forms, he still has no way of making the transition from organic structure to consciousness. Here his scientific realism collapses into a quasi-Kantian assertion of the subjective universality of moral law. In short, he founders on G. E. Moore's "naturalistic fallacy," the fallacy of seeking to identify *ought* with *is*.[36] And, one must add, his original project of a scientific aesthetic, insofar as it cannot transcend the association of artistic form with moral order (as Helmholtz, for example, does), necessarily founders on the same rock. How, then, does Lewes extricate himself from this difficulty? The answer, as I have suggested, lies in a reconsideration of the nature of symbolization, a reconsideration to which he is led by a side of Helmholtz's thought we have not yet adequately developed.

IV

There is a substantial Kantian residue in Helmholtz of which, as we have seen, Lewes is well aware: "we cannot take a step unless we admit that consciousness is an active reagent." One of the things that the study of Helmholtz—and the extensive rereading of Kant occasioned by that study[37]—does for Lewes is awaken in him a full recognition of the radically *constitutive* function of mind. On this issue he ponders increasingly in the late work, becoming more and more preoccupied with scientific epistemology and, specifically, with the formation and function of hypothesis in scientific discovery. This turn of thought we first see, significantly, in **"The Principles of Success in Literature"** (1865), his last serious dissertation on art and, at the same time, the beginning for him of a new way of perceiving the intersection between the aesthetic and scientific planes. Lewes, as we shall see, is a central nineteenth-century instance of Gillian Beer's argument in her essay that there is a profound conjunction in the work of scientist and creative writer.

The first principle of success in art is the one we have already noticed, the principle of vision. This, again, is a power of "insight" into the unapparent, typical structure of things. In my earlier discussion of this concept I was concerned to show how Lewes used it to develop the point that what the artist imitates is not empirical reality but its inner form. Now I want to turn to a different implication of the principle, one that reflects the new direction in which Helmholtz and Kant are taking him. As we examine what he says about aesthetic vision, we soon see that it is a faculty not only for detecting what is potentially there in nature but also for "inferring" or "constructing" what is "apparently" not there. From the most fundamental level of perception to the highest expression of reason and imagination, Lewes says, the mind in some sense constructs the order of nature, and this is equally true whether that mind belongs to artist or scientist: "both poet and [scientific] philosopher draw their power from the energy of their mental vision—an energy which disengages the mind from the somnolence of habit and from the pressure of obtrusive sensation" (*Principles* [*The Principles of Success in Literature*], p. 18). Here Lewes is almost certainly following Helmholtz, who identifies the essential process of scientific discovery as an "aesthetic" rather than "logical" induction. The scientist's hypothetical conclusions rest, finally, says the German, "on a certain psychological instinct [for order] not on conscious reasoning."[38]

Helmholtz, in fact, is initiating a significant shift in the concept of scientific method. By the 1870s, observes a recent historian of scientific method, "mechanistic materialism" with its reliance on inductivism was, "in the German scientific community," "gradually [giving] way to a neo-Kantian philosophy of science developed initially by Helmholtz."[39]

Lewes, who closely followed "the German scientific community," obviously had not missed the point. A decade after *Principles,* in the first volume of his uncompleted organon of scientific philosophy, *Problems of Life and Mind,* Lewes produced a far more extensive and sophisticated account of what amounts to the aesthetic "principle of vision," only now he talks of it exclusively as a principle of scientific discovery. "Science is fertile not because it is a tank but because it is a spring. The grandest discoveries . . . have not only outstripped the slow march of Observation, but have revealed by the telescope of Imagination what the microscope of Observation could never have seen" (*Problems,* 1st ser., 1: 315). We need only be careful—and here the positivist bent of mind reasserts itself—to make sure we distinguish between the artistic and the scientific process. The scientist, having made his imaginative construct, must then *verify* it against observation, the "logic of feeling," as Lewes calls it. "Flights of imagination" are "legitimate tentatives of scientific Research" only if "they submit to the one indispensable condition . . . of ultimate verification" (p. 317).

But what principle of verification does Lewes have in mind for art? Returning to *Principles,* we find under the heading of the "principle of sincerity" that the successful literary artist is one who writes only about what he has directly experienced and genuinely believes.

> It is always understood as an expression of condemnation when anything in Literature or Art is said to be done for effect. . . . It is desirable to clear up this moral ambiguity, as I may call it, and to show that the real method of securing the legitimate effect is not to aim at it, but to aim at truth, relying on that for securing effect. . . . Nothing but what is true, or is held to be true, can succeed.
>
> (p. 42)

Good intentions notwithstanding, Lewes, far from clearing up an ambiguity, is creating one. Truth in the present formula ceases to be one. It is both "what is" and "what is held to be." The former is presumably the scientist's concern, the latter, what Lewes elsewhere calls "subjective truth," the artist's. If we sincerely believe something to be true, then it is, in some sense, so. In precisely what sense? In the sense that one's sincere conviction creates conviction in others; "belief creates belief," says Lewes (*Principles,* p. 45). This represents a significant departure from what he was arguing throughout the essays of the 1840s and 1850s. Now "falsity" in art is not necessarily failure to conform to things as they are, but failure to conform to things *as we hold them to be.* By this new criterion, to be false in art is to be self-consciously rhetorical, to aim at an effect rather than sincerely to express what one believes to be true.

The difficulty with this distinction is apparent. Whether the artist intends to deceive or genuinely believes what he says is immaterial to the question of whether his interpretation of life is true. As Yeats says, "The rhetorician would deceive his neighbours, / The sentimentalist himself" ("Ego Dominus Tuus," lines 46-47), or, put another way, the sincere believer in mere "sentiment" is but marginally less deceptive than the rhetorician who sets out to deceive. The former is honest only by virtue of lying to himself. In more consistent, less transitional phases of his thinking, Lewes is aware enough of the problem. Discussing "the place of sentiment in philosophy" in **Problems,** he asks what we are to say about the role of "Sentiment or Emotion" in the construction of our beliefs. We have "Moral Instincts and Aesthetic Instincts which determine conduct and magnify existence," but we have absolutely no more ground for believing in their truth than our "conviction" that their effects are beneficial, and we cannot identify conviction with verification. Our moral beliefs can "in a last resort . . . only be justified by asserting the facts are so" (1st ser., 1:456-57). The principle of sincerity, which begins as a strategy for grounding artistic vision in reality, ends by leading Lewes to a bifurcation of truth into that which can be properly verified by scientific method and that which can be verified only by subjective assent. The second kind of truth, associated at first with the relatively innocuous category of aesthetic expression, eventually works its way into the far more critical category of ethical belief. At this point Lewes seems to say, in anticipation of William James, that "the desire for a certain kind of truth . . . brings about that special truth's existence,"[40] and insofar as he is saying this, he has placed himself at a considerable distance from the positivist faith that one can construct a new morality and hence a new social order by scientific means alone. Once in this position he is ready for a revaluation of the nature of symbolic discourse.

This is precisely what begins to happen at the close of **Principles.** The third and final principle of art, the "principle of beauty," Lewes effectively identifies with style and, more specifically, *symbolic* expression. The artist's vision and his sincerity are useless unless he can express what he sees and believes in "accurate" symbols.

> It is not enough that a man has clearness of Vision, and reliance on Sincerity, he must also have the art of Expression. . . . The power of seizing unapparent relations of things is not always conjoined with the power of *selecting the fittest verbal symbols by which they can be made apparent to others.*
>
> (p. 55, my emphasis)

What we notice immediately in this reinstatement of symbols as crucial to the artistic process is not simply the reversal of Lewes' previous position, but the fact that the symbolization he is talking about is still very much an arbitrary expression into which preconceived concepts are *thrust.* There is no pretense of an organic or "consubstantial" relation between symbolic medium and that to which it refers. The symbols Lewes is talking about are clearly not Romantic ones. They require no verification beyond that of their *effectiveness* in conveying the artist's beliefs. Effectiveness becomes, as it were, a substitute for presence or, in Lewes' terms, for verification. This new willingness to countenance symbolic expression in art is, as I have suggested, a direct consequence of the bifurcation of truth we have just noticed. Once introduce a notion of subjective truth as the basis of art's reality, and the idea of art as the direct nonsymbolic representation of "what is" gives way to that of art as a system of communication aimed at causing the audience to "hold as true" what the artist believes "is." In short, the symbol becomes a means of embodying and imparting an order that cannot be scientifically demonstrated to exist in nature.

The concept of symbolization developed here at the close of **Principles,** like his "principle of vision," returns in **Problems of Life and Mind** as a crucial element in Lewes' theory of scientific discovery. In the last volume of **Problems,** he turns to what he calls "the Sphere of Intellect and the Logic of Signs." The logic of signs he also calls the "logic of symbols," and the hesitation between the two terms "sign" and "symbol" no doubt reflects the tension between his conventional positivism and his growing awareness of the pragmatic force of symbolic expression.

The logic of symbols, he writes, is essentially the representation of concepts. It involves the "mental constructions" or "abstract general signs" of what we receive through the logic of feeling or remember through the logic of images. It is a "notation," in "artificial marks" or "verbal symbols," of a "class," which it "signifies and condenses." It is also "conventional," the "result of social influence." In the last analysis, the logic of symbols is what makes us human: "the power of thinking by means of symbols . . . demarcates man from animals" (**Problems,** 3d ser., pp. 485-96).

As we pursue this discussion, we find some striking developments beyond Lewes' earlier treatment of symbolization in **Principles.** First, symbolization is no longer a process peculiar to artistic production, but an essential component of scientific reasoning. Using the symbolic logic of algebra as a metaphor for scientific thought in general, he speaks of how with algebraic notation the mind enters a "new sphere," where "letters are symbols of any values we please," and "although the values are changeable, yet once assigned, they must remain fixed throughout the operations." The process of scientific discovery is just such an algebraic tentative:

> Although it is impossible to frame an image of Infinity, we can, and do, form the idea, and reason on it with precision. Nay the paradox is demonstrable that the chief part of our scientific knowledge, so accurate and so important in its direction of our conduct, consists of ideas which cannot be formed into corresponding images and sensations.
>
> (pp. 469-71)

The freedom from referentiality that characterized the symbol as an artistic notation in *Principles* now is carried over for use in a scientific process that had hitherto decisively excluded it. One may go further: Lewes seems at this point actually to be replacing the principle of vision as the primary means of scientific discovery with that of symbolization. The objective of both principles, identifying the typical, lawlike structures within the real, is the same, but the shift from the metaphor of vision to that of symbol is crucial. When Lewes speaks of the scientist's *vision* of a type, he implies its real existence. When he speaks of the scientist's *symbolic construction* of the type, he implies its fundamental fictivity.

In his final chapter, "The Potency of Symbols," Lewes turns briefly to what we may call the sociology of the symbol. So "mighty is the power of names" that it is "capable of determining action" even among "highly-cultivated people."

> Ideas are verbal symbols. The power such ideas have over feelings and actions is incalculable. . . . It is Language which records and generalises experience and opens a vista of experiences about to be. [The logic of symbols] underlies all our planning, connects our actions with the lives of those who are to succeed us, and moulds our conception of the world. . . . The invention of a new symbol is a step in the advancement of civilization.
>
> (pp. 494-95)

We might almost be reading Cassirer. Indeed, for all practical purposes we are, for Lewes—by way of Helmholtz and, again, within the positivist tradition that Cassirer deplores—has arrived at the same "immanent" concept of the symbol which forms the ground of Cassirer's own philosophy. Like Cassirer, he understands the symbol not as the embodiment of a transcendent, metaphysical presence, but as simply a tentative ordering of experience. Like Cassirer, he has come to see the artist's construction of symbolic form as a universal humanistic gesture that informs all cultural production.

What I have been describing is how one well-read and very sophisticated literary theorist arrived at this demystified concept of the symbol well before Cassirer and the advent of literary modernism, and arrived at it

from within a tradition that modernism believes to be inherently inimical to art. Partly Lewes makes this movement of mind under the influence of a scientific thinker who felt, even as he radically modified, the force of Kant's thought. But it is important to emphasize that influence is not the only issue here. Helmholtz, after all, has little to tell Lewes about the nature of symbolism. Lewes' thought develops as it does ultimately, I believe, because of his acute understanding, unusual in so accomplished a scientific philosopher, of the way aesthetic and, in particular, literary discourse functions. More precisely, the difficulty he has in bringing aesthetic phenomena within the scope of scientific method, as he originally conceived it, effectively compels him to examine the function of that in art which is least commensurable with the scientific ideal, namely, its radical fictivity. The more he examines this fictivity, the more he realizes that he is working with a form of symbolic discourse whose object is not to picture existent realities but to affect certain attitudes and beliefs in the beholder. This mature understanding of fictivity and its symbolic conveyance comes eventually to "contaminate" his concept of scientific method in the ways we have just seen. Having begun with the conventionally positivist notion of scientizing art, he ends by, in effect, aestheticizing science, and, in the process, redefining the positivist enterprise at its methodological core.

De Man and deconstructionists in general would not consider that the Lewes I have described—any more than the neo-Kantians they are, in effect, displacing as arbiters of contemporary literary theory—has finally liberated himself from the ideology of the symbol. They would argue that Lewes, having begun by "deconstructing" a Romantic ideology of the symbol in favor of a positivist "metaphysic" of organic presence, has, after all, ended by reconstructing the ideology of the symbol in its new Kantian or "immanent" form. The symbol thus redefined no longer refers to a transcendent spiritual presence, but it is still a centered structure, whose origin is the creative human intelligence and whose object, however distant, is still correspondence to the structure of the world.

Yet do we not see in Lewes' final move toward the aestheticization of the sacred category of science itself a gesture that looks toward our distinctly postmodernist concerns? The ultimate effect of the Derridean assault on the ideology of the symbol has been, as Geoffrey Hartman has suggested, the "foregrounding of the artistic as the philosophical, or the birth of philosophy out of the spirit of art."[41] It would be impertinent of me to cast Lewes in the role of protodeconstructionist. He is still firmly in the positivist camp. Yet in his late discovery of the spirit of art *in* science, if not at its origin, he has embarked on a path which, if pursued, might well lead to such "deconstructive" approaches to this heartland of rationality and objectivity as those offered in our own time by Paul Feyerabend, Thomas Kuhn, W. V. Quine, and others. The principal controversy among modern philosophers of sciences, as Richard Rorty has said, is "about whether science, as the discovery of what is really out there in the world, differs in its patterns of argumentation from discourses for which the notion of 'correspondence to reality' seems less apposite (e.g., . . . literary criticism)."[42] Lewes at his most aesthetic would never abandon science to the "conceptual relativism" that Rorty is alluding to. Yet, at the same time, he could not help probing that persistent discontinuity between world and word, or, as he called it, "life and mind," which has issued in our "postempiricist" skepticism over whether science, any more than art, can ever deliver on its promise to bring the two realms together, to make mind the mirror of life.

Notes

1. Ernst Cassirer, *An Essay on Man: An Introduction to a Philosophy of Human Culture* (New Haven: Yale University Press, 1944), p. 170.

2. Jonathan Culler, *On Deconstruction: Theory and Criticism after Structuralism* (Ithaca: Cornell University Press, 1982), p. 178.

3. Cited by Culler, *On Deconstruction,* p. 23.

4. There are any number of definitions of positivism. The most comprehensive is that developed by Leszek Kolakowski in his historical survey *The Alienation of Reason: A History of Positivist Thought,* trans. N. Guterman (Garden City: Doubleday, 1968). See especially chapter 1. Like Kolakowski I do not restrict "positivism" to its Victorian connotation of the philosophy developed by Comte.

5. The phrase I borrow from Christopher Norris' *The Deconstructive Turn: Essays in the Rhetoric of Philosophy* (London and New York: Methuen, 1983), which does much to show us how pervasive a move deconstruction is in modern thought.

6. Paul de Man, "Sign and Symbol in Hegel's Aesthetics," *Critical Inquiry* 8 (1982): 763. For a more general discussion of Romantic metaphysics as ideology, see Jerome J. McGann's *The Romantic Ideology: A Critical Investigation* (Chicago: University of Chicago Press, 1983).

7. Jacques Derrida, *Margins of Philosophy,* trans. Alan Bass (Chicago: University of Chicago Press, 1982), pp. 20, 11.

8. G. W. F. Hegel, *Aesthetics: Lectures on Fine Arts,* trans. T. M. Knox (Oxford: Clarendon Press, 1975), 1: 7-8, 19, 164.

9. George Lewes, "Hegel's Aesthetics," *British and Foreign Review* 13 (1842): 1-49.

10. G. H. Lewes, *A Biographical History of Philosophy* (London: Routledge and Sons, 1846), p. 650.

11. G. H. Lewes, *The History of Philosophy from Thales to Comte* (London: Longmans, Green, 1871), 2: 689-98.

12. From the title of one of Lewes' earliest critical essays, "The Errors and Abuses of English Criticism," *Westminster Review* 38 (1842): 466-86. Here he first refers to the "truly deplorable condition" of contemporary English criticism. As becomes clear in subsequent essays, Lewes considers the "romantic spirit" responsible for this situation and, in particular, Coleridge's importation (and, as Lewes was perhaps the first to note publicly, plagiarism) of German sources. See especially, "August William Schlegel," *Foreign Quarterly Review* 32 (1843): 160-81; "Shakespeare and His Editors," *Westminster Review* 43 (1845): 40-77.

13. G. H. Lewes, "Shakespeare's Critics: English and Foreign," *Edinburgh Review* 90 (1849). This is, one notes, an early statement of an aesthetic project which Lewes will at last accomplish some twenty-five years later in *The Principles of Success in Literature* (see Section 4 below).

14. G. H. Lewes, *The Life of Goethe,* 3d ed. (London; Smith Elder, 1875), pp. 408-10, 447-48.

15. Auguste Comte, *Système de politique positive, ou traité de sociologie instituant la religion de l'humanité* (Paris: Mathias, 1851-54), 2: 382. Cited by Lewes in *Problems of Life and Mind* (London: Trubner, 1874-79), 1st ser., 1: 195.

16. Rudolf Carnap, "The Elimination of Metaphysics through Logical Analysis of Language," in A. J. Ayer, ed., *Logical Positivism* (New York, 1959), pp. 60-61.

17. G. H. Lewes, "Balzac and George Sand," *Foreign Quarterly Review* 33 (1844): 269, 284-85.

18. G. H. Lewes, "Julia von Krudener, as Coquette and Mystic," *Westminster Review* 57 (1852): 162-64. George Eliot, one notes, follows Lewes closely in the priority she gives to subrational motivation; see my "'Brother Jacob': Fables and the Physiology of Common Life," *Philological Quarterly* 59 (1985): 17-35.

19. Herbert Marcuse, *Reason and Revolution: Hegel and the Rise of Social Theory* (Atlantic Highlands, N.J.: Humanities Press, 1983), pp. 323-30.

20. G. H. Lewes, *Comte's Philosophy of the Sciences: Being an Exposition of the Principles of the "Cours de Philosophie Positive" of Auguste Comte* (London: George Bell, 1875), section 21, "Psy-

chology: A New Cerebral Theory." Lewes' primary source in Comte is the *Politique positive* [Système de politique positive], vol. 1, "Introduction fondamentale," chap. 3.

21. Notably by Frederick Gregory, *Scientific Materialism in Nineteenth-Century Germany* (Dordrecht: Reidel, 1977); John T. Mertz, *A History of European Thought in the Nineteenth Century* (Edinburgh: Blackwood, 1928), Vol. 2; and Robert M. Young, *Mind, Brain, and Adaptation in the Nineteenth Century: Cerebral Localization and Its Biological Context from Gall to Ferrier* (Oxford: Clarendon, 1970).

22. G. H. Lewes, *The Physiology of Common Life* (Edinburgh: Blackwood, 1859-60); see especially chap. 8.

23. Beginning with *Comte's Philosophy of the Sciences,* pp. 217-24. See also note 32 below.

24. G. H. Lewes, "Realism in Art: Recent German Fiction," *Westminster Review* 70 (1858): 493-95.

25. G. H. Lewes, *The Principles of Success in Literature* (Westmead: Gregg International Publishers, 1969), pp. 40-41; these essays were first published in the *Fortnightly Review*, May-November 1865. Lewes' preoccupation with "types" and their ontological status begins with his close study of Goethe in the early 1850s. See, e.g., "Goethe as a Man of Science," *Westminster Review* 52 (1852): 497, and the further development of the thought in that essay in the later *Life of Goethe,* especially book 5, chapter 9, "The Poet as a Man of Science."

26. Melvin Konner, *The Tangled Wing: Biological Constraints on the Human Spirit* (New York: Harper Colophon Books, 1983), p. 61.

27. Goethe, of course, is himself reacting against the excesses of contemporary Romanticism. Lewes' scientific aesthetic shares with Matthew Arnold's neoclassicist one a view of Goethe as the poet for the modern, post-Romantic era.

28. Cited by Ernst Mayr, *The Growth of Biological Thought: Diversity, Evolution, and Inheritance* (Cambridge, Mass.: Harvard University Press, 1982), p. 455.

29. J. W. Goethe, *Werke,* ed. E. Beutler (Zurich: Artemis, 1952), 17: 233. The translation is E. S. Russell's from *Form and Function: A Contribution to the History of Animal Morphology* (Chicago: University of Chicago Press, 1982), p. 46.

30. See Mayr's and Russell's discussions of Goethe in the works cited above. For more detailed treatments see Heinrich Henel, "Type and Proto-

Phenomenon in Goethe's Science," *PMLA* 71 (1956): 652-68, and H. B. Nisbet, "Herder, Goethe, and the Natural 'Type,'" *Publications of the English Goethe Society* 37 (1966-67): 82-119.

31. The fullest development of Lewes' concept of the type of "germinal matter" and the relation of that type to evolution (not discussed in *Physiology* [*The Physiology of Common Life*]) is in *The Physiological Basis of Mind* (London: Trubner, 1877; this is the Second Series of *Problems of Life and Mind*), "Problem I: The Nature of Life," pp. 3-136.

32. The enterprise Lewes is engaged upon represents an important strain of Victorian efforts to discover a biological basis for, essentially, Christian ethics. See Ashley Montague, *Darwin: Competition and Cooperation* (New York: Henry Schuman, 1952) for a brief (and impressionistic) survey of the movement.

33. The earliest mention I find of Helmholtz in Lewes' work is in the 1855 *Life of Goethe* (p. 141) where he quotes him on Goethe's scientific method. Given Lewes' growing interest in physiology in the late 1850s, it is likely he would have looked into Helmholtz's best-known work, *Handbuch der physiologischen Optik,* which began coming out in 1856. In any case, he admired Helmholtz's work enough to make a special effort to visit him on his German trip of 1868 (*Journal* 12 [Beinecke Library], 10 January 1868) and was reading him regularly in 1869 while working on what was to become *Problems* [*Problems of Life and Mind*] ("Diaries" [Beinecke Library], January-February 1869).

34. Hermann von Helmholtz, *Treatise on Physiological Optics,* trans. from third German ed. by J. P. C. Southall (New York: Dover Publications, 1962), 3: 1.

35. Ernst Cassirer, *The Problem of Knowledge: Philosophy, Science, and History since Hegel,* trans. W. H. Woglom and C. W. Hendel (New Haven: Yale University Press, 1950), p. 4.

36. G. E. Moore, *Principia Ethica* (Cambridge, Eng.: Cambridge University Press, 1903), chap. 2. See also W. D. Hudson, *Modern Moral Philosophy* (Garden City: Doubleday, 1970), chap. 3, part 1, "Moore and the Rejection of Ethical Naturalism."

37. Both the Prolegomena to the 1867 edition of *History of Philosophy* and the chapter on Kant evidence a much more comprehensive grasp of Kant and his commentators than one finds in the 1857 edition.

38. Hermann von Helmholtz, "The Relation of the Natural Sciences to Science in General" (1862),

trans. H. W. Eve, *Selected Writings of Hermann von Helmholtz,* ed. Russell Kahl (Middletown, Conn.: Wesleyan University Press, 1971), pp. 131-32. Helmholtz, in turn, is inspired, as Lewes well knows, by Goethe's "aesthetic" approach to scientific method; see "The Scientific Researches of Goethe" (1853), trans. H. W. Eve, *ibid.,* pp. 64-69, and Lewes' comments on Helmholtz on Goethe in *Life of Goethe* (1875), p. 351.

39. Frederick Suppe, introduction, in Suppe, ed., *The Structure of Scientific Theories* (Urbana: University of Illinois Press, 1974), pp. 8-9.

40. William James, *The Will to Believe and Other Essays in Popular Philosophy* (New York: Longmans Green, 1897), p. 24.

41. Geoffrey Hartman, *Saving the Text: Literature/Derrida/Philosophy* (Baltimore: Johns Hopkins University Press, 1981), p. 72.

42. Richard Rorty, *Philosophy and the Mirror of Nature* (Princeton: Princeton University Press, 1979), p. 332. The postempiricist movement in science against positivist presuppositions about the nature of truth is discussed in detail by Frederick Suppe, Introduction to *Structure of Scientific Theories,* pp. 119-90. I refer to this movement as "deconstructionist" only with the qualification indicated by the quotation marks. The movement, in fact, preceded and developed independently of the rise of Derrida and continental deconstructionism.

Lynn M. Voskuil (essay date summer 1995)

SOURCE: Voskuil, Lynn M. "Acting Naturally: Brontë, Lewes, and the Problem of Gender Performance." *ELH* 62, no. 2 (summer 1995): 409-42.

[*In the following excerpt, Voskuil analyzes Lewes's theory of "natural acting" in relation to his realist theories, noting his pseudonym, "Vivian," and his reviews of the actress Rachel.*]

I

During the summer of 1851, Charlotte Brontë visited London and saw Rachel Felix, the famous French actress, perform in several plays. "Thackeray's lectures and Rachel's acting," she wrote to Elizabeth Gaskell, "are the two things in this great Babylon which have stirred and interested me most—simply because in them I found most of what was genuine whether for good or evil. . . ."[1] Brontë's adjective, "genuine," affiliates her assessment of Rachel with a mid-century theatrical discourse that increasingly represented the stage and the most favored acting styles as "natural." Although it

turns up in many texts and contexts, George Henry Lewes, in his role as drama critic, articulated principles of "natural acting" that influentially framed the discourse for both its onstage and offstage versions.[2] When he too saw Rachel on stage in 1851, Lewes, echoing Brontë, accordingly pronounced the actress "exquisitely natural" and set her up as a positive exemplar for what he perceived to be a theater in decline.[3]

Brontë's and Lewes's assessments register a paradoxical cultural impulse that led them both to specify a controversial actress as the embodiment of naturalness. Recent studies of theatricality have underscored its potential to upset traditional gender categories; in particular, such studies have recognized women's capacities to elude naturalized sexual and gender roles in the theatre and to construct their own identities on stage.[4] While these studies have influenced my arguments, I also suggest that the structure of mid-Victorian theatricality accommodated an essentialist version of gendered identity. In the context of the 1850s, moreover, a careful assessment of some such conceptions of identity must modify what we usually see as the restrictive tendencies of essentialism. Jonathan Dollimore has recently argued for the transgressive potential of certain appropriations of dominant ideologies, even essentialist ones, at specific historical moments.[5] My readings of Lewes and Brontë support Dollimore's point: while they both viewed Rachel as essentially "natural," they surveyed her from markedly different gendered positions within Victorian culture. Their affiliated constructions of theatricality thus instantiate nature in the service of divergent cultural goals.

The discourse of natural acting exhibits the prominent features of a high culture conception of Victorian theatricality. This conception distinguished "genuine" or "natural" essence from a material and artificial medium of performance, a distinction that speaks to our current theoretical debates about identity. In postmodern critiques of the coherent humanist subject, theatricality often functions to disrupt conceptions of an originary self and essential identity that ostensibly exist apart from the discourses and practices of specific cultures. Delineating this disruptive theatricality is a project integral to many feminist dismantlings of monolithic, ahistorical conceptions of "the Feminine." These welcome efforts at cultural concreteness, however, cannot fully explain the Victorians' yoking of theatricality and gender, for their theatricality prefigured but was not a prototype of the postmodern version. Unlike postmodernists, many Victorians believed in a theatricality that sometimes revealed and sometimes obscured a timeless, innate self; in this view, an authentic core identity is separated from an external, performing, artificial self.[6] If the portents of postmodern disintegration lurk in the fissures of this divided self, the binary construction nonetheless permitted the Victorians to privilege the "authentic core" in an effort to maintain what they saw as the integrity of a coherent identity.

As Lewes's assessment of Rachel suggests, adherents of natural acting aimed to save the stage from what many mid-century observers saw as the excesses of its own artifice, what playgoer Henry Morley called its "flashy stage-effects."[7] Natural actors avoided such excesses by acknowledging and exploiting the divide between essence and performance. In his 1859 biography of Charles Kean, for example, John William Cole uses the term "natural acting" to describe a joint performance of Charles and his father Edmund Kean. When the spectators responded to the "last pathetic interview" with "prolonged peals of approbation," the biographer approvingly reports that Edmund whispered to his son, "'Charley, we are doing the trick.'" Quoting Talma to gloss the anecdote, Cole explains that to turn the "trick" of acting, the player must "study from himself" and "produce nature."[8] In Cole's example, the natural actor wields the material tools of performance—gestures, props, declamation, scenery, bodies—with just the right mixture and amount of physical cues to materialize a character's essence. Natural actors, that is, represent rather than reveal nature.

But when players relied too heavily on these performative tools, some critics argued, they impaired not only the aesthetics of the performance but also, more critically, the spectators' "real" emotional and imaginative capacities. Critic W. B. Donne, paralleling what he saw as the over-refined society of his age to its over-materialized stage, lamented the loss of "strong and natural emotions" and the "lack of imagination in the spectators." Compared to their contemporaries in the audience, he complained, playgoers of a previous age, however "far astray [they] may have gone in the principles of good taste . . . at least brought to the theatre an antecedent faith and earnestness from which we now shrink. . . ."[9] Like Cole, Donne testifies to an emotive core distinct from its theatrical embodiment, a distinction that, in his mind, mattered decisively for the world beyond the stage. In this cultural context, what Brontë described as Rachel's "genuine" performance was more than high praise for her talent. While Brontë's letters finally align Thackeray with "good" and the actress with "evil," she and Lewes both believed that Rachel had dissolved the theatrical false fronts which could block the spectators' view of the "genuine" or "natural" in life as well as in the theatre. Natural acting on stage is thus linked to natural feeling offstage, a type of authenticity Victorians both believed in and prescribed.

Such links were crucial for both Brontë and Lewes. One of the central appeals of natural acting was its offstage relevance, what was seen as its capacity to reach and train the emotions of the audience. It was in the construction of these onstage/offstage links that Brontë and Lewes, to some degree, parted ways. For Lewes, the natural actor directed the spectator's gaze to an ideal, universal Nature that authenticated not only the impersonations of professional players but also the everyday roles of ordinary people. For Brontë, in contrast, the natural player refocused the audience's view on the essential, interiorized, individual subject. Both constructed within the essence/performance dichotomy of Victorian theatricality, these affiliated conceptions of subjectivity nonetheless display competing, gendered visions of the "natural" actress and feminine identity. Brontë's insistence on individual female experience counters the naturalizing tendency of Lewes's aesthetic, the tendency to anchor feminine identity to universal ideals detached from the actual conditions of women's ordinary lives. Such divergent visions open to our view the multiple and varied uses of essentialism at specific historical moments, an understanding that we must cultivate if we are to render women's experience in the mid-Victorian period with accuracy and richness.

II

During the early 1850s, as theater critic for *The Leader* and in the persona of "Vivian," G. H. Lewes was formulating a sophisticated theory of natural acting that was to help cement the gender categories that middle-class Victorian culture was increasingly understanding as "natural." In his *Leader* columns, Lewes had begun to define "natural acting" in opposition to what he called "conventional acting." Both concepts emerge from Lewes's idealist tendencies. "The Drama, as an Art," he wrote, "is the material representation of an ideal conception. It places before our eyes the progress and culmination of some passion, the story of some ideal life" (*L* [*Leader*], 22 February 1851, 181). Conventions allowed actors to materialize that ideal life. By "convention," Lewes meant the means of theatrical representation: the actor's literal embodiment of an "ideal conception" in facial expression, gesture, intonation and declamation; and the material extension of the actor's representation in costumes, staging, and props. An 1851 review shows how Lewes understood conventions as a medium for expressing emotion: "She drew the back of her hand across her forehead, and, with drooping eyes and faltering voice, expressed that joy itself was a sort of pain in its intensity—which we all know to be the effect of sudden joy" (*L*, 21 June 1851, 589).[10] Without conventions, there could be no theater, a point Lewes frequently celebrated in his insistence that drama was subject to "Representative Conditions" (*L*, 22 February 1851, 182). In Lewes's aesthetic, commonly understood conventions permitted both the player's art and the spectator's response: players materialized ideal nature in the gestural language that audiences commonly comprehended; spectators thus "know" that "drooping eyes and faltering voice" are "the effect of sudden joy."

Merely conventional actors, however, compromised the aims of art. Such players, he alleged, emphasized the theater at the expense of true art. They scorned drama's grounding in the ideal, preferring to accent the means of theatrical representation over the ideal conceptions those means bodied forth. The result was a "stagey" acting style that was, in the terms of Lewes's dialectic, conventional or theatrical rather than natural or dramatic.[11] Lewes's notion of a "stagey" theatricalism reveals his belief in an authentic subjectivity that is "natural" to the extent that it can be distinguished from representational conventions, whether on stage or off. One of his many comparisons between French and English acting underscores the opposition: "If our [English] actors wish to see the superiority of truth and nature over their conventional *stagey* modes of representation they should study Nathalie, Regnier, and Lafont" (*L,* 11 May 1850, 162). Lewes's point is not that French and English players manipulate culturally disparate theatrical conventions, but that French players, unlike the English, use those conventions to reveal ideal "truth and nature."

Unlike merely conventional acting, then, natural acting pointed not to its own mode but to the "ideal conception" materialized by that mode. Of course Lewes could not downplay the theatrical medium too much if he meant to avoid the pitfalls of idiosyncratic acting—acting whose reach for the ideal fails to exceed the grasp of the player's own consciousness. Like other theories of acting, Lewes's notion of natural acting necessarily relied on theatrical conventions as the means of representation. However, natural acting, he maintained, emphasizes neither the player's tools nor the player's personality: "'To represent a character naturally' means to represent it according to *its* nature, not according to your own" (*L,* 21 June 1851, 589). Here, "nature" seems to mean not an ideal realm but the character's "inner nature"; rather than representing that inner nature as an imagined one, a merely conventional actor would idiosyncratically represent his own. Instead of acting in a self-consciously theatrical way to highlight the distinction between idiosyncratic reality and the ideal, a natural actor strives for a seamless impersonation that obscures the line between his own personality and the character he represents. The natural actor, Lewes noted, "selects a Mask more or less *typical* of the character to be represented; and having selected it, does not once let it fall" (*L,* 21 June 1851, 589; emphasis added). Such type acting, Lewes believed, would best embody the ideal, natural truths on which he founded the dramatic arts.[12]

Lewes's emphasis on impersonating the typical traits of a character points to the central feature of his conception of "nature." For Lewes, nature, as represented on stage, signifies not the "real" world but the ideal. To illustrate this point, Lewes told the story of a Roman actor who, rather than simulate a pig's squeal, brought a live pig on stage. Lewes humorously objected to this ploy in his fabricated response to the player: "Your pig is truly a pig, and the squeak thereof is real; but although a real pig, it is not a Representative Pig . . . it is not a type,—it is not ideal,—it does not give articulate expression to the abstract possibilities of pork! On the stage I require Pig,—not *this* pig or *that* pig, but Pig *par excellence,*—Abstract Pig" (*L,* 4 June 1853, 549). As Lewes's theory plays itself out here, the actor acts conventionally but not naturally when he stages the real thing, for nature resides not in the actual example but in the ideal world represented by the platonic type. In this case, the simulated pig is a convention the player would use to embody the ideal Pig naturally; but the actual, live pig is a mere convention that cannot transcend its own materiality.

Lewes meant his tongue-in-cheek story to have a serious point. Identity in his aesthetic is not merely idiosyncratic or individualistic but rather is grounded in an authentic, ideal, abstract human nature that is uniform for all cultures and histories. As represented on stage, such universal identity must rely on conventions and types that all spectators can recognize and apply to their present-day reality. Using such conventions, the natural actor can thus embody representations that any human in any time or place can comprehend and enjoy. This fundamental notion is evinced in a review of one of Bouffé's performances: "Bouffé is *natural* in the highest sense; he represents the nature of the character; the 'stuff' of human nature is plastic in his hands, and out of it he carves images which all the world can recognize as true" (*L,* 9 August 1851, 758). Because Bouffé's comic representation is derived from an ideal world and is hence independent of culture and history, Lewes believes, "all the world can recognize it as true."

As his review of Bouffé demonstrates, the spectator as well as the actor is central to Lewes's dialectic. What we could call "natural viewing," in the terms of his theory, thus becomes as important as natural acting to understand the significance of his performance theory for mid-Victorian conceptions of gender and identity. Lewes's spectatorial principles seemingly ensue from his ideal of a gradually developing collaborative endeavor between and among players and their audience: spectators do not experience a shock of recognition but participate in an unfolding visual consensus. Theoretically, the goal of natural acting—that is, in Lewes's terms, of authentic dramatic art—is "to elevate the spectator's soul up to the poet's region—to arrest the wandering attention and fix it on great ideas" (*L,* 28 June 1851, 613). By impersonating the ideal type, the natural player ostensibly shifts the spectator's gaze from the staged representation to the ideal realm materialized by the player. Compliant and open to art's influence, Lewes's imaginary playgoers are led by natural actors to see and thus identify both emotionally and intellectually with the ideal types such players represent.

The partnership of feeling and judgment is key, for the "common heart of sympathy" (*L*, 9 August 1851, 758) enables authentic community in the theater while transcedent "majestic truths" (*L*, 28 June 1851, 613) give drama its moral force. As Lewes observed, continuing his review of Bouffé, "The comedy expands your heart with laughter, at which you are not afterward ashamed, for judgment approves what instinct caught at . . ." (*L*, 9 August 1851, 758). In Lewes's performance theory, nature and convention, the ideal and the real, feeling and judgment, should thus constantly balance each other in a delicate dialectic, each extreme moderating the other's excesses to register and regulate the spectators' aesthetic response.

Lewes theorized a reflective, even spiritualized audience, spectators who would ruminate on Art's "majestic truths" (*L*, 28 June 1851, 613) in partnership with natural players. As both Joseph Roach and John Stokes have noted, such joint sympathetic identification and absorption were hallmarks of Lewes's performance theory.[13] But although he carefully cultivated the balance of his theoretical dialectic, it was disturbed when actual spectators voiced their preferences for what he saw as conventional theater. Faced with the actual tastes of the theater-going public, Lewes sometimes lost sight of his central premise: that drama is a representational art. In some reviews, "typical" thus seems to mean not "ideal" but the range of "real" identities earthbound spectators might recognize from their actual experience. Practically speaking, the meaning of "natural" then changed as well, signifying not so much "ideal" as "familiar" or "actual." In such cases, Lewes idealizes real-life middle-class roles as "natural" and censures uncooperative spectators for preferring melodrama, burlesque, farce—the conventional theatre that, in Lewes's eyes, promoted unnatural acting.

Lewes's tendency to conflate his conceptions of real and ideal is clear from a review of a Lyceum performance: "Vestris and Charles Mathews were *natural*—nothing more, nothing less. They were," he observed, "a lady and gentleman such as we meet with in drawing-rooms, graceful, quiet, well-bred, perfectly dressed, perfectly oblivious of the footlights" (*L*, 7 December 1850, 882). In this case, the natural players represent not platonic types that will elevate the spectator to spiritual realms but familiar actual types, here identified by class, that the spectator might meet on the street or invite to his home. The Lyceum review underscores these theoretical shifts, Lewes now upholding his standard of natural acting as indistinguishable from nonacting: "Oh! what a contrast between the natural manner of these two [Vestris and Mathews] and the stage manner and stage life of all the rest! Yet the others *played* well

too. . . . But the contrast was between sunshine and the footlights—the ruddy cheek and rouged cheek—the grace of a graceful woman and that of an opera dancer" (*L*, 7 December 1850, 882). With this revised notion of natural acting, Lewes blames the public for preferring the theatrical over the actual, the opera dancer over the graceful woman, so equating authenticity with the norms of middle-class life. "I insist upon this point, for the public, the critics, and the actors may here read a valuable lesson as to what constitutes acting: a thing at present they seem to have the wildest notions of, and the ignorance of the public reacts upon the performer, forcing him often to disobey his own conceptions to gain their ignorant applause" (*L*, 7 December 1850, 882). Sometimes, in similar departures from his theoretical principles, Lewes recognized the actual, commercial role of the spectator in shaping theatrical tastes. Then, with other culture critics, he bemoaned the "good, stolid, stupid public": "they swagger about Shakspeare [*sic*] . . . but in their heart of hearts they like a Melodrama" (*L*, 22 February 1851, 182). In such instances, the measured spectatorial consensus he cultivated seems more like a prescriptive policy of public taste, a policy that censures certain kinds of actual responses and the theater that elicits them.

Such prescription is visible in the particular version of Victorian theatricality that infuses Lewes's theory of natural acting. In *Melodramatic Tactics*, Elaine Hadley articulates a notion of subjectivity that characterized large segments of eighteenth-century culture, a subjectivity that was perceived as publicly constituted in the sympathetic, social exchange of fellow-feeling and did not recognize a divide between inner essence and outer performance.[14] While Lewes's theories of type acting, spectatorial consensus, and sympathetic recognition may seem to derive from those older constructions of identity, their abstraction from actual social exchange in fact places them firmly within mid-Victorian notions of theatricality. By constructing and endorsing authenticity as an ideal, universal category prior to and distinct from the performative process, Lewes's concept of natural acting cannot accommodate either what he deemed to be idiosyncratic acting or idiosyncratic response. Because such idiosyncrasies are not ideal (in his terms, "natural"), they are necessarily seen as conventional—and hence suspect, along with the spectators who applaud them.

Lewes's theory thus has no place for actual social exchange, a central contradiction that becomes clearer as we examine the roles "natural actresses" were expected to fill. Lewes's ideal spectator—spiritualized, receptive, sometimes even passive—exhibits the traits of idealized Victorian femininity. Indeed, when constructed by middle-class ideologies, women also seem the ideal Lewesian natural player: as guardians of the realms of private feeling (religion, the home), they "naturally" in-fuse their domestic roles with the requisite Lewesian ideal "truth." Without such "genuine" feeling, however, even the most "natural" actress could quickly become "unnatural." Precisely because actresses act—because, ostensibly unlike housewives, they pretend and display themselves in public—the promise of nature could, for many observers, be transformed into the threat of artifice. In theatrical texts, such actresses are often portrayed as prostitutes—that is, as women falsely playing at love, bereft of authentic feeling. Such theatrical models helped constitute mid-Victorian conceptions of female inauthenticity beyond the actual stage, as revealed in some important texts on prostitution. In these texts, prostitutes are represented in the terms of Victorian theatricality, as actresses who are threateningly conventional in Lewes's sense. In each case, a critical part of the focus is on anxious spectator-clients whose viewing habits are implicated in the "unnatural" acting of such prostituted players.

III

Lewes's anxiety over his own spectatorial performances is registered in the character of "Vivian," his persona in the *Leader* columns and his representation of a "real" spectator. While his theorized ideal was a spiritual, passive spectator, he personified in Vivian a witty, always tasteful, carefree and womanizing bachelor—a personification that destabilized the careful balance of his theories. Resolutely unspiritual, Vivian noticed women's bodies and commented on their clothes, both onstage and off; unlike the properly reflective spectator, he was immediately affected by the actress's physical presence rather than the represented character. The Lewes/Vivian doubling replicates the structure of the divided theatrical identity. Yet, as the performative self, Vivian materialized not ideal nature but Lewes's own physical responses to drama, responses that, in Lewes's mind, threatened not just the stage but the social and moral order as well. Vivian thus embodies the contradictions at the heart of Lewes's performance theory.

The blend of Vivian and Lewes is most discordant in their reviews of actresses. In 1854 Vivian/Lewes applauded a new, young actress not for her dramatic talent but exclusively for her appearance, carriage, and manners: "Miss Talbot . . . is tall, with a figure of voluptuous grace, with adorable arms and wrists, blonde hair, brilliant teeth, and fair complexion. Her manner was natural, quite unstagy [*sic*] . . ." (*L*, 11 March 1854, 235). Vivian's praise focuses unabashedly on her body, a body that conforms to the conventions of Victorian feminine beauty. In theory, if Miss Talbot is a good natural actress, he should not notice her body, the "commonplace features" (*L*, 21 June 1851, 589) of the real person behind the represented character. As a good natural actress, she should be representing a type whose source lies in the ideal, poetic realm. Instead, her "type"

is portrayed as very "real": sensual, attractive, and very conventionally Victorian. The emphasis on the actress's actual body tempers Lewes's idealism, but the theoretical weightiness of that idealism serves in turn to authorize the culturally conditioned terms of Miss Talbot's appearance and moralize her conventional womanly charms. Unlike the Roman actor's actual pig but like Vestris' and Mathews' performance, the actual woman is here very "natural" in Lewes's eyes: in her "blonde hair . . . and fair complexion," he sees ideal Woman.[15]

The purpose of my critique, of course, is not to dispute the "actual" appeal of Miss Talbot's stage presence. Instead, I am interested in revealing the cultural moorings of that appeal and in analyzing the representational strategies by which the identities of such actresses were naturalized and extended to women offstage. I also aim to uncover the cultural anxiety that made Miss Talbot's spectators moralize their very bodily attraction to her performances. Though Lewes often used Vivian's voice to muffle his own physical responses, he was at least implicitly aware that such responses rocked the ideal foundations of the sympathetic spectatorial community he theorized. His final assessment of Miss Talbot underscores his uneasiness. Lewes had watched the actress in a full-length play, but still followed the Vivian-like notes on her appearance by asserting that he had not yet seen enough to comment convincingly on her acting ability: "I can't say whether she has any genius for acting . . ." (*L*, 11 March 1854, 235). That claim did not stop him, however, from justifying his praise by offering the actress as an antidote to what had become a widely lamented malaise: the decline of the Victorian theater. "At present," Lewes noted, "it is enough for me to record the appearance of a beautiful woman, who, if she never takes one step forward as an actress, will still be valuable in the ladylike characters. Is not that something? In the present state of theatricals, is it not a great deal?" (*L*, 11 March 1854, 235). This defense only widens the fault in his theoretical fortress. Lewes here attempts to shore up a declining Victorian stage on the very grounds he condemns in other places. Like the "good, stolid, stupid public," Lewes/Vivian watches Miss Talbot to have his senses gratified rather than his judgment improved.

Just as Lewes's categories of natural and conventional, ideal and real, were disordered in his assessment of Miss Talbot, so were they scrambled in his evaluations of cross-dressed actresses. In various reviews, he criticizes or condones cross-dressing for conflicting reasons. In a review of a popular actress playing a young officer, for instance, he argues that her male impersonation compromises the "reality" of the play's situation: "It necessarily destroys the reality of the scene in this most pathetically real of dramas, and it is, on that account, an inexcusable error in taste." Such "unreal" impersonations, he asserts, can only be sustained in plays that do not purport to refer to reality: "It may be all very well for ladies to appear in trousers in farces; but in such a play as [this], this sort of masquerade, however admirably it may be sustained, is utterly out of place" (*L*, 8 July 1854, 645). Here, the actress is "unreal" not by virtue of an unnatural impersonation but by virtue of her staged reversal of gender categories. Elsewhere, Lewes condones cross-dressing if it makes the woman behind the actress more attractive and titillating: "It is seldom an agreeable sight, that of a woman dressed up as a man, but when a woman does an ungraceful thing we insist upon her doing it gracefully; the only excuse for donning our attire is that she become more piquante in it" (*L*, 10 May 1851, 447; see also *L*, 21 February 1852, 185). If cross-dressing confirms conventional gender categories, it thus counts as natural.

If Miss Talbot and cross-dressed actresses could be mostly contained by Lewes's theories, Rachel, in some of her staged incarnations, could not. In his reviews of her 1850 and 1851 performances, Lewes commended Rachel for being "exquisitely natural" (*L*, 21 June 1851, 589) in her interpretations of Racine and Corneille. This assessment seems to reflect his theory of ideal performance art, but Rachel's "exhibition of mental agony" provoked in Lewes not a corresponding ideal response but a palpably physical one: he described both Rachel's performances and his own response in erotically charged terms. He wrote that as Phèdre, Rachel was "wasting away with the fire that consumed her, standing on the verge of the grave, her face pallid, her eyes hot . . ." (*L*, 6 July 1850, 355). In *Polyeucte,* he wrote, Rachel generated a stronger reaction, pleasing the audience even with Corneille's "lawyer-like poetry" (*L*, 13 July 1850, 378). Again, Lewes's account is sexually charged. The final scene "with its mounting exultation and radiant glory, her face lighted up with a fervour which was irresistible, her whole frame convulsed with fanaticism, produced such an effect upon the audience as we have seldom witnessed . . ." (*L*, 13 July 1850, 378). In response to Rachel's Phèdre, Lewes's "nerves were quivering with excitement almost insupportable" (*L*, 6 July 1850, 355).

In the language of Victorian criticism, the "quivering nerves" Rachel stimulated were the expected if unhealthy response to art that was "sensational," a term that a decade later would be applied to the fiction of Mary Elizabeth Braddon, Wilkie Collins, and other popular novelists in the cultural debate over "sensationalism." In the 1850s, Lewes anticipated that debate, roundly condemning the kind of art that could evoke such "sensational" responses. He himself, he testified, preferred the "austere simplicity of Racine, trusting more to lovely verses than to startling surprises, caring more for the *emotions* of his audience than for their *sensations* . . ." (*L*, 12 July 1851, 662). If the "insurgent senses" (*L*, 22 February 1851, 181), the feelings of

the body, came to replace the feeling of the heart, the outcome would indeed be serious. For Lewes, such a reversal heralded no less than the end of the theater, even of art itself. He notes, "I see an omen of inevitable decay: decay not only of Art, which is one of the sacred influences; but decay even of the vulgar artifice that takes its place" (*L*, 22 February 1851, 182). To Lewes, the triumph of the sensational over the emotional, the conventional over the natural, was indeed the harbinger of cultural Doomsday.

By linking sensations to conventionality ("vulgar artifice"), Lewes replicated the movements of a mid-Victorian discourse of sexuality, a discourse that, like Lewes's own idealistic performance theory, postulated an authentic subjectivity whose inner essences were categorically distinct from its outer enactments. The outlines of this discourse are clearly apparent in mid-century discussions of sexuality, most notably of prostitution. The association of the theater and prostitution is, of course, a commonplace in Victorian critiques of the theater; our own criticism habitually underscores that relationship by noticing Victorian condemnations of women who displayed themselves for pay. The context of mid-century theatricality shows us clearly why Victorians judged prostitutes harshly by revealing just what the money signified to them: the absence of genuine feeling at the emotional core of a love relationship. In this concern, they echo the adherents of natural acting who censured the kind of "mere" performance that lacked an authentic essence.

William Acton, one of the most influential mid-century experts on prostitution, states this view clearly. A prostitute, Acton asserts, "is a woman who gives for money that which she ought to give only for love. . . ."[16] He emphasizes here mercenary self-display as a sign of unfeeling sexuality—what Lewes might call "mere sensation." His dissection of the prostitute's identity exposes her affinity to Lewes's conventional player: "She is a woman with half the woman gone, and that half containing all that elevates her nature, leaving her a mere instrument of impurity . . ." (*P*, 166). Unlike Lewes's version of the natural actor who "elevate[s] the spectator's soul up to the poet's region" (*L*, 28 June 1851, 613) and reaffirms the audience's authentic humanity, the prostitute violates the "threefold organization of body, mind, and spirit" (*P* [*Prostitution*], 162) by miring herself and her partner in mere materiality. And like Lewes's vulgar player of sensations, she is an "instrument" that cannot transcend the bodily medium, "impure" because she is separated from "elevated nature." With a telling stage allusion, Acton notes her perversion of "essential" womanhood: "The prostitute is a sad burlesque of woman . . ." (*P*, 166). In her ruin, she plays not the grand failure of tragedy but the mocked downfall of burlesque, the theatrical form that for many critics most blatantly staged its own inauthenticity.

In its parody of what many Victorians saw as the authentic emotions of romance, prostitution, they believed, also intensified "unnatural" cravings for "perverted" sex. In these convictions are further parallels between Lewes's notions of vulgar, conventional theatricality and unfeeling sexuality. Acton noted that "each act of gratification [with a prostitute] stimulates desire and necessitates fresh indulgence . . ." (*P,* 166). Elsewhere, he narrowed the limits of acceptable sexuality to exclude masturbation and what he saw as too frequent sexual intercourse; transgressing these limits had enormous consequences for human health. Immoderate sexual behavior revealed itself, he asserted, in a cumulative process of decay, resulting finally in nothing less than the total breakdown of the human body. "It appears that, at last," he wrote, "nothing but the morbid excitement produced by the baneful practice [of masturbation] can give any sexual gratification, and that the *natural* stimulus fails to cause any pleasure whatever. . . ."[17] Lewes, using language very similar to Acton's, similarly chronicles the fate of the body public if unhealthy appetites are incontinently indulged by conventional, material theater.

> Whoever knows anything of the human organization knows that the more you excite the public by *sensuous* stimulants the more you destroy the palate and pervert its taste. The four hours of tumult and surprise on Monday night will render more tumult and more surprise necessary for the next piece; and so on till the whole stock is exhausted, and the fate of the bankrupt *Théâtre Historique* be universal. By substituting the material for the moral such is always the result.
>
> (*L,* 22 February 1851, 182)

Like the desires of women and men who masturbate or have sex too often, the appetites of recent theatergoers have been unnaturally whetted. Unless stimulated at ever higher and more unnatural pitches, Lewes believed, they would no longer be satisfied and even conventional theatre would finally cease to exist. In both the sexual and theatrical discourses, the body, whether individual or corporate, is maintained by a wholesomely moderate indulgence in emotion and none whatever in "sensations." With its parallels to Victorian discussions of unfeeling sexuality, Lewes's anxious history of potential decay in the theater betrays his concern not only over the vision of Woman engendered on stage but also for spectators who are unnaturally partnered to her in their constant clamoring for more theatric sensations.

Lewes's performance theory, especially his principles of sympathetic and authentic emotional exchange between natural players and their spectators, was most forcibly challenged by his own performance anxiety during Rachel's 1851 dual portrayal of the queen and the courtesan in Jules Lacroix and Auguste Maquet's *Valéria et Lycisca.* Analyzed as a natural actress, Rachel complemented Lewes's view of the ruminative specta-tor whose gaze sees beyond the limitations of the player's embodied representation. Together, he could claim, he and Rachel were engaged in a common pursuit to improve the theater and spread the sacred influence of art. But that ideal agenda was potentially jeopardized by his own physical responses—a lapse he knew he was capable of when he vaguely acknowledged and defended his reaction to Miss Talbot. Maquet and Lacroix's play motivated similar responses, responses that qualified his admiration for Rachel: he applauded her performance but questioned her authenticity. Rachel played, Lewes wrote, "enchantingly." In the role of the empress, he praised her "maternal tenderness." And playing Lycisca, the courtesan, she seemed to him the "ideal of the Greek and Roman courtezan" (*L,* 12 July 1851, 663). But as Lycisca, Rachel provoked him to respond with irresistible sensations, proving that she could perform "unnaturally" and engage Lewes/Vivian in the act.

Lewes and Vivian's description of Rachel is a story of seduction (Rachel's of Vivian) and betrayal (Lewes's of Rachel), beginning with their response to her as a siren.

> She flashed upon my sight as the realization of a Bacchante in her maddening inspiration and beauty, in her exquisite elegance. She looked bewitchingly beautiful, and yet with a something unearthly, unhealthy, feverish, bewildering. For her sake you could do anything, you could commit any folly, almost a crime—but you could not love her!
>
> "C'est Venus toute entierè à sa proie attachée;" but it is the grace and fascination of a [*sic*] orgie, not the gentle lovingness of a pure heart. Horace, Catullus, Tibullus, and Anacreon are brilliantly illustrated in Rachel's Lysisca [*sic*]—she is Lalage, Lydia, Lesbia, Lais—the ideal of the Greek and Roman courtezan!
>
> But when all is over, when you have wondered at the picture of that voluptuous Lysisca, applauded her expressive singing—the very voice having a certain feverish tremulousness in it—and marvelled at the talent of the actress, what remains? You leave the theatre admiring Rachel, but what do you carry away with you of *Valeria*? No more than if you had but just gaped at a tight rope dancer! Of all that bustle, all that situation, all that intrigue, all those effects that have kept you restless, curious, startled during four mortal hours, nothing remains but a sense of fatigue! And this they call the triumph of dramatic Art!
>
> (*L,* 12 July 1851, 663)

From the start, Rachel is a "feverish, bewildering" Bacchante. In contrast to his other positive evaluations of Rachel, Lewes here imagines himself not engaged to cooperate with her in a moral enterprise but, as Vivian, lured to "commit any folly"—to give himself over to the pleasures of Rachel and the orgiastic sensations of conventional theatre. Lewes/Vivian then surrenders to "four mortal hours" of intrigue, effects, and curiosities. But these sensations are unredeemed by the "gentle lovingness of a pure heart"; and after the "feverish tremulousness" is past and Vivian is in the throes of post-theatric fatigue, Lewes discredits Rachel by disowning Vivian's response. Alarmed by her "bewitching" and "fascinating" allure, Lewes now relegates Rachel to the realm of conventional theater. Finally, he decides, she is a spectacle, a mere tight rope dancer, the figure who embodied for Lewes the worst moral and aesthetic excesses of the Victorian stage. Like the prostitute who burlesques true love, Rachel, he suggests, now merely performs her sensations in the absence of true feeling. And, casting himself as the degraded partner, Lewes walks away from the encounter, masking his own performance anxiety in concern for the state of "dramatic art."[18]

For Lewes, Rachel's performance was threatening precisely because he perceived it as a "genuine role." I use Brontë's paradoxical term to highlight once again the freighted philosophy of the self that grounds Lewes's performance theory. Clearly vulnerable to Rachel's seductive power, Lewes describes his own involuntary sensations ("restless, curious, startled"), which are not the carefully cultivated and sympathetic responses of the ideal spectator. If he was led on, as his language suggests, those sensations would be all the more suspect in his mind because they have been aroused by Rachel's burlesque of romantic feeling. Amid the representational complexities of his performance theory, Lewes emphasized the "genuineness" of sympathetic exchange. But as Rachel's spectator, he sees and feels the sensations of his own body, sensations that have supplanted the "genuine" feeling and ideal nature that are at the heart of his theory. If Rachel finally prostituted her art, as Lewes intimates, he had been a partner in the act.

Notes

1. *The Brontës: Their Lives, Friendships & Correspondences in Four Volumes,* ed. Thomas James Wise and John Alexander Symington (Oxford: Blackwell, 1932), 3:248. Further references to the letters will be cited parenthetically in text and designated by the letter *B*.

2. My focus in this essay is on Lewes's relatively early formulations of "natural acting" in his *Leader* theatre columns. Lewes remained interested in the concept for many years, however. In 1865, he again discussed natural acting in a series of essays on drama for the *Pall Mall Gazette,* republished in 1875 as *On Actors and the Art of Acting* (London: Smith, Elder, & Co., 1875). In "Shakespeare as Actor and Critic" and "On Natural Acting," two essays in that series, he more systematically articulates the ideas he formulated earlier in *The Leader.*

3. [G. H. Lewes], "Mlle. de Belle Isle," *The Leader,* 21 June 1851, 589. Further references to Lewes's

articles in *The Leader* will be cited within the text of the essay designated by the letter *L* and the date of issue.

4. Several excellent recent studies of eighteenth-century theatre and masquerade incorporate versions of this kind of analysis. See, for example, Kristina Straub, *Sexual Suspects: Eighteenth-Century Players and Sexual Ideology* (Princeton: Princeton Univ. Press, 1992), especially chapters 5 and 7. In *Masquerade and Civilization: The Carnivalesque in Eighteenth-Century English Culture and Fiction* (Stanford: Stanford Univ. Press, 1986), Terry Castle analyzes eighteenth-century masquerade as "anti-nature, a world upside-down, an intoxicating reversal of ordinary sexual, social, and metaphysical hierarchies" (6). Nina Auerbach uses terms similar to mine—sincerity, authenticity, theatricality—but sees Victorian theatricality as wholly resisting rather than partially accommodating a conception of the genuine self: "Reverent Victorians shunned theatricality as the ultimate, deceitful mobility. It connotes not only lies, but a fluidity of character that decomposes the uniform integrity of the self" (*Private Theatricals: The Lives of the Victorians* [Cambridge: Harvard Univ. Press, 1990], 4). In *Vested Interests: Cross-Dressing and Cultural Anxiety* (New York: Routledge, 1992), Marjorie Garber takes as her project not merely the disruption of traditional gender categories but a critique of categorization itself; see especially 9.

5. See especially chapter three, "Becoming Authentic," in Dollimore's *Sexual Dissidence: Augustine to Wilde, Freud to Foucault* (Oxford: Clarendon Press, 1991). Dollimore makes the point explicitly: "it is sometimes the appropriation of nature that is the most disturbing to the dominant: to lay claim to be (in certain respects) the same may be to reveal the limits of nature in an especially damaging way . . ." (44-45).

6. I am grateful to Elaine Hadley who, in conversations about Victorian theatre, helped me see more fully the implications of my readings for an enhanced understanding of "Victorian theatricality." In *Melodramatic Tactics: The Social Constitution of English Melodrama, 1800-1885* (Stanford: Stanford Univ. Press, forthcoming), she identifies a similar construction of theatricality but focuses her attention on what she calls the "melodramatic mode," "a polemical response to the invasive effects of market culture in the nineteenth century" (5). See also her essay, "The Old Price Wars: Melodramatizing the Public Sphere in Early-Nineteenth-Century England," *PMLA* 107 (1992): 524-37.

7. Henry Morley, *The Journal of a London Playgoer from 1851 to 1866* (London: Routledge, 1891), 22.

8. John William Cole, *The Life and Theatrical Times of Charles Kean, F.S.A., Including a Summary of the English Stage for the Last Fifty Years, and a Detailed Account of the Management of the Princess's Theatre from 1850 to 1859,* 2 vols. (London, 1859; rpt. New York: Garland, 1986), 1:163, 164, 165.

9. "The Drama, Past and Present," in William Bodham Donne, *Essays on the Drama* (London: John W. Parker & Son, 1858), 205-206 (first published in *Fraser's Magazine,* July 1855).

10. Despite a theory of natural acting that, in Lewes's view, transcended "staginess," his idea of conventions owes much to earlier, more obviously stylized acting methods such as those outlined by Leman Thomas Rede in *The Road to the Stage; Or, the Performer's Preceptor* (London: Joseph Smith, 1827). Rede included prescriptions for embodying various emotions by means of very specific physical movements and expressions. Grief, for example, in Rede's terms, "expresses itself by beating the head or forehead, tearing the hair, and catching the breath, as if choking; also by screaming, weeping, stamping with the feet, lifting the eyes from time to time to heaven, and hurrying backwards and forwards. This is a passion which admits, like many others, of a great deal of stage-trick; if not well contrived, and equally as well executed, frequently fails of the desired effect" (78). In Lewes's terms, these kinds of melodramatic gestures were often the staple of "unnatural" or conventional acting.

11. The distinction Lewes makes between drama and theatre, a distinction central to his formulation of natural acting, was widespread during the nineteenth century. The preference for drama over theatre was exemplified perhaps most starkly by the closet dramas of the Romantics. See Jonas Barish, *The Antitheatrical Prejudice* (Berkeley: Univ. of California Press, 1981), 323-37. For a recent essay that compellingly analyzes Romantic antitheatricalism as a species of antifeminist discourse, see Julie Carlson, "Impositions of Form: Romantic Antitheatricalism and the Case Against Particular Women," *ELH* 60 (1993): 149-79.

12. Later, in "Shakspeare [*sic*] as Actor and Critic," Lewes explicitly stated the central paradox of his performance theory: "If [the actor] really feel, he cannot act; but he cannot act unless he feel" (*On Actors* [*On Actors and the Art of Acting*] [note 2], 100). In this essay, as in his *Leader* columns, Lewes characterizes acting as a representational art that relies on conventions of performance. In the later formulation, however, he depends more heavily on the idiosyncratic individual whose "individual consciousness" provides the "interpreting key." In language that, in this later version, sounds more like Brontë's notion of natural acting, he quotes Talma to explain the actor's exploitation of the divided self: "I have suffered cruel losses, and have often been assailed with profound sorrows; but after the first moment when grief vents itself in cries and tears, I have found myself involuntarily turning my gaze inwards . . . and found that the actor was unconsciously studying the man, and catching nature in the act" (*On Actors,* 103). In *The Player's Passion: Studies in the Science of Acting* (Newark, Delaware and Toronto: Univ. of Delaware Press; Associated University Presses, 1985), Joseph Roach analyzes Lewes's understanding of the theatrical medium in the context of his scientific theories. Although Roach argues that Lewes upheld an "absolute mind-body monism" (190), his descriptions of what he sees as Lewes's scientifically based acting theory also support my notion of a bifurcated theatrical subjectivity. As Roach maintains, "The physical enactment of these outward manifestations of emotion, Lewes believed, inexorably reacts on the inner fibres of the sensorium, producing the emotion itself" (192). Roach notes "that an inner impulse can ignite an outward manifestation as 'spontaneously' powerful as 'the lurid flame of vengeance flashing from [Kean's] eye' . . . obviously intrigued Lewes" (191). Roach's readings give a physiological basis to the essentialism that also grounds Lewes's performance theory.

13. John Stokes, "Rachel's Terrible Beauty': An Actress Among the Novelists," *ELH* 51 (1984): 776; and Joseph R. Roach, Jr., "G. H. Lewes and Performance Theory: Towards a 'Science of Acting,'" *Theatre Journal* 32 (1980): 316. See also Roach's *The Player's Passion* (note 12).

14. Hadley (note 6), especially 10-13, 16-17.

15. In her recent biography of Rachel, Rachel Brownstein describes other such artless "natural" actresses and what contemporaries noted as their difference from Rachel. For example, Brownstein observes, "Marie Dorval . . . was the epitome of artlessness, naturalness, femininity: Gautier wrote that when she performed, 'It was no longer art, it was nature itself, it was the essence of maternity distilled in one single woman.' In sharp contrast, Rachel was imagined as an avatar of austere literary art" (*Tragic Muse: Rachel of the Comédie-Francaise* [New York: Knopf, 1993], 61).

16. William Acton, *Prostitution, Considered in Its Moral, Social, and Sanitary Aspects In London and Other Large Cities with Prospects for the Mitigation and Prevention of Its Attendant Evils,*

2d ed. (London, 1870; first edition 1857), 166. Other references to this work will be cited in the text of the essay and designated by *P.*

17. William Acton, *The Functions and Disorders of the Reproductive Organs* (London, 1857), cited in Elizabeth Helsinger, Robin Lauterbach Sheets, and William Veeder, *The Woman Question: Society and Literature in Britain and America, 1837-1883,* 3 vols. (Chicago: Univ. of Chicago Press, 1983), vol. 2, *Social Issues,* 63; emphasis added.

18. Lewes's later evaluations and recollections of Rachel consistently applaud her performance abilities. In *On Actors and the Art of Acting* (note 2), he offers perhaps his best-known and strongest praise of Rachel as "the panther of the stage." But even there, he still responds ambiguously to what he sees as her unfeminine and thus inhuman qualities. "Her range, like Kean's, was very limited, but her expression was perfect within that range. Scorn, triumph, rage, lust and merciless malignity she could represent in symbols of irresistible power; but she had little tenderness, no womanly caressing softness, no gaiety, no heartiness" (see "Rachel," in *On Actors,* 23). Lewes's early evaluations of Rachel were shaped not only by his conceptions of essential femininity but also, as Brownstein and Stokes note, by anti-Semitism (Brownstein [note 15], 236-37; Stokes [note 13], 776).

Richard Menke (essay date summer 2000)

SOURCE: Menke, Richard. "Fiction as Vivisection: G. H. Lewes and George Eliot." *ELH* 67, no. 2 (summer 2000): 617-53.

[*In the following excerpt, Menke highlights the vivisectionist themes in both Lewes's scientific studies and his literary criticism. Menke also explores Goethe's influence on Lewes's scientific and philosophical thought.*]

Years after his transition from man of letters to man of science, George Henry Lewes brought his experience with neurophysiology to bear on contemporary fiction. In his 1872 essay **"Dickens in Relation to Criticism,"** Lewes tries to provide a balanced assessment of the strengths and shortcomings of the novelist, who had died two years before. Largely because of two unusual scientific comparisons, however, many readers regarded his article as an attack on Dickens, with whom Lewes had in fact been friendly—despite their public feud over the scientific verisimilitude of Mr. Krook's spontaneous combustion in *Bleak House* (1852-53). First Lewes compares the "vividness of imagination" in the novelist's work to the intensity of "hallucinations," a trait Lewes has found in "no other perfectly sane mind."[1]

Later, Lewes considers the problem of character and caricature in Dickens and produces an even more peculiar—and to many friends of Dickens peculiarly offensive—comparison:

> When one thinks of Micawber always presenting himself in the same situation, moved with the same springs, and uttering the same sounds, always confident on something turning up, always crushed and rebounding, always making punch . . . one is reminded of the frogs whose brains have been taken out for physiological purposes, and whose actions henceforth want the distinctive peculiarity of organic action, that of fluctuating spontaneity. Place one of these brainless frogs on his back, and he will at once recover the sitting posture; draw a leg from under him, and he will draw it back again; tickle or prick him and he will push away the object, or take *one* hop out of the way; stroke his back, and he will utter *one* croak. All these things resemble the actions of the unmutilated frog, but they differ in being *isolated* actions, and *always the same*: they are as uniform and calculable as the movements of a machine. The uninjured frog may or may not croak, may or may not hop away; the result is never calculable, and is rarely a single croak or a single hop. It is this complexity of the organism which Dickens wholly fails to conceive; his characters have nothing flexible and incalculable in them . . .

(**D** ["**Dickens in Relation to Criticism**"], 148-49)

With what seems to be a scientific revision of *The Pickwick Papers*'s (1836-37) "Ode to an Expiring Frog," Lewes castigates Dickens for producing characters who, like frogs whose brains have been removed by vivisecting physiologists, display the basic operations of a living organism without its inherent intricacy and contingency.[2] In part, perhaps, because of the uproar created by the scientific comparisons in the essay, in part because absorption in his *Problems of Life and Mind* (1874-79) left Lewes little time for writing about literature in his final years, **"Dickens in Relation to Criticism"** would be the last original work of literary criticism by a man who had first made his reputation as a critic, editor, and belletrist.

A few pages after Lewes makes his analogy between Micawber and the vivisected frog, the unspoken literary touchstone for his assessment of Dickens becomes clearer. Dickens, claims Lewes, represented "perceptions" with brilliance and with an intensity that approached the hallucinatory, but "[t]hought is strangely absent from his work"; Lewes doubts that "a single thoughtful remark on life or character could be found throughout the twenty volumes" (**D,** 151). Not altogether surprisingly, the implicit counterpoint to Dickens's phantasmagorical rendering of sensation and supposedly inflexible, calculable treatment of character seems to be the fiction of Lewes's companion, George Eliot, well known for its inclusion of weighty remarks on life and character. When Dickens creates characters, he creates brainless amphibians; when George Eliot creates characters, she performs a different, apparently more successful operation.

This essay discusses the relationship between vivisection and fiction for both G. H. Lewes and George Eliot. I wish to show first that the analogy between literature and vivisection is fundamental for Lewes, a veteran amateur physiologist known in the last years of his life as a defender of vivisection during widespread antivivisectionist agitation in Britain. (In practice, "vivisection" for the Victorians included a range of invasive or painful animal experiments.) George Eliot herself was far less outspoken on the subject. Nonetheless, I will argue that Eliot's evolving theory of the novel, developed in collaboration with Lewes and articulated in both the literary essays she wrote before she became a novelist and in her fiction itself, takes her close to Lewes's theory of *écriture* as vivisection. Lewes believed that the zone of contact between the two would offer "laws" for creating successful literature: a psychology, conceived of neither in the terms of Kantian introspection nor in those of static natural history, but along the lines of Claude Bernard's new physiology, whose central investigative tools were animal experiment and vivisection.[3] Both Lewes and Eliot understood fiction's capacity to explore what laboratory experiment could not, but this recognition led them not to reject physiological techniques as a model but instead to realize that even as fiction emulated experimental physiology it should also exceed it, a realization apparent not only in Lewes's critique of Micawber but also in both Eliot's early story "The Lifted Veil" and *Middlemarch.*

My claim is not merely that fiction may profess to be based on minute observation, even invasion, of the processes of life, and that vivisection offers a figure for such close investigation. For Eliot and Lewes, the connection between fiction and vivisection *was* analogical, but it was also something more. At the same time that Lewes was making explicit comparisons between vivisection and literature, Eliot was imaginatively appropriating laboratory techniques in her fiction in order to produce depth psychology along the model of experimental physiology. As Lewes devotes his physiological research to studying the nerves and the mind, and Eliot emphasizes the representation of moment-to-moment thought in her late fiction, their shared task becomes the vivisection of consciousness, a project that becomes especially apparent—and perhaps ambivalent—in the novel Eliot was composing even as Lewes testified before a Royal Commission on vivisection, *Daniel Deronda.*

I. The Vivisectionist as Man of Letters: G. H. Lewes

In an obituary notice on George Henry Lewes, James Sully records that as a young man Lewes had contemplated a medical career. In the mid-1830s Lewes attended lectures and "actually began to walk the hospitals, and was only stopped in his course by an invincible repugnance at the sight of physical pain."[4] Loath to witness pain, and presumably, in an age before the widespread use of anesthesia, to cause it in patients, Lewes abandoned the study of medicine in favor of a career in letters. Such a vocation would entail the production of far less pain, even in the unfortunate readers of his tedious philosophical novel *Ranthorpe* (1847), which in fact presents the antics of a group of boisterous medical students in London.

For nearly two decades Lewes labored as a literary journalist, hack playwright, reviewer, editor, and biographer of Goethe; this last project involved the 1854 trip to Weimar that semi-publicly announced the relationship between Marian Evans and the unhappily married Lewes, and cast Evans out of polite society for years to come. In the 1850s, under the influence of his friend Herbert Spencer and his mentor Richard Owen, perhaps the most eminent anatomist and paleontologist of his time, Lewes returned to his interest in biology. One might also adduce his 1852 essay **"Goethe as a Man of Science,"** in which Lewes praises Goethe's anatomical and botanical works and hails him as "a great Man of Science, no less than a Great Poet," as evidence that Lewes the literary essayist was beginning to shift from literature to science.[5] As his championing of Goethe and his interest in the scientific positivism of Auguste Comte indicate, one of the main strengths of Lewes as a man of science, as it had been when he was principally a man of letters, was his familiarity with European thought and his devotion to popularizing it in England. This cosmopolitan outlook was especially handy for a budding physiologist, since for many years English physiologists had lagged behind their continental counterparts, in part because of concern in England over the cruelty of animal experiments.[6]

In this move from belletrist to biologist, a move neatly foreshadowed by his argument with Dickens over spontaneous human combustion, Lewes was also aided by recent scientific developments that would accommodate his squeamishness in the face of pain. In 1846 Robert Liston became the first English surgeon to perform an operation using "sulfuric ether" (ethyl oxide) as an "anæsthetic" (the term suggested a few months previously by Oliver Wendell Holmes).[7] Along with chloroform and chloral hydrate, ether became a central drug in a gradually growing anesthetic pharmacopoeia that would come to include morphine, curare (mistakenly and, by the 1870s, controversially, since it paralyzes without eliminating sensation), and—later—cocaine. In general, the availability of anesthetics both made new sorts of experimentation possible by preventing the physical and biological effects of laboratory animals' pain, and made the field of experimental physiology more attractive to potential experimenters such as Lewes.[8] With anesthetics, Lewes could remove the pain of his animal subjects, a laboratory practice that he along with many British scientists would recommend whenever feasible.

Another indication of Lewes's growing interest in science was his publication of ***Comte's Philosophy of the Sciences*** (1853), based on a series of articles he had written for his journal *The Leader.* If Lewes was seeking to assess Comte's ideas and popularize them in England, and in the process to display his own knowledge of both science and European philosophy, the reception afforded ***Comte's Philosophy of the Sciences*** must truly have rankled. In a review of the book, the young T. H. Huxley attacked Lewes for lacking "the discipline and knowledge" of a professional scientist and for making scientific blunders that are "not excusable even on the plea of mere book-knowledge."[9] Smarting from this public rebuke, Lewes set to work in the 1850s to become an expert dissector and, by the end of the decade, a skilled microscopist.[10] In the summer of 1855, Marian Evans reported that the two of them were busy "writing hard, walking hard, reading Homer and science and rearing tadpoles" for Lewes's experiments.[11] After completing his biography of Goethe, Lewes began a study of the coastal life of southwestern England and Wales. Lewes's first publications on biology correspond to Marian Evans's first assays into fiction; the dual reinventions of Lewes as a man of science and of Evans as "George Eliot" mirror each other as much as the chronology of his publication of **"Sea-Side Studies"** (*Blackwood's Magazine,* beginning August 1856) and Eliot's of "Scenes of Clerical Life" (*Blackwood's,* beginning January 1857) might suggest.

Even after winning both Huxley's compliments on the book edition of **"Sea-Side Studies"** and his friendship, Lewes was still eager to develop and to demonstrate his physiological expertise. In 1858, writing from Munich, he crowed to John Blackwood that he had "been doing some capital work in the laboratories of my friends here, where an extensive apparatus and no end of frogs are at my disposal! When government establishes a physiological Institute professors (and amateurs) can work in clover" (*L* [*The George Eliot Letters*], 2:467). Back in England, without the benefit of government-sponsored physiological laboratories, Lewes had to hire boys to catch the frogs he required.[12] Nevertheless, Marian Evans could soon brag to one of Lewes's sons that his father was "wonderfully clever now at the dissection of these delicate things"—a dragonfly, in this case—"and has attained this cleverness entirely by devoted practice during the last three years" (*L*, 3:177).

In ***The Physiology of Common Life*** (1859-60), Lewes turned his hard-won expertise to account, reporting the results of his experiments in order to justify his theories about biology and physiology, most notably his idea "that the Brain is only *one* organ of the Mind, and not by any means the exclusive centre of Consciousness."[13] The spinal chord and somatic nerves, argues Lewes, have the same properties as the nerves that compose the brain—perhaps even including consciousness; therefore,

the removal of the brain "does not imply the absence of *all* consciousness," as Lewes tries to "prove by experiment" (**P** [***The Physiology of Common Life***], 2:12). At one point Lewes applies a "galvanic battery" to the still-living nerves of a leg severed from a freshly killed frog in order to demonstrate that bodily nerves are not merely passive carriers of "force" from a "nervous centre" but have a motive power of their own (**P**, 2:21-22). At another he performs the similar but more gruesome experiment of taking one frog's legs and lumbar nerves and attaching the muscles of these legs to the severed leg of a second frog; when Lewes applies a current from a battery to the lumbar nerves, all three legs contract in grisly unison (**P**, 2:243).

Lewes supports his speculations in ***The Physiology of Common Life*** not merely with dissection and galvanic reanimation but also with vivisection; he severs the spinal chord of a triton (an aquatic salamander or newt) and argues not that the parts of the animal below the cut have lost sensation by losing their connection to the brain but, in keeping with his theory of the distribution of consciousness, that the cut has created two separate centers of sensation, one at the creature's brain and the other at its tail-end. "There is no longer one seat of government, but two seats," he concludes with a metaphoric flourish that turns the vivisected amphibian body into the body politic of the British Isles. "There has been a 'repeal of the union.' Parliament sits in Dublin, as well as in Westminster" (**P**, 2:214).[14]

A postscript from an 1867 letter from Marian Evans to Cara Bray, one of her oldest friends, hints at the type of experiments Lewes was performing a decade later: "<Froggie continues to do better than even he expected without his head *brain* [*sic*] for months. He dies of starvation at last>" (*L*, 4:405). Curiously, as the editorial brackets indicate, these lines were written and then overscored, as if denial or omission had triumphed over facetiousness as a cognitive mode for dealing with what seems a cruel, and possibly rather gratuitous, experiment. As she was writing this note, the plight of the unfortunate creature might well have been suggested to Evans by her final statement to Cara Bray in the body of the letter above: "Best love to Sara [Hennell, Cara's sister, and another friend from Evans's Coventry days] and congratulations that the tortures of the rack are a little diminished." The "tortures of the rack," after all, had just diminished for Froggie as well. Eliot, we shall see, would later align a woman's emotional suffering with animals and physical torture in her fiction. Whatever her reasons for including and then excluding them, the crossed-out words about Froggie remain one of Marian Evans's few surviving statements about Lewes's animal experiments. Another is her report several months later to their publisher John Blackwood that "Mr. Lewes is happy in dissecting all sorts of molluscs, about whom he has the agreeable theory that they don't object to a little rough handling for the benefit of science" (*L*, 4:426)—a most convenient state of affairs, if true.

After Lewes perfected his laboratory technique, his experiments began to deal more and more with the brain and the nervous system, for reasons that he outlines in his ambitious five-volume *Problems of Life and Mind* in the 1870s.[15] Claiming that "every problem of Mind is necessarily a problem of Life," Lewes argues for the "indispensable union of the physiological with the psychological investigation."[16] He therefore seeks to replace or supplement the older introspective method of psychology with experimentation:

> If, then, it is indispensable that Psychology should formulate the laws of the human mind, and not simply classify the individual states, the feelings and thoughts of others must be accessible; and if these are not accessible on their subjective side, access must be sought on their objective side. We must quit Introspection for Observation. We must study the mind's operations in its expressions, as we study electrical operations in their effects. We must vary our observations of the actions of men and animals by experiment, filling up the gaps of observation with hypothesis.[17]

Lewes argues that "Literature and Art" offer one source of "objective" understanding of thoughts and emotions outside of our own minds. A properly experimental psychology would offer another, as observation and experiment give us admittance into "the feelings and thoughts of others."[18] The late fiction of George Eliot, we shall see, would fuse the two—art and experiment.

The Physical Basis of Mind (1877), the middle volume of *Problems of Life and Mind,* reiterates some of the experiments and illustrations cited in *The Physiology of Common Life.* It also elaborates Lewes's important theory of the relationship between—and in a specific and fundamental sense even the identity of—mind and body. Lewes contends that physiology and psychology, nerves and neuroses, are best understood as, respectively, the objective and subjective presentations of what are in fact the same phenomena, a position now known as dual-aspect monism.[19] What *looks* like physiological excitation to the objective observer may *feel* like thought or sensation to the subject, but neither point of view is secondary or reducible to the other. Here again Lewes cites dozens of experiments involving vivisection to make his points. For instance, to explain his contention that consciousness need not accompany sensation, Lewes compares consciousness to pain: analgesics deaden pain without affecting sensation; in the same way, "an animal, after removal of the brain" in physiological experiments, may produce "struggles and cries"—like the unflagging Micawber, one must assume—yet most physiologists would agree that this is merely a reflex action, triggered by sensation but unac-

companied by pain. "Now for the term Pain in the foregoing paragraph substitute the term Consciousness," directs Lewes; the characteristics of pain are coextensive with those of consciousness itself.[20] Research that employed vivisection could thus investigate the properties of both, "filling up the gaps of observation with hypothesis" and elaborating experimental data into speculative fictions.

However, by the final phase of Lewes's scientific career, such physiological experimentation was becoming highly controversial. In late 1873 Lewes sent a letter to the journal *Nature* recording experiments meant again to support his contention that the locus of the mind is the entire nervous system. As a response to previous experiments in which intact frogs became "agitated" by being boiled alive, while brainless frogs remained torpid (therefore, it was argued, indicating the primacy of the brain over the rest of the nervous system), Lewes made a series of experiments involving brainless and in some cases skinless frogs who were boiled alive or had their "limbs . . . pinched, pricked, cut, burnt with acids, and even burnt to a cinder with the flame of a wax taper," which he felt lent credence to his own claims.[21] When an anonymous letter to the editor of *Nature* objected to Lewes's experiments as "shocking," "torture," "of excessive cruelty," "a case in which the infliction of pain is not an unavoidable *attendant* on the experiments, but the very essence or object of them," Lewes weighed in with a short article justifying vivisection and recalling that his own "inability to witness pain" had kept him from a medical career.[22] Two weeks later, *Nature* published an editorial defending judicious vivisection.

Moreover, the dispute in *Nature* only echoed the growing public worry about vivisection, touched off in large part by the publication of a controversial *Handbook for the Physiological Laboratory* in 1873, and the notorious "Norwich affair," in which a French physiologist and several British doctors were prosecuted for injecting a dog with absinthe at the 1874 meeting of the British Medical Association.[23] The animal protection movement now counted a friend of Marian Evans among its members: Cara Bray, the recipient of the letter mentioning (and then un-mentioning) "Froggie," had become active in the Royal Society for the Prevention of Cruelty to Animals, a cause to which Evans dutifully contributed in 1874 (*L*, 6:52). The R.S.P.C.A. officially opposed only vivisection that caused pain; experiments that used anesthesia were not painful and therefore not cruel.[24] But in 1875 the writer, philanthropist, and feminist Frances Power Cobbe founded the more radical Society for the Protection of Animals Liable to Vivisection, known as the Victoria Street Society, expressly to campaign against all experimentation on live animals.

As the Victorian debate on vivisection grew strident first in the mid-1870s and again in the early 1880s, a formidable assemblage of eminent Victorians lined up on either side of the issue; indeed, few other Victorian causes could boast such an array of contending worthies. In favor of restricting or outlawing animal experimentation was a host of literary, religious, and political figures: Ruskin, Arnold, Christina Rossetti, Robert Browning, Tennyson (whose sister Matilda "exasperated" Lewes with "her nonsense and ignorance" [*L*, 6:364] during a luncheon in 1877), Lewis Carroll, Wilkie Collins, Charles Kingsley, Benjamin Jowett, Benjamin Disraeli, and even Queen Victoria herself; along with the Earl of Shaftesbury and Cardinal Manning, Carlyle was an officer of Cobbe's Victoria Street Society.[25] On the side of vivisection, or at least in favor of the freedom of physiologists to engage in "animal experiment," was a smaller group consisting chiefly of scientists and medical researchers, including Huxley, Owen, Spencer, Darwin, and Lewes.[26] In light of the length and acrimony of the debate, it seems fair to conclude that "[h]owever marginal England may have been for experimental physiology" in comparison to France and Germany, "it was a world leader in anti-vivisection agitations."[27]

In 1875 a "Royal Commission on the Practice of Subjecting Live Animals to Experiments for Scientific Purposes" interviewed more than fifty experts on the subject. Before the commission, which included both Huxley and R. H. Hutton, the antivivisectionist editor of the *Spectator*, Lewes testified that every experimenter should "consider the question of pain" when planning an experiment and should also be aware that the "extreme complexity of the organism" would render many experimental results inconclusive and therefore "useless," a waste of the researcher's pains and the animal's pain.[28] Students of physiology must be impressed with the difficulty of experiment, Lewes advised, and must approach the experimental process only after rigorous thought. Still, he asserted, animal experiment must remain unregulated by government; not Parliament but the "scientific public" itself must develop norms that would discourage fruitless or cruel vivisection (*R* [*Report of the Royal Commission on the Practice of Subjecting Live Animals to Experiments for Scientific Purposes*], 312).

Lewes also elaborated his theory about the molluses who supposedly wouldn't "object to a little rough handling for the benefit of science." Questioned about the pain produced by his experiments on frogs, he replied that "Personally, I do not believe that even when they have the brain frogs suffer pain at all; but I should not like to state that publicly, because it would seem like an attempt to justify our practice on equivocal grounds" (*R*, 313). Asked to account for this non-belief in amphibian pain, Lewes offered an explanation based on a sort of quasi-evolutionism:

> We know that among human beings, especially when you descend to the savages, the sensibility to pain becomes less and less. Coming to animals, we know that, for instance, a horse that has had his leg shattered in battle will crop the grass, which no animal in great pain could do. . . . On any evidence that I have before me I should say that the fishes and the reptiles have sensibility, but none of that which we call pain.
>
> [*Commission member:*] But your answer applies to horses quite as much as to the lower animals?
>
> [*Lewes:*]—I say they do not suffer the pain that we do; yet a horse's skin is excessively sensitive [to other sensations], as we know.

(R, 313)

The more highly developed and refined the organism, the greater its sensitivity to pain, from fish and reptiles, to the lower mammals, to "savages," to the civilized. Such beliefs were widely held in the nineteenth century; while "Negresses" were compared to animals in terms of alleged insensitivity to pain, white women of the upper classes were said to feel unusually severe pain in childbirth, and "[e]ven domesticated animals suffered more exquisitely [in labor] than did their wild sisters."[29] Thus variations in sensitivity to pain not only helped exonerate vivisectors from charges of cruelty but also provided an index to the development and complexity of beings ranging from molluscs and horses to people.

As the sole "private investigator" appearing before the commission, Lewes perhaps came closest to coinciding with one *bête noire* of the antivivisection movement, the independent amateur physiologist toiling away at home (*R*, 312). The members of the commission also examined Lewes about his controversial experiments that involved boiling brainless frogs. Yet their questions were respectful, and his answers largely equivalent to the British Association for the Advancement of Science's moderate 1871 resolution on vivisection, endorsed by Darwin, Huxley, and others, and read to the commission on its first day of hearings (*R*, 12). In any case, notwithstanding the advice of Lewes, the Royal Commission recommended moderate legislation to regulate animal experiments and license experimenters, a course of action taken by Parliament with the passage of the Cruelty to Animals Act of 1876.

As with his essay on Dickens three years previously, the most unusual and characteristic feature of Lewes's testimony before the commission is his inclination to compare physiological experiment and literature:

> It seems to me that the vivisection of which we are now speaking is very much like vivisection in another department, that of Literature, that is to say, criticism, which is also vivisection. There is a great deal of real torture inflicted upon authors by critics, which lasts for a considerable time in sensitive minds.

[*Commission member:*] And without anæsthetics?

[*Lewes:*]—And without anæsthetics . . .

[*Commission chairman:*] But I suppose you would scarcely compare [the vivisection done by critics] in point of necessity of control with the fact of living animals being cut up?

[*Lewes:*]—Why not?

(*R,* 311)

Authors, after all, are "human beings who suffer frightfully" under the torment of criticism. "I do not think you could control that," Lewes admits, "but then I do not think you could control vivisection profitably" (*R,* 311).[30]

"[R]eal torture," according to Lewes, may be psychological as well as somatic, especially when it affects not allegedly insensate animals but the "sensitive minds" of unusually susceptible human beings. Shelley's "Adonais" treats a derogatory review as the fatal poison of an anonymous serpent; with similar hyperbole but perhaps more discernment, Lewes calls it vivisection: a minute and painful inspection that leaves the victim alive and wriggling under the critical knife. As in the Dickens essay, the analogy between literature and vivisection is at once jocular and in earnest. Lewes was not only a former literary critic but also for twenty years the companion of an author whom he worked assiduously to protect from any shred of negative criticism.

But an even more startling similarity between his essay on Dickens and his testimony to the commission on vivisection is Lewes's emphasis on what he calls, in a phrase common to both, the "complexity of the organism." Animal experimenters must carefully consider "the extreme complexity of the organism" when planning their work, Lewes claims, or it will yield misleading results and prove futile; any experimenter who does not acknowledge and respect such organic complexity will fail. In **"Dickens in Relation to Criticism,"** Lewes observes that fully intact frogs or fully realized fictional characters would act in ways that are "never calculable," but "[i]t is *this complexity of the organism* which Dickens wholly fails to conceive" (**D,** 149; my emphasis).

The shortcomings of Dickens as a novelist are thus precisely the deficiencies of an incompetent vivisector. On the one hand, Lewes denounces vivisecting critics for torturing the minds of authors, but, on the other, he suggests that the attitude of a subtle novelist to her subject may resemble that of a skillful vivisector to his. Success in vivisection or fiction is hard to achieve; yet if undertaken with foresight and an imagination rooted in reality, difficult and even painful experiments might

provide objective access to complex subjective phenomena. What techniques, then, might characterize a novelist who respected what every qualified vivisector understands—the complexity of the organism—indeed, who had developed her fictional method in dialogue with Lewes's science? And what would competently vivisected characters look like, if they did not resemble poor, automatized Froggie?

Notes

1. George Henry Lewes, "Dickens in Relation to Criticism," *Fortnightly Review* 17 (1872): 144. Hereafter cited parenthetically in the text by page number and abbreviated *D.*

2. In chapter 15 of *The Pickwick Papers* (1836-37), Mr. Leo Hunter recites his wife's "Ode to an Expiring Frog" for Mr. Pickwick. According to Mr. Hunter, the poem "created an immense sensation" when it was published, "signed with an 'L' and eight stars . . . in a Lady's Magazine" (Charles Dickens, *The Posthumous Papers of the Pickwick Club,* ed. Robert L. Patten [London: Penguin, 1986], 275). Here is the ode, quoted in its entirety from chapter 15 (I have omitted Mr. Pickwick's interruptions to Mr. Hunter's recitation between the two stanzas):

> Can I view thee panting, lying
> On thy stomach, without sighing;
> Can I unmoved see thee dying
>   On a log,
>   Expiring frog!
> Say, have fiends in shape of boys,
> With wild halloo, and brutal noise,
> Hunted thee from marshy joys,
>   With a dog,
>   Expiring frog!

(Dickens, 275)

In *Pickwick* [*The Pickwick Papers*], the poetic frog provides an object for stereotypically maudlin effusions and comically inappropriate pathos in a burlesque of sentimental poetry. Lewes cleverly recasts a batrachian murder to underwrite his critique of Dickens's own recourse to stereotyped character, inappropriate pathos, and sentimental fiction; yet to this highly literary move, he adds his experience of laboratory science. (I am grateful to Rob Polhemus for pointing out this reference.)

3. Lewes, "The Principles of Success in Literature," *Fortnightly Review* 1 (1865): 86.

4. Quoted in Rosemary Ashton, *G. H. Lewes: A Life* (Oxford: Clarendon, 1991), 14.

5. Lewes, "Goethe as a Man of Science," *Westminster Review* 58 (1852): 506. On Lewes's treatment of the science of Goethe, see Peter Allan Dale, *In Pursuit of a Scientific Culture: Science, Art, and Society in the Victorian Age* (Madison: Univ. of Wisconsin Press, 1989), 76-79.

6. See Richard D. French, *Antivivisection and Medical Science in Victorian Society* (Princeton: Princeton Univ. Press, 1975), 18-23, 36-39.

7. Thomas E. Keys, *The History of Surgical Anesthesia* (New York: Schuman's, 1945), 29-30.

8. French, 40.

9. Thomas Henry Huxley, "Science," *Westminster Review* 61 (1854): 255, 256.

10. On Lewes's experiences with the microscope and *Middlemarch*'s discourse of microscopy, see Mark Wormald, "Microscopy and Semiotic in *Middlemarch*," *Nineteenth-Century Literature* 50 (1996): 501-24.

11. George Eliot to Charles Bray, East Sheen, 17 June 1855, in *The George Eliot Letters,* ed. Gordon S. Haight, 9 vols. (New Haven: Yale Univ. Press, 1954-78), 2:202. The *Letters* are hereafter cited parenthetically in the text by volume and page number and abbreviated *L*.

12. Ashton, 190.

13. Lewes, *The Physiology of Common Life,* 2 vols. (New York: Appleton, 1864), 2:11. Hereafter cited parenthetically in the text by volume and page number and abbreviated *P.*

14. Lewes makes a similar pronouncement, more expansively but with the same combination of flippancy and a sort of oblique appositeness, in a letter written to his eldest son in 1858: "You ask me what book I am writing—do you not guess that it can be no other than The Tadpoles of Peloponnessus [*sic*] Und ihre Beziehung zur Weltgeschichte!!! [And their relation to the history of the world!] I am sure that Thornie [Lewes's second son] as Rex Ranarum [King of the Frogs] will feel the deepest interest in this work" (*The Letters of George Henry Lewes,* ed. William Baker, 2 vols. [Victoria, B. C.: Univ. of Victoria Press, 1995], 1:275). As far as I know, the reference to young Thornton Lewes as *Rex Ranarum* remains obscure.

15. The publication of Lewes's five-volume *Problems of Life and Mind* took place in three stages, which the spines and title pages of the books call "series." The first series was *The Foundations of a Creed,* 2 vols. (Boston: Osgood, 1874); then came the single-volume second series, *The Physical Basis of Mind* (Boston: Houghton, 1877). The posthumously published third series comprised *The Study of Psychology: Its Object, Scope, and Method* (Boston: Houghton, 1879), and a second volume with no title other than *Problems of Life and Mind,* ser. 3, vol. 2 (Boston: Osgood, 1880). Subsequent citations of *Problems of Life and Mind* refer to these editions; I cite them by their individual titles and, where necessary, by series and volume number.

16. Lewes, *Physical Basis* [*The Physical Basis of Mind*], 3; *Study of Psychology,* 14.

17. Lewes, *Study of Psychology,* 99.

18. Lewes, *Study of Psychology,* 98.

On the significance of Lewes's approach to psychology, see Daniel N. Robinson, "Preface" to *"A Text-Book in Psychology" by Johann Friedrich Herbart, "The Study of Psychology" by George Henry Lewes, "Outlines of Psychology" by Hermann Lotze,* Significant Contributions to the History of Psychology, 1750-1920, vol. 6, ser. A: Orientations (Washington, DC: Univ. Publications of America, 1977), xxii-xxxviii. Also see Dale, 68-71, 107-13. Dale argues that the work of Lewes shows "a decisive break with the dominant paradigms of British psychology, paradigms of rationalism, associationism, and individualism" and thus "make[s] an epoch in the history of the discipline" (71).

19. That is, Lewes holds that "[m]ental and physical processes . . . are simply different aspects of one and the same series of psychophysical events" (Robert H. Wozniak, *Mind and Body: René Descartes to William James* [Washington, DC: National Library of Medicine/American Psychological Association, 1992], 12). The result for him is not physical reductionism, however; Lewes concludes that because each of them is merely a particular point of view, both psychology and physiology are necessary in the study of the mind. See especially Lewes, *Physical Basis,* 376-98. On the significance of Lewes's dual-aspect monism and its relationship to other nineteenth-century formulations of the mind/body question, see Wozniak.

As Athena Vrettos observes, Lewes's "theoretical shifts between psychological and physiological explanations for human behavior mark his attempt, like Eliot's own, to explore the tenuous middle ground between body and mind" ("From Neurosis to Narrative: The Private Life of the Nerves in *Villette* and *Daniel Deronda*," *Victorian Studies* 33 [1990]: 560).

20. Lewes, *Physical Basis,* 216 ("an animal" and "struggles"), 216-17 ("Now").

21. Lewes, "Sensation in the Spinal Cord," *Nature* 9 (1873): 83, 84.

22. X [pseud.], "Experiments on Frogs" (letter), *Nature* 9 (1873): 121; Lewes, "Vivisection," *Nature* 9 (1873): 144-45.

23. French, 47, 55-57.

24. French, 32-33.

25. Dougald B. MacEachen, "Wilkie Collins' *Heart and Science* and the Vivisection Controversy," *The Victorian Newsletter* 29 (1966): 23; French, 65, 73; Coral Lansbury, "Gynaecology, Pornography, and the Antivivisection Movement," *Victorian Studies* 28 (1985): 414.

26. See MacEachen, 24; French, 71, 103, 198, 358.

27. John V. Pickstone, "A Profession of Discovery: Physiology in Nineteenth-Century History," *British Journal for the History of Science* 23 (1990): 213.

28. *Report of the Royal Commission on the Practice of Subjecting Live Animals to Experiments for Scientific Purposes* (London: Eyre and Spottiswoode, 1876), 310. Hereafter cited parenthetically in the text by page number and abbreviated *R.*

29. Martin S. Pernick, *A Calculus of Suffering: Pain, Professionalism, and Anesthesia in Nineteenth-Century America* (New York: Columbia Univ. Press, 1985), 156-57, 150.

30. In its editorial response to the vivisection commission's final report, *Nature* singles out Lewes's comments and applies them to critics not of literature but of vivisection itself: "careful consideration is therefore wanted lest in the endeavour to prevent abuses which may hereafter creep into the practice of vivisection on animals we do not afford facilities for the mental vivisection so graphically described in the evidence of Mr. G. H. Lewes, of honourable, kind-hearted, and sensitive men, whose pursuits are not merely advantageous to science but productive, as the Report clearly shows, of great benefit, both to the human race and the lower animals" ("Legislation Regarding Vivisection," *Nature* 13 [1876]: 343).

FURTHER READING

Bibliographies

Hopkin, John. "George Henry Lewes as Playwright: A Register of Pieces." In *Essays on Nineteenth-Century*

British Theatre, edited by Kenneth Richards and Peter Thompson, pp. 111-23. London: Methuen, 1971.
   Presents a complete listing of Lewes's plays.

Scholtes, Joann. "Additions and Corrections to G. H. Lewes's Primary Bibliography." *George Eliot-George Henry Lewes Studies* 48-49 (September 2005): 8-18.
   Adds to the record of Lewes's published works.

Biographies

Ashton, Rosemary. *G. H. Lewes: A Life.* Oxford: Clarendon Press, 1991, 369 p.
   Argues that George Henry Lewes, though he lived an unconventional life, was typically Victorian in his insistence on the unity of intellectual thought.

Baker, William. *The Letters of George Henry Lewes.* Vol. 3, with New George Eliot Letters. English Literary Studies Monograph Series, no. 79. Victoria, B.C.: University of Victoria, 1999, 189 p.
   Augments Baker's previous two volumes of Lewes's letters significantly, representing more fully the important literary partnership of the two authors.

Newton, K. M. "Pre-Eminent Victorian: The Life and Letters of G. H. Lewes." *Review* 20 (1998): 73-86.
   Discusses Lewes's works in the context of the biographical details of Lewes's life.

Williams, David. *Mr. George Eliot,* New York: Franklin Watts, 1983, 289 p.
   Explores the life of George Henry Lewes, including his connections with George Eliot.

Criticism

Armstrong, Isobel. "G. H. Lewes." In *The German Idea: Four English Writers and the Reception of German Thought, 1800-1860,* pp. 105-146. London: Libris, 1994, 245 p.
   Highlights the importance of Lewes's role in introducing German thought into nineteenth-century England.

———. "The Microscope: Mediations of the Sub-Visible World." In *Transactions and Encounters: Science and Culture in the Nineteenth Century,* edited by Roger Luckhurst and Josephine McDonagh, pp. 30-54. Manchester, England: Manchester University Press, 2002.
   Documents new uses of and ideas about the microscope in the mid-nineteenth century by Lewes and others.

Ashton, Rosemary. *Dickens, George Eliot and George Henry Lewes: The Hilda Hulme Memorial Lecture, 3 December 1991*. London: University of London, 1992, 32 p.

Explores Lewes's professional and personal relationships with Charles Dickens and George Eliot and probes Lewes's emphasis on psychological realism in fiction.

Caine, Barbara. "G. H. Lewes and 'The Lady Novelists.'" *Sydney Studies in English* 7 (1981-82): 85-101.

Exposes Lewes's ambivalent attitude toward women writers, whose role he exalted while patronizing the practitioners.

Collins, K. K. "G. H. Lewes Revised: George Eliot and the Moral Sense." *Victorian Studies* 21, no. 4 (summer 1978): 463-93.

Probes Eliot's revisions of Lewes's groundbreaking series *Problems of Life and Mind*.

Collins, K. K., and Frederick Williams. "Lewes at Colonus: An Early Victorian View of Translation from the Greek." *Modern Language Review* 82, no. 2 (April 1987): 293-312.

Treats Lewes's ideals of faithful translation, using his work on Sophocles' Oedipus at Colonus.

Feltes, N. N. "Phrenology: From Lewes to George Eliot." *Studies in the Literary Imagination* 1, no. 2 (April 1968): 13-22.

Discusses Lewes and Eliot's views of the Victorian pseudoscience of phrenology, which read bumps and fissures in the skull to determine personality traits.

Greenhut, Morris. "George Henry Lewes as a Critic of the Novel." *Studies in Philology* 45 (1948): 491-511.

Appraises Lewes's approach to literary criticism, both practical and theoretical.

———. "George Henry Lewes and the Classical Tradition in English Criticism." *Review of English Studies* 24, no. 94 (April 1948): 126-37.

Contends that Lewes's critical theories were highly evolved and that they paved the way for the literary criticism of Matthew Arnold and T. S. Eliot.

Haight, Gordon S. "Dickens and Lewes on Spontaneous Combustion." *Nineteenth-Century Fiction* 10, no. 1 (June 1955): 53-63.

Recounts the dispute between Lewes and Charles Dickens over Dickens's portrayal of a death by spontaneous combustion in his novel *Bleak House* (1852).

———. "The Carlyles and the Leweses." In *John Carlyle and His Contemporaries,* pp. 181-204. Durham, N.C.: Duke University Press, 1976.

Investigates the difficult relationships between Scottish author and historian Thomas Carlyle, his wife Jane Welsh, Lewes, and his common-law wife George Eliot, whom the Carlyles refused to entertain in their home.

Harrison, Frederic. "George Henry Lewes." *Academy* 14 (7 December 1878): 543-44.

Offers a short eulogy on Lewes written immediately after his death by fellow positivist and historian Frederic Harrison.

Hirshberg, Edgar W. *George Henry Lewes.* New York: Twayne Publishers, 1970, 230 p.

Examines Lewes's life and writings, in particular his literary and dramatic work.

Kaminsky, Alice. "George Eliot, George Henry Lewes, and the Novel." *PMLA* 70, no. 5 (December 1955): 997-1013.

Discusses Lewes's critical approach to the novel and its significance in relation to the works of George Eliot.

Knoepflmacher, U. C. "On Exile and Fiction: The Leweses and Shelleys." In *Mothering the Mind: Twelve Studies of Writers and Their Silent Partners,* edited by Ruth Perry and Martine Watson Brownley, pp. 102-21 New York: Holmes and Meier, 1984.

Examines the relationships between Eliot and Lewes and between Percy Bysshe and Mary Shelley with respect to gender and writing.

Read, Carveth. "G. H. Lewes's Posthumous Volumes." *Mind* 6, no. 24 (October 1881): 483-98.

Summarizes and assesses Lewes's series *Problems of Life and Mind,* some volumes of which were published after Lewes's death.

Robertson, Linda K. "Who Is a Professional Scholar? George Eliot and George Henry Lewes Considered." In *Scholarship in Victorian Britain,* edited by Martin Hewitt, pp. 102-13. Leeds, England: Leeds Centre for Victorian Studies, 1998.

Evaluates the qualifications of scholarship in Victorian England in regards to training versus experience.

Roll-Hansen, Diderik. "George Henry Lewes and His Critics." *English Studies: A Journal of English Language and Literature* 60, no. 2 (April 1979): 159-65.

Evaluates Lewes scholarship since the 1930s and suggests that Lewes's reputation has been undervalued.

Smalley, Barbara. Introduction to *Ranthorpe,* by George Henry Lewes, pp. vii-lvi. Athens: Ohio University Press, 1974.

> Surveys the composition of *Ranthorpe,* characterizing Lewes's novel as an autobiographical work and comparing it to the writings of George Eliot and Charlotte Brontë.

White, Paul. "Cross-Cultural Encounters: The Co-production of Science and Literature in Mid-Victorian Periodicals." In *Transactions and Encounters: Science and Culture in the Nineteenth Century,* edited by Roger Luckhurst and Josephine McDonagh, pp. 75-95. Manchester, England: Manchester University Press, 2002.

> Shows how Lewes bridged the elite-popular divide by making his scientific studies accessible to a general audience. White also describes the cross-disciplinary coverage of art and science made possible by Victorian journals.

Additional coverage of Lewes's life and career is contained in the following sources published by Gale: *Dictionary of Literary Biography,* **Vols. 55, 144;** *Literature Resource Center***; and** *Nineteenth-Century Literature Criticism,* **Vol. 25.**

Anthony Trollope
1815-1882

English novelist, biographer, short story writer, playwright, essayist, critic, lecturer, and sketch writer.

The following entry presents an overview of Trollope's life and works. For discussion of the novel *Barchester Towers* (1857), see *NCLC,* Volume 33; for additional discussion of Trollope's complete career, see *NCLC,* Volumes 6 and 101.

INTRODUCTION

Anthony Trollope was one of the most prolific writers of the Victorian period and one of the most financially successful at his craft. Although his works are not as well known today as those of some of his contemporaries, such as Charles Dickens and George Eliot, Trollope produced more than 47 novels, as well as nonfiction sketches, travel books, biographies, an autobiography, and various shorter works. Firmly established in the realist tradition, Trollope's works revolve around domestic life in the mid- to late nineteenth century. He is recognized for two series: the Barsetshire Chronicles, about the fictional English county of Barsetshire, and the Palliser novels, which center on the lives of a fictitious noble family. As a writer, Trollope was adept at presenting the struggles of average people and everyday life. Scholar Courtney C. Berger describes him as "the master of tedium." Some of his best-loved characters are simple, unextraordinary men and "good" women (that is, those who represent idealized Victorian feminine virtues, such as maternity, charity, and passivity).

Trollope's social circle included many of the most prominent authors of his day, such as William Makepeace Thackeray, Eliot, and Wilkie Collins. He was a founding member of the *Fortnightly,* a popular periodical of the era. Trollope remained a favorite with readers throughout his career, though during the decades after his death, he fell in the esteem of many critics, who felt he had only one kind of story to tell and that he lacked the artistic vision of a truly great novelist. Today's scholars find in his wide and diverse corpus unique insights into Victorian issues, including class and gender politics, the role of the marketplace in everyday life, and British colonialism.

BIOGRAPHICAL INFORMATION

Trollope was born on April 24, 1815. The fifth of seven children, he spent his early years in poverty, an experience that shaped the perspective revealed in his novels. His father, though well educated, was unable to support his family, abandoning careers in both law and farming and eventually fleeing in financial ruin to Belgium, where the family joined him a few days later. Education was important to Trollope's parents, and he was sent to Harrow School and later to Winchester College. Because of his family's indigence, he was often the butt of his peers' jokes and did not make friends at school. In his autobiography he explains that this early alienation helped him develop into a writer. While his peers were engaged in sports and other group activities, he was busy building "castles in the air" through which he learned "to live in a world altogether outside the world of my own material life."

After a trip to the United States in the early 1830s, Trollope's mother, Frances, began a successful career as a writer. During the family's residence in Belgium, she provided their sole income while her husband's health degenerated. Her dedication to her career, which she maintained even while caring for two of her children who were dying from tuberculosis, left a lasting impression on Trollope. He later credited her for inspiring the discipline that became his hallmark as a writer.

In 1834 Trollope took a position with the General Post Office, where he worked until his retirement in 1867. The job took him to Ireland in 1841, and there he met Rose Heseltine, whom he married in 1844. The couple had two sons. Soon after his marriage, Trollope began to write novels to supplement his income. He found that the travel he undertook each day for his employers afforded him time to compose his works. Trollope continued to write as his post office career took him around the world, from Egypt to the West Indies and eventually to the United States, where he witnessed the upheaval of the Civil War. Besides his novels, he wrote a number of travel books describing the people and customs of the countries he visited. Trollope returned to England from Ireland in 1859, bringing his family with him. They took up residence at Waltham House in Hertfordshire, where Trollope joined the London literary community and became a regular at the famed Garrick Club, which also counted Thackeray and Dickens as prominent members. For the first time he found the kind of camaraderie that had eluded him as a child.

After leaving the post office in 1867, Trollope continued to write and also served as the editor of *St. Paul's Magazine,* a short-lived periodical. Since his earliest days with the post office, he had cherished a dream of becoming a member of Parliament, and in 1868 he ran for office but lost the election. In the later years of his life, Trollope's work became increasingly political and satirical. He continued to write until the time of his death from a paralytic stroke in 1882.

MAJOR WORKS

Trollope published his first novel, *The Macdermots of Ballycloran,* in 1847. A story about an ill-fated Irish family, the work failed to attract a readership or any critical attention. He continued to write, but it would be eight years and two other failed novels before *The Warden* (1855) brought him his first taste of literary success. The novel tells the story of Mr. Harding, a likable and honest clergyman whose income from the almshouse he manages is questioned by a zealous reformer and eventually by the warden himself. The book launched Trollope's popular Barsetshire series, introducing a diverse cast of characters, most notably the formidable Mrs. Proudie, who soon became a household name in Britain. Over time the Barsetshire series grew to include *Barchester Towers* (1857), *Doctor Thorne* (1858), *Framley Parsonage* (1861; first issued in installments in the *Cornhill Magazine*), *The Small House at Allington* (1862-63; also published in segments in *Cornhill*), and *The Last Chronicle of Barset* (1866-67; distributed by a publisher in weekly installments for sixpence each), which Trollope considered his best novel.

As his popularity as an author grew, Trollope maintained an almost unparalleled level of productivity, completing one to six works each year for twenty-seven years. In 1864-65 he published *Can You Forgive Her?* in monthly shilling installments, introducing Plantagenet Palliser, an aristocrat, and his wife, Lady Glencora. The rest of the Palliser series is made up of *Phineas Finn: The Irish Member* (1867-68), *The Eustace Diamonds* (1871-73), *Phineas Redux* (1873-74), *The Prime Minister* (1875-76), and *The Duke's Children* (1879-80). These novels, published in installments in, respectively, *St. Paul's Magazine,* the *Fortnightly Review,* and the *Graphic,* by a private publisher, and in the journal *All the Year Round,* solidified Trollope's reputation as an expert on the lives and mannerisms of the British upper and middle classes.

In 1874-75 Trollope published *The Way We Live Now,* again in monthly shilling installments; the novel is a biting satire of Victorian life. Exploring the world of hack writers, dubious financiers, and dishonest speculators, the novel chastised what Trollope found to be the disagreeable attitudes of the age, including a significant decline in the manners of the British upper classes. Although it was not particularly well received by Trollope's contemporaries, who felt it to be almost vulgar in its subject matter and satire, *The Way We Live Now* is generally recognized today as one of Trollope's best novels. Similarly, *An Autobiography* (1883), once considered to have harmed Trollope's reputation as an artist by exposing his preoccupation with the business side of novel writing, is now as widely studied as his fiction exactly because Trollope was not afraid to discuss the more mechanical aspects of his craft and the financial transactions associated with literary life.

CRITICAL RECEPTION

In *An Autobiography* Trollope claimed that he made it a point never to court the favor of literary critics. He was well aware of how his works were received, however. He recorded, for example, the dearth of critical attention paid to his first novels, which passed virtually unnoticed from the literary scene. Among modern critics, these early texts are often viewed as immature works that are nonetheless helpful in tracing Trollope's growth as an author. In her 1983 essay, "Anthony Trollope's Apprenticeship," scholar Karen Faulkner describes their composition as a learning period; in these novels, Faulkner asserts, Trollope experiments with the popular literary styles of the day and "discovers what will not work for him and in the process achieves insight into what will work." Although many of his contemporaries saw his early failures as a function of their Irish setting, Trollope later returned to Irish themes in more successful works, such as *Castle Richmond* (1860), *Phineas Finn, Phineas Redux,* and *The Landleaguers* (1883). Today these novels are the cornerstone of an important vein of Trollope criticism that explores their commentary on Victorian England's relationship with the rest of the world.

The Warden, which brought Trollope to the attention of both audiences and critics, remains a frequent subject of scholarship today. The immediate appeal of the text for many early reviewers was its realistic depiction of the ordinary individuals inhabiting the fictional county of Barsetshire. For nearly a century after Trollope's death, critics tended to focus on narrative structure and technique in his texts, examining them, for example, in terms of the success of their realism as opposed to analyzing their politics. Such a mode of criticism tended to favor such novels as *The Warden* over more fanciful novels, including *The Fixed Period.* In these analyses, primacy was generally given to Trollope's fictional works over his travel and other nonfiction writings.

As scholars began to take a broader variety of approaches to Trollope's texts, the emphasis of study settled on the works as reflections of the Victorian marketplace. This trend is unsurprising, given that *An Auto-biography* reveals Trollope to have been virtually obsessed with commercial transactions. Such scholarship has explored the role of work and the marketplace in the lives of ordinary men and women in nineteenth-century England and traces the emergence of a new professional class that fascinated Trollope. Even critics who see Trollope as a staunch defender of the status quo generally agree that his early poverty predisposed him to sympathy for those who suffered due to their social status; scholars believe that he was therefore more supportive of a class-mobile society than readers might imagine. At the same time, however, Trollope's novels generally reveal him to have been in awe of the aristocracy and of the most financially successful members of the middle classes.

Criticism that explores the role of the marketplace in Trollope's work often intersects with feminist analyses of the same texts. The two are related in part because during the time that Trollope was writing, Britain was engaged in debate over a married woman's right to own property. In her essay "Heterosexual Exchange and Other Victorian Fictions," scholar Kathy Alexis Psomiades argued that such novels as Trollope's worked to reconnect the heterosexual exchange of women between men (through marriage) with the commercial exchange of goods in the marketplace at a time when new legislation was beginning to call the necessity of that connection into question. Scholars often look to *The Eustace Diamonds,* which sets up a relationship between economic transactions and female sexuality, and *He Knew He Was Right,* a novel written while the Married Women's Property Act was being debated in Parliament, as reflections of the gender politics of the age. Trollope, who was lauded by his contemporaries for his ability to represent idealized women, is generally thought to have had some unique insights into the lives of the opposite sex while remaining, for the most part, ambivalent regarding the rights of women in society.

One of the most recent developments in Trollope studies arose in relation to postcolonial theory. Such scholarship tends to focus on Trollope's travel writings, as well as on such novels as *Harry Heathcote of Gangoil* and *The Fixed Period,* which are set outside of England (in Australia and the fictional Britannula, a former colony of Great Britain, respectively). Commentator Nicholas Birns contends that while Trollope is often seen as "the epitome of beefy Englishness," a reputation that would tend to associate him with a zeal for colonialism, his treatment of the British colonies in his writing was not typical of the Anglo-centric views of the time. Other critics, such as Helen Heineman, point to the open-mindedness with which Trollope accepted the lives and customs of those he met during his travels as evidence of his somewhat progressive stance. In part, Trollope's own childhood sufferings, coupled with his

experiences in Ireland, seem to have colored his outlook, creating a tolerance that he applied to all he observed. At the same time, however, postcolonial scholars are aware that despite his fine-tuned sympathies, Trollope was very much a product of Victorian Britain, and his stories of other parts of the world often erase the experiences of native peoples and emphasize those of the colonizers. As Birns points out, for example, the Australia of *Harry Heathcote of Gangoil* "is white, male, and British."

PRINCIPAL WORKS

The Macdermots of Ballycloran (novel) 1847

The Kellys and the O'Kellys; or, Landlords and Tenants: A Tale of Irish Life (novel) 1848

La Vendée: An Historical Romance (novel) 1850

The Warden (novel) 1855

Barchester Towers (novel) 1857

Doctor Thorne: A Novel (novel) 1858

The Three Clerks: A Novel (novel) 1858

The Bertrams: A Novel (novel) 1859

The West Indies and the Spanish Main (travel essay) 1859

Castle Richmond: A Novel (novel) 1860

Framley Parsonage (novel) 1860-61; published in journal *Cornhill Magazine*

Orley Farm: A Novel (novel) 1861-62; published in monthly shilling installments

The Struggles of Brown, Jones, and Robinson, by One of the Firm (novel) 1861-62; published in journal *Cornhill Magazine*

Tales of All Countries. 3 vols. (short stories) 1861-1870

North America (travel essay) 1862

The Small House at Allington (novel) 1862-63; published in journal *Cornhill Magazine*

Rachel Ray (novel) 1863

Can You Forgive Her? (novel) 1864-65; published in monthly shilling installments

Hunting Sketches (sketches) 1865; published in journal *Pall Mall Gazette*

Miss Mackenzie (novel) 1865

The Belton Estate (novel) 1865-66; published in journal *Fortnightly Review*

Clergymen of the Church of England (nonfiction) 1865-66; published in journal *Pall Mall Gazette*

Travelling Sketches (travel essay) 1865-66; published in journal *Pall Mall Gazette*

The Claverings (novel) 1866-67; published in journal *Cornhill Magazine*

The Last Chronicle of Barset (novel) 1866-67; published in weekly sixpenny installments

Nina Balatka: The Story of a Maiden of Prague [published anonymously] (novel) 1866-67; published in journal *Blackwood's Magazine*

Lotta Schmidt and Other Stories (short stories) 1867

Linda Tressel [published anonymously] (novel) 1867-68; published in journal *Blackwood's Magazine*

Phineas Finn: The Irish Member (novel) 1867-68; published in journal *St. Paul's Magazine*

He Knew He Was Right (novel) 1868-69; published in weekly sixpenny installments

The Vicar of Bullhampton (novel) 1869-1870; published in journal *Once a Week*

The Commentaries of Caesar (literary criticism) 1870

An Editor's Tales (short stories) 1870

Sir Harry Hotspur of Humblethwaite (novel) 1870; published in journal *MacMillan's Magazine*

Ralph the Heir (novel) 1870-71; published in journal *St. Paul's Magazine*

The Eustace Diamonds (novel) 1871-73; published in journal *Fortnightly Review*

The Golden Lion of Granpère (novel) 1872; published in journal *Good Words*

Australia and New Zealand (travel essay) 1873-74; published in journal *Australasian*

Harry Heathcote of Gangoil: A Tale of Australian Bush Life (novel) 1873-74; published in journal *The Graphic*

Lady Anna (novel) 1873-74; published in journal *Fortnightly Review*

Phineas Redux (novel) 1873-74; published in journal *The Graphic*

The Way We Live Now (novel) 1874-75; published in monthly shilling installments

The Prime Minister (novel) 1875-76; published in monthly shilling installments

The American Senator (novel) 1876-77; published in journal *Temple Bar*

Is He Popenjoy? A Novel (novel) 1877-78; published in journal *All the Year Round*

How the "Mastiffs" Went to Iceland (travel book) 1878

South Africa (travel book) 1878

An Eye for an Eye (novel) 1878-79; published in journal *Whitehall Review*

John Caldigate (novel) 1878-79; published in journal *Blackwood's Magazine*

Cousin Henry: A Novel (novel) 1879; published in *Manchester Weekly Times* and *North British Weekly Mail*

Thackeray (biography) 1879

The Duke's Children: A Novel (novel) 1879-80; published in journal *All the Year Round*

Dr. Wortle's School: A Novel (novel) 1880; published in journal *Blackwood's Magazine*

The Life of Cicero (biography) 1880

Ayala's Angel (novel) 1880-81; published in *Cincinnati Commercial*

The Fixed Period: A Novel (novel) 1881-82; published in journal *Blackwood's Magazine*

Marion Fay: A Novel (novel) 1881-82; published in journal *The Graphic* and in the *Illustrated Sydney News*

Kept in the Dark: A Novel (novel) 1882; published in journal *Good Words*

Lord Palmerston (biography) 1882

The Two Heroines of Plumpington (novella) 1882

Why Frau Frohmann Raised Her Prices, and Other Stories (short stories) 1882

The Landleaguers (unfinished novel) 1882-83; published in journal *Life Magazine*

Mr. Scarborough's Family (novel) 1882-83; published in journal *All the Year Round*

Alice Dugdale and Other Stories (short stories) 1883

An Autobiography (autobiography) 1883

La Mère Bauche and Other Stories (short stories) 1883

The Mistletoe Bough and Other Stories (short stories) 1883

An Old Man's Love (novel) 1884

The Noble Jilt: A Comedy (play) 1923

London Tradesmen (nonfiction) 1927

Four Lectures (lectures) 1938

The Tireless Traveler: Twenty Letters to the "Liverpool Mercury" (letters) 1941

Novels and Stories (short stories) 1946

The Parson's Daughter and Other Stories (short stories) 1949

The Spotted Dog and Other Stories (short stories) 1950

Mary Gresley and Other Stories (short stories) 1951

Did He Steal It? A Comedy in Three Acts (play) 1952

The New Zealander (essay) 1972

CRITICISM

National Review (review date January 1863)

SOURCE: "Orley Farm." *National Review* 16, no. 31 (January 1863): 27-40.

[*In the following essay, the anonymous reviewer introduces Trollope's novel* Orley Farm *(1861-62) as an example of refined British culture and society. The review was written in reaction to an 1862 article that appeared in the French journal* Revue des deux mondes *criticizing British novels and accusing them of providing evidence of a corrupt society.*]

M. Folgues has recently taken occasion, in the pages of the *Revue des Deux Mondes*, to express, under the unflattering title of "Dégénérescence du Roman," his views as to the present state of English fiction, and the future prospects of English morality. As he grounds his opinion in the one case on a survey of about a dozen of the most worthless stories of the day, and in the other on the revelations of Sir Cresswell Cresswell's court, it is natural enough that the account which he gives of us should be of a somewhat gloomy and humiliating character. With perfect good humour, and with a polite vindictiveness, the fruit evidently of prolonged provocation, he turns the laugh of his audience against the affected severity of our social code, the delicacy of our taste, and the boasted prudery of our literature. British mothers, he says, look upon a French novel as "the abomination of desolation," and British youths veil their faces in pious horror before the innuendos of Paul de Kock, the eager voluptuousness of Dumas, or the ingenious impurity of Ernest Feydau. And yet, continues our frank monitor, England stands a good chance of descending from her pinnacle, and proving herself, in outward demonstration, no better than her neighbours. Such exposures as the Windham trial show that profligacy is much the same on one side of the Channel as the other, and the activity of the Divorce Court bespeaks an unhallowed restlessness in the matrimonial world. On the other hand, free trade is likely enough to extend from material to intellectual productions: along with the vintage of Bordeaux and the silks of Lyons, the sturdy Puritans are day by day imbibing the lax notions of less austere communities; and England, whose *métier* it has been to lecture the rest of Europe on improprieties, already possesses a race of novelists who want only the liveliness of their neighbours and the tricks of the trade, to be as viciously entertaining, and to gratify their own and their readers' improper cravings and unchastened sensibilities, by delineations as daring, a levity as complete, a license as openly avowed, as any thing that Eve's latest and most degenerate daughters can pluck from the fruit-trees of forbidden knowledge in the lending libraries of Paris.

Such a work as **Orley Farm** is perhaps the most satisfactory answer that can be given to so disagreeable an imputation. Here, it may fairly be said, is the precise standard of English taste, sentiment, and conviction. Mr. Trollope has become almost a national institution. The *Cornhill* counts its readers by millions, and it is to his contributions, in ninety-nine cases out of a hundred, that the reader first betakes himself. So great is his popularity, so familiar are his chief characters to his countrymen, so wide-spread is the interest felt about his tales, that they necessarily form part of the common stock-in-trade with which the social commerce of the day is carried on. If there are some men in real life whom not to know argues oneself unknown, there are certainly imaginary personages on Mr. Trollope's canvas with whom every well-informed member of the community is expected to have at least a speaking acquaintance. The disappointment of Sir Peregrine, the boyish love of his grandson, the conceited transcendentalism of Lucius Mason, the undeserved prosperity of Graham, the matrimonial troubles of the Furnival establishment, and the high life below stairs to which Mr. Moulder and his travelling companion introduce us,—have probably been discussed at half the dinner-tables in London, as often and with as much earnestness as Royal Academies, International Exhibitions, the last

mail from America, Sir William Armstrong's newest discovery in the science of destruction, or any other of the standing conversational topics on which the conventional interchange of thought is accustomed to depend. The characters are public property, and the prolific imagination which has called them into existence is, without doubt, the most accurate exponent of the public feeling, and of that sort of social philosophy which exercises an unperceived, but not less actual, despotism over the life and conscience of every individual who forms a unit in the great aggregate of society. More than a million people habitually read Mr. Trollope, and they do so because the personages in his stories correspond to something in themselves: the hopes, fears, and regrets, are such as they are accustomed to experience; the thoughtfulness is such as they can appreciate; the standard of conduct just that to which they are prepared to submit. It becomes, therefore, an interesting inquiry to see what are the principal characteristics of an author in whom so large a section of the community sees as it were its own reflection, and who may himself unhesitatingly be accepted as the modern type of a successful novelist:—how far are we justified, with **Orley Farm** in our hands, in rebutting M. Forgues' accusations, and in maintaining that neither in literature nor morality has the period of English degeneracy as yet commenced.

One part of the charge may, we think, be very speedily disposed of. If the popularity of the portrait is the result of its truthfulness, and English life is at all what Mr. Trollope paints it, whatever its other failings may be, it is at any rate a very correct affair; writer and readers alike look at the performance from a strictly moral point of view: there is a general air of purity, innocence, and cheerfulness. The Bohemians that now and then flit across the stage are the tamest imaginable, and are only just sufficiently Bohemian to be picturesque without violating propriety. There are occasional villains of course, but they seem to belong to an outer world, with which the audience has so little in common that it can afford to treat their crimes as a matter of mere curiosity. The low Jewish attorney, the brass-browed Old Bailey practitioner, Mr. Moulder in his drunken moods, Dockwrath in his revengeful spite,—are none of them models of what gentlemen and Christians should be; but they are never brought sufficiently near to display the full proportions of their guilt, or to suggest the possibility of contamination. The real interest of the story is concentrated upon well-to-do, decorous, and deservedly prosperous people, who solve, with a good deal of contentment and self-satisfaction, the difficult problem of making the most both of this world and the next. The family of the Staveleys is in this way perhaps the most characteristic group which Mr. Trollope has as yet produced. They are thoroughly successful, and their success is well deserved; they have a calm, well-ordered, and healthily unobtrusive religion; they are quite above intrigue, shabbiness, or malevolence. Lady Staveley is a model as wife, mother, and mother-in-law; and Madeline, though she falls rather more precipitately in love than that *bien rangée* young lady should, is on the whole just such a daughter as a Lady Staveley would wish to have. The Christmas party at Noningsby could have been written only by a man who had experienced and appreciated the enjoyment of a well-ordered, hospitable, unpretentious country-house, where there are plenty of children, wealth enough to rob life of its embarrassments, simplicity enough to allow of a little romping and flirtation, and where every member of the family is on confidential terms with all the rest. Among the guests are a vulgar scheming young woman, the daughter of a London barrister; a nice simple lad, heir to a neighbouring baronet; and Felix Graham, clever, talkative, and agreeable, but ugly and penniless, and encumbered moreover with "an angel of light," in the shape of a young lady whom he has rescued from poverty, supplied with the rudiments of education, and promised, some day or other, to make his wife. Every thing is, however, perfectly innocent; and Graham, having been guilty of nothing but a generous indiscretion, proceeds forthwith to throw the angel of light into the background, and to fall in love with the young lady of the house. There are Christmas games in the evening for the children; and Graham is selected by one of them as her champion, and effects on her behalf a successful raid upon the snap-dragon, over which Miss Staveley is presiding as ghost and dragoness.

> 'Now Marian,' he says, bringing her up in his arms.
>
> 'But it will burn, Mr. Felix; look there, see, there are a great many at that end. You do it.'
>
> 'I must have another kiss, then.'
>
> 'Very well, yes, if you get five;' and then Felix dashed his hand in among the flames and brought out a fistful of fruit, which imparted to his fingers and wristband a smell of brandy for the rest of the evening.
>
> 'If you take so many at a time, I shall rap your knuckles with the spoon,' said the ghost, as she stirred up the flames to keep them alive.
>
> 'But the ghost shouldn't speak,' said Marian, who was evidently unacquainted with the best ghosts in tragedy.
>
> 'But the ghost must speak when such large hands invade the caldron;' and then another raid was effected, and the threatened blow was given. Had any one told her in the morning that she would that day have rapped Mr. Graham's knuckles with a kitchen-spoon, she would not have believed that person. But it is so that hearts are lost and won.

All the point in this sort of scene depends on the innocence of the performers; and it is because Mr. Trollope can manufacture passages of the kind in any quantity required, that he has made himself the favourite writer of the day. The people on whose behalf he interests one are thoroughly sterling, warm-hearted, and excellent.

Every body would be glad to spend Christmas at Noningsby, to go for a walk on Sunday afternoon with the good-natured old judge, to have a chat with Lady Staveley, and to receive a rap on the knuckles from Miss Madeline. What every body would be glad to do, every body likes to read about, and hence a universal popularity without either an exciting plot or forcible writing, or the least pretence at real thoughtfulness, to support it. Contrast Mr. Trollope in this respect with such a writer as the author of *Guy Livingston,* his superior certainly in melodramatic conception, in vivid scene-painting, brilliant dialogue, and in familiarity with several amusing phases of life. Not all the ability, however, of *Guy Livingston* and its successors can force them into popularity against the steady dislike and disapproval which their loose tone excites. Throughout them there is an aroma of indelicacy, a half-admiration of profligacy, a familiarity with crime, which an English audience finds it impossible to forgive. There are, no doubt, sets of people whose proceedings and sentiments they correctly represent; but the great mass of readers regard them with aversion, and if they consent, for the sake of an amusing story, to make a transient acquaintance with the personages who play it out, accord them no welcome to their memories, and reject the whole picture as a libel upon modern society. When M. Forgues assures us that we are corrupt, and that our novels prove it, it would be enough, as regards this country, to contrast the fate of such books as *Sword and Gown* with that of **Orley Farm,** and, with respect to France, to remind him that such a volume as has within the last few weeks proceeded from the pen of M. Edmond About, at one time the most decent as well as the wittiest of his profession, would be unhesitatingly refused admission to every English library or railway-stall, and would certainly forfeit for its author not only literary reputation and general popularity, but would make him an outcast from all respectable society.

But if we reject the imputation of one kind of degeneracy, it should be admitted that the success of Mr. Trollope's school of writing suggests the possibility of another. Such delineations are, to say the truth, but very low art; and while they do not corrupt the morals, they may degrade the tastes, and foster the weaknesses of those for whose edification they are contrived. Mr. Trollope, it has been truly said, is a mere photographer; he manipulates with admirable skill, he groups his sitters in the most favourable attitudes, he contrives an endless series of interesting positions; but he never attains to the dignity of an artist. He has a quick eye for external characteristics, and he paints exclusively from without. He does not make us intimate with his characters, for the excellent reason that he is very far from being intimate with them himself. He watches their behaviour, their dress, their tone of voice, their expression of countenance, and he makes very shrewd guesses at their dispositions; but there is a veil in each one of their characters, behind which he is not privileged to pass, and where real conceptive genius could alone suffice to place him. Almost every nature has depths about it somewhere, with all sorts of moral curiosities at the bottom, if one has plummet deep enough to sound them. It is the inclination to do this, and the mental energy to do it with ability and discrimination, that constitute poetic power, and which give to writers like Charlotte Brontë or the authoress of *Adam Bede* so deep a hold over the interests and affections of the reader. When they have finished a portrait, one seems to have seen it through and through: it is a conception, created in their minds and brought visibly before their readers, by scenes so contrived as to bring the most secret passions into play, "to try the very reins and the heart," and to show the true nature of the actor more clearly, even than he sees it himself. Mr. Trollope sets to work in quite another fashion. He arms himself, in the first place, with a number of commonplaces on religion, morals, politics, social and domestic philosophy. These supply his theory of life, and beyond them, in his most imaginative moments, he never raises his eye; but, accepting them as a creed, and as the ultimate explanation of all around him, he watches the society in which he lives, and elaborates a series of complications, which interest, partly from the sympathy one feels for pretty, nicely-dressed, and well-behaved young ladies, and partly from a natural curiosity to see how the author will get himself out of the scrape into which the evolution of the story has brought him. This sort of writing can never produce a profound emotion, and leaves us at last with a sense of dissatisfaction. Mr. Trollope himself seems to feel that it falls short of the requirements of a real emergency, and screens the defect by implying conversations, feelings, and expressions which he does not choose precisely to delineate. It is precisely these that we want to have, if we are to care in the least about the characters of the tale, and in their absence we feel a void exactly proportionate to the interest previously excited. Take, for instance, the case of Lady Mason: nothing could be more exciting than the position assigned to her. She is beautiful, engaging, refined; an old country gentleman of high standing is her accepted lover, and she has just confessed to him that she has for twenty years been living on the proceeds of perjury and forgery, for which she is about, in a few weeks, to be brought into a court of justice. Sir Peregrine Orme, who was to have been her husband, sees of course the impossibility of his marriage; and Mrs. Orme, his widow daughter, and Lady Mason's confidential friend, proceeds to offer advice, consolation, and forgiveness. "Many," says Mr. Trollope, "will think that she was wrong to do so, and I fear it must be acknowledged that she was not strong-minded. By forgiving her, I do not mean that she pronounced absolution for the sin of past years, or that she endeavoured to make the sinner think that she was no worse for her sin. Mrs. Orme was a

good churchwoman, but not strong individually in points of doctrine. All that she left mainly to the woman's conscience and her own dealings with her Saviour, merely saying a word of salutary counsel as to a certain spiritual pastor who might be of aid. But Mrs. Orme forgave her as regarded herself."

This seems to us about the most feeble way of getting through a striking scene that it is possible to conceive, and the suggestion of calling in the clergyman puts the finishing touch to the "mildness" of the whole. Contrast it, for instance, with the description of Miriam and Donatello, in *Transformation,* after the commission of the murder, or with that of the heroine of the *Scarlet Letter* after the discovery of her guilt. It is mere trifling to slur the scene over with hack religious phrases, to send for the parson just as one would for the parish engine, and calmly to pretermit the exact tragical *dénouement* to which the whole story has been leading up. Later on in the book we have a glimpse of the sort of consolation which, we suppose, the "certain spiritual pastor" administered on his arrival. "No lesson," the author more than once informs us, "is truer than that which teaches us that God does temper the wind to the shorn lamb." A shorn lamb! and this of a woman whose whole life has been one long lie, whose every act has been studied for a hypocritical purpose, and who is driven to reluctant confession at last, not from any sudden conviction of guilt, not because she finds the burden of her solitary crime becoming absolutely intolerable, not because in an agony of fatigue and remorse she tears off the mask she has worn with such suffering endurance,—but because she is not wretch enough to incur the infamy of involving a noble old man in the disgrace and ruin which she knows, and which other people know, is shortly about to break upon herself.

There are, no doubt, people going about the world with secrets locked up in their hearts, to the safe custody of which, as of some ferocious wild beast, their whole existence is devoted. The Spartan lad with the hidden fox gnawing his flesh is probably no exaggeration of the agonies they endure, and the heroic self-restraint which concealment necessitates. "Let the great gods," cries Lear in the thunder-storm,

> Find out their enemies now. Tremble, thou wretch,
> That hast within thee undivulged crimes,
> Unwhipped of justice: Hide thee, thou bloody hand;
> Thou perjured, and thou simular man of virtue,
> That art incestuous: Caitiff, to pieces shake,
> That under covert and convenient seeming
> Hast practised on man's life!

The tragedy of such careers is a dark one, and the artist who essays to paint it must be prepared with a courageous hand, intense colouring, and shades and lights in more striking contrast than are to be found in the mere conventional routine of ordinary society. Hypocrisy is a painful trade, and must make itself felt over an entire character, where once its employment has become essential. Lady Mason, after twenty years of it, would have been something very different from the calm, handsome, well-dressed, but impressible and half-coquettish woman to whom Mr. Trollope introduces us. Her experience would have put her beyond the reach of such gentle ministrations as Mrs. Orme's, and would have made it impossible for her in the crisis of her fate to behave like a silly impressible school-girl. Imposture "should be made of sterner stuff," and the sternness should be evidenced by a resolution, a courage, prepared nerves, a daring spirit, a readiness to run risk and encounter disaster, such as we find no trace of in Mr. Trollope's creation. Repentance, when it comes, must be the result of something more than accident, and remorse, if it is to be real, must require deeper comfort than little bits of texts, pet curates, and pretty proverbs.

How tragical does such a position become in the hands of a really pathetic writer! Who has not almost shuddered at Hood's description of the utter isolation, the nervous watchfulness, the growing horror of the secret criminal living alone amid the crowd of innocent school-boys?—

> Peace went with them one and all,
>   And each calm pillow spread;
> But Guilt was my grim chamberlain
>   That lighted me to bed,
> And drew my midnight curtains round
>   With fingers bloody red.

Eugene Aram lives in one's thoughts as a reality; Lady Mason fades into indistinctness as soon as Mr. Millais's pretty sketches of a graceful sentimental woman, always *bien mise* and always in an appropriate attitude, have ceased to enlist our sympathies or arouse our curiosity.

But if Mr. Trollope's position in the artistic world is not very high, it is to this very circumstance that he probably owes much of his reputation. He travels with great agility, it is true, but never in a region where the million readers of *The Cornhill* find the least difficulty in following him. He paints life in its easy, superficial, intelligible aspects. Felix Graham and Lucius Mason, who are intended to be originals, deviate in no essential quality from the ten thousand other young men who might with equal propriety have been introduced to fill their place. Lucius is on the whole a greater fool than Graham, and being less of a gentleman, lets his folly escape in more disagreeable ways; but neither of them suggests any real rebellion against the actual constitution of society, the theories by which life is shaped, and the maxims which the majority at once obey for themselves and inflict upon others. The whole picture is full of sunshine; the tragedy of life, of which every man is conscious in his graver moments, and which at some particular crisis absorbs his thoughts,—the grave doubts, the painful struggles, the miserable anxieties, the humiliating defeats, all that makes the world something else than a mere playground for children or a bed of roses for idlers,—find no place in the cheerful, sanguine, well-to-do philosophy which feeds the perennial font of Mr. Trollope's fictions. "Si vis me flere," says the Roman instructor in the art of influencing others, "dolendum est Primum ipsi tibi." People like Charlotte Brontë speak out of the fulness of their heart, when they depict the sufferings of our existence, and they infect us with sympathy for vicissitudes, disappointments, or regrets, with which each of us has something in common. They go nearer the truth, and they teach us a worthier lesson than he whom a good-natured superficiality and a perilous influx of success prevent from looking into the gloomy caverns which surround him, from visiting the chamber where he, like his neighbours, has a skeleton on guard, and from indulging in the aspirations to which suffering flies for refuge, and which alone saves the miserable from despair.

A world of Lady Staveleys would be, after all, a poor concern, and angels like Madeline would be the inhabitants of a duller heaven than even that which conventional theology has depicted as the future residence of the blest. Contentment is a noble achievement, but it must not be the content of a mere material well-being, of shallow thought, of slight insight, of narrow scope. It is to this sort of mood that Mr. Trollope's stories are calculated to minister; and by fostering it, they perhaps do as much towards lowering the dignity, enfeebling the energies, and coarsening the prevailing taste of the times, as if they in any tangible particular violated the conventional standard of decorum. The mass of second-rate people is preserved from corruption only by a leaven of genius, and the world goes its way in peace only because a few men here and there are sensitive enough to appreciate its catastrophes, and bold enough to infringe its rules, question its methods, and attack its abuses. Without them we should degenerate into that Lilliputian congeries of petty interests, timid thoughts, and unworthy ambitions, which Béranger, with a gloomy mirth, depicted as the approaching condition of his countrymen:

> Combien d'imperceptibles êtres!
> De petits jésuites bilieux!
> De milliers d'autres petits prêtres
> Qui portent de petits bons dieux!
> Béni par eux tout dégénère,
> Par eux la plus vieille des cours
> N'est plus qu'un petit séminaire:
> Mais les barbons regnent toujours!
>
> Tout est petit,—palais, usines,
> Science, commerce, beaux arts,—
> De bonnes petites famines
> Désolent de petits remparts;
> Sur la frontière mal fermée

Marche, au bruit de petits tambours,
Une pauvre petite armée:
Mais les barbons regnent toujours!

Some such danger seems to us, we confess, to impend over a generation for which such contrivances as *The Cornhill* secure an infinity of "Orley Farms," and which seduces an artist like Mr. Millais from his legitimate occupations to draw little commonplace sketches of commonplace life, with be-crinolined young ladies fresh from the pages of *Le Follet,* and incidents whose trivialities his pencil alone could rescue from being absolutely vulgar.

When we have said, however, that Mr. Trollope is incapable of conceiving a tragedy, or of doing justice to it when circumstances bring it in his way, we have well nigh exhausted the complaints that need be brought against him. It is a more agreeable task to touch upon the many excellent qualities which have concurred in recommending him to the good will of his countrymen. His pages are unsullied by a single touch of malice, unkindness, or revenge. His amusing sketch in *The Warden* of three bishops, given as a burlesque account of the three sons of the archdeacon, proves that he could, if he pleased, be personal to the greatest effect; and every author must have little spites and dislikes of his own, which only a resolute good feeling can prevent from intruding upon his canvas. Mr. Trollope never sins in this respect, and his immunity from this failing might well be accepted as an apology for a host of minor delinquencies. Another great charm is, that the author is for the most part kept well out of sight, and if he appears, shows himself thoroughly interested in the piece, and sincerely desirous that his audience should be so likewise. Mr. Thackeray's curious taste for careless, rambling, "round-about" writing, and the clever knack he has of making the most of "an infinite deal of nothing," has set the fashion to a host of imitators, who do not scruple to stop at every convenient point of their narration to indulge in a few personal confidences, and enunciate their views about their story, themselves, or the world in general. Mr. Thackeray, in particular, loses no opportunity of, so to speak, yawning in public; saying how dreadfully tiresome his novels are to him, how he falls asleep over them at the club, and strongly recommends his friends to do the same. Mr. Trollope has no touch of this affectation; he does his very best: he believes in the piece, he detests the villains, admires the heroes, and can scarcely refrain from caressing his pet heroine when she crosses his path. If he comes for a few moments on the stage, it is only to bustle about, to adjust the ropes, to hurry the scene-shifters, and to assure the beholders that no pains are being spared for their entertainment. Mr. Thackeray, on the contrary, lolls in dressed in a dressing-gown and slippers, stretches his arms, cries, "Eheu! fugaces,—monsieur, mon cher confrère;" and acknowledges that he has often done vilely before, but never so vilely as on the present occasion.

Mr. Trollope does not, however, invariably preserve the wholesome rule of impersonality. Though a thorough optimist, and believing in his heart that the world is the best of all possible worlds, he has one or two little grievances which keep us just short of absolute perfection. With characteristic carelessness and high spirits, he points out the tiny flaw which he has discovered, and adds a scarcely serious murmur to the general chorus of complaint. One of his troubles, for instance, is, that there should be such wicked people as lawyers in the world, and he grows quite sentimental over the circumstance that gentlemen should put off their consciences when they put on their wigs, and consent, for the small remuneration of one guinea, to make the worse appear the better cause. In support of his views, he has constructed an elaborate trial scene, with a proper apparatus of bullying counsel, lying attorneys, frightened witnesses, and, finally, frustrated justice. A discriminating critic, who appears to write with professional enthusiasm, has been at the pains to tear the whole thing to pieces, and to show that in every essential particular Mr. Trollope did not know what he was talking about, that no such facts as those on which he grounds his insinuation could possibly exist, and that all but a few black sheep in the profession do precisely what Mr. Trollope says that they ought. So much good labour seems to us in a large degree wasted upon a writer with whom instruction is necessarily subsidiary to amusement, and who scarcely pretends to any but the most superficial acquaintance with the evils of which he complains. Some of the details of the trial, especially the cross-examination by the counsel for the defence, are so ludicrously unlike real life, that it is evident Mr. Trollope's visits to a court of justice have been few and far between, and have left on his mind only a vague and indistinct impression, which nothing but the haze in which it is involved preserves from instant exposure. Ideas of this kind hardly admit of being definitely stated, but may be easily insinuated in the course of a story constructed for the purpose of exemplifying them. Witnesses, no doubt, are sometimes bullied into confusion and even forgetfulness; but Mr. Trollope cannot seriously mean that when a poor fool like Kenneby gets into the box to swear away another person's life or character, his capacity to remember any thing, and the degree in which he actually does remember the particular facts in question, ought not to be tested with the utmost severity. It is curious that, in the very case which Mr. Trollope frames in his own support, the performers do precisely that which justice required. Mr. Chaffanbrass; from the Old Bailey, may have been a great rogue; but he acted quite properly, and served the general interests of society in demonstrating that Dockwrath had private motives of the very strongest kind for supporting the prosecution, just as Mr. Furnival acted quite properly in showing that Kenneby had only half his wits about him, and had no such accurate recollection of a matter which happened twenty years before as to justify a conviction for perjury. Mr. Trollope probably meant nothing more than that barristers are sometimes vulgar and unscrupulous, and judges sometimes petulant and overbearing; but he should beware of discussing as a grievance that which is really a necessity, and of grounding on imaginary and impossible facts an imputation on the honour and good faith of a profession which certainly contains in its ranks as many scrupulous and high-minded gentlemen as any other.

It would be easy to multiply instances of the same sort of unsubstantial complaint thrown in without any real conviction, as a sort of sentimental garnishing to a matter-of-fact narrative. In his last tale, for instance, the author stops in the midst of the description of a village to contrast our present ideas of rural grandeur with those of our forefathers. In old times the good squire "sat himself down close to his God and his tenants," and placed his house so as "to afford comfort, protection, and patronage" to those around him; nowadays "a solitude in the centre of a park is the only eligible site; no cottage must be seen but the cottage *orné* of the gardener; the village, if it cannot be abolished, must be got out of sight; the sound of the church-bells is not desirable," &c.; in fact, the present race of country gentlemen are a sad falling away from the traditional benevolence of their race. Does Mr. Trollope, we wonder, really believe this? What is the golden age with which the present iron epoch is contrasted? Does he look back with a loving eye upon feudal times and the "droits de seigneurie"? or are we wrong in believing that the maxim, that property has duties as well as rights, has never been more thoroughly accepted than in our day, and that the squires of England, more perhaps than any other class of proprietors in existence, are alive to the responsibilities of their position, and struggling conscientiously "to afford comfort, protection, and patronage" of the most substantial sort to their poorer neighbours?

We can afford to touch only upon one other characteristic of Mr. Trollope's writings, to which he would, we think, do well to pay attention,—their occasional broad vulgarity. He drops every now and then with suspicious case into a society which is simply repulsive in its stupid coarseness; and as he has not the extravagant fun that Dickens pours over low life, and which has immortalised such personages as Mrs. Gamp, these parts of Mr. Trollope's writings are singularly tedious and unattractive. Some people have a genius for such descriptions: the authoress of *Adam Bede* can draw a set of countrymen drinking in a public-house so humorously that we forget every thing but the fun of the scene; but Mr. Trollope's commercial gentlemen, lodging-house keepers, and attorneys, are simply snobs, into whose proceedings one feels no wish to pry, and who might with great advantage be banished altogether from the picture. A stupid violent man like Moulder, coming home half tipsy, and proceeding to complete the process of intoxication before his wife and friends, must be very amusing indeed meanwhile, if we are to look on without disgust; in Mr. Trollope's hands he is any thing but amusing, and tries to atone for his dulness by being unnecessarily coarse. Mr. Trollope succeeds capitally in depicting nice young ladies like Madeline Staveley, and pleasant gentlemanly lads like Peregrine Orme; and he may contentedly resign the portraiture of Moulders, Kantwises, and Kennebys, to artists whose knowledge of life is more varied than his own, or whose conceptive ability enables them, as in some rare instances is the case, to dispense with the experience from which all but the very highest sort of artists are obliged to draw.

Harper's New Monthly Magazine (review date June-November 1877)

SOURCE: "Editor's Literary Record." *Harper's New Monthly Magazine* 55 (June-November 1877): 787-90.

[*In the following excerpt, the reviewer provides a brief critique of Trollope's* The American Senator (1876-77) *from an American point of view.*]

Perhaps it is impossible for an American to criticise without prejudice Mr. Anthony Trollope's last novel, **The American Senator** (Harper and Brothers). The scene is English, so are the characters, except the one who gives the name to the book. With that exception, they are drawn with that fidelity to nature which is the chief charm in Mr. Trollope's writings. None of the personages of the simple drama are of a kind to awaken one's enthusiasm. They are just such as one might meet in any English hunting party or country parish. The satire on the national fox-hunting is all the more enjoyable that the satirist has only pictured prosaically, and without the least participation in the exhilaration of its devotees, that extraordinary sport. But when he comes to the painting of the American Senator, his cunning deserts him, and he falls into the inevitable exaggerations of all Englishmen when they undertake to depict an American. If the portrait had been that of an Assemblyman, we should not have objected; we could even have borne with him as a member of the House of Representatives; but to make him a Senator! Surely the body which has given to the political world a Calhoun, a Webster, a Clay, a Sumner, and a Seward deserved some different typical man to represent it to the readers of English romance than Mr. Gotobed. The story is an entertaining one, and even the caricature is clever.

Affable Hawk [pseudonym of Desmond MacCarthy] (essay date 22 April 1922)

SOURCE: Hawk, Affable [pseudonym of Desmond MacCarthy]. "Books in General." *New Statesman* 19, no. 471 (22 April 1922): 67.

[*In the following essay, Hawk praises Trollope's novel* He Knew He Was Right (1868-69).]

Anthony Trollope: "His great, his inestimable merit was a complete appreciation of the usual. Trollope, therefore, with his eyes comfortably fixed on the familiar, the actual, was far from having invented a new category; his distinction is that in resting just there his vision took in so much of the field. And then he *felt* all daily and immediate things as well as saw them; felt them in a simple, direct, salubrious way, with their sadness, their gladness, their charm, their comicality, all their obvious and measurable meanings." (Henry James, *Partial Portraits.* Macmillan.)

* * *

Having just re-read three of Trollope's novels I fully appreciate the excellence of this criticism. It states the central facts about him; "a complete appreciation of the usual," solid, unpretentious presentment of facts, warm human sympathies—these are great merits in a novelist. I can understand an artist, a poet, or a young reader passionately curious about life, thinking Trollope small beer, but I cannot understand any mature, prosaic novel-reader despising him. I should like to add to the above list of his merits another item: consistency in his attitude towards his characters. His moral standards were, of course, conventional; had they not been, he would not have been the favourite novelist of so many readers, neither would he have been so sensible, for his mind was not of the calibre to make discoveries in common sense and morals. But it is not only this kind of consistency I have in mind. In investigating motives, in recording the thoughts and emotions of his characters, he consistently stopped analysis at a certain point. This is a most important factor in achieving what is called "unity" in fiction. It is fatal to "unity" to be superficial in analysis on one page and dig deep the next. One reason why psycho-analysis is likely to have a baleful effect on fiction is that it offers easy short-cuts to apparent psychological profundity for smatterers in human nature, who proceed, after a passage or two of scientific acuteness, to describe life on another level. To write a love story in which the "complexes" of one of the pair are analysed, while the other's feelings are described in terms, say, of Hardy or Henry James, is to commit an artistic howler of the worst description; nor can the mole-burrowings of Dostoievsky or the subtleties of Tchekov be introduced into stories which then quietly proceed on a George Eliot level.

* * *

Any well-read man or woman—any talented duffer—can be psychological in certain directions nowadays; what no duffer can do is to pull the world together in his head in which profundities occur. Not a few novelists recognise this, and there is a noticeable tendency now to get rid of "the story" altogether in fiction, that is to say, of the general survey of life which anything like a story implies, and to confine attention to what is going on in the head of one character during a given space of time. Such novels resemble geological sections rather than a landscape; geology and perspective can be combined in the novel, and perhaps that is its great point as an art form, but it needs an artist to do it. In Mr. Joyce's *Ulysses,* in which the mental experience of twenty-four hours is described in seven hundred pages, the geological interest is pushed as far as it can possibly go; it deals with nothing but superimposed strata of consciousness. This is the stuff twenty-four hours of "life" is made of, he seems to say; *Ulysses* is the climax of this tendency; there is no outlook, no perspective; everything is the same size and right up against your nose.

How far that tendency has carried us I have been reminded by Trollope. Trollope sets out to tell us a story, and in the course of it to give us a wide view over life. But one story does not enable him to give us a wide enough view of the world; so, in the manner of Dickens and his contemporaries, under the title of one novel he gives us, as a matter of fact, a bundle of stories. One of the novels I re-read was **He Knew He Was Right.** It is a very good Trollope. Here, as usual, his technical problem is to combine plausibly his different stories. The central theme is a quarrel between a jealous husband and an indignant, innocent wife, which gradually separates them completely, until he becomes a victim to suspicion-mania, and she, in despairing pity, at last pretends, too late however to comfort him or restore the balance of his mind, that he was in the right. Trevelyan is the nearest approach to pathological study I know in Trollope's novels; he is drawn as convincingly as Archdeacon Grantley or any of Trollope's famous characters who stand so firmly on their legs. The transition from egotistic obstinacy through a dangerous and lonely pride towards something very like monomania, is admirably traced, and the closing scenes of his physical and mental dilapidation have the solidity, if not the intensity, of a Balzac tragedy. But Emily Trevelyan has a sister Nora, and the story of her love affair (she has two suitors, one a rich lord and the other a radical journalist) bulks large in the book. Hugh Stanbury again, her successful suitor, has a sister Dorothy, who is adopted by a spirited, tyrannical, warm-hearted old aunt, and Dorothy's tribulations and ultimate happiness bulk larger still. She also has two suitors, and Trollope not only marries her off, at last, after her own heart, but, in addition, he takes us through the love predicaments of the sleek, ignoble Rev. Gibson whom she refused, and the story of the engagement of the sensible Lord Peterborough, whom her sister Nora refused. All this has nothing, of course, to do with the main theme. Life in Exeter Cathedral close where Dorothy lives with Miss Stanbury, has only the barest tangential relation to the Trevelyan tragedy, while Mr. Gibson's affairs with the sisters French and Lord Peterborough's marriage have still less to do with it. The reader cannot help sometimes exclaiming with impatience on finding himself perpetually switched off from one line of interest to another; yet this old-fashioned method of driving six stories abreast through a novel does achieve an effect it is very difficult to produce in any other way.

* * *

When one reads a novel one instinctively narrows one's sense of the world down to the author's field of vision. Nothing could be more piteous than the story of the Trevelyans; isolate it, elaborate it, throw in a little physiology, and you have one of those novels which you finish feeling life is indeed a drab and desperate business. The great advantage of this old-fashioned, artificial method in fiction is that it at once puts such cases in the general landscape of human fate, not only to the great advantage of your spirits, but of your judgment. If we were immersed for three hundred pages in the mind of the wretched Louis Trevelyan, and meanwhile saw nothing else, we would rise as from out a stagnant well, at the bottom of which might lie a truth, but certainly not the truth about life as a whole.

* * *

"I do not think it probable that my name will remain among those who in the next century will be known as writers of English prose fiction"; thus Trollope wrote in his admirable and—to use an old-fashioned adjective of which he was particularly fond—"manly" autobiography (1883). Propitiatory modesty did not prompt the judgment; he was incapable of such subtle dishonesties. He underrated his work; he thought it good but of temporary interest; his downright temperament compelled him to write plainly and eschew grace, and he knew he had not the æsthetic temperament. He held that in many ways he was a sounder novelist than Thackeray, but that there was an imaginative sweep and glamour in the work of Thackeray which put it in a different class to his own. He was wrong about his fame. We are nearly at the end of the first quarter of the twentieth century and Trollope is more appreciated than he was thirty years ago.

Russell A. Fraser (essay date September 1951)

SOURCE: Fraser, Russell A. "Anthony Trollope's Younger Characters." *Nineteenth-Century Fiction* 6, no. 2 (September 1951): 96-106.

[*In the following essay, Fraser investigates the younger characters in Trollope's fiction, making the claim that though many may seem somewhat ordinary, they are fully realized and come across just as Trollope intended.*]

Trollope's complaint that Dickens did not concern himself with "real" characters establishes a criterion by which Trollope himself may be judged. Actually, his younger characters have some affinity with the young people of Dickens. They are undistinguished and rarely eccentric. They are, however, fully realized; the younger characters of Dickens are seldom so.

Trollope's success in getting at his characters from all sides can be tested by examination. What is the nature of Mark Robarts, the vicar of Framley? He is agreeable enough, courteous, and decent. But he is smug, too. "Women did not understand such things," Trollope says, supplying the vicar's thoughts. "Even his own wife, good, and nice, and sensible, and intelligent as she was."[1] Mark is distinguished, too, by an occasional flash of humor. Miss Dunstable asks him what the bishop would do to him if he should hunt. "It would depend upon his mood at the time," he tells her. "If that were very stern, he might perhaps have me beheaded before the palace gates."[2] Though Trollope tells us that Mark is relatively free of self-conceit, he is still a bit fatuous and inclined sometimes to puff himself. His feelings on the position he has attained so young are revealing. "Of course he thought that all these good things had been the results of his own peculiar merits. Of course he felt that he was different from other parsons,—more fitted by nature for intimacy with great persons, more urbane, more polished, and more richly endowed."[3] His good nature, moreover, is self-conscious. "For Robarts," Trollope says, "was a man who made himself pleasant to all men."[4]

Yet all the different facets of the vicar's character are subordinate to one. There is no single fact about Mark Robarts so important as his complaisance. He is first and last a mover with the tide. The ease with which Sowerby plays on this dominant characteristic and cozens the vicar into giving his signature, the ease with which Mark himself is able to rationalize and excuse his unclerical activities,[5] his dilatory, vacillating conduct with regard to the compromising pre-bend he had accepted[6]—all these incidents and typical reactions hammer home the fact that Mark Robarts is a weak man. Yet he is not a bad man; his faults are venial and common to most ordinary people. The reader is always conscious of a fundamental sympathy and tolerant understanding on Trollope's part investing each character.[7] That Mark is ordinary is important, however, for if he is not the hero of *Framley Parsonage,* he is at least one of the central figures in the story: he is introduced, in fact, in the very first line, and is the mover, directly or otherwise, of every important incident. It is therefore hard to miss Trollope's position with respect to character. Of Squire Dale in *The Small House at Allington,* he says, "He rarely indulged any expectation that people would make themselves agreeable to him."[8] It seems possible to apply the same characterization to Trollope himself. He knows his own creations intimately and sees them whole, but the all-inclusiveness of his seeing makes for a judgment that is really more than sanguine. He goes beyond even the contemporary writers in his realism: he seems to deny the possibility of a full-fledged hero. He is not cynical, but rather, chary of beginning with anything more than a modest potential in his estimation of the heights to which character can rise. If this man or that comes up to those heights, he is quite gratified. Young Lufton and Johnny Eames seem to be as far as he will go in realizing the excellence of the male protagonist.[9]

His refusal to portray a villain who is no worse at one extreme than his modestly conceived "heroes" are noble at another seems almost a slap on his part at man's idea of man as the significant center of things. He seems to indicate disbelief in man's bigness (a feeling that people do not have stature enough to be thoroughly good or evil). Whether this observation is true or not, it is certain that Trollope's young people are almost always small people. Three important consequences take their rise from this fact.

An immediate result is that Trollope's novels are lifted out of the normal novel province and become a kind of *Comédie Humaine.* The triviality of most of the characters lends a perspective of distance to figures and incidents alike. It is as if one were looking through the wrong end of a microscope rather than through the magnifier which most novelists traditionally present. The people of Trollope's Barchester are thus akin to those of Hardy's Wessex: in both instances, there is a stage atmosphere that one cannot escape. The noteworthy difference, however, is that Hardy's people are puppets in the hands of an angry "Prince of The Immortals." Trollope affects nothing so grand. He merely exploits his characters to divert, and exploits them, moreover, in a genial manner. His habit—after Bunyan—of creating names like Spermoil, Dumbello, Quiverful, Fiasco, Optimist, descriptive of the personalities they represent, enhances the atmosphere of the play or puppet show. His practice of passing direct judgment on his characters or of commenting on their behavior diminishes them even further.[10] He even goes out of his way to remind the reader that the story he tells is only make-believe. This is an unnecessary burden on his characters, who are trying hard to be believable. The conclusion of *Framley Parsonage*—"How They Were All Married, Had Two Children, And Lived Happy Ever After"—is a remarkably casual and unconcerned piece of writing. Olivia Proudie, Griselda Grantly, Miss Dunstable, and, of course, Lucy Robarts are all properly joined with their respective choices. Trollope hardly tries at all to make his last chapter an organic part of the novel. It is as if he were saying directly, "'Dear, affectionate, sympathetic readers,' since you must have it this way, I will gratify your desire—but don't expect

me to work hard at making such nonsense believable." And of course, it isn't believable. The only note of realism is struck with the faint implication that Lucy and Lady Lufton may chafe each other a bit in the future over the disposition of the nursery, and indeed, over the management of all Framley Court. The ending is really the beginning—as the characters Trollope has exploited come together and adjust their personalities to rub with minimum friction. The *Comédie* does not end, but its protagonists carry on in the dream world Thackeray pictures at the conclusion of *The Newcomes.*

Finally, the stress of a single quality in each of Trollope's characters tends to absorb, in retrospect, all those qualities that complement it, and leaves the reader with the intense image of a single moral attribute. Mark Robarts has demonstrably more than one dimension, but as one remembers him, he is weakness. Other figures are as wholly drawn, but are remarkable, nevertheless, for a fixed single-mindedness which gives to their characters a fundamental bias. With Fanny Robarts, it is loyalty, with Griselda Grantly, consuming vanity. With truly dramatic brevity, Trollope gives the central fact of Griselda's character. It has just been intimated to her that she is desired as the wife of Lord Lufton. Her reaction to this staggering news is typical: "Before she retired to sleep she looked carefully to her different articles of dress, discovering what amount of damage the evening's wear and tear might have inflicted."[11]

Again, on receiving the hint from her mother that her marriage with Dumbello may be off (information which frightfully upsets Mrs. Grantly), she says simply: "Then, mamma, I had better give them orders not to go on with the marking [of her trousseau]."[12]

In the first chapter of *Framley Parsonage,* Trollope remarks: "But little has as yet been said, personally, as to our hero himself, and perhaps it may not be necessary to say much. Let us hope that by degrees he may come forth upon the canvas, showing to the beholder the nature of the man inwardly and outwardly." His hope, taken generally, was not always gratified. In presenting his characters, he is dramatic and concise at his best, but expository and prolix (though usually insightful) most of the time. Thus, he introduces each important character with the traditional physical description. In *The Small House* [*The Small House at Allington*], however, one feels that the frivolous description of Lily and Bell Dale is indicative of Trollope's contempt for externals and his preoccupation with other things. Occasionally, he presents character by its effect, thus keeping within the legitimately dramatic. One knows a good deal about Miss Dunstable when he learns that the bishop "never felt quite at his ease with [her], as he rarely could ascertain whether or no she was earnest in what she was saying."[13] Like his master, Thackeray, Trollope often obtrudes his own person to philosophize about his characters, thus taking up a median position between the expository and dramatic presentations. The long dissertation on the "hobble-dehoyhood" of Johnny Eames is a good example. It is keen, kindly, witty, shows insight. Johnny "is the most eloquent of beings . . . but this eloquence is heard only by his own inner ears, and these triumphs [which he achieves] are the triumphs of his imagination."[14]

The second consequence of Trollope's self-imposed limitation with regard to the stature of his characters is that it protects those characters from the disaster which overtakes many of Dickens's creations. Here Trollope's condemnation of caricature does have validity, not in the sense that he meant it, but rather because Dickens inevitably found it impossible to sustain his larger than life figures through the length of a long novel. They are wonderful eccentrics for a time, but because they exist side by side with real people, or at least, because they must go through the everyday routine of real people, they break down eventually: several dimensions are required of them if they are to react to varying stimuli, and these dimensions they do not possess. Thus Mr. Micawber is gone from *David Copperfield* before the novel's end, and another character who does things that Micawber could never do assumes his name. Even worse, Harold Skimpole, introduced as a delightful, satiric morality, becomes a low villain in the last pages of *Bleak House.* He, with many of Dickens's caricatures, cannot bear strong sunlight too long. When subjected to it, he is vulgarized, distorted, and at last breaks up entirely. So, too, the heroes of the picaresque tradition: they must continually rise above their previous efforts—to the ultimate point of parody.

Thackeray did not have to worry about keeping intact a Skimpole, but it is nevertheless true that even he stimulates the reader at once—with an explosive, unconventional Ethel Newcome, for instance—and forfeits interest in consequence when his character "reforms" and follows a more normal pattern of behavior.

Trollope had never to worry at all. His characters are on the prosaic level; many, indeed, are even beneath it. Any deviation from the norm is pure and unexpected gain for the reader; a retreat to it does not constitute a denouement. His characters, too, do not have to undergo violent change, as the caricatures of Dickens must. Instead, they may develop—unfold vertically—in logical fashion, from the facts one knows about them at the outset. This is exactly what they do. Mark and Fanny, Lucy, Crosbie, the Dales, Griselda Grantly, confirm the reader's understanding of them over and again. Their moral natures are made clear at once, and all subsequent action is founded on those natures. Thus the young people of Trollope are invested throughout with an integrity that would not be theirs were they less constant in character.

The final consequence of Trollope's unorthodox approach to character is the handicap it gave him over his contemporaries in the presentation of characters who are believable and even lovable. Lucy Robarts, for instance, is a young woman who towers over the conventional female props of Dickens, and she shines so splendidly because the young men and women who surround her are so very proper and dull. The essentially negative quality of Griselda Grantly and the Proudie girls, of Lord Dumbello, even of Lufton and Robarts is obvious. Griselda, reacting to the news that her father may become Bishop of Westminster, sets a pattern of shallow behavior that is constantly reaffirmed: "'A Bishop of Westminster will be higher than a Bishop of Barchester; won't he? I shall so like to be able to snub those Miss Proudies.' It will therefore be seen that there were matters on which even Griselda Grantly could be animated. Like the rest of her family, she was devoted to the Church."[15] In *The Small House,* Lily Dale is set off similarly by her cousin Bernard, by Plantagenet Palliser, by Crosbie, his friend Dobbs and his wife, Alexandrina. Bernard Dale, amazed at his rejection by a woman he admittedly did not care a great deal about, is led involuntarily to desire her *because* of the rejection. His reaction to Crosbie's betrayal of his cousin, Lily, is even more revealing: "How would the world expect that he should behave to Crosbie? and what should he do when he met Crosbie at the club?"[16] Plantagenet Palliser, like Bernard, falls in "love" when an obstacle is presented to him: the duke astounds him by hinting that society is talking of his friendship with Lady Dumbello. He therefore discovers that he *does* love the lady. Montgomerie Dobbs is given courage to stand up for Crosbie by Fowler Pratt's assertion that he will do so: "'So shall I,' said Montgomerie Dobbs, who considered that he would be safe in doing whatever Fowler Pratt did; and who remarked to himself that, after all, Crosbie was marrying the daughter of an earl."[17] Lady Alexandrina considers the possibility of marriage with Crosbie: "She had no conception of a very strong passion, but conceived that a married life was more pleasant than one of single bliss."[18] The marriage consummated, she takes her first journey with her new husband: "'Take care of my bonnet,' she said, as she felt the motion of the railway carriage when he kissed her."[19]

The commonplace nature of these people—never bad, but merely negative—increases a hundredfold the value of complementary positiveness. Lucy Robarts and Lily Dale are not standard heroines. The former is not introduced at all until the tenth chapter of *Framley Parsonage,* the latter, while present from the beginning and sincerely commended—"for my reader must know," Trollope says, "that she is to be very dear, and that my story will be nothing to him if he do not love Lily Dale"[20]—is not as attractive as the legitimate heroine, not of extravagant romance, but of serious writing and living. Her appeal is lessened by the unthinking treatment she gives Johnny Eames—knowing of his love for her, she even asks him to attend her projected marriage. But mostly, she suffers in the estimation of the reader because of her unhappy love affair with Crosbie. When Lily falls in love, her role, because of the nature of the story, becomes passive. She herself is therefore less interesting, more conventional. She is bound to suffer, too, for being taken in: the reader, after all, is acquainted with Crosbie and is unreasonable enough to snort a bit when Lily is duped by such a palpable fellow.

Yet when all objections have been urged, Lily Dale, and more so, Lucy Robarts, remain as the likeliest candidates for reader sympathy in the respective novels. They take central positions because, as has been shown, they are "heroines by relief." Trollope's use of Fanny Robarts as a foil to Lucy illustrates his technique in this respect. Fanny, astounded by her sister-in-law's deprecatory remarks on Lufton (the defensive nature of which she hardly understands), replies lamely, "He is an excellent son, I believe."[21] Fanny certainly is a fine person, but she is really rather prosaic and thus serves admirably to focus attention on Lucy's far greater acuteness and sensibility. "'You would have thought it sacrilege for me to marry Lord Lufton!' [Lucy says] . . . If Lord Lufton really loved Lucy Robarts [Fanny thinks], and was loved by Lucy Robarts, why should not they two become man and wife? And yet she did feel that it would be—perhaps not sacrilege, as Lucy had said, but something almost as troublesome."[22] And again [Lucy:] "'He must have been insane at the time; there can be no other excuse made for him. I wonder whether there is anything of that sort in the family?' 'What; madness?' said Mrs. Robarts, quite in earnest."[23] Lucy's desperate humor brings this rejoinder: "'Lucy, I cannot understand you,' said Fanny, very gravely. 'I am sometimes inclined to doubt whether you can have any deep feeling in the matter or not.'"[24] Trollope, then, achieves character by toning down his background, Dickens by lifting up the figures in an already-raised foreground to the height of caricature.

The emotional and intellectual sterility of most of Trollope's younger people, their stereotyped reactions and observations, contrast the more boldly with the unconventionality of those characters one remembers—Miss Dunstable is spirited, quick with her answers; her aliveness is enhanced by the dryness of the set she moves in. Missing her poodle, she says to the Duke of Omnium, "'I declare I must go and look for him,—only think if they were to put him among your grace's dogs,—how his morals would be destroyed!'"[25] At her *conversazione,* she tells Doctor Thorne, "'I would give anything for a glass of beer. . . .'"[26] Her simple remark illustrates to perfection Trollope's success in achieving heroines "by relief." There is nothing in the world extraordinary about a woman indicating her preference for beer, but because all the other ladies at the party are so

incredibly stuffy, this innocent sentence is like a breath of air, and gives Miss Dunstable an aura she certainly doesn't merit on the strength of her remark alone. Lucy is kindred to her. Replying to Fanny's question whether any harm has been done by the affair with Lufton, she says, "Oh!! by God's mercy, very little. As for me, I shall get over it in three or four years I don't doubt— that's if I can get ass's milk and change of air."[27] Lily Dale—when not in love—is of the same pattern. Slyly, she twists the words of Crosbie and Bernard Dale against them: "We stupid people can go to bed. Mamma, I wish you had a little smoking room here for us. I don't like being considered stupid."[28] Lily and Lucy are both less than beautiful, and this, paradoxically, endears them, for they are thus differentiated from the run of the mill lovelies of other novelists. They are not demure either, and therefore pay the price of being misunderstood by their contemporaries. Crosbie, Trollope says, "would have been better pleased had Lily shown more reticence. . . ."[29] The reader is delighted, however, with her normality, all too scarce in other contemporary heroines. In *Framley Parsonage,* Mary Gresham and Miss Dunstable avow to each other that they are talking "absolute nonsense; such as schoolgirls of eighteen talk to each other."[30] Their frankness in the avowal is as sophisticated as it is reasonable. Yet the younger women of Dickens *do* talk—almost always—like schoolgirls, and this is very *un*reasonable. Because the reader is accustomed to such mediocre rendering of character, he is charmed with the frankness of Trollope's Dunstables and Lucys and Lily Dales. Her forgets that it is his right to expect fidelity in dialogue and character. He is grateful where he might with justice be complacent. This artistic triumph is accomplished by contrast. It is the major consequence of Trollope's self-imposed limitation with regard to the stature of his younger characters.

Notes

1. *Framley Parsonage* (New York: Dutton, 1948), p. 21.

2. *Ibid.,* p. 23.

3. *Ibid.,* pp. 31-32.

4. *Ibid.,* p. 144.

5. "And then, being a man only too prone by nature to do as others did around him, he found by degrees that that could hardly be wrong for him which he admitted to be right for others." *Ibid.,* p. 134.

6. "As to that he had made up his mind; but then again he unmade it, as men always do in such troubles." *Ibid.,* p. 186.

7. Understanding is manifested in Trollope's comment on the postscript concluding Mark Robarts's

guilty letter from Gatherum: "And then there was written, on an outside scrap which was folded round the full-written sheet of paper, 'Make it as smooth at Framley Court as possible.' However strong, and reasonable, and unanswerable the body of Mark's letter may have been, all his hesitation, weakness, doubt, and fear, were expressed in this short postscript." (*Ibid.*, p. 39.) Even Lucy is self-pitying, but her fall from grace is treated with broad and smiling sympathy: "She cared for no one, and no one cared for her." (*Ibid.*, p. 113.) Trollope understands, though Lucy does not, what her disagreeable spell really means: "She turned her back to the music, for she was sick of seeing Lord Lufton watch the artistic motion of Miss Grantly's fingers. . . ." Crosbie, despite his offense, is never degraded to the level of the melo-dramatic villain. In his guilty remorse at discarding Lily, he says to himself, "I wish she had a dozen brothers." (*The Small House at Allington* [New York: Harper Bros., 1864], p. 116.) Trollope not only displays great understanding in presenting a mood so very difficult to depict dramatically, but he shows by Crosbie's statement that he is unwilling to condemn the man completely.

8. P. 91.

9. There are many examples of Trollope's fundamental—though scarcely cynical—disenchantment, a characteristic that would be almost Byronic were it at all self-conscious. Following the conversation of Mrs. Harold Smith with Miss Dunstable, he says: "Of course, she declared in a very strong manner that her brother could not think of accepting from Miss Dunstable any such pecuniary assistance as that offered—and, to give her her due, such was the feeling of her mind at the moment; but as she went to meet her brother and gave him an account of this interview, it did occur to her that possibly Miss Dunstable might be a better creditor than the Duke of Omnium for the Chaldicotes property." (*Framley Parsonage*, p. 239.) On Lufton's dual attachment for Griselda Grantly and Lucy Robarts: "'Your hero, then,' I hear some well-balanced critic say, 'is not worth very much.' In the first place Lord Lufton is not my hero; and in the next place, a man may be very imperfect and yet worth a great deal." (*Ibid.*, pp. 297-298.) On Robarts: "He had within him many aptitudes for good, but not the strengthened courage of a man to act up to them. The stuff of which his manhood was to be formed had been slow of growth, as it is with many men; and, consequently, when temptation was offered to him, he had fallen. But he deeply grieved over his own stumbling, and from time to time, as his periods of penitence came upon him, he resolved that he would once more put his shoulder to the wheel as

became one who fights upon earth that battle for which he had put on the armour." (*Ibid.*, p. 408.) Eames is a confessed hero, but not a very grand one: "Alas, alas! I fear that those two years in London have not improved John Eames; and yet I have to acknowledge that John Eames is one of the heroes of my story." (*The Small House at Allington*, p. 29.) The unwillingness to inflate a character to heroic size is paralleled by an aversion for unmitigated baseness. A less sophisticated writer would be more prodigal with his villainy, but Trollope disdains to believe in a villain, as he does in a hero. Again of Mrs. Smith: "As for Mrs. Harold Smith, whatever may be the view taken of her general character as a wife and a member of society, it must be admitted that as a sister she had virtues." (*Framley Parsonage*, p. 318.) Even Crosbie is spared: "Adolphus Crosbie was a clever man: and he meant also to be a true man, if only the temptations to falsehood might not be too great for him." (*The Small House at Allington*, p. 58.)

10. On Mark: "He was grateful to Lady Lufton for what she had done for him; but perhaps not so grateful as he should have been." (*Framley Parsonage*, p. 32.) "What could a young flattered fool of a parson do, but say that he would go?" (*Ibid.*, p. 37.)

11. *Ibid.*, p. 200.

12. *Ibid.*, p. 441.

13. *Ibid.*, p. 169.

14. *The Small House* [*The Small House at Allington*], pp. 22-23.

15. *Framley Parsonage*, p. 225.

16. *The Small House*, p. 128.

17. *Ibid.*, p. 205.

18. *Ibid.*, p. 105.

19. *Ibid.*, p. 207.

20. *Ibid.*, p. 14.

21. *Framley Parsonage*, p. 252.

22. *Ibid.*, p. 257.

23. *Ibid.*

24. *Ibid.*, p. 343.

25. *Ibid.*, p. 70.

26. *Ibid.*, p. 291.

27. *Ibid.*, p. 206.

28. *The Small House*, p. 21.

29. *Ibid.*, p. 46.

30. P. 371.

John Hagan (essay date June 1959)

SOURCE: Hagan, John. "The Divided Mind of Anthony Trollope." *Nineteenth-Century Fiction* 14, no. 1 (June 1959): 1-26.

[*In the following essay, Hagan contends that Trollope's seemingly ambivalent treatment of two topics in his fiction—the problem of individual social advancement and the problem of the marriage of convenience—provide deep insight into mid-Victorian culture.*]

From the time of their first appearance to the present day Anthony Trollope's novels have been justly regarded as marvelously clear, full, and accurate pictures of the mid-Victorian panorama of English society. But an early consequence of this view was the opinion that these novels were less works of art than sociological documents, and Trollope less a creative artist than a social historian or passive observer. While such an attitude would be seriously endorsed no longer, it remains true that many readers continue to locate the historical interest of the novels in their surface realism alone, rather than in what they may unwittingly reveal to us about the mind of their author. Yet the unconscious, unarticulated perplexities of that mind are often as much an index to the deeper currents of the age in which the novels appeared as are their overt record of customs and manners, so that we may profit in our understanding of the time as much by studying Trollope's attitudes toward the social phenomena he describes as by observing the phenomena themselves. His treatment of two closely related subjects, in particular, reveals with such arresting clarity some of the ambivalence and evasiveness which could be induced by the social and moral uncertainties of the period in even the most scrupulous and honest of commentators that the novels should be indispensable reading for any serious student of mid-Victorian culture on that score alone. These two subjects are the problem of individual social advancement, and, an aspect of this, the problem of the marriage of convenience. I shall examine each of these in turn.

Two passages central to an understanding of Trollope's difficulty in dealing with the first question occur in articles which appeared in the *Fortnightly Review* for August and October, 1865. In the earlier of these (a discussion of the disestablishment of the Irish Church), he writes:

> For myself I like the rustle of dead leaves, and am keenly alive to the pleasantness of having them round my feet. . . . We venerate things that are old because they are old; and gently remove our ruins, fragment by fragment, with hands which love while they destroy. . . . We cannot ruthlessly cut down the half-dead tree of the grove, and tear asunder the roots, and plough and sow the soil, where the spot has been hallowed by ancient piety. The work of removal has, in-

deed, to be done; but it must be done tenderly, not ruthlessly. With loving hands must the old timber be dragged away, and the ground cleared for purposes of new utility.[1]

In the later (a piece on **"Public Schools"**) he makes remarks to this effect again:

> It is the same with us Englishmen in all matters. At last, after long internal debate and painful struggle, reason within us gets the better of feeling. In almost every bosom there sits a parliament in which a conservative party is ever combating to maintain things old, while the liberal side of the house is striving to build things new. In this parliament, as in the other, the liberal side is always conquering, but its adversary is never conquered.[2]

These comments take us at once to the heart of a central feature of Trollope's mentality which has important consequences for some of his most significant novels. In a word, they reveal a basic ambivalence of attitude that he was never able to resolve. Throughout the whole body of his work instinctive or emotional conservatism continually clashes with what he felt was the more rational, utilitarian, and liberal bent of his temperament; and, these two opposing forces never being reconciled, there is often engendered in vital areas of his fiction uncertainty and ambiguity to a very high degree.

The tendency of critics has been to overlook this fact, and to make Trollope's opinions more one-dimensional than they really were. Indeed, books like *The Warden* and *Barchester Towers,* for example, give impetus to such a tendency, the first by issuing a seemingly blanket defense of ancient feudal privilege, and the second by revealing with embarrassing candor a typical piece of mid-Victorian aristocratic snobbery. In chapter v of *The Warden* there appears a passage in which Trollope appears irresistibly inclined to defend the whole practice of clerical sinecures (such as the one which Mr. Harding is accused of holding) merely on the grounds of their being time-honored, soaked in picturesqueness and nostalgic associations, and suggestive of solemn, orderly comfort.[3] Similarly, the intemperate attack on Evangelicals like Mr. Slope in *Barchester Towers* is grounded on a powerful anti-democratic animus against merchants and manufacturers—representatives of "trade"—among whom Evangelical opinions had taken their first decisive hold. Throughout the novel Trollope takes every opportunity to insist upon the fact that Slope is not a "gentleman,"[4] and though he never makes the chaplain's origins clear enough for us to ascribe his deficiency to early environmental contamination, it is clear that we are to regard him as having met an appropriate fate when at the end of the novel he is married to "a rich sugar-refiner's wife in Baker Street."[5] For what Thomas Adolphus Trollope said of himself applied to his younger brother too:

. . . I grew into boyhood with the notion that "evangelicalism," or "low churchism," was a note of vulgarity—a sort of thing that might be expected to be met with in tradesmen's back parlors, and "academies," where the youths who came from such places were instructed in English grammar and arithmetic, but was not to be met with, and was utterly out of place, among gentlemen and in gentlemanlike places of education, where nothing of the kind was taught.[6]

But this is by no means the whole story. Running counter to the explicit statements in chapter v of *The Warden* is the dramatic import of the novel as a whole which, far from amounting merely to an indiscriminate defense of social anomalies *in toto,* is a realistic, pragmatically-minded plea only for the merits of the special case. Likewise, our impression of Trollope's snobbery in *Barchester Towers* must be modified in the light of some of his later writings (especially the short story entitled **"The Chateau of Prince Polignac"** in *Tales of All Countries,* 1861, and the novel *Lady Anna,* 1874) wherein Trollope came to insist rather strongly that the qualities of "gentlemanliness," being essentially moral, were not necessarily contingent upon one's position in society, but might very well be found in a tailor as much as in a country squire or a baronet.[7]

The fact that he had already suggested this attitude at one point in his early novel *La Vendée*[8] shows that it must have been present to his mind when writing *Barchester Towers* too. Yet its existence could never be deduced solely from a reading of that novel, in which Trollope's position appears, even for its own time, highly old-fashioned. The fact of the matter is simply that his opinions on such social questions were so unsettled that he could swing from one side to another as the momentary whim moved him. In a crucial passage in the *Autobiography* (which should be read in conjunction with the well-known statement of his "Conservative-Liberal" creed in chapter xvi) he states that

> there are places in life which can hardly be well filled except by "Gentlemen." . . . It may be that the son of the butcher of the village shall become as well fitted for employments requiring gentle culture as the son of the parson. Such is often the case. When such is the case, no one has been more prone to give the butcher's son all the welcome he has merited than I myself; but the chances are greatly in favour of the parson's son. The gates of the one class should be open to the other; but neither to the one class nor to the other can good be done by declaring that there are no gates, no barrier, no difference.[9]

Now it is obvious that this outlook permits Trollope a great deal of latitude. If he chooses on one day to demonstrate that the butcher's son is just as qualified "for employments requiring gentle culture as the son of the parson," he can readily do so; but with equal facility, he can turn on the next to showing that "the chances are greatly in favour" of the other. The reader soon learns, in short, that Trollope's treatment of the whole question of individual social advancement answers fewer problems than it raises, and is not to be reduced to any coherent philosophy at all. In answer to the question as to *how* "the son of the butcher . . . shall become as well fitted . . . as the son of the parson," he had a ready reply: "I am of opinion," he told the electors of Beverley, "that every poor man should have brought within his reach the means of educating his children, and that those means should be provided by the State."[10] But to tell us, when the butcher's son has acquired this education, that "no one has been more prone to give [him] . . . all the welcome he has merited than I myself" is completely inadequate without an explanation of the systematic social arrangements by means of which this "welcome" is to be given; and no such explanation (Trollope strenuously opposed "the system of competitive examination" all his life)[11] is forthcoming. It is impossible, in other words, to escape the impression that Trollope is hedging—that the portion of his mind he thought of as rational and liberal is inclining him toward a democratization of English society, but that the "conservative party" in his "bosom" is preventing him from following his reasoning to its logical conclusions. For the most part he believes in a static, hierarchical society with a self-perpetuating ruling class (he is careful in a number of instances not to have his genteel characters marry "beneath" themselves, as witness Charley Tudor's escape from Norah Geraghty in *The Three Clerks,* Johnny Eames's from Amelia Roper in *The Small House at Allington,* and Ralph's from Polly Neefit in *Ralph the Heir*). On the other hand, his conscience is struck now and then by some gross form of inequality and he beats the drums for greater social mobility. But he does not do so consistently or in a predictable way; he writes at the mercy of a divided mind.

The result for the total body of his work is vagueness and ambiguity. An excellent example of this is in *Dr. Thorne.* The novel troubles us because we can never be quite sure what, in his picture of the Greshams and De Courcys, Trollope is really getting at. Is he ridiculing these families because they refuse to surrender to economic necessity with good grace, but must degrade themselves in the process by hypocrisy or self-deception? Is he acquiescing, in other words, in the weakening of the old class barriers? Or is he censuring these families for the surrender itself, and the imprudence which made it necessary? The answer to these questions is not as evident as one might at first think. Our initial impression, perhaps, is that Trollope regards blood-pride as no more than an outworn fetish, and feels that all the fuss made by the Greshams and the De Courcys in its name to disguise their mercenary motives is both foolish and contemptible. This interpretation would seem to be borne out by the fact that he censures the family pride of Dr. Thorne himself,[12] that he treats the bourgeois Miss Dunstable with great affection, and that ultimately (in *Framley Parsonage*) he unites the doctor with her in marriage. The requirements for social elevation Trollope would seem to insist upon are neither gentle blood nor money, but simply good-nature, sophistication, kindliness, intelligence, and lack of greed. Miss Dunstable's social equal, Mr. Moffat, the tailor's son, who has risen to be an M.P. and the possessor of a large fortune, is given short shrift by Trollope because the love of money dominates him; Miss Dunstable, on the other hand, is saved because, for her, money is necessary only as a means to enjoyment. Trollope would seem merely to be scrupulously depicting a "good" and a "bad" parvenu as he had depicted a "good" and a "bad" reformer, and a "good" and a "bad" churchman in *The Warden*. But the situation is not really as simple as this; other, contradictory criteria are operating too. For how can we reconcile the delight he takes in the brilliant eccentricities of the patent medicine tycoon's daughter with the sweeping aristocratic hostility toward trade he voices explicitly in chapter i? And how can we square his seeming liberalism with his ridicule of Dr. Thorne's "subversive professional democratic tendencies?"[13] Above all, is there not a contradiction between his mockery of the doctor's blood-pride and the emphasis he places upon the virtues of (partially) gentle birth and gentle nurture in the development of Mary? It is impossible to escape the implication that one of the reasons she will succeed in high society, whereas the Scatcherds will fail, is that the Scatcherd blood in her veins has been cancelled out by the purer element of the Thornes. There is a congenital inferiority in Sir Roger and his family (just as there had been, for example, in Norah Geraghty of *The Three Clerks*) that education is powerless to change.

But perhaps the clearest revelation of Trollope's uncertainty occurs in his treatment of the love story. He obviously considers it a social triumph that Mary should finally be accepted into the ranks of the Greshams and the De Courcys—and yet nothing in the context of the novel prepares us to understand why: these families, as they have been dramatically represented for us, are (with the exception of young Frank Gresham himself) weak, foolish, and cruel. Another difficulty is connected with the fact that Frank's disinterested loyalty to Mary in the face of her apparent poverty, like Miss Dunstable's disillusionment, Scatcherd's frustration, Moffat's treachery, the Duke of Omnium's overweening pride, and the scenes of election bribery, enforces the moral that wealth is a vanity or a snare, and, by implication, that the aristocracy has an ancient dignity which it is obliged to protect from incursions of plutocrats and their values. Lady Arabella, through her folly, so the moral seems to run, has betrayed her class to the philistines. And yet Trollope shows no qualms whatsoever about bestowing upon Frank and Mary the huge fortune earned by the contractor Scatcherd. The version of the

evil potentialities of wealth, or at least of its power to vulgarize, seems suddenly to evaporate, the moral problem to dissolve into thin air. Frank can be prudent without at the same time succumbing to the overt mercenary ambition of his mother and thereby derogating from his status as a gentleman. He can enjoy the rewards of ungentlemanly conduct without having to pay the price in vulgarity. He does not have to marry for money, because he can get it by marrying for love. Grubbing for money is not regarded as having a place among aristocratic virtues, but money itself is evidently not an unsuitable reward for the practice of those virtues. The ostensible chivalric moral that it is better for a gentleman to sacrifice his own and his family's financial position in obedience to pure and disinterested love than to derogate from his rank by selling himself in marriage for money is quietly exploded.

In short, Trollope does not know how to choose between his regard for the preservation of aristocratic dignity and his equally keen recognition of economic necessity. He refuses to show us how the equally strong claims of disinterested love and mundane financial need are to be satisfied at the same time—except by accident. He does not show us how one can love and still be prudent, and prudent without compromising aristocratic values with those of the rising bourgeoisie. He appreciated the pressure that was being exercised for social change, and to some degree welcomed it. His comic sense was aroused by the way in which the aristocracy made itself ridiculous and mean by its hypocritical or self-deceptive clinging to the old blood formulae. If it must yield to money powers, let it do so openly, with good grace. But in another part of his mind—the conservative, nostalgic part—Trollope feared encroaching democracy profoundly. To save themselves from ruin the upper classes would have to court the rich, and thus decline into mammon-worship. The blood of the old families would become tainted, their way of life vulgarized. And for many of those who climbed to the top on the strength of their money-bags alone there would be nothing in store but disillusionment and frustration.

Thus was Trollope's attitude one of profound ambivalence. With great clarity the novel reveals the confusions and unsettled opinions that could beset an observant, well-intentioned mind during an epoch when the whole structure of a highly stratified society was undergoing rapid and radical change. Nor was this a confusion Trollope ultimately outgrew, for it leaves its mark again in a later novel with a very similar plot, *Is He Popenjoy?* When the Lady Mary Germain returns lovingly and complacently to her husband at the end and joyfully becomes the mother of the future heir to the Popenjoy title, there is more than a failure in character consistency. There is a sudden alteration of the novel's entire premises. Trollope's attitude toward the whole

Germain family at Manor Cross softens and mellows; everyone appears in a kindlier light than before; and then, unexpectedly, to climax the proceedings, the Dean addresses a speech to his daughter that, in the light of all that we have been shown previously of Lord George, the Marquis, and their mother and sisters, is simply incredible:

> It is a grand thing to rise in the world. The ambition to do so is the very salt of the earth. It is the parent of all enterprise, and the cause of all improvement. They who know no such ambition are savages and remain savage. As far as I can see, among us Englishmen such ambition is, healthily and happily, almost universal, and on that account we stand high among the citizens of the world. But, owing to false teaching, men are afraid to own aloud a truth which is known to their own hearts. I am not afraid to do so, and I would not have you afraid. I am proud that, by one step after another, I have been able so to place you and so to form you, that you should have been found worthy of rank much higher than my own. And I would have you proud also and equally ambitious for your child . . . that he may be great, you should rejoice that you yourself are great already.[14]

We have known all the way through, of course, that the Dean is a snob; but heretofore his snobbery has been an object of ridicule. Now suddenly it is transformed into noble ambition phrased in terms that are little short of a paraphrase of passages in Trollope's *Autobiography*.[15] And to leave no doubt in the reader's mind that the Dean is being used here as a mouthpiece for his creator, his sentiments are seconded in no uncertain terms by Mary herself:

> . . . the upshot of his philosophy she did receive as true, and she declared to herself that she would harbour in her heart of hearts the lessons which he had given her as to her own child—lessons which must be noble, as they tended to the well-being of the world at large.[16]

Trollope can be furiously critical of individual aristocrats precisely because he has great respect for the aristocratic ideal; unlike Dickens who measures his aristocrats against the best standards of another class (the lower or lower middle), Trollope measures his against the best standards of their own. But when in a novel like *Popenjoy* [*Is He Popenjoy?*] he consistently limits himself to pictures of decadence—to representations of his aristocrats as (to use Matthew Arnold's term) "Barbarians"—the ideal ceases to be apprehensible to us, to have any solidity, any convincing reality. Nor on such occasions can we be sure that it has any reality for Trollope himself. We wonder from what source the best standards which serve as his implied criteria are derived; the context fails to provide us with adequate grounds for faith in them. We come away with the suspicion that Trollope does not wholly know his own mind, that he fails to see the situation steadily and whole. Though on some days he can portray admirable

aristocrats like Plantagenet Palliser and Roger Carbury, on others his belief in the efficacy (or, indeed, even the existence) of such types seems to be severely shaken—to have degenerated into mere lip service. His fear of expanding democracy makes him turn to the "institution" of aristocracy as a source of stability—the "institution" itself as distinct from the weak and erring individuals who may comprise it at any one historical moment; in this he was exactly like his own Dr. Thorne who "naturally hated a lord at first sight," but "would have expended his means, his blood, and spirit, in fighting for the upper house of Parliament." But in a book like *Popenjoy* so fixed is his attention upon the vices and follies of individuals, so rigorously does he refrain from representing a saving remnant, that any distinction between them and the institution of which they are a part appears largely mystical. We are unconvinced by it, and we cannot be sure that Trollope is not unconvinced either.

The same thing is revealed if we look at these books from the angle of their heroines. Whenever any sympathetic character like Mary Thorne or Mary Germain (or their descendent, Mary Masters in *The American Senator*) rises above her rank, she must always be innocent of any desire to do so lest Trollope seem to be condoning equalitarianism. The complete absence in these heroines of anything even approaching social ambition is remarkable; the motive in each case is pure love undefiled. That they all manage to obtain their social deserts is thus the crassest chance. But surely no one like Trollope, who professed the belief that "the gates of the one class should be open to the other," would wish to leave the weakening or dissolution of class distinctions to such an uncertain agent. What should be said about the woman of unfortunate circumstances who not only possesses the exceptional qualities that entitle her to greater social opportunity, but is thoroughly conscious of them and determined to fullfill herself? This was the test case for a novelist of Trollope's beliefs, but he could never face up to it. As we shall see later, he never painted such a woman with complete sympathy; she always emerged at best as a Julia Brabazon (*The Claverings*) or a Laura Standish (*Phineas Finn* and *Phineas Redux*)—a character of many admirable qualities, but tainted by the vice of mercenary ambition for which she is unequivocally punished. The girl who deserves reward must be the "nice" girl—the girl so improbably innocent of her personal merit that she achieves social elevation almost in spite of herself. What Trollope is saying, in effect, through these latter heroines is that social mobility could be a good thing—but that it should not be hastened prematurely or too consciously; class distinctions are still necessary. The transformation of the social structure, evidently, is to be left to the unpremeditated processes of "natural" evolution and a highly indefinite future. This was not hypocrisy on Trollope's part, but the far commoner failing of uncertainty and ambivalence. It was the plight in epitome of the mid-Victorian Conservative-Liberal.

Perhaps the finest example of this plight is offered by the treatment of the titular hero of **The American Senator.** The problem to be faced in connection with this character is the precise nature of Trollope's attitude toward him. Does he, sharing the Senator's standards of logic and rationality, accept the latter's critique of English "institutions" as just? Or is he essentially hostile to the foreigner's point of view, seeing in his single-minded criteria only a naive and fanatical blindness to the necessity of social anomalies? Or is he perhaps only the detached and amused spectator, witnessing the clash of different cultures with a tolerant, good-natured eye to the strengths and weaknesses of both?

Each of these positions can be supported with some show of truth. The Senator, one recent commentator argues, was intended basically as a sympathetic figure. In him we can see a similarity to Trollope himself as he was in America in 1862. The conclusion is that Trollope intended to do two things:

> first, to show that an American in England behaved very much like an Englishman in America, and thereby once again to explain . . . that his intentions in that volume [**North America**] had been good, but that he realized that it was not acceptable to the people of one nation to be criticized by those of another; and second, to point out to his English countrymen a few of their foibles as seen from the point of view of an intelligent, fair, well-meaning foreigner. . . . [In sum, the novel has] a didactic intent, clearly aimed at English institutions and customs; the American was not the subject of the sharpest satire, for he came off the better in all his disagreements with the "unreasonable" English, and was depicted in all his dealings as a man of honor and intelligence. Yet he did not succeed in convincing the English of the error of their ways, any more than Trollope had succeed in his effort made in 1862 to inform the Americans.[17]

In the Senator's closing speeches, this writer contends, all Americanisms are lost, and the character speaks forth in true "Trollopian rhetoric."[18] From this point of view the Senator's victory over the arguments of his English opponents might be regarded as Trollope's elaborate way of compensating his American readers for his own presumption in having ventured to criticize their way of life over a decade earlier in **North America.**

On the other hand, another commentator has argued forcefully for a view that is diametrically opposite, seeing Trollope's central intention as that of satirizing the Senator and defending the institutions he attacks. On the subject of the ethics of fox-hunting, for example, Trollope builds up an unfair case against the Senator by failing "to separate principles from personalities."

> Throughout the novel the conservative cause is represented by courteousness and fairmindedness, the opposition by boorishness, mental dishonesty, and whatever

Trollope considers to be counter to self-evident ethics. Whatever is wrong with the conservative is usually inherited . . . [and] in Trollope's eyes, one could hardly accuse a man of being actively evil simply because he remained within the confines of the *status quo*. The most that could be urged against Lord Rufford is that he is somewhat negative and, occasionally, even a little weak. But, in compensation, he is delightfully courteous, considerate, good-natured, impatient of humbug, and unfailingly fair and sportsmanlike. From nature, he has inherited natural goodness. . . . On the other hand, all grumblers against the system turn out to have fatal flaws in their character. . . . Trollope makes the farmer [Goarly] a thoroughgoing ruffian and his opponent, Lord Rufford, a just, but righteously angry man. Personalities obscure the issue.[19]

We can conclude only that "there is definitely in Trollope the easygoing intolerance of a good-natured man who is sure that he is right. . . ."[20] Evidently a critic of this persuasion must see Trollope's intention as not that of apologizing to Americans for his own presumption, but of countering their adverse reception of **North America** by demonstrating that in a capacity for judging others wrong-headedly Englishmen are not alone.

It is obvious, therefore, from the contradictory nature of these different interpretations that the novel is one whose surface simplicity conceals an unexpected complexity. The easy solution, of course, would be to accept the third interpretation I suggested above, and conclude that Trollope is trying to make the best of both worlds. That this was his true intention would seem to be borne out by a conscientiously placating passage which appears at the beginning of chapter lxxvii. But this interpretation, as we shall see, will no more suffice than the others.

The problem to be solved is to which side—that of Logic, Rationality, Utilitarianism, represented by the Senator, or that of Tradition, Custom, Picturesqueness, represented by Lord Rufford and a number of the citizens of Dillsborough—Trollope gives his allegiance. To assume with our first critic that simply because the Senator is more "reasonable" than Lord Rufford and his arguments more "logical" he is therefore in essential agreement with Trollope's own views is, of course, to beg the whole question at issue. Though the Senator may be, in the words of another commentator, "a figure of Reason incarnate,"[21] we cannot be sure that Trollope is defending Reason in the accepted sense at all. In order to arrive at an accurate idea of the values on which Trollope is resting his case in this novel, we must study the text itself and some other writings pertinent to it with the closest attention.

Considering first the position of the pro-Senator interpreters, we must discover exactly what indications are given by Trollope that the Senator arouses his sympathy. There are a number of them. It is perfectly obvious, for example, that Trollope takes great pains to establish that the Senator's curiosity about English culture is a purely disinterested one, and that he is conscientious, sensitive, intelligent, and always decently motivated by his sense of what he regards as justice and fair-play—that he is, in short, as one of Trollope's letters put it, "a thoroughly honest man wishing to do good."[22] He is deliberately set in contrast to those Dillsborough citizens who simply want "to fight a lord"[23] and the partisans of Lord Rufford who are plainly to be scoffed out of court because of their crude intolerance, unthinking loyalty, and ignorance. We are also told explicitly that "among educated men" the Senator "had produced for himself a general respect."[24] Indeed, if we wish to see how harshly Trollope could treat Americans when he wanted to, we have only to recall the characters of Frederic F. Frew, the wealthy Philadelphian who marries the heroine of the short story **"The Widow's Mite"** (*Lotta Schmidt and other Stories*), and Jonas Spaulding in *He Knew He Was Right,* alongside whom the Senator appears in a strikingly mellow light.

As for the latter's ideas, they too seem at times to receive Trollope's sanction. In one of his letters he tells us quite unequivocally that the Senator was intended to be "not . . . half so absurd as the things which he criticizes," and, even more specifically, that in the amusing scene between him and Parson Mainwaring in chapter xlii, in which the Senator's logic is at its most relentless, he intended "to ridicule the modes of patronage in our church."[25] This remark is confirmed by a statement in the novel itself that "Mr. Gotobed had hardly said a word about England [on this occasion] which Morton himself might not have said,"[26] by the fact that the Senator never hears it alleged that he has told a lie,[27] and by a sketch written a number of years earlier for *Clergymen of the Church of England* entitled **"The Normal Dean of the Present Day"** wherein Trollope displayed an awareness of the confusing anomalies of this hallowed English institution quite as keen as that of the Senator himself:

> We are often led to express our dismay, and sometimes our scorn, at the ignorance shown by foreigners as to our institutions; but when we ourselves consider their complications and irrationalistic modes of procedure, the wonder is that any one not to the manner born should be able to fathom aught of their significance.[28]

What could be a more unanswerable demonstration of this point than the troubles of poor Crawley in *The Last Chronicle of Barset*? And what better could reveal Trollope's alertness to undesirable or comic anomalies in other corners of English life, too, than the new Duke of Omnium's hostility to the continued existence of pocket-boroughs (*The Prime Minister*), and the various humorous or satirical treatments of the ethics and etiquette of fox-hunting in *The Last Chronicle* [*The Last Chronicle of Barset*] (chapter xxxiii), *Phineas Redux* (chapter lxxv), and *The Duke's Children* (chapters lxii-lxiii)?

All of these passages would seem quite unmistakably to confirm the view of the Senator as simply a "mouthpiece" for Trollope's own opinions. But we must not necessarily equate a writer's intentions as expressed in letters with the finished work itself, nor assume that statements found in one part of a novel or in other writings are always in agreement with those found elsewhere in that novel. With those qualities which make the Senator a man of intelligence and integrity we have to match others which emphasize his absurdity. His curious name, Elias Gotobed, for example, serves no other apparent purpose than that of poking fun at that large number of unusual names to be found in the United States which Trollope had already commented upon in *North America.* And a great deal of comic emphasis is put upon his bad manners, sententiousness, chauvinism, and presumption. Of the latter trait Trollope at one point writes almost bitterly:

> All those matters, which to ordinary educated Englishmen are almost as common as the breath of their nostrils, had been to him matter of long and serious study. And as the intent student, who has zealously buried himself for a week among commentaries and notes, feels himself qualified to question Porson and to Bentley Bentley, so did our Senator believe, while still he was groping among the rudiments, that he had all our political intricacies at his fingers' ends.[29]

In the same passage and elsewhere Trollope mocks the Senator's fanatical, almost Puritan sense of duty (which is not unaccompanied by a strong feeling of "pleasure in associating with those here of the highest rank").[30] He throws himself into his inquiries with as much energy as Arabella Trefoil does into snaring a husband. At the same time he seems often to be surprisingly obtuse—he is certainly no unerring judge of character, regarding Arabella as a poor afflicted young woman and "'a good type of the English aristocracy,'"[31] and grossly misreading the character of Lord Rufford's enemy, Goarly, and his cohorts (as even he himself has eventually to acknowledge).

Moreover, what can be said in favor of the Senator's logic when we view it in the light of a passage like the following from the short story **"The Widow's Mite"** already mentioned?

> . . . an American argues more closely on politics than does an Englishman. His convictions are not truer on that account; very often the less true, as are the conclusions of a logician, because he trusts to syllogisms which are often false, instead of to the experience of his life and daily workings of his mind. . . . [Furthermore, the American] considers that every intelligent be-

ing is bound to argue whenever matter of argument is offered to him; nor can he understand that any subject may be too sacred for argument.[32]

The perfect dramatization of this position is, of course, **The Warden.** As we have seen, one commentator argues that Trollope is unfair in his treatment of the Senator because he fails "to separate principles from personalities." But, as the story of Mr. Harding proves conclusively, in the complex, delicate questions surrounding social anomalies, that separation was precisely what was to be avoided: regarded abstractly, the anomaly of the Warden's sinecure was intolerable; but when considered pragmatically from the point of view of how the funds were actually administered by a man of Mr. Harding's special character, it was no longer objectionable. In **The American Senator** a similar situation arises in connection with the pocket-borough of Quinborough which the Senator visits during an election. In a very revealing passage we can see Trollope taking the identical stand of twenty years earlier:

> Quinborough was a little town of 3,000 inhabitants, clustering round the gates of a great Whig marquis, which had been spared—who can say why?—at the first Reform Bill, and having but one member, had come out scatheless from the second. Quinborough still returned its one member with something less than 500 constituents, and in spite of household suffrage and the ballot had always returned the member favoured by the marquis. This nobleman, driven no doubt by his conscience to make some return to the country for the favour shown to his family, had always sent to Parliament some useful and distinguished man, who without such patronage might have been unable to serve his country. On the present occasion, a friend of the people,—so called,—an unlettered demagogue, such as is in England distasteful to all classes, had taken himself down to Quinborough as a candidate in opposition to the nobleman's nominee. He had been backed by all the sympathies of the American Senator, who knew nothing of him or his unfitness, and nothing whatever of the patriotism of the marquis. But he did know what was the population and what the constituency of Liverpool, and also what were those of Quinborough. He supposed that he knew what was the theory of representation in England, and he understood correctly that hitherto the member for Quinborough had been the nominee of that great lord. These things were horrid to him. . . . To the gentleman who assured him that the Right Honble.—would make a much better member of Parliament than Tom Bobster the plasterer from Shoreditch, he in vain tried to prove that the respective merits of the two men had nothing to do with the question.[33]

With this passage in mind, and remembering too Trollope's life-long aversion to other "progressive" measures like Civil Service Reform, the ballot, and women's suffrage, it is possible to see in this novel and **The Warden** a striking analogy—to see in the Senator and Goarly counterparts of John Bold and Hiram's bedesmen, and in Lord Rufford a replica of the embarrassing situation of the innocent, victimized Mr. Harding. Nor should we overlook the equally strong defiance of "logic" that Trollope could exhibit in such a comparatively trivial matter as fox-hunting. Here again his feelings were mixed, for though, as we have already seen, he could show awareness of the absurd features of the sport, he could also enlist himself as a keen partisan, and take pains to make sympathetic landowners like the new Duke of Omnium in **Phineas Redux** (chapter lxxv) and Reginald Morton here in **The American Senator** (chapter lxxiii) lend it their full support.

In short, we are confronted in **The American Senator** with sets of attitudes which simply cannot be reconciled. It is not accurate to say with one critic that Trollope is simply putting sentiments he shares into the mouth of a character who is also absurd, for we have no way of knowing where the serious leaves off and the absurd begins. And this, of course, is precisely why we also cannot regard Trollope in this novel as the detached spectator of two cultures who appreciates the strengths and weaknesses of each equally: we simply cannot tell what he regards as a strength and what he regards as a weakness. If, as the commentators who support the Senator tell us, the strength of the Senator is his strict logic, then of course Trollope cannot simultaneously consider the absence of that quality as constituting the strength of the Senator's opponents; but that, according to the other interpreters is apparently just what he does. The truth of the matter is that when the Senator displays his logic in the letters he writes home to his fellow congressman (chapters xxix-li), or on the lecture platform where he berates his English listeners for the irrationalities in such "institutions" as the House of Lords, the franchise, primogeniture, fox-hunting, the Church, and the Army (chapters lxxvii-lxxviii), or when he argues time and again that Goarly's "right to his own land . . . was not lessened by the fact that he was a poor, ignorant, squalid, dishonest wretch,"[34] it is impossible to be certain of the standpoint of Trollope himself. Our doubt as to whether he is defending Logic against Tradition or Tradition against Logic was his own.[35] It was the plight of the Conservative-Liberal in the mid-and later decades of the nineteenth century. Drawn by his intellect to a realization of the necessity of Liberal reforms, Trollope was impelled at the same time by an unquenchable nostalgia for the past, a deep-seated emotional conservatism, in a direction diametrically opposite. The result was tension that the simple expedient of placing a hyphen between the terms Conservative and Liberal does more to make poignantly evident than ever to resolve.

For a moment, no doubt, a resolution seems clearly in sight. In **The Duke's Children** for the first time in Trollope's work the conflict within the writer himself between emotional loyalties and intellectual convictions seems to have been raised to a conscious plane, lucidly objectified, and worked out to a satisfactory solution. The ambiguous social attitudes of the preceding novels seem suddenly to have come sharply within his awareness, and their challenge to have been deliberately and courageously confronted. What at first sight could appear to be a clearer dramatic equivalent of Trollope's divided allegiance than that which exists in the mind of the Duke himself? Not only does the latter have many of Trollope's personality traits, as he had in earlier novels as well, but he is caught on the horns of an identical dilemma: in his public and rational moments, and in his official parliamentary role, he adheres to the tenets of the Liberals; but in private, intimately personal affairs he cherishes emotions appropriate only to the most diehard of Conservatives. Moreover, what could seem to be a clearer resolution of this difficulty than the Duke's final surrender to the will of his more "progressive" children when it appears that conviction and action are squared once and for all? Indeed, the *Spectator* censured Trollope for settling the conflict all too facilely—for cutting "the Gordian knot" rather than untying it. Trollope brings to bear on "one of the quaintest of modern problems," the critic argued, an "able and comparatively impartial mind"; but

> the total impression upon the reader's mind is somewhat depressing . . . ; the bonds of the past are arbitrarily broken; they are not modified into picturesque appendages. Mr. Trollope appears to suggest that the religion of caste is hopelessly and helplessly incompatible with the creed of progress. . . .[36]

But is this really what Trollope suggests? At first glance, perhaps, yes; but is such the impression left by the book as a whole? Do we come away convinced that Trollope has somehow resolved the confusions of a lifetime? The likelihood is prima facie against such an assumption, and the text itself more than adequately confutes it. If Trollope's celebration of the victory of Liberal over Conservative was to be effective, it certainly needed to be much more unequivocal than it actually is. For one thing, the Duke, in giving his consent to his children's marriages to their chosen mates, does not so much repudiate his aristocratic philosophy of class as merely make an exception to it—and even at that he cannot refrain from "reminding himself of all that he had suffered."[37] Indeed, the suffering the Duke has to undergo in order to bring himself to his final decision is underscored much too heavily by Trollope to be consistent with the simple and straightforward didactic aim which the *Spectator* ascribed to him. He plainly wants us to sympathize not merely with the outcome of the struggle, but with the struggle itself, and to do that we must obviously respect and acknowledge the strength of both the opponents. No one who believed in the unequivocal superiority of the destined victor could have treated the Duke's plight with such depth of tenderness, affection, and understanding. Nor, conversely, could such a writer have done such scant justice to the

Duke's son-in-law, Francis Oliphant Tregear. Much is made of the fact that the latter is a thorough "gentleman," but we have to accept this on the basis of the mere statement of it alone; very little is done to make the character attractive in deed; Trollope's attitude seems distant and even cold. He reacts curiously to Isabel Boncassen, too: when we look closely we discover that the Duke's concession on her behalf is not quite as startling and generous as it is supposed to appear, for Trollope has taken the bite out of the situation by making Isabel hardly more than nominally distinct from any well-bred English girl. As in the case of Caroline Spaulding in *He Knew He Was Right,* the critics for the *Spectator* observed,

> Mr. Trollope has made his republican heiress lay aside her republican irreverence [i.e., her belief in equality] altogether too easily and too soon. . . . [For this reason] essentially and at bottom she is as English as the Duke himself, and not American at all.[38]

In the end, therefore, far from offering a solution to that unresolved "internal debate and painful struggle" between "reason" and "feeling" which Trollope described in the *Fortnightly* articles, the Duke is simply the perfect dramatic representation of it.

Comparable to, and perhaps indeed stemming from, his ambiguous attitude toward class was the conflict engendered in Trollope's mind when he dealt with the subject of the marriage of convenience. The unhappy fate of Caroline Waddington, who in *The Bertrams* turned down her true but financially embarrassed lover, George Bertram, in order to satisfy her social ambition by marrying the brilliant Solicitor-General, Sir Henry Harcourt, set the pattern for stories to which Trollope was to recur time and again with tireless fascination. The Dowager Countess Desmond in *Castle Richmond,* Alice Vavasor in *Can You Forgive Her?,* Lady Mason in *Orley Farm,* Julia Brabazon in *The Claverings,* Lady Laura Standish in *Phineas Finn* and *Phineas Redux,* Lizzie Greystock in *The Eustace Diamonds,* Josephine Murray in *Lady Anna,* and Lady Mabel Grex in *The Duke's Children* are all, like Caroline, proud, handsome, ambitious, but impecunious women who, in marrying (or seeking to marry) for prudential reasons rather than love, invariably doom themselves to lifelong misery or disgrace. Trollope's moral is obvious and always the same: marriages based solely or principally on mercenary ambition, a desire for title or position, or other interested motives, are evil and can have only evil results; poetic justice inevitably wins the day. Our interest in these stories, however, does not lie in their acceptance of conventional morality, nor in the obvious limits which this acceptance imposes upon their verisimilitude. It lies, rather, in the way in which this morality clashes with Trollope's direct, realistic apprehension of life itself. Whether Trollope fully recognized the fact that the morality could conveniently serve the interests of the privileged classes (by dampening in the lower orders the ambition for social advancement) we cannot be sure; his treatment of Mary Thorne, as we have noted, would seem to imply some recognition, but it is difficult to know how fully conscious a one. In any event, the fact remains that in becoming a spokesman for the conventional morality of his day (for whatever reasons) he was no more wholehearted in his commitment to it than he was in his commitment to either Conservatism or Liberalism.

From the family calamities of his boyhood, the buffets he received as a youth in London, and his exposure in manhood to the harrowing sights of Ireland, the shabby stratagems and humiliations to which people could be reduced by the want of money or an equivocal social position were things which Trollope knew intimately and could represent with the least sentimentalization or melodrama of all his contemporaries. Some of the most convincing passages in his novels are those that seem most obviously to have been inspired by aspects of his own life: Mrs. Dale, the dependent poor relation of the Squire in **The Small House at Allington,** is a wonderfully successful character whose situation and personality are in certain respects similar to those of Trollope's mother; the vivid stories of desperate young men like Thady Macdermot (**The Macdermots of Ballycloran**), Charley Tudor (**The Three Clerks**), Johnny Eames (**The Small House at Allington** and **The Last Chronicle of Barset**), and Phineas Finn (**Phineas Finn** and **Phineas Redux**) are almost literal transcripts of uncomfortable experiences of his own. But though Trollope was thus acutely sensitized to important aspects of economic hardship, there was always a certain class of problems offered by poverty in encountering which his imagination and integrity broke down. When it came to the economics of love and marriage he could never bring the truth of his experience into harmony with his inherited morality. When exceptional but poor and handicapped young women of the type we have named marry for money or position they invariably suffer. Trollope does not hesitate to extend to them all kinds of sympathy; he could not help himself, for in the deepest regions of his personality he appreciated their frustrations keenly. But he refuses to allow his observations and feelings to modify his judgments. Hence, he punishes his aspirants without ever convincing us that there might have been a satisfactory alternative to their conduct. In the case of Lord George Germain, Adelaide Houghton, and Jack de Baron of **Is He Popenjoy?,** for example, we are expected to feel that the preoccupation of these characters with money and the marriage of convenience is ignoble; but we are never shown that for people of their social status and taste any real escape from such preoccupations exists. It is axiomatic with Trollope that young women should marry; but the way in which they should go about this is never faced by him realistically. They must definitely not hunt their husbands; that is

vulgar. Nor should they marry solely for money; that is evil. On the other hand, they should not marry a pauper; that is foolish. What they should do, it would seem, is simply wait patiently to be courted by a young man whom they can sincerely love, and who also is not as bad off at the end as he and the reader thought he was;[39] has money already; is anticipating it; or, best of all, will have it showered upon him unexpectedly.[40]

Needless to say, no "solution" could be more unsatisfactory. It stems entirely from Trollope's refusal (or inability) to face up to the complexities of the problem he has chosen to present—from his acceptance, in short, of a ready-made morality which he will not re-examine in the light of his own evidence. It is not the morality per se which is invalid, but Trollope's willingness to superimpose it facilely upon a body of facts and feelings which make it seem totally irrelevant. His representations show us that no such simple a priori answers as those provided by conventional morality are adequate; and yet it is precisely upon just such answers that Trollope ultimately falls back. This is why a number of his books prove disappointments. They begin promisingly, but before the end stagnate intellectually. The genuine tragedy potential in the lives of Caroline Waddington, Alice Vavasor, Laura Standish, and their successors is cheapened or obscured by the factitious tragedy superimposed upon it by the didactic requirements of stereotyped thinking.

Perhaps one of the clearest examples of this is the story of Lady Mabel Grex in **The Duke's Children.** Before the novel opens Lady Mabel was deeply in love with her cousin, Frank Tregear; but since they were both without money, they agreed to part and seek advantageous marriages elsewhere. In time Lady Mabel comes to attract the attention of the Duke's son, Lord Silverbridge, and he soon offers her his hand. But moved by a curious scrupulosity of conscience which tells her that it would be bad for him to marry one who could not regard him as "an Apollo upon earth,"[41] and by a reluctance "to grasp too eagerly at the prize,"[42] she turns him down. Shortly after, however, she realizes her mistake when he transfers his affections to Isabel Boncassen. Dreading the thought that she has thrown away her last opportunity to escape from poverty and spinsterdom, she confronts him in a climactic scene, and discarding the last vestiges of her carefully guarded gentility, demands that he renew his proposal. But the time for such drastic action has long passed, and with the young man's refusal she has no alternative but to retire to her gloomy country house, an embittered woman for the rest of her days.

There are potentialities of great power in this story, and Trollope often makes the best of them. A carefully arranged climactic progression (reminiscent of that in the story of Arabella Trefoil in **The American Senator**) shows us each step in Lady Mabel's degeneration from the beautiful, blasé girl of impeccable manners in the early pages to the haggard, desperate, despairing figure of near-madness at the close. All that in the beginning she dreaded becoming—worldly, cynical, unfeminine, deceitful, shameless—finally overtakes her. In the scene in which she reproaches Silverbridge for having deceived her and then suddenly turns about and confesses that she never loved him in the first place (chapter lxxiii), and in that in which she has her last bitter interview with Tregear (chapter lxxvii), she emerges as another portrait worthy of a place in Trollope's memorable gallery of obsessives and monomaniacs. But the story is ultimately unsatisfactory because Trollope's deepest intuitions and the dictates of a conventional moral formula work radically at odds with each other throughout. In creating Lady Mabel, Trollope showed his capacity of rising above mere stereotypes by drawing for his inspiration directly upon experience. She is a rare sort of character not only in his own fiction, but in that of his contemporaries as well—the penniless young woman of good family who will marry for money, but who, at the same time, is not devoid of modesty and conscience; the woman who wishes "to be pure and good and feminine, and at the same time wise."[43] Her schemes, unlike those of Arabella Trefoil, do not exclude the genuine desire to behave in a ladylike fashion; nor do they exclude a sense of obligation to the husband whom she is determined to serve loyally even though (because of her continuing love for Tregear) she cannot passionately love him. This is a difficult kind of character to conceive and portray, and it is all to Trollope's credit that he is able to do it well. It calls forth from him a genuine understanding and sympathy. He seems to know intimately just how such a woman thinks and behaves, and to appreciate her plight in all its complexities. Indeed, his compassion is so unstinting at those moments, for example, when Lady Mabel inveighs against the passivity of the rôle which is forced upon her sex by conventional morality,[44] that he seems to throw his old prejudice against feminine emancipation to the winds. But the story ultimately disappoints us precisely because Trollope does not allow this sympathy to work itself out to its logical conclusion.

Ostensibly Lady Mabel's is the tragedy of one who fails to take the tide at its flood, who at a crucial turning-point in life (in this case, the moment of Silverbridge's proposal) proves too cautious or scrupulous or imperceptive to seize the unique opportunity. Lady Mabel, it would seem, fell short of the game she herself had chosen to play: a little more vulgarity and callousness in the style of Arabella Trefoil, a little less enthrallment by a hopeless passion for her former lover, and she would have ended her days more happily. But the more we consider the novel the more we realize that this is not the point at all. No less than Lady Laura Standish or Julia Brabazon or Adelaide Houghton or

Arabella Trefoil, Lady Mabel has to suffer, regardless of her decision, simply because of the nature of her whole ambition. Conventional Victorian morality demands that whoever attempts to marry for money rather than love must be frustrated and punished, and Trollope follows out this code to the letter. A highly romantic concept of feminine innocence is brought into play so that Lady Mabel may be stigmatized at the end as "a manufactured article," a creature which has lost its "native bloom," and from whose "first fair surface" something has been "scratched and chipped."[45] She is reduced to a mere illustration of what the *Saturday Review* called "the demoralizing influences incident to her class."[46] But this is a judgment imposed from without, not developing organically within the story itself. So many extenuating circumstances have been presented, so much compassion has been lavished on the woman, that we can conceive of no legitimate reason why we should not see her married and happily settled. Had Trollope remained faithful to his sympathies, had he allowed his vision of the clear facts of experience to determine the outcome of Lady Mabel's tale as it determined his conception of the character itself, instead of superimposing upon that vision a preconceived moral requirement, he would have written one of the most unconventional and refreshing love stories in the whole range of Victorian fiction. To ask this is not, of course, to dictate to the writer his choice of subject-matter; it is simply to ask him to be consistent with the emotional premises and expectations which he himself has chosen to establish. Having shown in the early part of the novel an unusually clear and uninhibited comprehension of, and sympathy for, a particular kind of character and the predicament in which it finds itself, Trollope has no right to play false with his feelings by forcing upon us a conclusion that calls for the acceptance of a whole set of stereotyped conceptions and values, the complete repudiation of which has been the obvious effect of the original presentation. An incipient ability to seize experience boldly and freshly is stifled by a last minute return to the comforting security of a conventional formula.

Notes

1. II (August 15, 1865), 82-84.

2. II (October 1, 1865), 476.

3. (London: Oxford University Press, "World's Classics," 1918), pp. 53-54.

4. See *Barchester Towers* (London: Oxford University Press, "World's Classics," 1925), pp. 50-51, 56, 82, 109, 112.

5. *Ibid.,* p. 490.

6. *What I Remember* (New York: Harper's, 1888), I, 10. For a full-scale satire on "trade" see *The Struggles of Brown, Jones, and Robinson.* Though

not published in serial form until 1861-62 or as a book until 1870 (1862 in the United States), it was projected by Trollope soon after the publication of *Barchester Towers*.

7. Cf. the ostensible moral lesson of the famous mid-Victorian novel by Mrs. Craik, *John Halifax, Gentleman* (1856), and T. W. Robertson's drama, *Caste* (1867).

8. When the high-born Agatha Larochejaquelin falls in love with the low-born Cathelineau, the former postilion who has become general-in-chief of the Vendean army, she declares passionately not only that he is "'the prince of gentlemen,'" but that "'despite his birth and former low condition, he is worthy of any woman's love,'" including, of course, her own ([London: Chapman and Hall, "uniform edition," n.d.], p. 161).

9. *An Autobiography* (Berkeley and Los Angeles: University of California Press, 1947), p. 34. Cf. Anthony Trollope, *Thackeray* (New York: Harper's, "English Men of Letters," 1879), pp. 85-86, and *Miss Mackenzie* (London: Oxford University Press, "World's Classics," 1924), p. 71.

10. Quoted in Lance O. Tingay, "Trollope and the Beverley Election," *Nineteenth-Century Fiction*, V (June, 1950), 27; cf. p. 31.

11. *An Autobiography*, p. 34.

12. (London: Oxford University Press, "World's Classics," 1926), pp. 25-26.

13. *Ibid.*, pp. 33, 37.

14. (London: Oxford University Press, "World's Classics Double," 1944), II, 286-287.

15. Pp. 141-143.

16. *Is He Popenjoy?*, II, 287.

17. David Stryker, "The Significance of Trollope's *American Senator*," *Nineteenth-Century Fiction*, V (September, 1950), 148, 145.

18. *Ibid.*, p. 148. Cf. the views of Donald Smalley and Bradford A. Booth in their introduction to *North America* (New York: Knopf, 1951), p. xxx, and the opinion of Willard Thorp in *Trollope's America* (New York: Grolier Club, 1950), p. 18.

19. John Hazard Wildman, "Trollope Illustrates Distinction," *Nineteenth-Century Fiction*, IV (September, 1949), 105, 107.

20. *Ibid.*, p. 110.

21. Clement Greenberg, "A Victorian Novel," *Partisan Review*, II (Spring, 1944), 236.

22. Bradford A. Booth, ed., *The Letters of Anthony Trollope* (London/New York: Oxford University Press, 1951), letter no. 634.

23. *The American Senator* (London: Oxford University Press, "World's Classics," 1931), p. 476.

24. *Ibid.*, p. 531.

25. Booth, *loc. cit.*

26. *The American Senator*, p. 349.

27. *Ibid.*, p. 354.

28. (London: Chapman and Hall, 1866), p. 41

29. *The American Senator*, p. 352.

30. *Ibid.*, p. 195.

31. *Ibid.*, p. 470.

32. *Lotta Schmidt and other Stories* (London: Alexander Strahan, 1867), pp. 231, 254.

33. *The American Senator*, pp. 350-351.

34. *Ibid.*, p. 353.

35. To my knowledge only one critic of the novel, Clement Greenberg, has seen this fact clearly: "The author's attitude to the senator is highly ambiguous. He seems to have been intended primarily as a mouthpiece for Trollope's own strictures on English society; secondarily as a caricature. But the two aims are in contradiction. Criticism is attributed to the senator with which it is obvious that Trollope does not agree, designed as it is to characterize the senator rather than the objects of his criticism. But it is very difficult to draw the line between this and the criticism with which the author does agree" ("A Victorian Novel," *loc. cit.*). Greenberg goes on, however, to draw from this fact an erroneous conclusion: for him this ambiguity is a virtue, enabling the character of the senator to attain "an objectivity rare in Victorian English fiction" (*ibid.*). But this claim is unintelligible, for it fails to make a distinction between ambiguity which is artistically controlled and mere confusion. What we have in *The American Senator* is the latter.

36. LIII (June 12, 1880), 755.

37. (London: Oxford University Press, "World's Classics Double," 1946), II, 378.

38. LIII (June 12, 1880), 755.

39. The perfect example of this is Frank Greystock in *The Eustace Diamonds*: for close to seven hundred pages we follow the story of a specimen of that "middle class of men, who, by reason of their education, are peculiarly susceptible to the charms of womanhood, but who literally cannot marry for love, because their earnings will do no more than support themselves," only to be complacently told at the end that marriage with a penniless girl

merely "seemed" to threaten him with ruin (New York: Modern Library, n.d.), p. 683.

40. Such recipients of unexpected fortunes or security are numerous; in addition to Mary Thorne there are Clara Desmond and Herbert Fitzgerald in *Castle Richmond,* Bell Dale and Dr. Crofts in *The Small House,* Fanny Clavering and Mr. Saul in *The Claverings,* Nora Rowley and Hugh Stanbury in *He Knew He Was Right,* Dorothy Stanbury and Brooke Burgess in the same, Mary Lowther and Walter Marrable in *The Vicar of Bullhampton,* Mary Bonner and Ralph Newton in *Ralph the Heir,* and Marie Bromar and George Voss in *The Golden Lion of Granpère.*

41. II, 195.

42. II, 134.

43. I, 102.

44. I, 98-99, 337; II, 317.

45. II, 271.

46. XLIX (June 12, 1880), 767.

Helen Heineman (essay date January 1982)

SOURCE: Heineman, Helen. "Anthony Trollope: The Compleat Traveller." *ARIEL: A Review of International English Literature* 13, no. 1 (January 1982): 33-50.

[*In the following essay, Heineman asserts that Trollope's travel essays best represent the author's true character and voice, as well as that Trollope's ability to observe and write without judgment made him a fair and trustworthy travel companion.*]

> The grand defect in travellers, and the reason why scarcely one in a hundred gives no more useful or interesting information touching the countries they visit, than any of us could give of the moon, is this. Man—the true unsophisticated, two legged, unfeathered man, is naturally and prodigiously an egotist. Whether he call himself *I,* in the style egotistical, or *we,* in the style royal, number one is the hero, the subject, predicate, and conclusion, the beginning middle, and end, by which he measures and compares every thing that he sees, enjoys, or suffers. In a word, his own habits, tastes, and pursuits, are the common measure by which he settles every value. . . . Very few travellers possess the enlargement of thought, and the generosity of feeling, and the capability of generalizing, to qualify them for giving adequate and just views of the countries they undertake to describe.
>
> "Travellers in America," Timothy Flint, *Knickerbocker,* October 1833

> Of all travellers in the world, the English are the best and the worst. . . . Their insular manners stand in the way of that free intercourse which is the *passe-partout* to the life of a people; and certain lofty prejudices, which are not amiss at home in helping to impart self-reliance to the national character, lead them to depreciate or misjudge foreign customs exactly in proportion as they differ from their own.
>
> "Recent Travellers," *Fraser's,* July 1850

The prevailing voice and dominant attitudes of Anthony Trollope are perhaps best known to readers of Victorian fiction through his quiet and sensible intrusions as narrator in his many novels of English life and manners. Wary of finding the real man in a literary convention, others seek Trollope in his workmanlike and self-effacing *Autobiography.* But in these more self-conscious days, there are those who regard his utter frankness as simply another kind of literary pose. It has not occurred to many that the most broadly representative voice of Trollope might be heard in his lesser-known works of travel: ***The West Indies and the Spanish Main,*** 1859; ***Travelling Sketches,*** 1866; ***Australia and New Zealand,*** 1873; ***South Africa,*** 1878; and his most comprehensive and perceptive volume, ***North America,*** 1862.[1] While these volumes are in large part renderings of factual and external realities, the voice, personality, and experience of Anthony Trollope lie at their cores, making them unique among similar books in the popular nineteenth-century travel genre. Trollope's deepest and most fundamental trait was an eminent sense of fairness, developed no doubt, during his dark years of boyhood when he felt himself abandoned by his family and miserably persecuted by the rich and socially superior boys at Harrow School. Emerging from such unpromising beginnings to a secure and famous adulthood, Trollope eventually came to value fairness as the supreme informing sense a man could bring to his life, or a writer to his books. In his many novels, he is always compassionate toward the characters of his creation. Reluctant to portray any of them as mere villains, he spoke a word in behalf even of Mrs. Proudie, who although she was "a tyrant, a bully, a would-be priestess, a very vulgar woman, and one who would send headlong to the nethermost pit all who disagreed with her," was "at the same time . . . conscientious, by no means a hypocrite, really believing in the brimstone which she threatened, and anxious to save the souls around her from its horrors."[2]

In the travel books, this stance emerges as a prevailing willingness to evaluate other countries on their own terms and according to their own goals. The achievement of such supreme fairness brought a new dimension to the travel book genre, and is most remarkable in his lengthy volume ***North America.*** The criticism of America by Englishmen during the nineteenth century had not been distinguished either by fairness or objectivity; it was a touchy subject, at best, this judging of a rebellious "child" by its older parent. Beginning with the early volumes of his mother (*Domestic Manners of* *the Americans,* 1832), who, in Anthony's own words, "judged . . . from her standing-point," and extending to Dickens, who in his *American Notes* (1842) let his disgust with the inequities of the Copyright Law colour his reactions, traveller after traveller seemed disposed to "write up" the United States according to his own particular set of prejudices or preconceptions.[3] Both praise and blame were doled out according to what the traveller thought America *should* be doing. One early reviewer, tired of such methods, noted:

> In a strange country, considerable pains must be taken to obtain sound materials for an opinion. There is, besides, a certain *charity of nature,* which is not more favourable to our own happiness and influence with others, than indispensable for the strict and simple purposes of truth. These precautions would weed page after page out of most modern travels, especially out of travels in America.[4]

Trollope, who came during the most difficult of all times for a foreign observer—the Civil War—succeeded in seeing the country for what it was: a young country struggling toward a difficult maturity. His innate "charity of nature" enabled him to do what so many had failed to do before him: to judge the United States on its own terms and according to its own goals. Because of his fairness as a person, he emerges as one of the most dependable sources of information on nineteenth-century America. His writings were not merely a desire to repeat the "family occupation" of writing travel books, for he had something special to offer: he really was "the compleat traveller."

In addition to his fairness Trollope brought to his writings still another asset. In that great age of peripatetic Englishmen, Trollope boasted an impressive set of credentials. Long before he visited America in 1861, he had proven his mettle as an indomitable and highly experienced traveller.

Living in and about Ireland for ten years, he had also made several visits to Florence to see his mother and brother. His position in the London Post Office had helped to make him intimately acquainted with the southern and western counties of England and Wales. In 1858 his employer selected him to journey to Egypt to conclude a postal treaty with that country. In the process, he toured Egypt and the Holy Land, returning to England by way of Malta, Gibraltar, Spain, and France. He was so successful in his mission, that the Post Office, four days after his return, sent him to Scotland, and then, in November, to the West Indies, to reorganize the decrepit postal system of the Islands. Although his tours were official in nature, he soon learned how to use them as a means to sightseeing, and sightseeing as a means to authorship.[5]

Trollope's behaviour recalls that of the narrator in the earliest of his many novels, a man who, left to amuse himself one evening while in a strange town on a business trip, went out to see the countryside: "in such a situation, to take a walk is all the brightest man can do, and the dullest always does the same. There is a kind of gratification in seeing what one has never seen before, be it ever so little worth seeing; and the gratification is the greater if the chances be that one will never see it again."[6] The West Indian trip resulted not only in the completion of his official duties, but also in the first of his several travel books. In it, he described his insatiable curiosity about the world and his pleasure in travel. "How best to get about this world which God has given us is certainly one of the most interesting works on which men can employ themselves" (p. 316).

For Trollope, there was an innate value in the mere fact of travel; even in the face of many personal misadventures, he never doubted the wisdom of giving up his accustomed home comforts in favour of the uncertainties of foreign travel. Once, in a wintry western city of the United States, Trollope, in search of hotel accommodations, stumbled and fell in the frozen snow, making a ludicrous spectacle even in his own eyes. He recorded in *North America* his wryly humorous analysis:

> Why is it that a stout Englishman bordering on fifty finds himself in such a predicament as that? No Frenchman, no Italian, no German, would so place himself, unless under the stress of insurmountable circumstances. No American would do so under any circumstances. As I slipped about on the ice and groaned with that terrible fardle on my back, burdened with a dozen shirts, and a suit of dress clothes, and three pair of boots, and four or five thick volumes, and a set of maps, and a box of cigars, and a washing-tub, I confessed to myself that I was a fool. What was I doing in such a galley as that? Why had I brought all that useless lumber down to Rolla? Why had I come to Rolla, with no certain hope even of shelter for a night? But we did reach the hotel; we did get a room between us with two bedsteads. And, pondering over the matter in my mind, since that evening, I have been inclined to think that the stout Englishman is in the right of it.
>
> (p. 395)

Never bristling at the hardships of travel, the dirt, delays and inconveniences, Trollope on tour "was very thoroughly Trollope. The banging, jolting, bustling adventure of train, steamer, diligence and mule-back travel, so far from tiring or fretting him, set him banging and jolting in response; spurred him to greater energies. . . ."[7]

Physical endurance was matched by his ability to forget the miseries of past travel, and he often so cautioned his readers. It is true that he began his volume on the West Indies in an uncharacteristically captious manner, by complaining about the dreariness and inconvenience of travelling in sailing vessels and that he resolved never again to set forth in one of those ships. But by the time he reached the end of his Caribbean journey, he had so far forgotten his grievance that he returned from Bermuda to New York again on board a similar vessel:

> I had declared during my unlucky voyage from Kingston to Cuba that no consideration should again tempt me to try a sailing vessel, but such declarations always go for nothing. A man in his misery thinks much of his misery; but as soon as he is out of it is forgotten, or becomes matter for mirth. Of even a voyage in a sailing vessel one may say that at some future time it will perhaps be pleasant to remember that also.

(p. 365)

An undemanding traveller, Trollope toured the United States during the Civil War, when many facilities were subject to extraordinary delays and upheavals. Instead of complaining, he commented, when required to accept the company of some American private soldiers who were loud, noisy, dirty, and profane: "Of course I felt that if I chose to travel in a country while it had such a piece of business on its hands, I could not expect that everything should be found in exact order. The matter for wonder, perhaps, was that the ordinary affairs of life were so little disarranged, and that any travelling at all was practicable" (p. 365). This self-effacing tone and a genuine tolerance distinguishes *North America,* his American book, from so many other travel volumes of the time.

Trollope was able to adjust to the mores and manners of the country he was visiting, while at the same time maintaining his own robust English individuality. He was never afflicted with what Henry James has called "the baleful spirit of the cosmopolite—that uncomfortable consequence of seeing many lands and feeling at home in none."[8] Trollope always felt the sanctity of English habits, and yet he was able to compare, to look for the points of difference and, finally, to "think well of mankind."[9] At Grand Haven, Michigan, while waiting for a steamboat to get underway (delays were proverbial), he amused himself according to the custom of the country. After walking alone for a time, "I went down into the bar-room of the steamer, put my feet upon the counter, lit my cigar, and struck into the debate then proceeding on the subject of the war" (p. 125). Ironically, this casual American posture was the very one so often vilified by his mother in her famous travel book, *Domestic Manners of the Americans.* Still, Trollope always carried with him his books, his flask of port, his toothbrushes and combs, and always managed gracefully to retain the accoutrements of "a sturdy and sensible middle-class Englishman."[10] As the reviewer for *Harper's* magazine rightly noted:

> To be sure, he thinks an Englishman of middle age, sound digestion, comfortable income, and fair position—like himself—the luckiest and best man on earth. But as all men can not have all these blessings, he is quite ready to see what else the world has to offer to them.[11]

He was not shy about letting his readers know where he stood on such matters as parallelogrammical cities, walking habits, and heated rooms.[12] Although he berated the American love of central heating, he saw it with his usual tolerant perspective: "as the boats are made for Americans, and as Americans like hot air, I do not put it forward with any idea that a change ought to be effected."[13] Surely the Stebbinses were incorrect in calling him "an insular Englishman whose early sympathies and antipathies were unmodified by reason or by observation."[14] On the contrary, over the years, as he wrote his many novels, his imagination became ever more responsive and sensitive to all kinds of "otherness."

Bradford Booth has accurately called Trollope "a statistical Baedeker."[15] Trollope never tired of assembling pages of practical information and facts about a country in which he found himself. He was seldom content merely with impressionistic renderings of places; factual details inevitably followed any generalization. Portland, Maine, had "an air of supreme plenty," and he noted its quiet confidence as young girls returned from their tea parties at nine-o-clock, "many of them alone, and all with some basket in their hands which betokened an evening not passed absolutely in idleness" (p. 38). Beyond this impression, he noted too the size of the harbour, the number of inhabitants, and the great number of houses, "which must require an expenditure of from six to eight hundred a year to maintain them." He always reinforced his observations by well-chosen statistics which emphasized salient facts in the life of the community. At Buffalo, for example, instead of describing young ladies walking quietly home in the evenings, he noted the city's rapid urbanization, and that its "cars on tramways run all day, and nearly all night as well" (p. 170). The difference in the kind of observations and statistics he included tells the story of the difference in cities. *North America* abounds in statistics: the number of slaves in cities; the population count; the number of children educated in public free schools; the cost of corn in Bloomington and in Liverpool; the salaries of the military during the civil war; the gross revenues of the post office. Sometimes his facts were not always of the practical variety. On at least one occasion he went out of his way to ascertain a statistic which only his insatiable curiosity and bureaucratic love of figures did not permit him to overlook. On a visit to San Francisco, years after the first American trip, he told of how he stopped outside Yosemite Valley to measure some of the redwood trees, "finding the girth of the largest which I saw to be seventy-eight feet."[16]

He was always willing to perform the expected, and he patiently visited all those places usually viewed by travellers. In his reactions to fabled places and striking views, Trollope comes close to "the average man." He is not the gushing aesthete, but the man who confesses to feelings of disappointment when confronted with, say, the citadel of Quebec. He was reluctant when pressed to go out to see the rock over which Wolfe climbed to the plains of Abraham. "Nevertheless, and as a matter of course, I went to see the rock, and can only say, as so many have said before me, that it is very steep" (p. 52). He ascended Mt. Washington on a pony because "that is *de rigueur,*" but confessed that "I did not gain much myself by my labour" (p. 40). On the Falls of Minnehaha he said: "It is a pretty little cascade, and might do for a picnic in fine weather, but it is not a waterfall of which a man can make much when found so far away from home" (p. 149). At the Mountain House, he did "the one thing to be done," and scaled a dangerous peak with Rose, his wife, a trip which almost ended in serious mishap (p. 58). He did these things, not because he saw himself in any way as a man travelling to gather "literary" materials—indeed, he never sought his inspiration in strange scenes or striking places—but simply because they were expected of tourists.

When he sat down to write about what he saw, what emerged was, as Henry James called it, his genius for the usual. This "genius" was by far the one best suited for the writing of a solid and substantial book of travels. And when he came to describing America, he was more interested in viewing the grain elevators at Buffalo than in exulting over the Falls of Montmorency or Minnehaha. He knew his strength—and he also, characteristically, noted its limitations. In many of his travel stories and books, he reveals a strong sense of his own potential for absurdity (**"John Bull on the Guadalquivir," "Father Giles of Ballmoy,"** in his *Tales of all Countries* and *Lotta Schmidt and Other Stories*). In his *Travelling Sketches* he made great fun of "the tourist in search of knowledge," the man who so resembled Anthony himself:

> He will listen with wondrous patience to the details of guides, jotting down figures in a little book, and asking wonder-working questions which no guide can answer. And he looks into municipal matters wherever he goes, learning all details as to mayors, aldermen, and councillors, as to custom duties on provisions, as to import duties on manufactures, as to schools, convents, and gaols, to scholars, mendicants, and criminals. He does not often care much for scenery, but he will be careful to inquire how many passengers the steamboats carry on the lakes, and what average of souls is boarded and lodged at each large hotel that he passes. He would like to know how many eggs are consumed annually, and probably does ask some question as to the amount of soap used in the laundries.
>
> To the romance and transcendental ebullitions of enthusiastic admirers of nature he is altogether hostile, and dislikes especially all quotations from poetry.
>
> (pp. 79-30)

He saw such a traveller as "always thanking God that he is not as those idlers who pass from country to country learning nothing of the institutions of the people among whom they travel . . ." (*Sketches* [*Travelling Sketches*], p. 75).

He was always ready to see himself as a figure of fun—and often appears in *North America* as the bumbling but lovable foreigner stumbling over the usages of a country new to him. He describes himself on a New York omnibus, helpless and befuddled, with bells ringing at him because he has not paid in the proper manner:

> I knew I was not behaving as a citizen should behave, but could not compass the exact points of my delinquency. And then when I desired to escape, the door being strapped up tight, I would halloo vainly at the driver through the little hole; whereas, had I known my duty, I should have rung a bell, or pulled a strap, according to the nature of the omnibus in question.
>
> (p. 197)

This warm humour, so often directed at himself, pervades the pages of all his travel books—whether in the West Indies he is trapped behind a door in his nightgown while a black chambermaid dutifully seeks him out in order to curtsey,[17] or whether he is being crushed by the crinoline of some New York beauty on the street cars.[18] He manages always to see his misadventures as comical, or humorous, or even absurd, a kind of approach noticeably lacking in the more famous travel books of his mother and Charles Dickens, who, for all his talent at humorous effects, rarely saw himself as a comical figure.

Finally, Trollope brought to his travels a quality for which he praised his mother in his *Autobiography*: the capacity for joy. In one of those many passages in which he advises readers on how to travel properly, Anthony wrote: "In seeing the outer world, which is open to your eye, there may be great joy, almost happiness,—if you will only look at it with sincerity."[19] He deplored the fact that many tourists do not really enjoy their travels:

> To have been over the railroads of the Continent, to have touched at some of those towns whose names are known so widely, to have been told that such a summit was called by one name and such another summit by another name, to have crossed the mountains and heard the whistle of a steamer on an Italian lake,—to have done these things so that the past accomplishment of them may be garnered like a treasure, is very well.— but oh and alas, the doing of them!—the troubles, the cares, the doubts, the fears! Is it not almost a question whether it would not be better to live at home quietly and unambitiously, without the garnering of any treasure which cannot be garnered without so much discomfort and difficulty? But yet the tourists go.[20]

Trollope knew how and where to find amusement. Instead of bemoaning the proverbial discomforts of sleeping in American trains, on a trip from Niagara to Detroit, he was glad to be introduced to "the thoroughly American institution of sleeping-cars," remarking that "I confess I have always taken a delight in seeing these beds made up, and consider that the operations of the change are generally as well executed as the manoeuvres of any pantomime at Drury Lane."[21] This capacity for enjoyment extended to a genuine affection for a whole host of casual New World acquaintances. He met an old man on the train who instantly recognized Trollope as an Englishman. Trollope was surprised:

> "There is no mistaking you," he said, "with your round face and your red cheek. They don't look like that here," and he gave me another grip.

Trollope's reaction was typical. "I felt quite fond of the old man, and offered him a cigar" (p. 255). In Washington, he told of the gypsy-like appearance of the sentry, his "higgledly-piggledy state; the man was dirty and often splashed mud on Trollope's clothes as he trotted by, but still, "as I went . . . I felt for him a sort of affection, and wished in my heart of hearts that he might soon be enabled to return to some more congenial employment" (p. 364). He met some teamsters at an inn, dirty men, clumsy with their knives and forks. But Trollope thinks rather of their orderliness and intelligence. "I conceived rather an affection for those dirty teamsters; they answered me civilly when I spoke to them, and sat in quietness, smoking their pipes, with a dull and dirty, but orderly demeanour" (p. 379).

Perhaps Trollope's most significant and unusual ability as a traveller was his ability to project himself into the position of those peoples he had come to see. When he later wrote a book on Australia, he stated as a general rule for an Englishman visiting, say, the United States, that he "should be ever guarding himself against the natural habit of looking at things only from his own point of view. As he would not buy gloves for his friend by the measure of his own hand, so should he not presume that an American will be well-fitted or ill-fitted in the details of his life according as he may or may not wear the customs and manners of his life out after an English fashion."[22] Trollope consciously refused to adopt English standards of measurement by which to judge the accomplishments of other lands. In *North America* he constantly reiterated a warning against judging on the basis of wrong standards. When on a New York omnibus, Trollope was bothered by some women who were aggressively arrogant in demanding their rights to a seat, and his mind automatically went to London women of the same class who were so humble as to doubt that they were even good enough to sit near an upper-class gentleman. But Trollope cut through his conventional assumptions, seeking (and finding) the new assumptions necessary to understand and judge a new phenomenon.

> The question is which is best, the crouching and crawling or the impudent unattractive self-composure. Not,

my reader, which action on her part may the better conduce to my comfort or to yours! That is by no means the question. *Which is the better for the woman herself?* That I take it is the point to be decided. That there is something better than either we shall all agree;—but to my thinking the crouching and crawling is the lowest type of all.

(p. 211; italics mine)

He liked the "hat-touchers" as well as any refined Englishman of his time, but he did not let personal preferences interfere with his clarity of thought. He knew that "if a man can forget his own miseries in his journeyings, and think of the people he comes to see rather than of himself, I think he will find himself driven to admit that education has made life for the million in the Northern States of America better than life for the million is with us" (pp. 267-68). He knew, too, what Englishmen would reply to this position:

> They will declare that they do not want their paviours and hodmen to talk politics; that they are as well pleased that their coachmen and cooks should not always have a newspaper in their hands; that private soldiers will fight as well, and obey better, if they are not trained to discuss the causes which have brought them into the field. An English gentleman will think that his gardener will be a better gardener without any excessive political ardour; and the English lady will prefer that her housemaid shall not have a very pronounced opinion of her own as to the capabilities of the cabinet ministers. But I would submit to all Englishmen and Englishwomen who may look at these pages whether such an opinion or feeling on their part bears much, or even at all, upon the subject. I am not saying that the man who is driven in the coach is better off because his coachman reads the paper, but that the coachman himself who reads the paper is better off than the coachman who does not and cannot. I think that we are too apt, in considering the ways and habits of any people, to judge of them by the effect of those ways and habits on us, rather than by their effects on the owners of them.

(p. 276)

Trollope acknowledged his personal discomfiture among the American lower orders. "They tread on my corns and offend me. They make my daily life unpleasant. But I do respect them. I acknowledge their intelligence and personal dignity. I know that they are men and women worthy to be so called; I see that they are living as human beings in the possession of reasoning faculties; and I perceive that they owe this to the progress that education had made among them" (p. 276). A broader or more humane point of view will not be found among many English travellers of this period. Consistently, conscientiously, he rejected the standard of personal comfort and satisfaction. He once remarked that "New York I regard as the most thoroughly American of all American cities. It is by no means the one in which I should find myself the happiest, but I do not on that account condemn it" (p. 452). After all, he asked:

What is wanted in this world? Is it not that men should eat and drink, and read and write, and say their prayers? Does not that include everything . . . ? When we talk of the advances of civilization, do we mean anything but this, that men who now eat and drink badly shall eat and drink well, and that those who cannot read and write now shall learn to do so,—the prayers following, as prayers will follow upon such learning?

Distinguishing his own kind of evaluation from that of other, more critical assessors of the American achievement, he answered his own question:

Civilization does not consist in the eschewing of garlic or the keeping clean of a man's finger-nails. It may lead to such delicacies, and probably will do so. But the man who thinks that civilization cannot exist without them imagines that the church cannot stand without the spire. In the States of America men do eat and drink, and do read and write.

(p. 276)

This method of evaluation produces the quality which gives his travel books as wholes their prevalent tone of fair friendliness, the hallmark which distinguishes, for example, *North America* from other contemporary British accounts of American life. In being able to see things from another point of view, Trollope brought to the writing of his travel books the same qualities that prevailed in his fiction. Just as there are no villains or heroes in his novels, so too, there are none in the accounts of his travels. He depicted only men and women walking the earth of the world, "going about their daily business, and not suspecting that they were being made a show of."[23]

Trollope was truly able to project himself into the position of the people he had come to observe. He therefore sought to avoid an overemphasis on an anecdotal approach, clearly seeing the dangers inherent in such a method. "Who has ever travelled in foreign countries without meeting excellent stories against the citizens of such countries?"[24] Although he uses anecdotes, it is important to note that he frequently turns them on himself. The ability to do so indicates a self-confidence, as well as a genial awareness that no man is free of absurdities. Anthony Trollope asks: "How few can travel without hearing such stories against themselves?"[25] The overall result of this objectivity is that the author and his subjects seem to stand on equal ground. When he came to write his travel book on America, for once, the Americans did not face a judge who had come over to record their foibles and not his own as well.

Several qualities distinguish *North America,* Trollope's book describing his eight-month stay in the States, from other contemporary travel books. Trollope believed that a good book of travels should tell not only about what *is,* but also about what is yet to come. Returning from the West Indies to Europe via a stop in the United States, he contemplated the writing of his book on America, a volume about "that people who are our children." He found the Americans worthy of special attention because they afforded "the most interesting phenomena which we find as to the new world;—the best means of prophesying, if I may say so, what the world will next be, and what men will next do."[26] Many other travellers had regarded their observations as final and conclusive. But Anthony was convinced that things would not long remain as they were (pp. 5-6), and in his book he frequently spoke in the prophetic voice. He saw "the all but countless population which is before long to be fed from these regions . . . the cities which will grow here . . ." (p. 123). Dickens, when once viewing some monotonous scenery, let his mind wander back, with romantic longing, to the past; he peopled the land, in his imagination, with tribes of Indians in picturesque postures.[27] But Trollope saw in similar scenes "crowds which will grow sleek and talk loudly, and become aggressive on these wheat and meat producing levels." Here will come "men and women who . . . are ambitious, who eat beef, and who read and write, and understand the dignity of manhood" (p. 123).

Europeans had seen as ludicrous the way in which American cities built hotels to accommodate many more guests than were ever in evidence. Trollope heard jokes about the ambitious street plan of New York, but he commented: "I do not in the least doubt that they will occupy it all, and that 154th street will find itself too narrow a boundary for the population" (p. 123). He was never deceived by present inadequacies. He saw at Chicago that the hotel was too big, that the post office, though grand, could not properly deliver the mail, that the theatre, though handsome and convenient, was almost empty on the night of his attendance. But he was astute enough to predict that generations would come to fill up what now was empty. "Those taps of hot and cold water will be made to run by the next owner of the hotel, if not by the present owner. In another ten years the letters, I do not doubt, will all be delivered. Long before that time the theatre will probably be full" (pp. 165-66). Trollope had a vision of America's inevitable growth and development. It was not a mystical vision of blind faith, nor was it a poetic instinct. He had himself seen the productive power of the fertile plains and had been astounded by the amount of wheat in Chicagoan granaries. He had actually gone down to those granaries, and climbed up into the grain elevators. The rhetoric of his sentences ("I saw . . . I ascertained . . . I breathed . . . I believed . . .") gives ineluctable authority to the vision.

I saw the wheat running in rivers from one vessel into another, and from the railroad vans up into the huge bins on the top stores of the warehouses;—for these rivers of food run up hill as easily as they do down. I saw the corn measured by the forty bushel with as much ease as we measure an ounce of cheese, and with greater rapidity. I ascertained that the work went on, weekday and Sunday, day and night incessantly; rivers of wheat and rivers of maize ever running. I saw the men bathed in corn as they distributed it in its flow. I saw bins by the score laden with wheat, in each of which bins there was space for a comfortable residence. I breathed the flour, and drank the flour, and felt myself to be enveloped in a world of breadstuff. And then I believed, understood, and brought it home to myself as a fact, that here in the corn lands of Michigan, and amidst the bluffs of Wisconsin, and on the high table plains of Minnesota, and the prairies of Illinois, had God prepared the good for the increasing millions of the Eastern world, as also for the coming millions of the Western. . . . I began then to know what it was for a country to overflow with milk and honey, to burst with its own fruits, and be smothered by its own riches.

(p. 158)

Although Trollope's prophecies were not always correct—he did, after all, predict the disintegration of the Union—this one has surely been realized. De Tocqueville had prophesied for America in an ideological sense, and had not stressed her incipient material prosperity. Trollope's emphasis on the potential power, strength, and expansion of America is unique among English travellers of the period. Although he observed the rampant hero-worship and ostentatious patriotism which had so annoyed countless others, Trollope was convinced that despite the arrogance and impudence of the typical American, he was "at any rate a civilized being, and on the road to that cultivation which will sooner or later divest him of his arrogance" (p. 272).

Thus, in Trollope's travel books, the most important single ingredient is the informing personality and intelligence of the author playing over the objective reality of external scenes. Thus, the final appeal of **North America** (and of Trollope's other travel books and stories) is rooted firmly in the qualities of mind of its author. Following Trollope as he crossed and recrossed the globe on his many trips, one becomes gradually aware of fundamentals—his warm, genial tolerance, his resistance to judging things evil because they displeased or annoyed him personally, his prophetic voice, his patient good will and affection for those he saw—in short, of the full gamut of those talents which made him supremely "the compleat traveller."

Notes

1. Trollope, Anthony, *The West Indies and the Spanish Main,* 1 vol., (London: Chapman & Hall, 1859); *Travelling Sketches,* 1 vol. (London: Chapman & Hall, 1866); *Australia and New Zealand,* 2 vols. (London: Chapman & Hall, 1873); *South Africa,* 2 vols. (London: Chapman & Hall, 1878); *North America,* 2 vols. (London: Chapman & Hall, 1862). All subsequent references are to these editions, except for *North America,* where I use the definitive edition edited by Donald Smalley and Bradford Booth (New York: Alfred A. Knopf, 1951).

2. Trollope, Anthony, *An Autobiography* (London: OUP [Oxford University Press], 1961), p. 238.

3. Trollope, Frances, *Domestic Manners of the Americans,* ed. Donald Smalley (New York: Alfred A. Knopf, 1949); Dickens, Charles, *American Notes for General Circulation* (London: Chapman & Hall, 1842). Henry T. Tuckerman (*America and Her Commentators,* New York, 1864) found English treatments of America so uniform that he devoted a chapter to "these monotonous protests against the imperfect civilization prevalent in the United States," entitled "English Abuse of America" (p. 252 ff.). He does not see Anthony Trollope's account as any different, and calls it "the old leaven of self-love, self-importance, self-assertion of the Englishman . . ." (p. 234).

4. Unsigned review of *Domestic Manners,* italics mine, *Edinburgh Review,* vol. 55 (July 1832), 480.

5. Sadleir, Michael, *Trollope: A Commentary* (New York: Farrar, Strauss, 1947), p. 183.

6. Trollope, Anthony, *The Macdermots of Ballycloran* (Philadelphia, n.d.), p. 21.

7. Sadleir, *Trollope,* p. 183.

8. Henry James, "Occasional Paris," in *The Art of Travel: Scenes and Journeys in America, England, France and Italy from the Travel Writings* of Henry James, ed. Morton Dauwen Zabel (New York: Doubleday, 1958), p. 213.

9. *Ibid.,* p. 213. James considered this latter trait the one advantage of being a cosmopolite.

10. James, Henry, *Partial Portraits* (London: Macmillan, 1888), pp. 121-22.

11. Unsigned review of *North America, Harper's New Monthly Magazine,* XXV (July 1862), 263.

12. See *North America,* p. 71: "I prefer a street that is forced to twist itself about. I enjoy the narrowness of Temple Bar and the misshapen curvature of Pickett Street. The disreputable dinginess of Holywell Street is dear to me, and I love to thread my way up by the Olympic into Covent Garden. Fifth Avenue in New York is as grand as paint and glass can make it; but I would not live in a palace in Fifth Avenue if the corporation of the city would pay my baker's and butcher's bills." For Trollope's views on the American dislike of walking, see *North America,* pp. 101-02.

13. See *North America,* p. 178, for this diatribe against central heating; for the qualification, *North America,* p. 142.

14. Stebbins, Lucy Poate, and Richard Poate Stebbins, *The Trollopes: The Chronicle of a Writing Family* (New York: Columbia University Press, 1945), p. 321.

15. Trollope, Anthony, *The Tireless Traveller: Twenty Letters to the Liverpool Mercury,* ed. Bradford Allen Booth (Berkeley: University of California Press, 1941), introduction, pp. 2-3.

16. *Tireless Traveller,* Letter XX, p. 220.

17. *West Indies,* [*The West Indies and the Spanish Main*], chapter XII.

18. *North America,* p. 200.

19. *Travelling Sketches,* p. 108.

20. *Travelling Sketches,* pp. 99-100.

21. *North America,* pp. 119-20. See also *North America,* p. 166: "I found that these cars were universally mentioned with great horror and disgust by Americans of the upper class. They always declared that they would not travel in them on any account. Noise and dirt were the two objections. They are very noisy, but to us belonged the happy power of sleeping down noise. I invariably slept all through the night, and knew nothing about the noise. They are also very dirty,—extremely dirty,—dirty so as to cause much annoyance. But then they are not quite so dirty as the day cars. If dirt is to be a bar against travelling in America, men and women must stay at home. For myself I don't care much for dirt, having a strong reliance on soap and water and scrubbing brushes. No one regards poisons who carries antidotes in which he has perfect faith."

22. *Australia and New Zealand* I, 25.

23. Quoted in Anthony Trollope, *An Autobiography,* p. 125. The remark is Hawthorne's criticism of Trollope's novels.

24. *North America,* p. 4.

25. *North America,* p. 4.

26. *West Indies,* p. 366.

27. Walter Dexter, ed., *The Letters of Charles Dickens,* 3 vols., Nonesuch Edition (Bloomsbury, 1938), I, 418, Dickens to Daniel Maclise, March 22, 1842: "As to scenery, we really have seen very little as yet. It is the same thing over and over again. The railroads go through the low grounds and swamps, and it is all one eternal forest, with fallen trees mouldering away in stagnant water and decayed vegetable matter and heaps of timber in every aspect of decay and utter ruin. I dress up imaginary tribes of Indians, as we rattle

on, and scatter them among the trees as they used to be, sleeping in their blankets, cleaning their arms, nursing brown children, and so forth."

Sally Brown (essay date autumn 1982)

SOURCE: Brown, Sally. "'This So-Called Autobiography': Anthony Trollope, 1812-1882." *British Library Journal* 8, no. 2 (autumn 1982): 168-73.

[*In the following essay, Brown alleges that the largely negative response to Trollope's autobiography was groundless. Brown asserts that the work provides a window into Trollope's authentic nature.*]

'There is perhaps no career of life so charming as that of a successful man of letters', Trollope declares in a happy moment, adding that 'it is in the consideration which he enjoys that the successful author finds his richest reward'. A good deal of the interest and fascination of his *Autobiography* (now Add. MS. 42856) lies in its frank charting, by turns mournful, angry, and wryly amused, of the long and often painful progress towards this longed-for state. That the 'idle, desolate hanger-on', the 'hobbledehoy of nineteen' he once was has become the man of property and substance, the best-selling author and respected Post Office official he now is, seems to be Trollope's chief source of satisfaction and delight, although the joy is occasionally tinged with a superstitious dread: 'There is unhappiness so great that the very fear of it is an alloy to happiness'.

The first thirty-three pages of the work (it opens in a hand which is for Trollope peculiarly neat) were written aboard the steamship *Bothnia* in October 1875,[1] on the return voyage from a visit to his son Frederic, a brave but unsuccessful sheep-farmer in Australia. Early in 1876, Trollope took it up again, and finished it on 30 April, within a week of his sixty-first birthday. The 'self-imposed laws' by which he bound himself, even in old age, then permitted him one day of rest before beginning a new three-volume novel, *The Duke's Children,* on 2 May. The manuscript was entrusted to his son Henry, with a letter requesting that it should 'be published after my death, and be edited by you'. In 1883 the first edition duly appeared, in two volumes, with 'some few passages', which in the manuscript are heavily crossed through,[2] 'suppressed' by Henry, who sets forth in his rather stiff preface his wish to adhere as closely as possible to his father's instructions.

Although well-received in some quarters—one reviewer and friend, W. Lucas Collins, nevertheless mildly regretted that Trollope had not 'told us something more about himself'—[3] the *Autobiography* contributed to the dramatic collapse after its author's death of a reputation which was already in decline. The Aesthetic Movement despised him for his commercialism and down-to-earth complacency; for how could any true work of art be first drawn up as a diary or plan and then produced at the rate of two hundred and fifty words every quarter of an hour, whether at a desk or in a crowded railway-carriage? Trollope is in fact extremely forthcoming, and unsentimental, about such matters. After the early period of 'suffering, disgrace and inward remorse', the turning-point came with his years as a surveyor's clerk with the Post Office in Ireland and the establishment of a literary routine, in the observance of which he hardly faltered, even when the early novels were spectacularly unsuccessful: 'There has ever been the record before me, and a week passed with an insufficient number of pages has been a blister to my eye, and a month so disgraced would have been a sorrow to my heart.' He takes pleasure in detailing the sheer extent of his work (which amounted altogether to forty-seven novels and sixteen other works, as well as contributions to 'periodicals without number') and the amounts of money, great and small, which he earned by it (at the time of writing the ***Autobiography*** these earnings had reached the princely figure of £68,959. 17*s*. 5*d*.). 'It is a mistake', he claims, 'to suppose that a man is a better man because he despises money'. On the other hand, it is with just as much forceful pride that he congratulates himself that his long years in the Post Office have helped to make it possible that 'the public in little villages should be enabled to buy postage stamps; that they should have their letters delivered free and at an early hour; that pillar letter-boxes should be put up for them (of which accommodation in the streets and ways of England I was the originator . . .)'.

The ***Autobiography*** is at its most vivid and moving in its descriptions, or evocations, of Trollope's unhappy childhood and adolescence. These came as something of a surprise to his contemporaries, for the novels (unlike those of Dickens) had hardly prepared them for such revelations. The sad, grubby little 'charity boy' at Harrow, constantly beaten and derided, excluded from the friendships and pursuits which other pupils took for granted, and secretly craving them 'with an exceeding longing', never quite fades from the memory, or from Trollope's own consciousness. He confesses that 'something of the disgrace of my schooldays has clung to me all through life'; and a cheerful picture of convivial afternoons at the Garrick Club is clouded by the reflection that 'I have ever had a wish to be liked by those around me a wish that during the first half of my life was never gratified'. In a passage which develops into an *apologia* for his misspent years as a young clerk in the Post Office, years dogged by debt and made heavy by idleness, he explains that during his boyhood he 'had seen gay things, but never enjoyed them'.

If Trollope's father, the failed barrister whose life was 'one long tragedy' and who retreated into a twilight world of 'monks and nuns' (he laboured, Casaubon-like, over an *Encyclopaedia Ecclesiastica,* three volumes of which had been published at his death), served as a warning to his son of the misery which follows a failure of purpose, his strong-willed mother should, on the face of things, have been an inspiration to him. When the family fortunes were at their lowest ebb, she set off for America, returned home having written a book which proceeded to sell in great numbers,[4] and so embarked at the age of fifty on a literary career which lasted well over twenty years, produced one hundred and fourteen volumes, and did not fail throughout the terrible time when she was nursing a dying husband, daughter and son. From her Trollope must have inherited his extraordinary energy (they shared the habit of rising to write at dawn); and yet his praise of her here is slightly muted, marked occasionally by a note of resentment, although he states with pride that the Trollopes had the distinction of writing 'more books than were probably ever before produced by a single family'.

About his own creative instincts and processes Trollope is very revealing, if at times a little defensive. He writes of his time as a Post Office clerk that, although barely educated, poor at spelling, and with 'wretched' handwriting (a truth borne out by some of the later sections of the ***Autobiography***), 'If I had a thing to say, I could so say it in written words that the reader should know what I meant.' Later on, he expresses his pleasure at Nathaniel Hawthorne's praise of his work as 'just as real as if some giant had hewn a great lump out of the earth and put it under a glass case, with all its inhabitants going about their daily business . . .', stating that he has no wish that his readers should 'feel themselves to be carried away among gods or demons', rather that they should be led to recognize simple moral truths 'that things meanly done are ugly and odious', and so on. All this harks back to his descriptions of the 'castle-building' of his youth, when the outwardly clumsy and graceless child would take refuge in an imaginary world in which he, the hero of all stories, 'strove to be kind of heart, and open of hand, and noble in thought . . .' This 'dangerous' but fruitful habit persisted, the only difference being that Trollope himself ceased to feature in the stories, although they drew very frequently on his own experiences. 'Reality' is his touchstone; of ***The Last Chronicle of Barset*** he declares, 'The archdeacon at his rectory is very real. There is a true savour of English country life all through the book . . .', and occasionally he himself seems to suspend disbelief: in ***The Three Clerks***, 'The passage in which Kate Woodward, thinking that she will die, tries to take leave of the lad she loves, still brings tears to my eyes when I read it. I had not the heart to kill her . . . And I do not doubt, but that they are living happily together to this day'. He was, incidentally, stung into 'killing off' one of his favourite characters, Mrs. Proudie, by the harsh remarks of two clergymen overheard at the Athenacum.

'The further it recedes in time', Charles Morgan wrote in the introduction to his edition of the **Autobiography,**[5] 'the more remarkable it seems to become'. It has the power to make us reimagine our own experience in its light. Beneath Trollope's public façade—the fox-hunting, whist-playing, crusty but 'clubbable' Victorian we catch glimpses of a private, vulnerable, and sometimes melancholy figure. The work is a strange mixture of anecdote (occasionally, as in the description of the visits to the clerks' office at St. Martin's-le-Grand of a moneylender who 'had a habit of twisting his chin as he uttered his caution', almost Dickensian in flavour), tub-thumping digression, and self-conscious 'set-piece'. At the very end an elegiac note creeps in: 'Now I stretch out my hand, and from the further shore I bid adieu . . .' Elsewhere, in a letter to a friend, Trollope confides a fear that 'the disembodied and beatified spirits' in heaven 'will not want novels'.[6] He could hardly have guessed that a hundred years after his death, his **Autobiography** would, for many readers, rank still higher than those fictional works in which he strove so hard to give 'a picture of common life enlivened by humour and sweetened by pathos'.

Notes

Th[e] phrase ["This So-Called Autobiography"] is Trollope's own. It occurs towards the end of the *Autobiography,* on fol. 213[v]. All other quotations are also from the *Autobiography,* unless it is stated otherwise.

1. This information, which comes from one of Trollope's working diaries, now at Princeton University, was kindly supplied by Mr. N. John Hall, of the City University of New York.

2. The passages contain a discussion of a 'literary gutter-scraper's' malicious publication of Trollope's indiscreet repetition of a dinner-table remark by Thackeray; a criticism of a passage by Carlyle as being 'silly and arrogant'; and a complaint against Messrs. Longman, the publishers, whom Trollope feels dealt unfairly with him over the copyright of *The Last Chronicle of Barset.*

3. See *Blackwood's Magazine,* cxxxiv (November 1883), pp. 577-96.

4. Frances Trollope, *The Domestic Manners of the Americans* (London, 1832).

5. London, 1946.

6. Quoted in A. O. J. Cockshut, *Anthony Trollope, A Critical Study* (London, 1955), p. 23.

Jane Nardin (essay date autumn 1990)

SOURCE: Nardin, Jane. "The Social Critic in Anthony Trollope's Novels." *SEL: Studies in English Literature, 1500-1900* 30, no. 4 (autumn 1990): 679-96.

[*In the following essay, Nardin contends that a general criticism of Trollope—that he was never a great political or social critic—actually names one of Trollope's main strengths: Trollope's novels, rather than serving up cures for society's problems, offer an approach to the issues through realism and observation.*]

Though Anthony Trollope is often acknowledged to be a shrewd observer of practical politics, he is rarely described as a profound political thinker. In their discussions of the political issues raised by Victorian literature, several critics have argued that Trollope's distrust of abstract thought and fear of rapid change prevented him from analyzing England's social problems with the rigor the situation demanded. "The treatment of major social questions in Trollope's novels . . . though impressive at a documentary level, is finally uninteresting," argues one such critic. "[Trollope] lacks the imaginative courage to challenge on any level, formal, intellectual, or moral, his readers' conventional habits of mind."[1] In a major study of British literature and politics from 1832 to 1867, Patrick Brantlinger dismisses Trollope's political views as "pious cant" because Trollope refuses to articulate a program to solve England's social problems.[2] Trollope, Brantlinger claims, writes "political novels that contain very few political ideas. What takes their place is what always takes the place of the ideal and the theoretical in realism: the unanalyzed flow of sensation and event."[3] The richly detailed, highly realistic social world of Trollope's fiction conceals its own intellectual emptiness so well that "we are hardly aware of what is missing from his novels while we are reading them."[4]

Trollope's distrust of abstractions does indeed make him reluctant to offer a sweeping political agenda for England in his political novels. But the critics who have noted this feature of Trollope's writing have not—as they conceive—located the weakness of his political thought. Rather they have identified its greatest strength. Trollope's novels do not attempt—as Brantlinger and others think they should—to offer solutions to social problems. Instead, they examine the way such problems should be approached; they consider what social criticism ought to be. Further, because Trollope is hostile to abstract thought, it is appropriate that his consideration of the social critic's proper role should be imbedded in the dense texture of daily life that his novels convey so well. His realism is not a deceptive tactic by which means he can sidestep the need to offer a radical critique of English society; it is the well-chosen method through which he demonstrates the limited relevance of abstractions to the enterprise of social criticism rightly conceived. Trollope's analysis of social criticism itself has little precedent in the political thought of his contemporaries. We must turn to the work of two major political theorists of the twentieth century, Michael Oakeshott and Michael Walzer, for theoretical formulations adequate to reveal its complexities.

"Where do we have to stand to be social critics?" asks Michael Walzer in *Interpretation and Social Criticism.*[5] Is the ideal social critic an outsider, who has wrenched himself loose "emotionally or intellectually" from his own society, so that he can evaluate its parochial traditions according to external standards which reason has discovered (p. 37)? Or is he an insider disturbed by the hypocrisy or confusion of his fellow citizens, who demands "angrily and insistently" that they live up to the internal standards of their own moral tradition (p. 39)? Should the social critic appeal to "universal principles" (p. 38) or merely to "localized principles" (p. 39)? In answering these questions, Walzer makes a persuasive argument for the connected social critic. But the substance of Walzer's argument is not new. In a group of essays written during the late 1940s and 1950s and later collected under the title *Rationalism and Politics,* Michael Oakeshott anticipates Walzer's attack upon detached social criticism.[6] In discussing the social critics who appear in four of Trollope's novels, I shall draw upon Oakeshott's and Walzer's analyses of the critic's relationship to his society in order to illuminate what remains implicit in Trollope's fictional treatments and to demonstrate how original a political thinker the novelist was.[7]

Oakeshott argues that two fundamentally opposed approaches to understanding society and politics—he labels them "Rationalism" and "Conservatism"—give rise to the competing paradigms of detached and connected social criticism. His theory thus offers an explanation and a context for the two models of social criticism that Walzer analyzes without considering their intellectual origins—and that Trollope's novels articulate by implication through their characterizations of self-appointed social critics.

The proponent of Rationalism, as Oakeshott uses the term, believes in the sovereign power of "thought free from obligation to any authority save the authority of 'reason'" (p. 1). But reason can only function properly after "all prejudices and preconceptions [that might bias its workings] are removed" from the mind (p. 12). The rationalist approach to education springs from this conception of knowledge. Because he believes the mind to be "endowed with the capacity of knowing in advance of activity," the Rationalist thinks that it is possible to devise ideal rules for the pursuit of any activity by reflecting upon its nature (p. 93). Training the reason aids this process, but practical experience only evokes resis-

tance to improvements. Thus the Rationalist believes you can teach an activity best by inculcating rules for its performance; performing it is secondary and should come later.

Believing that he possesses a sound method of mastering the activities that politics involves, the Rationalist who turns his attention to social criticism is likely to find the "destruction and creation" of institutions more appealing than their "acceptance or reform" (p. 4). He is confident that his reason can invent a new institution to do any job. But to create new institutions, the rationalist critic must subject his society to the scrutiny of an outsider. Involvement would bias his results.

It is not surprising, therefore, that rationalist politics should be "the politics of the politically inexperienced" (p. 23). Newcomers to power are naturally attracted by a philosophy that devalues the links to tradition and the practical knowledge of political processes they lack. "The outstanding characteristic of European politics in the last four centuries is that they have suffered the incursion of at least three types of political inexperience— that of the new ruler, the new ruling class, and of the new political society," Oakeshott argues (p. 23). These recent arrivals embraced the congenial political style of rationalism.

Unlike the Rationalist, the Conservative is temperamentally inclined to prefer "the tried to the untried" (p. 169), and he justifies his preferences according to a theory of knowledge, education, and political action that opposes the one on which Rationalism is based. He rejects the proposition that the mind is "an apparatus for thinking" which works best when not encumbered with traditional beliefs. The mind is merely a mass of thoughts which come to it through experience. Remove these thoughts and you have, not "pure intelligence" as the Rationalist argues, but rather "nothing at all" (p. 90).

It follows from this that the rationalist project of subjecting tradition to the scrutiny of unbiased reason is a chimera. Every mind is the product of particular experiences; every judgment is the judgment of a particular mind. We can judge a tradition only by the standards implicit within it—or by those of some other tradition. Believing that every activity has its own internal standards and logic, the Conservative argues that to participate in an activity is the best way of gaining a feel for its logic and thus of learning to perform it well. The Conservative values practical experience that cannot be reduced to a set of rules more than he values technical training.

The Conservative is, of course, likely to come from the ranks of the politically experienced—to be an insider, rather than an outsider. He learns about politics through his own participation in political action. It is therefore congenial to him (as well as consistent with his educational theory) to think of political expertise as something picked up by osmosis. And because he debunks the idea of pure reason and the faith in innovation associated with it, the Conservative social critic is committed to caution.

In considering reform, he will prefer innovations intended to remedy specific defects to those which spring from "a notion of a generally improved condition of human circumstances" (p. 172). He believes proposals for change must be judged in "relation to the idiom of activity to which they belong" (p. 102). An institution may be (or have grown to be) so far out of line with the traditions of its society as to demand reform. Or the traditions themselves may reveal a troubling incoherence in need of attention. Or major social changes may require adjustments of the society's institutional inheritance.[8] But for the conservative critic, any proposal for political change should be "related to an already existing tradition of how to attend to our arrangements" (p. 123). Reform aims at "the amendment of existing arrangements by exploring and pursuing what is intimated in them" (p. 124). To look at our tradition from the standpoint of pure reason is impossible; to see it through the eyes of another people can do little more than "reveal significant passages . . . which might otherwise remain hidden" (p. 132). No alien tradition can provide a blueprint for altering our own.

Like Oakeshott, Walzer argues that it is the business of social criticism to interpret a tradition, rather than to discover or invent moral principles external to it, whereby it can be judged. The two philosophers also agree that the rationalist (or, in Walzer's terms, detached) approach to social criticism has been dominant for some time, while the conservative approach has steadily lost ground.

Even in conservative Britain the monitory example of the French Revolution did no permanent harm to the growing prestige of Rationalism. Though many thinkers feared that rationalist reform might go too far, it nonetheless became the central feature of nineteenth-century English politics. During the Victorian era, Bentham's disciples were intent upon reconstituting every aspect of society: its morals, its educational system, and its laws. Pursuing the "rational" goals of increased efficiency and uniformity, reformers turned their attention to the church, the civil service, the army, the navy, the electoral system.

Many English thinkers of the late eighteenth and nineteenth centuries resisted sweeping rationalist projects of reform by maintaining that existing institutions could be defended in rational terms. Edmund Burke, for example, often suggests that because social customs are

the product of mankind's collective wisdom, reason supports the established order. In his essay on Coleridge, John Stuart Mill argues that progressives "miss the truth which is [embodied] in the traditional opinions" of men, while conservatives see this truth, but overlook the truth that is "at variance with [tradition]."[9] Mill thought that the conservative position, like the progressive position, was defensible only insofar as reason could demonstrate its truth—and he defended Coleridge's conservatism on the grounds that it passed the test of reason, at least in part. Trollope, however, took issue with Burke, Mill, and many others by refusing to argue that reason could justify traditional arrangements. He preferred to proceed by questioning the notion of reason itself, and it is in his choice of this line of defense against the rationalist reformer that his originality lies.

As the years passed, Trollope used his novels to test the claims of social critics to speak for pure reason. Fictionalizing one's own political theory (as Trollope undoubtedly does) may seem a dubious project, but realistic fiction—with its density of social detail—offers a highly suitable mode for stating the case in favor of conservative or connected social criticism. The conservative social critic is suspicious of abstractions, thinks a society can best be understood by its own members, and defines reform as the process of pursuing the subtle intimations of a tradition. Realistic fiction thus has a more natural connection with conservative social criticism than philosophy does. Philosophy strives to abstract general principles from particulars which have no special value in themselves, while fiction looks intently at particular social situations that are instinct with intimations of general significance. But this significance tends to emerge by implication, for fiction never allows its readers to slight the value of felt experience and stubbornly resists reduction to a set of abstractions.

In *Politics and the Novel*, Irving Howe argues that it is difficult for any political novel to "absorb into its stream of movement the hard and perhaps insoluble pellets of modern ideology," which it seeks to explicate, refute, or justify. Howe is certainly correct that abstract, rationalist ideologies will resist merging with "the novel's stream of sensuous impression . . . its [sense of] immediacy and closeness."[10] But just the opposite happens when a rich novel like ***The American Senator*** uses fictional techniques to develop a conservative understanding of social criticism. In this novel, form and content merge effortlessly into a unified whole, for the ideology it defends is an ideology of immanence.

Before turning to the issue of social criticism in Trollope's fiction, however, I want to look at the view of society that emerges from his autobiography. Here Trollope describes himself as "an advanced, but still a Conservative-Liberal" (p. 266).[11] He sympathizes with the Radicals' dream of a society where all men would have an equal opportunity to pursue happiness. The "terrible inequalities" (p. 266) of Victorian England cannot be observed, Trollope writes, "without some feeling of injustice" (p. 267), because they offend traditional English notions of fairness. These inequalities evoke a "consciousness of wrong" (p. 267) that demands to be remedied. But at the same time Trollope claims to be quite as averse as any Tory to a "sudden disruption of society in quest of some Utopian blessedness" (p. 268). Though the status quo may be painful to contemplate, it is nonetheless impossible to "set all things right by a proclaimed equality" (p. 267). Institutions that offend against England's moral tradition must be reformed—but they should be reformed slowly and carefully.

A look at his response to civil service reform—a highly rationalist scheme to which both Oakeshott and Walzer pay careful attention[12]—will show how deeply skeptical Trollope is of rationalist assumptions about knowledge, education, and society. The project to introduce competitive examinations into the civil service displays the Rationalist's characteristic hostility to the kind of education that (in Oakeshott's words) initiates children into "the moral and intellectual habits and achievements of [their] society" and emphasizes "a sharing of concrete knowledge" gained by pursuing an activity (p. 32). It also displays the "respect for 'brains,' [and the] great belief in training them" (p. 32), which distinguish the rationalist approach to education. Competitive examinations were seen as a way of identifying the "best" candidate for a position. Their use was justified on the grounds that each job requires specific skills and abilities. Once these skills have been identified, they can and should be taught *before* their possessor gains any practical experience of the job for which they are intended to prepare him. Their acquisition can be measured by an examination—and increased efficiency will be the result.

Before the introduction of competitive examination, civil service appointments were usually given to young men with the right connections (sometimes after a supremely perfunctory investigation of their literacy—a process Trollope describes comically in his 1858 novel, **The Three Clerks**). Promotions were usually awarded on the basis of seniority. The old system was as clearly founded upon conservative notions of education as the examination system is upon rationalist notions. It assumed that young men with minimal skills would learn their jobs by doing them.

Trollope emphatically endorsed the conservative approach to allocating positions in the civil service. Taking up the issue in his autobiography, he attacks competitive examination on uncompromisingly conservative grounds:

> The rule of the present day is that every place shall be open to public competition, and that it shall be given to the best among the comers. I object to this that at present there exists no known method of learning who is best, and that the method employed has no tendency to elicit the best. That method pretends only to decide who among a certain number of lads will best answer a string of questions, for the answering of which they are prepared by tutors. . . . The lad is no better fitted after [such preparation] than he was before for the future work of his life.

> (p. 34)

Trollope here questions two basic assumptions of rationalism: the power of "reason" to solve a complex social problem and the efficacy of technical education.

After asking who should be given posts in the civil service if they are not to be awarded by examination, Trollope offers an ultra-conservative answer: these posts should go to "gentlemen." He knows that his contemporaries will find this answer offensive, and he claims that in offering it he is daring to say "what no one now does dare to say in print" (p. 36). Civil service posts, Trollope acknowledges, should not be filled by youths who need basic instruction in "geography, arithmetic, or French" (p. 35), and with these subjects most gentlemen are conversant. But this is only a subsidiary reason for making gentility the criterion of choice.

The true reason is that positions of trust are "employments requiring a gentle culture" (p. 36) in morals, manners, and the difficult task of communicating with others—a culture which is best absorbed in the course of a long upbringing among those who possess and exemplify it. Neither this culture itself, nor the nature of the "gentleman" who has assimilated it, can be analyzed into its component elements and satisfactorily defined. Anyone who tried to define the term "gentleman" adequately would fail, Trollope admits, but for all that "he would know what he meant and so very probably would they who [had] defied him" to define it (p. 36)—for experience is a perfectly satisfactory way to learn its meaning. Affirmation of the view that one learns best by participating in a tradition could not be more explicit or complete.

And Trollope's remarks about civil service reform reveal a conservative view of English society, as well as a conservative approach to education. England is unified by the subtle tradition of manners and morals that its ruling class, the gentry, shares. The proponents of civil service reform, Trollope implies, are mistaken in their assumption that because the moral standards distinguishing the gentleman cannot be reduced to abstractions, they are valueless, perhaps even imaginary. If these standards could be satisfactorily reduced to a set of rules, they would be less rich and valuable than they are. Their value resides in their being so deeply, so unconsciously, ingrained that an entire class can find in them the basis for assured communication and common action.

Trollope's 1855 novel, **The Warden,** begins with the divided impulse of exposing both a social evil—"the possession by the Church of certain funds and endowments which had been . . . allowed to become incomes for idle church dignitaries" (**Autobiography,** p. 86)—and the arrogance of the reformers who presume to correct that evil. According to the narrator, the young doctor John Bold is "a strong reformer. His passion is the reform of all abuses; state abuses, church abuses, corporation abuses. . . . It would be well if . . . he could be brought to believe that . . . changes may possibly be dangerous; but no; Bold . . . hurls his anathemas against time-honoured practices with the violence of a French Jacobin" (pp. 15-16).[13] Bold has the Rationalist's arrogance: his confidence in his own ability to identify and cure any evil is unbounded. The pure type of rationalist social critic must necessarily be self-appointed, detached from the abuses he proposes to remedy by the application of his unbiased reason. Bold too is personally unconcerned in the evils he attacks. Nothing in his position makes the reform of Hiram's Hospital his natural concern. On the contrary, his friendship with its warden, Mr. Harding, suggests some powerful moral reasons for leaving this particular abuse alone.

But though Bold has points of contact with the rationalist social critic, Trollope does not tackle the issue of rationalist social criticism head-on in **The Warden.** Bold is a rationalist in his motives and his social philosophy, but not in his methods of pursuing reform. The way Bold prosecutes his projects shows him to be much closer to the conservative social critic who reforms a tradition by investigating the intimations contained within it, than he is to the Rationalist who criticizes a tradition according to external standards. When Bold gains "a victory over a certain old turnpike woman in the neighborhood, of whose charges another old woman had complained" (p. 23), he does so by demonstrating that "the act of Parliament relating to the trust" (p. 23) has been disobeyed. When he decides to reform Hiram's Hospital, Bold gets "a copy of John Hiram's will" and makes himself "perfectly master" of its wording (p. 24), before proceeding to argue that too large a proportion of the income from the trust is going to the warden. His objection, he claims, is solely that "John Hiram's will is not carried out to the letter" (p. 33). By making his case in these terms, he ensures that the hospital debate will take form around a series of retrospective queries: What did John Hiram intend to be the purpose of the trust? How should his intentions be carried out in an altered society?

The Warden implies that these questions do need to be asked. And the discussion arising from Bold's rash and arrogant intervention shows us the process of conservative social reform in action. This investigation into a tradition, into the links between past and present, proves fruitful, despite the moral and intellectual inadequacies that hamper some of the investigators. The hospital is reconstituted, in **Barchester Towers,** according to principles that are more consonant both with Hiram's intentions and with time-honored views concerning the nature of charitable trusts than had been the arrangement which Bold disturbed.

It is Bold's arrogance—not his requirement that particular institutional arrangements conform to the moral and legal traditions within which they have their being—that the novel reprobates. Archdeacon Grantly, arrogant in his *refusal* to question established practices, is clearly just as blameable as Bold. Neither man can see that pursuing the intimations of a rich moral and legal tradition is not a simple matter, nor one in which certainty can ever be achieved. The task of keeping our institutions in line with our traditions gives rise to a debate that must necessarily be inconclusive.[14]

Mr. Arabin, who makes his first appearance in **Barchester Towers,** is a clergyman who nearly "went over" to Rome in a futile search for spiritual certainty. Having retreated at the eleventh hour, he appropriately becomes the spokesman for the moderate skepticism about interpreting, applying, and reforming tradition that the first two Barsetshire novels endorse. When Eleanor Bold complains to Arabin that disputes about interpreting *its* tradition "bring scandal on the church" (p. 151)[15], Arabin admits that perhaps they do. "But what would you have in place of it?," he asks; "There is no infallible head for a church on earth" (p. 151). Arabin tells Eleanor that the circumstances of our lives make debate inevitable: where doctrine and morality are at issue "easy paths have not been thought good for us" (p. 151). Arabin would doubtless be pleased with Walzer's affirmation that a moral tradition "is something we have to argue about. The argument implies common possession, but common possession does not imply agreement. There is a tradition, a body of moral knowledge, and there is this group of sages, arguing. . . . No discovery or invention can end the argument" (p. 32). Because of its emphasis on interpretation, conservative social criticism allows for the necessity of disagreement, for the validity of multiple viewpoints, and thus for the virtue of tolerance that Mr. Harding exemplifies. **The Warden** and **Barchester Towers** make a case for social criticism, but only in the conservative sense of the term.

Several of Trollope's later novels, however, do feature social critics who are genuinely positioned outside the tradition they propose to reform.[16] But the position they occupy is a matter of debate: they claim to speak for reason, but Trollope persistently questions this claim. Unlike John Bold, who plays a comparatively minor role in *The Warden,* two of the social critics in Trollope's later fiction are major characters: Senator Gotobed of *The American Senator* (1877) and President John Neverbend of *The Fixed Period* (1882). It is no accident that both men should be colonials, political newcomers in Oakeshott's terms. Trollope digs much deeper into the psyches of these two self-styled rationalist reformers than he did into Bold's; as a result he grows more sympathetic with their motives. But because Gotobed and Neverbend are far closer than Bold to the pure type of rationalist reformer whom Trollope fears, his critique of their methods and assumptions is far more devastating. Unlike Bold, they do no good, and Neverbend nearly manages to do considerable harm.

Senator Gotobed claims—with an egotism that would be monstrous if it were not so charmingly naive—to speak for pure reason. He visits England in order to subject its mores to the scrutiny of this powerful instrument. His lecture on British customs and institutions is uncompromisingly titled "The Irrationality of Englishmen" (p. 536).[17] Gotobed believes in universal standards of judgment, as his assertion that "justice is the same everywhere" (p. 128) suggests, and he is certain that the American political system has been designed in accordance with the dictates of rationality. As Oakeshott notes, Americans have never been "given over-much to reflection upon the habits of behavior they had in fact inherited . . . they seemed to begin with nothing, and to owe to themselves all they had come to possess. A civilization of pioneers is, almost unavoidably, a civilization of . . . Rationalists" (p. 27). So it is not surprising to find the senator asserting confidently that "nowhere on the Earth's surface was justice more purely administered than in the great Western State of Mickewa" (p. 484) from whence he comes. He dismisses the sort of piecemeal reform dear to the conservative critic's heart as ineffectual "cobbling" (p. 357).

The American Senator attacks Gotobed's claim to be reason's spokesman, but it does not attack his motives as *The Warden* attacked Bold's. Arrogant and rude though the Senator sometimes is, his motives are so pure that he gradually gains general credit for "courage, benevolence, and a steadfast purpose" (p. 536). Like Oakeshott, Trollope understands that "the Rationalist can [sometimes] appear a not unsympathetic character. He wants so much to be right" (*Rationalism and Politics,* p. 30). The senator's failings are intellectual, rather than moral. Gotobed's central error is, of course, his failure to see that he is criticizing England not (as he thinks) from the standpoint of reason, but merely from that of America's somewhat different moral and social tradition.

Yet because the American and English traditions are closer than he realizes, Gotobed's criticisms of England are not invariably irrelevant. His criticisms of the church

patronage system illustrate Oakeshott's point that it can be somewhat revealing to look at our tradition through the eyes of another people.[18] The sale of livings, though still practiced in mid-Victorian England, was offensive to much in English moral tradition and was in the process of reform even as the Senator delivered his lecture. Here American practice could prove instructive, and "this part of the lecture was allowed to pass without strong marks of disapprobation" by his English audience (p. 547). But the Senator's criticism of the church is well taken only because its "fit" with English traditions themselves is so close.

Where American practices differ more radically from English ones, his audience dissents violently from ideas that seem to ignore the internal logic of their own tradition—which, indeed, the senator has not mastered as thoroughly as he thinks. When he attacks primogeniture on the rationalist ground that "it is natural" for all men to wish to divide their property among children "who are equal in [their] love," his hearers shout him down: "You know nothing about it." "Go back and learn" (p. 544).

Gotobed looks particularly silly when he denounces the "irrational" English amusement of fox hunting, while practicing the "rational" American amusement of devouring cigars and spitting out their remains. For the only "reasonable" function amusements perform is to amuse: we learn to enjoy a game by playing it as participants in a culture where it is played; we learn to enjoy cigars by smoking (or eating) them in congenial company. How can one people, then, ever appreciate another's amusements? Walzer's remark that an "outsider can become a social critic only if he manages to get himself inside, enters imaginatively into local practices" (p. 39) helps explain the Senator's comic inadequacy as a critic of English recreation.

That the Senator's standards of judgment are derived from American traditions themselves becomes clearer as something in the English air begins to erode his self-confidence. In spite of his contempt for English ways, Gotobed feels that he is "surrounded [in England] by people who claimed and made good their claims to superiority" (p. 351). Even a hostile visitor cannot live for months in an alien culture without beginning to absorb its values. The Senator never goes native, yet his English sojourn leaves him with a divided mind.

Towards the close of *The American Senator,* the narrator announces that the novel should really have been called *The Chronicle of a Winter at Dillsborough* (p. 557). These competing titles suggest the book's cleverly divided focus: the Senator's supposedly rational critique of English custom shares the novel's foreground with its highly detailed portrayal of an English community, a portrayal that is structured to refute him by implication. Dillsborough is not a place in which any reasonable person would choose to live; indeed, its very existence defies reason. "The town has no attractions, and never had any" (p. 3). Like custom, Dillsborough is there because it is there. Its prosperity is declining and there is every reason for its inhabitants to leave; yet many of them choose to stay. This stagnant community, the novel demonstrates, is also a community with rich and vital traditions.

The American Senator depicts the Dillsborough community from top to bottom, from Lord Rufford to the disreputable farmer Goarley. It is for this reason that James Kincaid calls the novel "an anatomy," or descriptive classification, of rural society.[19] Plot and character interest are very diffused. Nothing much happens in any of the several subplots, while most of the characters are uninteresting individuals who achieve significance only as members of the community upon whose corporate existence the novel relentlessly concentrates. Initially this community is under stress and seems about to fracture, but in the end, the threatened social world of Dillsborough heals itself with surprising ease. Its irrational traditions turn out to have a magical power (which the senator overlooked) to restore harmony.

The novel's conclusion celebrates this power and has a fairy-tale quality that is by no means accidental. The ambitious and dissatisfied farmer, Larry Twentyman, finds a satisfying social position through his involvement in that most irrational, traditional, and delightful of activities: fox hunting. Because so many Englishmen love it, this historic pursuit promotes unity, though its appeal could never be explained to foreigners.[20] The novel's "evil stepmother," Mrs. Masters, reveals a trace of allegiance to conventional morality when she unexpectedly decides to respect her stepdaughter Mary's refusal to marry without love. Even the greedy Arabella Trefoil manages to reject a bribe, thus meriting a last-minute rescue from social disaster. Though the Dillsborough community is neither rationally planned, nor internally consistent, it can survive because it possesses a powerful moral tradition and the affection of its citizens.

The American Senator also attacks the rationalist viewpoint in its handling of character. The novel's two love triangles debunk the notion that reason is (or ever could be) the basis for human behavior. Both Mary and Arabella are faced with the choice between settling for a satisfactory marriage or pursuing the seemingly unattainable man of their dreams. Both women (irrationally) decide to go for the long shot. Nor does any reasonable motive impel the Senator to lecture the English on their failings. Like Mary and Arabella he follows an impulse of the heart—"that intense desire to express himself which . . . sometimes [amounts] to fury with Americans" (pp. 537-38). If the plot structure of *The American Senator* demonstrates the power of tradition, its handling of characterization proves that reason is not man's strongest motive.

Although *The American Senator* celebrates the power of a vital community to heal itself, the novel by no means denies the need for reform. The bestial ignorance of the poor, the moral mediocrity of the aristocracy, the sale of livings to unsuitable clergymen, the corrupting education given to upper-class girls, and the hostility between classes depicted in this novel prove that England is not a Utopia, and give point to the Senator's criticisms—but not to the solutions he offers. Although this tradition stands in need of attention, it can only be reformed from inside.

But the imaginary twentieth-century colony of Britannula in *The Fixed Period* is an idyllic spot, and the social project that obsesses its well-meaning president, John Neverbend, springs solely from his desire to improve man's lot by bringing custom into conformity with the dictates of reason. Such projects, as we have seen, attract rationalist social critics and horrify Conservatives. Neverbend's plan, however, is likely to chill readers of either persuasion, for it is a project to kill every inhabitant who reaches the age of sixty-seven. Since the newly founded colony enacts this law when all its citizens are under forty, it is clearly not responding to an existing grievance. Rather its legislators are fired by Neverbend's conviction that reason has discovered a new truth, universal in its application: "Manifest advantages . . . would attend the adoption of the Fixed Period in all countries" (p. 8).

Neverbend's close affinities with Oakeshott's Rationalist can be seen in his views of education as well as in the kind of reform that attracts him. Like the Rationalist, he believes that no one who is steeped in a moral tradition really has the use of his reason. He deplores the arrival of "a crowd of educated Englishmen" at the very moment when Britannula is in a ferment over the first mercy killing mandated by the fixed period law—adding casually that "when I say educated, I mean prejudiced. They would be Englishmen with no ideas beyond those current in the last century and would be altogether deaf to the wisdom of the Fixed Period" (p. 90). "The philosophical truth" (p. 18) that euthanasia benefits mankind by freeing the young of an economic burden, while relieving the old from poverty and suffering, would be acknowledged immediately, Neverbend thinks, were it not for the hostility generated by residual commitment to an outmoded moral tradition. But Neverbend believes that with the proper training "feelings . . . would be taught at last to comply with reason" (p. 13).

Neverbend, then, comes closer than the American senator to the pure type of rationalist social critic who, without regard for any existing tradition, proposes that a new society be constructed on the basis of unprecedented discoveries about human nature and human needs. Neverbend constantly compares himself to Galileo and Columbus because he believes that his moral "discovery" parallels their discoveries in astronomy and geography. But what, exactly, has Neverbend discovered? The answer is nothing much. He is merely applying to the problem of old age the utilitarian theories of Bentham and the Mills. Using methods of calculation that are reminiscent of Bentham's felicific calculus in their simplicity, Neverbend decides that the social benefits of euthanasia outweigh the costs.

But though Neverbend did not invent utilitarian morality, as he appears to believe, he is correct that this approach represents a radical break with moral tradition. Utilitarians, Walzer argues, claim to have discovered a new and revolutionary truth "about human desire and aversion"; their radically original psychology leads to "radically unfamiliar outcomes" in the moral realm (p. 7). And certainly the practical conclusion to which Neverbend's utilitarianism leads is as shocking as anything Bentham suggested. But Walzer adds that when moral argument generates conclusions that are "not recognizable as features of ordinary life" (p. 7), we find such conclusions hard to accept, because our moral traditions have a strong hold upon us. This is what happened to Bentham's disciples. "Frightened by the strangeness of their own arguments," Walzer writes, "most utilitarian philosophers fiddle with the felicific calculus so that it yields results closer to what we all think" (p. 7).

It is Neverbend's peculiarity that he never does bend in this manner the strange conclusion he reached as a young man. But the other Britannulists follow the pattern Walzer describes. They may not be able to refute Neverbend's arguments, but as the first mercy killing approaches, they gradually draw back from his conclusion, realizing that euthanasia is abhorrent to the moral convictions they hold all the more deeply because they cannot fully articulate them. Faced with a stubborn opposition that clearly derives from his constituents' commitment to traditional moral notions, Neverbend has no choice but to defend his project in conventional moral terms, rather than in the "rational" consequentialist terms he favors. His attempt to jettison the tradition fails, proving Walzer's point that moral questions are necessarily "pursued within a tradition of moral discourse—indeed, they only arise within that tradition—and they are pursued by interpreting the terms of that discourse" (p. 23).

Neverbend thus finds himself defending the fixed period with standard concepts from the English moral and legal traditions. But he does not prove very skilled in the use of these concepts. Stung by the frequent remark that the fixed period mandates murder, Neverbend falls back on the legal tradition to refute his critics: "Murder, to be murder, must be opposed to the law" (p. 12). He is quick to point out that neither executions, nor battlefield killings, are murder, because they are "done by the law" (p. 12). But the traditions within which Neverbend is forced to argue are, in fact, more complex than he realizes. Neither English morality, nor English law, ever sanctions the killing of the innocent (this is the logic behind the rules of warfare protecting non-combatant immunity). The kinds of killing that can receive legal sanction are limited by this principle, and euthanasia is not one of them. It seems appropriate that the inarticulate, conventional soldier, Lieutenant Crosstrees, should be the one to point this out to the intelligent, but dissociated Neverbend: "The Parliament in England might order a three-months-old baby to be slain, but could not possibly get the deed done. . . . Not to save Great Britain from destruction" (p. 269).

Neverbend's attempt to find a standing place outside conventional morality fails; forced to justify his project from within the English moral tradition, he loses the argument. But his fanatical commitment to euthanasia as *his* contribution to progress remains. Neverbend's response to this dilemma demonstrates, to use Walzer's words, that "the problem with disconnected criticism, and thus with criticism that derives from newly discovered or invented moral standards, is that it presses its practitioners toward manipulation and compulsion" (p. 64). Facing resistance from those who adhere to the moral tradition they hope to replace, such critics are "driven to one or another version of an unattractive politics" (p. 64). Unable to revive the fading enthusiasm of euthanasia's first victim, Gabriel Crasweller, Neverbend attempts to shame his friend into submission by reminding him that he once publicly supported the measure. Though he knows that he is "in the position of a shepherd driving sheep into a pasture which was distasteful to them" (p. 188), Neverbend hopes that if he can carry out the first few killings by guile or force, his project may yet succeed.

But in the end Trollope's most rationalist social critic meets more total defeat than any of his predecessors. Britannula is reannexed by Great Britain and its new morality is reabsorbed by the English moral tradition. Yet there is something eerily prophetic in Neverbend's abortive project. In a large institution—overshadowed by a huge crematorium—a burdensome group of people, the elderly, are to be "deposited" until the state imposes upon them a "fixed period" via the opening of a vein in a bath of warm water. These innocent people will be killed in the interests of the common good, for in Brittanula utility takes precedence over rights. In *The Fixed Period,* tendencies that we can call totalitarian emerge from the rationalist approach to social criticism and social change.

Notes

1. William Myers, "George Eliot: Politics and Personality," in *Literature and Politics in the Nineteenth Century,* ed. John Lucas (London: Methuen, 1971), p. 106.

2. Patrick Brantlinger, *The Spirit of Reform: British Literature and Politics, 1832-1867* (Cambridge, MA: Harvard Univ. Press, 1977), p. 209.

3. Brantlinger, p. 213.

4. Ibid.

5. All citations to Michael Walzer's work refer to *Interpretation and Social Criticism* (Cambridge, MA: Harvard Univ. Press, 1987).

6. These essays by Michael Oakeshott were published in book form as *Rationalism in Politics and Other Essays* (London: Methuen, 1962). All citations to Oakeshott's work refer to this edition. I am not the first to notice a close affinity between Trollope and Oakeshott. In *The Gentleman in Trollope: Individuality and Moral Conduct* (Cambridge, MA: Harvard Univ. Press, 1982), Shirley Letwin draws upon Oakeshott's work to illuminate Trollope's view of the relationship between the individual and society.

7. The Palliser novels are more likely to be cited by those interested in the political novel than Trollope's other works. But the Palliser series is less germane to my purpose than the novels on which I plan to focus here, for all its characters are deeply involved in practical politics. Trollope's detached social critics appear elsewhere.

8. It follows from this that conservative social critics may argue for significant social change. Like Trollope, Walzer is a critic of this type.

9. John Stuart Mill, "Coleridge," in *Essays on Literature and Society,* ed. J. B. Schneewind (New York: Collier Books, 1965), p. 292.

10. Irving Howe, *Politics and the Novel* (New York: Horizon Press, 1957), p. 20.

11. All citations refer to Anthony Trollope, *An Autobiography* (London: Oxford Univ. Press, 1923).

12. Oakeshott, *Rationalism in Politics,* p. 88, and Michael Walzer, *Spheres of Justice: A Defense of Pluralism and Equality* (New York: Basic Books, 1983), pp. 129-64.

13. All citations refer to *The Warden* (Oxford: Oxford Univ. Press, 1952).

14. In *The Moral Trollope* (Athens: Ohio Univ. Press, 1971), Ruth apRoberts also notes that Trollope was disturbed by the inability of the English moral tradition to refute relativist attacks on its authority and to provide answers to specific moral dilemmas. She thinks he responded by developing a theory of "situation ethics" whereby the individual uses reason to evaluate each moral dilemma in its own terms—without regard to ethical tradition. Though I agree with apRoberts that Trollope recognized both the relativity and the indeterminacy of tradition, I see no evidence that he therefore decided to jettison traditional morality in favor of a morality of "reason." I think he concluded that even with all its warts, tradition is the only guide we have.

15. All citations refer to Anthony Trollope, *Barchester Towers* (New York: Macmillan, 1923).

16. One kind of social critic who appears regularly in Trollope's later fiction is the radical feminist. I have chosen not to discuss Trollope's feminists in this essay, simply for lack of space. Trollope's treatment of these characters in such novels as *He Knew He Was Right* and *Is He Popenjoy?* is consistent with his treatment of other rationalist critics: admitting that feminists are addressing serious problems, he nonetheless ridicules the simplistic solutions they offer.

17. All citations refer to Anthony Trollope, *The American Senator* (New York: Dover, 1979).

18. Walzer makes a similar point about what can be gained when a connected social critic pretends to look at his society through the eyes of a foreigner, as Montesquieu does, for example. *Interpretation and Social Criticism,* p. 39.

19. James R. Kincaid, *The Novels of Anthony Trollope* (Oxford: Clarendon Press, 1979), p. 235.

20. In *The Fixed Period,* Trollope uses cricket to perform a similar function. The wacky, twentieth-century version of the game that the characters in this novel play is more important to them than any of the serious political problems facing their colony. In both novels, games symbolize the cohesive powers of "irrational" traditions. All citations refer to *The Fixed Period* (Leipzig: Bernhard Tauchnitz, 1882).

Denise Kohn (essay date winter 1993)

SOURCE: Kohn, Denise. "'The Journey to Panama': One of Trollope's Best 'Tarts'—or, Why You Should Read 'The Journey to Panama' to Develop Your Taste for Trollope." *Studies in Short Fiction* 30, no. 1 (winter 1993): 15-22.

[*In the following essay, Kohn discusses the significance of Trollope's short stories, in particular "The Journey to Panama," which Kohn considers a feminist piece.*]

Today's literary appetites don't care much for Trollope's short stories. Although his place, for now, in the canon is firm, his reputation rests solely upon his novels. Trollope-hungry Victorians, however, enjoyed his short stories, which were published in popular periodicals such as *Cornhill,* edited by William Thackeray. In a letter to Trollope, Thackeray encouraged Trollope to write short stories, which he compared to baking tarts:

> Don't understand me to disparage our craft, especially *your* wares. I often say I am like the pastrycook, and don't care for tarts, but prefer bread and cheese; but the public love the tarts (luckily for us), and we must bake and sell them.

> (*Autobiography* 137)

Unluckily for us, though, many modern critics seem to think of Trollope's short stories as unnourishing tarts that do not deserve a place on the literary menu. The publication in 1983 of the five-volume **Anthony Trollope: The Complete Short Stories** did not create much interest in Trollope's short fiction.[1] Perhaps this is because Trollope's 47 novels offer critics plenty of bread and cheese to feast upon. Yet not all pastry is puff—especially among Trollope's wares.

"The Journey to Panama," the last (but not least) story in the **Complete Short Stories,** serves as an excellent example of substantial Trollope. I agree with Rebecca West and other critics that Trollope was a feminist (West [*The Court and the Castle*] 167; Barickman, MacDonald, and Stark [*Corrupt Relations*] 203). Critics such as Rajiva Wijesinha, author of *The Androgynous Trollope,* and Richard Barickman, Susan MacDonald, and Myra Stark, authors of *Corrupt Relations,* have shown that his novels express a deep sympathy for women and the constraints Victorian society imposed on them. These critics find his feminist themes most evident in his Palliser and other later novels, which were published from the mid-1860s through 1880s. Feminist scholars, like most Trollope scholars, miss an important opportunity to study the artist at work because they ignore his 42 short stories. As early as 1861, Trollope had openly addressed the problems women face in a patriarchal society in his short story, **"A Journey to Panama."** This story should play an important role in feminist discussion of Trollope.

The story was first published in *Victoria Regia,* a collection of poetry and prose edited by Adelaide A. Proctor and published by the feminist Emily Faithfull. The circumstances of the publication of this short story alone should be important in a feminist study of Trollope. Faithfull, who founded the Victoria Press, believed that printing offered new career opportunities for women (Sadleir, *A Bibliography* [*Anthony Trollope: A Bibliography*] 214). The press was staffed by female compositors, and *Victoria Regia*'s title page includes the social

statement, "Victoria Press (for the Employment of Women)" (Sadleir, *A Bibliography* 213). Trollope donated **"The Journey to Panama"** to Faithfull for the book (Sadleir, *A Bibliography* 214, *Letters* [*The Letters of Anthony Trollope*] 211), which is surprising considering the fine detail he pays to his literary earnings in his autobiography.

Trollope is better known for his harsh criticism of feminism than his support of it (Barickman, MacDonald, and Stark 195). Yet emphasis on his vituperative comments have led critics to conclude that there was a sort of Dr. Jekyll/Mr. Hyde split between Trollope the man and Trollope the artist. In their study of Trollope, Barickman, MacDonald, and Stark conclude that there are "two Trollopes—the seemingly hostile critic of the Victorian women's movement and the sympathetic Victorian sociological novelist capturing in fiction the tensions being felt by upper-class men and women of his day" (196). The publication of **"The Journey to Panama,"** however, shows that Trollope the man did, like Trollope the writer, publicly support feminist causes. He was not always consistent in his support of women's rights, but criticism that focuses solely on his objections and not his support does not reflect a true picture of Trollope.

Considering the feminist purposes of the Victoria Press and Trollope's support of Faithfull and her cause,[2] the feminism of **"The Journey to Panama"** is not so surprising. The story chronicles the desperation of Miss Emily Viner, an English woman who has sold herself "as a beast of burden" (Trollope, **"Journey"** [**"The Journey to Panama"**] 217) into marriage as her only chance at a respectable existence within the constraints of Victorian society. Viner travels to Panama to marry her fiancé, and en route shocks the British passengers by engaging in a "dangerous alliance" (**"Journey"** 210) with a widower during her final days of "self and liberty" (**"Journey"** 212). She also shocks the widower, Ralph Forrest, who believes she should live in a poorhouse rather than marry without love. When she arrives at Panama, Viner finds that her fiancé has died and left her a small sum of money. For Viner, money means independence. Instead of marrying the chivalrous Forrest or allowing him to protect her, she shakes his hand and returns alone to England.

The story quite openly deals with economic injustice, sexual double-standards, and the callousness of the patriarchy. Yet it seems to have created no sensation in Victorian England. **"The Journey to Panama"** was later reprinted in 1867 in the Trollope collection **Lotta Schmidt and Other Stories.** In the Sept. 21, 1867, edition of the *Saturday Review,* a critic said that Trollope should be commended for "facile painting" in the **Lotta Schmidt** collection. (qtd. in Lyons [*Anthony Trollope: An Annotated Bibliography*] 48). The same critic characterized the collection as "the pleasantest fancies of the thinnest material worked up with the smallest expenditure of labour possible—not strong meat, by any means, but clean and wholesome milk" (qtd. in Lyons 48). Although such comments may show that the modern view of Victorians as prudes is surely overly simplistic, I can't help but wonder if the reviewer could have possibly read **"The Journey to Panama."**

Trollope scholar Michael Sadleir did read—and praise—it. In *Anthony Trollope: A Commentary,* he stated that **"The Journey to Panama":**

> stands high among Trollope's short stories, being not only the most courageously "unfinished" of them all, but also with those included in the volume *Why Frau Frohmann Raised Her Prices,* the most vital to an understanding of his full-length work.
>
> (177)

Although Sadleir helped to resurrect Trollope's reputation in 1927 with the publication of *A Commentary,* his comments seem to have done little for the short story. Most twentieth-century critics seem to ignore it.[3] Those who don't make misleading[4] or rather vague comments about it.[5]

Betty Jane Slemp Breyer, editor of *The Complete Short Stories,* is one of the few critics to praise the story and note Sadleir's comments. In the introduction to the fifth volume, she states: "Nowhere else has Trollope studied more closely or with more sensitivity the interaction of men and women released from the constraints of conventional society" (xi). She concurs with Sadleir's praise but not his comment that the story is "unfinished." Unfortunately, she misses an opportunity to add to the criticism and provides no history on the story except to note when and where it was first published.

Although neither Breyer nor Sadleir provides much elaboration for their praise of **"The Journey to Panama,"** I believe their praise is well founded. Sadleir probably did not have feminism in mind when he said the story was important in the understanding of Trollope's novels; nevertheless, his comment is applicable to feminist criticism.

The narrator plays an important role in most of Trollope's novels, and the narrator is also important in understanding **"The Journey to Panama."** As in the novels, the narrator in the short story possesses a distinctive personality and offers friendly observations and advice to the reader. Francine Navakas does not mention **"The Journey"** in her review of *The Complete Short Stories,* but her comments about Trollope's narrator in other stories also apply to this one: The narrator is "male or at least 'manly'" and possesses a genial tone and "sound moral values" (177). Although the gender

of the narrator in **"The Journey"** is never stated outright, the narrator assumes a "manly," fatherly tone. Trollope uses this "manly" narrator to befriend the reader and establish a relationship of trust. Then as the tale unfolds, the narrator exposes the problems caused by the very patriarchy that the reader would believe the narrator represents.

In the first sentence of the story, the narrator establishes his authority: "There is perhaps no form of life, in which men and women of the present day frequently find themselves for a time existing, so unlike their customary conventional life, as that experienced on board the large Ocean Steamers" (199). The qualifier "perhaps" saves the assertion from pomposity and adds a friendly tone. The narrator believes he is wise, yet also admits that he realizes his opinions are not infallible.

For the next several paragraphs, the narrator shares his general observations about the life of travelers aboard ships and specific routes, verifying his position of authority. He even offers a paternal warning: "Though they may be full of sweet romance,—for people become very romantic among the discomforts of a sea voyage,—such romance is generally short lived and delusive, and occasionally is dangerous" (200).

The chatty narrator then introduces the reader to "my hero" (202), Ralph Forrest, the young widower who is traveling to California and Vancouver. Mr. Forrest is a novice to life aboard ocean steamers, but he quickly meets Mr. Morris, "an old traveller" who knew how "to become intimate with his allies at a very short notice" (202). At first, Mr. Morris bears an unusual similarity to the narrator: both are knowledgeable about all aspects of ocean travel. Mr. Morris, like the narrator, knows everyone on board, their backgrounds, and travel plans. Mr. Morris is an observer, not a participant, in the main action of the story. The narrator offers advice to the reader, and Mr. Morris offers advice to Ralph Forrest.

For example, in the first paragraph the narrator tells the reader that after a few days at sea, "the men begin to think that the women are not so ugly, vulgar and insipid" (199) and "remarkable alliances" are formed (200). When Mr. Forrest first sees Miss Viner he tells Mr. Morris that he thinks she is "ugly" (203). Mr. Morris replies, "She'll brighten up wonderfully before we're in the tropics" (203). A few days later Mr. Forrest denies that he ever thought she was ugly. And the wiser Mr. Morris adds, "By the time you reach Panama, she'll be all that is perfect in woman. I know how these things go" (206).

Miss Viner soon begins to spend more time with Mr. Forrest than with her aptly named chaperones, Mr. and Mrs. Grumpy. Emily Viner, not the narrator, sums up the theme of the story in her first conversation with Mr.

Forrest: "A man never suffers in being alone" (205). When the widowed Mr. Forrest disagrees, Miss Viner adds, "But there are worse things, Mr. Forrest, than being alone. It is often a woman's lot to wish that she were let alone" (205).

As the passengers get to know each other better, so do the narrator and the reader. Mr. Forrest changes from "my hero" to "our hero" (207). The narrator, a gentleman, always respectfully refers to Emily Viner as "Miss Viner." The reader does not even learn her first name until more than halfway through the story. The narrator is clearly British in tone, but if any doubts about his nationality (or gender) exist, they are erased when the narrator uses the phrase "we Englishmen" (211). Although "Englishmen" could be used as a gender-neutral term, earlier the narrator had used the gender-specific terms "Englishmen" and "Englishwomen" (200).

As the story progresses, differences between the gentlemanly narrator and the gentlemanly Mr. Morris begin to surface. Mr. Morris has encouraged Mr. Forrest in his relationship with Miss Viner. But Miss Viner's and Mr. Forrest's evident pleasure in their relationship begins to shock the other passengers on board; most know that she is traveling to Panama to marry her fiancé, a wealthy Briton who owns a business in Peru. The narrator remarks, "Perhaps Miss Viner was imprudent, but who in Peru would be wiser? Perhaps indeed, it was the world that was wrong, and not Miss Viner" (207). These comments are followed by Mr. Morris's unsympathetic comments about Miss Viner to Mr. Forrest: "Don't go too fast, old fellow. . . . One gets into a hobble in such matters before one knows where one is" (207). The attitudes expressed are vastly different: The narrator believes society unfairly constrains women, and Mr. Morris believes women generally chain and fetter men.

The paternal narrator continues to criticize the patriarchal society with his own comments and by showing Mr. Forrest's critical reaction to Miss Viner's anguish. Her fiancé is a "hard man" who is 20 years older than she (209). She has put off marrying him for 10 years and is now forced to now marry him because the relative she has lived with has died. Her fiancé, Mr. Gorloch, has paid for her voyage and her traveling clothes. She frankly sums up the economic nature of many Victorian marriages: "I have taken his money and have no escape" (209). One of Miss Viner's and Mr. Forrest's brief conversations exposes the Victorian double-standards: Mr. Forrest can earn a living and choose to marry for love; she cannot do the former, which denies her the option of the latter. Mr. Forrest, although he claims he "did not mean to judge," nevertheless tells her, "A woman should never marry a man unless she loves him" (209). Miss Viner is not at all surprised by Mr. Forrest's attitude. "Of course you will condemn me. That is the way in which women are always treated.

They have no choice given them, and are then scolded for choosing wrongly" (209). Mr. Forrest can only continue to reply to her problems with more platitudes: "We are bound to bear our burdens of sorrow" (210).

In showing the reader this conversation, the narrator makes no comments—Miss Viner is capable of speaking for herself. In case the reader, like the passengers, are concerned about the "alliance," the narrator assures us that neither Mr. Forrest nor Miss Viner have committed "aught that was wrong" and that the passengers who frowned upon the friendship did so with "prudish caution" (210). At this point the difference between the narrator and Mr. Morris is heightened. The narrator is clearly sympathetic to Miss Viner and not her fiancé. Mr. Morris, however, shows concern only for men and the patriarchal system as he departs at St. Thomas and cautions Mr. Forrest: "Don't interfere with the rights of the gentleman in Peru, or he might run a knife into you" (211).

The sentence is a master stroke of narrative technique. The friendly, paternal narrator exposes the callousness of a friendly, paternal passenger—a man who seemed much like himself. The narrator lets the reader know that the benevolent patriarchy is a Victorian illusion; men like Mr. Morris are interested only in the rights of other men and not in the rights of women. Trollope has made his point slowly and cleverly.

The rest of the story continues to explore sexual double-standards for men and women. Although Mr. Forrest is falling in love with Miss Viner and wants to help her, he cannot refrain from critical judgments. When she frankly states that her upcoming marriage means she has only "five more days of self and liberty left," he begs her not to say "horrible" things (212). Instead, he urges her to be "good and true, and womanly," and submit to the horrors of an English poorhouse (212).

The end of the story emphasizes the inescapable inequality found in so many relationships between men and women in Victorian society. When Miss Viner receives word that her fiancé has died, Mr. Forrest offers to help her and Miss Viner accepts. He pushes further, asking for the "right to act" as her "protector" (218). Miss Viner exclaims in shock and frustration: "My protector! I do not want such aid as that. During the days that we are here together you shall be my friend" (218).

Emily Viner, who has just regained her self and liberty through the death of one man, does not want to become the ward of another. Ralph Forrest does not understand her desire for an equal friend, not a paternal protector, as she rejects his offer to accompany her back to England. Her fiancé had provided for her in his will "sufficiently" (but "not liberally"), so for the first time she has the economic means that give men the right to make choices in personal relationships (212). The link between her new-found independence and her new money is obvious.

The last sentence of the story is a straightforward statement of fact: "Thus alone she took her departure for England, and he went on his way to California." This sentence is entirely different in tone from the first sentence of the story. The narrator no longer needs to add his own philosophical comments because the characters' actions are making his point clear: In Victorian England, a woman cannot have "self or liberty" in most relationships with a man.

The story of Emily Viner and her courage is an excellent example of some "brave Trollope" (Breyer [ed., **Anthony Trollope: The Complete Short Stories.**] vii)— the brave, feminist Trollope. In this story, he uses the names and characters of Emily Viner and Ralph Forrest to subvert the Victorian view of a woman as a parasitical vine who clings to a man as a vine clings to a strong tree. Trollope's heroine chooses instead to grow by herself rather than cling to "our hero." This remarkable story of a remarkable alliance is one that feminist scholars cannot afford to overlook. When readers finish **"A Journey to Panama,"** their literary appetites will have been nourished by this small but excellent tart. They, too, will agree with Rebecca West that "Trollope was a feminist."

Notes

1. Trollope's short stories have been the subject of little critical analysis. Since the *Complete Short Stories* was published (the first volume was published in 1979; the fifth and final volume in 1983), the MLA [Modern Language Association] and ABELL [Annual Bibliography of English Language and Literature] bibliographies list only one article about a specific short story ("The Panjandrum"). The other articles listed are all review articles. The 1979 volume of the Christmas stories garnered two brief reviews. The entire five-volume set also received two reviews: "The Man of Feeling" by Marvin Mudrick in the *Hudson Review* and "The Case for Trollope's Short Stories" by Francine Navakas in *Modern Philology*. Navakas finds that Trollope's short stories are "uneven at best" (174). Mudrick, on the other hand, praises the short stories and discusses their emphasis on female characters and the "power of women" (757). Such commentary, however, does not seem to have sparked much interest in the stories.

2. Trollope's support of Faithfull by contributing "The Journey" ["The Journey to Panama"] was not an aberration. Two years later he donated another short story, "Miss Ophelia Gledd" to *A Wel-*

come, another anthology published by Faithfull (*Letters* [*The Letters of Anthony Trollope*] 211).

3. Along with searches in general bibliographies, I checked about a dozen books on Trollope. Those that do not mention "The Journey to Panama" include a Trollope bibliography, *The Reputation of Trollope* [1977] edited by John Charles Olmstead; *Trollope Centenary Essays* [1982] edited by John Halperin; *The Art of Anthony Trollope* [1980] by Geoffrey Harvey; *The Gentleman in Trollope* [1982] by Shirley Dobin Letwin; *The Reasonable Man* [1981] by Coral Lansbury; and *Anthony Trollope: Dream and Art* [1983] by Andrew Wright. The essay "Baking Tarts for Readers of Periodicals" in *The Victorian Short Story* [1986] by Harold Orel offers some praise for Trollope's short stories in general but does not mention "The Journey." None of the review articles of *The Complete Short Stories* mention "The Journey."

4. [Gerould and Gerould,] *A Guide to Trollope* is extremely useful but should be used with a little caution. It incorrectly states that Emily Viner is Irish (247) and that she has spent her last funds on boat passage to marry her fiancé (129). (She is English, and her fiancé has paid for her passage.) It also incorrectly states that Ralph Forrest helps Emily Viner arrange her return trip to England (88).

5. In *Anthony Trollope: The Artist in Hiding*, R. C. Terry states that in the Victorian period "spinsterhood is so dreaded that a woman is prepared to pursue a potential husband around the world as happens in the story 'The Journey to Panama'" (151). In *The Chronicler of Barsetshire: A Life*, R. H. Super states that the story draws upon "Trollope's knowledge of the Caribbean" (220).

Works Cited

Barickman, Richard, Susan MacDonald and Myra Stark. *Corrupt Relations: Dickens, Thackeray, Trollope, Collins, and the Victorian Sexual System.* New York: Columbia UP, 1982.

Gerould, Winifred Gregory and James Thayer Gerould. *A Guide to Trollope.* Princeton: Princeton UP, 1948.

Lyons, Anne. *Anthony Trollope: An Annotated Bibliography of Periodical Works By and About Him in the United States and Great Britain to 1900.* Greenwood, FL: Penkevill, 1985.

Mudrick, Marvin. "The Man of Feeling." Rev. of *Anthony Trollope: The Complete Short Stories.* Ed. Betty Jane Slemp Breyer. *The Hudson Review* 36 (1983): 755-65.

Navakas, Francine. "The Case for Trollope's Short Stories." Rev. of *Anthony Trollope: The Complete Short*

Stories. Ed. Betty Jane Slemp Breyer. *Modern Philology* 83 (1985): 172-78.

Sadleir, Michael. *Anthony Trollope: A Bibliography.* London: Dawsons, 1928.

———. *Anthony Trollope: A Commentary.* Cambridge: Riverside, 1927.

Super, R. H. *The Chronicler of Barsetshire: A Life.* Ann Arbor: U of Michigan P, 1988.

Terry, R. C. *Anthony Trollope: The Artist in Hiding.* Totowa: Rowman and Littlefield, 1977.

Trollope, Anthony. *An Autobiography.* [1883] Ed. Michael Sadleir. Oxford: Oxford UP, 1980.

———. *The Letters of Anthony Trollope.* Ed. N. John Hall. Stanford: Stanford UP, 1983. 2 vols.

———. "The Journey to Panama." [1861] *Anthony Trollope: The Complete Short Stories.* Vol. 5. Ed. Betty Jane Slemp Breyer. Fort Worth: Texas Christian UP, 1983. 199-219. 5 vols. 1979-83.

West, Rebecca. *The Court and the Castle.* New Haven: Yale UP, 1957.

Wijesinha, Rajiva. *The Androgynous Trollope: Attitudes to Women Amongst Early Victorian Novelists.* Washington: UP of America, 1982.

Wendy Jones (essay date summer 1994)

SOURCE: Jones, Wendy. "Feminism, Fiction and Contract Theory: Trollope's 'He Knew He Was Right.'" *Criticism: A Quarterly for Literature and the Arts* 36, no. 3 (summer 1994): 401-14.

[*In the following essay, Jones studies the issue of married women's rights in the nineteenth century as depicted in Trollope's novel* He Knew He Was Right.]

Anthony Trollope wrote *He Knew He Was Right* from November 1867 to June 1868, years during which a bill to grant property rights to married women under common law was being fiercely debated in both Parliament and the press. The first Married Women's Property Act passed in 1870.[1] As an editor and writer for popular periodicals, and as a politician manqué who actually stood for Parliament in November 1868, Trollope was certain to have been familiar with arguments on both sides of this issue. *He Knew He Was Right,* an exploration of male authority and women's rights within marriage—core issues in arguments over married women's property—is Trollope's timely contribution to this debate. I attempt to make explicit the nature of this contribution by showing how *He Knew He Was Right* intersects with the broader cultural discourse of contract, which informs Victorian Feminist arguments, and which was central to an ideal of married love.

He Knew He Was Right is about a marital quarrel that begins when Louis Trevelyan forbids his wife, Emily, to see Colonel Osborne, an aging but flirtatious bachelor friend of the family, thereby casting aspersions on her honor and bullying her in a way considered unacceptable among people of their class. Although Emily resentfully complies with her husband's orders, Trevelyan finds he cannot master his wife's spirit; she refuses to submit gracefully to his command, for to do so would be to countenance the insult. As Trevelyan becomes progressively more obsessed with his right to "mastery," the quarrel escalates and they separate. He eventually goes mad, demanding that his wife confess to her "infidelity," which he has come to allege in his disordered condition. In the end, debilitated by mental illness, Trevelyan dies, freeing both himself and his wife from his monomania. Yet despite such an escape, Emily has essentially lost the quarrel, for as a married woman, she is not only unable to divorce (or even legally separate from) her husband, but she also has no right to custody of their child, despite Trevelyan's inability to care properly for the boy.

At stake in the quarrel is the definition of marriage itself. In Trevelyan's view, Emily's insubordination threatens the very foundation of their union; in her view, his orders undermine their loving partnership. Trollope had of course written about marital unhappiness in earlier novels such as *The Bertrams* (1859) and *Phineas Finn* (1869), while the theme of female autonomy had been the focus most famously in *Can You Forgive Her?* (1864-5). But in no other novel did he concentrate so fully on the relationship between a husband's authority and the legal and social structures that undergird that authority, nor had he previously interrogated the relative merits and justice of patriarchal laws and customs as he does in *He Knew He Was Right.* And in no other novel did he concentrate so fully on the implications of marriage as a contract.

Contract theory and the ideal of marital love had been associated since early modern times. The rise of an ethical imperative to marry for love in late seventeenth- and eighteenth-century England was part of a new "structure of feeling" (in Raymond Williams's phrase) that emphasized a contractual ethic.[2] To a large extent, voluntarism came to be asserted as the legitimate basis of all relationships and institutions, including the founding moment of civilization itself. The valuation of love as a basis for marriage was not new, as earlier literature demonstrates. But as the idea of "married love" entered into the discourse of contract, it was transformed. Prior to (roughly) the eighteenth century, married love existed as an ideal, not available to or even desirable for all people. Marital love now became an expectation as well as a duty, and marriage was defined as a relationship voluntarily entered into for the benefit of each party. Marriage theoretically became a contract, like all the other contracts that held society together.[3]

According to John Locke, whose political writings came to define contract for the English, the decision to enter a contract must be voluntary.[4] People cannot contract their liberty away altogether; a self-destructive contract is not valid; and if either of the parties to a contract violates its terms, their agreement is dissolable.[5] Locke's theory thus posits a "self" who possesses certain inborn and inalienable rights and whose basic liberty is inviolable. If women were to marry on contractual grounds, then presumably they too had such a "self." But this version of female subjectivity was at odds with English marriage laws and institutions.

The law was aptly characterized by a maxim ascribed to William Blackstone, the great eighteenth-century English jurist: "in law a husband and wife are one person, and the husband is that person."[6] Marriage laws ensured the non-subjectivity of women in a variety of ways. A married women was classified in the same legal category as "criminals, idiots and minors," to use Frances Power Cobbe's well-known formulation.[7] A wife was completely in the power of her husband: he could beat her, lock her up, and live openly with his mistress, and she had no recourse at law. In some cases, upper- and middle-class women had a limited amount of protection since their families routinely made marriage settlements of separate property held in trust for them under the legal system of equity; if the money had been settled in such a way as to allow the woman access to it, her funds could function *de facto* as a form of alimony. But it was more often the case that women were denied direct access to their separate property. And working- and lower-class women were forced to cede all property to their husbands, including wages.[8] In fact, Parliament's growing recognition of the inequity of the law (i.e. the discrepancy between common law and equity), rather than the support of women's rights, was a primary motive for reform of married women's property laws.[9] The gendered control of property was consequently crucial to both feminists and their opponents: both realized that if women were allowed economic independence, they would have some rights and power within marriage, and hence some control over their lives. For feminists, therefore, separate property came to stand for a complex of other demands; indeed, they saw their arguments for reform of marriage law as the first step in an agenda that included such women's rights as suffrage, accessible divorce, equitable child custody laws, and respectable employment opportunities.

Thus the appeal to the principle of contract, which was seen as asserting female subjectivity in the face of its legal denial, pervades the discourse of women's rights throughout the nineteenth century. Activists repeatedly point out that marriage laws violate the allegedly contractual nature of marriage. In 1825 (early on in the struggle), William Thompson derided the contradiction in the phrase "marriage *contract*": "Each man yokes a woman to his establishment and calls it a *contract*. Audacious falsehood! A contract! Where are any of the attributes of contracts . . . to be found in this transaction? . . . Can even both the parties, man and woman, by agreement alter the terms as to the *indissolubility* and *inequality,* of this pretended contract?[10]" In 1855, Caroline Norton, urging the reform of the common law, similarly argued that marriage laws fail to evince the contractual logic that the wedding ceremony purports: "As *her husband,* he has a right to all that is hers; as *his wife,* she has no right to anything that is his. As her husband, he may divorce her (if truth or false swearing can do it): as his wife, the utmost "divorce" she could obtain, is permission to reside alone,—married to his name." Marriage is a contract, a "civil bond," for the husband, but not for the wife, for whom it is an "indissoluble sacrament."[11] And in 1869, on the eve of the passage of the first Married Women's Property Act, John Stuart Mill observed that although "the most frequent case of voluntary association, next to marriage, is partnership in business," marriage laws do not follow the laws of contract. "If the law dealt with other contracts as it does with marriage, it would ordain that one partner should administer the common business as if it were his private concern" and "that the others should have only delegated powers."[12]

If married love provided a framework for articulating marriage as a contractual ideal, then conversely, a contractual ideal enabled feminists to associate women's rights with marital happiness: "the highest possible union" between husband and wife is intrinsically a corollary of contract.[13] Of course, an ideal of marital love could be used to support conservative interests as well. Lord Penzance, who led the opposition to married women's property rights in the House of Lords, speculated that if a married woman could own property and was therefore able to participate in business, a man might be startled by the information that his wife had determined to set up a rival shop in his neighbourhood" or "still more startled at hearing that she had entered into partnership with her cousin, who need not be a woman."[14] But feminists disputed the logic of such claims, arguing that if love is by definition freely given, then domestic relations, founded on and sustained by love, ought to be voluntary rather than coerced: only then, as William Thompson notes, will marriage provide the "delights" of "esteem, of friendship, of intellectual and sympathetic intercourse."[15] Similarly, Cobbe argues that oppressive laws for women are in fact incompatible with wifely love and devotion. If men believe "that a woman's whole life and being, her soul, body, time, property, thought, and care ought to be given to her husband" and that "nothing short of such absorption in him and his interests makes her a true wife," then denying women their rights undermines rather than furthers this goal:

> Is perfect love to be called out by perfect dependence? Does an empty purse necessarily imply a full heart? Is a generous-natured woman likely to be won or rather to be alienated and galled by being made to feel she has no choice but submission? Surely, there is a great fallacy in this direction. . . . Real unanimity is not produced between two parties by forbidding one of them to have any voice at all.[16]

The consensual logic of contract thus enabled feminists to argue that the reforms they urged furthered the ideal and harmonious domestic relations valued by all. Not only does coercion hinder the development of a happy home, but it is also redundant where such a home exists. Frances Cornwallis therefore opposed denying women their civil rights in order to guarantee male authority on the grounds that loving and responsible women do not need to be forced into being good wives:

> We are taught from our childhood to value the civil rights of a free citizen as the best inheritance of an Englishman, and when our mothers, sisters, daughters, wives ask for this birthright of their nation, can we tell them, without offering an insult which our countrywomen have by no means merited, that they are unfit for exercising it?—that if they are not bound by no less a penalty than the loss of all personal identity, they would rend asunder all the dearest affections of the human heart . . . [that] they would at once abandon their best hopes, both here and hereafter, and defy both God and man in their licentious madness? Those who say this, we may venture to affirm, do not believe it.[17]

Feminists also drew on contract theory to claim that women's rights were a necessary consequence of progress. Locke and other contractarians had identified the beginnings of civilization with the initiation of a social contract—a move from a society governed by force to one governed by consent. Feminists extrapolated from this logic to argue that gender relations free of force ought to constitute the next episode in the story of human development. Cobbe observes that because the "feudal structure" of gender relations is outmoded in the modern world, granting women their rights is clearly in line with an overall scheme of moral development: "It is clear enough that we have come to one of those stages in human history which, like a youth's attainment of his majority, makes some change in the arrangements of past time desirable, if not imperative."[18] Along similar lines, Mill argues that "the law of force was the avowed rule of general conduct" through much of the world's history, and it is only recently "that the affairs of society have been even pretended to be regulated according to any moral law. . . . "[I]nequality of rights" is "a relic of the past . . . and must necessarily disappear" (134, 142).

To these feminists, marriage for love was evidence that the world was changing for the better. They might criticize marriage for failing to live up to its allegedly contractual character, but they also assert that the contemporary emphasis on married love was a sign of progress. Josephine Butler notes that in "an advanced and Christian community" marriage is based on "free and deliberate choice,—a decision of the judgment and of the heart."[19] Mill observes that "until a late period in European history, the father had the power to dispose of his daughter in marriage at his own will and pleasure, without any regard to hers"; we now adhere to a "better morality" (157-58).

What is Trollope's position *vis a vis* these feminist arguments? Given his focus on women's issues, it is not surprising that critics have often debated the extent and nature of Trollope's liberal views regarding women. In general, they conclude that despite the progressive tendencies in many of his novels (particularly those of the 1860s), he is fundamentally ambivalent about feminism.[20] But if **He Knew He Was Right** is not unambiguously valuable *as* feminist polemic, it is nevertheless valuable *to* feminist polemic. This is because it espouses an ideal of married love that, as we have seen, has *already* been articulated within the discourse of Lockean contract. Thus by wholeheartedly endorsing marriage for love, and by following through on the contractual implications for women of that endorsement, **He Knew He Was Right** exemplifies the connections between married love, the domestic ideal, progress, and liberty that Victorian feminists invoked. In this case, Trollope's "feminism" has less to do with his attitude toward women than with his attitude toward marriage.

Like nearly all of Trollope's novels, **He Knew He Was Right** shows that for those fortunate enough to find love in the world, marriage is a joy as well as a duty, while marrying without love is a sin. When Hugh Stanbury, the novel's hero, deliberates about whether or not to marry on his small income, "there came upon him some dim ideal of self-abnegation,—that . . . the poetry of his life, was, in fact, the capacity of caring more for other human beings than for himself."[21] Nora Rowley (the woman he loves and Emily's sister) reaches a similar conclusion, rejecting a brilliant match with the future Lord Peterborough because she does not love him. Characters who use marriage for economic or social advancement, such as the French sisters, come in for heavy punishment. It is better to lead the lonely and penurious life of a spinster, like Hugh's sister, Priscilla Stanbury, than to marry without love.

If marriage for love is a duty, it is also a right—a right that even justifies female rebellion, as the stories of Nora and Dorothy Stanbury show. Marriage for love, in other words, legitimates a woman's desires and choices, recognizing the very personhood and autonomy of which the law would deprive her after marriage. When Nora's parents forbid her to marry Hugh, she firmly insists both that she will marry the man she loves and that it is her right to do so: "There is a time when a girl must be supposed to know what is best for herself,— just as there is for a man" (658).

Dorothy also exercises her right to choose her husband freely. When her aunt and adoptive guardian, Miss Stanbury, informs her that plans have been readied for her marriage to a local clergyman, Mr. Gibson, Dorothy refuses. Miss Stanbury is shocked that Dorothy, with her meager fortune and poor prospects, would dare to reject such an offer, which includes her own generous gift of 2000 pounds: "An offer from an honest man, with her friends' approval, and a fortune at her back as though she had been born with a gold spoon in her mouth! And she tells me that she can't, and won't, and wouldn't, and shouldn't, as though I were asking her to walk the streets" (342). But Miss Stanbury is indeed asking Dorothy to "walk the streets" insofar as she is asking her to prostitute herself—to negate her desires (she shudders when she thinks of embracing Mr. Gibson) and to commodify herself, exchanging her person and devotion for a good establishment. Not only does Dorothy assert her right to veto her aunt's choice of husband, but later she engages herself to the man she loves despite her aunt's disapproval.

The polemics of married love frequently dovetailed with the feminists' account of moral evolution; as the arguments of feminists did, *He Knew He Was Right* emphasizes that the right of marital choice had not always existed and that it is in itself evidence of progress. Miss Stanbury clearly associates Dorothy's refusal of Mr. Gibson with the changing role of women: "I don't know what has come to the young women;—or what it is they want" (342) she says, after Dorothy rejects her arranged marriage. Moreover, the novel suggests that denying women the right of marital choice is retrograde and in the end impossible, given contemporary mores. When Nora's father finds she is determined to marry Hugh, he threatens to curse and disinherit her, like the unyielding father in Samuel Richardson's *Clarissa*. His wife points out the absurdity of such a threat in the modern world: "On the stage they do such things as that . . . and, perhaps, they used to do it once in reality. But you know that it's out of the question now. Fancy your standing up and cursing the dear girl, just as we are all starting from Southampton!" (844).

More importantly, *He Knew He Was Right* suggests that social expectations had changed with regard to the relationship between husband and wife as well as between child and guardian; such changes are inherent in a contractual view of marriage. The novel presents what we might call "gentle patriarchy" as a successor to a tyrannical version of male power. While a husband still ought to retain supreme authority in his household, such authority should manifest itself through persuasion rather than force. So Hugh tells Trevelyan that rather than insulting his wife by forbidding her Colonel Osborne's company, he ought to have hinted his disapproval (184). Trevelyan himself, on the brink of madness, hears the internal voice of a better, saner self, which urges this form of exercising authority: "A man should be master in his own house, but he should make his mastery palatable, equitable, smooth, soft to the touch, a thing almost unfelt" (44). Such a view receives official sanction within the novel when Dorothy reads aloud from Jeremy Taylor's sermon, "The Marriage Ring," (486) which advocates exercising patriarchal power in just this sort of way.[22]

Gentle patriarchy assumes compliance. A man can assert his authority in muted ways because he can depend on his wife to know what is expected of her. Emily's problems are due in part to the fact that as a colonial, she has incompletely internalized the laws of English etiquette. In one sense, such scrupulous attention to the rules on the part of both husband and wife exemplifies the self-policing that is always the mark of well-regulated society in Trollope's novels, as D. A. Miller has demonstrated.[23] But this kinder, gentler patriarchy also demonstrates Trollope's attempt, although one that is doomed to the failure of contradiction, to bring patriarchy into accord with the consensual nature of contract and with the world's evolution from the rule of force to the moral law of consent.

Gentle patriarchy thus demonstrates the progressive implications of contract theory for gender, opening a space for the redefinition of gender roles in ways that potentially challenge patriarchy, even as it simultaneously undermines its own subversive implications. By showing that gender roles can change, and by evoking a less forceful mode of male authority, gentle patriarchy raises the possibility—albeit *only* the possibility—of an equal division of power between men and women. Furthermore, the self-discipline it exacts from women grants the principle of a separate female subjectivity. Indeed, it is the possibility of Emily's autonomy that threatens Trevelyan more than his fear of her adultery, which he never believes wholeheartedly. For him, the quarrel is above all about obtaining Emily's capitulation and being able to control her. Thus, like the ultra-conservative Lord Penzance, who worried that a married woman with property would go into business with a lover-partner (192), Trevelyan imagines a causal relationship between female autonomy and wifely infidelity. And because he is unable to put his faith in the moral law of self-discipline where Emily is concerned, he resorts to the "rigours of surveillance" (254): unable to trust his wife to police her own behavior, he hires an ex-policeman to do it for her, even though this is degrading to himself and insulting to her. He is altogether unable to allow his love for his wife to temper his need for mastery, although he knows he ought to do so in order to resolve the quarrel.

At some level of awareness, Trollope is as threatened by the contractual ideals he endorses as is his character, Trevelyan. He attempts to resolve this dilemma by equating true masculinity with persuasion rather than power. Since he rejects authoritarianism, a conventional sign of manliness, he aligns masculine strength itself with gentle patriarchy, with the ability to rule without bluntly displaying force, but with a settled confidence in male authority. In this way, what might seem to be a ceding of power on the part of patriarchy is reinscribed as a more potent form of control. And Trevelyan, who exemplifies an older model of male power, is shown to be less than manly. Trevelyan has problems with "mastery" because he is not "man enough" to admit his fault, as Hugh makes clear when he reproaches him for his inept handling of the quarrel. You have only to bid her come back to you, and let bygones be bygones, and all would be right. Can't you be man enough to remember that you are a man?" (310). Emily also equates his petulant behavior with a lack of "manliness" (81).

To underscore the manliness of gentle patriarchy, the slur of effeminacy haunts the "masterful" Trevelyan throughout the novel. From the start, he possesses distinctly feminine characteristics. Inhabiting the domestic rather than the public sphere, he leads a life much like that of an intelligent Victorian lady. Rather than work at a profession, he chooses to lead a life of leisure, dilettantishly pursuing intellectual interests. He is unusually domestic. Unlike other men, he takes no joy in being able to dine at his club or in any similar "release from the constraint imposed by family ties"; on the contrary, he is one "to whom the ordinary comforts of domestic life were attractive and necessary" (174). Even Trevelyan's madness is the sign of an inherent effeminacy; women were supposedly more susceptible to insanity than men because "the instability of their reproductive systems interfered with their sexual, emotional, and rational control."[24] Trevelyan's behavior throughout the novel thus supports Hugh's charge that Trevelyan's autocratic character is evidence of a failure to be "man enough." Yet the novel's very need for this defensive strategy is an index of the potential threat posed by the concept of contract.

He Knew He Was Right represents gentle patriarchy (like married love) as an ideal that exemplifies progress, since it replaces an older model of social convention. In this sense, it also accords with the feminists' evolutionary account of social relations. *He Knew He Was Right* further underscores the progressive nature of the social norms it endorses by stressing that Trevelyan, whose view of the family is outmoded, is unable to change with the times. He is shown to be consistently nostalgic, longing for a past when, in his view, methods of social control were more direct and forceful. He laments the fact that "as wives are managed now-a-days, he could not forbid to her [Emily] the use of the post-office" (254).[25] Trevelyan believes that in an earlier age, his problems would have been quickly solved by a duel: "Gentleman of old, his own grandfather or his father, would have taken such a fellow as Colonel Osborne by the throat and have caned him, and afterwards would have shot him, or have stood to be shot. All that was changed now" (253-54).

In the end, Trevelyan, the most domestic of men, ironically destroys his home: such is the logical consequence of his retrograde attitude, played out to its most drastic possible conclusion. For the very concept of home as a refuge and haven, the kind of home that Trevelyan holds dear and that Victorian society idealizes, accords with a contractual ideal of domesticity, at odds with his intolerant style of mastery. Such a home depends on respect, complaisance, and above all trust. As Emily points out, "A wife does not feel that her chances of happiness are increased when she finds that her husband suspects her of being too intimate with another man" (100). Trevelyan's story thus tacitly endorses the feminists' equation of autonomy with domesticity, even if Trollope's gentle patriarchy simultaneously and paradoxically upholds male supremacy.

He Knew He Was Right undermines its subversive implications in other ways as well, even in the subplots where it most strongly asserts the progressive aspects of contractual relationships. Because Nora's parents and Miss Stanbury eventually capitulate, Trollope never has to take the part of parents against children, the logical telos of his advocacy of married love. Dorothy's "rebellion" is also muted, since Miss Stanbury is neither a father nor a parent. And both Nora and Dorothy are perfectly happy with their domestic fates and willing to look on their men as gods. Nevertheless, *He Knew He Was Right* reveals the feminist implications of the logic of contract. Starting from the premise that it is right to marry for love, it elaborates the implications of that premise for female subjectivity, and therefore necessarily arrives at the same conclusions as the Victorian feminists: that contract accords rights, and, in line with the world's moral progress, that relationships between men and women ought to be consensual.

I would like to conclude with a brief appeal to historical context in assessing the relationship between contract theory and feminism. In our own time, the two have been at odds. Feminists generally agree that contract theory is complicit with women's oppression. They point out that Locke asserts the natural subordination of women and that he rejects the notion that family and government are analogous, thereby authorizing a separate feminine sphere in which women are isolated and powerless.[26] Moreover, as Carole Pateman argues, contract theory takes for granted that political right originates in male sex-right or conjugal right, which ensures the subordination of women: in the seventeenth and eighteenth centuries, contractarians incorporated this right, implicit in the theories of their patriarchalist opponents, thereby transforming "the law of male sex right into its modern contractual form."[27] Moreover, contractarian ideals tacitly assume a male political subject, thereby denying specific political recognition and accommodation of women's needs. In our own day, the concept of equal, genderless (but really male) political subjects has been used to deny women maternity leave and to gain control of children from the mothers who bore them.[28]

Yet contract theory was nevertheless an important stepping-stone for feminism. By granting the premise of an independent female subjectivity, it opened a utopian space for feminists to argue against oppressive laws. If we now see the perniciousness of contract, which was formerly obscured, that knowledge does not negate its utility as a political tool for feminists in the past. Trollope's somber novel of marital unhappiness remains a memorable testament to such utility.

Notes

1. The legal information in this essay is indebted to Lee Holcombe's *Wives and Property: Reform of the Married Women's Property Law in Nineteenth-Century England* (Toronto: Toronto University Press, 1983) and Mary Lyndon Shanley's *Feminism, Marriage and the Law in Victorian England: 1850-1895* (Princeton: Princeton University Press, 1990).

2. Williams defines "structure of feeling" as a "cultural hypothesis" that enables us to define individual perception within a given period of culture without reducing it to either the individual or the collective (*Marxism and Literature* [Oxford: Oxford University Press, 1977], 132). The contractual as I define it falls into this category, since it embraces thought, feeling, theory, and ethical imperative.

3. For the history of the conceptualization of marriage as a contract, see Mary Lyndon Shanley, "Marriage Contract and Social Contract," *Western Political Quarterly* 32 (March 1979): 79-91. Although married love began as a middle-class ideal, by the nineteenth century it had been accepted by the aristocracy. See J. R. Gillis, *For Better, For Worse: British Marriages, 1600 to the Present* (Oxford: Oxford University Press, 1985), 105.

4. The history of Locke's reception in England is a complex subject, beyond the scope of this essay. See e.g. Hans Aarsleff, *From Locke to Saussure:*

Essays on the Study of Language and Intellectual History (Minneapolis: University of Minnesota Press, 1982), 120-45.

5. John Locke, *Two Treatises of Government*, ed. Peter Laslett (Cambridge: Cambridge University Press, 1987), 284, 367. I use "contract" to refer to a Lockean contractual ideal.

6. Cited by Holcombe, 18. Cf. Blackstone's less aphoristic expression of the same idea: "The very being or legal existence of the woman is suspended during marriage, or at least is incorporated and consolidated into that of the husband" (William Blackstone, *Commentaries on the Laws of England,* 4 vols., Book I [Oxford: Clarendon Press, 1765-66], 430).

7. Frances Power Cobbe, "Criminals, Idiots, Women and Minors: Is the Classification Sound?," *Fraser's Magazine* 78 (1868): 77-94.

8. The one exception in common law was real property, which a husband could not dispose of without his wife's consent, although he had a right to any income it generated.

9. Such reform came about slowly. The 1857 Divorce Act allowed for legal separation (but not divorce) for women physically abused by their husbands and also granted women who obtained judicial separations or divorces, or who were deserted by their husbands, the property rights of single women. This was limited relief, for the determination of physical abuse would be left to judges who were often biased, and in any case, poor women could not afford to apply to the Divorce courts for separation orders and/or to activate their independent status. The first Married Women's Property Act (1870) allowed three kinds of property to be treated as separate: earnings, investments, and legacies of less than 200 pounds. The Married Women's Property Act of 1882 allowed women to enter into contracts independently and to will property to beneficiaries of their choice. Both property acts and the law of equity nevertheless recognized the rights of a wife's property rather than her personal rights. The Matrimonial Causes Act of 1878 enabled a wife who was a victim of physical abuse to apply for a separation order from a local magistrate's court. But it was not until 1891 that the courts ruled that a man was not entitled to imprison his wife.

10. William Thompson, *Appeal of One Half of the Human Race, Women, Against the Pretensions of the Other Half, Men, To Retain Them in Political, and Thence in Civil and Domestic Slavery: in Reply to Mr. [James] Mill's Celebrated "Article on Government"* (London, 1825; New York: Source Book Press, 1970), 55.

11. Caroline Norton, *Selected Writings of Caroline Norton: Facsimile Reproductions with an Introduction and Notes by James O. Hoge and Jane Marcus,* (Delmar, NY: Scholars' Facsimiles and Reprints, 1978), 4, 13, cited by Mary Poovey, in *Uneven Developments; The Ideological Work of Gender in Mid-Victorian England* (Chicago: University of Chicago Press, 1988), 64.

12. John Start Mill, "The Subjection of Women," in *Essays on Sex Equality,* ed. Alice Rossi (Chicago: University of Chicago Press, 1970), 168-69. Future references will appear in the text.

13. Cobbe, 788.

14. *Hansard's Parliamentary Debates,* Third Series, vol. 192, June 21, 1870, Column 604. Future references to *Parliamentary Debates* will be cited by volume, date and column number and will appear in the text.

15. Thompson, 70.

16. Cobbe, 788, 790.

17. Frances Caroline Cornwallis, "The Property of Married Women: Report of the Personal Laws Committee (of the Law Amendment Society) on the Laws Relating to the Property of Married Women," *Westminster Review* 66 (1856): 358-59.

18. Cobbe, 791.

19. Josephine Butler, Introduction to *Woman's Work and Woman's Culture: A Series of Essays,* ed. Josephine Butler (London: Macmillan and Co., 1869), xxxii.

20. Discussions of Trollope's feminism include Richard Barickman, Susan MacDonald and Myra Stark, *Corrupt Relations: Dickens, Thackeray, Trollope, Collins, and the Victorian Sexual System* (New York: Columbia University Press, 1982); P. D. Edwards, *Anthony Trollope: His Art and Scope* (New York: St. Martin's Press, 1987); N. John Hall, A Feminist In Spite of Himself," *Trollopiana: The Journal of the Trollope Society* 10 (August 1990): 13-19; and Jean Nardin, *He Knew She Was Right: The Independent Woman in the Novels of Anthony Trollope* (Carbondale and Edwardsville: Southern Illinois University Press, 1989). Trollope's two extended discussions of women's rights appear in his "Higher Education of Women," *Four Lectures,* ed. Morris L. Parrish (London: Constable and Co., 1938), 67-88 and *North America* (New York: Knopf, 1951), 256-65. For summaries of Trollope's overtly expressed views on feminism, see Hall, 14-15; Nardin, 16-18, and John Sutherland's introduction to the novel (in the edition cited in note 21), xxi-xxii.

21. Anthony Trollope, *He Knew He Was Right* (Oxford: Oxford University Press, 1985), 237. Future references will appear in the text.

22. See Ruth apRoberts, "Emily and Nora and Dorothy and Priscilla and Jemima and Carry," in *The Victorian Experience: The Novelists,* ed. Richard A. Levine (Athens: Ohio University Press, 1976), 116. Taylor, a seventeenth-century divine, was an authoritative religious guide for the Victorians; most households possessed his sermons. As this reference indicates, the revision of ideals of masculinity implied by "gentle patriarchy" was not new to the Victorians. A similar ideal had been popular with the Puritans. But it was always in conflict with sterner models of masculinity, and at this particular time, would appear "new" once more since it followed closely on a resurgence of autocratic patriarchy at mid century. On ideals of masculinity in the Victorian era, see Leonore Davidoff and Catherine Hall, *Family Fortunes: Men and Women of the English Middle Class, 1780-1850* (Chicago: University of Chicago Press, 1987), 109-13.

23. D. A. Miller, "The Novel as Usual: Trollope's *Barchester Towers*," *The Novel and the Police* (Berkeley and Los Angeles: University of California Press, 1988), 107-45.

24. Elaine Showalter, *The Female Malady* (New York: Penguin, 1987), 55.

25. Robert Polhemus observes that Trevelyan is driven mad by the changing role of women (*The Changing World of Anthony Trollope* [Berkeley and Los Angeles: University of California Press, 1968], 164).

26. See Susan Moller Okin, "Women and the Making of the Sentimental Family," *Philosophy and Public Affairs* 11 (1982): 65-88 and Ruth Perry, "Mary Astell and the Feminist Critique of Possessive Individualism," *Eighteenth-Century Studies* 23 (Summer 1990): 449-50. However, Okin also suggests that Locke's theory, posits a version of patriarchy that is "very limited" when compared to contemporary laws and customs. For additional analyses of the feminist potential of Locke's theories and the limits thereof, see Theresa Brennan and Carole Pateman, "'Mere Auxiliaries to the Commonwealth': Women and the Origins of Liberalism," *Political Studies* 27 (1979): 183-200. Melissa Butler, "Early Liberal Roots of English Feminism," *The American Political Science Review* 72 (1978): 135-50; and Shanley, "Marriage Contact" ["Marriage Contract and Social Contract"], 87-91.

27. Carole Pateman, *The Sexual Contract* (Stanford: Stanford University Press, 1988), 3.

28. Susan Moller Okin, *Justice, Gender and the Family* (New York: Basic Books, 1989), chaps. 7 and 8; Pateman, chaps. 1, 6, 7 and 8.

William A. Cohen (essay date spring 1995)

SOURCE: Cohen, William A. "Trollope's Trollop." *Novel: A Forum on Fiction* 28, no. 3 (spring 1995): 235-56.

[*In the following essay, Cohen evaluates Trollope's novel* The Eustace Diamonds, *concentrating on its symbolic use of jewels to depict sexuality and the sexual differences between men and women.*]

> When a woman thinks that her house is on fire, her instinct is at once to rush to the thing which she values most. It is a perfectly overpowering impulse, and I have more than once taken advantage of it. . . . A married woman grabs at her baby—an unmarried one reaches for her jewel box.
>
> Sherlock Holmes, in "A Scandal in Bohemia" (Conan Doyle 12)

> [O]n that day she wore at her waist . . . a small reticule of a shape which had just come into fashion; and, as she lay on the sofa and talked, she kept playing with it—opening it, putting a finger into it, shutting it again, and so on.
>
> Sigmund Freud, *Dora: An Analysis of a Case of Hysteria* (94)

I.

Though it hardly seems to warrant the scrupulous attention of detectives as eminent as Holmes and Freud, the symbolic substitution of female genitals with receptacles for valuables nonetheless requires constant proof. Of course Dora's fingering her reticule signifies her desire to masturbate; and yet, of course, this interpretation can in no way be substantiated.[1] The concatenation of the glaringly obvious with the strictly unverifiable points at once in two directions: toward the sexual and toward the literary. First, not simply as the record of sexual censorship but as an active agent of it, this combination signals the particular linguistic status of sexuality in the late nineteenth century. Perhaps because of his critical attitude toward its repression, Freud could describe the situation of sexual signification so astutely: "He that has eyes to see and ears to hear may convince himself that no mortal can keep a secret. If his lips are silent, he chatters with his finger-tips; betrayal oozes out of him at every pore" (96). As if reflexively to corroborate the point, at the very moment he seeks to prove the unprovable meaning of the reticule, Freud's unctuous and purulent diction divulges—embarrassingly, but for that, no more verifiably—its own erotic investment in extricating others' secrets. Second, long before the theorization of an unconscious whose continual censorship serves continually to betray it, nineteenth-century literary texts had been the repository for the obvious-and-yet-unprovable symbol. The Victorian imagination of the literary, that is to say, is thoroughly vested in this particular brand of ambiguity, which I want to call the unspeakable.

Sexual unspeakability generates linguistic cruxes that lavishly draw attention to themselves, though they never repay that attention with self-disclosure. A vivid instance of the specifically linguistic compensations sponsored by sexual subjects arises in the principal entry under which a nineteenth-century slang dictionary lists the terms for female genitals: *monosyllable* (or, alternately, "the divine monosyllable" [Farmer [*A Dictionary of Slang*] 4: 336-45]).[2] In elevating this particular term to the lexicon's main heading for twelve hundred slang synonyms, the compiler pays a strange kind of tribute to the censorship that necessitated production of such a dictionary in the first place. Frankly euphemistic in its identification of the subject, the dictionary anticipates Freud's self-canceling insistence that he does not hesitate to "call bodily organs and processes by their technical names. . . . *J'appelle un chat un chat*" (65). In both cases, the expletive is occluded in the process of being explicated. The very effort to give a name to the subject constitutes it as unspeakable, for it draws attention to the materiality of the term under erasure, in the one case by referring to the apparently irrelevant quantity of its syllables, in the other by translating its "technical name" into a foreign tongue. Such a paradoxical linguistic occasion, I am suggesting, is one that, when writ large in the novel, contributes to the production of the literary itself.

Anthony Trollope's novel ***The Eustace Diamonds*** (1871-72) supplies an especially remunerative instance of such signification, not only because it encodes sexuality in relatively overt ways, but because its central figure—the eponymous jewels—reveals a great deal about the representation of sexuality *in addition* to the imperative to keep it silent. The jewels, that is to say, are so suggestive that, even as they stand in for sexual meanings, they make use of the opportunities availed by unspeakability and lend their own status as objects of monetary value back to sexuality. The gems at once metaphorize sexuality and literalize the economics of sexual difference.

In using the diamonds to render explicit the putative differences between male and female property, the novel relies on a distinction between two conflicting accounts of their legal status: one, which takes them to have a price determined in the marketplace, and the other, which values them according to absolute, immutable standards. The clash between these two paradigms pertains not only to the struggle, depicted in the novel's plot, of a widow to retain her property, however; it pervades the story as a whole through a conjoined conflict of values in regard to the very source of the narrative's authority. For the novel is everywhere concerned to establish a basis for its own authority, and this account is itself split between, on the one hand, an entitlement derived from an imaginary market in public opinion and, on the other, an appeal on the part of the narrator to precisely the sort of external authority that would seem to oppose the capricious sentiments of a public audience. The property contest over the jewels thus analogizes—and has serious consequences for—Trollope's imagination of his own license to produce works of literary art. The symbolic artifact that announces even as it effaces its sexualization—the diamonds—provides the novel extraordinary opportunities to reflect on that nineteenth-century project of generating texts whose demurrals and evasions appear most literary precisely when they are most sexual.

II.

Even if one did not entirely concur with the character in *The Eustace Diamonds* who calls the novel's protagonist, Lizzie Eustace, "false, dishonest, heartless, cruel, irreligious, ungrateful, mean, ignorant, greedy, and vile" (1: 311), one would probably still be suspicious of her. A general odor of iniquity envelops Lizzie, and for most of the novel this malevolence expresses itself in her refusal to cede the family jewels to her late husband's estate. Lizzie insists that the £10,000 worth of diamonds are her own, and just when the scandal of her possessing them seems in danger of flagging, the stakes in the property contest are raised: first, by the theft from Lizzie's hotel room in Carlisle of the iron box in which her jewels are supposed to be encased (and her actual, secret retention of them), and second, by the subsequent theft of the diamonds themselves from her lodgings in London. The novel focuses so pointedly both on this object of vast monetary and symbolic value and on its container that our first order of business, as Trollope might say, is to dispense with the diamonds and their box.

Like the women whom Freud and Holmes describe, Lizzie Eustace pays her jewel box an extravagant amount of attention. In order to safeguard the gems her husband presented to her, she orders an iron box on her own initiative; in its synecdochal relation to its precious contents, the box itself becomes a thing of value and accrues a potent sexual charge. Following Freud, we can indicate the (utterly conventional) genital attributes of the high-profile jewel box, here displaced downward:

> [T]hey were like a load upon her chest, a load as heavy as though she were compelled to sit with the iron box on her lap day and night. In her sobbing she felt the thing under her feet, and knew that she could not get rid of it. She hated the box, and yet she must cling to it now. She was thoroughly ashamed of the box, and yet she must seem to take a pride in it. She was horribly afraid of the box, and yet she must keep it in her own very bed-room.
>
> (1: 187-88)[3]

According to an elementary substitutive logic, the box is thus suggestive of female genitals. Its function as a repository for patrilineal property, moreover, augments

its appropriateness as a figure for female sexuality, whose traditional purpose is to transfer property between men of different generations. The contents of the box, the family jewels, in turn designate the supposedly scarce resource of reproductive male sexuality, materialized in the seat of spermatic production: the testes. Insinuating the testicular referent between two of its principal symbolic containers, one of Lizzie's suitors, Lord George de Bruce Carruthers, establishes the metaphoric utility of speaking of jewels as nuts: "You had got the kernel yourself, and thought that I had taken all the trouble to crack the nut and had found myself with nothing but the shell. Then, when you found you couldn't eat the kernel; that you couldn't get rid of the swag without assistance, you came to me to help you" (2: 326). If the jewels thus signify the male contribution to procreation, they also represent the uneasy dependence of patriarchy upon a female vessel to pass along wealth.

To a first glance, which aligns inanimate objects with human reproductive organs, jewels metaphorize the male genitals just as the box does the female. But such symbolic suggestions can sustain a literary interest only so long as they resist becoming ossified. Staying for the moment in the symbolic register, we note that Trollope's representation of female sexuality extends beyond the box itself: through its proximity to Lizzie's body, the protective contrivance suggests the metonymic relation of the diamonds and all their trappings to her sexual prowess—and to the false modesty in which she envelops her rather voracious charms.

> "Heaven and earth! To suppose that I should ever keep them under less than seven keys, and that there should be any of the locks that anybody should be able to open except myself!"
>
> "And where are the seven keys?" asked Frank.
>
> "Next to my heart," said Lizzie, putting her hand on her left side. "And when I sleep they are always tied round my neck in a bag, and the bag never escapes from my grasp. And I have such a knife under my pillow, ready for Mr. Camperdown, should he come to seize them!" Then she ran out of the room, and in a couple of minutes returned with the necklace, hanging loose in her hand. It was part of her little play to show by her speed that the close locking of the jewels was a joke, and that the ornament, precious as it was, received at her hands no other treatment than might any indifferent feminine bauble.
>
> (1: 285)

If in this case the keys touch Lizzie's skin, it does not take much reflection to recognize that, when the diamonds themselves arrive, their metonymic rubbing up against her body also signifies sexually: "I ain't noways sure as she ain't got them very diamonds themselves locked up, or, perhaps, tied round her person" (2: 91), suggests a policeman; and her confidant, Lord George, reassures her, "They would never ask to search your person. . . . Keep them in your pocket while you are in the house during the day. They will hardly bring a woman with them to search you" (2: 106). The safest bet, as any latter-day drug smuggler could affirm, is to encase contraband goods within a bodily "pocket," and thereby evade any but the most invasive personal search.

The jewels' metaphoric relation to male sexuality thus slides—by virtue of their always adorning women—into a metonymic representation of female sexuality as well. Female governance of the male-inflected jewels extends from the protective custody of the box to the very display upon the body, as though to render explicit the question of whether the woman possesses the necklace or the necklace (like a choker) possesses the woman. In appropriating the gems as her own property, Lizzie does not simply exhibit female self-assertiveness but enacts a wholesale symbolic revaluation of jewels themselves. The story forms an erotic drama of protecting, transporting, concealing, and revealing the necklace, and in every case its extraordinary value (never its beauty) is what fascinates the characters. In order to assert her rights to the property, Lizzie boldly wears it out in public:

> *Lady Glencora's rooms were already very full when Lizzie entered them, but she was without a gentleman, and room was made for her to pass quickly up the stairs. The diamonds had been recognised by many before she had reached the drawing-room;—not that these very diamonds were known, or that there was a special memory for that necklace;—but the subject had been so generally discussed, that the blaze of the stones immediately brought it to the minds of men and women.*
>
> (1: 158)

The public interest evinced in Lizzie's neck is matched by her private obsession with the security of her valuables—a concern that, once compounded by her retaining the jewels after claiming they have been stolen, blurs into a sexualized secret: "She could not keep herself from unlocking her desk and looking at it twenty times a day, although she knew the peril of such nervous solicitude. . . . And then she was aware of a morbid desire on her own part to tell the secret,—of a desire that amounted almost to a disease" (2: 80-81).

Lizzie's propensity for bibelots long antedates her acquisition of the Eustace diamonds, as does the association of her sexuality with jewelry. In the novel's first paragraph we learn that, "when she was little more than a child, [she] went about everywhere with jewels on her fingers, and red gems hanging round her neck, and yellow gems pendent from her ears, and white gems shining in her black hair" (1: 2). This prepossessing child's acquisitive instinct is coterminous with her sexual precocity: she knows how to use her bejewelled charms to

ensnare a wealthy husband—Sir Florian Eustace, who repays the pawn brokers for the gems she took out on credit even before he unwittingly bestows his family diamonds upon her. Assimilating Lizzie's jewelry to the more general blush of her sex appeal, the narrator notes, "[I]t was true that Sir Florian was at her feet; and that by a proper use of her various charms,—the pawned jewels included,—she might bring him to an offer" (1: 4). Through the circulation of credit that follows the path of her own circulation between men, Lizzie pawns the jewels that her father gave her in order to amass the funds necessary for acquiring a husband; she then craftily retrieves the jewels, in order to charm the young man, on the promise that her (as yet unaffianced) suitor will redeem them.

In addition to the connections I have adduced between the jewels and Lizzie's sexuality, a final link ensures the impossibility of disentangling the two. The narrative tracks Lizzie's criminal possession of the diamonds, and while this scandal for a long time bears a faint aroma of impropriety, the sexual aspect of her case eventually becomes overwhelming. The switchpoint between the property question and the sexual one arises in the plot of Lizzie's engagement to Lord Fawn, who cannot decide which scenario will be more shameful: marrying a woman whose reputation has been damaged by the accusation that she illegally possesses another man's family jewels, or withdrawing from an engagement that has been publicly announced. Fawn's sister, Mrs. Hittaway, raises the moral stakes by exposing Lizzie's indiscreet flirtation with Frank Greystock, her cousin and possible paramour; she is now openly accused of the whorishness that was previously only implied:

> Then had come Mrs. Hittaway's evidence as to Lizzie's wicked doings down in Scotland. . . . And that which had been at first, as it were, added to the diamonds, as a supplementary weight thrown into the scale, so that Lizzie's iniquities might bring her absolutely to the ground, had gradually assumed the position of being the first charge against her. Lady Fawn had felt no aversion to discussing the diamonds. . . . It was well that the fact should be known, so that everybody might be aware that her son was doing right in refusing to marry so wicked a lady. But when the other thing was added to it; when the story was told of what Mr. Gowran had seen among the rocks, and when gradually that became the special crime which was to justify her son in dropping the lady's acquaintance, then Lady Fawn became very unhappy, and found the subject to be, as Mrs. Hittaway had described it, very distasteful.
>
> (2: 179-80)

The sexual connotations hovering around the theft solidify into denotation, and the two crimes are yoked together under the rubric of scandal with as little concern for accuracy as is usual in such matters. The collapse of the two scandals into one is realized in the simple substitution, through Lady Fawn's imagination, of the sexual indiscretion that "Mr. Gowran had seen among the rocks" for Lizzie's misconduct with those other rocks, the diamonds. Sexual unspeakability germinates in the interstices between her crimes as a generalized and unspecifiable sense that "'Lizzie,' as she was not uncommonly called by people who had hardly ever seen her,—had something amiss with it all. 'I don't know where it is she's lame,' said that very clever man . . . 'but she don't go flat all round'" (1: 153).

We have seen how, by means of symbolic substitution, the diamond necklace represents forms of sexuality that would otherwise be inarticulable. Yet the necklace's status as an authentic repository of monetary value ensures that it functions not only as a symbol. For this lapidary emblem allows the heterosexual contract to be conceived in literal financial terms, manifesting, as it does, the economic realities of the Victorian marriage market. I now want to suggest that in the text's economy, this sexualized and gendered property vacillates between two opposing paradigms—one, which conforms to a model of commodity exchange, the other, which appears to resist it. The story distinguishes between these two property formations through the competing legal definitions ascribed to the jewels. The judicial question that preoccupies the characters throughout the novel is whether the diamonds constitute an "heirloom"—and therefore belong to the scion of the Eustace estate, Lizzie's son—or whether they are separable and exchangeable property, which can be given as a gift and which Lizzie could therefore retain as "paraphernalia." The learned barrister, Mr. Dove, supplies the opinion that a diamond necklace cannot be an heirloom because there is no guarantee that it will be "maintained in its original form":

> [It] is not only alterable, but constantly altered, and cannot easily be traced. . . . Heirlooms have become so, not that the future owners of them may be assured of so much wealth, whatever the value of the thing so settled may be,—but that the son or grandson or descendant may enjoy the satisfaction which is derived from saying, my father or my grandfather or my ancestor sat in that chair, or looked as he now looks in that picture, or was graced by wearing on his breast that very ornament which you now see lying beneath the glass.
>
> (1: 258-59)

Heirlooms, by this reasoning, preserve value through their originality and constancy, and lie outside an exchange economy; they are quintessentially male property, since they belong to the estate and are conveyed by primogeniture. Paraphernalia, on the other hand, is property belonging to a married woman exclusive of what her husband appropriates from her (her dowry); up until 1870, paraphernalia was virtually the only property a married woman possessed, and could dispose of, as her own.[4] Though Dove is uncertain whether the court would actually deem the jewels paraphernalia (that is, Lizzie's exclusive property), he is persuaded that the necklace *cannot* be an heirloom because it is mutable and divisible, and because its value therefore subsists in its potential for exchange. He does, however, argue that even if the jewels were considered "paraphernalia belonging to her station," Lizzie would still be "debarred from selling" them because of their extraordinary value (1: 228-29). Although the assurance that Lizzie will be prevented from cashing in the jewels should comfort the Eustace family attorney, Mr. Camperdown, he justifiably persists in fearing she will sell them: "Were she once to get hold of that word, paraphernalia, it would be as a tower of strength to her. . . . He was as certain as ever that the woman was robbing the estate which it was his duty to guard, and that should he cease to be active in the matter, the necklace would be broken up and the property sold and scattered before a year was out, and then the woman would have got the better of him!" (1: 231).

For the purposes of the Eustace estate, it would be far preferable to have the jewels adjudged an heirloom, and everyone in the novel (except Dove) is incredulous that they cannot be: "A pot or a pan might be an heirloom, but not a necklace! Mr. Camperdown could hardly bring himself to believe that this was law. And then as to paraphernalia! Up to this moment, though he had been called upon to arrange great dealings in reference to widows, he had never as yet heard of a claim made by a widow for paraphernalia" (1: 254). Camperdown's logic betrays the following contradiction: the only reason he wants the jewels treated as heirlooms—and thus excluded from an exchange economy—is because their worth, as determined by the market in diamonds, is so great. The official distinction, then, between the two types of property—that the worth of paraphernalia, like any commodity, is determined in the marketplace, and the value of an heirloom derives from its traditional associations and its immutability—is, in practice, undermined. On the one hand, the only heirloom worth designating as such is one with a high commodity valuation. On the other, Lizzie's original claim (however disingenuous) to possession of the diamonds as paraphernalia—that her late husband gave them to her as a sign of his affection—itself prevents her from selling them, since it effectively revalues them *as* heirlooms (that is, property whose value lies in its familial and chivalric associations). Despite her legal right to redeem them, the enormous symbolic value of the diamonds as expropriated patrilineal property thus virtually precludes the possibility of her doing so: "[S]he could not bring herself to let them out of her own hands. Ten thousand pounds! If she could only sell them and get the money, from what a world of trouble would she be relieved. And the sale, for another reason, would have been convenient; for Lady Eustace was already a little in debt. But she could not sell them, and therefore when she got into the carriage there was the box under her feet" (1: 185).

Although the terms of this opposition seem to break down, the plot nonetheless depends upon the appearance of a stable distinction in order for the property battle to be meaningful. Since, as I have suggested, the novel inextricably binds up the story of the diamonds with female sexuality, we can now ask what the status of the jewels has to teach us about the economy of gender relations. In other words, if the legal issue is whether jewels accord with or resist a model of commodity valuation, can the same be said of female sexual property? According to the paraphernalia model, women retain possession of their sexual goods and simply retail them to the highest bidder. Lizzie clearly conforms to this paradigm, even though she has several incommensurable markets in which to consider her prospects: wealth (Sir Florian), respectability (Lord Fawn), and sentiment (Frank Greystock). That she ends up with the odious Mr. Emilius simply suggests how little her worth has come to by the end of the story. If it were not clear enough from Trollope, the terms of Sherlock Holmes's formulation would indicate just how unnatural Lizzie's sexuality is (thanks to the diamonds) felt to be: she confounds Holmes's conventional morality since she reaches for her jewels, not her baby, when she is in danger. Acting like a single woman who knows the value of her sexual goods, the widow Lizzie finally makes those goods valueless precisely by putting them in circulation.

Lizzie thus serves as a negative exemplar, as the narrator's frankly hostile presentation of her suggests: "There shall be no whitewashing of Lizzie Eustace. She was abominable" (1: 321). She disturbs patriarchal institutions both through her recognition of her function within that order—as a vehicle for the transfer of property between her husband and her son—and through her attempt to subvert that process. The novel, however, also subscribes to a fantasy of female sexuality according to the heirloom pattern, embodied in its domestic heroine, Lucy Morris. Despite extraordinary tortures of doubt and discouragement, Lucy sustains her love for Frank Greystock; and by setting her in heavily underscored counterpoint to Lizzie, Trollope affirms the latter's status as a whore with respect to both jewels and men. To use Dove's words, Lucy's heart is steadfastly "maintained in its original form," while Lizzie's desire (as the long succession of her lovers indicates) "is not only alterable, but constantly altered." Jewels once again both metaphorize and literalize female worth, now serving the broad strokes of the contrast between the two women. In figurative terms, the formulation is quite simple: "Lucy held her ground because she was real. You may knock about a diamond, and not even scratch

it; whereas paste in rough usage betrays itself. Lizzie, with all her self-assuring protestations, knew that she was paste, and knew that Lucy was real stone" (2: 230). Literally speaking, Lucy supplies an ornament of genuine sentimental worth, as Frank informs Lizzie:

> "If you were to attempt to sell the diamonds they would stop you, and would not give you credit for the generous purpose afterwards."
>
> "They wouldn't stop you if you sold the ring you wear." The ring had been given to him by Lucy, after their engagement, and was the only present she had ever made him. It had been purchased out of her own earnings, and had been put on his finger by her own hand. . . . "Let me look at the ring," she said. . . . "What is the price?" she asked.
>
> "It is not in the market, Lizzie. Nor should your diamonds be there."
>
> (1: 283)

By contrast with Lizzie's diamonds, Lucy's ring has a worth—its affectional symbolism—far in excess of its strict market price. Since it has little monetary value, Lucy's jewelry ironically serves as a much better demonstration of heirloom economics than Lizzie's, whose contradictory status (an heirloom prized for its pecuniary worth) it thus exposes. Finally, the metaphoric and literal distinctions between the two women converge on a single jewel—the hundred-guinea brooch with which Lizzie attempts to bribe Lucy (1: 141). In offering her the bauble, Lizzie tries to infect Lucy with an imagination of both jewels and feminine wiles as commodities, an idea so anathema to the pristine governess that she rebuffs her former friend altogether.

The evidence for this bipolar construction of femininity is so overwhelming that it cannot but seem suspicious. It should therefore come as no surprise that, although the narrative superficially posits the opposition as the organizing principle in its representation of women, Lizzie and Lucy simply compose two sides of the same coin. The presentation of the two women taken together elucidates the ideology that directs women to imagine their desires on the heirloom model and yet treats them as commodities, condemning them when they seek to govern their own value in the exchange economy in which they really do circulate. Frank Greystock's classic romantic bind epitomizes this conundrum: his career demands a wealthy wife while his desire aims at the pure girl with no property. In the collapse of the literal and metaphorical aspects of Lucy-as-jewel, the economics of the marriage plot become clear to Frank: "There was no doubt about Lucy being as good as gold;—only that real gold, vile as it is, was the one thing that Frank so much needed" (1: 276).[5]

The gross binarism of the Lucy/Lizzie relation announces itself not only in the symbolism of their reciprocal relation to jewels, but also in the proto-Barthesian phonetic distinction between their given names. As with the jewels, the text again transcends the simple opposition, now through the complex phonemic interrelation of their full names: Lucy Morris and Lizzie Eustace. The sibilant placidity of Lucy's "uc" converges on the first syllable of Lizzie's married surname, while the brazen buzzing of Lizzie's "iz" almost—but does not quite—terminate Lucy's maiden name. Indeed, the failure of "Lucy Mor*ris*" to voice the final consonant and thus incorporate "Lizzie"—by analogy with the capacity of "Lizzie *Eus*tace" to assimilate "Lucy"—suggests the breakdown of the symmetry just where one might expect it to be secured. The non-complementarity of the characters' nomenclature belies the simple opposition between them. If this seems an excessive amount of attention to pay to proper names, it need merely be pointed out that their significance has the same status as that of the sexual connotations attaching to jewel boxes: their obviousness makes them appear unnoteworthy even as their meaning is strictly unprovable.

A genuine difference in the representation of female sexuality arises more pointedly midway through the novel, with that female figure apparently midway between Lizzie and Lucy: she is called Lucinda. The introduction of Lucinda both augments and muddles the embodiment of characterological distinctions in nominal ones. Just as her name begins like Lucy's, she too arrives as a penurious but highly marriageable young woman with a certain charm; but Lucinda rapidly veers away from the sentimentalized domesticity to which Lucy accedes—though not by the same route as Lizzie. While Lizzie's proto-feminist independence patently shores up the patriarchy it resists, Lucinda's hysterical refusal of heterosexual conformity is so pathological as to exceed the very norms that structure both Lucy's submission and Lizzie's rebellion. At first, her mediating role appears as if it may simply reinforce, rather than challenge, the Lizzie/Lucy binary:

> [I]t had seemed to her that all the men who came near her were men whom she could not fail to dislike. She was hurried here and hurried there, and knew nothing of real social intimacies. As she told her aunt in her wickedness, she would almost have preferred a shoemaker,—if she could have become acquainted with a shoemaker in a manner that should be unforced and genuine. There was a savageness of antipathy in her to the mode of life which her circumstances had produced for her.
>
> (2: 4)

The fantasy common to Lucy, Lizzie, and the ideology of the narrative as a whole—that a poor marriage is always and only a loving one, a rich marriage always and only mercenary—clearly organizes Lucinda's romantic imagination too. But Lucinda's history represents a fundamental break with the novel's other versions of female sexuality—a break with the romantic imagination

itself. At first, she conforms to conventions of the *femme fatale* (she is compared to Cleopatra and the French murderess Brinvilliers); her potential suitors, "so used to softness and flattery from women," are said to "have learned to think that a woman silent, arrogant, and hard of approach, must be always meditating murder" (1: 330). Her contemptuous hostility is soon turned inward until (like a forebear of Hardy's Sue Bridehead), in her frigid mortification, she refuses to put herself in circulation at all. After the first kiss from her fiancé: "Never before had she been thus polluted. The embrace had disgusted her. It made her odious to herself. . . . For the sake of this man who was to be her husband, she hated all men" (2: 24); and on her wedding day: "I will never trust myself alone in his presence. I could not do it. When he touches me my whole body is in agony. To be kissed by him is madness" (2: 273). Though she imagines at first that Sir Griffin Tewett is simply the wrong man, she ends by rejecting the whole of his sex: "I don't think I could feel to any man as though I loved him" (2: 273). Lucinda's frank repugnance for male sexuality, and for all the obligations of marriage, poses an alternative—however psychotic in its depiction—to the heterosexual order that organizes the other women's desire. Her refusal of heterosexuality can only be portrayed as a frigid lack of desire, as against Lizzie's candid libidinousness and Lucy's more respectable (but no less fierce) devotion to her man.[6]

Lucinda's aborted engagement makes for a scandal in miniature, as the plaint of her guardian, Mrs. Carbuncle, makes clear: "Oh, Lucinda, this is the unkindest and the wickedest, and the most horrible thing that anybody ever did! I shall never, never be able to hold up my head again" (2: 277). This scandal both corresponds to and revises the drama that Lizzie enacts on the novel's main stage. As in Lizzie's case, sexual misconduct aligns with property difficulties: the relation of Lucinda's frigidity to her poverty parallels that of Lizzie's nymphomania to her ill-gotten wealth. As in Lizzie's case, also, the scandal makes it unclear whether sexuality propels the other issues or masks them—whether, that is to say, Lucinda's sexual crisis is the cause or the effect of her sensational refusal to go through with the marriage. By virtue of this ambiguity, the story insinuates sexual meanings precisely by promoting their unspeakability.

If the novel's principal technique for encoding women's sexuality consists in the representation of female property, what property formation does the text attribute to Lucinda? The term associated most closely with her plight is *tribute,* the title of the chapter in which Mrs. Carbuncle exacts expensive wedding gifts for Lucinda from everyone she knows.

> The presents to be made to Lucinda were very much thought of in Hertford Street at this time, and Lizzie . . . did all she could to assist the collection of tribute.

It was quite understood that as a girl can only be married once . . . everything should be done to gather toll from the tax-payers of society. It was quite fair on such an occasion that men should be given to understand that something worth having was expected.

(2: 232)

Unlike the heirloom, this "toll" is mutable and exchangeable, but unlike paraphernalia, its female possessor has little to say about its disposition; it is both uninheritable and unregenerate property, which simply goes to pay off the accumulated debt of the impoverished women. Indeed, the ultimate fate of all this tribute indicates the dead end to which such property relations lead—not nuptial bliss, but merely remunerated creditors:

> It was rumoured that Mrs. Carbuncle, with her niece, had gone to join her husband at New York. At any rate, she disappeared altogether from London, leaving behind her an amount of debts which showed how extremely liberal in their dealings the great tradesmen of London will occasionally be. . . . One account, however, she had honestly settled. The hotel-keeper in Albemarle Street had been paid, and all the tribute had been packed and carried off from the scene of the proposed wedding banquet.

(2: 359)

As the stolen diamond necklace parallels Lizzie's story, and the sentimental ring Lucy's, so the fifty-pound silver service (and £150 cash), which Mrs. Carbuncle extorts from Lizzie on behalf of her niece, both bespeaks and silences Lucinda's sexuality.

The correlation between women's sexuality and objects of material value thus extends across the representation of female characters in the novel. The mobile symbolism of the jewels in particular makes manifest the economic relations that organize sexual difference in Victorian England—both the difference between men and women and differences within the imagination of female sexuality. The exigency, I have suggested, of portraying sexuality in mitigated and deflected form itself affords certain literary opportunities. The compulsion for encoding indicates the unspeakability of what is covered, while the transparency of the code suggests how manageable literature has nonetheless made it. The ideological incitement to such displacement, in the case of *The Eustace Diamonds,* lies in the simultaneous imperative and refusal to acknowledge the relationship between female sexuality and property. But when, as we will shortly see, a male author identifies himself in certain conspicuous ways with a cannily sexual woman, we have to ask whether the status of his own property—his literary work—is equally divided between the two models, heirloom and paraphernalia, on which the woman-as-jewel is constructed.

III.

The distinction between a text's fabricated author-function and its narrator enables us to locate a peculiar identification between the former—call it "Trollope"—and the story's protagonist. As if to complement or compensate for the narrator's contemptuous antipathy toward Lizzie, the author behind the narrator exhibits an uncanny likeness to her. From at least the evidence of the Lizzie/Lucy opposition, we know that names are scarcely coincidental in this work, and there is no reason to think that the common meaning of the author's proper name is lost upon the text: "trollop," a strumpet or harlot, clearly identifies the novel's anti-heroine, though the word is never used explicitly in reference to her.

It is by means of a term that encapsulates Lizzie's chief characteristics—her avarice and her lubricity—that the author nominally identifies himself with her. But is the connection merely onomastic, or do these attributes apply as aptly to the author as to the character? Is there also an analogy, that is to say, between the forms of property—authorial commodities and female sexual goods—according to which each "trollop" is defined?[7] One place to begin looking for an answer to this question is the text in which "Trollope," as a purveyor of literary properties, is most fully realized: the *Autobiography* (1883). In this work, the author in fact imagines his literary manuscripts to be his own jewels, which, as he attests, he had a habit of keeping locked up in an iron box at just the period during which he wrote *The Eustace Diamonds.* Before embarking on an eighteenth-months' sojourn in Australia, for instance, Trollope arranges the publication of works while he is away:

> I . . . left in the hands of the editor of *The Fortnightly,* ready for production on the 1st of July following, a story called *The Eustace Diamonds.* . . . I also left behind, in a strong box, the manuscript of *Phineas Redux* . . . [and,] in the same strong box, another novel, called *An Eye for an Eye,* which then had been some time written, and of which, as it has not even yet [in 1876] been published, I will not further speak. It will probably be published some day, though, looking forward, I can see no room for it, at any rate, for the next two years.
>
> If therefore The Great Britain, in which we sailed for Melbourne, had gone to the bottom, I had so provided that there would be new novels ready to come out under my name for some years to come.

(343-45)

While explicitly subordinating his work to his name, Trollope implicitly draws an analogy between his authorial labors and Lizzie's work at maintaining possession of the diamonds: like her, he circulates his valuables in a competitive marketplace, holding out for the highest bidder and reserving his merchandise in a strong box until the market can bear it.[8]

Also like his character's, the author's allegiances are divided between a self-professed desire for profit and self-aggrandizing claims for the moral authenticity of his production. The figurative congruence between literary property and female jewels suggests that both the novelist and the protagonist advertise themselves according to the heirloom model—his motivation is moral improvement through art, hers is affection—while their monetary incentives indicate that they function like paraphernalia. What the representation of women and jewels in *The Eustace Diamonds* has taught us to recognize, however, is that the ostensive antagonism between these two economic modes masks an underlying collusion. Verbal art and sexual desire are no less authentic for being marketed, that is to say, but neither are they worth more for being real.

Though the two models of female sexuality appeared chasmally divided under our initial analytic rubric, they finally showed themselves to be fundamentally confederate. And just as with the woman-as-jewel, so too with the novel-as-commodity. Even at the moment of its inception, in fact, the distinction between the two basic types of property (heirloom and paraphernalia) seems already to have collapsed. On the one hand, despite being foremost among major Victorian novelists to conceive of himself as a workman producing literary commodities for the market,[9] Trollope subscribes at least minimally to a Romantic ideology of original authorship: "I think that an author, when he uses either the words or the plot of another, should own as much, demanding to be credited with no more of the work than he has himself produced. I may say also that I have never printed as my own a word that has been written by others" (116). This valuation of work, which, in its indivisible integrity, belongs exclusively to its author, comports with a model of literature as heirloom. On the other hand, however, at precisely the moment that Trollope explicitly articulates the paraphernalia/heirloom distinction in the novel—that is, in the account of Dove's legal opinion—this claim on behalf of immutable authorial property falls apart around him. The rendition of Dove's opinion is unique in Trollope's literary output, he states in the *Autobiography,* as the sole case of his publishing someone else's material under his own name. In a footnote to the passage just quoted, he writes: "I must make one exception to this declaration. The legal opinion as to heirlooms in *The Eustace Diamonds* was written for me by Charles Merewether, the present Member for Northampton. I am told that it has become the ruling authority on the subject" (116).[10] Trollope appropriates Merewether's words without acknowledging their authorship, taking writing as one more exchangeable, changeable commodity whose worth is determined not by its originality but by the value that can be derived from it in the literary marketplace. In treating as paraphernalia the very passage that differentiates between forms of property, and then, in

his posthumously published *Autobiography,* renouncing such use of the passage in favor of an ideology of literature as heirloom, Trollope has it both ways with the distinction even in the course of proposing it.

The analogy between the novelist's property and the character's thus holds: divided by the terms of a putative difference and then reconsolidated, both sorts of assets are secured all the more firmly in both the heirloom and the paraphernalia models for value. We can now understand this bifurcated account, of how worth is assigned to property, to extend to one other arena as well: to the scandal narrative that composes the text. This less material but no less consequential realm of value—truth value—supplies the very medium through which the novel makes its assertions about other kinds of property. And just as lapidary and literary commodities are defined simultaneously in market-valued and extra-market terms, so is the narrative ground on which the novel establishes the validity of its own avowals. While the definition of female capital in the novel's plot takes shape through a dispute over *legal* authority, however, the material that constitutes the novel is organized around a parallel conflict over *narrative* authority. This epistemology of the novel determines the means by which information about sexuality, as both vehicle and tenor of the economic metaphors, is simultaneously conveyed and held back—in short, the means by which it is rendered unspeakable.

Within the novel's plot, assertions about the truth of things seem to derive entirely from what people—"the public"—believe them to be. Lizzie Eustace's scandal, for instance, accrues all the public attention of a case which it actually is not—a sex scandal—but which everyone in the novel wills it to be (and which, *a fortiori,* it eventually becomes). Lizzie herself recognizes that scandal concerns illegal or immoral private behavior far less than it does public perceptions of the case, and she regularly employs the rumor machine to achieve her purposes.[11] When Camperdown attempts to take the jewels from her in Mount Street, for example, Lizzie's problem is less the material one of losing her property than the *réclame* of exposure before everyone: "Hitherto there had been some secrecy, or at any rate some privacy attached to the matter; but now that odious lawyer had discussed the matter aloud, in the very streets, in the presence of the servants, and Lady Eustace had felt that it was discussed also by every porter on the railway from London down to Troon" (1: 189). While the audience from which Lizzie wishes to shield herself in this instance is altogether plebeian, she eventually takes to parading her drama before the public that composes high society, for the latter will defend her better than any lawyer can. The elite audience too is indifferent to truth, desiring only a scoop ("Upon the whole, the little mystery is quite delightful. . . . Nobody now cares for anything except the Eustace diamonds" [2:

72], writes Barrington Erle) or a fashion tip ("'Nobody will dare to wear a diamond at all next season,' said Lady Glencora" [2: 73]). Though fully realized as characters elsewhere in the Palliser series, the denizens of Matching Priory function in this novel merely as embodiments of "the world," engrossed by scandal sheets and eager to correspond with one another about Lizzie's tribulations.[12]

The novel depicts a world in which social values seem wholly determined by a scandal economy: devoid of political, moral, or even legal standards, the ethics of any action are entirely articulated upon its social reception, upon how public opinion comes down (or, what amounts to the same thing, how it is imagined to do) on questions of conduct. In this arena of competing individual interests, opinions function in a marketplace much like the system in which, as we have seen, Lizzie merchandises her sexual goods. Hence the phantasmatic entity of the general public behaves not only, according to a theatrical metaphor, as an audience for the scandal's drama, but also, according to an economic one, as the consumer of news. The public is a consumer not merely in the sense that it purchases newspapers and retails gossip, but also in the sense that it composes the customers of the market in opinion: public confidence in a particular position (say, Lizzie's rights to the jewels) enhances its value as against another (say, Fawn's justification in withdrawing from the engagement). Like today's public opinion polls, which inherit this impulse to calibrate social attitudes, the novel quantifies audience response as if on an affective barometer: "since the two robberies, public opinion had veered round three or four points in Lizzie's favour, and people were beginning to say that she had been ill-used" (2: 179).[13]

The Eustace Diamonds affirms that the significance of an event hinges upon the consensus of the public that judges it; such judgments cannot be referred to a higher authority, and the social institutions intended to regulate conduct (the courts, the Church, Parliament) must wait upon the tide of an imagined public opinion. Even Lady Eustace regards herself as a spectacle to evaluate, for she has trouble distinguishing herself as object of the public's scrutiny from its subject position. She "was upon the whole disposed to think as everybody thought" (2: 209), and when she attempts to confess her crime to her cousin, "she told him the whole story;—not the true story, but the story as it was believed by all the world. She found it to be impossible to tell him the true story" (2: 53). Lizzie is as prone to believing the fictions upon which public opinion is founded as everyone else— even when she is the subject presumed to know the truth distorted by those opinions.

Though the plot has convinced us that the truth of a story is entirely contingent upon the public's feelings about it, we will, by now, be suspicious of any assign-

ment of value that appears driven solely by the market. This last quotation itself begins to suggest an alternate current of belief that runs throughout the novel: namely, that such a thing as "the true story" exists objectively, and that the narrator has access to it. Indeed, even if, as I have been arguing, for the purposes of the plot, truth is imagined as a mutable social construction dependent on opinion, for the purposes of the enclosing narrative, such truth is understood to be absolute and determinable. The novel, that is to say, accommodates two conflicting models of truth-construction, one roughly identified with the plot, the other with the narrative voice. These paired models recapitulate the accounts of sexual and literary property whose structure we have already delineated: while the plot locates truth in the marketplace of opinion, like paraphernalia, the guiding narrative consciousness registers it outside of exchange, in a realm of immutable value, like the heirloom.[14]

Critics have associated the so-called realism of Trollope's fiction with the author's professed valuation of the actual (truth) over the possible (fiction).[15] The determination of truth *within* the story follows a different logic, whereby opinion—expectations based on probability—functions like a market: such is the paraphernalia model, as we have seen, of narrative truth. But the narrator of ***The Eustace Diamonds*** draws on the heirloom model, in which the representation corresponds directly to unchanging truths. Against the marketplace, in which the value of aesthetic representations (like other commodities) is artificially inflated, the narrator insists upon an author's responsibility to portray life in real, unidealized form:

> Go into the market, either to buy or sell, and name the thing you desire to part with or to get, as it is, and the market is closed against you. . . . No assurance short of A 1. betokens even a pretence to merit. . . . In those delineations of life and character which we call novels a similarly superlative vein is desired. Our own friends around us are not always merry and wise . . . but neither are our friends villains.
>
> (1: 319)

By contrast with such corrupted notions of literature, the narrator presents his model:

> The persons whom you cannot care for in a novel, because they are so bad, are the very same that you so dearly love in your life, because they are so good. To make them and ourselves somewhat better . . . is, we may presume, the object of all teachers, leaders, legislators, spiritual pastors, and masters. He who writes tales such as this, probably also has, very humbly, some such object distantly before him. . . . When such a picture is painted, as intending to show what a man should be, it is true. If painted to show what men are, it is false. The true picture of life as it is, if it could be adequately painted, would show men what they are, and how they might rise, not, indeed, to perfection, but one step first, and then another on the ladder.
>
> (1: 320)

As Walter Kendrick observes, in order to realize this claim for "truth" or "realism," the narrator assumes the prior existence of an objectively knowable world; he also depends upon an uncomplicated theory of representation, by which reality is translated almost automatically into language. Such assumptions paradoxically motivate the counter-realistic intrusions by the narrator into the telling of the story.

Trollope inscribes this heirloom model—of narrative truth that can be objectively cited—in certain rhetorical positions. One exemplary trope, a minute but pervasive instance, is the aphorism. The novel's innumerable aphorisms arise as if to justify the characters' and plot's motivations. "The world, in judging of people who are false and bad and selfish and prosperous to outward appearances, is apt to be hard upon them, and to forget the punishments which generally accompany such faults. Lizzie Eustace was very false and bad and selfish" (1: 191). Such aphoristic rhetoric makes the specific incidents of the plot seem merely illustrative, or epiphenomenal, of universal, general truths. The narrator consistently points to the world outside the novel in order to validate the assertions made within it, positing general claims that the plot at hand is then seen to corroborate ("A man captivated by wiles was only captivated for a time, whereas a man won by simplicity would be won for ever" [1: 194]). Yet while Trollope's assertion of absolutes ("in truth" [2: 76], and so on) might suggest a fundamental break with the socially determined, market-driven nature of truth portrayed *in* the story, his immutable truths nevertheless align rather neatly with the opinion of the general public.

Trollope relies on aphorism to establish the rectitude of the truths that flow from an extra-novelistic order. Unlike a Dickens or Collins, who holds plot secrets in reserve until the precise moment for *dénouement,* Trollope famously gives away nearly all suspense and intrigue with a toss of the narrative head: "He who recounts these details has scorned to have a secret between himself and his readers. The diamonds were at this moment locked up within Lizzie's desk" (2: 78-79). Only by virtue of his confidence in the story's prior existence, apart from this verbal rendering, can the narrator afford such flippancy. When, for instance, Lucinda Roanoke appears, a question arises for both characters and readers about her identity: "There was some difficulty about her,—as to who she was." Immediately "the world" inside the novel adduces its conviction: "That she was an American was the received opinion." Two sentences later, the reader learns the objective truth, which simply goes to show how accurate the public's assessment is: "The received opinion was correct" (1: 331). As this example indicates, the difference between a truth ascertained by consensus ("the received

opinion . . .") and one introduced by the ultimate authority of the narrator (". . . was correct") may in fact amount to very little.

Just as the distinction between paraphernalia and heirlooms elsewhere proved, however useful, to be spurious, so it seems to be in this case too. Witness the exemplary breakdown between the two modes of truth-determination in this epigrammatic form: "Everybody said so, and it was so" (2: 189). On the paraphernalia model, we can read "and" in this sentence as "therefore"; on the heirloom model, as "because." Ultimately, the difference matters very little, since the two come down to the same in any case. This collapse only demonstrates the efficacy of the ideology that subtends both paradigms: either truth-values lie beyond the social, and public opinion simply happens to affirm them in every case; or public opinion determines social truths, which are then enshrined in absolute principles. Either way, the status quo regenerates itself, shored up on the one side with an evacuated set of values that cannot quite be referred to a higher power (religion, ethics, or the law), on the other with the fantasy of a coherent public that always reaffirms the values that were assumed from the outset.[16]

If in the register of narrative truth the distinction between the paraphernalia model and the heirloom model collapses, we are left with a question of why the novel does not simply lapse into self-contradiction. The answer lies with the irony that regulates the relationship between the two paradigms, tempering both the narrator's appeal to absolutes and the story's cynicism about the contingency of opinion.[17] The narrator assumes an amoral, urbane distance from the plot he relates, and this determinedly anti-sensational style can treat its racy material as little more than the humdrum machinations of an ambitious and self-interested social elite. Yet the insouciant attitude that the narrator adopts screens a certain moralism, as if the ironic voice of indifference itself were being ironized. This double irony manages to evade the impasse of moral agnosticism and yet, at the same time, to avoid committing the novel to either of the two positions—absolutism or consensus—raised as possible bases for judgment. Take, for example, one of the many invocations of the reader: "That Lizzie Eustace had stolen the diamonds, as a pickpocket steals a watch, was a fact as to which Mr. Camperdown had in his mind no shadow of a doubt. And, as the reader knows, he was right. She had stolen them" (1: 252). The narrator's unshakable conviction about "the true story" ("Lizzie Eustace had stolen the diamonds") provides ironic leverage on the characters' partial knowledge. Yet the suave indifference that such aplomb enables nonetheless allows an appeal to the reader, with an assurance that we recognize and concur about the true moral corruption of Lizzie.[18]

Although its narrative posture—an ironic lack of interest in fundamental truths—helps the novel to reconcile the conflicting models of value it has presented, this irony itself represents a tactic already within the domain of Victorian sexual unspeakability. With his voice of cultivated nonchalance, Trollope's narrator can simultaneously invoke scandalous plot elements (thus appealing to his audience's taste) and assume a stance of haughty disdain for the public's interest in such affairs (thus keeping above the level of prurience).[19] In raising indifference to an art form, Trollope produces the illusion of an escape from philistine sensationalism, even as this resistance itself demonstrates the persistent fascination for his readers of salacious material.[20] This super-sophistication relegates sexual significations to the realm of the unspeakable by implying that they are so flagrantly conspicuous as not to require any further elaboration. The embarrassment one endures in rendering explicit the genital designation of the unmarried woman's jewel box, in Holmes's figure, or of Dora's reticule, arises in the face of just such a genteel disavowal: one *need not* register libidinous meanings, and therefore one *should not* do so. Drawing upon the reciprocal interdependence of public opinion and absolute standards, this process presents as already-agreed-upon what no one has discussed, and thereby lends to sexuality its peculiar linguistic status.

The pose that narrators such as Trollope's strike ("of course . . . everybody knows . . . so why bother saying so?") allows them to have it both ways with sexual meanings, and it marks a paradigmatic moment in the discourse of sexuality. For we can finally understand that the mutually reinforcing oppositions, which apply not only to property but to narrative language as well, constitute a principal means of defining sexuality as the unspeakable subject in nineteenth-century England. This strategy makes it possible to mean things without saying them, to play upon a readership's fascination while disavowing any appeal to base interests. Analogizing the Eustace diamonds to both female sexuality and literary property, Trollope's work demonstrates the reciprocal and inextricable relationship between the two principal arenas of linguistic ambiguity in Victorian culture—the sexual and the literary. That the author's ambitions should align with a trollop's simply reinforces the relationship. Trollope only minimally disguises this similitude—conceals it, that is to say, only about as well as a jewel box conceals female sexuality.

Notes

1. Freud clearly recognizes that the heavy-handedness of an interpretation has little bearing on its persuasiveness: "Dora found no difficulty in producing a motive: 'Why should I not wear a reticule like this, as it is now the fashion to do?' But a justification of this kind does not dismiss the possibility of the action in question having an unconscious origin. Though on the other hand the existence of such an origin and the meaning attributed to the act cannot be conclusively established. We must content ourselves with recording the fact that such a meaning fits in quite extraordinarily well with the situation as a whole and with the order of the day as laid down by the unconscious" (95).

2. One of Farmer's citations under the lemma *monosyllable,* an 1823 dictionary, itself suggests an abyssal regression into linguistic self-reference as the sign of sexual unspeakability: after making it clear that the reference is to *pudenda muliebris,* the earlier lexicon indicates, "Of all the thousand monosyllables in our language, this *one* only is designated by the definite article—THE MONOSYLLABLE; therefore do some men call it 'the article,' 'my article,' and 'her article,' as the case may be." Now no longer even a linguistic description of the slang term, the article itself—"the monosyllable," or perhaps simply "the"—functions as the periphrastic substantive. Another dictionary citation (from 1811) states more economically: "MONOSYLLABLE. A woman's commodity" (4: 345).

3. The overdetermination of the shameful, fearful, bedchamber box for Lizzie's pudendum is the primary dirty joke in the novel, but by no means the only one. Drawing on the conventional misogyny that maliciously associates female sexuality with rancid fish, the narrative introduces an invidious non-sequitur: "[W]hen rumours reached [Mr. Emilius] prejudicial to Lizzie in respect of the diamonds, he perceived that such prejudice might work weal for him. A gentleman once, on ordering a mackerel for dinner, was told that a fresh mackerel would come to a shilling. He could have a stale mackerel for sixpence. Then bring me a stale mackerel,' said the gentleman. Mr. Emilius coveted fish, but was aware that his position did not justify him in expecting the best fish on the market" (2: 239-40). Trollope employs an identical narrative strategy, though without the same putrescent overtones, in describing the doubts of another suitor: "There was very much in the whole affair of which he would not be proud as he led his bride to the altar;—but a man does not expect to get four thousand pounds a year for nothing. Lord George, at any rate, did not conceive himself to be in a position to do so. Had there not been something crooked about Lizzie,—a screw loose, as people say,—she would never have been within his reach. There are men who always ride lame horses, and yet see as much of the hunting as others" (2: 217-18).

4. *Paraphernalia* (etymologically, "beyond the dowry") is defined in the *Oxford English Dictionary* as "Those articles of personal property which the law allows a married woman to keep and, to a certain extent, deal with as her own." The dictionary then elaborates, in an explanatory note: "The word *parapherna* was used by the Roman jurists to indicate all property which a married woman *sui juris* held apart from her *dos* (dower). Over such property the husband could exercise no rights without his wife's consent. . . . In English and Scottish Common law, under which all personal or movable property of a wife vested *ipso jure* in the husband, the *paraphernalia* became restricted to such purely personal belongings of a wife as dress, jewels, and the like. These latter were regarded as, in a sense, appropriated to the wife, and on the husband's death they were not treated as part of his succession, and the right of a trustee over them, in the event of the husband's bankruptcy, was restricted. . . . The effect of the 'Married Women's Property Acts' of 1870, etc., was to deprive the term of all significance in English and Scottish legal practice" (11: 203). Though the 1870 law allowed married women certain property rights, significant legislative changes did not come about until 1882. For a history of the law, including the contemporary context for Trollope's novel, see Holcombe.

5. The parallel between Lizzie and Lucy in terms of their jewels also extends at one point to the box: comparable to Lizzie's jewels stored in the iron box, the object of greatest value to Lucy—Frank's letter proposing to marry her—resides in a much-emphasized "iron post": "If Lucy could only have known of the letter, which was already her own property though lying in the pillar letter-box in Fleet Street. . . . It was so hard upon her that she should be so interrogated while that letter was lying in the iron box!" (1: 132-33). The letter-box yokes together Lizzie's pervasive strong box with Trollope's professional career in the post office—and, in particular, his role as "originator" of the pillar letter-box (Trollope, *Autobiography* 282). The novel's narrator makes a joke on the subject, referring to "The post-office, with that accuracy in the performance of its duties for which it is conspicuous among all offices" (1: 134).

6. While Lucinda is revolted by a man's touch, Lizzie knows how to make use of a posture of supplication, laying her head on the breast of each of her lovers in succession (Sir Florian [1: 8], Lord Fawn [1: 74], Frank [1: 291], Lord George [2: 104]). Even when she settles for (and on) Emilius, she eroticizes the very qualities that make him repellent: "The man was a nasty, greasy, lying, squinting Jew preacher . . . but there was a cer-

tain manliness in him. . . . While he was making his speech she almost liked his squint. She certainly liked the grease and nastiness. Presuming, as she naturally did, that something of what he said was false, she liked the lies" (2: 314).

7. On the relations among women, jewels, and authorship in an exchange economy, I am indebted to Gallagher.

8. As does Lizzie, Trollope abjures a paradigm of genital procreativity for his work. According to Hall, his literary ingenuity flowed instead on an anal-expulsive model: Trollope is said to have remarked to George Eliot, "'[W]ith my mechanical stuff it's a sheer matter of industry. It's not the head that does it [i.e., produces "imaginative work"]—it's the cobbler's wax on the seat and the sticking to my chair!' And, according to another account, he drove home his point about the seat of inspiration with 'an inelegant vigour of gesture that sent a thrill of horror through the polite circle there assembled'" (363). For a fuller consideration of the mode of literary production theorized and exemplified in Trollope's autobiography, see Kendrick.

9. "There are those who would be ashamed to subject themselves to such a taskmaster, and who think that the man who works with his imagination should allow himself to wait till—inspiration moves him. When I have heard such doctrine preached, I have hardly been able to repress my scorn. To me it would not be more absurd if the shoemaker were to wait for inspiration, or the tallow-chandler for the divine moment of melting. . . . The author wants [inspiration] as does every other workman,—that and a habit of industry" (*Autobiography* 120-21).

10. Later in the same text, Trollope suggests "what we all mean when we talk of literary plagiarism and literary honesty. The sin of which the author is accused is not that of taking another man's property, but of passing off as his own creation that which he did not himself create. When an author puts his name to a book he claims to have written all that there is therein, unless he makes direct signification to the contrary" (254).

11. On the role of public opinion ("the world") as a "policing force" more efficacious in *The Eustace Diamonds* than the police force itself, see Miller 14-15.

12. Spacks writes: "To say that Trollope's novels contain a lot of gossip says nothing very interesting about them. Nor does detailed examination of how the gossip works shed much light on the novels as wholes. . . . Trollope's characters talk obses-

sively about one another's dubious behavior: Lizzie Eustace keeps everyone busy and happy for years by her reprehensible conduct. In precisely the same way, she provides the reader of *The Eustace Diamonds* with occupation and pleasure" (190).

13. See Poovey on the invention of statistical thinking earlier in the century (which was requisite to the production of an objective public opinion) and the relation of this discourse, claimed by its proponents to be based in fact, to the figures that it finds unrepresentable.

14. In a related analysis, Kincaid writes about the tension in Trollope's work between "moral purism" (absolute standards) and "empiricism" or "relativism" (what I have been calling social contingency—in short, public opinion). Kincaid revises the theory of "situation ethics" that apRoberts proposes, suggesting instead a notion of flexible consistency: "This is not to deny that empirical standards are present in Trollope, but they seldom if ever stand in a normative position. Ordinarily, empiricism is one extreme pole of the novel's value system, a position seductive but dangerous. It is usually played off against an opposite moral purism. . . . Trollope's method and his morality, then, appear to me very much tied to situations, but only because situations test and make solid an ethical code that would otherwise remain abstract and superficial. The situations can diversify, even break, codes, but the codes derive always from a civilized base independent of the situations" (14-16). While I agree that such a conflict arises in *The Eustace Diamonds,* my effort is not to resolve it dialectically but to show how the putative difference was ideologically determined from the outset.

15. Kendrick fully elaborates such an analysis, proposing that, for Trollope, literature would ideally convey "life" without mediation, and that only the inadequacies of the representational medium produce a reader's awareness of "textuality." Kendrick argues that "both the characters and the novelist's knowledge of them are complete before any writing is done" (27), and that "in Trollope's theory it is precisely the recognition of this difference"—between "the novel world" and "the real world"—"that the novelist's labor is intended to suppress" (50). With reference to Trollope's authorial intrusions, Kendrick writes, "It is a typical tactic of Trollope's fiction that when it obeys literary conventions, it does so blatantly, grudgingly. Literature is different from and only partially adequate to life, and literature itself announces its inferiority" (75).

16. In an effort to challenge the view of Trollope as an uncomplicated conservative, Kucich makes a persuasive case for the ability of "transgressive" dishonesty to shore up middle-class hegemony in the process of challenging it in Trollope's fiction. It remains a question, however, whether any transgression that serves bourgeois ideology so effectively is worthy of the name in the first place.

17. For a discussion of Trollope's narrative voice, and the relation between its irony and its believability, see Lyons, who reviews the considerable critical literature on Trollopian irony.

18. On the invocation of the reader, see Vernon's essays.

19. This is to amplify Spacks's comments on how novelists, "often reliant on morally dubious raw material, may wish to justify it in fictional or in ethical terms": "The reader (to say nothing of the writer) thus has it both ways, free to contemplate the kind of behavior one whispers about, while remaining superior to mere scandal" (204).

20. For a consideration of one of the possible consequences of this strategy—boredom—see Miller 107-45.

Works Cited

apRoberts, Ruth. *The Moral Trollope.* Athens: Ohio UP, 1971.

Conan Doyle, Arthur. "A Scandal in Bohemia." 1891. *The Complete Adventures and Memoirs of Sherlock Holmes.* New York: Bramhall, 1975.

Farmer, John S. *A Dictionary of Slang.* 1890. 7 vols. Ware, Hertfordshire: Wordsworth, 1987.

Freud, Sigmund. *Dora: An Analysis of a Case of Hysteria.* 1905. Ed. Philip Rieff. New York: Collier, 1963.

Gallagher, Catherine. "George Eliot and *Daniel Deronda*: The Prostitute and the Jewish Question." *Sex, Politics, and Science in the Nineteenth-Century Novel: Selected Papers from the English Institute, 1983-84.* Ed. Ruth Bernard Yeazell. Baltimore: Johns Hopkins UP, 1986. 39-62.

Hall, N. John. *Trollope: A Biography.* Oxford: Clarendon, 1991.

Holcombe, Lee. *Wives and Property: Reform of the Married Women's Property Law in Nineteenth-Century England.* Toronto: U of Toronto P, 1983.

Kendrick, Walter M. *The Novel-Machine: The Theory and Fiction of Anthony Trollope.* Baltimore: Johns Hopkins UP, 1980.

Kincaid, James R. *The Novels of Anthony Trollope.* Oxford: Clarendon, 1977.

Kucich, John. "Transgression in Trollope: Dishonesty and the Antibourgeois Elite." *ELH* 56.3 (1989): 593-618.

Lyons, Paul. "The Morality of Irony and Unreliable Narrative in Trollope's *The Warden* and *Barchester Towers*." *South Atlantic Review* 54.1 (1989): 41-54.

Miller, D. A. *The Novel and the Police*. Berkeley: U of California P, 1988.

Oxford English Dictionary. 2nd ed. 20 vols. Oxford: Clarendon, 1989.

Poovey, Mary. "Figures of Arithmetic, Figures of Speech: The Discourse of Statistics in the 1830s." *Critical Inquiry* 19.2 (1993): 256-76.

Spacks, Patricia Meyer. *Gossip*. New York: Knopf, 1985.

Trollope, Anthony. *An Autobiography*. 1883. Oxford: Oxford UP, 1980.

———. *The Eustace Diamonds*. 1871-72. 2 vols. Oxford: Oxford UP, 1973.

Vernon, Patricia A. "The Poor Fictionist's Conscience: Point of View in the Palliser Novels." *Victorian Newsletter* 71 (1987): 16-20.

———. "Reading and Misreading in *The Eustace Diamonds*." *VIJ* [*Victorian Institute Journal*] 12 (1984): 1-8.

Nicholas Birns (essay date July 1996)

SOURCE: Birns, Nicholas. "The Empire Turned Upside Down: The Colonial Fictions of Anthony Trollope." *ARIEL: A Review of International English Literature* 27, no. 3 (July 1996): 7-23.

[*In the following essay, Birns defends Trollope's imperial novels as important and insightful contributions to colonial fiction, though Trollope was not recognized as a colonial writer.*]

I Reversed Space

It is fairly common now for metropolitan British authors to be represented as part of the postcolonial canon. Critics have long since devoted attention to writers like Joseph Conrad and E. M. Forster, who of course set significant portions of their work in Asia and other then-colonized regions of the globe. Finding the hidden colonial echoes and traces in books such as Charlotte Bronte's *Jane Eyre* and Jane Austen's *Mansfield Park* has become a cottage industry.[1] And there have been wider-ranging studies such as Gauri Viswanathan's assertion that the entire existence of English as a literary discipline owes itself to Indian colonial institutions. In all this activity, though, the name of Anthony Trollope has seldom been heard, even though he devoted several works to countries that were at the time part of the British Empire. The reasons for this are fairly clear: first, Trollope is seen as the epitome of beefy Englishness and has so been used to buttress British patriotism in times of stress and more generally appropriated as a synecdoche for British national identity (Wolfreys [*Being English*] 152). Second, Trollope's imperial fictions have largely to do with what are now (Australia, New Zealand) or have been until recently (South Africa) largely white-dominated settler colonies; thus his works do not address questions of racial subjugation the way, for instance, Conrad's are seen as doing. And third, Trollope's colonial works are given short shrift by traditionally conservative Trollope scholars, and thus lack the visibility that would draw them to the eyes of critics involved in the post-colonial project.

This neglect is regrettable, though, because several of Trollope's later novels, especially **Harry Heathcote of Gangoil** and **The Fixed Period,** are vital to an understanding of what might be termed the changing literary demography of the English language in the nineteenth century. In 1800, English literature was being written in the British Isles and in certain of the far eastern portions of North America. The Anglophone canon was overwhelmingly dominated by writers who lived in England and whom, in most respects, only England knew. By 1900, North American literature had achieved such range and confidence that not only did North American writers such as Walt Whitman develop cults of fashion among the aristocracy in the mother country, but North American novelists like Henry James and Sara Jeannette Duncan had the confidence to address broader issues of British-colonial relations whose relevance and implications stretched to include the entire English-speaking world. By 1900, English was being written in five continents, and not only by expatriate Englishmen or white settlers, but by native Indians (Henry Derozio and Toru Dutt), by First Nations Canadians (Pauline Johnson), and, shortly after 1900, by black South Africans (Sol Plaatje) and Sri Lankans (Lucien De Zilwa). Trollope's colonial novels can be seen as an important index of this process of globalization. However English Trollope might have been in his own mind, his literary productions revealed that the English language was now no longer the exclusive property of Europeans, and that it would be used in very different ways from those envisioned by the metropolitan élite.

Although Trollope set a surprising amount of his fiction outside the British Isles, Australia and the Antipodes in general are by far the other territories most represented. Trollope's son Fred had emigrated to the colony in 1871, and the novelist subsequently paid two extended visits there. This biographical fact, and the literary production it occasioned, are no secrets; but they have seldom been explored to their full potential. It is due to the work of the Australian critic P. D. Edwards that this constellation has found its way into criticism at all. Edwards, in explicating Trollope's Australian fiction and its literary and historical relation to the Australia of his day, has virtually defined this area of study for the future. Edwards has not only elucidated the hidden Australianness of the Trollope canon; he has shown also how Trollope can be seen, if not exactly as a part of "Australian literature," then at least as part of the field of reflection on what a literature of Australia possibly could be. As Edwards points out, Australian scenes and references have many a place in Trollope's work, without taking into account his travelogue of Australia and New Zealand published in 1873. Two of Trollope's novels, *Harry Heathcote of Gangoil* and *The Fixed Period,* are set entirely in the South Pacific, and are at the centre of his colonial fictions.

As Edwards and other critics have noted, the situation of the book's eponymous protagonist Harry Heathcote, is based upon that of Trollope's Australian son. The novel, though, is not a piece of untransmuted realism. *Harry Heathcote of Gangoil* is a deeply thought-out book, one whose interest lies in its most premeditative aspects. The book is premised as both a tale of Australia and a Christmas story. There is an obvious clash in these generic classifications enacted by the reversal of the seasons in the Southern Hemisphere. It is to make this clash more dramatic that Trollope undertakes one of the book's few departures from apparent biographical truth: its setting in Queensland rather than in New South Wales, where his son's plantation was actually located. The temperate climate of New South Wales is too much an approximation of that of England; what Trollope needs to undergird his book's structure is an utter contrast. He found that in the equatorial climate of Queensland, where Christmas is a hot and fierce season. Trollope seems to exult in this unfamiliar Yule: "From all this I trust the reader will understand that the Christmas to which he is introduced is not the Christmas with which he is intimate on this side of the equator—a Christmas of blazing fires indoors, and sleet and snow and frost outside—but the Christmas of Australia, in which happy land the Christmas fires are apt to be lighted, or to light themselves, when they are by no means needed (3-4)." What in England is a necessary rite becomes in Australia a superfluous ritual; yet, it is implied, the incongruity, the superfluous excess, of an Australian Christmas possesses instabilities bound to be exhilarating for the reader to contemplate. Christmas, customarily the site of home and hearth, becomes instead a symbol of exile and displacement. Whether Trollope's Australian argument manipulates the reader or allows for truly vertiginous instability is the central questions criticism of *Harry Heathcote of Gangoil* must confront.

The few critics who have written on *Harry Heathcote of Gangoil* regard the surface disjunction of Australia and Christmas as concealing a far less surprising conservatism. Trollope, on this view, sets his novel so far away only in order to emphasize values near-at-hand and close to home. The stolid, domestic cheer of an English Christmas will still resonate even in an Antipodean clime. Whatever the spatial coordinates of the action, a customary moral axis is maintained. This is a misreading not just of *Harry Heathcote of Gangoil,* but of Trollope. It is infrequently perceived how much of an advocate of social change Trollope was. In nearly every novel of his, there is a decided shift in power and in the nature of the society depicted in the book. Even in novels where the action takes place exclusively within the ranks of the aristocracy, such as *The Claverings* or *The Duke's Children,* the nature of that aristocracy is so thoroughly changed by the end of the book as to call its fundamental identity into question. That these changes are not radical or complete does not annul their effect. In *Middlemarch,* for instance, Lydgate and Dorothea entertain prospects of social change far more all-embracing than anything envisioned (at least by a character depicted positively) in Trollope. Yet these envisioned changes are foiled and their proponents are forced to submit to a constraining, disillusioned defeatism by the end of Eliot's book. Trollope may write books such as *Barchester Towers* where Anglo-Catholic conservatism seems to triumph over zealous reform, but even there Trollope's plot does not manifest a reconstitution of the social past. Social change, however piecemeal, actually occurs in Trollope (this point has been made especially well by Julian Wolfreys when he asserts that rather than re-establishing the old order Trollope "'lets go' of control" [176]). This change is directed towards greater enfranchisement and social mobility and to the weakening of the entrenched order, which at the end of a Trollope novel is usually what Wolfreys terms a "decentred centre" (153). The mechanics of the plot in *Harry Heathcote of Gangoil,* however predictable, are no exception to this enfranchising and liberating practice. The title-character, the surrogate for Trollope's son, is a "squatter," whereas his nominal antagonist, Giles Medlicot, is a "free-selector." "Squatter," whatever its overtones of arbitrary encampment in the context of traditional tenured landholdings, means "man of property" in the less precedent-bound Australian milieu. "Free-selectors," on the other hand, are more roving types who approach the landholding game in a more scattershot and *ad hoc* manner. Trollope's terms are sociologically accurate with regard to 1870s Australia; yet they seem a recapitulation of the purely English class antagonisms of the author's more typical works. In a series of developments familiar to Trollope's readers, Heathcote and Medlicot encounter each other, quarrel, and eventually resolve their dispute and find that they are indeed gentlemen of each other's calibre. This alliance is cemented by the convenient presence of Heathcote's unmarried sister-in-law Kate, who soon conceives a tender passion for Medlicot that leads to the virtually obligatory marriage at the end of the novel.

This resolution seems a complete imposition of English plot on Australian terrain, an almost complete act of colonial erasure. It is as such that the novel has been attacked, on those few occasions that it has not been ignored by Australian critics from the novel's publication up till the present. As Edwards points out, Australians of the 1870s were infuriated that the novel was even serialized in an Australian newspaper, and suggested that a British expatriate who had actually had the gumption to settle permanently in Australia, such as the brawling convict-writer Marcus Clarke (a close friend, incongruously, of Gerard Manley Hopkins), was more equipped for the task. But all these reprimands, though they gauge correctly the inauthenticity of Trollope's engagement with his Australian setting, miss the liberating arbitrariness that Trollope invokes even as he seems to be at his maximum of parochial imperial mastery. Consider, for instance, the conflict between the squatter and the free-selector. Could not its resemblance to previous English social conflicts recorded by Trollope underscore in fact the superficiality, the ultimate exchangeability, of all these conflicts? Rather than represent some existent social formation, they reveal that these formations are textually postulated and constructed. The Heathcote-Medlicot conflict, indeed, bears as much resemblance to the wars between cowboys and sheepmen in any typical American Western as it does to Trollope's English class conflicts. By using the same scheme that he has used in limning English society to describe a very different Australian reality, Trollope exposes the mechanistic nature of his social vision, and thus prevents it from possessing a constraining definition of place and culture.

Here Trollope, far from being the hearty realist, is a forerunner of the postmodern, postnational floating signifier. This was anathema to the Australian readers of the novel at its time of publication and for many decades later: this was just the period of Australian national self-definition, marked by the emergence of Australian Federation at the turn of the twentieth century and the hegemony of the *Bulletin* school of writers, figures such as Henry Lawson and Banjo Paterson who affirmatively chronicled the emergence of a distinctively and autonomously Australian soul. Yet we are well positioned today to see the negative aspect of an ostensibly liberating nationalist autonomy, what Bob Hodge and Vijay Mishra label "the dark side of the dream." In being "propagandistic" (167) for an "Australian legend," the *Bulletin,* as described by Hodge and Mishra, set up a vitalist rhetoric that exalted charismatic white males while excluding women and Aborigines. Thus the anti-colonialism of the *Bulletin* school attacked British

rule only in order to construct a new settler hierarchy with its own methods of cultural subjugation. Trollope, certainly, is not an acceptable alternative; the "Kanaks" or Polynesian migrant workers are depicted derisively, the Aboriginal population is virtually ignored, and the women in the novel are among Trollope's least emancipated. The only foreigner in the book treated at all positively is a racially assimilable German, and even he is from the principality of Hanover, a former possession of the British royal family—so hardly a foreigner at all. Trollope's Australia is white, male, and British (not even Anglo-Celtic). But, considering the impure nature of Australian anti-colonial braggadocio, Trollope can hardly be denigrated on this score.

And even Trollope is not without his observations on the nature of colonialism. In a pre-engagement reverie, Kate and Medlicot talk musingly of home. Medlicot makes explicit the parallel between the squatters and the English country gentlemen at "home," and then Kate remarks that she can hardly imagine what things are like at home. The authorial overvoice then interposes, "Both Medlicot and Kate meant England when they spoke of home" (76). Given Trollope's customarily sardonic attitude towards his lovers, especially when their love concludes a plot, we can see in this something more than a reaffirmation that, no matter how far the geographical dislocation, Christmas will still be Christmas and home will remain home. Trollope is gently satirizing the couple's psychological inability to see Australia as home, even though they are Australians. This is the phenomenon that the Australian critic A. A. Phillips was to label "the cultural cringe," and the Australian historian Geoffrey Blainey was to attribute to "the tyranny of distance"—the constant tendency for Australians to see Britain as a reference point when in fact they were on the other side of the earth from Britain. Trollope, as his Australian travelogue shows, recognized the inevitability and desirability of Australian self-government. But he was aware of the gaps and pitfalls in an Australian national identity—much as he was aware of his own distance from anything "really" Australian. Trollope, as so often elsewhere in his fiction, knows his own inauthenticity. It is this inauthenticity that has kept him from being accepted by Australians even as an English chronicler of Australia. But is Trollope's inauthenticity really inferior to the cultural arrogance of a book such as D. H. Lawrence's *Kangaroo,* which attempts to appropriate and merge with its subject? Lawrence's mantic, machismo-laden imperialism, because it does not admit fictiveness, is more irredeemable than Trollope's; yet Lawrence's book is accepted as a para-Australian work the way Trollope's novel certainly is not.

Does anyone who writes a novel set in Australia become in some way a para-Australian? No, perhaps not; but it is interesting to trace the relations between the signifier "Trollope" and Australia. As mentioned before, Trollope's son settled in Australia, and his descendants continue there to this day. Indeed, the Australian Trollopes very early on became the only descendants in the male line of Anthony Trollope; when Trollope's descendants inherited a baronetcy that had been in another branch of the family, that baronetcy passed to the Australian branch. Ironically, Trollope, the chronicler so often of the English aristocracy but never himself of that group, did have descendants who assumed that honour—yet they were Australians (Glendenning 509). The identity of "Trollope" the family name became Australian even as "Trollope" the literary "signature" (as Derrida would say) became associated with the bedrock core of English national identity. Can there be a better demonstration of the shifting nature of national identity in an English-speaking world that is no longer English but Anglophone—where a Trollope can feel at home yet not be in England? Anthony Trollope is an English writer, yet by virtue of his books and this odd anecdote of family history, is not some corner of him Australian, or at least splayed between the national identities of colonizer and colonized? Does not he have the same mixture of British and Australian that British writers who actually settled in Australia, such as Marcus Clarke, have in more equal measure? These are questions about national identity similar, if on a much smaller scale, to those frequently asked concerning contemporary post-colonial writers: Is Bharati Mukherjee Indian, American, or Canadian? Is Salman Rushdie Indian, Pakistani, or British? Is Derek Walcott St. Lucian, American, or a general citizen of the African diaspora?

Trollope certainly cannot be considered to have the place in the postcolonial canon of Mukherjee, Rushdie, Walcott, or even their more neglected earlier predecessors. Yet the insights of post-colonial theory can illuminate the fissures and instabilities in Trollope's Antipodean fictions. The "pluralism of the national sign" that is one result of the colonial process in the view of Homi Bhabha (303) seems very reminiscent of Trollope's deployment of Christmas and of the idea of home. They are duplications of a colonial original, yet their very sameness generates a disruption that calls attention to the instabilities latent in the colonial relationship. In the reversed space of Trollope's Antipodes, both everything and nothing are different. Trollope's combination of delight in the fissures of place and identity with skepticism about the stability of deep cultural differences anticipates the work of contemporary postcolonials such as Janet Frame, Nuruddin Farah, Salman Rushdie, and Gerald Murnane. These upendings of fixed identities also give us a new Trollope, a Trollope who, in encompassing the globe, knows his own limitations yet uses those to see into the future with surprising prescience. Nearly a decade after the publication of *Harry Heathcote of Gangoil,* Trollope was to produce the greatest of his colonial fictions.

II PROJECTED TIME

The Fixed Period, published in 1882, is marginal in the Trollope canon, at least in terms of reception, simply because of what it is: a futuristic fantasy. Trollopians usually have been so threatened by the irrealism of the book, though, that they have constrained its thematic exposition as much as possible, making the book seem more a *jeu d'esprit* than a speculative voyage. The book concerns the effort of one Fidus Neverbend, the president of a fictitious future British ex-colony of Britannula, to legislate a "fixed period" of 65 years of life allotted to each citizen, beyond which they will be humanely put to death. The novel's depth, though, exceeds this theme, which has monopolized the few analyses of the book. The chief agent in this excess is, as with *Harry Heathcote of Gangoil,* the book's setting in the South Pacific. Britannula, unlike the meticulously sketched Queensland of *Harry Heathcote of Gangoil,* is fictional. It is described as a former dependency of New Zealand (referred to in the novel as its "elder sister" [5]), which, along with that country and Australia, have now "set out for themselves" with the overt permission of Britain. (Again, we see Trollope's yielding stance on the question of Antipodean nationalism). Although the apparatus of the fixed period provides the dominating conceit of the novel, it can be read more broadly as a diagnosis of the problem of colonial nationalism, a problem clarified by Trollope by projecting it a century into the future.

The point of Trollope's book is usually seen as satirizing euthanasia, and so it is described as "Swiftian" in the manner of "A Modest Proposal." But *The Fixed Period* is more truly Swiftian in the manner of *Gulliver's Travels. Gulliver's Travels,* as David Fausett points out, is the capstone of a centuries-long "mode of utopian writing . . . closely bound with travel and human geography," which had the South Pacific area as its setting. Most of these were written when the South Pacific was still (in European eyes, of course) *terra incognita* or subject of a bare minimum of European exploration; thus Swift can set his various allegorical lands at England's Antipodes cheerfully indifferent to geography; the Antipodes for Swift are just a fictive inversion of the given rather than anything real in themselves. This allegorical tradition did completely fade once what Fausett terms "the closure of the global circle" (171) had occurred and Australia and New Zealand had been charted and subject to the routinizing sway of British colonization, symbolic of an abstract European universality that had triumphed, willy-nilly, over the entire globe. Both *The Fixed Period* and an American work such as Herman Melville's *Mardi,* Swiftian in both tone and setting, demonstrate this, as do contemporary works such as Peter Carey's *Unusual Life of Tristan Smith,* which in many ways rewrites this *topos* from a consciously subaltern and anti-imperialist perspective.[2] Interestingly, both Trollope and Melville had spent extensive time in the South Pacific region, yet both chose to use it as a basis for fantasy or allegory as well as setting more firmly realistic works there. In many ways, paradoxically, Trollope is less imperialist than Melville, whose attitudes towards the Pacific often herald a vulgar American expansionism.

Trollope's fantasy, though, has realistic consequences. Britannula is a certain type of colony. "Little Britain" by name, it is also a future Britain, standing for what Britain will be like in a hundred years, or what will characterize the geographically transplanted successors to the British cultural traditions. Trollope had already used this device in one of his earliest works, the unpublished *The New Zealander,* in which a future New Zealander diagnoses what has gone wrong with a declined Britain. The Antipodes are a mirror of Britain, yet a mirror with the perspective of futurity. One of the necessities of being a mirror-future of Britain is racial homogeneity. Britannula resembles Canada, Australia, New Zealand, and, during its days of white minority rule, South Africa rather than other British colonies such as India and Kenya. It is a colony where whites are a homogeneous majority that constitute the body politic, not an administrative minority. Even the one exception to this homogeneity in the "real" Antipodean countries, the indigenous inhabitants (Aborigines in Australia, Maoris in New Zealand) are totally absent in *The Fixed Period* the way they had not been, albeit present only marginally, in *Harry Heathcote of Gangoil.* Britannula is what Stephen Slemon has termed a "Second World" country, neither fully imperial nor fully subaltern (31). President Neverbend is very much a product of a Second World mentality: overconfident in the righteousness of his own local notions, but also dependent on the residue of a "universal" Englishness, even if his own philosophy and Britain's itself eventually cross swords.

Neverbend should be assessed not just as the purveyor of an eccentric philosophy, but as a politician and national leader. There is an obvious "plot reason" for Neverbend to be President of his country rather than just a crackpot philosopher; the executive position gives him the efficacy to carry out his schemes. Yet Neverbend's conduct is precisely that of a militant settler nationalist. The innovation of the fixed period is not just an abstract reassessment of the nature and use of human life. It is an attempt to prune the aging husks of decadent Europe, to assert a youthful vigorous settler culture as superior to the aging imperial edifice which had produced this reassessment. Britannula may be allegorically the Britain of the future; but the Britain of 1882 is also present in *The Fixed Period,* very much the dominant imperial power, and always in sight throughout the actions in the book. Early on, Neverbend, the book's unreliable narrator, makes clear that his fixed period

legislation is a nationalist, anti-imperial gesture. Commenting on the ultimate failure of his scheme (which has already been disabled by the time he begins recounting the story), Neverbend orates, "But it has been because the old men are still alive in England that the young in Britannula are to be afflicted . . ." (10). England is associated with age and time-bound traditionalism, Britannula with the innovative breezes of fresh national vigour as represented in the euthanasiac legislation enacted by its "young Assembly" (5). Neverbend's experiment, although clearly heinous to anyone who thinks twice about it and opposed by every countrymen of his mentioned in the book save for the cravenly opportunistic Abraham Grundle, requires overt British armed intervention for its overthrow. The reason for this is, implicitly, not that the people of Britannula lack conscience, but that, as in the case of some revolutionary nationalist leaders in our own time, Neverbend is so identified, as the founding President of Britannula, with that nation's anti-colonial self-assertion as to make his ouster by his own people politically inconceivable.

Britannula, though a fictive and allegorical nation, is a nation nonetheless. It is important that there is both a Britannula and a Britain in the book. And Britain does not just emerge as the *deus ex machina* at the end, but figures throughout the book. Britannula has a decided inferiority-complex towards the mother country. Its capital city is Gladstonopolis, this being as clear an example of the cultural cringe and of postcolonial mimicry as Kate and Medlicot's yearning for "home." One of the few breathing-spaces in the book's rather relentless plot involves a cricket match between Britannula and Britain, complete with futuristic mechanical implements and colonial ironies that make the reader wish that the West Indian cultural critic and cricket fan C. L. R. James had been transported through time and fictional world in order to comment from the sidelines. And even Neverbend, symbol of Britannula, feels that his exile at the end gives him the greater opportunity—to go to England and propagandize for his beliefs; only in England will the ultimate merit of these beliefs be decided. Britain is, indeed, as much master of the world in Trollope's projected "1980" as in 1882.

Thus the irony of the book's denouement, when Britain, in order to prevent the enactment of the first death mandated by the fixed period legislation, repossesses Britannula and reduces it once again to a status of dependency, complete with colonial governor. The end of Neverbend's experiment is coextensive with the curtailment of his nation's autonomy, which will only be restored "with the agreement of England" (167). Given that an Englishman is writing the book, the casting of Britain in the role of liberal policeman of global wrongdoing may be seen simply as a product of cultural arrogance. Yet Trollope does not present Neverbend's ouster moralistically, and Sir Ferdinando Brown, the newly installed colonial governor, is not presented as a hero. Although Trollope's postulation that global predominance would still belong to Great Britain a hundred years after the Victorian era was hardly clairvoyant, much the same role is being played by an English-speaking power. (Interestingly, even Trollope's powerful late twentieth-century Britain is made possible only by the assumption of further Civil War-like divisions within the United States; for Trollope, the only conceivable variety of Anglophone imperialism would be British, a view the twentieth century did not come to share.) Kipling saw that imperialism would be ephemeral in the 1890s; Trollope may not have had this insight, but he was certainly no proponent of a triumphalist, unremitting imperialism. His satiric jibes at then-current British politicians (John Bright, Lord Salisbury, and of course Gladstone himself are all lampooned), or their remote "grandchildren," in the course of the book show a healthy irreverence for jingoistic claims. In truth, either British or Antipodean nationalists can find little to cheer for in *The Fixed Period.* Rather than celebrating imperialism as the only acceptable guarantor of liberal humanitarianism, Trollope is critiquing the arrogance of both British imperialism and local settler nationalism. Much like African writers such as Chinua Achebe in *Anthills of the Savannah,* Trollope does not see being opposed to an unjust old order as any excuse for perpetrating an unjust new one, as was arguably the result of *Bulletin*-era Australian nationalism. The political reverberations of the novel demonstrate that Neverbend's role as emancipator of his country from Britain is inextricably intertwined with his role as proponent of the fixed period theory.

Yet Neverbend is not just a political caricature. He is also involved in domestic complications owing to the fact that it is his best friend, and loyal seneschal in the founding of the Britannulan commonwealth, that is to be the first man who, having attained the requisite age, will be forcibly admitted to the "College" where life's termination will be administered. Thus Neverbend is torn between duty and friendship. To further muddle matters, Neverbend's friend, Gabriel Crasweller, has a daughter, Eva, who attracts the tender interest of Neverbend's own son Jack. Jack is thereby also torn between filial duty, which would prompt him to support the involuntary end to the life of the same man whose daughter he desires. These domestic entanglements are not, as critics have alleged, an incompetent contradiction to the novel's satiric-philosophical armature. They are necessary to flesh out the book, to give Britannula a local habitation and a name. Without them, the book would be a mere allegory or exemplum; with them, it is a thick and multi-textured work.

The novel's domestic aspect particularly deepens the character of Neverbend himself. By positioning Neverbend in myriad and conflicting roles—as President, as father, and, not to be overlooked, as first-person narrator—Trollope makes him more than a one-dimensional caricature. David Skilton, in his introduction to the new Oxford paperback edition, observes that the novel is not "ironic in the simple, everyday sense which implies a reversal of all views expressed in order to reveal the 'truth' of the author's own opinions" (xiv) and that we "are thrown back on our own resources in our negotiations with the text" (xvi). Neverbend is a man of complex motives embedded in a complex narrative situation. Paradoxically, at the same time he is trying to execute his best friend Crasweller he is serving as a benevolent godfather to the romance of his son with Crasweller's daughter Eva. Skilton comments that the romance of Jack and Eva is given "little importance" (xvii) by the book, but in fact it has great significance. Far from just tying up the division of opinion in Britannula over the fixed period, much as the marriage of Kate and Medlicot had done with respect to the dispute between squatters and free-selectors in *Harry Heathcote,* the romance between the children of Crasweller and Neverbend gives the reader a glimpse of what (a more benign) Britannula will be like in the future.

It is this futurity which is at the heart of the power exerted by *The Fixed Period,* a power which, unlike Britain's, has waxed rather than waned with time. The "1980" in which the book takes place was not seriously intended by Trollope as a futuristic prediction of what life would be like a century hence. Therefore, where Trollope does not affirm, he cannot be said to lie. But the futuristic setting of the book does mark its readerly reception in a way that would never occur with a book possessing an emplotment strictly contemporary to its authorship. When Trollope set his book in "1980" he was not guaranteeing that the book would necessarily be read in or after the "real" 1980. But, providing the book were still read, the empirical arrival of "1980" would stand as a prime meridian in the book's reception-history, a point where the book would be no longer a futuristic fantasy *per se* but a futuristic fantasy of the past.

We would think that most of the fun of comparing the two versions of "1980" would be at Trollope's expense. Yet this is not really true; Trollope never pretended to a predictive veracity; *The Fixed Period,* unlike Orwell's *1984,* does not lose its power once the future year depicted passes and the book's predictions are shown to be wildly wrong. *The Fixed Period,* as evidenced in the role Jack and Eva play in the plot, is not about a determinate future, but an openness to futurity and, more specifically, a speculative and rather prescient interest in the nature of the British colonies in the next century. How eerie then that for all of Trollope's own intentional short-circuiting of the status of his novel as prophecy, *The Fixed Period* did end up foreshadowing world events of the "real" 1980. In that year, the status of a former British colony was finally resolved. This colony had, some years before, unilaterally declared independence in order to retain patently unjust policies which otherwise would have been jettisoned by the colonial power. A just solution involving the repeal of the intolerable policies was only brought about by the temporary repossession of the colony by Britain.

The nation in question was Rhodesia, later Zimbabwe, which to preserve segregationist white minority rule unilaterally revolted in 1965 and, under the charismatic leadership of the white-supremacist zealot Ian Smith, held out against world opinion and the internal, black-led "Chimurenga" or resistance movement until British mediation engendered the election of an integrationist black majority government under the leadership of Robert Mugabe (see Verrier [*The Road to Zimbabwe*] 149). The Mugabe government assumed office (and Zimbabwe became independent) on 18 April 1980, only a scant month before Trollope's fictional "May 15" on which Sir Ferdinando Brown was instructed, in the name of Britain, to repossess authority over Britannula from Neverbend and his fixed-periodists. Perhaps this is much more coincidence than prediction; but it is a happenstance whose significance Trollope, who had travelled in South Africa and attendant regions and had written on the racial situation there, would have recognized. If the similarity between **The Fixed Period** and Zimbabwean history does not prove Trollope's merit as a literal forecaster, it does show how engaged he was with questions of Empire, and its future. In some oblique way, Trollope anticipated the theoretical conditions under which a writer such as the contemporary Zimbabwean novelist Tsitsi Dangarembga would come to write. A small achievement, perhaps; yet a noteworthy one.

The colonial Trollope may be only a small part of the metropole-centred Trollope canon, and its suppositions about imperialism, for all their forward-looking aspects, may be too conventional, too time-bound, and too anchored in codified racial and national assumptions of their era to be fully appreciated at the turn of the twenty-first century. Yet Trollope's South Pacific fictions are major contributions to the literature of Empire in the Victorian Age, whose significance has all too infrequently been recognized. After reading **Harry Heathcote of Gangoil** and **The Fixed Period,** no reader can suppose Trollope merely to have been the laureate of the parochially English. Indeed, Trollope emerges as a principal agent in the globalization of English literature and the English language—that is, the change-over, occurring more than has been realized within the nineteenth century, from English literature to Anglophone literature. This global process, carried out in the wake of imperialism, often contradicted and subverted imperial norms, lending impetus to the decolonizing tendencies whose consequences still reverberate for us today.

In turning Englishness upside down, Trollope does not close, but extends the global circle.

Notes

1. Of course, Said's analysis of *Mansfield Park* in *Culture and Imperialism* is not just a close reading or source-study, but a model for a comprehensive engagement of the colonial presence in the mainstream English canon.

2. Shortly after the publication of *The Fixed Period* there was a wave of futuristic fiction published by New Zealand settler writers of the late nineteenth century considering the position of New Zealand in a hypothetical twentieth century (or after). Lawrence Jones mentions "a large group of only nominally 'New Zealand' fictions . . . usually purporting to be written from a New Zealand of the future (any time from 1942 to 2990) and showing the decline of England and Europe and the rise of Australasia . . ." (115). What *The Fixed Period* may achieve is an interrogation of Jones's phrase, "only nominally"—even nominal tropes can theorize historical and linguistic change.

Works Cited

Adam, Ian, and Helen Tiffin, eds. *Past The Last Post: Theorizing Post-colonialism and Post-modernism.* Calgary: U of Calgary P, 1990.

Ashcroft, Bill, Gareth Griffiths, and Helen Tiffin. *The Empire Writes Back.* London: Routledge, 1989.

Bhabha, Homi, ed. *Nation and Narration.* London: Routledge, 1990.

Edwards, P. D. *Anthony Trollope: His Art and Scope.* St. Lucia: U of Queensland P, 1977.

———, and P. D. Joyce. *Anthony Trollope's Son in Australia.* St. Lucia: U of Queensland P, 1982.

Fausett, David. *Writing the New World: Imaginary Voyages and Utopias of the Great Southern Land.* Syracuse: Syracuse UP, 1993.

Glendenning, Victoria. *Trollope.* London: Hutchinson, 1992.

Herbert, Christopher. *Culture and Anomie: The Ethnographic Imagination in Nineteenth-Century England.* Chicago: U of Chicago P, 1991.

Hodge, Bob, and Vijay Mishra. *Dark Side of the Dream: Australian Literature and the Postcolonial Mind.* North Sydney: Allen and Unwin, 1991.

Jones, Lawrence. "The Novel." *The Oxford History of New Zealand Literature in English.* Ed. Terry Sturm. Auckland: Oxford UP, 1991.

Mullen, Richard. *Anthony Trollope: A Victorian in His World.* London: Duckworth, 1990.

Said, Edward. *Culture and Imperialism.* New York: Knopf, 1993.

Slemon, Stephen. "Unsettling the Empire: Resistance Theory for the Second World." *WLWE* [*World Literature Written in English*] 30.2 (1990): 30-41.

Trollope, Anthony. *The Fixed Period.* 1882. Oxford: Oxford UP, 1993.

———. *Harry Heathcote of Gangoil.* 1873. Oxford: Oxford UP, 1993.

Verrier, Anthony. *The Road to Zimbabwe, 1890-1980.* London: Jonathan Cape, 1986.

Viswanathan, Gauri. *Masks of Conquest: Literary Study and British Rule in India.* New York: Columbia UP, 1989.

Wolfreys, Julian. *Being English: Narratives, Idioms, and Performances of National Identity from Coleridge to Trollope.* Albany: State U of New York P, 1994.

Kathy Alexis Psomiades (essay date fall 1999)

SOURCE: Psomiades, Kathy Alexis. "Heterosexual Exchange and Other Victorian Fictions: *The Eustace Diamonds* and Victorian Anthropology." *Novel: A Forum on Fiction* 33, no. 1 (fall 1999): 93-118.

[*In the following excerpts, Psomiades explores the idea that women circulated in Victorian society as objects of heterosexual exchange. According to Psomiades, heterosexual exchange is a protean concept, one that in Trollope's* The Eustace Diamonds *takes on an economic and capitalistic meaning, essentially binding money and sex inextricably.*]

Victorian novels and the people who read them have long been fascinated with the intersections of money and sex. When the economic and erotic come together and seem to resemble, explain, or reflect upon one another, money makes sex important and sex makes money, well, sexy. In particular, the notion that women circulate in heterosexual exchange in the same way that commodities circulate in capitalist exchange and that words circulate in language has powerfully shaped the way we read novels. When we refer to women as "circulating," feminine sexuality as "on the market," the desire for commodities as resembling the desire for sexual objects, relations between men as the true force between struggles over goods and struggles over women, we draw upon theoretical approaches that see heterosexuality and capitalism as homologous social structures, money and sex as connected because they somehow work in the same way to organize the world in which we live.[1]

Anthropologists have criticized this notion of exchange as the governing force of social life, pointing out that it merely projects a Western market concept onto the interactions involving people and goods across the globe.[2] Yet for the readers of Victorian novels, heterosexual exchange still seems to hold explanatory power. Situated between the old world and the new, between a world organized by marriage and kinship and a world organized by the market, Victorian women seem to circulate both literally and figuratively. In the fact that married women cannot own property or earn money for most of the nineteenth century, we can see how the old structures of kinship and alliance trafficked in women; in the association of women with commodity culture, we can see how this old structure is written over with the new economic relations of the market.[3] Heterosexual exchange, with one foot in the past of kinship, and one foot in the present of capitalist circulation, seems the perfect device for explaining how desire and economics function in Victorian novels, and why they still function that way, albeit perhaps more metaphorically, today. What I want to add to this account of how the Victorians and we their heirs live in a world organized by heterosexual exchange, is an account of how they didn't and we don't. I don't mean to imply that this construct didn't and doesn't have material effects. But the great paradox of the idea of heterosexual exchange is that it describes with greater and greater clarity woman's position as circulated sign and commodity at precisely the historical moment in the West in which middle-class women and men to a greater and greater extent are seen as having a claim to equal economic and political agency. Investment in the notion that women circulate seems to increase in direct proportion to their no longer doing so; investment in the archaic nature of heterosexuality seems to increase in direct proportion to changes in marriage and property law that make marriage less like the marriages of alliance than ever before.

The alternative narrative I am hypothesizing goes like this: heterosexual exchange emerges as a concept in precisely the time and place at which a) the exclusion of women, and married women in particular, from economic life comes to seem irrational, b) capitalism thus begins to seem at odds with the economics and ideologies of gender difference, c) cross-sex object choice is in the process of being disconnected from the old institutions of alliance-marriage and articulated as embodied desire both for men and for women, d) cross-sex object choice is being articulated as a sexual identity among other sexual identities: what might at the beginning of the century be seen as the normative center from which the perversions are expelled has itself been altered by the articulation of the perverse, thus the emergence in the 1880s of the word "heterosexual" to provide a complement to "homosexual." Heterosexual exchange makes marriage, that old vestige of alliance, look compatible with the market once again by making a homology between the two. If in alliance money and sex are intimately connected through reproduction, in heterosexual exchange money and sex are intimately connected because they participate in two systems whose similar structure makes them equivalents. In this way, alliance may be collapsed back into sexuality by becoming a sort of market precursor, and what is actually a new sexual identity based in cross-sex object choice can be systemized, archaized, and universalized. Rather than providing an explanation of how heterosexuality has functioned across time and space, heterosexual exchange is part of the process whereby in a very specific time and place heterosexuality is invented.

In what follows, I will be using Anthony Trollope's *The Eustace Diamonds* and some of the early texts of Victorian anthropology—Henry Sumner Maine's *Ancient Law* and John McLennan's *Primitive Marriage*—to examine some of the labor that goes into that invention. Late-Victorian meditations on women as property do not, I am claiming, reflect a state of fact, analyze an existing social order, or even merely seek to provide an alternative economic system to the somewhat threatening circulations of capital, although they make claims to do all of these things. Rather, these meditations constitute an attempt to think through the relations between marriage and capital, the structures of alliance and the newly emergent structures of sexuality, the relations between the gendered individual and the market individual, and the changing relations between sexuality and reproduction in such a world. To see the trouble Trollope takes to produce a metaphorics of circulation that runs contrary to the economic activity he describes, to see how much wild speculation is necessary to make patriarchal marriage look civilized instead of primitive, is to see heterosexuality not as a constant across historical time, but as something that has to be invented and reinvented. While Maine, McLennan, and Trollope assume universal cross-sex object choice, their efforts to describe and systematize that choice and describe its relation to private property have as their biproduct the opening of a space in which sexuality may be thought apart from gender and reproduction, a space as necessary to imagining modern heterosexuality as it is to imagining any other modern sexual identity.

I. Reading Heterosexual Exchange in The Eustace Diamonds

Structured around two contrasting heroines and one very valuable diamond necklace, *The Eustace Diamonds* uses metaphors of treasure, real and fake jewels, gift, theft, and circulation to tie good and bad women to good and bad property. Lizzie Eustace, the novel's bad girl, is associated with ill-gotten gains. She is "not just all that she should be" (1: 270), "paste" rather than "real stone" (2: 230). Like the diamonds she has stolen

from her husband's family, she is made "to shine and glitter" (1: 159). When she offers herself to her cousin Frank Greystock, her "charms of feminine grace" are described as being "tendered openly in the market" (2: 127). Lizzie is bad not only because she openly places her charms on the marriage market, but because she doesn't have the value she claims to have. Her value is exchange value—as such it doesn't inhere in her, but in the systems of exchange in which she operates, the laws of supply and demand. Thus, like most things in the system of objects, she is associated with surfaces, games, and lies, "the outward shows of all those things of which the inward facts are valued by the good and steadfast ones of the earth" (1: 126).

If Lizzie is associated with the world of surfaces, appearances, and shifting values that commodity circulation creates, Lucy Morris, the novel's other heroine, is associated with true value, depth, use, and the real, but also through a language that links her to objects. She is repeatedly referred to as a "treasure," a "little thing," and "truth itself" (1: 23-5, 121). She is "good as gold," "real stone" (1: 271, 2: 230). If Lizzie puts herself on the market, Lucy gives her heart and continues to possess herself, she knows her own worth, even when the possession of herself is "wearisome" and "bitter" to her, when she thinks Frank Greystock has deserted her (2: 189). As Andrew Miller cogently explains, "Figured as an object, Lucy then has her virtue represented as the proper attitude towards and behavior with possessions" (171). Lucy protects the value of women, words, and things by bestowing herself as a gift upon Frank, a gift whose value he recognizes and that places him under an obligation he ultimately fulfills. Lucy thus holds a place for objects and possessions not subject to the vagaries of the market by participating in a mode of exchange, gift exchange, that predates and provides an alternative to commodity culture.

In *The Afterlife of Property,* Jeff Nunokawa points out the ubiquity of this Victorian version of heterosexual exchange and its usefulness for managing anxieties about how the expansion of capitalism changes the nature of property itself:

> The difference between the angel of the house and the prostitute of the parlor or the streets is the difference between a species of property thought safe, from one that can never be, the difference between forms and forces that expand indefinitely beyond the arena of the commodity and a kind of estate exempted from all its vicissitudes.

(13)

The market in women is thus both a double and an "other" to the market in goods: like commodities, bad women occupy the "zone of circulation," whereas good women remain in the "zone of possession" like the inalienable property of a precapitalist past. Although he makes his argument through readings of Charles Dickens and George Eliot, Nunokawa's terms usefully illuminate Trollope's novel as well. Lucy will be for her husband a form of inalienable property, always in the "zone of possession," which she preserves and represents. Lizzie, by contrast, like her diamonds, is always in the "zone of circulation": she can never be permanently held, but is forever in the process of slipping into the hands of another. The novel thus links economic circulation and the marriage market in order to create a safe place in which the hero's less noble desires—the desire for sex, for money, for things, for power—will be tempered by Lucy's self-regulation and desire not to have things but to "be effective in the object then before her" (1: 26). Frank is thus safe from the market world of appearances and arbitrary values, a world with which he dallies, but from which he eventually breaks free, recognizing that Lucy is not only "as good as gold" but actually better than "real gold" because she can be permanently possessed in a way that gold cannot.

Nunokawa is one of the most careful readers of Victorian heterosexual exchange: although he invokes the context of the debates about marriage law taking place in the 1860s, he is generally careful not to imply that married women can be thought of as property because their legal status prevents them from being property owners.[4] He does not use theories of heterosexual exchange to explain how Victorian marriage works: rather, he is concerned with the cultural work performed by the idea that heterosexuality is structured by the notion of woman as inalienable estate. But in his suggestion that we broaden our understanding of the economic to include all forms of circulation and possession, he does at least participate in one central operation of heterosexual exchange: to create homologies between the different spheres of social life by locating them in a common structure.

The consequences of such homology-making may be seen not only in Trollope's novel, but also in the ways we read that novel today. In one of the most perceptive readings of "the relationship between female sexuality and property" in *The Eustace Diamonds,* William Cohen argues that Lizzie's diamonds "at once metaphorize sexuality and literalize the economics of sexual difference" (175, 161). According to Cohen, because sex is constituted as the unspeakable in the Victorian realist novel, the sexual secret of *The Eustace Diamonds* must be encoded in the diamonds themselves. Lizzie may be able to divert the diamonds from masculine control by claiming they are her own and not part of her husband's family estate, but she ultimately can neither hold nor sell them, just as women cannot maintain control over their own sexuality. For Cohen, the legal question of whether the diamonds are an heirloom—inalienable

property with a value outside market exchange—or paraphernalia—alienable property that might be sold—is also a question in the register of sexuality.[5] Heirloom indicates a masculine property passed down from father to son, paraphernalia a specifically feminine form of property—what the widow gets to keep as her own. The necklace thus "allows the heterosexual contract to be conceived in literal financial terms, manifesting, as it does, the economic realities of the marriage market" (167). Property can thus represent feminine sexuality because feminine sexuality is actually on some level really property. Lucy may treat her sexuality as an heirloom and Lizzie as paraphernalia, but "[t]he presentation of the two women taken together elucidates the ideology that directs women to imagine their desires on the heirloom model and yet treats them as commodities, condemning them when they seek to govern their own value in the exchange economy in which they really do circulate" (171).

Cohen's essay demonstrates how the idea of heterosexual exchange organizes the fictional world of Trollope's novel: the sense of rightness and inevitability about his reading shows how thorough the fit is between modern and Victorian meditations on these themes. But while heterosexual exchange allows him to see how women's sexuality and economic position are connected because of the way in which women circulate in heterosexuality, it does not allow him to see how this metaphorical connection is paired with a literal disconnection, at least in the world of the novel. By using phrases like "really do circulate" and "literal financial terms," Cohen invites us to examine the economic conditions in which Trollope's characters find themselves. What such an examination reveals is that what Cohen calls "the relation between female sexuality and property" acts to figure and obscure female characters' actual economic activities. The novel's plot is carefully constructed so that the world of the novel cannot possibly work in the way heterosexual exchange implies that it works. For example, Trollope employs the standard metaphors of sexual exchange to describe Lizzie's declaration of love to Frank:

> It is inexpressibly difficult for a man to refuse the tender of a woman's love. We may almost say that a man should do so as a matter of course,—that the thing so offered becomes absolutely valueless by the offer,— that the woman who can make it has put herself out of court by her own abandonment of the privileges due to her as a woman—that stern rebuke and even expressed contempt are justified by such conduct—and that the fairest beauty and most alluring charms of feminine grace should lose their attraction when thus tendered openly in the market.
>
> (2: 126-27)

This passage seems utterly in accordance with the rules of heterosexual exchange—women are not to act as agents on the market. When they do, offering sex for money like so many Becky Sharps, they are no better than prostitutes. But the economic/erotic transaction it describes is not the offer of female sexuality to a masculine buyer. Lizzie's offer is not an offer of sex for money, but an offer of money for sex: "I want to see you a great man and a lord, and I know that you cannot become so without an income" (2: 128). The transaction Trollope describes is almost the opposite of what actually occurs: Lizzie doesn't offer herself to the highest bidder, instead she puts in bids on all of her suitors, all of whom have lower incomes than she does herself.

Now we could certainly say that this contradiction proves the point of heterosexual exchange, that even when women have the money to enter the market as buyers, the status of feminine sexuality as object means they always must be for sale. But the problem posed by the contradiction still remains: why figure circulable property in the figure of a woman who is explicitly set up in the novel's opening chapter as one who has already traded her sex for property and is now the owner of both property and sex? We need only compare the novel, as it is often compared, to *Vanity Fair* to see how very much more successful a trader Lizzie is than Becky Sharp, and how differently they are situated in relation to the marriage market. Becky acquires little property of her own, despite her scheming, whereas Lizzie, thanks to her husband's generous settlement, has an income of £4000 a year entirely at her own disposal during her lifetime, in addition to the use of an estate, and her stolen necklace. Furthermore, not only is Lizzie clearly and explicitly situated as economic agent, but the novel describes to us men—Lord Fawn, Mr. Emelius, even Frank Greystock—offering themselves and their assets on the marriage market for money.

Trollope's novel thus goes out of its way to create a world in which actual economic relations and activities run counter to metaphorical economic relations and activities. In so doing, it assigns to its actual and metaphorical economies two different temporalities and logics. On the one hand, there is the marriage market of heterosexual exchange, an ancient system in which men and women play very different roles; on the other, there is a world in which men and women alike buy and sell, and are alike defined by the same standards of yearly income figures. In this world, Lizzie, Lucy, Frank, and Lord Fawn no longer signify bad and good feminine and masculine sexuality, but £4000, £80, £2000, and £2500, their yearly incomes. In the older, metaphorical world of heterosexual exchange, Lizzie and Lucy circulate as bad and good objects, dangerous and proper property. In the newer world both Lizzie and Lucy have economic agency, Lizzie as the possessor of property and Lucy as a wage earner. A world organized by gender difference is in the process of being supplanted by the world of capital.

The Victorian story of heterosexual exchange in which we as cultural critics share is just this story of the supplanting of a society organized by kinship and alliance by a society of individual units who act as independent agents in the market. When we invoke this story, which, like anthropology itself, has its origins in the Victorian period, we invoke a set of assumptions that have attained the status of common sense: that heterosexual gender relations predate capitalism, that contemporary notions of sexuality and gender are still written over with this archaic formation, that women are figured as property because they once were, and still metaphorically are, although they now have economic agency. Reading *The Eustace Diamonds* as one of a series of Victorian theories about the connections between women and property allows us to see not only the ways in which the common sense of heterosexual exchange acts to manage anxieties about property in the society of capital, but also how it acts to disguise the challenge such a society poses to traditional gender relations. The language of women and property fills Victorian novels and the writings of Victorian feminists alike not because these are the existing terms through which the culture thinks gender difference, but because these terms themselves are a way of thinking though the increasing irrationality attached to the notion that men and women have different relations to property.[6] Or to put it another way, women circulate in *The Eustace Diamonds* not because in 1870 married women are still not legally able to own property, but because by 1882, they legally are.

II. WHY THE EUSTACE DIAMONDS ARE NOT AN HEIRLOOM: WOMEN AND PROPERTY IN HENRY MAINE'S ANCIENT LAW

Henry Maine's 1861 *Ancient Law* is one of the more memorable Victorian versions of the story of the supplanting of kinship society by market society and the consequent changes in how property is conceived.[7] Written in the years immediately after the Divorce Act of 1857 and the refusal to pass a married women's property bill in the same year, *Ancient Law* very clearly articulates the ways in which marriage and market society have begun to seem fundamentally incompatible, belonging to two different and mutually exclusive ways of organizing culture. For Maine, this incompatibility is never mediated by a theory of heterosexual exchange: *Ancient Law* thus illuminates *The Eustace Diamonds* both through the story it tells, and through the story it does not tell.

Ancient Law is organized around a binary opposition between primitive and civilized societies. The world of individuals, property, and contract that allows both capitalism and civilization to exist has a "before" marked by the absence of all its distinguishing features. The primitive world is stationary, rather than progressive;

one in which goods and people stay put, rather than circulate; a world of the group, rather than the individual; of the family, rather than the territorial state; of the unwritten law that is the parent's word, rather than written law. The mark left on written law by this early form of society is what the Romans called "Patria Potestas": the father's authority over the person and property of his descendants, essentially the same whether exercised "over flocks, herds, slaves, children or wife" (307). There is no distinction between people and property in primitive patriarchy, because there is no such thing as an individual, and no such thing as private property. The father's authority over the household comes from his status as representative of the family as a whole, not from individual proprietary power:

> [S]ociety in primitive times was not what it is assumed to be at present, a collection of individuals. *In fact, and in the view of the men who composed it, it was* an aggregation of families. *The contrast may be most forcibly expressed by saying that the* unit *of an ancient society was the Family, of a modern society the Individual.*
>
> (121)

The primary characteristic of this primitive society seems to be its static, immobile nature. The family is a corporation, Maine says, and thus it never dies. Individual family leaders die, and others inherit their positions and powers, but the family goes on. Even the kinship structure of agnation, in which men trace their descent through their fathers and married women are seen as part of their husband's families, is not imagined by Maine as a series of exchanges between families and blood lines, but as the maintenance of one bloodline over time. "The foundation of Agnation is not the marriage of Father and Mother, but the authority of the Father" (144). Thus Maine imagines kinship and blood relations in patriarchal society not as based in a heterosexual union, and not even as exchanges between men: the Father is not imagined as exchanging with other Fathers, but as holding power over descendants of his own blood, reproducing himself and the family he represents eternally.

The transition from the static past of kinship to a mobile modern present of civilization is, Maine argues, the exception and not the rule: only the Romans, and those cultures exposed to them, really experienced this shift from ancient to modern, "the gradual disentanglement of the separate rights of individuals from the blended rights of a community" (261). "The history of political ideas" begins "with the assumption that kinship in blood is the sole possible ground of community in political functions" (124). Families aggregate into the Gens or House, then the Tribe, then the Commonwealth. But in ancient Rome, as groups of families become larger and aristocracies form, claiming rights of blood for some members of a society and not others, those unincluded

members begin to see themselves as a community grounded not in consanguinity, but in "local contiguity": if members of a family are linked in time through blood, members of a modern society are linked by the spaces they share. This movement from consanguinity to contiguity is accompanied by a focus on exchanges between individuals: people are tied together less and less by "those forms of reciprocity in rights and duties which have their origin in the Family" and more and more by "Contract" or "the free agreement of individuals" (163). Gradually, contracting workers replace slaves, women who are not married get the right to contract, parents no longer have power over children who are of age except through contract. "The individual is steadily substituted for the Family, as the unit of which civil laws take account" (163). Children, orphans, and lunatics are left subject to extrinsic control, but no longer on the grounds of parental power: "they do not possess the faculty of forming a judgment on their own interests . . . they are wanting in the first essential of an engagement by contract" (164).

Maine famously formulates "the law of progress" by using the word "status" to signify the bonds of power and obligation linking members of the patriarchal family, and the world "contract" to indicate the agreements between individuals that even more than physical contiguity seem to tie together capitalist cultures: "the movement of the progressive societies has hitherto been a movement *from Status to Contract*" (165). By redefining marriage as an ancient social arrangement of status, like slavery, a holdover from a world without the benefit of contract, Maine primitivizes patriarchy. The laws governing "the proprietary disabilities of married females" he sees as having "deeply injured civilization" (153). They are "archaisms," remnants of a social organization essentially hostile to capitalism and thus hostile to the full development of contemporary societies. In a world of contract, gender difference, like the other old relations of status, is irrelevant: the only distinctions between individuals that matter are those that refer to competency to contract. Patriarchy cannot be imagined as exchange because its operations are antithetical to exchange: only the operations of contract can be imagined as exchange. There is thus no possibility of heterosexual exchange in this world because gender difference and exchange belong to two different, incompatible universes that cannot exist in the same place at the same time.

Maine's articulation of the relation between marriage and market as one of pure opposition illuminates *The Eustace Diamonds* in several ways. First, it partly explains why the good wife is articulated as property held, rather than property exchanged, as marriage is connected to the inalienable possessions of families, rather than the alienable private property of individuals. Second, it allows us to recast the legal question of the diamonds, and see the connection of that question to issues of gender and sexuality: are the diamonds and the women they figure part of the world of status, or the world of contract? Finally, and perhaps most importantly, it helps us to see the labor required to make the unlike like, the labor of producing a theory of heterosexual exchange, a labor in which the diamonds prove very useful.

The diamond plot of *The Eustace Diamonds* makes graphically visible the relation between status and contract. At the novel's beginning, the diamonds Lizzie Eustace refuses to return to her late husband's property figure both marital and property relations in the culture of status. Worn by women who marry into the Eustace family—the sign of their absorption into agnation—and designated an heirloom, that is, property that has a special relation to the undying corporation that is the Eustace family, the diamonds necessitate the novel's engagement with property law. Insofar as they are connected to a society of status, the diamonds reveal how agnation differentiates between men and women's property relations: they can either be an heirloom—masculine property whose symbolic significance is to represent the undying nature of masculine blood and its ability to reproduce itself through female vessels—or paraphernalia—property not necessarily alienable which a widow may claim and hold out of the masculine order of succession. Both forms are status forms: the basis on which the widow can claim paraphernalia is her "income and degree," i.e., her status as determined by the status of her late husband and of her father (1: 260). Like coverture, heirloom and paraphernalia are still legal forms at the time of the novel's composition, but as Maine and the novel itself make clear, these forms are increasingly archaic. Thus Mr. Dove's assertion that "the system of heirlooms, if there can be said to be such a system, was not devised for what you and I mean when we talk of the protection of property. . . . It was devised with the more picturesque idea of maintaining chivalric associations" (1: 258). A remnant from a culture before system and before private property, heirloom is about a form of possession alien to modern ideas of ownership.

The most important thing about the heirloom/paraphernalia question and the world of reproduction, blood, and patriarchal conceptions of gender difference to which it refers, is its ultimate irrelevance. Mr. Dove's disquisition makes it very clear that the diamonds are neither an heirloom nor paraphernalia, but simply private property in masquerade. Being alterable, they cannot represent the unalterable nature of the corporation. More importantly, being of immense value, and having been acquired by purchase in the bourgeois era, their ability to signify a relation constructed by contract—£10,000—cancels out their ability to signify relations constructed by status.[8] It is thus ultimately a contract,

Sir Florian's will, that will determine the ownership of the diamonds, and not a determination of gendered status property rights—the basis of Lizzie's claim to them is not the concept of paraphernalia, but the false claim that they were given to her at Portray before her husband wrote the will leaving her its contents. It is the inexact language of the contract that allows ownership to become an issue of location purely. Through that contract, we might say, consanguinity gives way to contiguity.

At this point, when the diamonds have been detached from the culture of status and revealed as creatures of the culture of contract, the operations of heterosexual exchange become visible. Heirloom and paraphernalia have nothing to do with heterosexual exchange or with sexuality: they are connected to the logic of reproduction and blood that organizes what Maine calls status, and Foucault calls alliance. They situate gender difference in the past. In order to recivilize gender difference, and bring it into the present in a form compatible with the society of contract and sexuality, gender and sexuality must be detached from the society of status, reshaped, and reattached to the society of contract. When they cease to signify Eustaceness, and come instead to signify £10,000, the diamonds have entered the society of contract. At this point, they can be used to reshape sex and gender in two ways: 1) through their attachment to bodies, they come to signify sexuality as a matter of the body's desires and 2) through their metaphorical attachment to femininity specifically, and to the articulation of femininity as a value form (real stone/paste), they recast sexuality as an operation of exchange. If women are like jewels, and men are like people in search of jewels to purchase, then there is a structural homology between marriage and the market that makes them compatible. Heterosexual exchange is the mechanism whereby this structural homology is brought into being; it then makes gender difference structurally assimilable into the society of contract.

In order that women may be imagined as "really circulating" in an exchange economy called heterosexuality, both sex and property have to be detached from the relations of status and alliance that formerly ordered them, and reconnected through imagining structural homology to the market. In such an imagining, traditional marriage ceases to seem antithetical to the market and a drag upon it and becomes a mirror-image of the market, a necessary escape that nevertheless supports in reverse the market's principles. The woman no longer denied economic agency in the society of the contract can be figured as lacking that agency in the marriage market, where her femininity renders her an object among other circulating objects. When Cohen claims that the heirloom/paraphernalia distinction is a distinction between inalienable property and commodities—do women belong to men to keep, or do they endlessly circulate themselves?—he participates in the novel's project of removing gender difference from the culture of status, and reattaching it to the culture of contract. What Maine makes visible are the operations required to produce this effect. Cohen's claim that the necklace "allows the heterosexual contract to be conceived in literal financial terms, manifesting as it does, the economic realities of the marriage market," is thus both right and wrong (167). The necklace allows heterosexuality to be imagined as a contract and marriage to be imagined as a market, but it does so not because it manifests a reality, but because it produces a homology. If women are either treasures or fakes, inalienable or alienable property, gifts or purchases, then sexual difference can be imagined as an economic relation, one that works to cover over the gender indifference of the society of contract. It is the insistence on this gender indifference that makes Trollope's plot run counter to his metaphors, and it is the spectacle of marriage made archaic by capital that necessitates the production of figures of heterosexual exchange. The final owner of the jewels is a woman, but it is her wealth ("enormously rich") and position ("Russian princess") rather than her gender that makes it impossible to extricate them from her grasp.

That Lizzie is metaphorically for sale, but literally buying, marks out the problematic relation between figurative and literal markets in Trollope's novel. To read Maine is to understand some of why this is so, and how the diamonds, in their dual status as sex and property, disguise this problem. As property to which Lizzie has no right, and which she cannot keep, they distract our attention from the property to which she does have a right, and which she does manage to keep.[9] . . .

Rejected by anthropologists in the 1920s, the idea of the priority of primitive matrilineage is now primarily of historical rather than theoretical interest. Yet the Victorian rationalization of the inequality of patriarchal relations in the 1860s, 70s, and 80s depends on primitive matrilineage to render irrational the notion of a structural equivalence between men and women as market individuals. The Victorian theory of heterosexual exchange is only half of an attempt to theorize the new conditions of cross-sex object choice: the Victorian theory of primitive matrilineage is the other half of that attempt. To recover primitive matrilineage is thus to recover the cultural material that a theory of heterosexual exchange must of necessity disavow in order to make a homology of what remains. To generalize about Victorian heterosexuality through the medium of heterosexual exchange alone is to take the part for the whole.

In the case of *The Eustace Diamonds,* primitive matrilineage enters the novel in the form of its third heroine, Lucinda Roanoke. Read from the perspective of heterosexual exchange, Lucinda can be seen only as a third

circulating object: the girl who rather than opting for the gift exchange of love, or attempting to manipulate the market for her own ends, is a reluctant participant in a mercenary marriage arrangement that eventually destroys her. She turns a structure of good girl/bad girl into what seems more like the Goldilocks structure: too hot/too cold/just right.[10] Yet by ultimately refusing the marriage she has always hated, even if that refusal occurs on the very day of the wedding, she does, as Cohen notes, provide "[a] genuine difference in the representation of female sexuality" in the novel, "an alternative—however psychotic in its depiction—to the heterosexual order that organizes the other women's desire" (172-73). Primitive matrilineage gives us a way of looking at the specificity of this alternative: as both a gesture towards sexualities conceived of as exterior to heterosexuality, and a gesture towards the disorder interior to the emergent category of heterosexuality. Read from this perspective, Lucinda is not a marginalized third term, but a figure for feminine sexuality constructed on a different model than that of circulating object.

Lucinda's difference is figured as a difference of the body. In heterosexual exchange, women's bodies are shaped like commodities: they have surfaces that indicate their exchange value and depths in which their use value resides. The surface of the body is a disguise—Lizzie's flashy exterior hides her shallow nature; Lucy's unremarkable exterior also disguises the treasure that is her depth. Lizzie and Lucy's bodies are always compared to one another, through the gazes of Frank Greystock and the narrator, masculine consumers who use a standard of value to read in them their relative worth. When we first meet Lucinda, whose body is sensationally visible, it seems that this body must be read according to the same standards of value: her beautiful exterior hides not a lack of depth, but the bad depth of a murderer. But Lucinda's body resists this reading. Her murderousness is as much a matter of surface as depth, since it can be seen by those who have viewed only a representation of her surface, "her portrait" which "caused much remark in the Exhibition" (1: 330). Viewers of this portrait turn not to the market, but to history in the form of famous fatal women—Brinvilliers, Cleopatra, the Queen of Sheba—to read Lucinda's body. That body thus almost always emerges from a different time and place, the more distant, the less criminal the femininity. Brinvilliers, the seventeenth century French Marquise who murdered her father and brothers and sought to murder her husband, is far more deviant than the Queen who engaged in gift exchange with Solomon. The black hair, "broad nose," and "thick lips" that Lucinda shares with her aunt; the epithet "savage" so frequently applied to her; the Native American word that stands as Lucinda's patronym all conspire to racialize, primitivize, and archaize her (1: 328). Gigantic alongside the "little thing" that is Lucy and the equally delicate and diminutive Lizzie, all of Lucinda's physical characteristics announce that "one of these things is not like the others."

But if Lucinda can only be read as the thing that doesn't belong in the Lizzie/Lucy market model of femininity, there is a context in which she most certainly does belong. Lucinda's body is, from the first, presented as a copy of Mrs. Carbuncle's body, and the shared content of these bodies is not "value" as constituted by heterosexual exchange, but "blood" as constituted by primitive matrilineage, the distinctly embodied, biological and sexualized blood of promiscuous polyandry.[11] The spectacular resemblance between Lucinda and her "aunt" is the open and yet unspoken sexual scandal of the novel: although there is much speculation on who Lucinda's father may be, that speculation is predicated on certainty about who her mother is. The brilliant color that flushes Lucinda's face, "deep on her cheeks as on her aunt's," the complexion shared by both women that is "a wonder" and "marvelous," is both a metaphorical and literal reference to common blood (1: 329). It allows for and figures the perception of what McLennan calls "the fact of consanguinity in the simplest case," that is, an individual's recognition, "that he has his mother's blood in his veins" (85). In the blush, mother's blood is wonderfully, marvelously, spectacularly visible.

Whereas value turns the body into a commodity in search of a consumer, blood makes the body a sign not of desirability, but of desire. Both Lucy and Lucinda find themselves looking at their bodies in mirrors during moments when they are troubled by their lovers. Lucy, nearly abandoned by Frank Greystock, casts a "glance at her features in the glass" and sees in her physical appearance the sign of her valuelessness in a market driven by exchange (2: 187). Lucinda, fresh from the horror of Sir Griffin's kisses, stands "before her glass," looking not at her exterior features but "at herself," at the body that through its physical sexual response to another body constitutes itself as the location of identity: "The embrace had disgusted her. It made her odious to herself. And if this, the beginning of it, were so bad, how was she to drink the cup to the bitter dregs?" (1: 24). The former looks to the body to tell her more about a man's feelings for her, the latter looks to the body to tell her about her embodied feelings towards a male body. Blood, in the form of the blush, is not only the sign of the illicit feminine desire (i.e., her mother's promiscuity) to which Lucinda owes her very existence, but also the sign of Lucinda's own desire, conceived of as an involuntary bodily response.[12]

The circulation of blood thus takes the place of the circulation of objects in a market, indeed something about that blood renders Mrs. Carbuncle and Lucinda's bodies uncirculable. The relation between value, body, blood,

and femininity is encapsulated in the word "carbuncle" which presumably both is and isn't Mrs. Carbuncle's name. "Carbuncle" has the archaic meaning of "red stone," and in that sense it ties Mrs. Carbuncle to the lapidary theme of the novel. Its contemporary meaning, however, is "blemish," "boil," or "sore." When jewel and body come together in heterosexual exchange, the jewel defines the body's value—Lizzie is paste, Lucy is real stone. When jewel and body come together in a figure of primitive matrilineage, the body incorporates the jewel and gives it the bodily value of health/disease—red stones circulate, but there is no currency in skin disease. Finally, not only does Mrs. Carbuncle's name historicize the refiguration of "blood" as a feature of the medicalized body, but it ultimately suggests that this narrative is itself a cover, associated as it is with a name that is only temporarily Mrs. Carbuncle's own. "Mrs. Carbuncle" is "Jane" seen from the perspective of patriarchal marriage, a system with which she does not comply and which is not sufficient to define her.[13]

Lucinda and her mother, then, figure the two sides of feminine sexual agency: desire and disgust conceived of as desire's reversal. Lucinda's disgust is not the absence of embodied desire, but a negative form of that desire. Just as Mrs. Carbuncle has listened to her body's promptings rather than adhering to the calculating logic of heterosexual exchange, so ultimately does Lucinda heed her body rather than her economic interests. To Lizzie, who cannot conceive of a sexuality apart from calculation and whose body, the narrator is at great pains to tell us, feels neither desire nor disgust, Lady Glencora's references to the mystery of Lucinda's parentage are unintelligible, as is Lucinda's claim that she is afraid she will murder Sir Griffin: "Lady Eustace, I really think that I should—kill him, if he really were,— were my husband" (2: 244). The dashes point to Lucinda's inappropriate sexual knowledge—the fantasy of killing is also a fantasy of the sexual intercourse for which it substitutes. As Lucinda whispers to Lizzie after her refusal, "if ever 'he' should come there again, she would 'give him a kiss with a vengeance'" (2: 283). That feminine sexual desire should take the form of murderousness towards men, that Lucinda should fulfill the promises her body makes when we first view it, is based in a translation of the social structures of matrilineage into the structures of Lucinda's psyche. By rendering men's blood untraceable, father's unknowable, and men incapable of reproducing themselves, matrilineage metaphorically kills men.

The feminine sexual agency that matrilineage makes imaginable gives Lucinda alone of the three heroines a sexual identity based in object choice. This identity is as yet neither heterosexual nor homosexual, but the motivation of disgust/desire opens up the possibility of either position, both for Lucinda and for the other characters in the novel to whom disgust spreads. From the perspective of heterosexual exchange, Lucinda must choose between economic gain in a corrupt system or a refusal of the system from the position of irrationality. From the perspective of primitive matrilineage she struggles between two truths of the body, her link to her mother, and her disgust. She proclaims to Sir Griffin that she prefers Mrs. Carbuncle to him, she tells Lizzie that Sir Griffin must be the one to break the marriage off because, "He is not bound to anybody as I am bound to my aunt. No one can have extracted an oath from him," and she says to Mrs. Carbuncle herself, "I have struggled so hard,—simply that you might be freed from me" (2: 243, 273). She will either marry for the sake of female-female bonds, or refuse marriage because of her body's response to the object of her desire. The two aspects of this choice—bonds between women and feminine sexual agency—are unimaginable in heterosexual exchange except as refusal, yet they are absolutely necessary to imagining feminine and masculine sexuality as alike structured around the question of the gender of object choice. Primitive matrilineage makes them visible.

Finally, disgust imagined as anti-desire is visible in two other locations in the novel where it points up the instability of desire-based identities. Just as Lucinda's disgust gestures both towards masculine object choice and towards the possibility of feminine objects one might like better, so too does Frank Greystock's final disgust at Lizzie's physical presence—"soiled, haggard, disheveled, and unclean . . . her long lock of hair was out of curl and untidy,—a thing that ought not to have been there during such a journey as this" (2: 336). He recoils from something masculine, reaffirming his own heterosexual object choice, but his recoil is from the phallic lock of hair that once fascinated and thrilled him, so it also gestures towards his own deviance. More remarkably, the narrator, while graphically describing Lizzie's lack of disgust for Mr. Emilius, seems overly eager to imagine himself in her place:

> it was nothing against him in her judgment that he was a greasy, fawning, pawing, creeping, black-browed rascal, who could not look her full in the face, and whose every word sounded like a lie. There was a twang in his voice which ought to have told her that he was utterly untrustworthy. There was an oily pretence at earnestness in his manner which ought to have told that he was not fit to associate with gentlemen. There was a foulness of demeanour about him which ought to have given to her, as a woman at any rate brought up among ladies, an abhorrence of his society. But all this Lizzie did not feel. . . . [s]he was neither angry, nor disgusted.. . . .
>
> (2: 241-42)

If Lizzie's body does not respond to Mr. Emilius's body, the narrator's most certainly does: his recoil requires that he imagine himself as a woman having congress with that body. What these scenes suggest is that gender and sexuality, as conceived of under the operations of object choice and identity, are less stable categories than gender and sexuality conceived as rejection of or accession to heterosexual exchange.

What I am suggesting finally, is not that the desiring body is the location of resistance to system, a resistance that "heterosexual exchange" obscures. Rather I think that the homologies of heterosexual exchange obscure the ways in which sexuality actually connects bodies to the economic "through numerous and subtle relays, the main one of which, however, is the body—the body that produces and consumes" (Foucault [*History of Sexuality*] 106-7). Heterosexual exchange may be refused, sexuality cannot be. Individuals with sexual agency who think of themselves as heterosexual or homosexual are regulated, although in different ways and through different means than women who enter into economic alliances: even Mrs. Carbuncle and Lucinda have their disgust and desire for sexual objects figured in their relations to feminine consumer goods.[14] Further, a vision of heterosexuality as women circulating archaizes feminine sexuality and obscures the facts primitive matrilineage reveals, namely, that the woman who sleeps with men *becomes* a female heterosexual at a specific historic moment and that this new creature, who is constituted by her preference for male sexual objects in a universe of many different kinds of objects, is a much stranger, more unstable, and more troublesome creature than the phrase "heterosexual order" would imply.

Notes

1. A by no means complete list of the texts about exchange influencing Victorian novel criticism might include Levi-Strauss, Rubin, Irigaray, Sedgwick. Also germane would be Mauss and Goux.

2. See, for example, Weiner, who stresses the ways in which the drive to exchange works alongside the drive to keep other objects out of circulation.

3. In using the word "alliance" and drawing upon a historical narrative in which alliance is a societal structure belonging to an earlier time than "sexuality," I am, of course, drawing on Foucault.

4. He does, however, attribute this connection to Victorian feminists, who "noted that the abbreviation or abrogation of married women's right to own property was concomitant with the conversion of such women into the property of their husbands" (128n24).

5. Cohen's definition of paraphernalia as necessarily alienable property is not entirely shared by the lawyers in Trollope's novel.

6. Mary Poovey writes, "It is important to emphasize, however, that even though the gender in-

equality of patriarchal relations . . . was initially carried over from the theological into the modern economic domain, this inequality soon manifested itself as *ir*rational in relation to the claim that economic individuals were structurally equivalent in the marketplace. . . . The failure of attempts to pass a married women's property bill in 1857 allowed one kind of rationality (theological) to persist, then, but only as an increasingly obvious *ir*rationality when judged in the context of emergent modern domains (the juridical, the economic)" (15). For the particulars of these attempts, see Shanley. For a reading of the propertied woman in the Victorian novel, see Dolin.

7. Maine's work had a significant impact on historical jurisprudence, on the new social sciences that would become sociology and anthropology, and on the government of India, where he later served as Legal member of the Governor-General's Council. For extensive consideration of Maine's writing and its impact in these fields, see Diamond. For his role in the history of anthropology, see Kuper and Stocking.

8. "The diamonds in question had been bought, with other jewels, by Sir Florian's grandfather, on the occasion of his marriage with the daughter of a certain duke,—on which occasion old family jewels, which were said to have been heirlooms, were sold or given in exchange as part value for those then purchased" (1: 149).

9. Later in the Palliser novels, Lizzie reappears unmarried, Mr. Emilius having been a bigamist after all. In *The Prime Minister,* she has realized that holding on to one's money is preferable to acquiring men with it.

10. Who is "too hot" and who "too cold" is a matter for debate. For Cohen, Lucinda would be too cold in her frigidity, and Lizzie too hot in her libidinousness. For McCormack, the editor of the Oxford edition, Lucinda is pure sex object (hot), Lucy asexual (cold), and Lizzie a woman in charge of her own sexuality. For me, Trollope's insistence on Lizzie's lack of desire/disgust sets her out as too cold, Lucinda's passionate disgust marks her as too hot.

11. "Blood" here is not the abstract blood of patrilineal alliance, like that signified by the Eustace name and the Eustace jewels: for a discussion of how primitive matrilineage redefines the terms "blood" and "kinship" so that they mean differently than they do under aristocratic alliance, see Levy 63-64.

12. Lizzie, of course, does not blush: "It was only when she simulated anger,—she was almost incapable of real anger,—that she would succeed in calling the thinnest streak of pink from her heart, to show that there was blood running in her veins" (1: 17). Whereas in Lucinda's case, "the colour would go and come and shift and change with every word and every thought" (1: 329).

13. "Roanoke" in addition to being a place name is also, oddly enough, a gesture towards non-capitalist exchange: it means "shell money."

14. Mrs. Carbuncle manifests a love of dress as an art form, Lucinda expresses her feelings about her marriage by running amok amidst the items in her trousseau.

Works Cited

Cohen, William A. *Sex Scandal: The Private Parts of Victorian Fiction.* Durham: Duke UP, 1996.

Diamond, Alan, ed. *The Victorian Achievement of Sir Henry Maine: A Centennial Reappraisal.* Cambridge: Cambridge UP, 1991.

Dolin, Tim. *Mistress of the House: Women of Property in the Victorian Novel.* Aldershot: Ashgate, 1997.

Engels, Friedrich. *The Origin of the Family, Private Property and the State.* New York: International, 1972.

Fabian, Johannes. *Time and the Other: How Anthropology Makes its Object.* New York: Columbia UP, 1983.

Fee, Elizabeth. "The Sexual Politics of Victorian Social Anthropology." Eds. Mary S. Hartman and Lois Banner. *Clio's Consciousness Raised: New Perspectives on the History of Women.* New York: Octagon, 1974. 86-102.

Foucault, Michel. *History of Sexuality. Volume I: An Introduction.* Trans. Robert Hurley. New York: Random House, 1990.

Goux, Jean-Joseph. *Symbolic Economies: After Marx and Freud.* Trans. Jennifer Curtiss Gage. Ithaca: Cornell UP, 1990.

Irigaray, Luce. *This Sex Which Is Not One.* Trans. Catherine Porter. Ithaca: Cornell UP, 1985.

Kuper, Adam. "The Rise and Fall of Maine's Patriarchal Society." Diamond. 99-110.

Lévi Strauss, Claude. *The Elementary Structures of Kinship.* Trans. James Harle Bell, et al. Boston: Beacon Press, 1969.

Levy, Anita. *Other Women: The Writing of Class, Race, and Gender, 1832-1898.* Princeton: Princeton UP, 1990.

Maine, Henry Sumner. *Ancient Law: its Connection with the Early History of Society and its Relation to Modern Ideas.* New York: Henry Holt, 1864.

Mauss, Marcel. *The Gift: Forms and Functions of Exchange in Archaic Societies.* Trans. Ian Cunnison. Glencoe: The Free Press, 1954.

McLennan, John. *Studies in Ancient History: Comprising a Reprint of Primitive Marriage.* London: Macmillan, 1886.

Miller, Andrew. *Novels Behind Glass: Commodity, Culture, and Victorian Narrative.* Cambridge: Cambridge UP, 1995.

Morgan, Lewis Henry. *Ancient Society: or Researches in the Lines of Human Progress from Savagery through Barbarism to Civilization.* 1877. New York: Meridian Books, 1969.

Nunokawa, Jeff. *The Afterlife of Property: Domestic Security and the Victorian Novel.* Princeton: Princeton UP, 1994.

Poovey, Mary. *Making a Social Body: British Cultural Formation 1830-1864.* Chicago: U of Chicago P, 1995.

Radner, Hilary. "Introduction: Queering the Girl." Eds. Hilary Radner and Moya Luckett. *Swinging Single: Representing Sexuality in the 1960s.* Minneapolis: U of Minnesota P, 1999. 1-35.

Rubin, Gayle. "The Traffic in Women: Notes on the 'Political Economy' of Sex." Ed. Rayna R. Reiter. *Toward an Anthropology of Women.* New York: Monthly Review Press, 1975. 157-210.

Sedgwick, Eve Kosofsky. *Between Men: English Literature and Male Homosocial Desire.* New York: Columbia UP, 1985.

Shanley, Mary Lyndon. *Feminism, Marriage, and the Law in Victorian England.* Princeton: Princeton UP, 1989.

Stocking, George W. *Victorian Anthropology.* New York: Macmillan, 1987.

Trollope, Anthony. *The Eustace Diamonds.* 2 Vols in 1. Oxford: Oxford UP, 1983.

Weiner, Annette B. *Inalienable Possessions: The Paradox of Keeping-While-Giving.* Berkeley: U of California P, 1992.

Henry N. Rogers III (essay date 1999)

SOURCE: Rogers, Henry N., III "*The Fixed Period*: Trollope's 'Modest Proposal.'" *Utopian Studies* 10, no. 2 (1999): 16-24.

[*In the following essay, Rogers assesses Trollope's* The Fixed Period, *an uncharacteristic novel written in Trollope's later years, and the influence of Cicero's writings on the work.*]

"My readers will perceive that I am an enthusiast" (5). So says John Neverbend, former President of the colony of Brittanula, as he steams toward England aboard HMS John Bright in the year 1980. Deposed but undaunted, he is determined to persuade the British of the efficacy of the Fixed Period, a plan for mandatory euthanasia which he had made into law and attempted to enforce in Brittanula. And the story—and the plan—of Neverbend are the creations of Anthony Trollope, with whom, Henry James said, we are always "safe" (100). It would hardly seem so, for no work of Trollope's is so immediately and overtly strange, so apparently out of character, as *The Fixed Period.* Though James said that with Trollope "there were sure to be no new experiments" (100), the novel, written in 1880, set in 1980, is a futuristic, ironically utopian fantasy. It is also the single novel among his 47 in which he employed a first person narrator, a perspective which the intensely private Trollope considered, as he wrote to Kate Field, "too egoistic" and "dangerous" to utilize (429). And the novel's ostensible subject is that mandatory euthanasia which narrator/protagonist Neverbend advocates with such passionate conviction. We are certainly not in Barsetshire anymore, and if a closer look reveals much that is more familiar Trollopian ground, it also discloses a writer who in old age never ceased to question, experiment, and grow, both in mind and artistry.

There were several factors which seem to have influenced Trollope's creation of *The Fixed Period.* One, as R. H. Super has pointed out, was the current vogue in futuristic utopian tales, such as Samuel Butler's *Erewhon,* a mode which was not only marketable but potentially afforded freedom and flexibility which a contemporary and more realistic context would not (v-viii). Just such flexibility enabled Trollope to "safely" introduce into *The Fixed Period*—sometimes seriously, sometimes humorously—such controversial issues as the feasibility and benefits of cremation—Trollope belonged to an advocacy group—the question of self-government for British colonies, the potential destructiveness of advancing technology, and the flaws of a one house government. Another and much more personal and immediate matter was Trollope's own old age—he was sixty-seven—and inevitably approaching death. His letters stress what for him was more fearful than death itself, the uselessness and loss of purpose which old age might bring. He wrote to his son Harry just before the novel was finished: "Nothing really frightens me but the idea of forced Idleness" (886). The concept, at least, of euthanasia undoubtedly had an attraction for him, even if the subject seemed to the *Times* reviewer of the novel "essentially ghastly" (Glendinning [*Anthony Trollope*], 491).

All these matters played a part in the writing of the novel, but certainly the life, work, and writings of Cicero emerge as the most significant personal and artistic influence on *The Fixed Period.* Trollope had been interested in Cicero for 30 years, and his admiration for him as statesman, orator, and man of letters was profound. He loves him "not only for the divine felicity of his style, but for the sanctity of his heart and morals" (I: 143). Ruth apRoberts, in *The Moral Trollope,* examines his affinities with and emulation of many of Cicero's personal qualities, actions, and ideals: his ability to see all sides of an issue, to engage in rational discourse, his refusal to adhere rigidly to any system because of his belief that moral perception must always be rooted in the study of individual cases, and the underlying certainty of humanity, of brotherhood, which Trollope believed informed Cicero's life and work (57-71). Evidence of such affinity has often been noted in Trollope's fiction: his political conservatism, his relativistic moral stance, the focus on individual moral situations, the rational and humane third person narrator, the correspondingly unadorned, direct prose style, and that fundamental "tenderness" beneath the presentation of even the worst of his characters. More specifically, the nature and possible misery of old age and approaching death which Cicero addresses in "On Old Age" are issues at the heart of *The Fixed Period.*

Ciceronian influence was at least potentially at its peak during the composition of the novel, for Trollope had completed his *Life of Cicero* less than a year earlier. Inspired by his "love of the man" (I: 2), and a corresponding desire to defend him against the criticism of such writers as Charles Merivale, Trollope's biography was first projected in a two part article he wrote for the *Fortnightly Review* in 1878. It is a work of serious classical scholarship, an effort to revive Cicero's faltering reputation and to establish Trollope's own name in a more "exalted" literary field than novel writing. Opinions concerning his achievement were and have remained mixed, though Ruth apRoberts states "that Trollope's sense of Cicero is altogether just" ("Intro." ["Introduction"], 5). Whatever its significance as scholarship, its primary value lies in what it reveals of its author rather than its subject. In apRoberts's words, Trollope's novels themselves "are certainly the richest statement of his views, but here, in the *Cicero,* one may find the literal and discursive formulation of the attitudes that make the novels what they are" (57). If this may be said of *The Life of Cicero, The Fixed Period* seems at first glance an unlikely example of Ciceronian influence. It is just that, however, and Trollope's singular use of first-person perspective is both indicative of his purpose in the novel and essential to his accomplishing it. Here he abandons the scope and flexibility, the "classic moderation," of his customary third-person perspective to concentrate upon the actions, motives, and character of Neverbend, the narrator and protagonist. And Neverbend's self-revelation, through his words, the story they tell, and the manner of the telling, exposes a man who for all his admirable, sympathetic,

potentially Ciceronian qualities, is at last an anti-Cicero—an anti-Trollope unable to relinquish his beloved "Fixed Period." As Robert Tracy points out, Trollope's primary concern lies not with the question of euthanasia but in the revealing of the abstract reformer obsessed with that issue—he is more interested in the doctrinaire than the doctrine (292). To that end, then, he writes a novel fundamentally unlike any of his others, his most sustained work of satiric irony.

Neverbend in his own words is an "Enthusiast." The term's connotations were often ambivalent during the 19th century, and clearly he means to describe himself favorably. But he proves to be an enthusiast in the highly pejorative 18th century sense of the word—a fanatic beyond the reach of reason and the realities of human nature. To portray him, and to dramatize all the implications of that portrayal, Trollope adopts a familiar 18th century method, one perfected and used to devastating effect by Jonathan Swift, the creation of an obsessed narrative persona who unveils and satirizes himself through his own words and arguments (502-509). Indeed, the "Introduction" with which Neverbend prefaces his tale is to a remarkable degree a "Modest Proposal" of powerful comic and satiric effect.

Neverbend's intention in his opening remarks is simple enough—to gain his readers' sympathy for his position and their support for his noble but misunderstood plan. His argument is intricate, couched in "moderate language," and infused with earnest conviction—and, as is the proposal of Swift's persona, a masterpiece of unconscious self-revelation. Neverbend enumerates the many benefits of the "Fixed Period" as carefully as Swift's creation unfolds his plan for the children of Ireland. It is politically wise—old and weak leaders will be eliminated. It is socially beneficial—society will be younger, healthier, and happier. Economic progress becomes inevitable—younger and more efficient workers produce more prosperity. Above all, the plan is humane. Neverbend's "unanswerable" argument rests with the relief from illness, senility, uselessness, and misery which his "Period" brings to the aged. Supporting his assertions with statistics and quotations from Scripture, he speaks with certainty and apparent sense, yet he can no more see his own faulty logic and false assumptions than can the "Modest Proposer." He asserts that Brittanula was a good country, that this country had the idea of the "Fixed Period," so since the country was good, the idea must be good. With dazzling obtuseness, he points out that the English leaders who interfered with the enactment of his plan are advanced into "effete old age," and, were that plan in effect in England, they wouldn't be alive to butt in. His major assumptions are more obviously erroneous—that mankind's passion for life and fear of death may be altered by reason, and that all are sick, imbecilic, useless, or miserable at a certain age. Above all, Neverbend dismisses as weak, illogical, and therefore finally insignificant such human realities as affection, love, and fear. Cicero's *humanitas* has no place in his plan. In sum, this is precisely the kind of argument—a parody of the open, rational, and humane Ciceronian discourse Trollope so admired—and proponent that he most disliked. At the conclusion of the "Introduction," Neverbend has utterly although unwittingly exposed both himself and his Fixed Period.

The parallels between Trollope's "Introduction" and Swift's "Modest Proposal," the supreme exemplar of that satiric form, are striking, both in method and effect. As David Skilton has noted, however, the work's irony "is not adequate to support a Swiftian satire . . ." (41). *The Fixed Period* is a novel, more than just a satiric "Proposal." Trollope's "Introduction" not only exposes the "Period"'s originator and its fallacies, but that it has already failed. Thus Neverbend's narrative is the retrospective account of his struggle with his people, his own family, the "tyrannical" British, and most importantly with himself, for he finds it hard work to sustain his faith in the great reform. His story is the dramatization of a "Proposer" trying to make his proposal become actuality, and since we know at the outset that he has failed in that attempt yet retains his belief in the plan, the implications of that effort, especially for Neverbend himself, become of primary significance. It follows that because the plan was defeated, not, according to him, by any of its own defects, but by opposition, circumstances, even Neverbend's admitted shortcomings, it remains in his eyes potentially, even inevitably, viable. His story, then, no less than his "Introduction," becomes an appeal, dramatic rather than purely argumentative, a part of the preparation necessary for his reform's eventual acceptance. It in fact exposes the enormity of that scheme and its consequences for himself even more powerfully than did his "Introduction."

Neverbend's struggle to enforce the "Fixed Period" is difficult, and if it often seems comic to us, it is serious and vexatious to him. He must, for example, overcome an aversion to "deposition and departure" based on the unsavory smell of incinerated pig which accidentally escapes during testing of the crematorium. Neverbend of course finds nothing funny in this—we see the humor and its implications, but he does not. More substantial problems rapidly arise, for the initial candidate for "deposition," Neverbend's best friend Crasweller, arrives at the designated age of 67—Trollope's age—in appallingly robust health and spirits, the happiest, most prosperous, and most useful man in Brittanula. His vigor and intellect not only belie all of the President's arguments, they make him one who finds, as Cicero did, that "old age sits lightly upon me" (138).[1] Not surprisingly, he becomes increasingly reluctant to serve as the country's first "departee." Neverbend's allies are either young and thoughtless, like most of his legislature, young and avaricious like Grundle, who wants

Crasweller dead so he can marry his daughter and fortune, or old and essentially dead like Graybody, the curator of the College of Deposition. To his credit and chagrin, Neverbend recognizes these for what they are, especially Grundle: "I myself had never liked him much" (17). More distressingly, his opponents are those whom he loves and respects: Crasweller, his own son, Jack, who leads the resistance, Eva Crasweller, Jack's beloved, and his wife, who confounds his theories by simply labeling them as "nonsense." All these, and the English who thwart him by superior force, are moved by those very factors of human emotion which Neverbend refuses to acknowledge as paramount. His adamance is dearly bought, however, for he must continually feel the power of love, affection, and human sympathy as the crisis over Crasweller's approaching deposition draws them forth. He suffers those human and humane vacillations because of conscience and feeling which Trollope felt so distinguished Cicero (I: 15). Eva Crasweller's indignant plea endears her to Neverbend: "I became more and more attached to her the more loudly she spoke on behalf of her father" (106). Such appeals move him and force him to re-examine his plan and himself and to acknowledge elements of pride and vanity that mingle with less selfish motives. In these crises, however, he remembers those other great reformers, Columbus and Galileo—ironically, heroes Trollope specifically compares to Cicero (I: 35)—and "better" thoughts return.

Thus Neverbend's narration makes him a fully realized, all-too-human character rather than a satiric mouthpiece like Swift's "Proposer" or a two dimensional satiric example of reason gone mad such as Gulliver in Book IV of *Gulliver's Travels.* If his presentation to some degree diffuses the satiric focus of *The Fixed Period,* it intensifies and enhances the ironic complexity of the novel. Unlike Swift's creations, Brittanula's President has a capacity for tenderness, for learning, for a measure of self-awareness; he could have become a model of Ciceronian—and Trollopian—values and qualities. He realizes his underestimation of man's "passion for life," and at last admits he would have been too "weak" to "depart" Crasweller himself. Yet although the tension between his sounder reason and human nature and the requirements of his proposal elicits our sympathy, his fanaticism proves too strong. All arguments, external and internal, rational and emotional, do not invalidate his idea—the world is just not yet "ripe" for it. Neverbend remains a satiric figure at his story's end, for his obsession is as absurd as ever. But he is also pathetic, a truly good man whose narrative reveals his capacity for love, suffering, and self-knowledge, but finally his inability to fully understand.

As Neverbend's account ends where it begins—he steams toward England, deposed, defeated, alienated from country and family, yet with his beloved Period theoretically intact—the ironic intricacy of Trollope's narrative method becomes evident. His protagonist has indeed brought us to a comprehension of his struggles and sufferings, but their dramatization has had the opposite of the desired effect. As Neverbend unconsciously piles irony upon irony, not only the rational flaws of his reform and the impossibility of its implementation but the dreadful consequences of his undying faith in it are unerringly exposed. So too is the artistry with which Trollope makes Neverbend the antithesis of Ciceronian—and Trollopian—attitudes and values. Brittanula's President complains of the tyranny of the interfering English, just as Cicero spoke and acted against the tyranny of first Catiline and later Caesar. As Trollope asserts, Cicero's one object in public life was to resist a single master with a strong hand (II, 252). Neverbend, however, has made the law itself a form of tyranny over his people and himself a tyrant as he attempts to enforce it. He never perceives, as we do, the inverted irony of the situation he has created; in Brittanula, guns come to defend humanity from a law—his law—which threatens it. There is little humor left as the novel reaches its conclusion. It is a fine irony that the "depositor" becomes the "depositee," that Neverbend, not Crasweller, ends up in effect "dead." He finds himself without all one would live for, not denied it by age or actual death, but by his choice of an abstract and inhuman system over human values and human reality—over the *humanitas* of Cicero. His is a self-imposed "Death-in-Life," for he is in truth alienated not by the British or the Brittanulans, but by his own fanaticism.

Nowhere is Trollope's narrative control more evident, the complexity of his Ciceronian parody more demonstrable and significant, than in Neverbend's use of language. Trollope felt that more important than Cicero's precepts on rhetoric was his "sweetness of language" (II: 319). Neverbend falls far short of such "sweetness." When the President addresses everyday matters, his style basically reflects his subject; it is essentially direct and relatively unpretentious. When he speaks in or writes of his role as president of his country or head of his household, however, his diction, syntax, and tone alter accordingly, increasing in elevation and formality. And as he advocates and defends his beloved "Fixed Period," his rhetoric and language become exaggeratedly elaborate, flowery, and cliché-ridden: "When they came to speak of the vices and the virtues of President Neverbend, to tell of his weakness and his strength, it should never be said of him that he had been deterred by fear of the people from carrying out the great measure which he had projected solely for their benefit" (47). In such often repeated instances, his use of language so far removed from that of normal human intercourse implies an equal distance between the ideas it espouses and human reality. Indeed, such language serves as protection for Neverbend, helping him avoid such reality by making his concept into the noble and humane plan he wishes it to be. In his *Orator* Cicero says the perfect orator is infinitely persuasive—as Trollope translates, "Then will he do with them as he would wish" (II. 328). So far from this ideal is Neverbend that he can at last persuade only himself. Crasweller quite accurately accuses him of talking of his plan so much that he falls in love with "deposition and departure." His rhetorical efforts in fact amount to a comic and sometimes painful attempt to make the word become actuality.

Neverbend's extreme sensitivity to the more mundane and direct language of others further indicates his psychological and linguistic dilemma. He is continually offended and frustrated by others' references to his plan, which he calls "an act of Grace," as "execution," "slaughter," or "putting an end to." He is completely and hilariously helpless before his wife, a woman incapable of abstract thought. Mrs. Neverbend wants to hear no more of "Columbus and Galileo" and asserts that, for all her husband's fancy talk, "English is English," and his great reform is "nonsense." Such comments strip the veneer from his plan; it is no longer a vision but an inhuman conception, both silly and monstrous. Neverbend's entire narrative thus becomes a defensive, finally desperate linguistic battle to avoid a truth, about himself and his obsession, which he cannot face and to continually reconstruct a desired reality which can only prevail in the mind of a fanatic. Finally, for all others in the novel and for us, the gap between human actuality and Neverbend's delusion becomes too great for his language to bridge; *how* he describes his plan cannot obscure and in fact helps to illuminate what it really is. In his narrative, any Ciceronian "felicity of style" vanishes because it no longer contains a true "sanctity of heart and morals." That style instead serves to convey the perversion of such sanctity, and its implications. There is no "sweetness" in his language and his plan is "nonsense." Exiled and alone at the novel's end, Neverbend finds himself left only with his words. They are not enough.

In *The Fixed Period,* then, Ciceronian ideals and influence are paradoxically implied by their absence, not from the novel, but from the character and narrative consciousness of the ironically deluded protagonist. By first creating a strikingly Swiftian persona, a "Modest Proposer" blind to the inhumanity and "wrong reason" of his proposal, Trollope satirizes the folly of the "Fixed Period" and the fanaticism of its originator. That satire, of course, suggests a better way, one predicated upon a Ciceronian model of basic humanity and truly rational discourse. Making Neverbend the narrator, making him the maker of his own story, both enlarges and diffuses the satire but intensifies and complicates the novel's irony. His account humanizes him; his noble intentions, his ability to feel, suffer, and learn, all make him a sympathetic, even a potentially Ciceronian figure. But that narration also exposes just how far from that ideal he is, and how crucial his failure proves to be. It is no accident that Sir Fernando Brown, the fatuous British diplomat sent to replace Neverbend as leader of Brittanula, explicitly, and ironically, compares him to Cicero, calling him the father of his country even as he removes him from that country. But Cicero became the father of his country by being the great conservative, by preserving the Roman Republic from the threat of Catiline's tyranny. In his delusion Neverbend forfeits that role to Brittanula's former "parent," England, for his obsession makes him a danger to his people, a would-be tyrant, the antithesis of a Ciceronian leader. His fate indicates how sorely such an ideal is needed, for if Neverbend ends as a sympathetic, even pathetic figure, he is also still a comic one, though that comedy may have become dark indeed. At last, fatally adherent to his "Fixed Period," Neverbend, unlike Cicero or Trollope, cannot sacrifice his system for an individual, see his plan for what it is, or accept the realities of human nature. He is like a madman or a child—beyond reason, a purveyor and follower of "Nonsense," a "Modest Proposer" after all. Gulliver ends talking to horses, not humans; Neverbend ends with only words and no one at all to talk to, only an unseen and uncertain audience for which he writes and which finally understands more than he. And what should be understood seems clear. No one in the novel, not Cicero, nor Trollope, nor the reader, can perfectly achieve those attributes of character, morality, reason, or literary merit which Trollope associated with the great orator. Our mingled lack and/or possession of them may make us right and wrong, wise and foolish, comic and admirable; it certainly renders us human. But as Neverbend's story demonstrates, to reject them at last, to cling to obsession and remain blind to the realities of self and of human nature is to court if not demand exclusion from those realities. It is fitting that Gulliver communes with horses; it is also sad but true that Neverbend deserves to be "deposited." The logic of his story and his unconsciously ironic narration, even the precepts of his own flawed plan require such a conclusion, for the fanatic denier of life *should* be removed from society. In the truest sense of the word, he is no longer "useful." We see, though he does not, that he is "hoist with his own petard." He is so, throughout the novel.

Thus in 1880, at the age of 67, Trollope creates, not one of his finest, but in various ways one of his most extraordinary novels. Throughout the work tension between the conflicting elements of obsessed Swiftian "Proposer" and humane Ciceronian leader informs his most innovative and impressive artistic achievement in ***The Fixed Period***—its protagonist's ironically self-revealing narration. Perhaps the most consistent and overriding irony of all is Neverbend's inability to see that he is *not* Columbus, Galileo, or Cicero, that he, not his family, his opponents, nor the English, is his own worst enemy. In spite of all his efforts and intentions, his narration is a continual digging beneath himself. When it is finished, he has blown himself to the moon. Trollope has arranged it all, of course, demonstrating through his fiction that he himself, not Neverbend, is like Cicero, not only morally, intellectually, and imaginatively, but in the amazing productivity and versatility of his last years. Whatever his fears of uselessness, Trollope's old age "sat lightly upon him" until very near the end.

Note

1. At the very end of "On Old Age," Cicero's spokesman, Cato, states, "Old age is the closing act of life, as of a drama, and we ought to leave when the play grows wearisome, especially if we have had our fill" (158). Taken out of context, his single remark might possibly be construed as suggesting that Neverbend's plan is not totally inconsistent with Cicero's own perspective on humanity. However, the comment more likely implies that we are to leave as nature takes its course. Cicero's entire essay extols the rightness and pleasure of living on through old age, and it is this emphasis which Trollope discusses in his consideration of the essay in his *Life of Cicero;* he never mentions the statement above. In addition, Cicero expressly speaks against suicide in both "Scipio's Dream" and his "Tusculan Disputations"; as Trollope translates from the "Disputations," "That God within us forbids us to depart hence without his permission" (*Cicero* [*Life of Cicero*], 2: 395). Neverbend's "period" would have received scant support from Cicero, as Trollope was certainly aware.

References

apRoberts, Ruth. *The Moral Trollope*. Athens: Ohio UP, 1971.

———. "Introduction." *The Life of Cicero*. Anthony Trollope. N.Y.: Arno P, 1981. I: 1-6.

Cicero. *The Basic Works of Cicero*. Ed. Moses Hadas. N.Y.: Random House, 1951.

Glendinning, Victoria. *Anthony Trollope*. N.Y.: Alfred A. Knopf, 1993.

James, Henry. "Anthony Trollope," in *Partial Portraits*. London: Macmillan, 1888; rpt. Westport, CT: Greenwood, 1970. 97-133.

Skilton, David. "*The Fixed Period:* Anthony Trollope's Novel of 1880," *Studies in the Literary Imagination* 6, no. 2 (Fall, 1973): 39-50.

Super, R. H. "Introduction." *The Fixed Period*. Anthony Trollope. Ann Arbor: U of Michigan P, 1990, v-xv.

Tracy, Robert. *Trollope's Later Novels*. Berkeley: California UP, 1978.

Trollope, Anthony. *The Fixed Period.* Ed. R. H. Super. Ann Arbor: Michigan P, 1990.

———. *The Letters of Anthony Trollope.* 2 Vols. Ed. N. John Hall. Stanford: Stanford UP, 1983.

———. *The Life of Cicero.* N.Y.: Arno P, 1981. 2 Vols.

Richard Mullen (essay date February 2001)

SOURCE: Mullen, Richard. "Trollope and the Pious Slippers of Cheltenham." *Contemporary Review* 278, no. 1621 (February 2001): 112-14.

[*In the following essay, Mullen ponders the literary manifestations of Trollope's contempt for the British resort town of Cheltenham.*]

Cheltenham, that cultivated spa town with its blend of elegant town houses inhabited by retired Anglo-Indian officers and officials, provided a good setting and target for Victorian novelists. To Thackeray it was a place where 'trumps and frumps were found together, wherever scandal was cackled'. That may seem bad enough but there was a novelist who was far more acerbic about Cheltenham. Strangely it was one who is normally regarded as the genial exponent of English life. Anthony Trollope had a curious contempt for the pleasant Gloucestershire town and subjected it to fierce attacks in several novels.

Before proceeding I should mention that at *Contemporary Review* we look on Anthony Trollope as one of our founders. He was the chairman and driving force in a group of Victorian writers and intellectuals who founded *The Fortnightly Review* in 1865. It eventually was incorporated into the *Contemporary Review* which had been founded a year later.

Trollope is not often seen as a writer who was strongly influenced by the 'spirit of place'. Yet it was a visit to Salisbury which inspired his most famous fiction, the six novels which make up the Barsetshire series. In his *Autobiography* he describes this 1852 visit to Salisbury and a walk round the great cathedral with it magnificent soaring spire: 'whilst wandering there on a midsummer evening round the purlieus of a cathedral, I conceived the story of *The Warden*—from whence came that series of novels of which Barchester, with its Bishops, Deans, and Archdeacon, was the central site'. The influence of place on Trollope's fiction is better seen in his neglected short stories or in some of the short continental novels he wrote.

For instance a visit in the mid-1860s to Vienna where he heard the great Johann Strauss conducting his waltzes in the Volksgarten gave Trollope the idea for a story called '**Lotta Schmidt**' (incidentally written for the founder of *Contemporary Review*) where a middle-aged bald conductor of the orchestra in the Volksgarten is in love with a Viennese girl. A visit to the old synagogue in Prague about the same time inspired his short anonymous novel, *Nina Balatka.* Yet both these examples, as well as numerous other ones, show how Trollope was inspired by cities that combined beauty and history to write a piece of fiction. Yet there is only one town that Trollope consistently unleashed fictional assaults on and that is Cheltenham.

In *The Bertrams* (1859) the main character visits 'Littlebath'—the name Trollope often used when attacking Cheltenham—and discovers its 'fast set', men who wear padded coats, to improve their figure, and idly 'talk about women much as a crafty knowing salmon might be presumed to talk about anglers'. The ladies in the 'fast set' are 'addicted to whist and false hair, but pursue their pleasures with a discreet economy'. Yet it was not the fast set that made Trollope dislike Cheltenham. The dislike sprang from his contempt for 'the predominant power' in the town, 'the pious set'. 'Of the pious set' says Trollope 'much needs not be said, as their light has never been hid under a bushel'. 'They live on the fat of the land. They are a strong, unctuous, moral, uncharitable people. The men never cease making money for themselves, nor the women making slippers for their clergymen'. The slippers provide the vital clue.

In the autumn of 1852 Trollope, an official of the General Post Office, and his wife Rose rented lodgings in the town for several months while he was arranging postal deliveries. Cheltenham was ruled by its Rector, the formidable Rev Francis Close, whom *The Times* called 'the Pope of Cheltenham'. His power was enormous and helped to make the town the centre for Evangelicals, whose activities resembled the modern American 'religious right'. Among the many crusades undertaken by Close was one against Sunday delivery of the post. When certain areas were granted the right to refuse Sunday deliveries, it caused havoc to Trollope's carefully drawn schedules. To him it was also a threat to a vital public service. Close was a powerful preacher renowned for his tirades against Catholicism and this further annoyed Trollope, who had seen the harm caused by such harangues during his long residence in Ireland. When the pious ladies of Littlebath knit slippers for their clergy in *The Bertrams,* Trollope was poking fun at Close who was said to have received 1500 of these from his devoted flock.

Trollope returned to the attack in *Miss Mackenzie* (1865). Margaret Mackenzie is a single woman in her thirties who, having inherited a pleasant fortune, comes to 'drink the waters' at Littlebath. She is taken into the 'pious set' and meets some of the same people who had appeared in **The Bertrams**. The dominant figure is the local clergyman, Mr Stumfold: 'a shining light . . . the man of men. If he was not something more than mere man, in the eyes of the devout inhabitants of that town'. Stumfold wages war on card-playing, dancing, and hunting: all pursuits enjoyed by Trollope.

Even worse was 'a Stumfoldian edict . . . ordaining that no Stumfoldian in Littlebath should be allowed to receive a letter on Sundays'; Margaret Mackenzie nearly misses her brother's death-bed because a letter is not delivered until the Monday. Trollope himself was an old fashioned High Churchman and clergymen who held views similar to his own, such as Barchester's Archdeacon Grantly, denounce attempts to stop Sabbath deliveries as the work of 'numskulls'.

Trollope saw the narrow religion of the 'Stumfoldians' as essentially spiteful and hypocritical. It is no accident that in **Framley Parsonage** when the Evangelical Proudies arrange for an anonymous letter to be sent to the Grantlys claiming that their daughter was being jilted, it bears a 'Littlebath' postmark. Mrs Grantly referred to the act as 'a part of the new Christianity'.

Trollope's last real attack comes in **The American Senator** (1877) where his target is not the town but Cheltenham College which he blames for a character's faulty grammar. After its publication he confided to a friend: 'Larry's early schooldays at Cheltenham with his subsequent somewhat illiterate language' came from the author's 'long-ago-entertained dislike of Dean Close *But that is quite for yourself*'. I do not know why Trollope was annoyed with Cheltenham College, but I suspect it could have something to do with the fact that he was looking for a school for his two sons and he may have tried Cheltenham before settling for the High Church Bradfield.

Cheltenham also appears in several Trollope novels under its own name and then he does not normally fire insults at it. This is the case in **Mr. Scarborough's Family** or **Can You Forgive Her?** In both he modelled various characters' lodgings on his own at No. 5, the Paragon Buildings.

There was another inherited reason why Trollope disliked Cheltenham. His youth had been darkened by his father's attempt to become a gentleman-farmer. The elder Trollope blamed his failure on his landlord, Lord Northwick, who was also well known for his property developments in Cheltenham. Anthony regarded Northwick as a 'cormorant who was eating us up'. In 1834 the nineteen year old Anthony drove his father in the family gig to the London docks so he could flee to Belgium to escape arrest for his debts to Lord Northwick. To confuse the peer's agent the Trollopes pretended they were leaving Harrow on a shorter journey—to Cheltenham.

Elsie B. Michie (essay date autumn 2001)

SOURCE: Michie, Elsie B. "Buying Brains: Trollope, Oliphant, and Vulgar Victorian Commerce." *Victorian Studies* 44, no. 1 (autumn 2001): 77-97.

[*In the following excerpt, Michie explores the shift in Victorian economics from production to consumption, using Trollope's novel* The Last Chronicle of Barset *as one piece of evidence.*]

> Poverty is the desire of ascetics, and this is not an ascetic age.
>
> —[Margaret Oliphant], **Phoebe Junior** (174)

Grant Allen's 1894 description of the shift from "the old asceticism [which] said, 'Be virtuous, and you will be happy' [to] the new hedonism [which] says, 'Be happy and you will be virtuous'" (377) applies to large-scale economic movements of the nineteenth century. During the era preceding the expansion of the credit economy, capital was hard to come by; in order to expand businesses, entrepreneurs had to save, borrow from relatives and friends who had also saved, or both save and borrow. "In these circumstances abstinence became a buttress of industrial expansion because what was not spent on personal account stayed in the business. Personal abstinence is one of the qualities most universally attributed to the entrepreneurs" (Mathias [*The First Industrial Nation*] 143). With the expansion and centralization of the banking industry in the 1860s and 70s, commerce was no longer based on saving but on the ability to borrow capital and amass credit, which led to the development of a "plutocracy of big business men and great landowners [. . .] in which the old virile, ascetic and radical ideal of active capital was submerged to the [. . .] supine, hedonistic and conservative ideal of passive property" (Perkin, *Origins* [*Origins of Modern English Society*] 436). These changes were associated with the emergence, in the early 1870s, of marginalist economics, which negotiated what Regenia Gagnier calls a "paradigm shift" (137), when it turned critical attention from production, and the habits of saving associated with it, to consumption, and the habits of expenditure associated with it. I examine here a pair of interconnected novels by Anthony Trollope and Margaret Oliphant, authors noted for their explicitness in dealing with money and money-making. Published in 1867 and 1876 respectively, **The Last Chronicle of Barset** and **Phoebe Junior: A Last Chronicle of Carlingford** bracket the moment when the philosophy of consumption and pleasure was articulated publicly in W. Stanley Jevons's *The Theory of Political Economy* (1871). Both novels function in a quasi-anthropological sense, evoking, through the drama of individual characters' financial problems, an entire culture's response to dramatic changes in economic practice and theory taking place in the last third of the nineteenth century.

Both these novels address anxieties about the expansiveness of late-Victorian commerce through the story of a clergyman who becomes inextricably involved with the mechanisms of the credit economy. Clergymen are especially effective for these stories because the Victorians wanted the church to be a "vocation [that] lies in such a very different direction" from the stock market and investing (L. Oliphant ["The Autobiography of a Joint-Stock Company"] 96), with the ideal clergyman exhibiting "his remoteness from mercantile life [. . .] his enthusiastic character, eager after things far less sublunary than money" (Bagehot, "Postulates" ["The Postulates of Political Economy"] 25). This description, however, is not of the clergy but of John Stuart Mill, and marks the way that, at mid-century, the unworldliness associated with religion was being attached to intellectuals as well, particularly those critical of monetary interests. Intellectual clergymen, thus, were seen as particularly remote from commerce. In *On the Constitution of Church and State* (1830), Samuel Taylor Coleridge had earlier posited the "clerisy" as that section of society which will be able to counter the increasingly powerful political and social influence of the commercial factions through the exercise of cultivation (36-38). Bringing a knowledge of Greek to his work with bricklayers, the highly educated Josiah Crawley in Trollope's *The Last Chronicle* [*The Last Chronicle of Barset*] perfectly embodies Coleridge's ideal cleric, "who is with his parishioners and among them; he is neither in the cloistered cell nor in the wilderness, but a neighbor and family-man, whose education and rank admit him to the mansions of the rich landholder, while his duties make him the frequent visitor of the farmhouse and the cottage" (60). Similarly, *Phoebe Junior*'s Reverend Mr. May, hired to tutor the son of the millionaire industrialist Copperhead, has been educated at Oxford. However, while both these clergymen do, to differing extents, represent the intellectual realm that Victorians thought of as outside commerce, neither is able to remain separate from commercial transactions. Charting the peculiar amalgam of pain, shame, and pleasure these intellectual clergymen feel as they become implicated in the credit economy allows Trollope and Oliphant to explore with special force the late-Victorian uneasiness about the intrusion of new financial mechanisms into individuals' personal lives.

The Last Chronicle of Barset occupies a pivotal position in Trollope's long novelistic career. As Richard Holt Hutton argued, the "old order had changed, giving place to the new. [. . .] Natural selection had brought speculating stockbrokers, American senators, and American heiresses into the foreground of Mr. Trollope's [. . .] and the advance of both plutocratic and democratic ideas might have been steadily traced in the vivid social pictures with which he so liberally supplied us" (1573). Hutton's references to American heiresses and senators identify *The Duke's Children* (1880), the

last of the Palliser novels, as the end point of a development that begins with the first of the Barsetshire novels. In the early novels, we see the clearest depiction both of what Hutton calls "the ardent admiration with which [Trollope] always painted humility and unworldliness, like Mr. Harding's, or even Dean Arabin's" and "the scorn which he felt for all the knavery of commercial Rings [. . .] the keen insight with which he contemplated the snares and toils of the speculative commercial life" (1573). The unworldly characters Hutton describes here, Harding and Arabin, to whose names could be added Frank Gresham (who chooses the apparently penniless Mary Thorne over the wealthy Miss Dunstable) and Mark Robarts (who finally chooses to have nothing to do with bills of exchange), all appear in the Barsetshire series. In starting the Palliser series, Trollope turns away from using the clergy to examine "the symbolic profits occurring from political unity" (Bourdieu [*Outline of a Theory of Practice*] 62) and focuses instead on parliamentary politics. In *The Last Chronicle of Barset,* a self-conscious coda to the Barsetshire series written after the Palliser novels had begun, Trollope uses the Reverend Mr. Crawley as a valedictory figure through whom to explore a set of ascetic values that were ceasing to be tenable in a culture where social interactions were depending more and more on the credit nexus.

In Crawley, Trollope emphasizes not just the lack of interest in worldly concerns he celebrated in characters like Mr. Harding but active self-denial, a conscious intellectual rejection of the seductions of the material world. The novel highlights that asceticism through a series of encounters between Crawley and clergymen who play prominent roles in the earlier Barsetshire novels—Mark Robarts, Archdeacon Grantly, and Dean Arabin—all of whom, though virtuous, are wealthier than Crawley and able to lead more materially comfortable lives. Through these encounters, Crawley emerges as what one reviewer called the most "intensely unworldly" of all Trollope's characters, having "nothing of the earth, earthy, about [him]." He is "Trollope's noblest and most unique acquaintance," "cast in a deeper and nobler, if also narrower, mould than most of Mr. Trollope's acquaintances," with "sins and [. . .] virtues [that] have a grander stamp upon them." "Mr. Trollope has never before drawn a character either so full of (indicated rather than delineated) intellectual power, or so devoted to the diviner ends of life" ("Review of *The Last Chronicle* [*of Barset*]," *Spectator* 779). With Crawley, Trollope has "struck a higher note than he has yet attempted" (Oliphant, "Novels" 277). Trollope's portrait of Crawley reinforced the image of "the gentleman [who] was by definition above the mercenary money-grubbing pursuits of the commercial classes" (Perkin, *Origins* 275). Crawley exhibits precisely those attributes that Samuel Smiles ascribes to "the true gentleman," who "has a keen sense of honor—scrupulously avoiding mean actions. His standard of probity in word and action is high. He does not shuffle or prevaricate, dodge or skulk; but is honest, upright and straightforward" (432).

As we shall see, Crawley displays his scrupulous sense of honor principally in relation to finances. His exquisitely honorable dealings with the men who surround him appealed so intensely to Victorian readers because they wished to believe that such an unworldly stance was possible in their commercial universe. But Trollope's novel also suggests that Crawley's "codes of honor" function as what John Kucich calls "distancing mechanisms" (20). Indeed, Crawley's story allows Trollope to explore what Pierre Bourdieu describes as "the collective misrecognition which is the basis of the ethic of honour, a collective denial of the economic reality of exchange" (195-96).

That denial is dramatized in the scene that lies at the heart of *The Last Chronicle*: driven by exigency, Crawley goes to Dean Arabin, asks for financial aid, and receives, unbeknownst to himself, the check that causes his subsequent legal problems. This interchange holds the key to the mysteries of the novel, but the truth of what happened in it is difficult to recover because its two main actors are unable to remember it clearly. Contemporary reviewers describe Crawley's relation to the check in psychological terms, asserting that the novel's main dilemma is "whether an eccentric clergyman of sensitive and noble nature [. . .] did or did not, consciously or unconsciously, steal or use as his own a cheque for 20*l*. that was not his" ("Review of *The Last Chronicle [of Barset]*," *Examiner* 453). To a post-Freudian reader the entire novel reads like a therapy session, as various characters seek to recover a scene of economic exchange in which the two male figures involved felt such an intense, almost sexualized, shame that both subsequently repressed or denied the financial aspects of the transaction. As Trollope's narrator explains in paraphrasing Crawley's testimony before the magistrate, "The dean had given him money, covered up, in an enclosure, 'so that the touch of the coin might not add to my disgrace in taking his alms,' [. . .]. He had not seen the dean's monies as they had been given, and he had thought that the cheque had been with them" (82). "The fact that the dean had given him money was very important, and he remembered it well. But the amount of the money, and its form, at a moment in which he had flattered himself that he might have strength to leave it unused, had not been important to him" (665). The dean is similarly divorced from the practical details of what is passing between them: "The interview had been so painful that Arabin would hardly have been able to count the money or to know of what it had consisted, had he taken the notes and cheque out of the envelope" (835).

Trollope situates this scene of individual pain about the contaminating touch of monetary transactions within a larger social framework that conforms to Bourdieu's observations of the societies he describes in *Outline of a Theory of Practice* (1977). In such societies, "the urge to calculate, repressed in men, finds more overt expression in women, who are structurally predisposed to be less concerned with the symbolic profits accruing from political unity, and to devote themselves more readily to strictly economic practices" (62). In *The Last Chronicle,* the difference between the attitudes of men and women toward economics emerges in their responses to the Reverend Crawley's financial dilemma. While the men in the novel think that Crawley should be tried as a matter of justice, arguing that "'Ladies will never understand that magistrates must act in accordance with the law'" (100), the women think he should be exonerated whether he committed the theft or not. In the words of the wealthy Mrs. Thorne, "'what does it matter about the trumpery check? Everybody knows it was a mistake, if he did take it'" (139). Women have a similarly pragmatic response to the Crawleys' economic plight; as Mrs. Crawley explains, "'the feeling of disgrace which does attach itself to being so poor as we are is deadened by the actual suffering which such poverty brings with it. At least it has become so with me. [. . .] His spirit is higher than mine, I think, and he suffers more from the natural disinclination which we all have to receiving alms'" (205). Mr. Crawley's exquisite sensitivity to their poverty means that Mrs. Crawley must manage the day-to-day details of the family's survival, which may be why Oliphant claimed feelingly both that "Mr. Trollope is about the only writer we know [. . .] who realizes the position of a sensible and right-minded woman among the ordinary affairs of the world," and that Mr. Crawley is "almost as exasperating to the reader as he must have been to his poor wife" ("Novels" 278, 277). Mr. Crawley not only refuses to accept direct aid from those who would help him and his family, he also tells his friend Dean Arabin, "'I request that nothing may pass from your hands to the hands of my wife'" (835). Crawley's request does not stop the flow of financial aid in the novel; it simply means that aid must come from women. As the narrator tells us, "After that the gifts had come from the hands of Mrs. Arabin" (835), as they come from the older or younger Lady Lufton, Mrs. Robarts, the Prettyman sisters, and Lily Dale and her mother.

If in Trollope's novel "[l]ending between women is regarded as the antithesis of the exchange of honour; and it is indeed closer to the economic truth of exchange than the men's dealings" (Bourdieu 62), then we can best identify the economic realities from which honorable men seek to distance themselves by looking at the function of women. Even the language of the final authoritative accounting of the scene between Crawley and Arabin reflects the differing relation of men and women to money. As long as the narrator is describing dealings between men, the references to money remain vague and euphemistic; after a woman is mentioned they become concrete (758-59). The woman mentioned is Eleanor Arabin, who is the source both of the assets that are given to Crawley in the envelope that passes between the two men, and later of the "truth" of what happened in the economic exchange between them. Significantly, she provides her authoritative account of the exchange from Venice, where she first learns the particulars of the accusation against Crawley—it has, until then, been kept an affair among men—and writes back to explain all. Venice is the perfect site for her revelation because it was the city the Victorians generally, and Trollope specifically, associated with banking and the commercial practices they feared were engulfing their society. As Trollope's narrator comments in the opening of *Doctor Thorne* (1858):

> England a commercial country! Yes; as Venice was. She may excel other nations in commerce, but yet it is not that in which she most prides herself, in which she most excels. Merchants as such are not the first men among us; though it perhaps be open, barely open, to a merchant to become one of them. Buying and selling is good and necessary; it is very necessary, and may, possibly, be very good; but it cannot be the noblest work of man; and let us hope that it may not in our time be esteemed the noblest work of an Englishman.
>
> (15)

In *The Last Chronicle,* Arabin and Crawley's actions exemplify what Trollope's narrator calls the noble work of Englishmen, while the check marks the presence of those excellent financial instruments threatening that nobility.

The Last Chronicle was written and published in the wake of the financial panic of 1866, which had been triggered by the collapse of the discount house Overend, Gurney and Co. In the period following that collapse, the British banking industry was consolidated. "[W]ith the Overend-Gurney cataclysm there closed the era of isolated, incoherent, and disunited finance. [. . .] [F]rom the close of this period onwards we shall see that the elements begin to act in a determinate relation, which becomes more intimate and—shall we say?—cordial, with every year that passes" (Powell [*The Evolution of the Money Market*] 409). During this time the system of banking as we now know it, with individual savings and checking accounts, began rapidly to develop: "by the 1860s [. . .] deposit banking was spreading through the commercial community, and more and more of the capital and savings of the nation were coming to rest in bank vaults" (Mathias 328).[1] As R. H. Patterson explained in "The Panic in the City" (1866), "no one nowadays keeps more than a few pounds in hand—seldom sufficient for a single day's expenditure—the cheque-book being used in payment of all

sums above £5" (86). In his 1869 book, *The Science of Finance,* Patterson emphasized the importance the Victorians ascribed to the use of checks, ranking checking (and the establishment of counting houses to clear checks) as the last of three revolutions that enabled the development of the commercial market that was currently benefitting the British economy (the first being the advent of banking, the second the shift to paper money).

Trollope describes the envelope Eleanor hands her husband as containing a "'rich but perilous freightage'" (795) because in 1867 checks were still a relatively unfamiliar financial instrument and therefore appeared potentially hazardous to the Victorian public. Patterson addresses anxieties about checking in his chapter "Our Invisible Capital," where he evokes an imaginary spectator who looks at contemporary commercial activities and says, "'I see no buying and selling [. . .]. Where is the money?'" (*Science* [*The Science of Finance*] 3). To assuage such anxieties, Walter Bagehot explains the complex mechanism of checking at length in *Lombard Street* (1870):

> The common course of business is this. A B having to receive 50,000*l.* from C D takes C D's cheque on a banker crossed, as it is called, and, therefore, only payable to another banker. He pays that cheque to his own credit with his own banker, who presents it to the banker on whom it is drawn, and if good it is an item between them in the general clearing or settlement of the afternoon. But this is evidently a very refined machinery, which a panic will be apt to destroy.
>
> (192)

The Last Chronicle of Barset depicts just such a complex negotiation when Eleanor Arabin gives Crawley a check "taken [. . .] as part of the rent due to her from the landlord of 'The Dragon of Wantly'" (759), a check that, unbeknownst to her, the landlord's brother has stolen from Lord Lufton's agent, an exchange which therefore leads Crawley to be falsely accused of theft. Trollope thus touches on Victorian anxieties about living in what Thomas Carlyle called "the Age of Script" (qtd. in [*The Hell of the English*] Weiss 139).

But Trollope acknowledges that living in a credit economy, though anxiety producing, might also be pleasurable. He does so through the figure of another woman who controls her own money, the wealthy Mrs. Thorne who first appeared in *Doctor Thorne* as the ointment heiress Miss Dunstable. In that earlier novel, Miss Dunstable, like the envelope that passes from Arabin to Crawley, is described in terms that evoke early Venetian sea-going commercial ventures: we hear of her that "ships so richly freighted were not to be run down in one summer morning's plain sailing" (225). In *Framley Parsonage* (1861), she is associated with the infamous bubbles of the speculative economy when

"Trollope has one of his impecunious aristocrats [. . .] 'teach her to blow soap-bubbles on scientific principles'" (Langbauer [*Novels of Everyday Life*] 110n72; *Framley Parsonage* 119). In *The Last Chronicle,* Trollope links her to joint-stock banking: "It was a way with Mrs. Thorne that they who came within the influence of her immediate sphere should be made to feel that the comforts and luxuries arising from her wealth belonged to a common stock, and were the joint property of them all" (551). Like Eleanor Arabin's association with checking, the symbolic link between Mrs. Thorne and joint-stock banking reflects the economic developments of the period. By the 1860s, as Peter Mathias explains,

> bank deposits grew to be several times the value of circulating media and currency as the banking habit spread over the nation. But a consequence was that inland transfers of credit were increasingly done by cheques and drafts drawn directly on other bank deposits. This was true of industrialists and merchants settling accounts in their normal way of trade, quite apart from private persons conducting their household expenditures. These transfers passed within the banking system, needing no financial intermediaries outside it like the bill brokers. The extension of multibranched joint stock banking with national networks encouraged this further.
>
> (328-29)[2]

Like a bank, Mrs. Thorne commands liquid capital that is easily put to use: "She had enormous wealth at her command, and had but few of those all-absorbing drains upon wealth which in this country make so many rich men poor. She had no family property,—no place to keep up in which she did not live. She had no retainers to be maintained because they were retainers. She had neither sons nor daughters" (551). In her world, as in the late-nineteenth-century credit economy more generally, it is no longer possible or even desirable to follow the old-fashioned practice of paying for things as you use them. Squire Dale, who practices the ascetic values of an earlier era, having saved enough through parsimonious living to protect his property, is frustrated when he attempts to recompense Mrs. Thorne for the horse she provides for his niece: "'when people are so rich and good-natured as Mrs. Thorne it is no good inquiring where things come from'" (552).

The issues raised in *The Last Chronicle of Barset* through the twin poles of the Reverend Mr. Crawley, with his poverty and asceticism, and Mrs. Thorne, with her liquid wealth and desire to give pleasure to others, reemerge in *An Autobiography.* "Now and then a man may arise among us," Trollope writes there, "who in any calling, whether it be law, in physic, in religious teaching, in art, or literature, may in his professional enthusiasm utterly disregard money" (106). It is this "utter disregard" that is represented in the scene where Crawley takes the envelope from Arabin. But in his au-

tobiography, Trollope also makes clear that, while we are drawn to such unworldliness, a position like Crawley's is finally not feasible in the modern world: "all will honour his enthusiasm, and if he be wifeless and childless, his disregard of the great object of men's work will be blameless. But it is a mistake to suppose that a man is a better man because he despises money. Few do so, and those few in doing so suffer a defect" (106). Trollope concludes by endorsing a position like the one taken by the generous Mrs. Thorne, asking, "Who does not desire to be hospitable to his friends, generous to the poor, liberal to all, munificent to his children, and to be himself free from the carking fears which poverty creates?" (106).

In *Can You Forgive Her?* (1864), the novel written immediately before *The Last Chronicle of Barset,* Plantagenet Palliser asserts that "'there is no vulgar error so vulgar,—that is to say, common or erroneous, as that by which men have been taught to say that mercenary tendencies are bad'" (283). As he shifts from the Barsetshire series to the Palliser novels Trollope moves toward this position. In his bridge novel, *The Last Chronicle,* he begins to represent mercenary tendencies as good or beneficial rather than bad. But his association of women with economics and men with asceticism in the novel allows him to cordon off an idea of honor. The gender split means that no matter how much Trollope emphasizes the pleasure and power of mercenary tendencies, his novel continues to locate intellectual and commercial impulses in two separate spheres, thereby underwriting what Harold Perkin describes as "an important vertical barrier, not always conscious or watertight, but in some ways more significant than the division between upper and lower middle class: the division between the business and the professional classes" (*Rise* [*The Rise of Professional Society*] 83). This strategy meant that while Victorian critics acknowledged Trollope's interest in vulgar commercial subjects they considered Trollope himself "neither vulgar nor mean" (qtd. in Skilton [*Anthony Trollope and His Contemporaries*] 22), able to "escape vulgarity" ("Review of *Barchester Towers*" 503), "a novelist who can paint vulgarity [. . .] [but] inspire a constant conviction that he himself is not in the least vulgar" ("Review of *Rachel Ray*" 555).[3]

Notes

1. By the time of *Phoebe Junior,* this consolidated banking system was firmly in place; "in 1875 [. . .] there were more than 50,000 shareholders in joint-stock banks" (Powell 398).

2. "Following the Joint Stock Bank Act (1844), the Bank Charter Act (1844), and the extension of limited liability to banking (1858), numerous joint-stock banks joined the critical and still dominant Bank of England" (Poovey 158).

3. David Skilton quotes this passage in discussing the general problem of vulgarity in the critical reception of Trollope and notes that the work Trollope produced in the mid-1870s tended to be seen as more vulgar than his earlier work (83, 31-32).

Works Cited

Allen, Grant. "The New Hedonism." *Fortnightly Review* Mar. 1894: 377-92.

Bagehot, Walter. *Lombard Street: A Description of the Money Market.* 1870. New York: John Wiley & Sons, 1999.

———. "The Postulates of Political Economy." *Economic Studies.* Ed. Richard Holt Hutton. London: Longmans, Green, 1911. 1-94.

Rev. [Review] of *Barchester Towers,* by Anthony Trollope. *Saturday Review* 30 May 1857: 503-04.

Bourdieu, Pierre. *Outline of a Theory of Practice.* Trans. Richard Nice. Cambridge: Cambridge UP, 1977.

Coleridge, Samuel Taylor. *On the Constitution of the Church and State According to the Idea of Each.* 1830. Ed. John Barrell. London: J. M. Dent, 1972.

Gagnier, Regenia. "On the Insatiability of Human Wants: Economic and Aesthetic Man." *Victorian Studies* 36:2 (Winter 1993): 125-53.

[Hutton, Richard Holt]. "Anthony Trollope." *Spectator* 9 Dec. 1882: 1573-74.

Jevons, W. Stanley. *The Theory of Political Economy.* London: Macmillan, 1888.

Kucich, John. *The Power of Lies: Transgression in Victorian Fiction.* Ithaca: Cornell UP, 1994.

Langbauer, Laurie. *Novels of Everyday Life: The Series in English Fiction, 1850-1930.* Ithaca: Cornell UP, 1999.

Rev. of *The Last Chronicle of Barset,* by Anthony Trollope. *Examiner* 20 July 1867: 452-53.

Rev. of *The Last Chronicle of Barset,* by Anthony Trollope. *Spectator* 13 July 1867: 778-80.

Mathias, Peter. *The First Industrial Nation: An Economic History of Britain 1700-1914.* London: Methuen, 1969.

[Oliphant, Lawrence]. "The Autobiography of a Joint-Stock Company (Limited)." *Blackwood's* July 1876: 96-122.

Oliphant, Margaret. "Novels." *Blackwood's* Sept. 1867: 257-80.

———. *Phoebe Junior: A Last Chronicle of Carlingford.* 1876. London: Virago, 1989.

Patterson, R. H. "The Panic in the City." *Blackwood's* July 1866: 78-93.

———. *The Science of Finance; A Practical Treatise.* Edinburgh: William Blackwood, 1868.

Perkin, Harold. *Origins of Modern English Society.* London: Routledge, 1969.

———. *The Rise of Professional Society: England since 1880.* London: Routledge, 1989.

Poovey, Mary. *Making a Social Body: British Cultural Formation 1830-1864.* Chicago: U of Chicago P, 1995.

Powell, Ellis T. *The Evolution of the Money Market (1385-1915).* 1915. New York: Augustus M. Kelley, 1966.

Rev. of *Rachel Ray,* by Anthony Trollope. *Saturday Review* 24 Oct. 1863: 554-55.

Skilton, David. *Anthony Trollope and His Contemporaries: A Study in the Theory and Conventions of Mid-Victorian Fiction.* New York: St. Martin's, 1972.

Trollope, Anthony. *An Autobiography.* 1883. Ed. Michael Sadleir and Frederic Page. Oxford: Oxford UP, 1950.

———. *Can You Forgive Her?* 1864. Ed. Stephen Wall. Harmondsworth: Penguin, 1972.

———. *Doctor Thorne.* 1858. Intro. and notes Ruth Rendell. Harmondsworth: Penguin, 1991.

———. *Framley Parsonage.* 1861. Ed. David Skilton and Peter Miles. Harmondsworth: Penguin, 1986.

———. *The Last Chronicle of Barset.* 1867. Ed. Stephen Gill. Oxford: Oxford UP, 1980.

Weiss, Barbara. *The Hell of the English: Bankruptcy and the Victorian Novel.* Lewisburg: Bucknell UP, 1986.

Audrey Jaffe (essay date autumn 2002)

SOURCE: Jaffe, Audrey. "Trollope in the Stock Market: Irrational Exuberance and *The Prime Minister.*" *Victorian Studies* 45, no. 1 (autumn 2002): 43-64.

[*In the following essay, Jaffe characterizes the ups and downs of the stock market as reflections of society and human emotions. In Jaffe's view, Trollope's 1876 novel* The Prime Minister *portrays complex connections between finance and romantic relationships.*]

A television advertisement for CNBC, aired frequently before the late-2000 stock-market decline, features a digital stock ticker projected across the chest of a railway commuter, its numbers coursing around him in a continuous, moving ribbon. Like an EKG, or some new kind of medical tracking device, this image—locating the numbers where the man's other ticker would be—captures the contemporary fascination with the stock market by identifying the movement of stock prices with life itself: physical and, especially, emotional life. The ad evokes the fantasy of connectedness that the stock market has become, as it pictures this commuter surrounded by—in effect, bound up in—a complex arrangement of digits that must, it seems, signify something crucial about him. The band across his chest registering both the intensity and banality of today's incessant market monitoring, the man with the ticker is a new everyman, a more intriguing version of the familiar work-a-day commuter, his internalization of the market (and the admiring gaze of his fellow commuter) singling him out as an enviable type: a vision of how connected we may all someday hope to become. In an age of such heightened attention to stock prices that they can be identified as vital signs, the man with the ticker is our better, more tuned-in self; watching the numbers, the ad intimates, we are simply watching ourselves.

But how, exactly, are those signs to be read? In both popular and academic discourse, the movement of stock-market prices, especially as symbolized by the jagged line of the stock-market graph, is amenable both to interpretation and to the failure of interpretation: it looks so much like a narrative, and yet no one can say for certain what it means. Or rather, everyone has something to say: an encyclopedia of "chart patterns" lists forty-seven variations, with such engaging names as "bump and run reversal," "hanging man," and "dead-cat bounce." The book also includes a chart identifying its own "failure rate": "Percentage of formations that do not work as expected" (Bulkowski [*Encyclopedia of Chart Patterns*] 655). A writer on day-trading cautions against selling on Mondays, with this caveat: "There is no pattern, relationship, or indicator in the market that will always be correct [. . .] Now, getting back to the Monday pattern" (Bernstein [*The Compleat Day Trader II*] 71). Nor does the graph's much-vaunted unpredictability, or "failure rate," inhibit interpretation; if its trajectory fails to confirm expectations, as it frequently does, that failure tends to be rationalized by the idea that the market knows us better than we know ourselves: more "sensitive" than any individual human being, it is said to respond to "unpredictable human impulses" (Carret [*The Art of Speculation*] 24). Indeed, most frequently, as the CNBC image suggests, the line's trajectory is assimilated to a narrative of feeling: universally apprehended as a picture of emotions—a snapshot of the national (or global) mood—it is understood as swinging between (for example) elation and depression, optimism and alarm. Looking to the numbers to see how we feel, we both personalize them—render them a projection of our individual and collective narratives—and depersonalize them, conceding our authority

to know ourselves to an abstract system that seems to have captured this knowledge. Do the numbers emerge from within the man's chest, or are they projected from without? Is the market a projection of the man, or is the man a projection of the market? Making sense of the numbers, we seek to discover, in that familiar phrase that registers the identification of economic with emotional well-being, how we are doing.

The market must have some authority of its own, it seems—it can't be just us, writ large, and yet it appears to be. The idea of the stock market as emotional projection bears on the question, addressed by market theorists, of whether stock prices are determined by facts about companies or commodities or by opinions, as reflected in the activity of investment. The contention that stocks in the dot.com economy of the 1990s were "overvalued" was tied to an assessment of investor emotion: "irrational exuberance" was Alan Greenspan's term for the relationship between the way companies were valued and the way investors felt about their stocks. According to Greenspan, investors used their positive feeling about the market as a basis for further investment, investing, in effect, in their own emotions. This phenomenon drove up prices, leading to further exuberance, all of which tended toward the creation of a "bubble"—a term whose own implicit narrative, itself a rhetorical projection of the stock-market graph, stands as an answer to at least one of the interpretative questions the graph is said to pose.[1] For Greenspan, the irrationality of irrational exuberance lies in the absence of a connection between feeling and value: irrational exuberance is feeling based "merely" on feeling.

But the circularity that made Greenspan nervous (and along with him, eventually, everyone else)—the idea that the market affects feeling, and feeling affects the market—merely reconfigures a discomfort that has existed at least since Anthony Trollope's time: an uneasiness about the unpredictability of investing in shares and about the attenuated relationship between investors and the objects of their investment. Because investors usually operate at a distance from the companies or commodities in which they invest, possessing at best limited knowledge of them, they invest in something other than facts: in narratives about companies and commodities, for instance, and in their own hopes and wishes about those narratives. The term "irrational exuberance," referring both to the market and to the feelings of those who invest in it, seeks to ward off the danger of too much happiness by gesturing toward its unlikely-sounding opposite, rational feeling: the idea that feeling could be an accurate gauge of value. But the attempt to separate rational from irrational feeling is only one of numerous futile attempts made during the course of stock-exchange history to remove instability from the market. Indeed, from Trollope to Greenspan, discussions about investment and the market have repeatedly sought to draw similar lines: between the solid and the ephemeral, between safety and risk—between, in general, value securely located in companies or commodities and value that is only imagined to be there—as a means of countering the uncertainty and unpredictability—indeed, the sheer uninterpretability—of the fluctuating value of shares.[2] In seeking to fix such lines, they merely point toward the uncertainties, and the movements of the heart with which we register them, that tie our identities to the market.

* * *

The CNBC commercial assimilates the movement of stock prices to the biological and metaphorical pulse, condensing in a single image—a videographic palimpsest—a connection that financial narratives from the Victorian period to the present have spelled out, and in doing so reinforced: that between money and the heart. Trollope's *The Prime Minister* (1876) might be said to present an uncontroversial understanding of the way this connection works: one can read a man's character, the novel has it, in the way he manages his money. But *The Prime Minister* also offers other ways of understanding our own assimilations of feeling and the market and the lines we continue to draw in their name, perhaps most strikingly in its status as a precursor of today's stock-market dramas: those episodes, played out in the daily newspapers and the nightly news, in which a violation of financial rules (or merely a suspected one, since such cases do not always involve legal wrongdoing) registers as a general social violation, an offense against middle-class culture and feeling.[3] In offering up as villains stock-market characters whose particular forms of exuberance are routinely characterized as reverberating beyond the market, contemporary culture demonstrates the persistence and the usefulness of a Victorian master narrative within which matters not otherwise easily regulated may be placed.

Similarities between the Victorian and contemporary stock markets are not hard to find. In both periods, an increase in the popular buying and selling of shares spurs widespread, vicarious interest in the movement of stock prices. Both periods are fascinated by the market's reverberations in everyday life: the potential for ordinary individuals to participate, via investment, in domestic and international commerce. New technologies—the railway and the Internet—allow for similarly phantasmatic relations between investor and investment: today's (or yesterday's) dot.com is the nineteenth century's railway to Vera Cruz. Less visible to contemporary thinking, however, is the way persistent belief in the market's dependence on emotional and characterological distinctions may be traced to the persuasive articulation of such distinctions in the Victorian novel.

The established, traditional families in Trollope's *The Prime Minister,* the Whartons and the Fletchers, rely on feeling as a means of gauging value, but the appearance of a new man—a man of the stock exchange—disrupts their ability to do so. Of the Whartons and the Fletchers, Trollope writes:

> As a class they are more impregnable, more closely guarded by their feelings and prejudices against strangers than any other. None keep their daughters to themselves with greater care, or are less willing to see their rules of life changed or abolished. And yet this man, half foreigner half Jew,—and as it now appeared,—whole pauper, had stepped in and carried off a prize of which such a one as Arthur Fletcher was contending!
>
> (662)[4]

It is precisely in relation to the feelings and prejudices of this class that the character Ferdinand Lopez poses a problem; about Lopez, throughout much of the first half of *The Prime Minister,* no one knows—though many suspect—what the appropriate feeling might be. Thus when trying to convince his daughter Emily, who has declared herself in love with Lopez, that the man is no gentleman, all Wharton can say with certainty is that "no one knows anything about him, or where to inquire even" (46). And while that ignorance, we are told, would be enough for Dr. Johnson, according to whom "any other derivation of this difficult word ['gentleman'] [. . .] than that which causes it to signify 'a man of ancestry' is whimsical" (10), what troubles Wharton's ability to make his case with conviction is the fact that, as the novel puts it, the nineteenth century admits exceptions. And Ferdinand Lopez is an exception: on the basis of his bearing, his clothing, his manner of sitting on a horse, and the lower half of his face (12), "It was admitted on all sides that Ferdinand Lopez was a 'gentleman'" (10).

The admission of Ferdinand Lopez as a gentleman—like Trollope's effacement of the quotation marks with which he briefly surrounds the term—constitutes an admission of the impossibility of keeping him out: like the markets, which cannot afford to invest only at home, English society is necessarily vulnerable to foreign charm.[5] What allows for Lopez's admission is this:

> We all know the man,—a little man generally, who moves seldom and softly,—who looks always as though he had just been sent home in a bandbox. Ferdinand Lopez was not a little man, and moved freely enough; but never, at any moment,—going into the city or coming out of it, on horseback or on foot, at home over his book or after the mazes of the dance,—was he dressed otherwise than with perfect care. Money and time did it, but folk thought that it grew with him, as did his hair and nails. And he always rode a horse which charmed good judges of what a park nag should be;—not a prancing, restless, giggling, sideway-going, useless garran, but an animal well made, well bitted, and with perfect paces, on whom a rider if it pleased him could be as quiet as a statue on a monument.
>
> (12-13)

It is of course known by Wharton and others that not knowing anything about Lopez is the same as knowing something about him, and that the suspicions hovering around him are likely to resolve into knowledge of a specific kind. Indeed, we are told that his father is Portuguese, and we are invited to suspect that he is a Jew.[6] The novel's gentlemen intuit, as it is the business of gentlemen to do, Lopez's lack of gentlemanly status; what "a gentleman knows" (30) above all is how to identify another gentleman. However, the allowance of exceptions to the rule means that gentlemanliness must be determined in each individual case; once exceptions are admitted, each candidate becomes, in effect, a stock, his value a function of the assessment of the group. In this case, what a gentleman knows has no practical effect on what Ferdinand Lopez does, for his admission as a gentleman is an admission that nothing can be done about him. And once the doors to Wharton/Fletcher society, along with questions of gentlemanly identity, are thrown open, the identities of the Whartons and Fletchers—formerly held in place by their strong feelings and prejudices—are also in play.

If the nineteenth century admits exceptions, there is nothing to keep the Ferdinand Lopezes of the world from attending one's social gatherings, meeting one's family, running for Parliament, and marrying one's daughter. Victorian novels typically rely on narratives of romantic love to adjudicate the relationship between feeling and value, the love relationship absorbing and disseminating the codes of ideological discourses such as those of race, nationality, and class. It makes sense, then, that the crisis signaled by Lopez's admission into the world of the Whartons and Fletchers should take shape as the novel's romantic plot. But the relation between romance and finance in *The Prime Minister* is more complex than the model of ideological mystification allows, since for Trollope and his readers, as for twentieth- and twenty-first-century subjects of market economies and the narratives that circulate within them, the stock exchange has provided a compellingly coherent set of terms within which familiar cultural narratives, and indeed familiar cultural identities, have been rewritten and reconceived. In the cultural narrative of the stock exchange whose terms are *The Prime Minister*'s, for instance, Emily's feeling for Lopez may be understood as the characteristic attitude of the speculator: she must therefore be taught to invest her emotions, as she would her money, wisely. The terms of romance and those of finance are interchangeable, universalized by gender difference: if feeling is a woman's capital (and its signifier, since she brings her father's wealth with her) then speculating with love is understandable in relation to, or as an analogy for, speculating with money. Feeling here is a form of currency, and feelings about money are a template for feelings in general: the truth about a character, Trollope implies, can be learned from the way that character feels about money. Thus

The Prime Minister's calibration of feeling and value has as much to do with Lopez's financial dealings as it does with his romantic ones; indeed, the former serve as the hallmark by which the true character of the latter will be judged. The marriage plot *is*, in fact, the financial plot: the lesson Emily Wharton learns about Lopez is taught by way of her increasing knowledge of his financial dealings. His value—more precisely, his lack of value—emerges for her, as it does in the novel as a whole, in a series of demonstrations of the nature of his feelings about money.

After his failed run for Parliament, Lopez accepts payment for his electioneering expenses twice—once from the Duke of Omnium and once from Wharton—without telling the second that he has already been paid by the first. His thoughts on the subject are these:

> It was not as he sat at the breakfast table that Ferdinand Lopez made up his mind to pocket the Duke's money and to say nothing about it to Mr. Wharton. He had been careful to conceal the cheque, but he had done so with the feeling that the matter was one to be considered in his own mind before he took any step. As he left the house, already considering it, he was inclined to think that the money must be surrendered. Mr. Wharton had very generously paid his electioneering expenses, but had not done so simply with the view of making him a present of the money. He wished the Duke had not taken him at his word. In handing this cheque over to Mr. Wharton he would be forced to tell the story of his letter to the Duke, and he was sure that Mr. Wharton would not approve of his having written such a letter. How could anyone approve of his having applied for a sum of money which had already been paid to him? How could such a one as Mr. Wharton—an old-fashioned English gentleman,—approve of such an application being made under any circumstances? Mr. Wharton would very probably insist on having the cheque sent back to the Duke,—which would be a sorry end to the triumph as at present achieved. And the more he thought of it the more sure he was that it would be imprudent to mention to Mr. Wharton his application to the Duke. The old men of the present day were, he said to himself, such fools that they understood nothing. And then the money was very convenient to him [. . .] By the time, therefore, that he had reached the city he had resolved that at any rate for the present he would say nothing about it to Mr. Wharton. Was it not spoil got from the enemy by his own courage and cleverness? When he was writing his acknowledgment for the money to Warburton he had taught himself to look upon the sum extracted from the Duke as a matter quite distinct from the payment made to him by his father-in-law.

(376-77)

In a process that enacts the business it describes—"the more he thought of it the more sure he was"—Lopez provides himself with a rationale for keeping both sums. Gentlemanly behavior matters, to his way of thinking, only to others; it is a performance ("How could anyone approve?") relevant only insofar as it supports or interferes with his plans. And as he teaches himself to look upon two identical payments as distinct, differentiating himself in the process from "the old men of the present day," he displays a characteristic the novel defines elsewhere as an inability to perceive appropriate distinctions: he is a man who "wouldn't mind whether he ate horseflesh or beef if horseflesh were as good as beef" (141)—one who has, more generally, no feeling for "the lines which separated right from wrong" (373). The movement of his thought—choreographed by the movement of his feet and bounded by his trip from home to city—displays, indeed, not an observance of that line but rather a mental fluidity, an ability to justify the merits of the position he wishes to take.

Not possessing the sensibilities held by the old men of the present day—not knowing what it is that a gentleman knows, but aspiring nevertheless to gentlemanliness—Ferdinand Lopez is necessarily in the position of "teaching" himself "to look upon" things. When his partner, Sexty Parker, expresses concern that "the coffee and guano [in which Lopez has invested] were not always real coffee and guano," Lopez teaches him, daily after lunch, to see things in a different way:

> "If I buy a ton of coffee and keep it six weeks, why do I buy it and keep it, and why does the seller sell it instead of keeping it? The seller sells it because he thinks he can do best by parting with it now at a certain price. I buy it because I think I can make money by keeping it. It is just the same as though we were to back our opinions. He backs the fall. I back the rise. You needn't have coffee and you needn't have guano to do this. Indeed the possession of the coffee and the possession of the guano is only a very clumsy addition to the trouble of your profession [. . .]." Coffee and guano still had to be bought because the world was dull and would not learn the tricks of trade as taught by Ferdinand Lopez [. . .] but our enterprising hero looked for a time in which no such dull burden should be imposed upon him.
>
> (377)

In fact, the world has since learned the tricks of the trade as taught by Ferdinand Lopez; for Trollope, however, Lopez's failure to distinguish between the guano that is not there and the guano that is further displays his status as a man who fails to make appropriate distinctions.[7] Repeatedly documenting Lopez's feelings about money, the novel illustrates in increasingly vivid detail the contention it finally makes explicit: "He knew how to speak, and how to look, how to use a knife and fork, how to dress himself, and how to walk. But he had not the faintest notion of the feelings of a gentleman" (497).

"Teaching to look upon," an activity that Trollope seems here to disparage, is also one whose necessity he admits—for despite the novel's insistence on the intuitive

quality of gentlemanly knowledge, Abel Wharton no less than Trollope himself had to make his way to it. And Trollope's awareness of the necessity of such activity leads not to anarchy, or to *avant-la-lettre* deconstruction, or even to an excessively threatened social fabric, but rather and in several ways to the novel: that vehicle par excellence both for teaching the nineteenth century how to look upon things and, in Trollope's case as in others, for securing the admission of middle-class authors into gentlemanly circles.[8] Indeed, that Lopez's ambition is also his author's suggests the importance of the lines this novel attempts to draw. For if the speculator and the novelist are both seeking to rise in the world by telling stories—stories Trollope referred to in his own case as his "castles in the air" (*Autobiography* 42)—then a certain strain accompanies the assertion that the true gentleman can be separated from the pretender by means of gentlemanly intuition.

In an atmosphere in which money seems to have appropriated the power to create gentlemen, Trollope makes it the business of his novels to delineate the distinctions in feeling that separate the gentleman from the nongentleman: to refine and elaborate the code for an age in which that elaboration is, he believes, sorely needed. Revealing the contents of Lopez's mind in order to illustrate distinctions between gentlemanly values and their absence, Trollope both dramatizes the need his novels are designed to fulfill and seeks to affirm his own possession of the discourse, his solid grasp of the nature and texture of gentlemanly ideals. But his contribution to a history of the emotions lies, beyond this, in his ability to bring money into the realm of feeling, and more significantly, to demonstrate that it is already there. For the feelings within which Trollope discerns distinctions are feelings about money: money is the proving ground within which distinctions in feeling appear. In the context of wealth made rapidly and often mysteriously through the buying and selling of shares (a context in which respectability might be built on a foundation of guano, or, even worse, its absence), and in which discourses about money sought to maintain the possibility that respectability and the stock exchange could coexist by marking boundaries between legitimate and illegitimate ways of reaping investment's rewards, the distinction between what was regarded approvingly as investment and what was reviled as speculation turns out, not surprisingly, to be a distinction in feeling as well.[9]

* * *

Trollope's emphasis on the role of gentlemanly feeling in financial matters informs his description of the way Wharton and Lopez came by their money. Wharton, we are told, "had begun his practice early, and had worked in a stuff gown till he was nearly sixty. At that time he had amassed a large fortune, mainly from his profession, but partly also by the careful use of his own small patrimony and by his wife's money. Men knew that he was rich, but no one knew the extent of his wealth" (*Prime Minister* 25-26). Here is the corresponding account of Lopez: "He had been on the Stock Exchange, and still in some manner, not clearly understood by his friends, did business in the City [. . .]. But nobody, not even his own bankers or his own lawyer,—not even the old woman who looked after his linen,—ever really knew the state of his affairs" (11). The difference between Wharton's gentlemanliness and Lopez's lies, in keeping with Johnson's dictum, in what is known of their ancestry, with the implication that what this particular lack of knowledge signifies for Lopez's "use" of money is an absence of care. And the line between care and the absence of care is, in general terms (though not always in the manner one would expect), from the nineteenth century to the twenty-first, the line that separates the investor from the speculator.

If the stock-market graph is generally aligned with the movement of feeling, then a close attention to fluctuations of value suggests an identification with impulse itself. Thus while the investor is typically imagined as detached from his money, able to ignore its day-to-day movements, the speculator is viewed as a creature of unregulated impulse and unruly emotion, in thrall, day and night, to his greed. (Thus while the investor may make more careful "use" of his money, the speculator is a more active caretaker of his.) The investor, able to wait for his "emotional payoff" (Schott [*Mind Over Money*] 25), is promised in the end an even greater reward, while the speculator serves as a useful embodiment of bad habits: mental depravity, idleness, deceitfulness, and greed.

But the image of the investor waiting patiently for his payoff should alert us to a certain wavering in conventional representations of the difference between speculators and investors—a difference that has long rested upon the premise that, when it comes to the business of making money from money, there is a right way and a wrong one. "Wealth accrues from generally right behavior," a commentator in 1998 writes, "not from trying to extract the maximum profit out of any situation" (Schott 24). "Generally right behavior," according to this formulation, refers not exactly to not trying to make money, but, as in Carlyle's formula for attaining happiness, to making money without appearing to try to make money—to making money, in effect, while looking carefully in another direction. "Speculation" routinely describes an energetic attention to fluctuations in value, as contrasted with the investor's long-term involvement with "safe" stocks; identified as the placing of money in the service of risky projects, speculation is associated with terms like "optimism," "hope," and "bubble." But if one seeks to define the term with any precision, and in particular to clarify the distinction between invest-

ment and speculation, what one discovers is not that distinctions cannot be made—on the contrary, everyone can make them—but rather that, in the context of Britain's economy in the nineteenth century no less than our contemporary one, there is hardly an investment that is not, according to the usual definitions, a speculation: "The practice of buying articles of merchandise, or any purchasable commodity whatever, in expectation of a rise of price and of selling the same at considerable advance" (S. Maunder, qtd. in Mottram [*A History of Financial Speculation*] 4).[10]

Distinctions between investment and speculation tend to be made on the basis of personal involvement: the investor is said to be more committed to the company or commodity to which he lends his money. But both activities posit an attenuated relationship to the substance or commodity being traded; neither investor nor speculator need ever see the coffee or the guano. Differences thus tend to be articulated as matters of degree, assessing the quantity and quality of such intangibles as duration (how long an investor plans to hold a stock before selling) and intent (is the investor primarily interested in building a railroad, or in making money from an expected rise in railway shares?). Moreover, the characteristic charge made against speculators—that their greed involves them in risky enterprises—is also a matter of degree, since the anxieties about risk and instability attached to the term "speculator" are simply amplifications or exaggerations of feelings that attend the buying and selling of shares in general. In the hair-splitting nature of these distinctions, and in particular the failure of academic discourse to arrive at any consensus on the meaning of the terms,[11] it is possible to see that the two categories are characteristically distinguished from one another not by any precise definition of the activities themselves, where difference to this day remains at the level of name-calling (the annals of respectable financial activity include venture capitalists, investment bankers, stockbrokers—anything but speculators), but rather according to particular constellations of feelings and attitudes—and that the character called the speculator, whose qualities were rapidly assimilated to the villains of nineteenth-century fiction at the same time that investment (or speculation) became the province of middle-class novel readers, served for the Victorians, as he does for us, as a bogeyman whose function it is to make speculation safe for everyone else: to assume for the national psyche the risks of involvement in the market.[12] The term "speculator" marks a boundary between right and wrong that cannot quite be aligned with the wavering pattern of the stock-market graph; in particular, it insists on a distinction between respectable and illicit behavior in relation to what has traditionally been represented as the dubious practice of making money from fluctuations in value.[13] The opposition between investment and speculation serves to shore up the belief that the system of values defining gentlemanly behavior coincides with, and will be revealed through, an individual's feelings about money.

Describing the source of Wharton's and Lopez's money, Trollope provides no specific account of the "care" Wharton has taken. But care is evident in the novel's quiet mystification of Wharton's financial activity, since for neither man is the source of his money revealed. And though we are told repeatedly that Wharton keeps his financial status and that of his children secret, to their detriment, these details are hidden from readers as well. Given the attention the novel devotes to each man's thinking when it comes to Emily, to one another's faults, and to Lopez's financial dealings, its silence about Wharton's wealth may be said to echo Wharton's own: to participate in the mystification of money and power intended to secure the line between right behavior and wrong. Trollope's non-divulgence of details here—the silence of a novelist whose signature, critics often remark, is the precise specification of his characters' income and capital—underscores the point that the distinction between investors and speculators lies less in what they do than in how they are said to feel about what they do, and in how we are taught to feel about them.

* * *

That Emily Wharton's feeling for Lopez resembles a speculator's hopes for his shares—that her feeling about him is irrationally exuberant—we, like her father, suspect but can do nothing about; such truths, like all speculations, can only be proved retrospectively, once the bubble has burst. While her initial feelings about him are supremely confident—"I do love him, and I shall never love anyone else in the same way" (46)—she must be taught to see that her feelings are as ungrounded as Lopez's own happiness upon receiving large sums of money. Indeed, for Emily, Lopez comes to personify the rapid fluctuations to which, living in the atmosphere of her father's apparently illimitable wealth, she has never before been subject: he proves to be the embodiment of fluctuating value, the man with a stock ticker for a heart. After receiving a requested loan of £3,000 from his father-in-law, for instance, Lopez is elated: "he was overjoyed,—so much so that for a while he lost that restraint over himself which was habitual to him. He ate his breakfast in a state of exultation" (224). And yet "almost immediately" he finds himself needing money again. Here is Emily's response: "She endeavoured to judge him kindly, but a feeling of insecurity in reference to his affairs struck her at once and made her heart cold [. . .] surely a large sum to have vanished in so short a time! Something of the uncertainty of business she could understand, but a business must be perilously uncertain if subject to such vicissitudes as these!" (301). The pattern of feeling she begins to observe in her husband and in her married life—a pattern that

causes her heart to grow cold, revealing it to be no less a ticker than her husband's—is that of the fluctuating value of shares, the pace of whose movement she cannot, though she tries, assimilate to the "better or worse" of her marriage vows (301). It is a pattern whose appropriate periodicity she has internalized in her father's house, along with the intuition that she need not—indeed, ought not—know the source of the money that supports her.

Lopez, we learn, is possessed of the power of compelling belief; to this is ascribed Emily's mistaken conviction "that she had found the good man in Ferdinand Lopez" (42). His financial success depends, as we see in his relationship with Sexty Parker, on perpetuating his beliefs: on selling himself. Thus his first order of business upon marrying Emily is to teach her to look as he does upon money: "She must be instructed in his ways. She must learn to look the world with his eyes. She must be taught the great importance of money." And, more seriously, "He had perceived that she had much influence with her father, and she must be taught to use this influence unscrupulously on her husband's behalf" (214). But she resists—indeed, recoils from—his teaching, which requires her to be the conduit of her father's wealth: "He demanded of her the writing of the letter almost immediately [. . .]. It seemed as though she were seizing the advantage of the first moment of her freedom to take a violent liberty with her father" (220).

That asking her father for money should resemble the "taking" of "a violent liberty" points toward the Oedipal nature of this scenario; in Emily's narrative the symbolic system that identifies money with guano includes sexuality among the categories from which respectability requires the keeping of a careful distance.[14] For Emily, knowing the source of her husband's money, and in particular having her father be that source, both demystifies and endangers the hygienic attitude toward money the Wharton/Fletcher class wishes to preserve. The atmosphere of wealth in which Whartons and Fletchers dwell—in which wealth *is* atmosphere, as in the "pretty things" with which Emily surrounds herself after her marriage—is transformed by Lopez into money: "she was told that her household gods had a price put upon them, and that they were to be sold" (337). What Wharton keeps secret from his children is not, of course, that he is wealthy, but rather by how much: not the fact of wealth but the details, the numbers invested with the mystery of parental power. Thus Emily's growing sense of degradation involves not just her husband's financial failure, but the fact that she cannot choose not to know about it: the book of life, once opened (and one might say this of Trollope's book as well), turns out to be the financial page. "Without a moment's hesitation he could catch at the idea of throwing upon her father the burden of maintaining both her and himself! She understood the meaning of this. She could read his mind so far. She endeavoured not to read the book too closely,—but there it was, opened to her wider day by day, and she knew that the lessons which it taught were vulgar and damnable" (338).

The irrationality of Emily's earlier exuberance is both confirmed and balanced by the otherwise inexplicable rush of degradation and self-loathing she experiences after Lopez's suicide: by her own account she is "the woman that he had thrust so far into the mire that she can never again be clean" (643). Her repulsion—and Lopez's Jewishness contributes here—viscerally reinforces the difference between speculator and investor. Moreover, the feelings about money embodied in each term take shape as paradigmatically different forms of masculinity and a lesson about manhood: "there would come upon her unbidden, unwelcome reminiscences of Arthur Fletcher [. . .] She remembered his light wavy hair, which she had loved as one loves the beauty of a dog, which had seemed to her young imagination, to her in the ignorance of her early years to lack something of a dreamed-of manliness [. . .]. But now,—now that it was all too late,—the veil had fallen from her eyes." And once feelings about money take shape in this way—are embodied as two men—they can be "seen" with absolute clarity: "She could now see the difference between manliness and 'deportment'" (338). Indeed, money appears to make everything clear, as Lopez's increasingly bad luck with it seems naturally to accompany and support the revelation that he is a thoroughly bad character. Thus the stock-market narrative substantiates, in an altogether unsurprising way, the differences between Lopez's character and Fletcher's. And it also enables the drawing of another much-needed distinction: that between one's father and the "good man" who will be one's husband. In Emily's desire not to know, as in her feeling of repulsion toward her husband and herself, the narrative of speculation, with its moral baggage about greed and the defiling touch of money—and of the Jew—is intertwined with a necessary cultural narrative whose trajectory demonstrates, with the unmistakable clarity of a plunging line on the stock-market graph, the irrationality of her investment in Ferdinand Lopez.

Wharton's failure to stop his daughter's marriage has been ascribed both to a failure of his prejudice—he is not quite prejudiced enough—and to its success: so concerned is he about Lopez's "foreignness" that he fails adequately to scrutinize the man's character. But like other characters in the novel, including his daughter and Lopez, Wharton in fact blunders because he is overidentified with his investment: his ability to evaluate Lopez is clouded by his feeling for his daughter. Indeed, as he considers Emily's feeling for Lopez he is unable to maintain the distinction of which he had previously been so certain:

But then was he sure that he was right? He of course had his own way of looking at life, but was it reasonable that he should force his girl to look at things with his eyes? The man was distasteful to him as being unlike his idea of an English gentleman, and as being without those far-reaching fibres and roots by which he thought that the stability and solidity of a human tree should be assured. But the world was changing around him every day. Royalty was marrying out of its degree. Peers' sons were looking only for money. And, more than that, peers' daughters were bestowing themselves on Jews and shopkeepers. Had he not better make the usual inquiry about the man's means, and, if satisfied on that head, let the girl do as she would? Added to all this, there was growing on him a feeling that ultimately youth would as usual triumph over age, and that he would be beaten. If that were so, why worry himself, or why worry her?

(75)

Wharton's thoughts display not the unwavering certainty of the clear moral line but rather the jittery peaks and valleys of the stock-market graph; his willingness to entertain the possibility of Ferdinand Lopez as a son-in-law—to overlook a distinction he had previously considered vital—takes shape as a mental wavering, one not wholly dissimilar from that manifested by Ferdinand Lopez in the process of teaching himself to distinguish between two identical payments. Tracing the fluctuating movements of characters' thoughts as they wend their way from one side of a question to the other, Trollope gives narrative form and identity to those peaks and valleys. But the identity such thoughts suggest, as they cross and re-cross the lines that separate right from wrong, is not organized enough to take a stand on one side or the other: it is identity that, finding no solid ground but its own conclusions, is in the position of backing itself, of founding feeling on feeling. Indeed, the pattern of Wharton's thoughts here mimics the uncertain status of Ferdinand Lopez himself, whose admission into polite society threatens its solid values: not because that society doesn't "know," as a gentleman knows, what kind of a man he is, but rather because it cannot locate the line he has crossed, nor can it draw one that will keep him out. It is up to the novel, then—and not only Trollope's, but the entire genre of evil-speculator novels of the period—to do what novels do best, which is to draw that line: to harden suspicion into narrative, to fix the trajectory of Lopez's life into a recognizable pattern, to render vivid distinctions and differences in character and feeling.

The beginning of *The Prime Minister* keeps the status of Lopez's Jewishness mysterious: it invites characters and readers to wonder whether he is, in fact, a Jew. Suspicion, as in those "disagreeable matters" Lopez hopes will not come up for discussion, creates a distinction waiting to be made, an outline that requires filling in, a potential awaiting fulfillment. So too, it turns out, does his status as speculator; Lopez's careless treatment of his wife, deceitfulness, and commission of the actual crime of forgery invite not so much the conclusion that speculators are evil as the suspicion that perhaps they are not quite evil enough. The series of mishaps that leads Lopez to suicide suggests on the part of the novelist what market analysts call "magical thinking"—something is so because I have wished it to be: a kind of thinking distinguishable from the novelist's usual business, if it is at all, by the palpability of its need. Making Lopez a Jew and a criminal is the equivalent of wanting the guano to be real, the equivalent of narratives that attempt to explain what the market is doing: it is a stock-market story, an attempt to secure feelings and beliefs in something outside the self.

Just as Lopez's Jewishness functions simultaneously as a figure for the unknown (no one knows his background) and as an image of absolute predictability (reinforcing the suspicion that he will, and deserves to, come to a bad end), so too does the novel's final section substantiate the suspicions it has aroused about him and, at the same time, devote itself to annihilating his identity. Having lost everything in speculation, he throws himself under a train and is "knocked into bloody atoms" (520). But his clothes reveal no signs of identity: he carries no papers, and his handkerchief and collar bear no marks. "The fragments of his body set identity at defiance, and even his watch had been crumpled into ashes" (523-24). Hammering his point home, as another nail in the coffin, Trollope has it discovered five months later that Lopez has signed Sexty Parker's name to a bill, effectively ruining Parker's wife and children: "He had been all a lie from head to foot" (606). But Lopez is not exactly a lie. Like the stories periodically found to circulate in the market—stories, designed to move stock prices, whose authors must be discovered, punished, and never allowed to trade again—his is not so much a false story as it is a shadow story, a trope for the market itself, which retains a cultural function as a clearinghouse for the separation of true narratives from false ones. And it is a trope for Trollope as well, as he tells us the story of a man who looks, dresses, and sits on a horse like a gentleman but is not one. And we know he is not, we are told, because the stories he tells are not the right kind of stories.[15]

Veering between exuberance and self-loathing, Emily Wharton defines the boundaries between which, Trollope suggests, feelings about money characteristically waver; that her feelings appear spontaneous and visceral, and are mediated through men, naturalizes emotion whose financial bearing the novel elaborates more directly elsewhere. Intertwining personal drama and financial crisis, Emily's story incorporates money into the familial narrative: just as she recoils from herself in horror, as from the contents of her husband's mind, so too may the state of one's money seem to echo—or does it produce?—the state of one's emotions. Such narratives facilitate the transfer of identity into numbers that is the market's lifeblood; in the elation or self-loathing that attends the fluctuation of the numbers, we pursue our own self-regulation, an ideal self embodied in the fantasy of an ideal number. Exploring the painful consciousness that signifies a failure to keep one's proper distance from money, however, Emily's narrative in fact suggests how attending to the numbers may help us avoid such a consciousness, structuring our proper relation to money and the market. For the numbers, possessing the lure of authenticity and simultaneously refusing to give anything away, offer us the feeling that we know even as they tell us nothing, even as they serve as substitutes for whatever it is they might tell. Thus while keeping us focused on the drama of their movement—on, for instance, what we have designated the roller-coaster ride of the market's ups and downs—they allow us to keep our feet, or so it seems, out of the guano. After the narrative of Lopez's exuberance, of Emily's mistake, and of the degradation that results from their entanglement comes the embrace of what might now have to be called rational exuberance: the ordinary emotions of the married, middle-class subject, whose choice, shaped by life's hard lessons, is articulated by that narrative as a choice of investment over speculation. One might choose otherwise; in some cases, one has done so, and may do so again. To know this is to know the compelling quality of the line we have learned to straddle and of the numbers whose path we continue to trace.

Notes

1. This paper was written toward the end of the "boom" of the late 1990s: before its end was officially designated. But what was then called the "slow-down" of winter 2000-01 was a slow-down only in the context of the bubble narrative. Writes Robert Shiller: "The present stock market displays the classic features of a speculative bubble, a situation in which temporarily high prices are sustained largely by investors' enthusiasm rather than by consistent estimation of real value" (xii). And: "We need to know if the value investors have imputed to the market is not really there, so that we can adjust our planning and thinking. But a bubble is only discernible as such once most investors have ceased to put their money on those 'overvalued' stocks—in other words, once it is perceived to have popped. Hence I tend to agree more with Peter Garber: "'Bubble' characterizations [. . .] are non-explanations of events, merely a name that we attach to a financial phenomenon that we have not invested sufficiently in understanding" (124).

2. As Tatiana Holway observes, the problem is noted by Adam Smith: money "cannot adequately represent value, though the market, which trades on

price, behaves as if it does, obscuring the distinction between the 'nominal' and the 'real.'" Holway goes on to discuss this distinction, writing that "speculation [. . .] served the interests of capitalism" (113). My point is that speculation *is* capitalism.

3. Contemporary examples include such figures as Ivan Boesky, Michael Milken, Martin Frankel, and Jonathan Lebed, the last discussed further below. Frankel's story is one of familial corruption and sexual debauchery as well as (the always-cited) greed; Boesky notoriously expressed the extent of his corruption when he commented—at a commencement address, no less—that "Greed is all right." When Lebed's case came to light, his relationship with his family was of much interest to reporters. In such cases, the Securities Exchange Commission appears (understandably) hapless.

4. On Victorian participation in the market, see Hennessy 51.

5. Trollope uses the term "admitted" similarly in relation to Augustus Melmotte: "Mr. Melmotte was admitted into society, because of some enormous power which was supposed to lie in his hands; but even by those who thus admitted him he was regarded as a thief and a scoundrel" (*The Way We Live Now* 247). On Britain's exportation of raw materials and goods and importation of manufactured goods from the mid-1870s on, see Checkland 62-64.

6. The suggestion is that Lopez's open admission of his foreignness might deflect Wharton's attention away from other, still-unspecified problems: "He could not get over the fact that he was the son of a Portugese parent, but by admitting that openly he thought he might avoid present discussion on matters which might, perhaps, be more disagreeable, but to which he need not allude if the accident of his birth were to be taken by the father as settling the question" (32-33). The "matters" remain unnamed: Lopez's financial activities and his Jewishness are, the implication is, equally and interchangeably disagreeable.

7. Thus while the definition of speculation is unstable, the insistence on a distinction between legitimate and illegitimate modes of investment is not. That stock-market discourse continues to insist on this difference even as the meanings of the terms shift (what Lopez does is now called options trading, for instance, and there is nothing illegitimate about it) both reveals the continuing presence of the nineteenth century in the twenty-first and explains why it is so easy not to see it. Any number of people today called "successful investors" are also contemporary versions of Ferdinand Lopez: Jim Rogers, for instance, who claims to "bet" on "whole countries," has this to say: "the only thing better is finding a country everybody's bullish on and shorting it" (qtd. in Train 3). There is Michael Milken, said to have considered finance an artform, and Jonathan Lebed, discussed below—both of whose activities, while widely considered immoral, were completely legal (see Lewis, *Money Culture* xiv). But perhaps the more salient point is that anyone involved in the market today is a Lopez figure in the sense that investment is the "backing" of opinion; our own Lopez-like qualities are obscured, however, by the speculator/investor dramas played out in public. When a good investment goes bad—as in the case of Enron, in December 2001—it becomes a speculation, and the search for culprits begins.

8. "My hope to rise had always been built on writing novels, and at last by writing novels I have risen" (Trollope, *Autobiography* 169).

9. Trollope's attention to "the business of life" has been discussed by Collins, who notes that, when introducing a character, Trollope "specifies his or her income or capital" (297). But to say this much is only to suggest, as Trollope criticism typically does, that in his novels and in his life the author displays an amusing and eccentric—and thus wholly "Victorian"—obsession with financial detail.

10. Mottram dates the term "speculation" from "about 1850," though the point of his book is that "The thing itself is of immemorial antiquity." He offers his own, succinct definition: "Dealing in fluctuating values" (41). Writes Michael Guth, "A speculator buys (sells) goods under uncertainty, with the intent to resell (repurchase) them after some anticipated favorable price change" (10).

11. Consider the fine shades of differentiation and judgment required by this definition: "The more a house purchaser weighs the capital gain potential of his investment, as opposed to wanting to capture the benefits from living in a house, the more he acts like a speculator *per se*" (Guth 10).

12. In Dickens's *Little Dorrit* (1855-57), speculation is a "fever" and an "infection." Dickens thus seems aware that a speculator is an investor by another, less decorous name: he or she is an ordinary person with a "disorder." Says Pancks of Clennam, "It was my misfortune to lead him into a ruinous investment' (Mr. Pancks still clung to that word, and never said speculation.)" (538).

The figure of the investor reinforces the characteristic Victorian division between work and home, while the speculator's imagined constant attention to his money attests to the unsavory nature of someone who has no "other" life. In this way, the speculator turns out to be a strangely unified figure, and Victorian discomfort about him reveals the undesirability of such unity in Victorian ideologies of identity. For another example, see Jaffe.

13. This dubiousness is, of course, emotional and moral as well as practical. Identifying someone as a speculator is thus analogous to diagnosing that person as having an "eating disorder" or finding him or her to be a "compulsive shopper." Such diagnoses, classifying the psychological and somatic effects of capitalism as "disorders," simultaneously define and disavow the mechanisms on which capitalism depends; they gesture toward an ideal balance in comparison with which individual subjects can only be said to waver.

14. My use of the term "Oedipal" refers to the way in which marriage invokes the specter of parental sexuality. Wharton's desire that Emily marry Arthur Fletcher—the candidate most like himself, and someone she has known her entire life—requires the drawing of a distinction between father and husband; this is accomplished, first by Emily's choice of an outsider as husband, and then by the association of that husband with everything illicit. Lopez is too close to the money, and that closeness is linked to racial and sexual impurity as well as moral degradation because marriage itself evokes the possibility of being too close to the money: to parental sexuality. (The intense odoriferousness of Lopez's chosen commodities—coffee and guano—figures in this symbolic constellation as well.) Emily's first marriage thus enables—requires—a return, in the second, to her father and her father's values; it allows for a marriage from which the dangers of illicit desire, whether imagined as involving sexuality or money, have been purged. Fletcher, it should be noted, is a lover on the investment model: he will wait for Emily indefinitely.

15. Here are some examples of the wrong kind of stories: "The stock price of Emulex, a maker of computer networking equipment, plunged early yesterday after a false negative report about the company was circulated" (Berenson). Also relevant is the story of Jonathan Lebed, a New Jersey teenager who made his avid attention to the CNBC numbers pay off by

> attend[ing] high school by day and, according to securities regulators, manipulat[ing] stocks by night on his computer. When he was apprehended for his scheme of promoting obscure stocks on the Internet that he had recently bought himself, then selling the shares at higher prices to those who

inexplicably acted on his anonymous tips, his response was 'Everybody does it.' In a world where analysts put outlandish price targets on stocks and money managers regularly promote the stocks they hold on CNBC, truer words were never spoken.

(Morgenson 9)

(This article hands out the annual "Augustus Melmotte Memorial Prize," which Lebed won for 2000.) The false report works, of course, because it looks exactly like a true one, and the "hair-trigger" state of the market reflects investors' awareness of their inability to tell the difference. A profile of Lebed by Michael Lewis makes a number of relevant points, including the idea that the Securities Exchange Commission was created because, "To the greater public in 1934, the numbers on the stock-market ticker no longer seemed to represent anything 'real,' but rather the result of manipulation by financial pros. So, how to make the market seem 'real'? The answer was to make new stringent laws against stock-market manipulation, whose job it was to make sure their machinations did not ever again unnerve the great sweaty rabble. That's not how the S. E. C. put it, of course" ("Extracurricular Activities" ["Jonathan Lebed's Extracurricular Activities"] 32-33).

Works Cited

Berenson, Alex. "On Hair-Trigger Wall Street, a Stock Plunges on Fake News." *The New York Times* 26 Aug. 2000: A1+.

Bernstein, Jake. *The Compleat Day Trader II.* New York: McGraw-Hill, 1998.

Bulkowski, Thomas N. *Encyclopedia of Chart Patterns.* New York: Wiley, 2000.

Carret, Phillip L. *The Art of Speculation.* New York: Wiley, 1930.

Checkland, S. G. *The Rise of Industrial Society in England, 1815-1885.* New York: St. Martin's, 1965.

Collins, Phillip. "Business and Bosoms: Some Trollopian Concerns." *Nineteenth-Century Fiction* 37.3 (December 1982): 293-315.

Dickens, Charles. *Little Dorrit.* 1855-57. Ed. H. P. Sucksmith. Oxford: Oxford UP, 1982.

Garber, Peter M. *Famous First Bubbles: The Fundamentals of Early Manias.* Cambridge: MIT P, 2000.

Guth, Michael A. S. *Speculative Behaviors and the Operation of Competitive Markets under Uncertainty.* Avebury: Ashgate, 1994.

Hennessy, Elizabeth. *Coffee House to Cyber Market: 200 Years of the London Stock Exchange.* London: Ebury, 2001.

Holway, Tatiana M. "The Game of Speculation: Economics and Representation." *Dickens Quarterly* 9 (1992): 103-14.

Jaffe, Audrey. "Detecting the Beggar: Arthur Conan Doyle, Henry Mayhew, and 'The Man with the Twisted Lip.'" *Representations* 31 (1990): 96-117.

Lewis, Michael. "Jonathan Lebed's Extracurricular Activities." *The New York Times Magazine* 25 Feb. 2001: 26+.

Lewis, Michael. *The Money Culture*. New York: Penguin, 1991.

Martin, Linda Carroll. "Live from New York, the Trading Day." *The New York Times* 9 July 2000: C7.

Morgenson, Gretchen. "Market Watch." *The New York Times* 31 Dec. 2000: C1.

Mottram, R. H. *A History of Financial Speculation*. Boston: Little, 1929.

Reed, John R. "A Friend to Mammon: Speculation in Victorian Literature." *Victorian Studies* 27 (1984): 179-202.

Schott, John. *Mind over Money*. Boston: Little, 1998.

Shiller, Robert. *Irrational Exuberance*. Princeton: Princeton UP, 2000.

Train, John. *The New Money Masters: Winning Investment Strategies of Soros, Lynch, Steinhardt, Rogers, Neff, Wanger, Michaelis, Carret*. New York: Harper, 1989.

Trollope, Anthony. *An Autobiography*. 1883. Ed. Michael Sadleir and Frederick Page. Oxford: Oxford UP, 1992.

———. *The Prime Minister*. 1876. Ed. David Skilton. Harmondsworth: Penguin, 1994.

———. *The Way We Live Now*. 1874-75. Ed. Frank Kermode. Harmondsworth: Penguin, 1994.

Nicholas Dames (essay date winter 2003)

SOURCE: Dames, Nicholas. "Trollope and the Career: Vocational Trajectories and the Management of Ambition." *Victorian Studies* 45, no. 2 (winter 2003): 247-78.

[*In the following essay, Dames discusses Trollope's careerism, examining how it filtered into and impacted his writing.*]

> The critic said to himself, "if it is written by Mr. Trollope, I shall soon meet with the phrase, 'made his way,' as applied to walking where there is no physical difficulty or embarrassment, but only a certain moral hesitation as to the end and aim of the walking in ques-

tion," and behold within a page at which the silent remark was made, came the very phrase in the peculiar sense indicated.

> —R. H. Hutton, review of *Nina Balatka*, *Spectator*, 23 March 1867 (qtd. in Smalley 268)

Hutton's shrewd detection of Anthony Trollope's authorship of *Nina Balatka* (1867) does more than reveal an identifiable tic within a prose style straining after the kind of innocuous, transparent ordinariness that might speak for society itself. More importantly, it points us to the cause of this symptomatic self-betrayal: a concern with "making one's way," with progressing toward a goal, about the value of which one remains, nonetheless, unsure—in plainer words, a concern with a *career*. Nothing less than Trollope's pervasive regard for individual paths and their various obstacles, with "making it," gives him away. Trollope's well-known careerism—his open interest in the growing market power of his fiction, an interest that has had such a deleterious impact on his reputation—is certainly in play here; that his vocational ambitions, capacious enough to spread to two separate careers, might find a voice in even the humblest of his style's habits is perhaps not surprising. Hutton's alert guess, however, directs us even farther than this. Taking his cue, it is possible to read Trollope as a central instance within the mid-Victorian development of the modern sense of "career": as the novelist whose narratives of professional upward mobility demonstrate the emergence of a discrete form of individual life-plan, a "making one's way" that is bound by new imperatives and new difficulties.

"There is, I suppose," Trollope writes in *The Claverings* (1867), published the same year as *Nina Balatka*, "no young man possessed of average talents and average education, who does not early in life lay out for himself some career with more or less precision,—some career which is high in its tendencies and noble in its aspirations and to which he is afterwards compelled to compare the circumstances of the life which he shapes for himself" (322). As a précis of his plots in the 1860s and 1870s this claim, which mediates so typically between a sense of "career" as specifically vocational and more broadly biographical, and which limits itself to a male careerism, is fairly accurate. It resonates with the somewhat colorless but nonetheless ambitious male careerists of his mature fiction: parliamentary careerists like Phineas Finn, Frank Greystock of *The Eustace Diamonds* (1873), and Frank Tregear of *The Duke's Children* (1880); Civil Service careerists like Alaric Tudor and Harry Norman of *The Three Clerks* (1859); careerists in the applied sciences and engineering, like *The Claverings*'s own Harry Clavering. These are careerists insofar as their ambition carries them not to extremes of success or degradation, like some Balzacian parvenu, but merely to the next rung on the ladder; their stories turn on a named progression of professional stations, how quickly those stations are traversed, and how that progression veers from suddenly fluid to insuperably blocked. Telling their stories is, I would suggest, tantamount to telling the story of the narrativization of professional labor itself in the Victorian period: how social and vocational ambition found itself newly structured by the figure of "career," and how the figure of "career" managed to create linear, ordered sequences out of the disruptive energies unleashed by the spread of professionalism itself in the early and mid-nineteenth century.

As such, this inquiry takes its impetus from the burgeoning field of work on Victorian professionalism and its various forms, but by way of inquiring how one crucial and understudied cognate term, "career," operated to create narratives, and forms of self-understanding, that both exposed the latent dilemmas of professionalism and managed their rhetorical and psychological solutions.[1] My intent here is to excavate the contours of this important Trollopian figure (the career, the careerist) and, more conjecturally, to situate the historical conditions of its emergence. The initial step will take us to Trollope's Palliser novels, which—despite their concentration on a putatively nonprofessional setting, parliamentary government—take up the idea of "career" with increasing urgency, as the various possibilities of living within a vocational trajectory are each explored. The second step, which will follow my consideration of the Palliser fictions, is more properly a genealogical one: to turn away from the metropolitan center where Trollope's careerists stage their progress, and toward the colonial and imperial settings where the emergent sense of "career" received its structuring principles and, in some fashion, its ethical justifications.[2] Two postulates, then, will govern my investigation of Trollope's career-plots: first, that the "career" is a mediating, even domesticating figure for social energy, making of "vocations" or "ambitions" a path more amenable to rationalization; second, that the emergence of this concept can be related, perhaps causally ascribed, to alterations in the form and style of imperial administration, alterations consequent upon the bureaucratization of imperial rule whose most notable instance is the 1858 Government of India Act and the Civil Service reforms that directly preceded it. Specific aspects of the imperial example, as this essay's concluding section will argue through texts by Walter Bagehot and Trollope himself, provided a compelling model of how irregular, profit-driven enterprises on a large scale could be reshaped, streamlined, and organized into the following: a preplanned trajectory for individuals with a set sequence and nameable steps along that sequence, or a career.

Trollope's own *Autobiography* (1883) might initially serve as an apt model: the unpredictable leaps and chasms of novel-writing as a pursuit are transmuted into the famously linear, almost bell-shaped progression of novel after novel matched to its increasing, and then slightly diminishing, rate of remuneration with which the text closes. Even today Trollope's eagerness to formulate his novelistic career in terms appropriate to bureaucratic labor (pay, time off, promotion) is slightly embarrassing to his commentators, even as—or particularly as—his popular readership grows.[3] Academic commentary is certainly not immune to this embarrassment, particularly as the academic "careerist" continues to exert a fascination within a profession where making one's way, or whether there even is a way to be made, remains so fraught. It is an embarrassment Trollope's own careerism not only generates but helps to elucidate. Situated at the moment when the "career" first receives its professionalized sense, and when the links between those professionalized "careers" and imperial careers are most exposed, Trollope's recurrent scripting of career-plots shows us the crucial role that the career played in managing otherwise barely coherent social tensions. One might say that Trollope's analysis of career activity was so preternaturally acute because it was expressed through a pursuit, novel-writing, which remained—despite his protestations—outside the bureaucratized career-world he otherwise inhabited. To paraphrase Max Weber, Trollope wanted to work within a career; his characters are forced to do so.

I. FROM VOCATION TO THE VOCATIONAL

Any semantic history of "career" must note the rupture that occurs in the middle decades of the nineteenth century, when a specialized meaning—"career" as a progress through professional employment—begins to supercede the older sense of "career" as a generalized course of life. The word's well-known roots, from the *carraria* or racecourse of late antiquity and the later French *carrière,* develop into the ruts and grooves of industrial and postindustrial labor, as the race of the human life span metamorphoses into the race of mature capitalist competition. Trollope's characteristic usage of the term is expressive of a rather muddled semantic overlap: at times preferring its precapitalist meaning, at others anticipating its specifically professional contours, the word acts in Trollope to suture the two semantic fields into one, making life-narrative and professional-narrative coalesce. The early Palliser novels are rife with this sort of confusion, as when in *Phineas Finn* (1869) the Earl of Brentford, a Whig eminence, taxes his son Chiltern with his idleness:

> "I have always worked, either in the one House or in the other, and those of my fellows with whom I have been most intimate have worked also. The same career is open to you."
>
> "You mean politics?"
>
> "Of course I mean politics."
>
> (2: 159)

That the Earl might mean a "career" of utility and labor—a style of life—instead of the more specific, vocational sense of a career in politics has to be explicitly denied. To have a career implies more than a life of useful work: it implies a necessary sense of the professional label and structure (politics, law, medicine) that gives direction and stability to that labor. The term can be detected in its passage, that is, from vaguely biographical to stringently specialized. "I think there was not much in his career of which he did not say something to Madame Goesler," Trollope writes of one of Phineas's typically self-indulgent confessions, "and that he received from her a good deal of excellent advice and encouragement in the direction of his political ambition" (2: 161). However much in the way of affective history Phineas has revealed, Madame Max responds strictly to the professional career he has mapped out for himself—turning the conversation in that "direction," as well as "directing" the political trajectory he has initiated.

As such the fortunes of the word "career" in Trollope might speak to his awareness of the situatedness of human agency in general, his tendency to investigate the external constraints and conditions of desire, or what James Kincaid has called his ability to "expose the system as a system" ("Unmannerly" ["Anthony Trollope and the Unmannerly Novel"] 90). At its most extreme in Trollope criticism this has taken the form of an analysis of his ethical situationism, or his interest in the contingencies that give action its shape rather than the abstract meanings of action.[4] The allure of such a reading of the Trollopian "career"—the eventual submerging of individual desire in exterior contingency, expressed in the word's professionalizing tendency—is the opening up, within a narrative style of such consistent equanimity, of a wounding, even tragic, split between what an individual wants and what that individual's practical social options might be. Fredric Jameson's critique of middle-class ennui, in which "to wonder what to do with your life is already to commit yourself in advance to a certain ontological dissatisfaction with any of the ultimate possibilities" (9), might express the trap of Trollope's careerists: the subjectivity that can think about career options is always in excess of what those options might offer. This is a story about middle-class labor, and middle-class subjectivity, that is a familiar aspect of canonical accounts of the bildungsroman, and that derives essentially from Weber's description, in *The Protestant Ethic and the Spirit of Capitalism* (1904-05), of the "calling."[5] If all labor must be a calling or vocation, a *Beruf*, then finally all labor must fall short of the tremendous imaginative and spiritual demands placed upon it. The result is pervasive disappointment.

The story—the tragic impact of "vocation" when it meets the division of labor of advanced capitalist society—is a compelling one. But it is not quite Trollope's story; nor does it accurately express the functions of the career-narrative as Trollope usually presents it. If Phineas's biographical career is collapsed by Madame Max into his professional career, or if the career suggested to Lord Chiltern is defined by one specific pursuit rather than any more broad style of life—if, in the Palliser series as a whole, Phineas will become a Whig functionary and Chiltern a Master of Hounds—Trollope does not permit us to read that process as a tragic divorce of inclination and possibility. Rather than exploring the dissatisfactions native to a Weberian *Beruf*, Trollope is far more interested in the mechanisms of how a "career" shapes, disciplines, and makes socially workable the desires and ambitions that (supposedly) precede it. "Vocation," with its dialectic of subjective demand and limiting objective options, expressed by the Stendhalian "Quel métier prendre?" that Jameson cites as central to bourgeois ennui, is in Trollope replaced by the career's central question: how does this "métier" work, and what adaptations do I have to learn to master it?

Thus the relatively minor amount of space Trollope devotes to the *choice* of a career, and the unexpectedly large amount he provides for an exploration of a given career's inner logic, specific procedures, and various subordinate career paths. The decision to become an MP is in *Phineas Finn* of far less moment than Phineas's necessary, and continually evolving, evaluation of what kind of an MP to be, where the choices range from party hack (Bonteen, Fawn, Ratler) to key functionary (Barrington Erle), to independent maverick (Joshua Monk), to models of eminent, if nonetheless rather staid, achievement (Plantagenet Palliser, or the Duke of St. Bungay, the Whig éminence grise). "He had made up his mind to be Whig Ministerial, and to look for his profession in that line," Trollope writes of one of Phineas's many initial, and provisional, decisions. "But now he began to reflect how far this ministerial profession would suit him. Would it be much to be a Lord of the Treasury, subject to the dominion of Mr. Ratler? Such lordship and such subjection would be the result of success" (*Phineas Finn* 1: 243). Each career path brings with it its own necessary consequences, its own vocational styles of success and failure, and its own narrow set of options; and Phineas's evaluative process is regularly in the narrative forefront. On this basis it is possible to explain the relative lack of forward narrative energy *Phineas Finn* displays; it is less concerned with narrative momentum than with mapping a syntagmatic field of various career possibilities. It would be possible, in fact, to devise a spatial schema for parliamentary career roles as Phineas faces them, from the most purely bureaucratic or functional possibilities—life as a secure Whig vote at the disposition of the party's leaders, with governmental office as the eventual reward—to the most radical independence. That most of the options Trollope depicts are various styles of compromise between these two poles is part of the difficulty initially confronting Phineas, who has to learn fine discriminations between closely adjacent modes of career activity. Furthermore, such a spatial schema would reveal the essentially allegorical nature of the choice Phineas faces, which could be extended to any profession: a choice between a secure, if undistinguished, presence within the given professional field, and a more perilous desire at least to partially transform that field.

The emphasis on what I have called a spatial narrative procedure, centered on the tactics of career choice and discrimination, nonetheless contains a temporality of its own, a gradualism that, while palpable throughout Trollope's canon, is most evident in his series fiction. What replaces the aesthetic appeal of forward propulsion (suspense, surprise, the denouement), all the rage in the sensationalistic 1860s and 1870s, is an aesthetics of slow accumulation. Unlike narratives of "vocation," where sudden epiphanies of devotion or failure are the norm, the career-narrative presents a sequence of tutelary examples whose full meaning can only be known once the entire sequence has been consumed and all the examples are present to compare to one another. The aesthetic appeal of the career narrative, aside from its deep familiarity to a middle-class readership, is perhaps this savoring of *tactical time*: the dilated, elongated temporality of careful choice, where each new piece of information slightly adjusts our sense of the previous choices made. And if the model of the vocation-narrative remained theatrical—melodrama, perhaps, or even tragedy—the model of the career narrative is closer to chess, where deliberate tactical maneuvers accrue over prolonged time. Such a narrative aesthetic would of course demand a wholly new size: the series.

Despite the inapplicability of Weberian "vocation" to Trollope's career plots, Weber is still of use here, as even at the moments when he theorizes most grandly the way subjectivity and work might mesh, he nonetheless rests the argument on an analysis of how various professions are structured. "Vocation" or *Beruf* is complemented in Weber by an analysis of the "career" or *Laufbahn*. In Weber's well-known "Science as a Vocation" (1919) the investigation of a "value-free objectivity" is prefaced by a close analysis of the career-paths in which German, and American, academics are likely to find themselves, or what Weber calls "the external conditions" of the scholarly vocation: possibilities for promotion, job security, teaching responsibilities. For Trollope these external conditions, what we might call the vocational aspect to a vocation, are virtually determinative of any satisfaction a career might offer. "There is perhaps no career of life so charming as that of a successful man of letters," his *Autobiography* confides. "Who else is free from all shackle as to hours?" (209-10). Flexible work conditions, and the relatively remote possibilities of regular remuneration,

define Trollope's analysis of the novelistic career; the work-conditions of Parliament in the mid-nineteenth century define Phineas's plot, as its irregular hours and lack of pay force him into an office-hunting path which will entail its own series of compromises and adaptations.

The result of this switch from "vocation" to "career" is the following: an abandonment of any interest in pre-vocational desire, and a stress instead on the disciplining of subjectivity exerted by career activity, even on the kinds of desire produced by that very discipline.[6] The stress is most visible when Trollope, generally wary of any but ironically invoked figural language, takes up the familiar metaphors of the career: the harness, the grooved racecourse. "There are but very few horses which you cannot put into harness," *Phineas Finn*'s narrator observes when Joshua Monk takes Whig office, "and those of the highest spirit will generally do your work the best" (1: 129). When Phineas later tells Laura Standish that he is tiring of office, she replies: "The ox desires the saddle. The charger wants to plough [. . .] Your career may combine the dignity of the one with the utility of the other" (2: 242). Even Palliser himself, upon rising to the top of the minsterial ladder in *The Prime Minister* (1876), laments that "I have put myself into a groove, and ground myself into a mould, and clipped and pared and pinched myself all round,—very ineffectually as I fear,—to fit myself for this thing" (1: 58). For a novelist who periodically extolled the virtues of "routine" labor, as in his chapter on the Civil Service in *The Three Clerks,* the routinization of career-discipline exerted a very real fascination, and Phineas's ability to adapt himself to the usual demands of a parliamentary career will almost entirely determine his staying power.

What vocational desire there is in Trollope is not excessive to the career-system but instead inheres in it; the vocational process in Trollope might be best expressed as the narrative of learning to want what you are in the way of getting. Thus Palliser, on the threatened demise of the ministry that he had initially not wanted to lead: "But, though he had never wished to be put into his present high office, now that he was there he dreaded the sense of failure which would follow his descent from it. It is this feeling rather than genuine ambition, rather than the love of power or patronage or pay, which induces men to cling to place" (*Prime Minister* 1: 250). A "genuine ambition," which desires the subsidiary effects of a career ("power, patronage, or pay"), is replaced by an ambition solely for the track itself; put another way, a desire that preexists the track is supplanted by the desire engendered by the track. "Failure" in the terms Trollope outlines here is regression along an accepted career sequence—a failure that is only relative to the extreme possibilities of failure that the Palliser novels do not take up; the pathos of that regression is the pathos of the Palliser series.[7] Failure is also a glitch in the career process, which in Trollope ensures that vocation and subjectivity find a perfect match through the socializing processes of career training; in terms borrowed from Bourdieu, entering a career in Trollope means the formation of a "disposition" for that very career. Bourdieu's term "trajectory"—the set of movements within a given field made by one agent, dictated by the state of the field, the individual's "disposition," and the individual's class origin, which determines the range of possible trajectories—is, insofar as it works toward a disenchantment of the "calling," highly expressive of Trollope's world: subjectivity and vocation fit because the kinds of investment required by career progression elicit precisely the subjectivity the vocation will require.[8] If Phineas Finn is a cipher prior to his immediate immersion in Whig politics, it is because his character, his set of dispositions, will only be found within those political machinations.

To say that desire, or ambition, is formed by the institutions and procedures that it is ordinarily supposed to precede is essentially to say that those desires are not particularly explosive or transformative. The kind of internecine tactical battles waged by the officeholders and office-seekers of Balzac's *Les Employés* (1838)—a useful counterexample to Trollope—express social ambitions channeled through bureaucratic processes; the darker side of the Trollopian careerist, such as **The Three Clerks**'s Undy Scott, **The Prime Minister**'s Ferdinand Lopez, or even Disraeli's fictional double in the Palliser series, Daubeny, similarly finds in career activity an outlet for the discharge of cathexes that preexist that activity. But the core of Trollope's interest is with those whose ambitions, formed by their career, are thereby much more amenable to rationalization, regularization, and compromise: Phineas and Palliser preeminently. That "career" could once, and even still, mean a course of reckless, chaotic progression is ignored in Trollope in favor of the far more modern sense of a career's systematized, rhythmic, grooved paths; not for him the already somewhat antiquated sense of "careering," which is best exemplified by George Meredith's *Beauchamp's Career* (1876), whose hero, denied admission to Parliament, can adhere to no stabilized path, and whose career is a series of unpredictable missteps. The "career" not only domesticates ambition—by placing it in a harness, as it were—but in fact replaces it altogether with a version that desires the career as an end, not a means.

Thus the spectacle, perhaps, of what D. A. Miller has called "a Parliament that, for all its politicking, has no politics" (116): a world where a parliamentary career seems a means to nothing but itself.[9] It is a world where the possible extra-professional ends are so technically detailed (Palliser's planned decimalization of the coinage, a comic donnée that runs through the series), or so

relentlessly abstract (Palliser's Whiggish desire for the gradual diminishment, but not elimination, of the space between classes), as to remain outside the narrative's interest. What does engage the Palliser series are instead the vocational aspects of the parliamentary career—its status as specialized labor, as Palliser himself claims:

> If I could have my way,—which is of course impossible, for I cannot put off my honours,—I would return to my old place. I would return to the Exchequer, where the work is hard and certain, where a man can do, or at any rate attempt to do, some special thing. A man there if he sticks to that and does not travel beyond it, need not be popular, need not be a partisan, need not be eloquent, need not be a courtier. He should understand his profession, as should a lawyer or a doctor.
>
> (**Duke's Children** 622-23)

As specialized as law or medicine, and as opaque to outsiders—Trollope is fond of reminding his readers, as in **Can You Forgive Her?** (1865), that the rules and customs of parliamentary procedure are not to be found in newspapers—effective government, like any effective labor, is a process of mastering vocational rules. Trollope's analysis of the political profession is more radical even than any means-over-ends analysis might suspect; like a monad, parliamentary professionalism is ultimately a tautology (what does an MP do? what an MP does) that nonetheless operates effectively in the real world by continually self-adjusting its procedures, by a gradual but persistent accommodation to what "the people" seem to demand.[10] Even when Trollope's high minded minsters, like Palliser, seek to defend their profession against a soulless technical proficiency like that wielded by Daubeny or Sir Timothy Beeswax, the rhetoric of "career" nonetheless intrudes:

> And then I would have you always remember the purport for which there is a Parliament elected in this happy and free country. It is not that some men may shine there, that some may acquire power, or that all may plume themselves on being the elect of the nation [. . .] It often appears to me that some members of Parliament so regard their success in life,—as the fellows of our colleges do too often, thinking that their fellowships were awarded for their comfort and not for the furtherance of any object as education or religion [. . .] A member of Parliament should feel himself to be the servant of his country,—and like every other servant, he should serve. If this be distasteful to a man he need not go into Parliament. If the harness gall him he need not wear it. But if he takes the trappings, then he should draw the coach [. . .].
>
> (**Duke's Children** 122)

An anti-career peroration, here to his son Silverbridge, can only borrow the metaphor of "career" to explain its meaning; there is no dream in Trollope of a labor that is both valuable and free of harness.

Here a paradox lurks: that Parliament, for Trollope and other observers British society's most august instance of nonprofessional activity, was nonetheless the site for Trollope's investigation of the conditions of professional careers.[11] We might rest easier with this paradox by paying attention to the frequency with which Trollope's parliamentarians explain harnessing, or grooving, with reference to professional activity *as such.* When Phineas says that any government official is a slave, Monk corrects him: "There I think you are wrong. If you mean that you cannot do joint work with other men altogether after your own fashion the same may be said of all work. If you have stuck to the Bar you must have pleaded your causes in conformity with instructions from the attorneys" (*Phineas Finn* 2: 252-53). If Parliament is the collectively wise action of amateurs, it is also increasingly a model of how professional careers work, in that the logic of the career—promotions, specializations, trajectories of achievement—supplants any overarching logic, to the overall benefit of the work to be done. If, in other words, it is still very much an enclave of nobility, it is nonetheless a model for how middle-class professional careerism might operate, in the manner that many middle-class norms are, in John Kucich's useful phrase, "rotated slightly upward in the social scale" by Trollope (51). Keeping that paradox in mind will go far toward explaining not only the deformations of Trollope's picture of Parliament, but also the stakes at play in the "career's" ability to domesticate and structure social ambition. For Trollope's Parliament, like its historical counterpart, is involved in keeping vast social upheavals at bay.

II. CONFLICT AND LINEARITY: CAREER SEQUENCES

Career activity is, to simplify, a linear narrative of technical, means-oriented, rule-bound activity whose sole desideratum is upward progression in a correct sequence—and sequence might be the crucial term. Consider the sweep, from *Phineas Finn* through *Phineas Redux* (1874) to *The Prime Minister,* of Phineas's own career sequence: first merely an Irish MP for the Galway constituency of Loughshane; then member for Loughton, an English borough; then in office, in the Irish seat on the Treasury Board; then Under-Secretary for the Colonies, upon the resignation of his friend Lawrence Fitzgibbon; then the first of his principled resignations, upon disagreement with his party over Irish tenant-right, followed by a consolatory prize of a sinecure post as Poor Law Inspector in Cork. Upon his return to Parliament as member for Tankerville, a seat won on petition, and after the scandal occasioned by his trial for murder, a sudden and rapid rise: to Chief Secretary for Ireland in the Omnium coalition government, to First Lord of the Admiralty, and finally to another sinecure post, Chancellor of the Duchy of Lancaster. Far from steady—interrupted, in fact, at several junctures, by accidents and decisive abstentions alike—the sequence is nonetheless remarkable for its very presence

in the series' narrative *as a sequence.* Unlike so many other professional heroes of Victorian fiction, what Trollope gives us is a named progression through various professional stations; although the process can seem to a reader somewhat stochastic (why these posts? why in this order?), it is, seen as a whole, an upward movement along a vertical hierarchy of vocational achievement and consequence. Furthermore, each step along this ladder, at least until the rapid rise in Phineas' fortunes occasioned by Palliser's rise to power, is susceptible to narrative dramatization: as various chapter titles attest, such as *Phineas Finn*'s "Promotion," or *The Prime Minister*'s "The Beginning of a New Career," the switch from one position in a professional sequence to another is a *topos* dear to Trollope, bringing with it the attendant anxiety, satisfaction, and renewed cathexis that promotion tends to offer. Each step along the ascent further binds the protagonist to the career activity undertaken, and each step provokes the question as to how much farther there is to go. Character, Trollope's well-known aesthetic priority, is in the Palliser novels presented as continually in transition: between suffering (or enjoying) the consequences of one decision and worrying about (or anticipating) necessarily subsequent decisions.

That Trollope's stress falls on hierarchical ascent rather than other aspects of professional activity is particularly curious given its parliamentary site. To use the language of contemporary sociologists of labor markets, Victorian parliamentary labor is surely an example of the "horizontal career": a career that "need not involve any increase in bureaucratic authority but involves instead an increase in reputation or prestige based on expertise," rather than the "vertical" or "bureaucratic" careers where "mobility involves promotion up a firm's hierarchy in 'careers of advancement'" (Freidson [*Professionalism, the Third Logic*] 76). In other words, the relative lack of a secure, established hierarchical ladder in British parliamentary government would seem to preclude it from a treatment along bureaucratic lines, a point that Weber continually made when differentiating German and British governmental styles. And yet, in Trollope, we find the opposite: parliament treated as a stage for advancement up vertical ladders, where office in a bureaucratic, or managerial-bureaucratic, post is the motive power behind all but the most detached participants in the game. Whether one reads this representation of Parliament as a critique or a celebration is finally less relevant than the ideological labor it performs: by "sequencing" a parliamentary career, as it were, Trollope erases any exterior, contending forces of social conflict that might enter the parliamentary arena in favor of a rigorously *serial* narrative procedure. Conflict, that is, is rewritten as sequence.

What Phineas's career sequence obscures is precisely any element of ethnic or class conflict; his Irishness, or his class status as son of a country doctor, is strangely washed out compared to the vividness of his vertical ascension. This might be, in fact, the central work of the career: the replotting of contending social forces through a progressive sequence of achievement. Such is the guess of one analyst of the professional ethos, Samuel Weber, who writes of the "career," or "the arrangement of the individual's professional life in terms of an ascending ladder of achievement," as follows:

> In place of the lateral ties of earlier local communities, as well as of emerging class structure, the progressive initiation, mastery, and exercise of a profession is presented in terms of upward mobility, the reward of rising achievement. Existing hierarchies of rank and privilege are associated with individual performance within an institutionally defined framework. Social and economic insecurity is thereby presented not as a function of conflict, not as the resultant of an agonistic field of forces, but as the linear order of ascending qualification, based on predictable, objective criteria.
>
> (31)

Career sequence displaces a sense of society as constituted by contending, and contentious, bases of power. Furthermore, the narrative emphasis upon the *individual's* upward progression obscures the larger class or ethnic trajectories that may be in play; what, for instance, can be learned of the mid-century state of the Catholic Irish through Phineas's rise through the Whig ranks? And insofar as the temporal weight of career sequence is always thrown toward the future (what promotion will come next?) past and present difficulties are relatively obscured; like Trollope's series fiction itself, the career sequence is an unrolling that rarely stops to consider where it began.

We might call this process "contextual rearranging": the process whereby linearity rearranges, by placing in sequential order, conflicts that are otherwise fairly entrenched or intractable. The first consequence of contextual rearranging is the way in which, throughout the Palliser novels, "faction" becomes a matter of timing—of place in a temporal sequence—rather than principle; as James Kincaid has noted, there are no consistent factions throughout the series: "Faction comes not from ideological clash but from blind change, simple fluidity" (*Novels* [*The Novels of Anthony Trollope*] 221). Whether Phineas's stand on Irish tenant-right will align him with, or against, his party is a matter of when it occurs; by the end of the series it places him firmly in the party's center. Similarly, whether espousing the disestablishment of the Established Church makes one Radical or Tory will be a function of when one chooses to take up the position; at the onset of ***Phineas Redux*** the unscrupulous Tory Prime Minister Daubeny cynically, but effectively, makes it his party's primary goal. The second consequence is perhaps more momentous for the form of Trollope's fiction: sequence becomes a

thematic of the first importance, most notably in ***Phineas Finn.*** Continually the novel revolves around the question of the order in which things are done; in fact, the figure of *hysteron proteron* seems to organize the novel's plot, as Phineas's decision to take a parliamentary seat prior to establishing himself in the law is critiqued as *doing things in the wrong order.* Mr. Low, Phineas's legal tutor, asserts as much:

> When he first heard that Finn intended to stand for Loughshane he was stricken with dismay, and strongly dissuaded him [. . .] But the electors of Loughshane had not rejected Mr. Low's pupil, and Mr. Low was now called upon to advise what Phineas should do in his present circumstances. There is nothing to prevent the work of a Chancery barrister being done by a member of Parliament. Indeed, the most successful barristers are members of Parliament. But Phineas Finn was beginning at the wrong end, and Mr. Low knew that no good would come of it.
>
> (1: 42)

Advice to Phineas usually takes the form of admonitions to keep the proper order in mind, as with Laura Standish's characteristic reminder: "You cannot begin, you know, by being Prime Minister [. . .] Pitt was Prime Minister at four-and-twenty, and that precedent has ruined half our young politicians" (1: 52). That disarray of sequence extends to Phineas's amatory career, as is demonstrated by his propensity for proposing marriage only when his chosen object—from Lady Laura to Violet Effingham—has already accepted, or at least intends to accept, another man. When not too late, he is too early: his proposal to Mary Flood Jones, his Irish sweetheart, prematurely cuts off his ability to marry money in the person of Madame Max Goesler, and therefore to stay in Parliament even after resigning office, a mistake that only Trollope's authorial murder of the first Mrs. Finn, at the beginning of ***Phineas Redux,*** can correct. The desire to skip rungs on the professional ladder; the fear that by beginning too high up descent is inevitable; the attempt to comprehend the rather opaque order of promotion within the Whig ranks: much of Phineas's time is spent attempting to master, correct, or alter sequences.

Properly speaking, therefore, Phineas—as well as his careerist counterparts in the Palliser series—is no adventurer. Seeking not an escape from the linearity of experience but merely its acceleration, his vocational desire is instead characteristic of the bureaucratic official.[12] Weber's sketch of the bureaucratic narrative is appropriate here: "The official is set for a '*career*' within the hierarchical order of the public service. He moves from the lower, less important, and lower paid to the higher positions. The average official naturally desires a mechanical fixing of the conditions of promotion; if not of the offices, at least of the salary levels. He wants these conditions fixed in terms of 'seniority,' or possibly according to grades achieved in a developed system of expert examinations" (*Economy and Society* 963). Trollope's well-known insistence upon the maintenance of formal civil service procedures, particularly promotion by seniority, is relevant in this connection.[13] Narrative momentum is spurred not by "adventures," which—like Phineas's duel with Chiltern over Violet—tend to have little impact, but instead by conflicts over promotions. Most notable among these nodes of energy is the controversy over who will ascend to Chancellor of the Exchequer once Palliser heads to the House of Lords; when one possible candidate, Mr. Bonteen, who "had been a junior Lord, a Vice-President, a Deputy Controller, a Chief Commissioner, and a Joint Secretary," and whose "hopes had been raised or abased among the places of £1,000, £1,200, or £1,500 a year" (*Phineas Redux* 284) is denied through the backdoor efforts of Lady Glencora on Phineas's behalf, the result is nothing less than a complete narrative trajectory: Bonteen's murder, Phineas's arrest and subsequent acquittal, and Phineas's (temporary) departure from Parliament in pique. Even if the murder was committed by a decidedly adventurous, and dangerous, figure—the shadowy preacher Emilius—its significance is wholly dependent on the prior difficulty over one promotion.

Sequence, as a thematic concern and method of narrative organization, does, however, present its own dilemmas. "With Nelson it was Westminster Abbey or a peerage," Phineas tells Lady Laura. "With me it is parliamentary success or sheep-skinning" (*Phineas Finn* 1: 35). We may doubt whether the options in Trollope are ever that extreme—a soft if disappointing landing in some sinecure is the likeliest possibility—but we are even less prone to believe that parliamentary "success" is so very terminal an option, insofar as the "career" offers no real solution to the problem of conclusions. Is any career-success final, and if it is, what would it look like? As a result, Trollope's career-narratives cannot end on any secure or lasting achievement, since the very temporal pull of "career" makes achievement itself a transitional stage to the next achievement. The two most complete career-plots in the Palliser series, Phineas's and Palliser's, conclude with a disappointed withdrawal; we leave Palliser a rather obsolescent Whig, the emergent, activist, and Gladstonian left-wing of his party having reduced his brief period of coalition leadership to a dim memory, and we leave Phineas in a somewhat humiliating, if impressive-sounding, sinecure. If Phineas wonders "whether the wonderful success which he had achieved would ever be of permanent value to him" (*Phineas Finn* 1: 299), we can only answer no—unless that "permanent value" can be expressed in monetary terms, as part of a sinecure appointment, which would represent nonetheless personal stasis or failure. Outside the parameters of the Palliser series, Trollope often solved this dilemma by allowing his career-seeking protagonists an avenue of escape: in-

heritance and landed leisure. In this manner *The Three Clerks*'s Harry Norman, *The Claverings*'s Harry Clavering, and *The Prime Minister*'s Everett Wharton are permitted an exemption from the inevitable dying fall that accompanies the career. "But to have done something was nothing to him,—nothing to his personal happiness,—unless there was also something left for him to do" (*Prime Minister* 2: 320), we are told of Palliser: a temporal bind that can lead nowhere but to disappointment. Phineas's many resignations are perhaps only illusory attempts to halt this recognition, as he several times forestalls Parliament's lack of desire to have anything to do with him by claiming that he wants nothing to do with it; his departures from Parliament coincide neatly with scandals that deplete his career capital. The "career," in other words, has a melancholy ability to hollow out agency, to prove that one only does what was required of one anyway. As Bourdieu puts it in relation to career choices: "All successful socialization tends to get agents to act as accomplices in their own destiny" (*State Nobility* 45).

If career sequences offer no conclusiveness, they are even less capable of extending their reach to a reasonably representative range of character types. As "career" itself begins its semantic shift in the direction of professional activity, the idea of a woman's career becomes grotesque; not primarily because of the innumerable actual barriers to female professional employment, although those barriers certainly have their impact in a realist fiction, but more specifically because Trollope cannot ascribe sequential narratives to female characters. Insofar as Trollope's women should have no sequence save the one promotion from *jeune fille à marier* to *femme* proper, the female careerist becomes an aberration at best, a criminal at worst. It is no small matter that only two women possess "careers" in the Palliser novels: Lizzie Eustace and Lady Glencora Palliser. On Lizzie: "She was rich, beautiful, and clever; and, though her marriage with Mr. Emilius had never been looked upon as a success, still, in the estimation of some people, it added an interest to her career" (*Phineas Redux* 2: 39-40). On Glencora's abandonment of her attempts to be the social leader of her husband's coalition government: "The system on which the Duchess had commenced her career as wife of the Prime Minister had now been completely abandoned" (*Prime Minister* 2: 299). The publicity attached to these "careers" is finally less damaging than the sequentiality they imply; if marriage remains the only "proper career" (*Prime Minister* 2: 340), as Abel Wharton tells his daughter Emily, it is because it would finally cancel the seriality that careers necessarily entail: there would be no more transitions to narrate. Refuge from story, particularly from the literally inconclusive kinds of stories careers generate, is the anti-career that remains the only safe career for Trollope's women, a career that can scarcely go under the name. The genealogy of the "career" is perhaps best understood as a series of exclusions: from the capaciousness of the antiquated sense of the word, potentially applicable to every human activity, "career" develops a series of rigid exclusions whose consequences can still be found in any discussion of professionalized labor.[14]

To situate the Palliser series at a key moment in the genealogy of "career" is not to ignore the equally detailed presentation of clerical careers in the earlier Barchester series; it is, instead, to recognize in the later series a set of key differences in the functioning of career activity, differences which are perhaps more responsive to the conditions of managerial-bureaucratic, or more broadly professional, labor of Trollope's time. It is a critical consensus that Trollope's Barsetshire clergymen are as devoted to careerist temporalities as their non-clerical brethren; as Philip Collins puts it: "Being a priest—to use an un-Trollopian locution—is for him a professional career" (294). Yet if the Barchester novels demonstrate a similar investment in the mechanics of promotion and advancement, their stress upon *faction,* and factional struggles for professional/clerical capital, is finally less pertinent to a genealogy of the career than the relentlessly individualistic pursuits of the Palliser careerists, who can depend on no secure factions to strategize for them, not even—especially not even—the political parties to which they belong.

What is perhaps most notable about the Barchester series is the recurrent tendency of even the most minor professional disagreements to immediately ramify into a series of larger-scale conflicts, conflicts which can then be re-sorted into a single stable binary of two familiar parties. When, for instance, a non-clerical battle breaks out in **Doctor Thorne** (1858) between the eponymous hero and his rival Dr. Fillgrave over an appropriate system of consulting fees, that battle first organizes other local physicians into one of the two parties, then is taken up by rival metropolitan centers of medical opinion (such as *The Lancet* and the *Journal of Medical Science*) which can be each allied to one side of the central political and theological conflict which rules the series. If such is the case in the medical profession, it is even more prevalent among Barset clergymen, who operate within a factional framework that immediately supplies professional allies and professional enemies. As a result, each career move—from the naming of the Bishop of Barchester to the filling of other less august clerical vacancies—brings into motion wheels within wheels of factional strategy. However crucial to their individual careers are such promotions as Mr. Quiverful to the wardenship of Hiram's Hospital in **Barchester Towers** (1857), or Josiah Crawley to the living of St. Ewold's in **The Last Chronicle of Barset** (1867), those promotions are narrated via a consideration of how rival factions have each engaged tactically and strategically for that individual's professional fate, to such an

extent that the individual's own agency is relatively helpless as compared to the business-as-usual warfare that will determine the matter. If Trollope's Palliser careerists can reliably depend upon only their own skill at manipulating their chosen "field," his Barchester professionals inhabit a rather more prelapsarian setting, in which their field is firmly anchored to two stable points. Whether we describe those points as political (Whig/Tory), geographical (West Barset/East Barset), personal (Proudie/Grantly), or theological (Low Church/High Church), their stability and mutual interconnectedness cannot be ignored. As a result, collective or party tactics take priority over individual tactics, factional conflict prevails over the post-to-post seriality more common in the Palliser series, and the longevity and reliability of the conflictual binary prevents the opening up of a more fluid, open career game such as Parliament presents. Trollope's Palliser careerists could only, one imagines, look back with longing to a world where the options are so firmly and openly partisan. The world they inhabit, the world of more flexible professional labor, is far less scrutable.

It is therefore important to mention that Trollope, in **Framley Parsonage** (1861), famously denied the relevance of "careers" at all to his Barset novels:

> I have written much of clergymen, but in doing so I have endeavoured to portray them as they bear on our social life rather than to describe the mode and working of their professional careers. Had I done the latter I could hardly have steered clear of subjects on which it has not been my intention to pronounce an opinion, and I should either have laden my fiction with sermons or I should have degraded my sermons into fiction.
>
> (503)

A similar disclaimer, at the end of **The Last Chronicle,** protests that "my object has been to paint the social and not the professional lives of clergymen" (890). The terms of these asides are not immediately clear: surely much of the Barset series is devoted to professional, or career, matters, such as appointments, promotions, and even (most notably with Crawley) remuneration? But what Trollope here insists upon is a barrier that the Palliser series will continually violate: the distinction between "social" aspects of labor, what I have called careers, and the "professional" aspects of labor, which bear a striking relation to the Weberian "calling." Beneath the social contentions over ecclesiastical temporalities, Trollope suggests, there is the more narrowly professional side of clerical labor, where the labor itself—sermons, teaching, ministrations—breaks free of its temporal constraints. Beneath the *Laufbahn,* Trollope claims, lies a *Beruf* too personal (or too spiritualized) for a properly social, comic fiction to describe. There are Archdeacon Grantlys or Mark Robartses, to be sure, whose relation to their labor is more or less restricted to its career aspects; but there are also Crawleys and Hardings, whose labor rides free of such encumbrances. Those who mix "social" and "professional," career advance with affective life, such as Robarts and his darker image Adolphus Crosbie in *The Small House at Allington* (1864), come in for punishment, while their procedure—to mix their social selves with their professional aspirations—becomes utterly normal in the Palliser series, particularly for such as Phineas. In the later series, what here go under the names "social" and "professional" are almost completely conflated, as the career-path itself becomes the site of all the various aspirations that in the Barsetshire series are reserved for those unconcerned with its workings. To put it simply: no "professional lives" exist in the Palliser series without their "social" context. The two have become indissoluble, and have merged in the figure of the career.

III. Careerists Abroad

Who then were the first careerists to be acknowledged as such? Trollope's own professional exertions outside of novel-writing provide us with a clue: his well-mapped battles over Post Office procedure, and the structure of civil service more generally, took place within a bureaucratic context that was to a large extent shaped by the example of imperial governance, and it might be there that we can find careerism forming its contours. Such, at least, will be my conjecture here—a conjecture that is at the same time an invitation to further research. That the laboratory of the Indian Civil Service offered the experimental results that would justify the 1855 Northcote-Trevelyan Report is well known; and the full-scale bureaucratization of Indian rule that followed the Government of India Act in 1858 offered an interesting, and eventually compelling, example for the metropole to consider.[15] What we can detect happening in the 1850s—the decade in which Trollope's first public opinions on the professions took shape—is a curious interchange of ideas and possibilities between imperial and domestic settings on the subject of the forms, and narratives, of professional labor. Amidst this complicated exchange, the figure of "career" developed into its modern form: the sequential ascension of one ambitious individual within a profession whose stations were carefully graded (by Civil Service procedure), whose intended public or client-range (imperial subjects) was distanced from the sources of professional expertise, and whose justification lay, importantly, in the boundaries that that distance, and those gradations, put around the ambition that initiated the entire sequence.

If, in other words, the "career" is born in imperial settings, that is not because the empire provided careerists with unlimited scope for vocational desires, but rather because the careers found within imperial governance provided an image of the way professional structures streamlined, and made predictably linear, the otherwise explosive ambitions of individual strivers. It is no accident that Trollope's most committed parliamentary "professionals" find themselves engaged in imperial matters—that both Phineas and Lord Fawn come to occupy the seat of Under-Secretary of State for the Colonies, or that *The Eustace Diamonds*'s Frank Greystock, in an attempt to make a splash, seizes rather cynically upon the slighted claims of the Sawab of Mygawb. But it is of greater significance that these careerists will find their professional options, and ambitions, limited by these subjects: that "the colonies," as an avenue of professional advancement, signifies in Trollope a necessary *specialization* that mitigates against any more all-encompassing ambition. Rise by way of the empire, Trollope seems to say, but be aware that that rise, like any career-sequence, puts a harness upon the horse. Phineas's stand on behalf of Irish tenant-right at the end of *Phineas Finn* is critiqued as a perilous stepping beyond the boundaries of professional expertise, as in Lord Cantrip's ventriloquized thoughts: "A man in office,—in an office which really imposed upon him as much work as he could possibly do with credit to himself or his cause,—was dispensed from the necessity of a conscience with reference to other matters. It was for Sir Walter Morrison to have a conscience about Irish tenant-right, as no doubt he had,—just as Phineas Finn had a conscience about Canada, and Jamaica, and the Cape" (2: 284). There is of course Trollope's familiar irony here, but that irony is powerless against the logic of the career, which permits no tales told out of school: Phineas loses both office and parliamentary seat as a result of transgressing the boundaries of his specialty. "You see, Finn," Cantrip admonishes him, "it's my idea that if a man wants to make himself useful he should stick to some special kind of work. With you it's a thousand pities that you should not do so" (2: 269).

The practice of colonial administration means, above all, limitation; as in Trollope's following meditation upon parliamentary skills, it becomes an image for professional specialization at its most technically detailed:

> We may say, perhaps, that the highest duty imposed upon us as a nation is the management of India; and we may also say that in a great national assembly personal squabbling among its members is the least dignified work in which it can employ itself. But the prospect of an explanation,—or otherwise of a fight,—between two leading politicians will fill the House; and any allusion to our Eastern Empire will certainly empty it. An aptitude for such encounters is almost a necessary qualification for a popular leader in Parliament, as is a capacity for speaking for three hours to the reporters, and to the reporters only,—a necessary qualification for an Under-Secretary for India.
>
> (*Phineas Redux* 322)

Despite the grandiosity of the professional object ("the management of India"), the labor of the Under-Secretary is anything but grandiose; it is instead an expertise recognized only by cognoscenti. The Palliser series continually deploys this kind of logic, evoking the myth of powers-that-be invisible to the untutored eye; the allure of that myth, of being permitted to be "in the know," explains much of the attraction these novels possess. At the center of the myth, at least in the Palliser novels, is the professional parliamentarian-as-careerist: the specialist whose ability, while highly professionally viable, is not immediately transferrable (or even perceptible) outside of the professional realm. Colonial administration, put more simply, is not a path to some sort of Napoleonic rise. It is nothing more or less than a career.[16]

All this flies in the face of Trollope's open tendency to depict colonial adminstrators as gentlemanly amateurs. But it would be more accurate to say that the more Trollope warned of the intrusions of professionals into colonial government—or any government for that matter—the more he turned government itself into a profession, defined like other professions by what sorts of expertise it excludes. Here Trollope's travel writings are useful: in his *Australia and New Zealand* (1873) he explains the continuing necessity of the veto power governors held over colonial assemblies, in such colonies as Queensland, as a result of the professionalism of the assembly's ministers:

> Among such a population the minister chosen will usually be a gentleman intent on his own profession,—whatever that may be; whose education and chances in life have made him a lawyer, a merchant, or a squatter. Such a man finds himself suddenly in parliament, and almost as suddenly a minister of state,—a colonial secretary or prime minister,—or perhaps a colonial treasurer or chancellor of the exchequer,—backed by a majority in parliament, and enabled, therefore, as far as the colonial parliament is concerned, to carry his own measures.
>
> (182)

A dangerous place for a professional from another field, Trollope feels; the correct response is to keep a professional in the correct field—governance—in a supervisory role over these colonial ministers. Implicit here is the claim that if no such dilettantism endangers British home government, it is because British ministers have become professionals in government; a British minister is no less "intent on his own profession," but that profession has become governance itself. The colonial governor, therefore, becomes the very principle of professionalization in the constitutions of British colonies.

He is therefore, not coincidentally, the first real image of careerism. Here a turn to Walter Bagehot, who since Asa Briggs's *Victorian People* (1954) has been continually linked to Trollope, is again instructive. In his *English Constitution* (1867)—which appeared in the Trollope-edited pages of the *Fortnightly Review* starting in 1865—Bagehot is one of the first to employ the con-

temporary sense of the word "career," and he does so within an analogous discussion of the colonial governor and his veto power over inexperienced colonial assemblies. Seeking for an "extrinsic, impartial, and capable authority" to rein in the tendency toward mild corruption, and less mild factionalism, of parliaments, Bagehot turns to the governor:

> They are always intelligent, for they have to live by a difficult trade; they are nearly sure to be impartial, for they come from the ends of the earth; they are sure not to participate in the selfish desires of any colonial class or body, for long before these desires can have attained fruition they will have passed to the other side of the world; be busy with other faces and minds [. . .] A colonial governor is a super-parliamentary authority, animated, by a wisdom which is probably in quantity considerable and is different from the local Parliament, even if not above it. But even in this case the advantage of this extrinsic authority is purchased at a heavy price—a price which must not be made light of, because it is often worth paying. A colonial governor is a ruler who has no permanent interest in the colony he governs; who perhaps had to look for it in the map when he was sent thither; who takes years before he really understands his parties and its controversies; who, though without prejudice himself, is apt to be a slave to the prejudices of local people near him; who inevitably, and almost laudably, governs not in the interest of the colony, which he may mistake, but in his own interest, which he sees and is sure of. The first desire of a colonial governor is not to get into a 'scrape,' not to do anything which may give trouble to his superiors—the colonial office—at home, which may cause an untimely and dubious recall, which may hurt his after career.
>
> (165)

A strange careerism this: cautious, possessed of an expertise that is less topical (the colony itself) and rather more procedural (how not to get into trouble), wise in a *techne* that has no particular reference to the specific needs of the public he serves, concerned above all with sequence ("his after career") rather than with immediate dilemmas. As most recent work on the colonial governor or proconsul has demonstrated, he is an intermediary figure, an agent "whose strategic-structural positions between the home and frontier societies combined with the conjuctions of personality and opportunity to give unexpected twists and real impetus to the expansionary and consolidatory forces known generically as 'imperialism'" (Benyon ["Overlords of the Empire?"] 194). But this intermediate position is suddenly the very definition of the career itself: an ambition that, trapped between the evaluations of superiors and the specifics of "clients," becomes ever more concerned with its own progress and less able to make wholesale revisions of any given situation. With limited time in one post, and limited ability to enter into the disputes and problems he faces, the governor-as-careerist attends finally to the management of his own career.

This is not, for Bagehot or Trollope, a fact to be lamented. It is instead the very work "career" performs: the harnessing of ambition. By limiting the chaotic, professionally uninformed, and possibly destructive energies of colonial populations, the governor-as-careerist only allegorizes his own process of career habituation, in which his ambitions were placed in the specific forms of accountability and hierarchy of a colonial career. What I am suggesting, then, is that the bureaucratized colonial governance of the mid-to-late nineteenth century provides British culture with its first image of the careerist; and that that image, rather than the primarily negative space it currently inhabits, was initially an image of domesticated social energy, of conflictual forces rearranged to form a linear narrative. To understand Trollope's Palliser novels as lengthy explorations of this condition is to deny them the label of novels of "vocation," insofar as the emerging semantic field of the "career" manages a fit between individual ambition and social exigency with rather less friction than any sense of "vocation" could ever achieve. It is also to understand them anew as among the first, and most successful, attempts to narrativize professional labor in the nineteenth century—as narratives not of the formation of a subjective "calling" for labor, but of the acclimatization of an individual to the exterior strictures and exigencies of a lifelong pursuit within a single hierarchy of accomplishment. Finally, such an understanding might permit us to reexamine the provenance of professional careers themselves, with reference to the imperial labors Trollope's careerists so symptomatically undertake.

Notes

1. While the material on Victorian professionalism is too large to rehearse in its entirety, the following have been of particular value to this study: Cohen, *Professional Domesticity*; Corfield, *Power and the Professions*; Daly, "Incorporated Bodies"; Larson, *The Rise of Professionalism*; Perkin, *The Rise of Professional Society*; Poovey, *Uneven Developments*; Robbins, "Telescopic Philanthropy."

2. The linkage of careerism to British colonial rule is most famously signaled by the line from Disraeli's *Tancred* (1847)—"The East is a career"—that served as epigraph in Said's *Orientalism*. But that there might be a necessary link between the later history of the word "career," particularly its shift into a specifically professional register, and the forms of vocational activity that "the East" could offer, has remained perhaps too professionally embarrassing to pursue, as Bruce Robbins, in his commentary on Disraeli's sentence and Said's work, has surmised: "There are good reasons why this sentence remains not quite sayable. But there is also at least one bad reason—a reason of some significance for the politics of intellectual work. This is the assumption that success in professional career-making is at best an embarrassment to any scholar who, like Said, makes a career while and by maintaining a commitment to radical social change" (*Vocations* [*Secular Vocations*] 152-53).

3. The tendency to mock Trollope's professionalism has recently encountered an interestingly inverse trend: to mock the professionalism of Trollope's readers. That most representative example of American belletristic gentility, *The New Yorker,* has twice in the last decade turned its attention to the Trollope Society, which is gently ridiculed for its commercialism (rooted in its publishing series) and for its staple audience (lawyers). See "Living Author" and Rebecca Mead's "The Bench: Lawyers Who Love Trollope."

4. The analysis of Trollope's "situationist ethics" comes from Ruth apRoberts's *The Moral Trollope*; James Kincaid has responded at length to apRoberts's thesis, claiming that "Trollope's method and his morality [. . .] appear to me very much tied to situations, but only because situations test and make solid an ethical code that would otherwise remain abstract and superficial" (*Novels* [*The Novels of Anthony Trollope*] 15). For a historicized contribution to this debate, see Nardin's *Trollope and Victorian Moral Philosophy.*

5. See particularly Franco Moretti's *The Way of the World,* especially his account of the bildungsroman's eventual collapse, in George Eliot, between the competing claims of labor and subjectivity: "For better or worse, vocation is depersonalized, objective, hostile to 'personal experience': to suggest that it can be fulfilled within everyday personal relationships implies a perversion of its meaning. It also implies a repression of the 'other half' of the novel: of the splendid and sorrowful account—short was the happy life of Tertius Lydgate—of the *conflict* between vocation and everyday life" (218). See also Mintz, *George Eliot and the Novel of Vocation.*

6. There is an echo here of Said's powerful account of the development of literary "careers"—a figure for the exile from secure conventions or any exterior agencies—out of literary "vocations" in *Beginnings.* For Said the fall from vocation into career is expressive of the unalterably subjectivist stance of the modern writer, without a home in literary precedent; in the Trollopian sense "career" expresses an analogous fall into a disconnected individuality that now can only compete with others, without the collectivist umbrella of "vocation." See also Arac's *Commissioned Spirits* for an analysis of the development of novelistic "careers" proper in the nineteenth century (23-27).

7. See Corfield's *Power and the Professions* for a sociological picture of "relative failure" in mid-

nineteenth-century British professional life, a picture that cites Trollope's father as an instance of the kind of stalled career-path which best expresses the term (224). For one acute version of the relation of sentimentality, or pathos, to social mobility, see Bailin.

8. Bourdieu's theory of the "disposition" explicitly responds to Weber: "The homogeneity of the dispositions associated with a position and their seemingly miraculous adjustment to the demands inscribed in it result partly from the mechanisms which channel toward positions individuals who are already adjusted to them, either because they feel 'made' for jobs that are 'made' for them—this is 'vocation,' the proleptic assumption of an objective destiny that is imposed by practical reference to the modal trajectory in the class of origin—or because they are seen in this light by the occupants of the posts—this is co-option based on the immediate harmony of dispositions—and partly from the dialectic which is established, throughout a lifetime, between dispositions and positions, aspirations and achievements" (*Distinction* 110). Bourdieu's theoretical apparatus is useful here particularly because of its attempt to formalize a theory of biography based on the *career,* on successive choices made within particular fields of power, which is remarkably close to the biographical procedure of Trollope in the Palliser novels and even in such brief studies as his *Lord Palmerston* (1882). For both, the vocational "aspiration" is of far less moment than the kinds of choices the individual faces in the midst of a vocational pursuit—choices that are always limiting, and limited. See also "The Field of Cultural Production" for further definitions of "trajectory" and what Bourdieu calls "constructed biography." Contemporary sociologies of careerism stress what is often called the investment effect: the increase of desire for what has been achieved, which turns career-paths into "a powerful factor of conformity with the existing social order and a source of basic conservatism" (Larson [*The Rise of Professionalism*] 229).

9. Miller's contention reflects a lively debate among Trollope critics as to how truly "political"—or, responsive to social changes outside of parliamentary tactics—the Palliser novels are; for a defense of Trollope's engagement with the issues of the 1860s and 1870s, see Halperin, *Trollope and Politics,* and for an acute analysis of Trollopian politics as a "spectacle of violence directed against another" (22), see Dellamora, "Stupid Trollope." One further useful account is Hillis Miller's in *The Ethics of Reading,* where Trollope's relation to the playing of games—cricket, whist, the novel—could be usefully extended to the game Trollope was finally excluded from playing, Parliament.

10. The similarity this analysis of Trollope's Parliament bears to contemporary accounts of the profession of literary criticism is intended; the monadic, self-enclosed nature of parliamentary government reflects Stanley Fish's account, in *Professional Correctness,* of disciplines and their boundaries, while the self-adjusting and self-critiquing quality of Parliament evokes the nuanced critique of Fish offered in Robbins's *Secular Vocations.* While any too-strict allegory of contemporary academic labor should be resisted, it is nonetheless curious how strikingly contemporary Trollope's account of parliamentary and clerical labor seems from the vantage point of the modern academy.

11. One of those observers was Weber himself, who in "Politics as a Vocation" (1918) analyzes the British parliamentary system as relatively safe from the bureaucratization that had overrun continental government. Yet when Weber lists those quasi-official figures who represent the gradual professionalizing of governance, it is interesting to note that each item on the list has its carefully drawn, and usually recurrent, companion in the Palliser series: the journalist (Quintus Slide, of the fictional *People's Banner*), the election agent (of which Trollope provides numerous examples, such as *Phineas Redux*'s Mr. Ruddles), the "whip" (Bonteen and Ratler), and the trade union representative (*Phineas Finn*'s Mr. Bunce).

12. My claim here borrows from Simmel's definition of the "adventurer," who seeks an entirely bounded experience cut off from sequential continuity: "The adventure [. . .] according to its intrinsic meaning, is independent of the 'before' and 'after': its boundaries are defined regardless of them [. . .] The adventure lacks that reciprocal interpenetration with adjacent parts of life which constitutes life-as-a-whole" (189).

13. Even if Trollope's much-discussed abhorrence of the civil service examinations instituted by the 1855 Northcote-Trevelyan Report, "On the Organization of the Permanent Civil Service," is taken into account, it nonetheless remains accurate to say that Trollope's polemical battles with his Post Office superiors, and his various intrusions into civil service matters more broadly, tended to have the intent of restoring bureaucratic normality in the face of "arbitrary" decisions. His insistence upon seniority as the one secure criterion for promotion is well mapped: his participation in an 1860 Committee of Inquiry into Post Office employment procedures, which recommended pro-

motion by seniority rather than ill-defined considerations of merit, is discussed in Hall (221) and Super (51); see also Shuman's account of Trollope's predilection for seniority, which "attests to his belief that value accrues from the worker's actual hours of labor, and that it is only labor that can be exchanged for money—not inalienable, indefinable qualities like merit" (106). By resisting examinations Trollope is not resisting bureaucratic fixity; he is, in fact, attempting a rearguard defense of established bureaucratic procedure in the face of unpredictable, and less easily quantifiable, reformist criteria.

14. One important location for the continuing fight over the word "career" and what it can or cannot include—a locus of no small relevance to Trollope's female careerists—is the debate over the possibility of a viably feminist careerism. Madelon Sprengnether's well-known critique of "careerist feminism," which "focuses on individual achievement as its primary goal, disavowing the very value of collectivity in its definition of feminism" (206), plays upon the sense of "career" as a personal trajectory masking, possibly even sacrificing, more sweeping trajectories; it similarly alludes to the central temporal problematic of the "career" as I've sketched it: the inability of a career-narrative to posit satisfactory conclusions. For one response to Sprengnether, see Langbauer, "Queen Victoria and Me"; see also Keller and Moglen, "Competition and Feminism," and Hirsch and Keller, "Conclusion: Practicing Conflict in Feminist Theory." Bruce Robbins's point about any such condemnations of what might be called a "left careerism" is worth citing: "Now if there *is* a logic linking 'careerism' to 'rhetorics of oppositional politics' [. . .] this would be a strange fact, and it would seem to call out for investigation. Of all the ways to make a career, this is surely the least predictable. Assuming the worst possible motives on the part of the individual careerist, it would still be interesting that careerist motives should have to be camouflaged by 'rhetoric of oppositional politics,' rather than by some other form of camouflage" (*Secular Vocations* 4).

15. For considerations of the "bureaucratization" of British rule in India centering on the reorganizations of 1858, see Misra, *The Bureaucracy in India*; Spangenberg, *British Bureaucracy in India*; Stokes, "Bureaucracy and Ideology: Britain and India in the Nineteenth Century." Misra's study pays particular attention to the development of "rationalized" administrative hierarchies in the I. C. S. [Indian Civil Service], hierarchies that virtually define the modern "career."

16. It should come as no surprise, therefore, that the language of "career"—expertise, possibilities for promotion, regular pay, and pension, the socialization of ambition—is increasingly, in the later decades of the nineteenth century, found in discussions of imperial labor. One typical example is "The Civil Service of India as a Career," an 1883 piece which analyzes for an untutored reader the structures of a professional life spent within the empire; the writer takes pains to analyze pension procedures, increases in salary, and probable speed of advancement, thereby displaying the distance the very word "career" had traveled since the early nineteenth century. Others have traced the genealogy of the professional "career" to colonial rule; see Elliott's *Sociology of the Professions* for an account of the "career system" that was begotten by reforms in the I. C. S. and Indian Army alike (50).

Works Cited

apRoberts, Ruth. *The Moral Trollope*. Athens: Ohio UP, 1971.

Arac, Jonathan. *Commissioned Spirits: The Shaping of Social Motion in Dickens, Carlyle, Melville, and Hawthorne*. New York: Columbia UP, 1989.

Bagehot, Walter. *The English Constitution*. 1867. Ed. Miles Taylor. Oxford: Oxford UP, 2001.

Bailin, Miriam. "'Dismal Pleasure': Victorian Sentimentality and the Pathos of the Parvenu." *ELH* 66 (1999): 1015-32.

Balzac, Honoré de. *The Bureaucrats*. Trans. [translation] of *Les Employés*. Trans. Charles Foulkes. Evanston: Northwestern UP, 1993.

Benyon, John. "Overlords of Empire? British 'Proconsular Imperialism' in Comparative Perspective." *The Journal of Imperial and Commonwealth History* 19 (1991): 164-202.

Bourdieu, Pierre. *Distinction: A Social Critique of the Judgment of Taste*. Trans. Richard Nice. Cambridge: Harvard UP, 1984.

———. "The Field of Cultural Production, or: The Economic World Reversed." *The Field of Cultural Production: Essays on Art and Literature*. Ed. Randal Johnson. New York: Columbia UP, 1993.

———. *The State Nobility: Elite Schools in the Field of Power*. Trans. Lauretta Clough. Stanford: Stanford UP, 1996.

Briggs, Asa. *Victorian People: A Reassessment of Persons and Themes, 1851-1867*. Chicago: U of Chicago P, 1954.

"The Civil Service of India as a Career." *Chambers's Journal* 60 (1883): 580-82.

Cohen, Monica. *Professional Domesticity in the Victorian Novel: Women, Work, and Home.* Cambridge: Cambridge UP, 1998.

Collins, Philip. "Business and Bosoms: Some Trollopian Concerns." *Nineteenth-Century Fiction* 37 (1982): 293-315.

Corfield, Penelope. *Power and the Professions in Britain 1700-1850.* London: Routledge, 1995.

Dellamora, Richard. "Stupid Trollope." *The Victorian Newsletter* 100 (2001): 22-26.

Daly, Nicholas. "Incorporated Bodies: Dracula and the Rise of Professionalism." *Texas Studies in Literature and Language* 39.2 (1997): 181-203.

Disraeli, Benjamin. *Tancred; or, The New Crusade.* London: Colburn, 1847.

Elliott, Philip. *The Sociology of the Professions.* London: Macmillan, 1972.

Fish, Stanley. *Professional Correctness: Literary Studies and Political Change.* Cambridge: Harvard UP, 1995.

Freidson, Eliot. *Professionalism, the Third Logic: On the Practice of Knowledge.* Chicago: U of Chicago P, 2001.

Hall, N. John. *Trollope: A Biography.* Oxford: Clarendon, 1991.

Halperin, John. *Trollope and Politics: A Study of the Pallisers and Others.* London: Macmillan, 1977.

Hirsch, Marianne, and Evelyn Fox Keller. "Conclusion: Practicing Conflict in Feminist Theory." *Conflicts in Feminism.* Ed. Marianne Hirsch and Evelyn Fox Keller. New York: Routledge, 1990. 370-85.

Jameson, Fredric. "The Vanishing Mediator: or, Max Weber as Storyteller." *The Syntax of History.* Vol. 2 of *The Ideologies of Theory, Essays 1971-1986.* Minneapolis: U of Minnesota P, 1988. 3-34.

Keller, Evelyn Fox, and Helene Moglen. "Competition and Feminism: Conflicts for Academic Women." *Signs* 12 (1987): 493-511.

Kincaid, James. "Anthony Trollope and the Unmannerly Novel." *Reading and Writing Women's Lives: A Study of the Novel of Manners.* Ed. Bege Bowers and Barbara Brothers. Ann Arbor: UMI Research P, 1990. 87-104.

———. *The Novels of Anthony Trollope.* Oxford: Clarendon, 1977.

Kucich, John. *The Power of Lies: Transgression in Victorian Fiction.* Ithaca: Cornell UP, 1994.

Langbauer, Laurie. "Queen Victoria and Me." *Victorian Afterlife: Postmodern Culture Rewrites the Nineteenth Century.* Ed. John Kucich and Dianne Sadoff. Minneapolis: U of Minnesota P, 2000. 211-33.

Larson, Magali Sarfatti. *The Rise of Professionalism: A Sociological Analysis.* Berkeley: U of California P, 1977.

"Living Author." *The New Yorker* 3 Dec. 1990: 40-41.

Mead, Rebecca. "The Bench: Lawyers Who Love Trollope." *The New Yorker* 17 Apr. 2001: 31.

Meredith, George. *Beauchamp's Career.* London: Chapman and Hall, 1876.

Miller, D. A. *The Novel and the Police.* Berkeley: U of California P, 1988.

Miller, J. Hillis. *The Ethics of Reading: Kant, de Man, Eliot, Trollope, James, and Benjamin.* New York: Columbia UP, 1987.

Mintz, Alan. *George Eliot and the Novel of Vocation.* Cambridge: Harvard UP, 1978.

Misra, B. B. *The Bureaucracy in India: A Historical Analysis of Development up to 1947.* Delhi: Oxford UP, 1977.

Moretti, Franco. *The Way of the World: The* Bildungsroman *in European Culture.* Trans. Albert Sbragia. London: Verso, 1987.

Nardin, Jane. *Trollope and Victorian Moral Philosophy.* Athens: Ohio UP, 1996.

Perkin, Harold. *The Rise of Professional Society: England Since 1880.* London: Routledge, 1989.

Poovey, Mary. *Uneven Developments: The Ideological Work of Gender in Mid-Victorian England.* Chicago: U of Chicago P, 1988.

Robbins, Bruce. *Secular Vocations: Intellectuals, Professionalism, Culture.* London: Verso, 1993.

———. "Telescopic Philanthropy: Professionalism and Responsibility in *Bleak House.*" *Nation and Narration.* Ed. Homi Bhabha. London: Routledge, 1990. 213-30.

Said, Edward. *Beginnings: Intention and Method.* New York: Basic, 1975.

———. *Orientalism.* New York: Pantheon, 1978.

Shuman, Cathy. *Pedagogical Economies: The Examination and the Victorian Literary Man.* Stanford: Stanford UP, 2000.

Simmel, Georg. "The Adventurer." *Georg Simmel on Individuality and Social Forms: Selected Writings.* Ed. Donald Levine. Chicago: U of Chicago P, 1971. 187-98.

Smalley, Donald, ed. *Trollope: The Critical Heritage.* London: Routledge, 1969.

Spangenberg, Bradley. *British Bureaucracy in India: Status, Policy, and the I. C. S. in the Late Nineteenth Century.* Columbia, MO: South Asia, 1976.

Sprengnether, Madelon. "Generational Differences: Reliving Mother-Daughter Conflicts." *Changing Subjects: The Making of Feminist Literary Criticism.* Ed. Gayle Greene and Coppelia Kahn. New York: Routledge, 1993. 201-08.

Stokes, Eric. "Bureaucracy and Ideology: Britain and India in the Nineteenth Century." *Transactions of the Royal Historical Society* 30 (1980): 131-56.

Super, R. H. *Trollope in the Post Office.* Ann Arbor: U of Michigan P, 1981.

Trevelyan, Charles, and Stafford Northcote. "On the Organization of the Permanent Civil Service." *English Historical Documents.* Ed. David Douglas. Vol. 12. Oxford: Oxford UP, 1956. 567-75.

Trollope, Anthony. *Australia.* 1873. Ed. P. D. Edwards and R. B. Joyce. St. Lucia: U of Queensland P, 1967.

———. *An Autobiography.* 1883. Ed. P. D. Edwards. Oxford: Oxford UP, 1980.

———. *Barchester Towers.* 1857. Ed. John Sutherland. Oxford: Oxford UP, 1996.

———. *Can You Forgive Her?* 1865. Ed. Andrew Swarbrick. Oxford: Oxford UP, 1982.

———. *The Claverings.* 1867. Ed. David Skilton. Oxford: Oxford UP, 1986.

———. *Doctor Thorne.* 1858. Ed. David Skilton. Oxford: Oxford UP, 2000.

———. *The Duke's Children.* 1880. Ed. Hermione Lee. Oxford: Oxford UP, 1982.

———. *The Eustace Diamonds.* 1873. Ed. W. J. McCormack. Oxford: Oxford UP, 1982.

———. *Framley Parsonage.* 1861. Ed. P. D. Edwards. Oxford: Oxford UP, 1980.

———. *The Last Chronicle of Barset.* 1867. Ed. Stephen Gill. Oxford: Oxford UP, 1980.

———. *Lord Palmerston.* 1882. Ed. John Halperin. New York: Arno, 1981.

———. *Phineas Finn: The Irish Member.* 1869. Ed. Jacques Berthoud. Oxford: Oxford UP, 1982.

———. *Phineas Redux.* 1874. Ed. John Whale. Oxford: Oxford UP, 1982.

———. *The Prime Minister.* 1876. Ed. Jennifer Uglow. Oxford: Oxford UP, 1982.

———. *The Small House at Allington.* 1864. Ed. James Kincaid. Oxford: Oxford UP, 1989.

———. *The Three Clerks.* 1859. Ed. Graham Handley. Oxford: Oxford UP, 1989.

Weber, Max. *Economy and Society.* Ed. Guenther Roth and Claus Wittich. Vol. 3. New York: Bedminster, 1968.

———. "Politics as a Vocation." *From Max Weber: Essays in Sociology.* Trans. H. H. Gerth and C. Wright Mills. Oxford: Oxford UP, 1946. 77-128.

———. *The Protestant Ethic and the Spirit of Capitalism.* Trans. Talcott Parsons. London: Routledge, 1930.

———. "Science as a Vocation." *From Max Weber: Essays in Sociology.* Trans. H. H. Gerth and C. Wright Mills. Oxford: Oxford UP, 1946. 129-56.

Weber, Samuel. *Institution and Interpretation.* Minneapolis: U of Minnesota P, 1987.

Phyllis Rose (essay date summer 2003)

SOURCE: Rose, Phyllis. "At Large and At Small: Embedding Trollope." *American Scholar* 72, no. 3 (summer 2003): 5-10.

[*In the following essay, Rose makes a case for reading Trollope with the purpose of better understanding and appreciating the intricacies of democracy and political reform.*]

Embedding journalists in Iraq alongside frontline troops was a fine idea. It guaranteed that the soldiers' own stories were told, so we did not repeat the Vietnam-era shame of blaming the troops for the war they were obliged to fight. We know now, better than at any time in history, what soldiers do. We have learned how unclear battle lines are, how often death and ruin are inflicted inadvertently. Of course, you would already know that if you had read the opening chapter of Stendhal's *The Charterhouse of Parma,* in which the hero goes heroically to war and finds himself stumbling about on some Napoleonic battlefield, unable to locate the side he means to join, uncertain even whether a battle is taking place. But how many people these days read a fictional depiction of the Battle of Waterloo to find out about the Battle of Baghdad?

Niall Ferguson, the historian of the British Empire, has suggested that Americans don't have the attention spans needed to manage an empire (or, if you prefer, to "foster democratic institutions around the globe"). And whether or not we embrace that enterprise abroad, for the better practice of democracy at home we need to appreciate the extended time line of our political institutions. But how are we to stretch attention spans that everything in our culture aims toward shortening? The average duration of an artistic experience these days is midway between that of a film and that of a TV show: an hour and a half at most. As for reading, average the length of a short magazine article with the length of an e-mail. That's the problem I hope to correct with my modest proposal. I want us to embed Victorian novels—specifically, Trollope's. Embedding of this sort should be easy and inexpensive to implement. I would suggest giving a paperback to every taxpayer, whether soldier or civilian. I want to encourage Americans at home, living our democratic lives, along with those abroad, spreading our democratic civilization, more of a sense of the past, of the slow growth of things in time. We all need training in patience.

Victorian novels make good embedding material because, for one thing, they're long. One volume will keep you occupied for weeks—helpful whether you're a democracy-builder trying to travel light, or just an ordinary citizen who might profit from the lesson that life does not resolve itself quickly. For another thing, they're peppy and, on the whole, upbeat. It's hard to imagine sending young people out nation-building with any of the classics of American literature. *Moby-Dick,* for example, might present too ironic a view of their quest. And none of the greats of modern American literature, from Hemingway's *The Sun Also Rises* to Robert Stone's *A Flag for Sunrise,* Norman Mailer's *The Executioner's Song,* and Jonathan Franzen's *The Corrections,* shows a nation that one would be inspired to fight for or replicate. Unlike British novels, American novels tend to derive their greatness from their oppositional stance.

That Victorian novels are distant and alien in trappings and references, which makes them hard to enter, works in the long run to help ensure their universality. *Jane Eyre,* published in 1847, has been claimed by girls everywhere who've felt themselves to be unloved, undervalued, and insufficiently beautiful. African-American girls in the South and Jewish girls in New York have read it well into the twentieth century and felt that Charlotte Brontë was writing about them. But we read Michael Chabon's *The Amazing Adventures of Kavalier and Clay* or Philip Roth's *The Human Stain,* to mention two contemporary novels I've particularly liked, and say to ourselves: That world is (or is not) my world. What may be true for those urban sophisticates (or college professors) may (or may not) be true for me. When we read about contemporary reality, we know the material too well to take "a" world as "our" world.

* * *

To exercise our attention spans, to teach us the lesson of time and the virtue of perseverance, and to keep before our eyes the blessings of a democratic society, we need the spacious, panoramic, and progressive Victorian novel, and my particular choice would be Trollope, who, we are told, was the novelist British soldiers in World War I turned to in order to be reminded of what they fought for. Remembering that, to help myself through a difficult situation recently, I read *Phineas Finn* and *Phineas Redux,* two of Trollope's Palliser novels, about power and politics in mid-nineteenth-century London. I think they would do very nicely for embedding, for they constitute a picture, as sustaining as snapshots of loved ones, of the face of democracy.

Phineas Finn, a young Irishman, son of a country doctor, goes to London to be trained in law without having any special interest in law. He really does not know what he wants to do with his life. Nonetheless, he is likable, intelligent honest, sincere, an interested listener, and a clear speaker, and, though he isn't much aware of it himself, because of a becoming absence of vanity, he is good-looking and highly attractive to women. The women of the liberal aristocracy take him up and introduce him to their fathers, brothers, and cousins. Soon he finds himself a member of Parliament and, not long after, a respected undersecretary of state for the colonies. He finds he loves the work. He becomes friends with the most serious reformer statesman in the land, Mr. Monk, and almost a member of the family of the powerful Earl of Brentford. Like every good democratic hero, he's at ease with a range of people, from his Cockney landlady, Mrs. Bunce, to titled lords and members of the cabinet.

The young man from the provinces who goes to the big city and makes good is not a currently fashionable type, but he was an indispensable fixture in French and English literature of the great period. Balzac had his Rastignac, Stendhal his Julien Sorel, Dickens his David Copperfield and his Pip. Each allowed the writer to portray that period of human life which is, from a narrative point of view, perhaps the most interesting—the transition from youth to adulthood, from potential to actual. What is so wonderful about Trollope's young men—and, in their own way, his young women, who are able to express their desires for the future only through their choice of husband—is that they so realistically don't know what they're doing. They don't see clear paths to choose between. They move from one interest to another, from one new acquaintance to another, by accident. Sometimes they make mistakes. Their parents think they're adrift and purposeless. And then something solidifies out of the chaos of possibilities. They cling to it, find they rather like it, become passionate about it, then devote their lives to it. Phineas finds his way into politics like that, while Lord Chiltern, his fiery, uncontrollable friend, so huge a disappointment to his father, the Earl of Brentford, finds his way in a similar fashion to the fulfillment of his talents as Master of the Brake hounds, a huntsman par excellence, sacrificing his energy and comfort that his countrymen may enjoy a good hunt in season. Trollope isn't a bit ironic about this use of Chiltern's life. He seems, with typical generosity of spirit, happy that his character has found some way to put his interests, gifts, and passion effectively to use.

Phineas Finn's success does not depend on his marrying an heiress or a lady of position, as so often happens in French novels. A man of strong feelings who really likes women, he is attracted successively to Mary Flood Jones, of his hometown in Ireland; Lady Laura Standish, a wealthy and well-placed young woman whose father is the Earl of Brentford; the extremely wealthy and well-born Violet Effingham; and the supremely wealthy but slightly louche (probably Jewish) widow Madame Max Goesler. He marries none of the wealthy ladies in the first book of which he is hero, and, returning to Ireland, chooses humble, devoted Mary Flood Jones. Trollope wants it clear that although women love Phineas and help him, he succeeds on his own merits and that his success consists in finding the way to use his talents and serve his country—not in establishing himself as a man of wealth and position. Ruthless about the demands of his narrative, Trollope will have no trouble killing Mary off in childbirth once his point is made.

Phineas is a beneficiary of the main principle for which, according to Napoleon, the French Revolution was fought: *la carrière ouverte aux talents*—positions to those who merit them, not to people born into a privileged family. To underline that further, Trollope makes Phineas Irish, a second-class citizen in Great Britain. People are constantly saying of him that he is smart (for an Irishman) and hardworking (for an Irishman). His success in the British Parliament is a pioneer's success. Like the first Roman Catholic in the U.S. presidency or the first African-American in the Senate, he scores a triumph that is more than personal; it represents another step forward for representative democracy.

The British effort to make its government represent people and not power or wealth went on for over a century. Reform bills aimed at widening the franchise and reducing hereditary power were passed in 1832, 1867, and 1884. Each extended the number of Britons entitled to vote: not just big property owners, but small property owners; not just property owners, but workers; not just industrial workers, but agricultural workers; not just members of the Church of England, but Dissenters and Catholics; not just men, but women.

At the same time that voting rights were widened, wealthy landowners' power to appoint members of Parliament was curtailed. Pocket boroughs (boroughs in the pockets of powerful men) were increasingly abolished. Big cities got more representation. Phineas's

story reflects these changes. Initially he represented Loughlane, the Irish district in which he grew up. He ran for office uncontested, because Lord Tulla, the local Conservative kingmaker, was mad at his brother, the usual MP, and refused to back him. When Phineas needed to be elected again, Loughlane had become unavailable, because Lord Tulla and his brother had made up. Phineas is then given the borough of Loughton, controlled by the Earl of Brentford and destined to be itself reformed out of existence in the course of the novel. The irony that a reformer like Phineas would stand for a rotten borough is of course explored, but it's always Trollope's view that imperfection must be lived with during the gradual process of improving things. There is not an extreme or revolutionary fiber in his body. When Loughton is gone and Phineas again needs election, he turns to the industrial town of Tankerville, where he faces an entrenched opponent against whom he has to fight hard. He loses the election by a slim margin but finally wins in court, proving illegalities in his opponent's victory. In other words, a modern democratic election! But the novel shows how recent a development in democracy that is.

Reform is the subject of many great Victorian novels. George Eliot's *Middlemarch* is set in the two or three years before the passage of the first reform bill, in 1832. Compared with the Palliser novels, even glorious *Middlemarch* is crude in its depiction of political change. The spirit of reform is represented by Will Ladislaw, dashing, romantic, vaguely Polish, and too sketchily drawn to have much impact. George Eliot is far more interested in showing the slow efforts toward medical reform, the frustration, setbacks, compromises, and finally defeat of the new young physician in town, Dr. Lydgate. And she is best of all at showing the slow changes in an individual's soul—Dorothea Brooke's painful education, Mr. Bulstrode's creeping self-deception, Fred Vincy's growth to maturity under the pressure of love for Mary Garth, Dr. Lydgate's descent into pettiness and mediocrity under the influence of his wife, Rosamond.

The Phineas Finn novels are set at the time of the second reform bill, 1867, a generation after *Middlemarch.* The work of basic political reform is still going on. What makes Trollope an ideal chronicler of political changes is that he appreciates how slow they must be. He understands how closed systems of human beings—organizations, communities, and governments—work, and how, within them, ideas go from being inconceivable to possible, to probable, to inevitable, to desirable, and, finally, to essential. Phineas resigns over an issue, Irish tenant rights, that is radical when he and his friend Mr. Monk take it up in *Phineas Finn,* a thing long since taken for granted in the next volume, *Phineas Redux.* The disestablishment of the Church of England is another such step. Everyone knows that government will eventually have to be cut loose from state religion. It is only a question of timing.

I am not the first—I wish I were—to connect the central achievement of the Victorian novel, the depiction of change over time, with the great scientific theory of the day, Darwin's theory of evolution. Darwin posited infinitely small variations in species that result in changes of great magnitude over inconceivably long periods of time. His theory did for biology what other nineteenth-century scientists had already done for geology, extending the time line of creation by vast factors, replacing older theories of cataclysmic change that posited tremendous upheavals in short periods of time. The biblical account of Creation is, of course, read literally, a cataclysmic theory. The static theories of pre-Darwinian science and the static presentation of character in eighteenth-century novels are no doubt connected, as are the psychological and political histories of the Victorian novel and the historical impulse of the new science.

Dickens differs from other Victorian novelists in continuing the older literary tradition, which emphasized enduring types and sudden changes rather than gradual progress. Filling his canvas with vivid if somewhat one-dimensional characters, he makes up in its size and variety for its lack of depth (as we think of depth) in the portrayal of individuals. He, too, is concerned with his characters' reform, but bad guys in Dickens have overnight changes of heart and turn into good guys cataclysmically. Think of Scrooge. Much as I love Dickens, I don't recommend embedding him. He would foster any instinctive love of melodrama and caricature, any desire for instant gratification, any emphasis on "hearts" rather than "minds." We Americans are, on the whole, already too Dickensian in our desire for instantaneous change and conversion.

* * *

For obvious reasons, I've been thinking for months about the connection between imaginative literature and public policy. Our current foreign policy, which produced the invasion of Iraq, seems so wildly imaginative that at times I am awed by its daring. Who could have thought this up?

Last September, the *New York Times Sunday Magazine* ran two profiles—one of Paul D. Wolfowitz, the deputy secretary of defense who created our Get Saddam policy, and the other of Joss Whedon, the television producer who created *Buffy, the Vampire Slayer.* I don't suppose the *Times* intended the two portraits as a pair, but I couldn't help seeing them as commenting on each other. Both these guys seemed brilliant, off the wall, nuts—visionaries on different playing fields.

Whedon, a third-generation script writer, has been trained to understand the power of fantasy. He was educated at Wesleyan University (where I myself teach) by the American studies scholar Richard Slotkin, an expert in history and popular culture and the way our dualistic mythology of violence serves as self-justification. His conversation with the *Times* reporter is punctuated by self-deprecating comments like "Oh, my God, I am a hack," which she recognizes as an artist's good manners. He insists he doesn't aspire to "transcend genre" (code for: being taken for more than a storyteller). He thinks storytelling an honorable occupation, fantasy nobler and deeper than realism. "'Law and Order' is the most enjoyable thing in the world!" he told the reporter. "But I do not go through life imagining myself as Sam Waterston, breakin' a case, prosecutin' a guy. I don't want to create responsible shows with lawyers in them. I want to invade people's dreams." Hence, Buffy, the slayer of evil and the sexiest girl in school, with a devoted following of teenage girls and college professors.

Wolfowitz is the son of a mathematician at Cornell. As an undergraduate, Wolfowitz, like his father, was a mathematician. After taking a course in political science with the conservative thinker Allan Bloom, Wolfowitz was inspired to go on to do graduate work in his new field at the University of Chicago. When he got interested in political science, according to the *Times* piece, his father was horrified. To the father, political "science" seemed little better than astrology. But Wolfowitz persisted, and now he has triumphed as a political scientist. Not only did he get the idea for replacing Saddam Hussein's regime with a democratic one, which would serve as a model for the whole Middle East, he persuaded others to implement it. Wolfowitz's vision of a democratic Iraq as a counterweight to Islamist extremism is the reason that billions of dollars' worth of armaments were used on Iraq and that thousands of our soldiers fought and some died there. What could be realer than that? Eh, Dad? Wolfowitz comes across as smart, likable, well-meaning, and deep, but clueless about fantasy. Not for him invading people's dreams. Humility might have made him laugh at his own global war game plans. Some other character trait forced him to see them enacted.

Coleridge had a theory, discussed in the second chapter of *Biographia Literaria,* of the sanity of genius. Genius, in his view, was a midpoint on a continuum. At one end of the continuum, there was fanaticism and superstition—people who had no ideas of their own. At the other, there was passing enthusiasm and inaction—people who got ideas but didn't bother turning them into reality, thinking the idea was enough. In the middle there was true genius, which had, according to Coleridge, supreme self-confidence, marrying ideas and action in a continuous flow of works of art. There was also what he called "Commanding Genius," a lesser form. Men with this kind of genius had to affect other people with their ideas in order to believe in them themselves. In tranquil times, says Coleridge, these are the men who build canals, aqueducts, palaces. "But alas! in times of tumult they are the men destined to come forth as the shaping spirit of Ruin, to destroy the wisdom of ages in order to substitute the fancies of the day, and to change kings and kingdoms, as the wind shifts and shapes clouds."

Like so many other writers in the early nineteenth century, Coleridge was trying to account for Napoleon, the most commanding public figure of the age. Clearly he was some sort of genius. But what sort? How did his dreams of liberation turn into dreams of conquest? How did he end up bringing disaster and ruin to so much of Europe that he had to be, at the end, confined to a remote island as a dangerous animal is confined to a cage? What made one person able to mobilize hundreds of thousands of others to fight? Byron called such people "the madmen . . . who have made men mad by their contagion." Most of the romantic poets who thought politically (which was most of them) saw a connection between their own creativity and that of popular leaders. They aspired to influence people in one way, statesmen in another. I don't think there's any doubt that when Shelley called poets "the unacknowledged legislators of the world," he meant to imply that the unacknowledged legislators were working at a deeper level and were, in the long run, more important than the acknowledged ones. The shapes the mind imposes on the chaotic materials of life, the force and direction of the imagination—these come from literature. Laws can merely affect behavior.

This habit of thinking about the power of literature versus the power of government continues into twentieth-century British literature, where, in the work of Virginia Woolf, it becomes, characteristically, associated with gender. *Mrs. Dalloway,* following a series of works in which Woolf mocked the rigidity of male authority, grew out of a contrast in her mind between the creativity of a woman like Clarissa Dalloway—a creativity of gifts, conversation, and party giving, one that affected the inner life—and that of male legislators and governors. Originally, the specific, individualized figure of Clarissa, the hostess, was to be balanced by the generic figure of the prime minister, a man equivalent to the clothes he wore and the car he was driven in, whose power, like his presentation, had to do with the externals of life. The novel grew into something much more subtle and complex, involving the shell-shocked soldier Septimus Warren Smith as another double for Clarissa, someone who acts out an urge to obliteration that she suppresses. But it's useful to remember that the book, published in 1925, was occasioned by World War I, by Woolf's thinking about the masculine kinds of creativity that produced wars, and by a contrast, however

crude, between masculine power over the external parts of life and feminine power over the interior life. If this notion seems strained or quaint, it's useful to remember, too, that women, and only women over thirty, had been voting in England for a mere seven years when *Mrs. Dalloway* was published, and women in their twenties wouldn't be allowed to vote, as men were, for another three years! It was a long way to Indira Gandhi, Margaret Thatcher, and Condoleezza Rice. Fantasies about what female influence on world affairs might be like needed few reality checks.

* * *

Today it seems unduly idealistic, if not downright naïve, to characterize power over the external circumstances of life as trivial. To consider the Holocaust, the firebombing of Dresden, the explosions at Hiroshima and Nagasaki, the destruction of Coventry and much of London in World War II as affecting "merely" the externals is callous to the point of stupidity. To consider Saddam Hussein's dictatorship—or that of Stalin, or of Idi Amin—as a perverted kind of genius, one that would have been better put to building canals or writing poetry, seems frivolous and unworthy of the gravity of their evil. Only from within a placid, stable, well-run democratic society do we have the luxury to consider such matters.

This seems to be a time to choose our values all over again. Call me an English professor, but this could be the moment to admire our connection to British culture and to remind ourselves of the ways in which we are like the English and not like the French. There are few more inspiring spectacles than the bloodless change from the rule of the privileged few to the rule of the people in nineteenth- and early-twentieth-century Britain. The French democratic revolution led to an attempt at world conquest and the self-installation of a dictator, Napoleon, whose own *carrière ouverte aux talents* became the inherited privilege of his children. And, incidentally, the French did not give women the vote until after World War II.

Democracy is not one instance of "majority rules," but incremental, consensual political change over time. The really important principle is time. One free election, one moment of popular sentiment prevailing, is not enough. Too often the prevailing inclination is to install a new kind of absolutism. Things change, and should. Any attempt to stop the clock leads to a kind of slavery. No party's members should stay in office so long that they forget what it's like to be out of office. They should govern as though they will be powerless tomorrow, making no enemies and preparing for their own futures. You can never reach a Final Solution. If you wipe out your enemies today, they will still come back and get you. To remind ourselves of time and of our Anglo-

American commitment to evolution, the great truth of Victorian culture, is my purpose in suggesting the embedding of Trollope.

I have more than my share of wonderful things from France in my life because my husband is French, and I do not intend, from loony consumerist patriotism, to dump my Beaujolais-Villages and L'Air du Temps or swear off Hermès scarves. These are things France does well. Why not make use of them? But I've been waiting twenty-five years to see the two Jacques, Lacan and Derrida, put back on the shelves, and to see people take down and brush off sensible, public-spirited, humorous, laconic, pragmatic British culture. If, in our current alliance with the British, we seem like a married couple in which the man has all the power and the woman has all the brains, we should all the more value the culture, the intelligence, the articulateness, and the humane values of the woman.

Courtney C. Berger (essay date autumn 2003)

SOURCE: Berger, Courtney C. "Partying with the Opposition: Social Politics in *The Prime Minister.*" *TSLL: Texas Studies in Literature and Language* 45, no. 3 (autumn 2003): 315-36.

[*In the following essay, Berger surveys the dissolution of boundaries between society and politics in Trollope's novel* The Prime Minister. *Berger appraises Trollope belief that a blending of the social realm and the political order was responsible for a loss of individual identity in society.*]

The critical reviews of Anthony Trollope's 1876 novel **The Prime Minister** resound with a single complaint. Trollope's characters have descended into the netherworld of "vulgarity." The reviewer for the *Spectator,* for example, sees in Trollope's story "the disposition to attribute to the majority of mankind an inherent vulgarity of thought."[1] Even previously dignified and aristocratic characters, such as Plantagenet Palliser (now the Duke of Omnium), have been dragged through the mud and made to seem like common people. The reviewer, however, saves her most severe censure for Glencora, Palliser's wife, noting that "She descends . . . to an impossible degree, and perspires with effort in the vulgar crowd till she is utterly unrecognizable."[2] The charge of vulgarity is not limited to the actions of the characters but applies equally to the aesthetic experience of reading the novel, as the *Saturday Review* notes: "To whatever part of the story he may turn, the reader of the **Prime Minister** is unable to escape the all-pervading sense of artistic vulgarity."[3]

Vulgarity, however, is not just an aesthetic problem *with* the novel; it proves to be a problem *within* the novel as well. Here the reviewers seem to be taking their cues from Palliser, who charges his wife with this very sin. Seeing the expensive changes that Glencora has made to their estate, Palliser deems the effort vulgar. Glencora, feeling the sting of this condemnation, thinks, "Vulgarity! There was no other word in the language so hard to bear as that."[4] For Palliser, vulgarity results from the assumption that money alone represents class. When he sees his redecorated home, with its useless porticos and its carefully designed archery field, he balks at the ostentatious "display." In Palliser's opinion, the flag announcing his arrival is the proper, dignified demonstration of his class position. Ducal flags cannot be purchased, while the "assumed and preposterous grandeur" of his altered home is "as much within the reach of some rich swindler or of some prosperous haberdasher as himself" (I, 175). This, for Palliser, is the root of vulgarity: the accessibility of aristocratic privileges to people who have no need to regard them as a duty.

Glencora, unlike her husband, cares little for the pomp of aristocratic tradition. She is concerned instead with providing the type of hospitality she thinks befits a Duke and which she believes will sustain her husband's new position as Prime Minister of the Coalition government. Glencora sees herself as *investing in* her husband's political position by way of her financial and social stature. For her, a bit of vulgarity is all part of the political game: she must placate and pander to innumerable ministers and politicos, each expecting aristocratic treatment. Her hospitality, then, stems from the opinion that socializing, not politicizing, will provide cohesion to the otherwise fractious Coalition government. She sees, as Palliser grudgingly acknowledges at one point, that "a ministry could best be kept together, not by parliamentary capacity, but by social arrangements, such as his Duchess, and his Duchess alone, could carry out" (I, 162).

Despite the moderate success of Glencora's political endeavors, by the end of the novel she finds herself repenting her behavior. The novel as a whole in fact rejects the very vulgarity it is charged with producing. What, then, we might ask, provoked critics to claim Trollope had committed such a moral and aesthetic breach of conduct? From Palliser's comments, it would seem that vulgarity is entirely an issue of economic class. Here, vulgarity suggests a lack of that ineffable something that constitutes aristocracy: culture, tradition, distinction. The word "vulgar," however, has another sense equally important to Trollope's literary reputation; it means simply "common," the everyday condition of ordinary people. The line between "vulgarity" and "commonness" is, in fact, quite thin. To be "common" suggests a likeness with others and an indistinguishability from the mass. It is this tendency towards commonness, as it turns out, that is for reviewers the most problematic aspect of Trollope's characters in this novel. Glencora "perspires with effort" thereby making herself "unrecognizable." Palliser is "vulgar in his unreasoning and exaggerated dread."[5] Ferdinand Lopez, the novel's antagonist and most blatantly vulgar character, is "a mere rogue, and a rogue of the most ordinary and feeble type," made vulgar not by audacious crimes but rather by the fact that he is a "cad."[6] In these examples, we see neither charges of personal ostentation nor of economic crudeness; rather, the reviewers suggest that the characters' manners and actions render them unexceptional or unworthy of the reader's attention.

What makes the reviewers' charges of vulgarity particularly striking is that ordinariness has generally been regarded as a positive quality in Trollope's novels. The critical heritage tends to highlight the "commonness" of his plots and characters. He gives extraordinary snapshots of completely banal events. He chronicles. He compiles. He sorts through the details of Victorian life. He is, in fact, the master of tedium. For the most part, Trollope's ordinariness does not translate into vulgarity. For example, in 1859, when Trollope was ascending the ladder of popular novelists, E. S. Dallas praised Trollope's status as "the most fertile, the most popular, the most successful author—that is to say, of the circulating library sort."[7] This qualification, "of the circulating library sort," marks Trollope not as a great artist but rather as a literary and economic success. The comment is not, however, condemnatory. That is, success amongst the crowd that subscribes to Mudie's circulating library is not "vulgar," it is simply "popular" or "general."

This strain of criticism, touting Trollope as the master of the mundane, has persisted. The common or ordinary, for most critics, is Trollope's most potent weapon as well as the tool of his trade. Moreover, the banal aspects of Trollope's novels have generally been regarded as the foundation of his moral and ethical claims—what critics have alternately referred to as tolerance, relativism, pluralism, or liberalism. Ruth apRoberts, in one of the most influential statements on Trollope's moral vision, praises his attention to the minute circumstances and details of events, claiming that this nonmetaphoric, anti-philosophical style constitutes a "casuistic," and therefore tolerant, approach to morality.[8] D. A. Miller, with a much more suspicious eye to Trollope's intentions and effects, agrees that Trollope's "boring" novels instantiate a type of pervasive tolerance, though he regards that tolerance as ultimately reinforcing a decidedly bourgeois form of "self-policing."[9] Whether regarded as happily liberal or disarmingly oppressive, however, according to the bulk of his critics, Trollope produces his middle-class morals through commonplace plots and events.[10]

If vulgarity is in part a product of both social and economic commonness, then *The Prime Minister* must be doing something different from the majority of Trollope's other uncontroversially common novels. What precisely causes commonness to lose its appealing quality and slide into vulgarity? The difference, I will argue, lies in the novel's representation of the relationship between political and social order, and more specifically, in the tendency for the two realms to become interchangeable, for politics to become subject to social rule. The eradication of formal distinctions both within the political arena as well as separating politics from the social world precipitates a crisis of identity within the novel. It is under the guise of political "unification" that this threat most forcefully emerges. A Coalition government, we learn at the novel's outset, is in the process of being formed, because neither the Liberal nor the Conservative party can muster the support necessary to form a Government of its own. In this case, coalition is made possible not out of any sense of agreement or harmony between the two groups, but rather from a lack of any sharp disagreement. In hopes that a temporary political hiatus would revive party division, the party heads ask Palliser to be Prime Minister, expecting that his social rank would lull members into momentary complacency. Thus, from the beginning of the story, a strange collapsing of boundaries has taken place. Otherwise divided parties have mingled, and otherwise separate spheres, such as economics and politics, have become indistinguishable.

It is the disintegration of the boundaries that separate and define people against one another, politically, but also socially and individually, that Trollope identifies as the most worrisome aspect of "the way we live now." Although it is tempting to read Trollope's concern with "order" as simply retrograde or traditionalist, the protection of an existing social hierarchy is not the novel's primary concern. Instead, it is a desire to sustain political differences, and by extension distinctions between individuals, that most crucially informs the novel's interest in a world structured by oppositions. For Trollope, political structure (in this case, the two-party, bicameral system) is not simply a comforting fiction allowing for the division of people into "us and them"; it also provides a platform upon which all other distinctions (social, economic, gender, national, religious) can be constructed. In particular, Trollope sees political division as highlighting the forms of belief and conviction that give order to social relations. The emergence of a new "social" realm, one able to contain all of those distinctions that once rendered the world partite and knowable, however, makes this political realm, as Trollope sees it, basically inert. In *The Prime Minister* the world-at-large encroaches on the previously protected political world, subjecting it to social rule. But, as Trollope demonstrates in the novel, this annexation of politics by the social world also threatens to undermine the very forms of individual identity which in fact sustain social order.

* * *

I want to pause here in order to set out more clearly what I see as Trollope's claim for a particularized politics that stands apart from the social realm. First, I should clarify the various definitions of "social" that I am deploying in this essay. Certainly the most obvious manifestation of society within Trollope is that of "high society." The novel, in fact, opens with just such a distinction when it introduces Ferdinand Lopez, generally assumed to be foreign and suspected to be of Jewish extraction. As Lopez makes his first foray into the inner circles of London social life, his conspicuous lack of ancestry marks him as suspicious. The narrator comments: "It is certainly of service to a man to know who were his grandfathers and who were his grandmothers if he entertain an ambition to move in the upper circles of society, and also of service to be able to speak of them as of persons who were themselves somebodies in their time" (I, 1). Society, in this form, is identified both with aristocracy and nationality. Not only does Lopez have no past, but any past he might have is vaguely non-English. Lacking a history, Lopez is unfit for high society, precisely because it is not apparent *where* he fits in genealogically.

Although this elitist notion of society certainly informs Trollope's world vision, in **The Prime Minister** disruptions in social class are of secondary concern. Trollope never abandons his conservative notion of social distinction. For example, the question of Lopez's suitability for Emily Wharton hinges upon his lack of pedigree. Yet, unlike the majority of Trollope's novels, **The Prime Minister** raises the more abstract question of how differences, both social and political, are essential mechanisms for the creation of individual identity. That is, in this novel, a broader and more all-encompassing version of the social—of which high society is only an expression—intrudes upon the novel's depiction of political order: that is, the social as the ordinary existence of human beings. Rather than being a catch-all category (that is, the boring or quotidian aspects of life brought together), this version of the social signifies the diffuse set of practices, institutions, and interpersonal relations which do not depend upon political association, but rather seem to exist prior to politics.[11] Although this definition of the social is not the same as vulgarity, for Trollope the two concepts do overlap. Vulgarity denotes not just a class sensibility (or a lack thereof); it also suggests a lack of distinction between one group and another, and ultimately between one person and another. In Trollope's view, pervasive sociality untethered from political structure can have a similar effect, subjecting everyone to the same rules of interaction, thereby doing away with the differences that help to formulate morals in the first place.

In his distrust of a freestanding and self-sufficient sociality, Trollope was indeed swimming against the tide of mid-Victorian social theory. For authors such as George Eliot, Herbert Spencer, and Charles Dickens, the notion that social relations could supplant political ones was quite appealing, and the realist novel was a primary site for demonstrating the full measure of the social world. Eliot, for instance, demonstrates quite vividly in her early novels (such as *Adam Bede* and *Silas Marner*) that the customs and beliefs which bind a community together bear more weight in the dispensation of justice, in distinguishing a "good" action from a "bad" one, than do any available legal apparatus; likewise, Dickens, in a much more cynical fashion, regards those same legal operations as not just cumbersome but lethal (for example, Roger Carstone's death in *Bleak House*). Spencer most fully expresses this view when he argues that the social body is constantly striving towards organic perfection, consisting of a free association of individuals, each accountable for him or herself. Government, for Spencer, serves only as a temporary measure until the "voluntary exertion" of individuals is fully realized.[12] Although the type of privileging of social relations I am attributing to both the realist novel and social theory was not the only working notion of the social in mid-century (Mill, for instance, was adamant about the place of politics in society), it was certainly becoming the predominant "liberal" version of how communities are formed, as well as how morals are transmitted from generation to generation, from person to person.

How and why, we might then ask, does Trollope regard the political realm as something that both exceeds and informs the "ordinary" aspects of social interaction? Why, in the face of arguments that social relations could do all of the work of politics without its more obvious forms, does Trollope insist that politics is absolutely essential to the social as we know it? First, while social distinctions are minute and subject to constant alteration (through marriage, newly given titles, and financial influence), political differences are rigid and enduring. The two-party system leaves little room for alternative positions. Within the Trollopean world of Parliamentary politics, members either fall with the party or they are banished from it. Although differences and quarrels may arise within the party, ultimately, the party stands as a whole; fracture brings about a loss of confidence and, in turn, the rise of the opposing party. Moreover, the formal rigidity of division is paramount for Trollope's notion of politics, because it embodies the principles of disagreement and difference that impel action and commitment. Partisanship not only requires that the individual member endorse one position, but also that he place himself in opposition to others. Within partisan politics, however, the acceptance and dismissal of positions is not infinite; for it to be so would damage the efficacy of government, making debates and decisions impossibly complex. In other words, politics cannot function along the lines of social differentiation. The process of distinguishing infinitely amongst individuals on a social level—manifest in the saying that one could arrange all of England in a single file line, according to each person's place within society—would only confound the political system. Politics, for Trollope, formalizes conviction through the open endorsement of positions, thereby demonstrating its necessity to both social cohesion and individual identity.

Coalition, because it collapses the relevant differences between two parties, tends to make politics look more like the diverse world of social interaction. The novel's greatest critic of this disintegration of political boundaries is in fact the Coalition's leader. Palliser advocates a "pure" politics that is informed by partisanship and ideas, not the social and economic concerns of its participants. Indeed, Palliser is so committed to "non-social" politics that he even regrets his ascent to Dukedom, because it bars him from sitting in the House of Commons. Title, wealth, social stature, all seem immaterial in the face of political duty. Though Palliser's "idealism" is characterized by many of his political cohorts as either naïveté or an utter lack of pragmatism, Palliser is quite literally committed to a politics of *ideas*. For him, ideas, not people, should drive political agendas. This form of impersonal politics derives from his belief that decisions pertaining to the English people as a whole cannot be directed by personal likes or dislikes, nor by the vagaries of a politician's personality, but rather must be the product of a conscious subscription to a set of principles informing political action.

In one respect, political impersonality is simply a form of professional demeanor.[13] The proper administration of law requires a cultivated detachment from one's personal views and opinions. Yet, in seeming contradiction, personal opinion and conviction are in fact central to Palliser's notion of political idealism, producing a curious interdependence of personal and impersonal belief. Impersonality is characterized by a commitment to an abstract whole, epitomized in Palliser's assertion that, "'I don't want a man to stick to me. I want a man to stick to his country'" (I, 55). Yet, for him, this impersonal attitude is only valid when underwritten by personal conviction. Lecturing his friend Phineas Finn, Palliser states: "'You should first know what Liberalism means, and then assure yourself that the thing itself is good'" (II, 262). Assuring the rightness of a position allows for whole-hearted advocacy, which means that an unselfish and idea-driven politics relies first on the personal convictions of its participants.[14]

Personal belief, however, is itself circumscribed by a preexisting set of options. In Trollope's parliamentary world, political beliefs, as genuinely felt as they may be, are dependent upon political parties. Convention, thus, dictates the possible forms of "personal" belief. Conservative or Liberal, Whig or Tory: These traditional divisions give shape to political debate through

opposition; but, also, by allying themselves with others, politicians are freed to act objectively for the nation based on their initial advocacy of a party. Palliser, in his final instructions to Finn, espouses this dual need for a conventional separation of parties along with a personally felt adoption of a political position. He says:

> It seems to me that many men . . . embrace the profession of politics not only without political convictions, but without seeing that it is proper that they should entertain them. Chance brings a young man under the guidance of this or that elder man. He has come from a Whig family as was my case,—or from some old Tory stock; and—loyalty keeps him true to the interests which have first pushed him forward into the world. There is no conviction there.
>
> (II, 261)

While the stage may already be set—parties, houses, policies alter only infrequently—individual advocacy of the ideas is no less a necessary ingredient for "pure" politics. Palliser does not deny the force of tradition; he knows that within his own family, "the political creed was fixed as adamant" (II, 262). And, yet, while tradition certainly informs belief, it cannot replace the decision to endorse that belief. Thus, Palliser resents the all-too-true implication that his appointment as Prime Minister pertains more to his social attributes as a person than to his ability to best represent the Liberal perspective.

Trollope is quick to reveal the limitations of Palliser's "ideal" and impersonal politics. Palliser soon finds that his refusal to foster a "community of feeling" within his Cabinet undermines any political agenda he may have (56). Moreover, his peculiar sense of political impersonality causes him to be excessively sensitive to other people's criticism of what Palliser regards as his "personal" behavior. In his **Autobiography,** composed around the time of **The Prime Minister**'s publication, Trollope claims that "To rid oneself of fine scruples, to fall into the tradition of the party, [. . .] to be able to be a bit, and at first only a very little bit,—these are the necessities of the growing Statesman."[15] Palliser, Trollope admits, was an attempt to show how the politician who combines an "inexhaustible love of country" with uncomplicated scrupulousness would ultimately fail. Despite the fact that Palliser's idealism is ineffectual, Trollope does continue to hope for that "glorious time" in which Palliser's brand of politics may in fact prevail.[16]

Palliser's lack of success as a statesman is not simply the result of inadequate charisma, though; it derives equally from the equivocal nature of coalition. Palliser's impersonal and combative politics depends upon the structural division of partisanship.[17] By doing away with any clear-cut opposition, in Palliser's view, Coalition eliminates politics itself. The unity of opposing parties breeds stagnation, leaving Palliser unable to produce a meaningful policy. He is instead simply a "stopgap," a "nominal Prime Minister," and a "gilded treasury log" (II, 308; I, 162). During the tenure of the Coalition Ministry, almost no law is passed and no larger plan of action is ever executed. "Thus it came to pass that the only real measure which the Government had in hand was one by Phineas Finn. . . . It was not a great measure, and poor Phineas himself hardly believed in it." (I, 346). The minor quality of Phineas's measure seems irrelevant in comparison to the fact that "poor Phineas himself hardly believed in it."[18] For Trollope, it is this lack of conviction, not just the lack of action, engendered by Coalition that truly marks its inadequacy as a political system. Belief, either in the form of conscientious decision-making or political conviction, coupled with debate and conflict, underwrite democratic politics for Trollope. Together they allow individuals to demonstrate their commitments while formalizing those commitments within a larger framework. Partisanship, thus, stands for more than the visible division of political parties; it plays a crucial role in the expression and affirmation of personal belief. Taking a political stance gives the individual a more pressing sense of what it means to endorse a position, and in effect, reminds individuals of the need to debate their positions conscientiously.

The uneasy unity forced by the Coalition eliminates the need for distinct positions, in turn making social negotiation, not debate, the new hallmark of political struggle. Members begin to vie for seats at dinner parties rather than seats in Government. Moreover, it is Palliser's wife, *not* his Parliamentary colleagues, who most vehemently takes up the form of "social" politics to which Palliser so strenuously objects. Unlike her husband, who compartmentalizes his political and social duties, Glencora regards the two as identical. First learning of her husband's appointment, Glencora determines it necessary to install a Cabinet of her own. She duly appoints her friend Marie Finn as Minister of Foreign Affairs. Then, with characteristic majesty, Glencora announces: "And I mean to be my own home secretary, and to keep my own conscience,—and to be my own master of ceremonies certainly. I think a small cabinet gets on best. Do you know,—I should like to put the Queen down" (I, 54). Glencora's decision to adopt her own "home rule" is comic yet meaningful. She wants to make her husband and herself the most popular, and therefore the most powerful, people in England. Furthermore, she believes that through such popularity, the Coalition government will prosper.

Glencora insists that social and political work naturally "go together," declaring that: "'Popularity is the staff on which alone Ministers can lean in this country with security'" (I, 105). This assessment of the modern political scene—what matters is who you are not what you think—directly contradicts Palliser's "ideal" politics. Whereas Glencora believes in the power of the individual person, in charisma, in the social world as an expanded version of the political one, her husband insists on the sanctity and separateness of political work, of its necessary isolation from the social world. Policy is meaningless, Glencora realizes, but social power can successfully sustain the Coalition. Palliser later acknowledges the inherently social qualities of coalition, ceding that his wife "with her dinner parties and receptions, with her crowded saloons, her music, her picnics, and social temptations, was the Prime Minister rather than himself" (I, 161).

Glencora's attempts to make the social and political worlds coincide is regarded by characters such as Phineas Finn as an atavistic gesture. Phineas tells his wife: "'the time has gone by for what one might call drawing-room influences'" (I, 265). In ***Phineas Redux,*** of course, Finn actually benefits from this type of influence, when Glencora and her female allies rally to have Finn recognized as a political player. While his circumstances certainly belie the statement, there is a truth in Finn's claim. The "drawing-room influences" he imagines suggest a type of courtly existence, where only the privileged few can gain audience with the monarch. While Glencora is certainly not beyond contemplating her power as sovereign (she does, admittedly, want to supplant the Queen as the central power of England), her approach to social politics tends to err on the side of inclusiveness rather than exclusiveness. She is actually a bit more "democratic" than her Parliamentary counterparts, quickly recognizing the benefit of soliciting everyone and anyone's help in her schemes and power plays. Glencora's ability to produce ad hoc alliances testifies to her political, as well as her social, savvy. She imagines her role in party politics to be one of coalescing power: "She was always making up the party,—meaning the coalition,—doing something to strengthen the buttresses, writing little letters to little people, who, little as they were, might become big by amalgamation" (I, 247). That is, Glencora functions somewhat like a democratic party machine, attempting to gather strength from the bottom up through favors and social attention. For her, rarified politics, composed of blue books and Cabinet meetings, is a luxury that can only be indulged in after the work of popularity has been achieved.

The "socializing" of politics evident in Glencora's attempts at popularity are reiterated in the novel's numerous descriptions of Coalition as akin to the world of commerce. At one point, hoping to ease Palliser's overwrought sense of duty, the Duke of St. Bungay, the Prime Minister's friend and mentor, suggests: "Think about your business as a shoemaker thinks of his. Do your best, and then let your customers judge for themselves. Caveat emptor" (I, 252). Needless to say, this piece of advice does little to placate Palliser, who regards this consumeristic philosophy as anathema to his belief that the politician has a duty to his public, not the other way around. To let others determine the rightness of one's actions is to discard the forms of conviction which underwrite the political system.

Without the internal sustenance of division which provides authority and creativity to Parliamentary politics, in Trollope's opinion, coalition devolves into simply being serviceable and, therefore, commercial.[19] As one politician comments: "'Everything must be dead when men holding different opinions on every subject under the sun come together in order that they may carry on a government as they would a trade business. The work may be done, but it must be done without spirit'" (II, 2). As a type of "trade," politics not only loses the "ideal" quality attributed to it by Palliser, it also begins to resemble a bureaucracy, where accountability as well as belief or commitment are thoroughly unnecessary to the smooth functioning of the system. To imagine Parliament as a form of bureaucracy suggests that it no longer matters what you think *or* who you are, only that you fill the appropriate space.

In aligning bureaucracy with commercialism, I am not suggesting that Trollope completely rejected either; he was, of course, famously bureaucratic both in his career as a civil servant and in his attitude towards writing.[20] He was, however, ambivalent about the interplay between efficient government and pure politics, concerned about how far the mechanisms of profit and efficiency could be allowed to infiltrate politics before jeopardizing its protected status as an arena for ideas.[21] By resisting the encroachment of commercial and social relations on the institution of politics, Trollope not only protects politics, but also guards against the potential social costs of a bureaucratic world where accountability and sincerity are irrelevant. The installation of a politics based on profit and popularity rather than duty and commitment would, according to Trollope, reverberate throughout the social body, taking its toll on all forms of identity and alliance.

It is in the character of Ferdinand Lopez that Trollope most thoroughly dramatizes the dangerous outcome of a nonpartisan world. More importantly, however, through Lopez Trollope demonstrates the ways in which partisanship helps to shape the world beyond politics. Of course, within the social arena partisanship does not follow the formalized and polarized structure of parliamentary politics; yet, the principles of personal conviction and belief underwriting politics also help form the groundwork for social and individual identity. The process of "taking a part" which animates Palliser's politics is treated with utter contempt by Lopez, who is the quintessential nonpartisan. Instead of subscribing to any particular custom or belief system, Lopez camouflages himself with the ideas and traditions of the people who

surround him. This ability to blend into any social environment is reinforced by Lopez's seeming lack of history, which renders him an autonomous and contained character who is difficult to comprehend because he is both unpredictable and uncategorizable. Because Lopez never discusses his past, his friend Everett Wharton imagines that he was born "self-sufficient," without the parentage that decides the social status of other people (I, 13). Lopez echoes the mystery surrounding his past when he describes himself as a sort of historical blank, saying in response to inquiries about his life, "But there is nothing to be known" (I, 126).[22] Lopez's attitude towards his past and his identity reflects a lack of concern with the rules and traditions which, Trollope believes, provide individuals with a sense of social belonging. Without any meaningful association, Lopez freefloats through London society, mimicking to advantage the ideas and beliefs of those surrounding him, but never adopting them as truth.

The rootlessness associated with Lopez's heritage is redoubled in his treatment of the political and commercial spheres. Here, Lopez's characteristics begin to echo the political situation that provides the backdrop for his story. His mutability fits perfectly into the goals and strategies of the Coalition government. When considering the possibility of running for Parliament, for instance, Lopez muses: "'And why shouldn't I support this party,—or that?'" (I, 205). Lopez's aspiration for a political career, we quickly learn, arises from his belief that the position will translate into social and financial success. A political career "assists a man in getting a seat as the director of certain companies. People are still such asses that they trust a Board of Directors made up of Members of Parliament" (I, 12). For Lopez, politics becomes a stepping stone towards commercial success, not the other way around. Rather than buying his way into politics (as Melmotte does in *The Way We Live Now*), he expects politics to endow him with a legitimate social identity that will strengthen his business. Although Lopez does not prosper in his financial speculations, his ability to habituate himself effortlessly with his surroundings makes him peculiarly effective for a short while. His willingness to endorse any advantageous position means that Lopez, like the Coalition, melds political and commercial strategies. Coupled with a "power of creating belief" in others, Lopez's lack of partisanship gives him exactly the qualities needed for uniting the Coalition which Palliser so notably lacks (I, 40).

Lopez's strength lies in making others believe in his self-representations (a literal "confidence man"), not from telling lies (until the end of the novel, he scrupulously refrains from outright fraud) but from simply appearing to be something. The ability to seem like a gentleman, for Lopez, serves as well as actually being one. To cultivate a genuine or sincere relationship to one's identity, such as Palliser does with his Whig heritage, would be burdensome to Lopez, who believes that the trappings of sincerity would only harness him to an unprofitable position. This commitment to "representation" not "reality" (I use the term loosely here) characterizes Lopez's entire attitude towards the world, and in particular, his view of commodity speculation. Here, Lopez seeks to shrug off the material world and to live by representation alone. The narrator half jokes: "Coffee and guano still had to be bought because the world was dull and would not learn the tricks of trade as taught by Ferdinand Lopez,—also possibly because somebody might want such articles, but our enterprising hero looked for a time in which no such dull burden should be imposed on him" (II, 31). A world based solely on representation—where a company's prospectuses refer not to some material result but are ends unto themselves—is the logical outcome of commodity speculation and the trade in "futures." Most strikingly, though, Lopez's commercial philosophy posits a form of "ideal" relations between participants; individuals commit to a scheme, win or lose, then continue to play the game with no material manifestation of the struggle. They also commit to what seems like the most profitable or the soundest idea, regardless of its execution. All in all, this strikes close to the heart of Palliser's "ideal" politics. Of course, Palliser would insist on the impact of politics on the "material" world of England; the politician's "duty" towards his country serves as a reminder that Parliamentary actions exert influence on the nation. Political duty for Trollope is not about self-interest; the politician adopts a disinterested attitude towards the moral decisions he makes for the country. Yet, disinterest, or a cultivated detachment from the effects of an action or policy, exists within the same spectrum as the *un*-attached comportment of Lopez; Lopez is, in some regards, simply a less evolved version of Palliser.

The proximity of this "ideal" (as opposed to "material") commercialism to "ideal" (as opposed to "personal") politics becomes a source of consternation for Trollope, because both speculation and democratic politics rely upon the same tool: representation. The elected politician stands in for the interests of the country or the constituency; similarly, shares are like financial votes of confidence for a company who acts in the interest of its own and thus its investors' profit. The basis for representation, of course, differs. Trollope's concept of political partisanship relies on the sincerity of its participants. The politician enlists to represent the interests of others and not his own personal concerns. Voters choose the candidate who best reflects their interests and those of the country. In finance, on the other hand, sincerity is beside the point. The investor expects the company to seek profit, not out of concern for the investors but out of self-interest. Because sincerity is a difficult sentiment to gauge, however, political representation seems as

though it could almost without detection slide into a mode of commercial representation. For Trollope the susceptibility of the political system to commercial tactics can be combated, but never entirely ensured, by the techniques of openness and self-declaration that underwrite Trollope's notion of Parliamentary politics.

Although Lopez's adeptness at feigning interest in others and their beliefs underscores the vulnerability of personal commitment, Trollope insists on its necessity, within both the political and social arenas. Trollope advocates sincerity; he wants individuals to *feel* their positions to be the correct ones. The real work of partisanship, however, does not lie in the unequivocal rightness of any one stance. Rather, it is through the experience of *bias* that individuals begin to experience themselves as coherent, and thus knowable, human beings. Lopez's complete detachment from belief extends beyond mere opportunism; he simply has no foundational beliefs. He neither identifies with any group, nor does he see himself as beholden to any tradition. For Trollope, this detachment promotes a form of relativism that undermines the ties that bind groups together, both morally and socially. In refusing traditions and beliefs, then, Lopez rejects any identification with other people, making him seem to be "'bound by none of the ordinary rules of mankind'" (II, 184). The character John Fletcher fully articulates the dangers of Lopez's autonomy when he says: "'He isn't of our sort. He's too clever, too cosmopolitan,—a sort of man whitewashed of all prejudices, who wouldn't mind whether he ate horseflesh or beef if horseflesh were as good as beef, and never had an association in his life. I'm not sure that he's not on the safest side'" (I, 152). Being "whitewashed of prejudice" translates into refusing not just morals, but also the coherency which a moral position lends to a group of people.[23] Superficial beliefs cause division, but they also remind individuals of their position in the world. While John Fletcher jokingly asserts that Lopez is "on the safest side," it becomes increasingly apparent throughout the novel that Lopez's refusal to take sides is in fact a dangerous ploy.

The novel's tacit rejection of Lopez's cosmopolitanism raises questions about the credo of tolerance which many critics, including Ruth apRoberts and David Miller, attribute to Trollope. If Trollope advocates the "tolerant appreciation" of other people's views, how do we read this obviously derogatory comment about Lopez's ability to adapt to anything?[24] In one respect, Lopez's chameleon-like impersonality has little to do with tolerance; he is so devoid of any belief of his own that it would be impossible for him to comprehend the merits of tolerating or appreciating the beliefs of others. John Fletcher sees the advantage of such a non-position; Lopez can without moral qualms accustom himself to any setting. But this indifference towards other people's mores and conventions hardly qualifies as tolerance. As a liberal virtue, tolerance does not require that people alter their views when confronted with differences but rather that they acknowledge the plausibility of other beliefs. In order to be tolerant, one must be aware of the means by which beliefs are acquired: through heredity, social context, and personal conviction. Like Palliser's assertion that he both accepts his tradition and feels it to be right, the doctrine of tolerance acknowledges that others have different traditions and different notions of rightness.

Lopez's brand of cosmopolitanism amounts to the simple rejection of belief as meaningful outside of its immediate context. He is in this respect an extreme relativist: all customs and cultures are equally good. But his relativism arises from a sense of its usefulness, not its morality, thereby distinguishing it from true tolerance. What complements tolerance in Trollope's novels is not permissiveness but rather partisanship or, in John Fletcher's terms, "prejudice." Here, I am disputing apRoberts's claim that Trollope's notion of moral tolerance is in fact "non-partisan" and "cosmopolitan." Her argument depends upon a notion of tolerance as the endless acceptance of differences between people and as the non-systematic negotiation of moral questions. In the case of a doctrine of extreme relativism, tolerance liberates individuals from belief and dogma and allows them to form moral judgments on a case-by-case basis. This form of relativism, apRoberts suggests, enables people to assume a universal perspective and thus universal tolerance.[25]

Ruth apRoberts argues that belief obstructs moral universalism, because it disbars them from being "multiperspectival."[26] Tolerance as I have defined it, though, exists quite comfortably alongside partisanship. People do not relinquish their beliefs simply because they accept the existence of other points of view. Rather, Trollope regards bias and tolerance to be of a piece. Cosmopolitanism, in the form given to it by Lopez, discards both, leaving the individual to aimlessly acquire and toss aside moral positions.[27] Parliamentary government proves to be the best example of the dynamic produced by bias and tolerance. An insurmountable difference in perspective energizes politics, and the goal of one party is not to eradicate the other position but to challenge it. Political parties must accept the plausibility of an opposing position while advocating the moral correctness of their own. Glencora taps into this double bind when she claims: "Anything is constitutional, or anything is unconstitutional, just as you choose to look at it" (I, 251). While this comment alarms Palliser, because Glencora advocates using it opportunistically, it is also an accurate reflection of how two different parties would regard constitutionality. Both groups believe that they adhere to the true meaning of the law; likewise, each accepts that the opposition holds the same conviction.

Political bipartisanship, as I argued earlier, anchors its participants by radically circumscribing the range of positions available. The rigidity of the system ensures the ability to act, because it is driven by dissent and decision and spurred by polarized conflict rather than by the dispersed energies of myriad, endlessly differentiated moments of disagreement. The protection of this highly structured political realm is important to Trollope not just because it is traditional (although that matters), but because it lends coherency to the nation. The social world, on the other hand, functions adequately without the rigid form of politics; its goals and needs are much more varied than those of politics and, therefore, so are its strategies. Partisanship, however, still plays an important role in the social world. As Lopez's refusal to accept a position demonstrates, Trollope's notion of social cohesion also relies on people "taking a part" or identifying themselves with a set of beliefs.

Furthermore, for Trollope, social identity inscribes individual identity. Not simply a matter of outwardly perceived and visible differences between people, social identity requires a reflective relationship between people and their various (given or self-nominated) identities. It matters how people relate to their own social class, gender, parentage, as much as it matters how others perceive them. When Lopez tells people that "there is nothing to be known" about his past, he both shields himself from social judgment *and* refuses to cultivate any personal relationship to his social identity (126). The only thing worse than having a disreputable past, according to Trollope, is to deny that past. The historical self must then form the basis of one's present self to be considered "genuine." Take, for instance, Glencora's assertion: "I am Duchess of Omnium, and I am the wife of the Prime Minister . . . and I am myself too,—Glencora M'Cluskie that was, and I've made for myself a character that I'm not ashamed of" (I, 350). Glencora envisions herself not as a single entity, but as a proliferation of selves, all of whom have meaning and purchase in the world. The term into which Glencora folds all of this—"character"—denotes not just the attributes evident to the public but the ones that make her an identifiable and knowable entity to herself as well.

In the case of Lopez, this delicate construction of social and personal identity crumbles. And, in Lopez's spectacular death, he illustrates the lethality of refusing to attach himself to a particular belief or position. Although Lopez's blanket nonpartisanship initially provides him with the power to traverse London society and commerce, as his operations are discovered and his options for the future begin to dwindle, Lopez realizes that he will have to leave England and begin again. With no inherited belief to hang his hat on, no custom to retreat to, Lopez flounders. He chooses—and, given the equivocal quality of his action, this word might be too strong—suicide.

The very tenuous identity Lopez has maintained throughout the novel is thoroughly discarded at the end of his life. On the pretense of taking a business trip, Lopez arrives at Tenway Junction, a "bewildering" and "pandemoniac" place, where he casually walks in front of an oncoming train. The station's pundits attempt to stop him, but "Lopez heeded not the call, and the rush was too late. With quick, but still with gentle and apparently unhurried steps, he walked down before the flying engine—and in a moment had been knocked into bloody atoms" (II, 194). This is not just a pedestrian suicide; it is an absolute obliteration. In life Lopez refuses to identify himself; likewise, in death he is denuded of a recognizable self and transformed into undifferentiated "atoms." Even in the aftermath of Lopez's death, nothing remains which points to his earlier self.

> It seemed as though the man had been careful to carry with him no record of identity, the nature of which would permit it to outlive the crash of the train. No card was found, no scrap of paper with his name; and it was discovered that when he left the house on the fatal morning he had been careful to dress himself in shirt and socks, with handkerchief and collar that had been newly purchased for his proposed journey and which bore no mark. The fragments of his body set identity at defiance, and even his watch had been crumpled into ashes.
>
> (I, 195)

Lopez himself is partly responsible for this radical effacement. All the traditional marks of identity—a name, initials, tailor tags—are suspiciously missing from his body. Lopez thus ensures that he departs the novel as he entered it: as a "nobody."

The problems of identity and partisanship raised by Lopez in **The Prime Minister** are intrinsically linked with the concept of difference raised by Trollope's version of politics. Lopez's reduction to physical non-identity parallels Palliser's growing attachment to his political status and, thus, the collapsing of his personal and impersonal beliefs. Like his contemporary, George Eliot, Trollope sees the individual's identity as emerging from a process of self-reflection in conjunction with tradition. However, while Eliot sees social relations as sufficient basis for identity, Trollope insists upon the existence of a separate political realm where differences can be cultivated and, in turn, provide a foundation for social identity.[28] That is, for Trollope, social relations without political ones would devolve into a world full of Lopezes, unable to commit to a place in the world and unwilling to be identified with a group. In a way Lopez is a casualty of the momentary identification of the social and the political realms, as well as the temporary erasure of political differences, within the novel.[29] Trollope certainly rejects Lopez's attempts to "set identity at defiance" in the novel, but he also sees Lopez's actions as the logical outcome of a world where no credence is given to authenticity and sincerity.

The question of vulgarity, which I raised at the beginning of this article, has new resonance when considered as a problem of identification and difference. Let us return to the comment one reviewer made about Glencora: "She descends . . . to an impossible degree, and perspires with effort in the vulgar crowd till she is utterly unrecognizable." What the reviewer points to as the problem with the novel—readers can no longer distinguish characters they thought they knew—is in fact the problem Trollope attempts to confront in **The Prime Minister.** Trollope registers his concern that without a formal system of differentiation—such as that provided by bipartisanship—people will no longer be distinguishable from one another. Lopez's nonidentity, both in his self-representation and in his ultimate destruction, points to the dangers of putting aside the differences that help to distinguish people from one another. To give everyone an equal part in the system—breaking the world down into interchangeable "atoms"—threatens to destroy the very structure which ensures that individuals have agency and can recognize agency in others. Political structure as Trollope imagines it—partisan, hierarchical, ideal—reinforces difference through division and the cultivation of conviction. Without these political tools, Trollope asserts, social and personal identities fall into disarray. When the social world attempts to co-opt politics, it undermines the very basis of sociality itself.

Notes

1. [Meredith White Townsend], *Spectator* (22 July 1876), *Trollope: The Critical Heritage,* ed. Donald Smalley (London: Routledge & Kegan Paul, 1969), 419.

2. *Spectator,* 422.

3. Unsigned notice, *Saturday Review* (14 October 1876), *Trollope: The Critical Heritage,* 426.

4. Anthony Trollope, *The Prime Minister* [1876], (Oxford: Oxford University Press, 1983), 177. All further references will be made parenthetically within the text.

5. *Spectator,* 421.

6. *Spectator,* 420.

7. E. S. Dallas, *The Times* (23 May 1859), *Trollope: The Critical Heritage,* 104. By the time *The Prime Minister* appeared in serial form, Trollope was no longer the financial success he once had been. Trollope earned £2500 for the novel, but as he says in his *Autobiography,* "It was worse spoken

of by the press than any novel I had written." Anthony Trollope, *An Autobiography* [1883] (New York: Oxford University Press, 1990), 360fn.

8. Ruth apRoberts, *The Moral Trollope* (Athens: University of Ohio Press, 1971), 17, 39. For other examples of such criticism, see George Levine, *Darwin and the Novelists;* Jane Nardin, *Trollope and Victorian Moral Philosophy;* Robert Polhemus, *The Changing World of Anthony Trollope;* and Peter Garrett, *The Victorian Multiplot Novel.*

9. D. A. Miller, "The Novel as Usual: Trollope's *Barchester Towers," The Novel and the Police* (Berkeley: University of California Press, 1988). Miller claims that Trollope's notion of tolerance is intertwined with a form of normalization that produces in individuals a "consciousness of behavior," thereby allowing individuals to police themselves and their own behavior (133-37).

10. See, in particular, Laurie Langbauer's chapter on Trollope, "The Everyday is Everything," *Novels of Everyday Life: The Series in English Fiction, 1850-1930* (Ithaca: Cornell University Press, 1999).

11. This is what Ruth apRoberts refers to when she discusses Trollope's casuistic morals. In the social world, right and wrong are determined in an ad hoc manner; each case brings with it new circumstances and, thus, varying standards. While I agree with this aspect of apRoberts's argument, I do not think that it successfully accounts for Trollope's version of politics and political ethics.

12. See Herbert Spencer, "The Proper Sphere of Government" [1843] and "The Man *versus* The State" [1860], *Political Writings,* ed. John Offer (Cambridge: Cambridge University Press, 1994); see also, *Social Statics* [1855] (New York: Robert Schalkenbach Foundation, 1970). In *Social Statics,* Spencer argues that in its more "developed" forms, society begins to exceed the confines of government and to operate more in accord with the "natural" laws of social organization (14, passim).

13. Charles Dickens, in particular, depicted the positive and negative qualities of professional disinterestedness. Compare, for example, the figures of Tulkinghorn (lawyer) and Woodcourt (doctor) in *Bleak House* (1853). While Tulkinghorn's detached behavior leads to a monomaniacal drive towards omniscience, Woodcourt's benevolent professionalism results in success.

14. Palliser butts heads with his colleague Sir Orlando over just such a difference in unselfish advocacy. Glencora summarizes her husband's position as such: "It is not the opposition he hates, but the cause in the man's mind which may produce it. When Sir Orlando opposed him, and he thought that Sir Orlando's opposition was founded on jealousy, then he despised Sir Orlando. But had he believed in Sir Orlando's belief in the new ships, he would have been capable of pressing Sir Orlando to his bosom, although he might have been forced to oppose Sir Orlando's ships in the Cabinet" (II, 211).

15. Trollope, *An Autobiography,* 359.

16. Trollope was keenly interested in what made a successful statesman. As George Butte points out, Trollope's studies of Cicero and Caesar reflect his interest in the conflict between the power of the past and the need for reform. See George Butte, "Trollope's Duke of Omnium and 'The Pain of History': A Study in the Novelist's Politics," *Victorian Studies* 24 (1981): 209-27.

17. Trollope's belief in the "openness" of politics—debate waged publicly and without rancor—is likewise evident in his opposition to the secret ballot. For a short account of Trollope's opposition to the Ballot Act, see Victoria Glendenning, *Trollope* (London: Hutchinson, 1992), 390. See also Trollope's own discussion of it in his *Autobiography,* 302.

18. Phineas shows himself, in his two earlier eponymous novels, to be absolutely full of convictions. In *Phineas Finn* he refuses to support a party policy, and consequently leaves politics, because of his convictions. His return to politics, in *Phineas Redux,* is equally linked to conviction in the form of a debate over Church Disestablishment.

19. Government, understood in commercial terms, does not possess the same authority and autonomy that a company would have. Instead, it is the center of "capital," a conduit not a source of commercial power. Arthur, for instance, describes a Parliamentary bill in this way: "It is one of the instances of the omnipotence of capital. Parliament can do such a thing, not because it has any creative power of its own, but because it has the command of unlimited capital" (I, 341). Here, Arthur suggests that government is purely formal, a mechanism for distributing and guiding raw economic power.

20. In his *Autobiography,* for example, Trollope provides a table detailing the profits he received for his novels (363-64). He was also known for keeping account books for the number of words he wrote each day.

21. Trollope's uneasiness with seeing politics as a "service industry" places him in conflict with the political theorist with whom he is most often aligned, Walter Bagehot. Asa Briggs sees Trollope

and Bagehot as equally committed to retaining "[d]eference and dignity" as the "safeguards of parliamentary government." Asa Briggs, "Trollope, Bagehot, and the English Constitution," in *Victorian People: A Reassessment of Persons and Themes* (Chicago: University of Chicago Press, 1973), 89. Indeed, in his 1867 *English Constitution,* Bagehot sets forth his ideas on the interplay between paternalistic and dignified aspects of the monarchy and the more efficacious and powerful qualities of Parliament and the Cabinet system. But whereas Trollope wants always to maintain an openness in political structure, Bagehot applauds Cabinet government as the "efficient secret" of the English system. He consistently describes the Cabinet as a form of corporate rule that allows for the dissipation of individual responsibility as well as the obfuscation of the source of political authority. Bagehot remarks: "So well is our real government concealed, that if you tell a cabman to drive to 'Downing Street,' he most likely will never have heard of it, and will not in the least know where to take you. It is only a 'disguised republic' which is suited to such a being as the Englishman in such a century as the nineteenth." Walter Bagehot, *The English Constitution* [1867] (Ithaca: Cornell University Press, 1995), 266.

22. It is easy to read Lopez's character as evidence of Trollope's anti-Semitism. Admittedly, Trollope employs a stereotypical depiction of the Jew as money-lender and of doubtful moral character. I want to push this analysis a bit further, however, because I think that Trollope (like George Eliot) identifies Judaism with the issue of heritage and conviction. In *The Way We Live Now,* for example, while Melmotte, Cohenlupe, and the other Jewish financiers appear stereotypical, Breghert, who openly embraces his Jewish identity, seems admirable in his sincerity. The discrepancy in these characterizations, I think, at least suggests that Jewish identity was not a completely straightforward issue for Trollope.

23. Juliet McMaster provides a good account of how prejudice has been regarded as a positive quality, particularly as it functions politically. Using Edmund Burke's *Reflections* as an example, she argues that prejudice was regarded as allowing individuals to put feeling into action by making it an habitual response. *Trollope's Palliser Novels* (New York: Oxford University Press, 1978), 111.

24. D. A. Miller, *The Novel and the Police,* 133. Miller argues that Trollope's version of tolerance is simply the flip side of normalization. By instilling in individuals a consciousness of their own actions, both norms and tolerance set limits on acceptable behaviors (136). In contrast to Miller's assumption that the give-and-take between self-consciousness and behavior is a form of surveillance and thus oppression, I am suggesting that in a less pernicious way, Trollope sees the relationship between the two as rescuing individuals from a form of identificatory alienation.

25. apRoberts, *The Moral Trollope,* 188.

26. apRoberts, *The Moral Trollope,* 115. Here apRoberts claims that in *The Warden* Trollope defuses controversy through his ability to show multiple perspectives on the same dilemma. These varied perspectives are quite important to Trollope, as is the issue of conscience in the case of Mr. Harding and Palliser, but it is not clear that the acknowledgement of differences amounts to non-advocacy or the relinquishment of belief. Controversy, as Miller argues, forms an important part of Trollope's novels, and while Trollope depicts a multiplicity of perspectives, he nevertheless feels free to accept one as more acceptable.

27. Ruth apRoberts's claim that Trollope is antisystematic relies on the notion that because moral positions for Trollope are historically determined rather than universal or inevitable, there could be no externally imposed structure for morality. While the range and kind of positions available at any given time may change (for example, Whig and Tory to Liberal and Conservative), Trollope does not see structure as incompatible with tradition. Structure may be cultivated from tradition, but it can also be given systematic functions (such as bureaucracy). Bagehot argues as well that the machinery of English government is imperfect and has transformed over time, but this does not make it any less organized.

28. Politics is a mechanism for formalizing differences, but as Palliser points out after the Coalition has dissolved and the two-party system is restored, politics is also the site for debating the appropriate "differences" and "distance" that should be maintained between people. The Liberal, he tells Phineas Finn, strives to lessen the inequalities between people and encourages the "continual improvement of the lower man" (II, 264). The Conservative, on the other hand, works "'to maintain the differences and the distances which separate the highly placed from their lower brethren," because he "thinks that God has divided the world as he finds it divided" (II, 264). Palliser's evolutionary posture is limited by his anxiety about what equality would mean.

> The Liberal, if he have any fixed idea at all must, I think, have conceived the idea of lessening distances,—of bringing the coachman and the duke nearer together,—

nearer and nearer, till a millennium shall be reached by—

(II, 265)

Here Palliser stops short of using the word "equality" for fear of sounding like a radical. He claims that he only shies away from advocating "equality" as it stands at the time, because he believes that "men's intellects are at present so various" that the majority of people could not fully take advantage, or employ properly, the rights accorded to them. Yet, the more overarching difficulty posed by the dream of equality is how to make it something other than "sameness" or contrary to identity. Liberalism, taken to its extreme, would eradicate all differences. So, for equality to be the "heaven" Palliser dreams of, it would have to combat the pseudo-democratic tendencies attributed to Lopez. Lopez feels that his lack of money, status, and family should not bar him from the pursuit of his goals.

29. At the end of the novel, Glencora likens herself to Lady Macbeth in her pursuit of power, but notes that "there hasn't been any absolute murder" (II, 383). Her allusion to murder refers back to her earlier statement that "among us we made the train run over him" (II, 348).

Works Cited

apRoberts, Ruth. *The Moral Trollope.* Athens: University of Ohio Press, 1971.

Bagehot, Walter. *The English Constitution.* 1867. Ithaca: Cornell University Press, 1995.

Briggs, Asa. *Victorian People: A Reassessment of Persons and Themes.* Chicago: University of Chicago Press, 1973.

Butte, George. "Trollope's Duke of Omnium and 'The Pain of History': A Study in the Novelist's Politics." *Victorian Studies* 24 (1981): 209-27.

Garrett, Peter. *The Victorian Multiplot Novel: Studies in Dialogical Form.* New Haven: Yale University Press, 1980.

Glendenning, Victoria. *Trollope.* London: Hutchinson, 1992.

Langbauer, Laurie. *Novels of Everyday Life: The Series in English Fiction, 1850-1930.* Ithaca: Cornell University Press, 1999.

Levine, George. *Darwin and the Novelists: Patterns of Science in Victorian Fiction.* Chicago: University of Chicago Press, 1988.

McMaster, Juliet. *Trollope's Palliser Novels.* New York: Oxford University Press, 1978.

Miller, D. A. *The Novel and the Police.* Berkeley: University of California Press, 1988.

Nardin, Jane. *Trollope and Victorian Moral Philosophy.* Athens: Ohio University Press, 1988.

Polhemus, Robert. *The Changing World of Anthony Trollope.* Berkeley: University of California Press, 1968.

Smalley, Donald, ed. *Trollope: The Critical Heritage.* London: Routledge & Kegan Paul, 1969.

Spencer, Herbert. *Political Writings.* Ed. John Offer. Cambridge: Cambridge University Press, 1994.

———. *Social Statics.* 1855. New York: Robert Schalkenbach Foundation, 1970.

Trollope, Anthony. *An Autobiography.* 1883. New York: Oxford University Press, 1990.

———. *The Prime Minister.* 1876. Oxford: Oxford University Press, 1983.

Cathrine O. Frank (essay date 2004)

SOURCE: Frank, Cathrine O. "Fictions of Justice: Testamentary Intention and the (Il)legitimate Heir in Trollope's *Ralph the Heir* and Forster's *Howards End.*" *English Literature in Transition, 1880-1920* 47, no. 3 (2004): 311-30.

[*In the following excerpt, Frank probes concepts of inheritance, as well as issues of legal and social views on illegitimacy, in Trollope's 1870-71 novel* Ralph the Heir.]

In 1766 William Blackstone wrote in volume II of his *Commentaries* "Of the Rights of Things" that the right to inherit actually predated the right to make a will. By confounding the individual's desire to direct the disposition of his goods (by submitting them to prescribed inheritance patterns), the law that had established the legal right to and protection of property in the first place was thus felt to infringe too closely upon individual autonomy. In response, the right of testation was introduced by which "the pleasure of the deceased" became the rule for succession through the document that, notes Blackstone, "we therefore emphatically stile [*sic*] his will."[1] He further observes, however, that this new dispensation was so obstructed by other regulations that the effect was to emphasize the law's "pleasure" rather than the individual's volition. By restricting the type of people who may write wills, the type who may benefit under them, the type of bequest that could be made—in short, everything that goes into a will and might be said to constitute freedom of testation—the law made what was "emphatically stile[d]" the testator's will seem largely a rhetorical turn of phrase.[2]

This concept of an individual's rights in things was to become a central subject of both legal and literary writing of the nineteenth century. The Wills Act of 1837, for example, repealed all previous wills acts and made the legal document a specifically Victorian text. For James Traill Christie, commenting on the Act in 1857, its third section effected perhaps the greatest change precisely in the degree to which it "enlarge[ed] the power of the testator."[3] Literary characters, too, ranging from John Harmon, Sr. to Mr. Scarborough invoked the idea laid out by J. S. Mill in *Principles of Political Economy* (1848): "The ownership of a thing cannot be looked upon as complete without the power of bestowing it, at death or during life, at the owner's pleasure: and all the reasons which recommend that private property should exist, recommend pro tanto, this extension of it."[4] As Mr. Scarborough in Trollope's **Mr. Scarborough's Family** (1883) asserts, "If a man has a property he should be able to leave it as he pleases; or—else he doesn't have it."[5]

The novel's response to this legal contest can illuminate literature's ability to offer a potentially more satisfying world than the one created through legal discourse. At the very least, by importing the "real" legal document into its fictional world, the novel creates a competing view of the law and an opportunity for readers to engage it in its symbolic capacity as a narrative that shapes experience. Just as the testator's will is regulated by the governing legal conventions of the time, however, so too does the novel's representation of it shift in rough allegiance to aesthetic standards. In this sense, the novel's rhetorical usage of the last will and testament can provide an index of the movement from realism towards modernism. The number of novels that adopt the last will and testament, whether as minor plot point or central incident, is too great to receive a full accounting here. In this article, then, I turn briefly to Anthony Trollope's **Ralph the Heir** (1871) in order to illustrate a growing Victorian ambivalence towards empirical emphasis on the law before focusing more fully on E. M. Forster's *Howards End* (1910) as an Edwardian revision of the general legal negotiation between a testator's intention and the law circumscribing it.

The more specific legal problem canvassed in these novels lies in the terms of this negotiation. By introducing the figure of the illegitimate child, both present two opposed, potential heirs whose legitimacy or eligibility as heirs is better determined by their stance towards property than by the legalities surrounding the circumstances of their birth or selection. In **Ralph the Heir,** the novel's focus oscillates between Squire Gregory's attempts to draft his will and the heirs' (identically named cousins: one legitimate by birth, the other not) responses. In the spirit of realism, Trollope gives equal attention to the will as an empirical document and an expression of personal identity. By contrast, in *Howards*

End the will-as-document is no more than a penciled scrawl, but the willed imperative of its testatrix presides over the entire book. Margaret Schlegel's spiritual connection with Ruth Wilcox and her understanding of the house's symbolic significance make her the proper heir in contrast to the Wilcox kin. Margaret's nephew is the only technically illegitimate heir, but like his aunt he is Mrs. Wilcox's spiritual successor. Forster's trope of the will and legitimacy is just that, a metaphor that revises Victorian methodologies through a more modern interpretation of the legitimate means of representation.

SINS OF THE FATHER: "BASTARDY" AND THE RIGHT TO NO NAME

Whether Heathcliff of *Wuthering Heights* (1847), Esther Summerson of *Bleak House* (1853), Norah and Magdalen Vanstone of *No Name* (1873), or Ralph Newton of **Ralph the Heir** (1871), the Victorian novel is frequently peopled by illegitimate children, whose unlocatability within the social structure makes them often pitiable and sometimes threatening figures. The novel's preoccupation with them reveals a cultural anxiety over the unnameable from which arises the ironic backlash that gives to these children of no paternal name the dubious title "bastard." By attaching this name to the socially fluid individual, the empiricist mind set laid the groundwork for knowing and controlling it.

Both the impulse to regulate and the mechanism through which such control became possible rest in the legal development of illegitimacy. Describing the rights of illegitimate children under Roman law, as compared to the "much superior" reason of the English system, William Blackstone refers to the folly of allowing any number of children born before their parents' marriage to be legitimated at any time by a subsequent union and to "be admitted to all the privileges of legitimate children." "This is plainly a great discouragement to the matrimonial state," he continues, "to which one main inducement is usually not only the desire of having children, but the desire of procreating lawful heirs." Blackstone's alarm at the possibility children born out of wedlock might have the same rights as "lawful heirs" is more nearly a fear that proper, familial inheritance patterns would be disrupted. The materialism of the nineteenth century and the coincident birth of the last will and testament as a written document align the transmission of goods with legal or social identity. The ability to pass on possessions, to control them even after death, is synonymous with shaping individual identity and conferring it to posterity. The preservation of property is thus a preservation of the self that is doubly confirmed by the procreation of lawful heirs of the body.[6]

For the illegitimate person, however, this equation creates a circular problem. Anny Sadrin's formulation that "one must have in order to be" finds its reverse here:

one must first be in order to have.[7] And to be the *filius nullius* or "nobody's child" Blackstone describes is to be disqualified from inheriting the very (real) property that carries with it social identity.[8] Thus in novels of Blackstone's time, such as *Tom Jones* (1749), the illegitimate child becomes the picaresque wanderer, the modern individual *par excellence* in search of an identity to call his own. The journey continues in the nineteenth century in novels about figures, who, though situated in the center of the home, are nonetheless dispossessed by the circumstances of their births and the laws of "bastardy."

England's so-called bastardy laws were notoriously strict and remained so far into the twentieth century.[9] During the nineteenth century, the law was guided mainly by the Bastardy Act of 1845. As "An Act for the Further Amendment of the Laws Relating to the Poor," it sought primarily to assist the mother in gaining support for her child's maintenance from the alleged father.[10] Less a matter of moral than fiscal concern, at least in the eyes of common law, the object was to defray the costs to the parish that arose when the child or *filius populii* was born within its precincts and thus eligible for its aid.

For fathers anxious to secure lawful heirs to their property, the Act could be particularly detrimental. If brought up by the mother in bastardy proceedings and confirmed by the court as the natural father, he became liable for care until the child reached the age of thirteen. Failure to do so resulted in the "distress and sale of [his] goods and chattels" to recuperate the sum and, where these proved insufficient, imprisonment for up to three months.[11] Subsequent amendments to the Act, notably the Bastardy Laws Amendment Acts of 1872 and 1873, extended both the time frame during which a woman could make an order for proceedings and the variety of expenses for which the father could be made responsible, inclusive of court costs and reimbursement to the parish.[12] Thus, the existence of an illegitimate child could severely undermine the integrity of its parents' assets and identity, which says nothing of the damage done to the child's rights in a society so contingent upon the possession of property.[13]

The child born out of wedlock inherits a social stigma that literally prevents him from inheriting property. Halsbury records that "the rule that a bastard is *nullius filius* applies only to the case of inheritance and cases analogous thereto."[14] The statutes show that, although his rights as an English citizen are the same as any legitimate person's (inclusive of the right to acquire property and to leave it to his children), his relationship to his own parents actively debars him, as well as his children through him, from inheriting by descent.[15] Though he may have a name "by reputation," he has no "surname by inheritance."

This focus on the parent-child or "natural relationship" is justified in one sense by laws that prohibit marriage within certain degrees of relationship, laws which after 1908 could subject the parties to the Punishment of Incest Act. However, the bulk of the law concentrates not on blood-lines (since the bastard is a "stranger in blood") but precisely on the issue of patrilineal inheritance.[16] Thus, even where a child is subsequently legitimized, he is not entitled to inherit by descent from his father, while the restrictive nature of married women's property laws frequently left the mother no property to bequeath.[17] So apart from preventing certain marriages, the rules of bastardy are designed primarily with a view towards the preservation of property for both the testator and his legal heirs, which in turn solidifies the patriarchal and material basis of social identity: no name equals no property equals no identity, save what one can cobble together oneself.

The question Trollope and Forster raise regarding such laws is whether they are just (or even practical) in respect both to the testator and his potential beneficiaries. The early bastardy laws paint a picture of wayward fathers, the "dead-beat dads" of the early nineteenth century who might well land in jail for failure or inability to maintain their children. But case law shows fathers who want to provide for their children, and under certain conditions may, yet are legally unable to give them a name. The testator's will-as-imperative is constrained, and the illegitimate child's worth, already complicated from a moral standpoint, is degraded in the material, social sense. Jenny Bourne-Taylor writes that by the nineteenth century, illegitimacy had become "both an excessive and predictable, even banal, plot device" in novels of the period whose effect was to question "the constitution of authority within the legitimate family."[18] The presence of this legal issue in novels was matched, she claims, by the fictional value of illegitimacy even within the law: albeit a "legal fiction," bastardy has real effects and "raises the question of how we think about the relationship between social and symbolic structures."[19]

To conceive of bastardy as a "legal fiction," one that has literal and metaphorical value, makes it a rhetorical strategy similar to the last will and testament. Like the will, bastardy serves the social function Bourne-Taylor links to the perpetuation of patriarchy and property, in this case as a deterrent to inheritance rather than a mechanism for it. And the law's definition of the bastard as "one born out of lawful wedlock" reveals its status as a legal category, not a biological fact;[20] as Trollope illustrates in *Ralph the Heir,* there is no question that Ralph Newton is the biological descendent of his grandfather Ralph or that he would inherit his estate, if only his parents had been lawfully joined. Trollope bares the "relationship between social and symbolic structures," the desire for continuity in the social arena and the creation of "illegitimacy" to safeguard it, and the potential injustice that can result by creating two Ralphs. Forster creates two families. By examining each one's fitness as heir along with the testator's wish to determine this for him or herself, both writers expose the disjunction between legitimacy and eligibility and between the will-as-imperative and the law.

"WHAT'S IN A NAME": PATRONYMS AND
PATRIMONY IN TROLLOPE

Ralph the Heir (1871) is a complicated familial and legal drama. It tells the story of a testator's attempt to circumvent one law through recourse to another and ultimately questions what constitutes justice and whether strict adherence to the law always produces it. Specifically, it recounts the story of Squire Gregory and his illegitimate son, Ralph. Ralph is a model child and would make a model squire of Newton Peele were the estate not entailed upon his younger, imprudent—but legitimate—cousin Ralph. "According to Trollope," writes Coral Lansbury, "the law establishes a society that bears only passing resemblance to reality but retains the power to impose this fictitious version of reality upon people."[21] In reality, the illegitimate Ralph should be "Ralph the heir." In reality, the Squire rightly perceives that the estate would be better maintained in his son's hands than his nephew's, but the legal reality dictates otherwise: Squire Gregory's will is not his own since the entail ties his hands in terms of how he may manage his property.[22] As Mrs. Mountjoy in *Mr. Scarborough's Family* succinctly states, "when a property was entailed the present owner had nothing to do with its future disposition."[23] Thus hampered by the imposition of his own father's will, Squire Gregory concocts a plan to buy out his nephew's interest.

The laws of bastardy declare that though the illegitimate child may not inherit by descent, he may "always do so by purchase."[24] If the Squire could possess Newton Priory outright, he could memorialize himself by his own good works and rest confidently in the knowledge that these would be perpetuated by his son, rather than squandered by his ne'er-do-well nephew. Even Sir Thomas, the Squire's attorney and guardian to Ralph the heir, admits that if Gregory's son were somehow to inherit instead of his ward "the estate [would] go to a better fellow, though out of the proper line."[25] However, just when it seems that the heavily indebted Ralph the heir will sell his interest, the Squire is killed before being legally entitled to draft a new will. The Squire's will-as-imperative fails. Ralph the heir remains the heir; Newton goes to him.

Trollope's decision to outline the Newton's legal conundrum, develop a loophole, and then close it in favor of the status quo entertains the possibility that what the law decrees from a distance may, upon closer examina-

tion, prove the less judicious course. Yet the novel also questions whether defiance or manipulation of the law would result in still greater losses. While Squire Gregory deserves attention as both an heir and a testator, the majority of the novel focuses on the two Ralphs. By giving them the same name, Trollope deliberately closes the gap between their titular identities in order to shift attention to their character. In effect he asks the question "what's in a name?" which, applied here to the legal categories of illegitimacy and inheritance rights, serves as an investigation of the law's preoccupation with potentially superficial markers of identity—the literal patronym versus the consciousness of belonging—that may ultimately damage the integrity of the property such laws are meant to protect. In this way he operates on the basis of a more individual ethic, as opposed to the edicts of a pre-ordained law, that considers the evidence of personal accountability and the reader's response to it as the final arbiter of justice.[26]

Trollope's play with naming in the novel illustrates this point. The senior Ralph Newton has two sons: Squire Gregory and Ralph, the Parson of Newton Priory. Squire Gregory is father to Ralph the bastard. The now-deceased Parson is father to his own namesake, Ralph the heir, and to the current Parson Gregory. This proliferation of names makes it difficult to distinguish between characters and generations, but sharing a name is the extent of the similarity between them, as the two living Ralphs and the two Gregories exhibit such divergent attitudes. In a move that further accentuates the centrality of a name to the novel, Trollope hones in on their attitudes about the family name and concomitantly the role that legitimacy plays in the correct distribution of property.

The law thus provides a framework, writes R. D. McMaster, in which Trollope can "pursue most effectively his interest in the tensions between public behavior and private scruple."[27] Informed by justice, expressed through law, and administered by professionals, the legal system is a hierarchy at the bottom of which lies the citizenry who may reasonably feel the weight of such tradition. By creating a narrative voice for the individual experience of the law, the novel reverses this hierarchy. Trollope suggests that a better rule for gauging the two Ralphs' eligibility as heirs lies more in their attitudes toward legal principles and practices than in the law itself. If in theory he favors the illegitimate Ralph, however, he does so in large part because of that man's sensitivity to English tradition and his own intuitive understanding that he is not the right man for the job. Thus, the fact that Ralph the heir is actuated by his shifting financial circumstances becomes a major point of contrast to his cousin's more constant sense of the order of things.

Pushed to extremities by expensive habits, Ralph the heir waffles between his long-term desire to keep his interest in the lucrative Newton estate and his immediate need for cash. Nearly dissuaded by his own brother's arguments that "Almost anything would be better than abandoning the property,"[28] Ralph nevertheless decides to sell. Lamenting his imminent loss, he vows never to visit the Priory again: "Nothing on earth could induce him to go there, now that it under no circumstances could be his own. It would still belong to a Newton, and he would try to take comfort in that."[29] Ralph's attitude to his cousin's inclusion in the Newton family, though likely to garner agreement and sympathy from twenty-first-century audiences, is neither entirely applauded nor supported by the novel. His negligent attitude toward the property, and in this instance towards the law, discourages the reader from accepting his judgment.

Indeed, neither his brother nor the illegitimate Ralph himself views the issue of the name in the same light. For example, Parson Gregory, who could be generous when the sale was only contemplated, is shocked by his brother's decision: "though he must have known that Ralph the base-born was in all respects a better man than his own brother, more of a man than the legitimate heir,—still to his feelings that legitimacy was everything."[30] Gregory even makes the astounding proposition that it would be best if "neither he nor his brother should have a child" so that the "proper line" of the Newtons should die out. In the context of the bastardy and inheritance laws, extinction is preferable to the ongoing injustice that would exist if "real" Newtons were to live dispossessed of their patrimony. Extreme as the younger Gregory's sentiments are, the reader is positioned to favor his opinion by virtue of his loyalty to the English system.

The base-born Ralph's feelings confirm this attitude. Even before the lawyers are consulted, Ralph squirms under his father's proposal: "Let what might be done in regard to the property, nothing could make him, who was illegitimate, capable of holding the position in the country which of right belonged to Newton of Newton."[31] By reputation only is Ralph a Newton, and, while this social concession may sustain a pleasant life-style within the family and the community, it cannot eradicate the fact that at law he has no name. His grandfather's will, not his father's, was correct and "more consistent with the English order of things."[32]

This order recalls England's feudal organization and is therefore a facet of traditional attitudes towards a squire's relationship to his tenants. When the "richest and most intelligent" of the Newton tenantry congratulates this Ralph on his new position, he reminds the new heir that "there will be a feeling."[33] And Ralph acknowledges that "After all, such a property as Newton does not in England belong altogether to the owner of it." Rather, he has a "part property" with those who

"make it what it is, and will not make it what it should be, unless in their hearts they are proud of it." Unlike his cousin, the illegitimate Ralph is a visible and active figure on the landscape, attuned to the mentality of the people with whom he lives. In contrast, Ralph the heir does not consider the land's social significance and views it as another personal possession. Significant here is what this clash of values means for Trollope's view of the justice of legal dictates and their impact on personal and national identity.

Trollope's fictional community and his readers can only regret the ultimate failure of Squire Gregory's will-as-imperative and Ralph's projected inheritance if it is clear that Ralph himself believes in his own ineligibility. That he has this conservative attitude places him in a traditional camp that values the land in its capacity as "a symbol of order and continuity."[34] As such, Ralph's theoretical position, like Roger Carbury's in *The Way We Live Now* (1875), further endorses the law's symbolic power as the engine that sustains familial and national identity. The closest Ralph comes to criticizing his "institutional identity" derives not from his inability simply to inherit what others have made, but from the possibility that it will impede him from making a life for himself.[35] Having engaged himself to Mary Bonner on the assumption that his new inheritance will alleviate the stigma of his birth, the dissolution of that prospect likewise blurs his marital outlook. Although in the end Ralph does marry, the fact that his personal identity suffers at the hands of the same law without prompting his own willful rejection of its values—a rejection made possible by his father's efforts—solidifies his traditionalism.

Ralph the heir's attitude, in contrast, tends towards a more liberal interpretation of the individual's personal rights, a modern sense of property as personal, not communal, wealth (Galsworthy's "Forsytism") and of the latitude to create one's own identity. The irony here is that, though otherwise opposed to one another, Ralph the heir and Squire Gregory share this willingness to subvert tradition for the sake of personal interests in contrast to Parson Gregory and Ralph the bastard, whose love for one another cannot efface their shared sense that the illegitimate Ralph should not inherit. Their close relationship in general and their unity on this point mends the rupture between their fathers and indicates that adherence to the law maintains familial order. Trollope's decision to support the status quo "in proper conformity with English habits and English feelings" suggests, moreover, that the law lies at the heart of English identity.[36] However, his painstaking efforts to create sympathy and respect for the illegitimate Ralph and for his father's efforts on his behalf reveal a troubled stance towards the law's equation of familial and cultural identity and its consequent right to define family.

Notes

1. William Blackstone, *Of the Rights of Things,* vol. 2 of *Commentaries on the Laws of England,* Stanley N. Katz, ed. (Chicago: University of Chicago Press, 1979), 12.

2. Ibid., 13.

3. James Traill Christie, *Concise Precedents of Wills* (London: Maxwell, 1857), 162.

4. John Stuart Mill, *Principles of Political Economy,* V. W. Braden and J. M. Robson, eds. (Toronto: University of Toronto Press, 1965), 223.

5. Anthony Trollope, *Mr. Scarborough's Family,* The Penguin Trollope (New York: Penguin, 1993), 389.

6. William Blackstone, *Of the Rights of Persons,* vol. 1 of *Commentaries on the Laws of England,* Stanley N. Katz, ed. (Chicago: University of Chicago Press, 1979), 443.

7. Anny Sadrin, *Parentage and Inheritance in the Novels of Charles Dickens* (Cambridge: Cambridge University Press, 1994), 4.

8. Blackstone, *Of the Rights of Persons,* 447.

9. The 1953 edition of *Halsbury's Laws of England* retains a chapter on "Bastardy," and it was not until the 1970s that the statutes abandoned the pejorative title in favor of the less inflammatory "illegitimate person."

10. For a comprehensive social history of illegitimacy, see Iva Pinchbeck and Margaret Hewitt's *Children in English Society,* vol. 2 (London: Routledge, 1973) and Jenny Bourne-Taylor, "Representing Illegitimacy in Victorian Culture," in *Victorian Identities: Social and Cultural Formations in Nineteenth-Century Literature,* Ruth Robbins and Julian Wolfreys, eds. (London: MacMillan, 1996).

11. Great Britain. Bastardy Act of 1845, 8 May 1845, (Stat. 8 & 9 Vict. c. 10).

12. See Great Britain. Bastardy Laws Amendment Act of 1872, 10 August 1872, (Stat. 35 & 36 Vict. c. 65) and Bastardy Laws Amendment Act of 1873, 24 April 1873, (Stat. 36 Vict. c. 9).

13. These provisions notwithstanding, the law's attitude towards paternal responsibility is lenient to say the least and places greatest responsibility on the mother. In *Seaborne v. Maddy* (1840), for example, the court determined that the father is "under no obligation to provide for the child, in the absence of any affiliation order [outlined above]." And in the 1861 case of *R. v. Brighton (Inhabitants),* it was determined that "the father of an illegitimate child is not recognized by the law of England for civil purposes" (Halsbury 1st ed. [see note 14] 441). The existence of measures to exhort paternal care for the child seem, then, to beg the question as to how frequently affiliations were granted. In terms of *Ralph the Heir* knowledge of the law reveals just how vigilant are Squire Gregory's efforts on his son's behalf in comparison to what was actually required of him.

14. Earl of Halsbury, *The Laws of England: Being a Complete Statement of the Whole Law of England* (London: Butterworth, 1908), 438.

15. Ibid., 439.

16. Ibid., 440.

17. For women of the lower socio-economic classes, the issue of how to provide for their children during their lives was more pressing than what they were unable to bequeath at their deaths. Bourne-Taylor points out that with the passage of the New Poor Law in 1834 mothers themselves were no longer able to sue the putative fathers so that the child became her sole responsibility, thus affirming the symbolic and material link between mother and child ("Representing Illegitimacy," 133). Ironically, the economic straits to which unwed mothers were subject often lead to a physical separation from their children. Because they could not afford to support their children, they were often sent either to the workhouse or to so-called baby farms. "Commissioners [of the Poor Law]," according to Jenny Teichman, "seemed to believe that the best . . . way to reduce illegitimacy was to subject the unmarried mother to the 'providential' operation of economic forces. . . . At all events, they were concerned to remove from the statute books those regulations which tended to ameliorate the economic plight of the unmarried mother, while adding new regulations that imposed the duty of support upon her" (*Illegitimacy: An Examination of Bastardy* [Ithaca: Cornell University Press, 1982], 66).

18. Jenny Bourne-Taylor, "Nobody's Secret: Illegitimate Inheritance and the Uncertainties of Memory," *Nineteenth-Century Contexts,* 21 (2000), 569.

19. Ibid., 570.

20. Halsbury, 426.

21. Coral Lansbury, *The Reasonable Man: Trollope's Legal Fiction* (Princeton: Princeton University Press, 1981), 85.

22. R. D. McMaster, *Trollope and the Law* (New York: St. Martin's Press, 1986). McMaster explains what he calls the conservative and liberal tendencies of bequeathing real property. The conservative ap-

proach, which derives from the original owner's desire to "keep the property intact and in the family" (13), informed the fee tail's restriction of descent to "a person and the heirs of his body." The liberal tendency is held most often by the heir who feels he "ought to be able to do what he likes with what he possesses." Thus, *Ralph the Heir* illustrates the way that the old Squire follows laws of primogeniture even where there is no entail, but then makes one to punish Gregory for his illegitimate son and to "preserve the English way" (13). The importance of primogeniture as a facet of English law and national identity continued until 1925. Quoting A. V. Dicey in 1905, McMaster identifies the paradox that "'the constitution of England . . . has become a democracy, but the land law of England remains the land law appropriate to an aristocratic state'" (15).

23. Trollope, *Mr. Scarborough's Family,* 24.

24. *Halsbury's Laws of England,* 3rd ed. (London: Butterworth, 1953), 105.

25. Anthony Trollope, *Ralph the Heir,* John Sunderland, ed. (Oxford: Oxford University Press, 1990), 17.

26. Lansbury, 24, 20. In terms "of language and of structure," Trollope was indebted to the law's forms and to the methods of legal reasoning. However, he "allowed [his fiction] to be governed by an ethic wholly different from that which the law was assumed to defend. His was a vision of a social order in which individuals knew success or failure as a result of free decisions reached in circumstances unaffected by external contingencies" (24). "External contingencies" strike me as one of the central components of this new ethic insofar as the characters' responses to them form the basis of the reader's evaluation. If, as Lansbury also affirms, reason is "the arbiter of his fiction in the persona of the reader" (20), then the reader needs to have some understanding of the significance of what's at stake in their behavior. In this lies the novel's symbolic value.

27. R. D. McMaster, "Trollope and the Terrible Meshes of the Law: *Mr. Scarborough's Family,*" *Nineteenth-Century Fiction,* 36 (1981), 155.

28. Trollope, *Ralph the Heir,* 215.

29. Ibid., 322.

30. Ibid., 339.

31. Ibid., 217-28.

32. Ibid., 29.

33. Ibid., 347.

34. Geoffrey Harvey, "A Parable of Justice: Drama and Rhetoric in *Mr. Scarborough's Family,*" *Nineteenth-Century Fiction,* 37 (1982), 420.

35. Lansbury, 95. "Institutional identity" is Lansbury's term for the literal role a person occupied in the public realm in contrast to the individual's private sense of self. The possibility for human agency in the Trollopian world are constituted by the relationship between the two. In a more ideological sense, one's interaction with the law is itself an act of identity formation. In other words, to document a person (whether it be through birth, death, or marriage certificates) is to assign an institutional or social identity. In the case of the will-as-document, that simplistic legal registration is enhanced by the testator's own exercise of the will-as-imperative.

36. Trollope, *Ralph the Heir,* 85.

Timothy Ziegenhagen (essay date summer 2006)

SOURCE: Ziegenhagen, Timothy. "Trollope's Professional Gentleman: Medical Training and Medical Practice in *Doctor Thorne* and *The Warden*." *Studies in the Novel* 38, no. 2 (summer 2006): 154-71.

[*In the following essay, Ziegenhagen comments on the ways in which Trollope's novels challenged the tradiional view of the professional gentleman. Ziegenhagen explores changes in the medical profession in the mid-1800s, pointing to Trollope's doctor characters as representations of the working professional and the working gentleman.*]

In his autobiography, Anthony Trollope says that the idea for *The Warden* came to him on a surveying trip near Winchester, "whilst wandering there on a midsummer evening round the purlieus of the cathedral." The ancient environs and the Anglican traditions they evoked brought to Trollope's mind "the story . . . from whence came that series of novels of which Barchester, with its bishops, deans, and archdeacon, was the central site" (92). In his account of this incident, Trollope seems to suggest that the central conflict depicted in *The Warden* is fictional—inspired by a scene or a place, not by the contemporary controversies, with which he presumably had some familiarity, over Church revenue, spending, and sinecures. Indeed, the scene inspiring the fiction may itself be fictional. R. S. Super has pointed out Trollope's "blunder" in reporting the date of this incident, calling into question—by implication, at least—the author's account of it (76-77), while John Sutherland suggests that Trollope may have invented his walk through the grounds of Winchester Cathedral to distance the events of *The Warden* from a highly public scandal surrounding the Earl of Guilford, who had collected 300,000£ as Master of Winchester's St. Cross Hospital. In order to protect Guilford from humiliation—but wanting to show the hypocrisy of Guilford's rabid attackers—Trollope created an analogous conflict in an imaginary city depicting his hero, Septimus Harding, as an ethical man caught in unfortunate circumstances. Thirty years later, Trollope re-imagined the genesis of **The Warden** to separate the story further from contemporary events, establishing an aesthetic claim for his fiction as disinterested, objective, and untainted by personal bias ("Trollope, the *Times* [and *The Warden*]," 68-69).

In this essay I want to argue that even if Trollope somehow thought he could set some imaginative distance between **The Warden** and Church controversies actually occurring in his day, this account of its inception remains true to an issue the confronting of which is crucially formative to Trollope's career as a novelist, a turning point in which he moved from writing somewhat obscure Irish novels to the commercially popular Barset series. For the surveyor strolling about the Cathedral grounds embodies an intersection of two professions, literature and public service. The General Post Office (GPO) surveyor engages in the narrative "castle building" of the author, making what we have come to think of as the two Trollopes quite indistinguishable from each other here. Despite the fact that Trollope worked so hard to keep these two spheres separate (at least in the mind of his reading public),[1] he was constantly examining what it meant to be a working professional—and a working gentleman—in both. In **The Warden** and later in **Doctor Thorne,** we see Trollope use medical men (whom I will very loosely refer to as "doctors") as a way of depicting a new, emerging kind of mid-Victorian professional figure—a character type resonant with his own experience as writer and government employee, one that balances the genteel with the professional. Drs. Thorne and Bold have different medical backgrounds—one has gentlemanly university training while the other more up-to-date technical training (walking the wards in the London hospitals). Each, in his way, embodies medical progress and reform, but Trollope is careful to avoid drawing an easy dichotomy between old and new, the physician and the surgeon, the traditional and the progressive. Dr. Thorne, a physician of good blood, is not an agent of reactionary medical practices, but is, in fact, quite innovative in some of his medical practices. Dr. Bold, a surgeon with superior technical training, is not, strictly speaking, a better doctor than Thorne, for all his cutting-edge knowledge. In examining these two figures closely, we see Trollope subverting readerly expectations about education and class, forging an ideal of professionalism that is inclusive of both tradition and progress. This ideal is consistent with Trollope's depictions of himself, in his *Autobiography,* in which he embraces literature—a genteel pursuit—and GPO careerism.

Credentials and Training

As Trollope was able to see in his tenure at the General Post Office, a new kind of professionalism was transforming the British Civil Service—getting a job in the Civil Service no longer depended solely on patronage but successfully completing a competitive exam, which required a certain amount of technical training and skill. Trollope felt that the Northcote-Trevelyan reforms were a simple fix for a complex problem; inefficiency within the Civil Service would not be solved by examinations only. Indeed, such examinations might prevent talented individuals from being considered for positions in the first place. In his **Autobiography,** Trollope emphasizes his own initial ill-preparedness for the Civil Service (he fictionalizes his lackluster interview with the GPO in **The Three Clerks**). Indeed, Trollope feared that competitive examinations might "keep out gentlemen" from government positions "in favour of swots" and grinds with ambition, perhaps, but little imagination ("Introduction," Sutherland xviii-xix). The new system required greater accountability, but—divorced from patronage—the Civil Service became less genteel, less the kind of work a gentleman would do. The author had mixed feelings about this shift, but he could see that it was inevitable, perhaps even necessary, given the growth of bureaucratic institutions in England during his time at the GPO. Work, on one level, was becoming a lot more like *work,* a laudable development, for Trollope, who believed "[m]en should be paid for their endeavour and abilities, [and] not their family name." On the other hand, competitive Civil Service examinations did not always successfully determine skill or merit, which is why Trollope opposed them in the first place (Durey [*Trollope and the Church of England*] 43), and credentials were not an absolute guarantee of professional fitness either (as will be shown shortly, in our examination of two of Trollope's doctors).

We see Trollope working through this idea of the professional gentleman in his many novels, and there are no easy categories demarcating a kind of ideal of this type; as always with Trollope, there is room for flexibility, for a middle ground. In **Doctor Thorne** and **The Warden,** Trollope uses doctors as a way to explore the effects of training and background on the practice of medicine. John Bold, the "doctor" in **The Warden,** in fact, is not technically a doctor at all, but a GP, or General Practitioner, a medical worker trained in the hospitals and with a different social status than a university-trained physician. Independently wealthy, Bold moves in good Barsetshire society, but he is nevertheless a reformer, positioning himself against institutional systems, tradition, and privilege. Doctor Thorne has been trained as a physician and is closely related to the genteel Thornes of Ullathorne, but he is not your typical physician, as the novel makes clear. A compounder and dispenser of drugs, he is ostracized from the community of physicians in Barchester—to his colleagues, he is little more than a grasping tradesman, expressly not a gentleman.

In Thorne and Bold, we are introduced to two medical workers who vary greatly in their medical training, practice, and ability, and these characters show the complex way in which Trollope hoped to depict the professional gentleman as a construct of various factors: family background, technical training, professional practices, even personal temperament. A medical practitioner like Thorne or Bold is a gentleman not by class or education alone, but also by the work of his hands. Perhaps Thorne's greatest strength is that he is flexible: he does what needs to be done to help his patients, dispensing drugs and charging reasonable rates for his services; when Lady Arabella banishes him from Greshamsbury, Thorne takes it in stride and continues the struggle to make a living. While proud of his family background, Thorne works modestly, with his patients' interests in mind. Bold's shortcomings, in fact, stem from his egotism; rather than serve the community with his medical training, he dreams of becoming a famous reformer, hobnobbing with the movers and shakers of Whig London. The educational background of Bold and Thorne—the hands-on training in a London hospital versus university education—is almost incidental to the Trollope narratives discussed here. Doctor Thorne is a professional gentleman because he is willing to sacrifice for the community. Willing to sell drugs like an apothecary and make seven-and-sixpence visits, he is a model for the other Barchester physicians who, the narrator tells us, would do well "if they consulted their own dignity a little less and the comforts of their customers somewhat more" (***Doctor Thorne*** 31).

Trollope used his depictions of these medical workers as a way to examine the changing nature of the medical professional in the 1850s and 1860s. The scholarly, university-trained physician had, by this time, been to some degree displaced by the technically-trained GP, or General Practitioner. I would like to suggest that in depicting the doctors in these novels, Trollope is working through complex attitudes towards the professions in general at a time when the definitions of a gentleman and a professional were in flux, the subject of broad socio-cultural debate. In "*Middlemarch* and the Doctors," Asa Briggs explores how crucial were debates revolving around medical reform in the 1830s and beyond, arguing the "health problem was a major Victorian problem" around which centered various other social issues: the role of philanthropy and the nature of the philanthropist; exploding populations and the problem of public health; the relationship between hospitals and re-

ligion; an evolving understanding of disease, including a fuller understanding of the germ theory of disease (755, 755-59), which was by no means established until the 1870s and beyond (Rosen [*A History of Public Health*] 280-91). A part of the issue of medical reform is medical training and practice; Lydgate is distrusted by the other doctors of Middlemarch, who attack his "new-fangled methods" (Briggs ["*Middlemarch* and the Doctors"] 759). In a period when the training of doctors was rapidly evolving, doctors themselves were irregularly credentialed. In Trollope, for instance, there are many kinds of "doctors"—some with MD degrees, and others with articles of apprenticeship (i.e., apothecaries). A doctor succeeded—and more often failed—on the visible success of his practice: whether his patients lived or died. Before reforms that brought educational consistency to the credentialing of medical workers, reputation was key: "personal integrity and unflinching determination were at a premium" (Briggs 759).

The flexibility in the training and practice of medical practitioners in the early to mid-Victorian period enabled Trollope to test and challenge assumptions about the professional medical gentleman, whose status as such is complex and—above all—not fixed. In presenting the characters of Thorne and Bold, Trollope is able to examine his own position as a hard-working and responsible clerk and surveyor for the General Post Office, but also a writer of literature who, crucially, did not absolutely depend upon the profits from his labors. In combining certain qualities of the practically-trained GP and the university-trained physician, Trollope establishes a new kind of professional—a medical gentleman of great personal integrity (to use Briggs's phrase)—one gratefully conscious of tradition and the reach of the past but favorably if cautiously disposed toward progress and change.

DR. THORNE AND THE TAINT OF THE APOTHECARY

Doctor Thorne is the third Barsetshire novel, begun in the fall of 1857 (about five months after the publication by Longman of ***Barchester Towers***). Like so many Trollope novels, ***Doctor Thorne*** dramatizes the struggles of upward and downward class mobility. In the opening the narrator describes the history of the Gresham family by comparing the successful old squire to his downwardly mobile son, Frank Gresham, who, by the opening pages of the novel, has burdened his Greshamsbury estate with debt. Like his future nephew-in-law Frank, Doctor Thorne comes from a genteel background, related to the venerable Thornes of Ullathorne, a family "in one sense as good, and at any rate as old, as that of Mr. Gresham" (19). Despite being of "a high family," Doctor Thorne is also "a poor man" (28) with an unstable social position, having been cut off from his relatives of Ullathorne because of his brother's bad behavior (and, it is true, his own stubbornness). A thorough gentleman with very good family connections, Thorne is forced to make his way in the world professionally without the patronage of his family. Not unlike Trollope in his early days at the General Post Office, the doctor must succeed according to his own energy and skill.

The title of Trollope's novel itself calls attention to Thorne's status as a professional man (even as it suggests something about his methods of medical practice). Like other physicians trained during early Victorian England, Thorne would have studied medicine at a university—possibly Oxford or Cambridge, or perhaps, more likely, Edinburgh. At this time, students training to become physicians had to read widely in the classics, because it was believed that "the character of a physician ought to be that of a gentleman, which cannot be maintained with dignity, but by a man of literature" (Newman [*The Evolution of Medical Education in the Nineteenth Century*] 5). While the physician's university education might still be very literary and theoretical in nature, "teachers of medicine felt . . . you could no longer learn medicine from ancient texts, which was the essence of medical education in eighteenth-century Oxford and Cambridge" (Loudon ["Medical Education and Medical Reform"] 231). Marie-Francois-Xavier Bichat's advice to "open up a few corpses" and see the internal workings of disease was part of an attempt to move medicine from the strictly theoretical to include the material (Foucault 129-37). As a result of rapidly changing pedagogy in the teaching hospitals and the universities at this time, the traditional boundaries demarcating medical professionals began to shift, taking methods of professional certification and accreditation with them. As Thomas Neville Bonner shows, there were still a "wide range of regional and professional bodies empowered to grant licenses to practice [medicine]. Nineteen such agencies, many of them overlapping in jurisdiction and varying in requirements, existed in Britain and Ireland" (167). Predictably, physicians holding a privileged place in the medical hierarchy could be very protective not only of certification procedures governing professional rights and practices but also of the perception of the profession in the eyes of the public. Physicians trained at Cambridge or Oxford were even suspicious of those who trained at Edinburgh, which had a less academic system of education, although a more anatomically-based one (Hamilton [*The Healers*] 141-43). Bonner has pointed out that while the traditional medical hierarchies—physicians, surgeons, apothecaries—still held during the mid-century, in practice the education and training of these three groups was beginning to merge and would continue to do so throughout the Victorian era (158-59, 166-75).[2]

Even with the changes in medical education, older practicing physicians still hesitated to acknowledge the efficacy of the training of their more recently-credentialed

counterparts, the "young fanatics" of progress, like Lydgate, in *Middlemarch* (Briggs 759). In Trollope's novel, for instance, the established practitioners greet Thorne's arrival to Barchester with great suspicion. It is not simply that he is a rival for patients in a market saturated with physicians and GPs but also that his methods of practice seem uncouth, ungentlemanly, even dangerous to them. They admit that the newcomer's credentials are "en regle" (32), but they feel he operates more as a tradesman than a professional:

> Dr. Thorne, though a graduated physician, though entitled beyond all dispute to call himself a doctor, according to all the laws of the colleges, made it known to the East Barsetshire world, very soon after he had seated himself at Greshamsbury, that his rate of pay was to be seven-and-sixpence a visit within a circuit of five miles, with a proportionately increased charge at proportionately increased distances. Now, there was something low, mean, unprofessional, and democratic in this; so, at least, said the children of Aesculapius gathered together in conclave at Barchester.
>
> (32)

Thorne's willingness to charge "by the mile" smacks of receipts and ledger sheets to his more traditionalist colleagues, whose connection to classical medicine (and university medical training) is signaled by the narrator's reference to them as "children of Aesculapius," the Roman god of medicine. In creating a "rate of pay," Thorne does not charge consultation fees in the manner of the traditional eighteenth-century physician—a system meant to preserve professional and gentlemanly status (consultation was not "work" per se). That Thorne's visits generate "seven-and-sixpence" payments underscores the seemingly low status of his type of work. A real professional, according to the Barchester physicians, barely even considers payment and "should take his fee without letting his left hand know what his right was doing; it should be taken without a thought, without a look, without a move of the facial muscles" (32-33).

But it is not just that Thorne is "always thinking of money, like an apothecary." He also dispenses drugs like one, further hazing the boundaries between the duties of a university-trained physician and an apprenticed, lower-status medical worker. He is seen as ruining the profession, while also being a traitor to his own social order:

> [I]t was clear that this man had no appreciation of the dignity of a learned profession. He might constantly be seen compounding medicines in the shop, at the left hand of his front door; not making experiments philosophically in materia medica for the benefit of coming ages—which, if he did, he should have done in the seclusion of his study, far from profane eyes—but positively putting together common powders for rural bowels, or spreading vulgar ointments for agricultural ailments.
>
> (33)

As always when referring to the "learned" doctors of Barchester, the narrator here brings an edge of irony to the description of Thorne's trade. Had Thorne compounded his drugs "philosophically," as an experiment in medical science for the future but abstract "benefit of coming ages," rather than for the specific (and somehow "vulgar") suffering of one local person, he would have been performing laudably as a professional. But Thorne's drug-making is linked with the crudest bodily functions of working class laborers, the "rural bowels" of men and women troubled with "agricultural ailments"—ailments caused, one assumes, by hard days of toil in the fields and rough diets.

Later in the novel we actually see Thorne manufacturing drugs, and the narrator plays with the notion that, for some, this might not be a gentlemanly activity. When Beatrice Gresham comes on a peace-making mission between her mother and the doctor, she sees Thorne "in his little shop . . . deeply engaged in some derogatory branch of an apothecary's mechanical trade; mixing a dose . . ." (436). Though Thorne has left the door to his office ajar, Beatrice sees his activity as a clandestine one and intends to pass by the door unnoticed, out of a sense of delicacy for his feelings. After all, she believes she has caught him at his "villainous compounds" (436), doing something shameful.[3] With typical irony, the narrator uses the phrase "villainous compounds" to reveal more about Beatrice's genteel attitude than the work Thorne is engaged in—she wishes to ignore the less gentlemanly aspects of what she does, however, perceive as his "trade." When Thorne realizes that Beatrice has seen him, he unselfconsciously greets her, unaware that he has been caught doing anything undignified. He has been performing the duties of a country doctor—a professional with traditional university training and a certain amount of technical (again, "mechanical") knowledge. Thorne's openness, Trollope wants us to understand, is a function of his honesty: he does not need to make a show of his "secret medical knowledge" (158) as does Dr. Fillgrave (who raises the rate of his services by presenting his knowledge as arcane, mysterious—beyond the common reach of men and women).

Doctor Thorne is in fact so open about his medical practices that he even duels Dr. Fillgrave in print over his "seven-and-sixpence" visits. While Fillgrave is backed by the conservative community of physicians in Barsetshire in this dispute, Thorne finds support in "the metropolis," the center of medical reform and the home of leading teaching hospitals like Guy's and St. Thomas. At the heart of this discussion is Fillgrave's notion that Thorne is debasing the professional image of the physician: "The guinea fee, the principle of *giving* advice and of selling no medicine, the great resolve to keep a distinct barrier between the physician and the apothecary, and, above all, the hatred of the contamina-

tion of a bill, were strong in the medical mind of Barsetshire" (35). As before, Thorne is criticized for the way he accepts payment for his services: a bill itemizes services rendered, giving a pre-established cost for specialized forms of labor. Ironically, Thorne's method of billing is figured by Fillgrave as potentially disease-inducing, a "contamination," dangerous to both patient and the medical profession in general. On the other hand, Fillgrave's consultation fee—a guinea—is seen by the Barchester medical community as a respectable amount, given for expertise (associated with university training), not labor per se; furthermore, this fee is "*given*" (the emphasis is Trollope's), not billed.

By asserting that the true physician gives "advice," Thorne's competitor establishes himself as learned, a professional—a gentleman. In "selling medicine," Fillgrave suggests, Thorne is reducing the physician's practice to the level of trade, becoming, by extension, little more than an apothecary. This is a serious accusation—or at least, it is meant to be—because apothecaries had long been accused of being money-hungry and dishonest, more concerned with profits than the welfare of their patients.[4] What is more, the apothecary traditionally struggled for that elusive title of gentleman, so important to professionals in the early nineteenth century (Lawrence ["Anatomy and Address"] 203). Thorne, Fillgrave seems to suggest, is no gentleman if he is willing to hand out drugs like some kind of tradesman. Despite his family background, he is a "pseudo-doctor" and "half-apothecary" (523)—an imposter attempting to usurp others' genteel status. The professional honesty of apothecaries is questioned in the literature of the medieval period, and even before that (Rawcliff 154-55). Fillgrave believes that even associating with Thorne could be potentially damaging to his reputation—his personal integrity will be called into question—and as he waits for Thorne to finish attending to Roger Scratcherd, Fillgrave angrily ruminates that he has acquired the taint, kept "as though he were some apothecary with a box of leeches in his pocket" (159). Ironically, Fillgrave here is presented as grasping for money—he is a leech himself—since moments before he was sizing up Scratcherd's wealth, "calculating the price of the furniture," thereby attempting to determine Sir Roger's ability to pay handsome fees (158).

Despite Thorne's "democratic," reformist medical practices (32), he is still very proud of his family's heritage and of tradition in general: "[n]o man plumed himself on good blood more than Dr. Thorne; no man had greater pride in his genealogical tree, and his hundred and thirty clearly proved descents from MacAdam." While "[o]ther doctors round the county had ditch-water in their veins; he could boast of a pure ichor, to which that of the great Omnium family was but a muddy puddle" (28). This seeming inconsistency in Thorne's character is crucial to his function in the novel; he is a mediator between the ancient (Tory) Gresham family, linked to an agrarian past, and families like the Scratcherds, whose new and immense wealth is based on the development of England as an industrial nation (and a market economy). With the knowledge that his niece is Roger Scratcherd's heir, Thorne is able to unite-literally, in the marriage of Mary and Frank—the old England with the new, the past with the future. The Scratcherd family gains blood and the Gresham family gains money. Thorne's love of blood and his democratic tendencies, in fact, are consistent with his professional status. A physician steeped in the traditional learning of the universities, he is also at the forefront in bringing medical reform to Barsetshire.

This balancing of tradition with progress has its echo in Trollope's autobiography. Describing his own political viewpoint as that of "an advanced, but still a conservative Liberal" (291), Trollope takes equally to task the conservative belief that inequality is utterly the work of God alone and the liberal view that a "continual diminution" of inequality equals a "series of steps towards that human millennium of which he dreams" (293-94). In this passage, we see Trollope's belief in the importance of gradual change; N. John Hall suggests that while Trollope often espouses a streak of conservatism in his writings, they also display a strong undercurrent of "theoretical liberalism" (Hall [*Trollope, a Biography*] 112). Thorne matches this pattern. A traditionalist in his love of family background, he nevertheless serves as a physician to the entire Greshambury community, including the poor, all too easily forgotten by his fellow practitioners. He is an effective doctor, in part, because he is defined by movement (and flexibility): Thorne regularly travels from Greshambury to Boxall Hill, to London, literally connecting all the (uneasily coexisting) Barsetshire factions. Thorne is the one character whose influence, in a rather sprawling narrative, touches all the other characters; without him, the various plotlines would spin away centrifugally, and each world would continue to exist unaffected by the others. (Just to give one example, Thorne brings Scratcherd and Gresham together in the first place.) Thorne's mobility, in fact, is key in preventing a crisis in Greshambury: Frank's estate is preserved, and "the race of Scratcherd" is saved from extinction.

JOHN BOLD AND THE REFORMING DOCTOR

Like *Doctor Thorne, The Warden* shows a conflict between forces of conservatism and those of progress. At its center, of course, is the living of Reverend Septimus Harding, Warden of Hiram's Hospital in Barchester, jeopardized and then destroyed by the reforming medical worker John Bold, who creates a firestorm in the Barchester community that costs both Harding his position as Warden and Bold's reputation as reformer. Nobody profits from the conflict until the novel's sequel,

Barchester Towers, when effective reform at once bestows the wardenship upon a person who badly needs the money and doubles the number of charity tenants. Without its sequel, however, *The Warden* suggests that reform, even when needed, must be done in the proper way—that is, tactfully, and with deference to the delays necessary in healing change. Or rather, to put it more precisely, *The Warden* makes such a suggestion most fully only when its sequel offers temporal proofs. In emphasizing the need for gradual rather than sudden change, Trollope carries out his thesis over the very time called for, delaying the positive results of reform past the conclusion of one novel and well into the conclusion of another. Even within *The Warden,* however, Trollope deftly manages both sides of the issue. Bold is not right in how he prosecutes his reform, but Archdeacon Grantly is not right in arguing for the status quo and Harding's right to such a comfortable sinecure.[5] Somehow, *The Warden* posits, change for the better must respect the past even in deciding against it. The customary rights of the clergy and the traditions of the Church both demand deference and, because of the very worth legitimating that demand, orient themselves toward difference in the future.[6]

If Dr. Thorne balances tradition and reform in his Greshamsbury methods of healing (that is, if he knows how much weight to assign to each), John Bold rejects the past, which he sees as the origin of present social ills. Bold comes to Barchester to reform "state abuses, church abuses, corporation abuses" (12). In keeping with his medical training, Bold hopes to "mend mankind" (12). Strictly speaking, Bold is a doctor, but he is no physician: He avoids studying medicine at the universities but learns medicine "in the London hospitals" (11), which were, in the mid-nineteenth century, the very epicenter of medical reform; these hospitals produced doctors like Ernest Hart, longtime editor of the *British Medical Journal* who launched an investigation into the medical care at poorhouses and who was an ardent anti-vivisectionist (Behlmer ["Ernest Hart and the Social Thrust of Victorian Medicine"] 711-12). Walking the wards of the hospitals of London, Bold gains licensure as a "surgeon and apothecary," obtaining the kind of hands-on experience that would have made him a useful doctor in Barchester (11). This type of clinical training was less theoretical—one could say more practical—than that of period physicians, and included lectures on anatomy and practice at dissection (Cope ["The Influence of the Royal College of Surgeons of England"] 47-51). Bold's role as reformer in *The Warden* is appropriate given that hospital teaching was the great medical reform in the nineteenth century, allowing for "immediate communication of teaching within the concrete field of experience." Such training commonly included "anatomy, physiology, and medical chemistry" as well as surgery and materia medica, in addition to "internal and external pathology" (Foucault 68, 71).

With the passage of the Apothecaries Act in 1815, the training of apothecaries became linked with the professional training of surgeons (as in Keats's case), and the surgeon-apothecary "seemed perfectly tailored to meet the wide-ranging needs of a public who could afford a single, reasonably cheap, multi-purpose practitioner" (Porter [*Patient's Progress*] 127). In a real sense, the rise of the surgeon-apothecary in the mid-Victorian period made access to medical care more democratic: health care became available to a larger segment of the British population.

As part of this movement—at least in his background and training—Bold would seem to be at the forefront of improvements in medical care and philanthropic medicine. Strangely, despite his immersion in the reformist atmosphere of the London teaching hospitals, Bold eschews the practice of medicine altogether. Upon his arrival in Barchester, he puts up a "large brass plate," advertising himself as a surgeon, but he fails to take "three fees" in as many years of practice (12). This does not mean that Bold has been working gratis among the lower classes of a cathedral city like some Victorian Mother Teresa. In fact, Bold considers the work he trained for to be tedious: "Having enough to live on, he has not been forced to work for bread; he has declined to subject himself to what he calls the drudgery of the profession, by which, I believe, he means the general work of practising surgeon." While Bold indeed sometimes "binds up the bruises and sets the limbs" of the "poorer classes" in Barchester, his real work is much broader in scope—he hopes to "mend mankind" (12).

If Bold's object is to "mend mankind," his failure as a church reformer can be traced back to the fact that he has acted in violation of his own medical training and the code of behavior mandated for physicians by the Hippocratic ethic. In short, Bold's biggest problem as a reformer is his lack of professionalism. Ludwig Edelstein points out that the Hippocratic ethic is a culmination of Pythagorean doctrine, which suggests that medicine is a means of regulating the physical processes according to the natural biological principles by which they would normally operate; thus the most effective medicine allows nature to run its course (22-24). The best way to heal a body, according to the Hippocratic corpus of writings, is by avoiding aggressive treatment regimens that will upset or disturb the body's natural impulse to dispel sickness on its own. The Church, according to this metaphor, must willingly undertake reforms—these reforms must come from within the Church itself, by conscientious individuals. However, Bold is not willing to wait and must take "bold" action; his attempts to "heal" the Church are extremely aggressive, involving the radical public press—the *Jupiter*—to shame Harding into resigning his position. This course of action, meant to bring about a quick and decisive reform, achieves little else than making Harding miser-

able and entrenching Archdeacon Grantly more deeply into a reactionary position, namely keeping the terms of the wardenship just as they always have been without any possibility of change. In short, Bold's public actions—taking his case to the popular press—actually make it less likely, according to the ethic implicitly at work here, that any reforms will occur.

Bold's desire to "mend mankind" is a grandiose aim, revealing his egotism; his attempts to mend the Church—which seems to be the place where he thinks he should begin—demonstrate that the doctor is more interested in his own reputation than the well-being of the Church itself, even if he has reduced it to a metonym. Despite all the delicacy required, Bold forges ahead with an invasive "treatment," using the pages of the *Jupiter* as a kind of violent purgative. Unfortunately, Bold quickly loses control of this healing regimen; Dr. Anticant and Mr. Popular Sentiment embrace the cause, depicting Harding as an evil opportunist in the sensational, serialized novel, the *Almshouse*. Neither does the Church benefit from the bad public relations. Jerome Meckier writes that the reforms, "begun too quickly, are impossible to stop: they acquire momentum of their own" (213). *Jupiter* editor Tom Towers, in particular, indicates that he is not interested in half-measures; true reform requires an institution like the Church to be torn down first, then rebuilt from the ground up: "The fire has gone too far to be quenched . . . the building must go now," Towers tells Bold, "and as the timbers are all rotten, why, I should be inclined to say, the sooner the better" (130). Such a solution strikes even Bold as going too far; if applied medically, it would mean killing the patient to stop the spread of disease, and then hoping to discover, before it is too late, the secret of resurrection.

In a sense, Bold's treatment regimen to "mend" the Church is what one might call heroic—an ideal category in which the physician takes a more aggressive role in the cure of disease (than simply relying on the body to heal itself). Heroic medicine of the nineteenth century often cast the doctor as a defender of empire in the fight against foreign disease (Otis [*Membranes*] 31-36); manliness and resolve, "the masculine power of will, self-regulation, and control was taken for granted" (Wood [*Passion and Pathology in Victorian Fiction*] 76) as a virtue for the medical practitioner. Indeed, Bold frames his own reforms in heroic terms, as we see in his "severe battle" with the "old turnpike woman in the neighbourhood" who unfairly taxes certain travelers who should be able to pass by her tollfree (17). In his battle with the Church, Bold regrets that he is not more steady, more heroic in his actions: "How weakly he had managed his business! He had already done the harm, and then stayed his hand when the good which he had in view was to be commenced" (130). This passage reflects Bold's interventionist medical stance. His reform was a kind of bungled surgery—not because his hand shook or slipped but because he "stayed" it when the time came for action. Bold never stops to consider that his aggressiveness might not have been the best strategy in the first place, though Trollope too does not rule out aggressiveness altogether. It is a matter of tact, of knowing when to act in a manner that will bring about positive change.

From the Church's perspective, Bold is hardly heroic, and his regimen of reform actually aggravates social ills. He is often depicted as an active agent of disease. Although Bold and Mr. Harding are friends, Archdeacon Grantly would have the Warden avoid Bold "as the plague" (13). After the initiation of the lawsuit, the Archdeacon refers to the "'pestilent' John Bold" (39). Even the kindly old Bishop refers to Bold as a "pestilent intruder" (28), while Sir Abraham Haphazard calls Bold and his allies "pestilent dissenters" (75). The recurrence of the figure of pestilence is linked to Bold's mobility, which helps make him so threatening: He moves in many circles and has many points of contact he can touch with his contagious ideas, which spread from the cadres of reform in Barchester to every drawing room in England. It is not strictly reform that Bold is spreading, however, but a factionalism that encourages ad hominem attacks and bad feeling, leading to more bad feeling and the further entrenchment of the Archdeacon's position. Like a disease, too, Bold is not choosy. He observes no niceties of class or party affiliation, and he is willing to compromise friendship for advancement in his career as a reformer by playing both sides. The intimate friend of Harding, he also knows Tom Towers, editor of the newspaper that makes the case against the Warden. This indiscrimination makes Bold all the more dangerous, and he is in fact pestilential, in that his attempts to "mend" the Church do more harm than good. What is more, in using information gained from his friendly dealings with Harding—and by passing that information on to Towers—Bold breaks another tenet of the Hippocratic ethic, disinterestedness: In taking the case of Hiram's Will before the public, Bold disregards his patient's welfare for his own gain. In this respect, he is very much like Dr. Fillgrave when he is sizing up the gaudy furniture of Sir Roger, in ***Doctor Thorne***.

Despite the ferocity of the attacks against the Warden, however, it is finally Harding's own conscience that makes him resign his position. He acts, Trollope seems to say, very much like a gentleman, while Bold does not. What gentleman means here has something to do with the interiority of the motivation to be and do good, and in this respect Trollope links Harding's behavior to the Hippocratic ethic of "Body, heal thyself." For neither the lawsuit nor the inflammatory print was necessary—change came on its own, from within, without any kind of radical surgery. Harding is not attempting

to take advantage of the system: once it has been pointed out to the Warden that he might not be entitled to the proceeds of Hiram's will, he begins to struggle with whether or not he should keep his position at the hospital. Much of the drama in the novel, in fact, derives precisely from Harding's horror at being accused of corrupt practices, but Trollope leaves little room for doubt that the Warden is a decent man, and he is decent, a gentleman, because he determines on his own—apart from the actual legalities of the will—that he is in the wrong. By establishing his own reckoning, Harding proves to be morally superior to the Archdeacon's interested partisanship and Bold's reformist social "medicine," which he practices only to enhance his reputation; his clumsy attempts to control the outcomes of his reforms underscore his inability to diagnose and heal the underlying social ills he hopes to mend.

Whether or not Bold has knowledge of the Hippocratic corpus (knowledge any physician, trained in classics at university would have), he proves not to be entirely a gentleman, even though Trollope rewards him at the end of the novel with marriage to Eleanor Harding.[7] It is not Bold's professional hospital training, rather than a university education, that makes his gentlemanly status suspect; as Trollope points out in the beginning of the novel, Bold has skills that make him potentially useful to society—he has cutting-edge knowledge that would enable him materially to help the sick in Barchester. (The inept Dr. Fillgrave's success in the town indicates there is a real unmet need for adequate medical care there.) What makes Bold suspect as a gentleman is precisely that he has no interior motivation to work—at least as a doctor. And Trollope stresses interiority, again, by relieving Bold of the extreme necessity to earn a livelihood—the very condition which would, in an older cultural setting, define the status of "gentleman." Here the telling contrast comes from Dr. Thorne, whose travels throughout Greshamsbury are heroic in a different sense, on par with a real-life country physician, Erasmus Darwin (thought to travel up to 10,000 miles a year visiting patients) (King-Hele [*Erasmus Darwin*] 64). Thorne's mobility enables him to minister to the health of his patients, while Bold's is merely a sign (and a pestilential one) that he has nothing better to do.

Work, in this context, finally and perhaps even apart from self-motivation, becomes a positive value in and of itself. Bold's refusal to practice medicine is condemned as ungentlemanly because he refuses to help the poor even as he harms revered institutions like the Church of England. While it is true that work is anathema to the aristocratic ideal held by the de Courceys of Barsetshire—i.e., they propose that a gentleman must never work—*Doctor Thorne* shows the de Courceys to be outmoded, looking too much to the past. As Walter Houghton points out, work had taken on tremendous significance by the mid-nineteenth century in England:

"the 'meaning of life'—came more and more to lie in strenuous labor for the good of society," and loss of religious faith incurred a new "religion of work" that "came to be, in fact, the actual faith of many Victorians" (251). In his book of social commentary, **The New Zealander,** Trollope writes that Adam's fall is perhaps fortunate for humanity, since work is not always a curse but often a blessing: "There is neither disgrace nor sorrow nor pain in labour well ordered and well done. If men could but be brought to love their labour, to do loving work, how nearly happy would they be even here below!" (14). That Bold views his medical work as "drudgery" indicates that he is not entirely to be trusted; worse, his work as a reformist is to put others to work, while he enjoys the leisure he hopes to deny Harding. Worse yet, this work is mostly legal maneuvering involving the parsing a 400-year-old will. Nothing is made, built, or accomplished: Bold wastes his time, wasting the time of others as well.[8]

As a medical professional, then, Bold compares poorly to Doctor Thorne, not because of training or background, but because Thorne makes himself useful, while Bold does not. Thorne, in fact, seems to embody Trollope's ideal professional—he works hard, and he provides a valuable service to the community, striving locally to heal local ills. Bold's desire to "mend mankind" is finally too abstract, and he seems too similar to the medical charlatan of **The New Zealander** who "takes out a brazen trumpet sufficiently loud, and blows forth to the world a lying promise that he can cure all the ills that flesh is heir to. He, and he alone, he being the only true and duly skilful son of Galen! He! he can cure nothing! has no intention of trying to cure anything" (73). Even after telling Tom Towers he is going to stop the lawsuit, Bold still fantasizes about having his name up in lights, "backed by the *Jupiter*." Bold muses, "what might it not have given rise? What delightful intimacies—what public praise—to what Athenian banquets and rich flavour of Attic salt?" (130). Motivations such as these, Trollope reminds us, are not honest. Work ought to be its own reward; work done for pleasure, for satisfaction, ceases to become exactly *work*, or labor, but it becomes, instead, a pursuit that is at once professional and gentlemanly. Indeed, even after Mary Thorne inherits Scratcherd's great wealth and marries Frank Gresham, the Doctor refuses the comforts of retirement, choosing instead to "extend his practice, to the great disgust of Dr. Fillgrave" (624). Thorne loves his work—it gives meaning to his day-to-day existence, helps define him.

While Doctor Thorne—the physician—proves to be a better medical practitioner than the surgeon-apothecary Bold, Trollope is in no way suggesting that a university education is necessary for a doctor to be a gentleman. After all, Trollope himself had no such education (even if he did attend Harrow school, like Byron). Although

Trollope was intended for Oxford, his father's financial difficulties made Oxford impossible; nevertheless, he was of "[g]entle [family] [o]rigins," his grandfather the son of a baronet (Hall 3). Like Doctor Thorne, Trollope himself straddled gentility and the working professionalism of the middle-class, Victorian man. In regarding his own work, Trollope admits that he has perhaps written too much, but adds: "I do lay claim to whatever merit should be accorded to me for persevering diligence in my profession" (**Autobiography** 364).[9] Despite his (perhaps disingenuous) modesty, Trollope stood by the value of his own work and the utility of novel writing, which could teach "true honour, true love, true worship, and true humanity" (218). Still, even with his work as a writer, Trollope valued his experiences at the General Post Office, which were anyway helpful to his writing—the travels gave him a view of the world, broadened his horizons, and brought him into contact with people who would often character his novels. In short, Trollope's depiction of Doctor Thorne as the ideal professional man reflects something about the author's own attitude to work and its ennobling influence. A professional gentleman—of literature or of medicine—works hard, takes pride in his work, and loves the routines of labor.

Writing near the end of his life, Trollope admits that "I could be really happy only when . . . at work." Interestingly, Trollope insists that his own professionalism relates to a form of mechanical work, that of the shoemaker, rather than the traditional gentlemanly fields of employment—the church, law, even medicine. Comparing his books to footwear, Trollope writes "I had now quite accustomed myself to begin a second pair as soon as the first was out of hand" (**Autobiography** 324). That Trollope should have chosen this metaphor is appropriate. The shoemaker's art is useful: people wear shoes every day. Shoes also enable their wearers to travel long distances, even as novels take readers to distant lands. Musing (unapologetically) on his industry, Trollope writes that he probably has written "more than any other living English author" and possibly more than any dead one (362). Thinking of the prolific Roman scholar Varro, who wrote 480 volumes, Trollope wistfully speculates on their length: "I comfort myself by reflecting that the amount of manuscript described as a book in Varro's time was not much. Varro . . . is dead, and Voltaire [too]; whereas I am still living, and may add to the pile" (**Autobiography** 363).

Notes

1. Even the prolific Stephen King, in his recent *On Writing,* notes Trollope's legendary industry, but the *Autobiography* insists that the novels were not written at the expense of his work at the GPO [General Post Office]. Trollope goes so far as to include a letter written by J. Tilley in response to

his own letter of resignation from the GPO. Tilley praises Trollope's industry and writes, "you have never permitted your other avocations to interfere with your Post Office work, which has always been faithfully and indeed energetically performed" (280-81). While Trollope admits that Tilley's letter is filled with "official flummery," he nevertheless presents it as evidence that he was hard-working as a public servant (281).

2. Dr. G. Burrows, speaking before the Select Committee on Medical Registration in 1847, suggests that physicians and GPs were trained similarly:

> physicians received theoretical training first, then hands-on clinical knowledge, while with surgeon-apothecaries (and related practitioners) the order is reversed: "A young man who intends to pursue the profession of general practitioner usually leaves school at about the age of sixteen, and is apprenticed to some practitioner of the same grade of the profession that he intends to enter himself, and he usually passes two or three years with that practitioner, and then comes to some of the great public institutions where medical education is going on, and he there remains during three years, or the greater part of three years; having remained that length of time, he undergoes his examination, and leaves his place of education, and commences practice, and pursues his profession in the best way that he can. . . . The course of education of a physician, in the present day, is twofold. There are some young men who intend to become physicians, who come from the English universities at the age of one or two and twenty, having graduated in arts, or not having graduated in arts. I myself graduated in arts, and most of them do so now. They come to St. Bartholomew's, and remain there for four or five years, sometimes longer, till they have arrived at the age of six and seven and twenty. Their business, in the earlier part of their career at the hospital, is to attend lectures, just in the same way as the man who is to become a general practitioner. They attend the same course of lectures, but the probability is that they attend more courses of lectures. They remain in the hospital five or six years before they go up for their examination."

> > (qtd. in *The Universities in the Nineteenth Century* [85-86])

3. The apothecary's status as gentleman is also later called into question at a party for the Duke of Omnium; old Bolus is referred to as a "doctor," and an "apothecary" by Mr. Athill, who is pointing out the other guests to Frank Gresham. When Frank asks Athill whether Bolus is "by way of a gentleman," Athill responds "Ha! ha! ha! Well, I suppose we must be charitable, and say that he is quite as good, at any rate, as many others there are here" (261).

4. It should be emphasized here that this is a very old debate. For some good accounts of the struggle between physicians and apothecaries, see Barrett 110-18 or Copeman 43-49. At the time of Fillgrave and Thorne's debate, there were in fact no final distinctions between the medical practices (despite educational variances) of apothecaries, physicians, and other medical practitioners [see n. 2]. Many apothecaries were also training as surgeons to become surgeon-apothecaries; John Keats, for instance, was apprenticed as an apothecary, then licensed as an apothecary-surgeon after a period of training at Guy's Hospital, London (Goellnicht 24-42). These surgeon-apothecaries received theoretical training and were more than simply pill-dispensers. See Loudon, particularly chapters 6-9, for a detailed analysis of the transformation of the eighteenth-century apothecary into the mid-Victorian GP.

5. For a discussion of philanthropy and the Church of England, see Durey 42-82.

6. Trollope describes his distaste of uncompromising extremism in relating how the idea of *The Warden* came to him, while he was walking the grounds of Winchester Cathedral. "I had been struck by two opposite evils [. . . or what seemed to me to be evils,—and with an absence of all art-judgement in such matters, I thought that I might be able to expose them, or rather to describe them, both in one and the same tale]. The first evil was the possession by the Church of certain funds and endowments which had been intended for charitable purposes, but which had been allowed to become incomes for idle Church dignitaries. . . . The second evil was its very opposite. Though I had been much struck by the injustice above described, I had also often been angered by the undeserved severity of the newspapers towards the recipients of such incomes, who could hardly be considered to be the chief sinners in the matter" (*An Autobiography* 93-94).

7. Of course, Trollope then kills Bold off-stage, so that Eleanor Bold is a widow at the beginning of his next Barset novel, *Barchester Towers*.

8. It could be argued that Harding, who is, by conventional wisdom, the novel's moral center, is also lazy, although Trollope makes a distinction

here between a "lazy priest," which Harding is not, and "retiring," which he is (60). Even if he is classed with Bold as not working, however, here the contrast between two characters only contributes to thematic variety, since Harding is not called on to work, which Bold is. Doubtless if Harding were medically trained and disliked medical practice he too would come in for Trollope's criticism. The point is that for Trollope liberalism in belief and caution in action are complementary, not contradictory, and their reciprocal status can be validated, testified to, only in work.

9. In his autobiography, Trollope claims to have written about 40 pages of material a week during his more productive periods (a Trollopian page containing 250 words). During his more "lazy" weeks, Trollope wrote as few as 20 pages, but during a particularly productive week, the number "has risen to 112" (119). Trollope wrote a grand total of sixty-five books, some running to 800 pages.

Works Cited

Barrett, C. R. B. *The History of the Society of Apothecaries of London.* London: Elliot Stock, 1905.

Behlmer, George K. "Ernest Hart and the Social Thrust of Victorian Medicine." *British Medical Journal* 301.3 (1990): 3-5.

Bonner, Thomas Neville. *Becoming a Physician: Medical Education in Britain, France, Germany, and the United States, 1750-1945.* Baltimore: Johns Hopkins UP, 1995.

Briggs, Asa. "*Middlemarch* and the Doctors." *Cambridge Journal* 1 (1948): 749-62.

Burrows, Dr. G. An extract from "Minutes of Evidence of the Select Committee on Medical Registration." *The Universities in the Nineteenth Century.* Ed. Michael Sanderson. London: Routledge, 1975. 85-86.

Cope, Zachary. "The Influence of the Royal College of Surgeons of England Upon the Evolution of Medical Practice in Britain." *The Evolution of Medical Practice in Britain.* Ed. F. N. L. Poynter. London: Pitman Medical, 1961. 47-55.

Copeman, Dr. W. S. C. *Apothecaries of London: A History, 1617-1967.* Oxford: Pergamon, 1967.

Durey, Jill Felicity. *Trollope and the Church of England.* Basingstoke: Palgrave, 2002.

Edelstein, Ludwig. *The Hippocratic Oath.* Baltimore: Johns Hopkins, 1943.

Glendinning, Victoria. *Anthony Trollope.* New York: Knopf, 1993.

Goellnicht, Donald G. *The Poet-Physician: Keats and Medical Science.* Pittsburgh: U of Pittsburgh P, 1984.

Hall, N. John. *Trollope, A Biography.* Oxford: Clarendon, 1991.

Hamilton, David. *The Healers: A History of Medical Education in Scotland.* Edinburgh: Canongate, 1987.

Houghton, Walter E. *The Victorian Frame of Mind, 1830-1870.* New Haven: Yale UP, 1985.

Kincaid, James R. *The Novels of Anthony Trollope.* Oxford: Clarendon, 1977.

King-Hele, Desmond. *Erasmus Darwin: A Life of Unequalled Achievement.* London: Giles de la Mare, 1999.

Lawrence, Susan C. "Anatomy and Address: Creating Medical Gentlemen in Eighteenth-Century London." *The History of Medical Education in Britain.* Ed. Vivian Nutton and Roy Porter. Amsterdam: Rodopi, 1995. 199-228.

Loudon, Irvine. "Medical Education and Medical Reform." *The History of Medical Education in Britain.* Ed. Vivian Nutton and Roy Porter. Amsterdam: Rodopi, 1995. 229-49.

Meckier, Jerome. "The Cant of Reform: Trollope Rewrites Dickens in *The Warden.*" *Studies in the Novel* 15.3 (1983): 202-23.

Newman, Charles. *The Evolution of Medical Education in the Nineteenth Century.* London: Oxford UP, 1957.

Otis, Laura. *Membranes: Metaphors of Invasion in Nineteenth-Century Literature, Science, and Politics.* Baltimore: Johns Hopkins, 1999.

Porter, Dorothy and Roy Porter. *Patient's Progress: Doctors and Doctoring in Eighteenth-Century England.* Stanford: Stanford UP, 1989.

Rosen, George. *A History of Public Health.* Expanded Edition. Baltimore: Johns Hopkins UP, 1993.

Super, R. H. "Truth and Fiction in Trollope's *Autobiography.*" *Nineteenth-Century Literature* 48.1 (1993): 74-88.

Sutherland, John. "Introduction." *Barchester Towers* by Anthony Trollope. New York: Oxford UP, 1998. vii-xxviii.

———. "Trollope, the *Times,* and *The Warden.*" *Victorian Journalism: Exotic and Domestic.* Ed. Barbara Garlick and Margaret Harris. Queensland, Australia: Queensland UP, 1998.

Trollope, Anthony. *An Autobiography.* 1883. Ed. Michael Sadleir and Frederick Page. Oxford: Oxford UP, 1999.

———. *Doctor Thorne.* 1858. Oxford: Oxford UP, 1980.

———. *The New Zealander.* Ed. N. John Hall. Oxford: Clarendon, 1972.

———. *The Warden.* 1855. London: Everyman, 1994.

Wood, Jane. *Passion and Pathology in Victorian Fiction.* Oxford: Oxford UP, 2001.

Marc Arkin (essay date October 2007)

SOURCE: Arkin, Marc. "Trollope and the Law." *New Criterion* 26, no. 2 (October 2007): 23-7.

[*In the following essay, Arkin studies Trollope's presentation of legal issues, including the morality of defending guilty parties, in his novels.*]

For the general public, criminal defense exercises all the tabloid fascination of the louche; defending a genuinely guilty client carries the extra frisson of a brush with Old Nick himself. Seated at a dinner party or with a drink in hand, the question a criminal defense attorney inevitably hears from a new acquaintance is "How can you defend someone who is guilty?" In fact, this is really two questions in one: How, consistent with legal and ethical obligations, can you advocate the innocence of someone whom you believe is guilty? And, why would you do so?

Lawyers, of course, have many ways of answering both questions, not all of them self-serving, and in that most humane of novels, *Orley Farm,* Anthony Trollope, the son of a failed barrister, did justice to most of them, almost despite himself. Indeed, at the heart of the story is the attorney's most challenging professional dilemma, presenting a full defense at trial of a client rightly thought by all involved to be guilty of the crime charged.

I say "almost despite himself" because *Orley Farm* is dominated by Trollope's scathing view of the legal profession in general and of the trial bar in particular. Trollope gave us his thoughts when, writing of the novel's impending trial, he complained,

> There were five lawyers concerned, not one of whom gave to the course of justice the credit that it would ascertain the truth, and not one of whom wished that the truth be ascertained. Surely had they been honest-minded in their profession they would all have so wished, or else have abstained from all professional intercourse in the matter. I cannot understand how any gentleman can be willing to use his intellect for the propagation of untruth, and to be paid for so doing.

This, of course, assumes that there is something like "absolute truth" as opposed to what one might call "legal truth"—the story that emerges from the clutter of witness testimony as each side presents its case in the crossfire of the adversary system.

It is particularly appropriate to revisit the traditional defense function at a time when Britain's Labour government is engaged, in its own words, in a "root and branch effort" to "rebalance the criminal justice system in favour of victims, witnesses, and communities." As the recent exoneration of the Duke lacrosse players from spurious charges of rape demonstrates, this is a dangerous business at best. In particular, British defense counsel face increasing pressure from the government to treat "efficient adminstration of justice" on a par with the interests of clients, pressure that is evident, for example, in the Law Society's recently adopted Code for Advocacy which states that counsel has "an overriding duty" to ensure efficiency even in the face of the "client's best interests." This is somewhat disturbing since the duty of "zealous advocacy," like the presumption of innocence and the right against self-incrimination, has always been thought to be among the hallmarks of the Anglo-American criminal justice system, distinguishing it from the continental "inquisitorial system." In the United States, these guarantees—including the right to counsel—are embedded in the federal constitution. In England, they are left to the increasingly malleable unwritten customary "constitution" and—heaven help us—to the vagaries of various United Nations and international conventions on human rights.

Thus, in the interests of "recalibrating" the criminal justice system, the Labour government now requires defendants to disclose the elements of their defense to the government during the investigative stage. Should they fail to do so, jurors may be instructed to draw an inference of guilt from their silence, arguably impinging upon the right against self-incrimination. And, if the defendant points to legal advice as an excuse for his silence at the police station, it may be treated as a waiver of the privilege of confidentiality between attorney and client.

* * *

This apparent encroachment on the attorney-client relationship has, in turn, re-energized discussion of the problem that most fascinated Trollope: the devices his legal characters use to shield themselves from certain knowledge of their client's guilt. For, then as now, a lawyer could not knowingly present perjured testimony or commit a fraud on the court. Thus, the defender must tread a fine line between learning as much as he can in order to present the vigorous defense to which the client is entitled and learning what lawyers call "the ultimate fact." In current terms, it is the tension between the lawyer's "duty of zealous advocacy" on behalf of his client and his obligations as "an officer of the court." In Trollope's day, the balance was struck decidedly on the side of the client.

Of course, once the cat gets out of the bag, there is little counsel can do within the constraints of law but withdraw, plea bargain, or put on a limited defense that effectively signals guilt. When Trollope was writing, a lawyer who learned of his client's guilt mid-trial was permitted to continue the defense but neither to suggest that his client was innocent nor to attempt to place the blame on anyone else known to be innocent. At least, Trollope's lawyers were spared that greatest of all professional perils: a guilty client who insists on testifying in his own defense. Not until 1898—more than a quarter-century after *Orley Farm* appeared—was the British criminal defendant given what one legal historian has called "the dangerous privilege" of being able to give evidence under oath. So great is the incentive to perjury—and so serious the prospect of damnation to a society that believed in the power of oaths—that for centuries the law protected the defendant from himself and the trial from his unreliable testimony.

Legal improbabilities aside, and there are many, the novel revolves around Lady Mason's forgery of a codicil to her late husband's will in order to ensure that her infant son Lucius—rather than her husband's son by a previous marriage, Joseph Mason of Groby Park—will inherit Orley Farm. Joseph Mason unsuccessfully contests the codicil, and Lady Mason settles into quiet occupancy of the property. Twenty years later, when Lucius comes of age, she turns the farm over to him. He immediately reclaims a field long rented to Samuel Dockwrath, a solicitor of distasteful character. In revenge for his loss of the property, Dockwrath revisits the will, finds new evidence of fraud, and instigates Joseph Mason to bring a prosecution against Lady Mason for her perjured testimony in the original civil trial. From very early on, Trollope leads the reader to suspect that the charges against Lady Mason are true; when she confesses guilt late in the novel, no one is surprised.

As Lady Mason's legal troubles mount, Trollope assembles for her a defense team that represents not only the entire spectrum of approaches to criminal defense, but its class divisions as well, ranging from the genteel Furnival to Mr. Chaffanbrass, the Old Bailey barrister who looks more like "a dirty old Jew" than Solomon Aram, the Jewish solicitor with whom he happily associates to the distaste of his fellow defenders. Indeed, just as the appearance of certain present-day attorneys in a case signals the defendant's guilt to the cognoscenti, so resort to Chaffanbrass and Aram is one more indication that Lady Mason is, in fact, guilty of forging the codicil. Both Chaffanbrass and Aram are well aware of this; when mulling over the case, they speak circumspectly of the prospects of acquittal or conviction; neither bothers to mention the question of factual guilt, since they know they would not be needed were the lady innocent.

* * *

The first to confront the prospect of defending Lady Mason is Furnival, the prominent barrister who represented her in the first trial and presumably elicited the perjurious testimony in the first place. She consults him

in his chambers in a highly irregular interview. Although he is susceptible to Lady Mason's considerable charms—as is Sir Peregrine Orme, the neighbor whose support she seeks in order to buttress her respectability and who ultimately proposes marriage—Furnival does not totally abandon his professional wits: he strongly suspects that Lady Mason is guilty and, like any sensible defense attorney, he steers his course accordingly.

In his conscious avoidance of what he increasingly assumes to be the truth, Furnival follows one of the great practical traditions of the defense bar. But his deepening suspicions, coupled with the personal complications, convince Furnival that he cannot act alone for Lady Mason at the upcoming trial; he must find a solicitor who will, in turn, bring the case to another barrister in the "usual way." Burdened with those suspicions, Furnival rejects the immensely respectable solicitors Slow and Bideawhile, Sir Peregrine's own attorneys, because "Old Slow would not conceal the truth for all the baronets in England—no, nor for all the pretty women."

But Old Slow is not quite such a brick as all that. When visited by Sir Peregrine, who hopes to buy off Lord Mason, Slow recognizes that the suggestions of the younger members of chambers as to the lady's guilt are justified. At the same time, he is in the awkward position of having acted for both Joseph Mason and Sir Peregrine over the years. Despite the conflict of interest, as a gentleman—a quality greatly valued in the novel—Slow assures Orme that nothing of the conversation will leave the room. Indeed, it is Old Slow who eventually stands at the center of the ambiguous moral resolution of the novel, at once refusing to represent the odious Groby Park contingent any longer, while effectuating the transfer of the farm to its rightful owner, Joseph Mason, after Chaffanbrass secures Lady Mason's acquittal.

The novel builds to the trial itself, with Furnival, Chaffanbrass, and Felix Graham, an iconoclastic young barrister, in the defense. Graham is presumably intended to be the voice of the future—and of the author. He attends interminable conferences on law reform and writes incendiary articles on the topic, but, like Lucius Mason, he is hampered by the self-righteous naïveté of youth. He is unwilling to represent Lady Mason unless convinced of her innocence and worries incessantly over "the absolute truth in this affair." The guilty deserve no defense. His vision of a trial is to "let every lawyer go into court with a mind resolved to make conspicuous to the light of day that which seems to him to be the truth." Needless to say, this makes for difficulties.

In a pretrial meeting in Furnival's chambers, Graham repeatedly asks the older barrister to assure him that "Lady Mason is really innocent,—that is, free from all fraud and falsehood" since Furnival has represented her from the beginning. Furnival is flummoxed by this faux pas—professional etiquette dictates that the question is out of place precisely because he *has* represented Lady Mason from the beginning. Caught in the dilemma—if he admits his suspicions, they both must withdraw—Furnival says he has "no doubt, none in the least" and "thus, the lie which he had been trying to avoid, was at last told." Youth and inexperience have backed him into falsehood. Following the unwritten professional dictate, Furnival has put loyalty to his client ahead of what he believes to be the truth.

* * *

But is Graham's position tenable, much less morally desirable, as Trollope seems to think? No less an authority than Dr. Johnson opined that "a lawyer has no business with the justice or injustice of the cause which he undertakes . . . [that] is to be decided by the judge." For the adversary system to work—for the government to be forced to prove its case beyond a reasonable doubt before depriving citizens of their lives or liberty—lawyers cannot restrict themselves to defending only clients whom they believe factually innocent. Simply put, as the early rush to judgment in the Duke case showed, a lawyer may be wrong and deprive an innocent party, particularly one already guilty in the court of public opinion, of a defense. In a later novel, *Phineas Redux,* Trollope recognizes this point. There, Chaffanbrass successfully defends Phineas Finn from a charge of murder founded on what seems to be airtight eyewitness testimony. He undertakes the defense despite his initial belief, like that of virtually all the other characters, that Finn committed the crime; in fact Phineas is innocent and the crime was committed by someone else. Without a lawyer willing to defend an apparently guilty man, great injustice would have been done.

As it turns out, Lady Mason's trial is everything Graham feared. Chaffanbrass and Aram orchestrate a successful defense. Despite his misgivings, like an old firehorse, Furnival responds to the bell. He so demolishes the essentially truthful witness Kenneby that the judge tells the jury in his summation that the man was "too stupid to be held of any account." Chaffanbrass takes on the dreadful Dockwrath and gives him the drubbing he deserves; although it is of no relevance to the case, it serves to plant doubt in the jury's mind. He then proceeds to goad a second reliable witness, Bridget Bolster, into responding with such truculence that the jury cannot but suspect her truthfulness. Graham is so disturbed by what he has seen that he barely tests the story of the prosecution witness assigned to him; because of his scruples, he fails his client and, quite possibly, the truth. Furnival sums up, beginning by telling the jury that "I never rose to plead a client's cause with more confidence than I now feel in pleading the case of Lady Mason" and then continuing for three hours. Without hesitation, he lends his own professional stature to the lie. After a long day of jury deliberations, Lady Mason is acquitted.

If professional technique, loyalty to one's client, and a strategic blind eye constitute an answer to how one defends the guilty, Chaffanbrass holds the key to the why. Perhaps because of this, to the present-day lawyer, the center of the legal drama is Chaffanbrass. Chaffanbrass is a gun-for-hire, "a great guardian of the innocence—or rather not-guiltiness of the public," like an "Irish assassin" "always true to the man whose money he had taken." Trollope famously couples Chaffanbrass with Moulder, a vulgar commercial traveler, who admires the barrister's courtroom ways: "You'll see a little fellow in a wig, and he'll get up; and there'll be a man in the box before him,—some swell dressed up to his eyes, who thinks no end of strong beer of himself; and in about ten minutes he'll be as flabby as wet paper, and he'll say—on his oath mind you,—just anything that that little fellow wants him to say. That's power, mind you, and I call it beautiful."

What is more, Moulder's mercenary morals seemingly align with those of Chaffanbrass. When challenged that Chaffanbrass's bullying doesn't produce justice, Moulder replies, "I say it is justice. You can have it if you choose to pay for it and so can I. If I buy a greatcoat against the winter, and you go out at night without having one, is it injustice because you're perished by the cold while I'm as warm as toast. I say it's a grand thing to live in a country where one can buy a greatcoat." Thus, as the jury deliberates Lady Mason's fate, and Chaffanbrass prepares to move on to the next case, he leaves Graham with a parting shot, "Mr. Graham, you are too great for this kind of work, I take it. If I were you I would keep out of it for the future. . . . If a man undertakes a duty, he should do it. That's my opinion, though I confess it's a little old fashioned; especially if he takes money for it."

There's no gainsaying that money is a great motivator—as well as a great equalizer, as Moulder recognizes. But that is not all there is to Chaffanbrass. In a reflective moment with Aram, he admits that the course of his life has unfitted him to be a judge; his legal knowledge is not of the broadest. In another life, he might not have chosen this course. Yet, he also muses, "I've done a great deal of good in my way." At a time when felonies were hanging offenses, he has "prevented unnecessary bloodshed"; he saved the country thousands in the cost of incarceration; and, he has "made the Crown lawyers very careful as to what sort of evidence they would send up to the Old Bailey."

This last is crucial to the defense function to this day and explains what is so unsettling about Labour's "recalibration" of the balance between the defendant and the state. As a matter of law, a plea of innocence is not a factual claim, but a challenge to the state to prove each and every element of its case against the defendant beyond a reasonable double. By putting the government to its burden of proof—even when the defendant is factually guilty—Chaffanbrass and his successors keep the government honest for the rest of us.

Not until his appearance in ***Phineas Redux,*** however, is Chaffanbrass allowed fully to explain himself—and by then Trollope had softened his views of the adversary system a good deal. We already know Chaffanbrass's dirty linen, his taste for the picaresque, his pleasure in courtroom combat, his professional ambition. But now we see more. When Phineas demands to see his lawyer to make sure Chaffanbrass believes in his innocence, the barrister quails. "I hate seeing a client," he says, "He'll tell me either one of two things. He'll swear he didn't murder the man . . . which can have no effect on me one way or the other; or else he'll say that he did,—which would cripple me altogether." In fact, like most attorneys, Chaffanbrass dreads client confidences: "There's no knowing what they'll say. A man will go on swearing by his God that he is innocent, till at last, in a moment of emotion, he breaks down, and out comes the truth." Any attorney who has ever had a client testify in his own defense can hear his own voice in that.

This empathy for fallen human nature cloaked in realism—not to say cynicism—is central to Chaffanbrass's persona as a defender of anyone who can pay his fee, even the guilty. If all politics is local, then all defense is personal. When, in ***Phineas Redux,*** his instructing solicitor suggests that his ferocious cross-examinations are the stuff of legend, Chaffanbrass replies, "It's just the trick of the trade that you learn, as a girl learns the notes of her piano. You forget it the next hour. But, when a man has been hung whom you have striven to save, you do remember that."

FURTHER READING

Bibliographies

Olmsted, John Charles, and Jeffrey Egan Welch. *The Reputation of Trollope: An Annotated Bibliography, 1925-1975.* New York: Garland, 1978, 212 p.

> Provides annotations for some 652 critical pieces on Trollope's work.

Sadleir, Michael. *Trollope: A Bibliography.* London: Constable & Co., 1928, 322 p.

> Presents a descriptive bibliography of Trollope's publications in their early editions. Includes data on the popularity of each of the author's works.

Biographies

Glendinning, Victoria. *Anthony Trollope.* New York: Knopf, 1992, 551 p.

> Offers a comprehensive look at Trollope's life and career.

Hall, N. John. *Trollope: A Biography.* Oxford, England: Clarendon Press, 1991, 581 p.

> Examines Trollope's autobiography and letters, as well as historical data, to provide a rich portrait of Trollope's life.

Criticism

Aguirre, Robert D. "Cold Print: Professing Authorship in Anthony Trollope's *An Autobiography.*" *Biography* 25, no. 4 (fall 2002): 269-92.

> Studies Trollope's autobiography to gain insight into authorial identity as it relates to Trollope.

Aitken, David. "'A Kind of Felicity': Some Notes about Trollope's Style." *Nineteenth-Century Fiction* 20, no. 4 (March 1966): 337-53.

> Investigates whether Trollope's writing style is practiced and learned or a result of natural talent.

apRoberts, Ruth. *The Moral Trollope.* Athens, Ohio: Ohio University Press, 1971, 203 p.

> Analyzes moral issues in *Barchester Towers* and other writings by Trollope.

Blythe, Helen Lucy. "*The Fixed Period* (1882): Euthanasia, Cannibalism, and Colonial Extinction in Trollope's Antipodes." *Nineteenth-Century Contexts* 25, no. 2 (June 2003): 161-80.

> Discusses Trollope's novel *The Fixed Period,* an often overlooked work, and its representation of British colonialism.

Christian, George Scott. "'Something Heroic Is Still Expected': Realism and Comic Heroism in *The Claverings.*" *LIT: Literature Interpretation Theory* 14, no. 3 (July-September 2003): 205-22.

> Argues that the literary realism in Trollope's little-read *The Claverings* departs from nineteenth-century realism and is more akin to the realism of eighteenth-century humorists.

Colella, Sylvana. "Sweet Money: Cultural and Economic Value in Trollope's *Autobiography.*" *Nineteenth-Century Contexts* 28, no. 1 (March 2006): 5-20.

> Examines Trollope's *Autobiography* and his views of the literary marketplace, along with his role in it.

Gilead, Sarah. "Trollope's *Autobiography*: The Strategies of Self-Production." *Modern Language Quarterly* 47, no. 3 (September 1986): 272-90.

Evaluates the narrative structure of Trollope's *Autobiography*.

Halperin, John. *Trollope and Politics: A Study of the Pallisers and Others.* New York: Barnes and Noble, 1977, 318 p.

Investigates Trollope's political novels to gain insight into his civic ideals and the political climate of his time.

Helling, Rafael. *A Century of Trollope Criticism.* Port Washington, N.Y.: Kennikat Press, Inc., 1956, 203 p.

Details literary criticism of Trollope's works from the time of publication of *The Warden* (1855) through the 1950s.

Hirsch, Gordon, and Louella Hirsch. "Trollope's *The Last Chronicle of Barset*: Memory, Depression, and Cognitive Science." *Mosaic: A Journal for the Interdisciplinary Study of Literature* 39, no. 1 (2006): 165-79.

Explores Trollope's *The Last Chronicle of Barset* in the context of cognitive neuroscience.

Lindner, Christoph. "Trollope's Material Girl." *Yearbook of English Studies* 32 (2002): 36-51.

Considers the role of the female in Trollope's writing; includes a look at sexual politics and the treatment of women as commodities.

Nardin, Jane. "Anthony Trollope and Common Morality." In *Trollope and Victorian Moral Philosophy,* pp. 1-16. Athens: Ohio University Press, 1996.

Proposes that Trollope's work upheld and celebrated the moral traditions of England, in contrast to other nineteenth-century literature that viewed British morality in a negative light.

Noonkester, Myron C. "Trollope's *Doctor Thorne.*" *The Explicator* 61, no. 1 (fall 2002): 25-7.

Reviews Trollope's *Doctor Thorne,* focusing in particular on the exile of character Frank Gresham.

O'Mealy, Joseph H. "Rewriting Trollope and Yonge: Mrs. Oliphant's *Phoebe Junior* and the Realism Wars." *Texas Studies in Language and Literature* 39, no. 2 (summer 1997): 125-37.

Discusses writer Margaret Oliphant's literary attacks on Trollope and other contemporaries. Oliphant rewrote novels penned by her literary rivals, including Trollope's *The Last Chronicle of Barset* and *The Warden.*

Pollard, Arthur. *Anthony Trollope.* London: Routledge & Kegan Paul, 1978, 208 p.

Provides an in-depth look at Trollope's life and career; includes criticism of Trollope's writings.

Reiter, Paula Jean. "Husbands, Wives, and Lawyers: Gender Roles and Professional Representation in Trollope and the Adelaide Bartlett Case." *College Literature* 25, no. 1 (winter 1998): 41-62.

Explores the roles and relationships of husbands, wives, and lawyers in relation to Trollope's *Orley Farm* and the 1886 murder trial of Adelaide Bartlett.

Skilton, David. *Anthony Trollope and His Contemporaries: A Study in the Theory and Conventions of Mid-Victorian Fiction.* London: Longman, 1972, 170 p.

Probes criticism by Trollope's contemporaries of his works to gain insight into nineteenth-century concerns, as well as to better understand Trollope's literary reputation.

Tintner, Adeline R. "James' 'The Patagonia': A Critique of Trollope's 'The Journey to Panama.'" *Studies in Short Fiction* 32, no. 1 (winter 1995): 59.

Investigates Henry James' reworking of Trollope's short story "The Journey to Panama" as "The Patagonia," a more tragic version than Trollope's.

Vernon, Patricia A. "The Poor Fictionist's Conscience: Point of View in the Palliser Novels." *Victorian Newsletter* 71 (spring 1987): 16-20.

Evaluates the complex role of the narrator in Trollope's Palliser novels.

Additional coverage of Trollope's life and career is contained in the following sources published by Gale: *British Writers,* **Vol. 5;** *Concise Dictionary of British Literary Biography, 1832-1890;* *Dictionary of Literary Biography,* **Vols. 21, 57, 159;** *DISCovering Authors;* *DISCovering Authors: British Edition;* *DISCovering Authors: Canadian Edition;* *DISCovering Authors Modules: Most-studied Authors* **and** *Novelists;* *DISCovering Authors 3.0;* *Literature Resource Center;* *Nineteenth-Century Literature Criticism,* **Vols. 6, 33, 101;** *Reference Guide to English Literature,* **Ed. 2;** *Reference Guide to Short Fiction,* **Ed. 2;** *Short Story Criticism,* **Vol. 28;** *Something About the Author,* **Vol. 22;** **and** *World Literature Criticism,* **Vol. 6.**

How to Use This Index

The main references

> **Calvino, Italo**
> 1923-1985 .... CLC 5, 8, 11, 22, 33, 39,
> 73; SSC 3, 48

list all author entries in the following Gale Literary Criticism series:

AAL = Asian American Literature
BG = The Beat Generation: A Gale Critical Companion
BLC = Black Literature Criticism
BLCS = Black Literature Criticism Supplement
CLC = Contemporary Literary Criticism
CLR = Children's Literature Review
CMLC = Classical and Medieval Literature Criticism
DC = Drama Criticism
FL = Feminism in Literature: A Gale Critical Companion
GL = Gothic Literature: A Gale Critical Companion
HLC = Hispanic Literature Criticism
HLCS = Hispanic Literature Criticism Supplement
HR = Harlem Renaissance: A Gale Critical Companion
LC = Literature Criticism from 1400 to 1800
NCLC = Nineteenth-Century Literature Criticism
NNAL = Native North American Literature
PC = Poetry Criticism
SSC = Short Story Criticism
TCLC = Twentieth-Century Literary Criticism
WLC = World Literature Criticism, 1500 to the Present
WLCS = World Literature Criticism Supplement

The cross-references

> See also CA 85-88, 116; CANR 23, 61;
> DAM NOV; DLB 196; EW 13; MTCW 1, 2;
> RGSF 2; RGWL 2; SFW 4; SSFS 12

list all author entries in the following Gale biographical and literary sources:

AAYA = Authors & Artists for Young Adults
AFAW = African American Writers
AFW = African Writers
AITN = Authors in the News
AMW = American Writers
AMWR = American Writers Retrospective Supplement
AMWS = American Writers Supplement
ANW = American Nature Writers
AW = Ancient Writers
BEST = Bestsellers
BPFB = Beacham's Encyclopedia of Popular Fiction: Biography and Resources
BRW = British Writers
BRWS = British Writers Supplement
BW = Black Writers
BYA = Beacham's Guide to Literature for Young Adults
CA = Contemporary Authors
CAAS = Contemporary Authors Autobiography Series
CABS = Contemporary Authors Bibliographical Series
CAD = Contemporary American Dramatists
CANR = Contemporary Authors New Revision Series
CAP = Contemporary Authors Permanent Series
CBD = Contemporary British Dramatists
CCA = Contemporary Canadian Authors
CD = Contemporary Dramatists
CDALB = Concise Dictionary of American Literary Biography

CDALBS = *Concise Dictionary of American Literary Biography Supplement*
CDBLB = *Concise Dictionary of British Literary Biography*
CMW = *St. James Guide to Crime & Mystery Writers*
CN = *Contemporary Novelists*
CP = *Contemporary Poets*
CPW = *Contemporary Popular Writers*
CSW = *Contemporary Southern Writers*
CWD = *Contemporary Women Dramatists*
CWP = *Contemporary Women Poets*
CWRI = *St. James Guide to Children's Writers*
CWW = *Contemporary World Writers*
DA = *DISCovering Authors*
DA3 = *DISCovering Authors 3.0*
DAB = *DISCovering Authors: British Edition*
DAC = *DISCovering Authors: Canadian Edition*
DAM = *DISCovering Authors: Modules*
    DRAM: *Dramatists Module;* **MST:** *Most-studied Authors Module;*
    MULT: *Multicultural Authors Module;* **NOV:** *Novelists Module;*
    POET: *Poets Module;* **POP:** *Popular Fiction and Genre Authors Module*
DFS = *Drama for Students*
DLB = *Dictionary of Literary Biography*
DLBD = *Dictionary of Literary Biography Documentary Series*
DLBY = *Dictionary of Literary Biography Yearbook*
DNFS = *Literature of Developing Nations for Students*
EFS = *Epics for Students*
EXPN = *Exploring Novels*
EXPP = *Exploring Poetry*
EXPS = *Exploring Short Stories*
EW = *European Writers*
FANT = *St. James Guide to Fantasy Writers*
FW = *Feminist Writers*
GFL = *Guide to French Literature,* Beginnings to 1789, 1798 to the Present
GLL = *Gay and Lesbian Literature*
HGG = *St. James Guide to Horror, Ghost & Gothic Writers*
HW = *Hispanic Writers*
IDFW = *International Dictionary of Films and Filmmakers: Writers and Production Artists*
IDTP = *International Dictionary of Theatre: Playwrights*
LAIT = *Literature and Its Times*
LAW = *Latin American Writers*
JRDA = *Junior DISCovering Authors*
MAICYA = *Major Authors and Illustrators for Children and Young Adults*
MAICYAS = *Major Authors and Illustrators for Children and Young Adults Supplement*
MAWW = *Modern American Women Writers*
MJW = *Modern Japanese Writers*
MTCW = *Major 20th-Century Writers*
NCFS = *Nonfiction Classics for Students*
NFS = *Novels for Students*
PAB = *Poets: American and British*
PFS = *Poetry for Students*
RGAL = *Reference Guide to American Literature*
RGEL = *Reference Guide to English Literature*
RGSF = *Reference Guide to Short Fiction*
RGWL = *Reference Guide to World Literature*
RHW = *Twentieth-Century Romance and Historical Writers*
SAAS = *Something about the Author Autobiography Series*
SATA = *Something about the Author*
SFW = *St. James Guide to Science Fiction Writers*
SSFS = *Short Stories for Students*
TCWW = *Twentieth-Century Western Writers*
WLIT = *World Literature and Its Times*
WP = *World Poets*
YABC = *Yesterday's Authors of Books for Children*
YAW = *St. James Guide to Young Adult Writers*

Literary Criticism Series
Cumulative Author Index

Appelfeld, Aharon 1932- ... **CLC 23, 47; SSC 42**
> See also CA 112; 133; CANR 86, 160; CWW 2; DLB 299; EWL 3; RGHL; RGSF 2; WLIT 6

Appelfeld, Aron
> See Appelfeld, Aharon

Apple, Max (Isaac) 1941- .... **CLC 9, 33; SSC 50**
> See also AMWS 17; CA 81-84; CANR 19, 54; DLB 130

Appleman, Philip (Dean) 1926- .... **CLC 51**
> See also CA 13-16R; CAAS 18; CANR 6, 29, 56

Appleton, Lawrence
> See Lovecraft, H. P.

Apteryx
> See Eliot, T(homas) S(tearns)

Apuleius, (Lucius Madaurensis) c. 125-c. 164 .... **CMLC 1, 84**
> See also AW 2; CDWLB 1; DLB 211; RGWL 2, 3; SUFW; WLIT 8

Aquin, Hubert 1929-1977 .... **CLC 15**
> See also CA 105; DLB 53; EWL 3

Aquinas, Thomas 1224(?)-1274 ..... **CMLC 33**
> See also DLB 115; EW 1; TWA

Aragon, Louis 1897-1982 .... **CLC 3, 22; TCLC 123**
> See also CA 69-72; 108; CANR 28, 71; DAM NOV, POET; DLB 72, 258; EW 11; EWL 3; GFL 1789 to the Present; GLL 2; LMFS 2; MTCW 1, 2; RGWL 2, 3

Arany, Janos 1817-1882 .... **NCLC 34**

Aranyos, Kakay 1847-1910
> See Mikszath, Kalman

Aratus of Soli c. 315B.C.-c. 240B.C. .... **CMLC 64**
> See also DLB 176

Arbuthnot, John 1667-1735 .... **LC 1**
> See also DLB 101

Archer, Herbert Winslow
> See Mencken, H(enry) L(ouis)

Archer, Jeffrey 1940- .... **CLC 28**
> See also AAYA 16; BEST 89:3; BPFB 1; CA 77-80; CANR 22, 52, 95, 136; CPW; DA3; DAM POP; INT CANR-22; MTFW 2005

Archer, Jeffrey Howard
> See Archer, Jeffrey

Archer, Jules 1915- .... **CLC 12**
> See also CA 9-12R; CANR 6, 69; SAAS 5; SATA 4, 85

Archer, Lee
> See Ellison, Harlan

Archilochus c. 7th cent. B.C.- .... **CMLC 44**
> See also DLB 176

Ard, William
> See Jakes, John

Arden, John 1930- .... **CLC 6, 13, 15**
> See also BRWS 2; CA 13-16R; CAAS 4; CANR 31, 65, 67, 124; CBD; CD 5, 6; DAM DRAM; DFS 9; DLB 13, 245; EWL 3; MTCW 1

Arenas, Reinaldo 1943-1990 .. **CLC 41; HLC 1; TCLC 191**
> See also CA 124; 128; 133; CANR 73, 106; DAM MULT; DLB 145; EWL 3; GLL 2; HW 1; LAW; LAWS 1; MTCW 2; MTFW 2005; RGSF 2; RGWL 3; WLIT 1

Arendt, Hannah 1906-1975 .... **CLC 66, 98; TCLC 193**
> See also CA 17-20R; 61-64; CANR 26, 60, 172; DLB 242; MTCW 1, 2

Aretino, Pietro 1492-1556 .... **LC 12, 165**
> See also RGWL 2, 3

Arghezi, Tudor
> See Theodorescu, Ion N.

Arguedas, Jose Maria 1911-1969 .... **CLC 10, 18; HLCS 1; TCLC 147**
> See also CA 89-92; CANR 73; DLB 113; EWL 3; HW 1; LAW; RGWL 2, 3; WLIT 1

Argueta, Manlio 1936- .... **CLC 31**
> See also CA 131; CANR 73; CWW 2; DLB 145; EWL 3; HW 1; RGWL 3

Arias, Ron 1941- .... **HLC 1**
> See also CA 131; CANR 81, 136; DAM MULT; DLB 82; HW 1, 2; MTCW 2; MTFW 2005

Ariosto, Lodovico
> See Ariosto, Ludovico

Ariosto, Ludovico 1474-1533 ... **LC 6, 87; PC 42**
> See also EW 2; RGWL 2, 3; WLIT 7

Aristides
> See Epstein, Joseph

Aristophanes 450B.C.-385B.C. .... **CMLC 4, 51; DC 2; WLCS**
> See also AW 1; CDWLB 1; DA; DA3; DAB; DAC; DAM DRAM, MST; DFS 10; DLB 176; LMFS 1; RGWL 2, 3; TWA; WLIT 8

Aristotle 384B.C.-322B.C. .... **CMLC 31; WLCS**
> See also AW 1; CDWLB 1; DA; DA3; DAB; DAC; DAM MST; DLB 176; RGWL 2, 3; TWA; WLIT 8

Arlt, Roberto (Godofredo Christophersen) 1900-1942 .... **HLC 1; TCLC 29**
> See also CA 123; 131; CANR 67; DAM MULT; DLB 305; EWL 3; HW 1, 2; IDTP; LAW

Armah, Ayi Kwei 1939- . **BLC 1:1, 2:1; CLC 5, 33, 136**
> See also AFW; BRWS 10; BW 1; CA 61-64; CANR 21, 64; CDWLB 3; CN 1, 2, 3, 4, 5, 6, 7; DAM MULT, POET; DLB 117; EWL 3; MTCW 1; WLIT 2

Armatrading, Joan 1950- .... **CLC 17**
> See also CA 114; 186

Armin, Robert 1568(?)-1615(?) .... **LC 120**

Armitage, Frank
> See Carpenter, John (Howard)

Armstrong, Jeannette (C.) 1948- .... **NNAL**
> See also CA 149; CCA 1; CN 6, 7; DAC; DLB 334; SATA 102

Arnette, Robert
> See Silverberg, Robert

Arnim, Achim von (Ludwig Joachim von Arnim) 1781-1831 .. **NCLC 5, 159; SSC 29**
> See also DLB 90

Arnim, Bettina von 1785-1859 ...... **NCLC 38, 123**
> See also DLB 90; RGWL 2, 3

Arnold, Matthew 1822-1888 ..... **NCLC 6, 29, 89, 126; PC 5, 94; WLC 1**
> See also BRW 5; CDBLB 1832-1890; DA; DAB; DAC; DAM MST, POET; DLB 32, 57; EXPP; PAB; PFS 2; TEA; WP

Arnold, Thomas 1795-1842 .... **NCLC 18**
> See also DLB 55

Arnow, Harriette (Louisa) Simpson 1908-1986 ...... **CLC 2, 7, 18; TCLC 196**
> See also BPFB 1; CA 9-12R; 118; CANR 14; CN 2, 3, 4; DLB 6; FW; MTCW 1, 2; RHW; SATA 42; SATA-Obit 47

Arouet, Francois-Marie
> See Voltaire

Arp, Hans
> See Arp, Jean

Arp, Jean 1887-1966 .... **CLC 5; TCLC 115**
> See also CA 81-84; 25-28R; CANR 42, 77; EW 10

Arrabal
> See Arrabal, Fernando

Arrabal (Teran), Fernando
> See Arrabal, Fernando

Arrabal, Fernando 1932- ... **CLC 2, 9, 18, 58**
> See also CA 9-12R; CANR 15; CWW 2; DLB 321; EWL 3; LMFS 2

Arreola, Juan Jose 1918-2001 .... **CLC 147; HLC 1; SSC 38**
> See also CA 113; 131; 200; CANR 81; CWW 2; DAM MULT; DLB 113; DNFS 2; EWL 3; HW 1, 2; LAW; RGSF 2

Arrian c. 89(?)-c. 155(?) .... **CMLC 43**
> See also DLB 176

Arrick, Fran
> See Angell, Judie

Arrley, Richmond
> See Delany, Samuel R., Jr.

Artaud, Antonin (Marie Joseph) 1896-1948 .... **DC 14; TCLC 3, 36**
> See also CA 104; 149; DA3; DAM DRAM; DFS 22; DLB 258, 321; EW 11; EWL 3; GFL 1789 to the Present; MTCW 2; MTFW 2005; RGWL 2, 3

Arthur, Ruth M(abel) 1905-1979 ..... **CLC 12**
> See also CA 9-12R; 85-88; CANR 4; CWRI 5; SATA 7, 26

Artsybashev, Mikhail (Petrovich) 1878-1927 .... **TCLC 31**
> See also CA 170; DLB 295

Arundel, Honor (Morfydd) 1919-1973 .... **CLC 17**
> See also CA 21-22; 41-44R; CAP 2; CLR 35; CWRI 5; SATA 4; SATA-Obit 24

Arzner, Dorothy 1900-1979 .... **CLC 98**

Asch, Sholem 1880-1957 .... **TCLC 3**
> See also CA 105; DLB 333; EWL 3; GLL 2; RGHL

Ascham, Roger 1516(?)-1568 .... **LC 101**
> See also DLB 236

Ash, Shalom
> See Asch, Sholem

Ashbery, John 1927- ... **CLC 2, 3, 4, 6, 9, 13, 15, 25, 41, 77, 125, 221; PC 26**
> See also AMWS 3; CA 5-8R; CANR 9, 37, 66, 102, 132, 170; CP 1, 2, 3, 4, 5, 6, 7; DA3; DAM POET; DLB 5, 165; DLBY 1981; EWL 3; GLL 1; INT CANR-9; MAL 5; MTCW 1, 2; MTFW 2005; PAB; PFS 11, 28; RGAL 4; TCLE 1:1; WP

Ashbery, John Lawrence
> See Ashbery, John

Ashbridge, Elizabeth 1713-1755 .... **LC 147**
> See also DLB 200

Ashdown, Clifford
> See Freeman, R(ichard) Austin

Ashe, Gordon
> See Creasey, John

Ashton-Warner, Sylvia (Constance) 1908-1984 .... **CLC 19**
> See also CA 69-72; 112; CANR 29; CN 1, 2, 3; MTCW 1, 2

Asimov, Isaac 1920-1992 ..... **CLC 1, 3, 9, 19, 26, 76, 92**
> See also AAYA 13; BEST 90:2; BPFB 1; BYA 4, 6, 7, 9; CA 1-4R; 137; CANR 2, 19, 36, 60, 125; CLR 12, 79; CMW 4; CN 1, 2, 3, 4, 5; CPW; DA3; DAM POP; DLB 8; DLBY 1992; INT CANR-19; JRDA; LAIT 5; LMFS 2; MAICYA 1, 2; MAL 5; MTCW 1, 2; MTFW 2005; NFS 29; RGAL 4; SATA 1, 26, 74; SCFW 1, 2; SFW 4; SSFS 17; TUS; YAW

Askew, Anne 1521(?)-1546 .... **LC 81**
> See also DLB 136

Assis, Joaquim Maria Machado de
> See Machado de Assis, Joaquim Maria

Astell, Mary 1666-1731 .... **LC 68**
> See also DLB 252, 336; FW

Bacon, Francis 1561-1626 ..... **LC 18, 32, 131**
See also BRW 1; CDBLB Before 1660;
DLB 151, 236, 252; RGEL 2; TEA
Bacon, Roger 1214(?)-1294 ... **CMLC 14, 108**
See also DLB 115
Bacovia, George 1881-1957 .... **TCLC 24**
See also CA 123; 189; CDWLB 4; DLB
220; EWL 3
Badanes, Jerome 1937-1995 .... **CLC 59**
See also CA 234
Bage, Robert 1728-1801 .... **NCLC 182**
See also DLB 39; RGEL 2
Bagehot, Walter 1826-1877 .... **NCLC 10**
See also DLB 55
Bagnold, Enid 1889-1981 .... **CLC 25**
See also AAYA 75; BYA 2; CA 5-8R; 103;
CANR 5, 40; CBD; CN 2; CWD; CWRI
5; DAM DRAM; DLB 13, 160, 191, 245;
FW; MAICYA 1, 2; RGEL 2; SATA 1, 25
Bagritsky, Eduard
See Dzyubin, Eduard Georgievich
Bagritsky, Edvard
See Dzyubin, Eduard Georgievich
Bagrjana, Elisaveta
See Belcheva, Elisaveta Lyubomirova
Bagryana, Elisaveta
See Belcheva, Elisaveta Lyubomirova
Bailey, Paul 1937- .... **CLC 45**
See also CA 21-24R; CANR 16, 62, 124;
CN 1, 2, 3, 4, 5, 6, 7; DLB 14, 271; GLL
2
Baillie, Joanna 1762-1851 ...... **NCLC 71, 151**
See also DLB 93, 344; GL 2; RGEL 2
Bainbridge, Beryl 1934- ...... **CLC 4, 5, 8, 10,
14, 18, 22, 62, 130**
See also BRWS 6; CA 21-24R; CANR 24,
55, 75, 88, 128; CN 2, 3, 4, 5, 6, 7; DAM
NOV; DLB 14, 231; EWL 3; MTCW 1,
2; MTFW 2005
Baker, Carlos (Heard)
1909-1987 .... **TCLC 119**
See also CA 5-8R; 122; CANR 3, 63; DLB
103
Baker, Elliott 1922-2007 .... **CLC 8**
See also CA 45-48; 257; CANR 2, 63; CN
1, 2, 3, 4, 5, 6, 7
Baker, Elliott Joseph
See Baker, Elliott
Baker, Jean H.
See Russell, George William
Baker, Nicholson 1957- .... **CLC 61, 165**
See also AMWS 13; CA 135; CANR 63,
120, 138; CN 6; CPW; DA3; DAM POP;
DLB 227; MTFW 2005
Baker, Ray Stannard 1870-1946 .... **TCLC 47**
See also CA 118; DLB 345
Baker, Russell 1925- .... **CLC 31**
See also BEST 89:4; CA 57-60; CANR 11,
41, 59, 137; MTCW 1, 2; MTFW 2005
Bakhtin, M.
See Bakhtin, Mikhail Mikhailovich
Bakhtin, M. M.
See Bakhtin, Mikhail Mikhailovich
Bakhtin, Mikhail
See Bakhtin, Mikhail Mikhailovich
Bakhtin, Mikhail Mikhailovich
1895-1975 .... **CLC 83; TCLC 160**
See also CA 128; 113; DLB 242; EWL 3
Bakshi, Ralph 1938(?)- .... **CLC 26**
See also CA 112; 138; IDFW 3
Bakunin, Mikhail (Alexandrovich)
1814-1876 .... **NCLC 25, 58**
See also DLB 277
Bal, Mieke (Maria Gertrudis)
1946- .... **CLC 252**
See also CA 156; CANR 99

Baldwin, James 1924-1987 ...... **BLC 1:1, 2:1;
CLC 1, 2, 3, 4, 5, 8, 13, 15, 17, 42, 50,
67, 90, 127; DC 1; SSC 10, 33, 98;
WLC 1**
See also AAYA 4, 34; AFAW 1, 2; AMWR
2; AMWS 1; BPFB 1; BW 1; CA 1-4R;
124; CABS 1; CAD; CANR 3, 24;
CDALB 1941-1968; CN 1, 2, 3, 4; CPW;
DA; DA3; DAB; DAC; DAM MST,
MULT, NOV, POP; DFS 11, 15; DLB 2,
7, 33, 249, 278; DLBY 1987; EWL 3;
EXPS; LAIT 5; MAL 5; MTCW 1, 2;
MTFW 2005; NCFS 4; NFS 4; RGAL 4;
RGSF 2; SATA 9; SATA-Obit 54; SSFS
2, 18; TUS
Baldwin, William c. 1515-1563 .... **LC 113**
See also DLB 132
Bale, John 1495-1563 .... **LC 62**
See also DLB 132; RGEL 2; TEA
Ball, Hugo 1886-1927 .... **TCLC 104**
Ballard, J.G. 1930-2009 ..... **CLC 3, 6, 14, 36,
137; SSC 1, 53**
See also AAYA 3, 52; BRWS 5; CA 5-8R;
CANR 15, 39, 65, 107, 133; CN 1, 2, 3,
4, 5, 6, 7; DA3; DAM NOV, POP; DLB
14, 207, 261, 319; EWL 3; HGG; MTCW
1, 2; MTFW 2005; NFS 8; RGEL 2;
RGSF 2; SATA 93; SCFW 1, 2; SFW 4
Balmont, Konstantin (Dmitriyevich)
1867-1943 .... **TCLC 11**
See also CA 109; 155; DLB 295; EWL 3
Baltausis, Vincas 1847-1910
See Mikszath, Kalman
Balzac, Guez de (?)-
See Balzac, Jean-Louis Guez de
Balzac, Honore de 1799-1850 ... **NCLC 5, 35,
53, 153; SSC 5, 59, 102; WLC 1**
See also DA; DA3; DAB; DAC; DAM
MST, NOV; DLB 119; EW 5; GFL 1789
to the Present; LMFS 1; RGSF 2; RGWL
2, 3; SSFS 10; SUFW; TWA
Balzac, Jean-Louis Guez de
1597-1654 .... **LC 162**
See also DLB 268; GFL Beginnings to 1789
Bambara, Toni Cade 1939-1995 ..... **BLC 1:1,
2:1; CLC 19, 88; SSC 35, 107; TCLC
116; WLCS**
See also AAYA 5, 49; AFAW 2; AMWS 11;
BW 2, 3; BYA 12, 14; CA 29-32R; 150;
CANR 24, 49, 81; CDALBS; DA; DA3;
DAC; DAM MST, MULT; DLB 38, 218;
EXPS; MAL 5; MTCW 1, 2; MTFW
2005; RGAL 4; RGSF 2; SATA 112; SSFS
4, 7, 12, 21
Bamdad, A.
See Shamlu, Ahmad
Bamdad, Alef
See Shamlu, Ahmad
Banat, D. R.
See Bradbury, Ray
Bancroft, Laura
See Baum, L(yman) Frank
Banim, John 1798-1842 .... **NCLC 13**
See also DLB 116, 158, 159; RGEL 2
Banim, Michael 1796-1874 .... **NCLC 13**
See also DLB 158, 159
Banjo, The
See Paterson, A(ndrew) B(arton)
Banks, Iain 1954- .... **CLC 34**
See also BRWS 11; CA 123; 128; CANR
61, 106, 180; DLB 194, 261; EWL 3;
HGG; INT CA-128; MTFW 2005; SFW 4
Banks, Iain M.
See Banks, Iain
Banks, Iain Menzies
See Banks, Iain
Banks, Lynne Reid
See Reid Banks, Lynne

Banks, Russell 1940- . **CLC 37, 72, 187; SSC
42**
See also AAYA 45; AMWS 5; CA 65-68;
CAAS 15; CANR 19, 52, 73, 118; CN 4,
5, 6, 7; DLB 130, 278; EWL 3; MAL 5;
MTCW 2; MTFW 2005; NFS 13
Banks, Russell Earl
See Banks, Russell
Banville, John 1945- .... **CLC 46, 118, 224**
See also CA 117; 128; CANR 104, 150,
176; CN 4, 5, 6, 7; DLB 14, 271, 326;
INT CA-128
Banville, Theodore (Faullain) de
1832-1891 .... **NCLC 9**
See also DLB 217; GFL 1789 to the Present
Baraka, Amiri 1934- .. **BLC 1:1, 2:1; CLC 1,
2, 3, 5, 10, 14, 33, 115, 213; DC 6; PC
4; WLCS**
See also AAYA 63; AFAW 1, 2; AMWS 2;
BW 2, 3; CA 21-24R; CABS 3; CAD;
CANR 27, 38, 61, 133, 172; CD 3, 5, 6;
CDALB 1941-1968; CN 1, 2; CP 1, 2, 3,
4, 5, 6, 7; CPW; DA; DA3; DAC; DAM
MST, MULT, POET, POP; DFS 3, 11, 16;
DLB 5, 7, 16, 38; DLBD 8; EWL 3; MAL
5; MTCW 1, 2; MTFW 2005; PFS 9;
RGAL 4; TCLE 1:1; TUS; WP
Baratynsky, Evgenii Abramovich
1800-1844 .... **NCLC 103**
See also DLB 205
Barbauld, Anna Laetitia
1743-1825 .... **NCLC 50, 185**
See also DLB 107, 109, 142, 158, 336;
RGEL 2
Barbellion, W. N. P.
See Cummings, Bruce F(rederick)
Barber, Benjamin R. 1939- .... **CLC 141**
See also CA 29-32R; CANR 12, 32, 64, 119
Barbera, Jack (Vincent) 1945- .... **CLC 44**
See also CA 110; CANR 45
Barbey d'Aurevilly, Jules-Amedee
1808-1889 .... **NCLC 1, 213; SSC 17**
See also DLB 119; GFL 1789 to the Present
Barbour, John c. 1316-1395 .... **CMLC 33**
See also DLB 146
Barbusse, Henri 1873-1935 .... **TCLC 5**
See also CA 105; 154; DLB 65; EWL 3;
RGWL 2, 3
Barclay, Alexander c. 1475-1552 .... **LC 109**
See also DLB 132
Barclay, Bill
See Moorcock, Michael
Barclay, William Ewert
See Moorcock, Michael
Barea, Arturo 1897-1957 .... **TCLC 14**
See also CA 111; 201
Barfoot, Joan 1946- .... **CLC 18**
See also CA 105; CANR 141, 179
Barham, Richard Harris
1788-1845 .... **NCLC 77**
See also DLB 159
Baring, Maurice 1874-1945 .... **TCLC 8**
See also CA 105; 168; DLB 34; HGG
Baring-Gould, Sabine 1834-1924 ... **TCLC 88**
See also DLB 156, 190
Barker, Clive 1952- .... **CLC 52, 205; SSC 53**
See also AAYA 10, 54; BEST 90:3; BPFB
1; CA 121; 129; CANR 71, 111, 133, 187;
CPW; DA3; DAM POP; DLB 261; HGG;
INT CA-129; MTCW 1, 2; MTFW 2005;
SUFW 2
Barker, George Granville
1913-1991 .... **CLC 8, 48; PC 77**
See also CA 9-12R; 135; CANR 7, 38; CP
1, 2, 3, 4, 5; DAM POET; DLB 20; EWL
3; MTCW 1
Barker, Harley Granville
See Granville-Barker, Harley

Beattie, Ann 1947- ..... **CLC 8, 13, 18, 40, 63, 146; SSC 11**
See also AMWS 5; BEST 90:2; BPFB 1; CA 81-84; CANR 53, 73, 128; CN 4, 5, 6, 7; CPW; DA3; DAM NOV, POP; DLB 218, 278; DLBY 1982; EWL 3; MAL 5; MTCW 1, 2; MTFW 2005; RGAL 4; RGSF 2; SSFS 9; TUS

Beattie, James 1735-1803 .... **NCLC 25**
See also DLB 109

Beauchamp, Kathleen Mansfield 1888-1923 . **SSC 9, 23, 38, 81; TCLC 2, 8, 39, 164; WLC 4**
See also BPFB 2; BRW 7; CA 104; 134; DA; DA3; DAB; DAC; DAM MST; DLB 162; EWL 3; EXPS; FW; GLL 1; MTCW 2; RGEL 2; RGSF 2; SSFS 2, 8, 10, 11; TEA; WWE 1

Beaumarchais, Pierre-Augustin Caron de 1732-1799 .... **DC 4; LC 61**
See also DAM DRAM; DFS 14, 16; DLB 313; EW 4; GFL Beginnings to 1789; RGWL 2, 3

Beaumont, Francis 1584(?)-1616 .. **DC 6; LC 33**
See also BRW 2; CDBLB Before 1660; DLB 58; TEA

Beauvoir, Simone de 1908-1986 .... **CLC 1, 2, 4, 8, 14, 31, 44, 50, 71, 124; SSC 35; WLC 1**
See also BPFB 1; CA 9-12R; 118; CANR 28, 61; DA; DA3; DAB; DAC; DAM MST, NOV; DLB 72; DLBY 1986; EW 12; EWL 3; FL 1:5; FW; GFL 1789 to the Present; LMFS 2; MTCW 1, 2; MTFW 2005; RGSF 2; RGWL 2, 3; TWA

Beauvoir, Simone Lucie Ernestine Marie Bertrand de
See Beauvoir, Simone de

Becker, Carl (Lotus) 1873-1945 ..... **TCLC 63**
See also CA 157; DLB 17

Becker, Jurek 1937-1997 .... **CLC 7, 19**
See also CA 85-88; 157; CANR 60, 117; CWW 2; DLB 75, 299; EWL 3; RGHL

Becker, Walter 1950- .... **CLC 26**

Becket, Thomas a 1118(?)-1170 .... **CMLC 83**

Beckett, Samuel 1906-1989 .... **CLC 1, 2, 3, 4, 6, 9, 10, 11, 14, 18, 29, 57, 59, 83; DC 22; SSC 16, 74; TCLC 145; WLC 1**
See also BRWC 2; BRWR 1; BRWS 1; CA 5-8R; 130; CANR 33, 61; CBD; CDBLB 1945-1960; CN 1, 2, 3, 4; CP 1, 2, 3, 4; DA; DA3; DAB; DAC; DAM DRAM, MST, NOV; DFS 2, 7, 18; DLB 13, 15, 233, 319, 321, 329; DLBY 1990; EWL 3; GFL 1789 to the Present; LATS 1:2; LMFS 2; MTCW 1, 2; MTFW 2005; RGSF 2; RGWL 2, 3; SSFS 15; TEA; WLIT 4

Beckford, William 1760-1844 .... **NCLC 16, 214**
See also BRW 3; DLB 39, 213; GL 2; HGG; LMFS 1; SUFW

Beckham, Barry (Earl) 1944- .... **BLC 1:1**
See also BW 1; CA 29-32R; CANR 26, 62; CN 1, 2, 3, 4, 5, 6; DAM MULT; DLB 33

Beckman, Gunnel 1910- .... **CLC 26**
See also CA 33-36R; CANR 15, 114; CLR 25; MAICYA 1, 2; SAAS 9; SATA 6

Becque, Henri 1837-1899 .... **DC 21; NCLC 3**
See also DLB 192; GFL 1789 to the Present

Becquer, Gustavo Adolfo 1836-1870 .... **HLCS 1; NCLC 106**
See also DAM MULT

Beddoes, Thomas Lovell 1803-1849 .. **DC 15; NCLC 3, 154**
See also BRWS 11; DLB 96

Bede c. 673-735 .... **CMLC 20**
See also DLB 146; TEA

Bedford, Denton R. 1907-(?) .... **NNAL**

Bedford, Donald F.
See Fearing, Kenneth (Flexner)

Beecher, Catharine Esther 1800-1878 .... **NCLC 30**
See also DLB 1, 243

Beecher, John 1904-1980 .... **CLC 6**
See also AITN 1; CA 5-8R; 105; CANR 8; CP 1, 2, 3

Beer, Johann 1655-1700 .... **LC 5**
See also DLB 168

Beer, Patricia 1924- .... **CLC 58**
See also BRWS 14; CA 61-64; 183; CANR 13, 46; CP 1, 2, 3, 4, 5, 6; CWP; DLB 40; FW

Beerbohm, Max
See Beerbohm, (Henry) Max(imilian)

Beerbohm, (Henry) Max(imilian) 1872-1956 .... **TCLC 1, 24**
See also BRWS 2; CA 104; 154; CANR 79; DLB 34, 100; FANT; MTCW 2

Beer-Hofmann, Richard 1866-1945 .... **TCLC 60**
See also CA 160; DLB 81

Beg, Shemus
See Stephens, James

Begiebing, Robert J(ohn) 1946- .... **CLC 70**
See also CA 122; CANR 40, 88

Begley, Louis 1933- .... **CLC 197**
See also CA 140; CANR 98, 176; DLB 299; RGHL; TCLE 1:1

Behan, Brendan (Francis) 1923-1964 ...... **CLC 1, 8, 11, 15, 79**
See also BRWS 2; CA 73-76; CANR 33, 121; CBD; CDBLB 1945-1960; DAM DRAM; DFS 7; DLB 13, 233; EWL 3; MTCW 1, 2

Behn, Aphra 1640(?)-1689 .. **DC 4; LC 1, 30, 42, 135; PC 13, 88; WLC 1**
See also BRWS 3; DA; DA3; DAB; DAC; DAM DRAM, MST, NOV, POET; DFS 16, 24; DLB 39, 80, 131; FW; TEA; WLIT 3

Behrman, S(amuel) N(athaniel) 1893-1973 .... **CLC 40**
See also CA 13-16; 45-48; CAD; CAP 1; DLB 7, 44; IDFW 3; MAL 5; RGAL 4

Bekederemo, J. P. Clark
See Clark Bekederemo, J.P.

Belasco, David 1853-1931 .... **TCLC 3**
See also CA 104; 168; DLB 7; MAL 5; RGAL 4

Belcheva, Elisaveta Lyubomirova 1893-1991 .... **CLC 10**
See also CA 178; CDWLB 4; DLB 147; EWL 3

Beldone, Phil "Cheech"
See Ellison, Harlan

Beleno
See Azuela, Mariano

Belinski, Vissarion Grigoryevich 1811-1848 .... **NCLC 5**
See also DLB 198

Belitt, Ben 1911- .... **CLC 22**
See also CA 13-16R; CAAS 4; CANR 7, 77; CP 1, 2, 3, 4, 5, 6; DLB 5

Belknap, Jeremy 1744-1798 .... **LC 115**
See also DLB 30, 37

Bell, Gertrude (Margaret Lowthian) 1868-1926 .... **TCLC 67**
See also CA 167; CANR 110; DLB 174

Bell, J. Freeman
See Zangwill, Israel

Bell, James Madison 1826-1902 ..... **BLC 1:1; TCLC 43**
See also BW 1; CA 122; 124; DAM MULT; DLB 50

Bell, Madison Smartt 1957- ..... **CLC 41, 102, 223**
See also AMWS 10; BPFB 1; CA 111, 183; CAAE 183; CANR 28, 54, 73, 134, 176; CN 5, 6, 7; CSW; DLB 218, 278; MTCW 2; MTFW 2005

Bell, Marvin (Hartley) 1937- ...... **CLC 8, 31; PC 79**
See also CA 21-24R; CAAS 14; CANR 59, 102; CP 1, 2, 3, 4, 5, 6, 7; DAM POET; DLB 5; MAL 5; MTCW 1; PFS 25

Bell, W. L. D.
See Mencken, H(enry) L(ouis)

Bellamy, Atwood C.
See Mencken, H(enry) L(ouis)

Bellamy, Edward 1850-1898 ..... **NCLC 4, 86, 147**
See also DLB 12; NFS 15; RGAL 4; SFW 4

Belli, Gioconda 1948- .... **HLCS 1**
See also CA 152; CANR 143; CWW 2; DLB 290; EWL 3; RGWL 3

Bellin, Edward J.
See Kuttner, Henry

Bello, Andres 1781-1865 .... **NCLC 131**
See also LAW

Belloc, (Joseph) Hilaire (Pierre Sebastien Rene Swanton) 1870-1953 .... **PC 24; TCLC 7, 18**
See also CA 106; 152; CLR 102; CWRI 5; DAM POET; DLB 19, 100, 141, 174; EWL 3; MTCW 2; MTFW 2005; SATA 112; WCH; YABC 1

Belloc, Joseph Peter Rene Hilaire
See Belloc, (Joseph) Hilaire (Pierre Sebastien Rene Swanton)

Belloc, Joseph Pierre Hilaire
See Belloc, (Joseph) Hilaire (Pierre Sebastien Rene Swanton)

Belloc, M. A.
See Lowndes, Marie Adelaide (Belloc)

Belloc-Lowndes, Mrs.
See Lowndes, Marie Adelaide (Belloc)

Bellow, Saul 1915-2005 ...... **CLC 1, 2, 3, 6, 8, 10, 13, 15, 25, 33, 34, 63, 79, 190, 200; SSC 14, 101; WLC 1**
See also AITN 2; AMW; AMWC 2; AMWR 2; BEST 89:3; BPFB 1; CA 5-8R; 238; CABS 1; CANR 29, 53, 95, 132; CDALB 1941-1968; CN 1, 2, 3, 4, 5, 6, 7; DA; DA3; DAB; DAC; DAM MST, NOV, POP; DLB 2, 28, 299, 329; DLBD 3; DLBY 1982; EWL 3; MAL 5; MTCW 1, 2; MTFW 2005; NFS 4, 14, 26; RGAL 4; RGHL; RGSF 2; SSFS 12, 22; TUS

Belser, Reimond Karel Maria de 1929- .... **CLC 14**
See also CA 152

Bely, Andrey
See Bugayev, Boris Nikolayevich

Belyi, Andrei
See Bugayev, Boris Nikolayevich

Bembo, Pietro 1470-1547 .... **LC 79**
See also RGWL 2, 3

Benary, Margot
See Benary-Isbert, Margot

Benary-Isbert, Margot 1889-1979 .... **CLC 12**
See also CA 5-8R; 89-92; CANR 4, 72; CLR 12; MAICYA 1, 2; SATA 2; SATA-Obit 21

Benavente (y Martinez), Jacinto 1866-1954 .... **DC 26; HLCS 1; TCLC 3**
See also CA 106; 131; CANR 81; DAM DRAM, MULT; DLB 329; EWL 3; GLL 2; HW 1, 2; MTCW 1, 2

Brontes
See Bronte, Anne; Bronte, (Patrick) Branwell; Bronte, Charlotte; Bronte, Emily (Jane)

Brooke, Frances 1724-1789 .... **LC 6, 48**
See also DLB 39, 99

Brooke, Henry 1703(?)-1783 .... **LC 1**
See also DLB 39

Brooke, Rupert (Chawner)
1887-1915 .. **PC 24; TCLC 2, 7; WLC 1**
See also BRWS 3; CA 104; 132; CANR 61; CDBLB 1914-1945; DA; DAB; DAC; DAM MST, POET; DLB 19, 216; EXPP; GLL 2; MTCW 1, 2; MTFW 2005; PFS 7; TEA

Brooke-Haven, P.
See Wodehouse, P(elham) G(renville)

Brooke-Rose, Christine 1923(?)- ..... **CLC 40, 184**
See also BRWS 4; CA 13-16R; CANR 58, 118, 183; CN 1, 2, 3, 4, 5, 6, 7; DLB 14, 231; EWL 3; SFW 4

Brookner, Anita 1928- . **CLC 32, 34, 51, 136, 237**
See also BRWS 4; CA 114; 120; CANR 37, 56, 87, 130; CN 4, 5, 6, 7; CPW; DA3; DAB; DAM POP; DLB 194, 326; DLBY 1987; EWL 3; MTCW 1, 2; MTFW 2005; NFS 23; TEA

Brooks, Cleanth 1906-1994 . **CLC 24, 86, 110**
See also AMWS 14; CA 17-20R; 145; CANR 33, 35; CSW; DLB 63; DLBY 1994; EWL 3; INT CANR-35; MAL 5; MTCW 1, 2; MTFW 2005

Brooks, George
See Baum, L(yman) Frank

Brooks, Gwendolyn 1917-2000 .... **BLC 1:1, 2:1; CLC 1, 2, 4, 5, 15, 49, 125; PC 7; WLC 1**
See also AAYA 20; AFAW 1, 2; AITN 1; AMWS 3; BW 2, 3; CA 1-4R; 190; CANR 1, 27, 52, 75, 132; CDALB 1941-1968; CLR 27; CP 1, 2, 3, 4, 5, 6, 7; CWP; DA; DA3; DAC; DAM MST, MULT, POET; DLB 5, 76, 165; EWL 3; EXPP; FL 1:5; MAL 5; MBL; MTCW 1, 2; MTFW 2005; PFS 1, 2, 4, 6; RGAL 4; SATA 6; SATA-Obit 123; TUS; WP

Brooks, Mel 1926-
See Kaminsky, Melvin
See also CA 65-68; CANR 16; DFS 21

Brooks, Peter 1938- .... **CLC 34**
See also CA 45-48; CANR 1, 107, 182

Brooks, Peter Preston
See Brooks, Peter

Brooks, Van Wyck 1886-1963 .... **CLC 29**
See also AMW; CA 1-4R; CANR 6; DLB 45, 63, 103; MAL 5; TUS

Brophy, Brigid (Antonia)
1929-1995 .... **CLC 6, 11, 29, 105**
See also CA 5-8R; 149; CAAS 6; CANR 25, 53; CBD; CN 1, 2, 3, 4, 5, 6; CWD; DA3; DLB 14, 271; EWL 3; MTCW 1, 2

Brosman, Catharine Savage 1934- ..... **CLC 9**
See also CA 61-64; CANR 21, 46, 149

Brossard, Nicole 1943- .... **CLC 115, 169; PC 80**
See also CA 122; CAAS 16; CANR 140; CCA 1; CWP; CWW 2; DLB 53; EWL 3; FW; GLL 2; RGWL 3

Brother Antoninus
See Everson, William (Oliver)

Brothers Grimm
See Grimm, Jacob Ludwig Karl; Grimm, Wilhelm Karl

The Brothers Quay
See Quay, Stephen; Quay, Timothy

Broughton, T(homas) Alan 1936- ..... **CLC 19**
See also CA 45-48; CANR 2, 23, 48, 111

Broumas, Olga 1949- .... **CLC 10, 73**
See also CA 85-88; CANR 20, 69, 110; CP 5, 6, 7; CWP; GLL 2

Broun, Heywood 1888-1939 .... **TCLC 104**
See also DLB 29, 171

Brown, Alan 1950- .... **CLC 99**
See also CA 156

Brown, Charles Brockden
1771-1810 .... **NCLC 22, 74, 122**
See also AMWS 1; CDALB 1640-1865; DLB 37, 59, 73; FW; GL 1; HGG; LMFS 1; RGAL 4; TUS

Brown, Christy 1932-1981 .... **CLC 63**
See also BYA 13; CA 105; 104; CANR 72; DLB 14

Brown, Claude 1937-2002 ..... **BLC 1:1; CLC 30**
See also AAYA 7; BW 1, 3; CA 73-76; 205; CANR 81; DAM MULT

Brown, Dan 1964- .... **CLC 209**
See also AAYA 55; CA 217; MTFW 2005

Brown, Dee 1908-2002 .... **CLC 18, 47**
See also AAYA 30; CA 13-16R; 212; CAAS 6; CANR 11, 45, 60, 150; CPW; CSW; DA3; DAM POP; DLBY 1980; LAIT 2; MTCW 1, 2; MTFW 2005; NCFS 5; SATA 5, 110; SATA-Obit 141; TCWW 1, 2

Brown, Dee Alexander
See Brown, Dee

Brown, George
See Wertmueller, Lina

Brown, George Douglas
1869-1902 .... **TCLC 28**
See also CA 162; RGEL 2

Brown, George Mackay 1921-1996 ... **CLC 5, 48, 100**
See also BRWS 6; CA 21-24R; 151; CAAS 6; CANR 12, 37, 67; CN 1, 2, 3, 4, 5, 6; CP 1, 2, 3, 4, 5, 6; DLB 14, 27, 139, 271; MTCW 1; RGSF 2; SATA 35

Brown, James Willie
See Komunyakaa, Yusef

Brown, James Willie, Jr.
See Komunyakaa, Yusef

Brown, Larry 1951-2004 .... **CLC 73**
See also CA 130; 134; 233; CANR 117, 145; CSW; DLB 234; INT CA-134

Brown, Moses
See Barrett, William (Christopher)

Brown, Rita Mae 1944- .... **CLC 18, 43, 79, 259**
See also BPFB 1; CA 45-48; CANR 2, 11, 35, 62, 95, 138, 183; CN 5, 6, 7; CPW; CSW; DA3; DAM NOV, POP; FW; INT CANR-11; MAL 5; MTCW 1, 2; MTFW 2005; NFS 9; RGAL 4; TUS

Brown, Roderick (Langmere) Haig-
See Haig-Brown, Roderick (Langmere)

Brown, Rosellen 1939- .... **CLC 32, 170**
See also CA 77-80; CAAS 10; CANR 14, 44, 98; CN 6, 7

Brown, Sterling Allen 1901-1989 ...... **BLC 1; CLC 1, 23, 59; HR 1:2; PC 55**
See also AFAW 1, 2; BW 1, 3; CA 85-88; 127; CANR 26; CP 3, 4; DA3; DAM MULT, POET; DLB 48, 51, 63; MAL 5; MTCW 1, 2; MTFW 2005; RGAL 4; WP

Brown, Will
See Ainsworth, William Harrison

Brown, William Hill 1765-1793 .... **LC 93**
See also DLB 37

Brown, William Larry
See Brown, Larry

Brown, William Wells 1815-1884 ... **BLC 1:1; DC 1; NCLC 2, 89**
See also DAM MULT; DLB 3, 50, 183, 248; RGAL 4

Browne, Clyde Jackson
See Browne, Jackson

Browne, Jackson 1948(?)- .... **CLC 21**
See also CA 120

Browne, Sir Thomas 1605-1682 .... **LC 111**
See also BRW 2; DLB 151

Browning, Robert 1812-1889 . **NCLC 19, 79; PC 2, 61, 97; WLCS**
See also BRW 4; BRWC 2; BRWR 2; CDBLB 1832-1890; CLR 97; DA; DA3; DAB; DAC; DAM MST, POET; DLB 32, 163; EXPP; LATS 1:1; PAB; PFS 1, 15; RGEL 2; TEA; WLIT 4; WP; YABC 1

Browning, Tod 1882-1962 .... **CLC 16**
See also CA 141; 117

Brownmiller, Susan 1935- .... **CLC 159**
See also CA 103; CANR 35, 75, 137; DAM NOV; FW; MTCW 1, 2; MTFW 2005

Brownson, Orestes Augustus
1803-1876 .... **NCLC 50**
See also DLB 1, 59, 73, 243

Bruccoli, Matthew J. 1931-2008 .... **CLC 34**
See also CA 9-12R; 274; CANR 7, 87; DLB 103

Bruccoli, Matthew Joseph
See Bruccoli, Matthew J.

Bruce, Lenny
See Schneider, Leonard Alfred

Bruchac, Joseph 1942- .... **NNAL**
See also AAYA 19; CA 33-36R, 256; CAAE 256; CANR 13, 47, 75, 94, 137, 161; CLR 46; CWRI 5; DAM MULT; DLB 342; JRDA; MAICYA 2; MAICYAS 1; MTCW 2; MTFW 2005; SATA 42, 89, 131, 176; SATA-Essay 176

Bruin, John
See Brutus, Dennis

Brulard, Henri
See Stendhal

Brulls, Christian
See Simenon, Georges (Jacques Christian)

Brunetto Latini c. 1220-1294 .... **CMLC 73**

Brunner, John (Kilian Houston)
1934-1995 .... **CLC 8, 10**
See also CA 1-4R; 149; CAAS 8; CANR 2, 37; CPW; DAM POP; DLB 261; MTCW 1, 2; SCFW 1, 2; SFW 4

Bruno, Giordano 1548-1600 .... **LC 27, 167**
See also RGWL 2, 3

Brutus, Dennis 1924- ...... **BLC 1:1; CLC 43; PC 24**
See also AFW; BW 2, 3; CA 49-52; CAAS 14; CANR 2, 27, 42, 81; CDWLB 3; CP 1, 2, 3, 4, 5, 6, 7; DAM MULT, POET; DLB 117, 225; EWL 3

Bryan, C(ourtlandt) D(ixon) B(arnes)
1936- .... **CLC 29**
See also CA 73-76; CANR 13, 68; DLB 185; INT CANR-13

Bryan, Michael
See Moore, Brian

Bryan, William Jennings
1860-1925 .... **TCLC 99**
See also DLB 303

Bryant, William Cullen 1794-1878 . **NCLC 6, 46; PC 20**
See also AMWS 1; CDALB 1640-1865; DA; DAB; DAC; DAM MST, POET; DLB 3, 43, 59, 189, 250; EXPP; PAB; PFS 30; RGAL 4; TUS

Bryusov, Valery Yakovlevich
1873-1924 .... **TCLC 10**
See also CA 107; 155; EWL 3; SFW 4

Buchan, John 1875-1940 .... **TCLC 41**
See also CA 108; 145; CMW 4; DAB; DAM POP; DLB 34, 70, 156; HGG; MSW; MTCW 2; RGEL 2; RHW; YABC 2

Butler, Samuel 1835-1902 .... **TCLC 1, 33; WLC 1**
See also BRWS 2; CA 143; CDBLB 1890-1914; DA; DA3; DAB; DAC; DAM MST, NOV; DLB 18, 57, 174; RGEL 2; SFW 4; TEA

Butler, Walter C.
See Faust, Frederick (Schiller)

Butor, Michel (Marie Francois)
1926- .... **CLC 1, 3, 8, 11, 15, 161**
See also CA 9-12R; CANR 33, 66; CWW 2; DLB 83; EW 13; EWL 3; GFL 1789 to the Present; MTCW 1, 2; MTFW 2005

Butts, Mary 1890(?)-1937 ... **SSC 124; TCLC 77**
See also CA 148; DLB 240

Buxton, Ralph
See Silverstein, Alvin; Silverstein, Virginia B(arbara Opshelor)

Buzo, Alex
See Buzo, Alexander (John)

Buzo, Alexander (John) 1944- .... **CLC 61**
See also CA 97-100; CANR 17, 39, 69; CD 5, 6; DLB 289

Buzzati, Dino 1906-1972 .... **CLC 36**
See also CA 160; 33-36R; DLB 177; RGWL 2, 3; SFW 4

Byars, Betsy 1928- .... **CLC 35**
See also AAYA 19; BYA 3; CA 33-36R, 183; CAAE 183; CANR 18, 36, 57, 102, 148; CLR 1, 16, 72; DLB 52; INT CANR-18; JRDA; MAICYA 1, 2; MAICYAS 1; MTCW 1; SAAS 1; SATA 4, 46, 80, 163; SATA-Essay 108; WYA; YAW

Byars, Betsy Cromer
See Byars, Betsy

Byatt, Antonia Susan Drabble
See Byatt, A.S.

Byatt, A.S. 1936- .... **CLC 19, 65, 136, 223; SSC 91**
See also BPFB 1; BRWC 2; BRWS 4; CA 13-16R; CANR 13, 33, 50, 75, 96, 133; CN 1, 2, 3, 4, 5, 6; DA3; DAM NOV, POP; DLB 14, 194, 319, 326; EWL 3; MTCW 1, 2; MTFW 2005; RGSF 2; RHW; SSFS 26; TEA

Byrd, William II 1674-1744 .... **LC 112**
See also DLB 24, 140; RGAL 4

Byrne, David 1952- .... **CLC 26**
See also CA 127

Byrne, John Keyes 1926-2009 .... **CLC 19**
See also CA 102; CANR 78, 140; CBD; CD 5, 6; DFS 13, 24; DLB 13; INT CA-102

Byron, George Gordon (Noel)
1788-1824 ..... **DC 24; NCLC 2, 12, 109, 149; PC 16, 95; WLC 1**
See also AAYA 64; BRW 4; BRWC 2; CD-BLB 1789-1832; DA; DA3; DAB; DAC; DAM MST, POET; DLB 96, 110; EXPP; LMFS 1; PAB; PFS 1, 14, 29; RGEL 2; TEA; WLIT 3; WP

Byron, Robert 1905-1941 .... **TCLC 67**
See also CA 160; DLB 195

C. 3. 3.
See Wilde, Oscar

Caballero, Fernan 1796-1877 .... **NCLC 10**

Cabell, Branch
See Cabell, James Branch

Cabell, James Branch 1879-1958 .... **TCLC 6**
See also CA 105; 152; DLB 9, 78; FANT; MAL 5; MTCW 2; RGAL 4; SUFW 1

Cabeza de Vaca, Alvar Nunez
1490-1557(?) .... **LC 61**

Cable, George Washington
1844-1925 .... **SSC 4; TCLC 4**
See also CA 104; 155; DLB 12, 74; DLBD 13; RGAL 4; TUS

Cabral de Melo Neto, Joao
1920-1999 .... **CLC 76**
See also CA 151; CWW 2; DAM MULT; DLB 307; EWL 3; LAW; LAWS 1

Cabrera Infante, G. 1929-2005 ... **CLC 5, 25, 45, 120; HLC 1; SSC 39**
See also CA 85-88; 236; CANR 29, 65, 110; CDWLB 3; CWW 2; DA3; DAM MULT; DLB 113; EWL 3; HW 1, 2; LAW; LAWS 1; MTCW 1, 2; MTFW 2005; RGSF 2; WLIT 1

Cabrera Infante, Guillermo
See Cabrera Infante, G.

Cade, Toni
See Bambara, Toni Cade

Cadmus and Harmonia
See Buchan, John

Caedmon fl. 658-680 .... **CMLC 7**
See also DLB 146

Caeiro, Alberto
See Pessoa, Fernando

Caesar, Julius
See Julius Caesar

Cage, John (Milton), (Jr.)
1912-1992 .... **CLC 41; PC 58**
See also CA 13-16R; 169; CANR 9, 78; DLB 193; INT CANR-9; TCLE 1:1

Cahan, Abraham 1860-1951 .... **TCLC 71**
See also CA 108; 154; DLB 9, 25, 28; MAL 5; RGAL 4

Cain, Christopher
See Fleming, Thomas

Cain, G.
See Cabrera Infante, G.

Cain, Guillermo
See Cabrera Infante, G.

Cain, James M(allahan) 1892-1977 .. **CLC 3, 11, 28**
See also AITN 1; BPFB 1; CA 17-20R; 73-76; CANR 8, 34, 61; CMW 4; CN 1, 2; DLB 226; EWL 3; MAL 5; MSW; MTCW 1; RGAL 4

Caine, Hall 1853-1931 .... **TCLC 97**
See also RHW

Caine, Mark
See Raphael, Frederic (Michael)

Calasso, Roberto 1941- .... **CLC 81**
See also CA 143; CANR 89

Calderon de la Barca, Pedro
1600-1681 . **DC 3; HLCS 1; LC 23, 136**
See also DFS 23; EW 2; RGWL 2, 3; TWA

Caldwell, Erskine 1903-1987 ... **CLC 1, 8, 14, 50, 60; SSC 19; TCLC 117**
See also AITN 1; AMW; BPFB 1; CA 1-4R; 121; CAAS 1; CANR 2, 33; CN 1, 2, 3, 4; DA3; DAM NOV; DLB 9, 86; EWL 3; MAL 5; MTCW 1, 2; MTFW 2005; RGAL 4; RGSF 2; TUS

Caldwell, (Janet Miriam) Taylor (Holland)
1900-1985 .... **CLC 2, 28, 39**
See also BPFB 1; CA 5-8R; 116; CANR 5; DA3; DAM NOV, POP; DLBD 17; MTCW 2; RHW

Calhoun, John Caldwell
1782-1850 .... **NCLC 15**
See also DLB 3, 248

Calisher, Hortense 1911-2009 .... **CLC 2, 4, 8, 38, 134; SSC 15**
See also CA 1-4R; CANR 1, 22, 117; CN 1, 2, 3, 4, 5, 6, 7; DA3; DAM NOV; DLB 2, 218; INT CANR-22; MAL 5; MTCW 1, 2; MTFW 2005; RGAL 4; RGSF 2

Callaghan, Morley Edward
1903-1990 ..... **CLC 3, 14, 41, 65; TCLC 145**
See also CA 9-12R; 132; CANR 33, 73; CN 1, 2, 3, 4; DAC; DAM MST; DLB 68; EWL 3; MTCW 1, 2; MTFW 2005; RGEL 2; RGSF 2; SSFS 19

Callimachus c. 305B.C.-c.
240B.C. .... **CMLC 18**
See also AW 1; DLB 176; RGWL 2, 3

Calvin, Jean
See Calvin, John

Calvin, John 1509-1564 .... **LC 37**
See also DLB 327; GFL Beginnings to 1789

Calvino, Italo 1923-1985 .... **CLC 5, 8, 11, 22, 33, 39, 73; SSC 3, 48; TCLC 183**
See also AAYA 58; CA 85-88; 116; CANR 23, 61, 132; DAM NOV; DLB 196; EW 13; EWL 3; MTCW 1, 2; MTFW 2005; RGHL; RGSF 2; RGWL 2, 3; SFW 4; SSFS 12; WLIT 7

Camara Laye
See Laye, Camara

Cambridge, A Gentleman of the University of
See Crowley, Edward Alexander

Camden, William 1551-1623 .... **LC 77**
See also DLB 172

Cameron, Carey 1952- .... **CLC 59**
See also CA 135

Cameron, Peter 1959- .... **CLC 44**
See also AMWS 12; CA 125; CANR 50, 117, 188; DLB 234; GLL 2

Camoens, Luis Vaz de 1524(?)-1580
See Camoes, Luis de

Camoes, Luis de 1524(?)-1580 . **HLCS 1; LC 62; PC 31**
See also DLB 287; EW 2; RGWL 2, 3

Camp, Madeleine L'Engle
See L'Engle, Madeleine

Campana, Dino 1885-1932 .... **TCLC 20**
See also CA 117; 246; DLB 114; EWL 3

Campanella, Tommaso 1568-1639 .... **LC 32**
See also RGWL 2, 3

Campbell, Bebe Moore 1950-2006 . **BLC 2:1; CLC 246**
See also AAYA 26; BW 2, 3; CA 139; 254; CANR 81, 134; DLB 227; MTCW 2; MTFW 2005

Campbell, John Ramsey
See Campbell, Ramsey

Campbell, John W(ood, Jr.)
1910-1971 .... **CLC 32**
See also CA 21-22; 29-32R; CANR 34; CAP 2; DLB 8; MTCW 1; SCFW 1, 2; SFW 4

Campbell, Joseph 1904-1987 .... **CLC 69; TCLC 140**
See also AAYA 3, 66; BEST 89:2; CA 1-4R; 124; CANR 3, 28, 61, 107; DA3; MTCW 1, 2

Campbell, Maria 1940- .... **CLC 85; NNAL**
See also CA 102; CANR 54; CCA 1; DAC

Campbell, Ramsey 1946- ... **CLC 42; SSC 19**
See also AAYA 51; CA 57-60, 228; CAAE 228; CANR 7, 102, 171; DLB 261; HGG; INT CANR-7; SUFW 1, 2

Campbell, (Ignatius) Roy (Dunnachie)
1901-1957 .... **TCLC 5**
See also AFW; CA 104; 155; DLB 20, 225; EWL 3; MTCW 2; RGEL 2

Campbell, Thomas 1777-1844 .... **NCLC 19**
See also DLB 93, 144; RGEL 2

Campbell, Wilfred
See Campbell, William

Campbell, William 1858(?)-1918 ..... **TCLC 9**
See also CA 106; DLB 92

Campbell, William Edward March
1893-1954 .... **TCLC 96**
See also CA 108; 216; DLB 9, 86, 316; MAL 5

Campion, Jane 1954- .... **CLC 95, 229**
See also AAYA 33; CA 138; CANR 87

Campion, Thomas 1567-1620 . **LC 78; PC 87**
See also CDBLB Before 1660; DAM POET; DLB 58, 172; RGEL 2

Casal, Julian del 1863-1893 .... **NCLC 131**
See also DLB 283; LAW
Casanova, Giacomo
See Casanova de Seingalt, Giovanni Jacopo
Casanova, Giovanni Giacomo
See Casanova de Seingalt, Giovanni Jacopo
Casanova de Seingalt, Giovanni Jacopo
1725-1798 .... **LC 13, 151**
See also WLIT 7
Casares, Adolfo Bioy
See Bioy Casares, Adolfo
Casas, Bartolome de las 1474-1566
See Las Casas, Bartolome de
Case, John
See Hougan, Carolyn
Casely-Hayford, J(oseph) E(phraim)
1866-1903 .... **BLC 1:1; TCLC 24**
See also BW 2; CA 123; 152; DAM MULT
Casey, John (Dudley) 1939- .... **CLC 59**
See also BEST 90:2; CA 69-72; CANR 23,
100
Casey, Michael 1947- .... **CLC 2**
See also CA 65-68; CANR 109; CP 2, 3;
DLB 5
Casey, Patrick
See Thurman, Wallace (Henry)
Casey, Warren (Peter) 1935-1988 .... **CLC 12**
See also CA 101; 127; INT CA-101
Casona, Alejandro
See Alvarez, Alejandro Rodriguez
Cassavetes, John 1929-1989 .... **CLC 20**
See also CA 85-88; 127; CANR 82
Cassian, Nina 1924- .... **PC 17**
See also CWP; CWW 2
Cassill, R(onald) V(erlin)
1919-2002 .... **CLC 4, 23**
See also CA 9-12R; 208; CAAS 1; CANR
7, 45; CN 1, 2, 3, 4, 5, 6, 7; DLB 6, 218;
DLBY 2002
Cassiodorus, Flavius Magnus c. 490(?)-c.
583(?) .... **CMLC 43**
Cassirer, Ernst 1874-1945 .... **TCLC 61**
See also CA 157
Cassity, (Allen) Turner 1929- .... **CLC 6, 42**
See also CA 17-20R, 223; CAAE 223;
CAAS 8; CANR 11; CSW; DLB 105
Cassius Dio c. 155-c. 229 .... **CMLC 99**
See also DLB 176
Castaneda, Carlos (Cesar Aranha)
1931(?)-1998 .... **CLC 12, 119**
See also CA 25-28R; CANR 32, 66, 105;
DNFS 1; HW 1; MTCW 1
Castedo, Elena 1937- .... **CLC 65**
See also CA 132
Castedo-Ellerman, Elena
See Castedo, Elena
Castellanos, Rosario 1925-1974 .... **CLC 66;
HLC 1; SSC 39, 68**
See also CA 131; 53-56; CANR 58; CD-
WLB 3; DAM MULT; DLB 113, 290;
EWL 3; FW; HW 1; LAW; MTCW 2;
MTFW 2005; RGSF 2; RGWL 2, 3
Castelvetro, Lodovico 1505-1571 .... **LC 12**
Castiglione, Baldassare 1478-1529 ..... **LC 12,
165**
See also EW 2; LMFS 1; RGWL 2, 3;
WLIT 7
Castiglione, Baldesar
See Castiglione, Baldassare
Castillo, Ana 1953- .... **CLC 151**
See also AAYA 42; CA 131; CANR 51, 86,
128, 172; CWP; DLB 122, 227; DNFS 2;
FW; HW 1; LLW; PFS 21
Castillo, Ana Hernandez Del
See Castillo, Ana
Castle, Robert
See Hamilton, Edmond

Castro (Ruz), Fidel 1926(?)- .... **HLC 1**
See also CA 110; 129; CANR 81; DAM
MULT; HW 2
Castro, Guillen de 1569-1631 .... **LC 19**
Castro, Rosalia de 1837-1885 ... **NCLC 3, 78;
PC 41**
See also DAM MULT
Castro Alves, Antonio de
1847-1871 .... **NCLC 205**
See also DLB 307; LAW
Cather, Willa (Sibert) 1873-1947 . **SSC 2, 50,
114; TCLC 1, 11, 31, 99, 132, 152;
WLC 1**
See also AAYA 24; AMW; AMWC 1;
AMWR 1; BPFB 1; CA 104; 128; CDALB
1865-1917; CLR 98; DA; DA3; DAB;
DAC; DAM MST, NOV; DLB 9, 54, 78,
256; DLBD 1; EWL 3; EXPN; EXPS; FL
1:5; LAIT 3; LATS 1:1; MAL 5; MBL;
MTCW 1, 2; MTFW 2005; NFS 2, 19;
RGAL 4; RGSF 2; RHW; SATA 30; SSFS
2, 7, 16, 27; TCWW 1, 2; TUS
Catherine II
See Catherine the Great
Catherine, Saint 1347-1380 .... **CMLC 27**
Catherine the Great 1729-1796 .... **LC 69**
See also DLB 150
Cato, Marcus Porcius
234B.C.-149B.C. .... **CMLC 21**
See also DLB 211
Cato, Marcus Porcius, the Elder
See Cato, Marcus Porcius
Cato the Elder
See Cato, Marcus Porcius
Catton, (Charles) Bruce 1899-1978 . **CLC 35**
See also AITN 1; CA 5-8R; 81-84; CANR
7, 74; DLB 17; MTCW 2; MTFW 2005;
SATA 2; SATA-Obit 24
Catullus c. 84B.C.-54B.C. .... **CMLC 18**
See also AW 2; CDWLB 1; DLB 211;
RGWL 2, 3; WLIT 8
Cauldwell, Frank
See King, Francis (Henry)
Caunitz, William J. 1933-1996 .... **CLC 34**
See also BEST 89:3; CA 125; 130; 152;
CANR 73; INT CA-130
Causley, Charles (Stanley)
1917-2003 .... **CLC 7**
See also CA 9-12R; 223; CANR 5, 35, 94;
CLR 30; CP 1, 2, 3, 4, 5; CWRI 5; DLB
27; MTCW 1; SATA 3, 66; SATA-Obit
149
Caute, (John) David 1936- .... **CLC 29**
See also CA 1-4R; CAAS 4; CANR 1, 33,
64, 120; CBD; CD 5, 6; CN 1, 2, 3, 4, 5,
6, 7; DAM NOV; DLB 14, 231
Cavafy, C. P.
See Kavafis, Konstantinos Petrou
Cavafy, Constantine Peter
See Kavafis, Konstantinos Petrou
Cavalcanti, Guido c. 1250-c.
1300 .... **CMLC 54**
See also RGWL 2, 3; WLIT 7
Cavallo, Evelyn
See Spark, Muriel
Cavanna, Betty
See Harrison, Elizabeth (Allen) Cavanna
Cavanna, Elizabeth
See Harrison, Elizabeth (Allen) Cavanna
Cavanna, Elizabeth Allen
See Harrison, Elizabeth (Allen) Cavanna
Cavendish, Margaret Lucas
1623-1673 .... **LC 30, 132**
See also DLB 131, 252, 281; RGEL 2
Caxton, William 1421(?)-1491(?) .... **LC 17**
See also DLB 170
Cayer, D. M.
See Duffy, Maureen (Patricia)

Cayrol, Jean 1911-2005 .... **CLC 11**
See also CA 89-92; 236; DLB 83; EWL 3
Cela (y Trulock), Camilo Jose
See Cela, Camilo Jose
Cela, Camilo Jose 1916-2002 .... **CLC 4, 13,
59, 122; HLC 1; SSC 71**
See also BEST 90:2; CA 21-24R; 206;
CAAS 10; CANR 21, 32, 76, 139; CWW
2; DAM MULT; DLB 322; DLBY 1989;
EW 13; EWL 3; HW 1; MTCW 1, 2;
MTFW 2005; RGSF 2; RGWL 2, 3
Celan, Paul
See Antschel, Paul
Celine, Louis-Ferdinand
See Destouches, Louis-Ferdinand
Cellini, Benvenuto 1500-1571 .... **LC 7**
See also WLIT 7
Cendrars, Blaise
See Sauser-Hall, Frederic
Centlivre, Susanna 1669(?)-1723 .... **DC 25;
LC 65**
See also DLB 84; RGEL 2
Cernuda (y Bidon), Luis
1902-1963 .... **CLC 54; PC 62**
See also CA 131; 89-92; DAM POET; DLB
134; EWL 3; GLL 1; HW 1; RGWL 2, 3
Cervantes, Lorna Dee 1954- ..... **HLCS 1; PC
35**
See also CA 131; CANR 80; CP 7; CWP;
DLB 82; EXPP; HW 1; LLW; PFS 30
Cervantes (Saavedra), Miguel de
1547-1616 .... **HLCS; LC 6, 23, 93; SSC
12, 108; WLC 1**
See also AAYA 56; BYA 1, 14; DA; DAB;
DAC; DAM MST, NOV; EW 2; LAIT 1;
LATS 1:1; LMFS 1; NFS 8; RGSF 2;
RGWL 2, 3; TWA
Cesaire, Aime
See Cesaire, Aime
Cesaire, Aime 1913-2008 .... **BLC 1:1; CLC
19, 32, 112; DC 22; PC 25**
See also BW 2, 3; CA 65-68; 271; CANR
24, 43, 81; CWW 2; DA3; DAM MULT,
POET; DLB 321; EWL 3; GFL 1789 to
the Present; MTCW 1, 2; MTFW 2005;
WP
Cesaire, Aime Fernand
See Cesaire, Aime
Chaadaev, Petr Iakovlevich
1794-1856 .... **NCLC 197**
See also DLB 198
Chabon, Michael 1963- ... **CLC 55, 149, 265;
SSC 59**
See also AAYA 45; AMWS 11; CA 139;
CANR 57, 96, 127, 138; DLB 278; MAL
5; MTFW 2005; NFS 25; SATA 145
Chabrol, Claude 1930- .... **CLC 16**
See also CA 110
Chairil Anwar
See Anwar, Chairil
Challans, Mary 1905-1983 ...... **CLC 3, 11, 17**
See also BPFB 3; BYA 2; CA 81-84; 111;
CANR 74; CN 1, 2, 3; DA3; DLBY 1983;
EWL 3; GLL 1; LAIT 1; MTCW 2;
MTFW 2005; RGEL 2; RHW; SATA 23;
SATA-Obit 36; TEA
Challis, George
See Faust, Frederick (Schiller)
Chambers, Aidan 1934- .... **CLC 35**
See also AAYA 27; CA 25-28R; CANR 12,
31, 58, 116; JRDA; MAICYA 1, 2; SAAS
12; SATA 1, 69, 108, 171; WYA; YAW
Chambers, James .... **CLC 21**
See also CA 124; 199
Chambers, Jessie
See Lawrence, D(avid) H(erbert Richards)

Child, Mrs.
See Child, Lydia Maria

Child, Philip 1898-1978 .... **CLC 19, 68**
See also CA 13-14; CAP 1; CP 1; DLB 68;
RHW; SATA 47

Childers, (Robert) Erskine
1870-1922 .... **TCLC 65**
See also CA 113; 153; DLB 70

Childress, Alice 1920-1994 .... **BLC 1:1; CLC 12, 15, 86, 96; DC 4; TCLC 116**
See also AAYA 8; BW 2, 3; BYA 2; CA 45-
48; 146; CAD; CANR 3, 27, 50, 74; CLR
14; CWD; DA3; DAM DRAM, MULT,
NOV; DFS 2, 8, 14, 26; DLB 7, 38, 249;
JRDA; LAIT 5; MAICYA 1, 2; MAIC-
YAS 1; MAL 5; MTCW 1, 2; MTFW
2005; RGAL 4; SATA 7, 48, 81; TUS;
WYA; YAW

Chin, Frank (Chew, Jr.) 1940- .... **AAL; CLC 135; DC 7**
See also CA 33-36R; CAD; CANR 71; CD
5, 6; DAM MULT; DLB 206, 312; LAIT
5; RGAL 4

Chin, Marilyn (Mei Ling) 1955- .... **PC 40**
See also CA 129; CANR 70, 113; CWP;
DLB 312; PFS 28

Chislett, (Margaret) Anne 1943- ...... **CLC 34**
See also CA 151

Chitty, Thomas Willes 1926- .... **CLC 6, 11**
See also CA 5-8R; CN 1, 2, 3, 4, 5, 6; EWL
3

Chivers, Thomas Holley
1809-1858 .... **NCLC 49**
See also DLB 3, 248; RGAL 4

Chlamyda, Jehudil
See Peshkov, Alexei Maximovich

Ch'o, Chou
See Shu-Jen, Chou

Choi, Susan 1969- .... **CLC 119**
See also CA 223; CANR 188

Chomette, Rene Lucien 1898-1981 .. **CLC 20**
See also CA 103

Chomsky, Avram Noam
See Chomsky, Noam

Chomsky, Noam 1928- .... **CLC 132**
See also CA 17-20R; CANR 28, 62, 110,
132, 179; DA3; DLB 246; MTCW 1, 2;
MTFW 2005

Chona, Maria 1845(?)-1936 .... **NNAL**
See also CA 144

Chopin, Kate
See Chopin, Katherine

Chopin, Katherine 1851-1904 .... **SSC 8, 68, 110; TCLC 127; WLCS**
See also AAYA 33; AMWR 2; BYA 11, 15;
CA 104; 122; CDALB 1865-1917; DA3;
DAB; DAC; DAM MST, NOV; DLB 12,
78; EXPN; EXPS; FL 1:3; FW; LAIT 3;
MAL 5; MBL; NFS 3; RGAL 4; RGSF 2;
SSFS 2, 13, 17, 26; TUS

Chretien de Troyes c. 12th cent. - . **CMLC 10**
See also DLB 208; EW 1; RGWL 2, 3;
TWA

Christie
See Ichikawa, Kon

Christie, Agatha (Mary Clarissa)
1890-1976 .. **CLC 1, 6, 8, 12, 39, 48, 110**
See also AAYA 9; AITN 1, 2; BPFB 1;
BRWS 2; CA 17-20R; 61-64; CANR 10,
37, 108; CBD; CDBLB 1914-1945; CMW
4; CN 1, 2; CPW; CWD; DA3; DAB;
DAC; DAM NOV; DFS 2; DLB 13, 77,
245; MSW; MTCW 1, 2; MTFW 2005;
NFS 8; RGEL 2; RHW; SATA 36; TEA;
YAW

Christie, Ann Philippa
See Pearce, Philippa

Christie, Philippa
See Pearce, Philippa

Christine de Pisan
See Christine de Pizan

Christine de Pizan 1365(?)-1431(?) ...... **LC 9, 130; PC 68**
See also DLB 208; FL 1:1; FW; RGWL 2,
3

Chuang-Tzu c. 369B.C.-c.
286B.C. .... **CMLC 57**

Chubb, Elmer
See Masters, Edgar Lee

Chulkov, Mikhail Dmitrievich
1743-1792 .... **LC 2**
See also DLB 150

Churchill, Caryl 1938- .... **CLC 31, 55, 157; DC 5**
See also BRWS 4; CA 102; CANR 22, 46,
108; CBD; CD 5, 6; CWD; DFS 25; DLB
13, 310; EWL 3; FW; MTCW 1; RGEL 2

Churchill, Charles 1731-1764 .... **LC 3**
See also DLB 109; RGEL 2

Churchill, Chick
See Churchill, Caryl

Churchill, Sir Winston (Leonard Spencer)
1874-1965 .... **TCLC 113**
See also BRW 6; CA 97-100; CDBLB
1890-1914; DA3; DLB 100, 329; DLBD
16; LAIT 4; MTCW 1, 2

Chute, Carolyn 1947- .... **CLC 39**
See also CA 123; CANR 135; CN 7

Ciardi, John (Anthony) 1916-1986 . **CLC 10, 40, 44, 129; PC 69**
See also CA 5-8R; 118; CAAS 2; CANR 5,
33; CLR 19; CP 1, 2, 3, 4; CWRI 5; DAM
POET; DLB 5; DLBY 1986; INT
CANR-5; MAICYA 1, 2; MAL 5; MTCW
1, 2; MTFW 2005; RGAL 4; SAAS 26;
SATA 1, 65; SATA-Obit 46

Cibber, Colley 1671-1757 .... **LC 66**
See also DLB 84; RGEL 2

Cicero, Marcus Tullius
106B.C.-43B.C. .... **CMLC 3, 81**
See also AW 1; CDWLB 1; DLB 211;
RGWL 2, 3; WLIT 8

Cimino, Michael 1943- .... **CLC 16**
See also CA 105

Cioran, E(mil) M. 1911-1995 .... **CLC 64**
See also CA 25-28R; 149; CANR 91; DLB
220; EWL 3

Circus, Anthony
See Hoch, Edward D.

Cisneros, Sandra 1954- .... **CLC 69, 118, 193; HLC 1; PC 52; SSC 32, 72**
See also AAYA 9, 53; AMWS 7; CA 131;
CANR 64, 118; CLR 123; CN 7; CWP;
DA3; DAM MULT; DLB 122, 152; EWL
3; EXPN; FL 1:5; FW; HW 1, 2; LAIT 5;
LATS 1:2; LLW; MAICYA 2; MAL 5;
MTCW 2; MTFW 2005; NFS 2; PFS 19;
RGAL 4; RGSF 2; SSFS 3, 13, 27; WLIT
1; YAW

Cixous, Helene 1937- .... **CLC 92, 253**
See also CA 126; CANR 55, 123; CWW 2;
DLB 83, 242; EWL 3; FL 1:5; FW; GLL
2; MTCW 1, 2; MTFW 2005; TWA

Clair, Rene
See Chomette, Rene Lucien

Clampitt, Amy 1920-1994 .... **CLC 32; PC 19**
See also AMWS 9; CA 110; 146; CANR
29, 79; CP 4, 5; DLB 105; MAL 5; PFS
27

Clancy, Thomas L., Jr. 1947- ... **CLC 45, 112**
See also AAYA 9, 51; BEST 89:1, 90:1;
BPFB 1; BYA 10, 11; CA 125; 131;
CANR 62, 105, 132; CMW 4; CPW;
DA3; DAM NOV, POP; DLB 227; INT
CA-131; MTCW 1, 2; MTFW 2005

Clancy, Tom
See Clancy, Thomas L., Jr.

Clare, John 1793-1864 .. **NCLC 9, 86; PC 23**
See also BRWS 11; DAB; DAM POET;
DLB 55, 96; RGEL 2

Clarin
See Alas (y Urena), Leopoldo (Enrique
Garcia)

Clark, Al C.
See Goines, Donald

Clark, Brian (Robert)
See Clark, (Robert) Brian

Clark, (Robert) Brian 1932- .... **CLC 29**
See also CA 41-44R; CANR 67; CBD; CD
5, 6

Clark, Curt
See Westlake, Donald E.

Clark, Eleanor 1913-1996 .... **CLC 5, 19**
See also CA 9-12R; 151; CANR 41; CN 1,
2, 3, 4, 5, 6; DLB 6

Clark, J. P.
See Clark Bekederemo, J.P.

Clark, John Pepper
See Clark Bekederemo, J.P.
See also AFW; CD 5; CP 1, 2, 3, 4, 5, 6, 7;
RGEL 2

Clark, Kenneth (Mackenzie)
1903-1983 .... **TCLC 147**
See also CA 93-96; 109; CANR 36; MTCW
1, 2; MTFW 2005

Clark, M. R.
See Clark, Mavis Thorpe

Clark, Mavis Thorpe 1909-1999 ...... **CLC 12**
See also CA 57-60; CANR 8, 37, 107; CLR
30; CWRI 5; MAICYA 1, 2; SAAS 5;
SATA 8, 74

Clark, Walter Van Tilburg
1909-1971 .... **CLC 28**
See also CA 9-12R; 33-36R; CANR 63,
113; CN 1; DLB 9, 206; LAIT 2; MAL 5;
RGAL 4; SATA 8; TCWW 1, 2

Clark Bekederemo, J.P. 1935- .... **BLC 1:1; CLC 38; DC 5**
See Clark, John Pepper
See also AAYA 79; BW 1; CA 65-68;
CANR 16, 72; CD 6; CDWLB 3; DAM
DRAM, MULT; DFS 13; DLB 117; EWL
3; MTCW 2; MTFW 2005

Clarke, Arthur
See Clarke, Arthur C.

Clarke, Arthur C. 1917-2008 .. **CLC 1, 4, 13, 18, 35, 136; SSC 3**
See also AAYA 4, 33; BPFB 1; BYA 13;
CA 1-4R; 270; CANR 2, 28, 55, 74, 130;
CLR 119; CN 1, 2, 3, 4, 5, 6, 7; CPW;
DA3; DAM POP; DLB 261; JRDA; LAIT
5; MAICYA 1, 2; MTCW 1, 2; MTFW
2005; SATA 13, 70, 115; SATA-Obit 191;
SCFW 1, 2; SFW 4; SSFS 4, 18; TCLE
1:1; YAW

Clarke, Arthur Charles
See Clarke, Arthur C.

Clarke, Austin 1896-1974 .... **CLC 6, 9**
See also CA 29-32; 49-52; CAP 2; CP 1, 2;
DAM POET; DLB 10, 20; EWL 3; RGEL
2

Clarke, Austin C. 1934- .... **BLC 1:1; CLC 8, 53; SSC 45, 116**
See also BW 1; CA 25-28R; CAAS 16;
CANR 14, 32, 68, 140; CN 1, 2, 3, 4, 5,
6, 7; DAC; DAM MULT; DLB 53, 125;
DNFS 2; MTCW 2; MTFW 2005; RGSF
2

Clarke, Gillian 1937- .... **CLC 61**
See also CA 106; CP 3, 4, 5, 6, 7; CWP;
DLB 40

Clarke, Marcus (Andrew Hislop)
1846-1881 .... **NCLC 19; SSC 94**
See also DLB 230; RGEL 2; RGSF 2

Clarke, Shirley 1925-1997 .... **CLC 16**
See also CA 189

Colum, Padraic 1881-1972 .... **CLC 28**
See also BYA 4; CA 73-76; 33-36R; CANR 35; CLR 36; CP 1; CWRI 5; DLB 19; MAICYA 1, 2; MTCW 1; RGEL 2; SATA 15; WCH

Colvin, James
See Moorcock, Michael

Colwin, Laurie (E.) 1944-1992 .... **CLC 5, 13, 23, 84**
See also CA 89-92; 139; CANR 20, 46; DLB 218; DLBY 1980; MTCW 1

Comfort, Alex(ander) 1920-2000 .... **CLC 7**
See also CA 1-4R; 190; CANR 1, 45; CN 1, 2, 3, 4; CP 1, 2, 3, 4, 5, 6, 7; DAM POP; MTCW 2

Comfort, Montgomery
See Campbell, Ramsey

Compton-Burnett, I(vy) 1892(?)-1969 .... **CLC 1, 3, 10, 15, 34; TCLC 180**
See also BRW 7; CA 1-4R; 25-28R; CANR 4; DAM NOV; DLB 36; EWL 3; MTCW 1, 2; RGEL 2

Comstock, Anthony 1844-1915 ...... **TCLC 13**
See also CA 110; 169

Comte, Auguste 1798-1857 .... **NCLC 54**

Conan Doyle, Arthur
See Doyle, Sir Arthur Conan

Conde (Abellan), Carmen 1901-1996 .... **HLCS 1**
See also CA 177; CWW 2; DLB 108; EWL 3; HW 2

Conde, Maryse 1937- .... **BLC 2:1; BLCS; CLC 52, 92, 247**
See also BW 2, 3; CA 110; 190; CAAE 190; CANR 30, 53, 76, 171; CWW 2; DAM MULT; EWL 3; MTCW 2; MTFW 2005

Condillac, Etienne Bonnot de 1714-1780 .... **LC 26**
See also DLB 313

Condon, Richard 1915-1996 ...... **CLC 4, 6, 8, 10, 45, 100**
See also BEST 90:3; BPFB 1; CA 1-4R; 151; CAAS 1; CANR 2, 23, 164; CMW 4; CN 1, 2, 3, 4, 5, 6; DAM NOV; INT CANR-23; MAL 5; MTCW 1, 2

Condon, Richard Thomas
See Condon, Richard

Condorcet
See Condorcet, marquis de Marie-Jean-Antoine-Nicolas Caritat

Condorcet, marquis de Marie-Jean-Antoine-Nicolas Caritat 1743-1794 .... **LC 104**
See also DLB 313; GFL Beginnings to 1789

Confucius 551B.C.-479B.C. .... **CMLC 19, 65; WLCS**
See also DA; DA3; DAB; DAC; DAM MST

Congreve, William 1670-1729 ... **DC 2; LC 5, 21; WLC 2**
See also BRW 2; CDBLB 1660-1789; DA; DAB; DAC; DAM DRAM, MST, POET; DFS 15; DLB 39, 84; RGEL 2; WLIT 3

Conley, Robert J. 1940- .... **NNAL**
See also CA 41-44R; CANR 15, 34, 45, 96; 186; DAM MULT; TCWW 2

Connell, Evan S., Jr. 1924- .... **CLC 4, 6, 45**
See also AAYA 7; AMWS 14; CA 1-4R; CAAS 2; CANR 2, 39, 76, 97, 140; CN 1, 2, 3, 4, 5, 6; DAM NOV; DLB 2, 335; DLBY 1981; MAL 5; MTCW 1, 2; MTFW 2005

Connelly, Marc(us Cook) 1890-1980 . **CLC 7**
See also CA 85-88; 102; CAD; CANR 30; DFS 12; DLB 7; DLBY 1980; MAL 5; RGAL 4; SATA-Obit 25

Connolly, Paul
See Wicker, Tom

Connor, Ralph
See Gordon, Charles William

Conrad, Joseph 1857-1924 ..... **SSC 9, 67, 69, 71; TCLC 1, 6, 13, 25, 43, 57; WLC 2**
See also AAYA 26; BPFB 1; BRW 6; BRWC 1; BRWR 2; BYA 2; CA 104; 131; CANR 60; CDBLB 1890-1914; DA; DA3; DAB; DAC; DAM MST, NOV; DLB 10, 34, 98, 156; EWL 3; EXPN; EXPS; LAIT 2; LATS 1:1; LMFS 1; MTCW 1, 2; MTFW 2005; NFS 2, 16; RGEL 2; RGSF 2; SATA 27; SSFS 1, 12; TEA; WLIT 4

Conrad, Robert Arnold
See Hart, Moss

Conroy, Pat 1945- .... **CLC 30, 74**
See also AAYA 8, 52; AITN 1; BPFB 1; CA 85-88; CANR 24, 53, 129; CN 7; CPW; CSW; DA3; DAM NOV, POP; DLB 6; LAIT 5; MAL 5; MTCW 1, 2; MTFW 2005

Constant (de Rebecque), (Henri) Benjamin 1767-1830 .... **NCLC 6, 182**
See also DLB 119; EW 4; GFL 1789 to the Present

Conway, Jill K. 1934- .... **CLC 152**
See also CA 130; CANR 94

Conway, Jill Kathryn Ker
See Conway, Jill K.

Conybeare, Charles Augustus
See Eliot, T(homas) S(tearns)

Cook, Michael 1933-1994 .... **CLC 58**
See also CA 93-96; CANR 68; DLB 53

Cook, Robin 1940- .... **CLC 14**
See also AAYA 32; BEST 90:2; BPFB 1; CA 108; 111; CANR 41, 90, 109, 181; CPW; DA3; DAM POP; HGG; INT CA-111

Cook, Roy
See Silverberg, Robert

Cooke, Elizabeth 1948- .... **CLC 55**
See also CA 129

Cooke, John Esten 1830-1886 .... **NCLC 5**
See also DLB 3, 248; RGAL 4

Cooke, John Estes
See Baum, L(yman) Frank

Cooke, M. E.
See Creasey, John

Cooke, Margaret
See Creasey, John

Cooke, Rose Terry 1827-1892 ...... **NCLC 110**
See also DLB 12, 74

Cook-Lynn, Elizabeth 1930- .... **CLC 93; NNAL**
See also CA 133; DAM MULT; DLB 175

Cooney, Ray .... **CLC 62**
See also CBD

Cooper, Anthony Ashley 1671-1713 .. **LC 107**
See also DLB 101, 336

Cooper, Dennis 1953- .... **CLC 203**
See also CA 133; CANR 72, 86; GLL 1; HGG

Cooper, Douglas 1960- .... **CLC 86**

Cooper, Henry St. John
See Creasey, John

Cooper, J. California (?)- .... **CLC 56**
See also AAYA 12; BW 1; CA 125; CANR 55; DAM MULT; DLB 212

Cooper, James Fenimore 1789-1851 .... **NCLC 1, 27, 54, 203**
See also AAYA 22; AMW; BPFB 1; CDALB 1640-1865; CLR 105; DA3; DLB 3, 183, 250, 254; LAIT 1; NFS 25; RGAL 4; SATA 19; TUS; WCH

Cooper, Susan Fenimore 1813-1894 .... **NCLC 129**
See also ANW; DLB 239, 254

Coover, Robert 1932- .. **CLC 3, 7, 15, 32, 46, 87, 161; SSC 15, 101**
See also AMWS 5; BPFB 1; CA 45-48; CANR 3, 37, 58, 115; CN 1, 2, 3, 4, 5, 6, 7; DAM NOV; DLB 2, 227; DLBY 1981; EWL 3; MAL 5; MTCW 1, 2; MTFW 2005; RGAL 4; RGSF 2

Copeland, Stewart (Armstrong) 1952- .... **CLC 26**

Copernicus, Nicolaus 1473-1543 .... **LC 45**

Coppard, A(lfred) E(dgar) 1878-1957 .... **SSC 21; TCLC 5**
See also BRWS 8; CA 114; 167; DLB 162; EWL 3; HGG; RGEL 2; RGSF 2; SUFW 1; YABC 1

Coppee, Francois 1842-1908 .... **TCLC 25**
See also CA 170; DLB 217

Coppola, Francis Ford 1939- ... **CLC 16, 126**
See also AAYA 39; CA 77-80; CANR 40, 78; DLB 44

Copway, George 1818-1869 .... **NNAL**
See also DAM MULT; DLB 175, 183

Corbiere, Tristan 1845-1875 .... **NCLC 43**
See also DLB 217; GFL 1789 to the Present

Corcoran, Barbara (Asenath) 1911- .... **CLC 17**
See also AAYA 14; CA 21-24R; 191; CAAE 191; CAAS 2; CANR 11, 28, 48; CLR 50; DLB 52; JRDA; MAICYA 2; MAICYAS 1; RHW; SAAS 20; SATA 3, 77; SATA-Essay 125

Cordelier, Maurice
See Giraudoux, Jean(-Hippolyte)

Cordier, Gilbert
See Scherer, Jean-Marie Maurice

Corelli, Marie
See Mackay, Mary

Corinna c. 225B.C.-c. 305B.C. ...... **CMLC 72**

Corman, Cid 1924-2004 .... **CLC 9**
See also CA 85-88; 225; CAAS 2; CANR 44; CP 1, 2, 3, 4, 5, 6, 7; DAM POET; DLB 5, 193

Corman, Sidney
See Corman, Cid

Cormier, Robert 1925-2000 .... **CLC 12, 30**
See also AAYA 3, 19; BYA 1, 2, 6, 8, 9; CA 1-4R; CANR 5, 23, 76, 93; CDALB 1968-1988; CLR 12, 55; DA; DAB; DAC; DAM MST, NOV; DLB 52; EXPN; INT CANR-23; JRDA; LAIT 5; MAICYA 1, 2; MTCW 1, 2; MTFW 2005; NFS 2, 18; SATA 10, 45, 83; SATA-Obit 122; WYA; YAW

Corn, Alfred (DeWitt III) 1943- .... **CLC 33**
See also CA 179; CAAE 179; CAAS 25; CANR 44; CP 3, 4, 5, 6, 7; CSW; DLB 120, 282; DLBY 1980

Corneille, Pierre 1606-1684 .. **DC 21; LC 28, 135**
See also DAB; DAM MST; DFS 21; DLB 268; EW 3; GFL Beginnings to 1789; RGWL 2, 3; TWA

Cornwell, David
See le Carre, John

Cornwell, David John Moore
See le Carre, John

Cornwell, Patricia 1956- .... **CLC 155**
See also AAYA 16, 56; BPFB 1; CA 134; CANR 53, 131; CMW 4; CPW; CSW; DAM POP; DLB 306; MSW; MTCW 2; MTFW 2005

Cornwell, Patricia Daniels
See Cornwell, Patricia

Cornwell, Smith
See Smith, David (Jeddie)

Crommelynck, Fernand 1885-1970 .. **CLC 75**
See also CA 189; 89-92; EWL 3
Cromwell, Oliver 1599-1658 .... **LC 43**
Cronenberg, David 1943- .... **CLC 143**
See also CA 138; CCA 1
Cronin, A(rchibald) J(oseph)
1896-1981 .... **CLC 32**
See also BPFB 1; CA 1-4R; 102; CANR 5;
CN 2; DLB 191; SATA 47; SATA-Obit 25
Cross, Amanda
See Heilbrun, Carolyn G(old)
Crothers, Rachel 1878-1958 .... **TCLC 19**
See also CA 113; 194; CAD; CWD; DLB
7, 266; RGAL 4
Croves, Hal
See Traven, B.
Crow Dog, Mary (?)- .... **CLC 93; NNAL**
See also CA 154
Crowfield, Christopher
See Stowe, Harriet (Elizabeth) Beecher
Crowley, Aleister
See Crowley, Edward Alexander
Crowley, Edward Alexander
1875-1947 .... **TCLC 7**
See also CA 104; GLL 1; HGG
Crowley, John 1942- .... **CLC 57**
See also AAYA 57; BPFB 1; CA 61-64;
CANR 43, 98, 138, 177; DLBY 1982;
FANT; MTFW 2005; SATA 65, 140; SFW
4; SUFW 2
Crowne, John 1641-1712 .... **LC 104**
See also DLB 80; RGEL 2
Crud
See Crumb, R.
Crumarums
See Crumb, R.
Crumb, R. 1943- .... **CLC 17**
See also CA 106; CANR 107, 150
Crumb, Robert
See Crumb, R.
Crumbum
See Crumb, R.
Crumski
See Crumb, R.
Crum the Bum
See Crumb, R.
Crunk
See Crumb, R.
Crustt
See Crumb, R.
Crutchfield, Les
See Trumbo, Dalton
Cruz, Victor Hernandez 1949- ... **HLC 1; PC
37**
See also BW 2; CA 65-68, 271; CAAE 271;
CAAS 17; CANR 14, 32, 74, 132; CP 1,
2, 3, 4, 5, 6, 7; DAM MULT, POET; DLB
41; DNFS 1; EXPP; HW 1, 2; LLW;
MTCW 2; MTFW 2005; PFS 16; WP
Cryer, Gretchen (Kiger) 1935- .... **CLC 21**
See also CA 114; 123
Csath, Geza
See Brenner, Jozef
Cudlip, David R(ockwell) 1933- .... **CLC 34**
See also CA 177
Cullen, Countee 1903-1946 ..... **BLC 1:1; HR
1:2; PC 20; TCLC 4, 37, 220; WLCS**
See also AAYA 78; AFAW 2; AMWS 4; BW
1; CA 108; 124; CDALB 1917-1929; DA;
DA3; DAC; DAM MST, MULT, POET;
DLB 4, 48, 51; EXPP; LMFS 2;
MAL 5; MTCW 1, 2; MTFW 2005; PFS
3; RGAL 4; SATA 18; WP
Culleton, Beatrice 1949- .... **NNAL**
See also CA 120; CANR 83; DAC
Culver, Timothy J.
See Westlake, Donald E.

Culver, Timothy J.
See Westlake, Donald E.
Cum, R.
See Crumb, R.
Cumberland, Richard
1732-1811 .... **NCLC 167**
See also DLB 89; RGEL 2
Cummings, Bruce F(rederick)
1889-1919 .... **TCLC 24**
See also CA 123
Cummings, E(dward) E(stlin)
1894-1962 .. **CLC 1, 3, 8, 12, 15, 68; PC
5; TCLC 137; WLC 2**
See also AAYA 41; AMW; CA 73-76;
CANR 31; CDALB 1929-1941; DA;
DA3; DAB; DAC; DAM MST, POET;
DLB 4, 48; EWL 3; EXPP; MAL 5;
MTCW 1, 2; MTFW 2005; PAB; PFS 1,
3, 12, 13, 19, 30; RGAL 4; TUS; WP
Cummins, Maria Susanna
1827-1866 .... **NCLC 139**
See also DLB 42; YABC 1
Cunha, Euclides (Rodrigues Pimenta) da
1866-1909 .... **TCLC 24**
See also CA 123; 219; DLB 307; LAW;
WLIT 1
Cunningham, E. V.
See Fast, Howard
Cunningham, J. Morgan
See Westlake, Donald E.
Cunningham, J(ames) V(incent)
1911-1985 .... **CLC 3, 31; PC 92**
See also CA 1-4R; 115; CANR 1, 72; CP 1,
2, 3, 4; DLB 5
Cunningham, Julia (Woolfolk)
1916- .... **CLC 12**
See also CA 9-12R; CANR 4, 19, 36; CWRI
5; JRDA; MAICYA 1, 2; SAAS 2; SATA
1, 26, 132
Cunningham, Michael 1952- .... **CLC 34, 243**
See also AMWS 15; CA 136; CANR 96,
160; CN 7; DLB 292; GLL 2; MTFW
2005; NFS 23
Cunninghame Graham, R. B.
See Cunninghame Graham, Robert
(Gallnigad) Bontine
**Cunninghame Graham, Robert (Gallnigad)
Bontine** 1852-1936 .... **TCLC 19**
See also CA 119; 184; DLB 98, 135, 174;
RGEL 2; RGSF 2
Curnow, (Thomas) Allen (Monro)
1911-2001 .... **PC 48**
See also CA 69-72; 202; CANR 48, 99; CP
1, 2, 3, 4, 5, 6, 7; EWL 3; RGEL 2
Currie, Ellen 19(?)- .... **CLC 44**
Curtin, Philip
See Lowndes, Marie Adelaide (Belloc)
Curtin, Phillip
See Lowndes, Marie Adelaide (Belloc)
Curtis, Price
See Ellison, Harlan
Cusanus, Nicolaus 1401-1464
See Nicholas of Cusa
Cutrate, Joe
See Spiegelman, Art
Cynewulf c. 770- .... **CMLC 23**
See also DLB 146; RGEL 2
Cyrano de Bergerac, Savinien de
1619-1655 .... **LC 65**
See also DLB 268; GFL Beginnings to
1789; RGWL 2, 3
Cyril of Alexandria c. 375-c. 430 . **CMLC 59**
Czaczkes, Shmuel Yosef Halevi
See Agnon, S.Y.
Dabrowska, Maria (Szumska)
1889-1965 .... **CLC 15**
See also CA 106; CDWLB 4; DLB 215;
EWL 3

Dabydeen, David 1955- .... **CLC 34**
See also BW 1; CA 125; CANR 56, 92; CN
6, 7; CP 5, 6, 7; DLB 347
Dacey, Philip 1939- .... **CLC 51**
See also CA 37-40R, 231; CAAE 231;
CAAS 17; CANR 14, 32, 64; CP 4, 5, 6,
7; DLB 105
Dacre, Charlotte c. 1772-1825(?) . **NCLC 151**
Dafydd ap Gwilym c. 1320-c. 1380 ..... **PC 56**
Dagerman, Stig (Halvard)
1923-1954 .... **TCLC 17**
See also CA 117; 155; DLB 259; EWL 3
D'Aguiar, Fred 1960- ..... **BLC 2:1; CLC 145**
See also CA 148; CANR 83, 101; CN 7;
CP 5, 6, 7; DLB 157; EWL 3
Dahl, Roald 1916-1990 ...... **CLC 1, 6, 18, 79;
TCLC 173**
See also AAYA 15; BPFB 1; BRWS 4; BYA
5; CA 1-4R; 133; CANR 6, 32, 37, 62;
CLR 1, 7, 41, 111; CN 1, 2, 3, 4; CPW;
DA3; DAB; DAC; DAM MST, NOV,
POP; DLB 139, 255; HGG; JRDA; MAI-
CYA 1, 2; MTCW 1, 2; MTFW 2005;
RGSF 2; SATA 1, 26, 73; SATA-Obit 65;
SSFS 4; TEA; YAW
Dahlberg, Edward 1900-1977 . **CLC 1, 7, 14;
TCLC 208**
See also CA 9-12R; 69-72; CANR 31, 62;
CN 1, 2; DLB 48; MAL 5; MTCW 1;
RGAL 4
Daitch, Susan 1954- .... **CLC 103**
See also CA 161
Dale, Colin
See Lawrence, T(homas) E(dward)
Dale, George E.
See Asimov, Isaac
d'Alembert, Jean Le Rond
1717-1783 .... **LC 126**
Dalton, Roque 1935-1975(?) ..... **HLCS 1; PC
36**
See also CA 176; DLB 283; HW 2
Daly, Elizabeth 1878-1967 .... **CLC 52**
See also CA 23-24; 25-28R; CANR 60;
CAP 2; CMW 4
Daly, Mary 1928- .... **CLC 173**
See also CA 25-28R; CANR 30, 62, 166;
FW; GLL 1; MTCW 1
Daly, Maureen 1921-2006 .... **CLC 17**
See also AAYA 5, 58; BYA 6; CA 253;
CANR 37, 83, 108; JRDA; MAI-
CYA 1, 2; SAAS 1; SATA 2, 129; SATA-
Obit 176; WYA; YAW
Damas, Leon-Gontran 1912-1978 ... **CLC 84;
TCLC 204**
See also BW 1; CA 125; 73-76; EWL 3
Dana, Richard Henry Sr.
1787-1879 .... **NCLC 53**
Dangarembga, Tsitsi 1959- .... **BLC 2:1**
See also BW 3; CA 163; NFS 28; WLIT 2
Daniel, Samuel 1562(?)-1619 .... **LC 24**
See also DLB 62; RGEL 2
Daniels, Brett
See Adler, Renata
Dannay, Frederic 1905-1982 .... **CLC 3, 11**
See also BPFB 3; CA 1-4R; 107; CANR 1,
39; CMW 4; DAM POP; DLB 137; MSW;
MTCW 1; RGAL 4
D'Annunzio, Gabriele 1863-1938 ... **TCLC 6,
40, 215**
See also CA 104; 155; EW 8; EWL 3;
RGWL 2, 3; TWA; WLIT 7
Danois, N. le
See Gourmont, Remy(-Marie-Charles) de
Dante 1265-1321 .... **CMLC 3, 18, 39, 70; PC
21; WLCS**
See also DA; DA3; DAB; DAC; DAM
MST, POET; EFS 1; EW 1; LAIT 1;
RGWL 2, 3; TWA; WLIT 7; WP

Deighton, Leonard Cyril 1929- ..... **CLC 4, 7, 22, 46**
    See also AAYA 57, 6; BEST 89:2; BPFB 1; CA 9-12R; CANR 19, 33, 68; CDBLB 1960- Present; CMW 4; CN 1, 2, 3, 4, 5, 6, 7; CPW; DA3; DAM NOV, POP; DLB 87; MTCW 1, 2; MTFW 2005

Dekker, Thomas 1572(?)-1632 ..... **DC 12; LC 22, 159**
    See also CDBLB Before 1660; DAM DRAM; DLB 62, 172; LMFS 1; RGEL 2

de Laclos, Pierre Ambroise Franois
    See Laclos, Pierre-Ambroise Francois

Delacroix, (Ferdinand-Victor-)Eugene
    1798-1863 .... **NCLC 133**
    See also EW 5

Delafield, E. M.
    See Dashwood, Edmee Elizabeth Monica de la Pasture

de la Mare, Walter (John)
    1873-1956 ..... **PC 77; SSC 14; TCLC 4, 53; WLC 2**
    See also CA 163; CDBLB 1914-1945; CLR 23; CWRI 5; DA3; DAB; DAC; DAM MST, POET; DLB 19, 153, 162, 255, 284; EWL 3; EXPP; HGG; MAICYA 1, 2; MTCW 2; MTFW 2005; RGEL 2; RGSF 2; SATA 16; SUFW 1; TEA; WCH

de Lamartine, Alphonse (Marie Louis Prat)
    See Lamartine, Alphonse (Marie Louis Prat) de

Delaney, Franey
    See O'Hara, John (Henry)

Delaney, Shelagh 1939- .... **CLC 29**
    See also CA 17-20R; CANR 30, 67; CBD; CD 5, 6; CDBLB 1960 to Present; CWD; DAM DRAM; DFS 7; DLB 13; MTCW 1

Delany, Martin Robison
    1812-1885 .... **NCLC 93**
    See also DLB 50; RGAL 4

Delany, Mary (Granville Pendarves)
    1700-1788 .... **LC 12**

Delany, Samuel R., Jr. 1942- .... **BLC 1:1; CLC 8, 14, 38, 141**
    See also AAYA 24; AFAW 2; BPFB 1; BW 2, 3; CA 81-84; CANR 27, 43, 116, 172; CN 2, 3, 4, 5, 6, 7; DAM MULT; DLB 8, 33; FANT; MAL 5; MTCW 1, 2; RGAL 4; SATA 92; SCFW 1, 2; SFW 4; SUFW 2

Delany, Samuel Ray
    See Delany, Samuel R., Jr.

de la Parra, (Ana) Teresa (Sonojo)
    1890(?)-1936 .... **HLCS 2; TCLC 185**
    See also CA 178; HW 2; LAW

Delaporte, Theophile
    See Green, Julien (Hartridge)

De La Ramee, Marie Louise
    1839-1908 .... **TCLC 43**
    See also CA 204; DLB 18, 156; RGEL 2; SATA 20

de la Roche, Mazo 1879-1961 .... **CLC 14**
    See also CA 85-88; CANR 30; DLB 68; RGEL 2; RHW; SATA 64

De La Salle, Innocent
    See Hartmann, Sadakichi

de Laureamont, Comte
    See Lautreamont

Delbanco, Nicholas 1942- ..... **CLC 6, 13, 167**
    See also CA 17-20R, 189; CAAE 189; CAAS 2; CANR 29, 55, 116, 150; CN 7; DLB 6, 234

Delbanco, Nicholas Franklin
    See Delbanco, Nicholas

del Castillo, Michel 1933- .... **CLC 38**
    See also CA 109; CANR 77

Deledda, Grazia (Cosima)
    1875(?)-1936 .... **TCLC 23**
    See also CA 123; 205; DLB 264, 329; EWL 3; RGWL 2, 3; WLIT 7

Deleuze, Gilles 1925-1995 .... **TCLC 116**
    See also DLB 296

Delgado, Abelardo (Lalo) B(arrientos)
    1930-2004 .... **HLC 1**
    See also CA 131; 230; CAAS 15; CANR 90; DAM MST, MULT; DLB 82; HW 1, 2

Delibes, Miguel
    See Delibes Setien, Miguel

Delibes Setien, Miguel 1920- .... **CLC 8, 18**
    See also CA 45-48; CANR 1, 32; CWW 2; DLB 322; EWL 3; HW 1; MTCW 1

DeLillo, Don 1936- ..... **CLC 8, 10, 13, 27, 39, 54, 76, 143, 210, 213**
    See also AMWC 2; AMWS 6; BEST 89:1; BPFB 1; CA 81-84; CANR 21, 76, 92, 133, 173; CN 3, 4, 5, 6, 7; CPW; DA3; DAM NOV, POP; DLB 6, 173; EWL 3; MAL 5; MTCW 1, 2; MTFW 2005; NFS 28; RGAL 4; TUS

de Lisser, H. G.
    See De Lisser, H(erbert) G(eorge)

De Lisser, H(erbert) G(eorge)
    1878-1944 .... **TCLC 12**
    See also BW 2; CA 109; 152; DLB 117

Deloire, Pierre
    See Peguy, Charles (Pierre)

Deloney, Thomas 1543(?)-1600 .... **LC 41; PC 79**
    See also DLB 167; RGEL 2

Deloria, Ella (Cara) 1889-1971(?) ..... **NNAL**
    See also CA 152; DAM MULT; DLB 175

Deloria, Vine, Jr. 1933-2005 .... **CLC 21, 122; NNAL**
    See also CA 53-56; 245; CANR 5, 20, 48, 98; DAM MULT; DLB 175; MTCW 1; SATA 21; SATA-Obit 171

Deloria, Vine Victor, Jr.
    See Deloria, Vine, Jr.

del Valle-Inclan, Ramon (Maria)
    See Valle-Inclan, Ramon (Maria) del

Del Vecchio, John M(ichael) 1947- .. **CLC 29**
    See also CA 110; DLBD 9

de Man, Paul (Adolph Michel)
    1919-1983 .... **CLC 55**
    See also CA 128; 111; CANR 61; DLB 67; MTCW 1, 2

de Mandiargues, Andre Pieyre
    See Pieyre de Mandiargues, Andre

DeMarinis, Rick 1934- .... **CLC 54**
    See also CA 57-60, 184; CAAE 184; CAAS 24; CANR 9, 25, 50, 160; DLB 218; TCWW 2

de Maupassant, (Henri Rene Albert) Guy
    See Maupassant, (Henri Rene Albert) Guy de

Dembry, R. Emmet
    See Murfree, Mary Noailles

Demby, William 1922- ...... **BLC 1:1; CLC 53**
    See also BW 1, 3; CA 81-84; CANR 81; DAM MULT; DLB 33

de Menton, Francisco
    See Chin, Frank (Chew, Jr.)

Demetrius of Phalerum c.
    307B.C.- .... **CMLC 34**

Demijohn, Thom
    See Disch, Thomas M.

De Mille, James 1833-1880 .... **NCLC 123**
    See also DLB 99, 251

Democritus c. 460B.C.-c. 370B.C. . **CMLC 47**

de Montaigne, Michel (Eyquem)
    See Montaigne, Michel (Eyquem) de

de Montherlant, Henry (Milon)
    See Montherlant, Henry (Milon) de

Demosthenes 384B.C.-322B.C. ...... **CMLC 13**
    See also AW 1; DLB 176; RGWL 2, 3; WLIT 8

de Musset, (Louis Charles) Alfred
    See Musset, Alfred de

de Natale, Francine
    See Malzberg, Barry N(athaniel)

de Navarre, Marguerite 1492-1549 .... **LC 61, 167; SSC 85**
    See also DLB 327; GFL Beginnings to 1789; RGWL 2, 3

Denby, Edwin (Orr) 1903-1983 .... **CLC 48**
    See also CA 138; 110; CP 1

de Nerval, Gerard
    See Nerval, Gerard de

Denham, John 1615-1669 .... **LC 73**
    See also DLB 58, 126; RGEL 2

Denis, Julio
    See Cortazar, Julio

Denmark, Harrison
    See Zelazny, Roger

Dennis, John 1658-1734 .... **LC 11, 154**
    See also DLB 101; RGEL 2

Dennis, Nigel (Forbes) 1912-1989 ...... **CLC 8**
    See also CA 25-28R; 129; CN 1, 2, 3, 4; DLB 13, 15, 233; EWL 3; MTCW 1

Dent, Lester 1904-1959 .... **TCLC 72**
    See also CA 112; 161; CMW 4; DLB 306; SFW 4

Dentinger, Stephen
    See Hoch, Edward D.

De Palma, Brian 1940- .... **CLC 20, 247**
    See also CA 109

De Palma, Brian Russell
    See De Palma, Brian

de Pizan, Christine
    See Christine de Pizan

De Quincey, Thomas 1785-1859 ..... **NCLC 4, 87, 198**
    See also BRW 4; CDBLB 1789-1832; DLB 110, 144; RGEL 2

De Ray, Jill
    See Moore, Alan

Deren, Eleanora 1908(?)-1961 .. **CLC 16, 102**
    See also CA 192; 111

Deren, Maya
    See Deren, Eleanora

Derleth, August (William)
    1909-1971 .... **CLC 31**
    See also BPFB 1; BYA 9, 10; CA 1-4R; 29-32R; CANR 4; CMW 4; CN 1; DLB 9; DLBD 17; HGG; SATA 5; SUFW 1

Der Nister 1884-1950 .... **TCLC 56**
    See also DLB 333; EWL 3

de Routisie, Albert
    See Aragon, Louis

Derrida, Jacques 1930-2004 ...... **CLC 24, 87, 225**
    See also CA 124; 127; 232; CANR 76, 98, 133; DLB 242; EWL 3; LMFS 2; MTCW 2; TWA

Derry Down Derry
    See Lear, Edward

Dersonnes, Jacques
    See Simenon, Georges (Jacques Christian)

Der Stricker c. 1190-c. 1250 .... **CMLC 75**
    See also DLB 138

Derzhavin, Gavrila Romanovich
    .... **NCLC 215**
    See also DLB 150

Desai, Anita 1937- . **CLC 19, 37, 97, 175, 271**
    See also BRWS 5; CA 81-84; CANR 33, 53, 95, 133; CN 1, 2, 3, 4, 5, 6, 7; CWRI 5; DA3; DAB; DAM NOV; DLB 271, 323; DNFS 2; EWL 3; FW; MTCW 1, 2; MTFW 2005; SATA 63, 126

EWL 3; LAIT 3; MAL 5; MTCW 1, 2;
MTFW 2005; NFS 6; RGAL 4; RGHL;
RHW; SSFS 27; TCLE 1:1; TCWW 1, 2;
TUS

Dodgson, Charles Lutwidge
See Carroll, Lewis

Dodsley, Robert 1703-1764 .... **LC 97**
See also DLB 95; RGEL 2

Dodson, Owen (Vincent)
1914-1983 .... **BLC 1:1; CLC 79**
See also BW 1; CA 65-68; 110; CANR 24;
DAM MULT; DLB 76

Doeblin, Alfred 1878-1957 .... **TCLC 13**
See also CA 110; 141; CDWLB 2; DLB 66;
EWL 3; RGWL 2, 3

Doerr, Harriet 1910-2002 .... **CLC 34**
See also CA 117; 122; 213; CANR 47; INT
CA-122; LATS 1:2

Domecq, H(onorio) Bustos
See Bioy Casares, Adolfo; Borges, Jorge
Luis

Domini, Rey
See Lorde, Audre

Dominic, R. B.
See Hennissart, Martha

Dominique
See Proust, (Valentin-Louis-George-Eugene)
Marcel

Don, A
See Stephen, Sir Leslie

Donaldson, Stephen R. 1947- ... **CLC 46, 138**
See also AAYA 36; BPFB 1; CA 89-92;
CANR 13, 55, 99; CPW; DAM POP;
FANT; INT CANR-13; SATA 121; SFW
4; SUFW 1, 2

Donleavy, J(ames) P(atrick) 1926- .... **CLC 1,
4, 6, 10, 45**
See also AITN 2; BPFB 1; CA 9-12R;
CANR 24, 49, 62, 80, 124; CBD; CD 5,
6; CN 1, 2, 3, 4, 5, 6, 7; DLB 6, 173; INT
CANR-24; MAL 5; MTCW 1, 2; MTFW
2005; RGAL 4

Donnadieu, Marguerite
See Duras, Marguerite

Donne, John 1572-1631 ... **LC 10, 24, 91; PC
1, 43; WLC 2**
See also AAYA 67; BRW 1; BRWC 1;
BRWR 2; CDBLB Before 1660; DA;
DAB; DAC; DAM MST, POET; DLB
121, 151; EXPP; PAB; PFS 2, 11; RGEL
3; TEA; WLIT 3; WP

Donnell, David 1939(?)- .... **CLC 34**
See also CA 197

Donoghue, Denis 1928- .... **CLC 209**
See also CA 17-20R; CANR 16, 102

Donoghue, Emma 1969- .... **CLC 239**
See also CA 155; CANR 103, 152; DLB
267; GLL 2; SATA 101

Donoghue, P.S.
See Hunt, E. Howard

Donoso (Yanez), Jose 1924-1996 ... **CLC 4, 8,
11, 32, 99; HLC 1; SSC 34; TCLC 133**
See also CA 81-84; 155; CANR 32, 73; CD-
WLB 3; CWW 2; DAM MULT; DLB 113;
EWL 3; HW 1, 2; LAW; LAWS 1; MTCW
1, 2; MTFW 2005; RGSF 2; WLIT 1

Donovan, John 1928-1992 .... **CLC 35**
See also AAYA 20; CA 97-100; 137; CLR
3; MAICYA 1, 2; SATA 72; SATA-Brief
29; YAW

Don Roberto
See Cunninghame Graham, Robert
(Gallnigad) Bontine

Doolittle, Hilda 1886-1961 . **CLC 3, 8, 14, 31,
34, 73; PC 5; WLC 3**
See also AAYA 66; AMWS 1; CA 97-100;
CANR 35, 131; DA; DAC; DAM MST,
POET; DLB 4, 45; EWL 3; FL 1:5; FW;
GLL 1; LMFS 2; MAL 5; MBL; MTCW
1, 2; MTFW 2005; PFS 6, 28; RGAL 4

Doppo
See Kunikida Doppo

Doppo, Kunikida
See Kunikida Doppo

Dorfman, Ariel 1942- .... **CLC 48, 77, 189;
HLC 1**
See also CA 124; 130; CANR 67, 70, 135;
CWW 2; DAM MULT; DFS 4; EWL 3;
HW 1, 2; INT CA-130; WLIT 1

Dorn, Edward (Merton)
1929-1999 .... **CLC 10, 18**
See also CA 93-96; 187; CANR 42, 79; CP
1, 2, 3, 4, 5, 6, 7; DLB 5; INT CA-93-96;
WP

Dor-Ner, Zvi .... **CLC 70**

Dorris, Michael 1945-1997 .... **CLC 109;
NNAL**
See also AAYA 20; BEST 90:1; BYA 12;
CA 102; 157; CANR 19, 46, 75; CLR 58;
DA3; DAM MULT, NOV; DLB 175;
LAIT 5; MTCW 2; MTFW 2005; NFS 3;
RGAL 4; SATA 75; SATA-Obit 94;
TCWW 2; YAW

Dorris, Michael A.
See Dorris, Michael

Dorsan, Luc
See Simenon, Georges (Jacques Christian)

Dorsange, Jean
See Simenon, Georges (Jacques Christian)

Dorset
See Sackville, Thomas

Dos Passos, John (Roderigo)
1896-1970 ... **CLC 1, 4, 8, 11, 15, 25, 34,
82; WLC 2**
See also AMW; BPFB 1; CA 1-4R; 29-32R;
CANR 3; CDALB 1929-1941; DA; DA3;
DAB; DAC; DAM MST, NOV; DLB 4,
9, 274, 316; DLBD 1, 15; DLBY 1996;
EWL 3; MAL 5; MTCW 1, 2; MTFW
2005; NFS 14; RGAL 4; TUS

Dossage, Jean
See Simenon, Georges (Jacques Christian)

Dostoevsky, Fedor Mikhailovich
1821-1881 .. **NCLC 2, 7, 21, 33, 43, 119,
167, 202; SSC 2, 33, 44; WLC 2**
See also AAYA 40; DA; DA3; DAB; DAC;
DAM MST, NOV; DLB 238; EW 7;
EXPN; LATS 1:1; LMFS 1, 2; NFS 28;
RGSF 2; RGWL 2, 3; SSFS 8; TWA

Dostoevsky, Fyodor
See Dostoevsky, Fedor Mikhailovich

Doty, Mark 1953(?)- .... **CLC 176; PC 53**
See also AMWS 11; CA 161, 183; CAAE
183; CANR 110, 173; CP 7; PFS 28

Doty, Mark A.
See Doty, Mark

Doty, Mark Alan
See Doty, Mark

Doty, M.R.
See Doty, Mark

Doughty, Charles M(ontagu)
1843-1926 .... **TCLC 27**
See also CA 115; 178; DLB 19, 57, 174

Douglas, Ellen 1921- .... **CLC 73**
See also CA 115; CANR 41, 83; CN 5, 6,
7; CSW; DLB 292

Douglas, Gavin 1475(?)-1522 .... **LC 20**
See also DLB 132; RGEL 2

Douglas, George
See Brown, George Douglas

Douglas, Keith (Castellain)
1920-1944 .... **TCLC 40**
See also BRW 7; CA 160; DLB 27; EWL
3; PAB; RGEL 2

Douglas, Leonard
See Bradbury, Ray

Douglas, Michael
See Crichton, Michael

Douglas, Michael
See Crichton, Michael

Douglas, (George) Norman
1868-1952 .... **TCLC 68**
See also BRW 6; CA 119; 157; DLB 34,
195; RGEL 2

Douglas, William
See Brown, George Douglas

Douglass, Frederick 1817(?)-1895 .. **BLC 1:1;
NCLC 7, 55, 141; WLC 2**
See also AAYA 48; AFAW 1, 2; AMWC 1;
AMWS 3; CDALB 1640-1865; DA; DA3;
DAC; DAM MST, MULT; DLB 1, 43, 50,
79, 243; FW; LAIT 2; NCFS 2; RGAL 4;
SATA 29

Dourado, (Waldomiro Freitas) Autran
1926- .... **CLC 23, 60**
See also CA 25-28R; 179; CANR 34, 81;
DLB 145, 307; HW 2

Dourado, Waldomiro Freitas Autran
See Dourado, (Waldomiro Freitas) Autran

Dove, Rita 1952- . **BLC 2:1; BLCS; CLC 50,
81; PC 6**
See also AAYA 46; AMWS 4; BW 2; CA
109; CAAS 19; CANR 27, 42, 68, 76, 97,
132; CDALBS; CP 5, 6, 7; CSW; CWP;
DA3; DAM MULT, POET; DLB 120;
EWL 3; EXPP; MAL 5; MTCW 2; MTFW
2005; PFS 1, 15; RGAL 4

Dove, Rita Frances
See Dove, Rita

Doveglion
See Villa, Jose Garcia

Dowell, Coleman 1925-1985 .... **CLC 60**
See also CA 25-28R; 117; CANR 10; DLB
130; GLL 2

Downing, Major Jack
See Smith, Seba

Dowson, Ernest (Christopher)
1867-1900 .... **TCLC 4**
See also CA 105; 150; DLB 19, 135; RGEL
2

Doyle, A. Conan
See Doyle, Sir Arthur Conan

Doyle, Sir Arthur Conan
1859-1930 ..... **SSC 12, 83, 95; TCLC 7;
WLC 2**
See also AAYA 14; BPFB 1; BRWS 2; BYA
4, 5, 11; CA 104; 122; CANR 131; CD-
BLB 1890-1914; CLR 106; CMW 4; DA;
DA3; DAB; DAC; DAM MST, NOV;
DLB 18, 70, 156, 178; EXPS; HGG;
LAIT 2; MSW; MTCW 1, 2; MTFW
2005; NFS 28; RGEL 2; RGSF 2; RHW;
SATA 24; SCFW 1, 2; SFW 4; SSFS 2;
TEA; WCH; WLIT 4; WYA; YAW

Doyle, Conan
See Doyle, Sir Arthur Conan

Doyle, John
See Graves, Robert

Doyle, Roddy 1958- .... **CLC 81, 178**
See also AAYA 14; BRWS 5; CA 143;
CANR 73, 128, 168; CN 6, 7; DA3; DLB
194, 326; MTCW 2; MTFW 2005

Doyle, Sir A. Conan
See Doyle, Sir Arthur Conan

Dr. A
See Asimov, Isaac; Silverstein, Alvin; Silverstein, Virginia B(arbara Opshelor)

Drabble, Margaret 1939- ...... **CLC 2, 3, 5, 8,
10, 22, 53, 129**
See also BRWS 4; CA 13-16R; CANR 18,
35, 63, 112, 131, 174; CDBLB 1960 to
Present; CN 1, 2, 3, 4, 5, 6, 7; CPW; DA3;
DAB; DAC; DAM MST, NOV, POP;
DLB 14, 155, 231; EWL 3; FW; MTCW
1, 2; MTFW 2005; RGEL 2; SATA 48;
TEA

Drakulic, Slavenka 1949- .... **CLC 173**
See also CA 144; CANR 92

Duong, Thu Huong 1947- .... **CLC 273**
See also CA 152; CANR 106, 166; DLB
348; NFS 23
Duong Thu Huong
See Duong, Thu Huong
du Perry, Jean
See Simenon, Georges (Jacques Christian)
Durang, Christopher 1949- .... **CLC 27, 38**
See also CA 105; CAD; CANR 50, 76, 130;
CD 5, 6; MTCW 2; MTFW 2005
Durang, Christopher Ferdinand
See Durang, Christopher
Duras, Claire de 1777-1832 .... **NCLC 154**
Duras, Marguerite 1914-1996 . **CLC 3, 6, 11,
20, 34, 40, 68, 100; SSC 40**
See also BPFB 1; CA 25-28R; 151; CANR
50; CWW 2; DFS 21; DLB 83, 321; EWL
3; FL 1:5; GFL 1789 to the Present; IDFW
4; MTCW 1, 2; RGWL 2, 3; TWA
Durban, (Rosa) Pam 1947- .... **CLC 39**
See also CA 123; CANR 98; CSW
Durcan, Paul 1944- .... **CLC 43, 70**
See also CA 134; CANR 123; CP 1, 5, 6, 7;
DAM POET; EWL 3
d'Urfe, Honore
See Urfe, Honore d'
Durfey, Thomas 1653-1723 .... **LC 94**
See also DLB 80; RGEL 2
Durkheim, Emile 1858-1917 .... **TCLC 55**
See also CA 249
Durrell, Lawrence (George)
1912-1990 ..... **CLC 1, 4, 6, 8, 13, 27, 41**
See also BPFB 1; BRWS 1; CA 9-12R; 132;
CANR 40, 77; CDBLB 1945-1960; CN 1,
2, 3, 4; CP 1, 2, 3, 4, 5; DAM NOV; DLB
15, 27, 204; DLBY 1990; EWL 3; MTCW
1, 2; RGEL 2; SFW 4; TEA
Durrenmatt, Friedrich
See Duerrenmatt, Friedrich
Dutt, Michael Madhusudan
1824-1873 .... **NCLC 118**
Dutt, Toru 1856-1877 .... **NCLC 29**
See also DLB 240
Dwight, Timothy 1752-1817 .... **NCLC 13**
See also DLB 37; RGAL 4
Dworkin, Andrea 1946-2005 ..... **CLC 43, 123**
See also CA 77-80; 238; CAAS 21; CANR
16, 39, 76, 96; FL 1:5; FW; GLL 1; INT
CANR-16; MTCW 1, 2; MTFW 2005
Dwyer, Deanna
See Koontz, Dean R.
Dwyer, K.R.
See Koontz, Dean R.
Dybek, Stuart 1942- .... **CLC 114; SSC 55**
See also CA 97-100; CANR 39; DLB 130;
SSFS 23
Dye, Richard
See De Voto, Bernard (Augustine)
Dyer, Geoff 1958- .... **CLC 149**
See also CA 125; CANR 88
Dyer, George 1755-1841 .... **NCLC 129**
See also DLB 93
Dylan, Bob 1941- .... **CLC 3, 4, 6, 12, 77; PC
37**
See also AMWS 18; CA 41-44R; CANR
108; CP 1, 2, 3, 4, 5, 6, 7; DLB 16
Dyson, John 1943- .... **CLC 70**
See also CA 144
Dzyubin, Eduard Georgievich
1895-1934 .... **TCLC 60**
See also CA 170; EWL 3
E. V. L.
See Lucas, E(dward) V(errall)
Eagleton, Terence (Francis) 1943- .. **CLC 63,
132**
See also CA 57-60; CANR 7, 23, 68, 115;
DLB 242; LMFS 2; MTCW 1, 2; MTFW
2005

Eagleton, Terry
See Eagleton, Terence (Francis)
Early, Jack
See Scoppettone, Sandra
East, Michael
See West, Morris L(anglo)
Eastaway, Edward
See Thomas, (Philip) Edward
Eastlake, William (Derry)
1917-1997 .... **CLC 8**
See also CA 5-8R; 158; CAAS 1; CANR 5,
63; CN 1, 2, 3, 4, 5, 6; DLB 6, 206; INT
CANR-5; MAL 5; TCWW 1, 2
Eastman, Charles A(lexander)
1858-1939 .... **NNAL; TCLC 55**
See also CA 179; CANR 91; DAM MULT;
DLB 175; YABC 1
Eaton, Edith Maude 1865-1914 .... **AAL**
See also CA 154; DLB 221, 312; FW
Eaton, (Lillie) Winnifred 1875-1954 .... **AAL**
See also CA 217; DLB 221, 312; RGAL 4
Eberhart, Richard 1904-2005 ...... **CLC 3, 11,
19, 56; PC 76**
See also AMW; CA 1-4R; 240; CANR 2,
125; CDALB 1941-1968; CP 1, 2, 3, 4, 5,
6, 7; DAM POET; DLB 48; MAL 5;
MTCW 1; RGAL 4
Eberhart, Richard Ghormley
See Eberhart, Richard
Eberstadt, Fernanda 1960- .... **CLC 39**
See also CA 136; CANR 69, 128
Ebner, Margaret c. 1291-1351 ...... **CMLC 98**
**Echegaray (y Eizaguirre), Jose (Maria
Waldo)** 1832-1916 .... **HLCS 1; TCLC 4**
See also CA 104; CANR 32; DLB 329;
EWL 3; HW 1; MTCW 1
Echeverria, (Jose) Esteban (Antonino)
1805-1851 .... **NCLC 18**
See also LAW
Echo
See Proust, (Valentin-Louis-George-Eugene)
Marcel
Eckert, Allan W. 1931- .... **CLC 17**
See also AAYA 18; BYA 2; CA 13-16R;
CANR 14, 45; INT CANR-14; MAICYA
2; MAICYAS 1; SAAS 21; SATA 29, 91;
SATA-Brief 27
Eckhart, Meister 1260(?)-1327(?) .. **CMLC 9,
80**
See also DLB 115; LMFS 1
Eckmar, F. R.
See de Hartog, Jan
Eco, Umberto 1932- .... **CLC 28, 60, 142, 248**
See also BEST 90:1; BPFB 1; CA 77-80;
CANR 12, 33, 55, 110, 131; CPW; CWW
2; DA3; DAM NOV, POP; DLB 196, 242;
EWL 3; MSW; MTCW 1, 2; MTFW
2005; NFS 22; RGWL 3; WLIT 7
Eddison, E(ric) R(ucker)
1882-1945 .... **TCLC 15**
See also CA 109; 156; DLB 255; FANT;
SFW 4; SUFW 1
Eddy, Mary (Ann Morse) Baker
1821-1910 .... **TCLC 71**
See also CA 113; 174
Edel, (Joseph) Leon 1907-1997 .. **CLC 29, 34**
See also CA 1-4R; 161; CANR 1, 22, 112;
DLB 103; INT CANR-22
Eden, Emily 1797-1869 .... **NCLC 10**
Edgar, David 1948- .... **CLC 42**
See also CA 57-60; CANR 12, 61, 112;
CBD; CD 5, 6; DAM DRAM; DFS 15;
DLB 13, 233; MTCW 1
Edgerton, Clyde (Carlyle) 1944- ...... **CLC 39**
See also AAYA 17; CA 118; 134; CANR
64, 125; CN 7; CSW; DLB 278; INT CA-
134; TCLE 1:1; YAW

Edgeworth, Maria 1768-1849 ... **NCLC 1, 51,
158; SSC 86**
See also BRWS 3; DLB 116, 159, 163; FL
1:3; FW; RGEL 2; SATA 21; TEA; WLIT
3
Edmonds, Paul
See Kuttner, Henry
Edmonds, Walter D(umaux)
1903-1998 .... **CLC 35**
See also BYA 2; CA 5-8R; CANR 2; CWRI
5; DLB 9; LAIT 1; MAICYA 1, 2; MAL
5; RHW; SAAS 4; SATA 1, 27; SATA-
Obit 99
Edmondson, Wallace
See Ellison, Harlan
Edson, Margaret 1961- ...... **CLC 199; DC 24**
See also AMWS 18; CA 190; DFS 13; DLB
266
Edson, Russell 1935- .... **CLC 13**
See also CA 33-36R; CANR 115; CP 2, 3,
4, 5, 6, 7; DLB 244; WP
Edwards, Bronwen Elizabeth
See Rose, Wendy
Edwards, Eli
See McKay, Festus Claudius
Edwards, G(erald) B(asil)
1899-1976 .... **CLC 25**
See also CA 201; 110
Edwards, Gus 1939- .... **CLC 43**
See also CA 108; INT CA-108
Edwards, Jonathan 1703-1758 .... **LC 7, 54**
See also AMW; DA; DAC; DAM MST;
DLB 24, 270; RGAL 4; TUS
Edwards, Sarah Pierpont 1710-1758 .. **LC 87**
See also DLB 200
Efron, Marina Ivanovna Tsvetaeva
See Tsvetaeva (Efron), Marina (Ivanovna)
Egeria fl. 4th cent. - .... **CMLC 70**
Eggers, Dave 1970- .... **CLC 241**
See also AAYA 56; CA 198; CANR 138;
MTFW 2005
Egoyan, Atom 1960- .... **CLC 151**
See also AAYA 63; CA 157; CANR 151
Ehle, John (Marsden, Jr.) 1925- ...... **CLC 27**
See also CA 9-12R; CSW
Ehrenbourg, Ilya (Grigoryevich)
See Ehrenburg, Ilya (Grigoryevich)
Ehrenburg, Ilya (Grigoryevich)
1891-1967 .... **CLC 18, 34, 62**
See Erenburg, Ilya (Grigoryevich)
See also CA 102; 25-28R; EWL 3
Ehrenburg, Ilyo (Grigoryevich)
See Ehrenburg, Ilya (Grigoryevich)
Ehrenreich, Barbara 1941- ..... **CLC 110, 267**
See also BEST 90:4; CA 73-76; CANR 16,
37, 62, 117, 167; DLB 246; FW; MTCW
1, 2; MTFW 2005
Ehrlich, Gretel 1946- .... **CLC 249**
See also ANW; CA 140; CANR 74, 146;
DLB 212, 275; TCWW 2
Eich, Gunter
See Eich, Gunter
Eich, Gunter 1907-1972 .... **CLC 15**
See also CA 111; 93-96; DLB 69, 124;
EWL 3; RGWL 2, 3
Eichendorff, Joseph 1788-1857 .... **NCLC 8**
See also DLB 90; RGWL 2, 3
Eigner, Larry
See Eigner, Laurence (Joel)
Eigner, Laurence (Joel) 1927-1996 ..... **CLC 9**
See also CA 9-12R; 151; CAAS 23; CANR
6, 84; CP 1, 2, 3, 4, 5, 6, 7; DLB 5; WP
Eilhart von Oberge c. 1140-c.
1195 .... **CMLC 67**
See also DLB 148
Einhard c. 770-840 .... **CMLC 50**
See also DLB 148

Engelhardt, Frederick
See Hubbard, L. Ron
Engels, Friedrich 1820-1895 .. **NCLC 85, 114**
See also DLB 129; LATS 1:1
Enquist, Per Olov 1934- .... **CLC 257**
See also CA 109; 193; CANR 155; CWW
2; DLB 257; EWL 3
Enright, D(ennis) J(oseph)
1920-2002 .... **CLC 4, 8, 31; PC 93**
See also CA 1-4R; 211; CANR 1, 42, 83;
CN 1, 2; CP 1, 2, 3, 4, 5, 6, 7; DLB 27;
EWL 3; SATA 25; SATA-Obit 140
Ensler, Eve 1953- .... **CLC 212**
See also CA 172; CANR 126, 163; DFS 23
Enzensberger, Hans Magnus
1929- .... **CLC 43; PC 28**
See also CA 116; 119; CANR 103; CWW
2; EWL 3
Ephron, Nora 1941- .... **CLC 17, 31**
See also AAYA 35; AITN 2; CA 65-68;
CANR 12, 39, 83, 161; DFS 22
Epicurus 341B.C.-270B.C. .... **CMLC 21**
See also DLB 176
Epinay, Louise d' 1726-1783 .... **LC 138**
See also DLB 313
Epsilon
See Betjeman, John
Epstein, Daniel Mark 1948- .... **CLC 7**
See also CA 49-52; CANR 2, 53, 90
Epstein, Jacob 1956- .... **CLC 19**
See also CA 114
Epstein, Jean 1897-1953 .... **TCLC 92**
Epstein, Joseph 1937- .... **CLC 39, 204**
See also AMWS 14; CA 112; 119; CANR
50, 65, 117, 164
Epstein, Leslie 1938- .... **CLC 27**
See also AMWS 12; CA 73-76, 215; CAAE
215; CAAS 12; CANR 23, 69, 162; DLB
299; RGHL
Equiano, Olaudah 1745(?)-1797 ..... **BLC 1:2;**
LC 16, 143
See also AFAW 1, 2; CDWLB 3; DAM
MULT; DLB 37, 50; WLIT 2
Erasmus, Desiderius 1469(?)-1536 ..... **LC 16,**
93
See also DLB 136; EW 2; LMFS 1; RGWL
2, 3; TWA
Erdman, Paul E. 1932-2007 .... **CLC 25**
See also AITN 1; CA 61-64; 259; CANR
13, 43, 84
Erdman, Paul Emil
See Erdman, Paul E.
Erdrich, Karen Louise
See Erdrich, Louise
Erdrich, Louise 1954- .... **CLC 39, 54, 120,**
176; NNAL; PC 52; SSC 121
See also AAYA 10, 47; AMWS 4; BEST
89:1; BPFB 1; CA 114; CANR 41, 62,
118, 138; CDALBS; CN 5, 6, 7; CP 6, 7;
CPW; CWP; DA3; DAM MULT, NOV,
POP; DLB 152, 175, 206; EWL 3; EXPP;
FL 1:5; LAIT 5; LATS 1:2; MAL 5;
MTCW 1, 2; MTFW 2005; NFS 5; PFS
14; RGAL 4; SATA 94, 141; SSFS 14,
22; TCWW 2
Erenburg, Ilya (Grigoryevich)
See Ehrenburg, Ilya (Grigoryevich)
See also DLB 272
Erickson, Stephen Michael
See Erickson, Steve
Erickson, Steve 1950- .... **CLC 64**
See also CA 129; CANR 60, 68, 136;
MTFW 2005; SFW 4; SUFW 2
Erickson, Walter
See Fast, Howard
Ericson, Walter
See Fast, Howard
Eriksson, Buntel
See Bergman, Ingmar

Eriugena, John Scottus c.
810-877 .... **CMLC 65**
See also DLB 115
Ernaux, Annie 1940- .... **CLC 88, 184**
See also CA 147; CANR 93; MTFW 2005;
NCFS 3, 5
Erskine, John 1879-1951 .... **TCLC 84**
See also CA 112; 159; DLB 9, 102; FANT
Erwin, Will
See Eisner, Will
Eschenbach, Wolfram von
See von Eschenbach, Wolfram
Eseki, Bruno
See Mphahlele, Es'kia
Esekie, Bruno
See Mphahlele, Es'kia
Esenin, S.A.
See Esenin, Sergei
Esenin, Sergei 1895-1925 .... **TCLC 4**
See also CA 104; EWL 3; RGWL 2, 3
Esenin, Sergei Aleksandrovich
See Esenin, Sergei
Eshleman, Clayton 1935- .... **CLC 7**
See also CA 33-36R, 212; CAAE 212;
CAAS 6; CANR 93; CP 1, 2, 3, 4, 5, 6,
7; DLB 5
Espada, Martin 1957- .... **PC 74**
See also CA 159; CANR 80; CP 7; EXPP;
LLW; MAL 5; PFS 13, 16
Espriella, Don Manuel Alvarez
See Southey, Robert
Espriu, Salvador 1913-1985 .... **CLC 9**
See also CA 154; 115; DLB 134; EWL 3
Espronceda, Jose de 1808-1842 ..... **NCLC 39**
Esquivel, Laura 1950(?)- ... **CLC 141; HLCS**
1
See also AAYA 29; CA 143; CANR 68, 113,
161; DA3; DNFS 2; LAIT 3; LMFS 2;
MTCW 2; MTFW 2005; NFS 5; WLIT 1
Esse, James
See Stephens, James
Esterbrook, Tom
See Hubbard, L. Ron
Esterhazy, Peter 1950- .... **CLC 251**
See also CA 140; CANR 137; CDWLB 4;
CWW 2; DLB 232; EWL 3; RGWL 3
Estleman, Loren D. 1952- .... **CLC 48**
See also AAYA 27; CA 85-88; CANR 27,
74, 139, 177; CMW 4; CPW; DA3; DAM
NOV, POP; DLB 226; INT CANR-27;
MTCW 1, 2; MTFW 2005; TCWW 1, 2
Etherege, Sir George 1636-1692 . **DC 23; LC**
78
See also BRW 2; DAM DRAM; DLB 80;
PAB; RGEL 2
Euclid 306B.C.-283B.C. .... **CMLC 25**
Eugenides, Jeffrey 1960- .... **CLC 81, 212**
See also AAYA 51; CA 144; CANR 120;
MTFW 2005; NFS 24
Euripides c. 484B.C.-406B.C. .... **CMLC 23,**
51; DC 4; WLCS
See also AW 1; CDWLB 1; DA; DA3;
DAB; DAC; DAM DRAM, MST; DFS 1,
4, 6, 25; DLB 176; LAIT 1; LMFS 1;
RGWL 2, 3; WLIT 8
Eusebius c. 263-c. 339 .... **CMLC 103**
Evan, Evin
See Faust, Frederick (Schiller)
Evans, Caradoc 1878-1945 ... **SSC 43; TCLC**
85
See also DLB 162
Evans, Evan
See Faust, Frederick (Schiller)
Evans, Marian
See Eliot, George
Evans, Mary Ann
See Eliot, George

Evarts, Esther
See Benson, Sally
Evelyn, John 1620-1706 .... **LC 144**
See also BRW 2; RGEL 2
Everett, Percival 1956- .... **CLC 57**
See Everett, Percival L.
See also AMWS 18; BW 2; CA 129; CANR
94, 134, 179; CN 7; MTFW 2005
Everett, Percival L.
See Everett, Percival
See also CSW
Everson, R(onald) G(ilmour)
1903-1992 .... **CLC 27**
See also CA 17-20R; CP 1, 2, 3, 4; DLB 88
Everson, William (Oliver)
1912-1994 .... **CLC 1, 5, 14**
See also BG 1:2; CA 9-12R; 145; CANR
20; CP 1; DLB 5, 16, 212; MTCW 1
Evtushenko, Evgenii Aleksandrovich
See Yevtushenko, Yevgeny (Alexandrovich)
Ewart, Gavin (Buchanan)
1916-1995 .... **CLC 13, 46**
See also BRWS 7; CA 89-92; 150; CANR
17, 46; CP 1, 2, 3, 4, 5, 6; DLB 40;
MTCW 1
Ewers, Hanns Heinz 1871-1943 ..... **TCLC 12**
See also CA 109; 149
Ewing, Frederick R.
See Sturgeon, Theodore (Hamilton)
Exley, Frederick (Earl) 1929-1992 .... **CLC 6,**
11
See also AITN 2; BPFB 1; CA 81-84; 138;
CANR 117; DLB 143; DLBY 1981
Eynhardt, Guillermo
See Quiroga, Horacio (Sylvestre)
Ezekiel, Nissim (Moses) 1924-2004 .. **CLC 61**
See also CA 61-64; 223; CP 1, 2, 3, 4, 5, 6,
7; DLB 323; EWL 3
Ezekiel, Tish O'Dowd 1943- .... **CLC 34**
See also CA 129
Fadeev, Aleksandr Aleksandrovich
See Bulgya, Alexander Alexandrovich
Fadeev, Alexandr Alexandrovich
See Bulgya, Alexander Alexandrovich
Fadeyev, A.
See Bulgya, Alexander Alexandrovich
Fadeyev, Alexander
See Bulgya, Alexander Alexandrovich
Fagen, Donald 1948- .... **CLC 26**
Fainzil'berg, Il'ia Arnol'dovich
See Fainzilberg, Ilya Arnoldovich
Fainzilberg, Ilya Arnoldovich
1897-1937 .... **TCLC 21**
See also CA 120; 165; DLB 272; EWL 3
Fair, Ronald L. 1932- .... **CLC 18**
See also BW 1; CA 69-72; CANR 25; DLB
33
Fairbairn, Roger
See Carr, John Dickson
Fairbairns, Zoe (Ann) 1948- .... **CLC 32**
See also CA 103; CANR 21, 85; CN 4, 5,
6, 7
Fairfield, Flora
See Alcott, Louisa May
Falco, Gian
See Papini, Giovanni
Falconer, James
See Kirkup, James
Falconer, Kenneth
See Kornbluth, C(yril) M.
Falkland, Samuel
See Heijermans, Herman
Fallaci, Oriana 1930-2006 .... **CLC 11, 110**
See also CA 77-80; 253; CANR 15, 58, 134;
FW; MTCW 1
Faludi, Susan 1959- .... **CLC 140**
See also CA 138; CANR 126; FW; MTCW
2; MTFW 2005; NCFS 3

Feuchtwanger, Lion 1884-1958 .... **TCLC 3**
    See also CA 104; 187; DLB 66; EWL 3;
    RGHL
Feuerbach, Ludwig 1804-1872 ..... **NCLC 139**
    See also DLB 133
Feuillet, Octave 1821-1890 .... **NCLC 45**
    See also DLB 192
Feydeau, Georges (Leon Jules Marie)
    1862-1921 .... **TCLC 22**
    See also CA 113; 152; CANR 84; DAM
    DRAM; DLB 192; EWL 3; GFL 1789 to
    the Present; RGWL 2, 3
Fichte, Johann Gottlieb
    1762-1814 .... **NCLC 62**
    See also DLB 90
Ficino, Marsilio 1433-1499 .... **LC 12, 152**
    See also LMFS 1
Fiedeler, Hans
    See Doeblin, Alfred
Fiedler, Leslie A(aron) 1917-2003 ..... **CLC 4,
    13, 24**
    See also AMWS 13; CA 9-12R; 212; CANR
    7, 63; CN 1, 2, 3, 4, 5, 6; DLB 28, 67;
    EWL 3; MAL 5; MTCW 1, 2; RGAL 4;
    TUS
Field, Andrew 1938- .... **CLC 44**
    See also CA 97-100; CANR 25
Field, Eugene 1850-1895 .... **NCLC 3**
    See also DLB 23, 42, 140; DLBD 13; MAI-
    CYA 1, 2; RGAL 4; SATA 16
Field, Gans T.
    See Wellman, Manly Wade
Field, Michael 1915-1971 .... **TCLC 43**
    See also CA 29-32R
Fielding, Helen 1958- .... **CLC 146, 217**
    See also AAYA 65; CA 172; CANR 127;
    DLB 231; MTFW 2005
Fielding, Henry 1707-1754 .... **LC 1, 46, 85,
    151, 154; WLC 2**
    See also BRW 3; BRWR 1; CDBLB 1660-
    1789; DA; DA3; DAB; DAC; DAM
    DRAM, MST, NOV; DLB 39, 84, 101;
    NFS 18; RGEL 2; TEA; WLIT 3
Fielding, Sarah 1710-1768 .... **LC 1, 44**
    See also DLB 39; RGEL 2; TEA
Fields, W. C. 1880-1946 .... **TCLC 80**
    See also DLB 44
Fierstein, Harvey (Forbes) 1954- ..... **CLC 33**
    See also CA 123; 129; CAD; CD 5, 6;
    CPW; DA3; DAM DRAM, POP; DFS 6;
    DLB 266; GLL; MAL 5
Figes, Eva 1932- .... **CLC 31**
    See also CA 53-56; CANR 4, 44, 83; CN 2,
    3, 4, 5, 6, 7; DLB 14, 271; FW; RGHL
Filippo, Eduardo de
    See de Filippo, Eduardo
Finch, Anne 1661-1720 ..... **LC 3, 137; PC 21**
    See also BRWS 9; DLB 95; PFS 30
Finch, Robert (Duer Claydon)
    1900-1995 .... **CLC 18**
    See also CA 57-60; CANR 9, 24, 49; CP 1,
    2, 3, 4, 5, 6; DLB 88
Findley, Timothy (Irving Frederick)
    1930-2002 .... **CLC 27, 102**
    See also CA 25-28R; 206; CANR 12, 42,
    69, 109; CCA 1; CN 4, 5, 6, 7; DAC;
    DAM MST; DLB 53; FANT; RHW
Fink, William
    See Mencken, H(enry) L(ouis)
Firbank, Louis 1942- .... **CLC 21**
    See also CA 117
Firbank, (Arthur Annesley) Ronald
    1886-1926 .... **TCLC 1**
    See also BRWS 2; CA 104; 177; DLB 36;
    EWL 3; RGEL 2
Firdaosi
    See Ferdowsi, Abu'l Qasem
Firdausi
    See Ferdowsi, Abu'l Qasem

Firdavsi, Abulqosimi
    See Ferdowsi, Abu'l Qasem
Firdavsii, Abulqosim
    See Ferdowsi, Abu'l Qasem
Firdawsi, Abu al-Qasim
    See Ferdowsi, Abu'l Qasem
Firdosi
    See Ferdowsi, Abu'l Qasem
Firdousi
    See Ferdowsi, Abu'l Qasem
Firdousi, Abu'l-Qasim
    See Ferdowsi, Abu'l Qasem
Firdovsi, A.
    See Ferdowsi, Abu'l Qasem
Firdovsi, Abulgasim
    See Ferdowsi, Abu'l Qasem
Firdusi
    See Ferdowsi, Abu'l Qasem
Fish, Stanley
    See Fish, Stanley Eugene
Fish, Stanley E.
    See Fish, Stanley Eugene
Fish, Stanley Eugene 1938- .... **CLC 142**
    See also CA 112; 132; CANR 90; DLB 67
Fisher, Dorothy (Frances) Canfield
    1879-1958 .... **TCLC 87**
    See also CA 114; 136; CANR 80; CLR 71;
    CWRI 5; DLB 9, 102, 284; MAICYA 1,
    2; MAL 5; YABC 1
Fisher, M(ary) F(rances) K(ennedy)
    1908-1992 .... **CLC 76, 87**
    See also AMWS 17; CA 77-80; 138; CANR
    44; MTCW 2
Fisher, Roy 1930- .... **CLC 25**
    See also CA 81-84; CAAS 10; CANR 16;
    CP 1, 2, 3, 4, 5, 6, 7; DLB 40
Fisher, Rudolph 1897-1934 ...... **BLC 1:2; HR
    1:2; SSC 25; TCLC 11**
    See also BW 1, 3; CA 107; 124; CANR 80;
    DAM MULT; DLB 51, 102
Fisher, Vardis (Alvero) 1895-1968 .... **CLC 7;
    TCLC 140**
    See also CA 5-8R; 25-28R; CANR 68; DLB
    9, 206; MAL 5; RGAL 4; TCWW 1, 2
Fiske, Tarleton
    See Bloch, Robert (Albert)
Fitch, Clarke
    See Sinclair, Upton
Fitch, John IV
    See Cormier, Robert
Fitzgerald, Captain Hugh
    See Baum, L(yman) Frank
FitzGerald, Edward 1809-1883 ...... **NCLC 9,
    153; PC 79**
    See also BRW 4; DLB 32; RGEL 2
Fitzgerald, F(rancis) Scott (Key)
    1896-1940 ... **SSC 6, 31, 75; TCLC 1, 6,
    14, 28, 55, 157; WLC 2**
    See also AAYA 24; AITN 1; AMW; AMWC
    2; AMWR 1; BPFB 1; CA 110; 123;
    CDALB 1917-1929; DA; DA3; DAB;
    DAC; DAM MST, NOV; DLB 4, 9, 86,
    219, 273; DLBD 1, 15, 16; DLBY 1981,
    1996; EWL 3; EXPN; EXPS; LAIT 3;
    MAL 5; MTCW 1, 2; MTFW 2005; NFS
    2, 19, 20; RGAL 4; RGSF 2; SSFS 4, 15,
    21, 25; TUS
Fitzgerald, Penelope 1916-2000 . **CLC 19, 51,
    61, 143**
    See also BRWS 5; CA 85-88; 190; CAAS
    10; CANR 56, 86, 131; CN 3, 4, 5, 6, 7;
    DLB 14, 194, 326; EWL 3; MTCW 2;
    MTFW 2005
Fitzgerald, Robert (Stuart)
    1910-1985 .... **CLC 39**
    See also CA 1-4R; 114; CANR 1; CP 1, 2,
    3, 4; DLBY 1980; MAL 5

FitzGerald, Robert D(avid)
    1902-1987 .... **CLC 19**
    See also CA 17-20R; CP 1, 2, 3, 4; DLB
    260; RGEL 2
Fitzgerald, Zelda (Sayre)
    1900-1948 .... **TCLC 52**
    See also AMWS 9; CA 117; 126; DLBY
    1984
Flanagan, Thomas (James Bonner)
    1923-2002 .... **CLC 25, 52**
    See also CA 108; 206; CANR 55; CN 3, 4,
    5, 6, 7; DLBY 1980; INT CA-108; MTCW
    1; RHW; TCLE 1:1
Flaubert, Gustave 1821-1880 .... **NCLC 2, 10,
    19, 62, 66, 135, 179, 185; SSC 11, 60;
    WLC 2**
    See also DA; DA3; DAB; DAC; DAM
    MST, NOV; DLB 119, 301; EW 7; EXPS;
    GFL 1789 to the Present; LAIT 2; LMFS
    1; NFS 14; RGSF 2; RGWL 2, 3; SSFS
    6; TWA
Flavius Josephus
    See Josephus, Flavius
Flecker, Herman Elroy
    See Flecker, (Herman) James Elroy
Flecker, (Herman) James Elroy
    1884-1915 .... **TCLC 43**
    See also CA 109; 150; DLB 10, 19; RGEL
    2
Fleming, Ian 1908-1964 ... **CLC 3, 30; TCLC
    193**
    See also AAYA 26; BPFB 1; BRWS 14; CA
    5-8R; CANR 59; CDBLB 1945-1960;
    CMW 4; CPW; DA3; DAM POP; DLB
    87, 201; MSW; MTCW 1, 2; MTFW
    2005; RGEL 2; SATA 9; TEA; YAW
Fleming, Ian Lancaster
    See Fleming, Ian
Fleming, Thomas 1927- .... **CLC 37**
    See also CA 5-8R; CANR 10, 102, 155;
    INT CANR-10; SATA 8
Fleming, Thomas James
    See Fleming, Thomas
Fletcher, John 1579-1625 . **DC 6; LC 33, 151**
    See also BRW 2; CDBLB Before 1660;
    DLB 58; RGEL 2; TEA
Fletcher, John Gould 1886-1950 .... **TCLC 35**
    See also CA 107; 167; DLB 4, 45; LMFS
    2; MAL 5; RGAL 4
Fleur, Paul
    See Pohl, Frederik
Flieg, Helmut
    See Heym, Stefan
Flooglebuckle, Al
    See Spiegelman, Art
Flying Officer X
    See Bates, H(erbert) E(rnest)
Fo, Dario 1926- .... **CLC 32, 109, 227; DC 10**
    See also CA 116; 128; CANR 68, 114, 134,
    164; CWW 2; DA3; DAM DRAM; DFS
    23; DLB 330; DLBY 1997; EWL 3;
    MTCW 1, 2; MTFW 2005; WLIT 7
Foden, Giles 1967- .... **CLC 231**
    See also CA 240; DLB 267; NFS 15
Fogarty, Jonathan Titulescu Esq.
    See Farrell, James T(homas)
Follett, Ken 1949- .... **CLC 18**
    See also AAYA 6, 50; BEST 89:4; BPFB 1;
    CA 81-84; CANR 13, 33, 54, 102, 156;
    CMW 4; CPW; DA3; DAM NOV, POP;
    DLB 87; DLBY 1981; INT CANR-33;
    MTCW 1
Follett, Kenneth Martin
    See Follett, Ken
Fondane, Benjamin 1898-1944 ..... **TCLC 159**
Fontane, Theodor 1819-1898 . **NCLC 26, 163**
    See also CDWLB 2; DLB 129; EW 6;
    RGWL 2, 3; TWA
Fonte, Moderata 1555-1592 .... **LC 118**

Fraser, Antonia 1932- .... **CLC 32, 107**
  See also AAYA 57; CA 85-88; CANR 44,
  65, 119, 164; CMW; DLB 276; MTCW 1,
  2; MTFW 2005; SATA-Brief 32

Fraser, George MacDonald
  1925-2008 .... **CLC 7**
  See also AAYA 48; CA 45-48, 180; 268;
  CAAE 180; CANR 2, 48, 74; MTCW 2;
  RHW

Fraser, Sylvia 1935- .... **CLC 64**
  See also CA 45-48; CANR 1, 16, 60; CCA
  1

Frater Perdurabo
  See Crowley, Edward Alexander

Frayn, Michael 1933- .... **CLC 3, 7, 31, 47,
  176; DC 27**
  See also AAYA 69; BRWC 2; BRWS 7; CA
  5-8R; CANR 30, 69, 114, 133, 166; CBD;
  CD 5, 6; CN 1, 2, 3, 4, 5, 6, 7; DAM
  DRAM, NOV; DFS 22; DLB 13, 14, 194,
  245; FANT; MTCW 1, 2; MTFW 2005;
  SFW 4

Fraze, Candida (Merrill) 1945- .... **CLC 50**
  See also CA 126

Frazer, Andrew
  See Marlowe, Stephen

Frazer, J(ames) G(eorge)
  1854-1941 .... **TCLC 32**
  See also BRWS 3; CA 118; NCFS 5

Frazer, Robert Caine
  See Creasey, John

Frazer, Sir James George
  See Frazer, J(ames) G(eorge)

Frazier, Charles 1950- .... **CLC 109, 224**
  See also AAYA 34; CA 161; CANR 126,
  170; CSW; DLB 292; MTFW 2005; NFS
  25

Frazier, Charles R.
  See Frazier, Charles

Frazier, Charles Robinson
  See Frazier, Charles

Frazier, Ian 1951- .... **CLC 46**
  See also CA 130; CANR 54, 93

Frederic, Harold 1856-1898 ... **NCLC 10, 175**
  See also AMW; DLB 12, 23; DLBD 13;
  MAL 5; NFS 22; RGAL 4

Frederick, John
  See Faust, Frederick (Schiller)

Frederick the Great 1712-1786 .... **LC 14**

Fredro, Aleksander 1793-1876 .... **NCLC 8**

Freeling, Nicolas 1927-2003 .... **CLC 38**
  See also CA 49-52; 218; CAAS 12; CANR
  1, 17, 50, 84; CMW 4; CN 1, 2, 3, 4, 5,
  6; DLB 87

Freeman, Douglas Southall
  1886-1953 .... **TCLC 11**
  See also CA 109; 195; DLB 17; DLBD 17

Freeman, Judith 1946- .... **CLC 55**
  See also CA 148; CANR 120, 179; DLB
  256

Freeman, Mary E(leanor) Wilkins
  1852-1930 .... **SSC 1, 47, 113; TCLC 9**
  See also CA 106; 177; DLB 12, 78, 221;
  EXPS; FW; HGG; MBL; RGAL 4; RGSF
  2; SSFS 4, 8, 26; SUFW 1; TUS

Freeman, R(ichard) Austin
  1862-1943 .... **TCLC 21**
  See also CA 113; CANR 84; CMW 4; DLB
  70

French, Albert 1943- .... **CLC 86**
  See also BW 3; CA 167

French, Antonia
  See Kureishi, Hanif

French, Marilyn 1929- .. **CLC 10, 18, 60, 177**
  See also BPFB 1; CA 69-72; CANR 3, 31,
  134, 163; CN 5, 6, 7; CPW; DAM DRAM,
  NOV, POP; FL 1:5; FW; INT CANR-31;
  MTCW 1, 2; MTFW 2005

French, Paul
  See Asimov, Isaac

Freneau, Philip Morin 1752-1832 .. **NCLC 1,
  111**
  See also AMWS 2; DLB 37, 43; RGAL 4

Freud, Sigmund 1856-1939 .... **TCLC 52**
  See also CA 115; 133; CANR 69; DLB 296;
  EW 8; EWL 3; LATS 1:1; MTCW 1, 2;
  MTFW 2005; NCFS 3; TWA

Freytag, Gustav 1816-1895 .... **NCLC 109**
  See also DLB 129

Friedan, Betty 1921-2006 .... **CLC 74**
  See also CA 65-68; 248; CANR 18, 45, 74;
  DLB 246; FW; MTCW 1, 2; MTFW
  2005; NCFS 5

Friedan, Betty Naomi
  See Friedan, Betty

Friedlander, Saul 1932- .... **CLC 90**
  See also CA 117; 130; CANR 72; RGHL

Friedman, B(ernard) H(arper)
  1926- .... **CLC 7**
  See also CA 1-4R; CANR 3, 48

Friedman, Bruce Jay 1930- .... **CLC 3, 5, 56**
  See also CA 9-12R; CAD; CANR 25, 52,
  101; CD 5, 6; CN 1, 2, 3, 4, 5, 6, 7; DLB
  2, 28, 244; INT CANR-25; MAL 5; SSFS
  18

Friel, Brian 1929- .. **CLC 5, 42, 59, 115, 253;
  DC 8; SSC 76**
  See also BRWS 5; CA 21-24R; CANR 33,
  69, 131; CBD; CD 5, 6; DFS 11; DLB
  13, 319; EWL 3; MTCW 1; RGEL 2; TEA

Friis-Baastad, Babbis Ellinor
  1921-1970 .... **CLC 12**
  See also CA 17-20R; 134; SATA 7

Frisch, Max 1911-1991 ...... **CLC 3, 9, 14, 18,
  32, 44; TCLC 121**
  See also CA 85-88; 134; CANR 32, 74; CD-
  WLB 2; DAM DRAM, NOV; DFS 25;
  DLB 69, 124; EW 13; EWL 3; MTCW 1,
  2; MTFW 2005; RGHL; RGWL 2, 3

Fromentin, Eugene (Samuel Auguste)
  1820-1876 .... **NCLC 10, 125**
  See also DLB 123; GFL 1789 to the Present

Frost, Frederick
  See Faust, Frederick (Schiller)

Frost, Robert 1874-1963 . **CLC 1, 3, 4, 9, 10,
  13, 15, 26, 34, 44; PC 1, 39, 71; WLC 2**
  See also AAYA 21; AMW; AMWR 1; CA
  89-92; CANR 33; CDALB 1917-1929;
  CLR 67; DA; DA3; DAB; DAC; DAM
  MST, POET; DLB 54, 284, 342; DLBD
  7; EWL 3; EXPP; MAL 5; MTCW 1, 2;
  MTFW 2005; PAB; PFS 1, 2, 3, 4, 5, 6,
  7, 10, 13; RGAL 4; SATA 14; TUS; WP;
  WYA

Frost, Robert Lee
  See Frost, Robert

Froude, James Anthony
  1818-1894 .... **NCLC 43**
  See also DLB 18, 57, 144

Froy, Herald
  See Waterhouse, Keith (Spencer)

Fry, Christopher 1907-2005 ... **CLC 2, 10, 14**
  See also BRWS 3; CA 17-20R; 240; CAAS
  23; CANR 9, 30, 74, 132; CBD; CD 5, 6;
  CP 1, 2, 3, 4, 5, 6, 7; DAM DRAM; DLB
  13; EWL 3; MTCW 1, 2; MTFW 2005;
  RGEL 2; SATA 66; TEA

Frye, (Herman) Northrop
  1912-1991 .... **CLC 24, 70; TCLC 165**
  See also CA 5-8R; 133; CANR 8, 37; DLB
  67, 68, 246; EWL 3; MTCW 1, 2; MTFW
  2005; RGAL 4; TWA

Fuchs, Daniel 1909-1993 .... **CLC 8, 22**
  See also CA 81-84; 142; CAAS 5; CANR
  40; CN 1, 2, 3, 4, 5; DLB 9, 26, 28;
  DLBY 1993; MAL 5

Fuchs, Daniel 1934- .... **CLC 34**
  See also CA 37-40R; CANR 14, 48

Fuentes, Carlos 1928- .. **CLC 3, 8, 10, 13, 22,
  41, 60, 113; HLC 1; SSC 24, 125; WLC
  2**
  See also AAYA 4, 45; AITN 2; BPFB 1;
  CA 69-72; CANR 10, 32, 68, 104, 138;
  CDWLB 3; CWW 2; DA; DA3; DAB;
  DAC; DAM MST, MULT, NOV; DLB
  113; DNFS 2; EWL 3; HW 1, 2; LAIT 3;
  LATS 1:2; LAW; LAWS 1; LMFS 2;
  MTCW 1, 2; MTFW 2005; NFS 8; RGSF
  2; RGWL 2, 3; TWA; WLIT 1

Fuentes, Gregorio Lopez y
  See Lopez y Fuentes, Gregorio

Fuertes, Gloria 1918-1998 .... **PC 27**
  See also CA 178; 180; DLB 108; HW 2;
  SATA 115

Fugard, (Harold) Athol 1932- . **CLC 5, 9, 14,
  25, 40, 80, 211; DC 3**
  See also AAYA 17; AFW; CA 85-88; CANR
  32, 54, 118; CD 5, 6; DAM DRAM; DFS
  3, 6, 10, 24; DLB 225; DNFS 1, 2; EWL
  3; LATS 1:2; MTCW 1; MTFW 2005;
  RGEL 2; WLIT 2

Fugard, Sheila 1932- .... **CLC 48**
  See also CA 125

Fujiwara no Teika 1162-1241 .... **CMLC 73**
  See also DLB 203

Fukuyama, Francis 1952- .... **CLC 131**
  See also CA 140; CANR 72, 125, 170

Fuller, Charles (H.), (Jr.) 1939- ..... **BLC 1:2;
  CLC 25; DC 1**
  See also BW 2; CA 108; 112; CAD; CANR
  87; CD 5, 6; DAM DRAM, MULT; DFS
  8; DLB 38, 266; EWL 3; INT CA-112;
  MAL 5; MTCW 1

Fuller, Henry Blake 1857-1929 .... **TCLC 103**
  See also CA 108; 177; DLB 12; RGAL 4

Fuller, John (Leopold) 1937- .... **CLC 62**
  See also CA 21-24R; CANR 9, 44; CP 1, 2,
  3, 4, 5, 6, 7; DLB 40

Fuller, Margaret
  See Ossoli, Sarah Margaret (Fuller)

Fuller, Roy (Broadbent) 1912-1991 ... **CLC 4,
  28**
  See also BRWS 7; CA 5-8R; 135; CAAS
  10; CANR 53, 83; CN 1, 2, 3, 4, 5; CP 1,
  2, 3, 4, 5; CWRI 5; DLB 15, 20; EWL 3;
  RGEL 2; SATA 87

Fuller, Sarah Margaret
  See Ossoli, Sarah Margaret (Fuller)

Fuller, Thomas 1608-1661 .... **LC 111**
  See also DLB 151

Fulton, Alice 1952- .... **CLC 52**
  See also CA 116; CANR 57, 88; CP 5, 6, 7;
  CWP; DLB 193; PFS 25

Furey, Michael
  See Ward, Arthur Henry Sarsfield

Furphy, Joseph 1843-1912 .... **TCLC 25**
  See also CA 163; DLB 230; EWL 3; RGEL
  2

Furst, Alan 1941- .... **CLC 255**
  See also CA 69-72; CANR 12, 34, 59, 102,
  159; DLBY 01

Fuson, Robert H(enderson) 1927- .... **CLC 70**
  See also CA 89-92; CANR 103

Fussell, Paul 1924- .... **CLC 74**
  See also BEST 90:1; CA 17-20R; CANR 8,
  21, 35, 69, 135; INT CANR-21; MTCW
  1, 2; MTFW 2005

Futabatei, Shimei 1864-1909 .... **TCLC 44**
  See also CA 162; DLB 180; EWL 3; MJW

Futabatei Shimei
  See Futabatei, Shimei

Futrelle, Jacques 1875-1912 .... **TCLC 19**
  See also CA 113; 155; CMW 4

GAB
  See Russell, George William

Gaberman, Judie Angell
See Angell, Judie

Gaboriau, Emile 1835-1873 .... **NCLC 14**
See also CMW 4; MSW

Gadda, Carlo Emilio 1893-1973 ...... **CLC 11;
TCLC 144**
See also CA 89-92; DLB 177; EWL 3;
WLIT 7

Gaddis, William 1922-1998 ... **CLC 1, 3, 6, 8,
10, 19, 43, 86**
See also AMWS 4; BPFB 1; CA 17-20R;
172; CANR 21, 48, 148; CN 1, 2, 3, 4, 5,
6; DLB 2, 278; EWL 3; MAL 5; MTCW
1, 2; MTFW 2005; RGAL 4

Gage, Walter
See Inge, William (Motter)

Gaiman, Neil 1960- .... **CLC 195**
See also AAYA 19, 42; CA 133; CANR 81,
129, 188; CLR 109; DLB 261; HGG;
MTFW 2005; SATA 85, 146, 197; SFW
4; SUFW 2

Gaiman, Neil Richard
See Gaiman, Neil

Gaines, Ernest J. 1933- ..... **BLC 1:2; CLC 3,
11, 18, 86, 181; SSC 68**
See also AAYA 18; AFAW 1, 2; AITN 1;
BPFB 2; BW 2, 3; BYA 6; CA 9-12R;
CANR 6, 24, 42, 75, 126; CDALB 1968-
1988; CLR 62; CN 1, 2, 3, 4, 5, 6, 7;
CSW; DA3; DAM MULT; DLB 2, 33,
152; DLBY 1980; EWL 3; EXPN; LAIT
5; LATS 1:2; MAL 5; MTCW 1, 2;
MTFW 2005; NFS 5, 7, 16; RGAL 4;
RGSF 2; RHW; SATA 86; SSFS 5; YAW

Gaitskill, Mary 1954- .... **CLC 69**
See also CA 128; CANR 61, 152; DLB 244;
TCLE 1:1

Gaitskill, Mary Lawrence
See Gaitskill, Mary

Gaius Suetonius Tranquillus
See Suetonius

Galdos, Benito Perez
See Perez Galdos, Benito

Gale, Zona 1874-1938 .... **DC 30; TCLC 7**
See also CA 105; 153; CANR 84; DAM
DRAM; DFS 17; DLB 9, 78, 228; RGAL
4

Galeano, Eduardo 1940- ... **CLC 72; HLCS 1**
See also CA 29-32R; CANR 13, 32, 100,
163; HW 1

Galeano, Eduardo Hughes
See Galeano, Eduardo

Galiano, Juan Valera y Alcala
See Valera y Alcala-Galiano, Juan

Galilei, Galileo 1564-1642 .... **LC 45**

Gallagher, Tess 1943- .... **CLC 18, 63; PC 9**
See also CA 106; CP 3, 4, 5, 6, 7; CWP;
DAM POET; DLB 120, 212, 244; PFS 16

Gallant, Mavis 1922- ..... **CLC 7, 18, 38, 172;
SSC 5, 78**
See also CA 69-72; CANR 29, 69, 117;
CCA 1; CN 1, 2, 3, 4, 5, 6, 7; DAC; DAM
MST; DLB 53; EWL 3; MTCW 1, 2;
MTFW 2005; RGEL 2; RGSF 2

Gallant, Roy A(rthur) 1924- .... **CLC 17**
See also CA 5-8R; CANR 4, 29, 54, 117;
CLR 30; MAICYA 1, 2; SATA 4, 68, 110

Gallico, Paul (William) 1897-1976 ..... **CLC 2**
See also AITN 1; CA 5-8R; 69-72; CANR
23; CN 1, 2; DLB 9, 171; FANT; MAI-
CYA 1, 2; SATA 13

Gallo, Max Louis 1932- .... **CLC 95**
See also CA 85-88

Gallois, Lucien
See Desnos, Robert

Gallup, Ralph
See Whitemore, Hugh (John)

Galsworthy, John 1867-1933 .... **SSC 22;
TCLC 1, 45; WLC 2**
See also BRW 6; CA 104; 141; CANR 75;
CDBLB 1890-1914; DA; DA3; DAB;
DAC; DAM DRAM, MST, NOV; DLB
10, 34, 98, 162, 330; DLBD 16; EWL 3;
MTCW 2; RGEL 2; SSFS 3; TEA

Galt, John 1779-1839 .... **NCLC 1, 110**
See also DLB 99, 116, 159; RGEL 2; RGSF
2

Galvin, James 1951- .... **CLC 38**
See also CA 108; CANR 26

Gamboa, Federico 1864-1939 .... **TCLC 36**
See also CA 167; HW 2; LAW

Gandhi, M. K.
See Gandhi, Mohandas Karamchand

Gandhi, Mahatma
See Gandhi, Mohandas Karamchand

Gandhi, Mohandas Karamchand
1869-1948 .... **TCLC 59**
See also CA 121; 132; DA3; DAM MULT;
DLB 323; MTCW 1, 2

Gann, Ernest Kellogg 1910-1991 ..... **CLC 23**
See also AITN 1; BPFB 2; CA 1-4R; 136;
CANR 1, 83; RHW

Gao Xingjian 1940-
See Xingjian, Gao

Garber, Eric 1943(?)- .... **CLC 38**
See also CA 144; CANR 89, 162; GLL 1

Garber, Esther
See Lee, Tanith

Garcia, Cristina 1958- .... **CLC 76**
See also AMWS 11; CA 141; CANR 73,
130, 172; CN 7; DLB 292; DNFS 1; EWL
3; HW 2; LLW; MTFW 2005

Garcia Lorca, Federico 1898-1936 ...... **DC 2;
HLC 2; PC 3; TCLC 1, 7, 49, 181,
197; WLC 2**
See also AAYA 46; CA 104; 131; CANR
81; DA; DA3; DAB; DAC; DAM DRAM,
MST, MULT, POET; DFS 4; DLB 108;
EW 11; EWL 3; HW 1, 2; LATS 1:2;
MTCW 1, 2; MTFW 2005; PFS 20;
RGWL 2, 3; TWA; WP

Garcia Marquez, Gabriel 1928- .... **CLC 2, 3,
8, 10, 15, 27, 47, 55, 68, 170, 254; HLC
1; SSC 8, 83; WLC 3**
See also AAYA 3, 33; BEST 89:1, 90:4;
BPFB 2; BYA 12, 16; CA 33-36R; CANR
10, 28, 50, 75, 82, 128; CDWLB 3; CPW;
CWW 2; DA; DA3; DAB; DAC; DAM
MST, MULT, NOV, POP; DLB 113, 330;
DNFS 1, 2; EWL 3; EXPN; EXPS; HW
1, 2; LAIT 2; LATS 1:2; LAW; LAWS 1;
LMFS 2; MTCW 1, 2; MTFW 2005;
NCFS 3; NFS 1, 5, 10; RGSF 2; RGWL
2, 3; SSFS 1, 6, 16, 21; TWA; WLIT 1

Garcia Marquez, Gabriel Jose
See Garcia Marquez, Gabriel

Garcilaso de la Vega, El Inca
1539-1616 .... **HLCS 1; LC 127**
See also DLB 318; LAW

Gard, Janice
See Latham, Jean Lee

Gard, Roger Martin du
See Martin du Gard, Roger

Gardam, Jane 1928- .... **CLC 43**
See also CA 49-52; CANR 2, 18, 33, 54,
106, 167; CLR 12; DLB 14, 161, 231;
MAICYA 1, 2; MTCW 1; SAAS 9; SATA
39, 76, 130; SATA-Brief 28; YAW

Gardam, Jane Mary
See Gardam, Jane

Gardner, Herb(ert George)
1934-2003 .... **CLC 44**
See also CA 149; 220; CAD; CANR 119;
CD 5, 6; DFS 18, 20

Gardner, John, Jr. 1933-1982 ... **CLC 2, 3, 5,
7, 8, 10, 18, 28, 34; SSC 7; TCLC 195**
See also AAYA 45; AITN 1; AMWS 6;
BPFB 2; CA 65-68; 107; CANR 33, 73;
CDALBS; CN 2, 3; CPW; DA3; DAM
NOV, POP; DLB 2; DLBY 1982; EWL 3;
FANT; LATS 1:2; MAL 5; MTCW 1, 2;
MTFW 2005; NFS 3; RGAL 4; RGSF 2;
SATA 40; SATA-Obit 31; SSFS 8

Gardner, John 1926-2007 .... **CLC 30**
See also CA 103; 263; CANR 15, 69, 127,
183; CMW 4; CPW; DAM POP; MTCW
1

Gardner, John Edmund
See Gardner, John

Gardner, Miriam
See Bradley, Marion Zimmer

Gardner, Noel
See Kuttner, Henry

Gardons, S.S.
See Snodgrass, W. D.

Garfield, Leon 1921-1996 .... **CLC 12**
See also AAYA 8, 69; BYA 1, 3; CA 17-
20R; 152; CANR 38, 41, 78; CLR 21;
DLB 161; JRDA; MAICYA 1, 2; MAIC-
YAS 1; SATA 1, 32, 76; SATA-Obit 90;
TEA; WYA; YAW

Garland, (Hannibal) Hamlin
1860-1940 .... **SSC 18, 117; TCLC 3**
See also CA 104; DLB 12, 71, 78, 186;
MAL 5; RGAL 4; RGSF 2; TCWW 1, 2

Garneau, (Hector de) Saint-Denys
1912-1943 .... **TCLC 13**
See also CA 111; DLB 88

Garner, Alan 1934- .... **CLC 17**
See also AAYA 18; BYA 3, 5; CA 73-76;
178; CAAE 178; CANR 15, 64, 134; CLR
20, 130; CPW; DAB; DAM POP; DLB
161, 261; FANT; MAICYA 1, 2; MTCW
1, 2; MTFW 2005; SATA 18, 69; SATA-
Essay 108; SUFW 1, 2; YAW

Garner, Hugh 1913-1979 .... **CLC 13**
See also CA 69-72; CANR 31; CCA 1; CN
1, 2; DLB 68

Garnett, David 1892-1981 .... **CLC 3**
See also CA 5-8R; 103; CANR 17, 79; CN
1, 2; DLB 34; FANT; MTCW 2; RGEL 2;
SFW 4; SUFW 1

Garnier, Robert c. 1545-1590 .... **LC 119**
See also DLB 327; GFL Beginnings to 1789

Garrett, George 1929-2008 ... **CLC 3, 11, 51;
SSC 30**
See also AMWS 7; BPFB 2; CA 1-4R; 202;
272; CAAE 202; CAAS 5; CANR 1, 42,
67, 109; CN 1, 2, 3, 4, 5, 6, 7; CP 1, 2, 3,
4, 5, 6, 7; CSW; DLB 2, 5, 130, 152;
DLBY 1983

Garrett, George P.
See Garrett, George

Garrett, George Palmer
See Garrett, George

Garrett, George Palmer, Jr.
See Garrett, George

Garrick, David 1717-1779 .... **LC 15, 156**
See also DAM DRAM; DLB 84, 213;
RGEL 2

Garrigue, Jean 1914-1972 .... **CLC 2, 8**
See also CA 5-8R; 37-40R; CANR 20; CP
1; MAL 5

Garrison, Frederick
See Sinclair, Upton

Garrison, William Lloyd
1805-1879 .... **NCLC 149**
See also CDALB 1640-1865; DLB 1, 43,
235

Garro, Elena 1920(?)-1998 .. **HLCS 1; TCLC
153**
See also CA 131; 169; CWW 2; DLB 145;
EWL 3; HW 1; LAWS 1; WLIT 1

Garth, Will
See Hamilton, Edmond; Kuttner, Henry

Garvey, Marcus (Moziah, Jr.)
1887-1940 ..... **BLC 1:2; HR 1:2; TCLC 41**
See also BW 1; CA 120; 124; CANR 79; DAM MULT; DLB 345

Gary, Romain
See Kacew, Romain

Gascar, Pierre
See Fournier, Pierre

Gascoigne, George 1539-1577 .... **LC 108**
See also DLB 136; RGEL 2

Gascoyne, David (Emery)
1916-2001 .... **CLC 45**
See also CA 65-68; 200; CANR 10, 28, 54; CP 1, 2, 3, 4, 5, 6, 7; DLB 20; MTCW 1; RGEL 2

Gaskell, Elizabeth Cleghorn
1810-1865 .... **NCLC 5, 70, 97, 137, 214; SSC 25, 97**
See also BRW 5; CDBLB 1832-1890; DAB; DAM MST; DLB 21, 144, 159; RGEL 2; RGSF 2; TEA

Gass, William H. 1924- . **CLC 1, 2, 8, 11, 15, 39, 132; SSC 12**
See also AMWS 6; CA 17-20R; CANR 30, 71, 100; CN 1, 2, 3, 4, 5, 6, 7; DLB 2, 227; EWL 3; MAL 5; MTCW 1, 2; MTFW 2005; RGAL 4

Gassendi, Pierre 1592-1655 .... **LC 54**
See also GFL Beginnings to 1789

Gasset, Jose Ortega y
See Ortega y Gasset, Jose

Gates, Henry Louis, Jr. 1950- ... **BLCS; CLC 65**
See also BW 2, 3; CA 109; CANR 25, 53, 75, 125; CSW; DA3; DAM MULT; DLB 67; EWL 3; MAL 5; MTCW 2; MTFW 2005; RGAL 4

Gatos, Stephanie
See Katz, Steve

Gautier, Theophile 1811-1872 .. **NCLC 1, 59; PC 18; SSC 20**
See also DAM POET; DLB 119; EW 6; GFL 1789 to the Present; RGWL 2, 3; SUFW; TWA

Gautreaux, Tim 1947- .... **CLC 270; SSC 125**
See also CA 187; CSW; DLB 292

Gay, John 1685-1732 .... **LC 49**
See also BRW 3; DAM DRAM; DLB 84, 95; RGEL 2; WLIT 3

Gay, Oliver
See Gogarty, Oliver St. John

Gay, Peter 1923- .... **CLC 158**
See also CA 13-16R; CANR 18, 41, 77, 147; INT CANR-18; RGHL

Gay, Peter Jack
See Gay, Peter

Gaye, Marvin (Pentz, Jr.)
1939-1984 .... **CLC 26**
See also CA 195; 112

Gebler, Carlo 1954- .... **CLC 39**
See also CA 119; 133; CANR 96, 186; DLB 271

Gebler, Carlo Ernest
See Gebler, Carlo

Gee, Maggie 1948- .... **CLC 57**
See also CA 130; CANR 125; CN 4, 5, 6, 7; DLB 207; MTFW 2005

Gee, Maurice 1931- .... **CLC 29**
See also AAYA 42; CA 97-100; CANR 67, 123; CLR 56; CN 2, 3, 4, 5, 6, 7; CWRI 5; EWL 3; MAICYA 2; RGSF 2; SATA 46, 101

Gee, Maurice Gough
See Gee, Maurice

Geiogamah, Hanay 1945- .... **NNAL**
See also CA 153; DAM MULT; DLB 175

Gelbart, Larry
See Gelbart, Larry (Simon)

Gelbart, Larry (Simon) 1928- .... **CLC 21, 61**
See also CA 73-76; CAD; CANR 45, 94; CD 5, 6

Gelber, Jack 1932-2003 ...... **CLC 1, 6, 14, 79**
See also CA 1-4R; 216; CAD; CANR 2; DLB 7, 228; MAL 5

Gellhorn, Martha (Ellis)
1908-1998 .... **CLC 14, 60**
See also CA 77-80; 164; CANR 44; CN 1, 2, 3, 4, 5, 6 7; DLBY 1982, 1998

Genet, Jean 1910-1986 .. **CLC 1, 2, 5, 10, 14, 44, 46; DC 25; TCLC 128**
See also CA 13-16R; CANR 18; DA3; DAM DRAM; DFS 10; DLB 72, 321; DLBY 1986; EW 13; EWL 3; GFL 1789 to the Present; GLL 1; LMFS 2; MTCW 1, 2; MTFW 2005; RGWL 2, 3; TWA

Genlis, Stephanie-Felicite Ducrest
1746-1830 .... **NCLC 166**
See also DLB 313

Gent, Peter 1942- .... **CLC 29**
See also AITN 1; CA 89-92; DLBY 1982

Gentile, Giovanni 1875-1944 .... **TCLC 96**
See also CA 119

Geoffrey of Monmouth c.
1100-1155 .... **CMLC 44**
See also DLB 146; TEA

George, Jean
See George, Jean Craighead

George, Jean Craighead 1919- .... **CLC 35**
See also AAYA 8, 69; BYA 2, 4; CA 5-8R; CANR 25; CLR 1, 80, 136; DLB 52; JRDA; MAICYA 1, 2; SATA 2, 68, 124, 170; WYA; YAW

George, Stefan (Anton) 1868-1933 . **TCLC 2, 14**
See also CA 104; 193; EW 8; EWL 3

Georges, Georges Martin
See Simenon, Georges (Jacques Christian)

Gerald of Wales c. 1146-c. 1223 ... **CMLC 60**

Gerhardi, William Alexander
See Gerhardie, William Alexander

Gerhardie, William Alexander
1895-1977 .... **CLC 5**
See also CA 25-28R; 73-76; CANR 18; CN 1, 2; DLB 36; RGEL 2

Gerome
See Thibault, Jacques Anatole Francois

Gerson, Jean 1363-1429 .... **LC 77**
See also DLB 208

Gersonides 1288-1344 .... **CMLC 49**
See also DLB 115

Gerstler, Amy 1956- .... **CLC 70**
See also CA 146; CANR 99

Gertler, T. .... **CLC 34**
See also CA 116; 121

Gertrude of Helfta c. 1256-c.
1301 .... **CMLC 105**

Gertsen, Aleksandr Ivanovich
See Herzen, Aleksandr Ivanovich

Ghalib
See Ghalib, Asadullah Khan

Ghalib, Asadullah Khan
1797-1869 .... **NCLC 39, 78**
See also DAM POET; RGWL 2, 3

Ghelderode, Michel de 1898-1962 ..... **CLC 6, 11; DC 15; TCLC 187**
See also CA 85-88; CANR 40, 77; DAM DRAM; DLB 321; EW 11; EWL 3; TWA

Ghiselin, Brewster 1903-2001 .... **CLC 23**
See also CA 13-16R; CAAS 10; CANR 13; CP 1, 2, 3, 4, 5, 6, 7

Ghose, Aurabinda 1872-1950 .... **TCLC 63**
See also CA 163; EWL 3

Ghose, Aurobindo
See Ghose, Aurabinda

Ghose, Zulfikar 1935- .... **CLC 42, 200**
See also CA 65-68; CANR 67; CN 1, 2, 3, 4, 5, 6, 7; CP 1, 2, 3, 4, 5, 6, 7; DLB 323; EWL 3

Ghosh, Amitav 1956- .... **CLC 44, 153**
See also CA 147; CANR 80, 158; CN 6, 7; DLB 323; WWE 1

Giacosa, Giuseppe 1847-1906 .... **TCLC 7**
See also CA 104

Gibb, Lee
See Waterhouse, Keith (Spencer)

Gibbon, Edward 1737-1794 .... **LC 97**
See also BRW 3; DLB 104, 336; RGEL 2

Gibbon, Lewis Grassic
See Mitchell, James Leslie

Gibbons, Kaye 1960- .... **CLC 50, 88, 145**
See also AAYA 34; AMWS 10; CA 151; CANR 75, 127; CN 7; CSW; DA3; DAM POP; DLB 292; MTCW 2; MTFW 2005; NFS 3; RGAL 4; SATA 117

Gibran, Kahlil 1883-1931 ..... **PC 9; TCLC 1, 9, 205**
See also CA 104; 150; DA3; DAM POET, POP; DLB 346; EWL 3; MTCW 2; WLIT 6

Gibran, Khalil
See Gibran, Kahlil

Gibson, Mel 1956- .... **CLC 215**

Gibson, William 1914-2008 .... **CLC 23**
See also CA 9-12R; CAD; CANR 9, 42, 75, 125; CD 5, 6; DA; DAB; DAC; DAM DRAM, MST; DFS 2; DLB 7; LAIT 2; MAL 5; MTCW 2; MTFW 2005; SATA 66; SATA-Obit 199; YAW

Gibson, William 1948- .... **CLC 39, 63, 186, 192; SSC 52**
See also AAYA 12, 59; AMWS 16; BPFB 2; CA 126; 133; CANR 52, 90, 106, 172; CN 6, 7; CPW; DA3; DAM POP; DLB 251; MTCW 2; MTFW 2005; SCFW 2; SFW 4; SSFS 26

Gibson, William Ford
See Gibson, William

Gide, Andre (Paul Guillaume)
1869-1951 ...... **SSC 13; TCLC 5, 12, 36, 177; WLC 3**
See also CA 104; 124; DA; DA3; DAB; DAC; DAM MST, NOV; DLB 65, 321, 330; EW 8; EWL 3; GFL 1789 to the Present; MTCW 1, 2; MTFW 2005; NFS 21; RGSF 2; RGWL 2, 3; TWA

Gifford, Barry 1946- .... **CLC 34**
See also CA 65-68; CANR 9, 30, 40, 90, 180

Gifford, Barry Colby
See Gifford, Barry

Gilbert, Frank
See De Voto, Bernard (Augustine)

Gilbert, W(illiam) S(chwenck)
1836-1911 .... **TCLC 3**
See also CA 104; 173; DAM DRAM, POET; DLB 344; RGEL 2; SATA 36

Gilbert of Poitiers c. 1085-1154 .... **CMLC 85**

Gilbreth, Frank B(unker), Jr.
1911-2001 .... **CLC 17**
See also CA 9-12R; SATA 2

Gilchrist, Ellen (Louise) 1935- .. **CLC 34, 48, 143, 264; SSC 14, 63**
See also BPFB 2; CA 113; 116; CANR 41, 61, 104; CN 4, 5, 6, 7; CPW; CSW; DAM POP; DLB 130; EWL 3; EXPS; MTCW 1, 2; MTFW 2005; RGAL 4; RGSF 2; SSFS 9

Gildas fl. 6th cent. - .... **CMLC 99**

Giles, Molly 1942- .... **CLC 39**
See also CA 126; CANR 98

Gill, Eric
See Gill, (Arthur) Eric (Rowton Peter Joseph)

Goldemberg, Isaac 1945- .... **CLC 52**
See also CA 69-72; CAAS 12; CANR 11,
32; EWL 3; HW 1; WLIT 1
Golding, Arthur 1536-1606 .... **LC 101**
See also DLB 136
Golding, William 1911-1993 . **CLC 1, 2, 3, 8,
10, 17, 27, 58, 81; WLC 3**
See also AAYA 5, 44; BPFB 2; BRWR 1;
BRWS 1; BYA 2; CA 5-8R; 141; CANR
13, 33, 54; CD 5; CDBLB 1945-1960;
CLR 94, 130; CN 1, 2, 3, 4; DA; DA3;
DAB; DAC; DAM MST, NOV; DLB 15,
100, 255, 326, 330; EWL 3; EXPN; HGG;
LAIT 4; MTCW 1, 2; MTFW 2005; NFS
2; RGEL 2; RHW; SFW 4; TEA; WLIT
4; YAW
Golding, William Gerald
See Golding, William
Goldman, Emma 1869-1940 .... **TCLC 13**
See also CA 110; 150; DLB 221; FW;
RGAL 4; TUS
Goldman, Francisco 1954- .... **CLC 76**
See also CA 162; CANR 185
Goldman, William 1931- .... **CLC 1, 48**
See also BPFB 2; CA 9-12R; CANR 29,
69, 106; CN 1, 2, 3, 4, 5, 6, 7; DLB 44;
FANT; IDFW 3, 4
Goldman, William W.
See Goldman, William
Goldmann, Lucien 1913-1970 .... **CLC 24**
See also CA 25-28; CAP 2
Goldoni, Carlo 1707-1793 .... **LC 4, 152**
See also DAM DRAM; EW 4; RGWL 2, 3;
WLIT 7
Goldsberry, Steven 1949- .... **CLC 34**
See also CA 131
Goldsmith, Oliver 1730(?)-1774 .... **DC 8; LC
2, 48, 122; PC 77; WLC 3**
See also BRW 3; CDBLB 1660-1789; DA;
DAB; DAC; DAM DRAM, MST, NOV,
POET; DFS 1; DLB 39, 89, 104, 109, 142,
336; IDTP; RGEL 2; SATA 26; TEA;
WLIT 3
Goldsmith, Peter
See Priestley, J(ohn) B(oynton)
Goldstein, Rebecca 1950- .... **CLC 239**
See also CA 144; CANR 99, 165; TCLE
1:1
Goldstein, Rebecca Newberger
See Goldstein, Rebecca
Gombrowicz, Witold 1904-1969 .... **CLC 4, 7,
11, 49**
See also CA 19-20; 25-28R; CANR 105;
CAP 2; CDWLB 4; DAM DRAM; DLB
215; EW 12; EWL 3; RGWL 2, 3; TWA
Gomez de Avellaneda, Gertrudis
1814-1873 .... **NCLC 111**
See also LAW
Gomez de la Serna, Ramon
1888-1963 .... **CLC 9**
See also CA 153; 116; CANR 79; EWL 3;
HW 1, 2
Goncharov, Ivan Alexandrovich
1812-1891 .... **NCLC 1, 63**
See also DLB 238; EW 6; RGWL 2, 3
Goncourt, Edmond (Louis Antoine Huot) de
1822-1896 .... **NCLC 7**
See also DLB 123; EW 7; GFL 1789 to the
Present; RGWL 2, 3
Goncourt, Jules (Alfred Huot) de
1830-1870 .... **NCLC 7**
See also DLB 123; EW 7; GFL 1789 to the
Present; RGWL 2, 3
Gongora (y Argote), Luis de
1561-1627 .... **LC 72**
See also RGWL 2, 3
Gontier, Fernande 19(?)- .... **CLC 50**
Gonzalez Martinez, Enrique
See Gonzalez Martinez, Enrique

Gonzalez Martinez, Enrique
1871-1952 .... **TCLC 72**
See also CA 166; CANR 81; DLB 290;
EWL 3; HW 1, 2
Goodison, Lorna 1947- .... **BLC 2:2; PC 36**
See also CA 142; CANR 88, 189; CP 5, 6,
7; CWP; DLB 157; EWL 3; PFS 25
Goodman, Allegra 1967- .... **CLC 241**
See also CA 204; CANR 162; DLB 244
Goodman, Paul 1911-1972 ..... **CLC 1, 2, 4, 7**
See also CA 19-20; 37-40R; CAD; CANR
34; CAP 2; CN 1; DLB 130, 246; MAL
5; MTCW 1; RGAL 4
Goodweather, Hartley
See King, Thomas
GoodWeather, Hartley
See King, Thomas
Googe, Barnabe 1540-1594 .... **LC 94**
See also DLB 132; RGEL 2
Gordimer, Nadine 1923- ...... **CLC 3, 5, 7, 10,
18, 33, 51, 70, 123, 160, 161, 263; SSC
17, 80; WLCS**
See also AAYA 39; AFW; BRWS 2; CA
5-8R; CANR 3, 28, 56, 88, 131; CN 1, 2,
3, 4, 5, 6, 7; DA; DA3; DAB; DAC; DAM
MST, NOV; DLB 225, 326, 330; EWL 3;
EXPS; INT CANR-28; LATS 1:2; MTCW
1, 2; MTFW 2005; NFS 4; RGEL 2;
RGSF 2; SSFS 2, 14, 19; TWA; WLIT 2;
YAW
Gordon, Adam Lindsay
1833-1870 .... **NCLC 21**
See also DLB 230
Gordon, Caroline 1895-1981 . **CLC 6, 13, 29,
83; SSC 15**
See also AMW; CA 11-12; 103; CANR 36;
CAP 1; CN 1, 2; DLB 4, 9, 102; DLBD
17; DLBY 1981; EWL 3; MAL 5; MTCW
1, 2; MTFW 2005; RGAL 4; RGSF 2
Gordon, Charles William
1860-1937 .... **TCLC 31**
See also CA 109; DLB 92; TCWW 1, 2
Gordon, Mary 1949- .. **CLC 13, 22, 128, 216;
SSC 59**
See also AMWS 4; BPFB 2; CA 102;
CANR 44, 92, 154, 179; CN 4, 5, 6, 7;
DLB 6; DLBY 1981; FW; INT CA-102;
MAL 5; MTCW 1
Gordon, Mary Catherine
See Gordon, Mary
Gordon, N. J.
See Bosman, Herman Charles
Gordon, Sol 1923- .... **CLC 26**
See also CA 53-56; CANR 4; SATA 11
Gordone, Charles 1925-1995 .... **BLC 2:2;
CLC 1, 4; DC 8**
See also BW 1, 3; CA 93-96; 180; 150;
CAAE 180; CAD; CANR 55; DAM
DRAM; DLB 7; INT CA-93-96; MTCW
1
Gore, Catherine 1800-1861 .... **NCLC 65**
See also DLB 116, 344; RGEL 2
Gorenko, Anna Andreevna
See Akhmatova, Anna
Gor'kii, Maksim
See Peshkov, Alexei Maximovich
Gorky, Maxim
See Peshkov, Alexei Maximovich
Goryan, Sirak
See Saroyan, William
Gosse, Edmund (William)
1849-1928 .... **TCLC 28**
See also CA 117; DLB 57, 144, 184; RGEL
2
Gotlieb, Phyllis (Fay Bloom) 1926- .. **CLC 18**
See also CA 13-16R; CANR 7, 135; CN 7;
CP 1, 2, 3, 4; DLB 88, 251; SFW 4
Gottesman, S. D.
See Kornbluth, C(yril) M.; Pohl, Frederik

Gottfried von Strassburg fl. c.
1170-1215 .... **CMLC 10, 96**
See also CDWLB 2; DLB 138; EW 1;
RGWL 2, 3
Gotthelf, Jeremias 1797-1854 .... **NCLC 117**
See also DLB 133; RGWL 2, 3
Gottschalk, Laura Riding
See Jackson, Laura (Riding)
Gould, Lois 1932(?)-2002 .... **CLC 4, 10**
See also CA 77-80; 208; CANR 29; MTCW
1
Gould, Stephen Jay 1941-2002 .... **CLC 163**
See also AAYA 26; BEST 90:2; CA 77-80;
205; CANR 10, 27, 56, 75, 125; CPW;
INT CANR-27; MTCW 1, 2; MTFW 2005
Gourmont, Remy(-Marie-Charles) de
1858-1915 .... **TCLC 17**
See also CA 109; 150; GFL 1789 to the
Present; MTCW 2
Gournay, Marie le Jars de
See de Gournay, Marie le Jars
Govier, Katherine 1948- .... **CLC 51**
See also CA 101; CANR 18, 40, 128; CCA
1
Gower, John c. 1330-1408 .... **LC 76; PC 59**
See also BRW 1; DLB 146; RGEL 2
Goyen, (Charles) William
1915-1983 .... **CLC 5, 8, 14, 40**
See also AITN 2; CA 5-8R; 110; CANR 6,
71; CN 1, 2, 3; DLB 2, 218; DLBY 1983;
EWL 3; INT CANR-6; MAL 5
Goytisolo, Juan 1931- .... **CLC 5, 10, 23, 133;
HLC 1**
See also CA 85-88; CANR 32, 61, 131, 182;
CWW 2; DAM MULT; DLB 322; EWL
3; GLL 2; HW 1, 2; MTCW 1, 2; MTFW
2005
Gozzano, Guido 1883-1916 .... **PC 10**
See also CA 154; DLB 114; EWL 3
Gozzi, (Conte) Carlo 1720-1806 .... **NCLC 23**
Grabbe, Christian Dietrich
1801-1836 .... **NCLC 2**
See also DLB 133; RGWL 2, 3
Grace, Patricia Frances 1937- .... **CLC 56**
See also CA 176; CANR 118; CN 4, 5, 6,
7; EWL 3; RGSF 2
Gracian, Baltasar 1601-1658 .... **LC 15, 160**
Gracian y Morales, Baltasar
See Gracian, Baltasar
Gracq, Julien 1910-2007 ..... **CLC 11, 48, 259**
See also CA 122; 126; 267; CANR 141;
CWW 2; DLB 83; GFL 1789 to the
present
Grade, Chaim 1910-1982 .... **CLC 10**
See also CA 93-96; 107; DLB 333; EWL 3;
RGHL
Grade, Khayim
See Grade, Chaim
Graduate of Oxford, A
See Ruskin, John
Grafton, Garth
See Duncan, Sara Jeannette
Grafton, Sue 1940- .... **CLC 163**
See also AAYA 11, 49; BEST 90:3; CA 108;
CANR 31, 55, 111, 134; CMW 4; CPW;
CSW; DA3; DAM POP; DLB 226; FW;
MSW; MTFW 2005
Graham, John
See Phillips, David Graham
Graham, Jorie 1950- .... **CLC 48, 118; PC 59**
See also AAYA 67; CA 111; CANR 63, 118;
CP 4, 5, 6, 7; CWP; DLB 120; EWL 3;
MTFW 2005; PFS 10, 17; TCLE 1:1
Graham, R(obert) B(ontine) Cunninghame
See Cunninghame Graham, Robert
(Gallnigad) Bontine
Graham, Robert
See Haldeman, Joe

Griffin, Gerald 1803-1840 .... **NCLC 7**
See also DLB 159; RGEL 2

Griffin, John Howard 1920-1980 ..... **CLC 68**
See also AITN 1; CA 1-4R; 101; CANR 2

Griffin, Peter 1942- .... **CLC 39**
See also CA 136

Griffith, David Lewelyn Wark
See Griffith, D.W.

Griffith, D.W. 1875(?)-1948 .... **TCLC 68**
See also AAYA 78; CA 119; 150; CANR 80

Griffith, Lawrence
See Griffith, D.W.

Griffiths, Trevor 1935- .... **CLC 13, 52**
See also CA 97-100; CANR 45; CBD; CD
5, 6; DLB 13, 245

Griggs, Sutton (Elbert)
1872-1930 .... **TCLC 77**
See also CA 123; 186; DLB 50

Grigson, Geoffrey (Edward Harvey)
1905-1985 .... **CLC 7, 39**
See also CA 25-28R; 118; CANR 20, 33;
CP 1, 2, 3, 4; DLB 27; MTCW 1, 2

Grile, Dod
See Bierce, Ambrose (Gwinett)

Grillparzer, Franz 1791-1872 .... **DC 14;**
NCLC 1, 102; SSC 37
See also CDWLB 2; DLB 133; EW 5;
RGWL 2, 3; TWA

Grimble, Reverend Charles James
See Eliot, T(homas) S(tearns)

Grimke, Angelina (Emily) Weld
1880-1958 .... **HR 1:2**
See also BW 1; CA 124; DAM POET; DLB
50, 54; FW

Grimke, Charlotte L(ottie) Forten
1837(?)-1914 .... **BLC 1:2; TCLC 16**
See also BW 1; CA 117; 124; DAM MULT,
POET; DLB 50, 239

Grimm, Jacob Ludwig Karl
1785-1863 .... **NCLC 3, 77; SSC 36, 88**
See also CLR 112; DLB 90; MAICYA 1, 2;
RGSF 2; RGWL 2, 3; SATA 22; WCH

Grimm, Wilhelm Karl 1786-1859 .. **NCLC 3,**
77; SSC 36
See also CDWLB 2; CLR 112; DLB 90;
MAICYA 1, 2; RGSF 2; RGWL 2, 3;
SATA 22; WCH

Grimm and Grim
See Grimm, Jacob Ludwig Karl; Grimm,
Wilhelm Karl

Grimm Brothers
See Grimm, Jacob Ludwig Karl; Grimm,
Wilhelm Karl

Grimmelshausen, Hans Jakob Christoffel
von
See Grimmelshausen, Johann Jakob Christoffel von

Grimmelshausen, Johann Jakob Christoffel
von 1621-1676 .... **LC 6**
See also CDWLB 2; DLB 168; RGWL 2, 3

Grindel, Eugene 1895-1952 .... **PC 38; TCLC**
7, 41
See also CA 104; 193; EWL 3; GFL 1789
to the Present; LMFS 2; RGWL 2, 3

Grisham, John 1955- .... **CLC 84, 273**
See also AAYA 14, 47; BPFB 2; CA 138;
CANR 47, 69, 114, 133; CMW 4; CN 6,
7; CPW; CSW; DA3; DAM POP; MSW;
MTCW 2; MTFW 2005

Grosseteste, Robert 1175(?)-1253 . **CMLC 62**
See also DLB 115

Grossman, David 1954- .... **CLC 67, 231**
See also CA 138; CANR 114, 175; CWW
2; DLB 299; EWL 3; RGHL; WLIT 6

Grossman, Vasilii Semenovich
See Grossman, Vasily (Semenovich)

Grossman, Vasily (Semenovich)
1905-1964 .... **CLC 41**
See also CA 124; 130; DLB 272; MTCW 1;
RGHL

Grove, Frederick Philip
See Greve, Felix Paul (Berthold Friedrich)

Grubb
See Crumb, R.

Grumbach, Doris 1918- .... **CLC 13, 22, 64**
See also CA 5-8R; CAAS 2; CANR 9, 42,
70, 127; CN 6, 7; INT CANR-9; MTCW
2; MTFW 2005

Grundtvig, Nikolai Frederik Severin
1783-1872 .... **NCLC 1, 158**
See also DLB 300

Grunge
See Crumb, R.

Grunwald, Lisa 1959- .... **CLC 44**
See also CA 120; CANR 148

Gryphius, Andreas 1616-1664 .... **LC 89**
See also CDWLB 2; DLB 164; RGWL 2, 3

Guare, John 1938- .... **CLC 8, 14, 29, 67; DC**
20
See also CA 73-76; CAD; CANR 21, 69,
118; CD 5, 6; DAM DRAM; DFS 8, 13;
DLB 7, 249; EWL 3; MAL 5; MTCW 1,
2; RGAL 4

Guarini, Battista 1538-1612 .... **LC 102**
See also DLB 339

Gubar, Susan 1944- .... **CLC 145**
See also CA 108; CANR 45, 70, 139, 179;
FW; MTCW 1; RGAL 4

Gubar, Susan David
See Gubar, Susan

Gudjonsson, Halldor Kiljan
1902-1998 .... **CLC 25**
See also CA 103; 164; CWW 2; DLB 293,
331; EW 12; EWL 3; RGWL 2, 3

Guedes, Vincente
See Pessoa, Fernando

Guenter, Erich
See Eich, Gunter

Guest, Barbara 1920-2006 ... **CLC 34; PC 55**
See also BG 1:2; CA 25-28R; 248; CANR
11, 44, 84; CP 1, 2, 3, 4, 5, 6, 7; CWP;
DLB 5, 193

Guest, Edgar A(lbert) 1881-1959 ... **TCLC 95**
See also CA 112; 168

Guest, Judith 1936- .... **CLC 8, 30**
See also AAYA 7, 66; CA 77-80; CANR
15, 75, 138; DA3; DAM NOV, POP;
EXPN; INT CANR-15; LAIT 5; MTCW
1, 2; MTFW 2005; NFS 1

Guevara, Che
See Guevara (Serna), Ernesto

Guevara (Serna), Ernesto
1928-1967 .... **CLC 87; HLC 1**
See also CA 127; 111; CANR 56; DAM
MULT; HW 1

Guicciardini, Francesco 1483-1540 ..... **LC 49**

Guido delle Colonne c. 1215-c.
1290 .... **CMLC 90**

Guild, Nicholas M. 1944- .... **CLC 33**
See also CA 93-96

Guillemin, Jacques
See Sartre, Jean-Paul

Guillen, Jorge 1893-1984 . **CLC 11; HLCS 1;**
PC 35
See also CA 89-92; 112; DAM MULT,
POET; DLB 108; EWL 3; HW 1; RGWL
2, 3

Guillen, Nicolas (Cristobal)
1902-1989 .... **BLC 1:2; CLC 48, 79;**
HLC 1; PC 23
See also BW 2; CA 116; 125; 129; CANR
84; DAM MST, MULT, POET; DLB 283;
EWL 3; HW 1; LAW; RGWL 2, 3; WP

Guillen y Alvarez, Jorge
See Guillen, Jorge

Guillevic, (Eugene) 1907-1997 .... **CLC 33**
See also CA 93-96; CWW 2

Guillois
See Desnos, Robert

Guillois, Valentin
See Desnos, Robert

Guimaraes Rosa, Joao 1908-1967 ... **CLC 23;**
HLCS 1
See also CA 175; 89-92; DLB 113, 307;
EWL 3; LAW; RGSF 2; RGWL 2, 3;
WLIT 1

Guiney, Louise Imogen
1861-1920 .... **TCLC 41**
See also CA 160; DLB 54; RGAL 4

Guinizelli, Guido c. 1230-1276 ...... **CMLC 49**
See also WLIT 7

Guinizzelli, Guido
See Guinizelli, Guido

Guiraldes, Ricardo (Guillermo)
1886-1927 .... **TCLC 39**
See also CA 131; EWL 3; HW 1; LAW;
MTCW 1

Gumilev, Nikolai (Stepanovich)
1886-1921 .... **TCLC 60**
See also CA 165; DLB 295; EWL 3

Gumilyov, Nikolay Stepanovich
See Gumilev, Nikolai (Stepanovich)

Gump, P. Q.
See Card, Orson Scott

Gump, P.Q.
See Card, Orson Scott

Gunesekera, Romesh 1954- .... **CLC 91**
See also BRWS 10; CA 159; CANR 140,
172; CN 6, 7; DLB 267, 323

Gunn, Bill
See Gunn, William Harrison

Gunn, Thom(son William)
1929-2004 . **CLC 3, 6, 18, 32, 81; PC 26**
See also BRWS 4; CA 17-20R; 227; CANR
9, 33, 116; CDBLB 1960 to Present; CP
1, 2, 3, 4, 5, 6, 7; DAM POET; DLB 27;
INT CANR-33; MTCW 1; PFS 9; RGEL
2

Gunn, William Harrison
1934(?)-1989 .... **CLC 5**
See also AITN 1; BW 1, 3; CA 13-16R;
128; CANR 12, 25, 76; DLB 38

Gunn Allen, Paula
See Allen, Paula Gunn

Gunnars, Kristjana 1948- .... **CLC 69**
See also CA 113; CCA 1; CP 6, 7; CWP;
DLB 60

Gunter, Erich
See Eich, Gunter

Gurdjieff, G(eorgei) I(vanovich)
1877(?)-1949 .... **TCLC 71**
See also CA 157

Gurganus, Allan 1947- .... **CLC 70**
See also BEST 90:1; CA 135; CANR 114;
CN 6, 7; CPW; CSW; DAM POP; GLL 1

Gurney, A. R.
See Gurney, A(lbert) R(amsdell), Jr.

Gurney, A(lbert) R(amsdell), Jr.
1930- .... **CLC 32, 50, 54**
See also AMWS 5; CA 77-80; CAD; CANR
32, 64, 121; CD 5, 6; DAM DRAM; DLB
266; EWL 3

Gurney, Ivor (Bertie) 1890-1937 ... **TCLC 33**
See also BRW 6; CA 167; DLBY 2002;
PAB; RGEL 2

Gurney, Peter
See Gurney, A(lbert) R(amsdell), Jr.

Guro, Elena (Genrikhovna)
1877-1913 .... **TCLC 56**
See also DLB 295

Gustafson, James M(oody) 1925- ... **CLC 100**
See also CA 25-28R; CANR 37

NOV, POP; DLB 2, 28, 227; DLBY 1980, 2002; EWL 3; EXPN; INT CANR-8; LAIT 4; MAL 5; MTCW 1, 2; MTFW 2005; NFS 1; RGAL 4; TUS; YAW

Hellman, Lillian 1905-1984 . **CLC 2, 4, 8, 14, 18, 34, 44, 52; DC 1; TCLC 119**
See also AAYA 47; AITN 1, 2; AMWS 1; CA 13-16R; 112; CAD; CANR 33; CWD; DA3; DAM DRAM; DFS 1, 3, 14; DLB 7, 228; DLBY 1984; EWL 3; FL 1:6; FW; LAIT 3; MAL 5; MBL; MTCW 1, 2; MTFW 2005; RGAL 4; TUS

Helprin, Mark 1947- .... **CLC 7, 10, 22, 32**
See also CA 81-84; CANR 47, 64, 124; CDALBS; CN 7; CPW; DA3; DAM NOV, POP; DLB 335; DLBY 1985; FANT; MAL 5; MTCW 1, 2; MTFW 2005; SSFS 25; SUFW 2

Helvetius, Claude-Adrien 1715-1771 .. **LC 26**
See also DLB 313

Helyar, Jane Penelope Josephine 1933- .... **CLC 17**
See also CA 21-24R; CANR 10, 26; CWRI 5; SAAS 2; SATA 5; SATA-Essay 138

Hemans, Felicia 1793-1835 ...... **NCLC 29, 71**
See also DLB 96; RGEL 2

Hemingway, Ernest (Miller) 1899-1961 .... **CLC 1, 3, 6, 8, 10, 13, 19, 30, 34, 39, 41, 44, 50, 61, 80; SSC 1, 25, 36, 40, 63, 117; TCLC 115, 203; WLC 3**
See also AAYA 19; AMW; AMWC 1; AMWR 1; BPFB 2; BYA 2, 3, 13, 15; CA 77-80; CANR 34; CDALB 1917-1929; DA; DA3; DAB; DAC; DAM MST, NOV; DLB 4, 9, 102, 210, 308, 316, 330; DLBD 1, 15, 16; DLBY 1981, 1987, 1996, 1998; EWL 3; EXPN; EXPS; LAIT 3, 4; LATS 1:1; MAL 5; MTCW 1, 2; MTFW 2005; NFS 1, 5, 6, 14; RGAL 4; RGSF 2; SSFS 17; TUS; WYA

Hempel, Amy 1951- .... **CLC 39**
See also CA 118; 137; CANR 70, 166; DA3; DLB 218; EXPS; MTCW 2; MTFW 2005; SSFS 2

Henderson, F. C.
See Mencken, H(enry) L(ouis)

Henderson, Mary
See Mavor, Osborne Henry

Henderson, Sylvia
See Ashton-Warner, Sylvia (Constance)

Henderson, Zenna (Chlarson) 1917-1983 .... **SSC 29**
See also CA 1-4R; 133; CANR 1, 84; DLB 8; SATA 5; SFW 4

Henkin, Joshua 1964- .... **CLC 119**
See also CA 161; CANR 186

Henley, Beth .... **CLC 23, 255; DC 6, 14**
See Henley, Elizabeth Becker
See also CABS 3; CAD; CD 5, 6; CSW; CWD; DFS 2, 21, 26; DLBY 1986; FW

Henley, Elizabeth Becker 1952- ...... **CLC 23, 255; DC 6, 14**
See Henley, Beth
See also AAYA 70; CA 107; CABS 3; CAD; CANR 32, 73, 140; CD 5, 6; CSW; DA3; DAM DRAM, MST; DFS 2, 21; DLBY 1986; FW; MTCW 1, 2; MTFW 2005

Henley, William Ernest 1849-1903 .. **TCLC 8**
See also CA 105; 234; DLB 19; RGEL 2

Hennissart, Martha 1929- .... **CLC 2**
See also BPFB 2; CA 85-88; CANR 64; CMW 4; DLB 306

Henry VIII 1491-1547 .... **LC 10**
See also DLB 132

Henry, O. 1862-1910 . **SSC 5, 49, 117; TCLC 1, 19; WLC 3**
See also AAYA 41; AMWS 2; CA 104; 131; CDALB 1865-1917; DA; DA3; DAB; DAC; DAM MST; DLB 12, 78, 79; EXPS;

MAL 5; MTCW 1, 2; MTFW 2005; RGAL 4; RGSF 2; SSFS 2, 18, 27; TCWW 1, 2; TUS; YABC 2

Henry, Oliver
See Henry, O.

Henry, Patrick 1736-1799 .... **LC 25**
See also LAIT 1

Henryson, Robert 1430(?)-1506(?) ..... **LC 20, 110; PC 65**
See also BRWS 7; DLB 146; RGEL 2

Henschke, Alfred
See Klabund

Henson, Lance 1944- .... **NNAL**
See also CA 146; DLB 175

Hentoff, Nat(han Irving) 1925- .... **CLC 26**
See also AAYA 4, 42; BYA 6; CA 1-4R; CAAS 6; CANR 5, 25, 77, 114; CLR 1, 52; DLB 345; INT CANR-25; JRDA; MAICYA 1, 2; SATA 42, 69, 133; SATA-Brief 27; WYA; YAW

Heppenstall, (John) Rayner 1911-1981 .... **CLC 10**
See also CA 1-4R; 103; CANR 29; CN 1, 2; CP 1, 2, 3; EWL 3

Heraclitus c. 540B.C.-c. 450B.C. ... **CMLC 22**
See also DLB 176

Herbert, Frank 1920-1986 ... **CLC 12, 23, 35, 44, 85**
See also AAYA 21; BPFB 2; BYA 4, 14; CA 53-56; 118; CANR 5, 43; CDALBS; CPW; DAM POP; DLB 8; INT CANR-5; LAIT 5; MTCW 1, 2; MTFW 2005; NFS 17; SATA 9, 37; SATA-Obit 47; SCFW 1, 2; SFW 4; YAW

Herbert, George 1593-1633 . **LC 24, 121; PC 4**
See also BRW 2; BRWR 2; CDBLB Before 1660; DAB; DAM POET; DLB 126; EXPP; PFS 25; RGEL 2; TEA; WP

Herbert, Zbigniew 1924-1998 ..... **CLC 9, 43; PC 50; TCLC 168**
See also CA 89-92; 169; CANR 36, 74, 177; CDWLB 4; CWW 2; DAM POET; DLB 232; EWL 3; MTCW 1; PFS 22

Herbst, Josephine (Frey) 1897-1969 .... **CLC 34**
See also CA 5-8R; 25-28R; DLB 9

Herder, Johann Gottfried von 1744-1803 .... **NCLC 8, 186**
See also DLB 97; EW 4; TWA

Heredia, Jose Maria 1803-1839 ...... **HLCS 2; NCLC 209**
See also LAW

Hergesheimer, Joseph 1880-1954 ... **TCLC 11**
See also CA 109; 194; DLB 102, 9; RGAL 4

Herlihy, James Leo 1927-1993 .... **CLC 6**
See also CA 1-4R; 143; CAD; CANR 2; CN 1, 2, 3, 4, 5

Herman, William
See Bierce, Ambrose (Gwinett)

Hermogenes fl. c. 175- .... **CMLC 6**

Hernandez, Jose 1834-1886 .... **NCLC 17**
See also LAW; RGWL 2, 3; WLIT 1

Herodotus c. 484B.C.-c. 420B.C. .. **CMLC 17**
See also AW 1; CDWLB 1; DLB 176; RGWL 2, 3; TWA; WLIT 8

Herr, Michael 1940(?)- .... **CLC 231**
See also CA 89-92; CANR 68, 142; DLB 185; MTCW 1

Herrick, Robert 1591-1674 .. **LC 13, 145; PC 9**
See also BRW 2; BRWC 2; DA; DAB; DAC; DAM MST, POP; DLB 126; EXPP; PFS 13, 29; RGAL 4; RGEL 2; TEA; WP

Herring, Guilles
See Somerville, Edith Oenone

Herriot, James 1916-1995 ..
See Wight, James Alfred

Herris, Violet
See Hunt, Violet

Herrmann, Dorothy 1941- .... **CLC 44**
See also CA 107

Herrmann, Taffy
See Herrmann, Dorothy

Hersey, John 1914-1993 .. **CLC 1, 2, 7, 9, 40, 81, 97**
See also AAYA 29; BPFB 2; CA 17-20R; 140; CANR 33; CDALBS; CN 1, 2, 3, 4, 5; CPW; DAM POP; DLB 6, 185, 278, 299; MAL 5; MTCW 1, 2; MTFW 2005; RGHL; SATA 25; SATA-Obit 76; TUS

Hervent, Maurice
See Grindel, Eugene

Herzen, Aleksandr Ivanovich 1812-1870 .... **NCLC 10, 61**
See also DLB 277

Herzen, Alexander
See Herzen, Aleksandr Ivanovich

Herzl, Theodor 1860-1904 .... **TCLC 36**
See also CA 168

Herzog, Werner 1942- .... **CLC 16, 236**
See also CA 89-92

Hesiod fl. 8th cent. B.C. .... **CMLC 5, 102**
See also AW 1; DLB 176; RGWL 2, 3; WLIT 8

Hesse, Hermann 1877-1962 ... **CLC 1, 2, 3, 6, 11, 17, 25, 69; SSC 9, 49; TCLC 148, 196; WLC 3**
See also AAYA 43; BPFB 2; CA 17-18; CAP 2; CDWLB 2; DA; DA3; DAB; DAC; DAM MST, NOV; DLB 66, 330; EW 9; EWL 3; EXPN; LAIT 1; MTCW 1, 2; MTFW 2005; NFS 6, 15, 24; RGWL 2, 3; SATA 50; TWA

Hewes, Cady
See De Voto, Bernard (Augustine)

Heyen, William 1940- .... **CLC 13, 18**
See also CA 33-36R; 220; CAAE 220; CAAS 9; CANR 98, 188; CP 3, 4, 5, 6, 7; DLB 5; RGHL

Heyerdahl, Thor 1914-2002 .... **CLC 26**
See also CA 5-8R; 207; CANR 5, 22, 66, 73; LAIT 4; MTCW 1, 2; MTFW 2005; SATA 2, 52

Heym, Georg (Theodor Franz Arthur) 1887-1912 .... **TCLC 9**
See also CA 106; 181

Heym, Stefan 1913-2001 .... **CLC 41**
See also CA 9-12R; 203; CANR 4; CWW 2; DLB 69; EWL 3

Heyse, Paul (Johann Ludwig von) 1830-1914 .... **TCLC 8**
See also CA 104; 209; DLB 129, 330

Heyward, (Edwin) DuBose 1885-1940 .... **HR 1:2; TCLC 59**
See also CA 108; 157; DLB 7, 9, 45, 249; MAL 5; SATA 21

Heywood, John 1497(?)-1580(?) .... **LC 65**
See also DLB 136; RGEL 2

Heywood, Thomas 1573(?)-1641 . **DC 29; LC 111**
See also DAM DRAM; DLB 62; LMFS 1; RGEL 2; TEA

Hiaasen, Carl 1953- .... **CLC 238**
See also CA 105; CANR 22, 45, 65, 113, 133, 168; CMW 4; CPW; CSW; DA3; DLB 292; MTCW 2; MTFW 2005

Hibbert, Eleanor Alice Burford 1906-1993 .... **CLC 7**
See also BEST 90:4; BPFB 2; CA 17-20R; 140; CANR 9, 28, 59; CMW 4; CPW; DAM POP; MTCW 1, 2; MTFW 2005; RHW; SATA 2; SATA-Obit 74

Hichens, Robert (Smythe) 1864-1950 .... **TCLC 64**
See also CA 162; DLB 153; HGG; RHW; SUFW

Hogarth, Charles
  See Creasey, John
Hogarth, Emmett
  See Polonsky, Abraham (Lincoln)
Hogarth, William 1697-1764 .... **LC 112**
  See also AAYA 56
Hogg, James 1770-1835 .... **NCLC 4, 109**
  See also BRWS 10; DLB 93, 116, 159; GL
  2; HGG; RGEL 2; SUFW 1
Holbach, Paul-Henri Thiry
  1723-1789 .... **LC 14**
  See also DLB 313
Holberg, Ludvig 1684-1754 .... **LC 6**
  See also DLB 300; RGWL 2, 3
Holbrook, John
  See Vance, Jack
Holcroft, Thomas 1745-1809 .... **NCLC 85**
  See also DLB 39, 89, 158; RGEL 2
Holden, Ursula 1921- .... **CLC 18**
  See also CA 101; CAAS 8; CANR 22
Holderlin, (Johann Christian) Friedrich
  1770-1843 .... **NCLC 16, 187; PC 4**
  See also CDWLB 2; DLB 90; EW 5; RGWL
  2, 3
Holdstock, Robert 1948- .... **CLC 39**
  See also CA 131; CANR 81; DLB 261;
  FANT; HGG; SFW 4; SUFW 2
Holdstock, Robert P.
  See Holdstock, Robert
Holinshed, Raphael fl. 1580- .... **LC 69**
  See also DLB 167; RGEL 2
Holland, Isabelle (Christian)
  1920-2002 .... **CLC 21**
  See also AAYA 11, 64; CA 21-24R; 205;
  CAAE 181; CANR 10, 25, 47; CLR 57;
  CWRI 5; JRDA; LAIT 4; MAICYA 1, 2;
  SATA 8, 70; SATA-Essay 103; SATA-Obit
  132; WYA
Holland, Marcus
  See Caldwell, (Janet Miriam) Taylor
  (Holland)
Hollander, John 1929- .... **CLC 2, 5, 8, 14**
  See also CA 1-4R; CANR 1, 52, 136; CP 1,
  2, 3, 4, 5, 6, 7; DLB 5; MAL 5; SATA 13
Hollander, Paul
  See Silverberg, Robert
Holleran, Andrew
  See Garber, Eric
Holley, Marietta 1836(?)-1926 .... **TCLC 99**
  See also CA 118; DLB 11; FL 1:3
Hollinghurst, Alan 1954- .... **CLC 55, 91**
  See also BRWS 10; CA 114; CN 5, 6, 7;
  DLB 207, 326; GLL 1
Hollis, Jim
  See Summers, Hollis (Spurgeon, Jr.)
Holly, Buddy 1936-1959 .... **TCLC 65**
  See also CA 213
Holmes, Gordon
  See Shiel, M(atthew) P(hipps)
Holmes, John
  See Souster, (Holmes) Raymond
Holmes, John Clellon 1926-1988 ...... **CLC 56**
  See also BG 1:2; CA 9-12R; 125; CANR 4;
  CN 1, 2, 3, 4; DLB 16, 237
Holmes, Oliver Wendell, Jr.
  1841-1935 .... **TCLC 77**
  See also CA 114; 186
Holmes, Oliver Wendell
  1809-1894 .... **NCLC 14, 81; PC 71**
  See also AMWS 1; CDALB 1640-1865;
  DLB 1, 189, 235; EXPP; PFS 24; RGAL
  4; SATA 34
Holmes, Raymond
  See Souster, (Holmes) Raymond
Holt, Samuel
  See Westlake, Donald E.
Holt, Victoria
  See Hibbert, Eleanor Alice Burford

Holub, Miroslav 1923-1998 .... **CLC 4**
  See also CA 21-24R; 169; CANR 10; CD-
  WLB 4; CWW 2; DLB 232; EWL 3;
  RGWL 3
Holz, Detlev
  See Benjamin, Walter
Homer c. 8th cent. B.C.- .... **CMLC 1, 16, 61;**
  PC 23; WLCS
  See also AW 1; CDWLB 1; DA; DA3;
  DAB; DAC; DAM MST, POET; DLB
  176; EFS 1; LAIT 1; LMFS 1; RGWL 2,
  3; TWA; WLIT 8; WP
Hong, Maxine Ting Ting
  See Kingston, Maxine Hong
Hongo, Garrett Kaoru 1951- .... **PC 23**
  See also CA 133; CAAS 22; CP 5, 6, 7;
  DLB 120, 312; EWL 3; EXPP; PFS 25;
  RGAL 4
Honig, Edwin 1919- .... **CLC 33**
  See also CA 5-8R; CAAS 8; CANR 4, 45,
  144; CP 1, 2, 3, 4, 5, 6, 7; DLB 5
Hood, Hugh (John Blagdon) 1928- . **CLC 15,**
  28, 273; SSC 42
  See also CA 49-52; CAAS 17; CANR 1,
  33, 87; CN 1, 2, 3, 4, 5, 6, 7; DLB 53;
  RGSF 2
Hood, Thomas 1799-1845 . **NCLC 16; PC 93**
  See also BRW 4; DLB 96; RGEL 2
Hooker, (Peter) Jeremy 1941- .... **CLC 43**
  See also CA 77-80; CANR 22; CP 2, 3, 4,
  5, 6, 7; DLB 40
Hooker, Richard 1554-1600 .... **LC 95**
  See also BRW 1; DLB 132; RGEL 2
Hooker, Thomas 1586-1647 .... **LC 137**
  See also DLB 24
hooks, bell 1952(?)- .... **BLCS; CLC 94**
  See also BW 2; CA 143; CANR 87, 126;
  DLB 246; MTCW 2; MTFW 2005; SATA
  115, 170
Hooper, Johnson Jones
  1815-1862 .... **NCLC 177**
  See also DLB 3, 11, 248; RGAL 4
Hope, A(lec) D(erwent) 1907-2000 .... **CLC 3,**
  51; PC 56
  See also BRWS 7; CA 21-24R; 188; CANR
  33, 74; CP 1, 2, 3, 4, 5; DLB 289; EWL
  3; MTCW 1, 2; MTFW 2005; PFS 8;
  RGEL 2
Hope, Anthony 1863-1933 .... **TCLC 83**
  See also CA 157; DLB 153, 156; RGEL 2;
  RHW
Hope, Brian
  See Creasey, John
Hope, Christopher 1944- .... **CLC 52**
  See also AFW; CA 106; CANR 47, 101,
  177; CN 4, 5, 6, 7; DLB 225; SATA 62
Hope, Christopher David Tully
  See Hope, Christopher
Hopkins, Gerard Manley
  1844-1889 .... **NCLC 17, 189; PC 15;**
  WLC 3
  See also BRW 5; BRWR 2; CDBLB 1890-
  1914; DA; DA3; DAB; DAC; DAM MST,
  POET; DLB 35, 57; EXPP; PAB; PFS 26;
  RGEL 2; TEA; WP
Hopkins, John (Richard) 1931-1998 .. **CLC 4**
  See also CA 85-88; 169; CBD; CD 5, 6
Hopkins, Pauline Elizabeth
  1859-1930 .... **BLC 1:2; TCLC 28**
  See also AFAW 2; BW 2, 3; CA 141; CANR
  82; DAM MULT; DLB 50
Hopkinson, Francis 1737-1791 .... **LC 25**
  See also DLB 31; RGAL 4
Hopley, George
  See Hopley-Woolrich, Cornell George
Hopley-Woolrich, Cornell George
  1903-1968 .... **CLC 77**
  See also CA 13-14; CANR 58, 156; CAP 1;
  CMW 4; DLB 226; MSW; MTCW 2

Horace 65B.C.-8B.C. .... **CMLC 39; PC 46**
  See also AW 2; CDWLB 1; DLB 211;
  RGWL 2, 3; WLIT 8
Horatio
  See Proust, (Valentin-Louis-George-Eugene)
  Marcel
Horgan, Paul (George Vincent
  O'Shaughnessy) 1903-1995 .. **CLC 9, 53**
  See also BPFB 2; CA 13-16R; 147; CANR
  9, 35; CN 1, 2, 3, 4, 5; DAM NOV; DLB
  102, 212; DLBY 1985; INT CANR-9;
  MTCW 1, 2; MTFW 2005; SATA 13;
  SATA-Obit 84; TCWW 1, 2
Horkheimer, Max 1895-1973 .... **TCLC 132**
  See also CA 216; 41-44R; DLB 296
Horn, Peter
  See Kuttner, Henry
Hornby, Nick 1957(?)- .... **CLC 243**
  See also AAYA 74; CA 151; CANR 104,
  151; CN 7; DLB 207
Horne, Frank (Smith) 1899-1974 ...... **HR 1:2**
  See also BW 1; CA 125; 53-56; DLB 51;
  WP
Horne, Richard Henry Hengist
  1802(?)-1884 .... **NCLC 127**
  See also DLB 32; SATA 29
Hornem, Horace Esq.
  See Byron, George Gordon (Noel)
Horne Tooke, John 1736-1812 ..... **NCLC 195**
Horney, Karen (Clementine Theodore
  Danielsen) 1885-1952 .... **TCLC 71**
  See also CA 114; 165; DLB 246; FW
Hornung, E(rnest) W(illiam)
  1866-1921 .... **TCLC 59**
  See also CA 108; 160; CMW 4; DLB 70
Horovitz, Israel 1939- .... **CLC 56**
  See also CA 33-36R; CAD; CANR 46, 59;
  CD 5, 6; DAM DRAM; DLB 7, 341;
  MAL 5
Horton, George Moses
  1797(?)-1883(?) .... **NCLC 87**
  See also DLB 50
Horvath, odon von 1901-1938
  See von Horvath, Odon
  See also EWL 3
Horvath, Oedoen von -1938
  See von Horvath, Odon
Horwitz, Julius 1920-1986 .... **CLC 14**
  See also CA 9-12R; 119; CANR 12
Horwitz, Ronald
  See Harwood, Ronald
Hospital, Janette Turner 1942- .... **CLC 42,**
  145
  See also CA 108; CANR 48, 166; CN 5, 6,
  7; DLB 325; DLBY 2002; RGSF 2
Hosseini, Khaled 1965- .... **CLC 254**
  See also CA 225; SATA 156
Hostos, E. M. de
  See Hostos (y Bonilla), Eugenio Maria de
Hostos, Eugenio M. de
  See Hostos (y Bonilla), Eugenio Maria de
Hostos, Eugenio Maria
  See Hostos (y Bonilla), Eugenio Maria de
Hostos (y Bonilla), Eugenio Maria de
  1839-1903 .... **TCLC 24**
  See also CA 123; 131; HW 1
Houdini
  See Lovecraft, H. P.
Houellebecq, Michel 1958- .... **CLC 179**
  See also CA 185; CANR 140; MTFW 2005
Hougan, Carolyn 1943-2007 .... **CLC 34**
  See also CA 139; 257
Household, Geoffrey (Edward West)
  1900-1988 .... **CLC 11**
  See also CA 77-80; 126; CANR 58; CMW
  4; CN 1, 2, 3, 4; DLB 87; SATA 14;
  SATA-Obit 59

Hunter, Mollie 1922- .... **CLC 21**
See also AAYA 13, 71; BYA 6; CANR 37, 78; CLR 25; DLB 161; JRDA; MAICYA 1, 2; SAAS 7; SATA 2, 54, 106, 139; SATA-Essay 139; WYA; YAW

Hunter, Robert (?)-1734 .... **LC 7**

Hurston, Zora Neale 1891-1960 ..... **BLC 1:2; CLC 7, 30, 61; DC 12; HR 1:2; SSC 4, 80; TCLC 121, 131; WLCS**
See also AAYA 15, 71; AFAW 1, 2; AMWS 6; BW 1, 3; BYA 12; CA 85-88; CANR 61; CDALBS; DA; DA3; DAC; DAM MST, MULT, NOV; DFS 6; DLB 51, 86; EWL 3; EXPN; EXPS; FL 1:6; FW; LAIT 3; LATS 1:1; LMFS 2; MAL 5; MBL; MTCW 1, 2; MTFW 2005; NFS 3; RGAL 4; RGSF 2; SSFS 1, 6, 11, 19, 21; TUS; YAW

Husserl, E. G.
See Husserl, Edmund (Gustav Albrecht)

Husserl, Edmund (Gustav Albrecht) 1859-1938 .... **TCLC 100**
See also CA 116; 133; DLB 296

Huston, John (Marcellus) 1906-1987 .... **CLC 20**
See also CA 73-76; 123; CANR 34; DLB 26

Hustvedt, Siri 1955- .... **CLC 76**
See also CA 137; CANR 149

Hutcheson, Francis 1694-1746 .... **LC 157**
See also DLB 252

Hutchinson, Lucy 1620-1675 .... **LC 149**

Hutten, Ulrich von 1488-1523 .... **LC 16**
See also DLB 179

Huxley, Aldous (Leonard) 1894-1963 .... **CLC 1, 3, 4, 5, 8, 11, 18, 35, 79; SSC 39; WLC 3**
See also AAYA 11; BPFB 2; BRW 7; CA 85-88; CANR 44, 99; CDBLB 1914-1945; DA; DA3; DAB; DAC; DAM MST, NOV; DLB 36, 100, 162, 195, 255; EWL 3; EXPN; LAIT 5; LMFS 2; MTCW 1, 2; MTFW 2005; NFS 6; RGEL 2; SATA 63; SCFW 1, 2; SFW 4; TEA; YAW

Huxley, T(homas) H(enry) 1825-1895 .... **NCLC 67**
See also DLB 57; TEA

Huygens, Constantijn 1596-1687 .... **LC 114**
See also RGWL 2, 3

Huysmans, Joris-Karl 1848-1907 ... **TCLC 7, 69, 212**
See also CA 104; 165; DLB 123; EW 7; GFL 1789 to the Present; LMFS 2; RGWL 2, 3

Hwang, David Henry 1957- .... **CLC 55, 196; DC 4, 23**
See also CA 127; 132; CAD; CANR 76, 124; CD 5, 6; DA3; DAM DRAM; DFS 11, 18; DLB 212, 228, 312; INT CA-132; MAL 5; MTCW 2; MTFW 2005; RGAL 4

Hyatt, Daniel
See James, Daniel (Lewis)

Hyde, Anthony 1946- .... **CLC 42**
See also CA 136; CCA 1

Hyde, Margaret O. 1917- .... **CLC 21**
See also CA 1-4R; CANR 1, 36, 137, 181; CLR 23; JRDA; MAICYA 1, 2; SAAS 8; SATA 1, 42, 76, 139

Hyde, Margaret Oldroyd
See Hyde, Margaret O.

Hynes, James 1956(?)- .... **CLC 65**
See also CA 164; CANR 105

Hypatia c. 370-415 .... **CMLC 35**

Ian, Janis 1951- .... **CLC 21**
See also CA 105; 187

Ibanez, Vicente Blasco
See Blasco Ibanez, Vicente

Ibarbourou, Juana de 1895(?)-1979 .... **HLCS 2**
See also DLB 290; HW 1; LAW

Ibarguengoitia, Jorge 1928-1983 ..... **CLC 37; TCLC 148**
See also CA 124; 113; EWL 3; HW 1

Ibn Arabi 1165-1240 .... **CMLC 105**

Ibn Battuta, Abu Abdalla 1304-1368(?) .... **CMLC 57**
See also WLIT 2

Ibn Hazm 994-1064 .... **CMLC 64**

Ibn Zaydun 1003-1070 .... **CMLC 89**

Ibsen, Henrik (Johan) 1828-1906 .. **DC 2, 30; TCLC 2, 8, 16, 37, 52; WLC 3**
See also AAYA 46; CA 104; 141; DA; DA3; DAB; DAC; DAM DRAM; MST; DFS 1, 6, 8, 10, 11, 15, 16, 25; EW 7; LAIT 2; LATS 1:1; MTFW 2005; RGWL 2, 3

Ibuse, Masuji 1898-1993 .... **CLC 22**
See also CA 127; 141; CWW 2; DLB 180; EWL 3; MJW; RGWL 3

Ibuse Masuji
See Ibuse, Masuji

Ichikawa, Kon 1915-2008 .... **CLC 20**
See also CA 121; 269

Ichiyo, Higuchi 1872-1896 .... **NCLC 49**
See also MJW

Idle, Eric 1943- .... **CLC 21**
See also CA 116; CANR 35, 91, 148

Idris, Yusuf 1927-1991 .... **SSC 74**
See also AFW; DLB 346; EWL 3; RGSF 2, 3; RGWL 3; WLIT 2

Ignatieff, Michael 1947- .... **CLC 236**
See also CA 144; CANR 88, 156; CN 6, 7; DLB 267

Ignatieff, Michael Grant
See Ignatieff, Michael

Ignatow, David 1914-1997 .... **CLC 4, 7, 14, 40; PC 34**
See also CA 9-12R; 162; CAAS 3; CANR 31, 57, 96; CP 1, 2, 3, 4, 5, 6; DLB 5; EWL 3; MAL 5

Ignotus
See Strachey, (Giles) Lytton

Ihimaera, Witi (Tame) 1944- .... **CLC 46**
See also CA 77-80; CANR 130; CN 2, 3, 4, 5, 6, 7; RGSF 2; SATA 148

Il'f, Il'ia
See Fainzilberg, Ilya Arnoldovich

Ilf, Ilya
See Fainzilberg, Ilya Arnoldovich

Illyes, Gyula 1902-1983 .... **PC 16**
See also CA 114; 109; CDWLB 4; DLB 215; EWL 3; RGWL 2, 3

Imalayen, Fatima-Zohra
See Djebar, Assia

Immermann, Karl (Lebrecht) 1796-1840 .... **NCLC 4, 49**
See also DLB 133

Ince, Thomas H. 1882-1924 .... **TCLC 89**
See also IDFW 3, 4

Inchbald, Elizabeth 1753-1821 ...... **NCLC 62**
See also DLB 39, 89; RGEL 2

Inclan, Ramon (Maria) del Valle
See Valle-Inclan, Ramon (Maria) del

Incogniteau, Jean-Louis
See Kerouac, Jack

Infante, G(uillermo) Cabrera
See Cabrera Infante, G.

Ingalls, Rachel 1940- .... **CLC 42**
See also CA 123; 127; CANR 154

Ingalls, Rachel Holmes
See Ingalls, Rachel

Ingamells, Reginald Charles
See Ingamells, Rex

Ingamells, Rex 1913-1955 .... **TCLC 35**
See also CA 167; DLB 260

Inge, William (Motter) 1913-1973 ..... **CLC 1, 8, 19**
See also CA 9-12R; CAD; CDALB 1941-1968; DA3; DAM DRAM; DFS 1, 3, 5, 8; DLB 7, 249; EWL 3; MAL 5; MTCW 1, 2; MTFW 2005; RGAL 4; TUS

Ingelow, Jean 1820-1897 .... **NCLC 39, 107**
See also DLB 35, 163; FANT; SATA 33

Ingram, Willis J.
See Harris, Mark

Innaurato, Albert (F.) 1948(?)- ... **CLC 21, 60**
See also CA 115; 122; CAD; CANR 78; CD 5, 6; INT CA-122

Innes, Michael
See Stewart, J(ohn) I(nnes) M(ackintosh)

Innis, Harold Adams 1894-1952 .... **TCLC 77**
See also CA 181; DLB 88

Insluis, Alanus de
See Alain de Lille

Iola
See Wells-Barnett, Ida B(ell)

Ionesco, Eugene 1912-1994 ... **CLC 1, 4, 6, 9, 11, 15, 41, 86; DC 12; WLC 3**
See also CA 9-12R; 144; CANR 55, 132; CWW 2; DA; DA3; DAB; DAC; DAM DRAM, MST; DFS 4, 9, 25; DLB 321; EW 13; EWL 3; GFL 1789 to the Present; LMFS 2; MTCW 1, 2; MTFW 2005; RGWL 2, 3; SATA 7; SATA-Obit 79; TWA

Iqbal, Muhammad 1877-1938 .... **TCLC 28**
See also CA 215; EWL 3

Ireland, Patrick
See O'Doherty, Brian

Irenaeus St. 130- .... **CMLC 42**

Irigaray, Luce 1930- .... **CLC 164**
See also CA 154; CANR 121; FW

Irish, William
See Hopley-Woolrich, Cornell George

Irland, David
See Green, Julien (Hartridge)

Iron, Ralph
See Schreiner, Olive (Emilie Albertina)

Irving, John 1942- . **CLC 13, 23, 38, 112, 175**
See also AAYA 8, 62; AMWS 6; BEST 89:3; BPFB 2; CA 25-28R; CANR 28, 73, 112, 133; CN 3, 4, 5, 6, 7; CPW; DA3; DAM NOV, POP; DLB 6, 278; DLBY 1982; EWL 3; MAL 5; MTCW 1, 2; MTFW 2005; NFS 12, 14; RGAL 4; TUS

Irving, John Winslow
See Irving, John

Irving, Washington 1783-1859 . **NCLC 2, 19, 95; SSC 2, 37, 104; WLC 3**
See also AAYA 56; AMW; CDALB 1640-1865; CLR 97; DA; DA3; DAB; DAC; DAM MST; DLB 3, 11, 30, 59, 73, 74, 183, 186, 250, 254; EXPS; GL 2; LAIT 1; RGAL 4; RGSF 2; SSFS 1, 8, 16; SUFW 1; TUS; WCH; YABC 2

Irwin, P. K.
See Page, P(atricia) K(athleen)

Isaacs, Jorge Ricardo 1837-1895 ... **NCLC 70**
See also LAW

Isaacs, Susan 1943- .... **CLC 32**
See also BEST 89:1; BPFB 2; CA 89-92; CANR 20, 41, 65, 112, 134, 165; CPW; DA3; DAM POP; INT CANR-20; MTCW 1, 2; MTFW 2005

Isherwood, Christopher 1904-1986 ... **CLC 1, 9, 11, 14, 44; SSC 56**
See also AMWS 14; BRW 7; CA 13-16R; 117; CANR 35, 97, 133; CN 1, 2, 3; DA3; DAM DRAM, NOV; DLB 15, 195; DLBY 1986; EWL 3; IDTP; MTCW 1, 2; MTFW 2005; RGAL 4; RGEL 2; TUS; WLIT 4

Ishiguro, Kazuo 1954- . **CLC 27, 56, 59, 110, 219**
See also AAYA 58; BEST 90:2; BPFB 2; BRWS 4; CA 120; CANR 49, 95, 133; CN 5, 6, 7; DA3; DAM NOV; DLB 194, 326; EWL 3; MTCW 1, 2; MTFW 2005; NFS 13; WLIT 4; WWE 1

Ishikawa, Hakuhin
See Ishikawa, Takuboku

Ishikawa, Takuboku 1886(?)-1912 ..... **PC 10; TCLC 15**
See Ishikawa Takuboku
See also CA 113; 153; DAM POET

Isidore of Seville c. 560-636 .... **CMLC 101**

Iskander, Fazil (Abdulovich) 1929- .. **CLC 47**
See also CA 102; DLB 302; EWL 3

Iskander, Fazil' Abdulevich
See Iskander, Fazil (Abdulovich)

Isler, Alan (David) 1934- .... **CLC 91**
See also CA 156; CANR 105

Ivan IV 1530-1584 .... **LC 17**

Ivanov, V.I.
See Ivanov, Vyacheslav

Ivanov, Vyacheslav 1866-1949 .... **TCLC 33**
See also CA 122; EWL 3

Ivanov, Vyacheslav Ivanovich
See Ivanov, Vyacheslav

Ivask, Ivar Vidrik 1927-1992 .... **CLC 14**
See also CA 37-40R; 139; CANR 24

Ives, Morgan
See Bradley, Marion Zimmer

Izumi Shikibu c. 973-c. 1034 .... **CMLC 33**

J. R. S.
See Gogarty, Oliver St. John

Jabran, Kahlil
See Gibran, Kahlil

Jabran, Khalil
See Gibran, Kahlil

Jaccottet, Philippe 1925- .... **PC 98**
See also CA 116; 129; CWW 2; GFL 1789 to the Present

Jackson, Daniel
See Wingrove, David

Jackson, Helen Hunt 1830-1885 .... **NCLC 90**
See also DLB 42, 47, 186, 189; RGAL 4

Jackson, Jesse 1908-1983 .... **CLC 12**
See also BW 1; CA 25-28R; 109; CANR 27; CLR 28; CWRI 5; MAICYA 1, 2; SATA 2, 29; SATA-Obit 48

Jackson, Laura (Riding) 1901-1991 .. **CLC 3, 7; PC 44**
See also CA 65-68; 135; CANR 28, 89; CP 1, 2, 3, 4, 5; DLB 48; RGAL 4

Jackson, Sam
See Trumbo, Dalton

Jackson, Sara
See Wingrove, David

Jackson, Shirley 1919-1965 . **CLC 11, 60, 87; SSC 9, 39; TCLC 187; WLC 3**
See also AAYA 9; AMWS 9; BPFB 2; CA 1-4R; 25-28R; CANR 4, 52; CDALB 1941-1968; DA; DA3; DAC; DAM MST; DLB 6, 234; EXPS; HGG; LAIT 4; MAL 5; MTCW 2; MTFW 2005; RGAL 4; RGSF 2; SATA 2; SSFS 1, 27; SUFW 1, 2

Jacob, (Cyprien-)Max 1876-1944 .... **TCLC 6**
See also CA 104; 193; DLB 258; EWL 3; GFL 1789 to the Present; GLL 2; RGWL 2, 3

Jacobs, Harriet A(nn) 1813(?)-1897 .... **NCLC 67, 162**
See also AFAW 1, 2; DLB 239; FL 1:3; FW; LAIT 2; RGAL 4

Jacobs, Jim 1942- .... **CLC 12**
See also CA 97-100; INT CA-97-100

Jacobs, W(illiam) W(ymark) 1863-1943 .... **SSC 73; TCLC 22**
See also CA 121; 167; DLB 135; EXPS; HGG; RGEL 2; RGSF 2; SSFS; SUFW 1

Jacobsen, Jens Peter 1847-1885 .... **NCLC 34**

Jacobsen, Josephine (Winder) 1908-2003 .... **CLC 48, 102; PC 62**
See also CA 33-36R; 218; CAAS 18; CANR 23, 48; CCA 1; CP 2, 3, 4, 5, 6, 7; DLB 244; PFS 23; TCLE 1:1

Jacobson, Dan 1929- ...... **CLC 4, 14; SSC 91**
See also AFW; CA 1-4R; CANR 2, 25, 66, 170; CN 1, 2, 3, 4, 5, 6, 7; DLB 14, 207, 225, 319; EWL 3; MTCW 1; RGSF 2

Jacopone da Todi 1236-1306 .... **CMLC 95**

Jacqueline
See Carpentier (y Valmont), Alejo

Jacques de Vitry c. 1160-1240 ...... **CMLC 63**
See also DLB 208

Jagger, Michael Philip
See Jagger, Mick

Jagger, Mick 1943- .... **CLC 17**
See also CA 239

Jahiz, al- c. 780-c. 869 .... **CMLC 25**
See also DLB 311

Jakes, John 1932- .... **CLC 29**
See also AAYA 32; BEST 89:4; BPFB 2; CA 57-60, 214; CAAE 214; CANR 10, 43, 66, 111, 142, 171; CPW; CSW; DA3; DAM NOV, POP; DLB 278; DLBY 1983; FANT; INT CANR-10; MTCW 1, 2; MTFW 2005; RHW; SATA 62; SFW 4; TCWW 1, 2

Jakes, John William
See Jakes, John

James I 1394-1437 .... **LC 20**
See also RGEL 2

James, Alice 1848-1892 .... **NCLC 206**
See also DLB 221

James, Andrew
See Kirkup, James

James, C(yril) L(ionel) R(obert) 1901-1989 .... **BLCS; CLC 33**
See also BW 2; CA 117; 125; 128; CANR 62; CN 1, 2, 3, 4; DLB 125; MTCW 1

James, Daniel (Lewis) 1911-1988 ..... **CLC 33**
See also CA 174; 125; DLB 122

James, Dynely
See Mayne, William (James Carter)

James, Henry Sr. 1811-1882 .... **NCLC 53**

James, Henry 1843-1916 .... **SSC 8, 32, 47, 108; TCLC 2, 11, 24, 40, 47, 64, 171; WLC 3**
See also AMW; AMWC 1; AMWR 1; BPFB 2; BRW 6; CA 104; 132; CDALB 1865-1917; DA; DA3; DAB; DAC; DAM MST, NOV; DLB 12, 71, 74, 189; DLBD 13; EWL 3; EXPS; GL 2; HGG; LAIT 2; MAL 5; MTCW 1, 2; MTFW 2005; NFS 12, 16, 19; RGAL 4; RGEL 2; RGSF 2; SSFS 9; SUFW 1; TUS

James, M. R.
See James, Montague (Rhodes)

James, Mary
See Meaker, Marijane

James, Montague (Rhodes) 1862-1936 .... **SSC 16, 93; TCLC 6**
See also CA 104; 203; DLB 156, 201; HGG; RGEL 2; RGSF 2; SUFW 1

James, P. D.
See White, Phyllis Dorothy James

James, Philip
See Moorcock, Michael

James, Samuel
See Stephens, James

James, Seumas
See Stephens, James

James, Stephen
See Stephens, James

James, T.F.
See Fleming, Thomas

James, William 1842-1910 .... **TCLC 15, 32**
See also AMW; CA 109; 193; DLB 270, 284; MAL 5; NCFS 5; RGAL 4

Jameson, Anna 1794-1860 .... **NCLC 43**
See also DLB 99, 166

Jameson, Fredric 1934- .... **CLC 142**
See also CA 196; CANR 169; DLB 67; LMFS 2

Jameson, Fredric R.
See Jameson, Fredric

James VI of Scotland 1566-1625 .... **LC 109**
See also DLB 151, 172

Jami, Nur al-Din 'Abd al-Rahman 1414-1492 .... **LC 9**

Jammes, Francis 1868-1938 .... **TCLC 75**
See also CA 198; EWL 3; GFL 1789 to the Present

Jandl, Ernst 1925-2000 .... **CLC 34**
See also CA 200; EWL 3

Janowitz, Tama 1957- .... **CLC 43, 145**
See also CA 106; CANR 52, 89, 129; CN 5, 6, 7; CPW; DAM POP; DLB 292; MTFW 2005

Jansson, Tove (Marika) 1914-2001 ... **SSC 96**
See also CA 17-20R; 196; CANR 38, 118; CLR 2, 125; CWW 2; DLB 257; EWL 3; MAICYA 1, 2; RGSF 2; SATA 3, 41

Japrisot, Sebastien 1931-
See Rossi, Jean-Baptiste

Jarrell, Randall 1914-1965 .... **CLC 1, 2, 6, 9, 13, 49; PC 41; TCLC 177**
See also AMW; BYA 5; CA 5-8R; 25-28R; CABS 2; CANR 6, 34; CDALB 1941-1968; CLR 6, 111; CWRI 5; DAM POET; DLB 48, 52; EWL 3; EXPP; MAICYA 1, 2; MAL 5; MTCW 1, 2; PAB; PFS 2; RGAL 4; SATA 7

Jarry, Alfred 1873-1907 .... **SSC 20; TCLC 2, 14, 147**
See also CA 104; 153; DA3; DAM DRAM; DFS 8; DLB 192, 258; EW 9; EWL 3; GFL 1789 to the Present; RGWL 2, 3; TWA

Jarvis, E.K.
See Ellison, Harlan; Silverberg, Robert

Jawien, Andrzej
See John Paul II, Pope

Jaynes, Roderick
See Coen, Ethan

Jeake, Samuel, Jr.
See Aiken, Conrad (Potter)

Jean-Louis
See Kerouac, Jack

Jean Paul 1763-1825 .... **NCLC 7**

Jefferies, (John) Richard 1848-1887 .... **NCLC 47**
See also DLB 98, 141; RGEL 2; SATA 16; SFW 4

Jeffers, John Robinson
See Jeffers, Robinson

Jeffers, Robinson 1887-1962 .... **CLC 2, 3, 11, 15, 54; PC 17; WLC 3**
See also AMWS 2; CA 85-88; CANR 35; CDALB 1917-1929; DA; DAC; DAM MST, POET; DLB 45, 212, 342; EWL 3; MAL 5; MTCW 1, 2; MTFW 2005; PAB; PFS 3, 4; RGAL 4

Jefferson, Janet
See Mencken, H(enry) L(ouis)

Jefferson, Thomas 1743-1826 . **NCLC 11, 103**
See also AAYA 54; ANW; CDALB 1640-1865; DA3; DLB 31, 183; LAIT 1; RGAL 4

Jeffrey, Francis 1773-1850 .... **NCLC 33**
See also DLB 107

Jelakowitch, Ivan
  See Heijermans, Herman
Jelinek, Elfriede 1946- .... **CLC 169**
  See also AAYA 68; CA 154; CANR 169;
  DLB 85, 330; FW
Jellicoe, (Patricia) Ann 1927- .... **CLC 27**
  See also CA 85-88; CBD; CD 5, 6; CWD;
  CWRI 5; DLB 13, 233; FW
Jelloun, Tahar ben
  See Ben Jelloun, Tahar
Jemyma
  See Holley, Marietta
Jen, Gish
  See Jen, Lillian
Jen, Lillian 1955- .... **AAL; CLC 70, 198, 260**
  See also AMWC 2; CA 135; CANR 89,
  130; CN 7; DLB 312
Jenkins, (John) Robin 1912- .... **CLC 52**
  See also CA 1-4R; CANR 1, 135; CN 1, 2,
  3, 4, 5, 6, 7; DLB 14, 271
Jennings, Elizabeth (Joan)
  1926-2001 .... **CLC 5, 14, 131**
  See also BRWS 5; CA 61-64; 200; CAAS
  5; CANR 8, 39, 66, 127; CP 1, 2, 3, 4, 5,
  6, 7; CWP; DLB 27; EWL 3; MTCW 1;
  SATA 66
Jennings, Waylon 1937-2002 .... **CLC 21**
Jensen, Johannes V(ilhelm)
  1873-1950 .... **TCLC 41**
  See also CA 170; DLB 214, 330; EWL 3;
  RGWL 3
Jensen, Laura (Linnea) 1948- .... **CLC 37**
  See also CA 103
Jerome, Saint 345-420 .... **CMLC 30**
  See also RGWL 3
Jerome, Jerome K(lapka)
  1859-1927 .... **TCLC 23**
  See also CA 119; 177; DLB 10, 34, 135;
  RGEL 2
Jerrold, Douglas William
  1803-1857 .... **NCLC 2**
  See also DLB 158, 159, 344; RGEL 2
Jewett, (Theodora) Sarah Orne
  1849-1909 . **SSC 6, 44, 110; TCLC 1, 22**
  See also AAYA 76; AMW; AMWC 2;
  AMWR 2; CA 108; 127; CANR 71; DLB
  12, 74, 221; EXPS; FL 1:3; FW; MAL 5;
  MBL; NFS 15; RGAL 4; RGSF 2; SATA
  15; SSFS 4
Jewsbury, Geraldine (Endsor)
  1812-1880 .... **NCLC 22**
  See also DLB 21
Jhabvala, Ruth Prawer 1927- . **CLC 4, 8, 29,**
  94, 138; SSC 91
  See also BRWS 5; CA 1-4R; CANR 2, 29,
  51, 74, 91, 128; CN 1, 2, 3, 4, 5, 6, 7;
  DAB; DAM NOV; DLB 139, 194, 323,
  326; EWL 3; IDFW 3, 4; INT CANR-29;
  MTCW 1, 2; MTFW 2005; RGSF 2;
  RGWL 2; RHW; TEA
Jibran, Kahlil
  See Gibran, Kahlil
Jibran, Khalil
  See Gibran, Kahlil
Jiles, Paulette 1943- .... **CLC 13, 58**
  See also CA 101; CANR 70, 124, 170; CP
  5; CWP
Jimenez (Mantecon), Juan Ramon
  1881-1958 .... **HLC 1; PC 7; TCLC 4,**
  183
  See also CA 104; 131; CANR 74; DAM
  MULT, POET; DLB 134, 330; EW 9;
  EWL 3; HW 1; MTCW 1, 2; MTFW
  2005; RGWL 2, 3
Jimenez, Ramon
  See Jimenez (Mantecon), Juan Ramon
Jimenez Mantecon, Juan
  See Jimenez (Mantecon), Juan Ramon

Jin, Ba 1904-2005 .... **CLC 18**
  See also CA 244; CWW 2; DLB 328; EWL
  3
Jin, Ha
  See Jin, Xuefei
Jin, Xuefei 1956- .... **CLC 109, 262**
  See also CA 152; CANR 91, 130, 184; DLB
  244, 292; MTFW 2005; NFS 25; SSFS 17
Jodelle, Etienne 1532-1573 .... **LC 119**
  See also DLB 327; GFL Beginnings to 1789
Joel, Billy
  See Joel, William Martin
Joel, William Martin 1949- .... **CLC 26**
  See also CA 108
John, St.
  See John of Damascus, St.
John of Damascus, St. c.
  675-749 .... **CMLC 27, 95**
John of Salisbury c. 1115-1180 ..... **CMLC 63**
John of the Cross, St. 1542-1591 .... **LC 18,**
  146
  See also RGWL 2, 3
John Paul II, Pope 1920-2005 .... **CLC 128**
  See also CA 106; 133; 238
Johnson, B(ryan) S(tanley William)
  1933-1973 .... **CLC 6, 9**
  See also CA 9-12R; 53-56; CANR 9; CN 1;
  CP 1, 2; DLB 14, 40; EWL 3; RGEL 2
Johnson, Benjamin F., of Boone
  See Riley, James Whitcomb
Johnson, Charles (Richard) 1948- . **BLC 1:2,**
  2:2; CLC 7, 51, 65, 163
  See also AFAW 2; AMWS 6; BW 2, 3; CA
  116; CAAS 18; CANR 42, 66, 82, 129;
  CN 5, 6, 7; DAM MULT; DLB 33, 278;
  MAL 5; MTCW 2; MTFW 2005; RGAL
  4; SSFS 16
Johnson, Charles S(purgeon)
  1893-1956 .... **HR 1:3**
  See also BW 1, 3; CA 125; CANR 82; DLB
  51, 91
Johnson, Denis 1949- . **CLC 52, 160; SSC 56**
  See also CA 117; 121; CANR 71, 99, 178;
  CN 4, 5, 6, 7; DLB 120
Johnson, Diane 1934- .... **CLC 5, 13, 48, 244**
  See also BPFB 2; CA 41-44R; CANR 17,
  40, 62, 95, 155; CN 4, 5, 6, 7; DLBY
  1980; INT CANR-17; MTCW 1
Johnson, E(mily) Pauline 1861-1913 . **NNAL**
  See also CA 150; CCA 1; DAC; DAM
  MULT; DLB 92, 175; TCWW 2
Johnson, Eyvind (Olof Verner)
  1900-1976 .... **CLC 14**
  See also CA 73-76; 69-72; CANR 34, 101;
  DLB 259, 330; EW 12; EWL 3
Johnson, Fenton 1888-1958 .... **BLC 1:2**
  See also BW 1; CA 118; 124; DAM MULT;
  DLB 45, 50
Johnson, Georgia Douglas (Camp)
  1880-1966 .... **HR 1:3**
  See also BW 1; CA 125; DLB 51, 249; WP
Johnson, Helene 1907-1995 .... **HR 1:3**
  See also CA 181; DLB 51; WP
Johnson, J. R.
  See James, C(yril) L(ionel) R(obert)
Johnson, James Weldon
  1871-1938 .... **BLC 1:2; HR 1:3; PC 24;**
  TCLC 3, 19, 175
  See also AAYA 73; AFAW 1, 2; BW 1, 3;
  CA 104; 125; CANR 82; CDALB 1917-
  1929; CLR 32; DA3; DAM MULT, POET;
  DLB 51; EWL 3; EXPP; LMFS 2; MAL
  5; MTCW 1, 2; MTFW 2005; NFS 22;
  PFS 1; RGAL 4; SATA 31; TUS
Johnson, Joyce 1935- .... **CLC 58**
  See also BG 1:3; CA 125; 129; CANR 102
Johnson, Judith (Emlyn) 1936- .... **CLC 7, 15**
  See also CA 25-28R; 153; CANR 34, 85;
  CP 2, 3, 4, 5, 6, 7; CWP

Johnson, Lionel (Pigot)
  1867-1902 .... **TCLC 19**
  See also CA 117; 209; DLB 19; RGEL 2
Johnson, Marguerite Annie
  See Angelou, Maya
Johnson, Mel
  See Malzberg, Barry N(athaniel)
Johnson, Pamela Hansford
  1912-1981 .... **CLC 1, 7, 27**
  See also CA 1-4R; 104; CANR 2, 28; CN
  1, 2, 3; DLB 15; MTCW 1, 2; MTFW
  2005; RGEL 2
Johnson, Paul 1928- .... **CLC 147**
  See also BEST 89:4; CA 17-20R; CANR
  34, 62, 100, 155
Johnson, Paul Bede
  See Johnson, Paul
Johnson, Robert .... **CLC 70**
Johnson, Robert 1911(?)-1938 .... **TCLC 69**
  See also BW 3; CA 174
Johnson, Samuel 1709-1784 . **LC 15, 52, 128;**
  PC 81; WLC 3
  See also BRW 3; BRWR 1; CDBLB 1660-
  1789; DA; DAB; DAC; DAM MST; DLB
  39, 95, 104, 142, 213; LMFS 1; RGEL 2;
  TEA
Johnson, Stacie
  See Myers, Walter Dean
Johnson, Uwe 1934-1984 .. **CLC 5, 10, 15, 40**
  See also CA 1-4R; 112; CANR 1, 39; CD-
  WLB 2; DLB 75; EWL 3; MTCW 1;
  RGWL 2, 3
Johnston, Basil H. 1929- .... **NNAL**
  See also CA 69-72; CANR 11, 28, 66;
  DAC; DAM MULT; DLB 60
Johnston, George (Benson) 1913- .... **CLC 51**
  See also CA 1-4R; CANR 5, 20; CP 1, 2, 3,
  4, 5, 6, 7; DLB 88
Johnston, Jennifer (Prudence)
  1930- .... **CLC 7, 150, 228**
  See also CA 85-88; CANR 92; CN 4, 5, 6,
  7; DLB 14
Joinville, Jean de 1224(?)-1317 ..... **CMLC 38**
Jolley, Elizabeth 1923-2007 ..... **CLC 46, 256,**
  260; SSC 19
  See also CA 127; 257; CAAS 13; CANR
  59; CN 4, 5, 6, 7; DLB 325; EWL 3;
  RGSF 2
Jolley, Monica Elizabeth
  See Jolley, Elizabeth
Jones, Arthur Llewellyn 1863-1947 . **SSC 20;**
  TCLC 4
  See Machen, Arthur
  See also CA 104; 179; DLB 36; HGG;
  RGEL 2; SUFW 1
Jones, D(ouglas) G(ordon) 1929- ..... **CLC 10**
  See also CA 29-32R; CANR 13, 90; CP 1,
  2, 3, 4, 5, 6, 7; DLB 53
Jones, David (Michael) 1895-1974 .... **CLC 2,**
  4, 7, 13, 42
  See also BRW 6; BRWS 7; CA 9-12R; 53-
  56; CANR 28; CDBLB 1945-1960; CP 1,
  2; DLB 20, 100; EWL 3; MTCW 1; PAB;
  RGEL 2
Jones, David Robert 1947- .... **CLC 17**
  See also CA 103; CANR 104
Jones, Diana Wynne 1934- .... **CLC 26**
  See also AAYA 12; BYA 6, 7, 9, 11, 13, 16;
  CA 49-52; CANR 4, 26, 56, 120, 167;
  CLR 23, 120; DLB 161; FANT; JRDA;
  MAICYA 1, 2; MTFW 2005; SAAS 7;
  SATA 9, 70, 108, 160; SFW 4; SUFW 2;
  YAW
Jones, Edward P. 1950- .. **BLC 2:2; CLC 76,**
  223
  See also AAYA 71; BW 2, 3; CA 142;
  CANR 79, 134; CSW; MTFW 2005; NFS
  26

Jones, Everett LeRoi
See Baraka, Amiri

Jones, Gayl 1949- .. **BLC 1:2; CLC 6, 9, 131, 270**
See also AFAW 1, 2; BW 2, 3; CA 77-80; CANR 27, 66, 122; CN 4, 5, 6, 7; CSW; DA3; DAM MULT; DLB 33, 278; MAL 5; MTCW 1, 2; MTFW 2005; RGAL 4

Jones, James 1921-1977 ...... **CLC 1, 3, 10, 39**
See also AITN 1, 2; AMWS 11; BPFB 2; CA 1-4R; 69-72; CANR 6; CN 1, 2; DLB 2, 143; DLBD 17; DLBY 1998; EWL 3; MAL 5; MTCW 1; RGAL 4

Jones, John J.
See Lovecraft, H. P.

Jones, LeRoi
See Baraka, Amiri

Jones, Louis B. 1953- .... **CLC 65**
See also CA 141; CANR 73

Jones, Madison 1925- .... **CLC 4**
See also CA 13-16R; CAAS 11; CANR 7, 54, 83, 158; CN 1, 2, 3, 4, 5, 6, 7; CSW; DLB 152

Jones, Madison Percy, Jr.
See Jones, Madison

Jones, Mervyn 1922- .... **CLC 10, 52**
See also CA 45-48; CAAS 5; CANR 1, 91; CN 1, 2, 3, 4, 5, 6, 7; MTCW 1

Jones, Mick 1956(?)- .... **CLC 30**

Jones, Nettie (Pearl) 1941- .... **CLC 34**
See also BW 2; CA 137; CAAS 20; CANR 88

Jones, Peter 1802-1856 .... **NNAL**

Jones, Preston 1936-1979 .... **CLC 10**
See also CA 73-76; 89-92; DLB 7

Jones, Robert F(rancis) 1934-2003 .... **CLC 7**
See also CA 49-52; CANR 2, 61, 118

Jones, Rod 1953- .... **CLC 50**
See also CA 128

Jones, Terence Graham Parry
1942- .... **CLC 21**
See also CA 112; 116; CANR 35, 93, 173; INT CA-116; SATA 67, 127; SATA-Brief 51

Jones, Terry
See Jones, Terence Graham Parry

Jones, Thom (Douglas) 1945(?)- ..... **CLC 81; SSC 56**
See also CA 157; CANR 88; DLB 244; SSFS 23

Jong, Erica 1942- .... **CLC 4, 6, 8, 18, 83**
See also AITN 1; AMWS 5; BEST 90:2; BPFB 2; CA 73-76; CANR 26, 52, 75, 132, 166; CN 3, 4, 5, 6, 7; CP 2, 3, 4, 5, 6, 7; CPW; DA3; DAM NOV, POP; DLB 2, 5, 28, 152; FW; INT CANR-26; MAL 5; MTCW 1, 2; MTFW 2005

Jonson, Ben(jamin) 1572(?)-1637 . **DC 4; LC 6, 33, 110, 158; PC 17; WLC 3**
See also BRW 1; BRWC 1; BRWR 1; CD-BLB Before 1660; DA; DAB; DAC; DAM DRAM, MST, POET; DFS 4, 10; DLB 62, 121; LMFS 1; PFS 23; RGEL 2; TEA; WLIT 3

Jordan, June 1936-2002 .. **BLCS; CLC 5, 11, 23, 114, 230; PC 38**
See also AAYA 2, 66; AFAW 1, 2; BW 2, 3; CA 33-36R; 206; CANR 25, 70, 114, 154; CLR 10; CP 3, 4, 5, 6, 7; CWP; DAM MULT, POET; DLB 38; GLL 2; LAIT 5; MAICYA 1, 2; MTCW 1; SATA 4, 136; YAW

Jordan, June Meyer
See Jordan, June

Jordan, Neil 1950- .... **CLC 110**
See also CA 124; 130; CANR 54, 154; CN 4, 5, 6, 7; GLL 2; INT CA-130

Jordan, Neil Patrick
See Jordan, Neil

Jordan, Pat(rick M.) 1941- .... **CLC 37**
See also CA 33-36R; CANR 121

Jorgensen, Ivar
See Ellison, Harlan

Jorgenson, Ivar
See Silverberg, Robert

Joseph, George Ghevarughese .... **CLC 70**

Josephson, Mary
See O'Doherty, Brian

Josephus, Flavius c. 37-100 ..... **CMLC 13, 93**
See also AW 2; DLB 176; WLIT 8

Josh
See Twain, Mark

Josiah Allen's Wife
See Holley, Marietta

Josipovici, Gabriel 1940- ...... **CLC 6, 43, 153**
See also CA 37-40R; 224; CAAE 224; CAAS 8; CANR 47, 84; CN 3, 4, 5, 6, 7; DLB 14, 319

Josipovici, Gabriel David
See Josipovici, Gabriel

Joubert, Joseph 1754-1824 .... **NCLC 9**

Jouve, Pierre Jean 1887-1976 .... **CLC 47**
See also CA 252; 65-68; DLB 258; EWL 3

Jovine, Francesco 1902-1950 .... **TCLC 79**
See also DLB 264; EWL 3

Joyaux, Julia
See Kristeva, Julia

Joyce, James (Augustine Aloysius)
1882-1941 .... **DC 16; PC 22; SSC 3, 26, 44, 64, 118, 122; TCLC 3, 8, 16, 35, 52, 159; WLC 3**
See also AAYA 42; BRW 7; BRWC 1; BRWR 1; BYA 11, 13; CA 104; 126; CD-BLB 1914-1945; DA; DA3; DAB; DAC; DAM MST, NOV; DLB 10, 19, 36, 162, 247; EWL 3; EXPN; EXPS; LAIT 3; LMFS 1, 2; MTCW 1, 2; MTFW 2005; NFS 7, 26; RGSF 2; SSFS 1, 19; TEA; WLIT 4

Jozsef, Attila 1905-1937 .... **TCLC 22**
See also CA 116; 230; CDWLB 4; DLB 215; EWL 3

Juana Ines de la Cruz, Sor
1651(?)-1695 ... **HLCS 1; LC 5, 136; PC 24**
See also DLB 305; FW; LAW; RGWL 2, 3; WLIT 1

Juana Inez de La Cruz, Sor
See Juana Ines de la Cruz, Sor

Juan Manuel, Don 1282-1348 .... **CMLC 88**

Judd, Cyril
See Kornbluth, C(yril) M.; Pohl, Frederik

Juenger, Ernst 1895-1998 .... **CLC 125**
See also CA 101; 167; CANR 21, 47, 106; CDWLB 2; DLB 56; EWL 3; RGWL 2, 3

Julian of Norwich 1342(?)-1416(?) . **LC 6, 52**
See also BRWS 1; DLB 146; LMFS 1

Julius Caesar 100B.C.-44B.C. .... **CMLC 47**
See also AW 1; CDWLB 1; DLB 211; RGWL 2, 3; WLIT 8

Jung, Patricia B.
See Hope, Christopher

Junger, Ernst
See Juenger, Ernst

Junger, Sebastian 1962- .... **CLC 109**
See also AAYA 28; CA 165; CANR 130, 171; MTFW 2005

Juniper, Alex
See Hospital, Janette Turner

Junius
See Luxemburg, Rosa

Junzaburo, Nishiwaki
See Nishiwaki, Junzaburo

Just, Ward 1935- .... **CLC 4, 27**
See also CA 25-28R; CANR 32, 87; CN 6, 7; DLB 335; INT CANR-32

Just, Ward Swift
See Just, Ward

Justice, Donald 1925-2004 ... **CLC 6, 19, 102; PC 64**
See also AMWS 7; CA 5-8R; 230; CANR 26, 54, 74, 121, 122, 169; CP 1, 2, 3, 4, 5, 6, 7; CSW; DAM POET; DLBY 1983; EWL 3; INT CANR-26; MAL 5; MTCW 2; PFS 14; TCLE 1:1

Justice, Donald Rodney
See Justice, Donald

Juvenal c. 60-c. 130 .... **CMLC 8**
See also AW 2; CDWLB 1; DLB 211; RGWL 2, 3; WLIT 8

Juvenis
See Bourne, Randolph S(illiman)

K., Alice
See Knapp, Caroline

Kabakov, Sasha .... **CLC 59**

Kabir 1398(?)-1448(?) .... **LC 109; PC 56**
See also RGWL 2, 3

Kacew, Romain 1914-1980 .... **CLC 25**
See also CA 108; 102; DLB 83, 299; RGHL

Kacew, Roman
See Kacew, Romain

Kadare, Ismail 1936- .... **CLC 52, 190**
See also CA 161; CANR 165; EWL 3; RGWL 3

Kadohata, Cynthia 1956(?)- ..... **CLC 59, 122**
See also AAYA 71; CA 140; CANR 124; CLR 121; SATA 155, 180

Kafka, Franz 1883-1924 ... **SSC 5, 29, 35, 60; TCLC 2, 6, 13, 29, 47, 53, 112, 179; WLC 3**
See also AAYA 31; BPFB 2; CA 105; 126; CDWLB 2; DA; DA3; DAB; DAC; DAM MST, NOV; DLB 81; EW 9; EWL 3; EXPS; LATS 1:1; LMFS 2; MTCW 1, 2; MTFW 2005; NFS 7; RGSF 2; RGWL 2, 3; SFW 4; SSFS 3, 7, 12; TWA

Kafu
See Nagai, Kafu

Kahanovitch, Pinchas
See Der Nister

Kahanovitsch, Pinkhes
See Der Nister

Kahanovitsh, Pinkhes
See Der Nister

Kahn, Roger 1927- .... **CLC 30**
See also CA 25-28R; CANR 44, 69, 152; DLB 171; SATA 37

Kain, Saul
See Sassoon, Siegfried (Lorraine)

Kaiser, Georg 1878-1945 .... **TCLC 9, 220**
See also CA 106; 190; CDWLB 2; DLB 124; EWL 3; LMFS 2; RGWL 2, 3

Kaledin, Sergei .... **CLC 59**

Kaletski, Alexander 1946- .... **CLC 39**
See also CA 118; 143

Kalidasa fl. c. 400-455 .... **CMLC 9; PC 22**
See also RGWL 2, 3

Kallman, Chester (Simon)
1921-1975 .... **CLC 2**
See also CA 45-48; 53-56; CANR 3; CP 1, 2

Kaminsky, Melvin .... **CLC 12, 217**
See Brooks, Mel
See also AAYA 13, 48; DLB 26

Kaminsky, Stuart M. 1934- .... **CLC 59**
See also CA 73-76; CANR 29, 53, 89, 161; CMW 4

Kaminsky, Stuart Melvin
See Kaminsky, Stuart M.

Kamo no Chomei 1153(?)-1216 .... **CMLC 66**
See also DLB 203

Kamo no Nagaakira
See Kamo no Chomei

Kandinsky, Wassily 1866-1944 .... **TCLC 92**
See also AAYA 64; CA 118; 155

Kane, Francis
See Robbins, Harold

Kane, Paul
See Simon, Paul

Kane, Sarah 1971-1999 .... **DC 31**
See also BRWS 8; CA 190; CD 5, 6; DLB 310

Kanin, Garson 1912-1999 .... **CLC 22**
See also CA 61-64; 73-76; CANR 60, 63; CN 1, 2; DLB 9, 102; MAL 5; MTCW 2; RHW; TCWW 1, 2

Kanze Motokiyo
See Zeami

Kaplan, David Michael 1946- .... **CLC 50**
See also CA 187

Kaplan, James 1951- .... **CLC 59**
See also CA 135; CANR 121

Karadzic, Vuk Stefanovic
1787-1864 .... **NCLC 115**
See also CDWLB 4; DLB 147

Karageorge, Michael
See Anderson, Poul

Karamzin, Nikolai Mikhailovich
1766-1826 .... **NCLC 3, 173**
See also DLB 150; RGSF 2

Karapanou, Margarita 1946- .... **CLC 13**
See also CA 101

Karinthy, Frigyes 1887-1938 .... **TCLC 47**
See also CA 170; DLB 215; EWL 3

Karl, Frederick R(obert)
1927-2004 .... **CLC 34**
See also CA 5-8R; 226; CANR 3, 44, 143

Karr, Mary 1955- .... **CLC 188**
See also AMWS 11; CA 151; CANR 100; MTFW 2005; NCFS 5

Kastel, Warren
See Silverberg, Robert

Kataev, Evgeny Petrovich
1903-1942 .... **TCLC 21**
See also CA 120; DLB 272

Kataphusin
See Ruskin, John

Katz, Steve 1935- .... **CLC 47**
See also CA 25-28R; CAAS 14, 64; CANR 12; CN 4, 5, 6, 7; DLBY 1983

Kauffman, Janet 1945- .... **CLC 42**
See also CA 117; CANR 43, 84; DLB 218; DLBY 1986

Kaufman, Bob (Garnell)
1925-1986 .... **CLC 49; PC 74**
See also BG 1:3; BW 1; CA 41-44R; 118; CANR 22; CP 1; DLB 16, 41

Kaufman, George S. 1889-1961 ...... **CLC 38; DC 17**
See also CA 108; 93-96; DAM DRAM; DFS 1, 10; DLB 7; INT CA-108; MTCW 2; MTFW 2005; RGAL 4; TUS

Kaufman, Moises 1964- .... **DC 26**
See also CA 211; DFS 22; MTFW 2005

Kaufman, Sue
See Barondess, Sue K(aufman)

Kavafis, Konstantinos Petrou
1863-1933 .... **PC 36; TCLC 2, 7**
See also CA 104; 148; DA3; DAM POET; EW 8; EWL 3; MTCW 2; PFS 19; RGWL 2, 3; WP

Kavan, Anna 1901-1968 .... **CLC 5, 13, 82**
See also BRWS 7; CA 5-8R; CANR 6, 57; DLB 255; MTCW 1; RGEL 2; SFW 4

Kavanagh, Dan
See Barnes, Julian

Kavanagh, Julie 1952- .... **CLC 119**
See also CA 163; CANR 186

Kavanagh, Patrick (Joseph)
1904-1967 .... **CLC 22; PC 33**
See also BRWS 7; CA 123; 25-28R; DLB 15, 20; EWL 3; MTCW 1; RGEL 2

Kawabata, Yasunari 1899-1972 ..... **CLC 2, 5, 9, 18, 107; SSC 17**
See also CA 93-96; 33-36R; CANR 88; DAM MULT; DLB 180, 330; EWL 3; MJW; MTCW 2; MTFW 2005; RGSF 2; RGWL 2, 3

Kawabata Yasunari
See Kawabata, Yasunari

Kaye, Mary Margaret
See Kaye, M.M.

Kaye, M.M. 1908-2004 .... **CLC 28**
See also CA 89-92; 223; CANR 24, 60, 102, 142; MTCW 1, 2; MTFW 2005; RHW; SATA 62; SATA-Obit 152

Kaye, Mollie
See Kaye, M.M.

Kaye-Smith, Sheila 1887-1956 .... **TCLC 20**
See also CA 118; 203; DLB 36

Kaymor, Patrice Maguilene
See Senghor, Leopold Sedar

Kazakov, Iurii Pavlovich
See Kazakov, Yuri Pavlovich

Kazakov, Yuri Pavlovich 1927-1982 . **SSC 43**
See also CA 5-8R; CANR 36; DLB 302; EWL 3; MTCW 1; RGSF 2

Kazakov, Yury
See Kazakov, Yuri Pavlovich

Kazan, Elia 1909-2003 .... **CLC 6, 16, 63**
See also CA 21-24R; 220; CANR 32, 78

Kazantzakis, Nikos 1883(?)-1957 .... **TCLC 2, 5, 33, 181**
See also BPFB 2; CA 105; 132; DA3; EW 9; EWL 3; MTCW 1, 2; MTFW 2005; RGWL 2, 3

Kazin, Alfred 1915-1998 ..... **CLC 34, 38, 119**
See also AMWS 8; CA 1-4R; CAAS 7; CANR 1, 45, 79; DLB 67; EWL 3

Keane, Mary Nesta (Skrine)
1904-1996 .... **CLC 31**
See also CA 108; 114; 151; CN 5, 6; INT CA-114; RHW; TCLE 1:1

Keane, Molly
See Keane, Mary Nesta (Skrine)

Keates, Jonathan 1946(?)- .... **CLC 34**
See also CA 163; CANR 126

Keaton, Buster 1895-1966 .... **CLC 20**
See also AAYA 79; CA 194

Keats, John 1795-1821 ...... **NCLC 8, 73, 121; PC 1, 96; WLC 3**
See also AAYA 58; BRW 4; BRWR 1; CD-BLB 1789-1832; DA; DA3; DAB; DAC; DAM MST, POET; DLB 96, 110; EXPP; LMFS 1; PAB; PFS 1, 2, 3, 9, 17; RGEL 2; TEA; WLIT 3; WP

Keble, John 1792-1866 .... **NCLC 87**
See also DLB 32, 55; RGEL 2

Keene, Donald 1922- .... **CLC 34**
See also CA 1-4R; CANR 5, 119

Keillor, Garrison 1942- ...... **CLC 40, 115, 222**
See also AAYA 2, 62; AMWS 16; BEST 89:3; BPFB 2; CA 111; 117; CANR 36, 59, 124, 180; CPW; DA3; DAM POP; DLBY 1987; EWL 3; MTCW 1, 2; MTFW 2005; SATA 58; TUS

Keith, Carlos
See Lewton, Val

Keith, Michael
See Hubbard, L. Ron

Kell, Joseph
See Burgess, Anthony

Keller, Gottfried 1819-1890 .... **NCLC 2; SSC 26, 107**
See also CDWLB 2; DLB 129; EW; RGSF 2; RGWL 2, 3

Keller, Nora Okja 1965- .... **CLC 109**
See also CA 187

Kellerman, Jonathan 1949- .... **CLC 44**
See also AAYA 35; BEST 90:1; CA 106; CANR 29, 51, 150, 183; CMW 4; CPW; DA3; DAM POP; INT CANR-29

Kelley, William Melvin 1937- .... **BLC 2:2; CLC 22**
See also BW 1; CA 77-80; CANR 27, 83; CN 1, 2, 3, 4, 5, 6, 7; DLB 33; EWL 3

Kellock, Archibald P.
See Mavor, Osborne Henry

Kellogg, Marjorie 1922-2005 .... **CLC 2**
See also CA 81-84; 246

Kellow, Kathleen
See Hibbert, Eleanor Alice Burford

Kelly, Lauren
See Oates, Joyce Carol

Kelly, M(ilton) T(errence) 1947- ...... **CLC 55**
See also CA 97-100; CAAS 22; CANR 19, 43, 84; CN 6

Kelly, Robert 1935- .... **SSC 50**
See also CA 17-20R; CAAS 19; CANR 47; CP 1, 2, 3, 4, 5, 6, 7; DLB 5, 130, 165

Kelman, James 1946- .... **CLC 58, 86**
See also BRWS 5; CA 148; CANR 85, 130; CN 5, 6, 7; DLB 194, 319, 326; RGSF 2; WLIT 4

Kemal, Yasar
See Kemal, Yashar

Kemal, Yashar 1923(?)- .... **CLC 14, 29**
See also CA 89-92; CANR 44; CWW 2; EWL 3; WLIT 6

Kemble, Fanny 1809-1893 .... **NCLC 18**
See also DLB 32

Kemelman, Harry 1908-1996 .... **CLC 2**
See also AITN 1; BPFB 2; CA 9-12R; 155; CANR 6, 71; CMW 4; DLB 28

Kempe, Margery 1373(?)-1440(?) ... **LC 6, 56**
See also BRWS 12; DLB 146; FL 1:1; RGEL 2

Kempis, Thomas a 1380-1471 .... **LC 11**

Kenan, Randall (G.) 1963- .... **BLC 2:2**
See also BW 2, 3; CA 142; CANR 86; CN 7; CSW; DLB 292; GLL 1

Kendall, Henry 1839-1882 .... **NCLC 12**
See also DLB 230

Keneally, Thomas 1935- .... **CLC 5, 8, 10, 14, 19, 27, 43, 117**
See also BRWS 4; CA 85-88; CANR 10, 50, 74, 130, 165; CN 1, 2, 3, 4, 5, 6, 7; CPW; DA3; DAM NOV; DLB 289, 299, 326; EWL 3; MTCW 1, 2; MTFW 2005; NFS 17; RGEL 2; RGHL

Keneally, Thomas Michael
See Keneally, Thomas

Kennedy, A. L. 1965- .... **CLC 188**
See also CA 168, 213; CAAE 213; CANR 108; CD 5, 6; CN 6, 7; DLB 271; RGSF 2

Kennedy, Adrienne (Lita) 1931- .... **BLC 1:2; CLC 66; DC 5**
See also AFAW 2; BW 2, 3; CA 103; CAAS 20; CABS 3; CAD; CANR 26, 53, 82; CD 5, 6; DAM MULT; DFS 9; DLB 38, 341; FW; MAL 5

Kennedy, Alison Louise
See Kennedy, A. L.

Kennedy, John Pendleton
1795-1870 .... **NCLC 2**
See also DLB 3, 248, 254; RGAL 4

CANR-34; MAL 5; MTCW 1, 2; MTFW 2005; PAB; PFS 9, 26; RGAL 4; TCLE 1:1; WP

Kinsella, Thomas 1928- .... **CLC 4, 19, 138, 274; PC 69**
See also BRWS 5; CA 17-20R; CANR 15, 122; CP 1, 2, 3, 4, 5, 6, 7; DLB 27; EWL 3; MTCW 1, 2; MTFW 2005; RGEL 2; TEA

Kinsella, W.P. 1935- .... **CLC 27, 43, 166**
See also AAYA 7, 60; BPFB 2; CA 97-100, 222; CAAE 222; CAAS 7; CANR 21, 35, 66, 75, 129; CN 4, 5, 6, 7; CPW; DAC; DAM NOV, POP; FANT; INT CANR-21; LAIT 5; MTCW 1, 2; MTFW 2005; NFS 15; RGSF 2

Kinsey, Alfred C(harles)
1894-1956 .... **TCLC 91**
See also CA 115; 170; MTCW 2

Kipling, (Joseph) Rudyard 1865-1936 . **PC 3, 91; SSC 5, 54, 110; TCLC 8, 17, 167; WLC 3**
See also AAYA 32; BRW 6; BRWC 1, 2; BYA 4; CA 105; 120; CANR 33; CDBLB 1890-1914; CLR 39, 65; CWRI 5; DA; DA3; DAB; DAC; DAM MST, POET; DLB 19, 34, 141, 156, 330; EWL 3; EXPS; FANT; LAIT 3; LMFS 1; MAICYA 1, 2; MTCW 1, 2; MTFW 2005; NFS 21; PFS 22; RGEL 2; RGSF 2; SATA 100; SFW 4; SSFS 8, 21, 22; SUFW 1; TEA; WCH; WLIT 4; YABC 2

Kircher, Athanasius 1602-1680 .... **LC 121**
See also DLB 164

Kirk, Russell (Amos) 1918-1994 .. **TCLC 119**
See also AITN 1; CA 1-4R; 145; CAAS 9; CANR 1, 20, 60; HGG; INT CANR-20; MTCW 1, 2

Kirkham, Dinah
See Card, Orson Scott

Kirkland, Caroline M. 1801-1864 . **NCLC 85**
See also DLB 3, 73, 74, 250, 254; DLBD 13

Kirkup, James 1918- .... **CLC 1**
See also CA 1-4R; CAAS 4; CANR 2; CP 1, 2, 3, 4, 5, 6, 7; DLB 27; SATA 12

Kirkwood, James 1930(?)-1989 .... **CLC 9**
See also AITN 2; CA 1-4R; 128; CANR 6, 40; GLL 2

Kirsch, Sarah 1935- .... **CLC 176**
See also CA 178; CWW 2; DLB 75; EWL 3

Kirshner, Sidney
See Kingsley, Sidney

Kis, Danilo 1935-1989 .... **CLC 57**
See also CA 109; 118; 129; CANR 61; CD-WLB 4; DLB 181; EWL 3; MTCW 1; RGSF 2; RGWL 2, 3

Kissinger, Henry A(lfred) 1923- ..... **CLC 137**
See also CA 1-4R; CANR 2, 33, 66, 109; MTCW 1

Kittel, Frederick August
See Wilson, August

Kivi, Aleksis 1834-1872 .... **NCLC 30**

Kizer, Carolyn 1925- ..... **CLC 15, 39, 80; PC 66**
See also CA 65-68; CAAS 5; CANR 24, 70, 134; CP 1, 2, 3, 4, 5, 6, 7; CWP; DAM POET; DLB 5, 169; EWL 3; MAL 5; MTCW 2; MTFW 2005; PFS 18; TCLE 1:1

Klabund 1890-1928 .... **TCLC 44**
See also CA 162; DLB 66

Klappert, Peter 1942- .... **CLC 57**
See also CA 33-36R; CSW; DLB 5

Klausner, Amos
See Oz, Amos

Klein, A(braham) M(oses)
1909-1972 .... **CLC 19**
See also CA 101; 37-40R; CP 1; DAB; DAC; DAM MST; DLB 68; EWL 3; RGEL 2; RGHL

Klein, Joe
See Klein, Joseph

Klein, Joseph 1946- .... **CLC 154**
See also CA 85-88; CANR 55, 164

Klein, Norma 1938-1989 .... **CLC 30**
See also AAYA 2, 35; BPFB 2; BYA 6, 7, 8; CA 41-44R; 128; CANR 15, 37; CLR 2, 19; INT CANR-15; JRDA; MAICYA 1, 2; SAAS 1; SATA 7, 57; WYA; YAW

Klein, T.E.D. 1947- .... **CLC 34**
See also CA 119; CANR 44, 75, 167; HGG

Klein, Theodore Eibon Donald
See Klein, T.E.D.

Kleist, Heinrich von 1777-1811 .... **DC 29; NCLC 2, 37; SSC 22**
See also CDWLB 2; DAM DRAM; DLB 90; EW 5; RGSF 2; RGWL 2, 3

Klima, Ivan 1931- .... **CLC 56, 172**
See also CA 25-28R; CANR 17, 50, 91; CDWLB 4; CWW 2; DAM NOV; DLB 232; EWL 3; RGWL 3

Klimentev, Andrei Platonovich
See Klimentov, Andrei Platonovich

Klimentov, Andrei Platonovich
1899-1951 .... **SSC 42; TCLC 14**
See also CA 108; 232; DLB 272; EWL 3

Klinger, Friedrich Maximilian von
1752-1831 .... **NCLC 1**
See also DLB 94

Klingsor the Magician
See Hartmann, Sadakichi

Klopstock, Friedrich Gottlieb
1724-1803 .... **NCLC 11**
See also DLB 97; EW 4; RGWL 2, 3

Kluge, Alexander 1932- .... **SSC 61**
See also CA 81-84; CANR 163; DLB 75

Knapp, Caroline 1959-2002 .... **CLC 99**
See also CA 154; 207

Knebel, Fletcher 1911-1993 .... **CLC 14**
See also AITN 1; CA 1-4R; 140; CAAS 3; CANR 1, 36; CN 1, 2, 3, 4, 5; SATA 36; SATA-Obit 75

Knickerbocker, Diedrich
See Irving, Washington

Knight, Etheridge 1931-1991 .... **BLC 1:2; CLC 40; PC 14**
See also BW 1, 3; CA 21-24R; 133; CANR 23, 82; CP 1, 2, 3, 4, 5; DAM POET; DLB 41; MTCW 2; MTFW 2005; RGAL 4; TCLE 1:1

Knight, Sarah Kemble 1666-1727 .... **LC 7**
See also DLB 24, 200

Knister, Raymond 1899-1932 .... **TCLC 56**
See also CA 186; DLB 68; RGEL 2

Knowles, John 1926-2001 ... **CLC 1, 4, 10, 26**
See also AAYA 10, 72; AMWS 12; BPFB 2; BYA 3; CA 17-20R; 203; CANR 40, 74, 76, 132; CDALB 1968-1988; CLR 98; CN 1, 2, 3, 4, 5, 6, 7; DA; DAC; DAM MST, NOV; DLB 6; EXPN; MTCW 1, 2; MTFW 2005; NFS 2; RGAL 4; SATA 8, 89; SATA-Obit 134; YAW

Knox, Calvin M.
See Silverberg, Robert

Knox, John c. 1505-1572 .... **LC 37**
See also DLB 132

Knye, Cassandra
See Disch, Thomas M.

Koch, C(hristopher) J(ohn) 1932- .... **CLC 42**
See also CA 127; CANR 84; CN 3, 4, 5, 6, 7; DLB 289

Koch, Christopher
See Koch, C(hristopher) J(ohn)

Koch, Kenneth 1925-2002 .... **CLC 5, 8, 44; PC 80**
See also AMWS 15; CA 1-4R; 207; CAD; CANR 6, 36, 57, 97, 131; CD 5, 6; CP 1, 2, 3, 4, 5, 6, 7; DAM POET; DLB 5; INT CANR-36; MAL 5; MTCW 2; MTFW 2005; PFS 20; SATA 65; WP

Kochanowski, Jan 1530-1584 .... **LC 10**
See also RGWL 2, 3

Kock, Charles Paul de 1794-1871 . **NCLC 16**

Koda Rohan
See Koda Shigeyuki

Koda Rohan
See Koda Shigeyuki

Koda Shigeyuki 1867-1947 .... **TCLC 22**
See also CA 121; 183; DLB 180

Koestler, Arthur 1905-1983 ... **CLC 1, 3, 6, 8, 15, 33**
See also BRWS 1; CA 1-4R; 109; CANR 1, 33; CDBLB 1945-1960; CN 1, 2, 3; DLBY 1983; EWL 3; MTCW 1, 2; MTFW 2005; NFS 19; RGEL 2

Kogawa, Joy Nozomi 1935- ..... **CLC 78, 129, 262, 268**
See also AAYA 47; CA 101; CANR 19, 62, 126; CN 6, 7; CP 1; CWP; DAC; DAM MST, MULT; DLB 334; FW; MTCW 2; MTFW 2005; NFS 3; SATA 99

Kohout, Pavel 1928- .... **CLC 13**
See also CA 45-48; CANR 3

Koizumi, Yakumo
See Hearn, (Patricio) Lafcadio (Tessima Carlos)

Kolmar, Gertrud 1894-1943 .... **TCLC 40**
See also CA 167; EWL 3; RGHL

Komunyakaa, Yusef 1947- . **BLC 2:2; BLCS; CLC 86, 94, 207; PC 51**
See also AFAW 2; AMWS 13; CA 147; CANR 83, 164; CP 6, 7; CSW; DLB 120; EWL 3; PFS 5, 20, 30; RGAL 4

Konigsberg, Alan Stewart
See Allen, Woody

Konrad, George
See Konrad, Gyorgy

Konrad, George
See Konrad, Gyorgy

Konrad, Gyorgy 1933- .... **CLC 4, 10, 73**
See also CA 85-88; CANR 97, 171; CD-WLB 4; CWW 2; DLB 232; EWL 3

Konwicki, Tadeusz 1926- .... **CLC 8, 28, 54, 117**
See also CA 101; CAAS 9; CANR 39, 59; CWW 2; DLB 232; EWL 3; IDFW 3; MTCW 1

Koontz, Dean
See Koontz, Dean R.

Koontz, Dean R. 1945- .... **CLC 78, 206**
See also AAYA 9, 31; BEST 89:3, 90:2; CA 108; CANR 19, 36, 52, 95, 138, 176; CMW 4; CPW; DA3; DAM NOV, POP; DLB 292; HGG; MTCW 1; MTFW 2005; SATA 92, 165; SFW 4; SUFW 2; YAW

Koontz, Dean Ray
See Koontz, Dean R.

Kopernik, Mikolaj
See Copernicus, Nicolaus

Kopit, Arthur (Lee) 1937- ...... **CLC 1, 18, 33**
See also AITN 1; CA 81-84; CABS 3; CAD; CD 5, 6; DAM DRAM; DFS 7, 14, 24; DLB 7; MAL 5; MTCW 1; RGAL 4

Kopitar, Jernej (Bartholomaus)
1780-1844 .... **NCLC 117**

Kops, Bernard 1926- .... **CLC 4**
See also CA 5-8R; CANR 84, 159; CBD; CN 1, 2, 3, 4, 5, 6, 7; CP 1, 2, 3, 4, 5, 6, 7; DLB 13; RGHL

Kornbluth, C(yril) M. 1923-1958 .... **TCLC 8**
See also CA 105; 160; DLB 8; SCFW 1, 2; SFW 4

La Fontaine, Jean de 1621-1695 .... **LC 50**
See also DLB 268; EW 3; GFL Beginnings to 1789; MAICYA 1, 2; RGWL 2, 3; SATA 18

LaForet, Carmen 1921-2004 .... **CLC 219**
See also CA 246; CWW 2; DLB 322; EWL 3

LaForet Diaz, Carmen
See LaForet, Carmen

Laforgue, Jules 1860-1887 . **NCLC 5, 53; PC 14; SSC 20**
See also DLB 217; EW 7; GFL 1789 to the Present; RGWL 2, 3

Lagerkvist, Paer (Fabian) 1891-1974 .. **CLC 7, 10, 13, 54; SSC 12; TCLC 144**
See also CA 85-88; 49-52; DA3; DAM DRAM, NOV; DLB 259, 331; EW 10; EWL 3; MTCW 1, 2; MTFW 2005; RGSF 2; RGWL 2, 3; TWA

Lagerkvist, Par
See Lagerkvist, Paer (Fabian)

Lagerloef, Selma (Ottiliana Lovisa)
See Lagerlof, Selma (Ottiliana Lovisa)

Lagerlof, Selma (Ottiliana Lovisa) 1858-1940 .... **TCLC 4, 36**
See also CA 108; 188; CLR 7; DLB 259, 331; MTCW 2; RGWL 2, 3; SATA 15; SSFS 18

La Guma, Alex 1925-1985 .. **BLCS; CLC 19; TCLC 140**
See also AFW; BW 1, 3; CA 49-52; 118; CANR 25, 81; CDWLB 3; CN 1, 2, 3; CP 1; DAM NOV; DLB 117, 225; EWL 3; MTCW 1, 2; MTFW 2005; WLIT 2; WWE 1

Lahiri, Jhumpa 1967- .... **SSC 96**
See also AAYA 56; CA 193; CANR 134, 184; DLB 323; MTFW 2005; SSFS 19, 27

Laidlaw, A. K.
See Grieve, C(hristopher) M(urray)

Lainez, Manuel Mujica
See Mujica Lainez, Manuel

Laing, R(onald) D(avid) 1927-1989 . **CLC 95**
See also CA 107; 129; CANR 34; MTCW 1

Laishley, Alex
See Booth, Martin

Lamartine, Alphonse (Marie Louis Prat) de 1790-1869 .... **NCLC 11, 190; PC 16**
See also DAM POET; DLB 217; GFL 1789 to the Present; RGWL 2, 3

Lamb, Charles 1775-1834 ..... **NCLC 10, 113; SSC 112; WLC 3**
See also BRW 4; CDBLB 1789-1832; DA; DAB; DAC; DAM MST; DLB 93, 107, 163; RGEL 2; SATA 17; TEA

Lamb, Lady Caroline 1785-1828 ... **NCLC 38**
See also DLB 116

Lamb, Mary Ann 1764-1847 ...... **NCLC 125; SSC 112**
See also DLB 163; SATA 17

Lame Deer 1903(?)-1976 .... **NNAL**
See also CA 69-72

Lamming, George (William) 1927- . **BLC 1:2, 2:2; CLC 2, 4, 66, 144**
See also BW 2, 3; CA 85-88; CANR 26, 76; CDWLB 3; CN 1, 2, 3, 4, 5, 6, 7; CP 1; DAM MULT; DLB 125; EWL 3; MTCW 1, 2; MTFW 2005; NFS 15; RGEL 2

L'Amour, Louis 1908-1988 .... **CLC 25, 55**
See also AAYA 16; AITN 2; BEST 89:2; BPFB 2; CA 1-4R; 125; CANR 3, 25, 40; CPW; DA3; DAM NOV, POP; DLB 206; DLBY 1980; MTCW 1, 2; MTFW 2005; RGAL 4; TCWW 1, 2

Lampedusa, Giuseppe (Tomasi) di
See Tomasi di Lampedusa, Giuseppe

Lampman, Archibald 1861-1899 .. **NCLC 25, 194**
See also DLB 92; RGEL 2; TWA

Lancaster, Bruce 1896-1963 .... **CLC 36**
See also CA 9-10; CANR 70; CAP 1; SATA 9

Lanchester, John 1962- .... **CLC 99**
See also CA 194; DLB 267

Landau, Mark Alexandrovich
See Aldanov, Mark (Alexandrovich)

Landau-Aldanov, Mark Alexandrovich
See Aldanov, Mark (Alexandrovich)

Landis, Jerry
See Simon, Paul

Landis, John 1950- .... **CLC 26**
See also CA 112; 122; CANR 128

Landolfi, Tommaso 1908-1979 .... **CLC 11, 49**
See also CA 127; 117; DLB 177; EWL 3

Landon, Letitia Elizabeth 1802-1838 .... **NCLC 15**
See also DLB 96

Landor, Walter Savage 1775-1864 .... **NCLC 14**
See also BRW 4; DLB 93, 107; RGEL 2

Landwirth, Heinz
See Lind, Jakov

Lane, Patrick 1939- .... **CLC 25**
See also CA 97-100; CANR 54; CP 3, 4, 5, 6, 7; DAM POET; DLB 53; INT CA-97-100

Lane, Rose Wilder 1887-1968 ...... **TCLC 177**
See also CA 102; CANR 63; SATA 29; SATA-Brief 28; TCWW 2

Lang, Andrew 1844-1912 .... **TCLC 16**
See also CA 114; 137; CANR 85; CLR 101; DLB 98, 141, 184; FANT; MAICYA 1, 2; RGEL 2; SATA 16; WCH

Lang, Fritz 1890-1976 .... **CLC 20, 103**
See also AAYA 65; CA 77-80; 69-72; CANR 30

Lange, John
See Crichton, Michael

Langer, Elinor 1939- .... **CLC 34**
See also CA 121

Langland, William 1332(?)-1400(?) .... **LC 19, 120**
See also BRW 1; DA; DAB; DAC; DAM MST, POET; DLB 146; RGEL 2; TEA; WLIT 3

Langstaff, Launcelot
See Irving, Washington

Lanier, Sidney 1842-1881 . **NCLC 6, 118; PC 50**
See also AMWS 1; DAM POET; DLB 64; DLBD 13; EXPP; MAICYA 1; PFS 14; RGAL 4; SATA 18

Lanyer, Aemilia 1569-1645 .... **LC 10, 30, 83; PC 60**
See also DLB 121

Lao-Tzu
See Lao Tzu

Lao Tzu c. 6th cent. B.C.-3rd cent. B.C. .... **CMLC 7**

Lapine, James (Elliot) 1949- .... **CLC 39**
See also CA 123; 130; CANR 54, 128; DFS 25; DLB 341; INT CA-130

Larbaud, Valery (Nicolas) 1881-1957 .... **TCLC 9**
See also CA 106; 152; EWL 3; GFL 1789 to the Present

Larcom, Lucy 1824-1893 .... **NCLC 179**
See also AMWS 13; DLB 221, 243

Lardner, Ring
See Lardner, Ring(gold) W(ilmer)

Lardner, Ring W., Jr.
See Lardner, Ring(gold) W(ilmer)

Lardner, Ring(gold) W(ilmer) 1885-1933 ..... **SSC 32, 118; TCLC 2, 14**
See also AMW; BPFB 2; CA 104; 131; CDALB 1917-1929; DLB 11, 25, 86, 171; DLBD 16; MAL 5; MTCW 1, 2; MTFW 2005; RGAL 4; RGSF 2; TUS

Laredo, Betty
See Codrescu, Andrei

Larkin, Maia
See Wojciechowska, Maia (Teresa)

Larkin, Philip (Arthur) 1922-1985 ... **CLC 3, 5, 8, 9, 13, 18, 33, 39, 64; PC 21**
See also BRWS 1; CA 5-8R; 117; CANR 24, 62; CDBLB 1960 to Present; CP 1, 2, 3, 4; DA3; DAB; DAM MST, POET; DLB 27; EWL 3; MTCW 1, 2; MTFW 2005; PFS 3, 4, 12; RGEL 2

La Roche, Sophie von 1730-1807 .... **NCLC 121**
See also DLB 94

La Rochefoucauld, Francois 1613-1680 .... **LC 108**
See also DLB 268; EW 3; GFL Beginnings to 1789; RGWL 2, 3

Larra (y Sanchez de Castro), Mariano Jose de 1809-1837 .... **NCLC 17, 130**

Larsen, Eric 1941- .... **CLC 55**
See also CA 132

Larsen, Nella 1893(?)-1963 ... **BLC 1:2; CLC 37; HR 1:3; TCLC 200**
See also AFAW 1, 2; AMWS 18; BW 1; CA 125; CANR 83; DAM MULT; DLB 51; FW; LATS 1:1; LMFS 2

Larson, Charles R(aymond) 1938- ... **CLC 31**
See also CA 53-56; CANR 4, 121

Larson, Jonathan 1960-1996 .... **CLC 99**
See also AAYA 28; CA 156; DFS 23; MTFW 2005

La Sale, Antoine de c. 1386-1460(?) . **LC 104**
See also DLB 208

Las Casas, Bartolome de 1474-1566 .... **HLCS; LC 31**
See also DLB 318; LAW; WLIT 1

Lasch, Christopher 1932-1994 .... **CLC 102**
See also CA 73-76; 144; CANR 25, 118; DLB 246; MTCW 1, 2; MTFW 2005

Lasker-Schueler, Else 1869-1945 ... **TCLC 57**
See also CA 183; DLB 66, 124; EWL 3

Lasker-Schuler, Else
See Lasker-Schueler, Else

Laski, Harold J(oseph) 1893-1950 . **TCLC 79**
See also CA 188

Latham, Jean Lee 1902-1995 .... **CLC 12**
See also AITN 1; BYA 1; CA 5-8R; CANR 7, 84; CLR 50; MAICYA 1, 2; SATA 2, 68; YAW

Latham, Mavis
See Clark, Mavis Thorpe

Lathen, Emma
See Hennissart, Martha

Lathrop, Francis
See Leiber, Fritz (Reuter, Jr.)

Lattany, Kristin
See Lattany, Kristin (Elaine Eggleston) Hunter

Lattany, Kristin (Elaine Eggleston) Hunter 1931- .... **CLC 35**
See also AITN 1; BW 1; BYA 3; CA 13-16R; CANR 13, 108; CLR 3; CN 1, 2, 3, 4, 5, 6; DLB 33; INT CANR-13; MAICYA 1, 2; SAAS 10; SATA 12, 132; YAW

Lattimore, Richmond (Alexander) 1906-1984 .... **CLC 3**
See also CA 1-4R; 112; CANR 1; CP 1, 2, 3; MAL 5

Laughlin, James 1914-1997 .... **CLC 49**
See also CA 21-24R; 162; CAAS 22; CANR 9, 47; CP 1, 2, 3, 4, 5, 6; DLB 48; DLBY 1996, 1997

Laurence, Jean Margaret Wemyss
See Laurence, Margaret
Laurence, Margaret 1926-1987 ..... **CLC 3, 6, 13, 50, 62; SSC 7**
See also BYA 13; CA 5-8R; 121; CANR 33; CN 1, 2, 3, 4; DAC; DAM MST; DLB 53; EWL 3; FW; MTCW 1, 2; MTFW 2005; NFS 11; RGEL 2; RGSF 2; SATA-Obit 50; TCWW 2
Laurent, Antoine 1952- .... **CLC 50**
Lauscher, Hermann
See Hesse, Hermann
Lautreamont 1846-1870 .... **NCLC 12, 194; SSC 14**
See also DLB 217; GFL 1789 to the Present; RGWL 2, 3
Lautreamont, Isidore Lucien Ducasse
See Lautreamont
Lavater, Johann Kaspar 1741-1801 .... **NCLC 142**
See also DLB 97
Laverty, Donald
See Blish, James (Benjamin)
Lavin, Mary 1912-1996 . **CLC 4, 18, 99; SSC 4, 67**
See also CA 9-12R; 151; CANR 33; CN 1, 2, 3, 4, 5, 6; DLB 15, 319; FW; MTCW 1; RGEL 2; RGSF 2; SSFS 23
Lavond, Paul Dennis
See Kornbluth, C(yril) M.; Pohl, Frederik
Lawes, Henry 1596-1662 .... **LC 113**
See also DLB 126
Lawler, Ray
See Lawler, Raymond Evenor
Lawler, Raymond Evenor 1922- .... **CLC 58**
See also CA 103; CD 5, 6; DLB 289; RGEL 2
Lawrence, D(avid) H(erbert Richards) 1885-1930 .... **PC 54; SSC 4, 19, 73; TCLC 2, 9, 16, 33, 48, 61, 93; WLC 3**
See also BPFB 2; BRW 7; BRWR 2; CA 104; 121; CANR 131; CDBLB 1914-1945; DA; DA3; DAB; DAC; DAM MST, NOV, POET; DLB 10, 19, 36, 98, 162, 195; EWL 3; EXPP; EXPS; GLL 1; LAIT 2, 3; MTCW 1, 2; MTFW 2005; NFS 18, 26; PFS 6; RGEL 2; RGSF 2; SSFS 2, 6; TEA; WLIT 4; WP
Lawrence, T(homas) E(dward) 1888-1935 .... **TCLC 18, 204**
See also BRWS 2; CA 115; 167; DLB 195
Lawrence of Arabia
See Lawrence, T(homas) E(dward)
Lawson, Henry (Archibald Hertzberg) 1867-1922 .... **SSC 18; TCLC 27**
See also CA 120; 181; DLB 230; RGEL 2; RGSF 2
Lawton, Dennis
See Faust, Frederick (Schiller)
Laxness, Halldor (Kiljan)
See Gudjonsson, Halldor Kiljan
Layamon fl. c. 1200- .... **CMLC 10, 105**
See also DLB 146; RGEL 2
Laye, Camara 1928-1980 .. **BLC 1:2; CLC 4, 38**
See also AFW; BW 1; CA 85-88; 97-100; CANR 25; DAM MULT; EWL 3; MTCW 1, 2; WLIT 2
Layton, Irving 1912-2006 ..... **CLC 2, 15, 164**
See also CA 1-4R; 247; CANR 2, 33, 43, 66, 129; CP 1, 2, 3, 4, 5, 6, 7; DAC; DAM MST, POET; DLB 88; EWL 3; MTCW 1, 2; PFS 12; RGEL 2
Layton, Irving Peter
See Layton, Irving
Lazarus, Emma 1849-1887 ...... **NCLC 8, 109**
Lazarus, Felix
See Cable, George Washington

Lazarus, Henry
See Slavitt, David R.
Lea, Joan
See Neufeld, John (Arthur)
Leacock, Stephen (Butler) 1869-1944 .... **SSC 39; TCLC 2**
See also CA 104; 141; CANR 80; DAC; DAM MST; DLB 92; EWL 3; MTCW 2; MTFW 2005; RGEL 2; RGSF 2
Lead, Jane Ward 1623-1704 .... **LC 72**
See also DLB 131
Leapor, Mary 1722-1746 .... **LC 80; PC 85**
See also DLB 109
Lear, Edward 1812-1888 ..... **NCLC 3; PC 65**
See also CA 48; BRW 5; CLR 1, 75; DLB 32, 163, 166; MAICYA 1, 2; RGEL 2; SATA 18, 100; WCH; WP
Lear, Norman (Milton) 1922- .... **CLC 12**
See also CA 73-76
Least Heat-Moon, William
See Trogdon, William (Lewis)
Leautaud, Paul 1872-1956 .... **TCLC 83**
See also CA 203; DLB 65; GFL 1789 to the Present
Leavis, F(rank) R(aymond) 1895-1978 .... **CLC 24**
See also BRW 7; CA 21-24R; 77-80; CANR 44; DLB 242; EWL 3; MTCW 1, 2; RGEL 2
Leavitt, David 1961- .... **CLC 34**
See also CA 116; 122; CANR 50, 62, 101, 134, 177; CPW; DA3; DAM POP; DLB 130; GLL 1; INT CA-122; MAL 5; MTCW 2; MTFW 2005
Leblanc, Maurice (Marie Emile) 1864-1941 .... **TCLC 49**
See also CA 110; CMW 4
Lebowitz, Fran(ces Ann) 1951(?)- ... **CLC 11, 36**
See also CA 81-84; CANR 14, 60, 70; INT CANR-14; MTCW 1
Lebrecht, Peter
See Tieck, (Johann) Ludwig
le Cagat, Benat
See Whitaker, Rod
le Carre, John
See le Carre, John
le Carre, John 1931- .... **CLC 9, 15**
See also AAYA 42; BEST 89:4; BPFB 2; BRWS 2; CA 5-8R; CANR 13, 33, 59, 107, 132, 172; CDBLB 1960 to Present; CMW 4; CN 1, 2, 3, 4, 5, 6, 7; CPW; DA3; DAM POP; DLB 87; EWL 3; MSW; MTCW 1, 2; MTFW 2005; RGEL 2; TEA
Le Clezio, J. M.G. 1940- . **CLC 31, 155; SSC 122**
See also CA 116; 128; CANR 147; CWW 2; DLB 83; EWL 3; GFL 1789 to the Present; RGSF 2
Le Clezio, Jean Marie Gustave
See Le Clezio, J. M.G.
Leconte de Lisle, Charles-Marie-Rene 1818-1894 .... **NCLC 29**
See also DLB 217; EW 6; GFL 1789 to the Present
Le Coq, Monsieur
See Simenon, Georges (Jacques Christian)
Leduc, Violette 1907-1972 .... **CLC 22**
See also CA 13-14; 33-36R; CANR 69; CAP 1; EWL 3; GFL 1789 to the Present; GLL 1
Ledwidge, Francis 1887(?)-1917 .... **TCLC 23**
See also CA 123; 203; DLB 20
Lee, Andrea 1953- .... **BLC 1:2; CLC 36**
See also BW 1, 3; CA 125; CANR 82; DAM MULT
Lee, Andrew
See Auchincloss, Louis

Lee, Chang-rae 1965- .... **CLC 91, 268, 274**
See also CA 148; CANR 89; CN 7; DLB 312; LATS 1:2
Lee, Don L.
See Madhubuti, Haki R.
Lee, George W(ashington) 1894-1976 .... **BLC 1:2; CLC 52**
See also BW 1; CA 125; CANR 83; DAM MULT; DLB 51
Lee, Harper 1926- ... **CLC 12, 60, 194; WLC 4**
See also AAYA 13; AMWS 8; BPFB 2; BYA 3; CA 13-16R; CANR 51, 128; CDALB 1941-1968; CSW; DA; DA3; DAB; DAC; DAM MST, NOV; DLB 6; EXPN; LAIT 3; MAL 5; MTCW 1, 2; MTFW 2005; NFS 2; SATA 11; WYA; YAW
Lee, Helen Elaine 1959(?)- .... **CLC 86**
See also CA 148
Lee, John .... **CLC 70**
Lee, Julian
See Latham, Jean Lee
Lee, Larry
See Lee, Lawrence
Lee, Laurie 1914-1997 .... **CLC 90**
See also CA 77-80; 158; CANR 33, 73; CP 1, 2, 3, 4, 5, 6; CPW; DAB; DAM POP; DLB 27; MTCW 1; RGEL 2
Lee, Lawrence 1941-1990 .... **CLC 34**
See also CA 131; CANR 43
Lee, Li-Young 1957- .... **CLC 164; PC 24**
See also AMWS 15; CA 153; CANR 118; CP 6, 7; DLB 165, 312; LMFS 2; PFS 11, 15, 17
Lee, Manfred B. 1905-1971 .... **CLC 11**
See also CA 1-4R; 29-32R; CANR 2, 150; CMW 4; DLB 137
Lee, Manfred Bennington
See Lee, Manfred B.
Lee, Nathaniel 1645(?)-1692 .... **LC 103**
See also DLB 80; RGEL 2
Lee, Nelle Harper
See Lee, Harper
Lee, Shelton Jackson
See Lee, Spike
Lee, Sophia 1750-1824 .... **NCLC 191**
See also DLB 39
Lee, Spike 1957(?)- .... **BLCS; CLC 105**
See also AAYA 4, 29; BW 2, 3; CA 125; CANR 42, 164; DAM MULT
Lee, Stan 1922- .... **CLC 17**
See also AAYA 5, 49; CA 108; 111; CANR 129; INT CA-111; MTFW 2005
Lee, Tanith 1947- .... **CLC 46**
See also AAYA 15; CA 37-40R; CANR 53, 102, 145, 170; DLB 261; FANT; SATA 8, 88, 134, 185; SFW 4; SUFW 1, 2; YAW
Lee, Vernon
See Paget, Violet
Lee, William
See Burroughs, William S.
Lee, Willy
See Burroughs, William S.
Lee-Hamilton, Eugene (Jacob) 1845-1907 .... **TCLC 22**
See also CA 117; 234
Leet, Judith 1935- .... **CLC 11**
See also CA 187
Le Fanu, Joseph Sheridan 1814-1873 .... **NCLC 9, 58; SSC 14, 84**
See also CMW 4; DA3; DAM POP; DLB 21, 70, 159, 178; GL 3; HGG; RGEL 2; RGSF 2; SUFW 1
Leffland, Ella 1931- .... **CLC 19**
See also CA 29-32R; CANR 35, 78, 82; DLBY 1984; INT CANR-35; SATA 65; SSFS 24

Leger, Alexis
 See Leger, (Marie-Rene Auguste) Alexis
 Saint-Leger

**Leger, (Marie-Rene Auguste) Alexis
 Saint-Leger** 1887-1975 .. **CLC 4, 11, 46;
 PC 23**
 See also CA 13-16R; 61-64; CANR 43;
 DAM POET; DLB 258, 331; EW 10;
 EWL 3; GFL 1789 to the Present; MTCW
 1; RGWL 2, 3

Leger, Saintleger
 See Leger, (Marie-Rene Auguste) Alexis
 Saint-Leger

Le Guin, Ursula K. 1929- ...... **CLC 8, 13, 22,
 45, 71, 136; SSC 12, 69**
 See also AAYA 9, 27; AITN 1; BPFB 2;
 BYA 5, 8, 11, 14; CA 21-24R; CANR 9,
 32, 52, 74, 132; CDALB 1968-1988; CLR
 3, 28, 91; CN 2, 3, 4, 5, 6, 7; CPW; DA3;
 DAB; DAC; DAM MST, POP; DLB 8,
 52, 256, 275; EXPS; FANT; FW; INT
 CANR-32; JRDA; LAIT 5; MAICYA 1,
 2; MAL 5; MTCW 1, 2; MTFW 2005;
 NFS 6, 9; SATA 4, 52, 99, 149, 194;
 SCFW 1, 2; SFW 4; SSFS 2; SUFW 1, 2;
 WYA; YAW

Lehmann, Rosamond (Nina)
 1901-1990 .... **CLC 5**
 See also CA 77-80; 131; CANR 8, 73; CN
 1, 2, 3, 4; DLB 15; MTCW 2; RGEL 2;
 RHW

Leiber, Fritz (Reuter, Jr.)
 1910-1992 .... **CLC 25**
 See also AAYA 65; BPFB 2; CA 45-48; 139;
 CANR 2, 40, 86; CN 2, 3, 4, 5; DLB 8;
 FANT; HGG; MTCW 1, 2; MTFW 2005;
 SATA 45; SATA-Obit 73; SCFW 1, 2;
 SFW 4; SUFW 1, 2

Leibniz, Gottfried Wilhelm von
 1646-1716 .... **LC 35**
 See also DLB 168

Leino, Eino
 See Lonnbohm, Armas Eino Leopold

Leiris, Michel (Julien) 1901-1990 ..... **CLC 61**
 See also CA 119; 128; 132; EWL 3; GFL
 1789 to the Present

Leithauser, Brad 1953- .... **CLC 27**
 See also CA 107; CANR 27, 81, 171; CP 5,
 6, 7; DLB 120, 282

le Jars de Gournay, Marie
 See de Gournay, Marie le Jars

Lelchuk, Alan 1938- .... **CLC 5**
 See also CA 45-48; CAAS 20; CANR 1,
 70, 152; CN 3, 4, 5, 6, 7

Lem, Stanislaw 1921-2006 ..... **CLC 8, 15, 40,
 149**
 See also AAYA 75; CA 105; 249; CAAS 1;
 CANR 32; CWW 2; MTCW 1; SCFW 1,
 2; SFW 4

Lemann, Nancy (Elise) 1956- .... **CLC 39**
 See also CA 118; 136; CANR 121

Lemonnier, (Antoine Louis) Camille
 1844-1913 .... **TCLC 22**
 See also CA 121

Lenau, Nikolaus 1802-1850 .... **NCLC 16**

L'Engle, Madeleine 1918-2007 .... **CLC 12**
 See also AAYA 28; AITN 2; BPFB 2; BYA
 2, 4, 5, 7; CA 1-4R; 264; CANR 3, 21,
 39, 66, 107; CLR 1, 14, 57; CPW; CWRI
 5; DA3; DAM POP; DLB 52; JRDA;
 MAICYA 1, 2; MTCW 1, 2; MTFW 2005;
 SAAS 15; SATA 1, 27, 75, 128; SATA-
 Obit 186; SFW 4; WYA; YAW

L'Engle, Madeleine Camp Franklin
 See L'Engle, Madeleine

Lengyel, Jozsef 1896-1975 .... **CLC 7**
 See also CA 85-88; 57-60; CANR 71;
 RGSF 2

Lenin 1870-1924 .... **TCLC 67**
 See also CA 121; 168

Lenin, N.
 See Lenin

Lenin, Nikolai
 See Lenin

Lenin, V. I.
 See Lenin

Lenin, Vladimir I.
 See Lenin

Lenin, Vladimir Ilyich
 See Lenin

Lennon, John (Ono) 1940-1980 .. **CLC 12, 35**
 See also CA 102; SATA 114

Lennox, Charlotte Ramsay
 1729(?)-1804 .... **NCLC 23, 134**
 See also DLB 39; RGEL 2

Lentricchia, Frank, Jr.
 See Lentricchia, Frank

Lentricchia, Frank 1940- .... **CLC 34**
 See also CA 25-28R; CANR 19, 106, 148;
 DLB 246

Lenz, Gunter .... **CLC 65**

Lenz, Jakob Michael Reinhold
 1751-1792 .... **LC 100**
 See also DLB 94; RGWL 2, 3

Lenz, Siegfried 1926- .... **CLC 27; SSC 33**
 See also CA 89-92; CANR 80, 149; CWW
 2; DLB 75; EWL 3; RGSF 2; RGWL 2, 3

Leon, David
 See Jacob, (Cyprien-)Max

Leonard, Dutch
 See Leonard, Elmore

Leonard, Elmore 1925- .... **CLC 28, 34, 71,
 120, 222**
 See also AAYA 22, 59; AITN 1; BEST 89:1,
 90:4; BPFB 2; CA 81-84; CANR 12, 28,
 53, 76, 96, 133, 176; CMW 4; CN 5, 6, 7;
 CPW; DA3; DAM POP; DLB 173, 226;
 INT CANR-28; MSW; MTCW 1, 2;
 MTFW 2005; RGAL 4; SATA 163;
 TCWW 1, 2

Leonard, Elmore John, Jr.
 See Leonard, Elmore

Leonard, Hugh
 See Byrne, John Keyes

Leonov, Leonid (Maximovich)
 1899-1994 .... **CLC 92**
 See also CA 129; CANR 76; DAM NOV;
 DLB 272; EWL 3; MTCW 1, 2; MTFW
 2005

Leonov, Leonid Maksimovich
 See Leonov, Leonid (Maximovich)

Leopardi, (Conte) Giacomo
 1798-1837 .... **NCLC 22, 129; PC 37**
 See also EW 5; RGWL 2, 3; WLIT 7; WP

Le Reveler
 See Artaud, Antonin (Marie Joseph)

Lerman, Eleanor 1952- .... **CLC 9**
 See also CA 85-88; CANR 69, 124, 184

Lerman, Rhoda 1936- .... **CLC 56**
 See also CA 49-52; CANR 70

Lermontov, Mikhail Iur'evich
 See Lermontov, Mikhail Yuryevich

Lermontov, Mikhail Yuryevich
 1814-1841 .... **NCLC 5, 47, 126; PC 18**
 See also DLB 205; EW 6; RGWL 2, 3;
 TWA

Leroux, Gaston 1868-1927 .... **TCLC 25**
 See also CA 108; 136; CANR 69; CMW 4;
 MTFW 2005; NFS 20; SATA 65

Lesage, Alain-Rene 1668-1747 .... **LC 2, 28**
 See also DLB 313; EW 3; GFL Beginnings
 to 1789; RGWL 2, 3

Leskov, N(ikolai) S(emenovich) 1831-1895
 See Leskov, Nikolai (Semyonovich)

Leskov, Nikolai (Semyonovich)
 1831-1895 ... **NCLC 25, 174; SSC 34, 96**
 See also DLB 238

Leskov, Nikolai Semenovich
 See Leskov, Nikolai (Semyonovich)

Lesser, Milton
 See Marlowe, Stephen

Lessing, Doris 1919- .. **CLC 1, 2, 3, 6, 10, 15,
 22, 40, 94, 170, 254; SSC 6, 61; WLCS**
 See also AAYA 57; AFW; BRWS 1; CA
 9-12R; CAAS 14; CANR 33, 54, 76, 122,
 179; CBD; CD 5, 6; CDBLB 1960 to
 Present; CN 1, 2, 3, 4, 5, 6, 7; CWD; DA;
 DA3; DAB; DAC; DAM MST, NOV;
 DFS 20; DLB 15, 139; DLBY 1985; EWL
 3; EXPS; FL 1:6; FW; LAIT 4; MTCW 1,
 2; MTFW 2005; NFS 27; RGEL 2; RGSF
 2; SFW 4; SSFS 1, 12, 20, 26; TEA;
 WLIT 2, 4

Lessing, Doris May
 See Lessing, Doris

Lessing, Gotthold Ephraim
 1729-1781 .... **DC 26; LC 8, 124, 162**
 See also CDWLB 2; DLB 97; EW 4; RGWL
 2, 3

Lester, Julius 1939- .... **BLC 2:2**
 See also AAYA 12, 51; BW 2; BYA 3, 9,
 11, 12; CA 17-20R; CANR 8, 23, 43, 129,
 174; CLR 2, 41, 143; JRDA; MAICYA 1,
 2; MAICYAS 1; MTFW 2005; SATA 12,
 74, 112, 157; YAW

Lester, Richard 1932- .... **CLC 20**

Levenson, Jay .... **CLC 70**

Lever, Charles (James)
 1806-1872 .... **NCLC 23**
 See also DLB 21; RGEL 2

Leverson, Ada Esther
 1862(?)-1933(?) .... **TCLC 18**
 See also CA 117; 202; DLB 153; RGEL 2

Levertov, Denise 1923-1997 .. **CLC 1, 2, 3, 5,
 8, 15, 28, 66; PC 11**
 See also AMWS 3; CA 1-4R; 178; 163;
 CAAE 178; CAAS 19; CANR 3, 29, 50,
 108; CDALBS; CP 1, 2, 3, 4, 5, 6; CWP;
 DAM POET; DLB 5, 165, 342; EWL 3;
 EXPP; FW; INT CANR-29; MAL 5;
 MTCW 1, 2; PAB; PFS 7, 17; RGAL 4;
 RGHL; TUS; WP

Levi, Carlo 1902-1975 .... **TCLC 125**
 See also CA 65-68; 53-56; CANR 10; EWL
 3; RGWL 2, 3

Levi, Jonathan .... **CLC 76**
 See also CA 197

Levi, Peter (Chad Tigar)
 1931-2000 .... **CLC 41**
 See also CA 5-8R; 187; CANR 34, 80; CP
 1, 2, 3, 4, 5, 6, 7; DLB 40

Levi, Primo 1919-1987 ...... **CLC 37, 50; SSC
 12, 122; TCLC 109**
 See also CA 13-16R; 122; CANR 12, 33,
 61, 70, 132, 171; DLB 177, 299; EWL 3;
 MTCW 1, 2; MTFW 2005; RGHL;
 RGWL 2, 3; WLIT 7

Levin, Ira 1929-2007 .... **CLC 3, 6**
 See also CA 21-24R; 266; CANR 17, 44,
 74, 139; CMW 4; CN 1, 2, 3, 4, 5, 6, 7;
 CPW; DA3; DAM POP; HGG; MTCW 1,
 2; MTFW 2005; SATA 66; SATA-Obit
 187; SFW 4

Levin, Ira Marvin
 See Levin, Ira

Levin, Ira Marvin
 See Levin, Ira

Levin, Meyer 1905-1981 .... **CLC 7**
 See also AITN 1; CA 9-12R; 104; CANR
 15; CN 1, 2, 3; DAM POP; DLB 9, 28;
 DLBY 1981; MAL 5; RGHL; SATA 21;
 SATA-Obit 27

Levine, Albert Norman
 See Levine, Norman

Liu, E. 1857-1909 .... **TCLC 15**
See also CA 115; 190; DLB 328

Lively, Penelope 1933- .... **CLC 32, 50**
See also BPFB 2; CA 41-44R; CANR 29,
67, 79, 131, 172; CLR 7; CN 5, 6, 7;
CWRI 5; DAM NOV; DLB 14, 161, 207,
326; FANT; JRDA; MAICYA 1, 2;
MTCW 1, 2; MTFW 2005; SATA 7, 60,
101, 164; TEA

Lively, Penelope Margaret
See Lively, Penelope

Livesay, Dorothy (Kathleen)
1909-1996 .... **CLC 4, 15, 79**
See also AITN 2; CA 25-28R; CAAS 8;
CANR 36, 67; CP 1, 2, 3, 4, 5; DAC;
DAM MST, POET; DLB 68; FW; MTCW
1; RGEL 2; TWA

Livius Andronicus c. 284B.C.-c.
204B.C. .... **CMLC 102**

Livy c. 59B.C.-c. 12 .... **CMLC 11**
See also AW 2; CDWLB 1; DLB 211;
RGWL 2, 3; WLIT 8

Li Yaotang
See Jin, Ba

Lizardi, Jose Joaquin Fernandez de
1776-1827 .... **NCLC 30**
See also LAW

Llewellyn, Richard
See Llewellyn Lloyd, Richard Dafydd Vivian

Llewellyn Lloyd, Richard Dafydd Vivian
1906-1983 .... **CLC 7, 80**
See also CA 53-56; 111; CANR 7, 71; DLB
15; SATA 11; SATA-Obit 37

Llosa, Jorge Mario Pedro Vargas
See Vargas Llosa, Mario

Llosa, Mario Vargas
See Vargas Llosa, Mario

Lloyd, Manda
See Mander, (Mary) Jane

Lloyd Webber, Andrew 1948- .... **CLC 21**
See also AAYA 1, 38; CA 116; 149; DAM
DRAM; DFS 7; SATA 56

Llull, Ramon c. 1235-c. 1316 .... **CMLC 12**

Lobb, Ebenezer
See Upward, Allen

Locke, Alain (Le Roy)
1886-1954 .... **BLCS; HR 1:3; TCLC 43**
See also AMWS 14; BW 1, 3; CA 106; 124;
CANR 79; DLB 51; LMFS 2; MAL 5;
RGAL 4

Locke, John 1632-1704 .... **LC 7, 35, 135**
See also DLB 31, 101, 213, 252; RGEL 2;
WLIT 3

Locke-Elliott, Sumner
See Elliott, Sumner Locke

Lockhart, John Gibson 1794-1854 .. **NCLC 6**
See also DLB 110, 116, 144

Lockridge, Ross (Franklin), Jr.
1914-1948 .... **TCLC 111**
See also CA 108; 145; CANR 79; DLB 143;
DLBY 1980; MAL 5; RGAL 4; RHW

Lockwood, Robert
See Johnson, Robert

Lodge, David 1935- .... **CLC 36, 141**
See also BEST 90:1; BRWS 4; CA 17-20R;
CANR 19, 53, 92, 139; CN 1, 2, 3, 4, 5,
6, 7; CPW; DAM POP; DLB 14, 194;
EWL 3; INT CANR-19; MTCW 1, 2;
MTFW 2005

Lodge, Thomas 1558-1625 .... **LC 41**
See also DLB 172; RGEL 2

Loewinsohn, Ron(ald William)
1937- .... **CLC 52**
See also CA 25-28R; CANR 71; CP 1, 2, 3,
4

Logan, Jake
See Smith, Martin Cruz

Logan, John (Burton) 1923-1987 .... **CLC 5**
See also CA 77-80; 124; CANR 45; CP 1,
2, 3, 4; DLB 5

Lo-Johansson, (Karl) Ivar
1901-1990 .... **TCLC 216**
See also CA 102; 131; CANR 20, 79, 137;
DLB 259; EWL 3; RGWL 2, 3

Lo Kuan-chung 1330(?)-1400(?) .... **LC 12**

Lomax, Pearl
See Cleage, Pearl

Lomax, Pearl Cleage
See Cleage, Pearl

Lombard, Nap
See Johnson, Pamela Hansford

Lombard, Peter 1100(?)-1160(?) ... **CMLC 72**

Lombino, Salvatore
See Hunter, Evan

London, Jack 1876-1916
See London, John Griffith

London, John Griffith 1876-1916 .... **SSC 4,**
49; TCLC 9, 15, 39; WLC 4
See also AAYA 13, 75; AITN 2; AMW;
BPFB 2; BYA 4, 13; CA 110; 119; CANR
73; CDALB 1865-1917; CLR 108; DA;
DA3; DAB; DAC; DAM MST, NOV;
DLB 8, 12, 78, 212; EWL 3; EXPS;
JRDA; LAIT 3; MAICYA 1, 2,; MAL 5;
MTCW 1, 2; MTFW 2005; NFS 8, 19;
RGAL 4; RGSF 2; SATA 18; SFW 4;
SSFS 7; TCWW 1, 2; TUS; WYA; YAW

Long, Emmett
See Leonard, Elmore

Longbaugh, Harry
See Goldman, William

Longfellow, Henry Wadsworth
1807-1882 .... **NCLC 2, 45, 101, 103; PC**
30; WLCS
See also AMW; AMWR 2; CDALB 1640-
1865; CLR 99; DA; DA3; DAB; DAC;
DAM MST, POET; DLB 1, 59, 235;
EXPP; PAB; PFS 2, 7, 17; RGAL 4;
SATA 19; TUS; WP

Longinus c. 1st cent. - .... **CMLC 27**
See also AW 2; DLB 176

Longley, Michael 1939- .... **CLC 29**
See also BRWS 8; CA 102; CP 1, 2, 3, 4, 5,
6, 7; DLB 40

Longstreet, Augustus Baldwin
1790-1870 .... **NCLC 159**
See also DLB 3, 11, 74, 248; RGAL 4

Longus fl. c. 2nd cent. - .... **CMLC 7**

Longway, A. Hugh
See Lang, Andrew

Lonnbohm, Armas Eino Leopold
See Lonnbohm, Armas Eino Leopold

Lonnbohm, Armas Eino Leopold
1878-1926 .... **TCLC 24**
See also CA 123; EWL 3

Lonnrot, Elias 1802-1884 .... **NCLC 53**
See also EFS 1

Lonsdale, Roger .... **CLC 65**

Lopate, Phillip 1943- .... **CLC 29**
See also CA 97-100; CANR 88, 157; DLBY
1980; INT CA-97-100

Lopez, Barry (Holstun) 1945- .... **CLC 70**
See also AAYA 9, 63; ANW; CA 65-68;
CANR 7, 23, 47, 68, 92; DLB 256, 275,
335; INT CANR-7; INT CANR-23; MTCW 1;
RGAL 4; SATA 67

Lopez de Mendoza, Inigo
See Santillana, Inigo Lopez de Mendoza,
Marques de

Lopez Portillo (y Pacheco), Jose
1920-2004 .... **CLC 46**
See also CA 129; 224; HW 1

Lopez y Fuentes, Gregorio
1897(?)-1966 .... **CLC 32**
See also CA 131; EWL 3; HW 1

Lorca, Federico Garcia
See Garcia Lorca, Federico

Lord, Audre
See Lorde, Audre

Lord, Bette Bao 1938- .... **AAL; CLC 23**
See also BEST 90:3; BPFB 2; CA 107;
CANR 41, 79; INT CA-107; SATA 58

Lord Auch
See Bataille, Georges

Lord Brooke
See Greville, Fulke

Lord Byron
See Byron, George Gordon (Noel)

Lord Dunsany
See Dunsany, Edward John Moreton Drax
Plunkett

Lorde, Audre 1934-1992 .... **BLC 1:2, 2:2;**
CLC 18, 71; PC 12; TCLC 173
See also AFAW 1, 2; BW 1, 3; CA 25-28R;
142; CANR 16, 26, 46, 82; CP 2, 3, 4, 5;
DA3; DAM MULT, POET; DLB 41; EWL
3; FW; GLL 1; MAL 5; MTCW 1, 2;
MTFW 2005; PFS 16; RGAL 4

Lorde, Audre Geraldine
See Lorde, Audre

Lord Houghton
See Milnes, Richard Monckton

Lord Jeffrey
See Jeffrey, Francis

Loreaux, Nichol .... **CLC 65**

Lorenzini, Carlo 1826-1890 .... **NCLC 54**
See also CLR 5, 120; MAICYA 1, 2; SATA
29, 100; WCH; WLIT 7

Lorenzo, Heberto Padilla
See Padilla (Lorenzo), Heberto

Loris
See Hofmannsthal, Hugo von

Loti, Pierre
See Viaud, (Louis Marie) Julien

Lottie
See Grimke, Charlotte L(ottie) Forten

Lou, Henri
See Andreas-Salome, Lou

Louie, David Wong 1954- .... **CLC 70**
See also CA 139; CANR 120

Louis, Adrian C. .... **NNAL**
See also CA 223

Louis, Father M.
See Merton, Thomas (James)

Louise, Heidi
See Erdrich, Louise

Lovecraft, H. P. 1890-1937 .... **SSC 3, 52;**
TCLC 4, 22
See also AAYA 14; BPFB 2; CA 104; 133;
CANR 106; DA3; DAM POP; HGG;
MTCW 1, 2; MTFW 2005; RGAL 4;
SCFW 1, 2; SFW 4; SUFW

Lovecraft, Howard Phillips
See Lovecraft, H. P.

Lovelace, Earl 1935- .... **CLC 51**
See also BW 2; CA 77-80; CANR 41, 72,
114; CD 5, 6; CDWLB 3; CN 1, 2, 3, 4,
5, 6, 7; DLB 125; EWL 3; MTCW 1

Lovelace, Richard 1618-1658 ..... **LC 24, 158;**
PC 69
See also BRW 2; DLB 131; EXPP; PAB;
RGEL 2

Low, Penelope Margaret
See Lively, Penelope

Lowe, Pardee 1904- .... **AAL**

Lowell, Amy 1874-1925 ... **PC 13; TCLC 1, 8**
See also AAYA 57; AMW; CA 104; 151;
DAM POET; DLB 54, 140; EWL 3;
EXPP; LMFS 2; MAL 5; MBL; MTCW
2; MTFW 2005; PFS 30; RGAL 4; TUS

Machen, Arthur Llewelyn Jones
  See Jones, Arthur Llewellyn

Machiavelli, Niccolo 1469-1527 ... **DC 16; LC 8, 36, 140; WLCS**
  See also AAYA 58; DA; DAB; DAC; DAM MST; EW 2; LAIT 1; NFS 9; RGWL 2, 3; TWA; WLIT 7

MacInnes, Colin 1914-1976 .... **CLC 4, 23**
  See also CA 69-72; 65-68; CANR 21; CN 1, 2; DLB 14; MTCW 1, 2; RGEL 2; RHW

MacInnes, Helen (Clark)
  1907-1985 .... **CLC 27, 39**
  See also BPFB 2; CA 1-4R; 117; CANR 1, 28, 58; CMW 4; CN 1, 2; CPW; DAM POP; DLB 87; MSW; MTCW 1, 2; MTFW 2005; SATA 22; SATA-Obit 44

Mackay, Mary 1855-1924 .... **TCLC 51**
  See also CA 118; 177; DLB 34, 156; FANT; RGEL 2; RHW; SUFW 1

Mackay, Shena 1944- .... **CLC 195**
  See also CA 104; CANR 88, 139; DLB 231, 319; MTFW 2005

Mackenzie, Compton (Edward Montague)
  1883-1972 .... **CLC 18; TCLC 116**
  See also CA 21-22; 37-40R; CAP 2; CN 1; DLB 34, 100; RGEL 2

Mackenzie, Henry 1745-1831 .... **NCLC 41**
  See also DLB 39; RGEL 2

Mackey, Nathaniel 1947- .... **BLC 2:3; PC 49**
  See also CA 153; CANR 114; CP 6, 7; DLB 169

Mackey, Nathaniel Ernest
  See Mackey, Nathaniel

MacKinnon, Catharine A. 1946- .... **CLC 181**
  See also CA 128; 132; CANR 73, 140, 189; FW; MTCW 2; MTFW 2005

Mackintosh, Elizabeth
  1896(?)-1952 .... **TCLC 14**
  See also CA 110; CMW 4; DLB 10, 77; MSW

Macklin, Charles 1699-1797 .... **LC 132**
  See also DLB 89; RGEL 2

MacLaren, James
  See Grieve, C(hristopher) M(urray)

MacLaverty, Bernard 1942- ..... **CLC 31, 243**
  See also CA 116; 118; CANR 43, 88, 168; CN 5, 6, 7; DLB 267; INT CA-118; RGSF 2

MacLean, Alistair (Stuart)
  1922(?)-1987 .... **CLC 3, 13, 50, 63**
  See also CA 57-60; 121; CANR 28, 61; CMW 4; CP 2, 3, 4, 5, 6, 7; CPW; DAM POP; DLB 276; MTCW 1; SATA 23; SATA-Obit 50; TCWW 2

Maclean, Norman (Fitzroy)
  1902-1990 .... **CLC 78; SSC 13**
  See also AMWS 14; CA 102; 132; CANR 49; CPW; DAM POP; DLB 206; TCWW 2

MacLeish, Archibald 1892-1982 ... **CLC 3, 8, 14, 68; PC 47**
  See also AMW; CA 9-12R; 106; CAD; CANR 33, 63; CDALBS; CP 1, 2; DAM POET; DFS 15; DLB 4, 7, 45; DLBY 1982; EWL 3; EXPP; MAL 5; MTCW 1, 2; MTFW 2005; PAB; PFS 5; RGAL 4; TUS

MacLennan, (John) Hugh
  1907-1990 .... **CLC 2, 14, 92**
  See also CA 5-8R; 142; CANR 33; CN 1, 2, 3, 4; DAC; DAM MST; DLB 68; EWL 3; MTCW 1, 2; MTFW 2005; RGEL 2; TWA

MacLeod, Alistair 1936- .. **CLC 56, 165; SSC 90**
  See also CA 123; CCA 1; DAC; DAM MST; DLB 60; MTCW 2; MTFW 2005; RGSF 2; TCLE 1:2

Macleod, Fiona
  See Sharp, William

MacNeice, (Frederick) Louis
  1907-1963 .... **CLC 1, 4, 10, 53; PC 61**
  See also BRW 7; CA 85-88; CANR 61; DAB; DAM POET; DLB 10, 20; EWL 3; MTCW 1, 2; MTFW 2005; RGEL 2

MacNeill, Dand
  See Fraser, George MacDonald

Macpherson, James 1736-1796 .... **CMLC 28; LC 29; PC 97**
  See also BRWS 8; DLB 109, 336; RGEL 2

Macpherson, (Jean) Jay 1931- .... **CLC 14**
  See also CA 5-8R; CANR 90; CP 1, 2, 3, 4, 6, 7; CWP; DLB 53

Macrobius fl. 430- .... **CMLC 48**

MacShane, Frank 1927-1999 .... **CLC 39**
  See also CA 9-12R; 186; CANR 3, 33; DLB 111

Macumber, Mari
  See Sandoz, Mari(e Susette)

Madach, Imre 1823-1864 .... **NCLC 19**

Madden, (Jerry) David 1933- .... **CLC 5, 15**
  See also CA 1-4R; CAAS 3; CANR 4, 45; CN 3, 4, 5, 6, 7; CSW; DLB 6; MTCW 1

Maddern, Al(an)
  See Ellison, Harlan

Madhubuti, Haki R. 1942- .... **BLC 1:2; CLC 2; PC 5**
  See also BW 2, 3; CA 73-76; CANR 24, 51, 73, 139; CP 2, 3, 4, 5, 6, 7; CSW; DAM MULT, POET; DLB 5, 41; DLBD 8; EWL 3; MAL 5; MTCW 2; MTFW 2005; RGAL 4

Madison, James 1751-1836 .... **NCLC 126**
  See also DLB 37

Maepenn, Hugh
  See Kuttner, Henry

Maepenn, K. H.
  See Kuttner, Henry

Maeterlinck, Maurice 1862-1949 .... **DC 32; TCLC 3**
  See also CA 104; 136; CANR 80; DAM DRAM; DLB 192, 331; EW 8; EWL 3; GFL 1789 to the Present; LMFS 2; RGWL 2, 3; SATA 66; TWA

Maginn, William 1794-1842 .... **NCLC 8**
  See also DLB 110, 159

Mahapatra, Jayanta 1928- .... **CLC 33**
  See also CA 73-76; CAAS 9; CANR 15, 33, 66, 87; CP 4, 5, 6, 7; DAM MULT; DLB 323

Mahfouz, Nagib
  See Mahfouz, Naguib

Mahfouz, Naguib 1911(?)-2006 . **CLC 52, 55, 153; SSC 66**
  See also AAYA 49; AFW; BEST 89:2; CA 128; 253; CANR 55, 101; DA3; DAM NOV; DLB 346; DLBY 1988; MTCW 1, 2; MTFW 2005; RGSF 2; RGWL 2, 3; SSFS 9; WLIT 2

Mahfouz, Naguib Abdel Aziz Al-Sabilgi
  See Mahfouz, Naguib

Mahfouz, Najib
  See Mahfouz, Naguib

Mahfuz, Najib
  See Mahfouz, Naguib

Mahon, Derek 1941- .... **CLC 27; PC 60**
  See also BRWS 6; CA 113; 128; CANR 88; CP 1, 2, 3, 4, 5, 6, 7; DLB 40; EWL 3

Maiakovskii, Vladimir
  See Mayakovski, Vladimir (Vladimirovich)

Mailer, Norman 1923-2007 ... **CLC 1, 2, 3, 4, 5, 8, 11, 14, 28, 39, 74, 111, 234**
  See also AAYA 31; AITN 2; AMW; AMWC 2; AMWR 2; BPFB 2; CA 9-12R; 266; CABS 1; CANR 28, 74, 77, 130; CDALB 1968-1988; CN 1, 2, 3, 4, 5, 6, 7; CPW; DA; DA3; DAB; DAC; DAM MST, NOV, POP; DLB 2, 16, 28, 185, 278; DLBD 3; DLBY 1980, 1983; EWL 3; MAL 5; MTCW 1, 2; MTFW 2005; NFS 10; RGAL 4; TUS

Mailer, Norman Kingsley
  See Mailer, Norman

Maillet, Antonine 1929- .... **CLC 54, 118**
  See also CA 115; 120; CANR 46, 74, 77, 134; CCA 1; CWW 2; DAC; DLB 60; INT CA-120; MTCW 2; MTFW 2005

Maimonides, Moses 1135-1204 ..... **CMLC 76**
  See also DLB 115

Mais, Roger 1905-1955 .... **TCLC 8**
  See also BW 1, 3; CA 105; 124; CANR 82; CDWLB 3; DLB 125; EWL 3; MTCW 1; RGEL 2

Maistre, Joseph 1753-1821 .... **NCLC 37**
  See also GFL 1789 to the Present

Maitland, Frederic William
  1850-1906 .... **TCLC 65**

Maitland, Sara (Louise) 1950- .... **CLC 49**
  See also BRWS 11; CA 69-72; CANR 13, 59; DLB 271; FW

Major, Clarence 1936- ...... **BLC 1:2; CLC 3, 19, 48**
  See also AFAW 2; BW 2, 3; CA 21-24R; CAAS 6; CANR 13, 25, 53, 82; CN 3, 4, 5, 6, 7; CP 2, 3, 4, 5, 6, 7; CSW; DAM MULT; DLB 33; EWL 3; MAL 5; MSW

Major, Kevin (Gerald) 1949- .... **CLC 26**
  See also AAYA 16; CA 97-100; CANR 21, 38, 112; CLR 11; DAC; DLB 60; INT CANR-21; JRDA; MAICYA 1, 2; MAICYAS 1; SATA 32, 82, 134; WYA; YAW

Maki, James
  See Ozu, Yasujiro

Makin, Bathsua 1600-1675(?) .... **LC 137**

Makine, Andrei 1957-
  See Makine, Andrei

Makine, Andrei 1957- .... **CLC 198**
  See also CA 176; CANR 103, 162; MTFW 2005

Malabaila, Damiano
  See Levi, Primo

Malamud, Bernard 1914-1986 .. **CLC 1, 2, 3, 5, 8, 9, 11, 18, 27, 44, 78, 85; SSC 15; TCLC 129, 184; WLC 4**
  See also AAYA 16; AMWS 1; BPFB 2; BYA 15; CA 5-8R; 118; CABS 1; CANR 28, 62, 114; CDALB 1941-1968; CN 1, 2, 3, 4; CPW; DA; DA3; DAB; DAC; DAM MST, NOV, POP; DLB 2, 28, 152; DLBY 1980, 1986; EWL 3; EXPS; LAIT 4; LATS 1:1; MAL 5; MTCW 1, 2; MTFW 2005; NFS 27; RGAL 4; RGHL; RGSF 2; SSFS 8, 13, 16; TUS

Malan, Herman
  See Bosman, Herman Charles; Bosman, Herman Charles

Malaparte, Curzio 1898-1957 .... **TCLC 52**
  See also DLB 264

Malcolm, Dan
  See Silverberg, Robert

Malcolm, Janet 1934- .... **CLC 201**
  See also CA 123; CANR 89; NCFS 1

Malcolm X
  See Little, Malcolm

Malebranche, Nicolas 1638-1715 .... **LC 133**
  See also GFL Beginnings to 1789

Malherbe, Francois de 1555-1628 .... **LC 5**
  See also DLB 327; GFL Beginnings to 1789

Mallarme, Stephane 1842-1898 ...... **NCLC 4, 41, 210; PC 4**
  See also DAM POET; DLB 217; EW 7; GFL 1789 to the Present; LMFS 2; RGWL 2, 3; TWA

Mallet-Joris, Francoise 1930- .... **CLC 11**
  See also CA 65-68; CANR 17; CWW 2; DLB 83; EWL 3; GFL 1789 to the Present

McGahern, John 1934-2006 .... **CLC 5, 9, 48, 156; SSC 17**
See also CA 17-20R; 249; CANR 29, 68, 113; CN 1, 2, 3, 4, 5, 6, 7; DLB 14, 231, 319; MTCW 1

McGinley, Patrick (Anthony) 1937- . **CLC 41**
See also CA 120; 127; CANR 56; INT CA-127

McGinley, Phyllis 1905-1978 .... **CLC 14**
See also CA 9-12R; 77-80; CANR 19; CP 1, 2; CWRI 5; DLB 11, 48; MAL 5; PFS 9, 13; SATA 2, 44; SATA-Obit 24

McGinniss, Joe 1942- .... **CLC 32**
See also AITN 2; BEST 89:2; CA 25-28R; CANR 26, 70, 152; CPW; DLB 185; INT CANR-26

McGivern, Maureen Daly
See Daly, Maureen

McGivern, Maureen Patricia Daly
See Daly, Maureen

McGrath, Patrick 1950- .... **CLC 55**
See also CA 136; CANR 65, 148; CN 5, 6, 7; DLB 231; HGG; SUFW 2

McGrath, Thomas (Matthew)
1916-1990 .... **CLC 28, 59**
See also AMWS 10; CA 9-12R; 132; CANR 6, 33, 95; CP 1, 2, 3, 4, 5; DAM POET; MAL 5; MTCW 1; SATA 41; SATA-Obit 66

McGuane, Thomas 1939- .. **CLC 3, 7, 18, 45, 127**
See also AITN 2; BPFB 2; CA 49-52; CANR 5, 24, 49, 94, 164; CN 2, 3, 4, 5, 6, 7; DLB 2, 212; DLBY 1980; EWL 3; INT CANR-24; MAL 5; MTCW 1; MTFW 2005; TCWW 1, 2

McGuane, Thomas Francis III
See McGuane, Thomas

McGuckian, Medbh 1950- .... **CLC 48, 174; PC 27**
See also BRWS 5; CA 143; CP 4, 5, 6, 7; CWP; DAM POET; DLB 40

McHale, Tom 1942(?)-1982 .... **CLC 3, 5**
See also AITN 1; CA 77-80; 106; CN 1, 2, 3

McHugh, Heather 1948- .... **PC 61**
See also CA 69-72; CANR 11, 28, 55, 92; CP 4, 5, 6, 7; CWP; PFS 24

McIlvanney, William 1936- .... **CLC 42**
See also CA 25-28R; CANR 61; CMW 4; DLB 14, 207

McIlwraith, Maureen Mollie Hunter
See Hunter, Mollie

McInerney, Jay 1955- .... **CLC 34, 112**
See also AAYA 18; BPFB 2; CA 116; 123; CANR 45, 68, 116, 176; CN 5, 6, 7; CPW; DA3; DAM POP; DLB 292; INT CA-123; MAL 5; MTCW 2; MTFW 2005

McIntyre, Vonda N. 1948- .... **CLC 18**
See also CA 81-84; CANR 17, 34, 69; MTCW 1; SFW 4; YAW

McIntyre, Vonda Neel
See McIntyre, Vonda N.

McKay, Claude
See McKay, Festus Claudius

McKay, Festus Claudius
1889-1948 ...... **BLC 1:3; HR 1:3; PC 2; TCLC 7, 41; WLC 4**
See also AFAW 1, 2; AMWS 10; BW 1, 3; CA 104; 124; CANR 73; DA; DAB; DAC; DAM MST, MULT, NOV, POET; DLB 4, 45, 51, 117; EWL 3; EXPP; GLL 2; LAIT 3; LMFS 2; MAL 5; MTCW 1, 2; MTFW 2005; PAB; PFS 4; RGAL 4; TUS; WP

McKuen, Rod 1933- .... **CLC 1, 3**
See also AITN 1; CA 41-44R; CANR 40; CP 1

McLoughlin, R. B.
See Mencken, H(enry) L(ouis)

McLuhan, (Herbert) Marshall
1911-1980 .... **CLC 37, 83**
See also CA 9-12R; 102; CANR 12, 34, 61; DLB 88; INT CANR-12; MTCW 1, 2; MTFW 2005

McMahon, Pat
See Hoch, Edward D.

McManus, Declan Patrick Aloysius
See Costello, Elvis

McMillan, Terry 1951- .. **BLCS; CLC 50, 61, 112**
See also AAYA 21; AMWS 13; BPFB 2; BW 2, 3; CA 140; CANR 60, 104, 131; CN 7; CPW; DA3; DAM MULT, NOV, POP; MAL 5; MTCW 2; MTFW 2005; RGAL 4; YAW

McMurtry, Larry 1936- .... **CLC 2, 3, 7, 11, 27, 44, 127, 250**
See also AAYA 15; AITN 2; AMWS 5; BEST 89:2; BPFB 2; CA 5-8R; CANR 19, 43, 64, 103, 170; CDALB 1968-1988; CN 2, 3, 4, 5, 6, 7; CPW; CSW; DA3; DAM NOV, POP; DLB 2, 143, 256; DLBY 1980, 1987; EWL 3; MAL 5; MTCW 1, 2; MTFW 2005; RGAL 4; TCWW 1, 2

McMurtry, Larry Jeff
See McMurtry, Larry

McNally, Terrence 1939- ... **CLC 4, 7, 41, 91, 252; DC 27**
See also AAYA 62; AMWS 13; CA 45-48; CAD; CANR 2, 56, 116; CD 5, 6; DA3; DAM DRAM; DFS 16, 19; DLB 7, 249; EWL 3; GLL 1; MTCW 2; MTFW 2005

McNally, Thomas Michael
See McNally, T.M.

McNally, T.M. 1961- .... **CLC 82**
See also CA 246

McNamer, Deirdre 1950- .... **CLC 70**
See also CA 188; CANR 163

McNeal, Tom .... **CLC 119**
See also CA 252; CANR 185; SATA 194

McNeile, Herman Cyril
1888-1937 .... **TCLC 44**
See also CA 184; CMW 4; DLB 77

McNickle, (William) D'Arcy
1904-1977 .... **CLC 89; NNAL**
See also CA 9-12R; 85-88; CANR 5, 45; DAM MULT; DLB 175, 212; RGAL 4; SATA-Obit 22; TCWW 1, 2

McPhee, John 1931- .... **CLC 36**
See also AAYA 61; AMWS 3; ANW; BEST 90:1; CA 65-68; CANR 20, 46, 64, 69, 121, 165; CPW; DLB 185, 275; MTCW 1, 2; MTFW 2005; TUS

McPhee, John Angus
See McPhee, John

McPherson, James Alan, Jr.
See McPherson, James Alan

McPherson, James Alan 1943- . **BLCS; CLC 19, 77; SSC 95**
See also BW 1, 3; CA 25-28R; 273; CAAE 273; CAAS 17; CANR 24, 74, 140; CN 3, 4, 5, 6; CSW; DLB 38, 244; EWL 3; MTCW 1, 2; MTFW 2005; RGAL 4; RGSF 2; SSFS 23

McPherson, William (Alexander)
1933- .... **CLC 34**
See also CA 69-72; CANR 28; INT CANR-28

McTaggart, J. McT. Ellis
See McTaggart, John McTaggart Ellis

McTaggart, John McTaggart Ellis
1866-1925 .... **TCLC 105**
See also CA 120; DLB 262

Mda, Zakes 1948- .... **BLC 2:3; CLC 262**
See also CA 205; CANR 151, 185; CD 5, 6; DLB 225

Mda, Zanemvula
See Mda, Zakes

Mda, Zanemvula Kizito Gatyeni
See Mda, Zakes

Mead, George Herbert 1863-1931 . **TCLC 89**
See also CA 212; DLB 270

Mead, Margaret 1901-1978 .... **CLC 37**
See also AITN 1; CA 1-4R; 81-84; CANR 4; DA3; FW; MTCW 1, 2; SATA-Obit 20

Meaker, M. J.
See Meaker, Marijane

Meaker, Marijane 1927- .... **CLC 12, 35**
See also AAYA 2, 23; BYA 1, 7, 8; CA 107; CANR 37, 63, 145, 180; CLR 29; GLL 2; INT CA-107; JRDA; MAICYA 1, 2; MAI-CYAS 1; MTCW 1; SAAS 1; SATA 20, 61, 99, 160; SATA-Essay 111; WYA; YAW

Meaker, Marijane Agnes
See Meaker, Marijane

Mechthild von Magdeburg c. 1207-c. 1282 .... **CMLC 91**
See also DLB 138

Medoff, Mark (Howard) 1940- .... **CLC 6, 23**
See also AITN 1; CA 53-56; CAD; CANR 5; CD 5, 6; DAM DRAM; DFS 4; DLB 7; INT CANR-5

Medvedev, P. N.
See Bakhtin, Mikhail Mikhailovich

Meged, Aharon
See Megged, Aharon

Meged, Aron
See Megged, Aharon

Megged, Aharon 1920- .... **CLC 9**
See also CA 49-52; CAAS 13; CANR 1, 140; EWL 3; RGHL

Mehta, Deepa 1950- .... **CLC 208**

Mehta, Gita 1943- .... **CLC 179**
See also CA 225; CN 7; DNFS 2

Mehta, Ved 1934- .... **CLC 37**
See also CA 1-4R, 212; CAAE 212; CANR 2, 23, 69; DLB 323; MTCW 1; MTFW 2005

Melanchthon, Philipp 1497-1560 .... **LC 90**
See also DLB 179

Melanter
See Blackmore, R(ichard) D(oddridge)

Meleager c. 140B.C.-c. 70B.C. ...... **CMLC 53**

Melies, Georges 1861-1938 .... **TCLC 81**

Melikow, Loris
See Hofmannsthal, Hugo von

Melmoth, Sebastian
See Wilde, Oscar

Melo Neto, Joao Cabral de
See Cabral de Melo Neto, Joao

Meltzer, Milton 1915- .... **CLC 26**
See also AAYA 8, 45; BYA 2, 6; CA 13-16R; CANR 38, 92, 107; CLR 13; DLB 61; JRDA; MAICYA 1, 2; SAAS 1; SATA 1, 50, 80, 128; SATA-Essay 124; WYA; YAW

Melville, Herman 1819-1891 ..... **NCLC 3, 12, 29, 45, 49, 91, 93, 123, 157, 181, 193; PC 82; SSC 1, 17, 46, 95; WLC 4**
See also AAYA 25; AMW; AMWR 1; CDALB 1640-1865; DA; DA3; DAB; DAC; DAM MST, NOV; DLB 3, 74, 250, 254; EXPN; EXPS; GL 3; LAIT 1, 2; NFS 7, 9; RGAL 4; RGSF 2; SATA 59; SSFS 3; TUS

Members, Mark
See Powell, Anthony

Membreno, Alejandro .... **CLC 59**

Menand, Louis 1952- .... **CLC 208**
See also CA 200

Menander c. 342B.C.-c. 293B.C. .... **CMLC 9, 51, 101; DC 3**
See also AW 1; CDWLB 1; DAM DRAM; DLB 176; LMFS 1; RGWL 2, 3

Menchu, Rigoberta 1959- .. **CLC 160; HLCS 2**
See also CA 175; CANR 135; DNFS 1; WLIT 1

Mencken, H(enry) L(ouis)
1880-1956 .... **TCLC 13, 18**
See also AMW; CA 105; 125; CDALB 1917-1929; DLB 11, 29, 63, 137, 222; EWL 3; MAL 5; MTCW 1, 2; MTFW 2005; NCFS 4; RGAL 4; TUS

Mendelsohn, Jane 1965- .... **CLC 99**
See also CA 154; CANR 94

Mendelssohn, Moses 1729-1786 .... **LC 142**
See also DLB 97

Mendoza, Inigo Lopez de
See Santillana, Inigo Lopez de Mendoza, Marques de

Menton, Francisco de
See Chin, Frank (Chew, Jr.)

Mercer, David 1928-1980 .... **CLC 5**
See also CA 9-12R; 102; CANR 23; CBD; DAM DRAM; DLB 13, 310; MTCW 1; RGEL 2

Merchant, Paul
See Ellison, Harlan

Meredith, George 1828-1909 .. **PC 60; TCLC 17, 43**
See also CA 117; 153; CANR 80; CDBLB 1832-1890; DAM POET; DLB 18, 35, 57, 159; RGEL 2; TEA

Meredith, William 1919-2007 ...... **CLC 4, 13, 22, 55; PC 28**
See also CA 9-12R; 260; CAAS 14; CANR 6, 40, 129; CP 1, 2, 3, 4, 5, 6, 7; DAM POET; DLB 5; MAL 5

Meredith, William Morris
See Meredith, William

Merezhkovsky, Dmitrii Sergeevich
See Merezhkovsky, Dmitry Sergeyevich

Merezhkovsky, Dmitry Sergeevich
See Merezhkovsky, Dmitry Sergeyevich

Merezhkovsky, Dmitry Sergeyevich
1865-1941 .... **TCLC 29**
See also CA 169; DLB 295; EWL 3

Merezhkovsky, Zinaida
See Gippius, Zinaida (Nikolaevna)

Merimee, Prosper 1803-1870 . **DC 33; NCLC 6, 65; SSC 7, 77**
See also DLB 119, 192; EW 6; EXPS; GFL 1789 to the Present; RGSF 2; RGWL 2, 3; SSFS 8; SUFW

Merkin, Daphne 1954- .... **CLC 44**
See also CA 123

Merleau-Ponty, Maurice
1908-1961 .... **TCLC 156**
See also CA 114; 89-92; DLB 296; GFL 1789 to the Present

Merlin, Arthur
See Blish, James (Benjamin)

Mernissi, Fatima 1940- .... **CLC 171**
See also CA 152; DLB 346; FW

Merrill, James 1926-1995 ...... **CLC 2, 3, 6, 8, 13, 18, 34, 91; PC 28; TCLC 173**
See also AMWS 3; CA 13-16R; 147; CANR 10, 49, 63, 108; CP 1, 2, 3, 4; DA3; DAM POET; DLB 5, 165; DLBY 1985; EWL 3; INT CANR-10; MAL 5; MTCW 1, 2; MTFW 2005; PAB; PFS 23; RGAL 4

Merrill, James Ingram
See Merrill, James

Merriman, Alex
See Silverberg, Robert

Merriman, Brian 1747-1805 .... **NCLC 70**

Merritt, E. B.
See Waddington, Miriam

Merton, Thomas (James)
1915-1968 . **CLC 1, 3, 11, 34, 83; PC 10**
See also AAYA 61; AMWS 8; CA 5-8R; 25-28R; CANR 22, 53, 111, 131; DA3; DLB 48; DLBY 1981; MAL 5; MTCW 1, 2; MTFW 2005

Merwin, W.S. 1927- ..... **CLC 1, 2, 3, 5, 8, 13, 18, 45, 88; PC 45**
See also AMWS 3; CA 13-16R; CANR 15, 51, 112, 140; CP 1, 2, 3, 4, 5, 6, 7; DA3; DAM POET; DLB 5, 169, 342; EWL 3; INT CANR-15; MAL 5; MTCW 1, 2; MTFW 2005; PAB; PFS 5, 15; RGAL 4

Metastasio, Pietro 1698-1782 .... **LC 115**
See also RGWL 2, 3

Metcalf, John 1938- .... **CLC 37; SSC 43**
See also CA 113; CN 4, 5, 6, 7; DLB 60; RGSF 2; TWA

Metcalf, Suzanne
See Baum, L(yman) Frank

Mew, Charlotte (Mary) 1870-1928 .. **TCLC 8**
See also CA 105; 189; DLB 19, 135; RGEL 2

Mewshaw, Michael 1943- .... **CLC 9**
See also CA 53-56; CANR 7, 47, 147; DLBY 1980

Meyer, Conrad Ferdinand
1825-1898 .... **NCLC 81; SSC 30**
See also DLB 129; EW; RGWL 2, 3

Meyer, Gustav 1868-1932 .... **TCLC 21**
See also CA 117; 190; DLB 81; EWL 3

Meyer, June
See Jordan, June

Meyer, Lynn
See Slavitt, David R.

Meyer-Meyrink, Gustav
See Meyer, Gustav

Meyers, Jeffrey 1939- .... **CLC 39**
See also CA 73-76, 186; CAAE 186; CANR 54, 102, 159; DLB 111

Meynell, Alice (Christina Gertrude Thompson) 1847-1922 .... **TCLC 6**
See also CA 104; 177; DLB 19, 98; RGEL 2

Meyrink, Gustav
See Meyer, Gustav

Mhlophe, Gcina 1960- .... **BLC 2:3**

Michaels, Leonard 1933-2003 ..... **CLC 6, 25; SSC 16**
See also AMWS 16; CA 61-64; 216; CANR 21, 62, 119, 179; CN 3, 45, 6, 7; DLB 130; MTCW 1; TCLE 1:2

Michaux, Henri 1899-1984 .... **CLC 8, 19**
See also CA 85-88; 114; DLB 258; EWL 3; GFL 1789 to the Present; RGWL 2, 3

Micheaux, Oscar (Devereaux)
1884-1951 .... **TCLC 76**
See also BW 3; CA 174; DLB 50; TCWW 2

Michelangelo 1475-1564 .... **LC 12**
See also AAYA 43

Michelet, Jules 1798-1874 .... **NCLC 31**
See also EW 5; GFL 1789 to the Present

Michels, Robert 1876-1936 .... **TCLC 88**
See also CA 212

Michener, James A. 1907(?)-1997 . **CLC 1, 5, 11, 29, 60, 109**
See also AAYA 27; AITN 1; BEST 90:1; BPFB 2; CA 5-8R; 161; CANR 21, 45, 68; CN 1, 2, 3, 4, 5, 6; CPW; DA3; DAM NOV, POP; DLB 6; MAL 5; MTCW 1, 2; MTFW 2005; RHW; TCWW 1, 2

Mickiewicz, Adam 1798-1855 . **NCLC 3, 101; PC 38**
See also EW 5; RGWL 2, 3

Middleton, (John) Christopher
1926- .... **CLC 13**
See also CA 13-16R; CANR 29, 54, 117; CP 1, 2, 3, 4, 5, 6, 7; DLB 40

Middleton, Richard (Barham)
1882-1911 .... **TCLC 56**
See also CA 187; DLB 156; HGG

Middleton, Stanley 1919- .... **CLC 7, 38**
See also CA 25-28R; CAAS 23; CANR 21, 46, 81, 157; CN 1, 2, 3, 4, 5, 6, 7; DLB 14, 326

Middleton, Thomas 1580-1627 ...... **DC 5; LC 33, 123**
See also BRW 2; DAM DRAM, MST; DFS 18, 22; DLB 58; RGEL 2

Mieville, China 1972(?)- .... **CLC 235**
See also AAYA 52; CA 196; CANR 138; MTFW 2005

Migueis, Jose Rodrigues 1901-1980 . **CLC 10**
See also DLB 287

Mihura, Miguel 1905-1977 .... **DC 34**
See also CA 214

Mikszath, Kalman 1847-1910 .... **TCLC 31**
See also CA 170

Miles, Jack .... **CLC 100**
See also CA 200

Miles, John Russiano
See Miles, Jack

Miles, Josephine (Louise)
1911-1985 .... **CLC 1, 2, 14, 34, 39**
See also CA 1-4R; 116; CANR 2, 55; CP 1, 2, 3, 4; DAM POET; DLB 48; MAL 5; TCLE 1:2

Militant
See Sandburg, Carl (August)

Mill, Harriet (Hardy) Taylor
1807-1858 .... **NCLC 102**
See also FW

Mill, John Stuart 1806-1873 ... **NCLC 11, 58, 179**
See also CDBLB 1832-1890; DLB 55, 190, 262; FW 1; RGEL 2; TEA

Millar, Kenneth 1915-1983 .. **CLC 1, 2, 3, 14, 34, 41**
See also AMWS 4; BPFB 2; CA 9-12R; 110; CANR 16, 63, 107; CMW 4; CN 1, 2, 3; CPW; DA3; DAM POP; DLB 2, 226; DLBD 6; DLBY 1983; MAL 5; MSW; MTCW 1, 2; MTFW 2005; RGAL 4

Millay, E. Vincent
See Millay, Edna St. Vincent

Millay, Edna St. Vincent 1892-1950 ..... **PC 6, 61; TCLC 4, 49, 169; WLCS**
See also AMW; CA 104; 130; CDALB 1917-1929; DA; DA3; DAB; DAC; DAM MST, POET; DLB 45, 249; EWL 3; EXPP; FL 1:6; GLL 1; MAL 5; MBL; MTCW 1, 2; MTFW 2005; PAB; PFS 3, 17; RGAL 4; TUS; WP

Miller, Arthur 1915-2005 ..... **CLC 1, 2, 6, 10, 15, 26, 47, 78, 179; DC 1, 31; WLC 4**
See also AAYA 15; AITN 1; AMW; AMWC 1; CA 1-4R; 236; CABS 3; CAD; CANR 2, 30, 54, 76, 132; CD 5, 6; CDALB 1941-1968; DA; DA3; DAB; DAC; DAM DRAM, MST; DFS 1, 3, 8; DLB 7, 266; EWL 3; LAIT 1, 4; LATS 1:2; MAL 5; MTCW 1, 2; MTFW 2005; RGAL 4; RGHL; TUS; WYAS 1

Miller, Henry (Valentine)
1891-1980 .... **CLC 1, 2, 4, 9, 14, 43, 84; TCLC 213; WLC 4**
See also AMW; BPFB 2; CA 9-12R; 97-100; CANR 33, 64; CDALB 1929-1941; CN 1, 2; DA; DA3; DAB; DAC; DAM MST, NOV; DLB 4, 9; DLBY 1980; EWL 3; MAL 5; MTCW 1, 2; MTFW 2005; RGAL 4; TUS

Miller, Hugh 1802-1856 .... **NCLC 143**
See also DLB 190

Miller, Jason 1939(?)-2001 .... **CLC 2**
See also AITN 1; CA 73-76; 197; CAD; CANR 130; DFS 12; DLB 7

Miller, Sue 1943- .... **CLC 44**
　　See also AMWS 12; BEST 90:3; CA 139;
　　CANR 59, 91, 128; DA3; DAM POP;
　　DLB 143
Miller, Walter M(ichael, Jr.)
　　1923-1996 .... **CLC 4, 30**
　　See also BPFB 2; CA 85-88; CANR 108;
　　DLB 8; SCFW 1, 2; SFW 4
Millett, Kate 1934- .... **CLC 67**
　　See also AITN 1; CA 73-76; CANR 32, 53,
　　76, 110; DA3; DLB 246; FW; GLL 1;
　　MTCW 1, 2; MTFW 2005
Millhauser, Steven 1943- ... **CLC 21, 54, 109;**
　　SSC 57
　　See also AAYA 76; CA 110; 111; CANR
　　63, 114, 133, 189; CN 6, 7; DA3; DLB 2;
　　FANT; INT CA-111; MAL 5; MTCW 2;
　　MTFW 2005
Millhauser, Steven Lewis
　　See Millhauser, Steven
Millin, Sarah Gertrude 1889-1968 ... **CLC 49**
　　See also CA 102; 93-96; DLB 225; EWL 3
Milne, A. A. 1882-1956 .... **TCLC 6, 88**
　　See also BRWS 5; CA 104; 133; CLR 1,
　　26, 108; CMW 4; CWRI 5; DA3; DAB;
　　DAC; DAM MST; DLB 10, 77, 100, 160;
　　FANT; MAICYA 1, 2; MTCW 1, 2;
　　MTFW 2005; RGEL 2; SATA 100; WCH;
　　YABC 1
Milne, Alan Alexander
　　See Milne, A. A.
Milner, Ron(ald) 1938-2004 .. **BLC 1:3; CLC**
　　56
　　See also AITN 1; BW 1; CA 73-76; 230;
　　CAD; CANR 24, 81; CD 5, 6; DAM
　　MULT; DLB 38; MAL 5; MTCW 1
Milnes, Richard Monckton
　　1809-1885 .... **NCLC 61**
　　See also DLB 32, 184
Milosz, Czeslaw 1911-2004 .... **CLC 5, 11, 22,**
　　31, 56, 82, 253; PC 8; WLCS
　　See also AAYA 62; CA 81-84; 230; CANR
　　23, 51, 91, 126; CDWLB 4; CWW 2;
　　DA3; DAM MST, POET; DLB 215, 331;
　　EW 13; EWL 3; MTCW 1, 2; MTFW
　　2005; PFS 16, 29; RGHL; RGWL 2, 3
Milton, John 1608-1674 ..... **LC 9, 43, 92; PC**
　　19, 29; WLC 4
　　See also AAYA 65; BRW 2; BRWR 2; CD-
　　BLB 1660-1789; DA; DA3; DAB; DAC;
　　DAM MST, POET; DLB 131, 151, 281;
　　EFS 1; EXPP; LAIT 1; PAB; PFS 3, 17;
　　RGEL 2; TEA; WLIT 3; WP
Min, Anchee 1957- .... **CLC 86**
　　See also CA 146; CANR 94, 137; MTFW
　　2005
Minehaha, Cornelius
　　See Wedekind, Frank
Miner, Valerie 1947- .... **CLC 40**
　　See also CA 97-100; CANR 59, 177; FW;
　　GLL 2
Minimo, Duca
　　See D'Annunzio, Gabriele
Minot, Susan (Anderson) 1956- ...... **CLC 44,**
　　159
　　See also AMWS 6; CA 134; CANR 118;
　　CN 6, 7
Minus, Ed 1938- .... **CLC 39**
　　See also CA 185
Mirabai 1498(?)-1550(?) .... **LC 143; PC 48**
　　See also PFS 24
Miranda, Javier
　　See Bioy Casares, Adolfo
Mirbeau, Octave 1848-1917 .... **TCLC 55**
　　See also CA 216; DLB 123, 192; GFL 1789
　　to the Present
Mirikitani, Janice 1942- .... **AAL**
　　See also CA 211; DLB 312; RGAL 4

Mirk, John (?)-c. 1414 .... **LC 105**
　　See also DLB 146
Miro (Ferrer), Gabriel (Francisco Victor)
　　1879-1930 .... **TCLC 5**
　　See also CA 104; 185; DLB 322; EWL 3
Misharin, Alexandr .... **CLC 59**
Mishima, Yukio
　　See Hiraoka, Kimitake
Mishima Yukio
　　See Hiraoka, Kimitake
Miss C. L. F.
　　See Grimke, Charlotte L(ottie) Forten
Mister X
　　See Hoch, Edward D.
Mistral, Frederic 1830-1914 .... **TCLC 51**
　　See also CA 122; 213; DLB 331; GFL 1789
　　to the Present
Mistral, Gabriela
　　See Godoy Alcayaga, Lucila
Mistry, Rohinton 1952- ... **CLC 71, 196, 274;**
　　SSC 73
　　See also BRWS 10; CA 141; CANR 86,
　　114; CCA 1; CN 6, 7; DAC; DLB 334;
　　SSFS 6
Mitchell, Clyde
　　See Ellison, Harlan; Silverberg, Robert
Mitchell, Emerson Blackhorse Barney
　　1945- .... **NNAL**
　　See also CA 45-48
Mitchell, James Leslie 1901-1935 .... **TCLC 4**
　　See also BRWS 14; CA 104; 188; DLB 15;
　　RGEL 2
Mitchell, Joni 1943- .... **CLC 12**
　　See also CA 112; CCA 1
Mitchell, Joseph (Quincy)
　　1908-1996 .... **CLC 98**
　　See also CA 77-80; 152; CANR 69; CN 1,
　　2, 3, 4, 5, 6; CSW; DLB 185; DLBY 1996
Mitchell, Margaret (Munnerlyn)
　　1900-1949 .... **TCLC 11, 170**
　　See also AAYA 23; BPFB 2; BYA 1; CA
　　109; 125; CANR 55, 94; CDALBS; DA3;
　　DAM NOV, POP; DLB 9; LAIT 2; MAL
　　5; MTCW 1, 2; MTFW 2005; NFS 9;
　　RGAL 4; RHW; TUS; WYAS 1; YAW
Mitchell, Peggy
　　See Mitchell, Margaret (Munnerlyn)
Mitchell, S(ilas) Weir 1829-1914 .... **TCLC 36**
　　See also CA 165; DLB 202; RGAL 4
Mitchell, W(illiam) O(rmond)
　　1914-1998 .... **CLC 25**
　　See also CA 77-80; 165; CANR 15, 43; CN
　　1, 2, 3, 4, 5, 6; DAC; DAM MST; DLB
　　88; TCLE 1:2
Mitchell, William (Lendrum)
　　1879-1936 .... **TCLC 81**
　　See also CA 213
Mitford, Mary Russell 1787-1855 ... **NCLC 4**
　　See also DLB 110, 116; RGEL 2
Mitford, Nancy 1904-1973 .... **CLC 44**
　　See also BRWS 10; CA 9-12R; CN 1; DLB
　　191; RGEL 2
Miyamoto, (Chujo) Yuriko
　　1899-1951 .... **TCLC 37**
　　See also CA 170, 174; DLB 180
Miyamoto Yuriko
　　See Miyamoto, (Chujo) Yuriko
Miyazawa, Kenji 1896-1933 .... **TCLC 76**
　　See also CA 157; EWL 3; RGWL 3
Miyazawa Kenji
　　See Miyazawa, Kenji
Mizoguchi, Kenji 1898-1956 .... **TCLC 72**
　　See also CA 167
Mo, Timothy (Peter) 1950- .... **CLC 46, 134**
　　See also CA 117; CANR 128; CN 5, 6, 7;
　　DLB 194; MTCW 1; WLIT 4; WWE 1
Modarressi, Taghi (M.) 1931-1997 ... **CLC 44**
　　See also CA 121; 134; INT CA-134

Modiano, Patrick (Jean) 1945- .... **CLC 18,**
　　218
　　See also CA 85-88; CANR 17, 40, 115;
　　CWW 2; DLB 83, 299; EWL 3; RGHL
Mofolo, Thomas (Mokopu)
　　1875(?)-1948 .... **BLC 1:3; TCLC 22**
　　See also AFW; CA 121; 153; CANR 83;
　　DAM MULT; DLB 225; EWL 3; MTCW
　　2; MTFW 2005; WLIT 2
Mohr, Nicholasa 1938- .... **CLC 12; HLC 2**
　　See also AAYA 8, 46; CA 49-52; CANR 1,
　　32, 64; CLR 22; DAM MULT; DLB 145;
　　HW 1, 2; JRDA; LAIT 5; LLW; MAICYA
　　2; MAICYAS 1; RGAL 4; SAAS 8; SATA
　　8, 97; SATA-Essay 113; WYA; YAW
Moi, Toril 1953- .... **CLC 172**
　　See also CA 154; CANR 102; FW
Mojtabai, A(nn) G(race) 1938- ..... **CLC 5, 9,**
　　15, 29
　　See also CA 85-88; CANR 88
Moliere 1622-1673 ..... **DC 13; LC 10, 28, 64,**
　　125, 127; WLC 4
　　See also DA; DA3; DAB; DAC; DAM
　　DRAM, MST; DFS 13, 18, 20; DLB 268;
　　EW 3; GFL Beginnings to 1789; LATS
　　1:1; RGWL 2, 3; TWA
Molin, Charles
　　See Mayne, William (James Carter)
Molnar, Ferenc 1878-1952 .... **TCLC 20**
　　See also CA 109; 153; CANR 83; CDWLB
　　4; DAM DRAM; DLB 215; EWL 3;
　　RGWL 2, 3
Momaday, N. Scott 1934- ...... **CLC 2, 19, 85,**
　　95, 160; NNAL; PC 25; WLCS
　　See also AAYA 11, 64; AMWS 4; ANW;
　　BPFB 2; BYA 12; CA 25-28R; CANR 14,
　　34, 68, 134; CDALBS; CN 2, 3, 4, 5, 6,
　　7; CPW; DA; DA3; DAB; DAC; DAM
　　MST, MULT, NOV, POP; DLB 143, 175,
　　256; EWL 3; EXPP; INT CANR-14;
　　LAIT 4; LATS 1:2; MAL 5; MTCW 1, 2;
　　MTFW 2005; NFS 10; PFS 2, 11; RGAL
　　4; SATA 48; SATA-Brief 30; TCWW 1,
　　2; WP; YAW
Monette, Paul 1945-1995 .... **CLC 82**
　　See also AMWS 10; CA 139; 147; CN 6;
　　GLL 1
Monroe, Harriet 1860-1936 .... **TCLC 12**
　　See also CA 109; 204; DLB 54, 91
Monroe, Lyle
　　See Heinlein, Robert A.
Montagu, Elizabeth 1720-1800 .... **NCLC 7,**
　　117
　　See also FW
Montagu, Mary (Pierrepont) Wortley
　　1689-1762 .... **LC 9, 57; PC 16**
　　See also DLB 95, 101; FL 1:1; RGEL 2
Montagu, W. H.
　　See Coleridge, Samuel Taylor
Montague, John (Patrick) 1929- ..... **CLC 13,**
　　46
　　See also CA 9-12R; CANR 9, 69, 121; CP
　　1, 2, 3, 4, 5, 6, 7; DLB 40; EWL 3;
　　MTCW 1; PFS 12; RGEL 2; TCLE 1:2
Montaigne, Michel (Eyquem) de
　　1533-1592 .... **LC 8, 105; WLC 4**
　　See also DA; DAB; DAC; DAM MST;
　　DLB 327; EW 2; GFL Beginnings to
　　1789; LMFS 1; RGWL 2, 3; TWA
Montale, Eugenio 1896-1981 ... **CLC 7, 9, 18;**
　　PC 13
　　See also CA 17-20R; 104; CANR 30; DLB
　　114, 331; EW 11; EWL 3; MTCW 1; PFS
　　22; RGWL 2, 3; TWA; WLIT 7
Montesquieu, Charles-Louis de Secondat
　　1689-1755 .... **LC 7, 69**
　　See also DLB 314; EW 3; GFL Beginnings
　　to 1789; TWA
Montessori, Maria 1870-1952 ...... **TCLC 103**
　　See also CA 115; 147

Newman, Charles 1938-2006 .... **CLC 2, 8**
See also CA 21-24R; 249; CANR 84; CN 3, 4, 5, 6

Newman, Charles Hamilton
See Newman, Charles

Newman, Edwin (Harold) 1919- ...... **CLC 14**
See also AITN 1; CA 69-72; CANR 5

Newman, John Henry 1801-1890 . **NCLC 38, 99**
See also BRWS 7; DLB 18, 32, 55; RGEL 2

Newton, (Sir) Isaac 1642-1727 ...... **LC 35, 53**
See also DLB 252

Newton, Suzanne 1936- .... **CLC 35**
See also BYA 7; CA 41-44R; CANR 14; JRDA; SATA 5, 77

New York Dept. of Ed. .... **CLC 70**

Nexo, Martin Andersen
1869-1954 .... **TCLC 43**
See also CA 202; DLB 214; EWL 3

Nezval, Vitezslav 1900-1958 .... **TCLC 44**
See also CA 123; CDWLB 4; DLB 215; EWL 3

Ng, Fae Myenne 1956- .... **CLC 81**
See also BYA 11; CA 146

Ngcobo, Lauretta 1931- .... **BLC 2:3**
See also CA 165

Ngema, Mbongeni 1955- .... **CLC 57**
See also BW 2; CA 143; CANR 84; CD 5, 6

Ngugi, James T.
See Ngugi wa Thiong'o

Ngugi, James Thiong'o
See Ngugi wa Thiong'o

Ngugi wa Thiong'o 1938- .... **BLC 1:3, 2:3; CLC 3, 7, 13, 36, 182, 275**
See also AFW; BRWS 8; BW 2; CA 81-84; CANR 27, 58, 164; CD 3, 4, 5, 6, 7; CD-WLB 3; CN 1, 2; DAM MULT, NOV; DLB 125; DNFS 2; EWL 3; MTCW 1, 2; MTFW 2005; RGEL 2; WWE 1

Niatum, Duane 1938- .... **NNAL**
See also CA 41-44R; CANR 21, 45, 83; DLB 175

Nichol, B(arrie) P(hillip) 1944-1988 . **CLC 18**
See also CA 53-56; CP 1, 2, 3, 4; DLB 53; SATA 66

Nicholas of Autrecourt c.
1298-1369 .... **CMLC 108**

Nicholas of Cusa 1401-1464 .... **LC 80**
See also DLB 115

Nichols, John 1940- .... **CLC 38**
See also AMWS 13; CA 9-12R, 190; CAAE 190; CAAS 2; CANR 6, 70, 121, 185; DLBY 1982; LATS 1:2; MTFW 2005; TCWW 1, 2

Nichols, Leigh
See Koontz, Dean R.

Nichols, Peter (Richard) 1927- .... **CLC 5, 36, 65**
See also CA 104; CANR 33, 86; CBD; CD 5, 6; DLB 13, 245; MTCW 1

Nicholson, Linda .... **CLC 65**

Ni Chuilleanain, Eilean 1942- .... **PC 34**
See also CA 126; CANR 53, 83; CP 5, 6, 7; CWP; DLB 40

Nicolas, F. R. E.
See Freeling, Nicolas

Niedecker, Lorine 1903-1970 ..... **CLC 10, 42; PC 42**
See also CA 25-28; CAP 2; DAM POET; DLB 48

Nietzsche, Friedrich (Wilhelm)
1844-1900 .... **TCLC 10, 18, 55**
See also CA 107; 121; CDWLB 2; DLB 129; EW 7; RGWL 2, 3; TWA

Nievo, Ippolito 1831-1861 .... **NCLC 22**

Nightingale, Anne Redmon 1943- .... **CLC 22**
See also CA 103; DLBY 1986

Nightingale, Florence 1820-1910 ... **TCLC 85**
See also CA 188; DLB 166

Nijo Yoshimoto 1320-1388 .... **CMLC 49**
See also DLB 203

Nik. T. O.
See Annensky, Innokenty (Fyodorovich)

Nin, Anais 1903-1977 ..... **CLC 1, 4, 8, 11, 14, 60, 127; SSC 10**
See also AITN 2; AMWS 10; BPFB 2; CA 13-16R; 69-72; CANR 22, 53; CN 1, 2; DAM NOV, POP; DLB 2, 4, 152; EWL 3; GLL 2; MAL 5; MBL; MTCW 1, 2; MTFW 2005; RGAL 4; RGSF 2

Nisbet, Robert A(lexander)
1913-1996 .... **TCLC 117**
See also CA 25-28R; 153; CANR 17; INT CANR-17

Nishida, Kitaro 1870-1945 .... **TCLC 83**

Nishiwaki, Junzaburo 1894-1982 .... **PC 15**
See also CA 194; 107; EWL 3; MJW; RGWL 3

Nissenson, Hugh 1933- .... **CLC 4, 9**
See also CA 17-20R; CANR 27, 108, 151; CN 5, 6; DLB 28, 335

Nister, Der
See Der Nister

Niven, Larry 1938- .... **CLC 8**
See also AAYA 27; BPFB 2; BYA 10; CA 21-24R, 207; CAAE 207; CAAS 12; CANR 14, 44, 66, 113, 155; CPW; DAM POP; DLB 8; MTCW 1, 2; SATA 95, 171; SCFW 1, 2; SFW 4

Niven, Laurence VanCott
See Niven, Larry

Nixon, Agnes Eckhardt 1927- .... **CLC 21**
See also CA 110

Nizan, Paul 1905-1940 .... **TCLC 40**
See also CA 161; DLB 72; EWL 3; GFL 1789 to the Present

Nkosi, Lewis 1936- .... **BLC 1:3; CLC 45**
See also BW 1, 3; CA 65-68; CANR 27, 81; CBD; CD 5, 6; DAM MULT; DLB 157, 225; WWE 1

Nodier, (Jean) Charles (Emmanuel)
1780-1844 .... **NCLC 19**
See also DLB 119; GFL 1789 to the Present

Noguchi, Yone 1875-1947 .... **TCLC 80**

Nolan, Brian
See O Nuallain, Brian

Nolan, Christopher 1965-2009 .... **CLC 58**
See also CA 111; CANR 88

Noon, Jeff 1957- .... **CLC 91**
See also CA 148; CANR 83; DLB 267; SFW 4

Norden, Charles
See Durrell, Lawrence (George)

Nordhoff, Charles Bernard
1887-1947 .... **TCLC 23**
See also CA 108; 211; DLB 9; LAIT 1; RHW 1; SATA 23

Norfolk, Lawrence 1963- .... **CLC 76**
See also CA 144; CANR 85; CN 6, 7; DLB 267

Norman, Marsha (Williams) 1947- . **CLC 28, 186; DC 8**
See also CA 105; CABS 3; CAD; CANR 41, 131; CD 5, 6; CSW; CWD; DAM DRAM; DFS 2; DLB 266; DLBY 1984; FW; MAL 5

Normyx
See Douglas, (George) Norman

Norris, (Benjamin) Frank(lin, Jr.)
1870-1902 . **SSC 28; TCLC 24, 155, 211**
See also AAYA 57; AMW; AMWC 2; BPFB 2; CA 110; 160; CDALB 1865-1917; DLB 12, 71, 186; LMFS 2; MAL 5; NFS 12; RGAL 4; TCWW 1, 2; TUS

Norris, Kathleen 1947- .... **CLC 248**
See also CA 160; CANR 113

Norris, Leslie 1921-2006 .... **CLC 14**
See also CA 11-12; 251; CANR 14, 117; CAP 1; CP 1, 2, 3, 4, 5, 6, 7; DLB 27, 256

North, Andrew
See Norton, Andre

North, Anthony
See Koontz, Dean R.

North, Captain George
See Stevenson, Robert Louis (Balfour)

North, Captain George
See Stevenson, Robert Louis (Balfour)

North, Milou
See Erdrich, Louise

Northrup, B. A.
See Hubbard, L. Ron

North Staffs
See Hulme, T(homas) E(rnest)

Northup, Solomon 1808-1863 ...... **NCLC 105**

Norton, Alice Mary
See Norton, Andre

Norton, Andre 1912-2005 .... **CLC 12**
See also AAYA 14; BPFB 2; BYA 4, 10, 12; CA 1-4R; 237; CANR 2, 31, 68, 108, 149; CLR 50; DLB 8, 52; JRDA; MAI-CYA 1, 2; MTCW 1; SATA 1, 43, 91; SUFW 1, 2; YAW

Norton, Caroline 1808-1877 .. **NCLC 47, 205**
See also DLB 21, 159, 199

Norway, Nevil Shute 1899-1960 .... **CLC 30**
See also BPFB 3; CA 102; 93-96; CANR 85; DLB 255; MTCW 2; NFS 9; RHW 4; SFW 4

Norwid, Cyprian Kamil
1821-1883 .... **NCLC 17**
See also RGWL 3

Nosille, Nabrah
See Ellison, Harlan

Nossack, Hans Erich 1901-1977 .... **CLC 6**
See also CA 93-96; 85-88; CANR 156; DLB 69; EWL 3

Nostradamus 1503-1566 .... **LC 27**

Nosu, Chuji
See Ozu, Yasujiro

Notenburg, Eleanora (Genrikhovna) von
See Guro, Elena (Genrikhovna)

Nova, Craig 1945- .... **CLC 7, 31**
See also CA 45-48; CANR 2, 53, 127

Novak, Joseph
See Kosinski, Jerzy

Novalis 1772-1801 .... **NCLC 13, 178**
See also CDWLB 2; DLB 90; EW 5; RGWL 2, 3

Novick, Peter 1934- .... **CLC 164**
See also CA 188

Novis, Emile
See Weil, Simone (Adolphine)

Nowlan, Alden (Albert) 1933-1983 ... **CLC 15**
See also CA 9-12R; CANR 5; CP 1, 2, 3; DAC; DAM MST; DLB 53; PFS 12

Noyes, Alfred 1880-1958 ...... **PC 27; TCLC 7**
See also CA 104; 188; DLB 20; EXPP; FANT; PFS 4; RGEL 2

Nugent, Richard Bruce
1906(?)-1987 .... **HR 1:3**
See also BW 1; CA 125; DLB 51; GLL 2

Nunez, Elizabeth 1944- .... **BLC 2:3**
See also CA 223

Nunn, Kem .... **CLC 34**
See also CA 159

Nussbaum, Martha Craven 1947- .. **CLC 203**
See also CA 134; CANR 102, 176

Nwapa, Flora (Nwanzuruaha)
1931-1993 .... **BLCS; CLC 133**
See also BW 2; CA 143; CANR 83; CD-WLB 3; CWRI 5; DLB 125; EWL 3; WLIT 2

Olson, Toby 1937- .... **CLC 28**
See also CA 65-68; CAAS 11; CANR 9, 31, 84, 175; CP 3, 4, 5, 6, 7

Olyesha, Yuri
See Olesha, Yuri (Karlovich)

Olympiodorus of Thebes c. 375-c. 430 .... **CMLC 59**

Omar Khayyam
See Khayyam, Omar

Ondaatje, Michael 1943- ..... **CLC 14, 29, 51, 76, 180, 258; PC 28**
See also AAYA 66; CA 77-80; CANR 42, 74, 109, 133, 172; CN 5, 6, 7; CP 1, 2, 3, 4, 5, 6, 7; DA3; DAB; DAC; DAM MST; DLB 60, 323, 326; EWL 3; LATS 1:2; LMFS 2; MTCW 2; MTFW 2005; NFS 23; PFS 8, 19; TCLE 1:2; TWA; WWE 1

Ondaatje, Philip Michael
See Ondaatje, Michael

Oneal, Elizabeth 1934- .... **CLC 30**
See also AAYA 5, 41; BYA 13; CA 106; CANR 28, 84; CLR 13; JRDA; MAICYA 1, 2; SATA 30, 82; WYA; YAW

Oneal, Zibby
See Oneal, Elizabeth

O'Neill, Eugene (Gladstone) 1888-1953 ... **DC 20; TCLC 1, 6, 27, 49; WLC 4**
See also AAYA 54; AITN 1; AMW; AMWC 1; CA 110; 132; CAD; CANR 131; CDALB 1929-1941; DA; DA3; DAB; DAC; DAM DRAM, MST; DFS 2, 4, 5, 6, 9, 11, 12, 16, 20, 26; DLB 7, 331; EWL 3; LAIT 3; LMFS 2; MAL 5; MTCW 1, 2; MTFW 2005; RGAL 4; TUS

Onetti, Juan Carlos 1909-1994 ... **CLC 7, 10; HLCS 2; SSC 23; TCLC 131**
See also CA 85-88; 145; CANR 32, 63; CD-WLB 3; CWW 2; DAM MULT, NOV; DLB 113; EWL 3; HW 1, 2; LAW; MTCW 1, 2; MTFW 2005; RGSF 2

O'Nolan, Brian
See O Nuallain, Brian

O Nuallain, Brian 1911-1966 .... **CLC 1, 4, 5, 7, 10, 47**
See also BRWS 2; CA 21-22; 25-28R; CAP 2; DLB 231; EWL 3; FANT; RGEL 2; TEA

Ophuls, Max
See Ophuls, Max

Ophuls, Max 1902-1957 .... **TCLC 79**
See also CA 113

Opie, Amelia 1769-1853 .... **NCLC 65**
See also DLB 116, 159; RGEL 2

Oppen, George 1908-1984 ..... **CLC 7, 13, 34; PC 35; TCLC 107**
See also CA 13-16R; 113; CANR 8, 82; CP 1, 2, 3; DLB 5, 165

Oppenheim, E(dward) Phillips 1866-1946 .... **TCLC 45**
See also CA 111; 202; CMW 4; DLB 70

Oppenheimer, Max
See Ophuls, Max

Opuls, Max
See Ophuls, Max

Orage, A(lfred) R(ichard) 1873-1934 .... **TCLC 157**
See also CA 122

Origen c. 185-c. 254 .... **CMLC 19**

Orlovitz, Gil 1918-1973 .... **CLC 22**
See also CA 77-80; 45-48; CN 1; CP 1, 2; DLB 2, 5

Orosius c. 385-c. 420 .... **CMLC 100**

O'Rourke, Patrick Jake
See O'Rourke, P.J.

O'Rourke, P.J. 1947- .... **CLC 209**
See also CA 77-80; CANR 13, 41, 67, 111, 155; CPW; DAM POP; DLB 185

Orris
See Ingelow, Jean

Ortega y Gasset, Jose 1883-1955 ...... **HLC 2; TCLC 9**
See also CA 106; 130; DAM MULT; EW 9; EWL 3; HW 1, 2; MTCW 1, 2; MTFW 2005

Ortese, Anna Maria 1914-1998 .... **CLC 89**
See also DLB 177; EWL 3

Ortiz, Simon
See Ortiz, Simon J.

Ortiz, Simon J. 1941- . **CLC 45, 208; NNAL; PC 17**
See also AMWS 4; CA 134; CANR 69, 118, 164; CP 3, 4, 5, 6, 7; DAM MULT, POET; DLB 120, 175, 256, 342; EXPP; MAL 5; PFS 4, 16; RGAL 4; SSFS 22; TCWW 2

Ortiz, Simon Joseph
See Ortiz, Simon J.

Orton, Joe
See Orton, John Kingsley

Orton, John Kingsley 1933-1967 .... **CLC 4, 13, 43; DC 3; TCLC 157**
See also BRWS 5; CA 85-88; CANR 35, 66; CBD; CDBLB 1960 to Present; DAM DRAM; DFS 3, 6; DLB 13, 310; GLL 1; MTCW 1, 2; MTFW 2005; RGEL 2; TEA; WLIT 4

Orwell, George
See Blair, Eric (Arthur)

Osborne, David
See Silverberg, Robert

Osborne, Dorothy 1627-1695 .... **LC 141**

Osborne, George
See Silverberg, Robert

Osborne, John 1929-1994 .... **CLC 1, 2, 5, 11, 45; TCLC 153; WLC 4**
See also BRWS 1; CA 13-16R; 147; CANR 21, 56; CBD; CDBLB 1945-1960; DA; DAB; DAC; DAM DRAM, MST; DFS 4, 19, 24; DLB 13; EWL 3; MTCW 1, 2; MTFW 2005; RGEL 2

Osborne, Lawrence 1958- .... **CLC 50**
See also CA 189; CANR 152

Osbourne, Lloyd 1868-1947 .... **TCLC 93**

Osceola
See Blixen, Karen (Christentze Dinesen)

Osgood, Frances Sargent 1811-1850 .... **NCLC 141**
See also DLB 250

Oshima, Nagisa 1932- .... **CLC 20**
See also CA 116; 121; CANR 78

Oskison, John Milton 1874-1947 .... **NNAL; TCLC 35**
See also CA 144; CANR 84; DAM MULT; DLB 175

Ossoli, Sarah Margaret (Fuller) 1810-1850 .... **NCLC 5, 50, 211**
See also AMWS 2; CDALB 1640-1865; DLB 1, 59, 73, 183, 223, 239; FW; LMFS 1; SATA 25

Ostriker, Alicia 1937- .... **CLC 132**
See also CA 25-28R; CAAS 24; CANR 10, 30, 62, 99, 167; CWP; DLB 120; EXPP; PFS 19, 26

Ostriker, Alicia Suskin
See Ostriker, Alicia

Ostrovsky, Aleksandr Nikolaevich
See Ostrovsky, Alexander

Ostrovsky, Alexander 1823-1886 .. **NCLC 30, 57**
See also DLB 277

Osundare, Niyi 1947- .... **BLC 2:3**
See also AFW; BW 3; CA 176; CDWLB 3; CP 7; DLB 157

Otero, Blas de 1916-1979 .... **CLC 11**
See also CA 89-92; DLB 134; EWL 3

O'Trigger, Sir Lucius
See Horne, Richard Henry Hengist

Otto, Rudolf 1869-1937 .... **TCLC 85**

Otto, Whitney 1955- .... **CLC 70**
See also CA 140; CANR 120

Otway, Thomas 1652-1685 ... **DC 24; LC 106**
See also DAM DRAM; DLB 80; RGEL 2

Ouida
See De La Ramee, Marie Louise

Ouologuem, Yambo 1940- .... **CLC 146**
See also CA 111; 176

Ousmane, Sembene 1923-2007 .... **BLC 1:3, 2:3; CLC 66**
See also AFW; BW 1, 3; CA 117; 125; 261; CANR 81; CWW 2; EWL 3; MTCW 1; WLIT 2

Ovid 43B.C.-17 .... **CMLC 7, 108; PC 2**
See also AW 2; CDWLB 1; DA3; DAM POET; DLB 211; PFS 22; RGWL 2, 3; WLIT 8; WP

Owen, Hugh
See Faust, Frederick (Schiller)

Owen, Wilfred (Edward Salter) 1893-1918 ... **PC 19; TCLC 5, 27; WLC 4**
See also BRW 6; CA 104; 141; CDBLB 1914-1945; DA; DAB; DAC; DAM MST, POET; DLB 20; EWL 3; EXPP; MTCW 2; MTFW 2005; PFS 10; RGEL 2; WLIT 4

Owens, Louis (Dean) 1948-2002 .... **NNAL**
See also CA 137, 179; 207; CAAE 179; CAAS 24; CANR 71

Owens, Rochelle 1936- .... **CLC 8**
See also CA 17-20R; CAAS 2; CAD; CANR 39; CD 5, 6; CP 1, 2, 3, 4, 5, 6, 7; CWD; CWP

Oz, Amos 1939- ...... **CLC 5, 8, 11, 27, 33, 54; SSC 66**
See also CA 53-56; CANR 27, 47, 65, 113, 138, 175; CWW 2; DAM NOV; EWL 3; MTCW 1, 2; MTFW 2005; RGHL; RGSF 2; RGWL 3; WLIT 6

Ozick, Cynthia 1928- . **CLC 3, 7, 28, 62, 155, 262; SSC 15, 60, 123**
See also AMWS 5; BEST 90:1; CA 17-20R; CANR 23, 58, 116, 160, 187; CN 3, 4, 5, 6, 7; CPW; DA3; DAM NOV, POP; DLB 28, 152, 299; DLBY 1982; EWL 3; EXPS; INT CANR-23; MAL 5; MTCW 1, 2; MTFW 2005; RGAL 4; RGHL; RGSF 2; SSFS 3, 12, 22

Ozu, Yasujiro 1903-1963 .... **CLC 16**
See also CA 112

Pabst, G. W. 1885-1967 .... **TCLC 127**

Pacheco, C.
See Pessoa, Fernando

Pacheco, Jose Emilio 1939- .... **HLC 2**
See also CA 111; 131; CANR 65; CWW 2; DAM MULT; DLB 290; EWL 3; HW 1, 2; RGSF 2

Pa Chin
See Jin, Ba

Pack, Robert 1929- .... **CLC 13**
See also CA 1-4R; CANR 3, 44, 82; CP 1, 2, 3, 4, 5, 6, 7; DLB 5; SATA 118

Packer, Vin
See Meaker, Marijane

Padgett, Lewis
See Kuttner, Henry

Padilla (Lorenzo), Heberto 1932-2000 .... **CLC 38**
See also AITN 1; CA 123; 131; 189; CWW 2; EWL 3; HW 1

Paerdurabo, Frater
See Crowley, Edward Alexander

Page, James Patrick 1944- .... **CLC 12**
See also CA 204

Page, Jimmy 1944-
See Page, James Patrick

Paterson, Katherine 1932- .... **CLC 12, 30**
See also AAYA 1, 31; BYA 1, 2, 7; CA 21-24R; CANR 28, 59, 111, 173; CLR 7, 50, 127; CWRI 5; DLB 52; JRDA; LAIT 4; MAICYA 1, 2; MAICYAS 1; MTCW 1; SATA 13, 53, 92, 133; WYA; YAW

Paterson, Katherine Womeldorf
See Paterson, Katherine

Patmore, Coventry Kersey Dighton
1823-1896 .... **NCLC 9; PC 59**
See also DLB 35, 98; RGEL 2; TEA

Paton, Alan 1903-1988 ..... **CLC 4, 10, 25, 55, 106; TCLC 165; WLC 4**
See also AAYA 26; AFW; BPFB 3; BRWS 2; BYA 1; CA 13-16; 125; CANR 22; CAP 1; CN 1, 2, 3, 4; DA; DA3; DAB; DAC; DAM MST, NOV; DLB 225; DLBD 17; EWL 3; EXPN; LAIT 4; MTCW 1, 2; MTFW 2005; NFS 3, 12; RGEL 2; SATA 11; SATA-Obit 56; TWA; WLIT 2; WWE 1

Paton Walsh, Gillian
See Paton Walsh, Jill

Paton Walsh, Jill 1937- .... **CLC 35**
See also AAYA 11, 47; BYA 1, 8; CA 262; CAAE 262; CANR 38, 83, 158; CLR 2, 6, 128; DLB 161; JRDA; MAICYA 1, 2; SAAS 3; SATA 4, 72, 109, 190; SATA-Essay 190; WYA; YAW

Patsauq, Markoosie 1942- .... **NNAL**
See also CA 101; CLR 23; CWRI 5; DAM MULT

Patterson, (Horace) Orlando (Lloyd)
1940- .... **BLCS**
See also BW 1; CA 65-68; CANR 27, 84; CN 1, 2, 3, 4, 5, 6

Patton, George S(mith), Jr.
1885-1945 .... **TCLC 79**
See also CA 189

Paulding, James Kirke 1778-1860 ... **NCLC 2**
See also DLB 3, 59, 74, 250; RGAL 4

Paulin, Thomas Neilson
See Paulin, Tom

Paulin, Tom 1949- .... **CLC 37, 177**
See also CA 123; 128; CANR 98; CP 3, 4, 5, 6, 7; DLB 40

Pausanias c. 1st cent. - .... **CMLC 36**

Paustovsky, Konstantin (Georgievich)
1892-1968 .... **CLC 40**
See also CA 93-96; 25-28R; DLB 272; EWL 3

Pavese, Cesare 1908-1950 .... **PC 13; SSC 19; TCLC 3**
See also CA 104; 169; DLB 128, 177; EW 12; EWL 3; PFS 20; RGSF 2; RGWL 2, 3; TWA; WLIT 7

Pavic, Milorad 1929- .... **CLC 60**
See also CA 136; CDWLB 4; CWW 2; DLB 181; EWL 3; RGWL 3

Pavlov, Ivan Petrovich 1849-1936 . **TCLC 91**
See also CA 118; 180

Pavlova, Karolina Karlovna
1807-1893 .... **NCLC 138**
See also DLB 205

Payne, Alan
See Jakes, John

Payne, Rachel Ann
See Jakes, John

Paz, Gil
See Lugones, Leopoldo

Paz, Octavio 1914-1998 . **CLC 3, 4, 6, 10, 19, 51, 65, 119; HLC 2; PC 1, 48; TCLC 211; WLC 4**
See also AAYA 50; CA 73-76; 165; CANR 32, 65, 104; CWW 2; DA; DA3; DAB; DAC; DAM MST, MULT, POET; DLB 290, 331; DLBY 1990, 1998; DNFS 1;

EWL 3; HW 1, 2; LAW; LAWS 1; MTCW 1, 2; MTFW 2005; PFS 18, 30; RGWL 2, 3; SSFS 13; TWA; WLIT 1

p'Bitek, Okot 1931-1982 . **BLC 1:3; CLC 96; TCLC 149**
See also AFW; BW 2, 3; CA 124; 107; CANR 82; CP 1, 2, 3; DAM MULT; DLB 125; EWL 3; MTCW 1, 2; MTFW 2005; RGEL 2; WLIT 2

Peabody, Elizabeth Palmer
1804-1894 .... **NCLC 169**
See also DLB 1, 223

Peacham, Henry 1578-1644(?) .... **LC 119**
See also DLB 151

Peacock, Molly 1947- .... **CLC 60**
See also CA 103, 262; CAAE 262; CAAS 21; CANR 52, 84; CP 5, 6, 7; CWP; DLB 120, 282

Peacock, Thomas Love
1785-1866 .... **NCLC 22; PC 87**
See also BRW 4; DLB 96, 116; RGEL 2; RGSF 2

Peake, Mervyn 1911-1968 .... **CLC 7, 54**
See also CA 5-8R; 25-28R; CANR 3; DLB 15, 160, 255; FANT; MTCW 1; RGEL 2; SATA 23; SFW 4

Pearce, Ann Philippa
See Pearce, Philippa

Pearce, Philippa 1920-2006 .... **CLC 21**
See also BYA 5; CA 5-8R; 255; CANR 4, 109; CLR 9; CWRI 5; DLB 161; FANT; MAICYA 1; SATA 1, 67, 129; SATA-Obit 179

Pearl, Eric
See Elman, Richard (Martin)

Pearson, Jean Mary
See Gardam, Jane

Pearson, Thomas Reid
See Pearson, T.R.

Pearson, T.R. 1956- .... **CLC 39**
See also CA 120; 130; CANR 97, 147, 185; CSW; INT CA-130

Peck, Dale 1967- .... **CLC 81**
See also CA 146; CANR 72, 127, 180; GLL 2

Peck, John (Frederick) 1941- .... **CLC 3**
See also CA 49-52; CANR 3, 100; CP 4, 5, 6, 7

Peck, Richard 1934- .... **CLC 21**
See also AAYA 1, 24; BYA 1, 6, 8, 11; CA 85-88; CANR 19, 38, 129, 178; CLR 15, 142; INT CANR-19; JRDA; MAICYA 1, 2; SAAS 2; SATA 18, 55, 97, 110, 158, 190; SATA-Essay 110; WYA; YAW

Peck, Richard Wayne
See Peck, Richard

Peck, Robert Newton 1928- .... **CLC 17**
See also AAYA 3, 43; BYA 1, 6; CA 81-84, 182; CAAE 182; CANR 31, 63, 127; CLR 45; DA; DAC; DAM MST; JRDA; LAIT 3; MAICYA 1, 2; NFS 29; SAAS 1; SATA 21, 62, 111, 156; SATA-Essay 108; WYA; YAW

Peckinpah, David Samuel
See Peckinpah, Sam

Peckinpah, Sam 1925-1984 .... **CLC 20**
See also CA 109; 114; CANR 82

Pedersen, Knut 1859-1952 .. **TCLC 2, 14, 49, 151, 203**
See also AAYA 79; CA 104; 119; CANR 63; DLB 297, 330; EW 8; EWL 8; MTCW 1, 2; RGWL 2, 3

Peele, George 1556-1596 .... **DC 27; LC 115**
See also BRW 1; DLB 62, 167; RGEL 2

Peeslake, Gaffer
See Durrell, Lawrence (George)

Peguy, Charles (Pierre)
1873-1914 .... **TCLC 10**
See also CA 107; 193; DLB 258; EWL 3; GFL 1789 to the Present

Peirce, Charles Sanders
1839-1914 .... **TCLC 81**
See also CA 194; DLB 270

Pelagius c. 350-c. 418 .... **CMLC 112**

Pelecanos, George P. 1957- .... **CLC 236**
See also CA 138; CANR 122, 165; DLB 306

Pelevin, Victor 1962- .... **CLC 238**
See also CA 154; CANR 88, 159; DLB 285

Pelevin, Viktor Olegovich
See Pelevin, Victor

Pellicer, Carlos 1897(?)-1977 .... **HLCS 2**
See also CA 153; 69-72; DLB 290; EWL 3; HW 1

Pena, Ramon del Valle y
See Valle-Inclan, Ramon (Maria) del

Pendennis, Arthur Esquir
See Thackeray, William Makepeace

Penn, Arthur
See Matthews, (James) Brander

Penn, William 1644-1718 .... **LC 25**
See also DLB 24

PEPECE
See Prado (Calvo), Pedro

Pepys, Samuel 1633-1703 ... **LC 11, 58; WLC 4**
See also BRW 2; CDBLB 1660-1789; DA; DA3; DAB; DAC; DAM MST; DLB 101, 213; NCFS 4; RGEL 2; TEA; WLIT 3

Percy, Thomas 1729-1811 .... **NCLC 95**
See also DLB 104

Percy, Walker 1916-1990 .... **CLC 2, 3, 6, 8, 14, 18, 47, 65**
See also AMWS 3; BPFB 3; CA 1-4R; 131; CANR 1, 23, 64; CN 1, 2, 3, 4; CPW; CSW; DA3; DAM NOV, POP; DLB 2; DLBY 1980, 1990; EWL 3; MAL 5; MTCW 1, 2; MTFW 2005; RGAL 4; TUS

Percy, William Alexander
1885-1942 .... **TCLC 84**
See also CA 163; MTCW 2

Perdurabo, Frater
See Crowley, Edward Alexander

Perec, Georges 1936-1982 .... **CLC 56, 116**
See also CA 141; DLB 83, 299; EWL 3; GFL 1789 to the Present; RGHL; RGWL 3

Pereda (y Sanchez de Porrua), Jose Maria de 1833-1906 .... **TCLC 16**
See also CA 117

Pereda y Porrua, Jose Maria de
See Pereda (y Sanchez de Porrua), Jose Maria de

Peregoy, George Weems
See Mencken, H(enry) L(ouis)

Perelman, S(idney) J(oseph)
1904-1979 .. **CLC 3, 5, 9, 15, 23, 44, 49; SSC 32**
See also AAYA 79; AITN 1, 2; BPFB 3; CA 73-76; 89-92; CANR 18; DAM DRAM; DLB 11, 44; MTCW 1, 2; MTFW 2005; RGAL 4

Peret, Benjamin 1899-1959 .... **PC 33; TCLC 20**
See also CA 117; 186; GFL 1789 to the Present

Peretz, Isaac Leib
See Peretz, Isaac Loeb

Peretz, Isaac Loeb 1851(?)-1915 ...... **SSC 26; TCLC 16**
See also CA 109; 201; DLB 333

Peretz, Yitzkhok Leibush
See Peretz, Isaac Loeb

Portillo (y Pacheco), Jose Lopez
See Lopez Portillo (y Pacheco), Jose

Portillo Trambley, Estela
1927-1998 .... **HLC 2; TCLC 163**
See also CA 77-80; CANR 32; DAM
MULT; DLB 209; HW 1; RGAL 4

Posey, Alexander (Lawrence)
1873-1908 .... **NNAL**
See also CA 144; CANR 80; DAM MULT;
DLB 175

Posse, Abel .... **CLC 70, 273**
See also CA 252

Post, Melville Davisson
1869-1930 .... **TCLC 39**
See also CA 110; 202; CMW 4

Postman, Neil 1931(?)-2003 .... **CLC 244**
See also CA 102; 221

Potok, Chaim 1929-2002 ... **CLC 2, 7, 14, 26, 112**
See also AAYA 15, 50; AITN 1, 2; BPFB 3;
BYA 1; CA 17-20R; 208; CANR 19, 35,
64, 98; CLR 92; CN 4, 5, 6; DA3; DAM
NOV; DLB 28, 152; EXPN; INT CANR-
19; LAIT 4; MTCW 1, 2; MTFW 2005;
NFS 4; RGHL; SATA 33, 106; SATA-Obit
134; TUS; YAW

Potok, Herbert Harold -2002
See Potok, Chaim

Potok, Herman Harold
See Potok, Chaim

Potter, Dennis (Christopher George)
1935-1994 .... **CLC 58, 86, 123**
See also BRWS 10; CA 107; 145; CANR
33, 61; CBD; DLB 233; MTCW 1

Pound, Ezra (Weston Loomis)
1885-1972 .. **CLC 1, 2, 3, 4, 5, 7, 10, 13, 18, 34, 48, 50, 112; PC 4, 95; WLC 5**
See also AAYA 47; AMW; AMWR 1; CA
5-8R; 37-40R; CANR 40; CDALB 1917-
1929; CP 1; DA; DA3; DAB; DAC; DAM
MST, POET; DLB 4, 45, 63; DLBD 15;
EFS 2; EWL 3; EXPP; LMFS 2; MAL 5;
MTCW 1, 2; MTFW 2005; PAB; PFS 2,
8, 16; RGAL 4; TUS; WP

Povod, Reinaldo 1959-1994 .... **CLC 44**
See also CA 136; 146; CANR 83

Powell, Adam Clayton, Jr.
1908-1972 .... **BLC 1:3; CLC 89**
See also BW 1, 3; CA 102; 33-36R; CANR
86; DAM MULT; DLB 345

Powell, Anthony 1905-2000 ... **CLC 1, 3, 7, 9, 10, 31**
See also BRW 7; CA 1-4R; 189; CANR 1,
32, 62, 107; CDBLB 1945-1960; CN 1, 2,
3, 4, 5, 6; DLB 15; EWL 3; MTCW 1, 2;
MTFW 2005; RGEL 2; TEA

Powell, Dawn 1896(?)-1965 .... **CLC 66**
See also CA 5-8R; CANR 121; DLBY 1997

Powell, Padgett 1952- .... **CLC 34**
See also CA 126; CANR 63, 101; CSW;
DLB 234; DLBY 01; SSFS 25

Power, Susan 1961- .... **CLC 91**
See also BYA 14; CA 160; CANR 135; NFS 11

Powers, J(ames) F(arl) 1917-1999 ..... **CLC 1, 4, 8, 57; SSC 4**
See also CA 1-4R; 181; CANR 2, 61; CN
1, 2, 3, 4, 5, 6; DLB 130; MTCW 1;
RGAL 4; RGSF 2

Powers, John R. 1945- .... **CLC 66**
See also CA 69-72

Powers, John
See Powers, John R.

Powers, Richard 1957- .... **CLC 93**
See also AMWS 9; BPFB 3; CA 148;
CANR 80, 180; CN 6, 7; MTFW 2005;
TCLE 1:2

Powers, Richard S.
See Powers, Richard

Pownall, David 1938- .... **CLC 10**
See also CA 89-92, 180; CAAS 18; CANR
49, 101; CBD; CD 5, 6; CN 4, 5, 6, 7;
DLB 14

Powys, John Cowper 1872-1963 ... **CLC 7, 9, 15, 46, 125**
See also CA 85-88; CANR 106; DLB 15,
255; EWL 3; FANT; MTCW 1, 2; MTFW
2005; RGEL 2; SUFW

Powys, T(heodore) F(rancis)
1875-1953 .... **TCLC 9**
See also BRWS 8; CA 106; 189; DLB 36,
162; EWL 3; FANT; RGEL 2; SUFW

Pozzo, Modesta
See Fonte, Moderata

Prado (Calvo), Pedro 1886-1952 ... **TCLC 75**
See also CA 131; DLB 283; HW 1; LAW

Prager, Emily 1952- .... **CLC 56**
See also CA 204

Pratchett, Terence David John
See Pratchett, Terry

Pratchett, Terry 1948- .... **CLC 197**
See also AAYA 19, 54; BPFB 3; CA 143;
CANR 87, 126, 170; CLR 64; CN 6, 7;
CPW; CWRI 5; FANT; MTFW 2005;
SATA 82, 139, 185; SFW 4; SUFW 2

Pratolini, Vasco 1913-1991 .... **TCLC 124**
See also CA 211; DLB 177; EWL 3; RGWL
2, 3

Pratt, E(dwin) J(ohn) 1883(?)-1964 . **CLC 19**
See also CA 141; 93-96; CANR 77; DAC;
DAM POET; DLB 92; EWL 3; RGEL 2;
TWA

Premacanda
See Srivastava, Dhanpat Rai

Premchand
See Srivastava, Dhanpat Rai

Premchand, Munshi
See Srivastava, Dhanpat Rai

Prem Chand, Munshi
See Srivastava, Dhanpat Rai

Prescott, William Hickling
1796-1859 .... **NCLC 163**
See also DLB 1, 30, 59, 235

Preseren, France 1800-1849 .... **NCLC 127**
See also CDWLB 4; DLB 147

Preussler, Otfried 1923- .... **CLC 17**
See also CA 77-80; SATA 24

Prevert, Jacques (Henri Marie)
1900-1977 .... **CLC 15**
See also CA 77-80; 69-72; CANR 29, 61;
DLB 258; EWL 3; GFL 1789 to the
Present; IDFW 3, 4; MTCW 1; RGWL 2,
3; SATA-Obit 30

Prevost, (Antoine Francois)
1697-1763 .... **LC 1**
See also DLB 314; EW 4; GFL Beginnings
to 1789; RGWL 2, 3

Price, Edward Reynolds
See Price, Reynolds

Price, Reynolds 1933- .. **CLC 3, 6, 13, 43, 50, 63, 212; SSC 22**
See also AMWS 6; CA 1-4R; CANR 1, 37,
57, 87, 128, 177; CN 1, 2, 3, 4, 5, 6, 7;
CSW; DAM NOV; DLB 2, 218, 278;
EWL 3; INT CANR-37; MAL 5; MTFW
2005; NFS 18

Price, Richard 1949- .... **CLC 6, 12**
See also CA 49-52; CANR 3, 147; CN 7;
DLBY 1981

Prichard, Katharine Susannah
1883-1969 .... **CLC 46**
See also CA 11-12; CANR 33; CAP 1; DLB
260; MTCW 1; RGEL 2; RGSF 2; SATA
66

Priestley, J(ohn) B(oynton)
1894-1984 .... **CLC 2, 5, 9, 34**
See also BRW 7; CA 9-12R; 113; CANR
33; CDBLB 1914-1945; CN 1, 2, 3; DA3;
DAM DRAM, NOV; DLB 10, 34, 77,
100, 139; DLBY 1984; EWL 3; MTCW
1, 2; MTFW 2005; RGEL 2; SFW 4

Prince 1958- .... **CLC 35**
See also CA 213

Prince, F(rank) T(empleton)
1912-2003 .... **CLC 22**
See also CA 101; 219; CANR 43, 79; CP 1,
2, 3, 4, 5, 6, 7; DLB 20

Prince Kropotkin
See Kropotkin, Peter (Aleksieevich)

Prior, Matthew 1664-1721 .... **LC 4**
See also DLB 95; RGEL 2

Prishvin, Mikhail 1873-1954 .... **TCLC 75**
See also DLB 272; EWL 3 !**

Prishvin, Mikhail Mikhailovich
See Prishvin, Mikhail

Pritchard, William H(arrison)
1932- .... **CLC 34**
See also CA 65-68; CANR 23, 95; DLB
111

Pritchett, V(ictor) S(awdon)
1900-1997 ... **CLC 5, 13, 15, 41; SSC 14**
See also BPFB 3; BRWS 3; CA 61-64; 157;
CANR 31, 63; CN 1, 2, 3, 4, 5, 6; DA3;
DAM NOV; DLB 15, 139; EWL 3;
MTCW 1, 2; MTFW 2005; RGEL 2;
RGSF 2; TEA

Private 19022
See Manning, Frederic

Probst, Mark 1925- .... **CLC 59**
See also CA 130

Procaccino, Michael
See Cristofer, Michael

Proclus c. 412-c. 485 .... **CMLC 81**

Prokosch, Frederic 1908-1989 ...... **CLC 4, 48**
See also CA 73-76; 128; CANR 82; CN 1,
2, 3, 4; CP 1, 2, 3, 4; DLB 48; MTCW 2

Propertius, Sextus c. 50B.C.-c.
16B.C. .... **CMLC 32**
See also AW 2; CDWLB 1; DLB 211;
RGWL 2, 3; WLIT 8

Prophet, The
See Dreiser, Theodore

Prose, Francine 1947- .... **CLC 45, 231**
See also AMWS 16; CA 109; 112; CANR
46, 95, 132, 175; DLB 234; MTFW 2005;
SATA 101, 149, 198

Protagoras c. 490B.C.-420B.C. ...... **CMLC 85**
See also DLB 176

Proudhon
See Cunha, Euclides (Rodrigues Pimenta)
da

Proulx, Annie
See Proulx, E. Annie

Proulx, E. Annie 1935- ...... **CLC 81, 158, 250**
See also AMWS 7; BPFB 3; CA 145;
CANR 65, 110; CN 6, 7; CPW 1; DA3;
DAM POP; DLB 335; MAL 5; MTCW 2;
MTFW 2005; SSFS 18, 23

Proulx, Edna Annie
See Proulx, E. Annie

Proust, (Valentin-Louis-George-Eugene)
Marcel 1871-1922 ..... **SSC 75; TCLC 7, 13, 33, 220; WLC 5**
See also AAYA 58; BPFB 3; CA 104; 120;
CANR 110; DA; DA3; DAB; DAC; DAM
MST, NOV; DLB 65; EW 8; EWL 3; GFL
1789 to the Present; MTCW 1, 2; MTFW
2005; RGWL 2, 3; TWA

Prowler, Harley
See Masters, Edgar Lee

Prudentius, Aurelius Clemens 348-c.
405 .... **CMLC 78**
See also EW 1; RGWL 2, 3

Romains, Jules 1885-1972 .... **CLC 7**
 See also CA 85-88; CANR 34; DLB 65, 321; EWL 3; GFL 1789 to the Present; MTCW 1
Romero, Jose Ruben 1890-1952 .... **TCLC 14**
 See also CA 114; 131; EWL 3; HW 1; LAW
Ronsard, Pierre de 1524-1585 . **LC 6, 54; PC 11**
 See also DLB 327; EW 2; GFL Beginnings to 1789; RGWL 2, 3; TWA
Rooke, Leon 1934- .... **CLC 25, 34**
 See also CA 25-28R; CANR 23, 53; CCA 1; CPW; DAM POP
Roosevelt, Franklin Delano 1882-1945 .... **TCLC 93**
 See also CA 116; 173; LAIT 3
Roosevelt, Theodore 1858-1919 ..... **TCLC 69**
 See also CA 115; 170; DLB 47, 186, 275
Roper, Margaret c. 1505-1544 .... **LC 147**
Roper, William 1498-1578 .... **LC 10**
Roquelaure, A. N.
 See Rice, Anne
Rosa, Joao Guimaraes 1908-1967
 See Guimaraes Rosa, Joao
Rose, Wendy 1948- . **CLC 85; NNAL; PC 13**
 See also CA 53-56; CANR 5, 51; CWP; DAM MULT; DLB 175; PFS 13; RGAL 4; SATA 12
Rosen, R.D. 1949- .... **CLC 39**
 See also CA 77-80; CANR 62, 120, 175; CMW 4; INT CANR-30
Rosen, Richard
 See Rosen, R.D.
Rosen, Richard Dean
 See Rosen, R.D.
Rosenberg, Isaac 1890-1918 .... **TCLC 12**
 See also BRW 6; CA 107; 188; DLB 20, 216; EWL 3; PAB; RGEL 2
Rosenblatt, Joe
 See Rosenblatt, Joseph
Rosenblatt, Joseph 1933- .... **CLC 15**
 See also CA 89-92; CP 3, 4, 5, 6, 7; INT CA-89-92
Rosenfeld, Samuel
 See Tzara, Tristan
Rosenstock, Sami
 See Tzara, Tristan
Rosenstock, Samuel
 See Tzara, Tristan
Rosenthal, M(acha) L(ouis) 1917-1996 .... **CLC 28**
 See also CA 1-4R; 152; CAAS 6; CANR 4, 51; CP 1, 2, 3, 4, 5, 6; DLB 5; SATA 59
Ross, Barnaby
 See Dannay, Frederic; Lee, Manfred B.
Ross, Bernard L.
 See Follett, Ken
Ross, J. H.
 See Lawrence, T(homas) E(dward)
Ross, John Hume
 See Lawrence, T(homas) E(dward)
Ross, Martin 1862-1915
 See Martin, Violet Florence
 See also DLB 135; GLL 2; RGEL 2; RGSF 2
Ross, (James) Sinclair 1908-1996 ... **CLC 13; SSC 24**
 See also CA 73-76; CANR 81; CN 1, 2, 3, 4, 5, 6; DAC; DAM MST; DLB 88; RGEL 2; RGSF 2; TCWW 1, 2
Rossetti, Christina 1830-1894 ... **NCLC 2, 50, 66, 186; PC 7; WLC 5**
 See also AAYA 51; BRW 5; BYA 4; CLR 115; DA; DA3; DAB; DAC; DAM MST, POET; DLB 35, 163, 240; EXPP; FL 1:3; LATS 1:1; MAICYA 1, 2; PFS 10, 14, 27; RGEL 2; SATA 20; TEA; WCH
Rossetti, Christina Georgina
 See Rossetti, Christina

Rossetti, Dante Gabriel 1828-1882 . **NCLC 4, 77; PC 44; WLC 5**
 See also AAYA 51; BRW 5; CDBLB 1832-1890; DA; DAB; DAC; DAM MST, POET; DLB 35; EXPP; RGEL 2; TEA
Rossi, Cristina Peri
 See Peri Rossi, Cristina
Rossi, Jean-Baptiste 1931-2003 .... **CLC 90**
 See also CA 201; 215; CMW 4; NFS 18
Rossner, Judith 1935-2005 .... **CLC 6, 9, 29**
 See also AITN 2; BEST 90:3; BPFB 3; CA 17-20R; 242; CANR 18, 51, 73; CN 4, 5, 6, 7; DLB 6; INT CANR-18; MAL 5; MTCW 1, 2; MTFW 2005
Rossner, Judith Perelman
 See Rossner, Judith
Rostand, Edmond (Eugene Alexis) 1868-1918 .... **DC 10; TCLC 6, 37**
 See also CA 104; 126; DA; DA3; DAB; DAC; DAM DRAM, MST; DFS 1; DLB 192; LAIT 1; MTCW 1; RGWL 2, 3; TWA
Roth, Henry 1906-1995 ..... **CLC 2, 6, 11, 104**
 See also AMWS 9; CA 11-12; 149; CANR 38, 63; CAP 1; CN 1, 2, 3, 4, 5, 6; DA3; DLB 28; EWL 3; MAL 5; MTCW 1, 2; MTFW 2005; RGAL 4
Roth, (Moses) Joseph 1894-1939 ... **TCLC 33**
 See also CA 160; DLB 85; EWL 3; RGWL 2, 3
Roth, Philip 1933- ... **CLC 1, 2, 3, 4, 6, 9, 15, 22, 31, 47, 66, 86, 119, 201; SSC 26, 102; WLC 5**
 See also AAYA 67; AMWR 2; AMWS 3; BEST 90:3; BPFB 3; CA 1-4R; CANR 1, 22, 36, 55, 89, 132, 170; CDALB 1968-1988; CN 3, 4, 5, 6, 7; CPW 1; DA; DA3; DAB; DAC; DAM MST, NOV, POP; DLB 2, 28, 173; DLBY 1982; EWL 3; MAL 5; MTCW 1, 2; MTFW 2005; NFS 25; RGAL 4; RGHL; RGSF 2; SSFS 12, 18; TUS
Roth, Philip Milton
 See Roth, Philip
Rothenberg, Jerome 1931- .... **CLC 6, 57**
 See also CA 45-48; CANR 1, 106; CP 1, 2, 3, 4, 5, 6, 7; DLB 5, 193
Rotter, Pat .... **CLC 65**
Roumain, Jacques (Jean Baptiste) 1907-1944 .... **BLC 1:3; TCLC 19**
 See also BW 1; CA 117; 125; DAM MULT; EWL 3
Rourke, Constance Mayfield 1885-1941 .... **TCLC 12**
 See also CA 107; 200; MAL 5; YABC 1
Rousseau, Jean-Baptiste 1671-1741 ...... **LC 9**
Rousseau, Jean-Jacques 1712-1778 .... **LC 14, 36, 122; WLC 5**
 See also DA; DA3; DAB; DAC; DAM MST; DLB 314; EW 4; GFL Beginnings to 1789; LMFS 1; RGWL 2, 3; TWA
Roussel, Raymond 1877-1933 .... **TCLC 20**
 See also CA 117; 201; EWL 3; GFL 1789 to the Present
Rovit, Earl (Herbert) 1927- .... **CLC 7**
 See also CA 5-8R; CANR 12
Rowe, Elizabeth Singer 1674-1737 ..... **LC 44**
 See also DLB 39, 95
Rowe, Nicholas 1674-1718 .... **LC 8**
 See also DLB 84; RGEL 2
Rowlandson, Mary 1637(?)-1678 .... **LC 66**
 See also DLB 24, 200; RGAL 4
Rowley, Ames Dorrance
 See Lovecraft, H. P.
Rowley, William 1585(?)-1626 .. **LC 100, 123**
 See also DFS 22; DLB 58; RGEL 2

Rowling, J.K. 1965- .... **CLC 137, 217**
 See also AAYA 34; BYA 11, 13, 14; CA 173; CANR 128, 157; CLR 66, 80, 112; MAICYA 2; MTFW 2005; SATA 109, 174; SUFW 2
Rowling, Joanne Kathleen
 See Rowling, J.K.
Rowson, Susanna Haswell 1762(?)-1824 .... **NCLC 5, 69, 182**
 See also AMWS 15; DLB 37, 200; RGAL 4
Roy, Arundhati 1960(?)- .... **CLC 109, 210**
 See also CA 163; CANR 90, 126; CN 7; DLB 323, 326; DLBY 1997; EWL 3; LATS 1:2; MTFW 2005; NFS 22; WWE 1
Roy, Gabrielle 1909-1983 .... **CLC 10, 14**
 See also CA 53-56; 110; CANR 5, 61; CCA 1; DAB; DAC; DAM MST; DLB 68; EWL 3; MTCW 1; RGWL 2, 3; SATA 104; TCLE 1:2
Royko, Mike 1932-1997 .... **CLC 109**
 See also CA 89-92; 157; CANR 26, 111; CPW
Rozanov, Vasilii Vasil'evich
 See Rozanov, Vassili
Rozanov, Vasily Vasilyevich
 See Rozanov, Vassili
Rozanov, Vassili 1856-1919 .... **TCLC 104**
 See also DLB 295; EWL 3
Rozewicz, Tadeusz 1921- ...... **CLC 9, 23, 139**
 See also CA 108; CANR 36, 66; CWW 2; DA3; DAM POET; DLB 232; EWL 3; MTCW 1, 2; MTFW 2005; RGHL; RGWL 3
Ruark, Gibbons 1941- .... **CLC 3**
 See also CA 33-36R; CAAS 23; CANR 14, 31, 57; DLB 120
Rubens, Bernice (Ruth) 1923-2004 . **CLC 19, 31**
 See also CA 25-28R; 232; CANR 33, 65, 128; CN 1, 2, 3, 4, 5, 6, 7; DLB 14, 207, 326; MTCW 1
Rubin, Harold
 See Robbins, Harold
Rudkin, (James) David 1936- .... **CLC 14**
 See also CA 89-92; CBD; CD 5, 6; DLB 13
Rudnik, Raphael 1933- .... **CLC 7**
 See also CA 29-32R
Ruffian, M.
 See Hasek, Jaroslav (Matej Frantisek)
Rufinus c. 345-410 .... **CMLC 111**
Ruiz, Jose Martinez
 See Martinez Ruiz, Jose
Ruiz, Juan c. 1283-c. 1350 .... **CMLC 66**
Rukeyser, Muriel 1913-1980 . **CLC 6, 10, 15, 27; PC 12**
 See also AMWS 6; CA 5-8R; 93-96; CANR 26, 60; CP 1, 2, 3; DA3; DAM POET; DLB 48; EWL 3; FW; GLL 2; MAL 5; MTCW 1, 2; PFS 10, 29; RGAL 4; SATA-Obit 22
Rule, Jane 1931-2007 .... **CLC 27, 265**
 See also CA 25-28R; 266; CAAS 18; CANR 12, 87; CN 4, 5, 6, 7; DLB 60; FW
Rule, Jane Vance
 See Rule, Jane
Rulfo, Juan 1918-1986 .. **CLC 8, 80; HLC 2; SSC 25**
 See also CA 85-88; 118; CANR 26; CD-WLB 3; DAM MULT; DLB 113; EWL 3; HW 1, 2; LAW; MTCW 1, 2; RGSF 2; RGWL 2, 3; WLIT 1
Rumi, Jalal al-Din 1207-1273 ...... **CMLC 20; PC 45**
 See also AAYA 64; RGWL 2, 3; WLIT 6; WP
Runeberg, Johan 1804-1877 .... **NCLC 41**

Runyon, (Alfred) Damon
1884(?)-1946 .... **TCLC 10**
See also CA 107; 165; DLB 11, 86, 171;
MAL 5; MTCW 2; RGAL 4

Rush, Norman 1933- .... **CLC 44**
See also CA 121; 126; CANR 130; INT CA-
126

Rushdie, Salman 1947- .... **CLC 23, 31, 55,
100, 191, 272; SSC 83; WLCS**
See also AAYA 65; BEST 89:3; BPFB 3;
BRWS 4; CA 108; 111; CANR 33, 56,
108, 133; CLR 125; CN 4, 5, 6, 7; CPW
1; DA3; DAB; DAC; DAM MST, NOV,
POP; DLB 194, 323, 326; EWL 3; FANT;
INT CA-111; LATS 1:2; LMFS 2; MTCW
1, 2; MTFW 2005; NFS 22, 23; RGEL 2;
RGSF 2; TEA; WLIT 4

Rushforth, Peter 1945-2005 .... **CLC 19**
See also CA 101; 243

Rushforth, Peter Scott
See Rushforth, Peter

Ruskin, John 1819-1900 .... **TCLC 63**
See also BRW 5; BYA 5; CA 114; 129; CD-
BLB 1832-1890; DLB 55, 163, 190;
RGEL 2; SATA 24; TEA; WCH

Russ, Joanna 1937- .... **CLC 15**
See also BPFB 3; CA 25-28; CANR 11, 31,
65; CN 4, 5, 6, 7; DLB 8; FW; GLL 1;
MTCW 1; SCFW 1, 2; SFW 4

Russ, Richard Patrick
See O'Brian, Patrick

Russell, George William
1867-1935 .... **TCLC 3, 10**
See also BRWS 8; CA 104; 153; CDBLB
1890-1914; DAM POET; DLB 19; EWL
3; RGEL 2

Russell, Jeffrey Burton 1934- .... **CLC 70**
See also CA 25-28R; CANR 11, 28, 52, 179

Russell, (Henry) Ken(neth Alfred)
1927- .... **CLC 16**
See also CA 105

Russell, William Martin 1947- .... **CLC 60**
See also CA 164; CANR 107; CBD; CD 5,
6; DLB 233

Russell, Willy
See Russell, William Martin

Russo, Richard 1949- .... **CLC 181**
AMWS 12; CA 127; 133; CANR
87, 114; NFS 25

Rutebeuf fl. c. 1249-1277 .... **CMLC 104**
See also DLB 208

Rutherford, Mark
See White, William Hale

Ruysbroeck, Jan van 1293-1381 ... **CMLC 85**

Ruyslinck, Ward
See Belser, Reimond Karel Maria de

Ryan, Cornelius (John) 1920-1974 ..... **CLC 7**
See also CA 69-72; 53-56; CANR 38

Ryan, Michael 1946- .... **CLC 65**
See also CA 49-52; CANR 109; DLBY
1982

Ryan, Tim
See Dent, Lester

Rybakov, Anatoli (Naumovich)
1911-1998 .... **CLC 23, 53**
See also CA 126; 135; 172; DLB 302;
RGHL; SATA 79; SATA-Obit 108

Rybakov, Anatolii (Naumovich)
See Rybakov, Anatoli (Naumovich)

Ryder, Jonathan
See Ludlum, Robert

Ryga, George 1932-1987 .... **CLC 14**
See also CA 101; 124; CANR 43, 90; CCA
1; DAC; DAM MST; DLB 60

Rymer, Thomas 1643(?)-1713 .... **LC 132**
See also DLB 101, 336

S. H.
See Hartmann, Sadakichi

S. L. C.
See Twain, Mark

S. S.
See Sassoon, Siegfried (Lorraine)

Sa'adawi, al- Nawal
See El Saadawi, Nawal

Saadawi, Nawal El
See El Saadawi, Nawal

Saadiah Gaon 882-942 .... **CMLC 97**

Saba, Umberto 1883-1957 .... **TCLC 33**
See also CA 144; CANR 79; DLB 114;
EWL 3; RGWL 2, 3

Sabatini, Rafael 1875-1950 .... **TCLC 47**
See also BPFB 3; CA 162; RHW

Sabato, Ernesto 1911- ... **CLC 10, 23; HLC 2**
See also CA 97-100; CANR 32, 65; CD-
WLB 3; CWW 2; DAM MULT; DLB 145;
EWL 3; HW 1, 2; LAW; MTCW 1, 2;
MTFW 2005

Sa-Carneiro, Mario de 1890-1916 . **TCLC 83**
See also DLB 287; EWL 3

Sacastru, Martin
See Bioy Casares, Adolfo

Sacher-Masoch, Leopold von
1836(?)-1895 .... **NCLC 31**

Sachs, Hans 1494-1576 .... **LC 95**
See also CDWLB 2; DLB 179; RGWL 2, 3

Sachs, Marilyn 1927- .... **CLC 35**
See also AAYA 2; BYA 6; CA 17-20R;
CANR 13, 47, 150; CLR 2; JRDA; MAI-
CYA 1, 2; SAAS 2; SATA 3, 68, 164;
SATA-Essay 110; WYA; YAW

Sachs, Marilyn Stickle
See Sachs, Marilyn

Sachs, Nelly 1891-1970 .. **CLC 14, 98; PC 78**
See also CA 17-18; 25-28R; CANR 87;
CAP 2; DLB 332; EWL 3; MTCW 2;
MTFW 2005; PFS 20; RGHL; RGWL 2,
3

Sackler, Howard (Oliver)
1929-1982 .... **CLC 14**
See also CA 61-64; 108; CAD; CANR 30;
DFS 15; DLB 7

Sacks, Oliver 1933- .... **CLC 67, 202**
See also CA 53-56; CANR 28, 50, 76, 146,
187; CPW; DA3; INT CANR-28; MTCW
1, 2; MTFW 2005

Sacks, Oliver Wolf
See Sacks, Oliver

Sackville, Thomas 1536-1608 .... **LC 98**
See also DAM DRAM; DLB 62, 132;
RGEL 2

Sadakichi
See Hartmann, Sadakichi

Sa'dawi, Nawal al-
See El Saadawi, Nawal

Sade, Donatien Alphonse Francois
1740-1814 .... **NCLC 3, 47**
See also DLB 314; EW 4; GFL Beginnings
to 1789; RGWL 2, 3

Sade, Marquis de
See Sade, Donatien Alphonse Francois

Sadoff, Ira 1945- .... **CLC 9**
See also CA 53-56; CANR 5, 21, 109; DLB
120

Saetone
See Camus, Albert

Safire, William 1929- .... **CLC 10**
See also CA 17-20R; CANR 31, 54, 91, 148

Sagan, Carl 1934-1996 .... **CLC 30, 112**
See also AAYA 2, 62; CA 25-28R; 155;
CANR 11, 36, 74; CPW; DA3; MTCW 1,
2; MTFW 2005; SATA 58; SATA-Obit 94

Sagan, Francoise
See Quoirez, Francoise

Sahgal, Nayantara (Pandit) 1927- .... **CLC 41**
See also CA 9-12R; CANR 11, 88; CN 1,
2, 3, 4, 5, 6, 7; DLB 323

Said, Edward W. 1935-2003 .... **CLC 123**
See also CA 21-24R; 220; CANR 45, 74,
107, 131; DLB 67, 346; MTCW 2; MTFW
2005

Saikaku, Ihara 1642-1693 .... **LC 141**
See also RGWL 3

Saikaku Ihara
See Saikaku, Ihara

Saint, H(arry) F. 1941- .... **CLC 50**
See also CA 127

St. Aubin de Teran, Lisa 1953- .... **CLC 36**
See also CA 118; 126; CN 6, 7; INT CA-
126

Saint Birgitta of Sweden c.
1303-1373 .... **CMLC 24**

St. E. A. of M. and S
See Crowley, Edward Alexander

Sainte-Beuve, Charles Augustin
1804-1869 .... **NCLC 5**
See also DLB 217; EW 6; GFL 1789 to the
Present

Saint-Exupery, Antoine de
1900-1944 .... **TCLC 2, 56, 169; WLC**
See also AAYA 63; BPFB 3; BYA 3; CA
108; 132; CLR 10, 142; DA3; DAM
NOV; DLB 72; EW 12; EWL 3; GFL
1789 to the Present; LAIT 3; MAICYA 1,
2; MTCW 1, 2; MTFW 2005; RGWL 2,
3; SATA 20; TWA

**Saint-Exupery, Antoine Jean Baptiste Marie
Roger de**
See Saint-Exupery, Antoine de

St. John, David
See Hunt, E. Howard

St. John, J. Hector
See Crevecoeur, Michel Guillaume Jean de

Saint-John Perse
See Leger, (Marie-Rene Auguste) Alexis
Saint-Leger

Saintsbury, George (Edward Bateman)
1845-1933 .... **TCLC 31**
See also CA 160; DLB 57, 149

Sait Faik
See Abasiyanik, Sait Faik

Saki
See Munro, H(ector) H(ugh)

Sala, George Augustus 1828-1895 . **NCLC 46**

Saladin 1138-1193 .... **CMLC 38**

Salama, Hannu 1936- .... **CLC 18**
See also CA 244; EWL 3

Salamanca, J(ack) R(ichard) 1922- .. **CLC 4,
15**
See also CA 25-28R, 193; CAAE 193

Salas, Floyd Francis 1931- .... **HLC 2**
See also CA 119; CAAS 27; CANR 44, 75,
93; DAM MULT; DLB 82; HW 1, 2;
MTCW 2; MTFW 2005

Sale, J. Kirkpatrick
See Sale, Kirkpatrick

Sale, John Kirkpatrick
See Sale, Kirkpatrick

Sale, Kirkpatrick 1937- .... **CLC 68**
See also CA 13-16R; CANR 10, 147

Salinas, Luis Omar 1937- ... **CLC 90; HLC 2**
See also AMWS 13; CA 131; CANR 81,
153; DAM MULT; DLB 82; HW 1, 2

Salinas (y Serrano), Pedro
1891(?)-1951 .... **TCLC 17, 212**
See also CA 117; DLB 134; EWL 3

Salinger, J.D. 1919- . **CLC 1, 3, 8, 12, 55, 56,
138, 243; SSC 2, 28, 65; WLC 5**
See also AAYA 2, 36; AMW; AMWC 1;
BPFB 3; CA 5-8R; CANR 39, 129;
CDALB 1941-1968; CLR 18; CN 1, 2, 3,
4, 5, 6, 7; CPW 1; DA; DA3; DAB; DAC;
DAM MST, NOV, POP; DLB 2, 102, 173;

EWL 3; EXPN; LAIT 4; MAICYA 1, 2; MAL 5; MTCW 1, 2; MTFW 2005; NFS 1; RGAL 4; RGSF 2; SATA 67; SSFS 17; TUS; WYA; YAW

Salisbury, John
See Caute, (John) David

Sallust c. 86B.C.-35B.C. .... **CMLC 68**
See also AW 2; CDWLB 1; DLB 211; RGWL 2, 3

Salter, James 1925- .... **CLC 7, 52, 59, 275; SSC 58**
See also AMWS 9; CA 73-76; CANR 107, 160; DLB 130; SSFS 25

Saltus, Edgar (Everton) 1855-1921 . **TCLC 8**
See also CA 105; DLB 202; RGAL 4

Saltykov, Mikhail Evgrafovich 1826-1889 .... **NCLC 16**
See also DLB 238:

Saltykov-Shchedrin, N.
See Saltykov, Mikhail Evgrafovich

Samarakis, Andonis
See Samarakis, Antonis

Samarakis, Antonis 1919-2003 .... **CLC 5**
See also CA 25-28R; 224; CAAS 16; CANR 36; EWL 3

Samigli, E.
See Schmitz, Aron Hector

Sanchez, Florencio 1875-1910 .... **TCLC 37**
See also CA 153; DLB 305; EWL 3; HW 1; LAW

Sanchez, Luis Rafael 1936- .... **CLC 23**
See also CA 128; DLB 305; EWL 3; HW 1; WLIT 1

Sanchez, Sonia 1934- . **BLC 1:3, 2:3; CLC 5, 116, 215; PC 9**
See also BW 2, 3; CA 33-36R; CANR 24, 49, 74, 115; CLR 18; CP 2, 3, 4, 5, 6, 7; CSW; CWP; DA3; DAM MULT; DLB 41; DLBD 8; EWL 3; MAICYA 1, 2; MAL 5; MTCW 1, 2; MTFW 2005; PFS 26; SATA 22, 136; WP

Sancho, Ignatius 1729-1780 .... **LC 84**

Sand, George 1804-1876 .... **DC 29; NCLC 2, 42, 57, 174; WLC 5**
See also DA; DA3; DAB; DAC; DAM MST, NOV; DLB 119, 192; EW 6; FL 1:3; FW; GFL 1789 to the Present; RGWL 2, 3; TWA

Sandburg, Carl (August) 1878-1967 . **CLC 1, 4, 10, 15, 35; PC 2, 41; WLC 5**
See also AAYA 24; AMW; BYA 1, 3; CA 5-8R; 25-28R; CANR 35; CDALB 1865-1917; CLR 67; DA; DA3; DAB; DAC; DAM MST, POET; DLB 17, 54, 284; EWL 3; EXPP; LAIT 2; MAICYA 1, 2; MAL 5; MTCW 1, 2; MTFW 2005; PAB; PFS 3, 6, 12; RGAL 4; SATA 8; TUS; WCH; WP; WYA

Sandburg, Charles
See Sandburg, Carl (August)

Sandburg, Charles A.
See Sandburg, Carl (August)

Sanders, (James) Ed(ward) 1939- .... **CLC 53**
See also BG 1:3; CA 13-16R; CAAS 21; CANR 13, 44, 78; CP 1, 2, 3, 4, 5, 6, 7; DAM POET; DLB 16, 244

Sanders, Edward
See Sanders, (James) Ed(ward)

Sanders, Lawrence 1920-1998 .... **CLC 41**
See also BEST 89:4; BPFB 3; CA 81-84; 165; CANR 33, 62; CMW 4; CPW; DA3; DAM POP; MTCW 1

Sanders, Noah
See Blount, Roy, Jr.

Sanders, Winston P.
See Anderson, Poul

Sandoz, Mari(e Susette) 1900-1966 .. **CLC 28**
See also CA 1-4R; 25-28R; CANR 17, 64; DLB 9, 212; LAIT 2; MTCW 1, 2; SATA 5; TCWW 1, 2

Sandys, George 1578-1644 .... **LC 80**
See also DLB 24, 121

Saner, Reg(inald Anthony) 1931- .... **CLC 9**
See also CA 65-68; CP 3, 4, 5, 6, 7

Sankara 788-820 .... **CMLC 32**

Sannazaro, Jacopo 1456(?)-1530 .... **LC 8**
See also RGWL 2, 3; WLIT 7

Sansom, William 1912-1976 . **CLC 2, 6; SSC 21**
See also CA 5-8R; 65-68; CANR 42; CN 1, 2; DAM NOV; DLB 139; EWL 3; MTCW 1; RGEL 2; RGSF 2

Santayana, George 1863-1952 .... **TCLC 40**
See also AMW; CA 115; 194; DLB 54, 71, 246, 270; DLBD 13; EWL 3; MAL 5; RGAL 4; TUS

Santiago, Danny
See James, Daniel (Lewis)

Santillana, Inigo Lopez de Mendoza, Marques de 1398-1458 .... **LC 111**
See also DLB 286

Santmyer, Helen Hooven 1895-1986 .... **CLC 33; TCLC 133**
See also CA 1-4R; 118; CANR 15, 33; DLBY 1984; MTCW 1; RHW

Santoka, Taneda 1882-1940 .... **TCLC 72**

Santos, Bienvenido N(uqui) 1911-1996 ... **AAL; CLC 22; TCLC 156**
See also CA 101; 151; CANR 19, 46; CP 1; DAM MULT; DLB 312, 348; EWL; RGAL 4; SSFS 19

Santos, Miguel
See Mihura, Miguel

Sapir, Edward 1884-1939 .... **TCLC 108**
See also CA 211; DLB 92

Sapper
See McNeile, Herman Cyril

Sapphire 1950- .... **CLC 99**
See also CA 262

Sapphire, Brenda
See Sapphire

Sappho fl. 6th cent. B.C.- ... **CMLC 3, 67; PC 5**
See also CDWLB 1; DA3; DAM POET; DLB 176; FL 1:1; PFS 20; RGWL 2, 3; WLIT 8; WP

Saramago, Jose 1922- .... **CLC 119, 275; HLCS 1**
See also CA 153; CANR 96, 164; CWW 2; DLB 287, 332; EWL 3; LATS 1:2; NFS 27; SSFS 23

Sarduy, Severo 1937-1993 .... **CLC 6, 97; HLCS 2; TCLC 167**
See also CA 89-92; 142; CANR 58, 81; CWW 2; DLB 113; EWL 3; HW 1, 2; LAW

Sargeson, Frank 1903-1982 ..... **CLC 31; SSC 99**
See also CA 25-28R; 106; CANR 38, 79; CN 1, 2, 3; EWL 3; GLL 2; RGEL 2; RGSF 2; SSFS 20

Sarmiento, Domingo Faustino 1811-1888 .... **HLCS 2; NCLC 123**
See also LAW; WLIT 1

Sarmiento, Felix Ruben Garcia
See Dario, Ruben

Saro-Wiwa, Ken(ule Beeson) 1941-1995 .... **CLC 114; TCLC 200**
See also BW 2; CA 142; 150; CANR 60; DLB 157

Saroyan, William 1908-1981 ... **CLC 1, 8, 10, 29, 34, 56; DC 28; SSC 21; TCLC 137; WLC 5**
See also AAYA 66; CA 5-8R; 103; CAD; CANR 30; CDALBS; CN 1, 2; DA; DA3; DAB; DAC; DAM DRAM, MST, NOV;

DFS 17; DLB 7, 9, 86; DLBY 1981; EWL 3; LAIT 4; MAL 5; MTCW 1, 2; MTFW 2005; RGAL 4; RGSF 2; SATA 23; SATA-Obit 24; SSFS 14; TUS

Sarraute, Nathalie 1900-1999 .... **CLC 1, 2, 4, 8, 10, 31, 80; TCLC 145**
See also BPFB 3; CA 9-12R; 187; CANR 23, 66, 134; CWW 2; DLB 83, 321; EW 12; EWL 3; GFL 1789 to the Present; MTCW 1, 2; MTFW 2005; RGWL 2, 3

Sarton, May 1912-1995 ... **CLC 4, 14, 49, 91; PC 39; TCLC 120**
See also AMWS 8; CA 1-4R; 149; CANR 1, 34, 55, 116; CN 1, 2, 3, 4, 5, 6; CP 1, 2, 3, 4, 5, 6; DAM POET; DLB 48; DLBY 1981; EWL 3; FW; INT CANR-34; MAL 5; MTCW 1, 2; MTFW 2005; RGAL 4; SATA 36; SATA-Obit 86; TUS

Sartre, Jean-Paul 1905-1980 . **CLC 1, 4, 7, 9, 13, 18, 24, 44, 50, 52; DC 3; SSC 32; WLC 5**
See also AAYA 62; CA 9-12R; 97-100; CANR 21; DA; DA3; DAB; DAC; DAM DRAM, MST, NOV; DFS 5, 26; DLB 72, 296, 321, 332; EW 12; EWL 3; GFL 1789 to the Present; LMFS 2; MTCW 1, 2; MTFW 2005; NFS 21; RGHL; RGSF 2; RGWL 2, 3; SSFS 9; TWA

Sassoon, Siegfried (Lorraine) 1886-1967 .... **CLC 36, 130; PC 12**
See also BRW 6; CA 104; 25-28R; CANR 36; DAB; DAM MST, NOV, POET; DLB 20, 191; DLBD 18; EWL 3; MTCW 1, 2; MTFW 2005; PAB; PFS 28; RGEL 2; TEA

Satterfield, Charles
See Pohl, Frederik

Satyremont
See Peret, Benjamin

Saul, John III
See Saul, John

Saul, John 1942- .... **CLC 46**
See also AAYA 10, 62; BEST 90:4; CA 81-84; CANR 16, 40, 81, 176; CPW; DAM NOV, POP; HGG; SATA 98

Saul, John W.
See Saul, John

Saul, John W. III
See Saul, John

Saul, John Woodruff III
See Saul, John

Saunders, Caleb
See Heinlein, Robert A.

Saura (Atares), Carlos 1932-1998 .... **CLC 20**
See also CA 114; 131; CANR 79; HW 1

Sauser, Frederic Louis
See Sauser-Hall, Frederic

Sauser-Hall, Frederic 1887-1961 ..... **CLC 18, 106**
See also CA 102; 93-96; CANR 36, 62; DLB 258; EWL 3; GFL 1789 to the Present; MTCW 1; WP

Saussure, Ferdinand de 1857-1913 .... **TCLC 49**
See also DLB 242

Savage, Catharine
See Brosman, Catharine Savage

Savage, Richard 1697(?)-1743 .... **LC 96**
See also DLB 95; RGEL 2

Savage, Thomas 1915-2003 .... **CLC 40**
See also CA 126; 132; 218; CAAS 15; CN 6, 7; INT CA-132; SATA-Obit 147; TCWW 2

Savan, Glenn 1953-2003 .... **CLC 50**
See also CA 225

Savonarola, Girolamo 1452-1498 ...... **LC 152**
See also LMFS 1

Sax, Robert
See Johnson, Robert

Scott, Sir Walter 1771-1832 .... **NCLC 15, 69, 110, 209; PC 13; SSC 32; WLC 5**
See also AAYA 22; BRW 4; BYA 2; CD-BLB 1789-1832; DA; DAB; DAC; DAM MST, NOV, POET; DLB 93, 107, 116, 144, 159; GL 3; HGG; LAIT 1; RGEL 2; RGSF 2; SSFS 10; SUFW 1; TEA; WLIT 3; YABC 2

Scribe, (Augustin) Eugene 1791-1861 . **DC 5; NCLC 16**
See also DAM DRAM; DLB 192; GFL 1789 to the Present; RGWL 2, 3

Scrum, R.
See Crumb, R.

Scudery, Georges de 1601-1667 .... **LC 75**
See also GFL Beginnings to 1789

Scudery, Madeleine de 1607-1701 .. **LC 2, 58**
See also DLB 268; GFL Beginnings to 1789

Scum
See Crumb, R.

Scumbag, Little Bobby
See Crumb, R.

Seabrook, John
See Hubbard, L. Ron

Seacole, Mary Jane Grant 1805-1881 .... **NCLC 147**
See also DLB 166

Sealy, I(rwin) Allan 1951- .... **CLC 55**
See also CA 136; CN 6, 7

Search, Alexander
See Pessoa, Fernando

Seare, Nicholas
See Whitaker, Rod

Sebald, W(infried) G(eorg) 1944-2001 .... **CLC 194**
See also BRWS 8; CA 159; 202; CANR 98; MTFW 2005; RGHL

Sebastian, Lee
See Silverberg, Robert

Sebastian Owl
See Thompson, Hunter S.

Sebestyen, Igen
See Sebestyen, Ouida

Sebestyen, Ouida 1924- .... **CLC 30**
See also AAYA 8; BYA 7; CA 107; CANR 40, 114; CLR 17; JRDA; MAICYA 1, 2; SAAS 10; SATA 39, 140; WYA; YAW

Sebold, Alice 1963- .... **CLC 193**
See also AAYA 56; CA 203; CANR 181; MTFW 2005

Second Duke of Buckingham
See Villiers, George

Secundus, H. Scriblerus
See Fielding, Henry

Sedges, John
See Buck, Pearl S(ydenstricker)

Sedgwick, Catharine Maria 1789-1867 .... **NCLC 19, 98**
See also DLB 1, 74, 183, 239, 243, 254; FL 1:3; RGAL 4

Sedulius Scottus 9th cent. -c. 874 .. **CMLC 86**

Seebohm, Victoria
See Glendinning, Victoria

Seelye, John (Douglas) 1931- .... **CLC 7**
See also CA 97-100; CANR 70; INT CA-97-100; TCWW 1, 2

Seferiades, Giorgos Stylianou 1900-1971 .... **CLC 5, 11; TCLC 213**
See also CA 5-8R; 33-36R; CANR 5, 36; DLB 332; EW 12; EWL 3; MTCW 1; RGWL 2, 3

Seferis, George
See Seferiades, Giorgos Stylianou

Segal, Erich (Wolf) 1937- .... **CLC 3, 10**
See also BEST 89:1; BPFB 3; CA 25-28R; CANR 20, 36, 65, 113; CPW; DAM POP; DLBY 1986; INT CANR-20; MTCW 1

Seger, Bob 1945- .... **CLC 35**

Seghers
See Radvanyi, Netty

Seghers, Anna
See Radvanyi, Netty

Seidel, Frederick 1936- .... **CLC 18**
See also CA 13-16R; CANR 8, 99, 180; CP 1, 2, 3, 4, 5, 6, 7; DLBY 1984

Seidel, Frederick Lewis
See Seidel, Frederick

Seifert, Jaroslav 1901-1986 . **CLC 34, 44, 93; PC 47**
See also CA 127; CDWLB 4; DLB 215, 332; EWL 3; MTCW 1, 2

Sei Shonagon c. 966-1017(?) ..... **CMLC 6, 89**

Sejour, Victor 1817-1874 .... **DC 10**
See also DLB 50

Sejour Marcou et Ferrand, Juan Victor
See Sejour, Victor

Selby, Hubert, Jr. 1928-2004 ..... **CLC 1, 2, 4, 8; SSC 20**
See also CA 13-16R; 226; CANR 33, 85; CN 1, 2, 3, 4, 5, 6, 7; DLB 2, 227; MAL 5

Selzer, Richard 1928- .... **CLC 74**
See also CA 65-68; CANR 14, 106

Sembene, Ousmane
See Ousmane, Sembene

Senancour, Etienne Pivert de 1770-1846 .... **NCLC 16**
See also DLB 119; GFL 1789 to the Present

Sender, Ramon (Jose) 1902-1982 ...... **CLC 8; HLC 2; TCLC 136**
See also CA 5-8R; 105; CANR 8; DAM MULT; DLB 322; EWL 3; HW 1; MTCW 1; RGWL 2, 3

Seneca, Lucius Annaeus c. 1B.C.-c. 65 .... **CMLC 6, 107; DC 5**
See also AW 2; CDWLB 1; DAM DRAM; DLB 211; RGWL 2, 3; TWA; WLIT 8

Senghor, Leopold Sedar 1906-2001 .. **BLC 1:3; CLC 54, 130; PC 25**
See also AFW; BW 2; CA 116; 125; 203; CANR 47, 74, 134; CWW 2; DAM MULT, POET; DNFS 2; EWL 3; GFL 1789 to the Present; MTCW 1, 2; MTFW 2005; TWA

Senior, Olive (Marjorie) 1941- .... **SSC 78**
See also BW 3; CA 154; CANR 86, 126; CN 6; CP 6, 7; CWP; DLB 157; EWL 3; RGSF 2

Senna, Danzy 1970- .... **CLC 119**
See also CA 169; CANR 130, 184

Sepheriades, Georgios
See Seferiades, Giorgos Stylianou

Serling, (Edward) Rod(man) 1924-1975 .... **CLC 30**
See also AAYA 14; AITN 1; CA 162; 57-60; DLB 26; SFW 4

Serna, Ramon Gomez de la
See Gomez de la Serna, Ramon

Serpieres
See Guillevic, (Eugene)

Service, Robert
See Service, Robert W(illiam)

Service, Robert W(illiam) 1874(?)-1958 ... **PC 70; TCLC 15; WLC 5**
See also BYA 4; CA 115; 140; CANR 84; DA; DAB; DAC; DAM MST, POET; DLB 92; PFS 10; RGEL 2; SATA 20

Seth, Vikram 1952- .... **CLC 43, 90**
See also BRWS 10; CA 121; 127; CANR 50, 74, 131; CN 6, 7; CP 5, 6, 7; DA3; DAM MULT; DLB 120, 271, 282, 323; EWL 3; INT CA-127; MTCW 2; MTFW 2005; WWE 1

Setien, Miguel Delibes
See Delibes Setien, Miguel

Seton, Cynthia Propper 1926-1982 .. **CLC 27**
See also CA 5-8R; 108; CANR 7

Seton, Ernest (Evan) Thompson 1860-1946 .... **TCLC 31**
See also ANW; BYA 3; CA 109; 204; CLR 59; DLB 92; DLBD 13; JRDA; SATA 18

Seton-Thompson, Ernest
See Seton, Ernest (Evan) Thompson

Settle, Mary Lee 1918-2005 .... **CLC 19, 61, 273**
See also BPFB 3; CA 89-92; 243; CAAS 1; CANR 44, 87, 126, 182; CN 6, 7; CSW; DLB 6; INT CA-89-92

Seuphor, Michel
See Arp, Jean

Sevigne, Marie (de Rabutin-Chantal) 1626-1696 .... **LC 11, 144**
See also DLB 268; GFL Beginnings to 1789; TWA

Sevigne, Marie de Rabutin Chantal
See Sevigne, Marie (de Rabutin-Chantal)

Sewall, Samuel 1652-1730 .... **LC 38**
See also DLB 24; RGAL 4

Sexton, Anne (Harvey) 1928-1974 ..... **CLC 2, 4, 6, 8, 10, 15, 53, 123; PC 2, 79; WLC 5**
See also AMWS 2; CA 1-4R; 53-56; CABS 2; CANR 3, 36; CDALB 1941-1968; CP 1, 2; DA; DA3; DAB; DAC; DAM MST, POET; DLB 5, 169; EWL 3; EXPP; FL 1:6; FW; MAL 5; MBL; MTCW 1, 2; MTFW 2005; PAB; PFS 4, 14, 30; RGAL 4; RGHL; SATA 10; TUS

Shaara, Jeff 1952- .... **CLC 119**
See also AAYA 70; CA 163; CANR 109, 172; CN 7; MTFW 2005

Shaara, Michael 1929-1988 .... **CLC 15**
See also AAYA 71; AITN 1; BPFB 3; CA 102; 125; CANR 52, 85; DAM POP; DLBY 1983; MTFW 2005; NFS 26

Shackleton, C.C.
See Aldiss, Brian W.

Shacochis, Bob
See Shacochis, Robert G.

Shacochis, Robert G. 1951- .... **CLC 39**
See also CA 119; 124; CANR 100; INT CA-124

Shadwell, Thomas 1641(?)-1692 .... **LC 114**
See also DLB 80; IDTP; RGEL 2

Shaffer, Anthony 1926-2001 .... **CLC 19**
See also CA 110; 116; 200; CBD; CD 5, 6; DAM DRAM; DFS 13; DLB 13

Shaffer, Anthony Joshua
See Shaffer, Anthony

Shaffer, Peter 1926- ... **CLC 5, 14, 18, 37, 60; DC 7**
See also BRWS 1; CA 25-28R; CANR 25, 47, 74, 118; CBD; CD 5, 6; CDBLB 1960 to Present; DA3; DAB; DAM DRAM, MST; DFS 5, 13; DLB 13, 233; EWL 3; MTCW 1, 2; MTFW 2005; RGEL 2; TEA

Shakespeare, William 1564-1616 . **PC 84, 89, 98; WLC 5**
See also AAYA 35; BRW 1; CDBLB Before 1660; DA; DA3; DAB; DAC; DAM DRAM, MST, POET; DLB 20, 62, 172, 263; EXPP; LAIT 1; LATS 1:1; LMFS 1; PAB; PFS 1, 2, 3, 4, 5, 8, 9; RGEL 2; TEA; WLIT 3; WP; WS; WYA

Shakey, Bernard
See Young, Neil

Shalamov, Varlam (Tikhonovich) 1907-1982 .... **CLC 18**
See also CA 129; 105; DLB 302; RGSF 2

Shamloo, Ahmad
See Shamlu, Ahmad

Shamlou, Ahmad
See Shamlu, Ahmad

Sidhwa, Bapsy (N.) 1938- .... **CLC 168**
See also CA 108; CANR 25, 57; CN 6, 7;
DLB 323; FW

Sidney, Mary 1561-1621 .... **LC 19, 39**
See also DLB 167

Sidney, Sir Philip 1554-1586 .... **LC 19, 39,
131; PC 32**
See also BRW 1; BRWR 2; CDBLB Before
1660; DA; DA3; DAB; DAC; DAM MST,
POET; DLB 167; EXPP; PAB; PFS 30;
RGEL 2; TEA; WP

Sidney Herbert, Mary
See Sidney, Mary

Siegel, Jerome 1914-1996 .... **CLC 21**
See also AAYA 50; CA 116; 169; 151

Siegel, Jerry
See Siegel, Jerome

Sienkiewicz, Henryk (Adam Alexander Pius)
1846-1916 .... **TCLC 3**
See also CA 104; 134; CANR 84; DLB 332;
EWL 3; RGSF 2; RGWL 2, 3

Sierra, Gregorio Martinez
See Martinez Sierra, Gregorio

Sierra, Maria de la O'LeJarraga Martinez
See Martinez Sierra, Maria

Sigal, Clancy 1926- .... **CLC 7**
See also CA 1-4R; CANR 85, 184; CN 1,
2, 3, 4, 5, 6, 7

Siger of Brabant 1240(?)-1284(?) . **CMLC 69**
See also DLB 115

Sigourney, Lydia H.
See Sigourney, Lydia Howard (Huntley)
See also DLB 73, 183

Sigourney, Lydia Howard (Huntley)
1791-1865 .... **NCLC 21, 87**
See Sigourney, Lydia H.
See also DLB 1, 42, 239, 243

Sigourney, Lydia Huntley
See Sigourney, Lydia Howard (Huntley)

Siguenza y Gongora, Carlos de
1645-1700 .... **HLCS 2; LC 8**
See also LAW

Sigurjonsson, Johann
See Sigurjonsson, Johann

Sigurjonsson, Johann 1880-1919 ... **TCLC 27**
See also CA 170; DLB 293; EWL 3

Sikelianos, Angelos 1884-1951 .... **PC 29;
TCLC 39**
See also EWL 3; RGWL 2, 3

Silkin, Jon 1930-1997 .... **CLC 2, 6, 43**
See also CA 5-8R; CAAS 5; CANR 89; CP
1, 2, 3, 4, 5, 6; DLB 27

Silko, Leslie 1948- ...... **CLC 23, 74, 114, 211;
NNAL; SSC 37, 66; WLCS**
See also AAYA 14; AMWS 4; ANW; BYA
12; CA 115; 122; CANR 45, 65, 118; CN
4, 5, 6, 7; CP 4, 5, 6, 7; CPW 1; CWP;
DA; DA3; DAC; DAM MST, MULT,
POP; DLB 143, 175, 256, 275; EWL 3;
EXPP; EXPS; LAIT 4; MAL 5; MTCW
2; MTFW 2005; NFS 4; PFS 9, 16; RGAL
4; RGSF 2; SSFS 4, 8, 10, 11; TCWW 1,
2

Sillanpaa, Frans Eemil 1888-1964 ... **CLC 19**
See also CA 129; 93-96; DLB 332; EWL 3;
MTCW 1

Sillitoe, Alan 1928- .. **CLC 1, 3, 6, 10, 19, 57,
148**
See also AITN 1; BRWS 5; CA 9-12R, 191;
CAAE 191; CAAS 2; CANR 8, 26, 55,
139; CDBLB 1960 to Present; CN 1, 2, 3,
4, 5; CP 1, 2, 3, 4, 5; DLB 14, 139;
EWL 3; MTCW 1, 2; MTFW 2005; RGEL
2; RGSF 2; SATA 61

Silone, Ignazio 1900-1978 .... **CLC 4**
See also CA 25-28; 81-84; CANR 34; CAP
2; DLB 264; EW 12; EWL 3; MTCW 1;
RGSF 2; RGWL 2, 3

Silone, Ignazione
See Silone, Ignazio

Siluriensis, Leolinus
See Jones, Arthur Llewellyn

Silver, Joan Micklin 1935- .... **CLC 20**
See also CA 114; 121; INT CA-121

Silver, Nicholas
See Faust, Frederick (Schiller)

Silverberg, Robert 1935- .... **CLC 7, 140**
See also AAYA 24; BPFB 3; BYA 7, 9; CA
1-4R, 186; CAAE 186; CAAS 3; CANR
1, 20, 36, 85, 140, 175; CLR 59; CN 6, 7;
CPW; DAM POP; DLB 8; INT CANR-
20; MAICYA 1, 2; MTCW 1, 2; MTFW
2005; SATA 13, 91; SATA-Essay 104;
SCFW 1, 2; SFW 4; SUFW 2

Silverstein, Alvin 1933- .... **CLC 17**
See also CA 49-52; CANR 2; CLR 25;
JRDA; MAICYA 1, 2; SATA 8, 69, 124

Silverstein, Shel 1932-1999 .... **PC 49**
See also AAYA 40; BW 3; CA 107; 179;
CANR 47, 74, 81; CLR 5, 96; CWRI 5;
JRDA; MAICYA 1, 2; MTCW 2; MTFW
2005; SATA 33, 92; SATA-Brief 27;
SATA-Obit 116

Silverstein, Virginia B(arbara Opshelor)
1937- .... **CLC 17**
See also CA 49-52; CANR 2; CLR 25;
JRDA; MAICYA 1, 2; SATA 8, 69, 124

Sim, Georges
See Simenon, Georges (Jacques Christian)

Simak, Clifford D(onald) 1904-1988 . **CLC 1,
55**
See also CA 1-4R; 125; CANR 1, 35; DLB
8; MTCW 1; SATA-Obit 56; SCFW 1, 2;
SFW 4

Simenon, Georges (Jacques Christian)
1903-1989 .... **CLC 1, 2, 3, 8, 18, 47**
See also BPFB 3; CA 85-88; 129; CANR
35; CMW 4; DA3; DAM POP; DLB 72;
DLBY 1989; EW 12; EWL 3; GFL 1789
to the Present; MSW; MTCW 1, 2; MTFW
2005; RGWL 2, 3

Simic, Charles 1938- .... **CLC 6, 9, 22, 49, 68,
130, 256; PC 69**
See also AAYA 78; AMWS 8; CA 29-32R;
CAAS 4; CANR 12, 33, 52, 61, 96, 140;
CP 2, 3, 4, 5, 6, 7; DA3; DAM POET;
DLB 105; MAL 5; MTCW 2; MTFW
2005; PFS 7; RGAL 4; WP

Simmel, Georg 1858-1918 .... **TCLC 64**
See also CA 157; DLB 296

Simmons, Charles (Paul) 1924- .... **CLC 57**
See also CA 89-92; INT CA-89-92

Simmons, Dan 1948- .... **CLC 44**
See also AAYA 16, 54; CA 138; CANR 53,
81, 126, 174; CPW; DAM POP; HGG;
SUFW 2

Simmons, James (Stewart Alexander)
1933- .... **CLC 43**
See also CA 105; CAAS 21; CP 1, 2, 3, 4,
5, 6, 7; DLB 40

Simmons, Richard
See Simmons, Dan

Simms, William Gilmore
1806-1870 .... **NCLC 3**
See also DLB 3, 30, 59, 73, 248, 254;
RGAL 4

Simon, Carly 1945- .... **CLC 26**
See also CA 105

Simon, Claude 1913-2005 ... **CLC 4, 9, 15, 39**
See also CA 89-92; 241; CANR 33, 117;
CWW 2; DAM NOV; DLB 83, 332; EW
13; EWL 3; GFL 1789 to the Present;
MTCW 1

Simon, Claude Eugene Henri
See Simon, Claude

Simon, Claude Henri Eugene
See Simon, Claude

Simon, Marvin Neil
See Simon, Neil

Simon, Myles
See Follett, Ken

Simon, Neil 1927- .... **CLC 6, 11, 31, 39, 70,
233; DC 14**
See also AAYA 32; AITN 1; AMWS 4; CA
21-24R; CAD; CANR 26, 54, 87, 126;
CD 5, 6; DA3; DAM DRAM; DFS 2, 6,
12, 18,, 24; DLB 7, 266; LAIT 4; MAL 5;
MTCW 1, 2; MTFW 2005; RGAL 4; TUS

Simon, Paul 1941(?)- .... **CLC 17**
See also CA 116; 153; CANR 152

Simon, Paul Frederick
See Simon, Paul

Simonon, Paul 1956(?)- .... **CLC 30**

Simonson, Rick .... **CLC 70**

Simpson, Harriette
See Arnow, Harriette (Louisa) Simpson

Simpson, Louis 1923- ... **CLC 4, 7, 9, 32, 149**
See also AMWS 9; CA 1-4R; CAAS 4;
CANR 1, 61, 140; CP 1, 2, 3, 4, 5, 6, 7;
DAM POET; DLB 5; MAL 5; MTCW 1,
2; MTFW 2005; PFS 7, 11, 14; RGAL 4

Simpson, Mona 1957- .... **CLC 44, 146**
See also CA 122; 135; CANR 68, 103; CN
6, 7; EWL 3

Simpson, Mona Elizabeth
See Simpson, Mona

Simpson, N(orman) F(rederick)
1919- .... **CLC 29**
See also CA 13-16R; CBD; DLB 13; RGEL
2

Sinclair, Andrew (Annandale) 1935- . **CLC 2,
14**
See also CA 9-12R; CAAS 5; CANR 14,
38, 91; CN 1, 2, 3, 4, 5, 6, 7; DLB 14;
FANT; MTCW 1

Sinclair, Emil
See Hesse, Hermann

Sinclair, Iain 1943- .... **CLC 76**
See also BRWS 14; CA 132; CANR 81,
157; CP 5, 6, 7; HGG

Sinclair, Iain MacGregor
See Sinclair, Iain

Sinclair, Irene
See Griffith, D.W.

Sinclair, Julian
See Sinclair, May

Sinclair, Mary Amelia St. Clair (?)-
See Sinclair, May

Sinclair, May 1865-1946 .... **TCLC 3, 11**
See also CA 104; 166; DLB 36, 135; EWL
3; HGG; RGEL 2; RHW; SUFW

Sinclair, Roy
See Griffith, D.W.

Sinclair, Upton 1878-1968 ...... **CLC 1, 11, 15,
63; TCLC 160; WLC 5**
See also CA 5-8R; 25-28R; CANR 7;
CDALB 1929-1941; DA; DA3; DAB;
DAC; DAM MST, NOV; DLB 9; EWL 3;
INT CANR-7; LAIT 3; MAL 5; MTCW
1, 2; MTFW 2005; NFS 6; RGAL 4;
SATA 9; TUS; YAW

Sinclair, Upton Beall
See Sinclair, Upton

Singe, (Edmund) J(ohn) M(illington)
1871-1909 .... **WLC**

Singer, Isaac
See Singer, Isaac Bashevis

Singer, Isaac Bashevis 1904-1991 .. **CLC 1, 3,
6, 9, 11, 15, 23, 38, 69, 111; SSC 3, 53,
80; WLC 5**
See also AAYA 32; AITN 1, 2; AMW;
AMWR 2; BPFB 3; BYA 1, 4; CA 1-4R;
134; CANR 1, 39, 106; CDALB 1941-
1968; CLR 1; CN 1, 2, 3, 4; CWRI 5;
DA; DA3; DAB; DAC; DAM MST, NOV;

Snyder, Zilpha Keatley 1927- .... **CLC 17**
See also AAYA 15; BYA 1; CA 9-12R; 252;
CAAE 252; CANR 38; CLR 31, 121;
JRDA; MAICYA 1, 2; SAAS 2; SATA 1,
28, 75, 110, 163; SATA-Essay 112, 163;
YAW

Soares, Bernardo
See Pessoa, Fernando

Sobh, A.
See Shamlu, Ahmad

Sobh, Alef
See Shamlu, Ahmad

Sobol, Joshua 1939- .... **CLC 60**
See also CA 200; CWW 2; RGHL

Sobol, Yehoshua 1939-
See Sobol, Joshua

Socrates 470B.C.-399B.C. .... **CMLC 27**

Soderberg, Hjalmar 1869-1941 ...... **TCLC 39**
See also DLB 259; EWL 3; RGSF 2

Soderbergh, Steven 1963- .... **CLC 154**
See also AAYA 43; CA 243

Soderbergh, Steven Andrew
See Soderbergh, Steven

Sodergran, Edith (Irene) 1892-1923
See Soedergran, Edith (Irene)

Soedergran, Edith (Irene)
1892-1923 .... **TCLC 31**
See also CA 202; DLB 259; EW 11; EWL
3; RGWL 2, 3

Softly, Edgar
See Lovecraft, H. P.

Softly, Edward
See Lovecraft, H. P.

Sokolov, Alexander V(sevolodovich)
1943- .... **CLC 59**
See also CA 73-76; CWW 2; DLB 285;
EWL 3; RGWL 2, 3

Sokolov, Raymond 1941- .... **CLC 7**
See also CA 85-88

Sokolov, Sasha
See Sokolov, Alexander V(sevolodovich)

Solo, Jay
See Ellison, Harlan

Sologub, Fedor
See Teternikov, Fyodor Kuzmich

Sologub, Feodor
See Teternikov, Fyodor Kuzmich

Sologub, Fyodor
See Teternikov, Fyodor Kuzmich

Solomons, Ikey Esquir
See Thackeray, William Makepeace

Solomos, Dionysios 1798-1857 .... **NCLC 15**

Solwoska, Mara
See French, Marilyn

Solzhenitsyn, Aleksandr 1918-2008 ... **CLC 1,
2, 4, 7, 9, 10, 18, 26, 34, 78, 134, 235;
SSC 32, 105; WLC 5**
See also AAYA 49; AITN 1; BPFB 3; CA
69-72; CANR 40, 65, 116; CWW 2; DA;
DA3; DAB; DAC; DAM MST, NOV;
DLB 302, 332; EW 13; EWL 3; EXPS;
LAIT 4; MTCW 1, 2; MTFW 2005; NFS
6; RGSF 2; RGWL 2, 3; SSFS 9; TWA

Solzhenitsyn, Aleksandr I.
See Solzhenitsyn, Aleksandr

Solzhenitsyn, Aleksandr Isayevich
See Solzhenitsyn, Aleksandr

Somers, Jane
See Lessing, Doris

Somerville, Edith Oenone
1858-1949 .... **SSC 56; TCLC 51**
See also CA 196; DLB 135; RGEL 2; RGSF
2

Somerville & Ross
See Martin, Violet Florence; Somerville,
Edith Oenone

Sommer, Scott 1951- .... **CLC 25**
See also CA 106

Sommers, Christina Hoff 1950- ...... **CLC 197**
See also CA 153; CANR 95

Sondheim, Stephen 1930- .. **CLC 30, 39, 147;
DC 22**
See also AAYA 11, 66; CA 103; CANR 47,
67, 125; DAM DRAM; DFS 25; LAIT 4

Sondheim, Stephen Joshua
See Sondheim, Stephen

Sone, Monica 1919- .... **AAL**
See also DLB 312

Song, Cathy 1955- .... **AAL; PC 21**
See also CA 154; CANR 118; CWP; DLB
169, 312; EXPP; FW; PFS 5

Sontag, Susan 1933-2004 ... **CLC 1, 2, 10, 13,
31, 105, 195**
See also AMWS 3; CA 17-20R; 234; CANR
25, 51, 74, 97, 184; CN 1, 2, 3, 4, 5, 6, 7;
CPW; DA3; DAM POP; DLB 2, 67; EWL
3; MAL 5; MBL; MTCW 1, 2; MTFW
2005; RGAL 4; RHW; SSFS 10

Sophocles 496(?)B.C.-406(?)B.C. .... **CMLC 2,
47, 51, 86; DC 1; WLCS**
See also AW 1; CDWLB 1; DA; DA3;
DAB; DAC; DAM DRAM, MST; DFS 1,
4, 8, 24; DLB 176; LAIT 1; LATS 1:1;
LMFS 1; RGWL 2, 3; TWA; WLIT 8

Sordello 1189-1269 .... **CMLC 15**

Sorel, Georges 1847-1922 .... **TCLC 91**
See also CA 118; 188

Sorel, Julia
See Drexler, Rosalyn

Sorokin, Vladimir .... **CLC 59**
See also CA 258; DLB 285

Sorokin, Vladimir Georgievich
See Sorokin, Vladimir

Sorrentino, Gilbert 1929-2006 .... **CLC 3, 7,
14, 22, 40, 247**
See also CA 77-80; 250; CANR 14, 33, 115,
157; CN 3, 4, 5, 6, 7; CP 1, 2, 3, 4, 5, 6,
7; DLB 5, 173; DLBY 1980; INT
CANR-14

Soseki
See Natsume, Soseki

Soto, Gary 1952- ... **CLC 32, 80; HLC 2; PC
28**
See also AAYA 10, 37; BYA 11; CA 119;
125; CANR 50, 74, 107, 157; CLR 38;
CP 4, 5, 6, 7; DAM MULT; DFS 26; DLB
82; EWL 3; EXPP; HW 1, 2; INT CA-
125; JRDA; LLW; MAICYA 2; MAIC-
YAS 1; MAL 5; MTCW 2; MTFW 2005;
PFS 7, 30; RGAL 4; SATA 80, 120, 174;
WYA; YAW

Soupault, Philippe 1897-1990 .... **CLC 68**
See also CA 116; 147; 131; EWL 3; GFL
1789 to the Present; LMFS 2

Souster, (Holmes) Raymond 1921- .... **CLC 5,
14**
See also CA 13-16R; CAAS 14; CANR 13,
29, 53; CP 1, 2, 3, 4, 5, 6, 7; DA3; DAC;
DAM POET; DLB 88; RGEL 2; SATA 63

Southern, Terry 1924(?)-1995 .... **CLC 7**
See also AMWS 11; BPFB 3; CA 1-4R;
150; CANR 1, 55, 107; CN 1, 2, 3, 4, 5,
6; DLB 2; IDFW 3, 4

Southerne, Thomas 1660-1746 .... **LC 99**
See also DLB 80; RGEL 2

Southey, Robert 1774-1843 .... **NCLC 8, 97**
See also BRW 4; DLB 93, 107, 142; RGEL
2; SATA 54

Southwell, Robert 1561(?)-1595 .... **LC 108**
See also DLB 167; RGEL 2; TEA

Southworth, Emma Dorothy Eliza Nevitte
1819-1899 .... **NCLC 26**
See also DLB 239

Souza, Ernest
See Scott, Evelyn

Soyinka, Wole 1934- .. **BLC 1:3, 2:3; CLC 3,
5, 14, 36, 44, 179; DC 2; WLC 5**
See also AFW; BW 2, 3; CA 13-16R;
CANR 27, 39, 82, 136; CD 5, 6; CDWLB
3; CN 6, 7; CP 1, 2, 3, 4, 5, 6 ,7; DA;
DA3; DAB; DAC; DAM DRAM, MST,
MULT; DFS 10, 26; DLB 125, 332; EWL
3; MTCW 1, 2; MTFW 2005; PFS 27;
RGEL 2; TWA; WLIT 2; WWE 1

Spackman, W(illiam) M(ode)
1905-1990 .... **CLC 46**
See also CA 81-84; 132

Spacks, Barry (Bernard) 1931- .... **CLC 14**
See also CA 154; CANR 33, 109; CP 3, 4,
5, 6, 7; DLB 105

Spanidou, Irini 1946- .... **CLC 44**
See also CA 185; CANR 179

Spark, Muriel 1918-2006 .... **CLC 2, 3, 5, 8,
13, 18, 40, 94, 242; PC 72; SSC 10, 115**
See also BRWS 1; CA 5-8R; 251; CANR
12, 36, 76, 89, 131; CDBLB 1945-1960;
CN 1, 2, 3, 4, 5, 6, 7; CP 1, 2, 3, 4, 5, 6,
7; DA3; DAB; DAC; DAM MST, NOV;
DLB 15, 139; EWL 3; FW; INT CANR-
12; LAIT 4; MTCW 1, 2; MTFW 2005;
NFS 22; RGEL 2; TEA; WLIT 4; YAW

Spark, Muriel Sarah
See Spark, Muriel

Spaulding, Douglas
See Bradbury, Ray

Spaulding, Leonard
See Bradbury, Ray

Speght, Rachel 1597-c. 1630 .... **LC 97**
See also DLB 126

Spence, J. A. D.
See Eliot, T(homas) S(tearns)

Spencer, Anne 1882-1975 ...... **HR 1:3; PC 77**
See also BW 2; CA 161; DLB 51, 54

Spencer, Elizabeth 1921- .... **CLC 22; SSC 57**
See also CA 13-16R; CANR 32, 65, 87; CN
1, 2, 3, 4, 5, 6, 7; CSW; DLB 6, 218;
EWL 3; MTCW 1; RGAL 4; SATA 14

Spencer, Leonard G.
See Silverberg, Robert

Spencer, Scott 1945- .... **CLC 30**
See also CA 113; CANR 51, 148; DLBY
1986

Spender, Stephen 1909-1995 ..... **CLC 1, 2, 5,
10, 41, 91; PC 71**
See also BRWS 2; CA 9-12R; 149; CANR
31, 54; CDBLB 1945-1960; CP 1, 2, 3, 4,
5, 6; DA3; DAM POET; DLB 20; EWL
3; MTCW 1, 2; MTFW 2005; PAB; PFS
23; RGEL 2; TEA

Spengler, Oswald (Arnold Gottfried)
1880-1936 .... **TCLC 25**
See also CA 118; 189

Spenser, Edmund 1552(?)-1599 ...... **LC 5, 39,
117; PC 8, 42; WLC 5**
See also AAYA 60; BRW 1; CDBLB Be-
fore 1660; DA; DA3; DAB; DAC; DAM
MST, POET; DLB 167; EFS 2; EXPP;
PAB; RGEL 2; TEA; WLIT 3; WP

Spicer, Jack 1925-1965 .... **CLC 8, 18, 72**
See also BG 1:3; CA 85-88; DAM POET;
DLB 5, 16, 193; GLL 1; WP

Spiegelman, Art 1948- .... **CLC 76, 178**
See also AAYA 10, 46; CA 125; CANR 41,
55, 74, 124; DLB 299; MTCW 2; MTFW
2005; RGHL; SATA 109, 158; YAW

Spielberg, Peter 1929- .... **CLC 6**
See also CA 5-8R; CANR 4, 48; DLBY
1981

Spielberg, Steven 1947- .... **CLC 20, 188**
See also AAYA 8, 24; CA 77-80; CANR
32; SATA 32

Spillane, Frank Morrison
See Spillane, Mickey

Sternberg, Josef von 1894-1969 .... **CLC 20**
See also CA 81-84

Sterne, Laurence 1713-1768 .. **LC 2, 48, 156; WLC 5**
See also BRW 3; BRWC 1; CDBLB 1660-1789; DA; DAB; DAC; DAM MST, NOV; DLB 39; RGEL 2; TEA

Sternheim, (William Adolf) Carl
1878-1942 .... **TCLC 8**
See also CA 105; 193; DLB 56, 118; EWL 3; IDTP; RGWL 2, 3

Stevens, Margaret Dean
See Aldrich, Bess Streeter

Stevens, Mark 1951- .... **CLC 34**
See also CA 122

Stevens, R. L.
See Hoch, Edward D.

Stevens, Wallace 1879-1955 . **PC 6; TCLC 3, 12, 45; WLC 5**
See also AMW; AMWR 1; CA 104; 124; CANR 181; CDALB 1929-1941; DA; DA3; DAB; DAC; DAM MST, POET; DLB 54, 342; EWL 3; EXPP; MAL 5; MTCW 1, 2; PAB; PFS 13, 16; RGAL 4; TUS; WP

Stevenson, Anne (Katharine) 1933- .. **CLC 7, 33**
See also BRWS 6; CA 17-20R; CAAS 9; CANR 9, 33, 123; CP 3, 4, 5, 6, 7; CWP; DLB 40; MTCW 1; RHW

Stevenson, Robert Louis (Balfour)
1850-1894 ...... **NCLC 5, 14, 63, 193; PC 84; SSC 11, 51; WLC 5**
See also AAYA 24; BPFB 3; BRW 5; BRWC 1; BRWR 1; BYA 1, 2, 4, 13; CD-BLB 1890-1914; CLR 10, 11, 107; DA; DA3; DAB; DAC; DAM MST, NOV; DLB 18, 57, 141, 156, 174; DLBD 13; GL 3; HGG; JRDA; LAIT 1, 3; MAICYA 1, 2; NFS 11, 20; RGEL 2; RGSF 2; SATA 100; SUFW; TEA; WCH; WLIT 4; WYA; YABC 2; YAW

Stewart, J(ohn) I(nnes) M(ackintosh)
1906-1994 .... **CLC 7, 14, 32**
See also CA 85-88; 147; CAAS 3; CANR 47; CMW 4; CN 1, 2, 3, 4, 5; DLB 276; MSW; MTCW 1, 2

Stewart, Mary (Florence Elinor)
1916- .... **CLC 7, 35, 117**
See also AAYA 29, 73; BPFB 3; CA 1-4R; CANR 1, 59, 130; CMW 4; CPW; DAB; FANT; RHW; SATA 12; YAW

Stewart, Mary Rainbow
See Stewart, Mary (Florence Elinor)

Stewart, Will
See Williamson, John Stewart

Stifle, June
See Campbell, Maria

Stifter, Adalbert 1805-1868 ... **NCLC 41, 198; SSC 28**
See also CDWLB 2; DLB 133; RGSF 2; RGWL 2, 3

Still, James 1906-2001 .... **CLC 49**
See also CA 65-68; 195; CAAS 17; CANR 10, 26; CSW; DLB 9; DLBY 01; SATA 29; SATA-Obit 127

Sting 1951- .... **CLC 26**
See also CA 167

Stirling, Arthur
See Sinclair, Upton

Stitt, Milan 1941-2009 .... **CLC 29**
See also CA 69-72

Stockton, Francis Richard
1834-1902 .... **TCLC 47**
See also AAYA 68; BYA 4, 13; CA 108; 137; DLB 42, 74; DLBD 13; EXPS; MAI-CYA 1, 2; SATA 44; SATA-Brief 32; SFW 4; SSFS 3; SUFW; WCH

Stockton, Frank R.
See Stockton, Francis Richard

Stoddard, Charles
See Kuttner, Henry

Stoker, Abraham 1847-1912 . **SSC 62; TCLC 8, 144; WLC 6**
See also AAYA 23; BPFB 3; BRWS 3; BYA 5; CA 105; 150; CDBLB 1890-1914; DA; DA3; DAB; DAC; DAM MST, NOV; DLB 304; GL 3; HGG; LATS 1:1; MTFW 2005; NFS 18; RGEL 2; SATA 29; SUFW; TEA; WLIT 4

Stoker, Bram
See Stoker, Abraham

Stolz, Mary 1920-2006 .... **CLC 12**
See also AAYA 8, 73; AITN 1; CA 5-8R; 255; CANR 13, 41, 112; JRDA; MAICYA 1, 2; SAAS 3; SATA 10, 71, 133; SATA-Obit 180; YAW

Stolz, Mary Slattery
See Stolz, Mary

Stone, Irving 1903-1989 .... **CLC 7**
See also AITN 1; BPFB 3; CA 1-4R; 129; CAAS 3; CANR 1, 23; CN 1, 2, 3, 4; CPW; DA3; DAM POP; INT CANR-23; MTCW 1, 2; MTFW 2005; RHW; SATA 3; SATA-Obit 64

Stone, Oliver 1946- .... **CLC 73**
See also AAYA 15, 64; CA 110; CANR 55, 125

Stone, Oliver William
See Stone, Oliver

Stone, Robert 1937- .... **CLC 5, 23, 42, 175**
See also AMWS 5; BPFB 3; CA 85-88; CANR 23, 66, 95, 173; CN 4, 5, 6, 7; DLB 152; EWL 3; INT CANR-23; MAL 5; MTCW 1; MTFW 2005

Stone, Robert Anthony
See Stone, Robert

Stone, Ruth 1915- .... **PC 53**
See also CA 45-48; CANR 2, 91; CP 5, 6, 7; CSW; DLB 105; PFS 19

Stone, Zachary
See Follett, Ken

Stoppard, Tom 1937- ... **CLC 1, 3, 4, 5, 8, 15, 29, 34, 63, 91; DC 6, 30; WLC 6**
See also AAYA 63; BRWC 1; BRWR 2; BRWS 1; CA 81-84; CANR 39, 67, 125; CBD; CD 5, 6; CDBLB 1960 to Present; DA; DA3; DAB; DAC; DAM DRAM, MST; DFS 2, 5, 8, 11, 13, 16; DLB 13, 233; DLBY 1985; EWL 3; LATS 1:2; MTCW 1, 2; MTFW 2005; RGEL 2; TEA; WLIT 4

Storey, David (Malcolm) 1933- . **CLC 2, 4, 5, 8**
See also BRWS 1; CA 81-84; CANR 36; CBD; CD 5, 6; CN 1, 2, 3, 4, 5, 6; DAM DRAM; DLB 13, 14, 207, 245, 326; EWL 3; MTCW 1; RGEL 2

Storm, Hyemeyohsts 1935- ... **CLC 3; NNAL**
See also CA 81-84; CANR 45; DAM MULT

Storm, (Hans) Theodor (Woldsen)
1817-1888 ... **NCLC 1, 195; SSC 27, 106**
See also CDWLB 2; DLB 129; EW; RGSF 2; RGWL 2, 3

Storni, Alfonsina 1892-1938 . **HLC 2; PC 33; TCLC 5**
See also CA 104; 131; DAM MULT; DLB 283; HW 1; LAW

Stoughton, William 1631-1701 .... **LC 38**
See also DLB 24

Stout, Rex (Todhunter) 1886-1975 ..... **CLC 3**
See also AAYA 79; AITN 2; BPFB 3; CA 61-64; CANR 71; CMW 4; CN 2; DLB 306; MSW; RGAL 4

Stow, (Julian) Randolph 1935- ... **CLC 23, 48**
See also CA 13-16R; CANR 33; CN 1, 2, 3, 4, 5, 6, 7; CP 1, 2, 3, 4; DLB 260; MTCW 1; RGEL 2

Stowe, Harriet (Elizabeth) Beecher
1811-1896 .... **NCLC 3, 50, 133, 195; WLC 6**
See also AAYA 53; AMWS 1; CDALB 1865-1917; CLR 131; DA; DA3; DAB; DAC; DAM MST, NOV; DLB 1, 12, 42, 74, 189, 239, 243; EXPN; FL 1:3; JRDA; LAIT 2; MAICYA 1, 2; NFS 6; RGAL 4; TUS; YABC 1

Strabo c. 64B.C.-c. 25 .... **CMLC 37**
See also DLB 176

Strachey, (Giles) Lytton
1880-1932 .... **TCLC 12**
See also BRWS 2; CA 110; 178; DLB 149; DLBD 10; EWL 3; MTCW 2; NCFS 4

Stramm, August 1874-1915 .... **PC 50**
See also CA 195; EWL 3

Strand, Mark 1934- .. **CLC 6, 18, 41, 71; PC 63**
See also AMWS 4; CA 21-24R; CANR 40, 65, 100; CP 1, 2, 3, 4, 5, 6, 7; DAM POET; DLB 5; EWL 3; MAL 5; PAB; PFS 9, 18; RGAL 4; SATA 41; TCLE 1:2

Stratton-Porter, Gene(va Grace)
1863-1924 .... **TCLC 21**
See also ANW; BPFB 3; CA 112; 137; CLR 87; CWRI 5; DLB 221; DLBD 14; MAI-CYA 1, 2; RHW; SATA 15

Straub, Peter 1943- .... **CLC 28, 107**
See also BEST 89:1; BPFB 3; CA 85-88; CANR 28, 65, 109; CPW; DAM POP; DLBY 1984; HGG; MTCW 1, 2; MTFW 2005; SUFW 2

Straub, Peter Francis
See Straub, Peter

Strauss, Botho 1944- .... **CLC 22**
See also CA 157; CWW 2; DLB 124

Strauss, Leo 1899-1973 .... **TCLC 141**
See also CA 101; 45-48; CANR 122

Streatfeild, Mary Noel
See Streatfeild, Noel

Streatfeild, Noel 1897(?)-1986 .... **CLC 21**
See also CA 81-84; 120; CANR 31; CLR 17, 83; CWRI 5; DLB 160; MAICYA 1, 2; SATA 20; SATA-Obit 48

Stribling, T(homas) S(igismund)
1881-1965 .... **CLC 23**
See also CA 189; 107; CMW 4; DLB 9; RGAL 4

Strindberg, (Johan) August
1849-1912 ... **DC 18; TCLC 1, 8, 21, 47; WLC 6**
See also CA 104; 135; DA; DA3; DAB; DAC; DAM DRAM, MST; DFS 4, 9; DLB 259; EW 7; EWL 3; IDTP; LMFS 2; MTCW 2; MTFW 2005; RGWL 2, 3; TWA

Stringer, Arthur 1874-1950 .... **TCLC 37**
See also CA 161; DLB 92

Stringer, David
See Roberts, Keith (John Kingston)

Stroheim, Erich von 1885-1957 ..... **TCLC 71**

Strugatskii, Arkadii (Natanovich)
1925-1991 .... **CLC 27**
See also CA 106; 135; DLB 302; SFW 4

Strugatskii, Boris (Natanovich)
1933- .... **CLC 27**
See also CA 106; DLB 302; SFW 4

Strugatsky, Arkadii Natanovich
See Strugatskii, Arkadii (Natanovich)

Strugatsky, Boris (Natanovich)
See Strugatskii, Boris (Natanovich)

Strummer, Joe 1952-2002 .... **CLC 30**

Strunk, William, Jr. 1869-1946 ...... **TCLC 92**
See also CA 118; 164; NCFS 5

Stryk, Lucien 1924- .... **PC 27**
See also CA 13-16R; CANR 10, 28, 55, 110; CP 1, 2, 3, 4, 5, 6, 7

Tesich, Steve 1943(?)-1996 .... **CLC 40, 69**
See also CA 105; 152; CAD; DLBY 1983

Tesla, Nikola 1856-1943 .... **TCLC 88**

Teternikov, Fyodor Kuzmich
1863-1927 .... **TCLC 9**
See also CA 104; DLB 295; EWL 3

Tevis, Walter 1928-1984 .... **CLC 42**
See also CA 113; SFW 4

Tey, Josephine
See Mackintosh, Elizabeth

Thackeray, William Makepeace
1811-1863 ...... **NCLC 5, 14, 22, 43, 169, 213; WLC 6**
See also BRW 5; BRWC 2; CDBLB 1832-1890; DA; DA3; DAB; DAC; DAM MST, NOV; DLB 21, 55, 159, 163; NFS 13; RGEL 2; SATA 23; TEA; WLIT 3

Thakura, Ravindranatha
See Tagore, Rabindranath

Thames, C. H.
See Marlowe, Stephen

Tharoor, Shashi 1956- .... **CLC 70**
See also CA 141; CANR 91; CN 6, 7

Thelwall, John 1764-1834 .... **NCLC 162**
See also DLB 93, 158

Thelwell, Michael Miles 1939- .... **CLC 22**
See also BW 2; CA 101

Theo, Ion
See Theodorescu, Ion N.

Theobald, Lewis, Jr.
See Lovecraft, H. P.

Theocritus c. 310B.C.- .... **CMLC 45**
See also AW 1; DLB 176; RGWL 2, 3

Theodorescu, Ion N. 1880-1967 .... **CLC 80**
See also CA 167; 116; CDWLB 4; DLB 220; EWL 3

Theriault, Yves 1915-1983 .... **CLC 79**
See also CA 102; CANR 150; CCA 1; DAC; DAM MST; DLB 88; EWL 3

Therion, Master
See Crowley, Edward Alexander

Theroux, Alexander 1939- .... **CLC 2, 25**
See also CA 85-88; CANR 20, 63; CN 4, 5, 6, 7

Theroux, Alexander Louis
See Theroux, Alexander

Theroux, Paul 1941- .... **CLC 5, 8, 11, 15, 28, 46, 159**
See also AAYA 28; AMWS 8; BEST 89:4; BPFB 3; CA 33-36R; CANR 20, 45, 74, 133, 179; CDALBS; CN 1, 2, 3, 4, 5, 6, 7; CP 1; CPW 1; DA3; DAM POP; DLB 2, 218; EWL 3; HGG; MAL 5; MTCW 1, 2; MTFW 2005; RGAL 4; SATA 44, 109; TUS

Theroux, Paul Edward
See Theroux, Paul

Thesen, Sharon 1946- .... **CLC 56**
See also CA 163; CANR 125; CP 5, 6, 7; CWP

Thespis fl. 6th cent. B.C.- .... **CMLC 51**
See also LMFS 1

Thevenin, Denis
See Duhamel, Georges

Thibault, Jacques Anatole Francois
1844-1924 .... **TCLC 9**
See also CA 106; 127; DA3; DAM NOV; DLB 123, 330; EWL 3; GFL 1789 to the Present; MTCW 1, 2; RGWL 2, 3; SUFW 1; TWA

Thiele, Colin 1920-2006 .... **CLC 17**
See also CA 29-32R; CANR 12, 28, 53, 105; CLR 27; CP 1, 2; DLB 289; MAICYA 1, 2; SAAS 2; SATA 14, 72, 125; YAW

Thiong'o, Ngugi Wa
See Ngugi wa Thiong'o

Thistlethwaite, Bel
See Wetherald, Agnes Ethelwyn

Thomas, Audrey (Callahan) 1935- .... **CLC 7, 13, 37, 107; SSC 20**
See also AITN 2; CA 21-24R, 237; CAAE 237; CAAS 19; CANR 36, 58; CN 2, 3, 4, 5, 6, 7; DLB 60; MTCW 1; RGSF 2

Thomas, Augustus 1857-1934 .... **TCLC 97**
See also MAL 5

Thomas, D.M. 1935- ..... **CLC 13, 22, 31, 132**
See also BPFB 3; BRWS 4; CA 61-64; CAAS 11; CANR 17, 45, 75; CDBLB 1960 to Present; CN 4, 5, 6, 7; CP 1, 2, 3, 4, 5, 6, 7; DA3; DLB 40, 207, 299; HGG; INT CANR-17; MTCW 1, 2; MTFW 2005; RGHL; SFW 4

Thomas, Dylan (Marlais) 1914-1953 .... **PC 2, 52; SSC 3, 44; TCLC 1, 8, 45, 105; WLC 6**
See also AAYA 45; BRWS 1; CA 104; 120; CANR 65; CDBLB 1945-1960; DA; DA3; DAB; DAC; DAM DRAM, MST; DLB 13, 20, 139; EWL 3; EXPP; LAIT 3; MTCW 1, 2; MTFW 2005; PAB; PFS 1, 3, 8; RGEL 2; RGSF 2; SATA 60; TEA; WLIT 4; WP

Thomas, (Philip) Edward 1878-1917 . **PC 53; TCLC 10**
See also BRW 6; BRWS 3; CA 106; 153; DAM POET; DLB 19, 98, 156, 216; EWL 3; PAB; RGEL 2

Thomas, J.F.
See Fleming, Thomas

Thomas, Joyce Carol 1938- .... **CLC 35**
See also AAYA 12, 54; BW 2, 3; CA 113; 116; CANR 48, 114, 135; CLR 19; DLB 33; INT CA-116; JRDA; MAICYA 1, 2; MTCW 1, 2; MTFW 2005; SAAS 7; SATA 40, 78, 123, 137; SATA-Essay 137; WYA; YAW

Thomas, Lewis 1913-1993 .... **CLC 35**
See also ANW; CA 85-88; 143; CANR 38, 60; DLB 275; MTCW 1, 2

Thomas, M. Carey 1857-1935 .... **TCLC 89**
See also FW

Thomas, Paul
See Mann, (Paul) Thomas

Thomas, Piri 1928- .... **CLC 17; HLCS 2**
See also CA 73-76; HW 1; LLW

Thomas, R(onald) S(tuart)
1913-2000 .... **CLC 6, 13, 48**
See also BRWS 12; CA 89-92; 189; CAAS 4; CANR 30; CDBLB 1960 to Present; CP 1, 2, 3, 4, 5, 6, 7; DAB; DAM POET; DLB 27; EWL 3; MTCW 1; RGEL 2

Thomas, Ross (Elmore) 1926-1995 .. **CLC 39**
See also CA 33-36R; 150; CANR 22, 63; CMW 4

Thompson, Francis (Joseph)
1859-1907 .... **TCLC 4**
See also BRW 5; CA 104; 189; CDBLB 1890-1914; DLB 19; RGEL 2; TEA

Thompson, Francis Clegg
See Mencken, H(enry) L(ouis)

Thompson, Hunter S. 1937(?)-2005 .. **CLC 9, 17, 40, 104, 229**
See also AAYA 45; BEST 89:1; BPFB 3; CA 17-20R; 236; CANR 23, 46, 74, 77, 111, 133; CPW; CSW; DA3; DAM POP; DLB 185; MTCW 1, 2; MTFW 2005; TUS

Thompson, James Myers
See Thompson, Jim

Thompson, Jim 1906-1977 .... **CLC 69**
See also BPFB 3; CA 140; CMW 4; CPW; DLB 226; MSW

Thompson, Judith (Clare Francesca)
1954- .... **CLC 39**
See also CA 143; CD 5, 6; CWD; DFS 22; DLB 334

Thomson, James 1700-1748 .... **LC 16, 29, 40**
See also BRWS 3; DAM POET; DLB 95; RGEL 2

Thomson, James 1834-1882 .... **NCLC 18**
See also DAM POET; DLB 35; RGEL 2

Thoreau, Henry David 1817-1862 .. **NCLC 7, 21, 61, 138, 207; PC 30; WLC 6**
See also AAYA 42; AMW; ANW; BYA 3; CDALB 1640-1865; DA; DA3; DAB; DAC; DAM MST; DLB 1, 183, 223, 270, 298; LAIT 2; LMFS 1; NCFS 3; RGAL 4; TUS

Thorndike, E. L.
See Thorndike, Edward L(ee)

Thorndike, Edward L(ee)
1874-1949 .... **TCLC 107**
See also CA 121

Thornton, Hall
See Silverberg, Robert

Thorpe, Adam 1956- .... **CLC 176**
See also CA 129; CANR 92, 160; DLB 231

Thorpe, Thomas Bangs
1815-1878 .... **NCLC 183**
See also DLB 3, 11, 248; RGAL 4

Thubron, Colin 1939- .... **CLC 163**
See also CA 25-28R; CANR 12, 29, 59, 95, 171; CN 5, 6, 7; DLB 204, 231

Thubron, Colin Gerald Dryden
See Thubron, Colin

Thucydides c. 455B.C.-c. 395B.C. . . **CMLC 17**
See also AW 1; DLB 176; RGWL 2, 3; WLIT 8

Thumboo, Edwin Nadason 1933- .... **PC 30**
See also CA 194; CP 1

Thurber, James (Grover)
1894-1961 .. **CLC 5, 11, 25, 125; SSC 1, 47**
See also AAYA 56; AMWS 1; BPFB 3; BYA 5; CA 73-76; CANR 17, 39; CDALB 1929-1941; CWRI 5; DA; DA3; DAB; DAC; DAM DRAM, MST, NOV; DLB 4, 11, 22, 102; EWL 3; EXPS; FANT; LAIT 3; MAICYA 1, 2; MAL 5; MTCW 1, 2; MTFW 2005; RGAL 4; RGSF 2; SATA 13; SSFS 1, 10, 19; SUFW; TUS

Thurman, Wallace (Henry)
1902-1934 .. **BLC 1:3; HR 1:3; TCLC 6**
See also BW 1, 3; CA 104; 124; CANR 81; DAM MULT; DLB 51

Tibullus c. 54B.C.-c. 18B.C. .... **CMLC 36**
See also AW 2; DLB 211; RGWL 2, 3; WLIT 8

Ticheburn, Cheviot
See Ainsworth, William Harrison

Tieck, (Johann) Ludwig
1773-1853 ..... **NCLC 5, 46; SSC 31, 100**
See also CDWLB 2; DLB 90; EW 5; IDTP; RGSF 2; RGWL 2, 3; SUFW

Tiger, Derry
See Ellison, Harlan

Tilghman, Christopher 1946- .... **CLC 65**
See also CA 159; CANR 135, 151; CSW; DLB 244

Tillich, Paul (Johannes)
1886-1965 .... **CLC 131**
See also CA 5-8R; 25-28R; CANR 33; MTCW 1, 2

Tillinghast, Richard (Williford)
1940- .... **CLC 29**
See also CA 29-32R; CAAS 23; CANR 26, 51, 96; CP 2, 3, 4, 5, 6, 7; CSW

Tillman, Lynne (?)- .... **CLC 231**
See also CA 173; CANR 144, 172

Timrod, Henry 1828-1867 .... **NCLC 25**
See also DLB 3, 248; RGAL 4

Tindall, Gillian (Elizabeth) 1938- ...... **CLC 7**
See also CA 21-24R; CANR 11, 65, 107; CN 1, 2, 3, 4, 5, 6, 7

Ting Ling
See Chiang, Pin-chin

Tiptree, James, Jr.
See Sheldon, Alice Hastings Bradley

Tirone Smith, Mary-Ann 1944- .... **CLC 39**
See also CA 118; 136; CANR 113; SATA 143

Tirso de Molina 1580(?)-1648 .... **DC 13; HLCS 2; LC 73**
See also RGWL 2, 3

Titmarsh, Michael Angelo
See Thackeray, William Makepeace

Tocqueville, Alexis (Charles Henri Maurice Clerel Comte) de 1805-1859 .. **NCLC 7, 63**
See also EW 6; GFL 1789 to the Present; TWA

Toe, Tucker
See Westlake, Donald E.

Toer, Pramoedya Ananta
1925-2006 .... **CLC 186**
See also CA 197; 251; CANR 170; DLB 348; RGWL 3

Toffler, Alvin 1928- .... **CLC 168**
See also CA 13-16R; CANR 15, 46, 67, 183; CPW; DAM POP; MTCW 1, 2

Toibin, Colm 1955- .... **CLC 162**
See also CA 142; CANR 81, 149; CN 7; DLB 271

Tolkien, John Ronald Reuel
See Tolkien, J.R.R

Tolkien, J.R.R 1892-1973 ...... **CLC 1, 2, 3, 8, 12, 38; TCLC 137; WLC 6**
See also AAYA 10; AITN 1; BPFB 3; BRWC 2; BRWS 2; CA 17-18; 45-48; CANR 36, 134; CAP 2; CDBLB 1914- 1945; CLR 56; CN 1; CPW 1; CWRI 5; DA; DA3; DAB; DAC; DAM MST, NOV, POP; DLB 15, 160, 255; EFS 2; EWL 3; FANT; JRDA; LAIT 1; LATS 1:2; LMFS 2; MAICYA 1, 2; MTCW 1, 2; MTFW 2005; NFS 8, 26; RGEL 2; SATA 2, 32, 100; SATA-Obit 24; SFW 4; SUFW; TEA; WCH; WYA; YAW

Toller, Ernst 1893-1939 .... **TCLC 10**
See also CA 107; 186; DLB 124; EWL 3; RGWL 2, 3

Tolson, M. B.
See Tolson, Melvin B(eaunorus)

Tolson, Melvin B(eaunorus)
1898(?)-1966 .... **BLC 1:3; CLC 36, 105; PC 88**
See also AFAW 1, 2; BW 1, 3; CA 124; 89- 92; CANR 80; DAM MULT, POET; DLB 48, 76; MAL 5; RGAL 4

Tolstoi, Aleksei Nikolaevich
See Tolstoy, Alexey Nikolaevich

Tolstoi, Lev
See Tolstoy, Leo (Nikolaevich)

Tolstoy, Aleksei Nikolaevich
See Tolstoy, Alexey Nikolaevich

Tolstoy, Alexey Nikolaevich
1882-1945 .... **TCLC 18**
See also CA 107; 158; DLB 272; EWL 3; SFW 4

Tolstoy, Leo (Nikolaevich)
1828-1910 . **SSC 9, 30, 45, 54; TCLC 4, 11, 17, 28, 44, 79, 173; WLC 6**
See also AAYA 56; CA 104; 123; DA; DA3; DAB; DAC; DAM MST, NOV; DLB 238; EFS 2; EW 7; EXPS; IDTP; LAIT 2; LATS 1:1; LMFS 1; NFS 10, 28; RGSF 2; RGWL 2, 3; SATA 26; SSFS 5; TWA

Tolstoy, Count Leo
See Tolstoy, Leo (Nikolaevich)

Tomalin, Claire 1933- .... **CLC 166**
See also CA 89-92; CANR 52, 88, 165; DLB 155

Tomasi di Lampedusa, Giuseppe
1896-1957 .... **TCLC 13**
See also CA 111; 164; DLB 177; EW 11; EWL 3; MTCW 2; MTFW 2005; RGWL 2, 3; WLIT 7

Tomlin, Lily 1939(?)- .... **CLC 17**
See also CA 117

Tomlin, Mary Jane
See Tomlin, Lily

Tomlin, Mary Jean
See Tomlin, Lily

Tomline, F. Latour
See Gilbert, W(illiam) S(chwenck)

Tomlinson, (Alfred) Charles 1927- .... **CLC 2, 4, 6, 13, 45; PC 17**
See also CA 5-8R; CANR 33; CP 1, 2, 3, 4, 5, 6, 7; DAM POET; DLB 40; TCLE 1:2

Tomlinson, H(enry) M(ajor)
1873-1958 .... **TCLC 71**
See also CA 118; 161; DLB 36, 100, 195

Tomlinson, Mary Jane
See Tomlin, Lily

Tonna, Charlotte Elizabeth
1790-1846 .... **NCLC 135**
See also DLB 163

Tonson, Jacob fl. 1655(?)-1736 .... **LC 86**
See also DLB 170

Toole, John Kennedy 1937-1969 ..... **CLC 19, 64**
See also BPFB 3; CA 104; DLBY 1981; MTCW 2; MTFW 2005

Toomer, Eugene
See Toomer, Jean

Toomer, Eugene Pinchback
See Toomer, Jean

Toomer, Jean 1894-1967 ... **BLC 1:3; CLC 1, 4, 13, 22; HR 1:3; PC 7; SSC 1, 45; TCLC 172; WLCS**
See also AFAW 1, 2; AMWS 3, 9; BW 1; CA 85-88; CDALB 1917-1929; DA3; DAM MULT; DLB 45, 51; EWL 3; EXPP; EXPS; LMFS 2; MAL 5; MTCW 1, 2; MTFW 2005; NFS 11; RGAL 4; RGSF 2; SSFS 5

Toomer, Nathan Jean
See Toomer, Jean

Toomer, Nathan Pinchback
See Toomer, Jean

Torley, Luke
See Blish, James (Benjamin)

Tornimparte, Alessandra
See Ginzburg, Natalia

Torre, Raoul della
See Mencken, H(enry) L(ouis)

Torrence, Ridgely 1874-1950 .... **TCLC 97**
See also DLB 54, 249; MAL 5

Torrey, E. Fuller 1937- .... **CLC 34**
See also CA 119; CANR 71, 158

Torrey, Edwin Fuller
See Torrey, E. Fuller

Torsvan, Ben Traven
See Traven, B.

Torsvan, Benno Traven
See Traven, B.

Torsvan, Berick Traven
See Traven, B.

Torsvan, Berwick Traven
See Traven, B.

Torsvan, Bruno Traven
See Traven, B.

Torsvan, Traven
See Traven, B.

Toson
See Shimazaki, Haruki

Tourneur, Cyril 1575(?)-1626 .... **LC 66**
See also BRW 2; DAM DRAM; DLB 58; RGEL 2

Tournier, Michel 1924- .... **CLC 6, 23, 36, 95, 249; SSC 88**
See also CA 49-52; CANR 3, 36, 74, 149; CWW 2; DLB 83; EWL 3; GFL 1789 to the Present; MTCW 1, 2; SATA 23

Tournier, Michel Edouard
See Tournier, Michel

Tournimparte, Alessandra
See Ginzburg, Natalia

Towers, Ivar
See Kornbluth, C(yril) M.

Towne, Robert (Burton) 1936(?)- ..... **CLC 87**
See also CA 108; DLB 44; IDFW 3, 4

Townsend, Sue
See Townsend, Susan Lilian

Townsend, Susan Lilian 1946- .... **CLC 61**
See also AAYA 28; CA 119; 127; CANR 65, 107; CBD; CD 5, 6; CPW; CWD; DAB; DAC; DAM MST; DLB 271; INT CA-127; SATA 55, 93; SATA-Brief 48; YAW

Townshend, Pete
See Townshend, Peter

Townshend, Peter 1945- .... **CLC 17, 42**
See also CA 107

Townshend, Peter Dennis Blandford
See Townshend, Peter

Tozzi, Federigo 1883-1920 .... **TCLC 31**
See also CA 160; CANR 110; DLB 264; EWL 3; WLIT 7

Trafford, F. G.
See Riddell, Charlotte

Traherne, Thomas 1637(?)-1674 .. **LC 99; PC 70**
See also BRW 2; BRWS 11; DLB 131; PAB; RGEL 2

Traill, Catharine Parr 1802-1899 .. **NCLC 31**
See also DLB 99

Trakl, Georg 1887-1914 .... **PC 20; TCLC 5**
See also CA 104; 165; EW 10; EWL 3; LMFS 2; MTCW 2; RGWL 2, 3

Trambley, Estela Portillo
See Portillo Trambley, Estela

Tranquilli, Secondino
See Silone, Ignazio

Transtroemer, Tomas Gosta
See Transtromer, Tomas

Transtromer, Tomas (Gosta)
See Transtromer, Tomas

Transtromer, Tomas 1931- .... **CLC 52, 65**
See also CA 117; 129; CAAS 17; CANR 115, 172; CWW 2; DAM POET; DLB 257; EWL 3; PFS 21

Transtromer, Tomas Goesta
See Transtromer, Tomas

Transtromer, Tomas Gosta
See Transtromer, Tomas

Transtromer, Tomas Gosta
See Transtromer, Tomas

Traven, B. 1882(?)-1969 .... **CLC 8, 11**
See also CA 19-20; 25-28R; CAP 2; DLB 9, 56; EWL 3; MTCW 1; RGAL 4

Trediakovsky, Vasilii Kirillovich
1703-1769 .... **LC 68**
See also DLB 150

Treitel, Jonathan 1959- .... **CLC 70**
See also CA 210; DLB 267

Trelawny, Edward John
1792-1881 .... **NCLC 85**
See also DLB 110, 116, 144

Tremain, Rose 1943- .... **CLC 42**
See also CA 97-100; CANR 44, 95, 186; CN 4, 5, 6, 7; DLB 14, 271; RGSF 2; RHW

Tremblay, Michel 1942- .... **CLC 29, 102, 225**
See also CA 116; 128; CCA 1; CWW 2; DAC; DAM MST; DLB 60; EWL 3; GLL 1; MTCW 1, 2; MTFW 2005

Underwood, Miles
See Glassco, John

Undset, Sigrid 1882-1949 .... **TCLC 3, 197; WLC 6**
See also AAYA 77; CA 104; 129; DA; DA3; DAB; DAC; DAM MST, NOV; DLB 293, 332; EW 9; EWL 3; FW; MTCW 1, 2; MTFW 2005; RGWL 2, 3

Ungaretti, Giuseppe 1888-1970 ... **CLC 7, 11, 15; PC 57; TCLC 200**
See also CA 19-20; 25-28R; CAP 2; DLB 114; EW 10; EWL 3; PFS 20; RGWL 2, 3; WLIT 7

Unger, Douglas 1952- .... **CLC 34**
See also CA 130; CANR 94, 155

Unsworth, Barry 1930- .... **CLC 76, 127**
See also BRWS 7; CA 25-28R; CANR 30, 54, 125, 171; CN 6, 7; DLB 194, 326

Unsworth, Barry Forster
See Unsworth, Barry

Updike, John 1932-2009 .... **CLC 1, 2, 3, 5, 7, 9, 13, 15, 23, 34, 43, 70, 139, 214; PC 90; SSC 13, 27, 103; WLC 6**
See also AAYA 36; AMW; AMWC 1; AMWR 1; BPFB 3; BYA 12; CA 1-4R; CABS 1; CANR 4, 33, 51, 94, 133; CDALB 1968-1988; CN 1, 2, 3, 4, 5, 6, 7; CP 1, 2, 3, 4, 5, 6, 7; CPW 1; DA; DA3; DAB; DAC; DAM MST, NOV, POET, POP; DLB 2, 5, 143, 218, 227; DLBD 3; DLBY 1980, 1982, 1997; EWL 3; EXPP; HGG; MAL 5; MTCW 1, 2; MTFW 2005; NFS 12, 24; RGAL 4; RGSF 2; SSFS 3, 19; TUS

Updike, John Hoyer
See Updike, John

Upshaw, Margaret Mitchell
See Mitchell, Margaret (Munnerlyn)

Upton, Mark
See Sanders, Lawrence

Upward, Allen 1863-1926 .... **TCLC 85**
See also CA 117; 187; DLB 36

Urdang, Constance (Henriette)
1922-1996 .... **CLC 47**
See also CA 21-24R; CANR 9, 24; CP 1, 2, 3, 4, 5, 6; CWP

Urfe, Honore d' 1567(?)-1625 .... **LC 132**
See also DLB 268; GFL Beginnings to 1789; RGWL 2, 3

Uriel, Henry
See Faust, Frederick (Schiller)

Uris, Leon 1924-2003 .... **CLC 7, 32**
See also AITN 1, 2; BEST 89:2; BPFB 3; CA 1-4R; 217; CANR 1, 40, 65, 123; CN 1, 2, 3, 4, 5, 6; CPW 1; DA3; DAM NOV, POP; MTCW 1, 2; MTFW 2005; RGHL; SATA 49; SATA-Obit 146

Urista (Heredia), Alberto (Baltazar)
1947- .... **HLCS 1; PC 34**
See also CA 45-48R; CANR 2, 32; DLB 82; HW 1; LLW

Urmuz
See Codrescu, Andrei

Urquhart, Guy
See McAlmon, Robert (Menzies)

Urquhart, Jane 1949- .... **CLC 90, 242**
See also CA 113; CANR 32, 68, 116, 157; CCA 1; DAC; DLB 334

Usigli, Rodolfo 1905-1979 .... **HLCS 1**
See also CA 131; DLB 305; EWL 3; HW 1; LAW

Usk, Thomas (?)-1388 .... **CMLC 76**
See also DLB 146

Ustinov, Peter (Alexander)
1921-2004 .... **CLC 1**
See also AITN 1; CA 13-16R; 225; CANR 25, 51; CBD; CD 5, 6; DLB 13; MTCW 2

U Tam'si, Gerald Felix Tchicaya
See Tchicaya, Gerald Felix

U Tam'si, Tchicaya
See Tchicaya, Gerald Felix

Vachss, Andrew 1942- .... **CLC 106**
See also CA 118, 214; CAAE 214; CANR 44, 95, 153; CMW 4

Vachss, Andrew H.
See Vachss, Andrew

Vachss, Andrew Henry
See Vachss, Andrew

Vaculik, Ludvik 1926- .... **CLC 7**
See also CA 53-56; CANR 72; CWW 2; DLB 232; EWL 3

Vaihinger, Hans 1852-1933 .... **TCLC 71**
See also CA 116; 166

Valdez, Luis (Miguel) 1940- ..... **CLC 84; DC 10; HLC 2**
See also CA 101; CAD; CANR 32, 81; CD 5, 6; DAM MULT; DFS 5; DLB 122; EWL 3; HW 1; LAIT 4; LLW

Valenzuela, Luisa 1938- .... **CLC 31, 104; HLCS 2; SSC 14, 82**
See also CA 101; CANR 32, 65, 123; CD-WLB 3; CWW 2; DAM MULT; DLB 113; EWL 3; FW; HW 1, 2; LAW; RGSF 2; RGWL 3

Valera y Alcala-Galiano, Juan
1824-1905 .... **TCLC 10**
See also CA 106

Valerius Maximus .... **CMLC 64**
See also DLB 211

Valery, (Ambroise) Paul (Toussaint Jules)
1871-1945 .... **PC 9; TCLC 4, 15**
See also CA 104; 122; DA3; DAM POET; DLB 258; EW 8; EWL 3; GFL 1789 to the Present; MTCW 1, 2; MTFW 2005; RGWL 2, 3; TWA

Valle-Inclan, Ramon (Maria) del
1866-1936 .... **HLC 2; TCLC 5**
See also CA 106; 153; CANR 80; DAM MULT; DLB 134, 322; EW 8; EWL 3; HW 2; RGSF 2; RGWL 2, 3

Vallejo, Antonio Buero
See Buero Vallejo, Antonio

Vallejo, Cesar (Abraham)
1892-1938 .... **HLC 2; TCLC 3, 56**
See also CA 105; 153; DAM MULT; DLB 290; EWL 3; HW 1; LAW; PFS 26; RGWL 2, 3

Valles, Jules 1832-1885 .... **NCLC 71**
See also DLB 123; GFL 1789 to the Present

Vallette, Marguerite Eymery
1860-1953 .... **TCLC 67**
See also CA 182; DLB 123, 192; EWL 3

Valle Y Pena, Ramon del
See Valle-Inclan, Ramon (Maria) del

Van Ash, Cay 1918-1994 .... **CLC 34**
See also CA 220

Vanbrugh, Sir John 1664-1726 .... **LC 21**
See also BRW 2; DAM DRAM; DLB 80; IDTP; RGEL 2

Van Campen, Karl
See Campbell, John W(ood, Jr.)

Vance, Gerald
See Silverberg, Robert

Vance, Jack 1916- .... **CLC 35**
See also CA 29-32R; CANR 17, 65, 154; CMW 4; DLB 8; FANT; MTCW 1; SCFW 1, 2; SFW 4; SUFW 1, 2

Vance, John Holbrook
See Vance, Jack

Van Den Bogarde, Derek Jules Gaspard Ulric Niven 1921-1999 .... **CLC 14**
See also CA 77-80; 179; DLB 14

Vandenburgh, Jane .... **CLC 59**
See also CA 168

Vanderhaeghe, Guy 1951- .... **CLC 41**
See also BPFB 3; CA 113; CANR 72, 145; CN 7; DLB 334

van der Post, Laurens (Jan)
1906-1996 .... **CLC 5**
See also AFW; CA 5-8R; 155; CANR 35; CN 1, 2, 3, 4, 5, 6; DLB 204; RGEL 2

van de Wetering, Janwillem
1931-2008 .... **CLC 47**
See also CA 49-52; 274; CANR 4, 62, 90; CMW 4

Van Dine, S. S.
See Wright, Willard Huntington

Van Doren, Carl (Clinton)
1885-1950 .... **TCLC 18**
See also CA 111; 168

Van Doren, Mark 1894-1972 .... **CLC 6, 10**
See also CA 1-4R; 37-40R; CANR 3; CN 1; CP 1; DLB 45, 284, 335; MAL 5; MTCW 1, 2; RGAL 4

Van Druten, John (William)
1901-1957 .... **TCLC 2**
See also CA 104; 161; DLB 10; MAL 5; RGAL 4

Van Duyn, Mona 1921-2004 .... **CLC 3, 7, 63, 116**
See also CA 9-12R; 234; CANR 7, 38, 60, 116; CP 1, 2, 3, 4, 5, 6, 7; CWP; DAM POET; DLB 5; MAL 5; MTFW 2005; PFS 20

Van Dyne, Edith
See Baum, L(yman) Frank

van Herk, Aritha 1954- .... **CLC 249**
See also CA 101; CANR 94; DLB 334

van Itallie, Jean-Claude 1936- .... **CLC 3**
See also CA 45-48; CAAS 2; CAD; CANR 1, 48; CD 5, 6; DLB 7

Van Loot, Cornelius Obenchain
See Roberts, Kenneth (Lewis)

van Ostaijen, Paul 1896-1928 .... **TCLC 33**
See also CA 163

Van Peebles, Melvin 1932- .... **CLC 2, 20**
See also BW 2, 3; CA 85-88; CANR 27, 67, 82; DAM MULT

van Schendel, Arthur(-Francois-Emile)
1874-1946 .... **TCLC 56**
See also EWL 3

Van See, John
See Vance, Jack

Vansittart, Peter 1920-2008 .... **CLC 42**
See also CA 1-4R; 278; CANR 3, 49, 90; CN 4, 5, 6, 7; RHW

Van Vechten, Carl 1880-1964 ... **CLC 33; HR 1:3**
See also AMWS 2; CA 183; 89-92; DLB 4, 9, 51; RGAL 4

van Vogt, A(lfred) E(lton) 1912-2000 . **CLC 1**
See also BPFB 3; BYA 13, 14; CA 21-24R; 190; CANR 28; DLB 8, 251; SATA 14; SATA-Obit 124; SCFW 1, 2; SFW 4

Vara, Madeleine
See Jackson, Laura (Riding)

Varda, Agnes 1928- .... **CLC 16**
See also CA 116; 122

Vargas Llosa, Jorge Mario Pedro
See Vargas Llosa, Mario

Vargas Llosa, Mario 1936- .. **CLC 3, 6, 9, 10, 15, 31, 42, 85, 181; HLC 2**
See also BPFB 3; CA 73-76; CANR 18, 32, 42, 67, 116, 140, 173; CDWLB 3; CWW 2; DA; DA3; DAB; DAC; DAM MST, MULT, NOV; DLB 145; DNFS 2; EWL 3; HW 1, 2; LAIT 5; LATS 1:2; LAW; LAWS 1; MTCW 1, 2; MTFW 2005; RGWL 2, 3; SSFS 14; TWA; WLIT 1

Varnhagen von Ense, Rahel
1771-1833 .... **NCLC 130**
See also DLB 90

Vasari, Giorgio 1511-1574 .... **LC 114**

von Daniken, Erich
See von Daeniken, Erich

von Eschenbach, Wolfram c. 1170-c.
1220 .... **CMLC 5**
See also CDWLB 2; DLB 138; EW 1;
RGWL 2, 3

von Hartmann, Eduard
1842-1906 .... **TCLC 96**

von Hayek, Friedrich August
See Hayek, F(riedrich) A(ugust von)

von Heidenstam, (Carl Gustaf) Verner
See Heidenstam, (Carl Gustaf) Verner von

von Heyse, Paul (Johann Ludwig)
See Heyse, Paul (Johann Ludwig von)

von Hofmannsthal, Hugo
See Hofmannsthal, Hugo von

von Horvath, Odon
See von Horvath, Odon

von Horvath, Odon
See von Horvath, Odon

von Horvath, Odon 1901-1938 .... **TCLC 45**
See also CA 118; 184, 194; DLB 85, 124;
RGWL 2, 3

von Horvath, Oedoen
See von Horvath, Odon

von Kleist, Heinrich
See Kleist, Heinrich von

Vonnegut, Kurt, Jr.
See Vonnegut, Kurt

Vonnegut, Kurt 1922-2007 .... **CLC 1, 2, 3, 4,
5, 8, 12, 22, 40, 60, 111, 212, 254; SSC
8; WLC 6**
See also AAYA 6, 44; AITN 1; AMWS 2;
BEST 90:4; BPFB 3; BYA 3, 14; CA
1-4R; 259; CANR 1, 25, 49, 75, 92;
CDALB 1968-1988; CN 1, 2, 3, 4, 5, 6,
7; CPW 1; DA; DA3; DAB; DAC; DAM
MST, NOV, POP; DLB 2, 8, 152; DLBD
3; DLBY 1980; EWL 3; EXPN; EXPS;
LAIT 4; LMFS 2; MAL 5; MTCW 1, 2;
MTFW 2005; NFS 3, 28; RGAL 4;
SCFW; SFW 4; SSFS 5; TUS; YAW

Von Rachen, Kurt
See Hubbard, L. Ron

von Sternberg, Josef
See Sternberg, Josef von

Vorster, Gordon 1924- .... **CLC 34**
See also CA 133

Vosce, Trudie
See Ozick, Cynthia

Voznesensky, Andrei (Andreievich)
1933- .... **CLC 1, 15, 57**
See also CA 89-92; CANR 37; CWW 2;
DAM POET; EWL 3; MTCW 1

Voznesensky, Andrey
See Voznesensky, Andrei (Andreievich)

Wace, Robert c. 1100-c. 1175 .... **CMLC 55**
See also DLB 146

Waddington, Miriam 1917-2004 .... **CLC 28**
See also CA 21-24R; 225; CANR 12, 30;
CCA 1; CP 1, 2, 3, 4, 5, 6, 7; DLB 68

Wade, Alan
See Vance, Jack

Wagman, Fredrica 1937- .... **CLC 7**
See also CA 97-100; CANR 166; INT CA-
97-100

Wagner, Linda W.
See Wagner-Martin, Linda (C.)

Wagner, Linda Welshimer
See Wagner-Martin, Linda (C.)

Wagner, Richard 1813-1883 ..... **NCLC 9, 119**
See also DLB 129; EW 6

Wagner-Martin, Linda (C.) 1936- .... **CLC 50**
See also CA 159; CANR 135

Wagoner, David (Russell) 1926- .... **CLC 3, 5,
15; PC 33**
See also AMWS 9; CA 1-4R; CAAS 3;
CANR 2, 71; CN 1, 2, 3, 4, 5, 6, 7; CP 1,
2, 3, 4, 5, 6, 7; DLB 5, 256; SATA 14;
TCWW 1, 2

Wah, Fred(erick James) 1939- .... **CLC 44**
See also CA 107; 141; CP 1, 6, 7; DLB 60

Wahloo, Per 1926-1975 .... **CLC 7**
See also BPFB 3; CA 61-64; CANR 73;
CMW 4; MSW

Wahloo, Peter
See Wahloo, Per

Wain, John (Barrington) 1925-1994 . **CLC 2,
11, 15, 46**
See also CA 5-8R; 145; CAAS 4; CANR
23, 54; CDBLB 1960 to Present; CN 1, 2,
3, 4, 5; CP 1, 2, 3, 4, 5; DLB 15, 27, 139,
155; EWL 3; MTCW 1, 2; MTFW 2005

Wajda, Andrzej 1926- .... **CLC 16, 219**
See also CA 102

Wakefield, Dan 1932- .... **CLC 7**
See also CA 21-24R, 211; CAAE 211;
CAAS 7; CN 4, 5, 6, 7

Wakefield, Herbert Russell
1888-1965 .... **TCLC 120**
See also CA 5-8R; CANR 77; HGG; SUFW

Wakoski, Diane 1937- ...... **CLC 2, 4, 7, 9, 11,
40; PC 15**
See also CA 13-16R, 216; CAAE 216;
CAAS 1; CANR 9, 60, 106; CP 1, 2, 3, 4,
5, 6, 7; CWP; DAM POET; DLB 5; INT
CANR-9; MAL 5; MTCW 2; MTFW
2005

Wakoski-Sherbell, Diane
See Wakoski, Diane

Walcott, Derek 1930- . **BLC 1:3, 2:3; CLC 2,
4, 9, 14, 25, 42, 67, 76, 160; DC 7; PC
46**
See also BW 2; CA 89-92; CANR 26, 47,
75, 80, 130; CBD; CD 5, 6; CDWLB 3;
CP 1, 2, 3, 4, 5, 6, 7; DA3; DAB; DAC;
DAM MST, MULT, POET; DLB 117,
332; DLBY 1981; DNFS 1; EFS 1; EWL
3; LMFS 2; MTCW 1, 2; MTFW 2005;
PFS 6; RGEL 2; TWA; WWE 1

Waldman, Anne (Lesley) 1945- .... **CLC 7**
See also BG 1:3; CA 37-40R; CAAS 17;
CANR 34, 69, 116; CP 1, 2, 3, 4, 5, 6, 7;
CWP; DLB 16

Waldo, E. Hunter
See Sturgeon, Theodore (Hamilton)

Waldo, Edward Hamilton
See Sturgeon, Theodore (Hamilton)

Walker, Alice 1944- .... **BLC 1:3, 2:3; CLC 5,
6, 9, 19, 27, 46, 58, 103, 167; PC 30;
SSC 5; WLCS**
See also AAYA 3, 33; AFAW 1, 2; AMWS
3; BEST 89:4; BPFB 3; BW 2, 3; CA 37-
40R; CANR 9, 27, 49, 66, 82, 131;
CDALB 1968-1988; CN 4, 5, 6, 7; CPW;
CSW; DA; DA3; DAB; DAC; DAM MST,
MULT, NOV, POET, POP; DLB 6, 33,
143; EWL 3; EXPN; EXPS; FL 1:6; FW;
INT CANR-27; LAIT 3; MAL 5; MBL;
MTCW 1, 2; MTFW 2005; NFS 5; PFS
30; RGAL 4; RGSF 2; SATA 31; SSFS 2,
11; TUS; YAW

Walker, Alice Malsenior
See Walker, Alice

Walker, David Harry 1911-1992 ...... **CLC 14**
See also CA 1-4R; 137; CANR 1; CN 1, 2;
CWRI 5; SATA 8; SATA-Obit 71

Walker, Edward Joseph 1934-2004 .. **CLC 13**
See also CA 21-24R; 226; CANR 12, 28,
53; CP 1, 2, 3, 4, 5, 6, 7; DLB 40

Walker, George F(rederick) 1947- .. **CLC 44,
61**
See also CA 103; CANR 21, 43, 59; CD 5,
6; DAB; DAC; DAM MST; DLB 60

Walker, Joseph A. 1935-2003 .... **CLC 19**
See also BW 1, 3; CA 89-92; CAD; CANR
26, 143; CD 5, 6; DAM DRAM, MST;
DFS 12; DLB 38

Walker, Margaret 1915-1998 .... **BLC 1:3;
CLC 1, 6; PC 20; TCLC 129**
See also AFAW 1, 2; BW 2, 3; CA 73-76;
172; CANR 26, 54, 76, 136; CN 1, 2, 3,
4, 5, 6; CP 1, 2, 3, 4, 5, 6; CSW; DAM
MULT; DLB 76, 152; EXPP; FW; MAL
5; MTCW 1, 2; MTFW 2005; RGAL 4;
RHW

Walker, Ted
See Walker, Edward Joseph

Wallace, David Foster 1962-2008 .... **CLC 50,
114, 271; SSC 68**
See also AAYA 50; AMWS 10; CA 132;
277; CANR 59, 133; CN 7; DA3; MTCW
2; MTFW 2005

Wallace, Dexter
See Masters, Edgar Lee

Wallace, (Richard Horatio) Edgar
1875-1932 .... **TCLC 57**
See also CA 115; 218; CMW 4; DLB 70;
MSW; RGEL 2

Wallace, Irving 1916-1990 .... **CLC 7, 13**
See also AITN 1; BPFB 3; CA 1-4R; 132;
CAAS 1; CANR 1, 27; CPW; DAM NOV,
POP; INT CANR-27; MTCW 1, 2

Wallant, Edward Lewis 1926-1962 ... **CLC 5,
10**
See also CA 1-4R; CANR 22; DLB 2, 28,
143, 299; EWL 3; MAL 5; MTCW 1, 2;
RGAL 4; RGHL

Wallas, Graham 1858-1932 .... **TCLC 91**

Waller, Edmund 1606-1687 .... **LC 86; PC 72**
See also BRW 2; DAM POET; DLB 126;
PAB; RGEL 2

Walley, Byron
See Card, Orson Scott

Walpole, Horace 1717-1797 ..... **LC 2, 49, 152**
See also BRW 3; DLB 39, 104, 213; GL 3;
HGG; LMFS 1; RGEL 2; SUFW 1; TEA

Walpole, Hugh (Seymour)
1884-1941 .... **TCLC 5**
See also CA 104; 165; DLB 34; HGG;
MTCW 2; RGEL 2; RHW

Walrond, Eric (Derwent) 1898-1966 . **HR 1:3**
See also BW 1; CA 125; DLB 51

Walser, Martin 1927- .... **CLC 27, 183**
See also CA 57-60; CANR 8, 46, 145;
CWW 2; DLB 75, 124; EWL 3

Walser, Robert 1878-1956 ..... **SSC 20; TCLC
18**
See also CA 118; 165; CANR 100; DLB
66; EWL 3

Walsh, Gillian Paton
See Paton Walsh, Jill

Walsh, Jill Paton
See Paton Walsh, Jill

Walter, Villiam Christian
See Andersen, Hans Christian

Walter of Chatillon c. 1135-c.
1202 .... **CMLC 111**

Walters, Anna L(ee) 1946- .... **NNAL**
See also CA 73-76

Walther von der Vogelweide c.
1170-1228 .... **CMLC 56**

Walton, Izaak 1593-1683 .... **LC 72**
See also BRW 2; CDBLB Before 1660;
DLB 151, 213; RGEL 2

Walzer, Michael (Laban) 1935- ...... **CLC 238**
See also CA 37-40R; CANR 15, 48, 127

Wambaugh, Joseph, Jr. 1937- ...... **CLC 3, 18**
See also AITN 1; BEST 89:3; BPFB 3; CA
33-36R; CANR 42, 65, 115, 167; CMW
4; CPW 1; DA3; DAM NOV, POP; DLB
6; DLBY 1983; MSW; MTCW 1, 2

Wright, Willard Huntington
1888-1939 .... **TCLC 23**
See also CA 115; 189; CMW 4; DLB 306;
DLBD 16; MSW

Wright, William 1930- .... **CLC 44**
See also CA 53-56; CANR 7, 23, 154

Wroth, Lady Mary 1587-1653(?) .... **LC 30,
139; PC 38**
See also DLB 121

Wu Ch'eng-en 1500(?)-1582(?) .... **LC 7**

Wu Ching-tzu 1701-1754 .... **LC 2**

Wulfstan c. 10th cent. -1023 .... **CMLC 59**

Wurlitzer, Rudolph 1938(?)- .... **CLC 2, 4, 15**
See also CA 85-88; CN 4, 5, 6, 7; DLB 173

Wyatt, Sir Thomas c. 1503-1542 . **LC 70; PC
27**
See also BRW 1; DLB 132; EXPP; PFS 25;
RGEL 2; TEA

Wycherley, William 1640-1716 .... **LC 8, 21,
102, 136**
See also BRW 2; CDBLB 1660-1789; DAM
DRAM; DLB 80; RGEL 2

Wyclif, John c. 1330-1384 .... **CMLC 70**
See also DLB 146

Wylie, Elinor (Morton Hoyt)
1885-1928 .... **PC 23; TCLC 8**
See also AMWS 1; CA 105; 162; DLB 9,
45; EXPP; MAL 5; RGAL 4

Wylie, Philip (Gordon) 1902-1971 ... **CLC 43**
See also CA 21-22; 33-36R; CAP 2; CN 1;
DLB 9; SFW 4

Wyndham, John
See Harris, John (Wyndham Parkes Lucas)
Beynon

Wyss, Johann David Von
1743-1818 .... **NCLC 10**
See also CLR 92; JRDA; MAICYA 1, 2;
SATA 29; SATA-Brief 27

Xenophon c. 430B.C.-c. 354B.C. ... **CMLC 17**
See also AW 1; DLB 176; RGWL 2, 3;
WLIT 8

Xingjian, Gao 1940- .... **CLC 167**
See also CA 193; DFS 21; DLB 330;
MTFW 2005; RGWL 3

Yakamochi 718-785 .... **CMLC 45; PC 48**

Yakumo Koizumi
See Hearn, (Patricio) Lafcadio (Tessima
Carlos)

Yamada, Mitsuye (May) 1923- .... **PC 44**
See also CA 77-80

Yamamoto, Hisaye 1921- .... **AAL; SSC 34**
See also CA 214; DAM MULT; DLB 312;
LAIT 4; SSFS 14

Yamauchi, Wakako 1924- .... **AAL**
See also CA 214; DLB 312

Yan, Mo
See Moye, Guan

Yanez, Jose Donoso
See Donoso (Yanez), Jose

Yanovsky, Basile S.
See Yanovsky, V(assily) S(emenovich)

Yanovsky, V(assily) S(emenovich)
1906-1989 .... **CLC 2, 18**
See also CA 97-100; 129

Yates, Richard 1926-1992 .... **CLC 7, 8, 23**
See also AMWS 11; CA 5-8R; 139; CANR
10, 43; CN 1, 2, 3, 4, 5; DLB 2, 234;
DLBY 1981, 1992; INT CANR-10; SSFS
24

Yau, John 1950- .... **PC 61**
See also CA 154; CANR 89; CP 4, 5, 6, 7;
DLB 234, 312; PFS 26

Yearsley, Ann 1753-1806 .... **NCLC 174**
See also DLB 109

Yeats, W. B.
See Yeats, William Butler

Yeats, William Butler 1865-1939 . **DC 33; PC
20, 51; TCLC 1, 11, 18, 31, 93, 116;
WLC 6**
See also AAYA 48; BRW 6; BRWR 1; CA
104; 127; CANR 45; CDBLB 1890-1914;
DA; DA3; DAB; DAC; DAM DRAM,
MST, POET; DLB 10, 19, 98, 156, 332;
EWL 3; EXPP; MTCW 1, 2; MTFW
2005; NCFS 3; PAB; PFS 1, 2, 5, 7, 13,
15; RGEL 2; TEA; WLIT 4; WP

Yehoshua, A.B. 1936- .... **CLC 13, 31, 243**
See also CA 33-36R; CANR 43, 90, 145;
CWW 2; EWL 3; RGHL; RGSF 2; RGWL
3; WLIT 6

Yehoshua, Abraham B.
See Yehoshua, A.B.

Yellow Bird
See Ridge, John Rollin

Yep, Laurence 1948- .... **CLC 35**
See also AAYA 5, 31; BYA 7; CA 49-52;
CANR 1, 46, 92, 161; CLR 3, 17, 54, 132;
DLB 52, 312; FANT; JRDA; MAICYA 1,
2; MAICYAS 1; SATA 7, 69, 123, 176;
WYA; YAW

Yep, Laurence Michael
See Yep, Laurence

Yerby, Frank G(arvin) 1916-1991 . **BLC 1:3;
CLC 1, 7, 22**
See also BPFB 3; BW 1, 3; CA 9-12R; 136;
CANR 16, 52; CN 1, 2, 3, 4, 5; DAM
MULT; DLB 76; INT CANR-16; MTCW
1; RGAL 4; RHW

Yesenin, Sergei Aleksandrovich
See Esenin, Sergei

Yevtushenko, Yevgeny (Alexandrovich)
1933- ...... **CLC 1, 3, 13, 26, 51, 126; PC
40**
See also CA 81-84; CANR 33, 54; CWW
2; DAM POET; EWL 3; MTCW 1; PFS
29; RGHL; RGWL 2, 3

Yezierska, Anzia 1885(?)-1970 .... **CLC 46;
TCLC 205**
See also CA 126; 89-92; DLB 28, 221; FW;
MTCW 1; NFS 29; RGAL 4; SSFS 15

Yglesias, Helen 1915-2008 .... **CLC 7, 22**
See also CA 37-40R; 272; CAAS 20; CANR
15, 65, 95; CN 4, 5, 6, 7; INT CANR-15;
MTCW 1

Y.O.
See Russell, George William

Yokomitsu, Riichi 1898-1947 .... **TCLC 47**
See also CA 170; EWL 3

Yolen, Jane 1939- .... **CLC 256**
See also AAYA 4, 22; BPFB 3; BYA 9, 10,
11, 14, 16; CA 13-16R; CANR 11, 29, 56,
91, 126, 185; CLR 4, 44; CWRI 5; DLB
52; FANT; INT CANR-29; JRDA; MAI-
CYA 1, 2; MTFW 2005; SAAS 1; SATA
4, 40, 75, 112, 158, 194; SATA-Essay 111;
SFW 4; SUFW 2; WYA; YAW

Yonge, Charlotte (Mary)
1823-1901 .... **TCLC 48**
See also CA 109; 163; DLB 18, 163; RGEL
2; SATA 17; WCH

York, Jeremy
See Creasey, John

York, Simon
See Heinlein, Robert A.

Yorke, Henry Vincent 1905-1974 ...... **CLC 2,
13, 97**
See also BRWS 2; CA 85-88, 175; 49-52;
DLB 15; EWL 3; RGEL 2

Yosano, Akiko 1878-1942 ... **PC 11; TCLC 59**
See also CA 161; EWL 3; RGWL 3

Yoshimoto, Banana
See Yoshimoto, Mahoko

Yoshimoto, Mahoko 1964- .... **CLC 84**
See also AAYA 50; CA 144; CANR 98, 160;
NFS 7; SSFS 16

Young, Al(bert James) 1939- .... **BLC 1:3;
CLC 19**
See also BW 2, 3; CA 29-32R; CANR 26,
65, 109; CN 2, 3, 4, 5, 6, 7; CP 1, 2, 3, 4,
5, 6, 7; DAM MULT; DLB 33

Young, Andrew (John) 1885-1971 ...... **CLC 5**
See also CA 5-8R; CANR 7, 29; CP 1;
RGEL 2

Young, Collier
See Bloch, Robert (Albert)

Young, Edward 1683-1765 .... **LC 3, 40**
See also DLB 95; RGEL 2

Young, Marguerite (Vivian)
1909-1995 .... **CLC 82**
See also CA 13-16; 150; CAP 1; CN 1, 2,
3, 4, 5, 6

Young, Neil 1945- .... **CLC 17**
See also CA 110; CCA 1

Young Bear, Ray A. 1950- ... **CLC 94; NNAL**
See also CA 146; DAM MULT; DLB 175;
MAL 5

Yourcenar, Marguerite 1903-1987 ... **CLC 19,
38, 50, 87; TCLC 193**
See also BPFB 3; CA 69-72; CANR 23, 60,
93; DAM NOV; DLB 72; DLBY 1988;
EW 12; EWL 3; GFL 1789 to the Present;
GLL 1; MTCW 1, 2; MTFW 2005;
RGWL 2, 3

Yuan, Chu 340(?)B.C.-278(?)B.C. . **CMLC 36**

Yu Dafu 1896-1945 .... **SSC 122**
See also DLB 328; RGSF 2

Yurick, Sol 1925- .... **CLC 6**
See also CA 13-16R; CANR 25; CN 1, 2,
3, 4, 5, 6, 7; MAL 5

Zabolotsky, Nikolai Alekseevich
1903-1958 .... **TCLC 52**
See also CA 116; 164; EWL 3

Zabolotsky, Nikolay Alekseevich
See Zabolotsky, Nikolai Alekseevich

Zagajewski, Adam 1945- .... **PC 27**
See also CA 186; DLB 232; EWL 3; PFS
25

Zakaria, Fareed 1964- .... **CLC 269**
See also CA 171; CANR 151, 188

Zalygin, Sergei -2000 .... **CLC 59**

Zalygin, Sergei (Pavlovich)
1913-2000 .... **CLC 59**
See also DLB 302

Zamiatin, Evgenii
See Zamyatin, Evgeny Ivanovich

Zamiatin, Evgenii Ivanovich
See Zamyatin, Evgeny Ivanovich

Zamiatin, Yevgenii
See Zamyatin, Evgeny Ivanovich

Zamora, Bernice (B. Ortiz) 1938- .. **CLC 89;
HLC 2**
See also CA 151; CANR 80; DAM MULT;
DLB 82; HW 1, 2

Zamyatin, Evgeny Ivanovich
1884-1937 .... **SSC 89; TCLC 8, 37**
See also CA 105; 166; DLB 272; EW 10;
EWL 3; RGSF 2; RGWL 2, 3; SFW 4

Zamyatin, Yevgeny Ivanovich
See Zamyatin, Evgeny Ivanovich

Zangwill, Israel 1864-1926 ... **SSC 44; TCLC
16**
See also CA 109; 167; CMW 4; DLB 10,
135, 197; RGEL 2

Zanzotto, Andrea 1921- .... **PC 65**
See also CA 208; CWW 2; DLB 128; EWL
3

Zappa, Francis Vincent, Jr. 1940-1993
See Zappa, Frank
See also CA 108; 143; CANR 57

Zappa, Frank .... **CLC 17**
See Zappa, Francis Vincent, Jr.

Zaturenska, Marya 1902-1982 ..... **CLC 6, 11**
See also CA 13-16R; 105; CANR 22; CP 1,
2, 3

Literary Criticism Series
Cumulative Topic Index

This index lists all topic entries in Gale's *Children's Literature Review* (CLR), *Classical and Medieval Literature Criticism* (CMLC), *Contemporary Literary Criticism* (CLC), *Drama Criticism* (DC), *Literature Criticism from 1400 to 1800* (LC), *Nineteenth-Century Literature Criticism* (NCLC), *Short Story Criticism* (SSC), and *Twentieth-Century Literary Criticism* (TCLC). The index also lists topic entries in the Gale Critical Companion Collection, which includes the following publications: *The Beat Generation* (BG), *Feminism in Literature* (FL), *Gothic Literature* (GL), and *Harlem Renaissance* (HR).

Topic Index

Topic Index

Topic Index

NCLC Cumulative Nationality Index

NCLC-215 Title Index